R. W. STALLMAN is Professor of English at The University of Connecticut. He received his M.A. and Ph.D. from the University of Wisconsin and formerly taught at Yale University, the University of Minnesota, and the University of Kansas.

R. E. WATTERS is Professor of English and Head of the Department at The Royal Military College of Canada. He received his M.A. from the University of Toronto and his Ph.D. from the University of Wisconsin. Dr. Watters previously taught at the University of Wisconsin, the University of Washington, Indiana University, and the University of British Columbia.

The
CREATIVE

An
Anthology of

R. W. STALLMAN and
University of Connecticut

SECOND EDITION

THE RONALD PRESS

READER

FICTION,
DRAMA,
POETRY

R. E. WATTERS
The Royal Military College of Canada

COMPANY ⋅ NEW YORK

Library of Congress Catalog Card Number: 62-9861
PRINTED IN THE UNITED STATES OF AMERICA

PREFACE

This anthology, designed for courses which introduce literature at the college level to first- and second-year students, contains a rich representation of fiction, drama, and poetry. It is distinguished from other anthologies by making available materials for studying literary works both in relation to the creative process by which they came into being and in relation to the interpretative process by which they are understood and appreciated.

In this volume a literary work may be studied individually, as a thing in itself; but it may also be studied in relation to its source, composition, or revision; in relation to critical appraisal by some experienced reader; or, finally, in relation to other works with which it bears points of comparison or contrast. Variant representations of the same subject are provided by paired texts. For example, Stephen Crane's "The Open Boat" is juxtaposed with newspaper reports of the sinking of the *Commodore,* R. L. Stevenson's story about François Villon is paired with his biographical essay on the same person, and Melville's short novel, *Billy Budd,* has its accompaniment in the play based on that work. Equally illuminating but less specific interrelationships are also to be found, as when a short story has its parallel in another because of similarities in method, structure, or substance, or when a group of poems shares the same nominal subject or uses the same symbol, ironic tone, or theme.

In each of the three divisions of the anthology—fiction, drama, poetry—sections are devoted to the processes of creation and interpretation. For studying literary works in relation to the creative process, the student is provided with materials showing something of the origin and growth of different works of literature and the transmutation of the work from one form or medium to another. Often the best way to understand the nature of something is to study the process by which it became what it is.

For studying literary works in relation to the interpretative process of reading and evaluating, the student is introduced to critical essays which interpret the given work with skilled insight. He can, then, reread with fresh understanding the work he thought he had already read. By being thus challenged, he should come to develop his own powers of interpretation.

Additional guidance is offered by our Notes and Questions. These are intended to elicit a closer reading of the text through the weighing of facts and hints provided about the work, and to stimulate the student into examining interrelationships between poem and poem, story and poem, or story and play. In sum, our Notes and Questions are aimed at assisting the student to prepare for participation in critical discourse during class discussion.

The Creative Reader contains thirty-three stories which exhibit a wide range in subject, technique, and period; five full-length plays; and more than one hundred and fifty poems, simply classified according to their dominant characteristics. An innovation in the Poetry division is the section The Poem as Translation, where the

original text of poems by such poets as Chaucer, Heine, and Rimbaud is followed by
at least two translations for each poem. Comparison of the original with the variant
translations may suggest something of the problems and possibilities in transforming
a literary work from one language to another. Finally, the anthology includes thirty-
five essays, in addition to editorial notes and comments, each of which is focussed
upon literary issues raised by the literary works in the book.

It is impossible for the editors to thank adequately all those who offered helpful
suggestions for the preparation of this second edition. Special gratitude, however, is
due the following for their valuable insights and recommendations, many of which
have been incorporated into the text: Professors Norman Friedman, Charles Owen,
F. Semmler, H. L. Dean, Gordon Elliott, Dorothy Healy, J. J. Tobin, and Wilmer
K. Trauger.

R. W. STALLMAN
R. E. WATTERS

March, 1962

CONTENTS

Part One

FICTION

I: THE SHORT STORY

II: THE SHORT STORY AND THE CREATIVE PROCESS

III: THE SHORT STORY AND THE READER

Part Two

DRAMA

I: THE PLAY

II: THE PLAY AND THE CREATIVE PROCESS

III: THE PLAY AND THE READER

Part Three

POETRY

I: THE POEM

i: The Poem as Picture

ii: The Poem as Subject and Theme

iii: The Poem as Comparison

vi: The Poem as Satire and Parody

CONTENTS

vii: The Poem as Translation

II: THE POEM AND THE CREATIVE PROCESS

i: The Origins of Poetry

•

CONTENTS

III. THE POEM AND THE READER

CONTENTS

ACKNOWLEDGMENTS

Thanks are due to our colleagues and to the librarians at the Universities of Connecticut and British Columbia for suggestions and assistance of various kinds, and to the following copyright owners and their publishers for permission to reprint the following copyrighted material:

Earle Birney: For the poems "David" and "From the Hazel Bough."

R. P. Blackmur: For his poem "Mirage."

Basil Blackwell & Mott, Ltd.: For "How a Poem Is Made" from *Poetry for You* by C. Day Lewis. Copyright 1944 by Basil Blackwell & Mott, Ltd., and 1947 by Oxford University Press.

The Bodley Head, Ltd.: For the translation by Arthur Symons of Paul Verlaine's "Chanson d'Automne."

Albert & Charles Boni, Inc.: For "An Occurrence at Owl Creek Bridge" by Ambrose Bierce.

Brandt & Brandt: For the story "Mr. Arcularis" from *Selected Short Stories* of Conrad Aiken. The World Publishing Company. Copyright 1931 by Conrad Aiken. Reprinted with permission.

Curtis Brown, Ltd.: For the story "The Demon Lover" from *Ivy Gripped the Steps* by Elizabeth Bowen, copyright 1941, 1946 by Elizabeth Bowen, reprinted by permission of Curtis Brown, Ltd., and Alfred A. Knopf, Inc.

The Clarendon Press: For the selection from *Keats' Craftsmanship* by M. R. Ridley. Copyright 1933 by The Clarendon Press. For the poem "I will not let thee go" from *The Poetical Works of Robert Bridges*. Published by the Clarendon Press; reprinted by permission of The Clarendon Press.

Walter Van Tilburg Clark: For the story "The Portable Phonograph" and for "The Ghost of an Apprehension."

Reginald L. Cook: For "Robert Frost: A Time to Listen."

Malcolm Cowley for his poem "Mine No. 6" from *Blue Juanita*. Copyright 1929 by Malcolm Cowley.

Earl Daniels: For his note from *The Explicator* and for the selection from *The Art of Reading Poetry* by Earl Daniels. Published by Farrar & Rinehart. Copyright 1941.

The John Day Company, Inc.: For the poem "The Sirens" from *Selected Verse* by John Manifold. Copyright 1946 by The John Day Company, Inc.

J. M. Dent & Sons, Ltd.: For "The force that through the green fuse drives" and "Fern Hill" from *The Collected Poems of Dylan Thomas*. Copyright © 1957 by New Directions and J. M. Dent & Sons, Ltd. Reprinted by permission of J. M. Dent & Sons, Ltd., and New Directions, publishers. For the story "Amy Foster" by Joseph Conrad. For a note from the Preface to *The Nigger of the Narcissus* by Joseph Conrad.

W. C. DeVane for his article from *P.M.L.A.*

Dodd, Mead & Company, Inc.: For the poem "Heaven" from *The Collected Poems of Rupert Brooke*. Copyright 1915 by Dodd, Mead & Company, Inc. Copyright 1943 by Edward Marsh. For the translation by Arthur Symons of Paul Verlaine's "Chanson d'Automne."

E. P. Dutton & Co., Inc.: For the poems "On the Vanity of Earthly Greatness" and "Sea Chill" from *Gaily the Troubadour* by Arthur Guiterman. Copyright 1936 by E. P. Dutton & Co., Inc. For a note from *The Background of Modern Poetry* by J. Isaacs.

Ralph Eberly: For his note from *The Explicator.*

Editor of *Accent:* For "Kafka's Cage" by R. W. Stallman.

Editor of *The Atlantic Monthly:* For "Dover Beach Revisited" by Theodore Morrison.

Editor of *College English:* For "Robert Frost: A Time to Listen" by Reginald L. Cook, and for "Humpty Dumpty and Symbolism" by Bernard Knieger.

Editors of *The Explicator:* For a note by Ralph D. Eberly, a note by Marshall McLuhan, a note by G. Giovannini, and two notes by S. F. Johnson.

Editor of *Forum* for "A Trip to Czardis" by Edwin Granberry.

Editor of *The Kenyon Review:* For "The Gloves" by Colette Audry.

Editor of *The New Republic:* For the essay by Theodore Spencer and the poem "The Figurehead" by R. W. Stallman.

Editor of *The New Yorker:* For "The Catbird Seat" by James Thurber. Copyright 1942 by James Thurber. For "The Demon Lover" by Elizabeth Bowen.

Editor of *The Pacific Spectator:* For "The Ghost of an Apprehension" by Walter Van Tilburg Clark.

Editors of *The Partisan Review:* For "The Making of a Poem" by Stephen Spender.

Editor of *Publications of the Modern Language Association:* For articles by Harold Golder and W. C. DeVane.

Editor of *Scrutiny:* For "Emotional Quality in Poetry" by F. R. Leavis.

Editor of *University of Kansas City Review:* For the essay on W. B. Yeats's "Sailing to Byzantium" by Elder Olson.

Editor of *The Western Review:* For "A Hunger-Artist" by Franz Kafka. Translated by M. L. Nielsen and published in *The Rocky Mountain Review.*

Editor of *Yale Literary Magazine* for the essay by Arthur Nelson.

Editor of *The Yale Review:* For "The Portable Phonograph" by Walter Van Tilburg Clark. Copyright by Yale University Press and the author.

Norma Millay Ellis: For "The Return" from *Collected Poems of Edna St. Vincent Millay.* Copyright 1920–1947 by Edna St. Vincent Millay.

Faber & Faber, Ltd.: For the poem "The Love Song of J. Alfred Prufrock" by T. S. Eliot. Copyright 1936 by Faber & Faber, Ltd., and Harcourt, Brace & World, Inc. For the poems "Musée des Beaux Arts" and "The Unknown Citizen" from *Collected Poems* by W. H. Auden. Copyright 1940 by W. H. Auden. Reprinted also by permission of Random House, Inc. For the poems "Landscape Near an Aerodrome" and "The Express" from *Poems* by Stephen Spender. Copyright 1934 by Modern Library, Inc.

Kenneth Fearing: For his poem "Dirge."

G. Giovannini for his explication of Dylan Thomas's "The Force That Through the Green Fuse Drives."

Marjory S. Golder: For the article by Harold Golder from *P.M.L.A.*

Edwin Granberry: For "A Trip to Czardis" from *The Forum.*

Harcourt, Brace & World, Inc.: For the translation of *Antigone* from *The Antigone of Sophocles,* an English version by Dudley Fitts and Robert Fitzgerald. Copyright 1939 by Harcourt, Brace & World, Inc. For the poem "White Christmas" from *Awake! and Other Wartime Poems* by W. R. Rodgers. Copyright 1942 by Harcourt, Brace & World, Inc. For the story "A Still Moment" from *The Wide Net and Other Stories* by Eudora Welty. Copyright 1943 by Eudora Welty. For the essay pp. 605–607 by John Holmes from *Preface to Poetry* by Charles W. Cooper and John Holmes. Copyright 1946 by Harcourt, Brace & World, Inc. The above reprinted by permission of Harcourt, Brace & World, Inc. For the poems "The Love Song of J. Alfred Prufrock" and "Aunt Helen" from *Collected Poems, 1909–1935* by T. S. Eliot. Copyright 1936 by Harcourt, Brace & World, Inc. Reprinted by permission of Harcourt, Brace & World, Inc., and Faber and Faber, Ltd. For the poem "anyone lived in a pretty how town" from *Poems: 1923–1954* by E. E. Cummings. Copyright 1940 by E. E. Cummings. Reprinted by permission of Harcourt, Brace & World, Inc. For the poem "next to of course god" from *Poems: 1923–1954* by E. E. Cummings. Copyright 1926 by Horace Liveright; renewed 1954 by E. E. Cummings. Reprinted by permission of Harcourt, Brace & World, Inc. For the poem "Poem, or Beauty Hurts Mr. Vinal" from *Poems 1923–1954* by E. E. Cummings. Copyright 1940 by E. E. Cummings. Reprinted by permission of Harcourt, Brace & World, Inc. For the poem "Juggler" from *Ceremony and Other Poems,* copyright 1948, 1949, 1950 by Richard Wilbur. Reprinted by permission of Harcourt, Brace & World, Inc. For the poems "The Message" and *"Ein Fichtenbaum steht einsam"* from *Poems of Heinrich Heine* translated by Louis Untermeyer, copyright 1923, by Harcourt, Brace & World, Inc.; renewed 1951 by Louis Untermeyer. Reprinted by permission of the publishers. For the short story "Sixteen: Winter" from *Cress Delahanty* by Jessamyn West. Copyright 1946 by Jessamyn West. Reprinted from her volume *Cress Delahanty* by permission of Harcourt, Brace & World, Inc.

Harper & Brothers: For the poem "Sunburned Ulysses" from *Death at Sea* by Frederic Prokosch. Copyright 1940 by Frederic Prokosch, reprinted by permission of Harper & Brothers. For the poem "The spider holds a silver ball" from *Bolts of Melody* by Emily Dickinson, edited by Mabel Loomis Todd and Millicent Todd Bingham. Copyright 1945 by Millicent Todd Bingham.

Harvard University Press: For the passage pp. 91–92, Vol. I, from *The Keats Circle.* Edited by Hyder E. Rollins. Copyright 1948 by the President and Fellows of Harvard College. For Melville's *Billy Budd.* Edited by Frederic Baron Freeman and corrected by Elizabeth Treeman. Copyright 1948, 1956 by the President and Fellows of Harvard College. Reprinted by permission of the publishers.

John Holmes: For his essay on Robert Frost's "Stopping by Woods on a Snowy Evening."

Holt, Rinehart and Winston, Inc.: For the essay "The Figure a Poem Makes" by Robert Frost and the poems "Birches," "Tree at My Window," "Stopping by Woods on a Snowy Evening," "Mending Wall," from *Complete Poems of Robert Frost.* Copyright 1930, 1949 by Holt, Rinehart and Winston, Inc. Reprinted by permission of Holt, Rinehart and Winston, Inc. For the poem "Desert Places" from *A Further Range* by Robert Frost. Copyright 1936 by Robert Frost. Reprinted by permission of Holt, Rinehart and Winston, Inc. For the poem "Come In" from *A Witness Tree* by Robert Frost. Copyright 1952 by Robert Frost. Reprinted by permission of Holt, Rinehart and Winston, Inc. For the poems "Is My Team Ploughing," "To an Athlete Dying Young," "Loveliest of Trees," and Poem No. XLIV from *A Shropshire Lad*—Authorised Edition—from *Complete Poems* by A. E. Housman. Copyright © 1959 by Holt, Rinehart and Winston, Inc. Reprinted by permission of Holt, Rinehart and Winston, Inc. For the essay on T. S. Eliot's "The Love Song of J. Alfred Prufrock" from *Understanding Poetry* by Cleanth Brooks and Robert Penn Warren. Copyright 1938, 1950 by Holt, Rinehart and Winston, Inc. Reprinted by permission of Holt, Rinehart and Winston, Inc. For the passage pp. 16–20 from *The Art of Reading Poetry* by Earl Daniels. Copyright 1941 by Farrar and Rinehart. For the translation of Franz Kafka's "A Hunger-Artist" by M. L. Nielsen and for the essay by R. W. Stallman on Franz Kafka's "A Hunger-Artist," both from *The Art of Modern Fiction,* edited by Ray B. West, Jr., and R. W. Stallman. Copyright 1949 by Rinehart & Company, Inc.

Hope Leresche & Steele: For the poem "What, still alive at twenty-two?" by Hugh Kingsmill.

Houghton Mifflin Company: For the poems "You, Andrew Marvell" and "Arts Poetica" from *Poems: 1924–1933* by Archibald MacLeish. Copyright 1933 by Houghton Mifflin Company. For the poem "Patterns" by Amy Lowell. The above reprinted by permission of and arrangement with Houghton Mifflin Company, the authorized publishers.

S. F. Johnson for his explications of Dylan Thomas's "The Force That Through the Green Fuse Drives."

Nannine Joseph: For the poem "This Amber Sunstream" from *Collected Poems* by Mark Van Doren.

Bernard Knieger: For his essay "Humpty Dumpty and Symbolism."

Alfred A. Knopf, Inc.: For the story "The Demon Lover" from *Ivy Gripped the Steps* by Elizabeth Bowen. Copyright 1941, 1946 by Elizabeth Bowen; reprinted by permission of Alfred A. Knopf, Inc., and Curtis Brown, Ltd. For the poem "Domination of Black" from *The Collected Poems of Wallace Stevens.* Copyright 1931, 1954 by Wallace Stevens; reprinted by permission of Alfred A. Knopf, Inc. For the poems "Here Lies a Lady," "Piazza Piece," and "Philomela" from *Selected Poems* by John Crowe Ransom. Copyright 1927, 1945 by Alfred A. Knopf, Inc. For the stories "The Fly" and "The Daughters of the Late Colonel" from *The Short Stories of Katherine Mansfield.* Copyright 1922, 1937 by Alfred A. Knopf, Inc. For the stories "The Upturned Face" and "The Open Boat" from *Stephen Crane: An Omnibus,* edited by R. W. Stallman. Copyright 1952 by Alfred A. Knopf, Inc. For "Stephen Crane's Own Story" and "Newspaper Reports of the Wreck of the *Commodore*" from *Stephen Crane: An Omnibus,* edited by R. W. Stallman. Copyright 1952 by Alfred A. Knopf, Inc. The above reprinted by permission of Alfred A. Knopf, Inc.

John Lane: The Bodley Head Ltd.: For Arthur Symons's translation of Paul Verlaine's *Chanson d'Automne.*

Philip Larkin: For his poem "Next Please" from *The Less Deceived.*

F. R. Leavis: For "Emotional Quality in Poetry" from *Scrutiny.*

J. B. Lippincott Company: For "Strange Comfort Afforded by the Profession" by Malcolm Lowry. Reprinted with the permission of the publisher, J. B. Lippincott Company. Copyright 1953 by Malcolm Lowry.

Little Brown & Company: For "Poet" from *Poems 1947–1957* by William Jay Smith, by permission of Little, Brown & Co. Copyright © 1957 by William Jay Smith.

Robert Loy: For his translation of "The Gloves" by Colette Audry. Reprinted from *The Kenyon Review* by permission of the Editor and Robert Loy.

The Macmillan Company: For the poems "The Sorrow of Love," "An Irish Airman Foresees His Death," "Leda and the Swan," and "Sailing to Byzantium" from *Collected Poems* by William Butler Yeats. Copyright 1906, 1934 by The Macmillan Company. Reprinted by permission of the publishers and A. P. Watt & Son, London. For the poems "New Year's Eve," "Darkling Thrush," and "Neutral Tones" from *Collected Poems* by Thomas Hardy. Copyright 1925 by The Macmillan Company. Reprinted by permission of the publishers. For the poem "Poetry" from *Collected Poems* by Marianne Moore. Copyright 1935 by The Macmillan Company. Reprinted by permission of the publishers. For the poem "Coleridge" from *Scrimshaw* by Winfield Townley Scott. Copyright 1959. For the poem "Mr. Flood's Party" from *Collected Poems* by Edwin Arlington Robinson. Copyright 1929 by The Macmillan Company. Reprinted by permission of the publishers. For the poems "Sea Fever" and "Cargoes" from *Collected Poems* by John Masefield. Copyright 1945 by The Macmillan Company. Reprinted by permission of the publishers. For "Paste" from *The Soft Side* by Henry James. Copyright 1900 by The Macmillan Company. Reprinted by permission of the publishers and Paul Revere Reynolds & Son.

Macmillan & Co., Ltd.: For the poems "New Year's Eve," "Darkling Thrush," and "Neutral Tones" from *Collected Poems* by Thomas Hardy. Copyright 1925 by Macmillan & Co., Ltd. Reprinted by permission of the publishers and the trustees of the Hardy estate. For the poem "Invictus" by W. E. Henley. Reprinted by permission of the publishers and the representative of the late W. E. Henley.

Dorothy Martin: For her translation of Charles Baudelaire's "Harmonie du Soir."

Harold Matson: For "How a Poem is Made" from *Poetry for You* by C. Day Lewis. Copyright 1944 by Basil Blackwell & Mott, Ltd., 1947 by Oxford University Press. For the poems "Nearing Again the Legendary Isle," "Newsreel," and "Come Live with Me and Be My Love" from *A Time to Dance* by C. Day Lewis. Copyright 1936.

McClellan and Stewart, Ltd.: For the poem "Heaven" from *The Collected Poems of Rupert Brooke.* Copyright 1943 by Edward Marsh.

Marshall McLuhan: For his article "Henley's 'Invictus'" from *The Explicator.*

Michigan State University Press: For the poem "To Hold in a Poem" from *A Sort of Ecstasy* by A. J. M. Smith. Reprinted by permission of Michigan State University Press.

William Morris Agency: For "The Later Yeats" from *A Coat of Many Colours* by Herbert Read. Published by Routledge, Kegan Paul, Ltd.

Theodore Morrison: For his "Dover Beach Revisited" from *The Atlantic Monthly*.

National Council of Teachers of English: For "Humpty Dumpty and Symbolism" by Bernard Knieger. For "Robert Frost: A Time to Listen" by Reginald L. Cook.

Mrs. Arthur Nelson: For the essay by Arthur Nelson from the *Yale Literary Magazine* and *The Art of Modern Fiction*, edited by Ray B. West, Jr. and R. W. Stallman. Copyright 1949 by Rinehart & Company, Inc.

New Directions: For the poem "Futility" from *The Poems of Wilfred Owen*. All rights reserved. Reprinted by permission of New Directions, publishers. For the poem "Winter Landscape" by John Berryman from *Five Young American Poets*. Copyright 1940 by New Directions. Reprinted by permission of New Directions, publishers. For the poems "Fern Hill" and "The force that through the green fuse drives" from *The Collected Poems of Dylan Thomas*. Copyright © 1957 by New Directions. Reprinted by permission of New Directions, publishers, and J. M. Dent & Sons, Ltd. For the poem "Ancient Music" from *Personae: The Collected Poems of Ezra Pound*. Copyright 1926 by Ezra Pound. Reprinted by permission of New Directions, publishers. For the translation by Louise Varèse of the poem "Song of the Highest Tower" from *A Season in Hell* by Arthur Rimbaud, p. 57. Copyright 1945 by New Directions. Reprinted by permission of New Directions, publishers. For the translation by Dorothy Martin of the poem "Evening Harmony" from *The Flowers of Evil* by Charles Baudelaire, selected and edited by Marthiel and Jackson Mathews, p. 60. Copyright 1955 by New Directions. Reprinted by permission of New Directions, publishers.

M. L. Nielsen: For his translation of "A Hunger-Artist" by Franz Kafka from *The Art of Modern Fiction*, edited by Ray B. West, Jr. and R. W. Stallman. Copyright 1949 by Rinehart & Company, Inc.

W. W. Norton & Company, Inc.: For "Poetry and the Poet," pp. 17–29, from *Discovering Poetry* by Elizabeth Drew. Copyright 1933, 1940 by W. W. Norton & Company, Inc.

Princeton University Press: For *Billy Budd,* A Play in Three Acts by Louis O. Coxe and Robert Chapman. Copyright 1951 by Princeton University Press.

Random House, Inc.: For the play "Antigone" by Jean Anouilh, adapted and translated by Lewis Galantiere. Copyright 1946 by Random House, Inc. Reprinted by permission of Random House, Inc. For "The Portable Phonograph" from *The Watchful Gods and Other Stories* by Walter Van Tilburg Clark. Copyright 1941 by Walter Van Tilburg Clark. Reprinted by permission of Random House, Inc. For "A Rose for Emily" from *Collected Stories of William Faulkner*. Copyright 1930 and renewed 1957 by William Faulkner. Reprinted by permission of Random House, Inc. For "The Bear" by William Faulkner. Copyright 1942 by The Curtis Publishing Company. Reprinted by permission of Random House, Inc. For the poems "The Landscape Near an Aerodrome" and "The Express" from *Collected Poems: 1928–1953,* by Stephen Spender. Copyright 1934 by Modern Library, Inc. Reprinted by permission of Random House, Inc. For the poems "The Unknown Citizen" and "Musée des Beaux Arts" by W. H. Auden. Copyright 1940 by W. H. Auden. Reprinted by permission of Random House, Inc.

Paul Revere Reynolds & Son: For the story "Paste" by Henry James.

Edgell Rickword: For his translation "Song of the Topmost Tower" from the French of Rimbaud's "Chanson de la plus Haute Tour" from *Une Saison en Enfer*.

Theodore Roethke: For his poem "My Papa's Waltz."

Routledge, Kegan Paul, Ltd.: For "The Later Yeats" from *A Coat of Many Colours* by Herbert Read.

The Ryerson Press: For "To Hold in a Poem" from *A Sort of Ecstasy* by A. J. M. Smith, reprinted by permission of The Ryerson Press.

W. T. Scott: For his note on the poem "Coleridge."

Scott, Foresman & Company: For the text of *The Tempest* as edited and annotated by Hardin Craig.

Charles Scribner's Sons: For "Perspectives Are Precipices," reprinted with the permission of Charles Scribner's Sons from *Now With His Love* by John Peale Bishop. Copyright 1933 Charles Scribner's Sons. For "A Clean, Well-Lighted Place" from *The Fifth Column and the First Forty-Nine Stories* by Ernest Hemingway. Copyright 1938 by Ernest Hemingway. For the poem "La Belle Dame Sans Merci" from *A Summer Landscape* by Rolfe Humphries. Copyright 1944 by Charles Scribner's Sons. For the poems "For a Dead Lady" and "Miniver Cheevy" from *The Town Down the River* by Edwin Arlington Robinson. Copyright 1910 by Charles Scribner's Sons, 1938 by Ruth Nivison. For "The Black Godmother" from *Caravan* by John Galsworthy. Copyright 1925 by Charles Scribner's Sons. For "To a Sinister Potato" from *Terror and Decorum* by Peter Viereck. Copyright 1948 by Peter Viereck. For "Hunters in the Snow: Brueghel" from *The Green Town: Poems* by Joseph Langland. Copyright 1951 by the University of New Mexico. The above reprinted by permission of Charles Scribner's Sons.

Martin Secker & Warburg, Ltd.: For the poem "White Christmas" by W. R. Rodgers.

Simon and Schuster, Inc.: For the Wife of Bath sketch from the Prologue, from *The Canterbury Tales,* translated by R. M. Lumiansky. Copyright 1948 by Simon and Schuster, Inc. Reprinted by permission of the publishers.

Maxwell Singer for his translation "Song of the Highest Tower" from the French of Rimbaud's "Chanson de la plus Haute Tour."

A. J. M. Smith: For his poem "To Hold in a Poem."

The Society of Authors: For "The Fly" and "The Daughters of the Late Colonel" by Katherine Mansfield. Reprinted by permission of The Society of Authors and J. Middleton Murry, O. B. E. For the poems "Is My Team Ploughing," "To an Athlete Dying Young," "Loveliest of Trees," and Poem No. XLIV in *A Shropshire Lad* by A. E. Housman. Reprinted by permission of The Society of Authors as the Literary Representative of the estate of the late A. E. Housman, and Messrs. Jonathan Cape, Ltd., publishers of A. E. Housman's *Collected Poems.* For "An Epitaph" and "The Listeners" by Walter de la Mare, by permission of the Literary Trustees of Walter de la Mare and the Society of Authors as their representative.

The University of Chicago Press: For the essay pp. 663-78 from *The Meaning of Shakespeare* by Harold Goddard.

Mark Van Doren: For the selection from his *Introduction to Poetry.* Published by William Sloan Associates and The Dryden Press. Copyright 1952 by Mark Van Doren.

Peter Viereck: For the poem "To a Sinister Potato."

The Viking Press: For "The Horse Dealer's Daughter" from *England, My England* by D. H. Lawrence. Copyright 1922 by Thomas Seltzer, Inc., 1950 by Frieda Lawrence. Reprinted by permission of The Viking Press, Inc. For the poems "The Snake" and "Piano" from *Collected Poems* by D. H. Lawrence. Copyright 1929 by Jonathan Cape and Harrison Smith, Inc., 1957 by Frieda Lawrence Ravagli. Reprinted by permission of The Viking Press, Inc. For the poem "I Hear an Army Charging" from *Collected Poems* by James Joyce. Copyright 1918 by B. W. Huebsch, 1946 by Nora Joyce. Reprinted by permission of The Viking Press, Inc. For "A Little Cloud" from *Dubliners* by James Joyce. Reprinted by permission of The Viking Press, Inc. All rights reserved. For the Wife of Bath sketch from the Prologue, from *The Viking Portable Chaucer.* Edited and translated by Theodore Morrison. Copyright 1949 by Theodore Morrison. Reprinted by permission of The Viking Press, Inc. For "The Second Death" from *Nineteen Stories* by Graham Greene. Copyright 1947 by Graham Greene. Reprinted by permission of The Viking Press, Inc. For "The First Death of Her Life" from *Hester Lilly and Twelve Short Stories* by Elizabeth Taylor. Copyright 1949 by Elizabeth Taylor. Originally published in *The New Yorker.* Reprinted by permission of The Viking Press, Inc.

Eloise B. Wade: For the essay by Theodore Spencer from *The New Republic*.

A. P. Watt, Ltd.: For the poem "Ulysses" from *Collected Poems* by Robert Graves, published by Doubleday & Co., Inc., and by Cassell & Co. Ltd. Copyright by Roturman, S. A. For the essay on Two Shakespeare Sonnets from *The Common Asphodel* by Robert Graves, published by Hamish Hamilton Ltd., 1949. Copyright by Roturman, S. A. For the poems "The Sorrow of Love," "An Irish Airman Foresees His Death," "Leda and the Swan," and "Sailing to Byzantium." Reprinted by permission of A. P .Watt, Ltd. and the publishers of *Collected Poems* by William Butler Yeats, The Macmillan Company. Copyright 1906, 1934 by The Macmillan Company.

Oscar Williams: For the poem "Soldiers Bathing" by F. T. Prince from *New Poems 1944*. Edited and copyrighted 1944 by Oscar Williams.

Windsor Press: For the poem "High Flight" from *High Flight* by John Gillespie Magee. Copyright 1940 by Windsor Press.

Yale University Press: For selections from *The American Notebooks of Nathaniel Hawthorne*. Edited by Randall Stewart. Copyright 1932.

Mrs. W. B. Yeats and the Macmillan Company of Canada, Ltd.: For "The Sorrow of Love," "An Irish Airman Foresees his Death," "Leda and the Swan," and "Sailing to Byzantium" from *The Collected Poems of W. B. Yeats*. Copyright 1906, 1934 by The Macmillan Company of Canada, Ltd. and Mrs. W. B. Yeats. Reprinted by permission of A. P. Watt, Ltd.

Part One

FICTION

I

The Short Story

A skilful literary artist has constructed a tale. If wise, he has not fashioned his thoughts to accommodate his incidents; but having conceived, with deliberate care, a certain unique or single effect to be wrought out, he then invents such incidents—he then combines such events as may best aid him in establishing this preconceived effect. If his very initial sentence tend not to the outbringing of this effect, then he has failed in his first step. In the whole composition there should be no word written, of which the tendency, direct or indirect, is not to the one pre-established design. And by such means, with such care and skill, a picture is at length painted which leaves in the mind of him who contemplates it with a kindred art, a sense of the fullest satisfaction.

—EDGAR ALLAN POE

I scarcely think we could any of us claim that in reading a novel we deliberately watch the book itself, rather than the scenes and figures it suggests, or that we seek to construct an image of the book, page by page, while its form is gradually exposed to us. We are much more inclined to forget, if we can, that the book is an object of art, and to treat it as a piece of the life around us; we fashion for ourselves, we objectify, the elements in it that happen to strike us most keenly. These things take shape in the mind of the reader; they are re-created and set up where the mind's eye can rest on them, but they are not the book which the author offers us. . . .
The reader of a novel—by which I mean the critical reader—is himself a novelist; he is the maker of a book which may or may not please his taste when it is finished, but of a book for which he must take his own share of responsibility. The author does his part, but he cannot transfer his book like a bubble into the brain of the critic; he cannot make sure that the critic will possess his work. The reader must therefore become, for his part, a novelist, never permitting himself to suppose that the creation of the book is solely the affair of the author.

—PERCY LUBBOCK

THE CATBIRD SEAT *

JAMES THURBER (1894–1961)

Mr. Martin bought the pack of Camels on Monday night in the most crowded cigar store on Broadway. It was theatre time and seven or eight men were buying cigarettes. The clerk didn't even glance at Mr. Martin, who put the pack in his overcoat pocket and went out. If any of the staff at F & S had seen him buy the cigarettes, they would have been astonished, for it was generally known that Mr. Martin did not smoke, and never had. No one saw him.

It was just a week to the day since Mr. Martin had decided to rub out Mrs. Ulgine Barrows. The term "rub out" pleased him because it suggested nothing more than the correction of an error—in this case an error of Mr. Fitweiler. Mr. Martin had spent each night of the past week working out his plan and examining it. As he walked home now he went over it again. For the hundredth time he resented the element of imprecision, the margin of guesswork that entered into the business. The project as he had worked it out was casual and bold, the risks were considerable. Something might go wrong anywhere along the line. And therein lay the cunning of his scheme. No one would ever see in it the cautious, painstaking hand of Erwin Martin, head of the filing department at F & S, of whom Mr. Fitweiler had once said, "Man is fallible but Martin isn't." No one would see his hand, that is, unless it were caught in the act.

Sitting in his apartment, drinking a glass of milk, Mr. Martin reviewed his case against Mrs. Ulgine Barrows, as he had every night for seven nights. He began at the beginning. Her quacking voice and braying laugh had first profaned the halls of F & S on March 7, 1941 (Mr. Martin had a head for dates). Old Roberts, the personnel chief, had introduced her as the newly appointed special adviser to the president of the firm, Mr. Fitweiler. The woman had appalled Mr. Martin instantly, but he hadn't shown it. He had given her his dry hand, a look of studious concentration, and a faint smile. "Well," she had said, looking at the papers on his desk, "are you lifting the oxcart out of the ditch?" As Mr. Martin recalled that moment, over his milk, he squirmed slightly. He must keep his mind on her crimes as a special adviser, not on her peccadillos as a personality. This he found difficult to do, in spite of entering an objection and sustaining it. The faults of the woman as a woman kept chattering on in his mind like an unruly witness. She had, for almost two years now, baited him. In the halls, in the elevator, even in his own office, into which she romped now and then like a circus horse, she was constantly shouting these silly questions at him. "Are you lifting the oxcart out of the ditch? Are you tearing up the pea patch? Are you hollering down the rain barrel? Are you scraping around the bottom of the pickle barrel? Are you sitting in the catbird seat?"

It was Joey Hart, one of Mr. Martin's two assistants, who had explained what the gibberish meant. "She must be a Dodger fan," he had said. "Red Barber announces the Dodger games over the radio and he uses those expressions—picked 'em up down South." Joey had gone on to explain one or two. "Tearing up the pea patch" meant going on a rampage; "sitting in the catbird seat" meant sitting pretty, like a batter with three balls and no strikes on him. Mr. Martin dismissed all this with an effort. It had been annoying, it had driven him near to distraction, but he was too solid a man to be moved to murder by anything so childish. It was fortunate, he reflected as he passed on to the important charges against Mrs. Barrows, that he had stood up under it so well. He had maintained always an outward appearance of polite tolerance. "Why, I even believe you like the woman," Miss Paird, his other assistant, had once said to him. He had simply smiled.

A gavel rapped in Mr. Martin's mind and the case proper was resumed. Mrs. Ulgine Barrows stood charged with willful, blatant, and persistent attempts to destroy the efficiency and system of F & S. It was competent, material, and relevant to review her advent and rise to power. Mr. Martin had got the story from Miss Paird, who seemed always able to find things out. According to her, Mrs. Barrows had met Mr. Fitweiler at a party, where she had rescued him from the embraces of a powerfully built drunken man who had mistaken the president of F & S for a famous retired Middle Western football coach. She had led him to a sofa and somehow worked upon him a monstrous magic. The aging gentleman had jumped to the conclusion there and then that this was a woman of singular attainments, equipped to bring out the best in him and in the firm. A week later he had introduced her into F & S as his special adviser. On that day confusion got its foot in the door. After Miss Tyson, Mr. Brundage, and Mr. Bartlett had been fired and Mr. Munson had taken his hat and stalked out, mailing in his resignation later, old Roberts had been emboldened to speak to Mr. Fitweiler. He mentioned that Mr. Munson's department had been "a little disrupted" and hadn't they perhaps better resume the old system there? Mr. Fitweiler had said certainly not. He had the greatest faith in Mrs. Barrows' ideas. "They require a little seasoning, a little seasoning, is all," he had added. Mr. Roberts had given it up. Mr. Martin reviewed in detail all the changes wrought by Mrs. Barrows. She had begun chipping at the cornices of the firm's edifice and now she was swinging at the foundation stones with a pickaxe.

Mr. Martin came now, in his summing up, to the afternoon of Monday, November 2, 1942—just one week ago. On that day, at 3 P.M., Mrs. Barrows had bounced into his office. "Boo!" she had yelled. "Are you scraping around the bottom of the pickle barrel?" Mr. Martin had looked at her from under his green eyeshade, saying nothing. She had begun to wander about the office, taking it in with her great, popping eyes. "Do you really need *all* these filing cabinets?" she had demanded suddenly. Mr. Martin's heart had jumped. "Each of these files," he had said, keeping his voice even, "plays an indispensable part in the system of F & S." She had brayed at him, "Well, don't tear up the pea patch!" and gone to the door. From there she had bawled, "But you sure have got a lot of fine scrap in here!" Mr. Martin could no longer doubt that the finger was on his beloved department. Her pickaxe was on the upswing, poised for the first blow. It had not come yet; he had received no blue memo from the enchanted Mr. Fitweiler bearing nonsensical instructions deriving from the obscene woman. But there was no doubt in Mr. Martin's mind that one would be forthcoming. He must act quickly. Already a precious week had gone by. Mr. Martin stood up in his living room, still holding his milk glass. "Gentlemen of the jury," he said to himself, "I demand the death penalty for this horrible person."

The next day Mr. Martin followed his routine, as usual. He polished his glasses more often and once sharpened an already sharp pencil, but not even Miss Paird noticed. Only once did he catch sight of his victim; she swept past him in the hall with a patronizing "Hi!" At five-thirty he walked home, as usual, and had a glass of milk, as usual. He had never drunk anything stronger in his life—unless you could count ginger ale. The late Sam Schlosser, the S of F & S, had praised Mr. Martin at a staff meeting several years before for his temperate habits. "Our most efficient worker neither drinks nor smokes," he had said. "The results speak for themselves." Mr. Fitweiler had sat by, nodding approval.

Mr. Martin was still thinking about that red-letter day as he walked over to the Schrafft's on Fifth Avenue near Forty-sixth Street. He got there, as he always did, at eight o'clock. He finished his dinner and the financial page of the *Sun* at a quarter to nine, as he always did. It was his custom after dinner to take a walk. This time he walked down Fifth Avenue at a casual pace. His gloved hands felt moist and warm, his forehead cold. He transferred the Camels from his overcoat to a jacket pocket. He wondered, as he did so, if they did not represent an unnecessary note of strain. Mrs. Barrows smoked only Luckies. It was his idea to puff a few puffs on a Camel (after the rubbing-out), stub it out in the ashtray holding her lipstick-stained Luckies, and thus drag a small red herring across the trail. Perhaps it was not a good idea. It would take time. He might even choke, too loudly.

Mr. Martin had never seen the house on West Twelfth Street where Mrs. Barrows lived, but he had a clear enough picture of it. Fortunately, she had bragged to every-body about her ducky first-floor apartment in the perfectly darling three-story red-brick. There would be no doorman or other attendants; just the tenants of the second and third floors. As he walked along, Mr. Martin realized that he would get there before nine-thirty. He had considered walking north on Fifth Avenue from Schrafft's to a point from which it would take him until ten o'clock to reach the house. At that hour people were less likely to be coming in or going out. But the procedure would have made an awkward loop in the straight thread of his casualness, and he had abandoned it. It was impossible to figure when people would be entering or leaving the house, anyway. There was a great risk at any hour. If he ran into anybody, he would simply have to place the rubbing-out of Ulgine Barrows in the inactive file forever. The same thing would hold true if there were someone in her apartment. In that case he would just say that he had been passing by, recognized her charming house, and thought to drop in.

It was eighteen minutes after nine when Mr. Martin turned into Twelfth Street. A man passed him, and a man and a woman, talking. There was no one within fifty paces when he came to the house, halfway down the block. He was up the steps and in the small vestibule in no time, pressing the bell under the card that said "Mrs. Ulgine Barrows." When the clicking in the lock started, he jumped forward against the door. He got inside fast, closing the door behind him. A bulb in a lantern hung from the hall ceiling on a chain seemed to give a monstrously bright light. There was nobody on the stair, which went up ahead of him along the left wall. A door opened down the hall in the wall on the right. He went toward it swiftly, on tiptoe.

"Well, for God's sake, look who's here!" bawled Mrs. Barrows, and her braying laugh rang out like the report of a shotgun. He rushed past her like a football tackle, bumping her. "Hey, quit shoving!" she said, closing the door behind them. They were in her living room, which seemed to Mr. Martin to be lighted by a hundred lamps. "What's after you?" she said. "You're as jumpy as a goat." He found he was unable to speak. His heart was wheezing in his throat. "I—yes," he finally brought out. She was jabbering and laughing as she started to help him off with his coat. "No, no," he said. "I'll put it here." He took it off and put it on a chair near the door. "Your hat and gloves, too," she said. "You're in a lady's house." He put his hat on top of the coat. Mrs. Barrows seemed larger than he had thought. He kept his gloves on. "I was passing by," he said. "I recognized—is there anyone here?" She laughed louder than ever. "No," she said, "we're all alone. You're as white as a sheet, you funny man. Whatever *has* come over you? I'll mix you a toddy." She started toward a door across the room. "Scotch-and-soda be all right? But say, you don't drink, do you?" She turned and gave him her amused look. Mr. Martin pulled himself together. "Scotch-and-soda will be all right," he heard himself say. He could hear her laughing in the kitchen.

Mr. Martin looked quickly around the living room for the weapon. He had counted on finding one there. There were andirons and a poker and something in a corner that looked like an Indian club. None of them would do. It couldn't be that way. He began to pace around. He came to a desk. On it lay a metal paper knife with an ornate handle. Would it be sharp enough? He reached for it and knocked over a small brass jar. Stamps spilled out of it and it fell to the floor with a clatter. "Hey," Mrs. Barrows yelled from the kitchen, "are you tearing up the pea patch?" Mr. Martin gave a strange laugh. Picking up the knife, he tried its point against his left wrist. It was blunt. It wouldn't do.

When Mrs. Barrows reappeared, carrying two highballs, Mr. Martin, standing there with his gloves on, became acutely conscious of the fantasy he had wrought. Cigarettes in his pocket, a drink prepared for him—it was all too grossly improbable. It was more than that; it was impossible. Somewhere in the back of his mind a vague idea stirred, sprouted. "For heaven's sake, take off those gloves," said Mrs. Barrows. "I always wear them in the house," said Mr. Martin. The idea began to bloom, strange and wonderful. She put the glasses on a coffee table in front of a sofa and sat on the sofa. "Come over here, you odd little man," she said. Mr. Martin went over and sat beside her. It was difficult getting a cigarette out of the pack of Camels, but he managed it. She held a match for him, laughing. "Well," she said, handing him his drink, "this is perfectly marvellous. You with a drink and a cigarette."

Mr. Martin puffed, not too awkwardly, and took a gulp of the highball. "I drink and smoke all the time," he said. He clinked his glass against hers. "Here's nuts to that old windbag, Fitweiler," he said, and gulped again. The stuff tasted awful, but he made no grimace. "Really, Mr. Martin," she said, her voice and posture changing, "you are insulting our employer." Mrs. Barrows was now all special adviser to the president. "I am preparing a bomb," said Mr. Martin, "which will blow the old goat higher than hell." He had only had a little of the drink, which was not strong. It couldn't be that. "Do you take dope or something?" Mrs. Barrows asked coldly. "Heroin," said Mr. Martin. "I'll be coked to the gills when I bump that old buzzard off." "Mr. Martin!" she shouted, getting to her feet. "That will be all of that. You must go at once." Mr. Martin took another swallow of his drink. He tapped his cigarette out in the ashtray and put the pack of Camels on the coffee table. Then he got up. She stood glaring at him. He walked over and put on his hat and coat. "Not a word about this," he said, and laid an index finger against his lips. All Mrs. Barrows could bring out was "Really!" Mr. Martin put his hand on the doorknob. "I'm sitting in the catbird seat," he said. He stuck his tongue out at her and left. Nobody saw him go.

Mr. Martin got to his apartment, walking, well before eleven. No one saw him go in. He had two glasses of milk after brushing his teeth, and he felt elated. It wasn't tipsiness, because he hadn't been tipsy. Anyway, the walk had worn off all effects of the whiskey. He got in bed and read a magazine for a while. He was asleep before midnight.

Mr. Martin got to the office at eight-thirty the next morning, as usual. At a quarter to nine, Ulgine Barrows, who had never before arrived at work before ten, swept into his office. "I'm reporting to Mr. Fitweiler now!" she shouted. "If he turns you over to the police, it's no more than you deserve!" Mr. Martin gave her a look of shocked surprise. "I beg your pardon?" he said. Mrs. Barrows snorted and bounced out of the room, leaving Miss Paird and Joey Hart staring after her. "What's the matter with that old devil now?" asked Miss Paird. "I have no idea," said Mr. Martin, resuming his work. The other two looked at him and then at each other. Miss Paird got up and went out. She walked slowly past the closed door of Mr. Fitweiler's office. Mrs. Barrows was yelling inside, but she was not braying. Miss Paird could not hear what the woman was saying. She went back to her desk.

Forty-five minutes later, Mrs. Barrows left the president's office and went into her own, shutting the door. It wasn't until half an hour later that Mr. Fitweiler sent for Mr. Martin. The head of the filing department, neat, quiet, attentive, stood in front of the old man's desk. Mr. Fitweiler was pale and nervous. He took his glasses off and twiddled them. He made a small, bruffing sound in his throat. "Martin," he said, "you have been with us more than twenty years." "Twenty-two, sir," said Mr. Martin. "In that time," pursued the president, "your work and your—uh—manner have been exemplary." "I trust so, sir," said Mr. Martin. "I have understood, Martin," said Mr. Fitweiler, "that you have never taken a drink or smoked." "That is correct, sir," said Mr. Martin. "Ah, yes." Mr. Fitweiler polished his glasses. "You may describe what you did after leaving the office yesterday, Martin," he said. Mr. Martin allowed less than a second for his bewildered pause. "Certainly, sir," he said. "I walked home. Then I went to Schrafft's for dinner. Afterward I walked home again. I went to bed early, sir, and read a magazine for a while. I was asleep before eleven." "Ah, yes," said Mr. Fitweiler again. He was silent for a moment, searching for the proper words to say to the head of the filing department. "Mrs. Barrows," he said finally, "Mrs. Barrows has worked hard, Martin, very hard. It grieves me to report that she has suffered a severe breakdown. It has taken the form of a persecution complex accompanied by distressing hallucinations." "I am very sorry, sir," said Mr. Martin. "Mrs. Barrows is under the delusion," continued Mr. Fitweiler, "that you visited her last evening and behaved yourself in an—uh—unseemly manner." He raised his hand to silence Mr. Martin's little pained outcry. "It is the nature of these psychological diseases," Mr. Fitweiler said, "to fix upon the least likely and most innocent party as the—uh—source of persecution. These matters are not for the lay mind to grasp, Martin. I've just had my psychiatrist, Dr. Fitch, on the phone. He would not, of course, commit himself, but he made enough generalizations to substantiate my suspicions. I suggested to Mrs. Barrows, when she had completed her—uh—story to me this morning, that she visit Dr. Fitch, for I suspected a condition at once. She flew, I regret to say, into a rage, and demanded—uh—requested that I call you on the carpet. You may not know, Martin, but Mrs. Barrows had planned a reorganization of your department—subject to my approval, of course, subject to my approval. This brought you, rather than anyone else, to her mind—but again that is a phenomenon for Dr. Fitch and not for us. So, Martin, I am afraid Mrs. Barrows' usefulness here is at an end." "I am dreadfully sorry, sir," said Mr. Martin.

It was at this point that the door to the office blew open with the suddenness of a gas-main explosion and Mrs. Barrows catapulted through it. "Is the little rat denying

it?" she screamed. "He can't get away with that!" Mr. Martin got up and moved discreetly to a point beside Mr. Fitweiler's chair. "You drank and smoked at my apartment," she bawled at Mr. Martin, "and you know it! You called Mr. Fitweiler an old
windbag and said you were going to blow him up when you got coked to the gills on
your heroin!" She stopped yelling to catch her breath and a new glint came into her
popping eyes. "If you weren't such a drab, ordinary little man," she said, "I'd think
you'd planned it all. Sticking your tongue out, saying you were sitting in the catbird
seat, because you thought no one would believe me when I told it! My God, it's really
too perfect!" She brayed loudly and hysterically, and the fury was on her again. She
glared at Mr. Fitweiler. "Can't you see how he has tricked us, you old fool? Can't you
see his little game?" But Mr. Fitweiler had been surreptitiously pressing all the buttons
under the top of his desk and employees of F & S began pouring into the room.
"Stockton," said Mr. Fitweiler, "you and Fishbein will take Mrs. Barrows to her home.
Mrs. Powell, you will go with them." Stockton, who had played a little football in
high school, blocked Mrs. Barrows as she made for Mr. Martin. It took him and Fishbein together to force her out of the door into the hall, crowded with stenographers
and office boys. She was still screaming imprecations at Mr. Martin, tangled and contradictory imprecations. The hubbub finally died out down the corridor.

"I regret that this has happened," said Mr. Fitweiler. "I shall ask you to dismiss it
from your mind, Martin." "Yes, sir," said Mr. Martin, anticipating his chief's "That
will be all" by moving to the door. "I will dismiss it." He went out and shut the
door, and his step was light and quick in the hall. When he entered his department
he had slowed down to his customary gait, and he walked quietly across the room to
the W20 file, wearing a look of studious concentration.

A TRIP TO CZARDIS

EDWIN GRANBERRY (1897–   )

It was still dark in the pine woods when the two brothers awoke. But it was plain
that day had come, and in a little while there would be no more stars. Day itself would
be in the sky and they would be getting along the road. Jim waked first, coming
quickly out of sleep and sitting up in the bed to take fresh hold of the things in his
head, starting them up again out of the corners of his mind where sleep had tucked
them. Then he waked Daniel and they sat up together in the bed. Jim put his arm
around his young brother, for the night had been dewy and cool with the swamp wind.
Daniel shivered a little and whimpered, it being dark in the room and his baby concerns still on him somewhat, making sleep heavy on his mind and slow to give understanding its way.

"Hit's the day, Dan'l. This day that's right here now, we are goen. You'll recollect
it all in a minute."

"I recollect. We are goen in the wagon to see papa—"

"Then hush and don't whine."

"I were dreamen, Jim."

"What dreamen did you have?"

"I can't tell. But it were fearful what I dreamt."

"All the way we are goen this time. We won't stop at any places, but we will go all the way to Czardis to see papa. I never see such a place as Czardis."

"I recollect the water tower—"

"Not in your own right, Dan'l. Hit's by my tellen it you see it in your mind."

"And lemonade with ice in it I saw—"

"That too I seen and told to you."

"Then I never seen it at all?"

"Hit's me were there, Dan'l. I let you play like, but hit's me who went to Czardis. Yet I never till this day told half how much I see. There's sights I never told."

They stopped talking, listening for their mother's stir in the kitchen. But the night stillness was unlifted. Daniel began to shiver again.

"Hit's dark," he said.

"Hit's your eyes stuck," Jim said. "Would you want me to drip a little water on your eyes?"

"Oh!" cried the young one, pressing his face into his brother's side, "don't douse me, Jim, no more. The cold aches me."

The other soothed him, holding him around the body.

"You won't have e're chill or malarie ache today, Dan'l. Hit's a fair day—"

"I won't be cold?"

"Hit's a bright day. I hear mournen doves starten a'ready. The sun will bake you warm. . . . Uncle Holly might buy us somethen new to eat in Czardis."

"What would it be?"

"Hit ain't decided yet. . . . He hasn't spoke. Hit might be somethen sweet. Maybe a candy ball fixed on to a rubber string."

"A candy ball!" Daniel showed a stir of happiness. "Oh, Jim!" But it was deceit of the imagination, making his eyes shine wistfully; the grain of his flesh was against it. He settled into a stillness by himself.

"My stomach would retch it up, Jim. . . . I guess I couldn't eat it."

"You might could keep a little down."

"No. . . . I would bring it home and keep it. . . ."

Their mother when they went to bed had laid a clean pair of pants and a waist for each on the chair. Jim crept out of bed and put on his clothes, then aided his brother on with his. They could not hear any noise in the kitchen, but hickory firewood burning in the kitchen stove worked a smell through the house, and in the forest guinea fowls were sailing down from the trees and poking their way along the half-dark ground toward the kitchen steps, making it known the door was open and that within someone was stirring about at the getting of food.

Jim led his brother by the hand down the dark way of yellow-pine stairs that went narrowly and without banisters to the rooms below. The young brother went huddling in his clothes, ague-like, knowing warmth was near, hungering for his place by the stove, to sit in peace on the bricks in the floor by the stove's side and watch the eating, it being his nature to have a sickness against food.

They came in silence to the kitchen, Jim leading and holding his brother by the hand. The floor was lately strewn with fresh bright sand and that would sparkle when the day-break got above the forest, though now it lay dull as hoarfrost and cold to the unshod feet of the brothers. The door to the firebox of the stove was open and in front of it their mother sat in a chair speaking low as they entered, muttering under her breath. The two boys went near and stood still, thinking she was blessing the food.

there being mush dipped up and steaming in two bowls. And they stood cast down until she lifted her eyes to them and spoke.

"Your clothes on already," she said. "You look right neat." She did not rise, but kept her chair, looking cold and stiff, with the cloth of her black dress sagging between her knees. The sons stood in front of her and she laid her hand on first one head and then the other and spoke a little about the day, charging them to be sober and of few words, as she had raised them.

Jim sat on the bench by the table and began to eat, mixing dark molasses sugar through his bowl of mush. But a nausea began in Daniel's stomach at the sight of the sweet and he lagged by the stove, gazing at the food as it passed into his brother's mouth.

Suddenly a shadow filled the back doorway and Holly, their uncle, stood there looking in. He was lean and big and dark from wind and weather, working in the timber as their father had done. He had no wife and children and would roam far off with the timber gangs in the Everglades. This latter year he did not go far, but stayed near them. Their mother stopped and looked at the man and he looked at her in silence. Then he looked at Jim and Daniel.

"You're goen to take them after all?"

She waited a minute, seeming to get the words straight in her mind before bringing them out, making them say what was set there.

"He asked to see them. Nobody but God-Almighty ought to tell a soul hit can or can't have."

Having delivered her mind, she went out into the yard with the man and they spoke more words in an undertone, pausing in their speech.

In the silence of the kitchen, Daniel began to speak out and name what thing among his possessions he would take to Czardis to give his father. But the older boy belittled this and that and everything that was called up, saying one thing was of too little consequence for a man, and that another was of no account because it was food. But when the older boy had abolished the idea and silence had regained, he worked back to the thought, coming to it roundabout and making it new as his own, letting it be decided that each of them would take their father a pomegranate from the tree in the yard.

They went to the kitchen door. The swamp fog had risen suddenly. They saw their mother standing in the lot while their uncle hitched the horse to the wagon. Leaving the steps, Jim climbed to the first crotch of the pomegranate tree. The reddest fruits were on the top branches. He worked his way higher. The fog was now curling up out of the swamp, making gray mountains and rivers in the air and strange ghost shapes. Landmarks disappeared in the billows, or half-seen, they bewildered the sight and an eye could so little mark the known or strange that a befuddlement took hold of the mind, like the visitations sailors beheld in the fogs of Okeechobee. Jim could not find the ground. He seemed to have climbed into the mountains. The light was unnatural and dark and the pines were blue and dark over the mountains.

A voice cried out of the fog:

"Are worms gnawen you that you skin up a pomegranate tree at this hour? Don't I feed you enough?"

The boy worked his way down. At the foot of the tree he met his mother. She squatted and put her arm around him, her voice tight and quivering, and he felt tears on her face.

"We ain't come to the shame yet of you and Dan'l hunten your food off trees and grass. People seein' you gnawen on the road will say Jim Cameron's sons are starved, foragen like cattle of the field."

"I were getten the pomegranates for papa," said the boy, resigned to his mother's concern. She stood up when he said this, holding him in front of her skirts. In a while she said:

"I guess we won't take any, Jim. . . . But I'm proud it come to you to take your papa somethen."

And after a silence, the boy said:

"Hit were Dan'l it come to, Mamma."

Then she took his hand, not looking down, and in her throat, as if in her bosom, she repeated:

"Hit were a fine thought and I'm right proud . . . though to-day we won't take anything. . . ."

"I guess there's better pomegranates in Czardis where we are goen—"

"There's no better pomegranates in Czardis than right here over your head," she said grimly. "If pomegranates were needed, we would take him his own. . . . You are older'n Dan'l, Jim. When we get to the place we are goen, you won't know your papa after so long. He will be pale, and he won't be as bright as you recollect. So don't labor him with questions but speak when it behooves you and let him see you are upright."

When the horse was harnessed and all was ready for the departure, the sons were seated on the shallow bed of hay in the back of the wagon and the mother took the driver's seat alone. The uncle had argued for having the top up over the seat, but she refused the shelter, remarking that she had always driven under the sky and would still do it today. He gave in silently and got upon the seat of his own wagon, which took the road first, their wagon following. This was strange and the sons asked:

"Why don't we all ride in Uncle Holly's wagon?"

But their mother made no reply.

For several miles they traveled in silence through their own part of the woods, meeting no one. The boys whispered a little to themselves, but their mother and their uncle sat without speaking, nor did they turn their heads to look back. At last the narrow road they were following left the woods and came out to the highway and it was seen that other wagons besides their own were going to Czardis. And as they got farther along, they began to meet many other people going to town, and the boys asked their mother what day it was. It was Wednesday. And then they asked her why so many wagons were going along the road if it wasn't Saturday and a market day. When she told them to be quiet, they settled down to watching the people go by. Some of them were faces that were strange and some of them were neighbors who lived in other parts of the woods. Some who passed them stared in silence and some went by looking straight to the front. But there were none of them who spoke, for their mother turned her eyes neither right nor left, but drove the horse on like a woman in her sleep. All was silent as the wagons passed, except the squeaking of the wheels and the thud of the horses' hoofs on the dry, packed sand.

At the edge of the town, the crowds increased and their wagon got lost in the press of people. All were moving in one direction.

Finally they were going along by a high brick wall on top of which ran a barbed-wire fence. Farther along the way in the middle of the wall was a tall, stone building with many people in front. There were trees along the outside of the wall and in the branches of one of the trees Daniel saw a man. He was looking over the brick wa.'

down into the courtyard. All the wagons were stopping here and hitching through the grove in front of the building. But their Uncle Holly's wagon and their own drove on, making way slowly as through a crowd at a fair, for under the trees knots of men were gathered, talking in undertone. Daniel pulled at his mother's skirts and whispered:

"What made that man climb up that tree?"

Again she told him to be quiet.

"We're not to talk today," said Jim. "Papa is sick and we're not to make him worse." But his high, thin voice made his mother turn cold. She looked back and saw he had grown pale and still, staring at the iron-barred windows of the building. When he caught her gaze, his chin began to quiver and she turned back front to dodge the knowledge of his eyes.

For the two wagons had stopped now and the uncle gotten down and left them sitting alone while he went to the door of the building and talked with a man standing there. The crowd fell silent, staring at their mother.

"See, Jim, all the men up the trees!" Daniel whispered once more, leaning close in to his brother's side.

"Hush, Dan'l. Be still."

The young boy obeyed this time, falling into a bewildered stare at all the things about him he did not understand, for in all the trees along the brick wall men began to appear perched high in the branches, and on the roof of a building across the way stood other men, all gaping at something in the yard back of the wall.

Their uncle returned and hitched his horse to a ring in one of the trees. Then he hitched their mother's horse and all of them got out and stood on the ground in a huddle. The walls of the building rose before them. Strange faces at the barred windows laughed aloud and called down curses at the men below.

Now they were moving, with a wall of faces on either side of them, their uncle going first, followed by their mother who held to each of them by a hand. They went up the steps of the building. The door opened and their uncle stepped inside. He came back in a moment and all of them went in and followed a man down a corridor and into a bare room with two chairs and a wooden bench. A man in a black robe sat on one of the chairs, and in front of him on the bench, leaning forward looking down between his arms, sat their father. His face was lean and gray, which made him look very tall. But his hair was black, and his eyes were blue and mild and strange as he stood up and held his two sons against his body while he stooped his head to kiss their mother. The man in black left the room and walked up and down outside in the corridor. A second stranger stood in the doorway with his back to the room. The father picked up one of the sons and then the other in his arms and looked at them and leaned their faces on his own. Then he sat down on the bench and held them against him. Their mother sat down beside them and they were all together.

A few low words were spoken and then a silence fell over them all. And in a little while the parents spoke a little more and touched one another. But the bare stone floor and the stone walls and the unaccustomed arms of their father hushed the sons with the new and strange. And when the time had passed, the father took his watch from his pocket:

"I'm goen to give you my watch, Jim. You are the oldest. I want you to keep it till you are a grown man. . . . And I want you to always do what mamma tells you. . . . I'm goen to give you the chain, Dan'l. . . ."

The young brother took the chain, slipped out of his father's arms, and went to his mother with it. He spread it out on her knee and began to talk to her in a whisper. She bent over him, and again all of them in the room grew silent.

A sudden sound of marching was heard in the corridor. The man rose up and took his sons in his arms, holding them abruptly. But their uncle, who had been standing with the man in the doorway, came suddenly and took them and went out and down through the big doorway by which they had entered the building. As the doors opened to let them pass, the crowd gathered round the steps pressed forward to look inside. The older boy cringed in his uncle's arms. His uncle turned and stood with his back to the crowd. Their mother came through the doors. The crowd fell back. Again through a passageway of gazing eyes, they reached the wagons. This time they sat on the seat beside their mother. Leaving their uncle and his wagon behind, they started off on the road that led out of town.

"Is papa coming home with Uncle Holly?" Jim asked in a still voice.

His mother nodded her head.

Reaching the woods once more and the silence he knew, Daniel whispered to his brother:

"We got a watch and chain instead, Jim."

But Jim neither answered nor turned his eyes.

TWO FRIENDS *

GUY de MAUPASSANT (1850–1893)

Paris was besieged, famished, in its death agony. Sparrows had become scarcer and scarcer on the roof-tops and the sewers were being depopulated. People ate anything they could get.

As he was strolling sadly along the outer boulevard one bright January morning, his hands in his pockets and his stomach empty, M. Morissot, watchmaker by trade but militiaman through circumstances, stopped short before a brother-in-arms whom he recognized as a friend. It was M. Sauvage, a riverside acquaintance.

Every Sunday, before the war, Morissot would set out at dawn with a bamboo rod in his hand and a tin box at his back. He would take the Argenteuil train, get off at Colombes, and make his way to Marante Island. The moment he reached this place of his dreams he would start fishing; and he would keep on fishing until nightfall.

Every Sunday he would meet there a stout, jovial little man, M. Sauvage, a haberdasher in Rue Notre-Dame-de-Lorette, another devout fisherman. They often spent half a day side by side, line in hand and feet dangling above the stream; and they had taken a liking for each other.

Some days they never spoke. Sometimes they would chat; but they understood each other perfectly without saying a word, for their tastes were similar and their feelings identical.

On spring mornings towards ten o'clock, when the early sun was drawing up from the quiet river those wisps of haze which glide downstream above the water, and was pouring down its spring warmth on the backs of the two fanatical anglers, Morissot

* Translation by R. E. Watters.

would sometimes say to his neighbor, "Nice, isn't it?" and M. Sauvage would answer, "I know nothing better." And that was enough for them to understand and value each other.

In autumn, towards evening, when the sky, blood red from the setting sun, would cast reflections of its scarlet clouds on the water, empurpling the whole river, enflaming the horizon, making the two friends look as red as fire, and gilding the trees which were already crimsoned and beginning to shiver with a wintry chill, M. Sauvage would look at Morissot with a smile and say, "There's a sight for you!" And Morissot, lost in astonishment, would answer, "Better than the boulevard, isn't it?" without lifting his eyes from his float.

On this morning, as soon as they had recognized each other, they shook hands vigorously, very much moved at meeting under such changed circumstances. M. Sauvage, with a sigh, muttered, "What goings-on!" Morissot groaned dismally: "And such weather! Today's the first fine day of the year."

The sky was, indeed, blue and brilliant.

They began to walk on side by side, two sorrowful dreamers. Morissot spoke again. "And fishing! Ah! Nothing but a beautiful memory."

"When'll we get back to it?" asked M. Sauvage.

They went into a little café and had an absinthe together, then resumed their stroll along the sidewalks.

Suddenly Morissot stopped. "Another one, eh?" M. Sauvage agreed: "If you wish." And they entered another wine-shop.

On leaving they felt giddy, muddled, as a man does after drinking on an empty stomach. The day was mild. A caressing breeze touched their faces.

M. Sauvage, whom the warm air had made quite tipsy, stopped short. "What if we go?"

"Go where?"

"Fishing, of course."

"But where?"

"Why, to our island. The French outposts are near Colombes. I know Colonel Dumoulin. They'll let us through without any difficulty."

Morissot shivered in his eagerness: "It's a go! I'm with you." And they separated, to get their tackle.

An hour later they were walking side by side along the highway. In a little while they reached the villa occupied by the Colonel. He smiled at their request and agreed to their whim. They started off again armed with a pass.

Soon they passed the outposts, went through the deserted village of Colombes, and found themselves on the edge of the little vineyards which slope towards the Seine. It was about eleven o'clock.

In front of them, the village of Argenteuil seemed dead. The heights of Orgemont and Sannois dominated the whole countryside. The great plain which stretches as far as Nanterre was empty, absolutely empty, with its leafless cherry trees and its gray soil.

Pointing up to the heights, M. Sauvage murmured, "The Prussians are up there!" And a feeling of uneasiness paralyzed the two friends as they beheld this deserted countryside.

"The Prussians!" They had never seen any, but for months they had felt their presence, around Paris, ruining France, plundering, massacring, starving the country, invisible and all-powerful. And a kind of superstitious terror was now added to the hatred they felt for these unknown and victorious people.

Morissot stammered, "Say, suppose we meet some of them?"

M. Sauvage answered with that Parisian jauntiness which nothing can entirely quench: "We'll offer them some fried fish."

But they hesitated to venture into the open, frightened by the silence all about them.

Finally M. Sauvage came to a decision: "Come on! Let's go! But cautiously." And they made their way down into a vineyard, bent double, crawling, taking advantage of thickets to screen themselves, eyes alert, ears straining.

A strip of bare ground had to be crossed to reach the river's edge. They took it on the run, and when they gained the bank they sank down among the dry reeds.

Morissot put his ear to the ground to listen for sounds of anyone walking in the vicinity. He heard nothing. They were alone, utterly alone.

Reassured, they set about fishing.

Across from them Marante Island, deserted, concealed them from the other bank. The little building which had been a restaurant was shut up and looked as if it had been abandoned for years.

M. Sauvage caught the first gudgeon, Morissot got the second, and, from then on, every minute or two they pulled in their lines with a silvery little creature writhing on the end. It was a truly miraculous catch of fish.

Gently they slipped the fish into a sack made of fine net which they hung in the water at their feet. And a delightful happiness pervaded their whole being, the happiness which takes hold of you when you rediscover a cherished pleasure of which you have been deprived for a long time.

The good sun was pouring down its warmth on their shoulders. They no longer listened for anything; they no longer thought about anything; they dismissed the rest of the world.—They were fishing!

But suddenly a heavy noise which seemed to come from underground made the earth tremble. The cannon were beginning to thunder.

Morissot turned his head, and above the bank to the left he saw the great silhouette of Mount Valerien wearing a white plume on its brow—powder-smoke which it had just spat out.

And at once a second puff of smoke rose from the summit of the fortress, and a few moments later a new explosion rumbled.

Then others followed, and time after time the mountain belched forth its death-dealing breath, exhaling milky-white vapor which rose slowly into the calm sky and formed a cloud above the summit.

M. Sauvage shrugged his shoulders. "There they go again," he said.

Morissot, who was anxiously watching his feathered float bob up and down, was suddenly seized by the wrath of a peace-loving man against madmen who fight. He growled, "What crazy fools to kill one another like that."

M. Sauvage answered, "They're worse than animals."

And Morissot, who had just pulled in a young herring, went on, "And to think that it will always be like this as long as there are governments."

M. Sauvage stopped him. "The Republic wouldn't have declared war—"

Morissot interrupted. "Under kings you have war abroad; under the Republic you have war at home."

And placidly they started talking, clearing up great political problems with the healthy good sense of easy-going, limited individuals, and coming to agreement on this point—that men would never be free. And Mount Valerien thundered on, demolishing French homes with its cannon, crushing out lives, putting an end to many a dream, to many a long-awaited joy, to many a hoped-for happiness, planting in the hearts of wives, of girls, of mothers, over there in other lands, suffering that would never end.

"That's life for you," asserted M. Sauvage.

"You'd better say 'That's death for you,'" replied Morissot with a laugh.

But an instant later they were shuddering with fright, for they suddenly sensed that someone had come up behind them. Looking around, they saw, standing almost at their elbows, four men, four big men, armed and bearded, dressed like liveried servants, with flat caps on their heads. They held four rifles at the ready.

The two fishing lines dropped from their hands and started to float away down stream.

In a few seconds they were seized, tied up, carried off, tossed into a boat, and taken over to the island.

And behind the building which they had thought abandoned they saw a score of German soldiers.

A kind of hairy giant, seated astride a chair and smoking a huge porcelain pipe, asked them in excellent French, "Well, gentlemen, was the fishing good?"

Just then a soldier put down at the officer's feet the sack full of fish which he had carefully brought along. The Prussian smiled. "Aha! I see that it wasn't too bad. But we have other matters to think of. Listen to me and don't get upset.

"As far as I know, you are two spies sent to keep an eye on me. I catch you and I shoot you. You have fallen into my hands—so much the worse for you. War's like that.

"But—since you came through the outposts you have, of course, the password in order to return. Give me that password and I will let you off."

The two friends, side by side and dead-white, kept silent, but a slight nervous trembling shook their hands.

The officer continued: "No one will ever know. You will go back in peace. The secret will vanish with you. If you refuse, it is immediate death. Take your choice."

They stood motionless, mouths shut.

The Prussian, waving his hand towards the river, went on, still calmly: "Remember that within five minutes you will be at the bottom of that river. Within five minutes! I suppose you have relatives?"

Mount Valerien was still thundering.

The two fishermen stood erect and silent. The German gave some orders in his own language. Then he moved his chair so as not to be too near the prisoners, and twelve men took their stand, twenty paces distant, rifles at rest.

The officer resumed: "I give you one minute, but not two seconds longer."

Then he rose suddenly, approached the two Frenchmen, took Morissot by the arm, drew him aside and said in a low voice, "Quick, the password? Your friend won't know. I'll pretend to relent."

Morissot answered not a word.

The Prussian drew M. Sauvage aside and put the same question.

M. Sauvage did not answer.

They found themselves side by side again.

And the officer began to give commands. The soldiers raised their rifles.

Then Morissot's glance happened to fall on the sack full of gudgeons which was lying on the grass a few steps away.

A ray of sunlight was gleaming on the little pile of still quivering fish. And weakness filled him. In spite of his efforts his eyes flooded with tears.

He stammered, "Good-bye, Monsieur Sauvage."

M. Sauvage answered, "Good-bye, Monsieur Morissot."

They shook hands, shaken from head to foot with a trembling they could not control. The officer shouted "Fire!"

The twelve shots rang as one.

M. Sauvage fell on his face, like a log. Morissot, who was taller, swayed, turned about, and fell across his comrade, his face to the sky, while the blood gushed from the breast of his riddled tunic.

The German gave further orders.

His men scattered, then returned with ropes and stones which they tied to the feet of the dead men. Then they carried them to the bank.

Mount Valerien continued to roar, its summit now crowned with a mountainous cloud of smoke.

Two soldiers took Morissot by the head and legs, two others seized M. Sauvage the same way. The two bodies, swung powerfully to and fro for a moment, were hurled far out; they described an arc and plunged upright into the river, for the stones pulled them in feet first.

The water splashed, boiled, trembled, then grew calm, while tiny wavelets widened to both banks.

A little blood floated on the surface.

The officer, unruffled as ever, spoke half aloud: "Now the fish will get their turn."

Then he went back towards the house.

All at once he caught sight of the sack of gudgeons in the grass. He picked it up, looked at it, smiled, shouted "Wilhelm!"

A soldier in a white apron ran out. And the Prussian, tossing him the catch of the two dead men, issued a command: "Fry these little creatures right away while they're still alive. They'll be delicious."

Then he resumed his smoking.

A LITTLE CLOUD

JAMES JOYCE (1882–1941)

Eight years before he had seen his friend off at the North Wall and wished him godspeed. Gallaher had got on. You could tell that at once by his travelled air, his well-cut tweed suit, and fearless accent. Few fellows had talents like his and fewer still could remain unspoiled by such success. Gallaher's heart was in the right place and he had deserved to win. It was something to have a friend like that.

Little Chandler's thoughts ever since lunchtime had been of his meeting with Gallaher, of Gallaher's invitation and of the great city London where Gallaher lived. He was called Little Chandler because, though he was but slightly under the average stature, he gave one the idea of being a little man. His hands were white and small, his frame was fragile, his voice was quiet and his manners were refined. He took the greatest care of his fair silken hair and moustache and used perfume discreetly on his handkerchief. The half-moons of his nails were perfect and when he smiled you caught a glimpse of a row of childish white teeth.

As he sat at his desk in the King's Inns he thought what changes those eight years had brought. The friend whom he had known under a shabby and necessitous guise had become a brilliant figure on the London Press. He turned often from his tiresome writing to gaze out of the office window. The glow of a late autumn sunset covered the grass plots and walks. It cast a shower of kindly golden dust on the untidy nurses and decrepit old men who drowsed on the benches; it flickered upon all the moving figures—on the children who ran screaming along the gravel paths and on everyone who passed through the gardens. He watched the scene and thought of life; and (as always happened when he thought of life) he became sad. A gentle melancholy took possession of him. He felt how useless it was to struggle against fortune, this being the burden of wisdom which the ages had bequeathed to him.

He remembered the books of poetry upon his shelves at home. He had bought them in his bachelor days and many an evening, as he sat in the little room off the hall, he had been tempted to take one down from the bookshelf and read out something to his wife. But shyness had always held him back; and so the books had remained on their shelves. At times he repeated lines to himself and this consoled him.

When his hour had struck he stood up and took leave of his desk and of his fellow-clerks punctiliously. He emerged from under the feudal arch of the King's Inns, a neat modest figure, and walked swiftly down Henrietta Street. The golden sunset was waning and the air had grown sharp. A horde of grimy children populated the street. They stood or ran in the roadway or crawled up the steps before the gaping doors or squatted like mice upon the thresholds. Little Chandler gave them no thought. He picked his way deftly through all that minute vermin-like life and under the shadow of the gaunt spectral mansions in which the old nobility of Dublin had roystered. No memory of the past touched him, for his mind was full of a present joy.

He had never been in Corless's but he knew the value of the name. He knew that people went there after the theatre to eat oysters and drink liqueurs; and he had heard that the waiters there spoke French and German. Walking swiftly by at night he had seen cabs drawns up before the door and richly dressed ladies, escorted by cavaliers, alight and enter quickly. They wore noisy dresses and many wraps. Their faces were powdered and they caught up their dresses, when they touched earth, like alarmed Atalantas. He had always passed without turning his head to look. It was his habit to walk swiftly in the street even by day and whenever he found himself in the city late at night he hurried on his way apprehensively and excitedly. Sometimes, however, he courted the causes of his fear. He chose the darkest and narrowest streets and, as he walked boldly forward, the silence that was spread about his footsteps troubled him, the wandering, silent figures troubled him; and at times a sound of low fugitive laughter made him tremble like a leaf.

He turned to the right towards Capel Street. Ignatius Gallaher on the London Press! Who would have thought it possible eight years before? Still, now that he reviewed the past, Little Chandler could remember many signs of future greatness in his friend. People used to say that Ignatius Gallaher was wild. Of course, he did mix with a rakish set of fellows at that time, drank freely and borrowed money on all sides. In the end he had got mixed up in some shady affair, some money transaction: at least, that was one version of his flight. But nobody denied him talent. There was always a certain . . . something in Ignatius Gallaher that impressed you in spite of yourself. Even when he was out at elbows and at his wits' end for money he kept up a bold face. Little Chandler remembered (and the remembrance brought a slight flush of pride to his cheek) one of Ignatius Gallaher's sayings when he was in a tight corner:

"Half time now, boys," he used to say lightheartedly. "Where's my considering cap?"

That was Ignatius Gallaher all out; and, damn it, you couldn't but admire him for it.

Little Chandler quickened his pace. For the first time in his life he felt himself superior to the people he passed. For the first time his soul revolted against the dull inelegance of Capel Street. There was no doubt about it: if you wanted to succeed you had to go away. You could do nothing in Dublin. As he crossed Grattan Bridge he looked down the river towards the lower quays and pitied the poor stunted houses. They seemed to him a band of tramps, huddled together along the river-banks, their old coats covered with dust and soot, stupefied by the panorama of sunset and waiting for the first chill of night to bid them arise, shake themselves and begone. He wondered whether he could write a poem to express his idea. Perhaps Gallaher might be able to get it into some London paper for him. Could he write something original? He was not sure what idea he wished to express but the thought that a poetic moment had touched him took life within him like an infant hope. He stepped onward bravely.

Every step brought him nearer to London, farther from his own sober inartistic life. A light began to tremble on the horizon of his mind. He was not so old— thirty-two. His temperament might be said to be just at the point of maturity. There were so many different moods and impressions that he wished to express in verse. He felt them within him. He tried to weigh his soul to see if it was a poet's soul. Melancholy was the dominant note of his temperament, he thought, but it was a melancholy tempered by recurrences of faith and resignation and simple joy. If he could give expression to it in a book of poems perhaps men would listen. He would never be popular: he saw that. He could not sway the crowd but he might appeal to a little circle of kindred minds. The English critics, perhaps, would recognise him as one of the Celtic school by reason of the melancholy tone of his poems; besides that, he would put in allusions. He began to invent sentences and phrases from the notice which his book would get. *"Mr. Chandler has the gift of easy and graceful verse."* . . . *"A wistful sadness pervades these poems."* . . . *"The Celtic note."* It was a pity his name was not more Irish-looking. Perhaps it would be better to insert his mother's name before the surname: Thomas Malone Chandler, or better still: T. Malone Chandler. He would speak to Gallaher about it.

He pursued his revery so ardently that he passed his street and had to turn back. As he came near Corless's his former agitation began to overmaster him and he halted before the door in indecision. Finally he opened the door and entered.

The light and noise of the bar held him at the doorways for a few moments. He looked about him, but his sight was confused by the shining of many red and green wine-glasses. The bar seemed to him to be full of people and he felt that the people were observing him curiously. He glanced quickly to right and left (frowning slightly to make his errand appear serious), but when his sight cleared a little he saw that nobody had turned to look at him: and there, sure enough, was Ignatius Gallaher leaning with his back against the counter and his feet planted far apart.

"Hallo, Tommy, old hero, here you are! What is it to be? What will you have? I'm taking whisky: better stuff than we get across the water. Soda? Lithia? No mineral? I'm the same. Spoils the flavour. . . . Here, *garçon*, bring us two halves of malt whisky, like a good fellow. . . . Well, and how have you been pulling along since I saw you last? Dear God, how old we're getting! Do you see any signs of aging in me—eh, what? A little grey and thin on the top—what?"

Ignatius Gallaher took off his hat and displayed a large closely cropped head. His face was heavy, pale and clean-shaven. His eyes, which were of bluish slate-colour, relieved his unhealthy pallor and shone out plainly above the vivid orange tie he wore. Between these rival features the lips appeared very long and shapeless and colourless. He bent his head and felt with two sympathetic fingers the thin hair at the crown. Little Chandler shook his head as a denial. Ignatius Gallaher put on his hat again.

"It pulls you down," he said, "press life. Always hurry and scurry, looking for copy and sometimes not finding it: and then, always to have something new in your stuff. Damn proofs and printers, I say, for a few days. I'm deuced glad, I can tell you, to get back to the old country. Does a fellow good, a bit of a holiday. I feel a ton better since I landed again in dear dirty Dublin. . . . Here you are, Tommy. Water? Say when."

Little Chandler allowed his whisky to be very much diluted.

"You don't know what's good for you, my boy," said Ignatius Gallaher. "I drink mine neat."

"I drink very little as a rule," said Little Chandler modestly. "An odd half-one or so when I meet any of the old crowd: that's all."

"Ah, well," said Ignatius Gallaher, cheerfully, "here's to us and to old times and old acquaintance."

They clinked glasses and drank the toast.

"I met some of the old gang today," said Ignatius Gallaher. "O'Hara seems to be in a bad way. What's he doing?"

"Nothing," said Little Chandler. "He's gone to the dogs."

"But Hogan has a good sit, hasn't he?"

"Yes; he's in the Land Commission."

"I met him one night in London and he seemed to be very flush. . . . Poor O'Hara! Boose, I suppose?"

"Other things, too," said Little Chandler shortly.

Ignatius Gallaher laughed.

"Tommy," he said, "I see you haven't changed an atom. You're the very same serious person that used to lecture me on Sunday mornings when I had a sore head and a fur on my tongue. You'd want to knock about a bit in the world. Have you never been anywhere even for a trip?"

"I've been to the Isle of Man," said Little Chandler.

Ignatius Gallaher laughed.

"The Isle of Man!" he said. "Go to London or Paris: Paris, for choice. That'd do you good."

"Have you seen Paris?"

"I should think I have! I've knocked about there a little."

"And is it really so beautiful as they say?" asked Little Chandler.

He sipped a little of his drink, while Ignatius Gallaher finished his boldly.

"Beautiful?" said Ignatius Gallaher, pausing on the word and on the flavour of his drink. "It's not so beautiful, you know. Of course, it is beautiful. . . . But it's the life of Paris; that's the thing. Ah, there's no city like Paris for gaiety, movement, excitement. . . ."

Little Chandler finished his whisky and, after some trouble, succeeded in catching the barman's eye. He ordered the same again.

"I've been to the Moulin Rouge," Ignatius Gallaher continued when the barman had removed their glasses, "and I've been to all the Bohemian cafés. Hot stuff! Not for a pious chap like you, Tommy."

Little Chandler said nothing until the barman returned with two glasses: then he touched his friend's glass lightly and reciprocated the former toast. He was beginning to feel somewhat disillusioned. Gallaher's accent and way of expressing himself did not please him. There was something vulgar in his friend which he had not observed before. But perhaps it was only the result of living in London amid the bustle and competition of the Press. The old personal charm was still there under this new gaudy manner. And, after all, Gallaher had lived, he had seen the world. Little Chandler looked at his friend enviously.

"Everything in Paris is gay," said Ignatius Gallaher. "They believe in enjoying life —and don't you think they're right? If you want to enjoy yourself properly you must go to Paris. And, mind you, they've a great feeling for the Irish there. When they heard I was from Ireland they were ready to eat me, man."

Little Chandler took four or five sips from his glass.

"Tell me," he said, "is it true that Paris is so . . . immoral as they say?"

Ignatius Gallaher made a catholic gesture with his right arm.

"Every place is immoral," he said. "Of course you do find spicy bits in Paris. Go to one of the students' balls, for instance. That's lively, if you like, when the *cocottes* begin to let themselves loose. You know what they are, I suppose?"

"I've heard of them," said Little Chandler.

Ignatius Gallaher drank off his whisky and shook his head.

"Ah," he said, "you may say what you like. There's no woman like the Parisienne— for style, for go."

"Then it is an immoral city," said Little Chandler, with timid insistence—"I mean, compared with London or Dublin?"

"London!" said Ignatius Gallaher. "It's six of one and half-a-dozen of the other. You ask Hogan, my boy. I showed him a bit about London when he was over there. He'd open your eye. . . . I say, Tommy, don't make punch of that whisky: liquor up."

"No, really. . . ."

"O, come on, another one won't do you any harm. What is it? The same again, I suppose?"

"Well . . . all right."

"*François*, the same again. . . . Will you smoke, Tommy?"

Ignatius Gallaher produced his cigar-case. The two friends lit their cigars and puffed at them in silence until their drinks were served.

"I'll tell you my opinion," said Ignatius Gallaher, emerging after some time from the clouds of smoke in which he had taken refuge, "it's a rum world. Talk of immorality! I've heard of cases—what am I saying?—I've known them: cases of . . . immorality. . . ."

Ignatius Gallaher puffed thoughtfully at his cigar and then, in a calm historian's tone, he proceeded to sketch for his friend some pictures of the corruption which was rife abroad. He summarised the vices of many capitals and seemed inclined to award the palm to Berlin. Some things he could not vouch for (his friends had told him), but of others he had had personal experience. He spared neither rank nor caste. He revealed many of the secrets of religious houses on the Continent and described some of the practices which were fashionable in high society and ended by telling, with details, a story about an English duchess—a story which he knew to be true. Little Chandler was astonished.

"Ah, well," said Ignatius Gallaher, "here we are in old jog-along Dublin where nothing is known of such things."

"How dull you must find it," said Little Chandler, "after all the other places you've seen!"

"Well," said Ignatius Gallaher, "it's a relaxation to come over here, you know. And, after all, it's the old country, as they say, isn't it? You can't help having a certain feeling for it. That's human nature. . . . But tell me something about yourself. Hogan told me you had . . . tasted the joys of connubial bliss. Two years ago, wasn't it?"

Little Chandler blushed and smiled.

"Yes," he said. "I was married last May twelve months."

"I hope it's not too late in the day to offer my best wishes," said Ignatius Gallaher. "I didn't know your address or I'd have done so at the time."

He extended his hand, which Little Chandler took.

"Well, Tommy," he said, "I wish you and yours every joy in life, old chap, and tons of money, and may you never die till I shoot you. And that's the wish of a sincere friend, an old friend. You know that?"

"I know that," said Little Chandler.

"Any youngsters?" said Ignatius Gallaher.

Little Chandler blushed again.

"We have one child," he said.

"Son or daughter?"

"A little boy."

Ignatius Gallaher slapped his friend sonorously on the back.

"Bravo," he said, "I wouldn't doubt you, Tommy."

Little Chandler smiled, looked confusedly at his glass and bit his lower lip with three childishly white front teeth.

"I hope you'll spend an evening with us," he said, "before you go back. My wife will be delighted to meet you. We can have a little music and—"

"Thanks awfully, old chap," said Ignatius Gallaher, "I'm sorry we didn't meet earlier. But I must leave tomorrow night."

"Tonight, perhaps . . . ?"

"I'm awfully sorry, old man. You see I'm over here with another fellow, clever young chap he is too, and we arranged to go to a little card-party. Only for that. . . ."

"O, in that case. . . ."

"But who knows?" said Ignatius Gallaher considerately. "Next year I may take a little skip over here now that I've broken the ice. It's only a pleasure deferred."

"Very well," said Little Chandler, "the next time you come we must have an evening together. That's agreed now, isn't it?"

"Yes, that agreed," said Ignatius Gallaher. "Next year if I come, *parole d'honneur.*"

"And to clinch the bargain," said Little Chandler, "we'll just have one more now."

Ignatius Gallaher took out a large gold watch and looked at it.

"Is it to be the last?" he said. "Because you know, I have an a.p."

"O, yes, positively," said Little Chandler.

"Very well, then," said Ignatius Gallaher, "let us have another one as a *deoc an doruis*—that's good vernacular for a small whisky, I believe."

Little Chandler ordered the drinks. The blush which had risen to his face a few moments before was establishing itself. A trifle made him blush at any time: and now he felt warm and excited. Three small whiskies had gone to his head and Gallaher's strong cigar had confused his mind, for he was a delicate and abstinent person. The adventure of meeting Gallaher after eight years, of finding himself with Gallaher in Corless's surrounded by lights and noise, of listening to Gallaher's stories and of sharing for a brief space Gallaher's vagrant and triumphant life, upset the equipoise of his sensitive nature. He felt acutely the contrast between his own life and his friend's, and it seemed to him unjust. Gallaher was his inferior in birth and education. He was sure that he could do something better than his friend had ever done, or could ever do, something higher than mere tawdry journalism if he only got the chance. What was it that stood in his way? His unfortunate timidity! He wished to vindicate himself in some way, to assert his manhood. He saw behind Gallaher's refusal of his invitation. Gallaher was only patronising him by his friendliness just as he was patronising Ireland by his visit.

The barman brought their drinks. Little Chandler pushed one glass towards his friend and took up the other boldly.

"Who knows?" he said, as they lifted their glasses. "When you come next year I may have the pleasure of wishing long life and happiness to Mr. and Mrs. Ignatius Gallaher."

Ignatius Gallaher in the act of drinking closed one eye expressively over the rim of his glass. When he had drunk he smacked his lips decisively, set down his glass and said:

"No blooming fear of that, my boy. I'm going to have my fling first and see a bit of life and the world before I put my head in the sack—if I ever do."

"Some day you will," said Little Chandler calmly.

Ignatius Gallaher turned his orange tie and slate-blue eyes full upon his friend.

"You think so?" he said.

"You'll put your head in the sack," repeated Little Chandler stoutly, "like everyone else if you can find the girl."

He had slightly emphasised his tone and he was aware that he had betrayed himself; but, though the colour had heightened in his cheek, he did not flinch from his friend's gaze. Ignatius Gallaher watched him for a few moments and then said:

"If ever it occurs, you may bet your bottom dollar there'll be no mooning and spooning about it. I mean to marry money. She'll have a good fat account at the bank or she won't do for me."

Little Chandler shook his head.

"Why, man alive," said Ignatius Gallaher, vehemently, "do you know what it is? I've only to say the word and tomorrow I can have the woman and the cash. You don't believe it? Well, I know it. There are hundreds—what am I saying?—thousands of rich Germans and Jews, rotten with money, that'd only be too glad. . . . You wait a while, my boy. See if I don't play my cards properly. When I go about a thing I mean business, I tell you. You just wait."

He tossed his glass to his mouth, finished his drink and laughed loudly. Then he looked thoughtfully before him and said in a calmer tone:

"But I'm in no hurry. They can wait. I don't fancy tying myself up to one woman, you know."

He imitated with his mouth the act of tasting and made a wry face.

"Must get a bit stale, I should think," he said. . . .

Little Chandler sat in the room off the hall, holding a child in his arms. To save money they kept no servant but Annie's young sister Monica came for an hour or so in the morning and an hour or so in the evening to help. But Monica had gone home long ago. It was a quarter to nine. Little Chandler had come home late for tea and, moreover, he had forgotten to bring Annie home the parcel of coffee from Bewley's. Of course she was in a bad humour and gave him short answers. She said she would do without any tea but when it came near the time at which the shop at the corner closed she decided to go out herself for a quarter of a pound of tea and two pounds of sugar. She put the sleeping child deftly in his arms and said:

"Here. Don't waken him."

A little lamp with a white china shade stood upon the table and its light fell over a photograph which was enclosed in a frame of crumpled horn. It was Annie's photograph. Little Chandler looked at it, pausing at the thin tight lips. She wore the pale blue summer blouse which he had brought her home as a present one Saturday. It had cost him ten and elevenpence; but what an agony of nervousness it had cost him! How he had suffered that day, waiting at the shop door until the shop was empty, standing at the counter and trying to appear at his ease while the girl piled ladies' blouses before him, paying at the desk and forgetting to take up the odd penny of his change, being called back by the cashier, and finally, striving to hide his blushes as he left the shop by examining the parcel to see if it was securely tied. When he brought the blouse home Annie kissed him and said it was very pretty and stylish; but when she heard the price she threw the blouse on the table and said it was a regular swindle to charge ten and elevenpence for it. At first she wanted to take it back but when she tried it on she was delighted with it, especially with the make of the sleeves, and kissed him and said he was very good to think of her.

Hm! . . .

He looked coldly into the eyes of the photograph and they answered coldly. Certainly they were pretty and the face itself was pretty. But he found something mean in it. Why was it so unconscious and ladylike? The composure of the eyes irritated him. They repelled him and defied him: there was no passion in them, no rapture. He thought of what Gallaher had said about rich Jewesses. Those dark Oriental eyes, he thought, how full they are of passion, of voluptuous longing! . . . Why had he married the eyes in the photograph?

He caught himself up at the question and glanced nervously round the room. He found something mean in the pretty furniture which he had bought for his house on the hire system. Annie had chosen it herself and it reminded him of her. It too was prim and pretty. A dull resentment against his life awoke within him. Could he not escape from his little house? Was it too late for him to try to live bravely like Gallaher? Could he go to London? There was the furniture still to be paid for. If he could only write a book and get it published that might open the way for him.

A volume of Byron's poems lay before him on the table. He opened it cautiously with his left hand lest he should waken the child and began to read the first poem in the book:

> Hushed are the winds and still the evening gloom,
> Not e'en a Zephyr wanders through the grove,
> Whilst I return to view my Margaret's tomb
> And scatter flowers on the dust I love.

He paused. He felt the rhythm of the verse about him in the room. How melancholy it was! Could he, too, write like that, express the melancholy of his soul in verse? There were so many things he wanted to describe: his sensation of a few hours before on Grattan Bridge, for example. If he could get back again into that mood. . . .

The child awoke and began to cry. He turned from the page and tried to hush it: but it would not be hushed. He began to rock it to and fro in his arms but its wailing cry grew keener. He rocked it faster while his eyes began to read the second stanza:

> Within this narrow cell reclines her clay,
> That clay where once . . .

It was useless. He couldn't read. He couldn't do anything. The wailing of the child pierced the drum of his ear. It was useless, useless! He was a prisoner for life. His arms trembled with anger and suddenly bending to the child's face he shouted: "Stop!"

The child stopped for an instant, had a spasm of fright and began to scream. He jumped up from his chair and walked hastily up and down the room with the child in his arms. It began to sob piteously, losing its breath for four or five seconds, and then bursting out anew. The thin walls of the room echoed the sound. He tried to soothe it but it sobbed more convulsively. He looked at the contracted and quivering face of the child and began to be alarmed. He counted seven sobs without a break between them and caught the child to his breast in fright. If it died! . . .

The door was burst open and a young woman ran in, panting.

"What is it? What is it?" she cried.

The child, hearing its mother's voice, broke out into a paroxysm of sobbing.

"It's nothing, Annie . . . it's nothing. . . . He began to cry . . ."

She flung her parcels on the floor and snatched the child from him.

"What have you done to him?" she cried, glaring into his face.

Little Chandler sustained for one moment the gaze of her eyes and his heart closed together as he met the hatred in them. He began to stammer.

"It's nothing. . . . He . . . he began to cry. . . . I couldn't . . . I didn't do anything. . . . What?"

Giving no heed to him she began to walk up and down the room, clasping the child tightly in her arms and murmuring:

"My little man! My little mannie! Was 'ou frightened, love? . . . There now, love! There now! . . . Lambabaun! Mamma's little lamb of the world! . . . There now!"

Little Chandler felt his cheeks suffused with shame and he stood back out of the lamplight. He listened while the paroxysm of the child's sobbing grew less and less; and tears of remorse started to his eyes.

THE GLOVES *

COLETTE AUDRY

The hand was superbly gloved—brownish back, fawn-colored palm, and the thumb half and half. The lovely, thick glacé leather was like custard, with the seams so beautifully hand-sewn that it made you want to count the stitches. Though snuggling comfortably, the hand was still nimble in them . . . ideal gloves for riding under the oaks on an autumn day.

The young woman watched her hand as it picked up bits of merchandise on display here and there. As it flexed, the glove stretched lightly over the graceful depressions of the knuckles, then, as the fingers stretched out farther, a completely different network of wrinkles sank across the gloves. They were really too pretty for her overly long hair, and for the tweedy tailored suit which showed signs of wear. From time to time a sales girl would break in: "You wanted something, Madam?"

And the lady would reply, "Thanks, just looking." She had the right to look, the right to touch things, for the movements of her gloves proclaimed a sort of royalty over these shining objects: the perfume bottles, the jars of cosmetics wrapped in cellophane. Even the nonchalance of her well-cut, old tailored suit confirmed her familiarity with luxury, her right to enjoy it carelessly.

But the gloves were just too pretty; irresistibly they drew attention to these hands which presumed to have a life of their own, completely divorced from hers. As if enchanted, they were unaccountable and alarming. Better, perhaps, to try nothing difficult with hands such as these over which you are never sure of mastery.

On a shelf for smokers' needs there was quite a selection of ceramic ash trays. She weighed a large, thick one of gentian blue in her hand; the running enamel had left a little caramel-colored spot on it.

The sales girl was busy . . . "But it's for a gift," the customer was saying, "I can't carry it away in my bare hands."

"Sorry, sir, but we have no more wrapping paper in stock."

Their voices echoed like voices of people in the next room when you're sick in bed.

With the blue ash tray still in her hand, the young woman kept walking between the counters, without slowing up until she came to the revolving door. On the threshold a great gust of fresh air helped her to catch her breath. The November fog had begun to burn off and a milky sunlight bathed the street. She reached her bicycle at the curb and slipped the ash tray into her saddlebag.

Just then, someone above her head said, "Are you quite sure, Madam, that you have paid for what you have there?"

A tall, thin fellow was standing there in front of her with sharp, squinting eyes, wearing a sea-blue sweater and a beret; he seemed a nasty customer. She felt rather stupid answering "No." But that's the way you answer questions sometimes. She said "no" shaking her head and smiling haughtily. The fellow didn't seem to mind a bit. "Come along with me to the manager's," he said.

* Translation by J. Robert Loy.

Crossing the store seemed much longer to her this time than when she had left, and yet, they crossed only about halfway. The man turned to the left, knocked on a door, opened without waiting, and they went in. Behind the desk was a fat, little man about fifty years old. Over the pince-nez the face appeared florid and fastidious, with crescent-like eyes.

"Madam was taking this ash tray along with her without paying for it."

"How's that?" cried the little man. "But there's a name for that sort of thing, Madam."

The same old sentence! At first he had tried to change it from time to time because it bothered him to keep saying the same thing all the time with the police inspector standing there. But now he paid no more attention to his words than he did when he stopped in front of some counter to show a new sales girl how to make a sale. And then, this morning, he was in a peaceful frame of mind, a little sleepy from the heat of the furnace they had just lit; he would have found it difficult to adjust himself to the proper pitch. He seemed to be listening to his own voice as he spoke.

"It's a pretty mess," said the detective, "and it could take you mighty far; you know that, don't you?"

They're trying to scare me, she thought. But they don't arrest you the first time. She had put the ash tray on the desk.

"I'm sorry," she replied.

"Why did you do it?" asked the old fellow.

"He asked you why you did it," shouted the detective. She felt the flush of his eyes like a gash in her skin; he was really furious. "It's a little late to be sorry," he added, lowering his voice. "The high-class women, who think they can get away with anything and think they ought to get thanked for being sorry."

"I made a bet," she said.

The old chap was really bowled over. "A bet?" he asked. "What kind of a bet?"

"Well, I bet I could steal something."

The detective thrust his hands into his pockets so violently that she felt she must explain further—further than she would have believed it possible to go. It was really quite messy, completely unforeseen. "And as you can see," she added sadly, "I couldn't even do it."

But nobody seemed to hear this last confession.

The detective paced the floor. "A bet," he said, "but you don't bet about things like that, you bet about things that might happen."

"But you can," she said abashed. "Why not? I don't see why you can't."

If she had to explain that any further, she wouldn't be up to it. She wiped her forehead with her hand, realizing immediately that that was exactly what everyone does in such a fix. The detective was staring at the well-gloved hand, the dilating nostrils, the half-opened mouth. She felt herself under male scrutiny, which only helped make the situation worse.

The assistant manager caught this cruel stare and felt uneasy about it. To be forced to employ people like that! After all, she was only a poor little woman, and a lady. He decided to hurry things up, then they could give her some peace.

"Do you have any identification on you?" he asked. She rummaged in her hand-bag slowly, on purpose. She would say what she had to, yes, but tremble in front of that crude person . . . she would rather die. The detective went around behind the desk and without apology looked over the old man's shoulder at the identity card. The manager, annoyed, closed it. But the detective had already seen what he wanted.

"You're the wife of M. Franchet, the manufacturer, aren't you?"

"Yes," she said, remembering that on the identification photo she was wearing a sport blouse and a flowing scarf which gave her a triumphant expression.

"That's the last straw!" said the detective.

"Whatever got into you, Madam?" cried the manager. "What's your husband going to say?—because he's going to know. Every day we arrest some of his women workers who plead to us that they have no more clothing ration-points and must have something to wear. Where does that put us if you set them such an example yourself?"

She didn't answer; she was picturing herself as she had come out of the garden in the fog that morning. The bicycle moved by itself, the tires hummed on the hot asphalt. And to have come to the point now where some old employee was preaching a sermon to her! Did he suppose that she played the patronizing great lady with the little working girls?

"Are you going to telephone the police station?" asked the detective.

"Oh, you wouldn't do that!" she begged. She didn't think they would for a minute.

"But I have to, Madam," said the old man. "It's not because we want to, you understand . . ."

"And so we'll likely end up not doing it, huh?" broke in the detective. "That would be too easy."

"But you can't really mean it."

"You'll see about that," he said, going to the telephone without taking his eyes off her. If only that stupid assistant manager weren't there. . . . But he always was, naturally. The same thing every time; you could never go the whole way. If he could only put one hand on the phone and the other . . . she wouldn't dare cry out; she would damned well have understood, she would, with her black market silk stockings. And then, afterwards?—well, telephone all the same. Except with that kind of a woman, she might lodge a complaint. No, no matter how you looked at it, you could never go the whole way.

All of a sudden, she was afraid. That guy with his cutting eyes was capable of phoning just to make an example of her. He was too wound up. And now the old fellow, with his bluish eyes, a little globular like soft-boiled eggs. . . . She felt her eyes shift from one to the other; each time the black eyes cut her, she took refuge in the clear blue-eyes, plunged into their cloudy lustre, but then she was caught there.

"This is the first time this has ever happened to me," she said.

"And how should we know that?" snapped the detective.

She recoiled toward the wall and leaned with her right hand on some shelves. "Careful," said the manager, "they've just painted; it's still wet."

She withdrew her hand madly; there were two little spots on the tawny leather. She began to wipe them with the index finger of her other hand. Then she gave it up, but she did feel grateful that the old man had warned her about the paint just as if she had been anybody else.

"It's my first time," she repeated, "and you can be sure I'm not about to do it again." She was talking to the old fellow now. To him she would say whatever he wanted, for she could appeal to him.

He felt lucky to be chosen. However painful the whole event, things were working out respectably for him. It was between the two of them now, between two cultured people and over the head of the other one, that they would discuss the matter. She had recognized her own class, and was asking his help. Only he must seem firm: the detective made himself so at home there.

"You don't realize the seriousness of your action, Madam," he said, "but it's my duty to call the police."

At that, she spoke of her husband's anger, of her two little children, told him he couldn't do such a thing. And, finally, he was touched. She had been so terse at the beginning, so calm that she seemed hardened, but now, it was all right. He guessed, however, that the detective wasn't cooling off—voracious, great, evil bird that he was. So what! Who was the assistant manager around here, anyhow?

"Please don't do that, sir. I promise you'll see no more of me." In her excitement, she leaned once again on the shelf, then pulled back her hand murmuring sadly, "That's right; I had forgotten—paint."

He was completely awakened now, felt himself becoming well-disposed toward her. "Why did you do it?" he asked.

"I told you it was a bet."

"You don't make bets like that," said the detective.

She closed her eyes, overcome. "With whom did you make this bet?"

"I won't tell you," she cried violently. "You want me to incriminate someone else, is that it? Arrest me if you want to."

At last, she was able to get mad! She hadn't bet with anyone, unless it was with herself. But she was sure that he believed this bet story. Even the other one believed it, and the angrier she got, the more they would believe it. "Go on, arrest me; I'd prefer that."

He thought he may have been a little indelicate; enough was enough. "Well, then, Madam, I'll try to trust you, but you must realize that you can't just walk off like that. This unfortunate event should at least benefit the more unfortunate. You will donate 500 francs to our orphanage."

"Yes," she said, opening her bag.

"In addition to the price of the ash tray which you will pay."

"But I don't want it," she retorted. "I just up and took it! I didn't want it."

"Of all the nerve!" he cried, suddenly furious. "You're going to pay for that ash tray and you're going to take it with you."

He was crimson; she looked at him, stupefied, realized that she had committed some mysterious offense and said hurriedly, "All right, all right."

She opened her wallet. The detective sniggered. The old man pulled out a large ledger. "Write there—500 francs, sign your name." And, when she hesitated, he added, "You can sign illegibly and be sure of our discretion."

She took off her right glove, then, mechanically, the left one and wrote in the ledger. He closed the book. "Now it's about over," she thought. But the old fellow re-opened the identity folder which had remained on the desk and drew out a filing card.

"I'm going to take your name and address."

"Oh no!" she cried, "but you just said. . . ."

"Madam," he continued, "it is absolutely necessary and I can't let you leave without doing so. We always do it. Anyhow this card will be shown to nobody, I give you my word of honor."

In the silence which followed while he recopied the information, she slid to the depths of shame . . . shame for having been caught, but particularly shame for being ashamed in front of these people. She didn't give a damn for what they thought of her. And yet, she had been ashamed because they were grilling her and wanting to punish her. Her cheeks were burning. Oh, how she hated the detective! Just to be able to kill him, wipe him off the face of the earth! Well, she was punished for feeling so proud of herself this morning, punished in the worst possible way.

"There you are," said the old man, giving back her card, "and rest assured that the matter is finished."

"You may leave alone," said the detective. He had been determined to have the last word. She heard *alone* as if he had said *naked*. And so did he.

It was over. But when would thinking about it be over . . . ?

When she had left, the assistant manager pretended to be filing papers. But the detective didn't leave. Hands in his pockets, his thin abdomen protruding, he stood fast in front of a diagram of the store which hung on the wall, absorbed in a contemplation which there was no reason to cut short.

The manager gave in first. "The funny thing," he said distractedly, while examining the bottom of a drawer, "is that it must have been true, that bet story."

"Possible," said the other, turning his head and shoulders slightly. "Anyhow it did her a lot of good."

"What do you mean?" asked the old man drily. Now that she was no longer here, that he no longer had to battle with her, he felt personally affronted by the policeman's attitude. . . . If only the detective hadn't aroused such uneasiness in him!

"Women like that," explained the inspector, "always think that police are not for them. They take us for dogs. Well, she saw. Aha! look there! she forgot her gloves."

They had remained there, side by side, on the table. The detective felt them instinctively, approved with a grimace, took them and drew them part-way onto his fingers while examining the paint spots. Then he shoved them into his pocket.

"What's the idea?" asked the old man, astonished.

"Oh, I can promise you she won't be back looking for them," replied the other walking toward the door.

Someone knocked at the door. "Come in," said the manager. And the young woman appeared.

"Excuse me," she said. "Didn't I leave my gloves here?"

Going through the store again; all those echoes of lost steps; that bluish, glistening atmosphere which was intolerable from now on—she had never done anything so courageous in her life. There was a silence that the detective did not break; he had lost himself again in the diagram.

"Your gloves?" said the old man, finally, absent-mindedly.

"Yes, gloves of two-toned leather, beige and brown. I put them on the table to write and I can't find them."

"I don't see them," said the manager. "Look for yourself."

She swept the table slowly with her eyes, as if a glance were not enough. You could see her pupils moving to and fro. The nakedness of the polished table hid something strange and accusing, like hands held behind the back.

"I put them on the table to sign the book," she said again, "and I don't remember having picked them up again."

"Maybe you dropped them somewhere in the store," said the manager. "Go ask at Lost and Found; it's in Office 4, near the entrance." He felt his hands grow wet and didn't dare wipe them. Here he was, the accomplice of the unscrupulous policeman. He had to protect him and lie without hope of being understood—would perhaps be taken for the thief himself. The detective stopped dead in front of the lady.

"If I were you, I'd go look a little more in my saddlebag," he said. "Or perhaps Madam finds she hasn't seen enough of us."

"You can come see for yourself, and search me," she replied.

She spoke slowly, in low tones. She experienced such relief, such a lightening of heart that everything functioned in her with extreme slowness, like life coming back into the heart of a drowned man. She looked for a moment at the toes of her shoes, then she added, obstinately, "Since I don't remember taking them, I don't see why I wouldn't come back to look for them."

"So all right, then; they're not here," shouted the policeman harshly. "Now, get out!"

She tossed her head back and covered him with a sombre stare. Under her half-closed eyelids her pupils seemed a heavy paste in suspension. If she stayed five more minutes, he would again threaten her with telephoning headquarters. But for the moment, he was powerless against her; she held him under her stare. As for the old fellow, she had forgotten him.

She backed away, easily, put her hand behind her back to open the door, then left, still facing them.

After she had gone, silence fell over the room again. But the assistant manager could no longer stand the presence of that man; he had to show his authority.

"You may go now," he said.

"Right," replied the other, and he left, dragging his feet.

The old man sank back a little in his armchair. There were noises in the pipes of the radiator . . . nearby popping followed by a plaintive ringing in the distance. And behind the door, the shuffling commotion of the store. Again he felt sleepy; his knees were tingling pleasantly. He pulled his file case toward him, looked for the card he had slipped in a few minutes before, and, when he had found it, tore it up, slowly, into very small pieces.

THE BLACK GODMOTHER

JOHN GALSWORTHY (1867-1933)

Sitting out on the lawn at tea with our friend and his retriever, we had been dis-cussing those massacres of the helpless which had of late occurred, and wondering that they should have been committed by the soldiery of so civilized a State, when, in a momentary pause of our astonishment, our friend, who had been listening in silence, crumpling the drooping soft ear of his dog, looked up and said, "The cause of atrocities is generally the violence of Fear. Panic's at the back of most crimes and follies."

Knowing that his philosophical statements were always the result of concrete in-stance, and that he would not tell us what that instance was if we asked him— such being his nature—we were careful not to agree.

He gave us a look out of those eyes of his, so like the eyes of a mild eagle, and said abruptly: "What do you say to this, then? . . . I was out in the dog-days last

year with this fellow of mine, looking for Osmunda, and stayed some days in a village
—never mind the name. Coming back one evening from my tramp, I saw some boys
stoning a mealy-coloured dog. I went up and told the young devils to stop it.
They only looked at me in the injured way boys do, and one of them called out,
'It's mad, guv'ner!' I told them to clear off, and they took to their heels. The dog
followed me. It was a young, leggy, mild-looking mongrel, cross—I should say—
between a brown retriever and an Irish terrier. There was froth about its lips, and
its eyes were watery; it looked indeed as if it might be in distemper. I was afraid
of infection for this fellow of mine, and whenever it came too close shooed it away,
till at last it slunk off altogether. Well, about nine o'clock, when I was settling down
to write by the open window of my sitting-room—still daylight, and very quiet and
warm—there began that most maddening sound, the barking of an unhappy dog. I
could do nothing with that continual 'Yap—yap!' going on, and it was too hot to
shut the window; so I went out to see if I could stop it. The men were all at the pub,
and the women just finished with their gossip; there was no sound at all but the continual barking of this dog, somewhere away out in the fields. I travelled by ear across
three meadows, till I came on a haystack by a pool of water. There was the dog sure
enough—the same mealy-coloured mongrel, tied to a stake, yapping, and making
frantic little runs on a bit of a rusty chain; whirling round and round the stake, then
standing quite still, and shivering. I went up and spoke to it, but it backed into the
hay-stack, and there it stayed shrinking away from me, with its tongue hanging out.
It had been heavily struck by something on the head; the cheek was cut, one eye half-
closed, and an ear badly swollen. I tried to get hold of it, but the poor thing was
beside itself with fear. It snapped and flew round so that I had to give it up and sit
down with this fellow here beside me to try and quiet it—a strange dog, you know,
will generally form his estimate of you from the way it sees you treat another dog. I
had to sit there quite half an hour before it would let me go up to it, pull the stake
out, and lead it away. The poor beast, though it was so feeble from the blows it had
received, was still half-frantic, and I didn't dare to touch it; and all the time I took
good care that this fellow here didn't come too near. Then came the question what
was to be done. There was no vet, of course, and I'd no place to put it except my
sitting-room, which didn't belong to me. But, looking at its battered head, and its
half-mad eyes, I thought: 'No trusting you with these bumpkins; you'll have to come
in here for the night!' Well, I got it in, and heaped two or three of those hairy little
red rugs landladies are so fond of, up in a corner, and got it on to them, and put
down my bread and milk. But it wouldn't eat—its sense of proportion was all gone,
fairly destroyed by terror. It lay there moaning, and every now and then it raised its
head with a 'yap' of sheer fright, dreadful to hear, and bit the air, as if its enemies
were on it again; and this fellow of mine lay in the opposite corner, with his head
on his paw, watching it. I sat up for a long time with that poor beast, sick enough,
and wondering how it had come to be stoned and kicked and battered into this state;
and next day I made it my business to find out." Our friend paused, scanned us a
little angrily, and then went on: "It had made its first appearance, it seems, following
a bicyclist. There are men, you know—save the mark—who, when their beasts get ill
or too expensive, jump on their bicycles and take them for a quick run, taking care
never to look behind them. When they get back home they say: 'Hullo! Where's
Fido?' Fido is nowhere, and that's the end! Well, this poor puppy gave up just as it
got to our village; and, roaming about in search of water, attached itself to a farm

labourer. The man—with excellent intentions, as he told me himself—tried to take hold of it, but too abruptly, so that it was startled, and snapped at him. Whereon he kicked it for a dangerous cur, and it went drifting back towards the village, and fell in with the boys coming home from school. It thought, no doubt, that they were going to kick it too, and nipped one of them who took it by the collar. Thereupon they hullabalooed and stoned it down the road to where I found them. Then I put in my little bit of torture, and drove it away, through fear of infection to my own dog. After that it seems to have fallen in with a man who told me: "Well, you see, he came sneakin' round my house, with the children playin', and snapped at them when they went to stroke him, so that they came running in to their mother, an' she called to me in a fine takin' about a mad dog. I ran out with a shovel and gave 'im one, and drove him out. I'm sorry if he wasn't mad; he looked it right enough. You can't be too careful with strange dogs.' Its next acquaintance was an old stone-breaker, a very decent sort. 'Well! you see,' the old man explained to me, 'the dog come smellin' round my stones, an' it wouldn' come near, an' it wouldn' go away; it was all froth and blood about the jaw, and its eyes glared green at me. I thought to meself, bein' the dog-days—I don't like the look o' you, you look funny! So I took a stone, an' got it here, just on the ear; an' it fell over. And I thought to meself: Well, you've got to finish it, or it'll go bitin' somebody, for sure! But when I come to it with my hammer, the dog it got up—an' you know how it is when there's somethin' you've 'alf killed, and you feel sorry, and yet you feel you must finish it, an' you hit at it blind, you hit at it agen an' agen. The poor thing, it wriggled and snapped, an' I was terrified it'd bit me, an' some'ow it got away.' " Again our friend paused, and this time we dared not look at him.

"The next hospitality it was shown," he went on presently, "was by a farmer, who, seeing it all bloody, drove it off, thinking it had been digging up a lamb that he's just buried. The poor harmless beast came sneaking back, so he told his men to get rid of it. Well, they got hold of it somehow—there was a hole in its neck that looked as if they'd used a pitchfork—and, mortally afraid of its biting them, but not liking, as they told me, to drown it, for fear the owner might come on them, they got a stake and a chain, and fastened it up, and left it in the water by the hay-stack where I found it. I had some conversation with that farmer. 'That's right,' he said, 'but who was to know? I couldn't have my sheep worried. The brute had blood on his muzzle. These curs do a lot of harm when they've once been blooded. You can't run risks.' " Our friend cut viciously at a dandelion with his stick. "Run risks!" he broke out suddenly. "That was it—from beginning to end of that poor beast's sufferings, fear! From that fellow on the bicycle, afraid of the worry and expense, as soon as it showed signs of distemper, to myself and the man with the pitchfolk—not one of us, I daresay, would have gone out of our way to do it a harm. But we felt fear, and so—by the law of self-preservation, or whatever you like—it all began, till there the poor thing was, with a battered head and a hole in its neck, ravenous with hunger, and too distraught even to lap my bread and milk. Yes, there's something uncanny about a suffering animal—we sat watching it, and again we were afraid, looking at its eyes and the way it bit the air. Fear! It's the black godmother of all damnable things!"

Our friend bent down, crumpling and crumpling at his dog's ears. We, too, gazed at the ground, thinking of that poor lost puppy, and the horrible inevitability of all that happens, seeing men are what they are; thinking of all the foul doings in the world, whose black godmother is Fear.

"And what became of the poor dog?" one of us asked at last.

"When," said our friend slowly, "I'd had my fill of watching, I covered it with a rug, took this fellow away with me, and went to bed. There was nothing else to do. At dawn I was awakened by three dreadful cries—not like a dog's at all. I hurried down. There was the poor beast—wriggled out from under the rug—stretched on its side, dead. This fellow of mine had followed me in, and he went and sat down by the body. When I spoke to him he just looked round, and wagged his tail along the ground, but would not come away; and there he sat till it was buried, very interested but not sorry at all."

Our friend was silent, looking angrily at something in the distance.

And we, too, were silent, seeing in spirit that vigil of early morning: The thin, lifeless, sandy-coloured body, stretched on those red mats; and this black creature—now lying at our feet—propped on its haunches like the dog in "The Death of Procris", patient, curious, ungrieved, staring down at it with his bright, interested eyes.

AMY FOSTER

JOSEPH CONRAD (1857–1924)

Kennedy is a country doctor, and lives in Colebrook, on the shores of Eastbay. The high ground rising abruptly behind the red roofs of the little town crowds the quaint High Street against the wall which defends it from the sea. Beyond the sea-wall there curves for miles in a vast and regular sweep the barren beach of shingle, with the village of Brenzett standing out darkly across the water, a spire in a clump of trees; 'and still further out the perpendicular column of a lighthouse, looking in the distance no bigger than a lead-pencil, marks the vanishing-point of the land. The country at the back of Brenzett is low and flat; but the bay is fairly well sheltered from the seas, and occasionally a big ship, windbound or through stress of weather, makes use of the anchoring ground a mile and a half due north from you as you stand at the back door of the "Ship Inn" in Brenzett. A dilapidated windmill near by lifting its shattered arms from a mound no loftier than a rubbish-heap, and a Martello tower squatting at the water's edge half a mile to the south of the Coastguard cottages, are familiar to the skippers of small craft. These are the official sea-marks for the patch of trustworthy bottom represented on the Admiralty charts by an irregular oval of dots enclosing several figures six, with a tiny anchor engraved among them, and the legend "mud and shells" over all.

The brow of the upland overtops the square tower of the Colebrook Church. The slope is green and looped by a white road. Ascending along this road, you open a valley broad and shallow, a wide green trough of pastures and hedges merging inland into a vista of purple tints and flowing lines closing the view.

In this valley down to Brenzett and Colebrook and up to Darnford, the market town fourteen miles away, lies the practice of my friend Kennedy. He had begun life as surgeon in the Navy, and afterwards had been the companion of a famous traveller, in the days when there were continents with unexplored interiors. His papers on the fauna and flora made him known to scientific societies. And now he had come to a country practice—from choice. The penetrating power of his mind, acting like a corrosive fluid, had destroyed his ambition, I fancy. His intelligence is of a scientific order, of an investigating habit, and of that unappeasable curiosity which believes that there is a particle of a general truth in every mystery.

A good many years ago now, on my return from abroad, he invited me to stay with him. I came readily enough, and as he could not neglect his patients to keep me company, he took me on his rounds—thirty miles or so of an afternoon, sometimes. I waited for him on the roads; the horse reached after the leafy twigs, and, sitting high in the dogcart, I could hear Kennedy's laugh through the half-open door of some cottage. He had a big, hearty laugh that would have fitted a man twice his size, a brisk manner, a bronzed face, and a pair of grey, profoundly attentive eyes. He had the talent of making people talk to him freely, and an inexhaustible patience in listening to their tales.

One day, as we trotted out of a large village into a shady bit of road, I saw on our left hand a low, black cottage, with diamond panes in the windows, a creeper on the end wall, a roof of shingle, and some roses climbing on the rickety trellis-work of the tiny porch. Kennedy pulled up to a walk. A woman, in full sunlight, was throwing a dripping blanket over a line stretched between two old apple-trees. And as the bob-tailed, long-necked chestnut, trying to get his head, jerked the left hand, covered by a thick dogskin glove, the doctor raised his voice over the hedge: "How's your child, Amy?"

I had the time to see her dull face, red, not with a mantling blush, but as if her flat cheeks had been vigorously slapped, and to take in the squat figure, the scanty, dusty brown hair drawn into a tight knot at the back of the head. She looked quite young. With a distinct catch in her breath, her voice sounded low and timid.

"He's well, thank you."

We trotted again. "A young patient of yours?" I said; and the doctor, flicking the chestnut absently, muttered, "Her husband used to be."

"She seems a dull creature," I remarked listlessly.

"Precisely," said Kennedy. "She is very passive. It's enough to look at the red hands hanging at the end of those short arms, at those slow, prominent brown eyes to know the inertness of her mind—an inertness that one would think made it ever-lastingly safe from all the surprises of imagination. And yet which of us is safe? At any rate, such as you see her, she had enough imagination to fall in love. She's the daughter of one Isaac Foster, who from a small farmer has sunk into a shepherd; the beginning of his misfortunes dating from his runaway marriage with the cook of his widowed father—a well-to-do, apoplectic grazier, who passionately struck his name off his will, and had been heard to utter threats against his life. But this old affair, scandalous enough to serve as a motive for a Greek tragedy, arose from the similarity of their characters. There are other tragedies, less scandalous and of a subtler poignancy, arising from irreconcilable differences and from that fear of the Incomprehensible that hangs over all our heads—over all our heads. . . ."

The tired chestnut dropped into a walk; and the rim of the sun, all red in a speckless sky, touched familiarly the smooth top of a ploughed rise near the road as I had seen it times innumerable touch the distant horizon of the sea. The uniform brownness of the harrowed field glowed with a rosy tinge, as though the powdered clods had sweated out in minute pearls of blood the toil of uncounted ploughmen. From the edge of a copse a waggon with two horses was rolling gently along the ridge. Raised above our heads upon the sky-line, it loomed up against the red sun, triumphantly big, enormous, like a chariot of giants drawn by two slow-stepping steeds of legendary proportions. And the clumsy figure of the man plodding at the head of the leading horse projected itself on the background of the Infinite with a heroic uncouthness. The end of his carter's whip quivered high up in the blue. Kennedy discoursed.

"She's the eldest of a large family. At the age of fifteen they put her out to service at the New Barns Farm. I attended Mrs. Smith, the tenant's wife, and saw that girl there for the first time. Mrs. Smith, a genteel person with a sharp nose, made her put on a black dress every afternoon. I don't know what induced me to notice her at all. There are faces that call your attention by a curious want of definiteness in their whole aspect, as, walking in a mist, you peer attentively at a vague shape which, after all, may be nothing more curious or strange than a signpost. The only peculiarity I perceived in her was a slight hesitation in her utterance, a sort of preliminary stammer which passes away with the first word. When sharply spoken to, she was apt to lose her head at once; but her heart was of the kindest. She had never been heard to express a dislike for a single human being, and she was tender to every living creature. She was devoted to Mrs. Smith, to Mr. Smith, to their dogs, cats, canaries; and as to Mrs. Smith's grey parrot, its peculiarities exercised upon her a positive fascination. Nevertheless, when that outlandish bird, attacked by the cat, shrieked for help in human accents, she ran out into the yard stopping her ears, and did not prevent the crime. For Mrs. Smith this was another evidence of her stupidity; on the other hand, her want of charm, in view of Smith's well-known frivolousness, was a great recommendation. Her short-sighted eyes would swim with pity for a poor mouse in a trap, and she had been seen once by some boys on her knees in the wet grass helping a toad in difficulties. If it's true, as some German fellow has said, that without phosphorous there is no thought, it is still more true that there is no kindness of heart without a certain amount of imagination. She had some. She had even more than is necessary to understand suffering and to be moved by pity. She fell in love under circumstances that leave no room for doubt in the matter; for you need imagination to form a notion of beauty at all, and still more to discover your ideal in an unfamiliar shape.

"How this aptitude came to her, what it did feed upon, is an inscrutable mystery. She was born in the village, and had never been further away from it than Colebrook or perhaps Darnford. She lived for four years with the Smiths. New Barns is an isolated farmhouse a mile away from the road, and she was content to look day after day at the same fields, hollows, rises; at the trees and the hedgerows; at the faces of the four men about the farm, always the same—day after day, month after month, year after year. She never showed a desire for conversation, and, as it seemed to me, she did not know how to smile. Sometimes of a fine Sunday afternoon she would put on her best dress, a pair of stout boots, a large grey hat trimmed with a black feather (I've seen her in that finery), seize an absurdly slender parasol, climb over two stiles, tramp over three fields and along two hundred yards of road—never further. There stood Foster's cottage. She would help her mother to give their tea to the younger children, wash up the crockery, kiss the little ones, and go back to the farm. That was all. All the rest, all the change, all the relaxation. She never seemed to wish for anything more. And then she fell in love. She fell in love silently, obstinately— perhaps helplessly. It came slowly, but when it came it worked like a powerful spell; it was love as the Ancients understood it: an irresistible and fateful impulse—a possession! Yes, it was in her to become haunted and possessed by a face, by a presence, fatally, as though she had been a pagan worshipper of form under a joyous sky—and to be awakened at last from that mysterious forgetfulness of self, from that enchantment, from that transport, by a fear resembling the unaccountable terror of a brute. . . ."

With the sun hanging low on its western limit, the expanse of the grass-lands framed in the counterscarps of the rising ground took on a gorgeous and sombre aspect. A sense of penetrating sadness, like that inspired by a grave strain of music, disengaged itself from the silence of the fields. The men we met walked past, slow, unsmiling, with downcast eyes, as if the melancholy of an over-burdened earth had weighted their feet, bowed their shoulders, borne down their glances.

"Yes," said the doctor to my remark, "one would think the earth is under a curse, since of all her children these that cling to her the closest are uncouth in body and as leaden of gait as if their very hearts were loaded with chains. But here on this same road you might have seen amongst these heavy men a being lithe, supple and long-limbed, straight like a pine, with something striving upwards in his appearance as though the heart within him had been buoyant. Perhaps it was only the force of the contrast, but when he was passing one of these villagers here, the soles of his feet did not seem to me to touch the dust of the road. He vaulted over the stiles, paced these slopes with a long elastic stride that made him noticeable at a great distance, and had lustrous black eyes. He was so different from the mankind around that, with his freedom of movement, his soft—a little startled—glance, his olive complexion and graceful bearing, his humanity suggested to me the nature of a woodland creature. He came from there."

The doctor pointed with his whip, and from the summit of the descent seen over the rolling tops of the trees in a park by the side of the road, appeared the level sea far below us, like the floor of an immense edifice inlaid with bands of dark ripple, with still trails of glitter, ending in a belt of glassy water at the foot of the sky. The light blurr of smoke, from an invisible steamer, faded on the great clearness of the horizon like the mist of a breath on a mirror; and, inshore, the white sails of a coaster, with the appearance of disentangling themselves slowly from under the branches, floated clear of the foliage of the trees.

"Shipwrecked in the bay?" I said.

"Yes; he was a castaway. A poor emigrant from Central Europe bound to America and washed ashore here in a storm. And for him, who knew nothing of the earth, England was an undiscovered country. It was some time before he learned its name; and for all I know he might have expected to find wild beasts or wild men here, when, crawling in the dark over the sea-wall, he rolled down the other side into a dyke, where it was another miracle he didn't get drowned. But he struggled instinctively like an animal under a net, and this blind struggle threw him out into a field. He must have been, indeed, of a tougher fibre than he looked to withstand without expiring such buffetings, the violence of his exertions, and so much fear. Later on, in his broken English that resembled curiously the speech of a young child, he told me himself that he put his trust in God, believing he was no longer in this world. And truly—he would add—how was he to know? He fought his way against the rain and the gale on all fours, and crawled at last among some sheep huddled close under the lee of a hedge. They ran off in all directions, bleating in the darkness, and he welcomed the first familiar sound he heard on these shores. It must have been two in the morning then. And this is all we know of the manner of his landing, though he did not arrive unattended by any means. Only his grisly company did not begin to come ashore till much later in the day. . . ."

The doctor gathered the reins, clicked his tongue; we trotted down the hill. Then turning, almost directly, a sharp corner into the High Street, we rattled over the stones and were home.

Late in the evening, Kennedy, breaking a spell of moodiness that had come over him, returned to the story. Smoking his pipe, he paced the long room from end to end. A reading-lamp concentrated all its light upon the papers on his desk; and, sitting by the open window, I saw, after the windless, scorching day, the frigid splendour of a hazy sea lying motionless under the moon. Not a whisper, not a splash, not a stir of the shingle, not a footstep, not a sigh came up from the earth below—never a sign of life but the scent of climbing jasmine: and Kennedy's voice, speaking behind me, passed through the wide casement, to vanish outside in a chill and sumptuous stillness.

". . . The relations of shipwrecks in the olden time tell us of much suffering. Often the castaways were only saved from drowning to die miserably from starvation on a barren coast; others suffered violent death or else slavery, passing through years of precarious existence with people to whom their strangeness was an object of suspicion, dislike or fear. We read about these things, and they are very pitiful. It is indeed hard upon a man to find himself a lost stranger, helpless, incomprehensible, and of a mysterious origin, in some obscure corner of the earth. Yet amongst all the adventurers shipwrecked in all the wild parts of the world, there is not one, it seems to me, that ever had to suffer a fate so simply tragic as the man I am speaking of, the most innocent of adventurers cast out by the sea in the bight of this bay, almost within sight from this very window.

"He did not know the name of his ship. Indeed, in the course of time we discovered he did not even know that ships had names—'like Christian people'; and when, one day, from the top of the Talfourd Hill, he beheld the sea lying open to his view, his eyes roamed afar, lost in an air of wild surprise, as though he had never seen such a sight before. And probably he had not. As far as I could make out, he had been hustled together with many others on board an emigrant-ship lying at the mouth of the Elbe, too bewildered to take note of his surroundings, too weary to see anything, too anxious to care. They were driven below into the 'tween-deck and battened down from the very start. It was a low timber dwelling—he would say—with wooden beams overhead, like the houses in his country, but you went into it down a ladder. It was very large, very cold, damp and sombre, with places in the manner of wooden boxes where people had to sleep one above another, and it kept on rocking all ways at once all the time. He crept into one of these boxes and lay down there in the clothes in which he had left his home many days before, keeping his bundle and his stick by his side. People groaned, children cried, water dripped, the lights went out, the walls of the place creaked, and everything was being shaken so that in one's little box one dared not lift one's head. He had lost touch with his only companion (a young man from the same valley, he said), and all the time a great noise of wind went on outside and heavy blows fell—boom! boom! An awful sickness overcame him, even to the point of making him neglect his prayers. Besides, one could not tell whether it was morning or evening. It seemed always to be night in that place.

"Before that he had been travelling a long, long time on the iron track. He looked out of the window, which had a wonderfully clear glass in it, and the trees, the houses, the fields, and the long roads seemed to fly round and round about him till his head swam. He gave me to understand that he had on his passage beheld uncounted multitudes of people—whole nations—all dressed in such clothes as the rich wear. Once he was made to get out of the carriage, and slept through a night on a bench in a house of bricks with his bundle under his head; and once for many hours he had to sit on a floor of flat stones dozing, with his knees up and with his bundle between his feet. There was a roof over him, which seemed made of glass, and was so high that the tallest mountain-pine he has ever seen would have had room to grow under it. Steam-machines rolled in at one end and out at the other. People swarmed more than you can see on a feast-day round the miraculous Holy Image in the yard of the Carmelite Convent down in the plains where, before he left his home, he drove his mother in a wooden cart:—a pious old woman who wanted to offer prayers and make a vow for his safety. He could not give me an idea of how large and lofty and full of noise and smoke and gloom, and clang of iron, the place was, but some one had told him it was called Berlin. Then they rang a bell, and another steam-machine came in, and again he was taken on and on through a land that wearied his eyes by its flatness without a single bit of a hill to be seen anywhere. One more night he spent shut up in a building like a good stable with a litter of straw on the floor, guarding his bundle amongst a lot of men, of whom not one could understand a single word he said. In the morning they were all led down to the stony shores of an extremely broad muddy river, flowing not between hills but between houses that seemed immense. There was a steam-machine that went on the water and they all stood upon it packed tight, only now there were with them many women and children who made much noise. A cold rain fell, the wind blew in his face; he was wet through, and his teeth chattered. He and the young man from the same valley took each other by the hand.

"They thought they were being taken to America straight away, but suddenly the steam-machine bumped against the side of a thing like a great house on the water. The walls were smooth and black, and there uprose, growing from the roof as it were, bare trees in the shape of crosses, extremely high. That's how it appeared to him then, for he had never seen a ship before. This was the ship that was going to swim all the way to America. Voices shouted, everything swayed; there was a ladder dipping up and down. He went up on his hands and knees in mortal fear of falling into the water below, which made a great splashing. He got separated from his companion, and when he descended into the bottom of that ship his heart seemed to melt suddenly within him.

"It was then also, as he told me, that he lost contact for good and all with one of those three men who the summer before had been going about through all the little towns in the foothills of his country. They would arrive on market-days driving in a peasant's cart, and would set up an office in an inn or some other Jew's house. There were three of them, of whom one with a long beard looked venerable; and they had red cloth collars round their necks and gold lace on their sleeves like Government officials. They sat proudly behind a long table; and in the next room, so that the common people shouldn't hear, they kept a cunning telegraph machine, through which they could talk to the Emperor of America. The fathers hung about the door, but the young men of the mountains would crowd up to the table asking many questions, for there was work to be got all the year round at three dollars a day in America, and no military service to do.

"But the American Kaiser would not take everybody. Oh no! He himself had a great difficulty in getting accepted, and the venerable man in uniform had to go out of the room several times to work the telegraph on his behalf. The American Kaiser engaged him at last at three dollars, he being young and strong. However, many able young men backed out, afraid of the great distance; besides, those only who had some money could be taken. There were some who sold their huts and their land because it cost a lot of money to get to America; but then, once there, you had three dollars a day, and if you were clever you could find places where true gold could be picked up on the ground. His father's house was getting over full. Two of his brothers were married and had children. He promised to send money home from America by post twice a year. His father sold an old cow, a pair of pie-bald mountain ponies of his own raising, and a cleared plot of fair pasture land on the sunny slope of a pine-clad pass to a Jew inn-keeper, in order to pay the people of the ship that took men to America to get rich in a short time.

"He must have been a real adventurer at heart, for how many of the greatest enterprises in the conquest of the earth had for their beginning just such a bargaining away of the paternal cow for the mirage of true gold far away! I have been telling you more or less in my own words what I learned fragmentarily in the course of two or three years, during which I seldom missed an opportunity of a friendly chat with him. He told me this story of his adventure with many flashes of white teeth and lively glances of black eyes, at first in a sort of anxious baby-talk, then, as he acquired the language, with great fluency, but always with that singing, soft, and at the same time vibrating intonation that instilled a strangely penetrating power into the sound of the most familiar English words, as if they had been the words of an unearthly language. And he always would come to an end, with many emphatic shakes of his head, upon that awful sensation of his heart melting within him directly he set foot on board that ship. Afterwards there seemed to come for him a period of blank ignorance, at any rate as to facts. No doubt he must have been abominably seasick and abominably unhappy—this soft and passionate adventurer, taken thus out of his knowledge, and feeling bitterly as he lay in his emigrant bunk his utter loneliness; for his was a highly sensitive nature. The next thing we know of him for certain is that he had been hiding in Hammond's pig-pound by the side of the road to Norton, six miles, as the crow flies, from the sea. Of these experiences he was unwilling to speak: they seemed to have seared into his soul a sombre sort of wonder and indignation. Through the rumours of the country-side, which lasted for a good many days after his arrival, we know that the fisherman of West Colebrook had been disturbed and startled by heavy knocks against the walls of weatherboard cottages, and by a voice crying piercingly strange words in the night. Several of them turned out even, but, no doubt, he had fled in sudden alarm at their rough angry tones hailing each other in the darkness. A sort of frenzy must have helped him up the steep Norton hill. It was he, no doubt, who early the following morning had been seen lying (in a swoon, I should say) on the roadside grass by the Brenzett carrier, who actually got down to have a nearer look, but drew back, intimidated by the perfect immobility, and by something queer in the aspect of that tramp, sleeping so still under the showers. As the day advanced, some children came dashing into school at Norton in such a fright that the schoolmistress went out and spoke indignantly to a 'horrid-looking man' on the road. He edged away, hanging his head, for a few steps, and then suddenly ran off with extraordinary fleetness. The driver of Mr. Bradley's milk-cart made no secret of it that he had lashed with his whip at a hairy sort of gipsy fellow who, jumping up at a turn of the road by the Vents, made a snatch at the pony's bridle. And he caught him a good one too, right over the face, he said, that made him drop down in the mud a jolly sight quicker than he had jumped up; but it was a good half a mile before he could stop the pony. Maybe that in his desperate endeavours to get help, and in need to get in touch with some one, the poor devil had tried to stop the cart. Also three boys confessed afterwards to throwing stones at a funny tramp, knocking about all wet and muddy, and, it seemed, very drunk, in the narrow deep lane by the limekilns. All this was the talk of three villages for days; but we have Mrs. Finn's (the wife of Smith's waggoner) unim-peachable testimony that she saw him get over the low wall of Hammond's pig-pound and lurch straight at her, babbling aloud in a voice that was enough to make one die of fright. Having the baby with her in a perambulator, Mrs. Finn called out to him to go away, and as he persisted in coming nearer, she hit him courageously with her umbrella over the head, and, without once looking back, ran like the wind with the perambulator as far as the first house in the village. She stopped then, out of breath, and spoke to old Lewis, hammering there at a heap of stones; and the old chap, taking off his immense black wire goggles, got up on his shaky legs to look where she pointed. Together they followed with their eyes the figure of the man running over a field; they saw him fall down, pick himself up, and run on again, staggering and waving his long arms above his head, in the direction of the New Barns Farm. From that moment he is plainly in the toils of his obscure and touching destiny. There is no doubt after this of what happened to him. All is certain now: Mrs. Smith's intense terror; Amy Foster's stolid conviction held against the other's nervous attack, that the man 'meant no harm'; Smith's exasperation (on his return from Darnford Market) at finding the dog barking himself into a fit, the back-door locked, his wife in hysterics; and all for an unfortunate dirty tramp, supposed to be even then lurking in his stackyard. Was he? He would teach him to frighten women.

"Smith is notoriously hot-tempered, but the sight of some nondescript and miry creature sitting cross-legged amongst a lot of loose straw, and swinging itself to and fro like a bear in a cage, made him pause. Then this tramp stood up silently before him, one mass of mud and filth from head to foot. Smith, alone amongst his stacks with this apparition, in the stormy twilight ringing with the infuriated barking of the dog, felt the dread of an inexplicable strangeness. But when that being, parting with his black hands the long matted locks that hung before his face, as you part the two halves of a curtain, looked out at him with glistening, wild, black-and-white eyes, the weirdness of this silent encounter fairly staggered him. He has admitted since (for the story has been a legitimate subject of conversation about here for years) that he made more than one step backwards. Then a sudden burst of rapid, senseless speech persuaded him at once that he had to do with an escaped lunatic. In fact, that impres-sion never wore off completely. Smith has not in his heart given up his secret convic-tion of the man's essential insanity to this very day.

"As the creature approached him, jabbering in a most discomposing manner, Smith (unaware that he was being addressed as 'gracious lord,' and adjured in God's name to afford food and shelter) kept on speaking firmly but gently to it, and retreating all the time into the other yard. At last, watching his chance, by a sudden charge he bundled him headlong into the wood-lodge, and instantly shot the bolt. Thereupon he wiped his brow, though the day was cold. He had done his duty to the community by shutting up a wandering and probably dangerous maniac. Smith isn't a hard man at all, but he had room in his brain only for that one idea of lunacy. He was not imaginative enough to ask himself whether the man might not be perishing with cold and hunger. Meantime, at first, the maniac made a great deal of noise in the lodge. Mrs. Smith was screaming upstairs, where she had locked herself in her bedroom; but Amy Foster sobbed piteously at the kitchen-door, wringing her hands and muttering,

'Don't! don't!' I daresay Smith had a rough time of it that evening with one noise and another, and this insane, disturbing voice crying obstinately through the door only added to his irritation. He couldn't possibly have connected this troublesome lunatic with the sinking of a ship in Eastbay, of which there had been a rumour in the Darnford market-place. And I daresay the man inside had been very near to insanity on that night. Before his excitement collapsed and he became unconscious he was throwing himself violently about in the dark, rolling on some dirty sacks, and biting his fists with rage, cold, hunger, amazement, and despair.

"He was a mountaineer of the eastern range of the Carpathians, and the vessel sunk the night before in Eastbay was the Hamburg emigrant-ship *Herzogin Sophia-Dorothea*, of appalling memory.

"A few months later we could read in the paper the accounts of the bogus 'Emigration Agencies' among the Sclavonian peasantry in the more remote provinces of Austria. The object of these scoundrels was to get hold of the poor ignorant people's homesteads, and they were in league with the local usurers. They exported their victims through Hamburg mostly. As to the ship, I had watched her out of this very window, reaching close-hauled under short canvas into the bay on a dark, threatening afternoon. She came to an anchor, correctly by the chart, off the Brenzett Coastguard station. I remember before the night fell looking out again at the outlines of her spars and rigging that stood out dark and pointed on a background of ragged, slaty clouds like another and a slighter spire to the left of the Brenzett church-tower. In the evening the wind rose. At midnight I could hear in my bed the terrific gusts and the sounds of a driving deluge.

"About that time the Coastguardmen thought they saw the lights of a steamer over the anchoring-ground. In a moment they vanished; but it is clear that another vessel of some sort had tried for shelter in the bay on that awful, blind night, had rammed the German ship amidships (a breach—as one of the divers told me afterwards—'that you could sail a Thames barge through'), and then had gone out either scathless or damaged, who shall say; but had gone out, unknown, unseen, and fatal, to perish mysteriously at sea. Of her nothing ever came to light, and yet the hue and cry that was raised all over the world would have found her out if she had been in existence anywhere on the face of the waters.

"A completeness without a clue, and a stealthly silence as of a neatly executed crime, characterize this murderous disaster, which, as you may remember, had its gruesome celebrity. The wind would have prevented the loudest outcries from reaching the shore; there had been evidently no time for signals of distress. It was death without any sort of fuss. The Hamburg ship, filling all at once, capsized as she sank, and at daylight there was not even the end of a spar to be seen above water. She was missed, of course, and at first the Coastguardmen surmised that she had either dragged her anchor or parted her cable some time during the night, and had been blown out to sea. Then, after the tide turned, the wreck must have shifted a little and released some of the bodies, because a child—a little fair-haired child in a red frock—came ashore abreast of the Martello tower. By the afternoon you could see along three miles of beach dark figures with bare legs dashing in and out of the tumbling foam, and rough-looking men, women with hard faces, children, mostly fair-haired, were being carried, stiff and dripping, on stretchers, on wattles, on ladders, in a long procession past the door of the 'Ship Inn,' to be laid out in a row under the north wall of the Brenzett Church.

"Officially, the body of the little girl in the red frock is the first thing that came ashore from that ship. But I have patients amongst the seafaring population of West Colebrook, and, unofficially, I am informed that very early that morning two brothers, who went down to look after their cobble hauled up on the beach, found, a good way from Brenzett, an ordinary ship's hencoop lying high and dry on the shore, with eleven drowned ducks inside. Their families ate the birds, and the hencoop was split into firewood with a hatchet. It is possible that a man (supposing he happened to be on the deck at the time of the accident) might have floated ashore on that hencoop. He might. I admit it is improbable, but there was the man—and for days, nay, for weeks—it didn't enter our heads that we had amongst us the only living soul that had escaped from that disaster. The man himself, even when he learned to speak intelligibly, could tell us very little. He remembered he had felt better (after the ship had anchored, I suppose), and that the darkness, the wind, and the rain took his breath away. This looks as if he had been on deck some time during that night. But we mustn't forget he had been taken out of his knowledge, that he had been sea-sick and battened down below for four days, that he had no general notion of a ship or of the sea, and therefore could have no definite idea of what was happening to him. The rain, the wind, the darkness he knew; he understood the bleating of the sheep, and he remembered the pain of his wretchedness and misery, his heartbroken astonishment that it was neither seen nor understood, his dismay at finding all the men angry and all the women fierce. He had approached them as a beggar, it is true, he said; but in his country, even if they gave nothing, they spoke gently to beggars. The children in his country were not taught to throw stones at those who asked for compassion. Smith's strategy overcame him completely. The wood-lodge presented the horrible aspect of a dungeon. What would be done to him next? . . . . . No wonder that Amy Foster appeared to his eyes with the aureole of an angel of light. The girl had not been able to sleep for thinking of the poor man, and in the morning, before the Smiths were up, she slipped out across the back yard. Holding the door of the wood-lodge ajar, she looked in and extended to him half a loaf of white bread—'such bread as the rich eat in my country,' he used to say.

"At this he got up slowly from amongst all sorts of rubbish, stiff, hungry, trembling, miserable, and doubtful. 'Can you eat this?' she asked in her soft and timid voice. He must have taken her for a 'gracious lady.' He devoured ferociously, and tears were falling on the crust. Suddenly he dropped the bread, seized her wrist, and imprinted a kiss on her hand. She was not frightened. Through his forlorn condition she had observed that he was good-looking. She shut the door and walked back slowly to the kitchen. Much later on, she told Mrs. Smith, who shuddered at the bare idea of being touched by that creature.

"Through this act of impulsive pity he was brought back again within the pale of human relations with his new surroundings. He never forgot it—never.

"That very same morning old Mr. Swaffer (Smith's nearest neighbour) came over to give his advice, and ended by carrying him off. He stood, unsteady on his legs, meek, and caked over in half-dried mud, while the two men talked around him in an incomprehensible tongue. Mrs. Smith had refused to come downstairs till the madman was off the premises; Amy Foster, from far within the dark kitchen, watched through the open back door; and he obeyed the signs that were made to him to the best of his ability. But Smith was full of mistrust. 'Mind, sir! It may be all his cunning,' he cried repeatedly in a tone of warning. When Mr. Swaffer started the mare, the deplorable being sitting humbly by his side, through weakness, nearly fell out over the back of the high two-wheeled cart. Swaffer took him straight home. And it is then that I come upon the scene.

"I was called in by the simple process of the old man beckoning to me with his forefinger over the gate of his house as I happened to be driving past. I got down, of course.

" 'I've got something here,' he mumbled, leading the way to an outhouse at a little distance from his other farm-buildings.

"It was there that I saw him first, in a long low room taken upon the space of that sort of coach-house. It was bare and whitewashed, with a small square aperture glazed with one cracked, dusty pane at its further end. He was lying on his back upon a straw pallet; they had given him a couple of horse-blankets, and he seemed to have spent the remainder of his strength in the exertion of cleaning himself. He was almost speechless; his quick breathing under the blankets pulled up to his chin, his glittering, restless black eyes reminded me of a wild bird caught in a snare. While I was examining him, old Swaffer stood silently by the door, passing the tips of his fingers along his shaven upper lip. I gave some directions, promised to send a bottle of medicine, and naturally made some inquiries.

" 'Smith caught him in the stackyard at New Barns,' said the old chap in his deliberate, unmoved manner, and as if the other had been indeed a sort of wild animal, 'That's how I came by him. Quite a curiosity, isn't it? Now tell me, doctor—you've been all over the world—don't you think that's a bit of a Hindoo we've got hold of here?'

"I was greatly surprised. His long black hair scattered over the straw bolster contrasted with the olive pallor of his face. It occurred to me he might be a Basque. It didn't necessarily follow that he should understand Spanish; but I tried him with the few words I know, and also with some French. The whispered sounds I caught by bending my ear to his lips puzzled me utterly. That afternoon the young ladies from the rectory (one of them read Goethe with a dictionary, and the other had struggled with Dante for years), coming to see Miss Swaffer, tried their German and Italian on him from the doorway. They retreated, just the least bit scared by the flood of passionate speech which, turning on his pallet, he let out at them. They admitted that the sound was pleasant, soft, musical—but, in conjunction with his looks perhaps, it was startling—so excitable, so utterly unlike anything one had ever heard. The village boys climbed up the bank to have a peep through the little square aperture. Everybody was wondering what Mr. Swaffer would do with him.

"He simply kept him.

"Swaffer would be called eccentric were he not so much respected. They will tell you that Mr. Swaffer sits up as late as ten o'clock at night to read books, and they will tell you also that he can write a cheque for two hundred pounds without thinking twice about it. He himself would tell you that the Swaffers had owned land between this and Darnford for these three hundred years. He must be eighty-five to-day, but he does not look a bit older than when I first came here. He is a great breeder of sheep, and deals extensively in cattle. He attends market days for miles around in every sort of weather, and drives sitting bowed low over the reins, his lank grey hair curling over the collar of his warm coat, and with a green plaid rug round his legs. The calmness of advanced age gives a solemnity to his manner. He is clean-shaved; his lips are thin and sensitive; something rigid and monarchial in the set of his features lends a certain elevation to the character of his face. He has been known to drive miles in the rain to see a new kind of rose in somebody's garden, or a monstrous cabbage grown by a cottager. He loves to hear tell of or to be shown something what he calls 'outlandish.' Perhaps it was just that outlandishness of the man which influenced old Swaffer. Perhaps it was only an inexplicable caprice. All I know is that at the end of three weeks I caught sight of Smith's lunatic digging in Swaffer's kitchen garden. They had found out he could use a spade. He dug barefooted.

"His black hair flowed over his shoulders. I suppose it was Swaffer who had given him the striped old cotton shirt; but he wore still the national brown cloth trousers (in which he had been washed ashore) fitting to the leg almost like tights; was belted with a broad leathern belt studded with little brass discs; and had never yet ventured into the village. The land he looked upon seemed to him kept neatly, like the grounds round a landowner's house; the size of the cart-horses struck him with astonishment; the roads resembled garden walks, and the aspect of the people, especially on Sundays, spoke of opulence. He wondered what made them so hardhearted and their children so bold. He got his food at the back door, carried it in both hands, carefully, to his outhouse, and, sitting alone on his pallet, would make the sign of the cross before he began. Beside the same pallet, kneeling in the early darkness of the short days, he recited aloud the Lord's Prayer before he slept. Whenever he saw old Swaffer he would bow with veneration from the waist, and stand erect while the old man, with his fingers over his upper lip, surveyed him silently. He bowed also to Miss Swaffer, who kept house frugally for her father—a broad-shouldered, big-boned woman of forty-five, with the pocket of her dress full of keys, and a grey, steady eye. She was Church—as people said (while her father was one of the trustees of the Baptist Chapel)—and wore a little steel cross at her waist. She dressed severely in black, in memory of one of the innumerable Bradleys of the neighbourhood, to whom she had been engaged some twenty-five years ago—a young farmer who broke his neck out hunting on the eve of the wedding-day. She had the unmoved countenance of the deaf, spoke very seldom, and her lips, thin like her father's, astonished one sometimes by a mysteriously ironic curl.

"These were the people to whom he owed allegiance, and an overwhelming loneliness seemed to fall from the leaden sky of that winter without sunshine. All the faces were sad. He could talk to no one, and had no hope of ever understanding anybody. It was as if these had been the faces of people from the other world—dead people—he used to tell me years afterwards. Upon my word, I wonder he did not go mad. He didn't know where he was. Somewhere very far from his mountains—somewhere over the water. Was this America? he wondered.

"If it hadn't been for the steel cross at Miss Swaffer's belt he would not, he confessed, have known whether he was in a Christian country at all. He used to cast stealthy glances at it, and feel comforted. There was nothing here the same as in his country! The earth and the water were different; there were no images of the Redeemer by the roadside. The very grass was different, and the trees. All the trees but the three old Norway pines on the bit of lawn before Swaffer's house, and these reminded him of his country. He had been detected once, after dusk, with his forehead against the trunk of one of them, sobbing, and talking to himself. They had been like brothers to him at that time, he affirmed. Everything else was strange. Conceive you the kind of an existence over-shadowed, oppressed, by the everyday material appearances, as if by the visions of a nightmare. At night, when he could not sleep, he kept on thinking of the girl who gave him the first piece of bread he had eaten in this foreign land. She had been neither fierce nor angry, nor frightened. Her face he remembered as the only comprehensible face amongst all these faces that were as closed, as mysterious, and as mute as the faces of the dead who are possessed of a knowledge beyond the comprehension of the living. I wonder whether the memory of her compassion prevented him from cutting his throat. But there! I suppose I am an old sentimentalist, and forget the instinctive love of life which it takes all the strength of an uncommon despair to overcome.

"He did the work which was given him with an intelligence which surprised old Swaffer. By-and-by it was discovered that he could help at the ploughing, could milk the cows, feed the bullocks in the cattle-yard, and was of some use with the sheep. He began to pick up words, too, very fast; and suddenly, one fine morning in spring, he rescued from an untimely death a grand-child of old Swaffer.

"Swaffer's younger daughter is married to Willcox, a solicitor and the Town Clerk of Colebrook. Regularly twice a year they come to stay with the old man for a few days. Their only child, a little girl not three years old at the time, ran out of the house alone in her little white pinafore, and, toddling across the grass of a terraced garden, pitched herself over a low wall head first into the horsepond in the yard below.

"Our man was out with the waggoner and the plough in the field nearest to the house, and as he was leading the team round to begin a fresh furrow, he saw, through the gap of a gate, what for anybody else would have been a mere flutter of something white. But he had straight-glancing, quick, far-reaching eyes, that only seemed to flinch and lose their amazing power before the immensity of the sea. He was barefooted, and looking as outlandish as the heart of Swaffer could desire. Leaving the horses on the turn, to the inexpressible disgust of the waggoner he bounded off, going over the ploughed ground in long leaps, and suddenly appeared before the mother, thrust the child into her arms, and strode away.

"The pond was not very deep; but still, if he had not had such good eyes, the child would have perished—miserably suffocated in the foot or so of sticky mud at the bottom. Old Swaffer walked out slowly into the field, waited till the plough came over to his side, had a good look at him, and without saying a word went back to the house. But from that time they laid out his meals on the kitchen table; and at first, Miss Swaffer, all in black and with an inscrutable face, would come and stand in the doorway of the living-room to see him make a big sign of the cross before he fell to. I believe that from that day, too, Swaffer began to pay him regular wages.

"I can't follow step by step his development. He cut his hair short, was seen in the village and along the road going to and fro to his work like any other man. Children ceased to shout after him. He became aware of social differences, but remained for a long time surprised at the bare poverty of the churches among so much wealth. He couldn't understand either why they were kept shut up on week-days. There was nothing to steal in them. Was it to keep people from praying too often? The rectory took much notice of him about that time, and I believe the young ladies attempted to prepare the ground for his conversion. They could not, however, break him of his habit of crossing himself, but he went so far as to take off the string with a couple of brass medals the size of a sixpence, a tiny metal cross, and a square sort of scapulary which he wore round his neck. He hung them on the wall by the side of his bed, and he was still to be heard every evening reciting the Lord's Prayer, in incomprehensible words and in a slow, fervent tone, as he had heard his old father do at the head of all the kneeling family, big and little, on every evening of his life. And though he wore corduroys at work, and a slop-made pepper-and-salt suit on Sundays, strangers would turn round to look after him on the road. His foreignness had a peculiar and indelible stamp. At last people became used to seeing him. But they never became used to him. His rapid, skimming walk; his swarthy complexion; his hat cocked on the left ear; his habit, on warm evenings, of wearing his coat over one shoulder, like a hussar's dolman; his manner of leaping over the stiles, not as a feat of agility, but in the ordinary course of progression—all these peculiarities were, as one may say, so many causes of scorn and offence to the inhabitants of the village. *They* wouldn't in their dinner hour lie flat on their backs on the grass to stare at the sky. Neither did they go about the fields screaming dismal tunes. Many times have I heard his high-pitched voice from behind the ridge of some sloping sheep-walk, a voice light and soaring, like a lark's, but with a melancholy human note, over our fields that hear only the song of birds. And I would be startled myself. Ah! He was different: innocent of heart, and full of good will, which nobody wanted, this castaway, that, like a man transplanted into another planet, was separated by an immense space from his past and by an immense ignorance from his future. His quick, fervent utterance positively shocked everybody. 'An excitable devil,' they called him. One evening, in the tap-room of the Coach and Horses (having drunk some whisky), he upset them all by singing a love-song of his country. They hooted him down, and he was pained; but Preble, the lame wheelwright, and Vincent, the fat blacksmith, and the other notables too, wanted to drink their evening beer in peace. On another occasion he tried to show them how to dance. The dust rose in clouds from the sanded floor; he leaped straight up amongst the deal tables, struck his heels together, squatted on one heel in front of old Preble, shooting out the other leg, uttered wild and exulting cries, jumped up to whirl one foot, snapping his fingers above his head—and a strange carter who was having a drink in there began to swear, and cleared out with his half-pint in his hand into the bar. But when suddenly he sprang upon a table and continued to dance among the glasses, the landlord interfered. He didn't want any 'acrobat tricks in the tap-room.' They laid their hands on him. Having had a glass or two, Mr. Swaffer's foreigner tried to expostulate: was ejected forcibly: got a black eye.

"I believe he felt the hostility of his human surroundings. But he was tough—tough in spirit, too, as well as in body. Only the memory of the sea frightened him, with that vague terror that is left by a bad dream. His home was far away; and he did not want now to go to America. I had often explained to him that there is no place on earth where true gold can be found lying ready and to be got for the trouble of the picking up. How then, he asked, could he ever return home with empty hands when there had been sold a cow, two ponies, and a bit of land to pay for his going? His eyes would fill with tears, and, averting them from the immense shimmer of the sea, he would throw himself face down on the grass. But sometimes, cocking his hat with a little conquering air, he would defy my wisdom. He had found his bit of true gold. That was Amy Foster's heart; which was 'a golden heart, and soft to people's misery,' he would say in the accents of overwhelming conviction.

"He was called Yanko. He had explained that this meant Little John; but as he would also repeat very often that he was a mountaineer (some word sounding in the dialect of his country like Goorall) he got it for his surname. And this is the only trace of him that the succeeding ages may find in the marriage register of the parish. There it stands—Yanko Goorall—in the rector's handwriting. The crooked cross made by the castaway, a cross whose tracing no doubt seemed to him the most solemn part of the whole ceremony, is all that remains now to perpetuate the memory of his name.

"His courtship had lasted some time—ever since he got his precarious footing in the community. It began by his buying for Amy Foster a green satin ribbon in Darnford. This was what you did in his country. You bought a ribbon at a Jew's stall on a fair-day. I don't suppose the girl knew what to do with it, but he seemed to think that his honourable intentions could not be mistaken.

"It was only when he declared his purpose to get married that I fully understood how, for a hundred futile and inappreciable reasons, how—shall I say odious?—he was to all the countryside. Every old woman in the village was up in arms. Smith, coming upon him near the farm, promised to break his head for him if he found him about again. But he twisted his little black moustache with such a bellicose air and rolled such big, black fierce eyes at Smith that this promise came to nothing. Smith, however, told the girl that she must be mad to take up with a man who was surely wrong in his head. All the same, when she heard him in the gloaming whistle from beyond the orchard a couple of bars of a weird and mournful tune, she would drop whatever she had in her hand—she would leave Mrs. Smith in the middle of a sentence—and she would run out to his call. Mrs. Smith called her a shameless hussy. She answered nothing. She said nothing at all to anybody, and went on her way as if she had been deaf. She and I alone in all the land, I fancy, could see his very real beauty. He was very good-looking, and most graceful in his bearing, with that something wild as of a woodland creature in his aspect. Her mother moaned over her dismally whenever the girl came to see her on her day out. The father was surly, but pretended not to know; and Mrs. Finn once told her plainly that 'this man, my dear, will do you some harm some day yet.' And so it went on. They could be seen on the roads, she tramping stolidly in her finery—grey dress, black feather, stout boots, prominent white cotton gloves that caught your eye a hundred yards away; and he, his coat slung picturesquely over one shoulder, pacing by her side, gallant of bearing and casting tender glances upon the girl with the golden heart. I wonder whether he saw how plain she was. Perhaps among types so different from what he had seen, he had not the power to judge; or perhaps he was seduced by the divine quality of her pity.

"Yanko was in great trouble meantime. In his country you get an old man for an ambassador in marriage affairs. He did not know how to proceed. However, one day in the midst of sheep in a field (he was now Swaffer's under-shepherd with Foster) he took off his hat to the father and declared himself humbly. 'I daresay she's fool enough to marry you,' was all Foster said. 'And then,' he used to relate, 'he puts his hat on his head, looks black at me as if he wanted to cut my throat, whistles the dog, and off he goes, leaving me to do the work.' The Fosters, of course, didn't like to lose the wages the girl earned: Amy used to give all her money to her mother. But there was in Foster a very genuine aversion to that match. He contended that the fellow was very good with sheep, but was not fit for any girl to marry. For one thing, he used to go along the hedges muttering to himself like a dam' fool; and then, these foreigners behave very queerly to women sometimes. And perhaps he would want to carry her off somewhere—or run off himself. It was not safe. He preached it to his daughter that the fellow might ill-use her in some way. She made no answer. It was, they said in the village, as if the man had done something to her. People discussed the matter. It was quite an excitement, and the two went on 'walking out' together in the face of opposition. Then something unexpected happened.

"I don't know whether old Swaffer ever understood how much he was regarded in the light of a father by his foreign retainer. Anyway the relation was curiously feudal.

So when Yanko asked formally for an interview—'and the Miss too' (he called the severe, deaf Miss Swaffer simply *Miss*)—it was to obtain their permission to marry. Swaffer heard him unmoved, dismissed him by a nod, and then shouted the intelligence into Miss Swaffer's best ear. She showed no surprise, and only remarked grimly, in a veiled blank voice, 'He certainly won't get any other girl to marry him.'

"It is Miss Swaffer who has all the credit of the munificence: but in a very few days it came out that Mr. Swaffer had presented Yanko with a cottage (the cottage you've seen this morning) and something like an acre of ground—had made it over to him in absolute property. Willcox expedited the deed, and I remember him telling me he had a great pleasure in making it ready. It recited: 'In consideration of saving the life of my beloved grandchild Bertha Willcox.'

"Of course, after that no power on earth could prevent them from getting married.

"Her infatuation endured. People saw her going out to meet him in the evening. She stared with unblinking, fascinated eyes up the road where he was expected to appear, walking freely, with a swing from the hip, and humming one of the love-tunes of his country. When the boy was born, he got elevated at the 'Coach and Horses,' essayed again a song and a dance, and was again ejected. People expressed their commiseration for a woman married to that Jack-in-the-box. He didn't care. There was a man now (he told me boastfully) to whom he could sing and talk in the language of his country, and show how to dance by-and-by.

"But I don't know. To me he appeared to have grown less springy of step, heavier in body, less keen of eye. Imagination, no doubt; but it seems to me now as if the net of fate had been drawn closer round him already.

"One day I met him on the footpath over the Talfourd Hill. He told me that 'women were funny.' I had heard already of domestic differences. People were saying that Amy Foster was beginning to find out what sort of man she had married. He looked upon the sea with indifferent, unseeing eyes. His wife had snatched the child out of his arms one day as he sat on the doorstep crooning to it a song such as the mothers sing to babies in his mountains. She seemed to think he was doing it some harm. Women are funny. And she had objected to him praying aloud in the evening. Why? He expected the boy to repeat the prayer aloud after him by-and-by, as he used to do after his old father when he was a child—in his own country. And I discovered he longed for their boy to grow up so that he could have a man to talk with in that language that to our ears sounded so disturbing, so passionate, and so bizarre. Why his wife should dislike the idea he couldn't tell. But that would pass, he said. And tilting his head knowingly, he tapped his breastbone to indicate that she had a good heart: not hard, not fierce, open to compassion, charitable to the poor!

"I walked away thoughtfully; I wondered whether his difference, his strangeness, were not penetrating with repulsion that dull nature they had begun by irresistibly attracting. I wondered. . . ."

The doctor came to the window and looked out at the frigid splendour of the sea, immense in the haze, as if enclosing all the earth with all the hearts lost among the passions of love and fear.

"Physiologically now," he said, turning away abruptly, "it was possible. It was possible."

He remained silent. Then went on—

"At all events, the next time I saw him he was ill—lung trouble. He was tough, but I daresay he was not acclimatized as well as I had supposed. It was a bad winter; and, of course, these mountaineers do get fits of homesickness; and a state of depression would make him vulnerable. He was lying half dressed on a couch downstairs.

"A table covered with a dark oilcloth took up all the middle of the little room. There was a wicker cradle on the floor, a kettle spouting steam on the hob, and some child's linen lay drying on the fender. The room was warm, but the door opens right into the garden, as you noticed, perhaps.

"He was very feverish, and kept on muttering to himself. She sat on a chair and looked at him fixedly across the table with her brown, blurred eyes. 'Why don't you have him upstairs?' I asked. With a start and a confused stammer she said, 'Oh! ah! I couldn't sit with him upstairs, sir.'

"I gave her certain directions; and going outside, I said again that he ought to be in bed upstairs. She wrung her hands. 'I couldn't. I couldn't. He keeps on saying something—I don't know what.' With the memory of all the talk against the man that had been dinned into her ears, I looked at her narrowly. I looked into her short-sighted eyes, at her dumb eyes that once in her life had seen an enticing shape, but seemed, staring at me, to see nothing at all now. But I saw she was uneasy.

" 'What's the matter with him?' she asked in a sort of vacant trepidation. 'He doesn't look very ill. I never did see anybody look like this before. . . .'

" 'Do you think,' I asked indignantly, 'he is shamming?'

" 'I can't help it, sir,' she said stolidly. And suddenly she clasped her hands and looked right and left. 'And there's the baby. I am so frightened. He wanted me just now to give him the baby. I can't understand what he says to it.'

" 'Can't you ask a neighbour to come in to-night?' I asked.

" 'Please, sir, nobody seems to care to come,' she muttered, dully resigned all at once.

"I impressed upon her the necessity of the greatest care, and then had to go. There was a good deal of sickness that winter. 'Oh, I hope he won't talk!' she exclaimed softly just as I was going away.

"I don't know how it is I did not see—but I didn't. And yet, turning in my trap, I saw her lingering before the door, very still, and as if meditating a flight up the miry road.

"Towards the night his fever increased.

"He tossed, moaned, and now and then muttered a complaint. And she sat with the table between her and the couch, watching every movement and every sound, with the terror, the unreasonable terror, of that man she could not understand creeping over her. She had drawn the wicker cradle close to her feet. There was nothing in her now but the maternal instinct and that unaccountable fear.

"Suddenly coming to himself, parched, he demanded a drink of water. She did not move. She had not understood, though he may have thought he was speaking in English. He waited, looking at her, burning with fever, amazed at her silence and immobility, and then he shouted impatiently, 'Water! Give me water!'

"She jumped to her feet, snatched up the child, and stood still. He spoke to her, and his passionate remonstrances only increased her fear of that strange man. I believe he spoke to her for a long time, entreating, wondering, pleading, ordering I suppose. She says she bore it as long as she could. And then a gust of rage came over him.

"He sat up and called out terribly one word—some word. Then he got up as though he hadn't been ill at all, she says. And as in fevered dismay, indignation, and wonder he tried to get to her round the table, she simply opened the door and ran out with the child in her arms. She heard him call twice after her down the road in a terrible voice—and fled. . . . Ah! but you should have seen stirring behind the dull, blurred glance of those eyes the spectre of the fear which had hunted her on that night three miles and a half to the door of Foster's cottage! I did the next day.

"And it was I who found him lying face down and his body in a puddle just outside the little wicker-gate.

"I had been called out that night to an urgent case in the village, and on my way home at daybreak passed by the cottage. The door stood open. My man helped me to carry him in. We laid him on the couch. The lamp smoked, the fire was out, the chill of the stormy night oozed from the cheerless yellow paper on the wall. 'Amy!' I called aloud, and my voice seemed to lose itself in the emptiness of this tiny house as if I had cried in a desert. He opened his eyes. 'Gone!' he said distinctly. 'I had only asked for water—only for a little water. . . .'

"He was muddy. I covered him up and stood waiting in silence, catching a painfully gasped word now and then. They were no longer in his own language. The fever had left him, taking with it the heat of life. And with his panting breast and lustrous eyes he reminded me again of a wild creature under the net; of a bird caught in a snare. She had left him. She had left him—sick—helpless—thirsty. The spear of the hunter had entered his very soul. 'Why?' he cried in the penetrating and indignant voice of a man calling to a responsible Maker. A gust of wind and a swish of rain answered.

"And as I turned away to shut the door he pronounced the word 'Merciful!' and expired.

"Eventually I certified heart-failure as the immediate cause of death. His heart must have indeed failed him, or else he might have stood this night of storm and exposure, too. I closed his eyes and drove away. Not very far from the cottage I met Foster walking sturdily between the dripping hedges with his collie at his heels.

" 'Do you know where your daughter is?' I asked.

" 'Don't I!' he cried. 'I am going to talk to him a bit. Frightening a poor woman like this.'

" 'He won't frighten her any more,' I said. 'He is dead.'

"He struck with his stick at the mud.

" 'And there's the child.'

"Then, after thinking deeply for a while—

" 'I don't know that it isn't for the best.'

"That's what he said. And she says nothing at all now. Not a word of him. Never. Is his image as utterly gone from her mind as his lithe and striding figure, his caroling voice are gone from our fields? He is no longer before her eyes to excite her imagination into a passion of love or fear; and his memory seems to have vanished from her dull brain as a shadow passes away upon a white screen. She lives in the cottage and works for Miss Swaffer. She is Amy Foster for everybody, and the child is 'Amy Foster's boy.' She calls him Johnny—which means Little John.

"It is impossible to say whether this name recalls anything to her. Does she ever think of the past? I have seen her hanging over the boy's cot in a very passion of maternal tenderness. The little fellow was lying on his back a little frightened at me, but very still, with his big black eyes, with his fluttered air of a bird in a snare. And looking at him I seemed to see again the other one—the father, cast out mysteriously by the sea to perish in the supreme disaster of loneliness and despair."

THE SECOND DEATH

GRAHAM GREENE (1904–   )

She found me in the evening under trees that grew outside the village. I had never cared for her and would have hidden myself if I'd seen her coming. She was to blame, I'm certain, for her son's vices. If they were vices, but I'm very far from admitting that they were. At any rate he was generous, never mean, like others in the village I could mention if I chose.

I was staring hard at a leaf or she would never have found me. It was dangling from its twig, its stalk torn across by the wind or else by a stone one of the village children had flung. Only the green tough skin of the stalk held it there suspended. I was watching closely, because a caterpillar was crawling across the surface, making the leaf sway to and fro. The caterpillar was aiming at the twig, and I wondered whether it would reach it in safety or whether the leaf would fall with it into the water. There was a pool underneath the trees, and the water always appeared red, because of the heavy clay in the soil.

I never knew whether the caterpillar reached the twig, for, as I've said, the wretched woman found me. The first I knew of her coming was her voice just behind my ear.

"I've been looking in all the pubs for you," she said in her old shrill voice. It was typical of her to say "all the pubs" when there were only two in the place. She always wanted credit for trouble she hadn't really taken.

I was annoyed and I couldn't help speaking a little harshly. "You might have saved yourself the trouble," I said, "you should have known I wouldn't be in a pub on a fine night like this."

The old vixen became quite humble. She was always smooth enough when she wanted anything. "It's for my poor son," she said. That meant that he was ill. When he was well I never heard her say anything better than "that dratted boy." She'd make him be in the house by midnight every day of the week, as if there were any serious mischief a man could get up to in a little village like ours. Of course we soon found a way to cheat her, but it was the principle of the thing I objected to—a grown man of over thirty ordered about by his mother, just because she hadn't a husband to control. But when he was ill, though it might be with only a small chill, it was "my poor son."

"He's dying," she said, "and God knows what I shall do without him."

"Well, I don't see how I can help you," I said. I was angry, because he'd been dying once before and she'd done everything but actually bury him. I imagined it was the same sort of dying this time, the sort a man gets over. I'd seen him about the week before on his way up the hill to see the big-breasted girl at the farm. I'd watched him till he was like a little black dot, which stayed suddenly by a square grey box in a field. That was the barn where they used to meet. I've very good eyes and it amuses me to try how far and how clearly they can see. I met him again some time after midnight and helped him get into the house without his mother knowing, and he was well enough then—only a little sleepy and tired.

The old vixen was at it again. "He's been asking for you," she shrilled at me

"If he's as ill as you make out," I said, "it would be better for him to ask for a doctor."

"Doctor's there, but he can't do anything." That startled me for a moment, I'll admit it, until I thought, "The old devil's malingering. He's got some plan or other." He was quite clever enough to cheat a doctor. I had seen him throw a fit that would have deceived Moses.

"For God's sake come," she said, "he seems frightened." Her voice broke quite genuinely, for I suppose in her way she was fond of him. I couldn't help pitying her a little, for I knew that he had never cared a mite for her and had never troubled to disguise the fact.

I left the trees and the red pool and the struggling caterpillar, for I knew that she would never leave me alone, now that her "poor boy" was asking for me. Yet a week ago there was nothing she wouldn't have done to keep us apart. She thought me responsible for his ways, as though any mortal man could have kept him off a likely woman when his appetite was up.

I think it must have been the first time I had entered their cottage by the front door since I came to the village ten years ago. I threw an amused glance at his window. I thought I could see the marks on the wall of the ladder we'd used the week before. We'd had a little difficulty in putting it straight, but his mother slept sound. He had brought the ladder down from the barn, and when he'd got safely in, I carried it up there again. But you could never trust his word. He'd lie to his best friend, and when I reached the barn I found the girl had gone. If he couldn't bribe you with his mother's money, he'd bribe you with other people's promises.

I began to feel uneasy directly I got inside the door. It was natural that the house should be quiet, for the pair of them never had any friends to stay, although the old woman had a sister-in-law living only a few miles away. But I didn't like the sound of the doctor's feet as he came downstairs to meet us. He'd twisted his face into a pious solemnity for our benefit, as though there was something holy about death, even about the death of my friend.

"He's conscious," he said, "but he's going. There's nothing I can do. If you want him to die in peace, better let his friend go along up. He's frightened about something."

The doctor was right. I could tell that as soon as I bent under the lintel and entered my friend's room. He was propped up on a pillow, and his eyes were on the door, waiting for me to come. They were very bright and frightened, and his hair lay across his forehead in sticky stripes. I'd never realized before what an ugly fellow he was. He had sly eyes that looked at you too much out of the corners, but when he was in ordinary health, they held a twinkle that made you forget the slyness. There was something pleasant and brazen in the twinkle, as much as to say "I know I'm sly and ugly. But what does that matter? I've got guts." It was that twinkle, I think, some women found attractive and stimulating. Now when the twinkle was gone, he looked a rogue and nothing else.

I thought it my duty to cheer him up, so I made a small joke out of the fact that he was alone in bed. He didn't seem to relish it, and I was beginning to fear that he too was taking a religious view of his death, when he told me to sit down, speaking quite sharply.

"I'm dying," he said, talking very fast, "and I want to ask you something. That doctor's no good—he'd think me delirious. I'm frightened, old man. I want to be reassured," and then after a long pause, "someone with common sense." He slipped a little farther down in his bed.

"I've only once been badly ill before," he said. "That was before you settled here. I wasn't much more than a boy. People tell me that I was even supposed to be dead. They were carrying me out to burial when a doctor stopped them just in time."

I'd heard plenty of cases like that, and I saw no reason why he should want to tell me about it. And then I thought I saw his point. His mother had not been too anxious once before to see if he were properly dead, though I had little doubt that she made a great show of grief—"My poor boy. I don't know what I shall do without him." And I'm certain that she believed herself then, as she believed herself now. She wasn't a murderess. She was only inclined to be premature.

"Look here, old man," I said, and I propped him a little higher on his pillow, "you needn't be frightened. You aren't going to die, and anyway I'd see that the doctor cut a vein or something before they moved you. But that's all morbid stuff. Why, I'd stake my shirt that you've got plenty more years in front of you. And plenty more girls too," I added to make him smile.

"Can't you cut out all that?" he said, and I knew then that he had turned religious. "Why," he said, "if I lived, I wouldn't touch another girl. I wouldn't, not one."

I tried not to smile at that, but it wasn't easy to keep a straight face. There's always something a bit funny about a sick man's morals. "Anyway," I said, "you needn't be frightened."

"It's not that," he said. "Old man, when I came round that other time, I thought that I'd been dead. It wasn't like sleep at all. Or rest in peace. There was someone there, all round me, who knew everything. Every girl I'd ever had. Even that young one who hadn't understood. It was before your time. She lived a mile down the road, where Rachel lives now, but she and her family went away afterwards. Even the money I'd taken from mother. I don't call that stealing. It's in the family. I never had a chance to explain. Even the thoughts I'd had. A man can't help his thoughts."

"A nightmare," I said.

"Yes, it must have been a dream, mustn't it? The sort of dream people do get when they are ill. And I saw what was coming to me too. I can't bear being hurt. It wasn't fair. And I wanted to faint and I couldn't, because I was dead."

"In the dream," I said. His fear made me nervous. "In the dream," I said again.

"Yes, it must have been a dream—mustn't it?—because I woke up. The curious thing was I felt quite well and strong. I got up and stood in the road, and a little farther down, kicking up the dust, was a small crowd, going off with a man—the doctor who had stopped them burying me."

"Well," I said.

"Old man," he said, "suppose it was true. Suppose I had been dead. I believed it then, you know, and so did my mother. But you can't trust her. I went straight for a couple of years. I thought it might be a sort of second chance. Then things got fogged and somehow . . . It didn't seem really possible. It's not possible. Of course it's not possible. You know it isn't, don't you?"

"Why no," I said. "Miracles of that sort don't happen nowadays. And anyway, they aren't likely to happen to you, are they? And here of all places under the sun."

"It would be so dreadful," he said, "if it had been true, and I'd got to go through all that again. You don't know what things were going to happen to me in that dream. And they'd be worse now." He stopped and then, after a moment, he added as though he were stating a fact, "When one's dead there's no unconsciousness any more for ever."

"Of course it was a dream," I said and squeezed his hand. He was frightening me with his fancies. I wished that he'd die quickly, so that I could get away from his sly, bloodshot and terrified eyes and see something cheerful and amusing, like the Rachel he had mentioned, who lived a mile down the road.

"Why," I said, "if there had been a man about working miracles like that, we should have heard of others, you may be sure. Even poked away in this god-forsaken spot," I said.

"There were some others," he said. "But the stories only went round among the poor, and they'll believe anything, won't they? There were lots of diseased and crippled they said he'd cured. And there was a man, who'd been born blind, and he came and just touched his eyelids and sight came to him. Those were old wives' tales, weren't they?" he asked me, stammering with fear, and then lying suddenly still and bunched up at the side of the bed.

I began to say, "Of course they were all lies," but I stopped, because there was no need. All I could do was to go downstairs and tell his mother to come up and close his eyes. I wouldn't have touched them for all the money in the world. It was a long time since I'd thought of that day ages and ages ago, when I felt a cold touch like spittle on my lids and opening my eyes had seen a man like a tree surrounded by other trees walking away.

THE DEMON LOVER

ELIZABETH BOWEN (1899–   )

Towards the end of her day in London Mrs. Drover went round to her shut-up house to look for several things she wanted to take away. Some belonged to herself, some to her family, who were by now used to their country life. It was late August; it had been a steamy, showery day: at the moment the trees down the pavement glittered in an escape of humid yellow afternoon sun. Against the next batch of clouds, already piling up ink-dark, broken chimneys and parapets stood out. In her once familiar street, as in any unused channel, an unfamiliar queerness had silted up; a cat wove itself in and out of railings, but no human eye watched Mrs. Drover's return. Shifting some parcels under her arm, she slowly forced round her latchkey in an unwilling lock, then gave the door, which had warped, a push with her knee. Dead air came out to meet her as she went in.

The staircase window having been boarded up, no light came down into the hall. But one door, she could just see, stood ajar, so she went quickly through into the room and unshuttered the big window in there. Now the prosaic woman, looking about her, was more perplexed than she knew by everything that she saw, by traces of her long former habit of life—the yellow smoke-stain up the white marble mantelpiece, the ring left by a vase on the top of the escritoire; the bruise in the wallpaper where, on the door being thrown open widely, the china handle had always hit the wall. The piano, having gone away to be stored, had left what looked like claw-marks on its part of the parquet. Though not much dust had seeped in, each object wore a film of another kind; and, the only ventilation being the chimney, the whole drawing-room smelled of the cold hearth. Mrs. Drover put down her parcels on the escritoire and left the room to proceed upstairs; the things she wanted were in a bedroom chest.

She had been anxious to see how the house was—the part-time caretaker she shared with some neighbours was away this week on his holiday, known to be not yet back. At the best of times he did not look in often, and she was never sure that she trusted him. There were some cracks in the structure, left by the last bombing, on which she was anxious to keep an eye. Not that one could do anything—

A shaft of refracted daylight now lay across the hall. She stopped dead and stared at the hall table—on this lay a letter addressed to her.

She thought first—then the caretaker *must* be back. All the same, who, seeing the house shuttered, would have dropped a letter in at the box? It was not a circular, it was not a bill. And the post office redirected, to the address in the country, everything for her that came through the post. The caretaker (even if he *were* back) did not know she was due in London to-day—her call here had been planned to be a surprise —so his negligence in the manner of this letter, leaving it to wait in the dusk and the dust, annoyed her. Annoyed, she picked up the letter, which bore no stamp. But it cannot be important, or they would know . . . She took the letter rapidly upstairs with her, without a stop to look at the writing till she reached what had been her bedroom, where she let in light. The room looked over the garden and other gardens: the sun had gone in; as the clouds sharpened and lowered, the trees and rank lawns seemed already to smoke with dark. Her reluctance to look again at the letter came from the fact that she felt intruded upon—and by someone contemptuous of her ways. However, in the tenseness preceding the fall of rain she read it: it was a few lines.

Dear Kathleen,
    You will not have forgotten that to-day is our anniversary, and the day we said. The years have gone by at once slowly and fast. In view of the fact that nothing has changed, I shall rely upon you to keep your promise. I was sorry to see you leave London, but was satisfied that you would be back in time. You may expect me, therefore, at the hour arranged.

Until then . . .
K.

Mrs. Drover looked for the date: it was to-day's. She dropped the letter on to the bed-springs, then picked it up to see the writing again—her lips, beneath the remains of lipstick, beginning to go white. She felt so much the change in her own face that she went to the mirror, polished a clear patch in it and looked at once urgently and stealthily in. She was confronted by a woman of forty-four, with eyes starting out under a hat-brim that had been rather carelessly pulled down. She had not put on any more powder since she left the shop where she ate her solitary tea. The pearls her husband had given her on their marriage hung loose round her now rather thinner throat, slipping into the V of the pink wool jumper her sister knitted last autumn as they sat round the fire. Mrs. Drover's most normal expression was one of controlled worry, but of assent. Since the birth of the third of her little boys, attended by a quite serious illness, she had had an intermittent muscular flicker to the left of her mouth, but in spite of this she could always sustain a manner that was at once energetic and calm.

Turning from her own face as precipitately as she had gone to meet it, she went to the chest where the things were, unlocked it, threw up the lid and knelt to search. But as rain began to come crashing down she could not keep from looking over her shoulder at the stripped bed on which the letter lay. Behind the blanket of rain the clock of the church that still stood struck six—with rapidly heightening apprehension she counted each of the slow strokes. "The hour arranged . . . My God," she said, "*what* hour? How should I . . . ? After twenty-five years. . . ."

The young girl talking to the soldier in the garden had not ever completely seen his face. It was dark; they were saying good-bye under a tree. Now and then—for it felt, from not seeing him at this intense moment, as though she had never seen him at all—she verified his presence for these few moments longer by putting out a hand, which he each time pressed, without very much kindness, and painfully, on to one of the breast buttons of his uniform. That cut of the button on the palm of her hand was, principally, what she was to carry away. This was so near the end of a leave from France that she could only wish him already gone. It was August 1916. Being not kissed, being drawn away from and looked at intimidated Kathleen till she imagined spectral glitters in the place of his eyes. Turning away and looking back up the lawn she saw, through branches of trees, the drawing-room window alight: she caught a breath for the moment when she could go running back there into the safe arms of her mother and sister, and cry: "What shall I do, what shall I do? He has gone."

Hearing her catch her breath, her fiancé said, without feeling: "Cold?"

"You're going away such a long way."

"Not so far as you think."

"I don't understand?"

"You don't have to," he said. "You will. You know what we said."

"But that was—suppose you—I mean, suppose."

"I shall be with you," he said, "sooner or later. You won't forget that. You need do nothing but wait."

Only a little more than a minute later she was free to run up the silent lawn. Looking in through the window at her mother and sister, who did not for the moment perceive her, she already felt that unnatural promise drive down between her and the rest of all human kind. No other way of having given herself could have made her feel so apart, lost and foresworn. She could not have plighted a more sinister troth.

Kathleen behaved well when, some months later, her fiancé was reported missing, presumed killed. Her family not only supported her but were able to praise her courage without stint because they could not regret, as a husband for her, the man they knew almost nothing about. They hoped she would, in a year or two, console herself —and had it been only a question of consolation things might have gone much straighter ahead. But her trouble, behind just a little grief, was a complete dislocation from everything. She did not reject other lovers, for these failed to appear: for years she failed to attract men—and with the approach of her 'thirties she became natural enough to share her family's anxiousness on this score. She began to put herself out, to wonder; and at thirty-two she was very greatly relieved to find herself being courted by William Drover. She married him, and the two of them settled down in this quiet, arboreal part of Kensington: in this house the years piled up, her children were born and they all lived till they were driven out by the bombs of the next war. Her movements as Mrs. Drover were circumscribed, and she dismissed any idea that they were still watched.

As things were—dead or living the letter-writer sent her only a threat. Unable, for some minutes, to go on kneeling with her back exposed to the empty room, Mrs. Drover rose from the chest to sit on an upright chair whose back was firmly against the wall. The desuetude of her former bedroom, her married London home's whole air of being a cracked cup from which memory, with its reassuring power, had either evaporated or leaked away, made a crisis—and at just this crisis the letter-writer had, knowledgeably, struck. The hollowness of the house this evening cancelled years on years of voices, habits and steps. Through the shut windows she only heard rain fall on the roofs around. To rally herself, she said she was in a mood—and, for two or three seconds shutting her eyes, told herself that she had imagined the letter. But she opened them—there it lay on the bed.

On the supernatural side of the letter's entrance she was not permitting her mind to dwell. Who, in London, knew she meant to call at the house to-day? Evidently, however, this had been known. The caretaker, *had* he come back, had had no cause to expect her: he would have taken the letter in his pocket, to forward it, at his own time, through the post. There was no other sign that the caretaker had been in—but, if not? Letters dropped in at doors of deserted houses do not fly or walk to tables in halls. They do not sit on the dust of empty tables with the air of certainty that they will be found. There is needed some human hand—but nobody but the caretaker had a key. Under circumstances she did not care to consider, a house can be entered without a key. It was possible that she was not alone now. She might be being waited for, downstairs. Waited for—until when? Until "the hour arranged." At least that was not six o'clock: six has struck.

She rose from the chair and went over and locked the door.

The thing was, to get out. To fly? No, not that: she had to catch her train. As a woman whose utter dependability was the keystone of her family life she was not willing to return to the country, to her husband, her little boys and her sister, without the objects she had come up to fetch. Resuming work at the chest she set about making up a number of parcels in a rapid, fumbling-decisive way. These, with her shopping parcels, would be too much to carry; these meant a taxi—at the thought of the taxi her heart went up and her normal breathing resumed. I will ring up the taxi now; the taxi cannot come too soon: I shall hear the taxi out there running its engine, till I walk calmly down to it through the hall. I'll ring up— But no: the telephone is cut off . . . She tugged at a knot she had tied wrong.

The idea of flight . . . He was never kind to me, not really. I don't remember him kind at all. Mother said he never considered me. He was set on me, that was what it was—not love. Not love, not meaning a person well. What did he do, to make me promise like that? I can't remember— But she found that she could.

She remembered with such dreadful acuteness that the twenty-five years since then dissolved like smoke and she instinctively looked for the weal left by the button on the palm of her hand. She remembered not only all that he said and did but the complete suspension of *her* existence during that August week. I was not myself—they all told me so at the time. She remembered—but with one white burning blank as where acid has dropped on a photograph: *under no conditions* could she remember his face.

So, wherever he may be waiting, I shall not know him. You have no time to run from a face you do not expect.

The thing was to get to the taxi before any clock struck what could be the hour. She would slip down the street and round the side of the square to where the square gave on the main road. She would return in the taxi, safe, to her own door, and bring the solid driver into the house with her to pick up the parcels from room to room. The idea of the taxi driver made her decisive, bold: she unlocked her door, went to the top of the staircase and listened down.

She heard nothing—but while she was hearing nothing the *passé* air of the staircase was disturbed by a draught that travelled up to her face. It emanated from the basement: down there a door or window was being opened by someone who chose this moment to leave the house.

The rain had stopped; the pavements steamily shone as Mrs. Drover let herself out by inches from her own front door into the empty street. The unoccupied houses opposite continued to meet her look with their damaged stare. Making towards the thoroughfare and the taxi, she tried not to keep looking behind. Indeed, the silence was so intense—one of those creeks of London silence exaggerated this summer by the damage of war—that no tread could have gained on hers unheard. Where her street debouched on the square where people went on living she grew conscious of and checked her unnatural pace. Across the open end of the square two buses impassively passed each other; women, a perambulator, cyclists, a man wheeling a barrow signalized, once again, the ordinary flow of life. At the square's most populous corner should be—and was—the short taxi rank. This evening, only one taxi—but this, although it presented its blank rump, appeared already to be alertly waiting for her. Indeed, without looking round the driver started his engine as she panted up from behind and put her hand on the door. As she did so, the clock struck seven. The taxi faced the main road: to make the trip back to her house it would have to turn—she had settled back on the seat and the taxi *had* turned before she, surprised by its knowing movement, recollected that she had not "said where." She leaned forward to scratch at the glass panel that divided the driver's head from her own.

The driver braked to what was almost a stop, turned round and slid the glass panel back: the jolt of this flung Mrs. Drover forward till her face was almost into the glass. Through the aperture driver and passenger, not six inches between them, remained for an eternity eye to eye. Mrs. Drover's mouth hung open for some seconds before she could issue her first scream. After that she continued to scream freely and to beat with her gloved hands on the glass all round as the taxi, accelerating without mercy, made off with her into the hinterland of deserted streets.

THE UPTURNED FACE

STEPHEN CRANE (1871–1900)

"What will we do now?" said the adjutant, troubled and excited.

"Bury him," said Timothy Lean.

The two officers looked down close to their toes where lay the body of their comrade. The face was chalk-blue; gleaming eyes stared at the sky. Over the two upright figures was a windy sound of bullets, and on the top of the hill Lean's prostrate company of Spitzbergen infantry was firing measured volleys.

"Don't you think it would be better—" began the adjutant. "We might leave him until to-morrow."

"No," said Lean. "I can't hold that post an hour longer. I've got to fall back, and we've got to bury old Bill."

"Of course," said the adjutant, at once. "Your men got entrenching tools?"

Lean shouted back to his little line, and two men came slowly, one with a pick, one with a shovel. They stared in the direction of the Rostina sharp-shooters. Bullets cracked near their ears. "Dig here," said Lean gruffly. The men, thus caused to lower their glances to the turf, became hurried and frightened merely because they could not look to see whence the bullets came. The dull beat of the pick striking the earth sounded amid the swift snap of close bullets. Presently the other private began to shovel.

"I suppose," said the adjutant, slowly, "we'd better search his clothes for—things."

Lean nodded. Together in curious abstraction they looked at the body. Then Lean stirred his shoulders suddenly, arousing himself.

"Yes," he said, "we'd better see what he's got." He dropped to his knees, and his hands approached the body of the dead officer. But his hands wavered over the buttons of the tunic. The first button was brick-red with drying blood, and he did not seem to dare touch it.

"Go on," said the adjutant, hoarsely.

Lean stretched his wooden hand, and his fingers fumbled the blood-stained buttons. At last he rose with ghastly face. He had gathered a watch, a whistle, a pipe, a tobacco-pouch, a handkerchief, a little case of cards and papers. He looked at the adjutant. There was a silence. The adjutant was feeling that he had been a coward to make Lean do all the grisly business.

"Well," said Lean, "that's all, I think. You have his sword and revolver?"

"Yes," said the adjutant, his face working, and then he burst out in a sudden strange fury at the two privates. "Why don't you hurry up with that grave? What are you doing, anyhow? Hurry, do you hear? I never saw such stupid—"

Even as he cried out in his passion the two men were laboring for their lives. Ever overhead the bullets were spitting.

The grave was finished. It was not a masterpiece—a poor little shallow thing. Lean and the adjutant again looked at each other in a curious silent communication.

Suddenly the adjutant croaked out a weird laugh. It was a terrible laugh, which had its origin in that part of the mind which is first moved by the singing of the nerves. "Well," he said, humorously to Lean, "I suppose we had best tumble him in."

"Yes," said Lean. The two privates stood waiting, bent over their implements. "I suppose," said Lean, "it would be better if we laid him in ourselves."

"Yes," said the adjutant. Then apparently remembering that he had made Lean search the body, he stooped with great fortitude and took hold of the dead officer's clothing. Lean joined him. Both were particular that their fingers should not feel the corpse. They tugged away; the corpse lifted, heaved, toppled, flopped into the grave, and the two officers, straightening, looked again at each other—they were always looking at each other. They sighed with relief.

The adjutant said, "I suppose we should—we should say something. Do you know the service, Tim?"

"They don't read the service until the grave is filled in," said Lean, pressing his lips to an academic expression.

"Don't they?" said the adjutant, shocked that he had made the mistake.

"Oh well," he cried, suddenly, "let us—let us say something—while he can hear us."

"All right," said Lean. "Do you know the service?"

"I can't remember a line of it," said the adjutant.

Lean was extremely dubious. "I can repeat two lines, but—"

"Well, do it," said the adjutant. "Go as far as you can. That's better than nothing. And the beasts have got our range exactly."

Lean looked to his two men. "Attention," he barked. The privates came to attention with a click, looking much aggrieved. The adjutant lowered his helmet to his knee. Lean, bareheaded, stood over the grave. The Rostina sharpshooters fired briskly.

"O Father, our friend has sunk in the deep waters of death, but his spirit has leaped toward Thee as the bubble arises from the lips of the drowning. Perceive, we beseech, O Father, the little flying bubble, and—"

Lean, although husky and ashamed, had suffered no hesitation up to this point, but he stopped with a hopeless feeling and looked at the corpse.

The adjutant moved uneasily. "And from Thy superb heights—" he began, and then he too came to an end.

"And from Thy superb heights," said Lean.

The adjutant suddenly remembered a phrase in the back part of the Spitzbergen burial service, and he exploited it with the triumphant manner of a man who has recalled everything and can go on.

"O God, have mercy—"

"O God, have mercy—" said Lean.

"Mercy," repeated the adjutant, in quick failure.

"Mercy," said Lean. And then he was moved by some violence of feeling, for he turned suddenly upon his two men and tigerishly said, "Throw the dirt in."

. . . .

The fire of the Rostina sharpshooters was accurate and continuous.

One of the aggrieved privates came forward with his shovel. He lifted his first shovel-load of earth, and for a moment of inexplicable hesitation it was held above this corpse, which from its chalk-blue face looked keenly out of the grave. Then the soldier emptied his shovel on—on the feet.

Timothy Lean felt as if tons had been swiftly lifted off his forehead. He had felt that perhaps the private might empty the shovel on—on the face. It had been emptied on the feet. There was a great point gained there—ha, ha!—the first shovelful had been emptied on the feet. How satisfactory!

The adjutant began to babble. "Well, of course—a man we've messed with all these years—impossible—you can't, you know, leave your intimate friends rotting on the field. Go on, for God's sake, and shovel, you!"

The man with the shovel suddenly ducked, grabbed his left arm with his right hand, and looked at his officer for orders. Lean picked the shovel from the ground. "Go to the rear," he said to the wounded man. He also addressed the other private. "You get under cover, too; I'll finish this business."

The wounded man scrambled hard still for the top of the ridge without devoting any glances to the direction whence the bullets came, and the other man followed at an equal pace; but he was different, in that he looked back anxiously three times.

This is merely the way—often—of the hit and unhit.

Timothy Lean filled the shovel, hesitated, and then in a movement which was like a gesture of abhorrence he flung the dirt into the grave, and as it landed it made a sound—plop. Lean suddenly stopped and mopped his brow—a tired laborer.

"Perhaps we have been wrong," said the adjutant. His glance wavered stupidly. "It might have been better if we hadn't buried him just at this time. Of course, if we advance to-morrow the body would have been—"

"Damn you," said Lean, "shut your mouth!" He was not the senior officer.

He again filled the shovel and flung the earth. Always the earth made that sound—plop. For a space Lean worked frantically, like a man digging himself out of danger.

Soon there was nothing to be seen but the chalk-blue face. Lean filled the shovel. "Good God," he cried to the adjutant. "Why didn't you turn him somehow when you put him in? This—" Then Lean began to stutter.

The adjutant understood. He was pale to the lips. "Go on, man," he cried, beseechingly, almost in a shout.

Lean swung back the shovel. It went forward in a pendulum curve. When the earth landed it made a sound—plop.

A CLEAN, WELL-LIGHTED PLACE

ERNEST HEMINGWAY (1898–1961)

It was late and every one had left the café except an old man who sat in the shadow the leaves of the tree made against the electric light. In the day time the street was dusty, but at night the dew settled the dust and the old man liked to sit late because he was deaf and now at night it was quiet and he felt the difference. The two waiters inside the café knew that the old man was a little drunk, and while he was a good client they knew that if he became too drunk he would leave without paying, so they kept watch on him.

"Last week he tried to commit suicide," one waiter said.

"Why?"

"He was in despair."

"What about?"

"Nothing."

"How do you know it was nothing?"

"He has plenty of money."

They sat together at a table that was close against the wall near the door of the café and looked at the terrace where the tables were all empty except where the old man sat in the shadow of the leaves of the tree that moved slightly in the wind. A girl and a soldier went by in the street. The street light shone on the brass number on his collar. The girl wore no head covering and hurried beside him.

"The guard will pick him up," one waiter said.

"What does it matter if he gets what he's after?"

"He had better get off the street now. The guard will get him. They went by five minutes ago."

The old man sitting in the shadow rapped on his saucer with his glass. The younger waiter went over to him.

"What do you want?"

The old man looked at him. "Another brandy," he said.

"You'll be drunk," the waiter said. The old man looked at him. The waiter went away.

"He'll stay all night," he said to his colleague. "I'm sleepy now. I never get into bed before three o'clock. He should have killed himself last week."

The waiter took the brandy bottle and another saucer from the counter inside the café and marched out to the old man's table. He put down the saucer and poured the glass full of brandy.

"You should have killed yourself last week," he said to the deaf man. The old man motioned with his finger. "A little more," he said. The waiter poured on into the glass so that the brandy slopped over and ran down the stem into the top saucer of the pile. "Thank you," the old man said. The waiter took the bottle back inside the café. He sat down at the table with his colleague again.

"He's drunk now," he said.

"He's drunk every night."

"What did he want to kill himself for?"

"How should I know."

"How did he do it?"

"He hung himself with a rope."

"Who cut him down?"

"His niece."

"Why did they do it?"

"Fear for his soul."

"How much money has he got?"

"He's got plenty."

"He must be eighty years old."

"Anyway I should say he was eighty."

"I wish he would go home. I never get to bed before three o'clock. What kind of hour is that to go to bed?"

"He stays up because he likes it."

"He's lonely. I'm not lonely. I have a wife waiting in bed for me."

"He had a wife once too."

"A wife would be no good to him now."

"You can't tell. He might be better with a wife."

"His niece looks after him."

"I know. You said she cut him down."

"I wouldn't want to be that old. An old man is a nasty thing."

"Not always. This old man is clean. He drinks without spilling. Even now, drunk. Look at him."

"I don't want to look at him. I wish he would go home. He has no regard for those who must work."

The old man looked from his glass across the square, then over at the waiters.

"Another brandy," he said, pointing to his glass. The waiter who was in a hurry came over.

"Finished," he said, speaking with that omission of syntax stupid people employ when talking to drunken people or foreigners. "No more tonight. Close now."

"Another," said the old man.

"No. Finished." The waiter wiped the edge of the table with a towel and shook his head.

The old man stood up, slowly counted the saucers, took a leather coin purse from his pocket and paid for the drinks, leaving half a peseta tip.

The waiter watched him go down the street, a very old man walking unsteadily but with dignity.

"Why didn't you let him stay and drink?" the unhurried waiter asked. They were putting up the shutters. "It is not half-past two."

"I want to go home to bed."

"What is an hour?"

"More to me than to him."

"An hour is the same."

"You talk like an old man yourself. He can buy a bottle and drink at home."

"It's not the same."

"No, it is not," agreed the waiter with a wife. He did not wish to be unjust. He was only in a hurry.

"And you? You have no fear of going home before your usual hour?"

"Are you trying to insult me?"

"No, hombre, only to make a joke."

"No," the waiter who was in a hurry said, rising from pulling down the metal shutters. "I have confidence. I am all confidence."

"You have youth, confidence, and a job," the old waiter said. "You have everything."

"And what do you lack?"

"Everything but work."

"You have everything I have."

"No. I have never had confidence and I am not young."

"Come on. Stop talking nonsense and lock up."

"I am of those who like to stay late at the café," the older waiter said. "With all those who do not want to go to bed. With all those who need a light for the night."

"I want to go home and into bed."

"We are of two different kinds," the older waiter said. He was now dressed to go home. "It is not only a question of youth and confidence although those things are very beautiful. Each night I am reluctant to close up because there may be some one who needs the café."

"Hombre, there are bodegas open all night long."

"You do not understand. This is a clean and pleasant café. It is well lighted. The light is very good and also, now, there are shadows of the leaves."

"Good night," said the younger waiter.

"Good night," the other said. Turning off the electric light he continued the conversation with himself. It is the light of course but it is necessary that the place be clean and pleasant. You do not want music. Certainly you do not want music. Nor can you stand before a bar with dignity although that is all that is provided for these hours. What did he fear? It was not fear or dread. It was a nothing that he knew too well. It was all a nothing and a man was nothing too. It was only that and light was all it needed and a certain cleanness and order. Some lived in it and never felt it but he knew it all was nada y pues nada y nada y pues nada. Our nada who art in nada, nada be thy name thy kingdom nada thy will be nada in nada as it is in nada. Give us this nada our daily nada and nada us our nada as we nada our nadas and nada us not into nada but deliver us from nada; pues nada. Hail nothing full of nothing, nothing is with thee. He smiled and stood before a bar with a shining steam pressure coffee machine.

"What's yours?" asked the barman.

"Nada."

"Otro loco mas," said the barman and turned away.

"A little cup," said the waiter.

The barman poured it for him.

"The light is very bright and pleasant but the bar is unpolished," the waiter said.

The barman looked at him but did not answer. It was too late at night for conversation.

"You want another copita?" the barman asked.

"No, thank you," said the waiter and went out. He disliked bars and bodegas. A clean, well-lighted café was a very different thing. Now, without thinking further, he would go home to his room. He would lie in the bed and finally, with daylight, he would go to sleep. After all, he said to himself, it is probably only insomnia. Many must have it.

PASTE

HENRY JAMES (1843–1916)

"I've found a lot more things," her cousin said to her the day after the second funeral; "they're up in her room—but they're things I wish *you'd* look at."

The pair of mourners, sufficiently stricken, were in the garden of the vicarage together, before luncheon, waiting to be summoned to that meal, and Arthur Prime had still in his face the intention, she was moved to call it rather than the expression, of feeling something or other. Some such appearance was in itself of course natural within a week of his stepmother's death, within three of his father's; but what was most present to the girl, herself sensitive and shrewd, was that he seemed somehow to brood without sorrow, to suffer without what she in her own case would have called pain. He turned away from her after this last speech—it was a good deal his habit to drop an observation and leave her to pick it up without assistance. If the vicar's widow, now in her turn finally translated, had not really belonged to him it was not for want of her giving herself, so far as he ever would take her; and she had lain for three days all alone at the end of the passage, in the great cold chamber of hospitality, the dampish, greenish room where visitors slept and where several of the ladies of the parish had, without effect, offered, in pairs and successions, piously to watch with her. His personal connection with the parish was now slighter than ever, and he had really not waited for this opportunity to show the ladies what he thought of them. She felt that she herself had, during her doleful month's leave from Bleet, where she was governess, rather taken her place in the same snubbed order; but it was presently, none the less, with a better little hope of coming in for some remembrance, some relic, that she went up to look at the things he had spoken of, the identity of which, as a confused cluster of bright objects on a table in the darkened room, shimmered at her as soon as she had opened the door.

They met her eyes for the first time, but in a moment, before touching them, she knew them as things of the theatre, as very much too fine to have been, with any verisimilitude, things of the vicarage. They were too dreadfully good to be true, for her aunt had had no jewels to speak of, and these were coronets and girdles, diamonds, rubies, and sapphires. Flagrant tinsel and glass, they looked strangely vulgar, but if, after the first queer shock of them, she found herself taking them up, it was for the very proof, never yet so distinct to her, of a far-off faded story. An honest widowed cleric with a small son and a large sense of Shakespeare had, on a brave latitude of habit as well as of taste—since it implied his having in very fact dropped deep into the "pit"—conceived for an obscure actress, several years older than himself, an admiration of which the prompt offer of his reverend name and hortatory hand was the sufficiently candid sign. The response had perhaps, in those dim years, in the way of eccentricity, even bettered the proposal, and Charlotte, turning the tale over, had long since drawn from it a measure of the career renounced by the undistinguished *comédienne*—doubtless also tragic, or perhaps pantomimic, at a pinch—of her late uncle's dreams. This career couldn't have been eminent and must much more probably have been comfortless.

"You see what it is—old stuff of the time she never liked to mention."

Our young woman gave a start; her companion had, after all, rejoined her and had apparently watched a moment her slightly scared recognition. "So I said to myself," she replied. Then, to show intelligence, yet keep clear of twaddle: "How peculiar they look!"

"They look awful," said Arthur Prime. "Cheap gilt, diamonds as big as potatoes. These are trappings of a ruder age than ours. Actors do themselves better now."

"Oh, now," said Charlotte, not to be less knowing, "actresses have real diamonds."

"Some of them." Arthur spoke dryly.

"I mean the bad ones—the nobodies too."

"Oh, some of the nobodies have the biggest. But mamma wasn't of that sort."

"A nobody?" Charlotte risked.

"Not a nobody to whom somebody—well, not a nobody with diamonds. It isn't all worth, this trash, five pounds."

There was something in the old gewgaws that spoke to her, and she continued to turn them over. "They're relics. I think they have their melancholy and even their dignity."

Arthur observed another pause. "Do you care for them?" he then asked. "I mean," he promptly added, "as a souvenir."

"Of you?" Charlotte threw off.

"Of me? What have I to do with it? Of your poor dead aunt who was so kind to you," he said with virtuous sternness.

"Well, I would rather have them than nothing."

"Then please take them," he returned in a tone of relief which expressed somehow more of the eager than of the gracious.

"Thank you." Charlotte lifted two or three objects up and set them down again. Though they were lighter than the materials they imitated they were so much more extravagant that they struck her in truth as rather an awkward heritage, to which she might have preferred even a matchbox or a pen-wiper. They were indeed shameless pinchbeck. "Had you any idea she had kept them?"

"I don't at all believe she *had* kept them or knew they were there, and I'm very sure my father didn't. They had quite equally worked off any tenderness for the connection. These odds and ends, which she thought had been given away or destroyed, had simply got thrust into a dark corner and been forgotten."

Charlotte wondered. "Where then did you find them?"

"In that old tin box"—and the young man pointed to the receptacle from which he had dislodged them and which stood on a neighbouring chair. "It's rather a good box still, but I'm afraid I can't give you *that*."

The girl took no heed of the box; she continued only to look at the trinkets. "What corner had she found?"

"She hadn't 'found' it," her companion sharply insisted; "she had simply lost it. The whole thing had passed from her mind. The box was on the top shelf of the old schoolroom closet, which, until one put one's head into it from a step-ladder, looked, from below, quite cleared out. The door's narrow and the part of the closet to the left goes well into the wall. The box had stuck there for years."

Charlotte was conscious of a mind divided and a vision vaguely troubled, and once more she took up two or three of the subjects of this revelation: a big bracelet in the form of a gilt serpent with many twists and beady eyes, a brazen belt studded with emeralds and rubies, a chain, of flamboyant architecture, to which, at the Theatre Royal, Little Peddlington, Hamlet's mother must have been concerned to attach the portrait of the successor to Hamlet's father. "Are you very sure they're not really worth something? Their mere weight alone—!" she vaguely observed, balancing a moment a royal diadem that might have crowned one of the creations of the famous Mrs. Jarley.

But Arthur Prime, it was clear, had already thought the question over and found the answer easy. "If they had been worth anything to speak of she would long ago have sold them. My father and she had unfortunately never been in a position to keep any considerable value locked up." And while his companion took in the obvious force of this he went on with a flourish just marked enough not to escape her: "If they're worth anything at all—why, you're only the more welcome to them."

Charlotte had now in her hand a small bag of faded figured silk—one of those antique conveniences that speak to us, in the terms of evaporated camphor and lavender, of the part they have played in some personal history; but, though she had for the first time drawn the string, she looked much more at the young man than at the questionable treasure it appeared to contain. "I shall like them. They're all I have."

"All you have—?"

"That belonged to her."

He swelled a little, then looked about him as if to appeal—as against her avidity—to the whole poor place. "Well, what else do you want?"

"Nothing. Thank you very much." With which she bent her eyes on the article wrapped, and now only exposed, in her superannuated satchel—a string of large pearls, such a shining circle as might once have graced the neck of a provincial Ophelia and borne company to a flaxen wig. "This perhaps *is* worth something. Feel it." And she passed him the necklace, the weight of which she had gathered for a moment into her hand.

He measured it in the same way with his own, but remained quite detached "Worth at most thirty shillings."

"Not more?"

"Surely not if it's paste?"

"But *is* it paste?"

He gave a small sniff of impatience. "Pearls nearly as big as filberts?"

"But they're heavy," Charlotte declared.

"No heavier than anything else." And he gave them back with an allowance for her simplicity. "Do you imagine for a moment they're real?"

She studied them a little, feeling them, turning them round. "Mightn't they possibly be?"

"Of that size—stuck away with that trash?"

"I admit it isn't likely," Charlotte presently said. "And pearls are so easily imitated."

"That's just what—to a person who knows—they're not. These have no lustre, no play."

"No—they *are* dull. They're opaque."

"Besides," he lucidly inquired, "how could she ever have come by them?"

"Mightn't they have been a present?"

Arthur stared at the question as if it were almost improper.

"Because actresses are exposed—?" He pulled up, however, not saying to what, and before she could supply the deficiency had, with the sharp ejaculation of "No, they mightn't!" turned his back on her and walked away. His manner made her feel that she had probably been wanting in tact, and before he returned to the subject, the last thing that evening, she had satisfied herself of the ground of his resentment. They had been talking of her departure the next morning, the hour of her train and the fly that would come for her, and it was precisely these things that gave him his effective chance. "I really can't allow you to leave the house under the impression that my stepmother was at *any* time of her life the sort of person to allow herself to be approached—"

"With pearl necklaces and that sort of thing?" Arthur had made for her somehow the difficulty that she couldn't show him she understood him without seeming pert.

It at any rate only added to his own gravity. "That sort of thing, exactly."

"I didn't think when I spoke this morning—but I see what you mean."

"I mean that she was beyond reproach," said Arthur Prime.

"A hundred times yes."

"Therefore if she couldn't, out of her slender gains, ever have paid for a row of pearls—"

"She couldn't, in that atmosphere, ever properly have had one? Of course she couldn't. I've seen perfectly since our talk," Charlotte went on, "that that string of beads isn't even, as an imitation, very good. The little clasp itself doesn't seem even gold. With false pearls, I suppose," the girl mused, "it naturally wouldn't be."

"The whole thing's rotten paste," her companion returned as if to have done with it. "If it were *not,* and she had kept it all these years hidden—"

"Yes?" Charlotte sounded as he paused.

"Why, I shouldn't know what to think!"

"Oh, I see." She had met him with a certain blankness, but adequately enough, it seemed, for him to regard the subject as dismissed; and there was no reversion to it between them before, on the morrow, when she had with difficulty made a place for them in her trunk, she carried off these florid survivals.

At Bleet she found small occasion to revert to them and, in an air charged with such quite other references, even felt, after she had laid them away, much enshrouded, beneath various piles of clothing, as if they formed a collection not wholly without its note of the ridiculous. Yet she was never, for the joke, tempted to show them to her pupils, though Gwendolen and Blanche, in particular, always wanted, on her return, to know what she had brought back; so that without an accident by which the case was quite changed they might have appeared to enter on a new phase of interment. The essence of the accident was the sudden illness, at the last moment, of Lady Bobby, whose advent had been so much counted on to spice the five days' feast laid out for the coming of age of the eldest son of the house; and its equally marked effect was the despatch of a pressing message, in quite another direction, to Mrs. Guy, who, could she by a miracle be secured—she was always engaged ten parties deep—might be trusted to supply, it was believed, an element of exuberance scarcely less active. Mrs. Guy was already known to several of the visitors already on the scene, but she wasn't yet known to our young lady, who found her, after many wires and counterwires had at last determined the triumph of her arrival, a strange, charming little red-haired, black-dressed woman, with the face of a baby and the authority of a commodore. She took on the spot the discreet, the exceptional young governess into the confidence of her designs and, still more, of her doubts; intimating that it was a policy she almost always promptly pursued.

"Tomorrow and Thursday are all right," she said frankly to Charlotte on the second day, "but I'm not half-satisfied with Friday."

"What improvement then do you suggest?"

"Well, my strong point, you know, is *tableaux vivants*."

"Charming. And what is your favourite character?"

"Boss!" said Mrs. Guy with decision; and it was very markedly under that ensign that she had, within a few hours, completely planned her campaign and recruited her troop. Every word she uttered was to the point, but none more so than, after a general survey of their equipment, her final inquiry of Charlotte. She had been looking about, but half appeased, at the muster of decoration and drapery. "We shall be dull. We shall want more colour. You've nothing else?"

Charlotte had a thought. "No—I've *some* things."

"Then why don't you bring them?"

The girl weighed it. "Would you come to my room?"

"No," said Mrs. Guy—"bring them tonight to mine." So Charlotte, at the evening's end, after candlesticks had flickered through brown old passages bedward, arrived at her friend's door with the burden of her aunt's relics. But she promptly expressed a fear. "Are they too garish?"

When she had poured them out on the sofa Mrs. Guy was but a minute, before the glass, in clapping on the diadem. "Awfully jolly—we can do Ivanhoe!"

"But they're only glass and tin."

"Larger than life they are, *rather!*"—which is exactly what's wanted for tableaux. *Our* jewels, for historic scenes, don't tell—the real thing falls short. Rowena must have rubies as big as eggs. Leave them with me," Mrs. Guy continued—"they'll inspire me. Good-night."

The next morning she was in fact—yet very strangely—inspired. "Yes, *I'll* do Rowena. But I don't, my dear, understand."

"Understand what?"

Mrs. Guy gave a very lighted stare. "How you come to have such things."

Poor Charlotte smiled. "By inheritance."

"Family jewels?"

"They belonged to my aunt, who died some months ago. She was on the stage a few years in early life, and these are a part of her trappings."

"She left them to you?"

"No; my cousin, her stepson, who naturally has no use for them, gave them to me for remembrance of her. She was a dear kind thing, always so nice to me, and I was fond of her."

Mrs. Guy had listened with frank interest. "But it's *he* who must be a dear kind thing!"

Charlotte wondered. "You think so?"

"Is *he*," her friend went on, "also 'always so nice' to you?"

The girl, at this, face to face there with the brilliant visitor in the deserted breakfast-room, took a deeper sounding. "What is it?"

"Don't you know?"

Something came over her. "The pearls—?" But the question fainted on her lips. "Doesn't *he* know?"

Charlotte found herself flushing. "They're *not* paste?"

"Haven't you looked at them?"

She was conscious of two kinds of embarrassment. "*You* have?"

"Very carefully."

"And they're real?"

Mrs. Guy became slightly mystifying and returned for all answer: "Come again, when you've done with the children, to my room."

Our young woman found she had done with the children that morning so promptly as to reveal to them a new joy, and when she reappeared before Mrs. Guy this lady had already encircled a plump white throat with the only ornament, surely, in all the late Mrs. Prime's—the effaced Miss Bradshaw's—collection, in the least qualified to raise a question. If Charlotte had never yet once, before the glass, tied the string of pearls about her own neck, this was because she had been capable of no such condescension to approved "imitation"; but she had now only to look at Mrs. Guy to see that, so disposed, the ambiguous objects might have passed for frank originals. "What in the world have you done to them?"

"Only handled them, understood them, admired them, and put them on. That's what pearls want; they want to be worn—it wakes them up. They're alive, don't you see? How *have* these been treated? They must have been buried, ignored, despised. They were half-dead. Don't you *know* about pearls?" Mrs. Guy threw off as she fondly fingered the necklace.

"How *should* I? Do *you*?"

"Everything. These were simply asleep, and from the moment I really touched them —well," said their wearer lovingly, "it only took one's eye!"

"It took more than mine—though I did just wonder; and then Arthur's," Charlotte brooded. She found herself almost panting. "Then their value—?"

"Oh, their value's excellent."

The girl, for a deep moment, took another plunge into the wonder, the beauty and mystery, of them. "Are you *sure*?"

Her companion wheeled round for impatience. "Sure? For what kind of an idiot, my dear, do you take me?"

It was beyond Charlotte Prime to say. "For the same kind as Arthur—and as myself," she could only suggest. "But my cousin didn't know. He thinks they're worthless."

"Because of the rest of the lot? Then your cousin's an ass. But what—if, as I understand you, he gave them to you—has he to do with it?"

"Why, if he gave them to me as worthless and they turn out precious—"

"You must give them back? I don't see that—if he was such a noodle. He took the risk."

Charlotte fed, in fancy, on the pearls, which, decidedly, were exquisite, but which at the present moment somehow presented themselves much more as Mrs. Guy's than either as Arthur's or as her own. "Yes—he did take it; even after I had distinctly hinted to him that they looked to me different from the other pieces."

"Well, then!" said Mrs. Guy with something more than triumph—with a positive odd relief.

But it had the effect of making our young woman think with more intensity. "Ah, you see he thought they couldn't be different, because—so peculiarly—they shouldn't be."

"Shouldn't? I don't understand."

"Why, how would she have got them?"—so Charlotte candidly put it.

"She? Who?" There was a capacity in Mrs. Guy's tone for a sinking of persons—!

"Why, the person I told you of: his stepmother, my uncle's wife—among whose poor old things, extraordinarily thrust away and out of sight, he happened to find them."

Mrs. Guy came a step nearer to the effaced Miss Bradshaw. "Do you mean she may have stolen them?"

"No. But she had been an actress."

"Oh, well then," cried Mrs. Guy, "wouldn't that be just how?"

"Yes, except that she wasn't at all a brilliant one, nor in receipt of large pay." The girl even threw off a nervous joke. "I'm afraid she couldn't have been our Rowena."

Mrs. Guy took it up. "Was she very ugly?"

"No. She may very well, when young, have looked rather nice."

"Well, then!" was Mrs. Guy's sharp comment and fresh triumph.

"You mean it was a present? That's just what he so dislikes the idea of her having received—a present from an admirer capable of going such lengths."

"Because she wouldn't have taken it for nothing? *Speriamo*—that she wasn't a brute. The 'length' her admirer went was the length of a whole row. Let us hope she was just a little kind!"

"Well," Charlotte went on, "that she was 'kind' might seem to be shown by the fact that neither her husband, nor his son, nor I, his niece, knew or dreamed of her possessing anything so precious; by her having kept the gift all the rest of her life beyond discovery—out of sight and protected from suspicion."

"As if, you mean"—Mrs. Guy was quick—"she had been wedded to it and yet was ashamed of it? Fancy," she laughed while she manipulated the rare beads, "being ashamed of *these*!"

"But you see she had married a clergyman."

"Yes, she must have been 'rum.' But at any rate he had married *her*. What did he suppose?"

"Why, that she had never been the sort by whom such offerings are encouraged."

"Ah, my dear, the sort by whom they are *not*—!" But Mrs. Guy caught herself up. "And her stepson thought the same?"

"Overwhelmingly."

"Was he, then, if only her stepson—"

"So fond of her as that comes to? Yes; he had never known, consciously, his real mother, and, without children of her own, she was very patient and nice with him. And *I* liked her so," the girl pursued, "that at the end of ten years, in so strange a manner, to 'give her away'—"

"Is impossible to you? Then don't!" said Mrs. Guy with decision.

"Ah, but if they're real I can't keep them!" Charlotte, with her eyes on them, moaned in her impatience. "It's too difficult."

"Where's the difficulty, if he has such sentiments that he would rather sacrifice the necklace than admit it, with the presumption it carries with it, to be genuine? You've only to be silent."

"And keep it? How can *I* ever wear it?"

"You'd have to hide it, like your aunt?" Mrs. Guy was amused. "You can easily sell it."

Her companion walked round her for a look at the affair from behind. The clasp was certainly, doubtless intentionally, misleading, but everything else was indeed lovely. "Well, I must think. Why didn't *she* sell them?" Charlotte broke out in her trouble.

Mrs. Guy had an instant answer. "Doesn't that prove what they secretly recalled to her? You've only to be silent!" she ardently repeated.

"I must think—I must think!"

Mrs. Guy stood with her hands attached but motionless.

"Then you want them back?"

As if with the dread of touching them Charlotte retreated to the door. "I'll tell you tonight."

"But may I wear them?"

"Meanwhile?"

"This evening—at dinner."

It was the sharp, selfish pressure of this that really, on the spot, determined the girl; but for the moment, before closing the door on the question, she only said: "As you like!"

They were busy much of the day with preparation and rehearsal, and at dinner, that evening, the concourse of guests was such that a place among them for Miss Prime failed to find itself marked. At the time the company rose she was therefore alone in the schoolroom, where, towards eleven o'clock, she received a visit from Mrs. Guy. This lady's white shoulders heaved, under the pearls, with an emotion that the very red lips which formed, as if for the full effect, the happiest opposition of colour, were not slow to translate. "My dear, you should have seen the sensation— they've had a success!"

Charlotte, dumb a moment, took it all in. "It *is* as if they knew it—they're more and more alive. But so much the worse for both of us! I can't," she brought out with an effort, "be silent."

"You mean to return them?"

"If I don't I'm a thief."

Mrs. Guy gave her a long, hard look: what was decidedly not of the baby in Mrs. Guy's face was a certain air of established habit in the eyes. Then, with a sharp little jerk of her head and a backward reach of her bare beautiful arms, she undid the clasp and, taking off the necklace, laid it on the table. "If you do, you're a goose."

"Well, of the two—!" said our young lady, gathering it up with a sigh. And as if to get it, for the pang it gave, out of sight as soon as possible, she shut it up, clicking the lock, in the drawer of her own little table; after which, when she turned again, her companion looked naked and plain without it. "But what will you say?" it then occurred to her to demand.

"Downstairs—to explain?" Mrs. Guy was, after all, trying at least to keep her temper. "Oh, I'll put on something else and say that the clasp is broken. And you won't of course name *me* to him," she added.

"As having undeceived me? No—I'll say that, looking at the thing more carefully, it's my own private idea."

"And does he know how little you really know?"

"As an expert—surely. And he has always much the conceit of his own opinion."

"Then he won't believe you—as he so hates to. He'll stick to his judgment and maintain his gift, and we shall have the darlings back!" With which reviving assurance Mrs. Guy kissed her young friend for good-night.

She was not, however, to be gratified or justified by any prompt event, for, whether or no paste entered into the composition of the ornament in question, Charlotte shrank from the temerity of despatching it to town by post. Mrs. Guy was thus disappointed of the hope of seeing the business settled—"by return," she had seemed to expect—before the end of the revels. The revels, moreover, rising to a frantic pitch, pressed for all her attention, and it was at last only in the general confusion of leave-taking that she made, parenthetically, a dash at the person in the whole company with whom her contact had been most interesting.

"Come, what will you take for them?"

"The pearls? Ah, you'll have to treat with my cousin."

Mrs. Guy, with quick intensity, lent herself. "Where then does he live?"

"In chambers in the Temple. You can find him."

"But what's the use, if *you* do neither one thing nor the other?"

"Oh, I *shall* do the 'other,' " Charlotte said; "I'm only waiting till I go up. You want them so awfully?" She curiously, solemnly again, sounded her.

"I'm dying for them. There's a special charm in them—I don't know what it is: they tell so their history."

"But what do you know of that?"

"Just what they themselves say. It's all *in* them—and it comes out. They breathe a tenderness—they have the white glow of it. My dear," hissed Mrs. Guy in supreme confidence and as she buttoned her glove—"they're things of love!"

"Oh!" our young woman vaguely exclaimed.

"They're things of passion!"

"Mercy!" she gasped, turning short off. But these words remained, though indeed their help was scarce needed, Charlotte being in private face to face with a new light, as she by this time felt she must call it, on the dear dead kind colourless lady whose career had turned so sharp a corner in the middle. The pearls had quite taken their place as a revelation. She might have received them for nothing—admit that; but she couldn't have kept them so long and so unprofitably hidden, couldn't have enjoyed them only in secret, for nothing; and she had mixed them in her reliquary with false things, in order to put curiosity and detection off the scent. Over this strange fact poor Charlotte interminably mused: it became more touching, more attaching for her than she could now confide to any ear. How bad or how happy—in the sophisticated sense of Mrs. Guy and the young man at the Temple—the effaced Miss Bradshaw must have been to have had to be so mute! The little governess at Bleet put on the necklace now in secret sessions; she wore it sometimes under her dress; she came to feel verily a haunting passion for it. Yet in her penniless state she would have parted with it for money; she gave herself also to dreams of what in this direction it would do for her. The sophistry of her so often saying to herself that Arthur had after all definitely pronounced her welcome to any gain from his gift that might accrue—this trick remained innocent, as she perfectly knew it for what it was. Then there was always the possibility of his—as she could only picture it— rising to the occasion. Mightn't he have a grand magnanimous moment?—mightn't he just say: "Oh, of course I couldn't have afforded to let you have it if I had known; but since you *have* got it, and have made out the truth by your own wit, I really can't screw myself down to the shabbiness of taking it back"?

She had, as it proved, to wait a long time—to wait till, at the end of several months, the great house of Bleet had, with due deliberation, for the season, transferred itself to town; after which, however, she fairly snatched at her first freedom to knock, dressed in her best and armed with her disclosure, at the door of her doubting kinsman. It was still with doubt and not quite with the face she had hoped that he listened to her story. He had turned pale, she thought, as she produced the necklace, and he appeared, above all, disagreeably affected. Well, perhaps there was reason, she more than ever remembered; but what on earth was one, in close touch with the fact, to do? She had laid the pearls on his table, where, without his having at first put so much as a finger to them, they met his hard, cold stare.

"I don't believe in them," he simply said at last.

"That's exactly, then," she returned with some spirit, "what I wanted to hear!"

She fancied that at this his colour changed; it was indeed vivid to her afterwards— for she was to have a long recall of the scene—that she had made him quite angrily flush. "'It's a beastly unpleasant imputation, you know!"—and he walked away from her as he had always walked at the vicarage.

"It's none of *my* making, I'm sure," said Charlotte Prime. "If you're afraid to believe they're real—"

"Well?"—and he turned, across the room, sharp round at her.

"Why, it's not my fault."

He said nothing more, for a moment, on this; he only came back to the table. "They're what I originally said they were. They're rotten paste."

"Then I may keep them?"

"No. I want a better opinion."

"Than your own?"

"Than *your* own." He dropped on the pearls another queer stare, then, after a moment, bringing himself to touch them, did exactly what she had herself done in the presence of Mrs. Guy at Bleet—gathered them together, marched off with them to a drawer, put them in and clicked the key. "You say I'm afraid," he went on as he again met her; "but I shan't be afraid to take them to Bond Street."

"And if the people say they're real—?"

He had a pause and then his strangest manner. "They won't say it! They shan't!"

There was something in the way he brought it out that deprived poor Charlotte, as she was perfectly aware, of any manner at all. "Oh!" she simply sounded, as she had sounded for her last word to Mrs. Guy; and, within a minute, without more conversation, she had taken her departure.

A fortnight later she received a communication from him, and towards the end of the season one of the entertainments in Eaton Square was graced by the presence of Mrs. Guy. Charlotte was not at dinner, but she came down afterwards, and this guest, on seeing her, abandoned a very beautiful young man on purpose to cross and speak to her. The guest displayed a lovely necklace and had apparently not lost her habit of overflowing with the pride of such ornaments.

"Do you see?" She was in high joy.

They were indeed splendid pearls—so far as poor Charlotte could feel that she knew, after what had come and gone, about such mysteries. The poor girl had a sickly smile. "They're almost as fine as Arthur's."

"Almost? Where, my dear, are your eyes? They *are* 'Arthur's'!" After which, to meet the flood of crimson that accompanied her young friend's start: "I tracked them —after your folly, and, by miraculous luck, recognised them in the Bond Street window to which he had disposed of them."

"*Disposed* of them?" the girl gasped. "He wrote me that I had insulted his mother and that the people had shown him he was right—had pronounced them utter paste."

Mrs. Guy gave a stare. "Ah, I told you he wouldn't bear it! No. But I had, I assure you," she wound up, "to drive my bargain!"

Charlotte scarce heard or saw; she was full of her private wrong. "He wrote me," she panted, "that he had smashed them."

Mrs. Guy could only wonder and pity. "He's really morbid!" But it wasn't quite clear which of the pair she pitied; though the young person felt really morbid too after they had separated and she found herself full of thought. She even went the length of asking herself what sort of a bargain Mrs. Guy had driven and whether the marvel of the recognition in Bond Street had been a veracious account of the matter. Hadn't she perhaps in truth dealt with Arthur directly? It came back to Charlotte almost luridly that she had had his address.

AN OCCURRENCE AT OWL CREEK BRIDGE

AMBROSE BIERCE (1842-1914?)

A man stood upon a railroad bridge in northern Alabama, looking down into the swift water twenty feet below. The man's hands were behind his back, the wrists bound with a cord. A rope closely encircled his neck. It was attached to a stout cross-timber above his head and the slack fell to the level of his knees. Some loose boards laid upon the sleepers supporting the metals of the railway supplied a footing for him and his executioners—two private soldiers of the Federal army, directed by a sergeant who in civil life may have been a deputy sheriff. At a short remove upon the same temporary platform was an officer in the uniform of his rank, armed. He was a captain. A sentinel at each end of the bridge stood with his rifle in the position known as "support," that is to say, vertical in front of the left shoulder, the hammer resting on the forearm thrown straight across the chest—a formal and unnatural position, enforcing an erect carriage of the body. It did not appear to be the duty of these two men to know what was occurring at the center of the bridge; they merely blockaded the two ends of the foot planking that traversed it.

Beyond one of the sentinels nobody was in sight; the railroad ran straight away into a forest for a hundred yards, then, curving, was lost to view. Doubtless there was an outpost farther along. The other bank of the stream was open ground—a gentle acclivity topped with a stockade of vertical tree trunks, loopholed for rifles, with a single embrasure through which protruded the muzzle of a brass cannon commanding the bridge. Midway of the slope between the bridge and fort were the spectators— a single company of infantry in line, at "parade rest," the butts of the rifles on the ground, the barrels inclining slightly backward against the right shoulder, the hands crossed upon the stock. A lieutenant stood at the right of the line, the point of his sword upon the ground, his left hand resting upon his right. Excepting the group of four at the center of the bridge, not a man moved. The company faced the bridge, staring stonily, motionless. The sentinels, facing the banks of the stream, might have been statues to adorn the bridge. The captain stood with folded arms, silent, observing the work of his subordinates, but making no sign. Death is a dignitary who when he comes announced is to be received with formal manifestations of respect, even by those most familiar with him. In the code of military etiquette silence and fixity are forms of deference.

The man who was engaged in being hanged was apparently about thirty-five years of age. He was a civilian, if one might judge from his habit, which was that of a planter. His features were good—a straight nose, firm mouth, broad forehead, from which his long, dark hair was combed straight back, falling behind his ears to the collar of his well-fitting frock coat. He wore a mustache and pointed beard, but no whiskers; his eyes were large and dark gray, and had a kindly expression which one would hardly have expected in one whose neck was in the hemp. Evidently this was no vulgar assassin. The liberal military code makes provision for hanging many kinds of persons, and gentlemen are not excluded.

The preparations being complete, the two private soldiers stepped aside and each drew away the plank upon which he had been standing. The sergeant turned to the captain, saluted and placed himself immediately behind that officer, who in turn moved apart one pace. These movements left the condemned man and the sergeant standing on the two ends of the same plank, which spanned three of the crossties of the bridge. The end upon which the civilian stood almost, but not quite, reached a fourth. This plank had been held in place by the weight of the captain; it was now held by that of the sergeant. At a signal from the former the latter would step aside, the plank would tilt and the condemned man go down between two ties. The arrangement commended itself to his judgment as simple and effective. His face had not been covered nor his eyes bandaged. He looked a moment at his "unsteadfast footing," then let his gaze wander to the swirling water of the stream racing madly beneath his feet. A piece of dancing driftwood caught his attention and his eyes followed it down the current. How slowly it appeared to move! What a sluggish stream!

He closed his eyes in order to fix his last thoughts upon his wife and children. The water, touched to gold by the early sun, the brooding mists under the banks at some distance down the stream, the fort, the soldiers, the piece of drift—all had distracted him. And now he became conscious of a new disturbance. Striking through the thought of his dear ones was a sound which he could neither ignore nor understand, a sharp, distinct, metallic percussion like the stroke of a blacksmith's hammer upon the anvil; it had the same ringing quality. He wondered what it was, and whether immeasurably distant or near by—it seemed both. Its recurrence was regular, but as slow as the tolling of a death knell. He awaited each stroke with impatience and—he knew not why—apprehension. The intervals of silence grew progressively longer; the delays became maddening. With their greater infrequency the sounds increased in strength and sharpness. They hurt his ear like the thrust of a knife; he feared he would shriek. What he heard was the ticking of his watch.

He unclosed his eyes and saw again the water below him. "If I could free my hands," he thought, "I might throw off the noose and spring into the stream. By diving I could evade the bullets and, swimming vigorously, reach the bank, take to the woods and get away home. My home, thank God, is as yet outside their lines; my wife and little ones are still beyond the invader's farthest advance."

As these thoughts, which have here to be set down in words, were flashed into the doomed man's brain rather than evolved from it the captain nodded to the sergeant. The sergeant stepped aside.

Peyton Farquhar was a well-to-do planter, of an old and highly respected Alabama family. Being a slave owner and like other slave owners a politician, he was naturally an original secessionist and ardently devoted to the Southern cause. Circumstances of an imperious nature, which it is unnecessary to relate here, had prevented him from taking service with the gallant army that had fought the disastrous campaigns ending with the fall of Corinth, and he chafed under the inglorious restraint, longing for the release of his energies, the larger life of the soldier, the opportunity for distinction. That opportunity, he felt, would come, as it comes to all in war time. Meanwhile he did what he could. No service was too humble for him to perform in aid of the South, no adventure too perilous for him to undertake if consistent with the character of a civilian who was at heart a soldier, and who in good faith and without too much qualification assented to at least a part of the frankly villainous dictum that all is fair in love and war.

One evening while Farquhar and his wife were sitting on a rustic bench near the entrance to his grounds, a gray-clad soldier rode up to the gate and asked for a drink of water. Mrs. Farquhar was only too happy to serve him with her own white hands. While she was fetching the water her husband approached the dusty horseman and inquired eagerly for news from the front.

"The Yanks are repairing the railroads," said the man, "and are getting ready for another advance. They have reached the Owl Creek bridge, put it in order and built a stockade on the north bank. The commandant has issued an order, which is posted everywhere, declaring that any civilian caught interfering with the railroad, its bridges, tunnels or trains will be summarily hanged. I saw the order."

"How far is it to the Owl Creek bridge?" Farquhar asked.

"About thirty miles."

"Is there no force on this side the creek?"

"Only a picket post half a mile out, on the railroad, and a single sentinel at this end of the bridge."

"Suppose a man—a civilian and student of hanging—should elude the picket post and perhaps get the better of the sentinel," said Farquhar, smiling, "what could he accomplish?"

The soldier reflected. "I was there a month ago," he replied. "I observed that the flood of last winter had lodged a great quantity of driftwood against the wooden pier at this end of the bridge. It is now dry and would burn like tow."

The lady had now brought the water, which the soldier drank. He thanked her ceremoniously, bowed to her husband and rode away. An hour later, after nightfall, he re-passed the plantation, going northward in the direction from which he had come. He was a Federal scout.

As Peyton Farquhar fell straight downward through the bridge he lost consciousness and was as one already dead. From this state he was awakened—ages later, it seemed to him—by the pain of a sharp pressure up in his throat, followed by a sense of suffocation. Keen, poignant agonies seemed to shoot from his neck downward through every fiber of his body and limbs. These pains appeared to flash along well-defined lines of ramification and to beat with an inconceivably rapid periodicity. They seemed like streams of pulsating fire heating him to an intolerable temperature. As to his head, he was conscious of nothing but a feeling of fullness—of congestion. These sensations were unaccompanied by thought. The intellectual part of his nature was already effaced; he had power only to feel, and feeling was torment. He was conscious of motion. Encompassed in a luminous cloud, of which he was now merely the fiery heart, without material substance, he swung through unthinkable arcs of oscillation, like a vast pendulum. Then all at once, with terrible suddenness, the light about him shot upward with the noise of a loud plash; a frightful roaring was in his ears, and all was cold and dark. The power of thought was restored; he knew that the rope had broken and he had fallen into the stream. There was no additional strangulation; the noose about his neck was already suffocating him and kept the water from his lungs. To die of hanging at the bottom of a river!—the idea seemed to him ludicrous. He opened his eyes in the darkness and saw above him a gleam of light, but how distant, how inaccessible! He was still sinking, for the light became fainter and fainter until it was a mere glimmer. Then it began to grow and brighten, and he knew that he was rising toward the surface—knew it with reluctance, for he was now very comfortable. "To be hanged and drowned," he thought, "that is not so bad; but I do not wish to be shot. No; I will not be shot; that is not fair."

He was not conscious of an effort, but a sharp pain in his wrist apprised him that he was trying to free his hands. He gave the struggle his attention, as an idler might observe the feat of a juggler, without interest in the outcome. What splendid effort! What magnificent, what superhuman strength! Ah, that was a fine endeavor! Bravo! The cord fell away; his arms parted and floated upward, the hands dimly seen on each side in the growing light. He watched them with a new interest as first one and then the other pounced upon the noose at his neck. They tore it away and thrust it fiercely aside, its undulations resembling those of a water snake. "Put it back, put it back!" He thought he shouted these words to his hands, for the undoing of the noose had been succeeded by the direst pang that he had yet experienced. His neck ached horribly; his brain was on fire; his heart, which had been fluttering faintly, gave a great leap, trying to force itself out at his mouth. His whole body was racked and wrenched with an insupportable anguish! But his disobedient hands gave no heed to the command. They beat the water vigorously with quick, downward strokes, forcing him to the surface. He felt his head emerge; his eyes were blinded by the sunlight; his chest expanded convulsively, and with a supreme and crowning agony his lungs engulfed a great draught of air, which instantly he expelled in a shriek!

He was now in full possession of his physical senses. They were, indeed, preternaturally keen and alert. Something in the awful disturbance of his organic system had so exalted and refined them that they made record of things never before perceived. He felt the ripples upon his face and heard their separate sounds as they struck. He looked at the forest on the bank of the stream, saw the individual trees, the leaves and the veining of each leaf—saw the very insects upon them: the locusts, the brilliant-bodied flies, the gray spiders stretching their webs from twig to twig. He noted the prismatic colors in all the dewdrops upon a million blades of grass.

The humming of the gnats that danced above the eddies of the stream, the beating of the dragonflies' wings, the strokes of the water spiders' legs, like oars which had lifted their boat—all these made audible music. A fish slid along beneath his eyes and he heard the rush of its body parting the water.

He had come to the surface facing down the stream; in a moment the visible world seemed to wheel slowly round, himself the pivotal point, and he saw the bridge, the fort, the soldiers upon the bridge, the captain, the sergeant, the two privates, his executioners. They were in silhouette against the blue sky. They shouted and gesticulated, pointing at him. The captain had drawn his pistol, but did not fire; the others were unarmed. Their movements were grotesque and horrible, their forms gigantic.

Suddenly he heard a sharp report and something struck the water smartly within a few inches of his head, spattering his face with spray. He heard a second report, and saw one of the sentinels with his rifle at his shoulder, a light cloud of blue smoke rising from the muzzle. The man in the water saw the eye of the man on the bridge gazing into his own through the sights of the rifle. He observed that it was a gray eye and remembered having read that gray eyes were keenest, and that all famous marksmen had them. Nevertheless, this one had missed.

A counter-swirl had caught Farquhar and turned him half round; he was again looking into the forest on the bank opposite the fort. The sound of a clear, high voice in a monotonous singsong now rang out behind him and came across the water with distinctness that pierced and subdued all other sounds, even the beating of the ripples in his ears. Although no soldier, he had frequented camps enough to know the dread significance of that deliberate, drawling, aspirated chant; the lieutenant on shore was taking a part in the morning's work. How coldly and pitilessly—with what an even, calm intonation, presaging, and enforcing tranquillity in the men—with what accurately measured intervals fell those cruel words:

"Attention, company! . . . Shoulder arms! . . . Ready! . . . Aim! . . . Fire!"

Farquhar dived—dived as deeply as he could. The water roared in his ears like the voice of Niagara, yet he heard the dulled thunder of the volley and, rising again toward the surface, met shining bits of metal, singularly flattened, oscillating slowly downward. Some of them touched him on the face and hands, then fell away, continuing their descent. One lodged between his collar and neck; it was uncomfortably warm and he snatched it out.

As he rose to the surface, gasping for breath, he saw that he had been a long time under water; he was perceptibly farther down stream—nearer to safety. The soldiers had almost finished reloading; the metal ramrods flashed all at once in the sunshine as they were drawn from the barrels, turned in the air, and thrust into their sockets. The two sentinels fired again, independently and ineffectually.

The hunted man saw all this over his shoulder; he was now swimming vigorously with the current. His brain was as energetic as his arms and legs; he thought with the rapidity of lightning.

"The officer," he reasoned, "will not make that martinet's error a second time. It is as easy to dodge a volley as a single shot. He has probably already given the command to fire at will. God help me, I cannot dodge them all!"

An appalling plash within two yards of him was followed by a loud, rushing sound, *diminuendo,* which seemed to travel back through the air to the fort and died in an explosion which stirred the very river to its deeps! A rising sheet of water curved over him, fell down upon him, blinded him, strangled him! The cannon had taken a hand in the game. As he shook his head free from the commotion of the smitten water he heard the deflected shot humming through the air ahead, and in an instant it was cracking and smashing the branches in the forest beyond.

"They will not do that again," he thought; "the next time they will use a charge of grape. I must keep my eye upon the gun; the smoke will apprise me—the report arrives too late; it lags behind the missile. That is a good gun."

Suddenly he felt himself whirled round and round—spinning like a top. The water, the banks, the forests, the now distant bridge, fort and men—all were commingled and blurred. Objects were represented by their colors only; circular horizontal streaks of color—that was all he saw. He had been caught in a vortex and was being whirled on with a velocity of advance and gyration that made him giddy and sick. In a few moments he was flung upon the gravel at the foot of the left bank of the stream—the southern bank—and behind a projecting point which concealed him from his enemies. The sudden arrest of his motion, the abrasion of one of his hands on the gravel, restored him, and he wept with delight. He dug his fingers into the sand, threw it over himself in handfuls and audibly blessed it. It looked like diamonds, rubies, emeralds; he could think of nothing beautiful which it did not resemble. The trees upon the bank were giant garden plants; he noted a definite order in their arrangement, inhaled the fragrance of their blooms. A strange, roseate light shone through the spaces among their trunks and the wind made in their branches the music of Aeolian harps. He had no wish to perfect his escape—was content to remain in that enchanting spot until retaken.

A whiz and rattle of grapeshot among the branches high above his head roused him from his dream. The baffled cannoneer had fired him a random farewell. He sprang to his feet, rushed up the sloping bank, and plunged into the forest.

All that day he traveled, laying his course by the rounding sun. The forest seemed interminable; nowhere did he discover a break in it, not even a woodman's road. He had not known that he lived in so wild a region. There was something uncanny in the revelation.

By nightfall he was fatigued, footsore, famishing. The thought of his wife and children urged him on. At last he found a road which led him in what he knew to be the right direction. It was as wide and straight as a city street, yet it seemed untraveled. No fields bordered it, no dwelling anywhere. Not so much as the barking of a dog suggested human habitation. The black bodies of the trees formed a straight wall on both sides, terminating on the horizon in a point, like a diagram in a lesson in perspective. Overhead, as he looked up through this rift in the wood, shone great golden stars looking unfamiliar and grouped in strange constellations. He was sure they were arranged in some order which had a secret and malign significance. The wood on either side was full of singular noises, among which—once, twice, and again—he distinctly heard whispers in an unknown tongue.

His neck was in pain and lifting his hand to it he found it horribly swollen. He knew that it had a circle of black where the rope had bruised it. His eyes felt congested; he could no longer close them. His tongue was swollen with thirst; he relieved its fever by thrusting it forward from between his teeth into the cold air. How softly the turf had carpeted the untraveled avenue—he could no longer feel the roadway beneath his feet!

Doubtless, despite his suffering, he had fallen asleep while walking, for now he sees another scene—perhaps he has merely recovered from a delirium. He stands at the gate of his own home. All is as he left it, and all bright and beautiful in the morning sunshine. He must have traveled the entire night. As he pushes open the gate and passes up the wide white walk, he sees a flutter of female garments; his wife, looking fresh and cool and sweet, steps down from the veranda to meet him. At the bottom of the steps she stands waiting, with a smile of ineffable joy, an attitude of matchless grace and dignity. Ah, how beautiful she is! He springs forward with extended arms. As he is about to clasp her he feels a stunning blow upon the back of the neck; a blinding white light blazes all about him with a sound like the shock of a cannon—then all is darkness and silence!

Peyton Farquhar was dead; his body, with a broken neck, swung gently from side to side beneath the timbers of the Owl Creek bridge.

MR. ARCULARIS

CONRAD AIKEN (1889–   )

Mr. Arcularis stood at the window of his room in the hospital and looked down at the street. There had been a light shower, which had patterned the sidewalks with large drops, but now again the sun was out, blue sky was showing here and there between the swift white clouds, a cold wind was blowing the poplar trees. An itinerant band had stopped before the building and was playing, with violin, harp, and flute, the finale of "Cavalleria Rusticana." Leaning against the window-sill—for he felt extraordinarily weak after his operation—Mr. Arcularis suddenly, listening to the wretched music, felt like crying. He rested the palm of one hand against a cold window pane and stared down at the old man who was blowing the flute, and blinked his eyes. It seemed absurd that he should be so weak, so emotional, so like a child— and especially now that everything was over at last. In spite of all their predictions, in spite, too, of his own dreadful certainty that he was going to die, here he was, as fit as a fiddle—but what a fiddle it was, so out of tune!—with a long life before him. And to begin with, a voyage to England ordered by the doctor. What could be more delightful? Why should he feel sad about it and want to cry like a baby? In a few minutes Harry would arrive with his car to take him to the wharf; in an hour he would be on the sea, in two hours he would see the sunset behind him, where Boston had been, and his new life would be opening before him. It was many years since he had been abroad. June, the best of the year to come—England, France, the Rhine—how ridiculous that he should already be homesick!

There was a light footstep outside the door, a knock, the door opened, and Harry came in.

"Well, old man, I've come to get you. The old bus actually got here. Are you ready? Here, let me take your arm. You're tottering like an octogenarian!"

Mr. Arcularis submitted gratefully, laughing, and they made the journey slowly along the bleak corridor and down the stairs to the entrance hall. Miss Hoyle, his nurse, was there, and the Matron, and the charming little assistant with freckles who had helped to prepare him for the operation. Miss Hoyle put out her hand.

"Good-by, Mr. Arcularis," she said, "and *bon voyage.*"

"Good-by, Miss Hoyle, and thank you for everything. You were very kind to me. And I fear I was a nuisance."

The girl with the freckles, too, gave him her hand, smiling. She was very pretty, and it would have been easy to fall in love with her. She reminded him of someone. Who was it? He tried in vain to remember while he said good-by to her and turned to the Matron.

"And not too many latitudes with the young ladies, Mr. Arcularis!" she was saying.

Mr. Arcularis was pleased, flattered, by all this attention to a middle-aged invalid, and felt a joke taking shape in his mind, and no sooner in his mind than on his tongue.

"Oh, no latitudes," he said, laughing. "I'll leave the latitudes to the ship!"

"Oh, come now," said the Matron, "we don't seem to have hurt him much, do we?"

"I think we'll have to operate on him again and *really* cure him," said Miss Hoyle.

He was going down the front steps, between the potted palmettoes, and they all laughed and waved. The wind was cold, very cold for June, and he was glad he had put on his coat. He shivered.

"Damned cold for June!" he said. "Why should it be so cold?"

"East wind," Harry said, arranging the rug over his knees. "Sorry it's an open car, but I believe in fresh air and all that sort of thing. I'll drive slowly. We've got plenty of time."

They coasted gently down the long hill towards Beacon Street, but the road was badly surfaced, and despite Harry's care Mr. Arcularis felt his pain again. He found that he could alleviate it a little by leaning to the right, against the arm-rest, and not breathing too deeply. But how glorious to be out again! How strange and vivid the world looked! The trees had innumerable green fresh leaves—they were all blowing and shifting and turning and flashing in the wind; drops of rainwater fell downward sparkling; the robins were singing their absurd, delicious little four-noted songs; even the street cars looked unusually bright and beautiful, just as they used to look when he was a child and had wanted above all things to be a motorman. He found himself smiling foolishly at everything, foolishly and weakly, and wanted to say something about it to Harry. It was no use, though—he had no strength, and the mere finding of words would be almost more than he could manage. And even if he should succeed in saying it, he would then most likely burst into tears. He shook his head slowly from side to side.

"Ain't it grand?" he said.

"I'll bet it looks good," said Harry.

"Words fail me."

"You wait till you get out to sea. You'll have a swell time."

"Oh, swell! . . . I hope not. I hope it'll be calm."

"Tut tut."

When they passed the Harvard Club Mr. Arcularis made a slow and somewhat painful effort to turn in his seat and look at it. It might be the last chance to see it for a long time. Why this sentimental longing to stare at it, though? There it was, with the great flag blowing in the wind, the Harvard seal now concealed by the swift folds and now revealed, and there were the windows in the library, where he had spent so many delightful hours reading—Plato, and Kipling, and the Lord knows what—and the balconies from which for so many years he had watched the finish of the Marathon. Old Talbot might be in there now, sleeping with a book on his knee, hoping forlornly to be interrupted by anyone, for anything.

"Good-by to the old club," he said.

"The bar will miss you," said Harry, smiling with friendly irony and looking straight ahead.

"But let there be no moaning," said Mr. Arcularis.

"What's *that* a quotation from?"

" 'The Odyssey.' "

In spite of the cold, he was glad of the wind on his face, for it helped to dissipate the feeling of vagueness and dizziness that came over him in a sickening wave from time to time. All of a sudden everything would begin to swim and dissolve, the houses would lean their heads together, he had to close his eyes, and there would be a curious and dreadful humming noise, which at regular intervals rose to a crescendo and then drawlingly subsided again. It was disconcerting. Perhaps he still had a trace of fever. When he got on the ship he would have a glass of whisky. . . . From one of these spells he opened his eyes and found that they were on the ferry, crossing to East Boston. It must have been the ferry's engines that he had heard. From another spell he woke to find himself on the wharf, the car at a standstill beside a pile of yellow packing-cases.

"We're here because we're here because we're here," said Harry.

"Because we're here," added Mr. Arcularis.

He dozed in the car while Harry—and what a good friend Harry was!—attended to all the details. He went and came with tickets and passports and baggage checks and porters. And at last he unwrapped Mr. Arcularis from the rugs and led him up the steep gangplank to the deck, and thence by devious windings to a small cold stateroom with a solitary porthole like the eye of a cyclops.

"Here you are," he said, "and now I've got to go. Did you hear the whistle?"

"No."

"Well, you're half asleep. It's sounded the all-ashore. Good-by, old fellow, and take care of yourself. Bring me back a spray of edelweiss. And send me a picture post card from the Absolute."

"Will you have it finite or infinite?"

"Oh, infinite. But with your signature on it. Now you'd better turn in for a while and have a nap. Cheerio!"

Mr. Arcularis took his hand and pressed it hard, and once more felt like crying. Absurd! Had he become a child again?

"Good-by," he said.

He sat down in the little wicker chair, with his overcoat still on, closed his eyes, and listened to the humming of the air in the ventilator. Hurried footsteps ran up and down the corridor. The chair was not too comfortable, and his pain began to bother him again, so he moved, with his coat still on, to the narrow berth and fell asleep. When he woke up, it was dark, and the porthole had been partly opened. He groped for the switch and turned on the light. Then he rang for the steward.

"It's cold in here," he said. "Would you mind closing the port?"

The girl who sat opposite him at dinner was charming. Who was it she reminded him of? Why, of course, the girl at the hospital, the girl with the freckles. Her hair was beautiful, not quite red, not quite gold, nor had it been bobbed; arranged with a sort of graceful untidiness, it made him think of a Melozzo da Forli angel. Her face was freckled, she had a mouth which was both humorous and voluptuous. And she seemed to be alone.

He frowned at the bill of fare and ordered the thick soup.

"No hors d'oeuvres?" asked the steward.

"I think not," said Mr. Arcularis. "They might kill me."

The steward permitted himself to be amused and deposited the menu card on the table against the water-bottle. His eyebrows were lifted. As he moved away, the girl followed him with her eyes and smiled.

"I'm afraid you shocked him," she said.

"Impossible," said Mr. Arcularis. "These stewards, they're dead souls. How could they be stewards otherwise? And they think they've seen and known everything. They suffer terribly from the *déjà vu*. Personally, I don't blame them."

"It must be a dreadful sort of life."

"It's because they're dead that they accept it."

"Do you think so?"

"I'm sure of it. I'm enough of a dead soul myself to know the signs!"

"Well, I don't know what you mean by that!"

"But nothing mysterious! I'm just out of hospital, after an operation. I was given up for dead. For six months I had given *myself* up for dead. If you've ever been seriously ill you know the feeling. You have a posthumous feeling—a mild, cynical tolerance for everything and everyone. What is there you haven't seen or done or understood? Nothing."

Mr. Arcularis waved his hands and smiled.

"I wish I could understand you," said the girl, "but I've never been ill in my life."

"Never?"

"Never."

"Good God!"

The torrent of the unexpressed and inexpressible paralyzed him and rendered him speechless. He stared at the girl, wondering who she was and then, realizing that he had perhaps stared too fixedly, averted his gaze, gave a little laugh, rolled a pill of bread between his fingers. After a second or two he allowed himself to look at her again and found her smiling.

"Never pay any attention to invalids," he said, "or they'll drag you to the hospital."

She examined him critically, with her head tilted a little to one side, but with friend-liness.

"You don't *look* like an invalid," she said.

Mr. Arcularis thought her charming. His pain ceased to bother him, the disagree-able humming disappeared, or rather, it was dissociated from himself and became merely, as it should be, the sound of the ship's engines, and he began to think the voyage was going to be really delightful. The parson on his right passed him the salt.

"I fear you will need this in your soup," he said.

"Thank you. Is it as bad as that?"

The steward, overhearing, was immediately apologetic and solicitous. He explained that on the first day everything was at sixes and sevens. The girl looked up at him and asked him a question.

"Do you think we'll have a good voyage?" she said.

He was passing the hot rolls to the parson, removing the napkins from them with a deprecatory finger.

"Well, madam, I don't like to be a Jeremiah, but—"

"Oh, come," said the parson, "I hope we have no Jeremiahs."

"What do you mean?" said the girl.

Mr. Arcularis ate his soup with gusto—it was nice and hot.

"Well, maybe I shouldn't say it, but there's a corpse on board, going to Ireland; and I never yet knew a voyage with a corpse on board that we didn't have bad weather."

"Why, steward, you're just superstitious! What nonsense."

"That's a very ancient superstition," said Mr. Arcularis. "I've heard it many times. Maybe it's true. Maybe we'll be wrecked. And what does it matter, after all?" He was very bland.

"Then let's be wrecked," said the parson coldly.

Nevertheless, Mr. Arcularis felt a shudder go through him on hearing the steward's remark. A corpse in the hold—a coffin? Perhaps it was true. Perhaps some disaster would befall them. There might be fogs. There might be icebergs. He thought of all the wrecks of which he had read. There was the *Titanic*, which he had read about in the warm newspaper room at the Harvard Club—it had seemed dreadfully real, even there. That band, playing "Nearer My God to Thee" on the after-deck while the ship sank! It was one of the darkest of his memories. And the *Empress of Ireland* —all those poor people trapped in the smoking-room, with only one door between them and life, and that door locked for the night by the deck-steward, and the deck-steward nowhere to be found! He shivered, feeling a draft, and turned to the parson.

"How do these strange delusions arise?" he said.

The parson looked at him searchingly, appraisingly—from chin to forehead, from forehead to chin—and Mr. Arcularis, feeling uncomfortable, straightened his tie.

"From nothing but fear," said the parson. "Nothing on earth but fear."

"How strange!" said the girl.

Mr. Arcularis again looked at her—she had lowered her face—and again tried to think of whom she reminded him. It wasn't only the little freckle-faced girl at the hospital—both of them had reminded him of someone else. Someone far back in his life: remote, beautiful, lovely. But he couldn't think. The meal came to an end, they all rose, the ship's orchestra played a feeble fox-trot, and Mr. Arcularis, once more alone, went to the bar to have his whisky. The room was stuffy, and the ship's engines were both audible and palpable. The humming and throbbing oppressed him, the rhythm seemed to be the rhythm of his own pain, and after a short time he found his way, with slow steps, holding on to the walls in his moments of weakness and dizziness, to his forlorn and white little room. The port had been—thank God!—closed for the night: it was cold enough anyway. The white and blue ribbons fluttered from the ventilator, the bottle and glasses clicked and clucked as the ship swayed gently to the long, slow motion of the sea. It was all very peculiar—it was all like something he had experienced somewhere before. What was it? Where was it? . . . He untied his tie, looking at his face in the glass, and wondered, and from time to time put his hand to his side to hold in the pain. It wasn't at Portsmouth, in his childhood, nor at Salem, nor in the rose-garden at his Aunt Julia's, nor in the schoolroom at Cambridge. It was something very queer, very intimate, very precious. The jackstones, the Sunday-School cards which he had loved when he was a child . . . He fell asleep.

The sense of time was already hopelessly confused. One hour was like another, the sea looked always the same, morning was indistinguishable from afternoon—and was it Tuesday or Wednesday? Mr. Arcularis was sitting in the smoking-room, in his favorite corner, watching the parson teach Miss Dean to play chess. On the deck outside he could see the people passing and repassing in their restless round of the ship. The red jacket went by, then the black hat with the white feather, then the purple scarf, the brown tweed coat, the Bulgarian mustache, the monocle, the Scotch cap with fluttering ribbons, and in no time at all the red jacket again, dipping past the windows with its own peculiar rhythm, followed once more by the black hat and the purple scarf. How odd to reflect on the fixed little orbits of these things—as definite and profound, perhaps, as the orbits of the stars, and as important to God or the Absolute. There was a kind of tyranny in this fixedness, too—to think of it too much made one uncomfortable. He closed his eyes for a moment, to avoid seeing for the fortieth time the Bulgarian mustache and the pursuing monocle. The parson was explaining the movements of knights. Two forward and one to the side. Eight possible moves, always ito the opposite color from that on which the piece stands. Two forward and one to the side: Miss Dean repeated the words several times with reflective emphasis. Here, too, was the terrifying fixed curve of the infinite, the creeping curve of logic which at last must become the final signpost at the edge of nothing. After that—the deluge. The great white light of annihilation. The bright flash of death. . . . Was it merely the sea which made these abstractions so insistent, so intrusive? The mere notion of *orbit* had somehow become extraordinarily naked; and to rid himself of the discomfort and also to forget a little the pain which bothered his side whenever he sat down, he walked slowly and carefully into the writing-room, and examined a pile of superannuated magazines and catalogues of travel. The bright colors amused him, the photographs of remote islands and mountains, savages in sampans or sarongs or both —it was all very far off and delightful, like something in a dream or a fever. But he found that he was too tired to read and was incapable of concentration. Dreams! Yes, that reminded him. That rather alarming business—sleep-walking!

Later in the evening—at what hour he didn't know—he was telling Miss Dean about it, as he had intended to do. They were sitting in deck-chairs on the sheltered side. The sea was black, and there was a cold wind. He wished they had chosen to sit in the lounge.

Miss Dean was extremely pretty—no, beautiful. She looked at him, too, in a very strange and lovely way, with something of inquiry, something of sympathy, something of affection. It seemed as if, between the question and the answer, they had sat thus for a very long time, exchanging an unspoken secret, simply looking at each other quietly and kindly. Had an hour or two passed? And was it at all necessary to speak?

"No," she said, "I never have."

She breathed into the low words a note of interrogation and gave him a slow smile.

"That's the funny part of it. I never had either until last night. Never in my life. I hardly ever even dream. And it really rather frightens me."

"Tell me about it, Mr. Arcularis."

"I dreamed at first that I was walking, alone, in a wide plain covered with snow. It was growing dark, I was very cold, my feet were frozen and numb, and I was lost. I came then to a signpost—at first it seemed to me there was nothing on it. Nothing but ice. Just before it grew finally dark, however, I made out on it the one word 'Polaris.' "

"The Pole Star."

"Yes—and you see, I didn't myself know that. I looked it up only this morning. I suppose I must have seen it somewhere? And of course it rhymes with my name."

"Why, so it does!"

"Anyway, it gave me—in the dream—an awful feeling of despair, and the dream changed. This time, I dreamed I was standing *outside* my stateroom in the little dark corridor, or *cul-de-sac*, and trying to find the door-handle to let myself in. I was in my pajamas, and again I was very cold. And at this point I woke up. . . . The extraordinary thing is that's exactly where I was!"

"Good heavens. How strange!"

"Yes. And now the question is, *where had I been?* I was frightened, when I came to—not unnaturally. For among other things I *did* have, quite definitely, the feeling that I *had been* somewhere. Somewhere where it was very cold. It doesn't sound very proper. Suppose I had been seen!"

"That might have been awkward," said Miss Dean.

"Awkward! It might indeed. It's very singular. I've never done such a thing before. It's this sort of thing that reminds one—rather wholesomely, perhaps, don't you think?"—and Mr. Arcularis gave a nervous little laugh—"how extraordinarily little we know about the workings of our own minds or souls. After all, what *do* we know?"

"Nothing—nothing—nothing—nothing," said Miss Dean slowly.

"Absolutely nothing."

Their voices had dropped, and again they were silent; and again they looked at each other gently and sympathetically, as if for the exchange of something unspoken and perhaps unspeakable. Time ceased. The orbit—so it seemed to Mr. Arcularis—once more became pure, became absolute. And once more he found himself wondering who it was that Miss Dean—Clarice Dean—reminded him of. Long ago and far away. Like those pictures of the islands and mountains. The little freckle-faced girl at the hospital was merely, as it were, the stepping-stone, the signpost, or, as in algebra, the "equals" sign. But what was it they both "equalled"? The jackstones came again into his mind and his Aunt Julia's rose-garden—at sunset; but this was ridiculous. It couldn't be simply that they reminded him of his childhood! And yet why not?

They went into the lounge. The ship's orchestra, in the oval-shaped balcony among faded palms, was playing the finale of "Cavalleria Rusticana," playing it badly.

"Good God!" said Mr. Arcularis, "can't I ever escape from that damned sentimental tune? It's the last thing I heard in America, and the last thing I *want* to hear."

"But don't you like it?"

"As music? No! It moves me too much, but in the wrong way."

"What, exactly, do you mean?"

"Exactly? Nothing. When I heard it at the hospital—when was it?—it made me feel like crying. Three old Italians tootling it in the rain. I suppose, like most people, I'm afraid of my feelings."

"Are they so dangerous?"

"Now then, young woman! Are you pulling my leg?"

The stewards had rolled away the carpets, and the passengers were beginning to dance. Miss Dean accepted the invitation of a young officer, and Mr. Arcularis watched them with envy. Odd, that last exchange of remarks—very odd; in fact, everything was odd. Was it possible that they were falling in love? Was that what it was all about—all these concealed references and recollections? He had read of such things. But at his age! And with a girl of twenty-two!

After an amused look at his old friend Polaris from the open door on the sheltered side, he went to bed.

The rhythm of the ship's engines was positively a persecution. It gave one no rest, it followed one like the Hound of Heaven, it drove one out into space and across the Milky Way and then back home by way of Betelgeuse. It was cold there, too. Mr. Arcularis, making the round trip by way of Betelgeuse and Polaris, sparkled with frost. He felt like a Christmas tree. Icicles on his fingers and icicles on his toes. He tinkled and spangled in the void, hallooed to the waste echoes, rounded the buoy on the verge of the Unknown, and tacked glitteringly homeward. The wind whistled. He was barefooted. Snowflakes and tinsel blew past him. Next time, by George, he would go farther still—for altogether it was rather a lark. Forward into the untrodden! as somebody said. Some intrepid explorer of his own backyard, probably, some middle-aged professor with an umbrella: those were the fellows for courage! But give us time, thought Mr. Arcularis, give us time, and we will bring back with us the night-rime of the Obsolute. Or was it Absolete? If only there weren't this perpetual throbbing, this iteration of sound, like a pain, these circles and repetitions of light—the feeling as of everything coiling inward to a center of misery . . .

Suddenly it was dark, and he was lost. He was groping, he touched the cold, white, slippery woodwork with his fingernails, looking for an electric switch. The throbbing, of course, was the throbbing of the ship. But he was almost home—almost home. Another corner to round, a door to be opened, and there he would be. Safe and sound. Safe in his father's home.

It was at this point that he woke up: in the corridor that led to the dining saloon. Such pure terror, such horror, seized him as he had never known. His heart felt as if it would stop beating. His back was towards the dining saloon; apparently he had just come from it. He was in his pajamas. The corridor was dim, all but two lights having been turned out for the night, and—thank God!—deserted. Not a soul, not a sound. He was perhaps fifty yards from his room. With luck he could get to it unseen. Holding tremulously to the rail that ran along the wall, a brown, greasy rail, he began to creep his way forward. He felt very weak, very dizzy, and his thoughts refused to concentrate. Vaguely he remembered Miss Dean—Clarice—and the freckled girl, as if they were one and the same person. But he wasn't in the hospital, he was on the ship. Of course. How absurd. The Great Circle. Here we are, old fellow . . . steady round the corner . . . hold hard to your umbrella . . .

In his room, with the door safely shut behind him, Mr. Arcularis broke into a cold sweat. He had no sooner got into his bunk, shivering, than he heard the night watchman pass.

"But where—" he thought, closing his eyes in agony—"have I been? . . ."

A dreadful idea had occurred to him.

"It's nothing serious—how could it be anything serious? Of course it's nothing serious," said Mr. Arcularis.

"No, it's nothing serious," said the ship's doctor urbanely.

"I knew you'd think so. But just the same—"

"Such a condition is the result of worry," said the doctor. "Are you worried—do you mind telling me—about something? Just try to think."

"Worried?"

Mr. Arcularis knitted his brows. *Was* there something? Some little mosquito of a cloud disappearing into the southwest, the northeast? Some little gnat-song of despair? But no, that was all over. All over.

"Nothing," he said, "nothing whatever."

"It's very strange," said the doctor.

"Strange! I should say so. I've come to sea for a rest, not for a nightmare! What about a bromide?"

"Well, I can give you a bromide, Mr. Arcularis—"

"Then, please, if you don't mind, give me a bromide."

He carried the little phial hopefully to his stateroom, and took a dose at once. He could see the sun through his porthole. It looked northern and pale and small, like a little peppermint, which was only natural enough, for the latitude was changing with every hour. But why was it that doctors were all alike? and all, for that matter, like his father, or that other fellow at the hospital? Smythe, his name was. Doctor Smythe. A nice, dry little fellow, and they said he was a writer. Wrote poetry, or something like that. Poor fellow—disappointed. Like everybody else. Crouched in there, in his cabin, night after night, writing blank verse or something—all about the stars and flowers and love and death; ice and the sea and the infinite; time and tide— well, every man to his own taste.

"But it's nothing serious," said Mr. Arcularis, later, to the parson. "How could it be?"

"Why, of course not, my dear fellow," said the parson, patting his back. "How could it be?"

"I know it isn't and yet I worry about it."

"It would be ridiculous to think it serious," said the parson.

Mr. Arcularis shivered: it was colder than ever. It was said that they were near icebergs. For a few hours in the morning there had been a fog, and the siren had blown—devastatingly—at three-minute intervals. Icebergs caused fog—he knew that.

"These things always come," said the parson, "from a sense of guilt. You feel guilty about something. I won't be so rude as to inquire what it is. But if you could rid yourself of the sense of guilt—"

And later still, when the sky was pink:

"But is it anything to worry about?" said Miss Dean. "Really?"

"No, I suppose not."

"Then don't worry. We aren't children any longer!"

"Aren't we? I wonder!"

They leaned, shoulders touching, on the deck-rail, and looked at the sea, which was multitudinously incarnadined. Mr. Arcularis scanned the horizon in vain for an iceberg.

"Anyway," he said, "the colder we are the less we feel!"

"I hope that's no reflection on *you*," said Miss Dean.

"Here . . . feel my hand," said Mr. Arcularis.

"Heaven knows it's cold!"

"It's been to Polaris and back! No wonder."

"Poor thing, poor thing!"

"Warm it."

"May I?"

"You can."

"I'll try."

Laughing, she took his hand between both of hers, one palm under and one palm over, and began rubbing it briskly. The decks were deserted, no one was near them, everyone was dressing for dinner. The sea grew darker, the wind blew colder.

"I wish I could remember who you are," he said.

"And you—who are you?"

"Myself."

"Then perhaps *I* am yourself."

"Don't be metaphysical!"

"But I *am* metaphysical!"

She laughed, withdrew, pulled the light coat about her shoulders.

The bugle blew the summons for dinner—"The Roast Beef of Old England"—and they walked together along the darkening deck toward the door, from which a shaft of soft light fell across the deck-rail. As they stepped over the brass door-sill Mr. Arcularis felt the throb of the engines again; he put his hand quickly to his side.

"Auf wiedersehen," he said. *"Tomorrow and tomorrow and tomorrow."*

Mr. Arcularis was finding it impossible, absolutely impossible, to keep warm. A cold fog surrounded the ship, had done so, it seemed, for days. The sun had all but disappeared, the transition from day to night was almost unnoticeable. The ship, too, seemed scarcely to be moving—it was as if anchored among walls of ice and rime. Monstrous, that merely because it was June, and supposed, therefore, to be warm, the ship's authorities should consider it unnecessary to turn on the heat! By day, he wore his heavy coat and sat shivering in the corner of the smoking-room. His teeth chattered, his hands were blue. By night, he heaped blankets on his bed, closed the porthole's black eye against the sea, and drew the yellow curtains across it, but in vain. Somehow, despite everything, the fog crept in, and the icy fingers touched his throat. The steward, questioned about it, merely said, "Icebergs." Of course—any fool knew that. But how long, in God's name, was it going to last? They surely ought to be past the Grand Banks by this time! And surely it wasn't necessary to sail to England by way of Greenland and Iceland!

Miss Dean—Clarice—was sympathetic.

"It's simply because," she said, "your vitality has been lowered by your illness. You can't expect to be your normal self so soon after an operation! When *was* your operation, by the way?"

Mr. Arcularis considered. Strange—he couldn't be quite sure. It was all a little vague—his sense of time had disappeared.

"Heaven knows!" he said. "Centuries ago. When I was a tadpole and you were a fish. I should think it must have been at about the time of the Battle of Teutoburg Forest. Or perhaps when I was a Neanderthal man with a club!"

"Are you sure it wasn't farther back still?"

What did she mean by that?

"Not at all. Obviously, we've been on this damned ship for ages—for eras—for aeons. And even on this ship, you must remember, I've had plenty of time, in my nocturnal wanderings, to go several times to Orion and back. I'm thinking, by the way, of going farther still. There's a nice little star off to the left, as you round Betelgeuse, which looks as if it might be right at the edge. The last outpost of the finite. I think I'll have a look at it and bring you back a frozen rime-feather."

"It would melt when you got it back."

"Oh, no, it wouldn't—not on *this* ship!"

Clarice laughed.

"I wish I could go with you," she said.

"If only you would! If only—"

He broke off his sentence and looked hard at her—how lovely she was, and how desirable! No such woman had ever before come into his life; there had been no one with whom he had at once felt so profound a sympathy and understanding. It was a miracle, simply—a miracle. No need to put his arm around her or to kiss her—delightful as such small vulgarities would be. He had only to look at her, and to feel, gazing into those extraordinary eyes, that she knew him, had always known him. It was as if, indeed, she might be his own soul.

But as he looked thus at her, reflecting, he noticed that she was frowning.
"What is it?" he said.
She shook her head, slowly.
"I don't know."
"Tell me."
"Nothing. It just occurred to me that perhaps you weren't looking quite so well."
Mr. Arcularis was startled. He straightened himself up.
"What nonsense! Of course this pain bothers me—and I feel astonishingly weak—"
"It's more than that—much more than that. Something is worrying you horribly."
She paused, and then with an air of challenging him, added, "Tell me, did you?"
Her eyes were suddenly asking him blazingly the question he had been afraid of.
He flinched, caught his breath, looked away. But it was no use, as he knew: he
would have to tell her. He had known all along that he would have to tell her.
"Clarice," he said—and his voice broke in spite of his effort to control it—"it's
killing me, it's ghastly! Yes, I did."
His eyes filled with tears, he saw that her own had done so also. She put her hand
on his arm.
"I knew," she said. "I knew. But tell me."
"It's happened twice again—*twice*—and each time I was farther away. The same
dream of going round a star, the same terrible coldness and helplessness. That awful
whistling curve . . ." He shuddered.
"And when you woke up—" she spoke quietly—"where were you when you woke
up? Don't be afraid!"
"The first time I was at the farther end of the dining saloon. I had my hand on the
door that leads into the pantry."
"I see. Yes. And the next time?"
Mr. Arcularis wanted to close his eyes in terror—he felt as if he were going mad.
His lips moved before he could speak, and when at last he did speak it was in a voice
so low as to be almost a whisper.
"I was at the bottom of the stairway that leads down from the pantry to the hold,
past the refrigerating-plant. It was dark, and I was crawling on my hands and knees
. . . *Crawling on my hands and knees!* . . ."
"Oh!" she said, and again, "Oh!"
He began to tremble violently; he felt the hand on his arm trembling also. And
then he watched a look of unmistakable horror come slowly into Clarice's eyes, and a
look of understanding, as if sne saw . . . She tightened her hold on his arm.
"Do you think . . ." she whispered.
They stared at each other.
"I know," he said. "And so do you . . . Twice more—three times—and I'll be
looking down into an empty . . ."
It was then that they first embraced—then, at the edge of the infinite, at the last
signpost of the finite. They clung together desperately, forlornly, weeping as they
kissed each other, staring hard one moment and closing their eyes the next. Passion-
ately, passionately, she kissed him, as if she were indeed trying to give him her
warmth, her life.
"But what nonsense!" she cried, leaning back and holding his face between her
hands, her hands which were wet with his tears. "What nonsense! It can't be!"
"It is," said Mr. Arcularis slowly.
"But how do you know? . . . How do you know where the—"

For the first time Mr. Arcularis smiled.

"Don't be afraid, darling—you mean the coffin?"

"How could you know where it is?"

"I don't need to," said Mr. Arcularis . . . "I'm already almost there."

Before they separated for the night, in the smoking-room, they had several whisky cocktails.

"We must make it gay!" Mr. Arcularis said. "Above all, we must make it gay. Perhaps even now it will turn out to be nothing but a nightmare from which both of us will wake! And even at the worst, at my present rate of travel, I ought to need two more nights! It's a long way, still, to that little star."

The parson passed them at the door.

"What! turning in so soon?" he said. "I was hoping for a game of chess."

"Yes, both turning in. But tomorrow?"

"Tomorrow, then, Miss Dean! And good-night!"

"Good-night."

They walked once round the deck, then leaned on the railing and stared into the fog. It was thicker and whiter than ever. The ship was moving barely perceptibly, the rhythm of the engines was slower, more subdued and remote, and at regular intervals, mournfully, came the long reverberating cry of the foghorn. The sea was calm, and lapped only very tenderly against the side of the ship, the sound coming up to them clearly, however, because of the profound stillness.

" 'On such a night as this—' " quoted Mr. Arcularis grimly.

" 'On such a night as this—' "

Their voices hung suspended in the night, time ceased for them, for an eternal instant they were happy. When at last they parted it was by tacit agreement on a note of the ridiculous.

"Be a good boy and take your bromide!" she said.

"Yes, mother, I'll take my medicine!"

In his stateroom, he mixed himself a strong potion of bromide, a very strong one, and got into bed. He would have no trouble in falling asleep: he felt more tired, more supremely exhausted, than he had ever been in his life; nor had bed ever seemed so delicious. And that long, magnificent, delirious swoop of dizziness . .   the Great Circle . . . the swift pathway to Arcturus . . .

It was all as before, but infinitely more rapid. Never had Mr. Arcularis achieved such phenomenal, such supernatural, speed. In no time at all he was beyond the moon, shot past the North Star as if it were standing still (which perhaps it was?), swooped in a long, bright curve round the Pleiades, shouted his frosty greetings to. Betelgeuse, and was off to the little blue star which pointed the way to the unknown. Forward into the untrodden! Courage, old man, and hold on to your umbrella! Have you got your garters on? Mind your hat! In no time at all we'll be back to Clarice with the frozen time-feather, the rime-feather, the snowflake of the Absolute, the Obsolete. If only we don't wake . . . if only we needn't wake . . . if only we don't wake in that—in that—time and space . . . somewhere or nowhere . . . cold and dark . . . "Cavalleria Rusticana" sobbing among the palms; if a lonely . . . if only . . . the coffers of the poor—not coffers, not coffers, not coffers. Oh, God, not coffers, but light, delight, supreme white and brightness, and above all whirling lightness, whirling lightness above all—and freezing—freezing—freezing . . .

At this point in the void the surgeon's last effort to save Mr. Arcularis's life had failed. He stood back from the operating table and made a tired gesture with a rubber-gloved hand.

"It's all over," he said. "As I expected."

He looked at Miss Hoyle, whose gaze was downward, at the basin she held. There was a moment's stillness, a pause, a brief flight of unexchanged comment, and then the ordered life of the hospital was resumed.

MY KINSMAN, MAJOR MOLINEUX

NATHANIEL HAWTHORNE (1804–1864)

After the kings of Great Britain had assumed the right of appointing the colonial governors, the measures of the latter seldom met with the ready and generous approbation which had been paid to those of their predecessors, under the original charters. The people looked with most jealous scrutiny to the exercise of power which did not emanate from themselves, and they usually rewarded their rulers with slender gratitude for the compliances by which, in softening their instructions from beyond the sea, they had incurred the reprehension of those who gave them. The annals of Massachusetts Bay will inform us, that of six governors in the space of about forty years from the surrender of the old charter, under James II., two were imprisoned by a popular insurrection; a third, as Hutchinson inclines to believe, was driven from the province by the whizzing of a musket-ball; a fourth, in the opinion of the same historian, was hastened to his grave by continual bickerings with the House of Representatives; and the remaining two, as well as their successors, till the Revolution, were favored with few and brief intervals of peaceful sway. The inferior members of the court party, in times of high political excitement, led scarcely a more desirable life. These remarks may serve as a preface to the following adventures, which chanced upon a summer night, not far from a hundred years ago. The reader, in order to avoid a long and dry detail of colonial affairs, is requested to dispense with an account of the train of circumstances that had caused much temporary inflammation of the popular mind.

It was near nine o'clock of a moonlight evening, when a boat crossed the ferry with a single passenger, who had obtained his conveyance at that unusual hour by the promise of an extra fare. While he stood on the landing-place, searching in either pocket for the means of fulfilling his agreement, the ferryman lifted a lantern, by the aid of which, and the newly risen moon, he took a very accurate survey of the stranger's figure. He was a youth of barely eighteen years, evidently country-bred, and now, as it should seem, upon his first visit to town. He was clad in a coarse gray coat, well worn, but in excellent repair; his under garments were durably constructed of leather, and fitted tight to a pair of serviceable and well-shaped limbs; his stockings of blue yarn were the incontrovertible work of a mother or a sister; and on his head was a three-cornered hat, which in its better days had perhaps sheltered the graver brow of the lad's father. Under his left arm was a heavy cudgel formed of an oak sapling, and retaining a part of the hardened root; and his equipment was completed by a wallet, not so abundantly stocked as to incommode the vigorous shoulders on which it hung.

Brown, curly hair, well-shaped features, and bright, cheerful eyes were nature's gifts, and worth all that art could have done for his adornment.

The youth, one of whose names was Robin, finally drew from his pocket the half of a little province bill of five shillings, which, in the depreciation in that sort of currency, did but satisfy the ferryman's demand, with the surplus of a sexangular piece of parchment, valued at three pence. He then walked forward into the town, with as light a step as if his day's journey had not already exceeded thirty miles, and with as eager an eye as if he were entering London city, instead of the little metropolis of a New England colony. Before Robin had proceeded far, however, it occurred to him that he knew not whither to direct his steps; so he paused, and looked up and down the narrow street, scrutinizing the small and mean wooden buildings that were scattered on either side.

"This low hovel cannot be my kinsman's dwelling," thought he, "nor yonder old house, where the moonlight enters at the broken casement; and truly I see none hereabouts that might be worthy of him. It would have been wise to inquire my way of the ferryman, and doubtless he would have gone with me, and earned a shilling from the Major for his pains. But the next man I meet will do as well."

He resumed his walk, and was glad to perceive that the street now became wider, and the houses more respectable in their appearance. He soon discerned a figure moving on moderately in advance, and hastened his steps to overtake it. As Robin drew nigh, he saw that the passenger was a man in years, with a full periwig of gray hair, a wide-skirted coat of dark cloth, and silk stockings rolled above his knees. He carried a long and polished cane, which he struck down perpendicularly before him at every step; and at regular intervals he uttered two successive hems, of a peculiarly solemn and sepulchral intonation. Having made these observations, Robin laid hold of the skirt of the old man's coat, just when the light from the open door and windows of a barber's shop fell upon both their figures.

"Good evening to you, honored sir," said he, making a low bow, and still retaining his hold of the skirt. "I pray you tell me whereabouts is the dwelling of my kinsman, Major Molineux."

The youth's question was uttered very loudly; and one of the barbers, whose razor was descending on a well-soaped chin, and another who was dressing a Ramillies wig, left their occupations, and came to the door. The citizen, in the mean time, turned a long-favored countenance upon Robin, and answered him in a tone of excessive anger and annoyance. His two sepulchral hems, however, broke into the very centre of his rebuke, with most singular effect, like a thought of the cold grave obtruding among wrathful passions.

"Let go my garment, fellow! I tell you, I know not the man you speak of. What! I have authority, I have—hem, hem—authority; and if this be the respect you show for your betters, your feet shall be brought acquainted with the stocks by daylight, tomorrow morning!"

Robin released the old man's skirt, and hastened away, pursued by an ill-mannered roar of laughter from the barber's shop. He was at first considerably surprised by the result of his question, but, being a shrewd youth, soon thought himself able to account for the mystery.

"This is some country representative," was his conclusion, "who has never seen the inside of my kinsman's door, and lacks the breeding to answer a stranger civilly. The man is old, or verily—I might be tempted to turn back and smite him on the nose.

Ah, Robin, Robin! even the barber's boys laugh at you for choosing such a guide! You will be wiser in time, friend Robin."

He now became entangled in a succession of crooked and narrow streets, which crossed each other, and meandered at no great distance from the water-side. The smell of tar was obvious to his nostrils, the masts of vessels pierced the moonlight above the tops of the buildings, and the numerous signs, which Robin paused to read, informed him that he was near the centre of business. But the streets were empty, the shops were closed, and lights were visible only in the second stories of a few dwelling-houses. At length, on the corner of a narrow lane, through which he was passing, he beheld the broad countenance of a British hero swinging before the door of an inn, whence proceeded the voices of many guests. The casement of one of the lower windows was thrown back, and a very thin curtain permitted Robin to distinguish a party at supper, round a well-furnished table. The fragrance of the good cheer steamed forth into the outer air, and the youth could not fail to recollect that the last remnant of his travelling stock of provision had yielded to his morning appetite, and that noon had found and left him dinnerless.

"Oh, that a parchment three-penny might give me a right to sit down at yonder table!" said Robin, with a sigh. "But the Major will make me welcome to the best of his victuals; so I will even step boldly in, and inquire my way to his dwelling."

He entered the tavern, and was guided by the murmur of voices and the fumes of tobacco to the public-room. It was a long and low apartment, with oaken walls, grown dark in the continual smoke, and a floor which was thickly sanded, but of no immaculate purity. A number of persons—the larger part of whom appeared to be mariners, or in some way connected with the sea—occupied the wooden benches, or leather-bottomed chairs, conversing on various matters, and occasionally lending their attention to some topic of general interest. Three or four little groups were draining as many bowls of punch, which the West India trade had long since made a familiar drink in the colony. Others, who had the appearance of men who lived by regular and laborious handicraft, preferred the insulated bliss of an unshared potation, and became more taciturn under its influence. Nearly all, in short, evinced a predilection for the Good Creature in some of its various shapes, for this is a vice to which, as Fast Day sermons of a hundred years ago will testify, we have a long hereditary claim. The only guests to whom Robin's sympathies inclined him were two or three sheepish countrymen, who were using the inn somewhat after the fashion of a Turkish caravansary; they had gotten themselves into the darkest corner of the room, and heedless of the Nicotian atmosphere, were supping on the bread of their own ovens, and the bacon cured in their own chimney-smoke. But though Robin felt a sort of brotherhood with these strangers, his eyes were attracted from them to a person who stood near the door, holding whispered conversation with a group of ill-dressed associates. His features were separately striking almost to grotesqueness, and the whole face left a deep impression on the memory. The forehead bulged out into a double prominence, with a vale between; the nose came boldly forth in an irregular curve, and its bridge was of more than a finger's breadth; the eyebrows were deep and shaggy, and the eyes glowed beneath them like fire in a cave.

While Robin deliberated of whom to inquire respecting his kinsman's dwelling, he was accosted by the innkeeper, a little man in a stained white apron, who had come to pay his professional welcome to the stranger. Being in the second generation from a French Protestant, he seemed to have inherited the courtesy of his parent nation;

but no variety of circumstances was ever known to change his voice from the one shrill note in which he now addressed Robin.

"From the country, I presume, sir?" said he, with a profound bow. "Beg leave to congratulate you on your arrival, and trust you intend a long stay with us. Fine town here, sir, beautiful buildings, and much that may interest a stranger. May I hope for the honor of your commands in respect to supper?"

"The man sees a family likeness! the rogue has guessed that I am related to the Major!" thought Robin, who had hitherto experienced little superfluous civility.

All eyes were now turned on the country lad, standing at the door, in his worn three-cornered hat, gray coat, leather breeches, and blue yarn stockings, leaning on an oaken cudgel, and bearing a wallet on his back.

Robin replied to the courteous innkeeper, with such an assumption of confidence as befitted the Major's relative. "My honest friend," he said, "I shall make it a point to patronize your house on some occasion, when"—here he could not help lowering his voice—"when I may have more than a parchment three-pence in my pocket. My present business," continued he, speaking with lofty confidence, "is merely to inquire my way to the dwelling of my kinsman, Major Molineux."

There was a sudden and general movement in the room, which Robin interpreted as expressing the eagerness of each individual to become his guide. But the innkeeper turned his eyes to a written paper on the wall, which he read, or seemed to read, with occasional recurrences to the young man's figure.

"What have we here?" said he, breaking his speech into little, dry fragments. " 'Left the house of the subscriber, bounden servant, Hezekiah Mudge,—had on, when he went away, gray coat, leather breeches, master's third-best hat. One pound currency reward to whosoever shall lodge him in any jail of the providence.' Better trudge, boy; better trudge!"

Robin had begun to draw his hand towards the lighter end of the oak cudgel, but a strange hostility in every countenance induced him to relinquish his purpose of breaking the courteous innkeeper's head. As he turned to leave the room, he encountered a sneering glance from the bold-featured personage whom he had before noticed; and no sooner was he beyond the door, than he heard a general laugh, in which the innkeeper's voice might be distinguished, like the dropping of small stones into a kettle.

"Now, is it not strange," thought Robin, with his usual shrewdness,—"is it not strange that the confession of an empty pocket should outweigh the name of my kinsman, Major Molineux? Oh, if I had one of those grinning rascals in the woods, where I and my oak sapling grew up together, I would teach him that my arm is heavy though my purse be light!"

On turning the corner of the narrow lane, Robin found himself in a spacious street, with an unbroken line of lofty houses on each side, and a steepled building at the upper end, whence the ringing of a bell announced the hour of nine. The light of the moon, and the lamps from the numerous shop-windows, discovered people promenading on the pavement, and amongst them Robin had hoped to recognize his hitherto inscrutable relative. The result of his former inquiries made him unwilling to hazard another, in a scene of such publicity, and he determined to walk slowly and silently up the street, thrusting his face close to that of every elderly gentleman, in search of the Major's lineaments. In his progress, Robin encountered many gay and gallant figures. Embroidered garments of showy colors, enormous periwigs, gold-laced hats, and silver-hilted swords glided past him and dazzled his optics. Travelled youths, imitators of the European fine gentlemen of the period, trod jauntily along, half dancing to the fashionable tunes which they hummed, and making poor Robin ashamed of his quiet and natural gait. At length, after many pauses to examine the gorgeous display of goods in the shop-windows, and after suffering some rebukes for the impertinence of his scrutiny into people's faces, the Major's kinsman found himself near the steepled building, still unsuccessful in his search. As yet, however, he had seen only one side of the thronged street; so Robin crossed, and continued the same sort of inquisition down the opposite pavement, with stronger hopes than the philosopher seeking an honest man, but with no better fortune. He had arrived about midway towards the lower end, from which his course began, when he overheard the approach of some one who struck down a cane on the flag-stones at every step, uttering at regular intervals, two sepulchral hems.

"Mercy on us!" quoth Robin, recognizing the sound.

Turning a corner, which chanced to be close at his right hand, he hastened to pursue his researches in some other part of the town. His patience now was wearing low, and he seemed to feel more fatigue from his rambles since he crossed the ferry, than from his journey of several days on the other side. Hunger also pleaded loudly within him, and Robin began to balance the propriety of demanding, violently, and with lifted cudgel, the necessary guidance from the first solitary passenger whom he should meet. While a resolution to this effect was gaining strength, he entered a street of mean appearance, on either side of which a row of ill-built houses was straggling towards the harbor. The moonlight fell upon no passenger along the whole extent, but in the third domicile which Robin passed there was a half-opened door, and his keen glance detected a woman's garment within.

"My luck may be better here," he said to himself.

Accordingly, he approached the door, and beheld it shut closer as he did so; yet an open space remained, sufficing for the fair occupant to observe the stranger, without a corresponding display on her part. All that Robin could discern was a strip of scarlet petticoat, and the occasional sparkle of an eye, as if the moonbeams were trembling on some bright thing.

"Pretty mistress," for I may call her so with a good conscience, thought the shrewd youth, since I know nothing to the contrary,—"my sweet pretty mistress, will you be kind enough to tell me whereabouts I must seek the dwelling of my kinsman, Major Molineux?"

Robin's voice was plaintive and winning, and the female, seeing nothing to be shunned in the handsome country youth, thrust open the door, and came forth into the moonlight. She was a dainty little figure, with a white neck, round arms, and a slender waist, at the extremity of which her scarlet petticoat jutted out over a hoop, as if she were standing in a balloon. Moreover, her face was oval and pretty, her hair dark beneath the little cap, and her bright eyes possessed a sly freedom, which triumphed over those of Robin.

"Major Molineux dwells here," said this fair woman.

Now, her voice was the sweetest Robin had heard that night, yet he could not help doubting whether that sweet voice spoke Gospel truth. He looked up and down the mean street, and then surveyed the house before which they stood. It was a small, dark edifice of two stories, the second of which projected over the lower floor, and the front apartment had the aspect of a shop for petty commodities.

"Now, truly, I am in luck," replied Robin, cunningly, "and so indeed is my kinsman, the Major, in having so pretty a housekeeper. But I prithee trouble him to step to the door; I will deliver him a message from his friends in the country, and then go back to my lodgings at the inn."

"Nay, the Major has been abed this hour or more," said the lady of the scarlet petticoat; "and it would be to little purpose to disturb him to-night, seeing his evening draught was the strongest. But he is a kind-hearted man, and it would be as much as my life's worth to let a kinsman of his turn away from the door. You are the good old gentleman's very picture, and I could swear that was his rainy-weather hat. Also he has garments very much resembling those leather small-clothes. But come in, I pray, for I bid you hearty welcome in his name."

So saying, the fair and hospitable dame took our hero by the hand; and the touch was light, and the force was gentleness, and though Robin read in her eyes what he did not hear in her words, yet the slender-waisted woman in the scarlet petticoat proved stronger than the athletic country youth. She had drawn his half-willing footsteps nearly to the threshold, when the opening of a door in the neighborhood startled the Major's housekeeper, and, leaving the Major's kinsman, she vanished speedily into her own domicile. A heavy yawn preceded the appearance of a man, who, like the Moonshine of Pyramus and Thisbe, carried a lantern, needlessly aiding his sister luminary in the heavens. As he walked sleepily up the street, he turned his broad, dull face on Robin, and displayed a long staff, spiked at the end.

"Home, vagabond, home!" said the watchman, in accents that seemed to fall asleep as soon as they were uttered. "Home, or we'll set you in the stocks by peep of day!"

"This is the second hint of the kind," thought Robin. "I wish they would end my difficulties, by setting me there to-night."

Nevertheless, the youth felt an instinctive antipathy towards the guardian of midnight order, which at first prevented him from asking his usual question. But just when the man was about to vanish behind the corner, Robin resolved not to lose the opportunity, and shouted lustily after him,—

"I say, friend! will you guide me to the house of my kinsman, Major Molineux?"

The watchman made no reply, but turned the corner and was gone; yet Robin seemed to hear the sound of drowsy laughter stealing along the solitary street. At that moment, also, a pleasant titter saluted him from the open window above his head; he looked up, and caught the sparkle of a saucy eye; a round arm beckoned to him, and next he heard light footsteps descending the staircase within. But Robin, being of the household of a New England clergyman, was a good youth, as well as a shrewd one; so he resisted temptation, and fled away.

He now roamed desperately, and at random, through the town, almost ready to believe that a spell was on him, like that by which a wizard of his country had once kept three pursuers wandering, a whole winter night, within twenty paces of the cottage which they sought. The streets lay before him, strange and desolate, and the lights were extinguished in almost every house. Twice, however, little parties of men, among whom Robin distinguished individuals in outlandish attire, came hurrying along; but, though on both occasions, they paused to address him, such intercourse did not at all enlighten his perplexity. They did but utter a few words in some language of which Robin knew nothing, and perceiving his inability to answer, bestowed a curse upon him in plain English and hastened away. Finally, the lad determined to knock at the door of every mansion that might appear worthy to be occupied by his kinsman, trusting that perserverance would overcome the fatality that had hitherto thwarted him. Firm in this resolve, he was passing beneath the walls of a church, which formed the corner of two streets, when, as he turned into the shade of its steeple, he encountered a bulky stranger, muffled in a cloak. The man was proceeding with the speed of earnest business, but Robin planted himself full before him, holding the oak cudgel with both hands across his body as a bar to further passage.

"Halt, honest man, and answer me a question," said he, very resolutely. "Tell me, this instant, whereabouts is the dwelling of my kinsman, Major Molineux!"

"Keep your tongue between your teeth, fool, and let me pass!" said a deep, gruff voice, which Robin partly remembered. "Let me pass, or I'll strike you to the earth!"

"No, no, neighbor!" cried Robin, flourishing his cudgel and then thrusting its larger end close to the man's muffled face. "No, no, I'm not the fool you take me for, nor do you pass till I have an answer to my question. Whereabouts is the dwelling of my kinsman, Major Molineux?"

The stranger, instead of attempting to force his passage, stepped back into the moonlight, unmuffled his face, and stared full into that of Robin.

"Watch here an hour, and Major Molineux will pass by," said he.

Robin gazed with dismay and astonishment on the unprecedented physiognomy of the speaker. The forehead with its double prominence, the broad hooked nose, the shaggy eyebrows, and fiery eyes were those which he had noticed at the inn, but the man's complexion had undergone a singular, or, more properly, a twofold change. One side of the face blazed an intense red, while the other was black as midnight, the division line being in the broad bridge of the nose; and a mouth which seemed to extend from ear to ear was black or red, in contrast to the color of the cheek. The effect was as if two individual devils, a fiend of fire and a fiend of darkness, had united themselves to form this infernal visage. The stranger grinned in Robin's face, muffled his parti-colored features, and was out of sight in a moment.

"Strange things we travellers see!" ejaculated Robin.

He seated himself, however, upon the steps of the church-door, resolving to wait the appointed time for his kinsman. A few moments were consumed in philosophical speculations upon the species of man who had just left him; but having settled this point shrewdly, rationally, and satisfactorily, he was compelled to look elsewhere for his amusement. And first he threw his eyes along the street. It was of more respectable appearance than most of those into which he had wandered; and the moon, creating, like the imaginative power, a beautiful strangeness in familiar objects, gave something of romance to a scene that might not have possessed it in the light of day. The irregular and often quaint architecture of the houses, some of whose roofs were broken into numerous little peaks, while others ascended, steep and narrow, into a single point, and others again were square; the pure snow-white of some of their complexions, the aged darkness of others, and the thousand sparklings, reflected from bright substances in the walls of many; these matters engaged Robin's attention for a while, and then began to grow wearisome. Next he endeavored to define the forms of distant objects, starting away, with almost ghostly indistinctness, just as his eye appeared to grasp them; and finally he took a minute survey of an edifice which stood on the opposite side of the street, directly in front of the church-door, where he was stationed. It was a large, square mansion, distinguished from its neighbors by a balcony, which rested on tall pillars, and by an elaborate Gothic window, communicating therewith.

"Perhaps this is the very house I have been seeking," thought Robin.

Then he strove to speed away the time, by listening to a murmur which swept continually along the street, yet was scarcely audible, except to an unaccustomed ear like his; it was a low, dull, dreamy sound, compounded of many noises, each of which was at too great a distance to be separately heard. Robin marvelled at this snore of a sleeping town, and marvelled more whenever its continuity was broken by now and then a distant shout, apparently loud where it originated. But altogether it was a sleep-inspiring sound, and, to shake off its drowsy influence, Robin arose, and climbed a window-frame, that he might view the interior of the church. There the moonbeams came trembling in, and fell down upon the deserted pews, and extended along the quiet aisles. A fainter yet more awful radiance was hovering around the pulpit, and one solitary ray had dared to rest upon the open page of the great Bible. Had nature, in that deep hour, become a worshipper in the house which man had builded? Or was that heavenly light the visible sanctity of the place,—visible because no earthly and impure feet were within the walls? The scene made Robin's heart shiver with a sensation of loneliness stronger than he had ever felt in the remotest depths of his native woods; so he turned away and sat down again before the door. There were graves around the church, and now an uneasy thought obtruded into Robin's breast. What if the object of his search, which had been so often and so strangely thwarted, were all the time mouldering in his shroud? What if his kinsman should glide through yonder gate, and nod and smile to him in dimly passing by?

"Oh that any breathing thing were here with me!" said Robin.

Recalling his thoughts from this uncomfortable track, he sent them over forest, hill, and stream, and attempted to imagine how that evening of ambiguity and weariness had been spent by his father's household. He pictured them assembled at the door, beneath the tree, the great old tree, which had been spared for its huge twisted trunk and venerable shade, when a thousand leafy brethren fell. There, at the going down of the summer sun, it was his father's custom to perform domestic worship, that the neighbors might come and join with him like brothers of the family, and that the wayfaring man might pause to drink at that fountain, and keep his heart pure by freshening the memory of home. Robin distinguished the seat of every individual of the little audience; he saw the good man in the midst, holding the Scriptures in the golden light that fell from the western clouds; he beheld him close the book and all rise up to pray. He heard the old thanksgivings for daily mercies, the old supplications for their continuance, to which he had so often listened in weariness, but which were now among his dear remembrances. He perceived the slight inequality of his father's voice when he came to speak of the absent one; he noted how his mother turned her face to the broad and knotted trunk; how his elder brother scorned, because the beard was rough upon his upper lip, to permit his features to be moved; how the younger sister drew down a low hanging branch before her eyes; and how the little one of all, whose sports had hitnerto broken the decorum of the scene, understood the prayer for her playmate, and burst into clamorous grief. Then he saw them go in at the door; and when Robin would have entered also, the latch tinkled into its place, and he was excluded from his home.

"Am I here, or there?" cried Robin, starting; for all at once, when his thoughts had become visible and audible in a dream, the long, wide, solitary street shone out before him.

He aroused himself, and endeavored to fix his attention steadily upon the large edifice which he had surveyed before. But still his mind kept vibrating between fancy and reality; by turns, the pillars of the balcony lengthened into the tall, bare stems of pines, dwindled down to human figures, settled again into their true shape and size, and then commenced a new succession of changes. For a single moment, when he deemed himself awake, he could have sworn that a visage—one which he seemed to remember, yet could not absolutely name as his kinsman's—was looking towards him from the Gothic window. A deeper sleep wrestled with and nearly overcame him, but fled at the sound of footsteps along the opposite pavement. Robin rubbed his eyes, discerned a man passing at the foot of the balcony, and addressed him in a loud, peevish, and lamentable cry.

"Hallo, friend! must I wait here all night for my kinsman, Major Molineux?"

The sleeping echoes awoke, and answered the voice; and the passenger, barely able to discern a figure sitting in the oblique shade of the steeple, traversed the street to obtain a nearer view. He was himself a gentleman in his prime, of open, intelligent, cheerful, and altogether prepossessing countenance. Perceiving a country youth, apparently homeless and without friends, he accosted him in a tone of real kindness, which had become strange to Robin's ears.

"Well, my good lad, why are you sitting here?" inquired he. "Can I be of service to you in any way?"

"I am afraid not, sir," replied Robin, despondingly; "yet I shall take it kindly if you'll answer me a single question. I've been searching, half the night, for one Major Molineux; now, sir, is there really such a person in these parts, or am I dreaming?"

"Major Molineux! The name is not altogether strange to me," said the gentleman, smiling. "Have you any objection to telling me the nature of your business with him?"

Then Robin briefly related that his father was a clergyman, settled on a small salary, at a long distance back in the country, and that he and Major Molineux were brothers' children. The Major, having inherited riches, and acquired civil and military rank, had visited his cousin, in great pomp, a year or two before; had manifested much interest in Robin and an elder brother, and, being childless himself, had thrown out hints respecting the future establishment of one of them in life. The elder brother was destined to succeed to the farm which his father cultivated in the interval of sacred duties; it was therefore determined that Robin should profit by his kinsman's generous intentions, especially as he seemed to be rather the favorite, and was thought to possess other necessary endowments.

"For I have the name of being a shrewd youth," observed Robin, in this part of his story.

"I doubt not you deserve it," replied his new friend, good-naturedly; "but pray proceed."

"Well, sir, being nearly eighteen years old, and well grown, as you see," continued Robin, drawing himself up to his full height, "I thought it high time to begin in the world. So my mother and sister put me in handsome trim, and my father gave me half the remnant of his last year's salary, and five days ago I started for this place, to pay the Major a visit. But, would you believe it, sir! I crossed the ferry a little after dark, and have yet found nobody that would show me the way to his dwelling; only, an hour or two since, I was told to wait here, and Major Molineux would pass by."

"Can you describe the man who told you this?" inquired the gentleman.

"Oh, he was a very ill-favored fellow, sir," replied Robin, "with two great bumps on his forehead, a hook nose, fiery eyes; and, what struck me as the strangest, his face was of two different colors. Do you happen to know such a man, sir?"

"Not intimately," answered the stranger, "but I chanced to meet him a little time previous to your stopping me. I believe you may trust his word, and that the Major will very shortly pass through this street. In the mean time, as I have a singular curiosity to witness your meeting, I will sit down here upon the steps and bear you company."

He seated himself accordingly, and soon engaged his companion in animated discourse. It was but of brief continuance, however, for a noise of shouting, which had long been remotely audible, drew so much nearer that Robin inquired its cause.

"What may be the meaning of this uproar?" asked he. "Truly, if your town be always as noisy, I shall find little sleep while I am an inhabitant."

"Why, indeed, friend Robin, there do appear to be three or four riotous fellows abroad to-night," replied the gentleman. "You must not expect all the stillness of your native woods here in our streets. But the watch will shortly be at the heels of these lads and"—

"Ay, and set them in the stocks by peep of day," interrupted Robin, recollecting his own encounter with the drowsy lantern-bearer. "But, dear sir, if I may trust my ears, an army of watchmen would never make head against such a multitude of rioters. There were at least a thousand voices went up to make that one shout."

"May not a man have several voices, Robin, as well as two complexions?" said his friend.

"Perhaps a man may; but Heaven forbid that a woman should!" responded the shrewd youth, thinking of the seductive tones of the Major's housekeeper.

The sounds of a trumpet in some neighboring street now became so evident and continual, that Robin's curiosity was strongly excited. In addition to the shouts, he heard frequent bursts from many instruments of discord, and a wild and confused laughter filled up the intervals. Robin rose from the steps, and looked wistfully towards a point whither people seemed to be hastening.

"Surely some prodigious merry-making is going on," exclaimed he. "I have laughed very little since I left home, sir, and should be sorry to lose an opportunity. Shall we step round the corner by that darkish house, and take our share of the fun?"

"Sit down again, sit down, good Robin," replied the gentleman, laying his hand on the skirt of the gray coat. "You forget that we must wait here for your kinsman; and there is reason to believe that he will pass by, in the course of a very few moments."

The near approach of the uproar had now disturbed the neighborhood; windows flew open on all sides; and many heads, in the attire of the pillow, and confused by sleep suddenly broken, were protruded to the gaze of whoever had leisure to observe them. Eager voices hailed each other from house to house, all demanding the explanation, which not a soul could give. Half-dressed men hurried towards the unknown commotion, stumbling as they went over the stone steps that thrust themselves into the narrow foot-walk. The shouts, the laughter, and the tuneless bray, the antipodes of music, came onwards with increasing din, till scattered individuals, and then denser bodies, began to appear round a corner at the distance of a hundred yards.

"Will you recognize your kinsman, if he passes in this crowd?" inquired the gentleman.

"Indeed, I can't warrant it, sir; but I'll take my stand here, and keep a bright lookout," answered Robin, descending to the outer edge of the pavement.

A mighty stream of people now emptied into the street, and came rolling slowly towards the church. A single horseman wheeled the corner in the midst of them, and close behind him came a band of fearful wind-instruments, sending forth a fresher discord now that no intervening buildings kept it from the ear. Then a redder light disturbed the moonbeams, and a dense multitude of torches shone along the

street, concealing, by their glare, whatever object they illuminated. The single horseman, clad in a military dress, and bearing a drawn sword, rode onward as the leader,
and, by his fierce and variegated countenance, appeared like war personified; the red
of one cheek was an emblem of fire and sword; the blackness of the other betokened
the mourning that attends them. In his train were wild figures in the Indian dress,
and many fantastic shapes without a model, giving the whole march a visionary air,
as if a dream had broken forth from some feverish brain, and were sweeping visibly
through the midnight streets. A mass of people, inactive, except as applauding spectators, hemmed the procession in; and several women ran along the sidewalk, piercing
the confusion of heavier sounds with their shrill voices of mirth or terror.

"The double-faced fellow has his eye upon me," muttered Robin, with an indefinite but an uncomfortable idea that he was himself to bear a part in the pag-
eantry.

The leader turned himself in the saddle, and fixed his glance full upon the country
youth, as the steed went slowly by. When Robin had freed his eyes from those fiery
ones, the musicians were passing before him, and the torches were close at hand; but
the unsteady brightness of the latter formed a veil which he could not penetrate. The
rattling of wheels over the stones sometimes found its way to his ear, and confused
traces of a human form appeared at intervals, and then melted into the vivid light. A
moment more, and the leader thundered a command to halt: the trumpets vomited a
horrid breath, and then held their peace; the shouts and laughter of the people died
away, and there remained only a universal hum, allied to silence. Right before Robin's
eyes was an uncovered cart. There the torches blazed the brightest, there the moon
shone out like day, and there, in tar-and-feathery dignity, sat his kinsman, Major
Molineux!

He was an elderly man, of large and majestic person, and strong, square features,
betokening a steady soul; but steady as it was, his enemies had found means to shake
it. His face was pale as death, and far more ghastly; the broad forehead was contracted in his agony, so that his eyebrows formed one grizzled line; his eyes were red
and wild, and the foam hung white upon his quivering lip. His whole frame was
agitated by a quick and continual tremor, which his pride strove to quell, even in
those circumstances of overwhelming humiliation. But perhaps the bitterest pang of
all was when his eyes met those of Robin; for he evidently knew him on the instant,
as the youth stood witnessing the foul disgrace of a head grown gray in honor. They
stared at each other in silence, and Robin's knees shook, and his hair bristled, with a
mixture of pity and terror. Soon, however, a bewildering excitement began to seize
upon his mind; the preceding adventures of the night, the unexpected appearance
of the crowd, the torches, the confused din and the hush that followed, the spectre
of his kinsman reviled by that great multitude,—all this, and, more than all, a perception of tremendous ridicule in the whole scene, affected him with a sort of mental
inebriety. At that moment a voice of sluggish merriment saluted Robin's ears; he
turned instinctively, and just behind the corner of the church stood the lantern-bearer,
rubbing his eyes, and drowsily enjoying the lad's amazement. Then he heard a peal of
laughter like the ringing of silvery bells; a woman twitched his arm, a saucy eye met
his, and he saw the lady of the scarlet petticoat. A sharp, dry cachinnation appealed
to his memory, and, standing on tiptoe in the crowd, with his white apron over his
head, he beheld the courteous little innkeeper. And lastly, there sailed over the heads
of the multitude a great, broad laugh, broken in the midst by two sepulchral hems;
thus, "Haw, haw, haw,—hem, hem,—haw, haw, haw, haw!"

The sound proceeded from the balcony of the opposite edifice and thither Robin turned his eyes. In front of the Gothic window stood the old citizen, wrapped in a wide gown, his gray periwig exchanged for a nightcap, which was thrust back from his forehead, and his silk stockings hanging about his legs. He supported himself on his polished cane in a fit of convulsive merriment, which manifested itself on his solemn old features like a funny inscription on a tombstone. Then Robin seemed to hear the voices of the barbers, of the guests of the inn, and of all who had made sport of him that night. The contagion was spreading among the multitude, when all at once, it seized upon Robin, and he sent forth a shout of laughter that echoed through the street,—every man shook his sides, every man emptied his lungs, but Robin's shout was the loudest there. The cloud-spirits peeped from their silvery islands, as the congregated mirth went roaring up the sky! The Man in the Moon heard the far bellow. "Oho," quoth he, "the old earth is frolicsome to-night!"

When there was a momentary calm in that tempestuous sea of sound, the leader gave the sign, the procession resumed its march. On they went, like fiends that throng in mockery around some dead potentate, mighty no more, but majestic still in his agony. On they went, in counterfeited pomp, in senseless uproar, in frenzied merriment, trampling all on an old man's heart. On swept the tumult, and left a silent street behind.

.   .   .   .

"Well, Robin, are you dreaming?" inquired the gentleman, laying his hand on the youth's shoulder.

Robin started, and withdrew his arm from the stone post to which he had instinctively clung, as the living stream rolled by him. His cheek was somewhat pale, and his eye not quite as lively as in the earlier part of the evening.

"Will you be kind enough to show me the way to the ferry?" said he, after a moment's pause.

"You have, then, adopted a new subject of inquiry?" observed his companion, with a smile.

"Why, yes, sir," replied Robin, rather dryly. "Thanks to you, and to my other friends, I have at last met my kinsman, and he will scarce desire to see my face again. I begin to grow weary of a town life, sir. Will you show me the way to the ferry?"

"No, my good friend Robin,—not to-night, at least," said the gentleman. "Some few days hence, if you wish it, I will speed you on your journey. Or, if you prefer to remain with us, perhaps, as you are a shrewd youth, you may rise in the world without the help of your kinsman, Major Molineux."

LIGEIA

EDGAR ALLAN POE (1809–1849)

And the will therein lieth, which dieth not. Who knoweth the mysteries of the will, with its vigor? For God is but a great will pervading all things by nature of its intentness. Man doth not yield himself to the angels, nor unto death utterly, save only through the weakness of his feeble will.

JOSEPH GLANVILL

I cannot, for my soul, remember how, when, or even precisely where, I first became acquainted with the lady Ligeia. Long years have since elapsed, and my memory is feeble through much suffering. Or, perhaps, I cannot *now* bring these points to mind, because, in truth, the character of my beloved, her rare learning, her singular yet placid cast of beauty, and the thrilling and enthralling eloquence of her low musical language, made their way into my heart by paces so steadily and stealthily progressive that they have been unnoticed and unknown. Yet I believe that I met her first and most frequently in some large, old, decaying city near the Rhine. Of her family—I have surely heard her speak. That it is of a remotely ancient date cannot be doubted. Ligeia! Ligeia! Buried in studies of a nature more than all else adapted to deaden impressions of the outward world, it is by that sweet word alone—by Ligeia—that I bring before mine eyes in fancy the image of her who is no more. And now, while I write, a recollection flashes upon me that I have *never known* the paternal name of her who was my friend and my betrothed, and who became the partner of my studies, and finally the wife of my bosom. Was it a playful charge on the part of my Ligeia? or was it a test of my strength of affection, that I should institute no inquiries upon this point? or was it rather a caprice of my own—a wildly romantic offering on the shrine of the most passionate devotion? I but indistinctly recall the fact itself—what wonder that I have utterly forgotten the circumstances which originated or attended it? And, indeed, if ever that spirit which is entitled *Romance*—if ever she, the wan and the misty-winged Ashtophet of idolatrous Egypt, presided, as they tell, over marriages ill-omened, then most surely she presided over mine.

There is one dear topic, however, on which my memory fails me not. It is the *person* of Ligeia. In stature she was tall, somewhat slender, and, in her latter days, even emaciated. I would in vain attempt to portray the majesty, the quiet ease, of her demeanor, or the incomprehensible lightness and elasticity of her footfall. She came and departed as a shadow. I was never made aware of her entrance into my closed study, save by the dear music of her low sweet voice, as she placed her marble hand upon my shoulder. In beauty of face no maiden ever equalled her. It was the radiance of an opium-dream—an airy and spirit-lifting vision more wildly divine than the fantasies which hovered about the slumbering souls of the daughters of Delos. Yet her features were not of that regular mould which we have been falsely taught to worship in the classical labors of the heathen. "There is no exquisite beauty," says Bacon, Lord Verulam, speaking truly of all the forms and genera of beauty.

"without some *strangeness* in the proportion." Yet, although I saw that the features of Ligeia were not of a classic regularity—although I perceived that her loveliness was indeed "exquisite," and felt that there was much of "strangeness" pervading it, yet I have tried in vain to detect the irregularity and to trace home my own perception of "the strange." I examined the contour of the lofty and pale forehead: it was faultless—how cold indeed that word when applied to a majesty so divine!—the skin rivalling the purest ivory, the commanding extent and repose, the gentle prominence of the regions above the temples; and then the raven-black, the glossy, the luxuriant, and naturally-curling tresses, setting forth the full force of the Homeric epithet, "hyacinthine!" I looked at the delicate outlines of the nose—and nowhere but in the graceful medallions of the Hebrews had I beheld a similar perfection. There were the same luxurious smoothness of surface, the same scarcely perceptible tendency to the aquiline, the same harmoniously curved nostrils speaking the free spirit. I regarded the sweet mouth. Here was indeed the triumph of all things heavenly—the magnificent turn of the short upper lip—the soft, voluptuous slumber of the under—the dimples which sported, and the color which spoke—the teeth glancing back, with a brilliancy almost startling, every ray of the holy light which fell upon them in her serene and placid, yet most exultingly radiant of all smiles. I scrutinized the formation of the chin: and here, too, I found the gentleness of breadth, the softness and the majesty, the fulness and the spirituality, of the Greek—the contour which the god Apollo revealed but in a dream to Cleomenes, the son of the Athenian. And then I peered into the large eyes of Ligeia.

For eyes we have no models in the remotely antique. It might have been, too, that in these eyes of my beloved lay the secret to which Lord Verulam alludes. They were, I must believe, far larger than the ordinary eyes of our own race. They were even fuller than the fullest of the gazelle eyes of the tribe of the valley of Nourjahad. Yet it was only at intervals—in moments of intense excitement—that this peculiarity became more than slightly noticeable in Ligeia. And at such moments was her beauty—in my heated fancy thus it appeared perhaps—the beauty of beings either above or apart from the earth, the beauty of the fabulous Houri of the Turk. The hue of the orbs was the most brilliant of black, and, far over them, hung jetty lashes of great length. The brows, slightly irregular in outline, had the same tint. The "strangeness," however, which I found in the eyes, was of a nature distinct from the formation, or the color, or the brilliancy of the features, and must, after all, be referred to the *expression*. Ah, word of no meaning! behind whose vast latitude of mere sound we intrench our ignorance of so much of the spiritual. The expression of the eyes of Ligeia! How for long hours have I pondered upon it! How have I, through the whole of a midsummer night, struggled to fathom it! What was it—that something more profound than the well of Democritus—whch lay far within the pupils of my beloved? What *was* it? I was possessed with a passion to discover. Those eyes! those large, those shining, those divine orbs! became to me twin stars of Leda, and I to them devoutest of astrologers.

There is no point, among the many incomprehensible anomalies of the science of mind, more thrillingly exciting than the fact—never, I believe, noticed in the schools —that in our endeavors to recall to memory something long forgotten, we often find ourselves *upon the very verge* of remembrance, without being able, in the end, to remember. And thus how frequently, in my intense scrutiny of Ligeia's eyes, have I felt approaching the full knowledge of their expression—felt it approaching—yet not quite be mine—and so at length entirely depart! And (strange, oh strangest mystery of all!) I found, in the commonest objects of the universe, a circle of analogies to that expression. I mean to say that, subsequently to the period when Ligeia's beauty passed into my spirit, there dwelling as in a shrine, I derived, from many existences in the material world, a sentiment such as I felt always aroused within me by her large and luminous orbs. Yet not the more could I define that sentiment, or analyze, or even steadily view it. I recognized it, let me repeat, sometimes in the survey of a rapidly growing vine—in the contemplation of a moth, a butterfly, a chrysalis, a stream of running water. I have felt it in the ocean; in the falling of a meteor. I have felt it in the glances of unusually aged people. And there are one or two stars in heaven, (one especially, a star of the sixth magnitude, double and changeable, to be found near the large star in Lyra,) in a telescopic scrutiny of which I have been made aware of the feeling. I have been filled with it by certain sounds from stringed instruments, and not unfrequently by passages from books. Among innumerable other instances, I well remember something in a volume of Joseph Glanvill, which (perhaps merely from its quaintness—who shall say?) never failed to inspire me with the sentiment: "And the will therein lieth, which dieth not. Who knoweth the mysteries of the will, with its vigor? For God is but a great will pervading all things by nature of its intentness. Man doth not yield him to the angels, nor unto death utterly, save only through the weakness of his feeble will."

Length of years and subsequent reflection have enabled me to trace, indeed, some remote connection between this passage in the English moralist and a portion of the character of Ligeia. An *intensity* in thought, action, or speech, was possibly, in her, a result, or at least an index, of that gigantic volition which, during our long intercourse, failed to give other and more immediate evidence of its existence. Of all the women whom I have ever known, she, the outwardly calm, the ever-placid Ligeia, was the most violently a prey to the tumultuous vultures of stern passion. And of such passion I could form no estimate, save by the miraculous expansion of those eyes which at once so delighted and appalled me—by the almost magical melody, modulation, distinctness, and placidity of her very low voice—and by the fierce energy (rendered doubly effective by contrast with her manner of utterance) of the wild words which she habitually uttered.

I have spoken of the learning of Ligeia: it was immense—such as I have never known in women. In the classical tongues was she deeply proficient, and as far as my own acquaintance extended in regard to the modern dialects of Europe, I have never known her at fault. Indeed upon any theme of the most admired, because simply the most abstruse of the boasted erudition of the academy, have I *ever* found Ligeia at fault? How singularly, how thrillingly, this one point in the nature of my wife has forced itself, at this late period only, upon my attention! I said her knowledge was such as I have never known in woman—but where breathes the man who has traversed, and successfully, *all* the wide areas of moral, physical, and mathematical science? I saw not then what I now clearly perceive, that the acquisitions of Ligeia were gigantic, were astounding; yet I was sufficiently aware of her infinite supremacy to resign myself, with a child-like confidence, to her guidance through the chaotic world of metaphysical investigation at which I was most busily occupied during the earlier years of our marriage. With how vast a triumph, with how vivid a delight, with how much of all that is ethereal in hope, did I *feel,* as she bent over me in studies but little sought—but less known—that delicious vista by slow degrees expanding before me, down whose long, gorgeous, and all untrodden path, I might at length pass onward to the goal of a wisdom too divinely precious not to be forbidden!

How poignant, then, must have been the grief with which, after some years, I beheld my well-grounded expectations take wings to themselves and fly away! Without Ligeia I was but as a child groping benighted. Her presence, her readings alone, rendered vividly luminous the many mysteries of the transcendentalism in which we were immersed. Wanting the radiant lustre of her eyes, letters, lambent and golden, grew duller than Saturnian lead. And now those eyes shone less and less frequently upon the pages over which I pored. Ligeia grew ill. The wild eyes blazed with a too—too glorious effulgence; the pale fingers became of the transparent waxen hue of the grave; and the blue veins upon the lofty forehead swelled and sank impetuously with the tides of the most gentle emotion. I saw that she must die—and I struggled desperately in spirit with the grim Azrael. And the struggles of the passionate wife were, to my astonishment, even more energetic than my own. There had been much in her stern nature to impress me with the belief that, to her, death would have come without its terrors; but not so. Words are impotent to convey any just idea of the fierceness of resistance with which she wrestled with the Shadow. I groaned in anguish at the pitiable spectacle. I would have soothed—I would have reasoned; but, in the intensity of her wild desire for life—for life—*but* for life— solace and reason were alike the uttermost of folly. Yet not until the last instance, amid the most convulsive writhings of her fierce spirit, was shaken the external placidity of her demeanor. Her voice grew more gentle—grew more low—yet I would not wish to dwell upon the wild meaning of the quietly uttered words. My brain reeled as I hearkened, entranced, to a melody more than mortal—to assumptions and aspirations which mortality had never before known.

That she loved me I should not have doubted; and I might have been easily aware that, in a bosom such as hers, love would have reigned no ordinary passion. But in death only was I fully impressed with the strength of her affection. For long hours, detaining my hand, would she pour out before me the overflowing of a heart whose more than passionate devotion amounted to idolatry. How had I deserved to be so blessed by such confessions? How had I deserved to be so cursed with the removal of my beloved in the hour of her making them? But upon this subject I cannot bear to dilate. Let me say only, that in Ligeia's more than womanly abandonment to a love, alas! all unmerited, all unworthily bestowed, I at length recognized the principle of her longing, with so wildly earnest a desire, for the life which was now fleeing so rapidly away. It is this wild longing, it is this eager vehemence of desire for life—*but* for life, that I have no power to portray, no utterance capable of expressing.

At high noon of the night in which she departed, beckoning me peremptorily to her side, she bade me repeat certain verses composed by herself not many days before. I obeyed her. They were these:

[THE CONQUEROR WORM]

Lo! 'tis a gala night
   Within the lonesome latter years!
An angel throng, bewinged, bedight
   In veils, and drowned in tears,
Sit in a theatre, to see
   A play of hopes and fears,
While the orchestra breathes fitfully
   The music of the spheres.

Mimes, in the form of God on high,
  Mutter and mumble low,
And hither and thither fly—
  Mere puppets they, who come and go
At bidding of vast formless things
  That shift the scenery to and fro,
Flapping from out their condor wings
  Invisible Woe!

That motley drama—oh, be sure
  It shall not be forgot!
With its Phantom chased for evermore,
  By a crowd that seize it not,
Through a circle that ever returneth in
  To the self-same spot,
And much of Madness, and more of Sin,
  And Horror the soul of the plot.

But see, amid the mimic rout
  A crawling shape intrude!
A blood-red thing that writhes from out
  The scenic solitude!
It writhes—it writhes! with mortal pangs
  The mimes become its food,
And seraphs sob at vermin fangs
  In human gore imbued.

Out—out are the lights—out all!
  And over each quivering form
The curtain, a funeral pall,
  Comes down with the rush of a storm,
While the angels, all pallid and wan,
  Uprising, unveiling, affirm
That the play is the tragedy, "Man,"
  And its hero, the Conqueror Worm.

"O God!" half shrieked Ligeia, leaping to her feet and extending her arms aloft with a spasmodic movement, as I made an end of these lines—"O God! O Divine Father! shall these things be undeviatingly so? shall this Conqueror be not once conquered? Are we not part and parcel in Thee? Who—who knoweth the mysteries of the will with its vigor? 'Man doth not yield him to the angels, *nor unto death utterly* save only through the weakness of his feeble will.'"

And now, as if exhausted with emotion, she suffered her white arms to fall, and returned solemnly to her bed of death. And as she breathed her last sighs, there came mingled with them a low murmur from her lips. I bent to them my ear, and distinguished, again, the concluding words of the passage in Glanvill: "*Man doth not yield him to the angels, nor unto death utterly, save only through the weakness of his feeble will.*"

She died: and I, crushed into the very dust with sorrow, could no longer endure the lonely desolation of my dwelling in the dim and decaying city by the Rhine. I had no lack of what the world calls wealth. Ligeia had brought me far more, very far more, than ordinarily falls to the lot of mortals. After a few months, therefore, of weary and aimless wandering, I purchased, and put in some repair, an abbey, which I shall not name, in one of the wildest and least frequented portions of fair England. The gloomy and dreary grandeur of the building, that almost savage aspect of the domain, the many melancholy and time-honored memories connected with both, had much in unison with the feelings of utter abandonment which had driven me into that remote and unsocial region of the country. Yet although the external abbey, with its verdant decay hanging about it, suffered but little alteration, I gave way with a child-like perversity, and perchance with a faint hope of alleviating my sorrows, to a display of more than regal magnificence within. For such follies, even in child-hood, I had imbibed a taste, and now they came back to me as if in the dotage of grief. Alas, I feel how much even of incipient madness might have been discovered in the gorgeous and fantastic draperies, in the solemn carvings of Egypt, in the wild cornices and furniture, in the Bedlam patterns of the carpets of tufted gold! I had become a bounden slave in the trammels of opium, and my labors and my orders had taken a coloring from my dreams. But these absurdities I must not pause to detail. Let me speak only of that one chamber, ever accursed, whither, in a moment of mental alienation, I led from the altar as my bride—as the successor of the unforgotten Ligeia—the fair-haired and blue-eyed Lady Rowena Trevanion, of Tremaine.

There is no individual portion of the architecture and decoration of that bridal chamber which is not now visibly before me. Where were the souls of the haughty family of the bride, when, through thirst of gold, they permitted to pass the threshold of an apartment *so* bedecked, a maiden and a daughter so beloved? I have said that I minutely remember the details of the chamber—yet I am sadly forgetful on topics of deep moment; and here there was no system, no keeping, in the fantastic display, to take hold upon the memory. The room lay in a high turret of the castellated abbey, was pentagonal in shape, and of capacious size. Occupying the whole southern face of the pentagon was the sole window—an immense sheet of unbroken glass from Venice —a single pane, and tinted of a leaden hue, so that the rays of either the sun or moon, passing through it, fell with a ghastly lustre on the objects within. Over the upper portion of this huge window extended the trellis-work of an aged vine, which clam-bered up the massy walls of the turret. The ceiling, of gloomy-looking oak, was ex-cessively lofty, vaulted, and elaborately fretted with the wildest and most grotesque specimens of a semi-Gothic, semi-Druidical device. From out the most central recess of this melancholy vaulting depended, by a single chain of gold with long links, a huge censer of the same metal, Saracenic in pattern, and with many perforations so contrived that there writhed in and out of them, as if endued with a serpent vitality, a continual succession of parti-colored fires.

Some few ottomans and golden candelabra, of Eastern figure, were in various sta-tions about; and there was the couch, too—the bridal couch—of an Indian model, and low, and sculptured of solid ebony, with a pall-like canopy above. In each of the angles of the chamber stood on end a gigantic sarcophagus of black granite, from the tombs of the kings over against Luxor, with their aged lids full of immemorial sculpture. But in the draping of the apartment lay, alas! the chief fantasy of all. The lofty walls, gigantic in height, even unproportionably so, were hung from summit to foot, in vast folds, with a heavy and massive-looking tapestry—tapestry of a material which was found alike as a carpet on the floor, as a covering for the ottomans and the ebony bed, as a canopy for the bed, and as the gorgeous volutes of the curtains which partially shaded the window. The material was the richest cloth of gold. It was spotted all over, at irregular intervals, with arabesque figures, about a foot in diameter, and wrought upon the cloth in patterns of the most jetty black. But these figures partook of the true character of the arabesque only when regarded from a single point of view. By a contrivance now common, and indeed traceable to a very remote period of antiquity, they were made changeable in aspect. To one entering the room, they bore the appearance of simple monstrosities; but upon a farther advance, this appearance gradually departed; and, step by step, as the visitor moved his station in the chamber, he saw himself surrounded by an endless succession of the ghastly forms which belong to the superstition of the Norman, or arise in the guilty slumbers of the monk. The phantasmagoric effect was vastly heightened by the artificial introduction of a strong continual current of wind behind the draperies, giving a hideous and uneasy animation to the whole.

In halls such as these, in a bridal chamber such as this, I passed, with the Lady of Tremaine, the unhallowed hours of the first month of our marriage—passed them with but little disquietude. That my wife dreaded the fierce moodiness of my temper —that she shunned me, and loved me but little—I could not help perceiving; but it gave me rather pleasure than otherwise. I loathed her with a hatred belonging more to demon than to man. My memory flew back (oh, with what intensity of regret!) to Ligeia, the beloved, the august, the beautiful, the entombed. I revelled in recollections of her purity, of her wisdom, of her lofty, her ethereal nature, of her passionate, her idolatrous love. Now, then, did my spirit fully and freely burn with more than all the fires of her own. In the excitement of my opium dreams (for I was habitually fettered in the shackles of the drug), I would call aloud upon her name, during the silence of the night, or among the sheltered recesses of the glens by day, as if, through the wild eagerness, the solemn passion, the consuming ardor of my longing for the departed, I could restore her to the pathway she had abandoned—ah, *could* it be forever?—upon the earth.

About the commencement of the second month of the marriage, the Lady Rowena was attacked with sudden illness, from which her recovery was slow. The fever which consumed her, rendered her nights uneasy; and in her perturbed state of half-slumber, she spoke of sounds, and of motions, in and about the chamber of the turret, which I concluded had no origin save in the distemper of her fancy, or perhaps in the phantasmagoric influences of the chamber itself. She became at length convalescent—finally, well. Yet but a brief period elapsed, ere a second more violent disorder again threw her upon a bed of suffering; and from this attack her frame, at all times feeble, never altogether recovered. Her illnesses were, after this epoch, of alarming character, and of more alarming recurrence, defying alike the knowledge and the great exertions of her physicians. With the increase of the chronic disease, which had thus apparently taken too sure hold upon her constitution to be eradicated by human means, I could not fail to observe a similar increase in the nervous irritation of her temperament, and in her excitability by trivial causes of fear. She spoke again, and now more frequently and pertinaciously, of the sounds—of the slight sounds— and of the unusual motions among the tapestries, to which she had formerly alluded.

One night, near the closing in of September, she pressed this distressing subject with more than usual emphasis upon my attention. She had just awakened from an unquiet slumber, and I had been watching, with feelings half of anxiety, half of vague terror, the workings of her emaciated countenance. I sat by the side of her ebony bed, upon one of the ottomans of India. She partly arose, and spoke, in an earnest low whisper, of sounds which she *then* heard, but which I could not hear—of motions which she *then* saw, but which I could not perceive. The wind was rushing hurriedly behind the tapestries, and I wished her to show her (what, let me confess it, I could not *all* believe) that those almost inarticulate breathings, and those very gentle variations of the figures upon the wall, were but the natural effects of that customary rushing of the wind. But a deadly pallor, overspreading her face, had proved to me that my exertions to reassure her would be fruitless. She appeared to be fainting, and no attendants were within call. I remembered where was deposited a decanter of light wine which had been ordered by her physicians, and hastened across the chamber to procure it. But, as I stepped beneath the light of the censer, two circumstances of a startling nature attracted my attention. I had felt that some palpable although invisible object had passed lightly by my person; and I saw that there lay upon the golden carpet, in the very middle of the rich lustre thrown from the censer, a shadow —a faint, indefinite shadow of angelic aspect—such as might be fancied for the shadow of a shade But I was wild with the excitement of an immoderate dose of opium, and heeded these things but little, nor spoke of them to Rowena. Having found the wine, I recrossed the chamber, and poured out a gobletful, which I held to the lips of the fainting lady. She had now partially recovered, however, and took the vessel herself, while I sank upon an ottoman near me, with my eyes fastened upon her person. It was then that I became distinctly aware of a gentle footfall upon the carpet, and near the couch; and in a second thereafter, as Rowena was in the act of raising the wine to her lips, I saw, or may have dreamed that I saw, fall within the goblet, as if from some invisible spring in the atmosphere of the room, three or four large drops of a brilliant and ruby-colored fluid. If this I saw—not so Rowena. She swallowed the wine unhesitatingly, and I forbore to speak to her of a circumstance which must after all, I considered, have been but the suggestion of a vivid imagination, rendered morbidly active by the terror of the lady, by the opium, and by the hour.

Yet I cannot conceal it from my own perception that, immediately subsequent to the fall of the ruby-drops, a rapid change for the worse took place in the disorder of my wife; so that, on the third subsequent night, the hands of her menials prepared her for the tomb, and on the fourth, I sat alone, with her shrouded body, in that fantastic chamber which had received her as my bride. Wild visions, opium-engendered, flitted shadow-like before me. I gazed with unquiet eye upon the sarcophagi in the angles of the room, upon the varying figures of the drapery, and upon the writhing of the parti-colored fires in the censer overhead. My eyes then fell, as I called to mind the circumstances of a former night, to the spot beneath the glare of the censer where I had seen the faint traces of the shadow. It was there, however, no longer; and breathing with greater freedom, I turned my glances to the pallid and rigid figure upon the bed. Then rushed upon me a thousand memories of Ligeia—and then came back upon my heart, with the turbulent violence of a flood, the whole of that unutterable woe with which I had regarded *her* thus enshrouded. The night waned; and still, with a bosom full of bitter thoughts of the one only and supremely beloved, I remained gazing upon the body of Rowena.

It might have been midnight, or perhaps earlier, or later, for I had taken no note of time, when a sob, low, gentle, but very distinct, startled me from my revery. I *felt* that it came from the bed of ebony—the bed of death. I listened in an agony of superstitious terror—but there was no repetition of the sound. I strained my vision to detect any motion in the corpse—but there was not the slightest perceptible. Yet I could not have been deceived. I *had* heard the noise, however faint, and my soul was awakened within me. I resolutely and perseveringly kept my attention riveted upon the body. Many minutes elapsed before any circumstance occurred tending to throw light upon the mystery. At length it became evident that a slight, a very feeble, and barely noticeable tinge of color had flushed up within the cheeks, and along the sunken small veins of the eyelids. Through a species of unutterable horror and awe, for which the language of mortality has no sufficiently energetic expression, I felt my heart cease to beat, my limbs grow rigid where I sat. Yet a sense of duty finally operated to restore my self-possession. I could no longer doubt that we had been precipitate in our preparations—that Rowena still lived. It was necessary that some immediate exertion be made; yet the turret was altogether apart from the portion of the abbey tenanted by the servants—there were none within call—I had no means of summoning them to my aid without leaving the room for many minutes—and this I could not venture to do. I therefore struggled alone in my endeavors to call back the spirit still hovering. In a short period it was certain, however, that a relapse had taken place; the color disappeared from both eyelid and cheek, leaving a wanness even more than that of marble; the lips became doubly shrivelled and pinched up in the ghastly expression of death; a repulsive clamminess and coldness overspread rapidly the surface of the body; and all the usual rigorous stiffness immediately supervened. I fell back with a shudder upon the couch from which I had been so startlingly aroused, and again gave myself up to passionate waking visions of Ligeia.

An hour thus elapsed, when (could it be possible?) I was a second time aware of some vague sound issuing from the region of the bed. I listened—in extremity of horror. The sound came again—it was a sigh. Rushing to the corpse, I saw—distinctly saw—a tremor upon the lips. In a minute afterwards they relaxed, disclosing a bright line of the pearly teeth. Amazement now struggled in my bosom with the profound awe which had hitherto reigned there alone. I felt that my vision grew dim, that my reason wandered; and it was only by a violent effort that I at length succeeded in nerving myself to the task which duty thus once more had pointed out. There was now a partial glow upon the forehead and upon the cheek and throat; a perceptible warmth pervaded the whole frame; there was even a slight pulsation at the heart. The lady *lived;* and with redoubled ardor I betook myself to the task of restoration. I chafed and bathed the temples and the hands, and used every exertion which experience, and no little medical reading, could suggest. But in vain. Suddenly, the color fled, the pulsation ceased, the lips resumed the expression of the dead, and, in an instant afterward, the whole body took upon itself the icy chilliness, the livid hue, the intense rigidity, the sunken outline, and all the loathsome peculiarities of that which has been, for many days, a tenant of the tomb.

And again I sunk into visions of Ligeia—and again, (what marvel that I shudder while I write?) *again* there reached my ears a low sob from the region of the ebony bed. But why shall I minutely detail the unspeakable horrors of that night? Why shall I pause to relate how, time after time, until near the period of the gray dawn, this hideous drama of revivification was repeated; how each terrific relapse was only into a sterner and apparently more irredeemable death; how each agony wore the aspect of a struggle with some invisible foe; and how each struggle was succeeded by I know not what of wild change in the personal appearance of the corpse? Let me hurry to a conclusion.

The greater part of the fearful night had worn away, and she who had been dead, once again stirred—and now more vigorously than hitherto, although arousing from a dissolution more appalling in its utter helplessness than any. I had long ceased to struggle or to move, and remained sitting rigidly upon the ottoman, a helpless prey to a whirl of violent emotions, of which extreme awe was perhaps the least terrible, the least consuming. The corpse, I repeat, stirred, and now more vigorously than before. The hues of life flushed up with unwonted energy into the countenance— and limbs relaxed—and, save that the eyelids were yet pressed heavily together, and that the bandages and draperies of the grave still imparted their charnel character to the figure, I might have dreamed that Rowena had indeed shaken off, utterly, the fetters of Death. But if this idea was not, even then, altogether adopted, I could at least doubt no longer, when, arising from the bed, tottering, with feeble steps, with closed eyes, and with the manner of one bewildered in a dream, the thing that was enshrouded advanced bodily and palpably into the middle of the apartment.

I trembled not—I stirred not—for a crowd of unutterable fancies connected with the air, the stature, the demeanor of the figure, rushing hurriedly through my brain, had paralyzed—had chilled me into stone. I stirred not—but gazed upon the apparition. There was a mad disorder in my thoughts—a tumult unappeasable. Could it, indeed, be the *living* Rowena who confronted me? Could it indeed be Rowena *at all*—the fair-haired, the blue-eyed Lady Rowena Trevanion of Tremaine? Why, *why* should I doubt it? The bandage lay heavily about the mouth—but then might it not be the mouth of the breathing Lady of Tremaine? And the cheeks—yes, these might indeed be the fair cheeks of the living Lady of Tremaine. And the chin, with its dimples, as in health, might it not be hers? but *had she then grown taller since her malady?* What inexpressible madness seized me with that thought? One bound, and I had reached her feet! Shrinking from my touch, she let fall from her head the ghastly cerements which had confined it, and there streamed forth, into the rushing atmosphere of the chamber, huge masses of long and dishevelled hair; *it was blacker than the raven wings of the midnight!* And now slowly opened *the eyes* of the figure which stood before me. "Here then, at least," I shrieked aloud, "can I never—can I never be mistaken—these are the full, and the black, and the wild eyes—of my lost love—of the lady—of the LADY LIGEIA."

A ROSE FOR EMILY

WILLIAM FAULKNER (1897–   )

I

When Miss Emily Grierson died, our whole town went to her funeral: the men through a sort of respectful affection for a fallen monument, the women mostly out of curiosity to see the inside of her house, which no one save an old manservant—a combined gardener and cook—had seen in at least ten years.

It was a big, squarish frame house that had once been white, decorated with cupolas and spires and scrolled balconies in the heavily lightsome style of the Seventies, set on what had once been our most select street. But garages and cotton gins had encroached and obliterated even the august names of that neighborhood; only Miss Emily's house was left, lifting its stubborn and coquettish decay above the cotton wagons and the gasoline pumps—an eyesore among eyesores. And now Miss Emily had gone to join the representatives of those august names where they lay in the cedar-bemused cemetery among the ranked and anonymous graves of Union and Confederate soldiers who fell at the battle of Jefferson.

Alive, Miss Emily had been a tradition, a duty, and a care; a sort of hereditary obligation upon the town, dating from that day in 1894 when Colonel Sartoris, the mayor —he who fathered the edict that no Negro woman should appear on the streets without an apron—remitted her taxes, the dispensation dating from the death of her father on into perpetuity. Not that Miss Emily would have accepted charity. Colonel Sartoris invented an involved tale to the effect that Miss Emily's father had loaned money to the town, which the town, as a matter of business, preferred this way of repaying. Only a man of Colonel Sartoris' generation and thought could have invented it, and only a woman could have believed it.

When the next generation, with its more modern ideas, became mayors and aldermen, this arrangement created some little dissatisfaction. On the first of the year they mailed her a tax notice. February came, and there was no reply. They wrote her a formal letter, asking her to call at the sheriff's office at her convenience. A week later the mayor wrote her himself, offering to call or to send his car for her, and received in reply a note on paper of an archaic shape, in a thin, flowing calligraphy in faded ink, to the effect that she no longer went out at all. The tax notice was also enclosed, without comment.

They called a special meeting of the Board of Aldermen. A deputation waited upon her, knocked at the door through which no visitor had passed since she ceased giving china-painting lessons eight or ten years earlier. They were admitted by the old Negro into a dim hall from which a stairway mounted into still more shadow. It smelled of dust and disuse—a close, dank smell. The Negro led them into the parlor. It was furnished in heavy, leather-covered furniture. When the Negro opened the blinds of one window, they could see that the leather was cracked; and when they sat down, a faint dust rose sluggishly about their thighs, spinning with slow motes in the single sun-ray. On a tarnished gilt easel before the fireplace stood a crayon portrait of Miss Emily's father.

They rose when she entered—a small, fat woman in black, with a thin gold chain descending to her waist and vanishing into her belt, leaning on an ebony cane with a tarnished gold head. Her skeleton was small and spare; perhaps that was why what would have been merely plumpness in another was obesity in her. She looked bloated, like a body long submerged in motionless water, and of that pallid hue. Her eyes, lost in the fatty ridges of her face, looked like two small pieces of coal pressed into a lump of dough as they moved from one face to another while the visitors stated their errand.

She did not ask them to sit. She just stood in the door and listened quietly until the spokesman came to a stumbling halt. Then they could hear the invisible watch ticking at the end of the gold chain.

Her voice was dry and cold. "I have no taxes in Jefferson. Colonel Sartoris explained it to me. Perhaps one of you can gain access to the city records and satisfy yourselves."

"But we have. We are the city authorities, Miss Emily. Didn't you get a notice from the sheriff, signed by him?"

"I received a paper, yes," Miss Emily said. "Perhaps he considers himself the sheriff . . . I have no taxes in Jefferson."

"But there is nothing on the books to show that, you see. We must go by the—"

"See Colonel Sartoris. I have no taxes in Jefferson."

"But, Miss Emily—"

"See Colonel Sartoris." (Colonel Sartoris had been dead almost ten years.) "I have no taxes in Jefferson. Tobe!" The Negro appeared. "Show these gentlemen out."

II

So she vanquished them, horse and foot, just as she had vanquished their fathers thirty years before about the smell. That was two years after her father's death and a short time after her sweetheart—the one we believed would marry her—had deserted her. After her father's death she went out very little; after her sweetheart went away, people hardly saw her at all. A few of the ladies had the temerity to call, but were not received, and the only sign of life about the place was the Negro man—a young man then—going in and out with a market basket.

"Just as if a man—any man—could keep a kitchen properly," the ladies said; so they were not surprised when the smell developed. It was another link between the gross, teeming world and the high and mighty Griersons.

A neighbor, a woman, complained to the mayor, Judge Stevens, eighty years old.

"But what will you have me do about it, madam?" he said.

"Why, send her word to stop it," the woman said. "Isn't there a law?"

"I'm sure that won't be necessary," Judge Stevens said. "It's probably just a snake or a rat that nigger of hers killed in the yard. I'll speak to him about it."

The next day he received two more complaints, one from a man who came in diffident deprecation. "We really must do something about it, Judge. I'd be the last one in the world to bother Miss Emily, but we've got to do something." That night the Board of Aldermen met—three graybeards and one younger man, a member of the rising generation.

"It's simple enough," he said. "Send her word to have her place cleaned up. Give her a certain time to do it in, and if she don't . . ."

"Dammit, sir," Judge Stevens said, "will you accuse a lady to her face of smelling bad?"

So the next night, after midnight, four men crossed Miss Emily's lawn and slunk about the house like burglars, sniffing along the base of the brickwork and at the cellar openings while one of them performed a regular sowing motion with his hand out of a sack slung from his shoulder. They broke open the cellar door and sprinkled lime there, and in all the outbuildings. As they recrossed the lawn, a window that had been dark was lighted and Miss Emily sat in it, the light behind her, and her upright torso motionless as that of an idol. They crept quietly across the lawn and into the shadow of the locusts that lined the street. After a week or two the smell went away.

That was when people had begun to feel really sorry for her. People in our town, remembering how Old Lady Wyatt, her great-aunt, had gone completely crazy at last, believed that the Griersons held themselves a little too high for what they really were. None of the young men were quite good enough for Miss Emily and such. We had long thought of them as a tableau: Miss Emily a slender figure in white in the background, her father a spraddled silhouette in the foreground, his back to her and clutching a horse-whip, the two of them framed by the back-flung front door. So when she got to be thirty and was still single, we were not pleased exactly, but vindicated; even with insanity in the family she wouldn't have turned down all of her chances if they had really materialized.

When her father died, it got about that the house was all that was left to her; and in a way, people were glad. At last they could pity Miss Emily. Being left alone, and a pauper, she had become humanized. Now she too would know the old thrill and the old despair of a penny more or less.

The day after his death all the ladies prepared to call at the house and offer condolence and aid, as is our custom. Miss Emily met them at the door, dressed as usual and with no trace of grief on her face. She told them that her father was not dead. She did that for three days, with the ministers calling on her, and the doctors, trying to persuade her to let them dispose of the body. Just as they were about to resort to law and force, she broke down, and they buried her father quickly.

We did not say she was crazy then. We believed she had to do that. We remembered all the young men her father had driven away, and we knew that with nothing left, she would have to cling to that which had robbed her, as people will.

III

She was sick for a long time. When we saw her again, her hair was cut short, making her look like a girl, with a vague resemblance to those angels in colored church windows—sort of tragic and serene.

The town had just let the contracts for paving the sidewalks, and in the summer after her father's death they began the work. The construction company came with niggers and mules and machinery, and a foreman named Homer Barron, a Yankee—a big, dark, ready man, with a big voice and eyes lighter than his face. The little boys would follow in groups to hear him cuss the niggers, and the niggers singing in time to the rise and fall of picks. Pretty soon he knew everybody in town. Whenever you heard a lot of laughing anywhere about the square, Homer Barron would be in the center of the group. Presently we began to see him and Miss Emily on Sunday afternoons driving in the yellow-wheeled buggy and the matched team of bays from the livery stable.

At first we were glad that Miss Emily would have an interest, because the ladies all said, "Of course a Grierson would not think seriously of a Northerner, a day laborer." But there were still others, older people, who said that even grief could not cause a real lady to forget *noblesse oblige*—without calling it *noblesse oblige*. They just said, "Poor Emily. Her kinsfolk should come to her." She had some kin in Alabama; but years ago her father had fallen out with them over the estate of Old Lady Wyatt, the crazy woman, and there was no communication between the two families. They had not even been represented at the funeral.

And as soon as the old people said, "Poor Emily," the whispering began. "Do you suppose it's really so?" they said to one another. "Of course it is. What else could . . ." This behind their hands; rustling of craned silk and satin behind jalousies closed upon the sun of Sunday afternoon as the thin, swift clop-clop-clop of the matched team passed: "Poor Emily."

She carried her head high enough—even when we believed that she was fallen. It was as if she demanded more than ever the recognition of her dignity as the last

Grierson; as if it had wanted that touch of earthiness to reaffirm her imperviousness. Like when she bought the rat poison, the arsenic. That was over a year after they had begun to say "Poor Emily," and while the two female cousins were visiting her.

"I want some poison," she said to the druggist. She was over thirty then, still a slight woman, though thinner than usual, with cold, haughty black eyes in a face the flesh of which was strained across the temples and about the eye-sockets as you imagine a lighthouse-keeper's face ought to look. "I want some poison," she said.

"Yes, Miss Emily. What kind? For rats and such? I'd recom—"

"I want the best you have. I don't care what kind."

The druggist named several. "They'll kill anything up to an elephant. But what you want is—"

"Arsenic," Miss Emily said. "Is that a good one?"

"Is . . . arsenic? Yes, ma'am. But what you want—"

"I want arsenic."

The druggist looked down at her. She looked back at him, erect, her face like a strained flag. "Why, of course," the druggist said. "If that's what you want. But the law requires you to tell what you are going to use it for."

Miss Emily just stared at him, her head tilted back in order to look him eye for eye, until he looked away and went and got the arsenic and wrapped it up. The Negro delivery boy brought her the package; the druggist didn't come back. When she opened the package at home there was written on the box, under the skull and bones: "For rats."

IV

So the next day we all said, "She will kill herself"; and we said it would be the best thing. When she had first begun to be seen with Homer Barron, we had said, "She will marry him." Then we said, "She will persuade him yet," because Homer himself had remarked—he liked men, and it was known that he drank with the younger men in the Elks' Club—that he was not a marrying man. Later we said, "Poor Emily" behind the jalousies as they passed on Sunday afternoon in the glittering buggy, Miss Emily with her head high and Homer Barron with his hat cocked and a cigar in his teeth, reins and whip in a yellow glove.

Then some of the ladies began to say that it was a disgrace to the town and a bad example to the young people. The men did not want to interfere, but at last the ladies forced the Baptist minister—Miss Emily's people were Episcopal—to call upon her. He would never divulge what happened during that interview, but he refused to go back again. The next Sunday they again drove about the streets, and the following day the minister's wife wrote to Miss Emily's relations in Alabama.

So she had blood-kin under her roof again and we sat back to watch developments. At first nothing happened. Then we were sure that they were to be married. We learned that Miss Emily had been to the jeweler's and ordered a man's toilet set in silver, with the letter H. B. on each piece. Two days later we learned that she had bought a complete outfit of men's clothing, including a nightshirt, and we said, "They are married." We were really glad. We were glad because the two female cousins were even more Grierson than Miss Emily had ever been.

So we were not surprised when Homer Barron—the streets had been finished some time since—was gone. We were a little disappointed that there was not a public blowing-off, but we believed that he had gone on to prepare for Miss Emily's coming, or to give her a chance to get rid of the cousins. (By that time it was a cabal, and we were all Miss Emily's allies to help circumvent the cousins.) Sure enough, after another week they departed. And, as we had expected all along, within three days Homer Barron was back in town. A neighbor saw the Negro man admit him at the kitchen door at dusk one evening.

And that was the last we saw of Homer Barron. And of Miss Emily for some time. The Negro man went in and out with the market basket, but the front door remained closed. Now and then we would see her at a window for a moment, as the men did that night when they sprinkled the lime, but for almost six months she did not appear on the streets. Then we knew that this was to be expected too; as if that quality of her father which had thwarted her woman's life so many times had been too virulent and too furious to die.

When we next saw Miss Emily, she had grown fat and her hair was turning gray. During the next few years it grew grayer and grayer until it attained an even pepper-and-salt iron-gray, when it ceased turning. Up to the day of her death at seventy-four it was still that vigorous iron-gray, like the hair of an active man.

From that time on her front door remained closed, save for a period of six or seven years, when she was about forty, during which she gave lessons in china-painting. She fitted up a studio in one of the downstairs rooms, where the daughters and grand-daughters of Colonel Sartoris' contemporaries were sent to her with the same regularity and in the same spirit that they were sent to church on Sundays with a twenty-five-cent piece for the collection plate. Meanwhile her taxes had been remitted.

Then the newer generation became the backbone and the spirit of the town, and the painting pupils grew up and fell away and did not send their children to her with boxes of color and tedious brushes and pictures cut from the ladies' magazines. The front door closed upon the last one and remained closed for good. When the town got free postal delivery, Miss Emily alone refused to let them fasten the metal numbers above her door and attach a mailbox to it. She would not listen to them.

Daily, monthly, yearly we watched the Negro grow grayer and more stooped, going in and out with the market basket. Each December we sent her a tax notice, which would be returned by the post office a week later, unclaimed. Now and then we would see her in one of the downstairs windows—she had evidently shut up the top floor of the house—like the carven torso of an idol in a niche, looking or not looking at us, we could never tell which. Thus she passed from generation to generation—dear, inescapable, impervious, tranquil, and perverse.

And so she died. Fell ill in the house filled with dust and shadows, with only a doddering Negro man to wait on her. We did not even know she was sick; we had long since given up trying to get any information from the Negro. He talked to no one, probably not even to her, for his voice had grown harsh and rusty, as if from disuse.

She died in one of the downstairs rooms, in a heavy walnut bed with a curtain, her gray head propped on a pillow yellow and moldy with age and lack of sunlight.

V

The Negro met the first of the ladies at the front door and let them in, with their hushed, sibilant voices and their quick, curious glances, and then he disappeared. He walked right through the house and out the back and was not seen again.

The two female cousins came at once. They held the funeral on the second day, with the town coming to look at Miss Emily beneath a mass of bought flowers, with the crayon face of her father musing profoundly above the bier and the ladies sibilant and macrabre; and the very old men—some in their brushed Confederate uniforms—on the porch and the lawn, talking of Miss Emily as if she had been a contemporary of theirs, believing that they had danced with her and courted her perhaps, confusing time with its mathematical progression, as the old do, to whom all the past is not a diminishing road but, instead, a huge meadow which no winter ever quite touches, divided from them now by the narrow bottle-neck of the most recent decade of years.

Already we knew that there was one room in that region above stairs which no one had seen in forty years, and which would have to be forced. They waited until Miss Emily was decently in the ground before they opened it.

The violence of breaking down the door seemed to fill this room with pervading dust. A thin, acrid pall as of the tomb seemed to lie everywhere upon this room decked and furnished as for a bridal: upon the valence curtains of faded rose color, upon the rose-shaded lights, upon the dressing table, upon the delicate array of crystal and the man's toilet things backed with tarnished silver, silver so tarnished that the monogram was obscured. Among them lay a collar and tie, as if they had just been removed, which, lifted, left upon the surface a pale crescent in the dust. Upon a chair hung the suit, carefully folded; beneath it the two mute shoes and the discarded socks.

The man himself lay in the bed.

For a long while we just stood there, looking down at the profound and fleshless grin. The body had apparently once lain in the attitude of an embrace, but now the long sleep that outlasts love, that conquers even the grimace of love, had cuckolded him. What was left of him, rotted beneath what was left of the nightshirt, had become inextricable from the bed in which he lay; and upon him and upon the pillow beside him lay that even coating of the patient and biding dust.

Then we noticed that in the second pillow was the indentation of a head. One of us lifted something from it, and leaning forward, that faint and invisible dust dry and acrid in the nostrils, we saw a long strand of iron-gray hair.

THE BEAR

WILLIAM FAULKNER (1897–   )

He was ten. But it had already begun, long before that day when at last he wrote his age in two figures and he saw for the first time the camp where his father and Major de Spain and old General Compson and the others spent two weeks each November and two weeks again each June. He had already inherited then, without ever having seen it, the tremendous bear with one trap-ruined foot which, in an area almost a hundred miles deep, had earned itself a name, a definite designation like a living man.

He had listened to it for years: the long legend of corncribs rifled, of shotes and grown pigs and even calves carried bodily into the woods and devoured, of traps and dead-falls overthrown and dogs mangled and slain, and shotgun and even rifle charges delivered at point-blank range and with no more effect than so many peas blown through a tube by a boy—a corridor of wreckage and destruction beginning back before he was born, through which sped, not fast but rather with the ruthless and irresistible deliberation of a locomotive, the shaggy tremendous shape.

It ran in his knowledge before he ever saw it. It looked and towered in his dreams before he even saw the unaxed woods where it left its crooked print, shaggy, huge, red-eyed, not malevolent but just big—too big for the dogs which tried to bay it, for the horses which tried to ride it down, for the men and the bullets they fired into it, too big for the very country which was its constricting scope. He seemed to see it entire with a child's complete divination before he ever laid eyes on either—the doomed wilderness whose edges were being constantly and punily gnawed at by men with axes and plows who feared it because it was wilderness, men myriad and name-less even to one another in the land where the old bear had earned a name, through which ran not even a mortal animal but an anachronism, indomitable and invincible, out of an old dead time, a phantom, epitome and apotheosis of the old wild life at which the puny humans swarmed and hacked in a fury of abhorrence and fear, like pygmies about the ankles of a drowsing elephant: the old bear solitary, indomitable and alone, widowered, childless, and absolved of mortality—old Priam reft of his old wife and having outlived all his sons.

Until he was ten, each November he would watch the wagon containing the dogs and the bedding and food and guns and his father and Tennie's Jim, the Negro, and Sam Fathers, the Indian, son of a slave woman and a Chickasaw chief, depart on the road to town, to Jefferson, where Major de Spain and the others would join them. To the boy, at seven, eight, and nine, they were not going into the Big Bottom to hunt bear and deer, but to keep yearly rendezvous with the bear which they did not even intend to kill. Two weeks later they would return, with no trophy, no head and skin. He had not expected it. He had not even been afraid it would be in the wagon. He believed that even after he was ten and his father would let him go too, for those two weeks in November, he would merely make another one, along with his father and Major de Spain and General Compson and the others, the dogs which feared to bay at it and the rifles and shotguns which failed even to bleed it, in the yearly pageant of the old bear's furious immortality.

Then he heard the dogs. It was in the second week of his first time in the camp. He stood with Sam Fathers against a big oak beside the faint crossing where they had stood each dawn for nine days now, hearing the dogs. He had heard them once before, one morning last week—a murmur, sourceless, echoing through the wet woods, swelling presently into separate voices which he could recognize and call by name. He had raised and cocked the gun as Sam told him and stood motionless again while the uproar, the invisible course, swept up and past and faded; it seemed to him that he could actually see the deer, the buck, blond, smoke-colored, elongated with speed, fleeing, vanishing, the woods, the gray solitude, still ringing even when the cries of the dogs had died away.

"Now let the hammers down," Sam said.

"You knew they were not coming here too," he said.

"Yes," Sam said. "I want you to learn how to do when you didn't shoot. It's after the chance for the bear or the deer has done already come and gone that men and dogs get killed."

"Anyway," he said, "it was just a deer."

Then on the tenth morning he heard the dogs again. And he readied the too-long, too-heavy gun as Sam had taught him, before Sam even spoke. But this time it was no deer, no ringing chorus of dogs running strong on a free scent, but a moiling yapping an octave too high, with something more than indecision and even abjectness in it, not even moving very fast, taking a long time to pass completely out of hearing, leaving then somewhere in the air that echo, thin, slightly hysterical, abject, almost grieving, with no sense of a fleeing, unseen, smoke-colored, grass-eating shape ahead of it, and Sam, who had taught him first of all to cock the gun and take position where he could see everywhere and then never move again, had himself moved up beside him; he could hear Sam breathing at his shoulder, and he could see the arched curve of the old man's inhaling nostrils.

"Hah," Sam said. "Not even running. Walking."

"Old Ben!" the boy said. "But up here!" he cried. "Way up here!"

"He do it every year," Sam said. "Once. Maybe to see who in camp this time, if he can shoot or not. Whether we got the dog yet that can bay and hold him. He'll take them to the river, then he'll send them back home. We may as well go back too; see how they look when they come back to camp."

When they reached the camp the hounds were already there, ten of them crouching back under the kitchen, the boy and Sam squatting to peer back into the obscurity where they had huddled, quiet, the eyes luminous, glowing at them and vanishing, and no sound, only that effluvium of something more than dog, stronger than dog and not just animal, just beast, because still there had been nothing in front of that abject and almost painful yapping save the solitude, the wilderness, so that when the eleventh hound came in at noon and with all the others watching—even old Uncle Ash, who called himself first a cook—Sam daubed the tattered ear and the raked shoulder with turpentine and axle grease, to the boy it was still no living creature, but the wilderness which, leaning for the moment down, had patted lightly once the hound's temerity.

"Just like a man," Sam said. "Just like folks. Put off as long as she could having to be brave, knowing all the time that sooner or later she would have to be brave to keep on living with herself, and knowing all the time beforehand what was going to happen to her when she done it."

That afternoon, himself on the one-eyed wagon mule which did not mind the smell of blood nor, as they told him, of bear, and with Sam on the other one, they rode for more than three hours through the rapid, shortening winter day. They followed no path, no trail even that he could see; almost at once they were in a country which he had never seen before. Then he knew why Sam had made him ride the mule which would not spook. The sound one stopped short and tried to whirl and bolt even as Sam got down, blowing its breath, jerking and wrenching at the rein, while Sam held it, coaxing it forward with his voice, since he could not risk tying it, drawing it forward while the boy got down from the marred one.

Then, standing beside Sam in the gloom of the dying afternoon, he looked down at the rotted over-turned log, gutted and scored with claw marks and, in the wet earth beside it, the print of the enormous warped two-toed foot. He knew now what he had smelled when he peered under the kitchen where the dogs huddled. He realized for the first time that the bear which had run in his listening and loomed in his dreams since before he could remember to the contrary, and which, therefore, must have existed in the listening and dreams of his father and Major de Spain and even old General Compson, too, before they began to remember in their turn, was a mortal animal, and that if they had departed for the camp each November without any actual hope of bringing its trophy back, it was not because it could not be slain, but because so far they had had no actual hope to.

"Tomorrow," he said.

"We'll try tomorrow," Sam said. "We ain't got the dog yet."

"We've got eleven. They ran him this morning."

"It won't need but one," Sam said. "He ain't here. Maybe he ain't nowhere. The only other way will be for him to run by accident over somebody that has a gun."

"That wouldn't be me," the boy said. "It will be Walter or Major or—"

"It might," Sam said. "You watch close in the morning. Because he's smart. That's how come he had lived this long. If he gets hemmed up and has to pick out somebody to run over, he will pick out you."

"How?" the boy said. "How will he know—" He ceased. "You mean he already knows me, that I ain't never been here before, ain't had time to find out yet whether I—" He ceased again, looking at Sam, the old man whose face revealed nothing until it smiled. He said humbly, not even amazed, "It was me he was watching. I don't reckon he did need to come but once."

The next morning they left the camp three hours before daylight. They rode this time because it was too far to walk, even the dogs in the wagon; again the first gray light found him in a place which he had never seen before, where Sam had placed him and told him to stay and then departed. With the gun which was too big for him, which did not even belong to him, but to Major de Spain, and which he had fired only once—at a stump on the first day, to learn the recoil and how to reload it— he stood against a gum tree beside a little bayou whose black still water crept without movement out of a canebrake and crossed a small clearing and into cane again, where, invisible, a bird—the big woodpecker called Lord-to-God by Negroes—clattered at a dead limb.

It was a stand like any other, dissimilar only in incidentals to the one where he had stood each morning for ten days; a territory new to him, yet no less familiar than that other one which, after almost two weeks, he had come to believe he knew a little —the same solitude, the same loneliness through which human beings had merely passed without altering it, leaving no mark, no scar, which looked exactly as it must have looked when the first ancestor of Sam Father's Chickasaw predecessors crept into it and looked about, club or stone ax or bone arrow drawn and poised; different only because, squatting at the edge of the kitchen, he smelled the hounds huddled and cringing beneath it and saw the raked ear and shoulder of the one who, Sam said, had had to be brave once in order to live with herself, and saw yesterday in the earth beside the gutted log the print of the living foot.

He heard no dogs at all. He never did hear them. He only heard the drumming of the woodpecker stop short off and knew that the bear was looking at him. He never saw it. He did not know whether it was in front of him or behind him. He did not move, holding the useless gun, which he had not even had warning to cock and which even now he did not cock, tasting in his saliva that taint as of brass which he knew now because he had smelled it when he peered under the kitchen at the huddled dogs

Then it was gone. As abruptly as it had ceased, the woodpecker's dry, monotonous clatter set up again, and after a while he even believed he could hear the dogs—a murmur, scarce a sound even, which he had probably been hearing for some time before he even remarked it, drifting into hearing and then out again, dying away. They came nowhere near him. If it was a bear they ran, it was another bear. It was Sam himself who came out of the cane and crossed the bayou, followed by the injured bitch of yesterday. She was almost at heel, like a bird dog, making no sound. She came and crouched against his leg, trembling, staring off into the cane.

"I didn't see him," he said. "I didn't, Sam!"

"I know it," Sam said. "He done the looking. You didn't hear him neither, did you?"

"No," the boy said. "I—"

"He's smart," Sam said. "Too smart." He looked down at the hound, trembling faintly and steadily against the boy's knee. From the raked shoulder a few drops of fresh blood oozed and clung. "Too big. We ain't got the dog yet. But maybe someday. Maybe not next time. But someday."

So I must see him, he thought. *I must look at him.* Otherwise, it seemed to him that it would go on like this forever, as it had gone on with his father and Major de Spain, who was older than his father, and even with old General Compson, who had been old enough to be a brigade commander in 1865. Otherwise, it would go on so forever, next time and next time, after and after and after. It seemed to him that he could never see the two of them, himself and the bear, shadowy in the limbo from which time emerged, becoming time; the old bear absolved of mortality and himself partaking, sharing a little of it, enough of it. And he knew now what he had smelled in the huddled dogs and tasted in his saliva. He recognized fear. *So I will have to see him,* he thought, without dread or even hope. *I will have to look at him.*

It was in June of the next year. He was eleven. They were in camp again, celebrating Major de Spain's and General Compson's birthdays. Although the one had been born in September and the other in the depth of winter and in another decade, they had met for two weeks to fish and shoot squirrels and turkey and run coons and wildcats with the dogs at night. That is, he and Boon Hoggenbeck and the Negroes fished and shot squirrels and ran the coons and cats, because the proved hunters, not only Major de Spain and old General Compson, who spent those two weeks sitting in a rocking chair before a tremendous iron pot of Brunswick stew, stirring and tasting, with old Ash to quarrel with about how he was making it and Tennie's Jim to pour whiskey from the demijohn into the tin dipper from which he drank it, but even the boy's father and Walter Ewell, who were still young enough, scorned such, other than shooting the wild gobblers with pistols for wagers on their marksmanship.

Or, that is, his father and the others believed he was hunting squirrels. Until the third day, he thought that Sam Fathers believed that too. Each morning he would leave the camp right after breakfast. He had his own gun now, a Christmas present. He went back to the tree beside the bayou where he had stood that morning. Using the compass which old General Compson had given him, he ranged from that point; he was teaching himself to be a better-than-fair woodsman without knowing he was doing it. On the second day he even found the gutted log where he had first seen the crooked print. It was almost completely crumbled now, healing with unbelievable speed, a passionate and almost visible relinquishment, back into the earth from which the tree had grown.

He ranged the summer woods now, green with gloom; if anything, actually dimmer than in November's gray dissolution, where, even at noon, the sun fell only in intermittent dappling upon the earth, which never completely dried out and which crawled with snakes—moccasins and water snakes and rattlers, themselves the color of the dappling gloom, so that he would not always see them until they moved, returning later and later, first day, second day, passing in the twilight of the third evening the little log pen enclosing the log stable where Sam was putting up the horses for the night.

"You ain't looked right yet," Sam said.

He stopped. For a moment he didn't answer. Then he said peacefully, in a peaceful rushing burst as when a boy's miniature dam in a little brook gives way, "All right. But how? I went to the bayou. I even found that log again. I—"

"I reckon that was all right. Likely he's been watching you. You never saw his foot?"

"I," the boy said—"I didn't—I never thought—"

"It's the gun," Sam said. He stood beside the fence, motionless—the old man, the Indian, in the battered faded overalls and the five-cent straw hat which in the Negro's race had been the badge of his enslavement and was now the regalia of his freedom. The camp—the clearing, the house, the barn and its tiny lot with which Major de Spain in his turn had scratched punily and evanescently at the wilderness—faded in the dusk, back into the immemorial darkness of the woods. *The gun*, the boy thought. *The gun.*

"Be scared," Sam said. "You can't help that. But don't be afraid. Ain't nothing in the woods going to hurt you unless you corner it, or it smells that you are afraid. A bear or a deer, too, has got to be scared of a coward the same as a brave man has got to be."

The gun, the boy thought.

"You will have to choose," Sam said.

He left the camp before daylight, long before Uncle Ash would wake in his quilts on the kitchen floor and start the fire for breakfast. He had only the compass and a stick for snakes. He could go almost a mile before he would begin to need the compass. He sat on a log, the invisible compass in his invisible hand, while the secret night sounds, fallen still at his movements, scurried again and then ceased for good, and the owls ceased and gave over to the waking of day birds, and he could see the compass. Then he went fast yet still quietly; he was becoming better and better as a woodsman, still without having yet realized it.

He jumped a doe and a fawn at sunrise, walked them out of the bed, close enough to see them—the crash of undergrowth, the white scut, the fawn scudding behind her faster than he had believed it could run. He was hunting right, upwind, as Sam had taught him; not that it mattered now. He had left the gun; of his own will and relinquishment he had accepted not a gambit, not a choice, but a condition in which not only the bear's heretofore inviolable anonymity but all the old rules and balances of hunter and hunted had been abrogated. He would not even be afraid, not even in the moment when the fear would take him completely—blood, skin, bowels, bones, memory from the long time before it became his memory—all save that thin, clear, immortal lucidity which alone differed him from this bear and from all the other bear and deer he would ever kill in the humility and pride of his skill and endurance, to which Sam had spoken when he leaned in the twilight on the lot fence yesterday.

By noon he was far beyond the little bayou, farther into the new and alien country than he had ever been. He was traveling now not only by the old, heavy, biscuit-thick silver watch which had belonged to his grandfather. When he stopped at last, it was for the first time since he had risen from the log at dawn when he could see the compass. It was far enough. He had left the camp nine hours ago; nine hours from now, dark would have already been an hour old. But he didn't think that. He thought, *All right. Yes. But what?* and stood for a moment, alien and small in the green and topless solitude, answering his own question before it had formed and ceased. It was the watch, the compass, the stick—the three lifeless mechanicals with which for nine hours he had fended the wilderness off; he hung the watch and compass carefully on a bush and leaned the stick beside them and relinquished completely to it.

He had not been going very fast for the last two or three hours. He went no faster now, since distance would not matter even if he could have gone fast. And he was trying to keep a bearing on the tree where he had left the compass, trying to complete a circle which would bring him back to it or at least intersect itself, since direction would not matter now either. But the tree was not there, and he did as Sam had schooled him—made the next circle in the opposite direction, so that the two patterns would bisect somewhere, but crossing no print of his own feet, finding the tree at last, but in the wrong place—no bush, no compass, no watch—and the tree not even the tree, because there was a down log beside it and he did what Sam Fathers had told him was the next thing and the last.

As he sat down on the log he saw the crooked print—the warped, tremendous, two-toed indentation which, even as he watched it, filled with water. As he looked up, the wilderness coalesced, solidified—the glade, the tree he sought, the bush, the watch and the compass glinting where a ray of sunshine touched them. Then he saw the bear. It did not emerge, appear; it was just there, immobile, solid, fixed in the hot dappling of the green and windless noon, not as big as he had dreamed it, but as big as he had expected it, bigger, dimensionless, against the dappled obscurity, looking at him where he sat quietly on the log and looked back at it.

Then it moved. It made no sound. It did not hurry. It crossed the glade, walking for an instant into the full glare of the sun; when it reached the other side it stopped again and looked back at him across one shoulder while his quiet breathing inhaled and exhaled three times.

Then it was gone. It didn't walk into the woods, the undergrowth. It faded, sank back into the wilderness as he had watched a fish, a huge old bass, sink and vanish into the dark depths of its pool without even any movement of its fins.

He thought, *It will be next fall.* But it was not next fall, nor the next nor the next. He was fourteen then. He had killed his buck, and Sam Fathers had marked his face with the hot blood, and in the next year he killed a bear But even before that accolade he had become as competent in the woods as many grown men with the same experience; by his fourteenth year he was a better woodsman than most grown men with more. There was no territory within thirty miles of the camp that he did not know— bayou, ridge, brake, landmark, tree and path. He could have led anyone to any point in it without deviation, and brought them out again. He knew the game trails that even Sam Fathers did not know; in his thirteenth year he found a buck's bedding place, and unbeknown to his father he borrowed Walter Ewell's rifle and lay in wait at dawn and killed the buck when it walked back to the bed, as Sam had told him how the old Chickasaw fathers did.

But not the old bear, although by now he knew its footprints better than he did his own, and not only the crooked one. He could see any one of the three sound ones and distinguish it from any other, and not only by its size. There were other bears within these thirty miles which left tracks almost as large, but this was more than that. If Sam Fathers had been his mentor and the back-yard rabbits and squirrels at home his kindergarten, then the wilderness the old bear ran was his college, the old male bear itself, so long unwifed and childless as to have become its own ungendered progenitor, was his alma mater. But he never saw it.

He could find the crooked print now almost whenever he liked, fifteen or ten or five miles, or sometimes nearer the camp than that. Twice while on stand during the three years he heard the dogs strike its trail by accident; on the second time they jumped it seemingly, the voices high, abject, almost human in hysteria, as on that first morning two years ago. But not the bear itself. He would remember that noon three years ago, the glade, himself and the bear fixed during that moment in the windless and dappled blaze, and it would seem to him that it had never happened, that he had dreamed that too. But it had happened. They had looked at each other, they had emerged from the wilderness old as earth, synchronized to the instant by something more than the blood that moved the flesh and bones which bore them, and touched, pledged something, affirmed, something more lasting than the frail web of bones and flesh which any accident could obliterate.

Then he saw it again. Because of the very fact that he thought of nothing else, he had forgotten to look for it. He was still hunting with Walter Ewell's rifle. He saw it cross the end of a long blow-down, a corridor where a tornado had swept, rushing through rather than over the tangle of trunks and branches as a locomotive would have, faster than he had ever believed it could move, almost as fast as a deer even, because a deer would have spent most of that time in the air, faster than he could bring the rifle sights up with it. And now he knew what had been wrong during all the three years. He sat on a log, shaking and trembling as if he had never seen the woods before nor anything that ran them, wondering with incredulous amazement how he could have forgotten the very thing which Sam Fathers had told him and which the bear itself had proved the next day and had now returned after three years to reaffirm.

And now he knew what Sam Fathers had meant about the right dog, a dog in which size would mean less than nothing. So when he returned alone in April—school was out then, so that the sons of farmers could help with the land's planting, and at last his father had granted him permission, on his promise to be back in four days—he had the dog. It was his own, a mongrel of the sort called by Negroes a fyce, a ratter, itself not much bigger than a rat and possessing that bravery which had long since stopped being courage and had become foolhardiness.

It did not take four days. Alone again, he found the trail on the first morning. It was not a stalk; it was an ambush. He timed the meeting almost as if it were an appointment with a human being. Himself holding the fyce muffled in a feed sack and Sam Fathers with two of the hounds on a piece of plowline rope, they lay down wind of the trail at dawn of the second morning. They were so close that the bear turned without even running, as if in surprised amazement at the shrill and frantic up-roar of the released fyce, turning at bay against the trunk of a tree, on its hind feet; it seemed to the boy that it would never stop rising, taller and taller, and even the two hounds seemed to take a desperate and despairing courage from the fyce, following it as it went in.

Then he realized that the fyce was actually not going to stop. He flung, threw the gun away, and ran; when he overtook and grasped the frantically pin-wheeling little dog, it seemed to him that he was directly under the bear

He could smell it, strong and hot and rank. Sprawling, he looked up to where it loomed and towered over him like a cloudburst and colored like a thunderclap, quite familiar, peacefully and even lucidly familiar, until he remembered: This was the way he had used to dream about it. Then it was gone. He didn't see it go. He knelt, holding the frantic fyce with both hands, hearing the abashed wailing of the hounds drawing farther and farther away, until Sam came up. He carried the gun. He laid it down quietly beside the boy and stood looking down at him.

"You've done seed him twice now with a gun in your hands," he said. "This time you couldn't have missed him."

The boy rose. He still held the fyce. Even in his arms and clear of the ground, it yapped frantically, straining and surging after the fading uproar of the two hounds like a tangle of wire springs. He was panting a little, but he was neither shaking nor trembling now.

"Neither could you!" he said. "You had the gun! Neither did you!"

"And you didn't shoot," his father said. "How close were you?"

"I don't know, sir," he said. "There was a big wood tick inside his right hind leg. I saw that. But I didn't have the gun then."

"But you didn't shoot when you had the gun," his father said. "Why?"

But he didn't answer, and his father didn't wait for him to, rising and crossing the room, across the pelt of the bear which the boy had killed two years ago and the larger one which his father had killed before he was born, to the bookcase beneath the mounted head of the boy's first buck. It was the room which his father called the office, from which all the plantation business was transacted; in it for the fourteen years of his life he had heard the best of all talking. Major de Spain would be there and sometimes old General Compson, and Walter Ewell and Boon Hoggenback and Sam Fathers and Tennie's Jim, too, were hunters, knew the woods and what ran them.

He would hear it, not talking himself but listening—the wilderness, the big woods, bigger and older than any recorded document of white man fatuous enough to believe he had bought any fragment of it or Indian ruthless enough to pretend that any fragment of it had been his to convey. It was of the men, not white nor black nor red, but men, hunters with the will and hardihood to endure and the humility and skill to survive, and the dogs and the bear and deer juxtaposed and reliefed against it, ordered and compelled by and within the wilderness in the ancient and unremitting contest by the ancient and immitigable rules which voided all regrets and brooked no quarter, the voices quiet and weighty and deliberate for retrospection and recollection and exact remembering, while he squatted in the blazing firelight as Tennie's Jim squatted, who stirred only to put more wood on the fire and to pass the bottle from one glass to another. Because the bottle was always present, so that after a while it seemed to him that those fierce instants of heart and brain and courage and wiliness and speed were concentrated and distilled into that brown liquor which not women, not boys and children, but only hunters drank, drinking not of the blood they had spilled but some condensation of the wild immortal spirit, drinking it moderately, humbly even, not with the pagan's base hope of acquiring the virtues of cunning and strength and speed, but in salute to them.

His father returned with the book and sat down again and opened it. "Listen," he said. He read the five stanzas aloud, his voice quiet and deliberate in the room where there was no fire now because it was already spring. Then he looked up. The boy watched him. "All right," his father said. "Listen." He read again, but only the second stanza this time, to the end of it, the last two lines, and closed the book and put it on the table beside him. "She cannot fade, though thou hast not thy bliss, for ever wilt thou love, and she be fair," he said.

"He's talking about a girl," the boy said.

"He had to talk about something," his father said. Then he said, "He was talking about truth. Truth doesn't change. Truth is one thing. It covers all things which touch the heart—honor and pride and pity and justice and courage and love. Do you see now?"

He didn't know. Somehow it was simpler than that. There was an old bear, fierce and ruthless, not merely just to stay alive, but with the fierce pride of liberty and freedom, proud enough of the liberty and freedom to see it threatened without fear or even alarm; nay, who at times even seemed deliberately to put that freedom and liberty in jeopardy in order to savor them, to remind his old strong bones and flesh to keep supple and quick to defend and preserve them. There was an old man, son of a Negro slave and an Indian king, inheritor on the one side of the long chronicle of a people who had learned humility through suffering, and pride through the endurance which survived the suffering and injustice, and on the other side, the chronicle of a people even longer in the land than the first, yet who no longer existed in the land at all save in the solitary brotherhood of an old Negro's alien blood and the wild and invincible spirit of an old bear. There was a boy who wished to learn humility and pride in order to become skillful and worthy in the woods, who suddenly found himself becoming so skillful so rapidly that he feared he would never become worthy because he had not learned humility and pride, although he had tried to, until one day and as suddenly he discovered that an old man who could not have defined either had led him, as though by the hand, to that point where an old bear and a little mongrel of a dog showed him that, by possessing one thing other, he would possess them both.

And a little dog, nameless and mongrel and many-fathered, grown, yet weighing less than six pounds, saying as if to itself, "I can't be dangerous, because there's nothing much smaller than I am; I can't be fierce, because they would call it just a noise; I can't be humble, because I'm already too close to the ground to genuflect; I can't be proud, because I wouldn't be near enough to it for anyone to know who was casting the shadow, and I don't even know that I'm not going to heaven, because they have already decided that I don't possess an immortal soul. So all I can be is brave. But it's all right. I can be that, even if they still call it just noise."

That was all. It was simple, much simpler than somebody talking in a book about youth and a girl he would never need to grieve over, because he could never approach any nearer her and would never have to get any farther away. He had heard about a bear, and finally got big enough to trail it, and he trailed it four years and at last met it with a gun in his hands and he didn't shoot. Because a little dog— But he could have shot long before the little dog covered the twenty yards to where the bear waited, and Sam Fathers could have shot at any time during that interminable minute while Old Ben stood on his hind feet over them. He stopped. His father was watching him gravely across the spring-rife twilight of the room; when he spoke, his words were as quiet as the twilight, too, not loud, because they did not need to be because they would last, "Courage, and honor, and pride," his father said, "and pity, and love of justice and of liberty. They all touch the heart, and what the heart holds to becomes truth, as far as we know the truth. Do you see now?"

Sam, and Old Ben, and Nip, he thought. And himself too. He had been all right too. His father had said so. "Yes, sir," he said.

THE HORSE DEALER'S DAUGHTER

D. H. LAWRENCE (1885–1930)

"Well, Mabel, and what are you going to do with yourself?" asked Joe, with foolish flippancy. He felt quite safe himself. Without listening for an answer, he turned aside, worked a grain of tobacco to the tip of his tongue, and spat it out. He did not care about anything, since he felt safe himself.

The three brothers and the sister sat round the desolate breakfast table, attempting some sort of desultory consultation. The morning's post had given the final tap to the family fortune, and all was over. The dreary dining-room itself, with its heavy mahogany furniture, looked as if it were waiting to be done away with.

But the consultation amounted to nothing. There was a strange air of ineffectuality about the three men, as they sprawled at table, smoking and reflecting vaguely on their own condition. The girl was alone, a rather short, sullen-looking young woman of twenty-seven. She did not share the same life as her brothers. She would have been good-looking, save for the impassive fixity of her face, "bull-dog," as her brothers called it.

There was a confused tramping of horses' feet outside. The three men all sprawled round in their chairs to watch. Beyond the dark holly-bushes that separated the strip of lawn from the highroad, they could see a cavalcade of shire horses swinging out of their own yard, being taken for exercise. This was the last time. These were the last horses that would go through their hands. The young men watched with critical, callous look. They were all frightened at the collapse of their lives, and the sense of disaster in which they were involved left them no inner freedom.

Yet they were three fine, well-set fellows enough. Joe, the eldest, was a man of thirty-three, broad and handsome in a hot, flushed way. His face was red, he twisted his black moustache over a thick finger, his eyes were shallow and restless. He had a sensual way of uncovering his teeth when he laughed, and his bearing was stupid. Now he watched the horses with a glazed look of helplessness in his eyes, a certain stupor of downfall.

The great draught-horses swung past. They were tied head to tail, four of them, and they heaved along to where a lane branched off from the highroad, planting their great hoofs floutingly in the fine black mud, swinging their great rounded haunches sumptuously, and trotting a few sudden steps as they were led into the lane, round the corner. Every movement showed a massive, slumbrous strength, and a stupidity which held them in subjection. The groom at the head looked back, jerking the leading rope. And the cavalcade moved out of sight up the lane, the tail of the last horse, bobbed up tight and stiff, held out taut from the swinging great haunches as they rocked behind the hedges in a motion-like sleep.

Joe watched with glazed hopeless eyes. The horses were almost like his own body to him. He felt he was done for now. Luckily he was engaged to a woman as old as himself, and therefore her father, who was steward of a neighbouring estate, would provide him with a job. He would marry and go into harness. His life was over, he would be a subject animal now.

He turned uneasily aside, the retreating steps of the horses echoing in his ears. Then, with foolish restlessness, he reached for the scraps of bacon-rind from the plates, and making a faint whistling sound, flung them to the terrier that lay against the fender. He watched the dog swallow them, and waited till the creature looked into his eyes. Then a faint grin came on his face, and in a high, foolish voice he said:

"You won't get much more bacon, shall you, you little bitch?"

The dog faintly and dismally wagged its tail, then lowered its haunches, circled round, and lay down again.

There was another helpless silence at the table. Joe sprawled uneasily in his seat, not willing to go till the family conclave was dissolved. Fred Henry, the second brother, was erect, clean-limbed, alert. He had watched the passing of the horses with more sang-froid. If he was an animal, like Joe, he was an animal which controls, not one which is controlled. He was master of any horse, and he carried himself with a well-tempered air of mastery. But he was not master of the situations of life. He pushed his coarse brown moustache upwards, off his lip, and glanced irritably at his sister, who sat impassive and inscrutable.

"You'll go and stop with Lucy for a bit, shan't you?" he asked. The girl did not answer.

"I don't see what else you can do," persisted Fred Henry.

"Go as a skivvy," Joe interpolated laconically.

The girl did not move a muscle.

"If I was her, I should go in for training for a nurse," said Malcolm, the youngest of them all. He was the baby of the family, a young man of twenty-two, with a fresh, jaunty *museau*.

But Mabel did not take any notice of him. They had talked at her and round her for so many years, that she hardly heard them at all.

The marble clock on the mantelpiece softly chimed the half-hour, the dog rose uneasily from the hearthrug and looked at the party at the breakfast table. But still they sat on in ineffectual conclave.

"Oh, all right," said Joe suddenly, apropos of nothing. "I'll get a move on."

He pushed back his chair, straddled his knees with a downward jerk, to get them free, in horsey fashion, and went to the fire. Still he did not go out of the room; he was curious to know what the others would do or say. He began to charge his pipe, looking down at the dog and saying, in a high, affected voice:

"Going wi' me? Going wi' me are ter? Tha'rt goin' further than tha counts on just now, dost hear?"

The dog faintly wagged its tail, the man stuck out his jaw and covered his pipe with his hands, and puffed intently, losing himself in the tobacco, looking down all the while at the dog with an absent brown eye. The dog looked up at him in mournful distrust. Joe stood with his knees stuck out, in real horsey fashion.

"Have you had a letter from Lucy?" Fred Henry asked of his sister.

"Last week," came the neutral reply.

"And what does she say?"

There was no answer.

"Does she *ask* you to go and stop there?" persisted Fred Henry.

"She says I can if I like."

"Well, then, you'd better. Tell her you'll come on Monday."

This was received in silence.

"That's what you'll do then, is it?" said Fred Henry, in some exasperation.

But she made no answer. There was a silence of futility and irritation in the room. Malcolm grinned fatuously.

"You'll have to make up your mind between now and next Wednesday," said Joe loudly, "or else find yourself lodgings on the kerbstone."

The face of the young woman darkened, but she sat on immutable.

"Here's Jack Fergusson!" exclaimed Malcolm, who was looking aimlessly out of the window.

"Where?" exclaimed Joe, loudly.

"Just gone past."

"Coming in?"

Malcolm craned his neck to see the gate.

"Yes," he said.

There was a silence. Mabel sat on like one condemned, at the head of the table. Then a whistle was heard from the kitchen. The dog got up and barked sharply. Joe opened the door and shouted:

"Come on."

After a moment a young man entered. He was muffled up in overcoat and a purple woollen scarf, and his tweed cap, which he did not remove, was pulled down on his head. He was of medium height, his face was rather long and pale, his eyes looked tired.

"Hello, Jack! Well, Jack!" exclaimed Malcolm and Joe. Fred Henry merely said, "Jack."

"What's doing?" asked the newcomer, evidently addressing Fred Henry.

"Same. We've got to be out by Wednesday. Got a cold?"

"I have—got it bad, too."

"Why don't you stop in?"

"*Me* stop in? When I can't stand on my legs, perhaps I shall have a chance." The young man spoke huskily. He had a slight Scotch accent.

"It's a knock-out, isn't it," said Joe, boisterously, "if a doctor goes round croaking with a cold. Looks bad for the patients, doesn't it?"

The young doctor looked at him slowly.

"Anything the matter with *you*, then?" he asked sarcastically.

"Not as I know of. Damn your eyes, I hope not. Why?"

"I thought you were very concerned about the patients, wondered if you might be one yourself."

"Damn it, no, I've never been patient to no flaming doctor, and hope I never shall be," returned Joe.

At this point Mabel rose from the table, and they all seemed to become aware of her existence. She began putting the dishes together. The young doctor looked at her, but did not address her. He had not greeted her. She went out of the room with the tray, her face impassive and unchanged.

"When are you off then, all of you?" asked the doctor.

"I'm catching the eleven-forty," replied Malcolm. "Are you goin' down wi' th' trap, Joe?"

"Yes, I've told you I'm going down wi' th' trap, haven't I?'

"We'd better be getting her in then. So long, Jack, if I don't see you before I go," said Malcolm, shaking hands.

He went out, followed by Joe, who seemed to have his tail between his legs.

"Well, this is the devil's own," exclaimed the doctor, when he was left alone with Fred Henry. "Going before Wednesday, are you?"

"That's the orders," replied the other.

"Where, to Northampton?"

"That's it."

"The devil!" exclaimed Fergusson, with quiet chagrin.

And there was silence between the two.

"All settled up, are you?" asked Fergusson.

"About."

There was another pause.

"Well, I shall miss yer, Freddy, boy," said the young doctor.

"And I shall miss thee, Jack," returned the other.

"Miss you like hell," mused the doctor.

Fred Henry turned aside. There was nothing to say. Mabel came in again, to finish clearing the table.

"What are *you* going to do, then, Miss Pervin?" asked Fergusson. "Going to your sister's, are you?"

Mabel looked at him with her steady, dangerous eyes, that always made him uncomfortable, unsettling his superficial ease.

"No," she said.

"Well, what in the name of fortune *are* you going to do? Say what you mean to do," cried Fred Henry, with futile intensity.

But she only averted her head, and continued her work. She folded the white table-cloth, and put on the chenille cloth.

"The sulkiest bitch that ever trod!" muttered her brother.

But she finished her task with perfectly impassive face, the young doctor watching her interestedly all the while. Then she went out.

Fred Henry stared after her, clenching his lips, his blue eyes fixing in sharp antagonism, as he made a grimace of sour exasperation.

"You could bray her into bits, and that's all you'd get out of her," he said in a small, narrowed tone.

The doctor smiled faintly.

"What's she *going* to do, then?" he asked.

"Strike me if *I* know!" returned the other.

There was a pause. Then the doctor stirred.

"I'll be seeing you to-night, shall I?" he said to his friend.

"Ay—where's it to be? Are we going over to Jessdale?"

"I don't know. I've got such a cold on me. I'll come round to the Moon and Stars, anyway."

"Let Lizzie and May miss their night for once, eh?"

"That's it—if I feel as I do now."

"All's one—"

The two young men went through the passage and down to the back door together. The house was large, but it was servantless now, and desolate. At the back was a small bricked house-yard, and beyond that a big square, gravelled fine and red, and having stables on two sides. Sloping, dank, winter-dark fields stretched away on the open sides.

But the stables were empty. Joseph Pervin, the father of the family, had been a man of no education, who had become a fairly large horse dealer. The stables had been full of horses, there was a great turmoil and come-and-go of horses and of dealers and grooms. Then the kitchen was full of servants. But of late things had declined. The old man had married a second time, to retrieve his fortunes. Now he was dead and everything was gone to the dogs, there was nothing but debt and threatening.

For months, Mabel had been servantless in the big house, keeping the home together in penury for her ineffectual brothers. She had kept house for ten years. But previously it was with unstinted means. Then, however brutal and coarse everything was, the sense of money had kept her proud, confident. The men might be foul-mouthed, the women in the kitchen might have bad reputations, her brothers might have illegitimate children. But so long as there was money, the girl felt herself established, and brutally proud, reserved.

No company came to the house, save dealers and coarse men. Mabel had no associates of her own sex, after her sister went away. But she did not mind. She went regularly to church, she attended to her father. And she lived in the memory of her mother, who had died when she was fourteen, and whom she had loved. She had loved her father, too, in a different way, depending upon him, and feeling secure in him, until at the age of fifty-four he married again. And then she had set hard against him. Now he had died and left them all hopelessly in debt.

She had suffered badly during the period of poverty. Nothing, however, could shake the curious sullen, animal pride that dominated each member of the family. Now, for Mabel, the end had come. Still she would not cast about her. She would follow her own way just the same. She would always hold the keys of her own situation. Mindless and persistent, she endured from day to day. Why should she think? Why should she answer anybody? It was enough that this was the end, and there was no way out. She need not pass any more darkly along the main street of the small town, avoiding every eye. She need not demean herself any more, going into the shops and buying the cheapest food. This was at an end. She thought of nobody, not even of herself. Mindless and persistent, she seemed in a sort of ecstasy to be coming nearer to her fulfilment, her own glorification, approaching her dead mother, who was glorified.

In the afternoon she took a little bag, with shears and sponge and a small scrubbing brush, and went out. It was a grey, wintry day, with saddened, dark green fields and an atmosphere blackened by the smoke of foundries not far off. She went quickly, darkly along the causeway, heeding nobody, through the town to the churchyard.

There she always felt secure, as if no one could see her, although as a matter of fact she was exposed to the stare of every one who passed along under the churchyard wall. Nevertheless, once under the shadow of the great looming church, among the graves, she felt immune from the world, reserved within the thick churchyard wall as in another country.

Carefully she clipped the grass from the grave, and arranged the pinky white, small chrysanthemums in the tin cross. When this was done, she took an empty jar from a neighbouring grave, brought water, and carefully, most scrupulously sponged the marble head-stone and the coping-stone.

It gave her sincere satisfaction to do this. She felt in immediate contact with the world of her mother. She took minute pains, went through the park in a state bordering on pure happiness, as if in performing this task she came into a subtle, intimate connection with her mother. For the life she followed here in the world was far less real than the world of death she inherited from her mother.

The doctor's house was just by the church. Fergusson, being a mere hired assistant, was slave to the country-side. As he hurried now to attend to the outpatients in the surgery, glancing across the graveyard with his quick eye, he saw the girl at her task at the grave. She seemed so intent and remote, it was like looking into another world. Some mystical element was touched in him. He slowed down as he walked, watching her as if spell-bound.

She lifted her eyes, feeling him looking. Their eyes met. And each looked away again at once, each feeling, in some way, found out by the other. He lifted his cap and passed on down the road. There remained distinct in his consciousness, like a vision, the memory of her face, lifted from the tombstone in the churchyard, and looking at him with slow, large, portentous eyes. It *was* portentous, her face. It seemed to mesmerize him. There was a heavy power in her eyes which laid hold of his whole being, as if he had drunk some powerful drug. He had been feeling weak and done before. Now the life came back into him, he felt delivered from his own fretted, daily self.

He finished his duties at the surgery as quickly as might be, hastily filling up the bottle of the waiting people with cheap drugs. Then, in perpetual haste, he set off again to visit several cases in another part of his round, before teatime. At all times he preferred to walk if he could, but particularly when he was not well. He fancied the motion restored him.

The afternoon was falling. It was grey, deadened, and wintry, with a slow, moist, heavy coldness sinking in and deadening all the faculties. But why should he think or notice? He hastily climbed the hill and turned across the dark green fields, following the black cinder-track. In the distance, across a shallow dip in the country, the small town was clustered like smouldering ash, a tower, a spire, a heap of low, raw, extinct houses. And on the nearest fringe of the town, sloping into the dip, was Oldmeadow, the Pervins' house. He could see the stables and the outbuildings distinctly, as they lay towards him on the slope. Well, he would not go there many more times! Another resource would be lost to him, another place gone: the only company he cared for in the alien, ugly little town he was losing. Nothing but work, drudgery, constant hastening from dwelling to dwelling among the colliers and the iron-workers. It wore him out, but at the same time he had a craving for it. It was a stimulant to him to be in the homes of the working people, moving as it were through the innermost body of their life. His nerves were excited and gratified. He could come so near, into the very lives of the rough, inarticulate, powerfully emotional men and women. He grumbled, he said he hated the hellish hole. But as a matter of fact it excited him, the contact with the rough, strongly-feeling people was a stimulant applied direct to his nerves.

Below Oldmeadow, in the green, shallow, soddened hollow of fields, lay a square, deep pond. Roving across the landscape, the doctor's quick eye detected a figure in black passing through the gate of the field, down towards the pond. He looked again. It would be Mabel Pervin. His mind suddenly became alive and attentive.

Why was she going down there? He pulled up on the path on the slope above, and stood staring. He could just make sure of the small black figure moving in the hollow of the failing day. He seemed to see her in the midst of such obscurity, that he was like a clairvoyant, seeing rather with the mind's eye than with ordinary sight. Yet he could see her positively enough, whilst he kept his eye attentive. He felt, if he looked away from her, in the thick, ugly falling dusk, he would lose her altogether.

He followed her minutely as she moved, direct and intent, like something transmitted rather than stirring in voluntary activity, straight down the field towards the pond. There she stood on the bank for a moment. She never raised her head. Then she waded slowly into the water.

He stood motionless as the small black figure walked slowly and deliberately towards the centre of the pond, very slowly, gradually moving deeper into the motionless water, and still moving forward as the water got up to her breast. Then he could see her no more in the dusk of the dead afternoon.

"There!" he exclaimed. "Would you believe it?"

And he hastened straight down, running over the wet, soddened fields, pushing through the hedges, down into the depression of callous wintry obscurity. It took him several minutes to come to the pond. He stood on the bank, breathing heavily. He could see nothing. His eyes seemed to penetrate the dead water. Yes, perhaps that was the dark shadow of her black clothing beneath the surface of the water.

He slowly ventured into the pond. The bottom was deep, soft clay, he sank in, and the water clasped dead cold round his legs. As he stirred he could smell the cold, rotten clay that fouled up into the water. It was objectionable in his lungs. Still, repelled and yet not heeding, he moved deeper into the pond. The cold water rose over his thighs, over his loins, upon his abdomen. The lower part of his body was all sunk in the hideous cold element. And the bottom was so deeply soft and uncertain, he was afraid of pitching with his mouth underneath. He could not swim, and was afraid.

He crouched a little, spreading his hands under the water and moving them round, trying to feel for her. The dead cold pond swayed upon his chest. He moved again, a little deeper, and again, with his hands underneath, he felt all around under the water. And he touched her clothing. But it evaded his fingers. He made a desperate effort to grasp it.

And so doing he lost his balance and went under, horribly, suffocating in the foul earthy water, struggling madly for a few moments. At last, after what seemed an eternity, he got his footing, rose again into the air and looked around. He gasped, and knew he was in the world. Then he looked at the water. She had risen near him. He grasped her clothing, and drawing her nearer, turned to take his way to land again.

He went very slowly, carefully, absorbed in the slow progress. He rose higher, climbing out of the pond. The water was now only about his legs; he was thankful, full of relief to be out of the clutches of the pond. He lifted her and staggered on to the bank, out of the horror of wet, grey clay.

He laid her down on the bank. She was quite unconscious and running with water. He made the water come from her mouth, he worked to restore her. He did not have to work very long before he could feel the breathing begin again in her; she was breathing naturally. He worked a little longer. He could feel her live beneath his hands; she was coming back. He wiped her face, wrapped her in his overcoat, looked round into the dim, dark grey world, then lifted her and staggered down the bank and across the fields.

It seemed an unthinkably long way, and his burden so heavy he felt he would never get to the house. But at last he was in the stable-yard, and then in the house-yard.

He opened the door and went into the house. In the kitchen he laid her down on the hearthrug, and called. The house was empty. But the fire was burning in the grate.

Then again he kneeled to attend to her. She was breathing regularly, her eyes were wide open and as if conscious, but there seemed something missing in her look. She was conscious in herself, but unconscious of her surroundings.

He ran upstairs, took blankets from a bed, and put them before the fire to warm. Then he removed her saturated, earthy-smelling clothing, rubbed her dry with a towel, and wrapped her naked in the blankets. Then he went into the dining-room, to look for spirits. There was a little whisky. He drank a gulp himself, and put some into her mouth.

The effect was instantaneous. She looked full into his face, as if she had been seeing him for some time, and yet had only just become conscious of him.

"Dr. Fergusson?" she said.

"What?" he answered.

He was divesting himself of his coat, intending to find some dry clothing upstairs. He could not bear the smell of the dead, clayey water, and he was mortally afraid for his own health.

"What did I do?" she asked.

"Walked into the pond," he replied. He had begun to shudder like one sick, and could hardly attend to her. Her eyes remained full on him, he seemed to be going dark in his mind, looking back at her helplessly. The shuddering became quieter in him, his life came back in him, dark and unknowing, but strong again.

"Was I out of my mind?" she asked, while her eyes were fixed on him all the time.

"Maybe, for the moment," he replied. He felt quiet, because his strength had come back. The strange fretful strain had left him.

"Am I out of my mind now?" she asked.

"Are you?" He reflected a moment. "No," he answered truthfully, "I don't see that you are." He turned his face aside. He was afraid now, because he felt dazed, and felt dimly that her power was stronger than his, in this issue. And she continued to look at him fixedly all the time. "Can you tell me where I shall find some dry things to put on?" he asked.

"Did you dive into the pond for me?" she asked.

"No," he answered. "I walked in. But I went in overhead as well."

There was silence for a moment. He hesitated. He very much wanted to go upstairs to get into dry clothing. But there was another desire in him. And she seemed to hold him. His will seemed to have gone to sleep, and left him, standing there slack before her. But he felt warm inside himself. He did not shudder at all, though his clothes were sodden on him.

"Why did you?" she asked.

"Because I didn't want you to do such a foolish thing," he said.

"It wasn't foolish," she said, still gazing at him as she lay on the floor, with a sofa cushion under her head. "It was the right thing to do. *I* knew best, then."

"I'll go and shift these wet things," he said. But still he had not the power to move out of her presence, until she sent him. It was as if she had the life of his body in her hands, and he could not extricate himself. Or perhaps he did not want to.

Suddenly she sat up. Then she became aware of her own immediate condition. She felt the blankets about her, she knew her own limbs. For a moment it seemed as if her reason were going. She looked round, with wild eye, as if seeking something. He stood still with fear. She saw her clothing lying scattered.

"Who undressed me?" she asked, her eyes resting full and inevitable on his face.

"I did," he replied, "to bring you round."

For some moments she sat and gazed at him awfully, her lips parted.

"Do you love me, then?" she asked.

He only stood and stared at her, fascinated. His soul seemed to melt.

She shuffled forward on her knees, and put her arms round him, round his legs, as he stood there, pressing her breasts against his knees and thighs, clutching him with strange, convulsive certainty, pressing his thighs against her, drawing him to her face, her throat, as she looked up at him with flaring, humble eyes of transfiguration, triumphant in first possession.

"You love me," she murmured, in strange transport, yearning and triumphant and confident. "You love me. I know you love me, I know."

And she was passionately kissing his knees, through the wet clothing, passionately and indiscriminately kissing his knees, his legs, as if unaware of everything.

He looked down at the tangled wet hair, the wild, bare, animal shoulders. He was amazed, bewildered, and afraid. He had never thought of loving her. He had never wanted to love her. When he rescued her and restored her, he was a doctor, and she was a patient. He had had no single personal thought of her. Nay, this introduction of the personal element was very distasteful to him, a violation of his professional honour. It was horrible to have her there embracing his knees. It was horrible. He revolted from it, violently. And yet—and yet—he had not the power to break away.

She looked at him again, with the same supplication of powerful love, and that same transcendent, frightening light of triumph. In view of the delicate flame which seemed to come from her face like a light, he was powerless. And yet he had never intended to love her. He had never intended. And something stubborn in him could not give way.

"You love me," she repeated, in a murmur of deep, rhapsodic assurance. "You love me."

Her hands were drawing him, drawing him down to her. He was afraid, even a little horrified. For he had, really, no intention of loving her. Yet her hands were drawing him towards her. He put out his hand quickly to steady himself, and grasped her bare shoulder. A flame seemed to burn the hand that grasped her soft shoulder. He had no intention of loving her: his whole will was against his yielding. It was horrible. And yet wonderful was the touch of her shoulders, beautiful the shining of her face. Was she perhaps mad? He had a horror of yielding to her. Yet something in him ached also.

He had been staring away at the door, away from her. But his hand remained on her shoulder. She had gone suddenly very still. He looked down at her. Her eyes were now wide with fear, with doubt, the light was dying from her face, a shadow of terrible greyness was returning. He could not bear the touch of her eyes' question upon him, and the look of death behind the question.

With an inward groan he gave way, and let his heart yield towards her. A sudden gentle smile came on his face. And her eyes, which never left his face, slowly, slowly filled with tears. He watched the strange water rise in her eyes, like some slow fountain coming up. And his heart seemed to burn and melt away in his breast.

He could not bear to look at her any more. He dropped on his knees and caught her head with his arms and pressed her face against his throat. She was very still. His heart, which seemed to have broken, was burning with a kind of agony in his breast. And he felt her slow, hot tears wetting his throat. But he could not move.

He felt the hot tears wet his neck and the hollows of his neck, and he remained motionless, suspended through one of man's eternities. Only now it had become indispensable to him to have her face pressed close to him; he could never let her go again. He could never let her head go away from the close clutch of his arm. He wanted to remain like that for ever, with his heart hurting him in a pain that was also life to him. Without knowing, he was looking down on her damp, soft brown hair.

Then, as it were suddenly, he smelt the horrid stagnant smell of that water. And at the same moment she drew away from him and looked at him. Her eyes were wistful and unfathomable. He was afraid of them, and he fell to kissing her, not knowing what he was doing. He wanted her eyes not to have that terrible, wistful, unfathomable look.

When she turned her face to him again, a faint delicate flush was glowing, and there was again dawning that terrible shining of joy in her eyes, which really terrified him, and yet which he now wanted to see, because he feared the look of doubt still more.

"You love me?" she said, rather faltering.

"Yes." The word cost him a painful effort. Not because it wasn't true. But because it was too newly true, the *saying* seemed to tear open again his newly-torn heart. And he hardly wanted it to be true, even now.

She lifted her face to him, and he bent forward and kissed her on the mouth, gently, with the one kiss that is an eternal pledge. And as he kissed her his heart strained again in his breast. He never intended to love her. But now it was over. He had crossed over the gulf to her, and all that he had left behind had shrivelled and become void.

After the kiss, her eyes again slowly filled with tears. She sat still, away from him, with her face drooped aside, and her hands folded in her lap. The tears fell very slowly. There was complete silence. He too sat there motionless and silent on the hearthrug. The strange pain of his heart that was broken seemed to consume him. That he should love her? That this was love! That he should be ripped open in this way! Him, a doctor! How they would all jeer if they knew! It was agony to him to think they might know.

In the curious naked pain of the thought he looked again to her. She was sitting there drooped into a muse. He saw a tear fall, and his heart flared hot. He saw for the first time that one of her shoulders was quite uncovered, one arm bare, he could see one of her small breasts; dimly, because it had become almost dark in the room.

"Why are you crying?" he asked, in an altered voice.

She looked up at him, and behind her tears the consciousness of her situation for the first time brought a dark look of shame to her eyes.

"I'm not crying, really," she said, watching him half frightened.

He reached his hand, and softly closed it on her bare arm.

"I love you! I love you!" he said in a soft, low vibrating voice, unlike himself.

She shrank, and dropped her head. The soft, penetrating grip of his hand on her arm distressed her. She looked up at him.

"I want to go," she said. "I want to go and get you some dry things."

"Why?" he said. "I'm all right."

"But I want to go," she said. "And I want you to change your things.'

He released her arm, and she wrapped herself in the blanket, looking at him rather frightened. And still she did not rise.

"Kiss me," she said wistfully.

He kissed her, but briefly, half in anger.

Then, after a second, she rose nervously, all mixed up in the blanket. He watched her in her confusion, as she tried to extricate herself and wrap herself up so that she could walk. He watched her relentlessly, as she knew. And as she went, the blanket trailing, and as he saw a glimpse of her feet and her white leg, he tried to remember her as she was when he had wrapped her in the blanket. But then he didn't want to remember, because she had been nothing to him then, and his nature revolted from remembering her as she was when she was nothing to him.

A tumbling, muffled noise from within the dark house startled him. Then he heard her voice:—"There are clothes." He rose and went to the foot of the stairs, and gathered up the garments she had thrown down. Then he came back to the fire to rub himself down and dress. He grinned at his own appearance when he had finished.

The fire was sinking, so he put on coal. The house was now quite dark, save for the light of a street-lamp that shone in faintly from beyond the holly trees. He lit the gas with matches he found on the mantelpiece. Then he emptied the pockets of his own clothes, and threw all his wet things in a heap into the scullery. After which he gathered up her sodden clothes, gently, and put them in a separate heap on the copper-top in the scullery.

It was six o'clock on the clock. His own watch had stopped. He ought to go back to the surgery. He waited, and still she did not come down. So he went to the foot of the stairs and called:

"I shall have to go."

Almost immediately he heard her coming down. She had on her best dress of black voile, and her hair was tidy, but still damp. She looked at him—and in spite of herself, smiled.

"I don't like you in those clothes," she said.

"Do I look a sight?" he answered.

They were shy of one another.

"I'll make you some tea," she said.

"No, I must go."

"Must you?" And she looked at him again with the wide, strained, doubtful eyes. And again, from the pain of his breast, he knew how he loved her. He went and bent to kiss her, gently, passionately, with his heart's painful kiss.

"And my hair smells so horrible," she murmured in distraction. "And I'm so awful, I'm so awful! Oh, no, I'm too awful." And she broke into bitter, heart-broken sobbing. "You can't want to love me, I'm horrible."

"Don't be silly, don't be silly," he said, trying to comfort her, kissing her, holding her in his arms. "I want you, I want to marry you, we're going to be married, quickly, quickly—tomorrow if I can."

But she only sobbed terribly, and cried:

"I feel awful. I feel awful. I feel I'm horrible to you."

"No, I want you, I want you," was all he answered, blindly, with that terrible intonation which frightened her almost more than her horror lest he should *not* want her.

SIXTEEN

JESSAMYN WEST (1903–   )

The steam from the kettle had condensed on the cold window and was running down the glass in tear-like trickles. Outside in the orchard the man from the smudge company was refilling the pots with oil. The greasy smell from last night's burning was still in the air. Mr. Delahanty gazed out at the bleak darkening orange grove; Mrs. Delahanty watched her husband eat, nibbling up to the edges of the toast, then stacking the crusts about his tea cup in a neat fence-like arrangement.

"We'll have to call Cress," Mr. Delahanty said, finally. "Your father's likely not to last out the night. She's his only grandchild. She ought to be here."

Mrs. Delahanty pressed her hands to the bones above her eyes. "Cress isn't going to like being called away from college," she said.

"We'll have to call her anyway. It's the only thing to do." Mr. Delahanty swirled the last of his tea around in his cup so as not to miss any sugar.

"Father's liable to lapse into unconsciousness any time," Mrs. Delahanty argued. "Cress'll hate coming and Father won't know whether she's here or not. Why not let her stay at Woolman?"

Neither wanted, in the midst of their sorrow for the good man whose life was ending, to enter into any discussion of Cress. What was the matter with Cress? What had happened to her since she went away to college? She, who had been open and loving? And who now lived inside a world so absolutely fitted to her own size and shape that she felt any intrusion, even that of the death of her own grandfather, to be an unmerited invasion of her privacy. Black magic could not have changed her more quickly and unpleasantly and nothing except magic, it seemed, would give them back their lost daughter.

Mr. Delahanty pushed back his cup and saucer. "Her place is here, Gertrude. I'm going to call her long distance now. She's a bright girl and it's not going to hurt her to miss a few days from classes. What's the dormitory number?"

"I know it as well as our number," Mrs. Delahanty said. "But at the minute it's gone. It's a sign of my reluctance, I suppose. Wait a minute and I'll look it up."

Mr. Delahanty squeezed out from behind the table. "Don't bother. I can get it."

Mrs. Delahanty watched her husband, his usually square shoulders sagging with weariness, wipe a clear place on the steamy windowpane with his napkin. Some of the green twilight appeared to seep into the warm dingy little kitchen. "I can't ever remember having to smudge before in February. I expect you're right," he added as he went toward the phone. "Cress isn't going to like it."

Cress didn't like it. It was February, the rains had been late and the world was burning with a green fire; a green smoke rolled down the hills and burst shoulder-high in the cover crops that filled the spaces between the trees in the orange orchards. There had been rain earlier in the day and drops still hung from the grass blades, sickle-shaped with their weight. Cress, walking across the campus with Edwin, squatted to look into one of these crystal globes.

"Green from the grass and red from the sun," she told him. "The whole world right there in one raindrop."

"As Blake observed earlier about a grain of sand," said Edwin.

"O.K., show off," Cress told him. "You know it—but I saw it." She took his hand and he pulled her up, swinging her in a semicircle in front of him. "Down there in the grass the world winked at me."

"Don't be precious, Cress," Edwin said.

"I will," Cress said, "just to tease you. I love to tease you, Edwin."

"Why?" Edwin asked.

"Because you love to have me," Cress said confidently, taking his hand. Being older suited Edwin. She remembered when she had liked him in spite of his looks; but now spindly had become spare, and the dark shadow of his beard—Edwin had to shave every day while other boys were still just fuzzy—lay under his pale skin; and the opinions, which had once been so embarrassingly unlike anyone else's, were now celebrated at Woolman as being "Edwinian." Yes, Edwin had changed since that day when she had knocked his tooth out trying to rescue him from the mush pot. And had she changed? Did she also look better to Edwin, almost slender now and the freckles not noticeable except at the height of summer? And with her new-found ability for light talk? They were passing beneath the eucalyptus trees and the silver drops, falling as the wind shook the leaves, stung her face, feeling at once both cool and burning. Meadow larks in the fields which edged the campus sang in the quiet way they have after the rain has stopped.

"Oh, Edwin," Cress said, "no one in the world loves the meadow lark's song the way I do!"

"It's not a competition," Edwin said, "you against the world in an 'I-love-meadow-larks' contest. Take it easy, kid. Love 'em as much as in you lieth, and let it go at that."

"No," she said. "I'm determined to overdo it. Listen," she exclaimed, as two birds sang together. "Not grieving, nor amorous, nor lost. Nothing to read into it. Simply music. Like Mozart. Complete. Finished. Oh, it is rain to listening ears." She glanced at Edwin to see how he took this rhetoric. He took it calmly. She let go his hand and capered amidst the fallen eucalyptus leaves.

"The gardener thinks you've got St. Vitus' dance," Edwin said.

Old Boat Swain, the college gardener whose name was really Swain, was leaning on his hoe, watching her hopping and strutting. She didn't give a hoot about him or what he thought.

"He's old," she told Edwin. "He doesn't exist." She felt less akin to him than to a bird or toad.

There were lights already burning in the dorm windows. Cress could see Ardis and Nina still at their tables, finishing their *Ovid* or looking up a final logarithm. But between five and six most of the girls stopped trying to remember which form of the sonnet Milton had used or when the Congress of Vienna had met, and dressed for dinner. They got out of their sweaters and jackets and into their soft bright dresses. She knew just what she was going to wear when she came downstairs at six to meet Edwin—green silk like the merman's wife. They were going to the Poinsettia for dinner, escaping salmon-wiggle night in the college dining room.

"At six," she told him, "I'll fly down the stairs to meet you like a green wave."

"See you in thirty minutes," Edwin said, leaving her at the dorm steps.

The minute she opened the door, she began to hear the dorm sounds and smell the dorm smells—the hiss and rush of the showers, the thud of the iron, a voice singing, "Dear old Woolman we love so well," the slap of bare feet down the hall, the telephone ringing.

And the smells! Elizabeth Arden and Cashmere Bouquet frothing in the showers; talcum powder falling like snow; *Intoxication* and *Love Me* and *Devon Violet;* rubbersoled sneakers, too, and gym T-shirts still wet with sweat after basketball practice, and the smell of the hot iron on damp wool.

But while she was still listening and smelling, Edith shouted from the top of the stairs, "Long distance for you, Cress. Make it snappy."

Cress took the stairs three at a time, picked up the dangling receiver, pressed it to her ear.

"Tenant calling Crescent Delahanty," the operator said. It was her father: "Grandfather is dying, Cress. Catch the 7:30 home. I'll meet you at the depot."

"What's the matter—Cressie?" Edith asked.

"I have to catch the 7:30 Pacific Electric. Grandfather's dying."

"Oh, poor Cress," Edith cried and pressed her arm about her.

Cress scarcely heard her. Why were they calling her home to watch Grandpa die, she thought, angrily and rebelliously. An old man, past eighty. He'd never been truly alive for her, never more than a rough, hot hand, a scraggly mustache that repelled her when he kissed her, an old fellow who gathered what he called "likely-looking" stones and kept them washed and polished, to turn over and admire. It was silly and unfair to make so much of his dying.

But before she could say a word, Edith was telling the girls. They were crowding about her. "Don't cry," they said. "We'll pack for you. Be brave, darling Cress. Remember your grandfather has had a long happy life. He wouldn't want you to cry."

"Brave Cress—brave Cress," they said. "Just frozen."

She wasn't frozen. She was determined. She was not going to go. It did not make sense. She went downstairs to meet Edwin as she had planned, in her green silk, ready for dinner at the Poinsettia. The girls had told him.

"Are you wearing that home?" he asked.

"I'm not going home," she said. "It's silly and useless. I can't help Grandfather. It's just a convention. What *good* can I do him, sitting there at home?"

"He might do you some good," Edwin said. "Had you thought about that?"

"Why Edwin!" Cress said. "Why Edwin!" She had the girls tamed, eating out of her hand, and here was Edwin who loved her—he said so, anyway—cold and disapproving. Looking at herself through Edwin's eyes, she hesitated.

"Go on," Edwin said. "Get what you need and I'll drive you to the station."

She packed her overnight bag and went with him; there didn't seem—once she'd had Edwin's view of herself—anything else to do. But once on the train her resentment returned. The Pacific Electric was hot and smelled of metal and dusty plush. It clicked past a rickety Mexican settlement, through La Habra and Brea, where the pool hall signs swung in the night wind off the ocean. An old man in a spotted corduroy jacket, and his wife, with her hair straggling through the holes in her broken net, sat in front of her.

Neat, thought Cress, anyone can be neat, if he wants to.

Her father, bareheaded, but in his big sheepskin jacket, met her at the depot. It was after nine, cold and raw.

"This is a sorry time, Cress," he said. He put her suitcase in the back of the car and climbed into the driver's seat without opening the door for her.

Cress got in, wrapped her coat tightly about herself. The sky was clear, the wind had died down.

"I don't see any sense in my having to come home," she said at last. "What good can I do Grandpa? If he's dying, how can I help?"

"I was afraid that was the way you might feel about it. So was your mother."

"Oh, Mother," Cress burst out. "Recently she's always trying to put me . . ."

Her father cut her off. "That'll be about enough, Cress. Your place is at home and you're coming home and keeping your mouth shut, whatever you think. I don't know what's happened to you recently. If college does this to you, you'd better stay home permanently."

There was nothing more said until they turned up the palm-lined driveway that led to the house. "Here we are," Mr. Delahanty told her.

Mrs. Delahanty met them at the door, tired and haggard in her Indian design bathrobe.

"Cress," she said, "Grandfather's conscious now. I told him you were coming and he's anxious to see you. You'd better go in right away—this might be the last time he'd know you."

Cress was standing by the fireplace holding first one foot then the other toward the fire. "Oh, Mother, what am I to say?" she asked. "What can I say? Or does Grandfather just want to see me?"

Her father shook his head as if with pain. "Aren't you sorry your grandfather's dying, Cress? Haven't you any pity in your heart? Don't you understand what death means?"

"He's an old man," Cress said obstinately. "It's what we must expect when we grow old," though she, of course, would never grow old.

"Warm your hands, Cress," her mother said. "Grandfather's throat bothers him and it eases him to have it rubbed. I'll give you the ointment and you can rub it in. You won't need to say anything."

Cress slid out of her coat and went across the hall with her mother to visit her grandfather's room. His thin old body was hardly visible beneath the covers; his head, with its gray skin and sunken eyes, lay upon the pillow as if bodiless. The night light frosted his white hair but made black caverns of his closed eyes.

"Father," Mrs. Delahanty said. "Father." But the old man didn't move. There was nothing except the occasional hoarse rasp of an indrawn breath to show that he was alive.

Mrs. Delahanty pulled the cane-bottomed chair a little closer to the bed. "Sit here," she said to Cress, "and rub this into his throat and chest." She opened her father's nightshirt so that an inch or two of bony grizzled chest was bared. "He says that this rubbing relieves him, even if he's asleep or too tired to speak. Rub it in with a slow steady movement." She went out to the living room leaving the door a little ajar.

Cress sat down on the chair and put two squeamish fingers into the jar of gray ointment; but she could see far more sense to this than to any talking or being talked to. If they had brought her home from school because she was needed in helping to care for Grandpa, that she could understand—but not simply to be present at his death. What had death to do with her?

She leaned over him, rubbing, but with eyes shut, dipping her fingers often into the gray grease. The rhythm of the rubbing, the warmth and closeness of the room, after the cold drive, had almost put her to sleep when the old man startled her by lifting a shaking hand to the bunch of yellow violets Edith had pinned to the shoulder of her dress before she left Woolman. She opened her eyes suddenly at his touch, but the old man said nothing, only stroked the violets awkwardly with a trembling fore-finger.

Cress unpinned the violets and put them in his hand. "There, Grandpa," she said, "there. They're for you."

The old man's voice was a harsh and faltering whisper and to hear what he said Cress had to lean very close.

"I used to—pick them—on Reservoir Hill. I was always sorry to—plow them up. Still—so sweet. Thanks," he said, "to bring them. To remember. You're like her. Your grandmother," he added after a pause. He closed his eyes, holding the bouquet against his face, letting the wilting blossoms spray across one cheek like a pulled-up sheet of flowering earth. He said one more word, not her name but her grand-mother's.

The dikes about Cress's heart broke. "Oh, Grandpa, I love you," she said. He heard her. He knew what she said, his fingers returned the pressure of her hand. "You were always so good to me. You were young and you loved flowers." Then she said what was her great discovery. "And you still do. You still love yellow violets, Grandpa, just like me."

At the sound of her uncontrolled crying, Mr. and Mrs. Delahanty came to the door. "What's the matter, Cress?"

Cress turned, lifted a hand toward them. "Why didn't you tell me?" she demanded. And when they didn't answer, she said, "Edwin knew."

Then she dropped her head on to her grandfather's outstretched hand and said something, evidently to him, which neither her father nor her mother understood.

"It's just the same."

THE FIRST DEATH OF HER LIFE

ELIZABETH TAYLOR (1912–   )

Suddenly, tears poured from Lucy's eyes. She rested her forehead against her mother's hand and let the tears soak into the counterpane.

Dear Mr. Wilcox, she began, for her mind was always composing letters, I shall not be at the shop for the next four days, as my mother has passed away and I shall not be available until after the funeral. My mother passed away very peacefully. . . .

The nurse came in. She took her patient's wrist for a moment, replaced it on the bed, removed a jar of white lilac from the table, as if this were no longer necessary, and went out again.

The girl kneeling by the bed had looked up, but Dear Mr. Wilcox, she resumed, her eyes returning to the counterpane, My mother has died. I shall come back to work the day after tomorrow. Yours sincerely, Lucy Mayhew.

Her father was late. She imagined him hurrying from work, bicycling through the darkening streets, dogged, hunched up, slush thrown up by his wheels. Her mother did not move. Lucy stroked her mother's hand, with its loose gold ring, the calloused palm, the fine, long fingers. Then she stood up stiffly, her knees bruised from the waxed floor, and went to the window.

Snowflakes turned idly, drifting down over the hospital gardens. It was four o'clock in the afternoon and already the day seemed over. So few sounds came from this muffled and discolored world. In the hospital itself, there was a deep silence.

Her thoughts came to her in words, as if her mind spoke them first, understood them later. She tried to think of her childhood—little scenes she selected to prove how she and her mother had loved one another. Other scenes, especially last week's quarrel, she chose to forget, not knowing that in this moment she sent them away forever. Only loving-kindness remained. But, all the same, intolerable pictures broke through—her mother at the sink; her mother ironing; her mother standing between the lace curtains, staring out at the dreary street with a wounded look in her eyes; her mother tying the same lace curtains with yellow ribbons; attempts at lightness, gaiety, which came to nothing; her mother gathering her huge black cat to her, burying her face in its fur while a great, shivering sigh—of despair, of boredom—escaped her.

Her mother no longer sighed. She lay very still and sometimes took a little sip of air. Her arms were neatly at her side. Her eyes, which all day long had been turned to the white lilacs, were closed. Her cheekbones rose sharply from her bruised, exhausted face. She smelled faintly of wine. A small lilac flower floated on a glass of champagne, now discarded on the table at her side.

The champagne, with which they hoped to stretch out the thread of her life minute by minute, the lilac, the room of her own, all came to her at the end of a life of drabness and denial, just as, all along the mean street of the small English town where they lived, the dying and the dead were able to claim a lifetime's savings from the bereaved.

She is no longer there, Lucy thought, standing beside the bed. All day, her mother had stared at the white lilac; now she had sunk away. Outside, beyond the hospital gardens, mist settled over the town, blurred the street lamps.

The nurse returned with the matron. Lucy tautened, ready to be on her best behavior. In her heart, she trusted her mother to die without frightening her, and when the matron, deftly drawing Lucy's head to rest on her own shoulder, said in her calm voice, "She has gone," Lucy felt she had met this happening halfway.

A little bustle began, quick footsteps along the empty passages, and for a moment she was left alone with her dead mother. She laid her hand timidly on the soft, dark hair, so often touched, played with, when she was a child, standing on a stool behind her mother's chair while she sewed.

There were still the smell of wine and the hospital smell. It was growing dark in the room. She went to the dressing table and took her mother's handbag, very worn and shiny, and a book, a library book that she had chosen carefully, believing her mother would read it. Then she had a quick sip from the glass on the table, a mouthful of champagne, which she had never tasted before, and, looking wounded and aloof, walked down the middle of the corridor, feeling nurses falling away to left and right. Opening the glass doors onto the snowy gardens, she thought that it was like the end of a film. But no music rose up and engulfed her. Instead, there was her father turning in at the gates. He propped his bicycle against the wall and began to run clumsily across the wet gravel.

THE LAMENT

ANTON CHEKHOV (1860–1904)

It is twilight. A thick wet snow is slowly twirling around the newly lighted street lamps, and lying in soft thin layers on roofs, on horses' backs, on people's shoulders and hats. The cabdriver Iona Potapov is quite white, and looks like a phantom; he is bent double as far as a human body can bend double; he is seated on his box; he never makes a move. If a whole snowdrift fell on him, it seems as if he would not find it necessary to shake it off. His little horse is also quite white, and remains motionless; its immobility, its angularity, and its straight wooden-looking legs, even close by, give it the appearance of a gingerbread horse worth a *kopek*. It is, no doubt, plunged in deep thought. If you were snatched from the plow, from your usual gray surroundings, and were thrown into this slough full of monstrous lights, unceasing noise, and hurrying people, you too would find it difficult not to think.

Iona and his little horse have not moved from their place for a long while. They left their yard before dinner, and up to now, not a fare. The evening mist is descending over the town, the white lights of the lamps replacing brighter rays, and the hubbub of the street getting louder. "Cabby for Viborg way!" suddenly hears Iona. "Cabby!"

Iona jumps, and through his snow-covered eyelashes sees an officer in a greatcoat, with his hood over his head.

"Viborg way!" the officer repeats. "Are you asleep, eh? Viborg way!"

With a nod of asent Iona picks up the reins, in consequence of which layers of snow slip off the horse's back and neck. The officer seats himself in the sleigh, the cabdriver smacks his lips to encourage his horse, stretches out his neck like a swan, sits up, and, more from habit than necessity, brandishes his whip. The little horse also stretches its neck, bends its wooden-looking legs, and makes a move undecidedly.

"What are you doing, werewolf!" is the exclamation Iona hears from the dark mass moving to and fro, as soon as they have started.

"Where the devil are you going? To the r-r-right!"

"You do not know how to drive. Keep to the right!" calls the officer angrily.

A coachman from a private carriage swears at him; a passerby, who has run across the road and rubbed his shoulder against the horse's nose, looks at him furiously as he sweeps the snow from his sleeve. Iona shifts about on his seat as if he were on needles, moves his elbows as if he were trying to keep his equilibrium, and gapes about like someone suffocating, who does not understand why and wherefore he is there.

"What scoundrels they all are!" jokes the officer; "one would think they had all entered into an agreement to jostle you or fall under your horse."

Iona looks round at the officer, and moves his lips. He evidently wants to say something, but the only sound that issues is a snuffle.

"What?" asks the officer.

Iona twists his mouth into a smile, and with an effort says hoarsely:

"My son, *barin,* died this week."

"Hm! What did he die of?"

Iona turns with his whole body toward his fare, and says:

"And who knows! They say high fever. He was three days in the hospital, and then died. . . . God's will be done."

"Turn around! The devil!" sounds from the darkness. "Have you popped off, old doggie, eh? Use your eyes!"

"Go on, go on," says the officer, "otherwise we shall not get there by tomorrow. Hurry up a bit!"

The cabdriver again stretches his neck, sits up, and, with a bad grace, brandishes his whip. Several times again he turns to look at his fare, but the latter has closed his eyes, and apparently is not disposed to listen. Having deposited the officer in the Viborg, he stops by the tavern, doubles himself up on his seat, and again remains motionless, while the snow once more begins to cover him and his horse. An hour, and another. . . . Then, along the footpath, with a squeak of galoshes, and quarreling, come three young men, two of them tall and lanky, the third one short and humpbacked.

"Cabby, to the Police Bridge!" in a cracked voice calls the humpback. "The three of us for two *griveniks!*"

Iona picks up his reins, and smacks his lips. Two *griveniks* is not a fair price, but he does not mind whether it is a *rouble* or five *kopeks*—to him it is all the same now, so long as they are fares. The young men, jostling each other and using bad language, approach the sleigh, and all three at once try to get onto the seat; then begins a discussion as to which two shall sit and who shall be the one to stand. After wrangling, abusing each other, and much petulance, it is at last decided that the humpback shall stand, as he is the smallest.

"Now then, hurry up!" says the humpback in a twanging voice, as he takes his place and breathes in Iona's neck. "Old furry! Here, mate, what a cap you have! There is not a worse one to be found in all Petersburg! . . ."

"He-he!—he-he!" giggles Iona. "Such a . . ."

"Now you, 'such a,' hurry up, are you going the whole way at this pace? Are you? . . . Do you want it in the neck?"

"My head feels like bursting," says one of the lanky ones. "Last night at the Donkmasovs, Vaska and I drank the whole of four bottles of cognac."

"I don't understand what you lie for," says the other lanky one angrily; "you lie like a brute."

"God strike me, it's the truth!"

"It's as much the truth as that a louse coughs!"

"He, he," grins Iona, "what gay young gentlemen!"

"Pshaw, go to the devil!" says the humpback indignantly.

"Are you going to get on or not, you old pest? Is that the way to drive? Use the whip a bit! Go on, devil, go on, give it to him well!"

Iona feels at his back the little man wriggling, and the tremble in his voice. He listens to the insults hurled at him, sees the people, and little by little the feeling of loneliness leaves him. The humpback goes on swearing until he gets mixed up in some elaborate six-foot oath, or chokes with coughing. The lankies begin to talk about a certain Nadejda Petrovna. Iona looks round at them several times; he waits for a temporary silence, then, turning round again, he murmurs:

"My son . . . died this week."

"We must all die," sighs the humpback, wiping his lips after an attack of coughing. "Now, hurry up, hurry up! Gentlemen, I really cannot go any farther like this! When will he get us there?"

"Well, just you stimulate him a little in the neck!"

"You old pest, do you hear, I'll bone your neck for you! If one treated the like of you with ceremony one would have to go on foot! Do you hear, old serpent Gorinytch! Or do you not care a spit?"

Iona hears rather than feels the blows they deal him.

"He, he," he laughs. "They are gay young gentlemen, God bless 'em!"

"Cabby, are you married?" asks a lanky one.

"I? He, he, gay young gentlemen! Now I have only a wife and the moist ground. . . . He, ho, ho . . . that is to say, the grave. My son has died, and I am alive. . . . A wonderful thing, death mistook the door . . . instead of coming to me, it went to my son. . . ."

Iona turns round to tell them how his son died, but at this moment, the humpback, giving a little sigh, announces, "Thank God, we have at last reached our destination," and Iona watches them disappear through the dark entrance. Once more he is alone, and again surrounded by silence. . . . His grief, which has abated for a short while, returns and rends his heart with greater force. With an anxious and hurried look, he searches among the crowds passing on either side of the street to find whether there may be just one person who will listen to him. But the crowds hurry by without noticing him or his trouble. Yet it is such an immense, illimitable grief. Should his heart break and the grief pour out, it would flow over the whole earth, so it seems, and yet no one sees it. It has managed to conceal itself in such an insignificant shell that no one can see it even by day and with a light.

Iona sees a hall porter with some sacking, and decides to talk to him.

"Friend, what sort of time is it?" he asks.

"Past nine. What are you standing here for? Move on."

Iona moves on a few steps, doubles himself up, and abandons himself to his grief. He sees it is useless to turn to people for help. In less than five minutes he straightens himself, holds up his head as if he felt some sharp pain, and gives a tug at the reins; he can bear it no longer. "The stables," he thinks, and the little horse, as if it understood, starts off at a trot.

About an hour and a half later Iona is seated by a large dirty stove. Around the stove, on the floor, on the benches, people are snoring; the air is thick and suffocatingly hot. Iona looks at the sleepers, scratches himself, and regrets having returned so early.

"I have not even earned my fodder," he thinks. "That's what's my trouble. A man who knows his job, who has had enough to eat, and his horse too, can always sleep peacefully."

A young cabdriver in one of the corners half gets up, grunts sleepily, and stretches towards a bucket of water.

"Do you want a drink?" Iona asks him.

"Don't I want a drink!"

"That's so? Your good health! But listen, mate—you know, my son is dead. . . . Did you hear? This week, in the hospital. . . . It's a long story."

Iona looks to see what effect his words have, but he sees none—the young man has hidden his face and is fast asleep again. The old man sighs, and scratches his head. Just as much as the young one wants to drink, the old man wants to talk. It will soon be a week since his son died, and he has not been able to speak about it properly to anyone. One must tell it slowly and carefully; how his son fell ill, how he suffered, what he said before he died, how he died. One must describe every detail of the funeral, and the journey to the hospital to fetch the dead son's clothes. His daughter Anissia has remained in the village—one must talk about her too. Is it nothing he has to tell? Surely the listener would gasp and sigh, and sympathize with him? It is better, too, to talk to women; although they are stupid, two words are enough to make them sob.

"I'll go and look after my horse," thinks Iona; "there's always time to sleep. No fear of that!"

He puts on his coat, and goes to the stables to his horse; he thinks of the corn, the hay, the weather. When he is alone, he dares not think of his son; he can speak about him to anyone, but to think of him, and picture him to himself, is unbearably painful.

"Are you tucking in?" Iona asks his horse, looking at its bright eyes; "go on, tuck in, though we've not earned our corn, we can eat hay. Yes! I am too old to drive— my son could have, not I. He was a first-rate cabdriver. If only he had lived!"

Iona is silent for a moment, then continues:

"That's how it is, my old horse. There's no more Kuzma Ionitch. He has left us to live, and he went off pop. Now let's say, you had a foal, you were the foal's mother, and suddenly, let's say, that foal went and left you to live after him. It would be sad, wouldn't it?"

The little horse munches, listens, and breathes over its master's hand. . . .

Iona's feelings are too much for him, and he tells the little horse the whole story.

THE FLY

KATHERINE MANSFIELD (1888–1923)

"Y'are very snug in here," piped old Mr. Woodifield, and he peered out of the great, green leather armchair by his friend, the boss's desk, as a baby peers out of its pram. His talk was over; it was time for him to be off. But he did not want to go. Since he had retired, since his . . . stroke, the wife and the girls kept him boxed up in the house every day of the week except Tuesday. On Tuesday he was dressed up and brushed and allowed to cut back to the City for the day. Though what he did there the wife and girls couldn't imagine. Made a nuisance of himself to his friends, they supposed. . . . Well, perhaps so. All the same, we cling to our last pleasures as the tree clings to its last leaves. So there sat old Woodifield, smoking a cigar and staring almost greedily at the boss, who rolled in his office chair, stout, rosy, five years older than he, and still going strong, still at the helm. It did one good to see him.

Wistfully, admiringly, the old voice added, "It's snug in here, upon my word!"

"Yes, it's comfortable enough," agreed the boss, and he flipped *The Financial Times* with a paper knife. As a matter of fact he was proud of his room; he liked to have it admired, especially by old Woodifield. It gave him a feeling of deep, solid satisfaction to be planted there in the midst of it in full view of that frail old figure in the muffler.

"I've had it done up lately," he explained, as he had explained for the past—how many?—weeks. "New carpet," and he pointed to the bright red carpet with a pattern of large white rings. "New furniture," and he nodded towards the massive bookcase and the table with legs like twisted treacle. "Electric heating!" He waved almost exultantly towards the five transparent, pearly sausages glowing so softly in the tilted copper pan.

But he did not draw old Woodifield's attention to the photograph over the table of a grave-looking boy in uniform standing in one of those spectral photographers' parks with photographers' storm clouds behind him. It was not new. It had been there for over six years.

"There was something I wanted to tell you," said old Woodifield, and his eyes grew dim remembering. "Now what was it? I had it in mind when I started out this morning." His hands began to tremble, and patches of red showed above his beard.

Poor old chap, he's on his last pins, thought the boss. And, feeling kindly, he winked at the old man, and said jokingly, "I tell you what. I've got a little drop of something here that'll do you good before you go out into the cold again. It's beautiful stuff. It wouldn't hurt a child." He took a key off his watch-chain, unlocked a cupboard below his desk, and drew forth a dark, squat bottle. "That's the medicine," said he. "And the man from whom I got it told me on the strict Q.T. it came from the cellars at Windsor Castle."

Old Woodifield's mouth fell open at the sight. He couldn't have looked more surprised if the boss had produced a rabbit.

"It's whisky, ain't it?" he piped, feebly.

The boss turned the bottle and lovingly showed him the label. Whisky it was.

"D'you know," said he, peering up at the boss wonderingly, "they won't let me touch it at home." And he looked as though he was going to cry.

"Ah, that's where we know a bit more than the ladies," cried the boss, swooping across for two tumblers that stood on the table with the water bottle, and pouring a generous finger into each. "Drink it down. It'll do you good. And don't put any water with it. It's sacrilege to tamper with stuff like this. Ah!" He tossed off his, pulled out his handkerchief, hastily wiped his moustaches, and cocked an eye at old Woodifield, who was rolling his in his chaps.

The old man swallowed, was silent a moment, and then said faintly, "It's nutty!" But it warmed him; it crept into his chill old brain—he remembered.

"That was it," he said, heaving himself out of his chair. "I thought you'd like to know. The girls were in Belgium last week having a look at poor Reggie's grave, and they happened to come across your boy's. They are quite near each other, it seems."

Old Woodifield paused, but the boss made no reply. Only a quiver of his eyelids showed that he heard.

"The girls were delighted with the way the place is kept," piped the old voice. "Beautifully looked after. Couldn't be better if they were at home. You've not been across, have yer?"

"No, no!" For various reasons the boss had not been across.

"There's miles of it," quavered old Woodifield, "and it's all as neat as a garden Flowers growing on all the graves. Nice broad paths." It was plain from his voice how much he liked a nice broad path.

The pause came again. Then the old man brightened wonderfully.

"D'you know what the hotel made the girls pay for a pot of jam?" he piped. "Ten francs! Robbery, I call it. It was a little pot, so Gertrude says, no bigger than a half-crown. And she hadn't taken more than a spoonful when they charged her ten francs. Gertrude brought the pot away with her to teach 'em a lesson. Quite right, too; it's trading on our feelings. They think because we're over there having a look around we're ready to pay anything. That's what it is." And he turned towards the door.

"Quite right, quite right!" cried the boss, though what was quite right he hadn't the least idea. He came round by his desk, followed the shuffling footsteps to the door, and saw the old fellow out. Woodifield was gone.

For a long moment the boss stayed, staring at nothing, while the gray-haired office messenger, watching him, dodged in and out of his cubbyhole like a dog that expects to be taken for a run: "I'll see nobody for half an hour, Macey," said the boss. "Understand? Nobody at all."

"Very good, sir."

The door shut, the firm, heavy steps recrossed the bright carpet, the fat body plumped down in the spring chair, and leaning forward, the boss covered his face with his hands. He wanted, he intended, he had arranged to weep. . . .

It had been a terrible shock to him when old Woodifield sprang that remark upon him about the boy's grave. It was exactly as though the earth had opened and he had seen the boy lying there with Woodifield's girls staring down at him. For it was strange. Although over six years had passed away, the boss never thought of the boy except as lying unchanged, unblemished in his uniform, asleep for ever. "My son!" groaned the boss. But no tears came yet. In the past, in the first months and even years after the boy's death, he had only to say those words to be overcome by such grief that nothing short of a violent fit of weeping could relieve him. Time, he had declared then, he had told everybody, could make no difference. Other men perhaps might recover, might live their loss down, but not he. How was it possible? His boy was an only son. Ever since his birth the boss had worked at building up this business for him; it had no other meaning if it was not for the boy. Life itself had come to have no other meaning. How on earth could he have slaved, denied himself, kept going all these years without the promise for ever before him of the boy's stepping into his shoes and carrying on where he left off?

And that promise had been so near being fulfilled. The boy had been in the office learning the ropes for a year before the war. Every morning they had started off together; they had come back by the same train. And what congratulations he had received as the boy's father! No wonder; he had taken to it marvelously. As to his popularity with the staff, every man jack of them down to old Macey couldn't make enough of the boy. And he wasn't in the least spoiled. No, he was just his bright, natural self, with the right word for everybody, with that boyish look and his habit of saying, "Simply splendid!"

But all that was over and done with as though it never had been. The day had come when Macey had handed him the telegram that brought the whole place crashing about his head. "Deeply regret to inform you . . ." And he had left the office a broken man, with his life in ruins.

Six years ago, six years . . . How quickly time passed! It might have happened yesterday. The boss took his hands from his face; he was puzzled. Something seemed to be wrong with him. He wasn't feeling as he wanted to feel. He decided to get up and have a look at the boy's photograph. But it wasn't a favorite photograph of his; the expression was unnatural. It was cold, even stern-looking. The boy had never looked like that.

At that moment the boss noticed that a fly had fallen into his broad inkpot, and was trying feebly but desperately to clamber out again. Help! help! said those struggling legs. But the sides of the inkpot were wet and slippery; it fell back again and began to swim. The boss took up a pen, picked the fly out of the ink, and shook it on to a piece of blotting paper. For a fraction of a second it lay still on the dark patch that oozed round it. Then the front legs waved, took hold, and, pulling its small sodden body up it began the immense task of cleaning the ink from its wings. Over and under, over and under, went a leg along a wing, as the stone goes over and under the scythe. Then there was a pause, while the fly, seeming to stand on the tips of its toes, tried to expand first one wing and then the other. It succeeded at last, and, sitting down, it began, like a minute cat, to clean its face. Now one could imagine that the little front legs rubbed against each other lightly, joyfully. The horrible danger was over; it had escaped; it was ready for life again.

But just then the boss had an idea. He plunged his pen back into the ink, leaned his thick wrist on the blotting paper, and as the fly tried its wings down came a great heavy blot. What would it make of that? What indeed! The little beggar seemed absolutely cowed, stunned, and afraid to move because of what would happen next. But then, as if painfully, it dragged itself forward. The front legs waved, caught hold and, more slowly this time, the task began from the beginning.

"He's a plucky little devil," thought the boss, and he felt a real admiration for the fly's courage. That was the way to tackle things; that was the right spirit. Never say die; it was only a question of . . . But the fly had again finished its laborious task, and the boss had just time to refill his pen, to shake fair and square on the new-cleaned body yet another dark drop. What about it this time? A painful moment of suspense followed. But behold, the front legs were again waving; the boss felt a rush of relief. He leaned over the fly and said to it tenderly, "You artful little b. . . ." And he actually had the brilliant notion of breathing on it to help the drying process. All the same, there was something timid and weak about its efforts now, and the boss decided that this time should be the last, as he dipped the pen into the inkpot.

It was. The last blot fell on the soaked blotting paper, and the draggled fly lay in it and did not stir. The back legs were stuck to the body; the front legs were not to be seen.

"Come on," said the boss. "Look sharp!" And he stirred it with his pen—in vain. Nothing happened or was likely to happen. The fly was dead.

The boss lifted the corpse on the end of the paper knife and flung it into the waste-paper basket, but such a grinding feeling of wretchedness seized him that he felt positively frightened. He started forward and pressed the bell for Macey.

"Bring me some fresh blotting paper," he said, sternly, "and look sharp about it."
And while the old dog padded away he fell to wondering what it was he had been
thinking about before. What was it? It was . . . He took out his handkerchief and
passed it inside his collar. For the life of him he could not remember.

A STILL MOMENT

EUDORA WELTY (1909–   )

Lorenzo Dow rode the Old Natchez Trace at top speed upon a race horse, and the
cry of the itinerant Man of God, "I must have souls! And souls I must have!" rang
in his own windy ears. He rode as if never to stop, toward his night's appointment.

It was the hour of sunset. All the souls that he had saved and all those he had not
took dusky shapes in the mist that hung between the high banks, and seemed by their
great number and density to block his way, and showed no signs of melting or changing back into mist, so that he feared his passage was to be difficult forever. The poor
souls that were not saved were darker and more pitiful than those that were, and still
there was not any of the radiance he would have hoped to see in such a congregation.

"Light up, in God's name!" he called, in the pain of his disappointment.

Then a whole swarm of fireflies instantly flickered all around him, up and down,
back and forth, first one golden light and then another, flashing without any of the
weariness that had held back the souls. These were the signs sent from God that he
had not seen the accumulated radiance of saved souls because he was not able, and
that his eyes were more able to see the fireflies of the Lord than His blessed souls.

"Lord, give me the strength to see the angels when I am in Paradise," he said. "Do
not let my eyes remain in this failing proportion to my loving heart always."

He gasped and held on. It was that day's complexity of horse-trading that had left
him in the end with a Spanish race horse for which he was bound to send money in
November from Georgia. Riding faster on the beast and still faster until he felt
as if he were flying he sent thoughts of love with matching speed to his wife Peggy
in Massachusetts. He found it effortless to love at a distance. He could look at the
flowering trees and love Peggy in fullness, just as he could see his visions and love
God. And Peggy, to whom he had not spoken until he could speak fateful words
("Would she accept of such an object as him?"), Peggy, the bride, with whom he had
spent a few hours of time, showing of herself a small round handwriting, declared
all in one letter, her first, that she felt the same as he, and that the fear was never of
separation, but only of death.

Lorenzo well knew that it was Death that opened underfoot, that rippled by at
night, that was the silence the birds did their singing in. He was close to death,
closer than any animal or bird. On the back of one horse after another, winding them
all, he was always riding toward it or away from it, and the Lord sent him directions
with protection in His mind.

Just then he rode into a thicket of Indians taking aim with their new guns. One
stepped out and took the horse by the bridle, it stopped at a touch, and the rest made
a closing circle. The guns pointed.

"Incline!" The inner voice spoke sternly and with its customary lightning-quickness.

Lorenzo inclined all the way forward and put his head to the horse's silky mane, his body to its body, until a bullet meant for him would endanger the horse and make his death of no value. Prone he rode out through the circle of Indians, his obedience to the voice leaving him almost fearless, almost careless with joy.

But as he straightened and pressed ahead, care caught up with him again. Turning half-beast and half-divine, dividing himself like a heathen Centaur, he had escaped his death once more. But was it to be always by some metamorphosis of himself that he escaped, some humiliation of his faith, some admission to strength and argumentation and not frailty? Each time when he acted so it was at the command of an instinct that he took at once as the word of an angel, until too late, when he knew it was the word of the devil. He had roared like a tiger at Indians, he had submerged himself in water blowing the savage bubbles of the alligator, and they skirted him by. He had prostrated himself to appear dead, and deceived bears. But all the time God would have protected him in His own way, less hurried, more divine.

Even now he saw a serpent crossing the Trace, giving out knowing glances.

He cried, "I know you now!", and the serpent gave him one look out of which all the fire had been taken, and went away in two darts into the tangle.

He rode on, all expectation, and the voices in the throats of the wild beasts went, almost without his noticing when, into words. "Praise God," they said. "Deliver us from one another." Birds especially sang of divine love which was the one ceaseless protection. "Peace, in peace," were their words so many times when they spoke from the briars, in a courteous sort of inflection, and he turned his countenance toward all perched creatures with a benevolence striving to match their own.

He rode on past the little intersecting trails, letting himself be guided by voices and by lights. It was battlesounds he heard most, sending him on, but sometimes ocean sounds, that long beat of waves that would make his heart pound and retreat as heavily as they, and he despaired again in his failure in Ireland when he took a voyage and persuaded with the Catholics with his back against the door, and then ran away to their cries of "Mind the white hat!" But when he heard singing it was not the militant and sharp sound of Wesley's hymns, but a soft, tireless and tender air that had no beginning and no end, and the softness of distance, and he had pleaded with the Lord to find out if all this meant that it was wicked, but no answer had come.

Soon night would descend, and a camp-meeting ground ahead would fill with its sinners like the sky with its stars. How he hungered for them! He looked in prescience with a longing of love over the throng that waited while the flames of the torches threw change, change, change over their faces. How could he bring them enough, if it were not divine love and sufficient warning of all that could threaten them? He rode on faster. He was a filler of appointments, and he filled more and more, until his journeys up and down creation were nothing but a shuttle, driving back and forth upon the rich expanse of his vision. He was homeless by his own choice, he must be everywhere at sometime, and somewhere soon. There hastening in the wilderness on his flying horse he gave the night's torch-lit crowd a premature benediction, he could not wait. He spread his arms out, one at a time for safety, and he wished, when they would all be gathered in by his tin horn blasts and the inspired words would go out over their heads, to brood above the entire and passionate life of the wide world, to become its rightful part.

He peered ahead. "Inhabitants of Time! The wilderness is your souls on earth!" he shouted ahead into the treetops. "Look about you, if you would view the condi tions of your spirit, put here by the good Lord to show you and affright you. These wild places and these trails of awesome loneliness lie nowhere, nowhere, but in your heart."

A dark man, who was James Murrell the outlaw, rode his horse out of a cane brake and began going along beside Lorenzo without looking at him. He had the alternately proud and aggrieved look of a man believing himself to be an instrument in the hands of a power, and when he was young he said at once to strangers that he was being used by Evil, or sometimes he stopped a traveler by shouting, "Stop! I'm the Devil!" He rode along now talking and drawing out his talk, by some deep control of the voice gradually slowing the speed of Lorenzo's horse down until both the horses were softly trotting. He would have wondered that nothing he said was heard, not knowing that Lorenzo listened only to voices of whose heavenly origin he was more certain.

Murrell riding along with his victim-to-be, Murrell riding, was Murrell talking. He told away at his long tales, with always a distance and a long length of time flowing through them, and all centered about a silent man. In each the silent man would have done a piece of evil, a robbery or a murder, in a place of long ago, and it was all made for the revelation in the end that the silent man was Murrell himself, and the long story had happened yesterday, and the place *here*—the Natchez Trace. It would only take one dawning look for the victim to see that all of this was another story and he himself had listened his way into it, and that he too was about to recede in time (to where the dread was forgotten) for some listener and to live for a listener in the long ago. Destroy the present!—that must have been the first thing that was whispered in Murrell's heart—the living moment and the man that lives in it must die before you can go on. It was his habit to bring the journey—which might even take days—to a close with a kind of ceremony. Turning his face at last into the face of the victim, for he had never seen him before now, he would tower up with the sudden height of a man no longer the tale teller but the speechless protagonist, silent at last, one degree nearer the hero. Then he would murder the man.

But it would always start over. This man going forward was going backward with talk. He saw nothing, observed no world at all. The two ends of his journey pulled at him always and held him in a nowhere, half asleep, smiling and witty, dangling his predicament. He was a murderer whose final stroke was over-long postponed, who had to bring himself through the greatest tedium to act, as if the whole wilderness, where he was born, were his impediment. But behind him and before him he kept in sight a victim, he saw a man fixed and stayed at the point of death—no matter how the man's eyes denied it, a victim, hands spreading to reach as if for the first time for life. Contempt! That is what Murrell gave that man.

Lorenzo might have understood, if he had not been in haste, that Murrell in laying hold of a man meant to solve his mystery of being. It was as if other men, all but himself, would lighten their hold on the secret, upon assault, and let it fly free at death. In his violence he was only treating of enigma. The violence shook his own body first, like a force gathering, and now he turned in the saddle.

Lorenzo's despair had to be kindled as well as his ecstasy, and could not come without that kindling. Before the awe-filled moment when the faces were turned up under the flares, as though an angel hand tipped their chins, he had no way of telling whether he would enter the sermon by sorrow or by joy. But at this moment the face of Murrell was turned toward him, turning at last, all solitary, in its full, and Lorenzo would have seized the man at once by his black coat and shaken him like prey for a lost soul, so instantly was he certain that the false fire was in his heart instead of the true fire. But Murrell, quick when he was quick, had put his own hand out, a restraining hand, and laid it on the wavelike flesh of the Spanish race horse, which quivered and shuddered at the touch.

They had come to a great live-oak tree at the edge of a low marsh-land. The burning sun hung low, like a head lowered on folded arms, and over the long reaches of violet trees the evening seemed still with thought. Lorenzo knew the place from having seen it among many in dreams, and he stopped readily and willingly. He drew rein, and Murrell drew rein, he dismounted and Murrell dismounted, he took a step, and Murrell was there too; and Lorenzo was not surprised at the closeness, how Murrell in his long dark coat and over it his dark face darkening still, stood beside him like a brother seeking light.

But in that moment instead of two men coming to stop by the great forked tree, there were three.

From far away, a student, Audubon, had been approaching lightly on the wilderness floor, disturbing nothing in his lightness. The long day of beauty had led him this certain distance. A flock of purple finches that he tried for the first moment to count went over his head. He made a spelling of the soft *pet* of the ivory-billed woodpecker. He told himself always: remember.

Coming upon the Trace, he looked at the high cedars, azure and still as distant smoke overhead, with their silver roots trailing down on either side like the veins of deepness in this place, and he noted some fact to his memory—this earth that wears but will not crumble or slide or turn to dust, they say it exists in one other spot in the world, Egypt—and then forgot it. He walked quietly. All life used this Trace, and he liked to see the animals move along it in direct, oblivious journeys, for they had begun it and made it, the buffalo and deer and the small running creatures before man ever knew where he wanted to go, and birds flew a great mirrored course above.

Walking beneath them Audubon remembered how in the cities he had seen these very birds in his imagination, calling them up whenever he wished, even in the hard and glittering outer parlors where if an artist were humble enough to wait, some idle hand held up promised money. He walked lightly and he went as carefully as he had started at two that morning, crayon and paper, a gun, and a small bottle of spirits disposed about his body. (*Note: "The mocking birds so gentle that they would scarcely move out of the way."*) He looked with care; great abundance had ceased to startle him, and he could see things one by one. In Natchez they had told him of many strange and marvelous birds that were to be found here. Their descriptions had been exact, complete, and wildly varying, and he took them for inventions and believed that like all the worldly things that came out of Natchez, they would be disposed of and shamed by any man's excursion into the reality of Nature.

In the valley he appeared under the tree, a sure man, very sure and tender, as if the touch of all the earth rubbed upon him and the stains of the flowery swamp had made him so.

Lorenzo welcomed him and turned fond eyes upon him. To transmute a man into an angel was the hope that drove him all over the world and never let him flinch from a meeting or withhold good-byes for long. This hope insistently divided his life into only two parts, journey and rest. There could be no night and day and love and despair and longing and satisfaction to make partitions in the single ecstasy of this alternation. All things were speech.

"God created the world," said Lorenzo, "and it exists to give testimony. Life is the tongue: speak."

But instead of speech there happened a moment of deepest silence.

Audubon said nothing because he had gone without speaking a word for days. He did not regard his thoughts for the birds and animals as susceptible, in their first change, to words. His long playing on the flute was not in its origin a talking to himself. Rather than speak to order or describe, he would aways draw a deer with a stroke across it to communicate his need of venison to an Indian. He had only found words when he discovered that there is much otherwise lost that can be noted down each item in its own day, and he wrote often now in a journal, not wanting anything to be lost the way it had been, all the past, and he would write about a day, "Only sorry that the Sun Sets."

Murrell, his cheated hand hiding the gun, could only continue to smile at Lorenzo, but he remembered in malice that he had disguised himself once as an Evangelist, and his final words to this victim would have been, "One of my disguises was what you are."

Then in Murrell Audubon saw what he thought of as "acquired sorrow"—that cumbrousness and darkness from which the naked Indian, coming just as he was made from God's hand, was so lightly free. He noted the eyes—the dark kind that loved to look through chinks, and saw neither closeness nor distance, light nor shade, wonder nor familiarity. They were narrowed to contract the heart, narrowed to make an averting plan. Audubon knew the finest-drawn tendons of the body and the working of their power, for he had touched them, and he supposed then that in man the enlargement of the eye to see started a motion in the hands to make or do, and that the narrowing of the eye stopped the hand and contracted the heart, Now Murrell's eyes followed an ant on a blade of grass, up the blade and down, many times in the single moment. Audubon had examined the Cave-In Rock where one robber had lived his hiding life, and the air in the cave was the cavelike air that enclosed this man, the same odor, flinty and dark. O secret life, he thought—is it true that the secret is withdrawn from the true disclosure, that man is a cave man, and that the openness I see, the ways through forests, the rivers brimming light, the wide arches where the birds fly, are dreams of freedom? If my origin is withheld from me, is my end to be unknown too? Is the radiance I see closed into an interval between two darks, or can it not illuminate them both and discover at last, though it cannot be spoken, what was thought hidden and lost?

In that quiet moment a solitary snowy heron flew down not far away and began to feed beside the marsh water.

At the single streak of flight, the ears of the race horse lifted, and the eyes of both horses filled with the soft lights of sunset, which in the next instant were reflected in the eyes of the men too as they all looked into the west toward the heron, and all eyes seemed infused with a sort of wildness.

Lorenzo gave the bird a triumphant look, such as a man may bestow upon his own vision, and thought, Nearness is near, lighted in a marsh-land, feeding at sunset. Praise God, His love has come visible.

Murrell, in suspicion pursuing all glances, blinking into a haze, saw only whiteness ensconced in darkness, as if it were a little luminous shell that drew in and held the eyesight. When he shaded his eyes, the brand "H.T." on his thumb thrust itself into his own vision, and he looked at the bird with the whole plan of the Mystic Rebellion darting from him as if in rays of the bright reflected light, and he stood looking proudly, leader as he was bound to become of the slaves, the brigands and outcasts of the entire Natchez country, with plans, dates, maps burning like a brand into his brain, and he saw himself proudly in a moment of prophecy going down rank after rank of successsively bowing slaves to unroll and flaunt an awesome great picture of the Devil colored on a banner.

Audubon's eyes embraced the object in the distance and he could see it as carefully as if he held it in his hand. It was a snowy heron alone out of its flock. He watched it steadily, in his care noting the exact inevitable things. When it feeds it muddies the water with its foot. . . . It was as if each detail about the heron happened slowly in time, and only once. He felt again the old stab of wonder—what structure of life bridged the reptile's scale and the heron's feather? That knowledge too had been lost. He watched without moving. The bird was defenseless in the world except for the intensity of its life, and he wondered, how can heat of blood and speed of heart defend it? Then he thought, as always as if it were new and unbelievable, it has nothing in space or time to prevent its flight. And he waited, knowing that some birds will wait for a sense of their presence to travel to men before they will fly away from them.

Fixed in its pure white profile it stood in the precipitous moment, a plumicorn on its head, its breeding dress extended in rays, eating steadily the little water creatures. There was a little space between each man and the others, where they stood overwhelmed. No one could say the three had ever met, or that this moment of intersection had ever come in their lives, or its promise fulfilled. But before them the white heron rested in the grasses with the evening all around it, lighter and more serene than the evening, flight closed in its body, the circuit of its beauty closed, a bird seen and a bird still, its motion calm as if it were offered: Take my flight. . . .

What each of them had wanted was simply *all*. To save all souls, to destroy all men, to see and to record all life that filled this world—all, all—but now a single frail yearning seemed to go out of the three of them for a moment and to stretch toward this one snowy, shy bird in the marshes. It was as if three whirlwinds had drawn together at some center, to find there feeding in peace a snowy heron. Its own slow spiral of flight could take it away in its own time, but for a little it held them still, it laid quiet over them, and they stood for a moment unburdened. . . .

Murrell wore no mask, for his face was that, a face that was aware while he was somnolent, a face that watched for him, and listened for him, alert and nearly brutal, the guard of a planner. He was quick without that he might be slow within, he staved off time, he wandered and plotted, and yet his whole desire mounted in him toward the end (was this the end—the sight of a bird feeding at dusk?), toward the instant of confession. His incessant deeds were thick in his heart now, and flinging himself to the ground he thought wearily, when all these trees are cut down, and the Trace lost, then my Conspiracy that is yet to spread itself will be disclosed, and all the stone-loaded bodies of murdered men will be pulled up, and all everywhere will know poor Murrell. His look pressed upon Lorenzo, who stared upward, and Audubon, who was taking out his gun, and his eyes squinted up to them in pleading as if to say, "How soon may I speak, and how soon will you pity me?" Then he looked back to the bird, and he thought if it would look at him a dread penetration would fill and gratify his heart.

Audubon in each act of life was aware of the mysterious origin he half-concealed and half-sought for. People along the way asked him in their kindness or their rudeness if it were true, that he was born a prince, and was the Lost Dauphin, and some

said it was his secret, and some said that that was what he wished to find out before
he died. But if it was his identity that he wished to discover, or if it was what a man
had to seize beyond that, the way for him was by endless examination, by the care for
every bird that flew in his path and every serpent that shone underfoot. Not one
was enough; he looked deeper and deeper, on and on, as if for a particular beast or
some legendary bird. Some men's eyes persisted in looking outward when they opened
to look inward, and to their delight, there outflung was the astonishing world under
the sky. When a man at last brought himself to face some mirror-surface he still saw
the world looking back at him, and if he continued to look, to look closer and closer,
what then? The gaze that looks outward must be trained without rest, to be indomitable. It must see as slowy as Murrell's ant in the grass, as exhaustively as Lorenzo's
angel of God, and then, Audubon dreamed, with his mind going to his pointed brush,
it must see like this, and he tightened his hand on the trigger of the gun and pulled
it, and his eyes went closed. In memory the heron was all its solitude, its total
beauty. All its whiteness could be seen from all sides at once, its pure feathers were
as if counted and known and their array one upon the other would never be lost.
But it was not from that memory that he could paint.

His opening eyes met Lorenzo's, close and flashing, and it was on seeing horror deep
in them, like fires in abysses, that he recognized it for the first time. He had never
seen horror in its purity and clarity until now, in bright blue eyes. He went and picked
up the bird. He had thought it to be a female, just as one sees the moon as female; and
so it was. He put it in his bag, and started away. But Lorenzo had already gone on,
leaning a-tilt on the horse which went slowly.

Murrell was left behind, but he was proud of the dispersal, as if he had done it, as
if he had always known that three men in simply being together and doing a thing
can, by their obstinacy, take the pride out of one another. Each must go away alone,
each send the others away alone. He himself had purposely kept to the wildest country in the world, and would have sought it out, the loneliest road. He looked about
with satisfaction, and hid. Travelers were forever innocent, he believed: that was his
faith. He lay in wait; his faith was in innocence and his knowledge was of ruin;
and had these things been shaken? Now, what could possibly be outside his grasp?
Churning all about him like a cloud about the sun was the great folding descent of his
thought. Plans of deeds made his thoughts, and they rolled and mingled about his
ears as if he heard a dark voice that rose up to overcome the wilderness voice, or was
one with it. The night would soon come, and he had gone through the day.

Audubon, splattered and wet, turned back into the wilderness with the heron warm
under his hand, his head still light in a kind of trance. It was undeniable, on some
Sunday mornings, when he turned over and over his drawings they seemed beautiful
to him, through what was dramatic in the conflict of life, or what was exact. What he
would draw, and what he had seen, became for a moment one to him then. Yet soon
enough, and it seemed to come in that same moment, like Lorenzo's horror and the
gun's firing, he knew that even the sight of the heron which surely he alone had appreciated, had not been all his belonging, and that never could any vision, even any
simple sight, belong to him or to any man. He knew that the best he could make
would be, after it was apart from his hand, a dead thing and not a live thing, never
the essence, only a sum of parts; and that it would always meet with a stranger's sight,
and never be one with the beauty in any other man's head in the world. As he had

seen the bird most purely at its moment of death, in some fatal way, in his care for looking outward, he saw his long labor most revealingly at the point where it met its limit. Still carefully, for he was trained to see well in the dark, he walked on into the deeper woods, noting all sights, all sounds, and was gentler than they as he went.

In the woods that echoed yet in his ears, Lorenzo riding slowly looked back. The hair rose on his head and his hands began to shake with cold, and suddenly it seemed to him that God Himself, just now, thought of the Idea of Separateness. For surely He had never thought of it before, when the little white heron was flying down to feed. He could understand God's giving Separateness first and then giving Love to follow and heal in its wonder; but God had reversed this, and given Love first and then Separateness, as though it did not matter to Him which came first. Perhaps it was that God never counted the moments of Time; Lorenzo did that, among his tasks of love. Time did not occur to God. Therefore—did He even know of it? How to explain Time and Separateness back to God, Who had never thought of them, Who could let the whole world come to grief in a scattering moment?

Lorenzo brought his cold hands together in a clasp and stared through the distance at the place where the bird had been as if he saw it still; as if nothing could really take away what had happened to him, the beautiful little vision of the feeding bird. Its beauty had been greater than he could account for. The sweat of rapture poured down from his forehead, and then he shouted into the marshes:

"Tempter!"

He whirled forward in the saddle and began to hurry the horse to its high speed. His camp ground was far away still, though even now they must be lighting the torches and gathering in the multitudes, so that at the appointed time he would duly appear in their midst, to deliver his address on the subject of "In that day when all hearts shall be disclosed."

Then the sun dropped below the trees, and the new moon, slender and white, hung shyly in the west.

STRANGE COMFORT AFFORDED BY THE PROFESSION

MALCOLM LOWRY (1909–1957)

Sigbjørn Wilderness, an American writer in Rome on a Guggenheim Fellowship, paused on the steps above the flower stall and wrote, glancing from time to time at the house before him, in a black notebook:

> Il poeta inglese Giovanni Keats mente maravigliosa quanto precoce mori in questa casa il 24 Febraio 1821 nel ventiseisimo anno dell' eta sua.

Here, in a sudden access of nervousness, glancing now not only at the house, but behind him at the church of Trinità dei Monti, at the woman in the flower stall, the Romans drifting up and down the steps, or passing in the Piazza di Spagna below (for though it was several years after the war he was afraid of being taken for a spy), he drew, as well as he was able, the lyre, similar to the one on the poet's tomb, that appeared on the house between the Italian and its translation:

Then he added swiftly the words below the lyre:

The young English poet, John Keats, died in this house on the 24th of February 1821, aged 26.

This accomplished, he put the notebook and pencil back in his pocket, glanced round him again with a heavier, more penetrating look—that in fact was informed by such a malaise he saw nothing at all but which was intended to say "I have a perfect right to do this," or "If you saw me do that, very well then, I *am* some sort of detective, perhaps even some kind of a painter"—descended the remaining steps, looked around wildly once more, and entered, with a sigh of relief like a man going to bed, the comforting darkness of Keats's house.

Here, having climbed the narrow staircase, he was almost instantly confronted by a legend in a glass case which said:

Remnants of aromatic gums used by Trelawny when cremating the body of Shelley.

And these words, for his notebook with which he was already rearmed felt ratified in this place, he also copied down, though he failed to comment on the gums themselves, which largely escaped his notice, as indeed did the house itself—there had been those stairs, there was a balcony, it was dark, there were many pictures, and these glass cases, it was a bit like a library—in which he saw no books of his—these made about the sum of Sigbjørn's unrecorded perceptions. From the aromatic gums he moved to the enshrined marriage licence of the same poet, and Sigbjørn transcribed this document too, writing rapidly as his eyes became more used to the dim light:

Percy Bysshe Shelley of the Parish *of* Saint Mildred, Bread Street, London, Widower, *and* Mary Wollstonecraft Godwin *of* the City of Bath, Spinster, a minor, *were married in this* Church *by* Licence *with Consent of* William Godwin her father *this* Thirtieth *Day of December in the year one thousand eight hundred and sixteen.* By me Mr. Heydon, Curate. This marriage was solemnized between us.
                                        Percy Bysshe Shelley
                                        Mary Wollstonecraft Godwin

        In the presence of:

                                        William Godwin
                                        M. J. Godwin.

Beneath this Sigbjørn added mysteriously:

Nemesis. Marriage of drowned Phoenician sailor. A bit odd here at all. Sad— feel swine to look at such things.

Then he passed on quickly—not so quickly he hadn't time to wonder with a remote twinge why, if there was no reason for any of his own books to be there on the shelves above him, the presence was justified of *In Memoriam, All Quiet on the Western Front, Green Light,* and the *Field Book of Western Birds*—to another glass case in which appeared a framed and unfinished letter, evidently from Severn, Keats's friend, which Sigbjørn copied down as before:

> My dear Sir:
>   Keats has changed somewhat for the worse—at least his mind has much—very much—yet the blood has ceased to come, his digestion is better and but for a cough he must be improving, that is as respects his body—but the fatal prospect of consumption hangs before his mind yet—and turns everything to despair and wretchedness—he will not hear a word about living—nay, I seem to lose his confidence by trying to give him this hope [the following lines had been crossed out by Severn but Sigbjørn ruthlessly wrote them down just the same: *for his knowledge of internal anatomy enables him to judge of any change accurately and largely adds to his torture*], he will not think his future prospect favorable—he says the continued stretch of his imagination has already killed him and were he to recover he would not write another line—he will not hear of his good friends in England except for what they have done—and this is another load—but of their high hopes of him— his certain success—his experience—he will not hear a word—then the want of some kind of hope to feed his vivacious imagination—

The letter having broken off here, Sigbjørn, notebook in hand, tiptoed lingeringly to another glass case where, another letter from Severn appearing, he wrote:

> My dear Brown—He is gone—he died with the most perfect ease—he seemed to go to sleep. On the 23rd at half past four the approaches of death came on. "Severn—lift me up for I am dying—I shall die easy—don't be frightened, I thank God it has come." I lifted him upon my arms and the phlegm seemed boiling in his throat. This increased until 11 at night when he gradually sank into death so quiet I still thought he slept—But I cannot say more now. I am broken down beyond my strength. I cannot be left alone. I have not slept for nine days—the days since. On Saturday a gentleman came to cast his hand and foot. On Thursday the body was opened. The lungs were completely gone. The doctors would not—

Much moved, Sigbjørn reread this as it now appeared in his notebook, then added beneath it:

> *On Saturday a gentleman came to cast his hand and foot*—that is the most sinister line to me. Who is this gentleman?

Once outside Keats's house Wilderness did not pause nor look to left or right, not even at the American Express, until he had reached a bar which he entered, however, without stopping to copy down its name. He felt he had progressed in one movement, in one stride, from Keats's house to this bar, partly just because he had wished to avoid signing his own name in the visitor's book. Sigbjørn Wilderness! The very sound of his name was like a bell-buoy—or more euphoniously a light-ship—broken adrift, and washing in from the Atlantic on a reef. Yet how he hated to write it down (loved to see it in print?)—though like so much else with him it had little reality unless he did. Without hesitating to ask himself why, if he was so disturbed by it, he did not choose another name under which to write, such as his second name which was Henry, or his mother's, which was Sanderson-Smith, he selected the most isolated booth he could find in the bar, that was itself an underground grotto, and drank two grappas in quick succession. Over his third he began to experience some of the emotions one might have expected him to undergo in Keats's house. He felt fully the surprise which had barely affected him that some of Shelley's relics were to be found there, if a fact no more astonishing than that Shelley—whose skull moreover had narrowly escaped appropriation by Byron as a drinking goblet, and whose heart, snatched out of the flames by Trelawny, he seemed to recollect from Proust, was interred in England— should have been buried in Rome at all (where the bit of Ariel's song inscribed on his gravestone might have anyway prepared one for the rich and strange), and he was touched by the chivalry of those Italians who, during the war, it was said, had preserved, at considerable risk to themselves, the contents of that house from the Germans. Moreover he now thought he began to see the house itself more clearly, though no doubt not as it was, and he produced his notebook again with the object of adding to the notes already taken these impressions that came to him in retrospect.

"Mamertine Prison," he read . . . He'd opened it at the wrong place, at some observations made yesterday upon a visit to the historic dungeon, but being gloomily entertained by what he saw, he read on as he did so feeling the clammy confined horror of that underground cell, or other underground cell, not, he suspected, really sensed at the time, rise heavily about him.

MAMERTINE PRISON [ran the heading]
   The lower is the true prison
of Mamertine, the state prison of ancient Rome.

The lower cell called Tullianus is probably the most ancient building in Rome. The prison was used to imprison malefactors and enemies of the State. In the lower cell is seen the well where according to tradition St. Peter miraculously made a spring to baptise the gaolers Processus and Martinianus. Victims: politicians. Pontius, King of the Sanniti. Died 290 B.C. Giurgurath (Jugurtha), Aristobulus, Vercingetorix.—The Holy Martyrs, Peter and Paul. Apostles imprisoned in the reign of Nero.—Processus, Abondius, *and many others unknown* were:
                        decapitato
                        suppliziato (suffocated)
                        strangolato
                        morto per fame.

Vercingetorix, the King of the Gauls, was certainly strangolato 49 B.C. and Jugurtha, King of Numidia, dead by starvation 104 B.C.

The lower is the true prison—why had he underlined that? Sigbjørn wondered. He ordered another grappa and, while awaiting it, turned back to his notebook where, beneath his remarks on the Mamertine prison, and added as he now recalled in the dungeon itself, this memorandum met his eyes:

Find Gogol's house—where wrote part of *Dead Souls*—1838. Where died Vielgorsky? "They do not heed me, nor see me, nor listen to me," wrote Gogol. "What have I done to them? Why do they torture me? What do they want of poor me? What can I give them? I have nothing. My strength is gone. I cannot endure all this." Suppliziato. Strangolato. In wonderful-horrible book of Nabokov's when Gogol was dying—he says—"you could feel his spine through his stomach." Leeches dangling from nose: "Lift them up, keep them away . . ." Henrik Ibsen, Thomas Mann, ditto brother: Buddenbrooks and Pippo Spano. A—where lived? became sunburned? Perhaps happy here. Prosper Mérimée and Schiller. Suppliziato. Fitzgerald in Forum. Eliot in Colosseum?

And underneath this was written enigmatically:

And many others.

And beneath this:

Perhaps Maxim Gorky too. This is funny. Encounter between Volga Boatman and saintly Fisherman.

What was funny? While Sigbjørn, turning over his pages toward Keats's house again was wondering what he had meant, beyond the fact that Gorky, like most of those other distinguished individuals, had at one time lived in Rome, if not in the Mamertine prison—though with another part of his mind he knew perfectly well—he realized that the peculiar stichometry of his observations, jotted down as if he imagined he were writing a species of poem, had caused him prematurely to finish the notebook:

On Saturday a gentleman came to cast his hand and foot—that is the most sinister line to me—who is this gentleman?

With these words his notebook concluded.

That didn't mean there was no more space, for his notebooks, he reflected avuncularly, just like his candles, tended to consume themselves at both ends; yes, as he thought, there was some writing at the beginning. Reversing this, for it was upside down, he smiled and forgot about looking for space, since he immediately recognized these notes as having been taken in America two years ago upon a visit to Richmond, Virginia, a pleasant time for him. So, amused, he composed himself to read, delighted also, in an Italian bar, to be thus transported back to the South. He had made nothing of these notes, hadn't even known they were there, and it was not always easy accurately to visualize the scenes they conjured up:

The wonderful slanting square in Richmond and the tragic silhouette of interlaced leafless trees.
On a wall: *dirty stinking Degenerate Bobs was here from Boston, North End, Mass. Warp son of a bitch.*

Sigbjørn chuckled. Now he clearly remembered the biting winter day in Richmond, the dramatic courthouse in the precipitous park, the long climb up to it, and the caustic attestation to solidarity with the North in the (white) men's wash room. Smiling he read on:

In Poe's shrine, strange preserved newsclipping: CAPACITY CROWD HEARS TRIBUTE TO POE'S WORKS. *University student, who ended life, buried at Wytherville.*

Yes, yes, and this he remembered too, in Poe's house, or one of Poe's houses, the one with the great dark wing of shadow on it at sunset, where the dear old lady who kept it, who'd showed him the news clipping, had said to him in a whisper: "So you see, *we* think these stories of his drinking can't *all* be true." He continued:

Opposite Craig House, where Poe's Helen lived, these words, upon façade, windows, stoop of the place from which E.A.P.—if I am right—must have watched the lady with the agate lamp: Headache—A.B.C.—Neuralgia: LIC-OFF-PREM— enjoy Pepsi—Drink Royal Crown Cola—Dr. Swell's Root Beer—"Furnish room for rent": did Poe really live here? Must have, could only have spotted Psyche from the regions which are Lic-Off-Prem.—Better than no Lic at all though. Bet Poe does not still live in Lic-Off-Prem. Else might account for "Furnish room for rent"?
Mem: Consult Talking Horse Friday.
—Give me Liberty or give me death [Sigbjørn now read]. In churchyard, with Patrick Henry's grave; a notice: No smoking within ten feet of the church;

then:

Outside Robert E. Lee's house:
Please pull the bell
To make it ring.
—Inside Valentine Museum, with Poe's relics—

Sigbjørn paused. Now he remembered that winter day still more clearly. Robert E. Lee's house was of course far below the courthouse, remote from Patrick Henry and the Craig house and the other Poe shrine, and it would have been a good step hence to the Valentine Museum, even had not Richmond, a city whose Hellenic character was not confined to its architecture, but would have been recognized in its gradients by a Greek mountain goat, been grouped about streets so steep it was painful to think of Poe toiling up them. Sigbjørn's notes were in the wrong order, and it must have been morning then, and not sunset as it was in the other house with the old lady, when he went to the Valentine Museum. He saw Lee's house again, and a faint feeling of the beauty of the whole frostbound city outside came to his mind, then a picture of a Confederate white house, near a gigantic red-brick factory chimney, with far below a glimpse of an old cobbled street, and a lone figure crossing a waste, as between three centuries, from the house toward the railway tracks and this chimney, which belonged to the Bone Dry Fertilizer Company. But in the sequence of his notes "Please pull the bell, to make it ring," on Lee's house, had seemed to provide a certain musical effect of solemnity, yet ushering him instead into the Poe museum which Sigbjørn now in memory re-entered.

Inside Valentine Museum, with Poe's relics [he read once more]
Please
Do not smoke
Do not run
Do not touch walls or exhibits
Observation of these rules will insure your own and other's enjoyment of the museum.
—Blue silk coat and waistcoat, gift of the Misses Boykin, that belonged to one of George Washington's dentists.

Sigbjørn closed his eyes, in his mind Shelley's crematory gums and the gift of the Misses Boykin struggling for a moment helplessly, then he returned to the words that followed. They were Poe's own, and formed part of some letters once presumably written in anguished and private desperation, but which were now to be perused at leisure by anyone whose enjoyment of them would be "insured" so long as they neither smoked nor ran nor touched the glass case in which, like the gums (on the other side of the world), they were preserved. He read:

Excerpt from a letter by Poe—after having been dismissed from West Point—to his foster father. Feb. 21, 1831.
"It will however be the last time I ever trouble any human being—I feel I am on a sick bed from which I shall never get up."

Sigbjørn calculated with a pang that Poe must have written these words almost seven years to the day after Keats's death, then, that far from never having got up from his sick bed, he had risen from it to change, thanks to Baudelaire, the whole course of European literature, yes, and not merely to trouble, but to frighten the wits out of several generations of human beings with such choice pieces as "King Pest," "The Pit and the Pendulum," and "A Descent into the Maelstrom," not to speak of the effect produced by the compendious and prophetic *Eureka*.

My *ear* has been too shocking for any description—I am wearing away every day, even if my last sickness had not completed it.

Sigbjørn finished his grappa and ordered another. The sensation produced by reading these notes was really very curious. First, he was conscious of himself read-

ing them here in this Roman bar, then of himself in the Valentine Museum in Richmond, Virginia, reading the letters through the glass case and copying fragments from
these down, then of poor Poe sitting blackly somewhere writing them. Beyond this
was the vision of Poe's foster father likewise reading some of these letters, for all he
knew unheedingly, yet solemnly putting them away for what turned out to be posterity,
these letters which, whatever they might not be, were certainly—he thought again—
intended to be private. But were they indeed? Even here at this extremity Poe must
have felt that he was transcribing the story that was E. A. Poe, at this very moment of
what he conceived to be his greatest need, his final—however consciously engineered
—disgrace, felt a certain reluctance, perhaps, to send what he wrote, as if he were
thinking: Damn it, I could use some of that, it may not be so hot, but it is at least too
good to waste on my foster father. Some of Keats's own published letters were not
different. And yet it was almost bizarre how, among these glass cases, in these mu-
seums, to what extent one revolved about, was hemmed in by, this cinereous evidence
of anguish. Where was Poe's astrolabe, Keats's tankard of claret, Shelley's "Useful
Knots for the Yachtsman"? It was true that Shelley himself might not have been
aware of the aromatic gums, but even that beautiful and irrelevant circumstantiality
that was the gift of the Misses Boykin seemed not without its suggestion of suffering,
at least for George Washington.

> Baltimore, April 12, 1833.
> I am perishing—absolutely perishing for want of aid. And yet I am not idle—
> nor have I committed any offence against society which would render me deserving
> of so hard a fate. For God's sake pity me and save me from destruction.
> E. A. Poe

Oh, God, thought Sigbjørn. But Poe had held out another sixteen years. He had
died in Baltimore at the age of forty. Sigbjørn himself was nine behind on that game
so far, and—with luck—should win easily. Perhaps if Poe had held out a little longer
—perhaps if Keats—he turned over the pages of his notebook rapidly, only to be confronted by the letter from Severn:

> My dear Sir:
> Keats has changed somewhat for the worse—at least his mind has much—very
> much—yet the blood has ceased to come . . . but the fatal prospect hangs . . .
> for his knowledge of internal anatomy . . . largely adds to his torture.

Suppliziato, strangolato, he thought . . . The lower is the true prison. And many
others. Nor have I committed any offence against society. Not much you hadn't,
brother. Society might pay you the highest honors, even to putting your relics in the
company of the waistcoat belonging to George Washington's dentist, but in its heart
it cried: —dirty stinking Degenerate Bobs was here from Boston, North End, Mass.
Warp son of a bitch! . . . "On Saturday a gentleman came to cast his hand and
foot . . ." Had anybody done that, Sigbjørn wondered, tasting his new grappa, and
suddenly cognizant of his diminishing Guggenheim, compared, that was, Keats and
Poe?—But compare in what sense, Keats, with what, in what sense, with Poe? What
was it he wanted to compare? Not the aesthetic of the two poets, nor the breakdown
of Hyperion, in relation to Poe's conception of the short poem, nor yet the philosophic
ambition of the one, with the philosophic achievement of the other. Or could that more
properly be discerned as negative capability, as opposed to negative achievement? Or
did he merely wish to relate their melancholias? potations? hangovers? Their sheer
guts—which commentators so obligingly forgot!—character, in a high sense of that

word, the sense in which Conrad sometimes understood it, for were they not in their souls like hapless shipmasters, determined to drive their leaky commands full of valuable treasure at all costs, somehow, into port, and always against time, yet through all but interminable tempest, typhoons that so rarely abated? Or merely what seemed funereally analogous within the mutuality of their shrines? Or he could even speculate, starting with Baudelaire again, upon what the French movie director Epstein who had made *La Chute de la Maison Usher* in a way that would have delighted Poe himself, might have done with *The Eve of St. Agnes: And they are gone!* . . . "For God's sake pity me and save me from destruction!"

Ah ha, now he thought he had it: did not the preservation of such relics betoken—beyond the filing cabinet of the malicious foster father who wanted to catch one out—less an obscure revenge for the poet's nonconformity, than for his magical monopoly, his possession of words? On the one hand he could write his translunar "Ulalume," his enchanted "To a Nightingale" (which might account for the *Field Book of Western Birds*), on the other was capable of saying, simply, "I am perishing . . . For God's sake pity me . . ." You see, after all, he's just like folks . . . What's this? . . . Conversely there might appear almost a tragic condescension in remarks such as Flaubert's often quoted "Ils sont dans le vrai" perpetuated by Kafka—Kaf—and others, and addressed to child-bearing rosy-cheeked and jolly humanity at large. Condescension, nay, inverse self-approval, something downright unnecessary. And Flaub— Why should they be dans le vrai any more than the artist was dans le vrai? All people and poets are much the same but some poets are more the same than others, as George Orwell might have said. George Or— And yet, what modern poet would be caught dead (though they'd do their best to catch him all right) with his "For Christ's sake send aid," unrepossessed, unincinerated, to be put in a glass case? It was a truism to say that poets not only were, but looked like folks these days. Far from ostensible nonconformists, as the daily papers, the very writers themselves—more shame to them—took every opportunity triumphantly to point out, they dressed like, and as often as not were bank clerks, or, marvellous paradox, engaged in advertising. It was true. He, Sigbjørn, dressed like a bank clerk himself—how else should he have courage to go into a bank? It was questionable whether poets especially, in uttermost private, any longer allowed themselves to say things like "For God's sake pity me!" Yes, they had become more like folks even than folks. And the despair in the glass case, all private correspondence carefully destroyed, yet destined to become ten thousand times more public than ever, viewed through the great glass case of art, was now transmuted into hieroglyphics, masterly compressions, obscurities to be deciphered by experts—yes, and poets—like Sigbjørn Wilderness. Wil—

And many others. Probably there was a good idea somewhere, lurking among these arrant self-contradictions; pity could not keep him from using it, nor a certain sense of horror that he felt all over again that these mummified and naked cries of agony should lie thus exposed to human view in permanent incorruption, as if embalmed evermore in their separate eternal funeral parlors: separate, yet not separate, for was it not as if Poe's cry from Baltimore, in a mysterious manner, in the manner that the octet of a sonnet, say, is answered by its sestet, had already been answered, seven years before, by Keats's cry from Rome; so that according to the special reality of Sigbjørn's notebook at least, Poe's own death appeared like something extraformal, almost extraprofessional, an afterthought. Yet inerrably it was part of the same poem, the same story. "And yet the fatal prospect hangs . . ." "Severn, lift me up, for I am dying." "Lift them up, keep them away." Dr. Swell's Root Beer.

Good idea or not, there was no more room to implement his thoughts within this notebook (the notes on Poe and Richmond ran, through Fredericksburg, into his remarks upon Rome, the Mamertine Prison, and Keats's house, and vice versa), so Sigbjørn brought out another one from his trousers pocket.

This was a bigger notebook altogether, its paper stiffer and stronger, showing it dated from before the war, and he had brought it from America at the last minute, fearing that such might be hard to come by abroad.

In those days he had almost given up taking notes: every new notebook bought represented an impulse, soon to be overlaid, to write afresh; as a consequence he had accumulated a number of notebooks like this one at home, yet which were almost empty, which he had never taken with him on his more recent travels since the war, else a given trip would have seemed to start off with a destructive stoop, from the past, in its soul: this one had looked an exception so he'd packed it.

Just the same, he saw, it was not innocent of writing: several pages at the beginning were covered with his handwriting, so shaky and hysterical of appearance, that Sigbjørn had to put on his spectacles to read it. Seattle, he made out. July? 1939. Seattle! Sigbjørn swallowed some grappa hastily. Lo, death hath reared himself a throne in a strange city lying alone far down within the dim west, where the good and the bad and the best and the rest, have gone to their eternal worst! The lower is the true Seattle . . . Sigbjørn felt he could be excused for not fully appreciating Seattle, its mountain graces, in those days. For these were not notes he had found but the draft of a letter, written in the notebook because it was that type of letter possible for him to write only in a bar. A bar? Well, one might have called it a bar. For in those days, in Seattle, in the state of Washington, they still did not sell hard liquor in bars—as, for that matter to this day they did not, in Richmond, in the state of Virginia—which was half the gruesome and pointless point of his having been in the state of Washington. LIC-OFF-PREM, he thought. No, no, go not to Virginia Dare . . . Neither twist Pepso—tight-rooted!—for its poisonous bane. The letter dated—no question of his recognition of it, though whether he'd made another version and posted it he had forgotten—from absolutely the lowest ebb of those low tides of his life, a time marked by the baleful circumstance that the small legacy on which he then lived had been suddenly put in charge of a Los Angeles lawyer, to whom this letter indeed was written, his family, who considered him incompetent, having refused to have anything further to do with him, as, in effect, did the lawyer, who had sent him to a religious-minded family of Buchmanite tendencies in Seattle on the understanding he be entrusted with not more than 25c a day.

Dear Mr. Van Bosch:
   It is, psychologically, apart from anything else, of extreme urgency that I leave Seattle and come to Los Angeles to see you. I fear a complete mental collapse else. I have co-operated far beyond what I thought was the best of my ability here in the matter of liquor and I have also tried to work hard, so far, alas, without selling anything. I cannot say either that my ways have been as circumscribed exactly as I thought they would be by the Mackorkindales, who at least have seen my point of view on some matters, and if they pray for guidance on the very few occasions when they do see fit to exceed the stipulated 25c a day, they are at least sympathetic with my wishes to return. This may be because the elder Mackorkindale is literally and physically worn out following me through Seattle, or because you have failed to supply sufficient means for my board, but this is certainly as far as the sympathy goes. In short, they sympathize, but cannot honestly agree; nor will they advise you I should return. And in anything that applies to my writing—and this I find

almost the hardest to bear—I am met with the opinion that I "should put all that behind me." If they merely claimed to be abetting yourself or my parents in this it would be understandable, but this judgment is presented to me independently, somewhat blasphemously in my view—though without question they believe it—as coming directly from God, who stoops daily from on high to inform the Mackorkindales, if not in so many words, that as a serious writer I am lousy. Scenting some hidden truth about this, things being what they are, I would find it discouraging enough if it stopped there, and were not beyond that the hope held out, miracuously congruent also with that of my parents and yourself, that I could instead turn myself into a successful writer of advertisements. Since I cannot but feel, I repeat, and feel respectfully, that they are sincere in their beliefs, all I can say is that in this daily rapprochement with their Almighty in Seattle I hope some prayer that has slipped in by mistake to let the dreadful man for heaven's sake return to Los Angeles may eventually be answered. For I find it impossible to describe my spiritual isolation in this place, nor the gloom into which I have sunk. I enjoyed of course the seaside—the Mackorkindales doubtless reported to you that the Group were having a small rally in Bellingham (I wish you could go to Bellingham one day) but I have completely exhausted any therapeutic value in my stay. God knows I ought to know, I shall never recover in this place, isolated as I am from Primrose who, whatever you may say, I want with all my heart to make my wife. It was with the greatest of anguish that I discovered that her letters to me were being opened, finally, even having to hear lectures on her moral character by those who had read these letters, which I had thus been prevented from replying to, causing such pain to her as I cannot think of. This separation from her would be an unendurable agony, without anything else, but as things stand I can only say I would be better off in a prison, in the worst dungeon that could be imagined, than to be incarcerated in this damnable place with the highest suicide rate in the Union. Literally I am dying in this macabre hole and I appeal to you to send me, out of the money that is after all mine, enough that I may return. Surely I am not the only writer, there have been others in history whose ways have been misconstrued and who have failed . . . who have won through . . . success . . . publicans and sinners . . . I have no intention—

Sigbjørn broke off reading, and resisting an impulse to tear the letter out of the notebook, for that would loosen the pages, began meticulously to cross it out, line by line.

And now this was half done he began to be sorry. For now, damn it, he wouldn't be able to use it. Even when he'd written it he must have thought it a bit too good for poor old Van Bosch, though one admitted that wasn't saying much. Wherever or however he could have used it. And yet, what if they had found this letter—whoever "they" were—and put it, glass-encased, in a museum among *his* relics? Not much— Still, you never knew!—Well, they wouldn't do it now. Anyhow, perhaps he would remember enough of it . . . . "I am dying, absolutely perishing." "What have I done to them?" "My dear Sir." "The worst dungeon." And many others: and *dirty stinking Degenerate Bobs was here from Boston, North End, Mass. Warp son—!*

Sigbjørn finished his fifth unregenerate grappa and suddenly gave a loud laugh, a laugh which, as if it had realized itself it should become something more respectable, turned immediately into a prolonged—though on the whole relatively pleasurable—fit of coughing. . . .

II

The Short Story and the Creative Process

There are, so far as I know, three ways, and three ways only, of writing a story. You may take a plot and fit characters to it, or you may take a character and choose incidents and situations to develop it, or lastly . . . you may take a certain atmosphere and get action and persons to express it and realize it. I'll give you an example—The Merry Men. There I began with the feeling of one of those islands on the west coast of Scotland, and I gradually developed the story to express the sentiment with which that coast affected me.

—ROBERT LOUIS STEVENSON

The power to guess the unseen from the seen, to trace the implication of things, to judge the whole piece by the pattern, the condition of feeling life in general so completely that you are well on your way to knowing any particular corner of it—this cluster of gifts may almost be said to constitute experience. . . . Therefore, if I should certainly say to a novice, "Write from experience and experience only," I should feel that this was rather a tantalizing monition if I were not careful immediately to add, "Try to be one of the people on whom nothing is lost!"

—HENRY JAMES

ETHAN BRAND

A Chapter From an Abortive Romance

NATHANIEL HAWTHORNE (1804–1864)

Bartram the lime-burner, a rough, heavy-looking man, begrimed with charcoal, sat watching his kiln at nightfall, while his little son played at building houses with the scattered fragments of marble, when, on the hill-side below them, they heard a roar of laughter, not mirthful, but slow, and even solemn, like a wind shaking the boughs of the forest.

"Father, what is that?" asked the little boy, leaving his play, and pressing betwixt his father's knees.

"Oh, some drunken man, I suppose," answered the lime-burner; "some merry fellow from the bar-room in the village, who dared not laugh loud enough within doors lest he should blow the roof of the house off. So here he is, shaking his jolly sides at the foot of Graylock."

"But, father," said the child, more sensitive than the obtuse, middle-aged clown, "he does not laugh like a man that is glad. So the noise frightens me!"

"Don't be a fool, child!" cried his father, gruffly. "You will never make a man, I do believe; there is too much of your mother in you. I have known the rustling of a leaf startle you. Hark! Here comes the merry fellow now. You shall see that there is no harm in him."

Bartram and his little son, while they were talking thus, sat watching the same lime-kiln that had been the scene of Ethan Brand's solitary and meditative life, before he began his search for the Unpardonable Sin. Many years, as we have seen, had now elapsed, since that portentous night when the IDEA was first developed. The kiln, however, on the mountain-side, stood unimpaired, and was in nothing changed since he had thrown his dark thoughts into the intense glow of its furnace, and melted them, as it were, into the one thought that took possession of his life. It was a rude, round, tower-like structure about twenty feet high, heavily built of rough stones, and with a hillock of earth heaped about the larger part of its circumference; so that the blocks and fragments of marble might be drawn by cart-loads, and thrown in at the top. There was an opening at the bottom of the tower, like an oven-mouth, but large enough to admit a man in a stooping posture, and provided with a massive iron door. With the smoke and jets of flame issuing from the chinks and crevices of this door, which seemed to give admittance into the hill-side, it resembled nothing so much as the private entrance to the infernal regions, which the shepherds of the Delectable Mountains were accustomed to show to pilgrims.

There are many such lime-kilns in that tract of country, for the purpose of burning the white marble which composes a large part of the substance of the hills. Some of them, built years ago, and long deserted, with weeds growing in the vacant round of the interior, which is open to the sky, and grass and wild-flowers rooting themselves into the chinks of the stones, look already like relics of antiquity, and may yet be over-spread with the lichens of centuries to come. Others, where the lime-burner still feeds his daily and night-long fire, afford points of interest to the wanderer among the hills, who seats himself on a log of wood or a fragment of marble, to hold a chat with the solitary man. It is a lonesome, and, when the character is inclined to thought, may be an intensely thoughtful occupation; as it proved in the case of Ethan Brand, who had mused to such strange purpose, in days gone by, while the fire in this very kiln was burning.

The man who now watched the fire was of a different order, and troubled himself with no thoughts save the very few that were requisite to his business. At frequent intervals, he flung back the clashing weight of the iron door, and, turning his face from the insufferable glare, thrust in huge logs of oak, or stirred the immense brands with a long pole. Within the furnace were seen the curling and riotous flames, and the burning marble, almost molten with the intensity of heat; while without, the reflection of the fire quivered on the dark intricacy of the surrounding forest, and showed in the foreground a bright and ruddy little picture of the hut, the spring beside its door, the athletic and coal-begrimed figure of the lime-burner, and the half-frightened child, shrinking into the protection of his father's shadow. And when, again, the iron door was closed, then reappeared the tender light of the half-full moon, which vainly strove to trace out the indistinct shapes of the neighboring mountains; and, in the upper sky, there was a flitting congregation of clouds, still faintly tinged with the rosy sunset, though thus far down into the valley the sunshine had vanished long and long ago.

The little boy now crept still closer to his father, as footsteps were heard ascending the hill-side, and a human form thrust aside the bushes that clustered beneath the trees.

"Halloo! who is it?" cried the lime-burner, vexed at his son's timidity, yet half infected by it. "Come forward, and show yourself, like a man, or I'll fling this chunk of marble at your head!"

"You offer me a rough welcome," said a gloomy voice, as the unknown man drew nigh. "Yet I neither claim nor desire a kinder one, even at my own fireside."

To obtain a distincter view, Bartram threw open the iron door of the kiln, whence immediately issued a gush of fierce light, that smote full upon the stranger's face and figure. To a careless eye there appeared nothing very remarkable in his aspect, which was that of a man in a coarse, brown, country-made suit of clothes, tall and thin, with the staff and heavy shoes of a wayfarer. As he advanced, he fixed his eyes—which were very bright—intently upon the brightness of the furnace, as if he beheld, or expected to behold, some object worthy of note within it.

"Good evening, stranger," said the lime-burner; "whence come you, so late in the day?"

"I come from my search," answered the wayfarer; "for, at last, it is finished."

"Drunk!—or crazy!" muttered Bartram to himself. "I shall have trouble with the fellow. The sooner I drive him away, the better."

The little boy, all in a tremble, whispered to his father, and begged him to shut the door of the kiln, so that there might not be so much light; for that there was something in the man's face which he was afraid to look at, yet could not look away from. And, indeed, even the lime-burner's dull and torpid sense began to be impressed by an indescribable something in that thin, rugged, thoughtful visage, with the grizzled hair hanging wildly about it, and those deeply sunken eyes, which gleamed like fires within the entrance of a mysterious cavern. But, as he closed the door, the stranger turned towards him, and spoke in a quiet, familiar way, that made Bartram feel as if he were a sane and sensible man, after all.

"Your task draws to an end, I see," said he. "This marble has already been burning three days. A few hours more will convert the stone to lime."

"Why, who are you?" exclaimed the lime-burner. "You seem as well acquainted with my business as I am myself."

"And well I may be," said the stranger; "for I followed the same craft many a long year, and here, too, on this very spot. But you are a new-comer in these parts. Did you never hear of Ethan Brand?"

"The man that went in search of the Unpardonable Sin?" asked Bartram, with a laugh.

"The same," answered the stranger. "He has found what he sought, and therefore he comes back again."

"What! then you are Ethan Brand himself?" cried the lime-burner, in amazement. "I am a new-comer here, as you say, and they call it eighteen years since you left the foot of Graylock. But, I can tell you, the good folks still talk about Ethan Brand, in the village yonder, and what a strange errand took him away from his lime-kiln. Well, and so you have found the Unpardonable Sin?"

"Even so!" said the stranger, calmly.

"If the question is a fair one," proceeded Bartram, "where might it be?"

Ethan Brand laid his finger on his own heart.

"Here!" replied he.

And then, without mirth in his countenance, but as if moved by an involuntary recognition of the infinite absurdity of seeking throughout the world for what was the closest of all things to himself, and looking into every heart, save his own, for what was hidden in no other breast, he broke into a laugh of scorn. It was the same slow, heavy laugh, that had almost appalled the lime-burner when it heralded the wayfarer's approach.

The solitary mountain-side was made dismal by it. Laughter, when out of place, mistimed, or bursting forth from a disordered state of feeling, may be the most terrible modulation of the human voice. The laughter of one asleep, even if it be a little child,—the madman's laugh,—the wild, screaming laugh of a born idiot,—are sounds that we sometimes tremble to hear, and would always willingly forget. Poets have imagined no utterance of fiends or hobgoblins so fearfully appropriate as a laugh. And even the obtuse lime-burner felt his nerves shaken, as this strange man looked inward at his own heart, and burst into laughter that rolled away into the night, and was indistinctly reverberated among the hills.

"Joe," said he to his little son, "scamper down to the tavern in the village, and tell the jolly fellows there that Ethan Brand has come back, and that he has found the Unpardonable Sin!"

The boy darted away on his errand, to which Ethan Brand made no objection, nor seemed hardly to notice it. He sat on a log of wood, looking steadfastly at the iron door of the kiln. When the child was out of sight, and his swift and light footsteps ceased to be heard treading first on the fallen leaves and then on the rocky mountain-path, the lime-burner began to regret his departure. He felt that the little fellow's presence had been a barrier between his guest and himself, and that he must now deal, heart to heart, with a man who, on his own confession, had committed the one only crime for which Heaven could afford no mercy. That crime, in its indistinct blackness, seemed to overshadow him. The lime-burner's own sins rose up within him, and made his memory riotous with a throng of evil shapes that asserted their kindred with the Master Sin, whatever it might be, which it was within the scope of man's corrupted nature to conceive and cherish. They were all of one family; they went to and fro between his breast and Ethan Brand's, and carried dark greetings from one to the other.

Then Bartram remembered the stories which had grown traditionary in reference to this strange man, who had come upon him like a shadow of the night, and was making himself at home in his old place, after so long absence, that the dead people, dead and buried for years, would have had more right to be at home, in any familiar spot, than he. Ethan Brand, it was said, had conversed with Satan himself in the lurid blaze of this very kiln. The legend had been matter of mirth heretofore, but looked grisly now. According to this tale, before Ethan Brand departed on his search, he had been accustomed to evoke a fiend from the hot furnace of the lime-kiln, night after night, in order to confer with him about the Unpardonable Sin; the man and the fiend each laboring to frame the image of some mode of guilt which could neither be atoned for nor forgiven. And, with the first gleam of light upon the mountain-top, the fiend crept in at the iron door, there to abide the intensest element of fire until again summoned forth to share in the dreadful task of extending man's possible guilt beyond the scope of Heaven's else infinite mercy.

While the lime-burner was struggling with the horror of these thoughts, Ethan Brand rose from the log, and flung open the door of the kiln. The action was in such accordance with the idea in Bartram's mind, that he almost expected to see the Evil One issue forth, red-hot, from the raging furnace.

"Hold! hold!" cried he, with a tremulous attempt to laugh; for he was ashamed of his fears, although they overmastered him. "Don't, for mercy's sake, bring out your Devil now!"

"Man!" sternly replied Ethan Brand, "what need have I of the Devil? I have left him behind me, on my track. It is with such half-way sinners as you that he busies himself. Fear not, because I open the door. I do but act by old custom, and am going to trim your fire, like a lime-burner, as I was once."

He stirred the vast coals, thrust in more wood, and bent forward to gaze into the hollow prison-house of the fire, regardless of the fierce glow that reddened upon his face. The lime-burner sat watching him, and half suspected this strange guest of a purpose, if not to evoke a fiend, at least to plunge bodily into the flames, and thus vanish from the sight of man. Ethan Brand, however, drew quietly back, and closed the door of the kiln.

"I have looked," said he, "into many a human heart that was seven times hotter with sinful passions than yonder furnace is with fire. But I found not there what I sought. No, not the Unpardonable Sin!"

"What is the Unpardonable Sin?" asked the lime-burner; and then he shrank farther from his companion, trembling lest his question should be answered.

"It is a sin that grew within my own breast," replied Ethan Brand, standing erect, with a pride that distinguishes all enthusiasts of his stamp. "A sin that grew nowhere else! The sin of an intellect that triumphed over the sense of brotherhood with man and reverence for God, and sacrificed everything to its own mighty claims! The only sin that deserves a recompense of immortal agony! Freely, were it to do again, would I incur the guilt. Unshrinkingly I accept the retribution!"

"The man's head is turned," muttered the lime-burner to himself. "He may be a sinner like the rest of us,—nothing more likely,—but, I'll be sworn, he is a madman too."

Nevertheless, he felt uncomfortable at his situation, alone with Ethan Brand on the wild mountain-side, and was right glad to hear the rough murmur of tongues, and the footsteps of what seemed a pretty numerous party, stumbling over the stones and rustling through the underbrush. Soon appeared the whole lazy regiment that was wont to infest the village tavern, comprehending three or four individuals who had drunk flip beside the bar-room fire through all the winters, and smoked their pipes beneath the stoop through all the summers, since Ethan Brand's departure. Laughing boisterously, and mingling all their voices together in unceremonious talk, they now burst into the moonshine and narrow streaks of firelight that illuminated the open space before the lime-kiln. Bartram set the door ajar again, flooding the spot with light, that the whole company might get a fair view of Ethan Brand, and he of them.

There, among other old acquaintances, was a once ubiquitous man, now almost extinct, but whom we were formerly sure to encounter at the hotel of every thriving village throughout the country. It was the stage-agent. The present specimen of the genus was a wilted and smoke-dried man, wrinkled and red-nosed, in a smartly cut, brown, bob-tailed coat, with brass buttons, who for a length of time unknown, had kept his desk and corner in the bar-room, and was still puffing what seemed to be the same cigar that he had lighted twenty years before. He had great fame as a dry joker, though, perhaps, less on account of any intrinsic humor than from a certain flavor of brandy-toddy and tobacco-smoke, which impregnated all his ideas and expressions, as well as his person. Another well-remembered, though strangely altered, face was that of Lawyer Giles, as people still called him in courtesy; an elderly ragamuffin, in his soiled shirt-sleeves and tow-cloth trousers. This poor fellow had been an attorney, in what he called his better days, a sharp practitioner, and in great vogue among the village litigants; but flip, and sling, and toddy, and cocktails, imbibed at all hours, morning, noon, and night, had caused him to slide from intellectual to various kinds and degrees of bodily labor, till at last, to adopt his own phrase, he slid into a soap-vat. In other words, Giles was now a soap-boiler, in a small way. He had come to be but the fragment of a human being, a part of one foot having been chopped off by an axe, and an entire hand torn away by the devilish grip of a steam-engine. Yet, though the corporeal hand was gone, a spiritual member remained; for, stretching forth the stump, Giles steadfastly averred that he felt an invisible thumb and fingers with as vivid a sensation as before the real ones were amputated. A maimed and miserable wretch he was; but one, nevertheless, whom the world could not trample on, and had no right to scorn, either in this or any previous stage of his misfortunes, since he had still kept up the courage and spirit of a man, asking nothing in charity, and with his one hand—and that the left one—fought a stern battle against want and hostile circumstances.

Among the throng, too, came another personage, who, with certain points of similarity to Lawyer Giles, had many more of difference. It was the village doctor; a man of some fifty years, whom, at an earlier period of his life, we introduced as paying a professional visit to Ethan Brand during the latter's supposed insanity. He was now a purple-visaged, rude, and brutal, yet half-gentlemanly figure, with something wild, ruined, and desperate in his talk, and in all the details of his gesture and manners. Brandy possessed this man like an evil spirit, and made him as surly and savage as a wild beast, and as miserable as a lost soul; but there was supposed to be in him such wonderful skill, such native gifts of healing, beyond any which medical science could impart, that society caught hold of him, and would not let him sink out of its reach. So, swaying to and fro upon his horse, and grumbling thick accents at the bedside, he visited all the sick-chambers for miles about among the mountain towns, and sometimes raised a dying man, as it were, by miracle, or quite as often, no doubt, sent his patient to a grave that was dug many a year too soon. The doctor had an everlasting pipe in his mouth, and, as somebody said, in allusion to his habit of swearing, it was always alight with hell-fire.

These three worthies pressed forward, and greeted Ethan Brand each after his own fashion, earnestly inviting him to partake of the contents of a certain black bottle, in which, as they averred, he would find something far better worth seeking for than the Unpardonable Sin. No mind, which has wrought itself by intense and solitary meditation into a high state of enthusiasm, can endure the kind of contact with low and vulgar modes of thought and feeling to which Ethan Brand was now subjected. It made him doubt—and, strange to say, it was a painful doubt—whether he had indeed found the Unpardonable Sin, and found it within himself. The whole question on which he had exhausted life, and more than life, looked like a delusion.

"Leave me," he said bitterly, "ye brute beasts, that have made yourselves so, shrivelling up your souls with fiery liquors! I have done with you. Years and years ago, I groped into your hearts and found nothing there for my purpose. Get ye gone!"

"Why, you uncivil scoundrel," cried the fierce doctor, "is that the way you respond to the kindness of your best friends? Then let me tell you the truth. You have no more found the Unpardonable Sin than yonder boy Joe has. You are but a crazy fellow,—I told you so twenty years ago,—neither better nor worse than a crazy fellow, and the fit companion of old Humphrey, here!"

He pointed to an old man, shabbily dressed, with long white hair, thin visage, and unsteady eyes. For some years past this aged person had been wandering about among the hills, inquiring of all travelers whom he met for his daughter. The girl, it seemed, had gone off with a company of circus-performers, and occasionally tidings of her came to the village, and fine stories were told of her glittering appearance as she rode on horseback in the ring, or performed marvelous feats on the tight-rope.

The white-haired father now approached Ethan Brand, and gazed unsteadily into his face.

"They tell me you have been all over the earth," said he, wringing his hands with earnestness. "You must have seen my daughter, for she makes a grand figure in the world, and everybody goes to see her. Did she send any word to her old father, or say when she was coming back?"

Ethan Brand's eye quailed beneath the old man's. That daughter, from whom he so earnestly desired a word of greeting, was the Esther of our tale, the very girl whom, with such cold and remorseless purpose, Ethan Brand had made the subject of a psychological experiment, and wasted, absorbed, and perhaps annihilated her soul, in the process.

"Yes," murmured he, turning away from the hoary wanderer, "it is no delusion. There is an Unpardonable Sin!"

While these things were passing, a merry scene was going forward in the area of cheerful light, beside the spring and before the door of the hut. A number of the youth of the village, young men and girls, had hurried up the hill-side, impelled by curiosity to see Ethan Brand, the hero of so many a legend familiar to their childhood.

Finding nothing, however, very remarkable in his aspect,—nothing but a sunburnt wayfarer, in plain garb and dusty shoes, who sat looking into the fire as if he fancied pictures among the coals,—these young people speedily grew tired of observing him. As it happened, there was other amusement at hand. An old German Jew, traveling with a diorama on his back, was passing down the mountain-road towards the village just as the party turned aside from it, and, in hopes of eking out the profits of the day, the showman had kept them company to the lime-kiln.

"Come, old Dutchman," cried one of the young men, "let us see your pictures, if you can swear they are worth looking at!"

"Oh yes, Captain," answered the Jew,—whether as a matter of courtesy or craft, he styled everybody Captain,—"I shall show you, indeed, some very superb pictures!"

So, placing his box in a proper position, he invited the young men and girls to look through the glass orifices of the machine, and proceeded to exhibit a series of the most outrageous scratchings and daubings, as specimens of the fine arts, that ever an itinerant showman had the face to impose upon his circle of spectators. The pictures were worn out, moreover, tattered, full of cracks and wrinkles, dingy with tobacco-smoke, and otherwise in a most pitiable condition. Some purported to be cities, public edifices, and ruined castles in Europe; others represented Napoleon's battles and Nelson's sea-fights; and in the midst of these would be seen a gigantic, brown, hairy hand,—which might have been mistaken for the Hand of Destiny, though, in truth, it was only the showman's,—pointing its forefinger to various scenes of the conflict, while its owner gave historical illustrations. When, with much merriment at its abominable deficiency of merit, the exhibition was concluded, the German bade little Joe put his head into the box. Viewed through the magnifying-glasses, the boy's round, rosy visage assumed the strangest imaginable aspect of an immense Titanic child, the mouth grinning broadly, and the eyes and every other feature overflowing with fun at the joke. Suddenly, however, that merry face turned pale, and its expression changed to horror, for this easily impressed and excitable child had become sensible that the eye of Ethan Brand was fixed upon him through the glass.

"You make the little man to be afraid, Captain," said the German Jew, turning up the dark and strong outline of his visage from his stooping posture. "But look again, and, by chance, I shall cause you to see somewhat that is very fine, upon my word!"

Ethan Brand gazed into the box for an instant, and then starting back, looked fixedly at the German. What had he seen? Nothing, apparently; for a curious youth, who had peeped in almost at the same moment, beheld only a vacant space of canvas.

"I remember you now," muttered Ethan Brand to the showman.

"Ah, Captain," whispered the Jew of Nuremberg, with a dark smile, "I find it to be a heavy matter in my show-box,—this Unpardonable Sin! By my faith, Captain, it has wearied my shoulders, this long day, to carry it over the mountain."

"Peace," answered Ethan Brand, sternly, "or get thee into the furnace yonder!"

The Jew's exhibition had scarcely concluded, when a great, elderly dog—who seemed to be his own master, as no person in the company laid claim to him—saw fit to render himself the object of public notice. Hitherto, he had shown himself a very quiet, well-disposed old dog, going round from one to another, and, by way of being sociable, offering his rough head to be patted by any kindly hand that would take so much trouble. But now, all of a sudden, this grave and venerable quadruped, of his own mere motion, and without the slightest suggestion from anybody else, began to run round after his tail, which, to heighten the absurdity of the proceeding, was a great deal shorter than it should have been. Never was seen such headlong eagerness in pursuit of an object that could not possibly be attained; never was heard such a tremendous outbreak of growling, snarling, barking, and snapping,—as if one end of the ridiculous brute's body were at deadly and most unforgivable enmity with the other. Faster and faster, round about went the cur; and faster and still faster fled the unapproachable brevity of his tail; and louder and fiercer grew his yells of rage and animosity; until, utterly exhausted, and as far from the goal as ever, the foolish old dog ceased his performance as suddenly as he had begun it. The next moment he was as mild, quiet, sensible, and respectable in his deportment, as when he first scraped acquaintance with the company.

As may be supposed, the exhibition was greeted with universal laughter, clapping of hands, and shouts of encore, to which the canine performer responded by wagging all that there was to wag of his tail, but appeared totally unable to repeat his very successful effort to amuse the spectators.

Meanwhile, Ethan Brand had resumed his seat upon the log, and moved, it might be, by a perception of some remote analogy between his own case and that of this self-pursuing cur, he broke into the awful laugh, which, more than any other token, expressed the condition of his inward being. From that moment, the merriment of the party was at an end; they stood aghast, dreading lest the inauspicious sound should be reverberated around the horizon, and that mountain would thunder it to mountain, and so the horror be prolonged upon their ears. Then, whispering one to another that it was late,—that the moon was almost down,—that the August night was growing chill,—they hurried homewards, leaving the lime-burner and little Joe to deal as they might with their unwelcome guest. Save for these three human beings, the open space on the hill-side was a solitude, set in a vast gloom of forest. Beyond that darksome verge, the firelight glimmered on the stately trunks and almost black foliage of pines, intermixed with the lighter verdure of sapling oaks, maples, and poplars, while here and there lay the gigantic corpses of dead trees, decaying on the leaf-strewn soil. And it seemed to little Joe—a timorous and imaginative child—that the silent forest was holding its breath until some fearful thing should happen.

Ethan Brand thrust more wood into the fire, and closed the door of the kiln; then looking over his shoulder at the lime-burner and his son, he bade, rather than advised, them to retire to rest.

"For myself, I cannot sleep," said he. "I have matters that it concerns me to meditate upon. I will watch the fire, as I used to do in the old time."

"And call the Devil out of the furnace to keep you company, I suppose," muttered Bartram, who had been making intimate acquaintance with the black bottle above mentioned. "But watch, if you like, and call as many devils as you like! For my part, I shall be all the better for a snooze. Come, Joe!"

As the boy followed his father into the hut, he looked back at the wayfarer, and the tears came into his eyes, for his tender spirit had an intuition of the bleak and terrible loneliness in which this man had enveloped himself.

When they had gone, Ethan Brand sat listening to the crackling of the kindled wood, and looking at the little spirts of fire that issued through the chinks of the door. These trifles, however, once so familiar, had but the slightest hold of his attention, while deep within his mind he was reviewing the gradual but marvelous change that had been wrought upon him by the search to which he had devoted himself. He remembered how the night dew had fallen upon him,—how the dark forest had whispered to him,—how the stars had gleamed upon him,—a simple and loving man, watching his fire in the years gone by, and ever musing as it burned. He remembered with what tenderness, with what love and sympathy for mankind, and what pity for human guilt and woe, he had first begun to contemplate those ideas which afterwards became the inspiration of his life; with what reverence he had then looked into the heart of man, viewing it as a temple originally divine, and, however desecrated, still to be held sacred by a brother; with what awful fear he had deprecated the success of his pursuit, and prayed that the Unpardonable Sin might never be revealed to him. Then ensued that vast intellectual development, which, in its progress, disturbed the counterpoise between his mind and heart. The Idea that possessed his life had operated as a means of education; it had gone on cultivating his powers to the highest point of which they were susceptible; it had raised him from the level of an unlettered laborer to stand on a star-lit eminence, whither the philosophers of the earth, laden with the lore of universities, might vainly strive to clamber after him. So much for the intellect! But where was the heart? That, indeed, had withered,—had contracted,—had hardened,—had perished! It had ceased to partake of the universal throb. He had lost his hold of the magnetic chain of humanity. He was no longer a brother-man, opening the chambers or the dungeons of our common nature by the key of holy sympathy, which gave him a right to share in all its secrets; he was now a cold observer, looking on mankind as the subject of his experiment, and, at length, converting man and woman to be his puppets, and pulling the wires that moved them to such degrees of crime as were demanded for his study.

Thus Ethan Brand became a fiend. He began to be so from the moment that his moral nature had ceased to keep the pace of improvement with his intellect. And now, as his highest effort and inevitable development,—as the bright and gorgeous flower, and rich, delicious fruit of his life's labor,—he had produced the Unpardonable Sin!

"What more have I to seek? what more to achieve?" said Ethan Brand to himself. "My task is done, and well done!"

Starting from the log with a certain alacrity in his gait and ascending the hillock of earth that was raised against the stone circumference of the lime-kiln, he thus reached the top of the structure. It was a space of perhaps ten feet across, from edge to edge, presenting a view of the upper surface of the immense mass of broken marble with which the kiln was heaped. All these innumerable blocks and fragments of marble were red-hot and vividly on fire, sending up great spouts of blue flame, which quivered aloft and danced madly, as within a magic circle, and sank and rose again, with continual and multitudinous activity. As the lonely man bent forward over this terrible body of fire, the blasting heat smote up against his person with a breath that, it might be supposed, would have scorched and shrivelled him up in a moment.

Ethan Brand stood erect, and raised his arms on high. The blue flames played upon his face, and imparted the wild and ghastly light which alone could have suited its expression; it was that of a fiend on the verge of plunging into his gulf of intensest torment.

"O Mother Earth," cried he, "who art no more my Mother, and into whose bosom this frame shall never be resolved! O mankind, whose brotherhood I have cast off, and trampled thy great heart beneath my feet! O stars of heaven, that shone on me of old, as if to light me onward and upward!—farewell all, and forever. Come, deadly element of Fire,—henceforth my familiar friend! Embrace me, as I do thee!"

That night the sound of a fearful peal of laughter rolled heavily through the sleep of the lime-burner and his little son; dim shapes of horror and anguish haunted their dreams, and seemed still present in the rude hovel, when they opened their eyes to the daylight.

"Up, boy, up!" cried the lime-burner, staring about him. "Thank Heaven, the night is gone, at last; and rather than pass such another, I would watch my lime-kiln, wide awake, for a twelvemonth. This Ethan Brand, with his humbug of an Unpardonable Sin, has done me no such mighty favor, in taking my place!"

He issued from the hut, followed by little Joe, who kept fast hold of his father's hand. The early sunshine was already pouring its gold upon the mountain-tops, and though the valleys were still in shadow, they smiled cheerfully in the promise of the bright day that was hastening onward. The village, completely shut in by hills, which swelled away gently about it, looked as if it had rested peacefully in the hollow of the great hand of Providence. Every dwelling was distinctly visible; the little spires of the two churches pointed upwards, and caught a fore-glimmering of brightness from the sun-gilt skies upon their gilded weathercocks. The tavern was astir, and the figure of the old, smoke-dried stage-agent, cigar in mouth, was seen beneath the stoop. Old Graylock was glorified with a golden cloud upon his head. Scattered likewise over the breasts of the surrounding mountains, there were heaps of hoary mist, in fantastic shapes, some of them far down into the valley, others high up towards the summits, and still others, of the same family of mist or cloud, hovering in the gold radiance of the upper atmosphere. Stepping from one to another of the clouds that rested on the hills, and thence to the loftier brotherhood that sailed in air, it seemed almost as if a mortal man might thus ascend into the heavenly regions. Earth was so mingled with sky that it was a day-dream to look at it.

To supply that charm of the familiar and homely, which Nature so readily adopts into a scene like this, the stage-coach was rattling down the mountain-road, and the driver sounded his horn, while Echo caught up the notes, and intertwined them into a rich and varied and elaborate harmony, of which the original performer could lay claim to little share. The great hills played a concert among themselves, each contributing a strain of airy sweetness.

Little Joe's face brightened at once.

"Dear father," cried he, skipping cheerily to and fro, "that strange man is gone, and the sky and the mountains all seem glad of it!"

"Yes," growled the lime-burner, with an oath, "but he has let the fire go down, and no thanks to him if five hundred bushels of lime are not spoiled. If I catch the fellow hereabouts again, I shall feel like tossing him into the furnace!"

With his long pole in his hand, he ascended to the top of the kiln. After a moment's pause, he called to his son.

"Come up here, Joe!" said he.

So little Joe ran up the hillock, and stood by his father's side. The marble was all burnt into perfect, snow-white lime. But on its surface, in the midst of the circle,— snow-white too, and thoroughly converted into lime,—lay a human skeleton, in the attitude of a person who, after long toil, lies down to long repose. Within the ribs— strange to say—was the shape of a human heart.

"Was the fellow's heart made of marble?" cried Bartram, in some perplexity at this phenomenon. "At any rate, it is burnt into what looks like special good lime; and, taking all the bones together, my kiln is half a bushel the richer for him."

So saying, the rude lime-burner lifted his pole, and, letting it fall upon the skeleton, the relics of Ethan Brand were crumbled into fragments.

SOURCE MATERIAL FOR "ETHAN BRAND"

FROM THE NOTEBOOKS OF NATHANIEL HAWTHORNE*

1835.—Amid the seeming confusion of our mysterious world, individuals are so nicely adjusted to a system, and systems to one another and to a whole, that, by stepping aside for a moment, a man exposes himself to a fearful risk of losing his place forever. Like Wakefield, he may become, as it were, the Outcast of the Universe.

1835.—It might be stated, as the closing circumstance of a tale, that the body of one of the characters had been petrified, and still existed in that state.

1837.— . . . Like all other men around whom an engrossing purpose wreathes itself, he [the portrait painter] was insulated from the mass of human kind. He had no aim—no pleasure—no sympathies—but what were ultimately connected with his art. Though gentle in manner and upright in intent and action, he did not possess kindly feelings; his heart was cold. . . . It is not good for man to cherish a solitary ambition. Unless there be those around him by whose example he may regulate himself, his thoughts, desires, and hopes will become extravagant, and he the semblance, perhaps the reality, of a madman. Reading other bosoms with an acuteness almost preternatural, the painter failed to see the disorder of his own. . . .

July 26, 1838.— . . . This morning an under-witted old man met me on a walk, and held a pretty long conversation, insisting upon shaking hands (to which I was averse, lest his hand should not be clean), and insisting on his right to do so, as being a "friend of mankind." He was an old gray, bald-headed, wrinkle-visaged figure, decently dressed, with cowhide shoes, a coat on one arm, and an umbrella on the other; and said that he was going to see a widow in the neighborhood. Finding that I was not provided with a wife, he recommended a certain "maid" of forty years, who had 300 acres of land. He spoke of his children, who are proprietors of a circus establishment, and have taken a granddaughter to bring up in their way of life; and he gave me a message to tell them, in case we should meet. While this old man is wandering among the hills, his children are in the gaze of multitudes. He told me the place where he was born, directing me to it by pointing to a wreath of mist which lay on the side of a mountain ridge, which he termed the "smoke yonder." Speaking of the widow, he said, "My wife has been dead these seven years, and why should not I enjoy myself a little." His manner was full of quirks and quips and eccentricities, waving his umbrella and gesticulating strangely, with a great deal of action. I suppose, to help his natural foolishness, he had been drinking. We parted, he exhorting me not to forget his message to his sons, and I shouting after him a request to be remembered to the widow. Conceive something tragical to be talked about; and much might be made of this interview, in a wild road among the hills; with Graylock at no great distance, looking sombre and angry by reason of the gray, heavy mist upon his head. . . .

July 29, 1838.—Remarkable characters:—a disagreeable figure, waning from middle-age, clad in a pair of tow homespun pantaloons and very dirty shirt, bare-foot, and

* For notes on the source material of "Ethan Brand" see *Notes and Questions,* page 364.

with one of his feet maimed by an axe; also, an arm amputated two or three inches below the elbow. His beard of a week's growth, grim and grisly, with a general effect of black;—altogether a filthy and disgusting object. Yet he has signs of having been a handsome man in his idea; though now such a beastly figure that, probably, no living thing but his great dog would touch him without an effort. Coming to the stoop, where several persons were sitting,—"Good morning, gentlemen," said the wretch. Nobody answered for a time, till at last one said, "I don't know who you speak to;—not me, I'm sure;" meaning that he did not claim to be a gentleman. "Why, I thought you'd all speak at once," replied the figure laughing. So he sat himself down on the lower step of the stoop, and began to talk; and the conversation being turned upon his bare feet, by one of the company, he related the story of his losing his toes by the glancing aside of an axe, and with what grim fortitude he bore it. Then he made a transition to the loss of his arm; and setting his teeth and drawing in his breath, said that the pain was dreadful; but this, too, he seems to have borne like an Indian; and a person testified to his fortitude by saying that he did not suppose that there was any feeling in him, from observing how he bore it. The man spoke of the pain of cutting the muscles, and the particular agony at one moment, while the bone was being sawed asunder; and there was a strange expression of remembered agony, as he shrugged his half-limb, and described the matter. Afterwards, in a reply to a question of mine whether he still seemed to feel the hand that had been amputated, he answered that he did, always—and baring the stump, he moved the severed muscles, saying, "There is the thumb, there the forefinger" &c. Then he talked to me about phrenology, of which he seems a firm believer and skilful practitioner, telling how he had hit upon the true characters of many people. There was a great deal of sense and acuteness in his talk, and something of elevation in his expression; perhaps a studied elevation—and a sort of courtesy in his manner; but his sense had something out of the way in it; something wild, and ruined, and desperate, in his talk, though I can hardly say what it was. There was something of the gentleman and man of intellect in his deep degradation; and a pleasure in intellectual pursuits, and an acuteness and trained judgment, which bespoke a mind once strong and cultivated. "My study is man," said he. And looking at me "I do not know your name," said he, "but there is something of the hawk-eye about you too." This man was formerly a lawyer in good practice, but taking to drinking, was reduced to this lowest state. Yet not the lowest; for, after the amputation of his arm, being advised by divers persons to throw himself upon the public for support, he told them that, even if he should lose his other arm, he would still be able to support himself and a waiter. Certainly he is a strong minded and iron-constitutioned man; but, looking at the stump of his arm, he said "that the pain of the mind was a thousand times greater than the pain of the body—That hand could make the pen go fast," said he. Among people in general, he does not seem to have any greater consideration in his ruin, for the sake of his former standing in society. He supports himself by making soap; and on account of the offals used in that business, there is probably rather an evil smell in his domicile. Talking about a dead horse, near his house, he said that he could not bear the scent of it. "I should not think you could smell carrion in that house," said a stage-agent. Whereupon the soap-maker dropped his head, with a little snort, as it were, of wounded feeling; but immediately said that he took all in good part. There was an old squire of the village, a lawyer probably, whose demeanor was different—with a distance, yet a kindliness; for he remembered the times when they met on equal terms. "You and I," said the squire, alluding to their respective troubles and sicknesses, "would have died long ago, if we had not had the courage to live." The poor devil kept talking to me long after everybody else had left the stoop, giving vent to much practical philosophy and just observation on the ways of men, mingled with rather more assumption of literature and cultivation, than belonged to the present condition of his mind. Meantime his great dog—a cleanly looking, and not ill-bred dog, being the only decent attribute appertaining to his master—a well natured dog, too, and receiving civilly any demonstration of courtesy from other people, though preserving a certain distance of deportment—this great dog grew weary of his master's lengthy talk, and expressed his impatience to be gone, by thrusting himself between his legs, rolling over on his back, seizing his ragged trowsers, or playfully taking his maimed bare foot into his mouth—using, in short, the kindly and humorous freedom of a friend, with a wretch to whom all are free enough, but none other kind. His master rebuked him, but with kindness too, and not so that the dog felt himself bound to desist, though he seemed willing to allow his master all the time that could possibly be spared. And, at last, having said many times that he must go and shave and dress himself—and as his beard had been at least a week growing, it might have seemed almost a week's work to get rid of it—he rose from the stoop, and went his way, a forlorn and miserable thing in the light of the cheerful summer Sabbath morning. Yet he seems to keep his spirits up, and still preserves himself a man among men, asking nothing from them—nor is it clearly perceptible what right they have to scorn him, though he seems to acquiesce, in a sort, in their doing so. And yet he cannot wholly have lost his self-respect· and doubtless there were persons on the stoop more grovelling than himself. . . .

July 30, 1838.— . . . A little boy, named Joe, who haunts about the bar-room and the stoop, about four years old, in a thin short jacket, and full-breeched trowsers, and bare feet. The men plague him, and put quids of tobacco in his mouth, under pretence of giving him a fig, and he gets enraged, and utters a peculiar sharp, spiteful cry, and strikes at them with a stick, to their great mirth. He is always in trouble, yet will not keep away. They dispatch him with two or three cents to buy candy, and nuts and raisins. They set him down in a niche of the door, and tell him to remain there a day and a half; he sits down very demurely, as if he really meant to fulfil his penance;—but, a moment after, behold there is little Joe, capering across the street to join two or three boys who are playing in a wagon. Take this boy as the germ of a tavern-haunter, a country roué, to spend a wild and brutal youth, ten years of his prime in the State-Prison, and his age in the poor-house. . . .

July 31, 1838.— . . . In the deep valleys of this neighborhood, where the shadows at sunset are thrown from mountain to mountain, the clouds have a beautiful effect, flitting high over the valley, bright with heavenly gold;—it seems as if the soul might soar up from the gloom, and alight upon them, and soar away. Walking along one of the valleys, the other evening, while a pretty fresh breeze blew along it, the clouds that were skimming the length of the valley, over my head, seemed to conform themselves to the valley's shape. . . .

A steam engine in a factory to be supposed to possess a malignant spirit; it catches one man's arm, and pulls it off; seizes another by the coat-tails, and almost grapples him bodily;—catches a girl by the hair, and scalps her;—and finally draws a man, and crushes him to death. . . .

The one-armed soap-maker, lawyer Haynes, wears an iron hook, which serves him instead of a hand for the purposes of holding on. They nickname him Black Hawk. . . .

Doctors walk about the village with their saddle-bags on their arms. One always with a pipe in his mouth. . . .

August 11, 1838.— ... A doctor, a stout, tall, round-paunched, red-faced, brutal looking old fellow, who gets drunk daily. He sat down on the step of our stoop, looking surly, and speaking to nobody; then got up and walked homeward, with a surly swagger, and a slight unevenness of track, attended by a fine Newfoundland dog. . . .

August 31, 1838.—A ride, on Tuesday, to Shelburne Falls—twenty-two miles, or thereabouts, distant. Started at about eight o'clock in a wagon with Mr. Leach and Mr. Buck. Our road lay over the Green Mountain; the long ridge of which was made awful by a dark, heavy, threatening cloud, apparently rolled and condensed along the whole summit. As we ascended the zig-zag road, we looked behind, at every opening through the forest, and beheld a wide landscape of mountain-swells, and valleys intermixt, and old Graylock, and the whole of Saddle-back. Over this wide scene, there was a general gloom; but there was a continual vicissitude of bright sunshine flitting over it; now resting for a brief space on portions of the heights, now flooding the valleys with green brightness, now marking out distinctly each dwelling, and the hotels, and then two small brick churches of the distant village—denoting its prosperity, while all around seemed under adverse fortunes. But we, who stood so elevated above mortal things, and saw so wide and far, could see the sunshine of prosperity departing from one spot and rolling toward another; so that we could not think it much matter which spot were sunny or gloomy at any one moment.

The top of this Green Mountain is a long ridge, marked on the county map as 2160 ft. above the sea; the summit is occupied by a valley, not very deep, but one or two miles wide, composing the town of Lebrida. Here there are respectable farmers, though it is a rough, and must be a bleak place. The first house, after reaching the summit, is a small, homely tavern, kept by P. Witt. We left our horse in the shed; and entering the little unpainted bar-room, we heard a voice, in a strange outlandish accent, explaining a diorama. It was an old man, with a full, gray-bearded countenance; and Mr. Leach exclaimed "Ah here's the old Dutchman again!" And he answered "Yes, Captain, here's the old Dutchman,"—tho' by the way, he is a German, and travels the country with this diorama, in a wagon; and had recently been at South Adams, and was now returning from Saratoga Springs. We looked through the glass orifice of his machine, while he exhibited a succession of the very worst scratchings and daubings that can be imagined—worn out, too, and full of cracks and wrinkles, besmeared with tobacco smoke, and every otherwise dilapidated. There were none in a later fashion than thirty years since, except some figures that had been cut from tailors' show-bills. There were views of cities and edifices in Europe, and ruins,—and of Napoleon's battles and Nelson's sea-fights; in the midst of which would be seen a gigantic, brown, hairy hand—the Hand of Destiny—pointing at the principal points of the conflict, while the old Dutchman explained. He gave considerable dramatic effect to his descriptions, but his accent and intonation cannot be written. He seemed to take an interest and pride in his exhibition; yet when the utter and ludicrous miserability thereof made us laugh, he joined in the joke very readily. When the last picture had been exhibited, he caused a country boor, who stood gaping beside the machine, to put his head within it, and thrust his tongue out. The head becoming gigantic, a singular effect was produced.

The old Dutchman's exhibition over, a great dog—apparently an elderly dog—suddenly made himself the object of notice, evidently in rivalship of the Dutchman. He had seemed to be a good-natured, quiet kind of dog, offering his head to be patted by those kindly disposed towards him. This great, old dog, suddenly and of his own

motion, began to run round after his own not very long tail, with the utmost eagerness; and catching hold of it, he growled furiously at it, and still continued to circle
round, growling and snarling, with increasing rage, as if one half of his body were
at deadly enmity with the other. Faster and faster went he round and round-about,
growling still fiercer, till at last he ceased in a state of utter exhaustion; but no sooner
had his exhibition finished, than he became the same mild, quiet, sensible old dog as
before; and no one could have suspected him of such nonsense as getting enraged with
his own tail. He was first taught this trick by attaching a bell to the end of his tail;
but he now commences entirely of his own accord, and I really believe feels vain at
the attention he excites.

It was chill and bleak on the mountain-top, and a fire was burning in the bar-room.
The old Dutchman bestowed on everybody the title of Captain—perhaps because such
a title has a great chance of suiting an American. . . .

September 7, 1838.—Mr. Leach and I took a walk by moonlight, last evening, on
the road that leads over the mountain. Remote from houses, far up on the hill side,
we found a lime kiln burning near the road side; and approaching it, a watcher started
from the ground, where he had been lying at his length. There are several of these
lime-kilns in this vicinity; they are built circular with stones, like a round tower,
eighteen or twenty feet high; having a hillock heaped around a considerable of their
circumference, so that the marble may be brought and thrown in by cart loads at the
top. At the bottom there is a doorway large enough to admit a man in a stooping
posture. Thus an edifice of great solidity is composed, which will endure for centuries, unless needless pains are taken to tear it down. There is one on the hill side
close to the village, wherein weeds grow at the bottom, and grass, and shrubs too are
rooted in the interstices of the stones; and its low doorway had a dungeonlike aspect;
and we look down from the top as into a roofless tower. It apparently has not been
used for many years; and the lime, and weather-stained fragments of marble are scattered about.

But in the one we saw last night, a hard wood fire was burning merrily beneath the
superincumbent marble—the kiln being heaped full; and shortly after we came, the
man (a dark, black-bearded figure in shirt-sleeves) opened the iron door, through the
chinks of which the fire was gleaming, and thrust in huge logs of wood, and stirred
the immense coals with a long pole; and showed us the glowing lime-stone,—the
lower layer of it. The glow of the fire was powerful, at the distance of several yards
from the open door. He talked very sociably with us,—being doubtless glad to have
two visitors to vary his solitary night-watch; for it would not do for him to get asleep;
since the fire should be refreshed as often as every twenty minutes. We ascended the
hillock to the top of the kiln; and the marble was red-hot and burning with a bluish
lambent flame, quivering up, sometimes, nearly a yard high, and resembling the flame
of anthracite coal—only, the marble being in larger fragments, the flame was higher.
The kiln was perhaps six or eight feet across. Four hundred bushels of marble were
then in a state of combustion. The expense of converting this quantity into lime is
about fifty dollars; and it sells for 25 cts per bushel at the kiln. We talked with the
man about whether he would run across the top of the intensely burning kiln for a
thousand dollars, barefooted; and he said he would for ten;—he said that the lime
had been burning 48 hours, and would be finished in 36 more, and cooled sufficiently
to handle in 12 more. He liked the business of watching it better by night than day;
because the days were often hot; but such a mild and beautiful night as the last was
just right. Here a poet might make verses, with moonlight in them—and a gleam of

fierce firelight flickering through them. It is a shame to use this brilliant, white, almost transparent marble, in this way. A man said of it, the other day, that into some pieces of it, when polished, one could see a considerable distance; and instanced a certain gravestone.

Mr. Leach told me how a girl, to whom he was once paying attention, with some idea of marrying her, made a confession of having forfeited her chastity. He had heard rumors of her having been indiscreet, with reference to a man who was formerly attentive to her—but had no idea of anything more than a merely pardonable indiscretion, in having trusted herself in long and solitary walk with this man. He began to talk with her on this subject, intending gently to reprehend her; but she became greatly agitated, and fell aweeping bitterly—her thoughts flying immediately to her guilt, and probably thinking that he was aware or suspicious of the full extent of it. She told so much, or betrayed so much, that he besought her to say no more. "That was the only time, Mr. Leach," sobbed she, "that I ever strayed from the path of virtue." Much might be made of such a scene—the lover's astoundment, at discovering so much more than he expected. Mr. Leach spoke to me as if one deviation from chastity might not be an altogether insuperable objection to making a girl his wife!! . . .

1842.—To trace out the influence of a frightful and disgraceful crime in debasing and destroying a character naturally high and noble—the guilty person being alone conscious of the crime.

1844.—". . . Rappaccini, it is said, . . . cares infinitely more for science than for mankind. His patients are interesting to him only as subjects for some new experiment. He would sacrifice human life, his own among the rest, or whatever else was dearest to him, for the sake of adding so much as a grain of mustard seed to the great heap of his accumulated knowledge. . . . "

1844.—The search of an investigator for the Unpardonable Sin;—he at last finds it in his own heart and practice. . . .

1844.—The Unpardonable Sin might consist in a want of love and reverence for the Human Soul; in consequence of which, the investigator pried into its dark depths, not with a hope or purpose of making it better, but from a cold philosophical curiosity, —content that it should be wicked in whatever kind or degree, and only desiring to study it out. Would not this, in other words, be the separation of the intellect from the heart? . . .

July 29, 1849.— . . . Julian has too much tenderness, love, and sensibility in his nature; he needs to be hardened and tempered. I would not take a particle of the love out of him; but methinks it is highly desirable that some sterner quality should be interfused throughout the softness of his heart; else, in course of time, the hard intercourse of the world, and the many knocks and bruises he will receive, will cause a morbid crust of callousness to grow over his heart; so that, for at least a portion of his life, he will have less sympathy and love for his fellow-beings than those who began life with a much smaller portion. After a lapse of years, indeed, if he have native vigor enough, there may be a second growth of love and benevolence; but the first crop, with its wild luxuriance, stands a good chance of being blighted. . . .

A LODGING FOR THE NIGHT

ROBERT LOUIS STEVENSON (1850–1894)

It was late in November, 1456. The snow fell over Paris with rigorous, relentless persistence; sometimes the wind made a sally and scattered it in flying vortices; sometimes there was a lull, and flake after flake descended out of the black night air, silent, circuitous, interminable. To poor people, looking up under moist eyebrows, it seemed a wonder where it all came from. Master Francis Villon had propounded an alternative that afternoon, at a tavern window: was it only Pagan Jupiter plucking geese upon Olympus, or were the holy angels moulting? He was only a poor Master of Arts, he went on; and as the question somewhat touched upon divinity, he durst not venture to conclude. A silly old priest from Montargis, who was among the company, treated the young rascal to a bottle of wine in honor of the jest and grimaces with which it was accompanied, and swore on his own white beard that he had been just such another irreverent dog when he was Villon's age.

The air was raw and pointed, but not far below freezing; and the flakes were large, damp, and adhesive. The whole city was sheeted up. An army might have marched from end to end and not a footfall given the alarm. If there were any belated birds in heaven, they saw the island like a large white patch, and the bridges like slim white spars, on the black ground of the river. High up overhead the snow settled among the tracery of the cathedral towers. Many a niche was drifted full; many a statue wore a long white bonnet on its grotesque or sainted head. The gargoyles had been transformed into great false noses, drooping toward the point. The crockets were like upright pillows swollen on one side. In the intervals of the wind there was a dull sound of dripping about the precincts of the church.

The cemetery of St. John had taken its own share of the snow. All the graves were decently covered; tall, white housetops stood around in grave array; worthy burghers were long ago in bed, benightcapped like their domiciles; there was no light in all the neighborhood but a little peep from a lamp that hung swinging in the church choir, and tossed the shadows to and fro in time to its oscillations. The clock was hard on ten when the patrol went by with halberds and a lantern, beating their hands; and they saw nothing suspicious about the cemetery of St. John.

Yet there was a small house, backed up against the cemetery wall, which was still awake, and awake to evil purpose, in that snoring district. There was not much to betray it from without; only a stream of warm vapor from the chimney top, a patch where the snow melted on the roof, and a few half-obliterated footprints at the door. But within, behind the shuttered windows, Master Francis Villon, the poet, and some of the thieving crew with whom he consorted, were keeping the night alive and passing around the bottle.

A great pile of living embers diffused a strong and ruddy glow from the arched chimney. Before this straddled Dom Nicolas, the Picardy monk, with his skirts picked up and his fat legs bared to the comfortable warmth. His dilated shadow cut the room in half; and the firelight only escaped on either side of his broad person, and in a little pool between his outspread feet. His face had the beery, bruised appearance of the continual drinker's; it was covered with a network of congested veins, purple in ordinary circumstances, but now pale violet, for even with his back to the fire the cold pinched him on the other side. His cowl had half fallen back, and made a strange excrescence on either side of his bull neck. So he straddled, grumbling, and cut the room in half with the shadow of his portly frame.

On the right, Villon and Guy Tabary were huddled together over a scrap of parchment; Villon making a ballade which he was to call the *Ballade of Roast Fish,* and Tabary spluttering admiration at his shoulder. The poet was a rag of a man, dark, little, and lean, with hollow cheeks and thin black locks. He carried his four-and-twenty years with feverish animation. Greed had made folds about his eyes, evil smiles had puckered his mouth. The wolf and pig struggled together in his face. It was an eloquent, sharp, ugly, earthly countenance. His hands were small and prehensile, with fingers knotted like a cord; and they were continually flickering in front of him in violent and expressive pantomime. As for Tabary, a broad, complacent, admiring imbecility breathed from his squash nose and slobbering lips: he had become a thief, just as he might have become the most decent of burgesses, by the imperious chance that rules the lives of human geese and human donkeys.

At the monk's other hand, Montigny and Thevenin Pensete played a game of chance. About the first there clung some flavor of good birth and training, as about a fallen angel; something long, lithe, and courtly in the person; something aquiline and darkling in the face. Thevenin, poor soul, was in great feather: he had done a good stroke of knavery that afternoon in the Faubourg St. Jacques, and all night he had been gaining from Montigny. A flat smile illuminated his face; his bald head shone rosily in a garland of red curls; his little protuberant stomach shook with silent chucklings as he swept in his gains.

"Doubles or quits?" said Thevenin.

Montigny nodded grimly.

"Some may prefer to dine in state," wrote Villon, *"On bread and cheese on silver plate.* Or—or—help me out, Guido!"

Tabary giggled.

"Or parsley on a golden dish," scribbled the poet.

The wind was freshening without; it drove the snow before it, and sometimes raised its voice in a victorious whoop, and made sepulchral grumblings in the chimney. The cold was growing sharper as the night went on. Villon, protruding his lips, imitated the gust with something between a whistle and a groan. It was an eerie, uncomfortable talent of the poet's, much detested by the Picardy monk.

"Can't you hear it rattle in the gibbet?" said Villon. "They are all dancing the devil's jig on nothing, up there. You may dance, my gallants, you'll be none the warmer! Whew, what a gust! Down went somebody just now! A medlar the fewer on the three-legged medlar-tree!—I say, Dom Nicolas, it'll be cold tonight on the St. Denis Road?" he asked.

Dom Nicolas winked both his big eyes, and seemed to choke upon his Adam's apple. Montfaucon, the great grisly Paris gibbet, stood hard by the St. Denis Road, and the pleasantry touched him on the raw. As for Tabary, he laughed immoderately over the medlars; he had never heard anything more light-hearted; and he held his sides and crowed. Villon fetched him a fillip on the nose, which turned his mirth into an attack of coughing.

"Oh, stop that row," said Villon, "and think of rhymes to 'fish.' "

"Doubles or quits," said Montigny doggedly.

"With all my heart," quoth Thevenin.

"Is there any more in that bottle?" asked the monk.

"Open another," said Villon. "How do you ever hope to fill that big hogshead, your body, with little things like bottles? And how do you expect to get to heaven? How many angels, do you fancy, can be spared to carry up a single monk from Picardy? Or do you think yourself another Elias—and they'll send the coach for you?"

"*Hominibus impossibile*," replied the monk, as he filled his glass.

Tabary was in ecstasies.

Villon filliped his nose again.

"Laugh at my jokes, if you like," he said.

"It was very good," objected Tabary.

Villon made a face at him. "Think of rhymes to 'fish,' " he said. "What have you to do with Latin? You'll wish you knew none of it at the great assizes, when the devil calls for Guido Tabary, *clericus*—the devil with the hump-back and red-hot finger-nails. Talking of the devil," he added in a whisper, "look at Montigny!"

All three peered covertly at the gamester. He did not seem to be enjoying his luck. His mouth was a little to a side; one nostril nearly shut, and the other much inflated. The black dog was on his back, as people say, in terrifying nursery metaphor; and he breathed hard under the gruesome burden.

"He looks as if he could knife him," whispered Tabary, with round eyes.

The monk shuddered, and turned his face and spread his open hands to the red embers. It was the cold that thus affected Dom Nicolas, and not any excess of moral sensibility.

"Come now," said Villon—"about this ballade. How does it run so far?" And beating time with one hand, he read it aloud to Tabary.

They were interrupted at the fourth rhyme by a brief and fatal movement among the gamesters. The round was completed, and Thevenin was just opening his mouth to claim another victory, when Montigny leaped up, swift as an adder, and stabbed him to the heart. The blow took effect before he had time to utter a cry, before he had time to move. A tremor or two convulsed his frame; his hands opened and shut, his heels rattled on the floor; then his head rolled backward over one shoulder with the eyes open, and Thevenin Pensete's spirit had returned to Him who made it.

Every one sprang to his feet; but the business was over in two twos. The four living fellows looked at each other in rather a ghastly fashion; the dead man contemplating a corner of the roof with a singular and ugly leer.

"My God!" said Tabary, and he began to pray in Latin.

Villon broke out into hysterical laughter. He came a step forward and ducked a ridiculous bow at Thevenin, and laughed still louder. Then he sat down suddenly, all of a heap, upon a stool, and continued laughing bitterly as though he would shake himself to pieces.

Montigny recovered his composure first.

"Let's see what he has about him," he remarked; and he picked the dead man's pockets with a practised hand, and divided the money into four equal portions on the table. "There's for you," he said.

The monk received his share with a deep sigh, and a single stealthy glance at the dead Thevenin, who was beginning to sink into himself and topple sideways off the chair.

"We're all in for it," cried Villon, swallowing his mirth. "It's a hanging job for every man jack of us that's here—not to speak of those who aren't." He made a shocking gesture in the air with his raised right hand, and put out his tongue and threw his head on on side, so as to counterfeit the appearance of one who has been hanged. Then he pocketed his share of the spoil, and executed a shuffle with his feet as if to restore the circulation.

Tabary was the last to help himself; he made a dash at the money, and retired to the other end of the apartment.

Montigny stuck Thevenin upright in the chair, and drew out the dagger, which was followed by a jet of blood.

"You fellows had better be moving," he said, as he wiped the blade on the victim's doublet.

"I think we had," returned Villon with a gulp. "Damm his fat head!" he broke out. "It sticks in my throat like phlegm. What right has a man to have red hair when he is dead?" And he fell all of a heap again upon the stool, and fairly covered his face with his hands.

Montigny and Dom Nicolas laughed aloud, even Tabary feebly chiming in.

"Cry baby," said the monk.

"I always said he was a woman," added Montigny with a sneer. "Sit up, can't you?" he went on, giving another shake to the murdered body. "Tread out that fire, Nick."

But Nick was better employed; he was quietly taking Villon's purse, as the poet sat, limp and trembling, on the stool where he had been making a ballade not three minutes before. Montigny and Tabary dumbly demanded a share of the booty, which the monk silently promised as he passed the little bag into the bosom of his gown. In many ways an artistic nature unfits a man for practical existence.

No sooner had the theft been accomplished than Villon shook himself, jumped to himself, and began helping to scatter and extinguish the embers. Meanwhile Montigny opened the door and cautiously peered into the street. The coast was clear; there was no meddlesome patrol in sight. Still it was judged wiser to slip out severally; and as Villon was himself in a hurry to escape from the neighborhood of the dead Thevenin, and the rest were in a still greater hurry to get rid of him before he should discover the loss of his money, he was the first by general consent to issue forth into the street.

The wind had triumphed and swept all the clouds from heaven. Only a few vapors, as thin as moonlight, fleeted rapidly across the stars. It was bitter cold; and by a common optical effect, things seemed almost more definite than in the broadest daylight. The sleeping city was absolutely still: a company of white hoods, a field full of little Alps, below the twinkling stars. Villon cursed his fortune. Would it were still snowing! Now, wherever he went he left an indelible trail behind him on the glittering streets; wherever he went he was still tethered to the house by the cemetery of St. John; wherever he went he must weave, with his own plodding feet, the rope that bound him to the crime and would bind him to the gallows. The leer of the dead man came back to him with a new significance. He snapped his fingers as if to pluck up his own spirits, and choosing a street at random, stepped boldly forward in the snow.

Two things preoccupied him as he went: the aspect of the gallows at Montfaucon in this bright windy phase of the night's existence, for one; and for another, the look of the dead man with his bald head and garland of red curls. Both struck cold upon his heart, and he kept quickening his pace as if he could escape from unpleasant thoughts by mere fleetness of foot. Sometimes he looked back over his shoulder with a sudden nervous jerk; but he was the only moving thing in the white streets, except when the wind swept around a corner and threw up the snow, which was beginning to freeze, in spouts of glittering dust.

Suddenly he saw, a long way before him, a black clump and a couple of lanterns. The clump was in motion, and the lanterns swung as though carried by men walking. It was a patrol. And though it was merely crossing his line of march, he judged it wiser to get out of eyeshot as speedily as he could. He was not in the humor to be challenged, and he was conscious of making a very conspicuous mark upon the snow. Just on his left hand there stood a great hotel, with some turrets and a large porch before the door; it was half-ruinous, he remembered, and had stood long empty; and so he made three steps of it and jumped inside the shelter of the porch. It was pretty dark inside, after the glimmer of the snowy streets, and he was groping forward with outspread hands, when he stumbled over some substance which offered an indescribable mixture of resistances, hard and soft, firm and loose. His heart gave a leap, and he sprang two steps back and stared dreadfully at the object. Then he gave a little laugh of relief. It was only a woman, and she dead. He knelt beside her to make sure upon this latter point. She was freezing cold, and rigid like a stick. A little ragged finery fluttered in the wind about her hair, and her cheeks had been heavily rouged that same afternoon. Her pockets were quite empty; but in her stocking, underneath the garter, Villon found two small coins that went by the name of whites. It was little enough; but it was always something; and the poet was moved with a deep sense of pathos that she should have died before she had spent her money. That seemed to him a dark and pitiable mystery; and he looked from the coins in his hand to the dead woman, and back again to the coins, shaking his head over the riddle of man's life. Henry V of England, dying at Vincennes just after he had conquered France, and this poor jade cut off by a cold draught in a great man's doorway, before she had time to spend her couple of whites—it seemed a cruel way to carry on the world. Two whites would have taken such a little while to squander; and yet it would have been one more good taste in the mouth, one more smack of the lips, before the devil got the soul, and the body was left to birds and vermin. He would like to use all his tallow before the light was blown out and the lantern broken.

While these thoughts were passing through his mind, he was feeling, half-mechanically, for his purse. Suddenly his heart stopped beating; a feeling of cold scales passed up the back of his legs, and a cold blow seemed to fall upon his scalp. He stood petrified for a moment; then he felt again with one feverish motion; and then his loss burst upon him, and he was covered with perspiration. To spendthrifts money is so living and actual—it is such a thin veil between them and their pleasures! There is only one limit to their fortune—that of time; and a spendthrift with only a few crowns is the Emperor of Rome until they are spent. For such a person to lose his money is to suffer the most shocking reverse, and fall from heaven to hell, from all to nothing, in a breath. And all the more if he has put his head in the halter for it; if he may be hanged to-morrow for that same purse, so dearly earned, so foolishly departed. Villon stood and cursed; he threw the two whites into the street; he shook his fist at heaven; he stamped, and was not horrified to find himself trampling the poor corpse. Then he began rapidly to retrace his steps toward the house beside the cemetery. He had forgotten all fear of the patrol, which was long gone by at any rate, and he had no idea but that of his lost purse. It was in vain that he looked right and left upon the snow; nothing was to be seen. He had not dropped it in the streets. Had it fallen in the house? He would have liked dearly to go in and see; but the idea of the grisly occupant unmanned him. And he saw besides, as he drew near, that their efforts to put out the fire had been unsuccessful; on the contrary, it had broken into a blaze, and a changeful light played in the chinks of the door and window, and revived his terror for the authorities and Paris gibbet.

He returned to the hotel with the porch, and groped about in the snow for the money he had thrown away in his childish passion. But he could only find one white; the other had probably struck sideways and sunk deeply in. With a single white in his pocket, all his projects for a rousing night in some wild tavern vanished utterly away. And it was not only pleasure that fled laughing from his grasp; positive discomfort, positive pain, attacked him as he stood ruefully before the porch. His perspiration had dried upon him; and though the wind had now fallen, a binding frost was setting in stronger with every hour, and he felt benumbed and sick at heart. What was to be done? Late as was the hour, improbable as was success, he would try the house of his adopted father, the chaplain of St. Benoît.

He ran there all the way, and knocked timidly. There was no answer. He knocked again and again, taking heart with every stroke; and at last steps were heard approaching from within. A barred wicket fell open in the iron-studded door, and emitted a gush of yellow light.

"Hold up your face to the wicket," said the chaplain from within.

"It's only me," whimpered Villon.

"Oh, it's only you, is it?" returned the chaplain; and he cursed him with foul unpriestly oaths for disturbing him at such an hour, and bade him be off to hell, where he came from.

"My hands are blue to the wrists," pleaded Villon; "my feet are dead and full of twinges; my nose aches with the sharp air; the cold lies at my heart. I may be dead before morning. Only this once, father, and before God I will never ask again!"

"You should have come earlier," said the ecclesiastic, coolly. "Young men require a lesson now and then." He shut the wicket and retired deliberately into the interior of the house.

Villon was beside himself; he beat upon the door with his hands and feet, and shouted hoarsely after the chaplain.

"Wormy old fox!" he cried. "If I had my hand under your twist, I would send you flying into the bottomless pit."

A door shut in the interior, faintly audible to the poet down long passages. He passed his hand over his mouth with an oath. And then the humor of the situation struck him, and he laughed and looked lightly up to heaven, where the stars seemed to be winking over his discomfiture.

What was to be done? It looked very like a night in the frosty streets. The idea of the dead woman popped into his imagination, and gave him a hearty fright; what had happened to her in the early night might very well happen to him before morning. And he so young! and with such immense possibilities of disorderly amusement before him! He felt quite pathetic over the notion of his own fate, as if it had been some one else's, and made a little imaginative vignette of the scene in the morning when they should find his body.

He passed all his chances under review, turning the white between his thumb and forefinger. Unfortunately he was on bad terms with some old friends who would once have taken pity on him in such a plight. He had lampooned them in verses, he had beaten and cheated them; and yet now, when he was in so close a pinch, he thought there was at least one who might perhaps relent. It was a chance. It was worth trying at least, and he would go and see.

On the way, two little accidents happened to him which colored his musings in a very different manner. For, first, he fell in with the track of a patrol, and walked in it for some hundred yards, although it lay out of his direction. And this spirited him up; at least he had confused his trail; for he was still possessed with the idea of people tracking him all about Paris over the snow, and collaring him next morning before he was awake. The other matter affected him quite differently. He passed a street corner, where, not so long before, a woman and her child had been devoured by wolves. This was just the kind of weather, he reflected, when wolves might take it into their heads to enter Paris again; and a lone man in these deserted streets would run the chance of something worse than a mere scare. He stopped and looked upon the place with an unpleasant interest—it was a centre where several lanes intersected each other; and he looked down them all one after another, and held his breath to listen, lest he should detect some galloping black things on the snow or hear the sound of howling between him and the river. He remembered his mother telling him the story and pointing out the spot, while he was yet a child. His mother! If he only knew where she lived, he might make sure at least of shelter. He determined he would inquire upon the morrow; nay, he would go and see her, too, poor old girl! So thinking, he arrived at his destination—his last hope for the night.

The house was quite dark, like its neighbors; and yet after a few taps, he heard a movement overhead, a door opening, and a cautious voice asking who was there. The poet named himself in a loud whisper, and waited, not without some trepidation, the result. Nor had he to wait long. A window was suddenly opened, and a pailful of slops splashed down upon the doorstep. Villon had not been unprepared for something of the sort, and had put himself as much in shelter as the nature of the porch admitted; but for all that, he was deplorably drenched below the waist. His hose began to freeze almost at once. Death from cold and exposure stared him in the face; he remembered he was of phthisical tendency, and began coughing tentatively. But the gravity of the danger steadied his nerves. He stopped a few hundred yards from the door where he had been so rudely used, and reflected with his finger to his nose. He could only see one way of getting a lodging, and that was to take it. He had noticed a house not far away which looked as if it might be easily broken into, and thither he betook himself promptly, entertaining himself on the way with the idea of a room still hot, with a table still loaded with the remains of a supper, where he might pass the rest of the black hours, and whence he should issue, on the morrow, with an armful of valuable plate. He even considered on what viands and wines he should prefer; and as he was calling the roll of his favorite dainties, roast fish presented itself with an odd mixture of amusement and horror.

"I shall never finish that ballade," he thought to himself; and then, with another shudder at the recollection, "Oh, damn his fat head!" he repeated fervently, and spat upon the snow.

The house in question looked dark at first sight; but as Villon made a preliminary inspection in search of the handiest point of attack, a little twinkle of light caught his eye from behind a curtained window.

"The devil!" he thought. "People awake! Some student or some saint, confound the crew! Can't they get drunk and lie in bed snoring like their neighbors! What's the good of a curfew, and poor devils of bell-ringers jumping at a rope's-end in bell-towers? What's the use of day, if people sit up all night? The gripes to them!" He grinned as he saw where his logic was leading him. "Every man to his business, after all," added he, "and if they're awake, by the Lord, I may come by a supper honestly for once, and cheat the devil."

He went boldly to the door, and knocked with an assured hand. On both previous occasions he had knocked timidly and with some dread of attracting notice but now, when he had just discarded the thought of a burglarious entry, knocking at a door seemed a mighty simple and innocent proceeding. The sound of his blows echoed through the house with thin, phantasmal reverberations, as though it were quite empty; but these had scarcely died away before a measured tread drew near, a couple of bolts were withdrawn, and one wing was opened broadly, as though no guile or fear of guile were known to those within. A tall figure of a man, muscular and spare, but a little bent, confronted Villon. The head was massive in bulk, but finely sculptured; the nose blunt at the bottom but refining upward to where it joined a pair of strong and honest eyebrows; the mouth and eyes surrounded with delicate markings, and the whole face based upon a thick white beard, boldly and squarely trimmed. Seen as it was by the light of a flickering hand-lamp, it looked perhaps nobler than it had a right to do; but it was a fine face, honorable rather than intelligent, strong, simple, and righteous.

"You knock late, sir," said the old man in resonant, courteous tones.

Villon cringed, and brought up many servile words of apology; at a crisis of this sort, the beggar was uppermost in him, and the man of genius hid his head with confusion.

"You are cold," repeated the old man, "and hungry? Well, step in." And he ordered him into the house with a noble enough gesture.

"Some great seigneur," thought Villon, as his host, setting down the lamp on the flagged pavement of the entry, shot the bolts once more into their places.

"You will pardon me if I go in front," he said, when this was done; and he preceded the poet up-stairs into a large apartment, warmed with a pan of charcoal and lit by a great lamp hanging from the roof. It was very bare of furniture; only some gold plate on a sideboard; some folios; and a stand of armor between the windows. Some smart tapestry hung upon the walls, representing the crucifixion of our Lord in one piece, and in another a scene of shepherds and shepherdesses by a running stream. Over the chimney was a shield of arms.

"Will you seat yourself," said the old man, "and forgive me if I leave you? I am alone in my house tonight, and if you are to eat I must forage for you myself."

No sooner was his host gone than Villon leaped from the chair on which he had just seated himself, and began examining the room, with the stealth and passion of a cat. He weighed the gold flagons in his hand, opened all the folios, and investigated the arms upon the shield, and the stuff with which the seats were lined. He raised the window-curtains, and saw that the windows were set with rich stained glass in figures, so far as he could see, of martial import. Then he stood in the middle of the room, drew a long breath, and retaining it with puffed cheeks, looked round and round him, turning on his heels, as if to impress every feature of the apartment on his memory.

"Seven pieces of plate," he said. "If there had been ten I would have risked it. A fine old house, and a fine old master, so help me all the saints!"

And just then, hearing the old man's tread returning along the corridor, he stole back to his chair, and began toasting his wet legs before the charcoal pan.

His entertainer had a plate of meat in one hand and a jug of wine in the other. He set down the plate upon the table, motioning Villon to draw in his chair, and going to the sideboard, brought back two goblets, which he filled.

"I drink to your better fortune," he said, gravely touching Villon's cup with his own.

"To our better acquaintance," said the poet, growing bold. A mere man of the people would have been awed by the courtesy of the old seigneur, but Villon was hardened in that matter; he had made mirth for great lords before now, and found them as black rascals as himself. And so he devoted himself to the viands with a ravenous gusto, while the old man, leaning backward, watched him with steady, curious eyes.

"You have blood on your shoulder, my man," he said.

Montigny must have laid his wet right hand upon his shoulder as he left the house. He cursed Montigny in his heart.

"It was none of my shedding," he stammered.

"I had not supposed so," returned his host quietly. "A brawl?"

"Well, something of that sort," Villon admitted with a quaver.

"Perhaps a fellow murdered?"

"Oh, no, not murdered," said the poet more and more confused. "It was all fair play—murdered by accident. I had no hand in it, God strike me dead!" he added fervently.

"One rogue the fewer, I dare say," observed the master of the house.

"You may dare to say that," agreed Villon, infinitely relieved. "As big a rogue as there is between here and Jerusalem. He turned up his toes like a lamb. But it was a nasty thing to look at. I dare say you've seen dead men in your time, my lord?" he added, glancing at the armor.

"Many," said the old man. "I have followed the wars, as you imagine."

Villon laid down his knife and fork, which he had just taken up again.

"Were any of them bald?" he asked.

"Oh yes, and with hair as white as mine."

"I don't think I would mind the white so much," said Villon. "His was red." And he had a return of his shuddering and tendency to laughter, which he drowned with a great draught of wine. "I'm a little put out when I think of it," he went on. "I knew him—damn him! And the cold gives a man fancies—or the fancies give a man cold, I don't know which."

"Have you any money?" asked the old man.

"I have one white," returned the poet laughing. "I got it out of a dead jade's stocking in a porch. She was as dead as Caesar, poor wench, and as cold as a church, with bits of ribbon sticking in her hair. This is a hard world in winter for wolves and wenches and poor rogues like me."

"I," said the old man, "am Enguerrand de la Feuillée, seigneur de Brisetout, bailly du Patatrac. Who and what may you be?"

Villon rose and made a suitable reverence. "I am called Francis Villon," he said, "a poor Master of Arts of this university. I know some Latin, and a deal of vice. I can make chansons, ballades, lais, virelais, and roundels, and I am very fond of wine. I was born in a garret, and I shall not improbably die upon the gallows. I may add, my lord, that from this night forward I am your lordship's very obsequious servant to command."

"No servant of mine," said the knight; "my guest for this evening, and no more."

"A very grateful guest," said Villon politely; and he drank in dumb show to his entertainer.

"You are shrewd," began the old man, tapping his forehead, "very shrewd; you have learning; you are a clerk; and yet you take a small piece of money off a dead woman in the street. Is it not a kind of theft?"

"It is a kind of a theft much practiced in the wars, my lord."

"The wars are the field of honor," returned the old man proudly. "There a man plays his life upon the cast; he fights in the name of his lord, the king, his Lord God, and all their lordships the holy saints and angels."

"Put it," said Villon, "that I were really a thief, should I not play my life also, and against heavier odds?"

"For gain, and not for honor."

"Gain?" repeated Villon with a shrug. "Gain! The poor fellow wants supper, and takes it. So does the soldier in a campaign. Why, what are all these requisitions we hear so much about? If they are not gain to those who take them, they are loss enough to others. The men-at-arms drink by a good fire, while the burgher bites his nails to buy them wine and wood. I have seen a good many ploughmen swinging on trees about the country; ay, I have seen thirty on one elm, and a very poor figure they made; and when I asked some one how all these came to be hanged, I was told it was because they could not scrape together enough crowns to satisfy the men-at-arms."

"These things are a necessity of war, which the low-born must endure with constancy. It is true that some captains drive overhard; there are spirits in every rank not easily moved by pity; and, indeed, many follow arms who are no better than brigands."

"You see," said the poet, "you cannot separate the soldier from the brigand; and what is a thief but an isolated brigand with circumspect manners? I steal a couple of mutton chops, without so much as disturbing people's sleep; the farmer grumbles a bit, but sups none the less wholesomely on what remains. You come up blowing gloriously on a trumpet, take away the whole sheep, and beat the farmer pitifully into the bargain. I have no trumpet; I am only Tom, Dick, or Harry; I am a rogue and a dog, and hanging's too good for me—with all my heart—but just you ask the farmer which of us he prefers, just find out which of us he lies awake to curse on cold nights."

"Look at us two," said his lordship. "I am old, strong, and honored. If I were turned from my house tomorrow, hundreds would be proud to shelter me. Poor people would go out and pass the night in the streets with their children, if I merely hinted that I wished to be alone And I find you up, wandering homeless, and picking farthings off dead women by the wayside! I fear no man and nothing; I have seen you tremble and lose countenance at a word. I wait God's summons contentedly in my own house, or, if it please the king to call me out again, upon the field of battle. You look for the gallows; a rough, swift death, without hope or honor. Is there no difference between these two?"

"As far as to the moon," Villon acquiesced. "But if I had been born lord of Brisetout, and you had been the poor scholar Francis, would the difference have been any less? Should not I have been warming my knees at this charcoal pan, and would not you have been groping for farthings in the snow? Should not I have been the soldier, and you the thief?"

"A thief!" cried the old man. "I a thief! If you understood your words, you would repent them."

Villon turned out his hands with a gesture of inimitable impudence. "If your lordship had done me the honor to follow my argument!" he said.

"I do you too much honor in submitting to your presence," said the knight. "Learn to curb your tongue when you speak with old and honorable men, or some one hastier than I may reprove you in a sharper fashion." And he rose and paced the lower end of the apartment, struggling with anger and antipathy. Villon surreptitiously filled his cup, and settled himself more comfortably in his chair, crossing his knees and leaning his head upon one hand and the elbow against the back of the chair. He was now replete and warm; and he was in no wise frightened of his host, having gauged him as justly as was possible between two such different characters. The night was far spent, and in very comfortable fashion after all; and he felt morally certain of a safe departure on the morrow.

"Tell me one thing," said the old man, pausing in his walk. "Are you really a thief?"

"I claim the sacred rights of hospitality," returned the poet. "My lord, I am."

"You are very young," the knight continued.

"I should never have been so old," replied Villon, showing his fingers, "if I had not helped myself with these ten talents. They have been my nursing mothers and my nursing fathers."

"You may still repent and change."

"I repent daily," said the poet. "There are few people more given to repentance than poor Francis. As for change, let somebody change my circumstances. A man must continue to eat, if it were only that he may continue to repent."

"The change must begin in the heart," returned the old man solemnly.

"My dear lord," answered Villon, "do you really fancy that I steal for pleasure? I hate stealing, like any other piece of work or danger. My teeth chatter when I see the gallows. But I must eat, I must drink, I must mix in society of some sort. What the devil! Man is not a solitary animal—*Cui Deus foeminam tradit*. Make me king's pantler—make me abbot of St. Denis; make me bailly of the Patatrac; and then I shall be changed indeed. But as long as you leave me the poor scholar Francis Villon, without a farthing, why, of course, I remain the same."

"The grace of God is all-powerful."

"I should be a heretic to question it," said Francis. "It has made you lord of Brisetout, and bailly of the Patatrac; it has given me nothing but the quick wits under my hat and these ten toes upon my hands. May I help myself to wine? I thank you respectfully. By God's grace, you have a very superior vintage."

The lord of Brisetout walked to and fro with his hands behind his back. Perhaps he was not quite settled in his mind about the parallel between thieves and soldiers; perhaps Villon had interested him by some cross-thread of sympathy; perhaps his wits were simply muddled by so much unfamiliar reasoning; but whatever the cause, he somehow yearned to convert the young man to a better way of thinking, and could not make up his mind to drive him forth again into the street.

"There is something more than I can understand in this," he said, at length. "Your mouth is full of subtleties, and the devil has led you far astray; but the devil is only a very weak spirit before God's truth, and all his subtleties vanish at a word of true honor, like darkness at morning. Listen to me once more. I learned long ago that a gentleman should live chivalrously and lovingly to God, and the king, and his lady; and though I have seen many strange things done, I have still striven to command my ways upon that rule. It is not only written in all noble histories, but in every man's heart, if he will take care to read. You speak of food and wine, and I know very well that hunger is a difficult trial to endure; but you do not speak of other wants; you say nothing of honor, of faith to God and other men, of courtesy, of love without reproach. It may be that I am not very wise—and yet I think I am—but you seem to me like one who has lost his way and made a great error in life. You are attending to the little wants, and you have totally forgotten the great and only real ones, like a man who should be doctoring a toothache on the Judgment Day. For such things as honor and love and faith are not only nobler than food and drink, but, indeed, I think that we desire them more, and suffer more sharply for their absence. I speak to you as I think you will most easily understand me. Are you not, while careful to fill your belly, disregarding another appetite in your heart, which spoils the pleasure of your life and keeps you continually wretched?"

Villon was sensibly nettled under all this sermonizing. "You think I have no sense of honor!" he cried. "I'm poor enough, God knows! It's hard to see rich people with their gloves, and you blowing in your hands. An empty belly is a bitter thing, although you speak so lightly of it. If you had had as many as I, perhaps you would change your tune. Anyway, I'm a thief—make the most of that—but I'm not a devil from hell, God strike me dead. I would have you to know that I've an honor of my own, as good as yours, though I don't prate about it all day long, as if it were a God's miracle to have any. It seems quite natural to me; I keep it in its box till it's wanted. Why now, look you here, how long have I been in this room with you? Did you not tell me you were alone in this house? Look at your gold plate! You're strong, if you like, but you're old and unarmed, and I have my knife. What did I want but a jerk of the elbow, and here would have been you with the cold steel in your bowels, and there would have been me, linking in the streets, with an armful of gold cups! Did you suppose I hadn't wit enough to see that? And I scorned the action. There are your damned goblets, as safe as in a church; there are you, with your heart ticking as good as new; and here am I, ready to go out again as poor as I came in, with my one white that you threw in my teeth! And you think I have no sense of honor—God strike me dead!"

The old man stretched out his right arm. "I will tell you what you are," he said. "You are a rogue, my man, an impudent and black-hearted rogue and vagabond. I have passed an hour with you. Oh! believe me, I feel myself disgraced! And you have eaten and drunk at my table. But now I am sick at your presence; the day has come, and the night-bird should be off to his roost. Will you go before, or after?"

"Which you please," returned the poet, rising. "I believe you to be strictly honorable." He thoughtfully emptied his cup. "I wish I could add you were intelligent," he went on, knocking on his head with his knuckles. "Age, age, the brains stiff and rheumatic."

The old man preceded him from a point of self-respect; Villon followed, whistling, with his thumbs in his girdle.

"God pity you," said the lord of Brisetout at the door.

"Good-bye, papa," returned Villon, with a yawn. "Many thanks for the cold mutton."

The door closed behind him. The dawn was breaking over the white roofs. A chill, uncomfortable morning ushered in the day. Villon stood and heartily stretched himself in the middle of the road.

"A very dull old gentleman," he thought. "I wonder what his goblets may be worth."

FRANÇOIS VILLON
Student, Poet, and Housebreaker

ROBERT LOUIS STEVENSON (1850–1894)

Perhaps one of the most curious revolutions in literary history is the sudden bull's-eye light cast by M. Longnon on the obscure existence of François Villon.* His book is not remarkable merely as a chapter of biography exhumed after four centuries. To readers of the poet it will recall, with a flavor of satire, that characteristic passage in which he bequeaths his spectacles—with a humorous reservation of the case—to the hospital for blind paupers known as the Fifteen-Score. Thus equipped, let the blind paupers go and separate the good from the bad in the cemetery of the Innocents! For his own part the poet can see no distinction. Much have the dead people made of their advantages. What does it matter now that they have lain in state beds and nourished portly bodies upon cakes and cream! Here they all lie, to be trodden in the mud; the large estate and the small, sounding virtue and adroit or powerful vice, in very much the same condition; and a bishop not to be distinguished from a lamp-lighter with even the strongest spectacles.

Such was Villon's cynical philosophy. Four hundred years after his death, when surely all danger might be considered at an end, a pair of critical spectacles have been applied to his own remains; and though he left behind him a sufficiently ragged reputation from the first, it is only after these four hundred years that his delinquencies have been finally tracked home, and we can assign him to his proper place among the good or wicked. It is a staggering thought, and one that affords a fine figure of the imperishability of men's acts, that the stealth of the private inquiry office can be carried so far back into the dead and dusty past. We are not so soon quit of our concerns as Villon fancied. In the extreme of dissolution, when not so much as a man's name is remembered, when his dust is scattered to the four winds, and perhaps the very grave and the very graveyard where he was laid to rest have been forgotten, desecrated, and buried under populous towns—even in this extreme let an antiquary fall across a sheet of manuscript, and the name will be recalled, the old infamy will pop out into daylight like a toad out of a fissure in the rock, and the shadow of the shade of what was once a man will be heartily pilloried by his descendants. A little while ago and Villon was almost totally forgotten; then he was revived for the sake of his verses; and now he is being revived with a vengeance in the detection of his misdemeanors. How unsubstantial is this projection of a man's existence, which can lie in abeyance for centuries and then be brushed up again and set forth for the consideration of posterity by a few dips in an antiquary's inkpot! This precarious tenure of fame goes a long way to justify those (and they are not few) who prefer cakes and cream in the immediate present.

A WILD YOUTH.—François de Montcorbier, *alias* François des Loges, *alias* François Villon, *alias* Michel Mouton, Master of Arts in the University of Paris, was born in

* "Etude Biographique sur François Villon." Paris: H. Menu. [All footnotes are those of Stevenson himself.]

that city in the summer of 1431. It was a memorable year for France on other and higher considerations. A great-hearted girl and a poor-hearted boy made, the one her last, the other his first appearance on the public stage of that unhappy country. On the 30th of May the ashes of Joan of Arc were thrown into the Seine, and on the 2d of December our Henry Sixth made his Joyous Entry dismally enough into disaffected and depopulating Paris. Sword and fire still ravaged the open country. On a single April Saturday twelve hundred persons, besides children, made their escape out of the starving capital. The hangman, as is not uninteresting to note in connection with Master Francis, was kept hard at work in 1431; on the last of April and on the 4th of May alone, sixty-two bandits swung from Paris gibbets.* A more confused or troublous time it would have been difficult to select for a start in life. Not even a man's nationality was certain; for the people of Paris there was no such thing as a Frenchman. The English were the English indeed, but the French were only the Armagnacs, whom, with Joan of Arc at their head, they had beaten back from under their ramparts not two years before. Such public sentiment as they had centered about their dear Duke of Burgundy, and the dear Duke had no more urgent business than to keep out of their neighborhood. . . . At least, and whether he liked it or not, our disreputable troubadour was tubbed and swaddled as a subject of the English crown.

We hear nothing of Villon's father except that he was poor and of mean extraction. His mother was given piously, which does not imply very much in an old Frenchwoman, and quite uneducated. He had an uncle, a monk in an abbey at Angers, who must have prospered beyond the family average, and was reported to be worth five or six hundred crowns. Of this uncle and his money-box the reader will hear once more. In 1448 Francis became a student of the University of Paris; in 1450 he took the degree of Bachelor, and in 1452 that of Master of Arts. His *bourse,* or the sum paid weekly for his board, was of the amount of two sous. Now two sous was about the price of a pound of salt butter in the bad times of 1417; it was the price of half-a-pound in the worse times of 1419; and in 1444, just four years before Villon joined the University, it seems to have been taken as the average wage for a day's manual labor.† In short, it cannot have been a very profuse allowance to keep a sharp-set lad in breakfast and supper for seven mortal days; and Villon's share of the cakes and pastry and general good cheer, to which he is never weary of referring, must have been slender from the first.

The educational arrangements of the University of Paris were, to our way of thinking, somewhat incomplete. Worldly and monkish elements were presented in a curious confusion, which the youth might disentangle for himself. If he had an opportunity, on the one hand, of acquiring much hair-drawn divinity and a taste for formal disputation, he was put in the way of much gross and flaunting vice upon the other. The lecture room of a scholastic doctor was sometimes under the same roof with establishments of a very different and peculiarly unedifying order. The students had extraordinary privileges, which by all accounts they abused extraordinarily. And while some condemned themselves to an almost sepulchral regularity and seclusion, others fled the schools, swaggered in the street "with their thumbs in their girdle," passed the night in riot, and behaved themselves as the worthy forerunners of Jehan Frollo in the romance of *Notre-Dame de Paris.* Villon tells us himself that he was among the truants, but we hardly needed his avowal. The burlesque erudition in which he sometimes indulged implies no more than the merest smattering of knowledge;

* "Bourgeois de Paris," ed. Panthéon, pp. 688, 689.
† "Bourgeois," pp. 627, 636, and 725.

whereas his acquaintance with blackguard haunts and industries could only have been acquired by early and consistent impiety and idleness. He passed his degrees, it is true; but some of us who have been to modern universities will make their own reflections on the value of the test. As for his three pupils, Colin Laurent, Girard Gossouyn, and Jehan Marceau—if they were really his pupils in any serious sense—what can we say but God help them! And sure enough, by his own description, they turned out as ragged, rowdy, and ignorant as was to be looked for from the views and manners of their rare preceptor.

At some time or other, before or during his university career, the poet was adopted by Master Guillaume de Villon, chaplain of Saint Benoît-de-Betourne near the Sorbonne. From him he borrowed the surname by which he is known to posterity. It was most likely from his house, called the *Porte Rouge,* and situated in a garden in the cloister of St. Benoît, that Master Francis heard the bell of the Sorbonne ring out the Angelus while he was finishing his "Small Testament" at Christmastide in 1456. Toward this benefactor he usually gets credit for a respectable display of gratitude. But with his trap and pitfall style of writing, it is easy to make too sure. His sentiments are about as much to be relied on as those of a professional beggar; and in this, as in so many other matters, he comes toward us whining and piping the eye, and goes off again with a whoop and his finger to his nose. Thus, he calls Guillaume de Villon his "more than father," thanks him with a great show of sincerity for having helped him out of many scrapes, and bequeaths him his portion of renown. But the portion of renown which belonged to a young thief, distinguished (if, at the period when he wrote this legacy, he was distinguished at all) for having written some more or less obscene and scurrilous ballads, must have been little fitted to gratify the self-respect or increase the reputation of a benevolent ecclesiastic. The same remark applies to a subsequent legacy of the poet's library, with specification of one work which was plainly neither decent nor devout. We are thus left on the horns of a dilemma. If the chaplain was a godly, philanthropic personage, who had tried to graft good principles and good behavior on this wild slip of an adopted son, these jesting legacies would obviously cut him to the heart. The position of an adopted son toward his adoptive father is one full of delicacy; where a man lends his name he looks for great consideration. And this legacy of Villon's portion of renown may be taken as the mere fling of an unregenerate scapegrace who has wit enough to recognize in his own shame the readiest weapon of offense against a prosy benefactor's feelings. The gratitude of Master Francis figures, on this reading, as a frightful *minus* quantity. If, on the other hand, those jests were given and taken in good humor, the whole relation between the pair degenerates into the unedifying complicity of a debauched old chaplain and a witty and dissolute young scholar. At this rate the house with the red door may have rung with the most mundane minstrelsy; and it may have been below its roof that Villon, through a hole in the plaster, studied, as he tells us, the leisures of a rich ecclesiastic.

It was, perhaps, of some moment in the poet's life that he should have inhabited the cloister of Saint Benoît. Three of the most remarkable among his early acquaintances are Catherine de Vausselles, for whom he entertained a short-lived affection and an enduring and most unmanly resentment; Regnier de Montigny, a young blackguard of good birth; and Colin de Cayeux, a fellow with a marked aptitude for picking locks. Now we are on a foundation of mere conjecture, but it is at least curious to find that two of the canons of Saint Benoît answered respectively to the names of Pierre de Vaucel and Etienne de Montigny, and that there was a householder called

Nicolas de Cayeux in a street—the Rue des Poirees—in the immediate neighborhood of the cloister. M. Longnon is almost ready to identify Catherine as the niece of Pierre; Regnier as the nephew of Etienne, and Colin as the son of Nicolas. Without going so far, it must be owned that the approximation of names is significant. As we go on to see the part played by each of these persons in the sordid melodrama of the poet's life, we shall come to regard it as even more notable. Is it not Clough who has remarked that, after all, everything lies in juxtaposition? Many a man's destiny has been settled by nothing apparently more grave than a pretty face on the opposite side of the street and a couple of bad companions round the corner.

Catherine de Vausselles (or de Vaucel—the change is within the limits of Villon's license) had plainly delighted in the poet's conversation; near neighbors or not, they were much together; and Villon made no secret of his court, and suffered himself to believe that his feeling was repaid in kind. This may have been an error from the first, or he may have estranged her by subsequent misconduct or temerity. One can easily imagine Villon an impatient wooer. One thing, at least, is sure: that the affair terminated in a manner bitterly humiliating to Master Francis. In presence of his lady-love, perhaps under her window and certainly with her connivance, he was unmercifully thrashed by one Noë le Joly—beaten, as he says himself, like dirty linen on the washing-board. It is characteristic that his malice had notably increased between the time when he wrote the "Small Testament" immediately on the back of the occurrence, and the time when he wrote the "Large Testament" five years after. On the latter occasion nothing is too bad for his "damsel with the twisted nose," as he calls her. She is spared neither hint nor accusation, and he tells his messenger to accost her with the vilest insults. Villon, it is thought, was out of Paris when these amenities escaped his pen; or perhaps the strong arm of Noë le Joly would have been again in requisition. So ends the love story, if love story it may properly be called. Poets are not necessarily fortunate in love; but they usually fall among more romantic circumstances and bear their disappointment with a better grace.

The neighborhood of Regnier de Montigny and Colin de Cayeux was probably more influential on his after life than the contempt of Catherine. For a man who is greedy of all pleasures, and provided with little money and less dignity of character, we may prophesy a safe and speedy voyage downward. Humble or even truckling virtue may walk unspotted in this life. But only those who despise the pleasures can afford to despise the opinion of the world. A man of a strong, heady temperament, like Villon, is very differently tempted. His eyes lay hold on all provocations greedily, and his heart flames up at a look into imperious desire; he is snared and broached-to by anything and everything, from a pretty face to a piece of pastry in a cookshop window; he will drink the rinsing of the wine cup, stay the latest at the tavern party; tap at the lighted windows, follow the sound of singing, and beat the whole neighborhood for another reveler, as he goes reluctantly homeward; and grudge himself every hour of sleep as a black empty period in which he cannot follow after pleasure. Such a person is lost if he have not dignity, or, failing that, at least pride, which is its shadow and in many ways its substitute. Master Francis, I fancy, would follow his own eager instincts without much spiritual struggle. And we soon find him fallen among thieves in sober, literal earnest, and counting as acquaintances the most disreputable people he could lay his hands on: fellows who stole ducks in Paris Moat; sergeants of the criminal court, and archers of the watch; blackguards who slept at night under the butchers' stalls, and for whom the aforesaid archers peered about carefully with lanterns; Regnier de Montigny, Colin de Cayeux, and their crew, all bound on a favoring breeze toward the gallows; the disorderly abbess of Port Royal, who went about at fair time with soldiers and thieves, and conducted her abbey on the queerest principles; and most likely Perette Mauger, the great Paris receiver of stolen goods, not yet dreaming, poor woman! of the last scene of her career when Henry Cousin, executor of the high justice, shall bury her, alive and most reluctant, in front of the new Montigny gibbet.* Nay, our friend soon began to take a foremost rank in this society. He could string off verses, which is always an agreeable talent; and he could make himself useful in many other ways. The whole ragged army of Bohemia, and whosoever loved good cheer without at all loving to work and pay for it, are addressed in contemporary verses as the "Subjects of François Villon." He was a good genius to all hungry and unscrupulous persons; and became the hero of a whole legendary cycle of tavern tricks and cheateries. At best, these were doubtful levities, rather too thievish for a schoolboy, rather too gamesome for a thief. But he would not linger long in this equivocal border land. He must soon have complied with his surroundings. He was one who would go where the cannikin clinked, not caring who should pay; and from supping in the wolves' den, there is but a step to hunting with the pack. And here, as I am on the chapter of his degradation, I shall say all I mean to say about its darkest expression, and be done with it for good. Some charitable critics see no more than a *jeu d'esprit*, a graceful and trifling exercise of the imagination, in the grimy ballad of Fat Peg ("Grosse Margot"). I am not able to follow these gentlemen to this polite extreme. Out of all Villon's works that ballad stands forth in flaring reality, gross and ghastly, as a thing written in a contraction of disgust. M. Longnon shows us more and more clearly at every page that we are to read our poet literally, that his names are the names of real persons, and the events he chronicles were actual events. But even if the tendency of criticism had run the other way, this ballad would have gone far to prove itself. I can well understand the reluctance of worthy persons in this matter; for of course it is unpleasant to think of a man of genius as one who held, in the words of Marina to Boult—

> "A place, for which the pained'st fiend
> Of Hell would not in reputation change."

But beyond this natural unwillingness, the whole difficulty of the case springs from a highly virtuous ignorance of life. Paris now is not so different from the Paris of then; and the whole of the doings of Bohemia are not written in the sugar-candy pastorals of Murger. It is really not at all surprising that a young man of the fifteenth century, with a knack of making verses, should accept his bread upon disgraceful terms. The race of those who do is not extinct; and some of them to this day write the prettiest verses imaginable. . . . After this, it were impossible for Master Francis to fall lower: to go and steal for himself would be an admirable advance from every point of view, divine or human.

And yet it is not as a thief, but as a homicide, that he makes his first appearance before angry justice. On June 5, 1455, when he was about twenty-four, and had been Master of Arts for a matter of three years, we behold him for the first time quite definitely. Angry justice had, as it were, photographed him in the act of his homicide; and M. Longnon, rummaging among old deeds, has turned up the negative and printed it off for our instruction. Villon had been supping—copiously we may

* "Chronique Scandaleuse," ed. Panthéon, p. 237.

believe—and sat on a stone bench in front of the Church of St. Benoît, in company with a priest called Gilles and a woman of the name of Isabeau. It was nine o'clock, a mighty late hour for the period, and evidently a fine summer's night. Master Francis carried a mantle, like a prudent man, to keep him from the dews, and had a sword below it dangling from his girdle. So these three dallied in front of St. Benoît, taking their pleasure. Suddenly there arrived upon the scene a priest, Philippe Chermoye or Sermaise, also with sword and cloak, and accompanied by one Master Jehan le Mardi. Sermaise, according to Villon's account, which is all we have to go upon, came up blustering and denying God; as Villon rose to make room for him upon the bench, thrust him rudely back into his place; and finally drew his sword and cut open his lower lip, by what I should imagine was a very clumsy stroke. Up to this point, Villon professes to have been a model of courtesy, even of feebleness: and the brawl, in his version, reads like the fable of the wolf and the lamb. But now the lamb was roused; he drew his sword, stabbed Sermaise in the groin, knocked him on the head with a big stone, and then, leaving him to his fate, went away to have his own lip doctored by a barber of the name of Fouquet. In one version, he says that Gilles, Isabeau, and Le Mardi ran away at the first high words, and that he and Sermaise had it out alone; in another, Le Mardi is represented as returning and wresting Villon's sword from him: the reader may please himself. Sermaise was picked up, lay all that night in the prison of Saint Benoît, where he was examined by an official of the châtelet and expressly pardoned Villon, and died on the following Saturday in the Hotel Dieu.

This, as I have said, was in June. Not before January of the next year could Villon extract a pardon from the king; but while his hand was in, he got two. One is for "François des Loges, *alias* de Villon;" and the other runs in the name of François de Montcorbier. Nay, it appears there was a further complication; for in the narrative of the first of these documents, it is mentioned that he passed himself off upon Fouquet, the barber-surgeon, as one Michel Mouton. M. Longnon has a theory that this unhappy accident with Sermaise was the cause of Villon's subsequent irregularities; and that up to that moment he had been the pink of good behavior. But the matter has to my eyes a more dubious air. A pardon necessary for Des Loges and another for Montcorbier? and these two the same person? and one or both of them known by the *alias* of Villon, however honestly come by? and lastly, in the heat of the moment, a fourth name thrown out with an assured countenance? A ship is not to be trusted that sails under so many colors. This is not the simple bearing of innocence. No—the young master was already treading crooked paths; already, he would start and blench at a hand upon his shoulder, with the look we know so well in the face of Hogarth's Idle Apprentice; already, in the blue devils, he would see Henry Cousin, the executor of high justice, going in dolorous procession toward Montfaucon, and hear the wind and the birds crying around Paris gibbet.

A GANG OF THIEVES.—In spite of the prodigious number of people who managed to get hanged, the fifteenth century was by no means a bad time for criminals. A great confusion of parties and great dust of fighting favored the escape of private housebreakers and quiet fellows who stole ducks in Paris Moat. Prisons were leaky; and as we shall see, a man with a few crowns in his pocket and perhaps some acquaintance among the officials, could easily slip out and become once more a free marauder. There was no want of a sanctuary where he might harbor until troubles blew by; and accomplices helped each other with more or less good faith. Clerks, above all, had remarkable facilities for a criminal way of life; for they were privileged, except in cases of notorious incorrigibility, to be plucked from the hands of rude secular justice and tried by a tribunal of their own. In 1402, a couple of thieves, both clerks of the University, were condemned to death by the Provost of Paris. As they were taken to Montfaucon, they kept crying "high and clearly" for their benefit of clergy, but were none the less pitilessly hanged and gibbeted. Indignant Alma Mater interfered before the king; and the Provost was deprived of all royal offices, and condemned to return the bodies and erect a great stone cross, on the road from Paris to the gibbet, graven with the effigies of these two holy martyrs.* We shall hear more of the benefit of clergy; for after this the reader will not be surprised to meet with thieves in the shape of tonsured clerks, or even priests and monks.

To a knot of such learned pilferers our poet certainly belonged; and by turning over a few more of M. Longnon's negatives, we shall get a clear idea of their character and doings. Montigny and De Cayeux are names already known; Guy Tabary, Petit-Jehan, Dom Nicolas, little Thibault, who was both clerk and goldsmith, and who made picklocks and melted plate for himself and his companions—with these the reader has still to become acquainted. Petit-Jehan and De Cayeux were handy fellows and enjoyed a useful pre-eminence in honor of their doings with the picklock. But the flower of the flock was little Thibault; it was reported that no lock could stand before him; he had a persuasive hand; let us salute capacity wherever we may find it. Perhaps the term *gang* is not quite properly applied to the persons whose fortunes we are now about to follow; rather they were independent malefactors, socially intimate, and occasionally joining together for some serious operation, just as modern stockjobbers form a syndicate for an important loan. Nor were they at all particular to any branch of misdoing. They did not scrupulously confine themselves to a single sort of theft, as I hear is common among modern thieves. They were ready for anything, from pitch-and-toss to manslaughter. Montigny, for instance, had neglected neither of these extremes, and we find him accused of cheating at games of hazard on the one hand and on the other of the murder of one Thevenin Pensete in a house by the Cemetery of St. John. If time had only spared us some particulars, might not this last have furnished us with the matter of a grisly winter's tale?

At Christmas-time in 1456, readers of Villon will remember that he was engaged on the "Small Testament." About the same period, he took part in a memorable supper at the Mule Tavern, in front of the Church of St. Mathurin. Tabary, who seems to have been very much Villon's creature, had ordered the supper in the course of the afternoon. He was a man who had had troubles in his time and languished in the Bishop of Paris's prisons on a suspicion of picking locks; confiding, convivial, not very astute—who had copied out a whole improper romance with his own right hand. This supper-party was to be his first introduction to De Cayeux and Petit-Jehan, which was probably a matter of some concern to the poor man's muddy wits; in the sequel, at least, he speaks of both with an undisguised respect, based on professional inferiority in the matter of picklocks. Dom Nicolas, a Picardy monk, was the fifth and last at table. When supper had been dispatched and fairly washed down, we may suppose, with white Baigneux or red Beaune, which were favorite wines among the fellowship, Tabary was solemnly sworn over to secrecy on the night's performances; and the party left the Mule and proceeded to an unoccupied house belonging to Robert de Saint-Simon. This, over a low wall, they entered without difficulty. All but Tabary took off their upper garments: a

* Monstrelet: "Panthéon Littéraire," p. 26.

ladder was found and applied to the high wall which separated Saint-Simon's house from the court of the College of Navarre; the four fellows in their shirt-sleeves (as we might say) clambered over in a twinkling; and Master Guy Tabary remained alone beside the overcoats. From the court the burglars made their way into the vestry of the chapel, where they found a large chest, strengthened with iron bands and closed with four locks. One of these locks they picked, and then, by levering up the corner, forced the other three. Inside was a small coffer, of walnut wood, also barred with iron, but fastened with only three locks, which were all comfortably picked by way of the keyhole. In the walnut coffer—a joyous sight by our thieves' lantern—were five hundred crowns of gold. There was some talk of opening the aumries, where, if they had only known, a booty eight or nine times greater lay ready to their hand; but one of the party (I have a humorous suspicion it was Dom Nicolas, the Picardy monk) hurried them away. It was ten o'clock when they mounted the ladder; it was about midnight before Tabary beheld them coming back. To him they gave ten crowns, and promised a share of a two-crown dinner on the morrow; whereat we may suppose his mouth watered. In course of time, he got wind of the real amount of their booty and understood how scurvily he had been used; but he seems to have borne no malice. How could he, against such superb operators as Petit-Jehan and De Cayeux; or a person like Villon, who could have made a new improper romance out of his own head, instead of merely copying an old one with mechanical right hand?

The rest of the winter was not uneventful for the gang. First they made a demonstration against the Church of St. Mathurin after chalices, and were ignominiously chased away by barking dogs. Then Tabary fell out with Casin Chollet, one of the fellows who stole ducks in Paris Moat, who subsequently became a sergeant of the Châtelet and distinguished himself by misconduct, followed by imprisonment and public castigation, during the wars of Louis Eleventh. The quarrel was not conducted with a proper regard to the king's peace, and the pair publicly belabored each other until the police stepped in, and Master Tabary was cast once more into the prisons of the Bishop. While he still lay in durance, another job was cleverly executed by the band in broad daylight, at the Augustine Monastery. Brother Guillaume Coiffier was beguiled by an accomplice to St. Mathurin to say mass; and during his absence, his chamber was entered and five or six hundred crowns in money and some silver plate successfully abstracted. A melancholy man was Coiffier on his return! Eight crowns from this adventure were forwarded by little Thibault to the incarcerated Tabary; and with these he bribed the jailer and reappeared in Paris taverns. Some time before or shortly after this, Villon set out for Angers, as he had promised in the "Small Testament." The object of this excursion was not merely to avoid the presence of his cruel mistress or the strong arm of Noë le Joly, but to plan a deliberate robbery on his uncle the monk. As soon as he had properly studied the ground, the others were to go over in force from Paris—picklocks and all— and away with my uncle's strongbox! This throws a comical sidelight on his own accusation against his relatives, that they had "forgotten natural duty" and disowned him because he was poor. A poor relation is a distasteful circumstance at the best, but a poor relation who plans deliberate robberies against those of his blood, and trudges hundreds of weary leagues to put them into execution, is surely a little on the wrong side of toleration. The uncle at Angers may have been monstrously undutiful; but the nephew from Paris was upsides with him.

On the 23d April, that venerable and discreet person, Master Pierre Marchand, Curate and Prior of Paray-le-Monial, in the diocese of Chartres, arrived in Paris and put up at the sign of the Three Chandeliers, in the Rue de la Huchette. Next day, or the day after, as he was breakfasting at the sign of the Armchair, he fell into talk with two customers, one of whom was a priest and the other our friend Tabary. The idiotic Tabary became mighty confidential as to his past life. Pierre Marchand, who was an acquaintance of Guillaume Coiffier's and had sympathized with him over his loss, pricked up his ears at the mention of picklocks, and led on the transcriber of improper romances from one thing to another, until they were fast friends. For picklocks the Prior of Paray professed a keen curiosity; but Tabary, upon some late alarm, had thrown all his into the Seine. Let that be no difficulty, however, for was there not little Thibault, who could make them of all shapes and sizes, and to whom Tabary, smelling an accomplice, would be only too glad to introduce his new acquaintance? On the morrow, accordingly, they met; and Tabary, after having first wet his whistle at the Prior's expense, led him to Notre Dame and presented him to four or five "young companions," who were keeping sanctuary in the church. They were all clerks, recently escaped, like Tabary himself, from the episcopal prisons. Among these we may notice Thibault, the operator, a little fellow of twenty-six, wearing long hair behind. The Prior expressed, through Tabary, his anxiety to become their accomplice and altogether such as they were. Mighty polite they showed themselves, and made him many fine speeches in return. But for all that, perhaps because they had longer heads than Tabary, perhaps because it is less easy to wheedle men in a body, they kept obstinately to generalities and gave him no information as to their exploits, past, present, or to come. I suppose Tabary groaned under this reserve; for no sooner were he and the Prior out of the church than he fairly emptied his heart to him, gave him full details of many hanging matters in the past, and explained the future intentions of the band. The scheme of the hour was to rob another Augustine monk, Robert de la Porte, and in this the Prior agreed to take a hand with simulated greed. Thus, in the course of two days, he had turned this wineskin of a Tabary inside out. For a while longer the farce was carried on; the Prior was introduced to Petit-Jehan, whom he describes as a little, very smart man of thirty, with a black beard and a short jacket; an appointment was made and broken in the de la Porte affair; Tabary had some breakfast at the Prior's charge and leaked out more secrets under the influence of wine and friendship; and then all of a sudden, on the 17th day of May, an alarm sprang up, the Prior picked up his skirts and walked quietly over to the Châtelet to make a deposition, and the whole band took to their heels and vanished out of Paris and the sight of the police.

Vanish as they like, they all go with a clog about their feet. Sooner or later, here or there, they will be caught in the fact, and ignominiously sent home. From our vantage of four centuries afterward, it is odd and pitiful to watch the order in which the fugitives are captured and dragged in.

Montigny was the first. In August of that same year, he was laid by the heels on many grievous counts; sacrilegious robberies, frauds, incorrigibility, and that bad business about Thevenin Pensete in the house by the Cemetery of St. John. He was reclaimed by the ecclesiastical authorities as a clerk; but the claim was rebutted on the score of incorrigibility, and ultimately fell to the ground; and he was condemned to death by the Provost of Paris. It was a very rude hour for Montigny, but hope was not yet over. He was a fellow of some birth; his father had been king's pantler;

his sister, probably married to some one about the Court, was in the family way, and her health would be endangered if the execution was proceeded with. So down comes Charles the Seventh with letters of mercy, commuting the penalty to a year in a dungeon on bread and water, and a pilgrimage to the shrine of St. James in Galicia. Alas! the document was incomplete; it did not contain the full tale of Montigny's enormities; it did not recite that he had been denied benefit of clergy, and it said nothing about Thevenin Pensete. Montigny's hour was at hand. Benefit of clergy, honorable descent from king's pantler, sister in the family way, royal letters of commutation—all were of no avail. He had been in prison in Rouen, in Tours, in Bordeaux, and four times already in Paris; and out of all these he had come scatheless; but now he must make a little excursion as far as Montfaucon with Henry Cousin, executor of high justice. There let him swing among the carrion crows.

About a year later, in July 1458, the police laid hands on Tabary. Before the ecclesiastical commissary he was twice examined, and, on the latter occasion, put to the question ordinary and extraordinary. What a dismal change from pleasant suppers at the Mule, where he sat in triumph with expert operators and great wits! He is at the lees of life, poor rogue; and those fingers which once transcribed improper romances are now agonizingly stretched upon the rack. We have no sure knowledge, but we may have a shrewd guess of the conclusion. Tabary, the admirer, would go the same way as those whom he admired.

The last we hear of is Colin de Cayeux. He was caught in autumn 1460, in the great Church of St. Leu d'Esserens, which makes so fine a figure in the pleasant Oise Valley between Creil and Beaumont. He was reclaimed by no less than two bishops; but the Procureur for the Provost held fast by incorrigible Colin. 1460 was an ill-starred year: for justice was making a clean sweep of "poor and indigent persons, thieves, cheats, and lockpickers," in the neighborhood of Paris;[*] and Colin de Cayeux, with many others, was condemned to death and hanged.[†]

VILLON AND THE GALLOWS.—Villon was still absent on the Angers expedition when the Prior of Paray sent such a bombshell among his accomplices; and the dates of his return and arrest remain undiscoverable. M. Campaux plausibly enough opined for the autumn of 1457, which would make him closely follow on Montigny, and the first of those denounced by the Prior to fall into the toils. We may suppose, at least, that it was not long thereafter; we may suppose him competed for between lay and clerical Courts; and we may suppose him alternately pert and impudent, humble and fawning, in his defense. But at the end of all supposing, we come upon some nuggets of fact. For first, he was put to the question by water. He who had tossed off so many cups of white Baigneux or red Beaune, now drank water through linen folds, until his bowels were flooded and his heart stood still. After so much raising of the elbow, so much outcry of fictitious thirst, here at last was enough drinking for a lifetime. Truly, of our pleasant vices, the gods make whips to scourge us. And secondly he was condemned to be hanged. A man may have been expecting a catastrophe for years, and yet find himself unprepared when it arrives. Certainly, Villon found, in this legitimate issue of his career, a very staggering and grave

* "Chron. Scand.," ut supra.
† Here and there, principally in the order of events, this article differs from M. Longnon's own reading of his material. The ground on which he defers the execution of Montigny and De Cayeux beyond the date of their trials seems insufficient. There is a law of parsimony for the construction of historical documents; simplicity is the first duty of narration; and hanged they were.

consideration. Every beast, as he says, clings bitterly to a whole skin. If everything is lost, and even honor, life still remains; nay, and it becomes, like the ewe lamb in Nathan's parable, as dear as all the rest. "Do you fancy," he asks, in a lively ballad, "that I had not enough philosophy under my hood to cry out: 'I appeal'? If I had made any bones about the matter, I should have been planted upright in the fields, by the St. Denis Road"—Montfaucon being on the way to St. Denis. An appeal to Parliament, as we saw in the case of Colin de Cayeux, did not necessarily lead to an acquittal or a commutation; and while the matter was pending, our poet had ample opportunity to reflect on his position. Hanging is a sharp argument, and to swing with many others on the gibbet adds a horrible corollary for the imagination. With the aspect of Montfaucon he was well acquainted; indeed, as the neighborhood appears to have been sacred to junketing and nocturnal picnics of wild young men and women, he had probably studied it under all varieties of hour and weather. And now, as he lay in prison waiting the mortal push, these different aspects crowded back on his imagination with a new and startling significance; and he wrote a ballad, by way of epitaph for himself and his companions, which remains unique in the annals of mankind. It is, in the highest sense, a piece of his biography:

> "La pluye nous a debuez et lavez,
> Et le soleil dessechez et noirciz;
> Pies, corbeaulx, nous ont les yeux cavez,
> Et arrachez la barbe et les sourcilz.
> Jamais, nul temps, nous ne sommes rassis;
> Puis çà, puis là, comme le vent varie,
> A son plaisir sans cesser nous charie,
> Plus becquetez d'oiseaulx que dez à couldre.
> Ne soyez donc de nostre confrairie,
> Mais priez Dieu que tous nous vueille absouldre."

Here is some genuine thieves' literature after so much that was spurious; sharp as an etching, written with a shuddering soul. There is an intensity of consideration in the piece that shows it to be the transcript of familiar thoughts. It is the quintessence of many a doleful nightmare on the straw, when he felt himself swing helpless in the wind, and saw the birds turn about him, screaming and menacing his eyes.

And, after all, the Parliament changed his sentence into one of banishment; and to Roussillon, in Dauphiny, our poet must carry his woes without delay. Travelers between Lyons and Marseilles may remember a station on the line, some way below Vienne, where the Rhone fleets seaward between vine-clad hills. This was Villon's Siberia. It would be a little warm in summer perhaps, and a little cold in winter in that draughty valley between two great mountain fields; but what with the hills, and the racing river, and the fiery Rhone wines, he was little to be pitied on the conditions of his exile. Villon, in a remarkably bad ballad, written in a breath, heartily thanked and fulsomely belauded the Parliament; the *envoi*, like the proverbial postscript of a lady's letter, containing the pith of his performance in a request for three days' delay to settle his affairs and bid his friends farewell. He was probably not followed out of Paris, like Antoine Fradin, the popular preacher, another exile of a few years later, by weeping multitudes;* but I daresay one or two rogues of his acquaintance would keep him company for a mile or so on the south road, and drink

* "Chron. Scand.," p. 338.

a bottle with him before they turned. For banished people, in those days, seem to have set out on their own responsibility, in their own guard, and at their own expense. It was no joke to make one's way from Paris to Roussillon alone and penniless in the fifteenth century. Villon says he left a rag of his tails on every bush. Indeed, he must have had many a weary tramp, many a slender meal, and many a to-do with blustering captains of the Ordonnance. But with one of his light fingers, we may fancy that he took as good as he gave; for every rag of his tail, he would manage to indemnify himself upon the population in the shape of food, or wine, or ringing money; and his route would be traceable across France and Burgundy by housewives and innkeepers lamenting over petty thefts, like the track of a single human locust. A strange figure he must have cut in the eyes of the good country people: this ragged, blackguard city poet, with a smack of the Paris student, and a smack of the Paris street arab, posting along the highways, in rain or sun, among the green fields and vineyards. For himself, he had no taste for rural loveliness; green fields and vineyards would be mighty indifferent to Master Francis; but he would often have his tongue in his cheek at the simplicity of rustic dupes, and often, at city gates, he might stop to contemplate the gibbet with its swinging bodies, and hug himself on his escape.

How long he stayed at Roussillon, how far he became the protege of the Bourbons, to whom that town belonged, or when it was that he took part, under the auspices of Charles of Orleans, in a rhyming tournament, are matters that still remain in darkness, in spite of M. Longnon's diligent rummaging among archives. When we next find him, in summer 1461, alas! he is once more in durance: this time at Meun-sur-Loire, in the prisons of Thibault d'Aussigny, Bishop of Orleans. He had been lowered in a basket into a noisome pit, where he lay, all summer, gnawing hard crusts and railing upon fate. His teeth, he says, were like the teeth of a rake: a touch of haggard portraiture all the more real for being excessive and burlesque, and all the more proper to the man for being a caricature of his own misery. His eyes were "bandaged with thick walls." It might blow hurricanes overhead; the lightning might leap in high heaven; but no word of all this reached him in his noisome pit. Above all, he was fevered with envy and anger at the freedom of others; and his heart flowed over into curses as he thought of Thibault d'Aussigny, walking the streets in God's sunlight, and blessing people with extended fingers. So much we find sharply lined in his own poems. Why he was cast again into prison —how he had again managed to shave the gallows—this we know not, nor, from the destruction of authorities, are we ever likely to learn. But on October 2, 1461, or some day immediately preceding, the new King, Louis Eleventh, made his joyous entry into Meun. Now it was a part of the formality on such occasions for the new King to liberate certain prisoners; and so the basket was let down into Villon's pit, and hastily did Master Francis scramble in, and was most joyfully hauled up, and shot out, blinking and tottering, but once more a free man, into the blessed sun and wind. Now or never is the time for verses! Such a happy revolution would turn the head of a stocking-weaver, and set him jingling rhymes. And so—after a voyage to Paris, where he finds Montigny and De Cayeux clattering their bones upon the gibbet, and his three pupils roistering in Paris streets, "with their thumbs under their girdles"—down sits Master Francis to write his "Large Testament," and perpetuate his name in a sort of glorious ignominy.

THE "LARGE TESTAMENT."—Of this capital achievement and, with it, of Villon's style in general, it is here the place to speak. The "Large Testament" is a hurly-burly of cynical and sentimental reflections about life, jesting legacies to friends and enemies, and, interspersed among these, many admirable ballades, both serious and absurd. With so free a design, no thought that occurred to him would need to be dismissed without expression; and he could draw at full length the portrait of his own bedeviled soul, and of the bleak and blackguardly world which was the theater of his exploits and sufferings. If the reader can conceive something between the slap-dash inconsequence of Byron's "Don Juan" and the racy humorous gravity and brief noble touches that distinguish the vernacular poems of Burns, he will have formed some idea of Villon's style. To the latter writer—except in the ballades, which are quite his own, and can be paralleled from no other language known to me—he bears a particular resemblance. In common with Burns he has a certain rugged compression, a brutal vivacity of epithet, a homely vigor, a delight in local personalities, and an interest in many sides of life, that are often despised and passed over by more effete and cultured poets. Both also, in their strong, easy colloquial way, tend to become difficult and obscure; the obscurity in the case of Villon passing at times into the absolute darkness of cant language. They are perhaps the only two great masters of expression who keep sending their readers to a glossary.

"Shall we not dare to say of a thief," asks Montaigne, "that he has a handsome leg?" It is a far more serious claim that we have to put forward in behalf of Villon. Beside that of his contemporaries, his writing, so full of color, so eloquent, so picturesque, stands out in an almost miraculous isolation. If only one or two of the chroniclers could have taken a leaf out of his book, history would have been a pastime, and the fifteenth century as present to our minds as the age of Charles Second. This gallow's-bird was the one great writer of his age and country, and initiated modern literature for France. Boileau, long ago, in the period of perukes and snuff-boxes, recognized him as the first articulate poet in the language; and if we measure him, not by priority of merit, but living duration of influence, not on a comparison with obscure forerunners, but with great and famous successors, we shall install this ragged and disreputable figure in a far higher niche in glory's temple than was ever dreamed of by the critic. It is, in itself, a memorable fact that, before 1542, in the very dawn of printing, and while modern France was in the making, the works of Villon ran through seven different editions. Out of him flows much of Rabelais; and through Rabelais, directly and indirectly, a deep, permanent, and growing inspiration. Not only his style, but his callous pertinent way of looking upon the sordid and ugly sides of life, becomes every day a more specific feature in the literature of France. And only the other year, a work of some power appeared in Paris, and appeared with infinite scandal, which owed its whole inner significance and much of its outward form to the study of our rhyming thief.

The world to which he introduces us is, as before said, blackguardly and bleak. Paris swarms before us, full of famine, shame, and death; monks and the servants of great lords hold high wassail upon cakes and pastry; the poor man licks his lips before the baker's window; people with patched eyes sprawl all night under the stalls; chuckling Tabary transcribes an improper romance; bare-bosomed lasses and ruffling students swagger in the streets; the drunkard goes stumbling homeward; the graveyard is full of bones; and away on Montfaucon, Colin de Cayeux and Montigny hang draggled in the rain. Is there nothing better to be seen than sordid misery and worthless joys? Only where the poor old mother of the poet kneels in church below painted windows, and makes tremulous supplication to the Mother of God.

In our mixed world, full of green fields and happy lovers, where not long before Joan of Arc had led one of the highest and noblest lives in the whole story of mankind, this was all worth chronicling that our poet could perceive. His eyes were indeed sealed with his own filth. He dwelt all his life in a pit more noisome than the dungeon at Meun. In the moral world, also, there are large phenomena not cognizable out of holes and corners. Loud winds blow, speeding home deep-laden ships and sweeping rubbish from the earth; the lightning leaps and cleans the face of heaven; high purposes and brave passions shake and sublimate men's spirits; and meanwhile, in the narrow dungeon of his soul, Villon is mumbling crusts and picking vermin.

Along with this deadly gloom of outlook, we must take another characteristic of his work: its unrivaled insincerity. I can give no better similitude of this quality than I have given already: that he comes up with a whine, and runs away with a whoop and his finger to his nose. His pathos is that of a professional mendicant who should happen to be a man of genius; his levity that of a bitter street arab, full of bread. On a first reading, the pathetic passages pre-occupy the reader, and he is cheated out of an alms in the shape of sympathy. But when the thing is studied the illusion fades away: in the transitions, above all, we can detect the evil, ironical temper of the man; and instead of a flighty work, where many crude but genuine feelings tumble together for the mastery as in the lists of tournament, we are tempted to think of the "Large Testament" as of one long-drawn epical grimace, pulled by a merry-andrew, who has found a certain despicable eminence over human respect and human affections by perching himself astride upon the gallows. Between these two views, at best, all temperate judgments will be found to fall; and rather, as I imagine, toward the last.

There were two things on which he felt with perfect and, in one case, even threatening sincerity.

The first of these was an undisguised envy of those richer than himself. He was forever drawing a parallel, already exemplified from his own words, between the happy life of the well-to-do and the miseries of the poor. Burns, too proud and honest not to work, continued through all reverses to sing of poverty with a light, defiant note. Beranger waited till he was himself beyond the reach of want, before writing the "Old Vagabond" or "Jacques." Samuel Johnson, although he was very sorry to be poor, "was a great arguer for the advantages of poverty" in his ill days. Thus it is that brave men carry their crosses, and smile with the fox burrowing in their vitals. But Villon, who had not the courage to be poor with honesty, now whiningly implores our sympathy, now shows his teeth upon the dung-heap with an ugly snarl. He envies bitterly, envies passionately. Poverty, he protests, drives men to steal, as hunger makes the wolf sally from the forest. The poor, he goes on, will always have a carping word to say, or, if that outlet be denied, nourish rebellious thoughts. It is a calumny on the noble army of the poor. Thousands in a small way of life, ay, and even in the smallest, go through life with tenfold as much honor and dignity and peace of mind, as the rich gluttons whose dainties and state-beds awakened Villon's covetous temper. And every morning's sun sees thousands who pass whistling to their toil. But Villon was the "mauvais pauvre" defined by Victor Hugo, and in its English expression, so admirably stereotyped by Dickens. He was the first wicked sansculotte. He is the man of genius with the moleskin cap. He is mighty pathetic and beseeching here in the street, but I would not go down a dark road with him for a large consideration.

The second of the points on which he was genuine and emphatic was common to the Middle Ages; a deep and somewhat sniveling conviction of the transitory nature of this life and the pity and horror of death. Old age and the grave, with some dark and yet half-skeptical terror of an after-world—these were ideas that clung about his bones like a disease. An old ape, as he says, may play all the tricks in its repertory, and none of them will tickle an audience into good humor. It is not the old jester who receives most recognition at a tavern party, but the young fellow, fresh and handsome, who knows the new slang, and carries off his vice with a certain air. Of this, as a tavern jester himself, he would be pointedly conscious. As for the women with whom he was best acquainted, his reflections on their old age, in all their harrowing pathos, shall remain in the original for me. Horace has disgraced himself to something the same tune; but what Horace throws out with an ill-favored laugh, Villon dwells on with an almost maudlin whimper.

It is in death that he finds his truest inspiration; in the swift and sorrowful change that overtakes beauty; in the strange revolution by which great fortunes and renowns are diminished to a handful of churchyard dust; and in the utter passing away of what was once lovable and mighty. It is in this that the mixed texture of his thought enables him to reach such poignant and terrible effects, and to enhance pity with ridicule, like a man cutting capers to a funeral march. It is in this, also, that he rises out of himself into the higher spheres of art. So, in the ballade by which he is best known, he rings the changes on names that once stood for beautiful and queenly women, and are now no more than letters and a legend. "Where are the snows of yester year?" runs the burden. And so, in another not so famous, he passes in review the different degrees of bygone men, from the Holy Apostles and the golden Emperor of the East, down to the heralds, pursuivants, and trumpeters, who also bore their part in the world's pageantries and ate greedily at great folks' tables: all this to the refrain of "So much carry the winds away!" Probably, there was some melancholy in his mind for a yet lower grade, and Montigny and Colin de Cayeux clattering their bones on Paris gibbet. Alas, and with so pitiful an experience of life, Villon can offer us nothing but terror and lamentation about death! No one has ever more skillfully communicated his own disenchantment; no one ever blown a more ear-piercing note of sadness. This unrepentant thief can attain neither to Christian confidence, nor to the spirit of the bright Greek saying, that whom the gods love die early. It is a poor heart, and a poorer age, that cannot accept the conditions of life with some heroic readiness.

.   .   .   .

The date of the "Large Testament" is the last date in the poet's biography. After having achieved that admirable and despicable performance, he disappears into the night from whence he came. How or when he died, whether decently in bed or trussed up to a gallows, remains a riddle for foolhardy commentators. It appears his health had suffered in the pit at Meun; he was thirty years of age and quite bald; with the notch in his under lip where Sermaise had struck him with the sword, and what wrinkles the reader may imagine. In default of portraits, this is all I have been able to piece together, and perhaps even the baldness should be taken as a figure of his destitution. A sinister dog, in all likelihood, but with a look in his eye, and the loose flexile mouth that goes with wit and an over-weening sensual temperament. Certainly the sorriest figure on the rolls of fame.

THE OPEN BOAT

A Tale intended to be after the fact. Being the Experience of Four Men
from the Sunk Steamer "Commodore"

STEPHEN CRANE (1871–1900)

I

None of them knew the colour of the sky. Their eyes glanced level, and were fastened upon the waves that swept toward them. These waves were of the hue of slate, save for the tops, which were of foaming white, and all of the men knew the colours of the sea. The horizon narrowed and widened, and dipped and rose, and at all times its edge was jagged with waves that seemed thrust up in points like rocks.

Many a man ought to have a bath-tub larger than the boat which here rode upon the sea. These waves were most wrongfully and barbarously abrupt and tall, and each froth-top was a problem in small boat navigation.

The cook squatted in the bottom and looked with both eyes at the six inches of gunwale which separated him from the ocean. His sleeves were rolled over his fat forearms, and the two flaps of his unbuttoned vest dangled as he bent to bail out the boat. Often he said: "Gawd! That was a narrow clip." As he remarked it he invariably gazed eastward over the broken sea.

The oiler, steering with one of the two oars in the boat, sometimes raised himself suddenly to keep clear of water that swirled in over the stern. It was a thin little oar and it seemed often ready to snap.

The correspondent, pulling at the other oar, watched the waves and wondered why he was there.

The injured captain, lying in the bow, was at this time buried in that profound dejection and indifference which comes, temporarily at least, to even the bravest and most enduring when, willy nilly, the firm fails, the army loses, the ship goes down. The mind of the master of a vessel is rooted deep in the timbers of her, though he command for a day or a decade, and this captain had on him the stern impression of a scene in the greys of dawn of seven turned faces, and later a stump of a top-mast with a white ball on it that slashed to and fro at the waves, went low and lower, and down. Thereafter there was something strange in his voice. Although steady, it was deep with mourning, and of a quality beyond oration or tears.

"Keep 'er a little more south, Billie," said he.

"A little more south, sir," said the oiler in the stern.

A seat in this boat was not unlike a seat upon a bucking broncho, and, by the same token, a broncho is not much smaller. The craft pranced and reared, and plunged like an animal. As each wave came, and she rose for it, she seemed like a horse making at a fence outrageously high. The manner of her scramble over these walls of water is a mystic thing, and, moreover, at the top of them were ordinarily these problems in white water, the foam racing down from the summit of each wave, requiring a new leap, and a leap from the air. Then, after scornfully bumping a crest, she would slide, and race, and splash down a long incline, and arrive bobbing and nodding in front of the next menace.

A singular disadvantage of the sea lies in the fact that after successfully surmounting one wave you discover that there is another behind it just as important and just as nervously anxious to do something effective in the way of swamping boats. In a ten-foot dingey one can get an idea of the resources of the sea in the line of waves that is not probable to the average experience which is never at sea in a dingey. As each slaty wall of water approached, it shut all else from the view of the men in the boat, and it was not difficult to imagine that this particular wave was the final outburst of the ocean, the last effort of the grim water. There was a terrible grace in the move of the waves, and they came in silence, save for the snarling of the crests.

In the wan light, the faces of the men must have been grey. Their eyes must have glinted in strange ways as they gazed steadily astern. Viewed from a balcony, the whole thing would doubtless have been weirdly picturesque. But the men in the boat had no time to see it, and if they had had leisure there were other things to occupy their minds. The sun swung steadily up the sky, and they knew it was broad day because the colour of the sea changed from slate to emerald-green, streaked with amber lights, and the foam was like tumbling snow. The process of the breaking day was unknown to them. They were aware only of this effect upon the colour of the waves that rolled toward them.

In disjointed sentences the cook and the correspondent argued as to the difference between a life-saving station and a house of refuge. The cook had said: "There's a house of refuge just north of the Mosquito Inlet Light, and as soon as they see us, they'll come off in their boat and pick us up."

"As soon as who see us?" said the correspondent.

"The crew," said the cook.

"Houses of refuge don't have crews," said the correspondent. "As I understand them, they are only places where clothes and grub are stored for the benefit of shipwrecked people. They don't carry crews."

"Oh yes, they do," said the cook.

"No, they don't," said the correspondent.

"Well, we're not there yet, anyhow," said the oiler, in the stern.

"Well," said the cook, "perhaps it's not a house of refuge that I'm thinking of as being near Mosquito Inlet Light. Perhaps it's a life-saving station."

"We're not there yet," said the oiler, in the stern.

II

As for the boat bounced from the top of each wave, the wind tore through the hair of the hatless men, and as the craft plopped her stern down again the spray slashed past them. The crest of each of these waves was a hill, from the top of which the men surveyed, for a moment, a broad tumultuous expanse, shining and wind-driven. It was probably splendid. It was probably glorious, this play of the free sea, wild with lights of emerald and white and amber.

"Bully good thing it's an on-shore wind," said the cook. "If not, where would we be? Wouldn't have a show."

"That's right," said the correspondent.

The busy oiler nodded his assent.

Then the captain, in the bow, chuckled in a way that expressed humour, contempt, tragedy, all in one. "Do you think we've got much of a show now, boys?" said he.

Whereupon the three were silent, save for a trifle of hemming and hawing. To express any particular optimism at this time they felt to be childish and stupid, but they all doubtless possessed this sense of the situation in their mind. A young man thinks doggedly at such times. On the other hand, the ethics of their condition was decidedly against any open suggestion of hopelessness. So they were silent.

"Oh, well," said the captain, soothing his children, "we'll get ashore all right."

But there was that in his tone which made them think, so the oiler quoth: "Yes! If this wind holds!"

The cook was bailing: "Yes! If we don't catch hell in the surf."

Canton flannel gulls flew near and far. Sometimes they sat down on the sea, near patches of brown seaweed that rolled over the waves with a movement like carpets on a line in a gale. The birds sat comfortably in groups, and they were envied by some in the dingey, for the wrath of the sea was no more to them than it was to a covey of prairie chickens a thousand miles inland. Often they came very close and stared at the men with black bead-like eyes. At these times they were uncanny and sinister in their unblinking scrutiny, and the men hooted angrily at them, telling them to be gone. One came, and evidently decided to alight on the top of the captain's head. The bird flew parallel to the boat and did not circle, but made short sidelong jumps in the air in chicken-fashion. His black eyes were wistfully fixed upon the captain's head. "Ugly brute," said the oiler to the bird. "You look as if you were made with a jackknife." The cook and the correspondent swore darkly at the creature. The captain naturally wished to knock it away with the end of the heavy painter; but he did not dare to do it, because anything resembling an emphatic gesture would have capsized this freighted boat, and so with his open hand, the captain gently and carefully waved the gull away. After it had been discouraged from the pursuit the captain breathed easier on account of his hair, and others breathed easier because the bird struck their minds at this time as being somehow gruesome and ominous.

In the meantime the oiler and the correspondent rowed. And also they rowed.

They sat together in the same seat, and each rowed an oar. Then the oiler took both oars; then the correspondent took both oars; then the oiler; then the correspondent. They rowed and they rowed. The very ticklish part of the business was when the time came for the reclining one in the stern to take his turn at the oars. By the very last star of truth, it is easier to steal eggs from under a hen than it was to change seats in the dingey. First the man in the stern slid his hand along the thwart and moved with care, as if he were of Sèvres. Then the man in the rowing seat slid his hand along the other thwart. It was all done with the most extraordinary care. As the two sidled past each other, the whole party kept watchful eyes on the coming wave, and the captain cried: "Look out now! Steady there!"

The brown mats of seaweed that appeared from time to time were like islands, bits of earth. They were travelling, apparently, neither one way nor the other. They were, to all intents, stationary. They informed the men in the boat that it was making progress slowly toward the land.

The captain, rearing cautiously in the bow, after the dingey soared on a great swell, said that he had seen the lighthouse at Mosquito Inlet. Presently the cook remarked that he had seen it. The correspondent was at the oars then, and for some reason he too wished to look at the lighthouse, but his back was toward the far shore and the waves were important, and for some time he could not seize an opportunity to turn his head. But at last there came a wave more gentle than the others, and when at the crest of it he swiftly scoured the western horizon.

"See it?" said the captain.

"No," said the correspondent slowly. "I didn't see anything."

"Look again," said the captain. He pointed. "It's exactly in that direction."

At the top of another wave, the correspondent did as he was bid, and this time his eyes chanced on a small still thing on the edge of the swaying horizon. It was precisely like the point of a pin. It took an anxious eye to find a lighthouse so tiny.

"Think we'll make it, captain?"

"If this wind holds and the boat don't swamp, we can't do much else," said the captain.

The little boat, lifted by each towering sea, and splashed viciously by the crests, made progress that in the absence of seaweed was not apparent to those in her. She seemed just a wee thing wallowing, miraculously top up, at the mercy of five oceans. Occasionally, a great spread of water, like white flames, swarmed into her.

"Bail her, cook," said the captain serenely.

"All right, captain," said the cheerful cook.

III

It would be difficult to describe the subtle brotherhood of men that was here established on the seas. No one said that it was so. No one mentioned it. But it dwelt in the boat, and each man felt it warm him. They were a captain, an oiler, a cook, and a correspondent, and they were friends, friends in a more curiously iron-bound degree than may be common. The hurt captain, lying against the water-jar in the bow, spoke always in a low voice and calmly, but he could never command a more ready and swiftly obedient crew than the motley three of the dingey. It was more than a mere recognition of what was best for the common safety. There was surely in it a quality that was personal and heartfelt. And after this devotion to the commander of the boat there was this comradeship that the correspondent, for instance, who had been taught to be cynical of men, knew even at the time was the best experience of his life. But no one said that it was so. No one mentioned it.

"I wish we had a sail," remarked the captain. "We might try my overcoat on the end of an oar and give you two boys a chance to rest." So the cook and the correspondent held the mast and spread wide the overcoat. The oiler steered, and the little boat made good way with her new rig. Sometimes the oiler had to scull sharply to keep a sea from breaking into the boat, but otherwise sailing was a success.

Meanwhile the lighthouse had been growing slowly larger. It had now almost assumed colour, and appeared like a little grey shadow on the sky. The man at the oars could not be prevented from turning his head rather often to try for a glimpse of this little grey shadow.

At last, from the top of each wave the men in the tossing boat could see land. Even as the lighthouse was an upright shadow on the sky, this land seemed but a long black shadow on the sea. It certainly was thinner than paper. "We must be about opposite New Smyrna," said the cook, who had coasted this shore often in schooners. "Captain, by the way, I believe they abandoned that life-saving station there about a year ago."

"Did they?" said the captain.

The wind slowly died away. The cook and the correspondent were not now obliged to slave in order to hold high the oar. But the waves continued their old impetuous swooping at the dingey, and the little craft, no longer under way, struggled woundily over them. The oiler or the correspondent took the oars again.

Shipwrecks are apropos of nothing. If men could only train for them and have them occur when the men had reached pink condition, there would be less drowning at sea. Of the four in the dingey none had slept any time worth mentioning for two days and two nights previous to embarking in the dingey, and in the excitement of clambering about the deck of a foundering ship they had also forgotten to eat heartily.

For these reasons, and for others, neither the oiler nor the correspondent was fond of rowing at this time. The correspondent wondered ingenuously how in the name of all that was sane could there be people who thought it amusing to row a boat It was not an amusement; it was a diabolical punishment, and even a genius of mental aberrations could never conclude that it was anything but a horror to the muscles and a crime against the back. He mentioned to the boat in general how the amusement of rowing struck him, and the weary-faced oiler smiled in full sympathy. Previously to the foundering, by the way, the oiler had worked double-watch in the engine-room of the ship.

"Take her easy, now, boys," said the captain. "Don't spend yourselves. If we have to run a surf you'll need all your strength, because we'll sure have to swim for it. Take your time."

Slowly the land arose from the sea. From a black line it became a line of black and a line of white, trees and sand. Finally, the captain said that he could make out a house on the shore. "That's the house of refuge, sure," said the cook. "They'll see us before long, and come out after us."

The distant lighthouse reared high. "The keeper ought to be able to make us out now, if he's looking through a glass," said the captain. "He'll notify the life-saving people."

"None of those other boats could have got ashore to give word of the wreck," said the oiler, in a low voice. "Else the lifeboat would be out hunting us."

Slowly and beautifully the land loomed out of the sea. The wind came again. It had veered from the north-east to the south-east. Finally, a new sound struck the ears of the men in the boat. It was the low thunder of the surf on the shore. "We'll never be able to make the lighthouse now," said the captain. "Swing her head a little more north, Billie."

"A little more north, sir," said the oiler.

Whereupon the little boat turned her nose once more down the wind, and all but the oarsman watched the shore grow. Under the influence of this expansion doubt and direful apprehension was leaving the minds of the men. The management of the boat was still most absorbing, but it could not prevent a quiet cheerfulness. In an hour, perhaps, they would be ashore.

Their backbones had become thoroughly used to balancing in the boat, and they now rode this wild colt of a dingey like circus men. The correspondent thought that he had been drenched to the skin, but happening to feel in the top pocket of his coat, he found therein eight cigars. Four of them were soaked with sea-water; four were perfectly scatheless. After a search, somebody produced three dry matches, and thereupon the four waifs rode impudently in their little boat, and with an assurance of an impending rescue shining in their eyes, puffed at the big cigars and judged well and ill of all men. Everybody took a drink of water.

IV

"Cook," remarked the captain, "there don't seem to be any signs of life about your house of refuge."

"No," replied the cook. "Funny they don't see us!"

A broad stretch of lowly coast lay before the eyes of the men. It was of low dunes topped with dark vegetation. The roar of the surf was plain, and sometimes they could see the white lip of a wave as it spun up the beach. A tiny house was blocked out black upon the sky. Southward, the slim lighthouse lifted its little grey length.

Tide, wind, and waves were swinging the dingey northward. "Funny they don't see us," said the men.

The surf's roar was here dulled, but its tone was, nevertheless, thunderous and mighty. As the boat swam over the great rollers, the men sat listening to this roar. "We'll swamp sure," said everybody.

It is fair to say here that there was not a life-saving station within twenty miles in either direction, but the men did not know this fact, and in consequence they made dark and opprobrious remarks concerning the eyesight of the nation's live-savers. Four scowling men sat in the dingey and surpassed records in the invention of epithets.

"Funny they don't see us."

The light-heartedness of a former time had completely faded. To their sharpened minds it was easy to conjure pictures of all kinds of incompetency and blindness and, indeed, cowardice. There was the shore of the populous land, and it was bitter and bitter to them that from it came no sign.

"Well," said the captain, ultimately, "I suppose we'll have to make a try for ourselves. If we stay out here too long, we'll none of us have strength left to swim after the boat swamps."

And so the oiler, who was at the oars, turned the boat straight for the shore. There was a sudden tightening of muscles. There was some thinking.

"If we don't all get ashore—" said the captain. "If we don't all get ashore, I suppose you fellows know where to send news of my finish?"

They then briefly exchanged some addresses and admonitions. As for the reflections of the men, there was a great deal of rage in them. Perchance they might be formulated thus: "If I am going to be drowned—if I am going to be drowned—if I am going to be drowned, why, in the name of the seven mad gods who rule the sea, was I allowed to come thus far and contemplate sand and trees? Was I brought here merely to have my nose dragged away as I was about to nibble the sacred cheese of life? It is preposterous. If this old ninny-woman, Fate, cannot do better than this, she should be deprived of the management of men's fortunes. She is an old hen who knows not her intention. If she has decided to drown me, why did she not do it in the beginning and save me all this trouble? The whole affair is absurd. . . . But no, she cannot mean to drown me. She dare not drown me. She cannot drown me. Not after all this work." Afterward the man might have had an impulse to shake his fist at the clouds: "Just you drown me, and then hear what I call you!"

The billows that came at this time were more formidable. They seemed always just about to break and roll over the little boat in a turmoil of foam. There was a preparatory and long growl in the speech of them. No mind unused to the sea would have concluded that the dingey could ascend these sheer heights in time. The shore was still afar. The oiler was a wily surfman. "Boys," he said swiftly, "she won't live three minutes more, and we're too far out to swim. Shall I take her to sea again, captain?"

"Yes! Go ahead!" said the captain.

This oiler, by a series of quick miracles, and fast and steady oarsmanship, turned the boat in the middle of the surf and took her safely to sea again.

There was a considerable silence as the boat bumped over the furrowed sea to deeper water. Then somebody in gloom spoke. "Well, anyhow, they must have seen us from the shore by now."

The gulls went in slanting flight up the wind toward the grey desolate east. A squall, marked by dingy clouds, and clouds brick-red, like smoke from a burning building, appeared from the south-east.

"What do you think of those life-saving people? Ain't they peaches?"

"Funny they haven't seen us."

"Maybe they think we're out here for sport! Maybe they think we're fishin'. Maybe they think we're damned fools."

It was a long afternoon. A changed tide tried to force them southward, but wind and wave said northward. Far ahead, where coastline, sea and sky formed their mighty angle, there were little dots which seemed to indicate a city on the shore.

"St. Augustine?"

The captain shook his head. "Too near Mosquito Inlet."

And the oiler rowed, and then the correspondent rowed. Then the oiler rowed. It was a weary business. The human back can become the seat of more aches and pains than are registered in books for the composite anatomy of a regiment. It is a limited area, but it can become the theatre of innumerable muscular conflicts, tangles, wrenches, knots, and other comforts.

"Did you ever like to row, Billie?" asked the correspondent.

"No," said the oiler. "Hang it."

When one exchanged the rowing-seat for a place in the bottom of the boat, he suffered a bodily depression that caused him to be careless of everything save an obligation to wiggle one finger. There was cold sea-water swashing to and fro in the boat, and he lay in it. His head, pillowed on a thwart, was within an inch of the swirl of a wave crest, and sometimes a particularly obstreperous sea came in-board and drenched him once more. But these matters did not annoy him. It is almost certain that if the boat had capsized he would have tumbled comfortably out upon the ocean as if he felt sure that it was a great soft mattress.

"Look! There's a man on the shore!"

"Where?"

"There! See 'im? See 'im?"

"Yes, sure! He's walking along."

"Now he's stopped. Look! He's facing us!"

"He's waving at us!"

"So he is! By thunder!"

"Ah, now we're all right! Now we're all right! There'll be a boat out here for us in half an hour."

"He's going on. He's running. He's going up to that house there."

The remote beach seemed lower than the sea, and it required a searching glance to discern the little black figure. The captain saw a floating stick and they rowed to it. A bath-towel was by some weird chance in the boat, and, tying this on the stick, the captain waved it. The oarsman did not dare turn his head, so he was obliged to ask questions.

"What's he doing now?"

"He's standing still again. He's looking, I think. . . . There he goes again. Toward the house. . . . Now he's stopped again."

"Is he waving at us?"

"No, not now! he was, though."

"Look! There comes another man!"

"He's running."

"Look at him go, would you."

"Why, he's on a bicycle. Now he's met the other man. They're both waving at us. Look!"

"There comes something up the beach."

"What the devil is that thing?"

"Why, it looks like a boat."

"Why, certainly it's a boat."

"No, it's on wheels."

"Yes, so it is. Well, that must be the life-boat. They drag them along shore on a wagon.

"That's the life-boat, sure."

"No, by—, it's—it's an omnibus."

"I tell you it's a life-boat."

"It is not! It's an omnibus. I can see it plain. See? One of these big hotel omnibuses."

"By thunder, you're right. It's an omnibus, sure as fate. What do you suppose they are doing with an omnibus? Maybe they are going around collecting the life-crew, hey?"

"That's it, likely. Look! There's a fellow waving a little black flag. He's standing on the steps of the omnibus. There comes those other two fellows. Now they're all talking together. Look at the fellow with the flag. Maybe he ain't waving it."

"That ain't a flag, is it? That's his coat. Why, certainly, that's his coat."

"So it is. It's his coat. He's taken it off and is waving it around his head. But would you look at him swing it."

"Oh, say, there isn't any life-saving station there. That's just a winter resort hotel omnibus that has brought over some of the boarders to see us drown."

"What's that idiot with the coat mean? What's he signalling, anyhow?"

"It looks as if he were trying to tell us to go north. There must be a life-saving station up there."

"No! He thinks we're fishing. Just giving us a merry hand. See? Ah, there, Willie."

"Well, I wish I could make something out of those signals. What do you suppose he means?"

"He don't mean anything. He's just playing."

"Well, if he'd just signal us to try the surf again, or to go to sea and wait, or go north, or go south, or go to hell—there would be some reason in it. But look at him. He just stands there and keeps his coat revolving like a wheel. The ass!"

"There come more people."

"Now there's quite a mob. Look! Isn't that a boat?"

"Where? Oh, I see where you mean. No, that's no boat."

"That fellow is still waving his coat."

"He must think we like to see him do that. Why don't he quit it? It don't mean anything."

"I don't know. I think he is trying to make us go north. It must be that there's a life-saving station there somewhere."

"Say, he ain't tired yet. Look at 'im wave."

"Wonder how long he can keep that up. He's been revolving his coat ever since he caught sight of us. He's an idiot. Why aren't they getting men to bring a boat out? A fishing boat—one of those big yawls—could come out here all right. Why don't he do something?"

"Oh, it's all right, now."

"They'll have a boat out here for us in less than no time, now that they've seen us."

A faint yellow tone came into the sky over the low land. The shadows on the sea slowly deepened. The wind bore coldness with it, and the men began to shiver.

"Holy smoke!" said one, allowing his voice to express his impious mood, "if we keep on monkeying out here! If we've got to flounder out here all night!"

"Oh, we'll never have to stay here all night! Don't you worry. They've seen us now, and it won't be long before they'll come chasing out after us."

The shore grew dusky. The man waving a coat blended gradually into this gloom, and it swallowed in the same manner the omnibus and the group of people. The spray, when it dashed uproariously over the side, made the voyagers shrink, and swear like men who were being branded.

"I'd like to catch the chump who waved that coat. I feel like soaking him one, just for luck."

"Why? What did he do?"

"Oh, nothing, but then he seemed so damned cheerful."

In the meantime the oiler rowed, and then the correspondent rowed, and then the oiler rowed. Grey-faced and bowed forward, they mechanically, turn by turn, plied the leaden oars. The form of the lighthouse had vanished from the southern horizon, but finally a pale star appeared, just lifting from the sea. The streaked saffron in the west passed before the all-merging darkness, and the sea to the east was black. The land had vanished, and was expressed only by the low and drear thunder of the surf.

"If I am going to be drowned—if I am going to be drowned—if I am going to be drowned, why, in the name of the seven mad gods who rule the sea, was I allowed to come thus far and contemplate sand and trees? Was I brought here merely to have my nose dragged away as I was about to nibble the sacred cheese of life?"

The patient captain, drooped over the water-jar, was sometimes obliged to speak to the oarsman.

"Keep her head up! Keep her head up!"

" 'Keep her head up,' sir." The voices were weary and low.

This was surely a quiet evening. All save the oarsman lay heavily and listlessly in the boat's bottom. As for him, his eyes were just capable of noting the tall black waves that swept forward in a most sinister silence, save for an occasional subdued growl of a crest.

The cook's head was on a thwart, and he looked without interest at the water under his nose. He was deep in other scenes. Finally he spoke. "Billie," he murmured, dreamfully, "what kind of pie do you like best?"

V

"Pie," said the oiler and the correspondent, agitatedly. "Don't talk about those things, blast you!"

"Well," said the cook, "I was just thinking about ham sandwiches, and—"

A night on the sea in an open boat is a long night. As darkness settled finally, the shine of the light, lifting from the sea in the south, changed to full gold. On the northern horizon a new light appeared, a small bluish gleam on the edge of the waters. These two lights were the furniture of the world. Otherwise there was nothing but waves.

Two men huddled in the stern, and distances were so magnificent in the dingey that the rower was enabled to keep his feet partly warmed by thrusting them under his companions. Their legs indeed extended far under the rowing-seat until they touched the feet of the captain forward. Sometimes, despite the efforts of the tired oarsman, a wave came piling into the boat, an icy wave of the night, and the chilling water soaked them anew. They would twist their bodies for a moment and groan, and sleep the dead sleep once more, while the water in the boat gurgled about them as the craft rocked.

The plan of the oiler and the correspondent was for one to row until he lost the ability, and then arouse the other from his sea-water couch in the bottom of the boat.

The oiler plied the oars until his head drooped forward, and the overpowering sleep blinded him. And he rowed yet afterward. Then he touched a man in the bottom of the boat, and called his name. "Will you spell me for a little while?" he said, meekly.

"Sure, Billie," said the correspondent, awakening and dragging himself to a sitting position. They exchanged places carefully, and the oiler, cuddling down in the sea-water at the cook's side, seemed to go to sleep instantly.

The particular violence of the sea had ceased. The waves came without snarling. The obligation of the man at the oars was to keep the boat headed so that the tilt of the rollers would not capsize her, and to preserve her from filling when the crests rushed past. The black waves were silent and hard to be seen in the darkness. Often one was almost upon the boat before the oarsman was aware.

In a low voice the correspondent addressed the captain. He was not sure that the captain was awake, although this iron man seemed to be always awake. "Captain, shall I keep her making for that light north, sir?"

The same steady voice answered him. "Yes. Keep it about two points off the port bow."

The cook had tied a life-belt around himself in order to get even the warmth which this clumsy cork contrivance could donate, and he seemed almost stove-like when a rower, whose teeth invariably chattered wildly as soon as he ceased his labour, dropped down to sleep.

The correspondent, as he rowed, looked down at the two men sleeping under-foot. The cook's arm was around the oiler's shoulders, and, with their fragmentary clothing and haggard faces, they were the babes of the sea, a grotesque rendering of the old babes in the wood.

Later he must have grown stupid at his work, for suddenly there was a growling of water, and a crest came with a roar and a swash into the boat, and it was a wonder that it did not set the cook afloat in his life-belt. The cook continued to sleep, but the oiler sat up, blinking his eyes and shaking with the new cold.

"Oh, I'm awful sorry, Billie," said the correspondent, contritely.

"That's all right, old boy," said the oiler, and lay down again and was asleep.

Presently it seemed that even the captain dozed, and the correspondent thought that he was the one man afloat on all the oceans. The wind had a voice as it came over the waves, and it was sadder than the end.

There was a long, loud swishing astern of the boat, and a gleaming trail of phosphorescence, like blue flame, was furrowed on the black waters. It might have been made by a monstrous knife.

Then there came a stillness, while the correspondent breathed with the open mouth and looked at the sea.

Suddenly there was another swish and another long flash of bluish light, and this time it was alongside the boat, and might almost have been reached with an oar. The correspondent saw an enormous fin speed like a shadow through the water, hurling the crystalline spray and leaving the long glowing trail.

The correspondent looked over his shoulder at the captain. His face was hidden, and he seemed to be asleep. He looked at the babes of the sea. They certainly were asleep. So, being bereft of sympathy, he leaned a little way to one side and swore softly into the sea.

But the thing did not then leave the vicinity of the boat. Ahead or astern, on one side or the other, at intervals long or short, fled the long sparkling streak, and there was to be heard the whiroo of the dark fin. The speed and power of the thing was greatly to be admired. It cut the water like a gigantic and keen projectile.

The presence of this biding thing did not affect the man with the same horror that it would if he had been a picnicker. He simply looked at the sea dully and swore in an undertone.

Nevertheless, it is true that he did not wish to be alone with the thing. He wished one of his companions to awaken by chance and keep him company with it. But the captain hung motionless over the water-jar, and the oiler and the cook in the bottom of the boat were plunged in slumber.

VI

"If I am going to be drowned—if I am going to be drowned—if I am going to be drowned, why, in the name of the seven mad gods who rule the sea, was I allowed to come thus far and contemplate sand and trees?"

During this dismal night, it may be remarked that a man would conclude that it was really the intention of the seven mad gods to drown him, despite the abominable injustice of it. For it was certainly an abominable injustice to drown a man who had worked so hard, so hard. The man felt it would be a crime most unnatural. Other people had drowned at sea since galleys swarmed with painted sails, but still—

When it occurs to a man that nature does not regard him as important, and that she feels she would not maim the universe by disposing of him, he at first wishes to throw bricks at the temple, and he hates deeply the fact that there are no bricks and no temples. Any visible expression of nature would surely be pelleted with his jeers.

Then, if there be no tangible thing to hoot he feels, perhaps, the desire to confront a personification and indulge in pleas, bowed to one knee, and with hands supplicant, saying: "Yes, but I love myself."

A high cold star on a winter's night is the word he feels that she says to him. Thereafter he knows the pathos of his situation.

The men in the dingey had not discussed these matters, but each had, no doubt, reflected upon them in silence and according to his mind. There was seldom any expression upon their faces save the general one of complete weariness. Speech was devoted to the business of the boat.

To chime the notes of his emotion, a verse mysteriously entered the correspondent's head. He had even forgotten that he had forgotten this verse, but it suddenly was in his mind.

> A soldier of the Legion lay dying in Algiers,
> There was lack of woman's nursing, there was dearth of woman's tears;
> But a comrade stood beside him, and he took that comrade's hand,
> And he said: "I shall never see my own, my native land."

In his childhood, the correspondent had been made acquainted with the fact that a soldier of the Legion lay dying in Algiers, but he had never regarded the fact as important. Myriads of his school-fellows had informed him of the soldier's plight, but the dinning had naturally ended by making him perfectly indifferent. He had never considered it his affair that a soldier of the Legion lay dying in Algiers, nor had it appeared to him as a matter for sorrow. It was less to him than the breaking of a pencil's point.

Now, however, it quaintly came to him as a human, living thing. It was no longer merely a picture of a few throes in the breast of a poet, meanwhile drinking tea and warming his feet at the grate; it was an actuality—stern, mournful, and fine.

The correspondent plainly saw the soldier. He lay on the sand with his feet out straight and still. While his pale left hand was upon his chest in an attempt to thwart the going of his life, the blood came between his fingers. In the far Algerian distance, a city of low square forms was set against a sky that was faint with the last sunset hues. The correspondent, plying the oars and dreaming of the slow and slower movements of the lips of the soldier, was moved by a profound and perfectly impersonal comprehension. He was sorry for the soldier of the Legion who lay dying in Algiers.

The thing which had followed the boat and waited had evidently grown bored at the delay. There was no longer to be heard the slash of the cutwater, and there was no longer the flame of the long trail. The light in the north still glimmered, but it was apparently no nearer to the boat. Sometimes the boom of the surf rang in the correspondent's ears, and he turned the craft seaward then and rowed harder. Southward, someone had evidently built a watch-fire on the beach. It was too low and too far to be seen, but it made a shimmering, roseate reflection upon the bluff back of it, and this could be discerned from the boat. The wind came stronger, and sometimes a wave suddenly raged out like a mountain-cat, and there was to be seen the sheen and sparkle of a broken crest.

The captain, in the bow, moved on his water-jar and sat erect. "Pretty long night," he observed to the correspondent. He looked at the shore. "Those life-saving people take their time."

"Did you see that shark playing around?"

"Yes, I saw him. He was a big fellow, all right."

"Wish I had known you were awake."

Later the correspondent spoke into the bottom of the boat.

"Billie!" There was a slow and gradual disentanglement. "Billie, will you spell me?"

"Sure," said the oiler.

As soon as the correspondent touched the cold comfortable sea-water in the bottom of the boat, and had huddled close to the cook's life-belt he was deep in sleep, despite the fact that his teeth played all the popular airs. This sleep was so good to him that it was but a moment before he heard a voice call his name in a tone that demonstrated the last stages of exhaustion. "Will you spell me?"

"Sure, Billie."

The light in the north had mysteriously vanished, but the correspondent took his course from the wide-awake captain.

Later in the night they took the boat farther out to sea, and the captain directed the cook to take one oar at the stern and keep the boat facing the seas. He was to call out if he should hear the thunder of the surf. This plan enabled the oiler and the correspondent to get respite together. "We'll give those boys a chance to get into shape again," said the captain. They curled down and, after a few preliminary chatterings and trembles, slept once more the dead sleep. Neither knew they had bequeathed to the cook the company of another shark, or perhaps the same shark.

As the boat caroused on the waves, spray occasionally bumped over the side and gave them a fresh soaking, but this had no power to break their repose. The ominous slash of the wind and the water affected them as it would have affected mummies.

"Boys," said the cook, with the notes of every reluctance in his voice, "she's drifted in pretty close. I guess one of you had better take her to sea again." The correspondent, aroused, heard the crash of the toppled crests.

As he was rowing, the captain gave him some whisky-and-water, and this steadied the chills out of him. "If I ever get ashore and anybody shows me even a photograph of an oar—"

At last there was a short conversation.

"Billie . . . Billie, will you spell me?"

"Sure," said the oiler.

VII

When the correspondent again opened his eyes, the sea and the sky were each of the grey hue of the dawning. Later, carmine and gold was painted upon the waters. The morning appeared finally, in its splendour, with a sky of pure blue, and the sunlight flamed on the tips of the waves.

On the distant dunes were set many little black cottages, and a tall white windmill reared above them. No man, nor dog, nor bicycle appeared on the beach. The cottages might have formed a deserted village.

The voyagers scanned the shore. A conference was held in the boat. "Well," said the captain, "if no help is coming, we might better try a run through the surf right away. If we stay out here much longer we will be too weak to do anything for ourselves at all." The others silently acquiesced in this reasoning. The boat was headed for the beach. The correspondent wondered if none ever ascended the tall windtower, and if then they never looked seaward. This tower was a giant, standing with its back to the plight of the ants. It represented in a degree, to the correspondent, the serenity of nature amid the struggles of the individual—nature in the wind, and nature in the vision of men. She did not seem cruel to him then, nor beneficent, nor treacherous, nor wise. But she was indifferent, flatly indifferent. It is, perhaps, plausible that a man in this situation, impressed with the unconcern of the universe, should see the innumerable flaws of his life, and have them taste wickedly in his mind and wish for another chance. A distinction between right and wrong seems absurdly clear to him, then, in this new ignorance of the grave-edge, and he understands that if he were given another opportunity he would mend his conduct and his words, and be better and brighter during an introduction or at a tea.

"Now, boys," said the captain, "she is going to swamp sure. All we can do is to work her in as far as possible, and then when she swamps, pile out and scramble for the beach. Keep cool now, and don't jump until she swamps sure."

The oiler took the oars. Over his shoulders he scanned the surf. "Captain," he said, "I think I'd better bring her about, and keep her head-on to the seas and back her in."

"All right, Billie," said the captain. "Back her in." The oiler swung the boat then and, seated in the stern, the cook and the correspondent were obliged to look over their shoulders to contemplate the lonely and indifferent shore.

The monstrous in-shore rollers heaved the boat high until the men were again enabled to see the white sheets of water scudding up the slanted beach. "We won't get in very close," said the captain. Each time a man could wrest his attention from the rollers, he turned his glance toward the shore, and in the expression of the eyes during this contemplation there was a singular quality. The correspondent, observing the others, knew that they were not afraid, but the full meaning of their glances was shrouded.

As for himself, he was too tired to grapple fundamentally with the fact. He tried to coerce his mind into thinking of it, but the mind was dominated at this time by the muscles, and the muscles said they did not care. It merely occurred to him that if he should drown it would be a shame.

There were no hurried words, no pallor, no plain agitation. The men simply looked at the shore. "Now, remember to get well clear of the boat when you jump," said the captain.

Seaward the crest of a roller suddenly fell with a thunderous crash, and the long white comber came roaring down upon the boat.

"Steady now," said the captain. The men were silent. They turned their eyes from the shore to the comber and waited. The boat slid up the incline, leaped at the furious top, bounced over it, and swung down the long back of the waves. Some water had been shipped and the cook bailed it out.

But the next crest crashed also. The tumbling, boiling flood of white water caught the boat and whirled it almost perpendicular. Water swarmed in from all sides. The correspondent had his hands on the gunwale at this time, and when the water entered at that place he swiftly withdrew his fingers, as if he objected to wetting them.

The little boat, drunken with this weight of water, reeled and snuggled deeper into the sea.

"Bail her out, cook! Bail her out," said the captain.

"All right, captain," said the cook.

"Now, boys, the next one will do for us, sure," said the oiler. "Mind to jump clear of the boat."

The third wave moved forward, huge, furious, implacable. It fairly swallowed the dingey, and almost simultaneously the men tumbled into the sea. A piece of life-belt had lain in the bottom of the boat, and as the correspondent went overboard he held this to his chest with his left hand.

The January water was icy, and he reflected immediately that it was colder than he had expected to find it off the coast of Florida. This appeared to his dazed mind as a fact important enough to be noted at the time. The coldness of the water was sad; it was tragic. This fact was somehow so mixed and confused with his opinion of his own situation that it seemed almost a proper reason for tears. The water was cold.

When he came to the surface he was conscious of little but the noisy water. Afterward he saw his companions in the sea. The oiler was ahead in the race. He was swimming strongly and rapidly. Off to the correspondent's left, the cook's great white and corked back bulged out of the water, and in the rear the captain was hanging with his one good hand to the keel of the overturned dingey.

There is a certain immovable quality to a shore, and the correspondent wondered at it amid the confusion of the sea.

It seemed also very attractive, but the correspondent knew that it was a long journey, and he paddled leisurely. The piece of life-preserver lay under him, and sometimes he whirled down the incline of a wave as if he were on a hand-sled.

But finally he arrived at a place in the sea where travel was beset with difficulty. He did not pause swimming to inquire what manner of current had caught him, but there his progress ceased. The shore was set before him like a bit of scenery on a stage, and he looked at it and understood with his eyes each detail of it.

As the cook passed, much farther to the left, the captain was calling to him, "Turn over on your back, cook! Turn over on your back and use the oar."

"All right, sir." The cook turned on his back, and, paddling with an oar, went ahead as if he were a canoe.

Presently the boat also passed to the left of the correspondent with the captain clinging with one hand to the keel. He would have appeared like a man raising himself to look over a board fence, if it were not for the extraordinary gymnastics of the boat. The correspondent marvelled that the captain could still hold to it.

They passed on, nearer to shore—the oiler, the cook, the captain—and following them went the water-jar, bouncing gaily over the seas.

The correspondent remained in the grip of this strange new enemy—a current. The shore, with its white slope of sand and its green bluff, topped with little silent cottages, was spread like a picture before him. It was very near to him then, but he was impressed as one who in a gallery looks at a scene from Brittany or Algiers.

He thought: "I am going to drown? Can it be possible? Can it be possible? Can it be possible?" Perhaps an individual must consider his own death to be the final phenomenon of nature.

But later a wave perhaps whirled him out of this small deadly current, for he found suddenly that he could again make progress toward the shore. Later still, he was aware that the captain, clinging with one hand to the keel of the dingey, had his face turned away from the shore and toward him, and was calling his name. "Come to the boat! Come to the boat!"

In his struggle to reach the captain and the boat, he reflected that when one gets properly wearied, drowning must really be a comfortable arrangement, a cessation of hostilities accompanied by a large degree of relief, and he was glad of it, for the main thing in his mind for some moments had been horror of the temporary agony. He did not wish to be hurt.

Presently he saw a man running along the shore. He was undressing with most remarkable speed. Coat, trousers, shirt, everything flew magically off him.

"Come to the boat," called the captain.

"All right, captain." As the correspondent paddled, he saw the captain let himself down to bottom and leave the boat. Then the correspondent performed his one little marvel of the voyage. A large wave caught him and flung him with ease and supreme speed completely over the boat and far beyond it. It struck him even then as an event in gymnastics, and a true miracle of the sea. An overturned boat in the surf is not a plaything to a swimming man.

The correspondent arrived in water that reached only to his waist, but his condition did not enable him to stand for more than a moment. Each wave knocked him into a heap, and the under-tow pulled at him.

Then he saw the man who had been running and undressing, and undressing and running, come bounding into the water. He dragged ashore the cook, and then waded toward the captain, but the captain waved him away, and sent him to the correspondent. He was naked, naked as a tree in winter, but a halo was about his head, and he shone like a saint. He gave a strong pull, and a long drag, and a bully heave at the correspondent's hand. The correspondent, schooled in the minor formulæ, said: "Thanks, old man." But suddenly the man cried: "What's that?" He pointed a swift finger. The correspondent said: "Go."

In the shallows, face downward, lay the oiler. His forehead touched sand that was periodically, between each wave, clear of the sea.

The correspondent did not know all that transpired afterward. When he achieved safe ground he fell, striking the sand with each particular part of his body. It was as if he had dropped from a roof, but the thud was grateful to him.

It seems that instantly the beach was populated with men, with blankets, clothes, and flasks, and women with coffee-pots and all the remedies sacred to their minds. The welcome of the land to the men from the sea was warm and generous, but a still and dripping shape was carried slowly up the beach, and the land's welcome for it could only be the different and sinister hospitality of the grave.

When it came night, the white waves paced to and fro in the moonlight, and the wind brought the sound of the great sea's voice to the men on shore, and they felt that they could then be interpreters.

NEWSPAPER REPORTS OF THE WRECK OF THE *COMMODORE*

I

[*New York Press*, Monday, January 4, 1897]

MORE OF THE FILIBUSTERS SAFE

COMMODORE'S WRECKED SEAMEN STRUGGLE FOR LIFE IN A HEAVY SURF

STEPHEN CRANE, NOVELIST, SWIMS ASHORE

YOUNG NEW YORK WRITER ASTONISHES THE SEA DOGS BY HIS COURAGE
IN THE FACE OF DEATH

CUBANS ASSERT A TRAITOR SUNK THE VESSEL

FEDERAL AUTHORITIES ORDER OUT THE THREE FRIENDS TO AID IN THE WORK OF RESCUE

JACKSONVILLE, Fla., Jan. 3.—Seventeen men accounted for out of the twenty-eight on the Cuban filibuster Commodore is the record here to-night, with a slight chance of seven more yet alive. Five men came ashore at Daytona this noon—Captain Murphy, Stephen Crane, the novelist, the cook and two sailors. One of the latter, William Higgins of Rhode Island, died soon after reaching land from the effects of severe wounds received while landing through the high surf. His family live in Boston. One of the survivors gives the following graphic details:

STORY OF A SURVIVOR

"The tug sank at 7 o'clock Saturday morning, twenty miles off New Smyrna, and the Americans on board remained till the last moment. A traitor in Spanish pay was the cause of the leak. Should he be found he will be dealt with severely. The leak was discovered at about 3 a.m. The pumps would not work long, though they did good service for a while.

"Finding that the water gained on us, the captain called all hands and at 3 the vessel was turned shoreward. As she still continued to sink, two boat loads of Cubans, twelve men in all, were first sent off. One boat containing six men was capsized, and I am afraid that the men were lost. The Americans all remained on the tug till she sank. One of the lifeboats containing nine men was swamped and a hastily constructed raft was made up from materials thrown to them, and they then disappeared from our sight. Captain Murphy, Stephen Crane, the novelist and correspondent, Higgins, myself and one other sailor took to the ten-foot dingy at the last moment. We tried to save the men in the water around us, but the heavy seas and blinding wind swept them from us. The spray was so thick that we could see only a few rods. Their cries were heartrending, but we could do nothing, it requiring all our efforts to keep our small boat right side up.

THROWN INTO THE BREAKERS

"For twenty-four hours we battled with the heavy seas, constantly bailing, and at last land was sighted. As we attempted to land the wind drove us into the breakers and in an instant the boat was overturned and we were struggling for life. For an hour almost we battled for life, and then managed to crawl out on the sands, almost dead. Captain Murphy saved Mr. Crane by helping him when a cramp caught him. Higgins was struck on the head by floating timbers and he died soon after landing. He was a good sailor and a brave man. He worked to save his comrades." . . .

PRAISE FOR CRANE

DAYTONA, Fla., Jan. 3.—"That newspaper feller was a nervy man," said the cook of the ill-fated Commodore to-night in reference to Stephen Crane, the novelist, who is after material for stories. "He didn't seem to know what fear was. He was down on the ship's papers as an able seaman at $20 a month. When we started out he insisted upon doing a seaman's work, and he did it well, too. When aroused Saturday morning he never quailed when he came on deck and saw the foaming and raging billows and knew that the vessel was sinking and that it was only a question of time when we would be at the mercy of the terrible sea in a small ten-foot dingy.

"He stood on the bridge with glasses in hand, sweeping the horizon in an effort to get a glimpse of land. He had one of the sailor lads above him on the short mast, and once he mounted the rigging to get a better view. I thought sure that he would be swept off as the vessel rolled from side to side, her yards almost touching the water as she rolled down. One of the Cubans got rattled and tried to run out one of the boats before time, and Crane let him have it right from the shoulder, and the man rolled down the leeway, stunned for the moment.

"When the boats were launched he was the last one, except Captain Murphy, to get in, and his nerve greatly encouraged all hands. In the small dingy he rowed as well as the others, notwithstanding he was so worn out that he could hardly hold his oar straight in the terrific seas. At the last moment he rose on his seat, and, seeing the big wave coming that overthrew us, cried out, 'Look out, boys, there's trouble for us. Jump, captain!'

SAVES A DROWNING MAN

"Both he and Captain Murphy were thrown out on the same side. Crane was partially thrown under the overturned boat and but for Captain Murphy's readiness in catching him by the collar he would have gone under. We all battled there in the water for hours, it seemed to us. Crane was a good swimmer, and he really saved one of the sailors, as the man could not swim a stroke, and Crane had to keep him up by the aid of an oar. These newspaper fellers have got spunk, if they do tell such awful woppers at times," concluded the cook, as he took another big swig of the "life preserver" provided by the good people here.

II

[*New York Press,* Tuesday, January 5, 1897]

COMMODORE SAID TO BE OVERLADEN

MANY THINK THAT FACT, AND NOT TREACHERY, SUNK HER

FOUR MORE MEN RESCUED

HALF-FAMISHED FILIBUSTERS LAND AT PORT ORANGE—CAPTAIN MURPHY COMPLIMENTS CRANE. . . .

CAPTAIN MURPHY TALKS

. . . Captain Murphy had his arm in a sling, but otherwise seemed all right. All of them looked tired and worn out.

The captain paid a marked compliment to his men for their orderly conduct. He said that Higgins was a game man, and fought hard for his life and to aid his ship-mates. Higgins was buried at Daytona yesterday.

Captain Murphy, in response to a direct question, answered evasively as to the report of the treachery, and stated that the leaks were not there early Friday evening, but were there at midnight.

Cubans here feel much dispirited over the sad affair, and the terrible ending of the expedition from which so much was expected.

CRANE'S SPLENDID GRIT

"That man Crane is the spunkiest fellow out," said Captain Murphy to-night to The Press correspondent, in speaking of the wreck and incidents pertaining to it. "The sea was so rough that even old sailors got seasick when we struck the open sea after leaving the bar, but Crane behaved like a born sailor. He and I were about the only ones not affected by the big seas which tossed us about. As we went south he sat in the pilot house with me, smoking and telling yarns. When the leak was discovered he was the first man to volunteer aid.

JOKES AMID DANGER

"His shoes, new ones, were slippery on the deck, and he took them off and tossed them overboard, saying, with a laugh: 'Well, captain, I guess I won't need them if we have to swim.' He stood on the deck by me all the while, smoking his cigarette, and aided me greatly while the boats were getting off. When in the dingey he suggested putting up the overcoat for a sail, and he took his turn at the oars or holding up the oar mast.

TRIES TO SAVE HIGGINS

"When we went over I called to him to see that his life preserver was on all right and he replied in his usual tones, saying that he would obey orders. He was under the boat once, but got out in some way. He held up Higgins when the latter got so terribly tired and endeavored to bring him in but the sailor was so far gone that he could hardly help himself. When we were thrown up by the waves, Crane was the first man to stagger up the beach looking for houses. He's a thoroughbred," concluded the captain, "and a brave man, too, with plenty of grit."

III

[*Florida Times-Union,* Tuesday, January 5, 1897]

CAPTAIN MURPHY'S SHIPWRECKED CREW

TWENTY MEN ARE NOW SAFE IN JACKSONVILLE WITH FRIENDS.

BUT EIGHT OTHERS MAY BE AT THE BOTTOM

STORY OF THE WRECK OF THE COMMODORE TOLD BY THE COMMANDER OF THE ILL-FATED VESSEL

THERE IS STILL SOME TALK OF TREACHERY

THREE MEN WERE DROWNED AS THE STEAMER SUNK—ONE DIED ON THE BEACH AND FIVE ARE AT SEA ON A RAFT—THE NEWARK AND THREE FRIENDS ARE STILL LOOKING FOR THEM, BUT THERE IS LITTLE OR NO HOPE THAT ANY MORE WILL BE SAVED.

. . . Captain Murphy's story is as follows:

"The engineer reported to me, about midnight, that the vessel was gaining water in her hold and that he was unable to get the pumps to work. They had tried to get the water out, but the pumps would not heave the water. The pipe was evidently choked or the suction gone. It is customary to keep the water clear of the hold. All necessary was to run the steam pumps now and then. If the water is allowed to get up into the coal, the coal is washed down and chokes the pumps. All the water that entered the ship was in the engine room."

"Was it treachery, do you think?" asked the Times-Union reporter.

"No, I don't think so. It was neglect, more than anything else.

"I gave the order to use the buckets: also an order to pile into the furnace wood, oil and alcohol, hoping to get up sufficient steam to run into Mosquito Inlet, about eighteen miles almost due west of us. The men used the buckets with a will. None stood back, but to our chagrin the water gained upon us slowly and surely, and we had not proceeded three miles when the fires were quenched. There was no hope then of saving the ship. I let go the anchor to get her head to the sea and told the men to quietly proceed to man the boats. We got two of the boats off. They contained all the Cubans.

"One boat was in command of Julio Rodriguez Baz, and those with him were Manuel Gonzalez, Luis Sierra Mederos and Jesus Alvarez.

"The other, in command of Paul F. Rojo, contained Ricardo Delgado, Felix de los Rios, Emelio Marquez, Ventura Linares, Romeo Hernandez, J. Francisco Blanco, Jose Hernandez, T. Benecenor, Lion Soldera, Gabriel Martinez and Santingo Diaz. Senor Baz's boat stood by for a considerable time to render us assistance, but finally, as we had boats sufficient for the rescue of all those left aboard, we told them to go ahead. Later on we launched the ship's boat, with seven men, in charge of Mate Grane. I told all those to go who desired to do so. All went except Mr. Crane, a brave little gentleman, Steward Montgomery and William Higgins. I intended to stand by the ship and then put ashore in the dingy. Later on we also embarked. We had proceeded but a few yards when we heard a cry from the ship:

ONE BOAT STOVE IN

" 'The big boat is stove!' They were also flying a distress flag.

"I don't know how this happened unless the mate returned and attempted to get some article that he had forgotten. We immediately put back in the dingy, and I told the men to construct a raft. They made three and got on these. Meanwhile, our little boat was remaining distant about 200 yards.

"Finally, they begged us to take them in tow. We put back against the waves and wind and made a towline fast. The first sea nearly filled our boat, and we were compelled to let go and bail our own craft dry. We went back again and once more made fast, but the first sea parted the rafts and broke our towline. The rafts all parted and were scattered. I told them to return to the vessel and make another raft while I bailed out. When fifty yards away, the vessel went down broadside. Three men went down with her, like heroes, with no cry of despair, not a murmur. I remained by the rafts twenty minutes longer, but as the boat was being filled by almost every sea, and as the wind was constantly increasing in force, we allowed our boat to go whither the elements carried her.

HOW THEY LANDED

"Saturday afternoon at 4 o'clock, we came in sight of the coast north of Mosquito Inlet. We saw people on shore and I flew a flag of distress, and repeatedly fired my pistol to attract their attention. I do not see how they could have failed to see us and appreciate our perilous position, for we were only a half mile from shore. Feeling certain that we had been seen, and thinking that they would send to us a staunch surf boat, we waited at the spot, pulling like Trojans against the heavy sea and wind all that afternoon and all that night. I do not see now, looking back upon it, how human strength could have successfully contended against the fierce odds of nature. We had a little store of brandy and this stood us in good stead. The next morning we found ourselves off the beach opposite Daytona, and seeing no one, resolved to make one last desperate effort with our little remaining strength to reach shore through the breakers. I gave one life belt to the steward and one to Mr. Crane. (The captain does not say that he, with a badly injured arm and shoulder, took none himself.) The sea upset the boat and washed us all away. I grabbed it and got on the bottom, but she was rolled over again. Higgins tried to swim, but sank. I tried to encourage him, and he made another attempt. The boat went over again, and I saw no more of him until his corpse came up on the beach.

DEATH OF HIGGINS

"John Getchell, one of nature's noblemen, who lives upon the beach, saw our dreadful predicament. He stripped to the skin and plunged into the surf and helped the steward and Mr. Crane in. I was safe in shallow water. I then saw Higgins' body on the wet sand. We rolled him and made every effort to bring him to life, but unfortunately failed. Poor fellow, he was brave and did his duty faithfully.

"We had not been on the beach long before the good women of the town came to us with hot coffee and all kinds of restoratives. Their attentions warmed a man's heart to the appreciation of human charity. Not one of these women came to us without some present of food, clothing, and all with offers of shelter. The people of Daytona buried poor Higgins at their own expense."

IV

[*New York Press,* Thursday, January 7, 1897]

STEPHEN CRANE'S OWN STORY

HE TELLS HOW THE COMMODORE WAS WRECKED AND HOW HE ESCAPED

FEAR-CRAZED NEGRO NEARLY SWAMPS BOAT

YOUNG WRITER COMPELLED TO WORK IN STIFLING ATMOSPHERE OF THE FIRE ROOM

BRAVERY OF CAPTAIN MURPHY AND HIGGINS

TRIED TO TOW THEIR COMPANIONS WHO WERE ON THE RAFT— LAST DASH FOR THE SHORE THROUGH THE SURF.

JACKSONVILLE, Fla., Jan. 6.—It was the afternoon of New Year's. The Commodore lay at her dock in Jacksonville and negro stevedores processioned steadily toward her with box after box of ammunition and bundle after bundle of rifles. Her hatch, like the mouth of a monster, engulfed them. It might have been the feeding time of some legendary creature of the sea. It was in broad daylight and the crowd of gleeful Cubans on the pier did not forbear to sing the strange patriotic ballads of their island.

Everything was perfectly open. The Commodore was cleared with a cargo of arms and munition for Cuba. There was none of that extreme modesty about the proceeding which had marked previous departures of the famous tug. She loaded up as placidly as if she were going to carry oranges to New York, instead of Remingtons to Cuba. Down the river, furthermore, the revenue cutter Boutwell, the old isosceles triangle that protects United States interests in the St. John's, lay at anchor, with no sign of excitement aboard her.

EXCHANGING FAREWELLS

On the decks of the Commodore there were exchanges of farewells in two languages. Many of the men who were to sail upon her had many intimates in the old Southern town, and we who had left our friends in the remote North received our first touch of melancholy on witnessing these strenuous and earnest good-bys.

It seems, however, that there was more difficulty at the custom house. The officers of the ship and the Cuban leaders were detained there until a mournful twilight settled upon the St. John's, and through a heavy fog the lights of Jacksonville blinked dimly. Then at last the Commodore swung clear of the dock, amid a tumult of goodbys. As she turned her bow toward the distant sea the Cubans ashore cheered and cheered. In response the Commodore gave three long blasts of her whistle, which even to this time impressed me with their sadness. Somehow, they sounded as wails.

Then at last we began to feel like filibusters. I don't suppose that the most stolid brain could contrive to believe that there is not a mere trifle of danger in filibustering, and so as we watched the lights of Jacksonville swing past us and heard the regular thump, thump, thump of the engines we did considerable reflecting.

But I am sure that there were no hifalutin emotions visible upon any of the faces which confronted the speeding shore. In fact, from cook's boy to captain, we were all enveloped in a gentle satisfaction and cheerfulness. But less than two miles from Jacksonville, this atrocious fog caused the pilot to ram the bow of the Commodore hard upon the mud and in this ignominious position we were compelled to stay until daybreak.

HELP FROM THE BOUTWELL

It was to all of us more than a physical calamity. We were now no longer filibusters. We were men on a ship stuck in the mud. A certain mental somersault was made once more necessary.

But word had been sent to Jacksonville to the captain of the revenue cutter Boutwell, and Captain Kilgore turned out promptly and generously fired up his old triangle, and came at full speed to our assistance. She dragged us out of the mud, and again we headed for the mouth of the river. The revenue cutter pounded along a half mile astern of us, to make sure that we did not take on board at some place along the river men for the Cuban army.

This was the early morning of New Year's Day, and the fine golden southern sunlight fell full upon the river. It flashed over the ancient Boutwell, until her white sides gleamed like pearl, and her rigging was spun into little threads of gold.

Cheers greeted the old Commodore from passing ship and from the shore. It was a cheerful, almost merry, beginning to our voyage. At Mayport, however, we changed our river pilot for a man who could take her to open sea, and again the Commodore was beached. The Boutwell was fussing around us in her venerable way, and, upon seeing our predicament, she came again to assist us, but this time, with engines reversed, the Commodore dragged herself away from the grip of the sand and again headed for the open sea.

The captain of the revenue cutter grew curious. He hailed the Commodore: "Are you fellows going to sea to-day?"

Captain Murphy of the Commodore called back: "Yes, sir."

And then as the whistle of the Commodore saluted him, Captain Kilgore doffed his cap and said: "Well, gentlemen, I hope you have a pleasant cruise," and this was our last word from shore.

When the Commodore came to enormous rollers that flee over the bar a certain lightheartedness departed from the ship's company.

SLEEP IMPOSSIBLE

As darkness came upon the waters, the Commodore was a broad, flaming path of blue and silver phosphorescence, and as her stout bow lunged at the great black waves she threw flashing, roaring cascades to either side. And all that was to be heard was the rhythmical and mighty pounding of the engines. Being an inexperienced filibuster, the writer had undergone considerable mental excitement since the starting of the ship, and in consequence he had not yet been to sleep and so I went to the first mate's bunk to indulge myself in all the physical delights of holding one's-self in bed. Every time the ship lurched I expected to be fired through a bulkhead, and it was neither amusing nor instructive to see in the dim light a certain accursed valise aiming itself at the top of my stomach with every lurch of the vessel.

THE COOK IS HOPEFUL

The cook was asleep on a bench in the galley. He is of a portly and noble exterior, and by means of a checker board he had himself wedged on this bench in such a manner the motion of the ship would be unable to dislodge him. He woke as I entered the galley and delivered himself of some dolorous sentiments: "God," he said in the course of his observations, "I don't feel right about this ship, somehow. It strikes me that something is going to happen to us. I don't know what it is, but the old ship is going to get it in the neck, I think."

"Well, how about the men on board of her?" said I. "Are any of us going to get out, prophet?"

"Yes," said the cook. "Sometimes I have these damned feelings come over me, and they are always right, and it seems to me, somehow, that you and I will both get and meet again somewhere, down at Coney Island, perhaps, or some place like that."

ONE MAN HAS ENOUGH

Finding it impossible to sleep, I went back to the pilot house. An old seaman, Tom Smith, from Charleston, was then at the wheel. In the darkness I could not see Tom's face, except at those times when he leaned forward to scan the compass and the dim light from the box came upon his weatherbeaten features.

"Well, Tom," said I, "how do you like filibustering?"

He said "I think I am about through with it. I've been in a number of these expeditions and the pay is good, but I think if I ever get back safe this time I will cut it."

I sat down in the corner of the pilot house and almost went to sleep. In the meantime the captain came on duty and he was standing near me when the chief engineer rushed up the stairs and cried hurriedly to the captain that there was something wrong in the engine room. He and the captain departed swiftly.

I was drowsing there in my corner when the captain returned, and, going to the door of the little room directly back of the pilot-house, he cried to the Cuban leader:

"Say, can't you get those fellows to work. I can't talk their language and I can't get them started. Come on and get them going."

HELPS IN THE FIREROOM

The Cuban leader turned to me and said: "Go help in the fireroom. They are going to bail with buckets."

The engine room, by the way, represented a scene at this time taken from the middle kitchen of hades. In the first place, it was insufferably warm, and the lights burned faintly in a way to cause mystic and grewsome shadows. There was a quantity of soapish sea water swirling and sweeping and swirling among machinery that roared and banged and clattered and steamed, and, in the second place, it was a devil of a way down below.

Here I first came to know a certain young oiler named Billy Higgins. He was sloshing around this inferno filling buckets with water and passing them to a chain of men

that extended up the ship's side. Afterward we got orders to change our point of attack on water and to operate through a little door on the windward side of the ship that led into the engine room.

NO PANIC ON BOARD

During this time there was much talk of pumps out of order and many other statements of a mechanical kind, which I did not altogether comprehend but understood to mean that there was a general and sudden ruin in the engine room.

There was no particular agitation at this time, and even later there was never a panic on board the Commodore. The party of men who worked with Higgins and me at this time were all Cubans, and we were under the direction of the Cuban leaders. Presently we were ordered again to the afterhold, and there was some hesitation about going into the abominable fireroom again, but Higgins dashed down the companionway with a bucket.

LOWERING BOATS

The heat and hard work in the fireroom affected me and I was obliged to come on deck again. Going forward, I heard as I went talk of lowering the boats. Near the corner of the galley the mate was talking with a man.

"Why don't you send up a rocket?" said this unknown man. And the mate replied: "What the hell do we want to send up a rocket for? The ship is all right."

Returning with a little rubber and cloth overcoat, I saw the first boat about to be lowered. A certain man was the first person in this first boat, and they were handing him in a valise about as large as a hotel. I had not entirely recovered from astonishment and pleasure in witnessing this noble deed when I saw another valise go to him.

HUMAN HOG APPEARS

This valise was not perhaps so large as a hotel, but it was a big valise anyhow. Afterward there went to him something which looked to me like an overcoat.

Seeing the chief engineer leaning out of his little window, I remarked to him:

"What do you think of that blank, blank, blank?"

"Oh, he's a bird," said the old chief.

It was now that was heard the order to get away the lifeboat, which was stowed on top of the deckhouse. The deckhouse was a mighty slippery place, and with each roll of the ship, the men there thought themselves likely to take headers into the deadly black sea.

Higgins was on top of the deckhouse, and, with the first mate and two colored stokers, we wrestled with that boat, which, I am willing to swear, weighed as much as a Broadway cable car. She might have been spiked to the deck. We could have pushed a little brick schoolhouse along a corduroy road as easily as we could have moved this boat. But the first mate got a tackle to her from a leeward davit, and on the deck below the captain corralled enough men to make an impression upon the boat.

We were ordered to cease hauling then, and in this lull the cook of the ship came to me and said: "What are you going to do?"

I told him of my plans, and he said:

"Well, by God, that's what I am going to do."

A WHISTLE OF DESPAIR

Now the whistle of the Commodore had been turned loose, and if there ever was a voice of despair and death, it was in the voice of this whistle. It had gained a new tone. It was as if its throat was already choked by the water, and this cry on the sea at night, with a wind blowing the spray over the ship, and the waves roaring over the bow, and swirling white along the decks, was to each of us probably a song of man's end.

It was now that the first mate showed a sign of losing his grip. To us who were trying in all stages of competence and experience to launch the lifeboat he raged in all terms of fiery satire and hammerlike abuse. But the boat moved at last and swung down toward the water.

Afterward, when I went aft, I saw the captain standing, with his arm in a sling, holding on to a stay with his one good hand and directing the launching of the boat. He gave me a five-gallon jug of water to hold, and asked me what I was going to do. I told him what I thought was about the proper thing, and he told me then that the cook had the same idea, and ordered me to go forward and be ready to launch the ten-foot dingy.

IN THE TEN-FOOT DINGY

I remember well that he turned then to swear at a colored stoker who was prowling around, done up in life preservers until he looked like a feather bed. I went forward with my five-gallon jug of water, and when the captain came we launched the dingy, and they put me over the side to fend her off from the ship with an oar.

They handed me down the water jug, and then the cook came into the boat, and we sat there in the darkness, wondering why, by all our hopes of future happiness, the captain was so long in coming over to the side and ordering us away from the doomed ship.

The captain was waiting for the other boat to go. Finally he hailed in the darkness: "Are you all right, Mr. Graines?"

The first mate answered: "All right, sir."

"Shove off, then," cried the captain.

The captain was just about to swing over the rail when a dark form came forward and a voice said: "Captain, I go with you."

The captain answered: "Yes, Billy; get in."

HIGGINS LAST TO LEAVE SHIP

It was Billy Higgins, the oiler. Billy dropped into the boat and a moment later the captain followed, bringing with him an end of about forty yards of lead line. The other end was attached to the rail of the ship.

As we swung back to leeward the captain said: "Boys, we will stay right near the ship till she goes down."

This cheerful information, of course, filled us all with glee. The line kept us headed properly into the wind, and as we rode over the monstrous waves we saw upon each rise the swaying lights of the dying Commodore.

When came the gray shade of dawn, the form of the Commodore grew slowly clear to us as our little ten-foot boat rose over each swell. She was floating with such an air of buoyancy that we laughed when we had time, and said "What a gag it would be on those other fellows if she didn't sink at all."

But later we saw men aboard of her, and later still they began to hail us.

HELPING THEIR MATES

I had forgot to mention that previously we had loosened the end of the lead line and dropped much further to leeward. The men on board were a mystery to us, of course, as we had seen all the boats leave the ship. We rowed back to the ship, but did not approach too near, because we were four men in a ten-foot boat, and we knew that the touch of a hand on our gunwale would assuredly swamp us.

The first mate cried out from the ship that the third boat had foundered alongside. He cried that they had made rafts, and wished us to tow them.

The captain said, "All right."

Their rafts were floating astern. "Jump in!" cried the captain, but there was a singular and most harrowing hesitation. There were five white men and two negroes. This scene in the gray light of morning impressed one as would a view into some place where ghosts move slowly. These seven men on the stern of the sinking Commodore were silent. Save the words of the mate to the captain there was no talk. Here was death, but here also was a most singular and indefinable kind of fortitude.

Four men, I remember, clambered over the railing and stood there watching the cold, steely sheen of the sweeping waves.

"Jump," cried the captain again.

The old chief engineer first obeyed the order. He landed on the outside raft and the captain told him how to grip the raft and he obeyed as promptly and as docilely as a scholar in riding school.

THE MATE'S MAD PLUNGE

A stoker followed him, and then the first mate threw his hands over his head and plunged into the sea. He had no life belt and for my part, even when he did this horrible thing, I somehow felt that I could see in the expression of his hands, and in the very toss of his head, as he leaped thus to death, that it was rage, rage, rage unspeakable that was in his heart at the time.

And then I saw Tom Smith, the man who was going to quit filibustering after this expedition, jump to a raft and turn his face toward us. On board the Commodore three men strode, still in silence and with their faces turned toward us. One man had his arms folded and was leaning against the deckhouse. His feet were crossed, so that the toe of his left foot pointed downward. There they stood gazing at us, and neither from the deck nor from the rafts was a voice raised. Still was there this silence.

TRIED TO TOW THE RAFTS

The colored stoker on the first raft threw us a line and we began to tow. Of course,

we perfectly understood the absolute impossibility of any such thing; our dingy was within six inches of the water's edge, there was an enormous sea running, and I knew that under the circumstances a tugboat would have no light task in moving these rafts.

But we tried it, and would have continued to try it indefinitely, but that something critical came to pass. I was at an oar and so faced the rafts. The cook controlled the line. Suddenly the boat began to go backward and then we saw this negro on the first raft pulling on the line hand over hand and drawing us to him.

He had turned into a demon. He was wild—wild as a tiger. He was crouched on this raft and ready to spring. Every muscle of him seemed to be turned into an elastic spring. His eyes were almost white. His face was the face of a lost man reaching upward, and we knew that the weight of his hand on our gunwale doomed us.

THE COMMODORE SINKS

The cook let go of the line. We rowed around to see if we could not get a line from the chief engineer, and all this time, mind you, there were no shrieks, no groans, but silence, silence and silence, and then the Commodore sank.

She lurched to windward, then swung afar back, righted and dove into the sea, and the rafts were suddenly swallowed by this frightful maw of the ocean. And then by the men on the ten-foot dingy were words that were still not words—something far beyond words.

The lighthouse of Mosquito Inlet stuck up above the horizon like the point of a pin. We turned our dingy toward the shore.

The history of life in an open boat for thirty hours would no doubt be instructive for the young, but none is to be told here and now. For my part I would prefer to tell the story at once, because from it would shine the splendid manhood of Captain Edward Murphy and of William Higgins, the oiler, but let it suffice at this time to say that when we were swamped in the surf and making the best of our way toward the shore the captain gave orders amid the wildness of the breakers as clearly as if he had been on the quarter deck of a battleship.

John Kitchell of Daytona came running down the beach, and as he ran the air was filled with clothes. If he had pulled a single lever and undressed, even as the fire horses harness, he could not seem to me to have stripped with more speed. He dashed into the water and dragged the cook. Then he went after the captain, but the captain sent him to me, and then it was that he saw Billy Higgins lying with his forehead on sand that was clear of the water, and he was dead.

STEPHEN CRANE.

THE PORTABLE PHONOGRAPH

WALTER VAN TILBURG CLARK (1909–   )

The red sunset, with narrow, black cloud strips like threats across it, lay on the curved horizon of the prairie. The air was still and cold, and in it settled the mute darkness and greater cold of night. High in the air there was wind, for through the veil of the dusk the clouds could be seen gliding rapidly south and changing shapes. A queer sensation of torment, of two-sided, unpredictable nature, arose from the stillness of the earth air beneath the violence of the upper air. Out of the sunset, through the dead, matted grass and isolated weed stalks of the prairie, crept the narrow and deeply rutted remains of a road. In the road, in places, there were crusts of shallow, brittle ice. There were little islands of an old oiled pavement in the road too, but most of it was mud, now frozen rigid. The frozen mud still bore the toothed impress of great tanks, and a wanderer on the neighboring undulations might have stumbled, in this light, into large, partially filled-in and weed-grown cavities, their banks channelled and beginning to spread into badlands. These pits were such as might have been made by falling meteors, but they were not. They were the scars of gigantic bombs, their rawness already made a little natural by rain, seed, and time. Along the road, there were rakish remnants of fence. There was also, just visible, one portion of tangled and multiple barbed wire still erect, behind which was a shelving ditch with small caves, now very quiet and empty, at intervals in its back wall. Otherwise there was no structure or remnant of a structure visible over the dome of the darkling earth, but only, in sheltered hollows, the darker shadows of young trees trying again.

Under the wuthering arch of the high wind a V of wild geese fled south. The rush of their pinions sounded briefly, and the faint, plaintive notes of their expeditionary talk. Then they left a still greater vacancy. There was the smell and expectation of snow, as there is likely to be when the wild geese fly south. From the remote distance, towards the red sky, came faintly the protracted howl and quick yap-yap of a prairie wolf.

North of the road, perhaps a hundred yards, lay the parallel and deeply intrenched course of a small creek, lined with leafless alders and willows. The creek was already silent under ice. Into the bank above it was dug a sort of cell, with a single opening, like the mouth of a mine tunnel. Within the cell there was a little red of fire, which showed dully through the opening, like a reflection or a deception of the imagination. The light came from the chary burning of four blocks of poorly aged peat, which gave off a petty warmth and much acrid smoke. But the precious remnants of wood, old fence posts and timbers from the long-deserted dugouts, had to be saved for the real cold, for the time when a man's breath blew white, the moisture in his nostrils stiffened at once when he stepped out, and the expansive blizzards paraded for days over the vast open, swirling and settling and thickening, till the dawn of the cleared day when the sky was thin blue-green and the terrible cold, in which a man could not live for three hours unwarmed, lay over the uniformly drifted swell of the plain.

Around the smoldering peat, four men were seated cross-legged. Behind them, traversed by their shadows, was the earth bench, with two old and dirty army blankets, where the owner of the cell slept. In a niche in the opposite wall were a few tin utensils which caught the glint of the coals. The host was rewrapping in a piece of daubed burlap four fine, leather-bound books. He worked slowly and very carefully, and at last tied the bundle securely with a piece of grass-woven cord. The other three looked intently upon the process, as if a great significance lay in it. As the host tied the cord, he spoke. He was an old man, his long, matted beard and hair gray to nearly white. The shadows made his brows and cheekbones appear gnarled, his eyes and cheeks deeply sunken. His big hands, rough with frost and swollen by rheumatism, were awkward but gentle at their task. He was like a prehistoric priest performing a fateful ceremonial rite. Also his voice had in it a suitable quality of deep, reverent despair, yet perhaps at the moment, a sharpness of selfish satisfaction.

"When I perceived what was happening," he said, "I told myself, 'It is the end. I cannot take much; I will take these.'

"Perhaps I was impractical," he continued. "But for myself, I do not regret, and what do we know of those who will come after us? We are the doddering remnant of a race of mechanical fools. I have saved what I love; the soul of what was good in us is here; perhaps the new ones will make a strong enough beginning not to fall behind when they become clever."

He rose with slow pain and placed the wrapped volumes in the niche with his utensils. The others watched him with the same ritualistic gaze.

"Shakespeare, the Bible, *Moby Dick,* the *Divine Comedy,*" one of them said softly. "You might have done worse, much worse."

"You will have a little soul left until you die," said another harshly. "That is more than is true of us. My brain becomes thick, like my hands." He held the big, battered hands, with their black nails, in the glow to be seen.

"I want paper to write on," he said. "And there is none."

The fourth man said nothing. He sat in the shadow farthest from the fire, and sometimes his body jerked in its rags from the cold. Although he was still young, he was sick and coughed often. Writing implied a greater future than he now felt able to consider.

The old man seated himself laboriously, and reached out, groaning at the movement, to put another block of peat on the fire. With bowed heads and averted eyes, his three guests acknowledged his magnanimity.

"We thank you, Doctor Jenkins, for the reading," said the man who had named the books.

They seemed then to be waiting for something. Doctor Jenkins understood, but was loath to comply. In an ordinary moment he would have said nothing. But the words of *The Tempest,* which he had been reading, and the religious attention of the three made this an unusual occasion.

"You wish to hear the phonograph," he said grudgingly.

The two middle-aged men stared into the fire, unable to formulate and expose the enormity of their desire.

The young man, however, said anxiously, between suppressed coughs, "Oh, please," like an excited child.

The old man rose again in his difficult way, and went to the back of the cell. He returned and placed tenderly upon the packed floor, where the firelight might fall upon it, an old portable phonograph in a black case. He smoothed the top with his hand, and then opened it. The lovely green-felt-covered disk became visible.

"I have been using thorns as needles," he said. "But tonight, because we have a musician among us"—he bent his head to the young man, almost invisible in the shadow—"I will use a steel needle. There are only three left."

The two middle-aged men stared at him in speechless adoration. The one with the big hands, who wanted to write, moved his lips, but the whisper was not audible.

"Oh, don't!" cried the young man, as if he were hurt. "The thorns will do beautifully."

"No," the old man said. "I have become accustomed to the thorns, but they are not really good. For you, my young friend, we will have good music tonight."

"After all," he added generously, and beginning to wind the phonograph, which creaked, "they can't last forever."

"No, nor we," the man who needed to write said harshly. "The needle, by all means."

"Oh, thanks," said the young man. "Thanks," he said again in a low, excited voice, and then stifled his coughing with a bowed head.

"The records, though," said the old man when he had finished winding, "are a different matter. Already they are very worn. I do not play them more than once a week. One, once a week, that is what I allow myself.

"More than a week I cannot stand it; not to hear them," he apologized.

"No, how could you?" cried the young man. "And with them here like this."

"A man can stand anything," said the man who wanted to write, in his harsh antagonistic voice.

"Please, the music," said the young man.

"Only the one," said the old man. "In the long run, we will remember more that way."

He had a dozen records with luxuriant gold and red seals. Even in that light the others could see that the threads of the records were becoming worn. Slowly he read out the titles and the tremendous, dead names of the composers and the artists and the orchestras. The three worked upon the names in their minds, carefully. It was difficult to select from such a wealth what they would at once most like to remember. Finally, the man who wanted to write named Gershwin's "New York."

"Oh, no," cried the sick young man, and then could say nothing more because he had to cough. The others understood him, and the harsh man withdrew his selection and waited for the musician to choose.

The musician begged Doctor Jenkins to read the titles again, very slowly, so that he could remember the sounds. While they were read, he lay back against the wall, his eyes closed, his thin, horny hand pulling at his light beard, and listened to the voices and the orchestras and the single instruments in his mind.

When the reading was done he spoke despairingly. "I have forgotten," he complained; "I cannot hear them clearly.

"There are things missing," he explained.

"I know," said Doctor Jenkins. "I thought that I knew all of Shelley by heart. I should have brought Shelley."

"That's more soul than we can use," said the harsh man. "*Moby Dick* is better.

"By God, we can understand that," he emphasized.

The Doctor nodded.

"Still," said the man who had admired the books, "we need the absolute if we are to keep a grasp on anything.

"Anything but these sticks and peat clods and rabbit snares," he said bitterly.

"Shelley desired an ultimate absolute," said the harsh man. "It's too much," he said. "It's no good; no earthly good."

The musician selected a Debussy nocturne. The others considered and approved. They rose to their knees to watch the Doctor prepare for the playing, so that they appeared to be actually in an attitude of worship. The peat glow showed the thinness of their bearded faces, and the deep lines in them, and revealed the condition of their garments. The other two continued to kneel as the old man carefully lowered the needle onto the spinning disk, but the musician suddenly drew back against the wall again, with his knees up, and buried his face in his hands.

At the first notes of the piano the listeners were startled. They stared at each other. Even the musician lifted his head in amazement, but then quickly bowed it again, strainingly, as if he were suffering from a pain he might not be able to endure. They were all listening deeply, without movement. The wet, blue-green notes tinkled forth from the old machine, and were individual, delectable presences in the cell. The individual, delectable presences swept into a sudden tide of unbearably beautiful dissonance, and then continued fully the swelling and ebbing of that tide, the dissonant inpourings, and the resolutions, and the diminishments, and the little, quiet wavelets of interlude lapping between. Every sound was piercing and singularly sweet. In all the men except the musician, there occurred rapid sequences of tragically heightened recollection. He heard nothing but what was there. At the final, whispering disappearance, but moving quietly so that the others would not hear him and look at him, he let his head fall back in agony, as if it were drawn there by the hair, and clenched the fingers of one hand over his teeth. He sat that way while the others were silent, and until they began to breathe again normally. His drawn-up legs were trembling violently.

Quickly Doctor Jenkins lifted the needle off, to save it and not to spoil the recollection with scraping. When he had stopped the whirling of the sacred disc, he courteously left the phonograph open and by the fire, in sight.

The others, however, understood. The musician rose last, but then abruptly, and went quickly out at the door without saying anything. The others stopped at the door and gave their thanks in low voices. The Doctor nodded magnificently.

"Come again," he invited, "in a week. We will have the 'New York.'"

When the two had gone together, out towards the rimed road, he stood in the entrance, peering and listening. At first, there was only the resonant boom of the wind overhead, and then far over the dome of the dead, dark plain, the wolf cry lamenting. In the rifts of clouds the Doctor saw four stars flying. It impressed the Doctor that one of them had just been obscured by the beginning of a flying cloud at the very moment he heard what he had been listening for, a sound of suppressed coughing. It was not near-by, however. He believed that down against the pale alders he could see the moving shadow.

With nervous hands he lowered the piece of canvas which served as his door, and pegged it at the bottom. Then quickly and quietly, looking at the piece of canvas frequently, he slipped the records into the case, snapped the lid shut, and carried the phonograph to his couch. There, pausing often to stare at the canvas and listen, he dug earth from the wall and disclosed a piece of board. Behind this there was a deep hole in the wall, into which he put the phonograph. After a moment's consideration, he went over and reached down his bundle of books and inserted it also. Then, guardedly, he once more sealed up the hole with the board and the earth. He also changed his blankets, and the grass-stuffed sack which served as a pillow, so that he could lie facing the entrance. After carefully placing two more blocks of peat upon the fire, he stood for a long time watching the stretched canvas, but it seemed to billow naturally with the first gusts of a lowering wind. At last he prayed, and got in under his blankets, and closed his smoke-smarting eyes. On the inside of the bed, next the wall, he could feel with his hand the comfortable piece of lead pipe.

THE GHOST OF AN APPREHENSION

WALTER VAN TILBURG CLARK (1909–   )

It being the declared purpose of this series to offer examples of the writing process rather than critical appraisals, I have chosen to expose myself by way of a little piece called "The Portable Phonograph," first because it was more than ordinarily conscious in its inception, and so may be reconsidered with a minimum of discovery after the fact, and secondly because it is readily accessible in full should the reader wish to apply the comment more specifically than a synopsis will allow.

Since the story took shape in my mind somewhat as a play might, the intention producing the scene, the scene and the intention selecting the cast, and all three, by means of certain guiding principles which developed with them, dictating the action, and since this approach has occurred often with me, in novels as well as in stories, it will help both to shape the discussion to follow and in a measure to widen its application, if we put the synopsis itself into something like dramatic form. To brief the brief, then (the story is only seven pages long):

THE SCENE. Interior of a dugout above a creek thinly lined with alders. A small, smoky, peat fire in the center. In one wall a niche containing a few battered cooking utensils. In the opposite wall an earth bunk with two old Army blankets on it. Above the entrance, a rolled canvas, which is the door. Outside (the backdrop, so to speak) a desolate prairie, pitted by craters and grooved by the frozen ruts of huge wheels and caterpillar treads. Here and there a remnant of highway pavement, a spidery entanglement of barbed wire, and, in the depressions, a few small, shadowy trees. On the far horizon, a red sunset with bars of black cloud across it. Overhead, changing clouds gliding rapidly south before a high, booming wind. A single wedge of wild geese passes over, going southward more swiftly than the clouds and conversing faintly among themselves. A prairie wolf yaps in the distance. There is no other sound or motion. The air near the ground is still and full of the cold promise of winter.

THE CAST. Four men, all dirty, ragged, and bearded: Dr. Jenkins, a former professor and the host, and three visitors: a powerful, sardonic man, once a writer; a polite, conciliatory soul, whose past is not revealed; and a very thin, nervous young man with a bad cough, who has been a musician. The writer and the conciliatory soul have evidently been here before, though not often, but the musician is making his first call.

THE ACTION. Dr. Jenkins has just finished reading *The Tempest* aloud, and while he wraps up his library, Shakespeare, the Bible, *The Divine Comedy,* and *Moby Dick,* is discussing with the writer and the anonymous one, the present, and possibly future, worth of the books. When he has put the books into the niche with the pots, there is a brief, coercive silence, after which he reluctantly produces an old portable phonograph and twelve records. They may hear one record; one record, once a week, is his rule. He reads the titles. A Gershwin named by the writer is rejected as too sharp a reminder. The musician is given the choice, and after hearing the titles again, and complaining that there are parts he can't remember, he selects a Debussy Nocturne. Dr. Jenkins, in a sudden, penitent gesture, takes out one of his three remaining steel needles, though he has been using thorns himself. The visitors rise to their knees in a reverent semicircle to watch him insert the needle and set the record on. At the first note of the piano, however, the musician shrinks back against the wall, where he struggles silently against his cough and the agony of hearing music again.

When the record is finished, the visitors rise. The musician is the last to rise, but then he goes out at once, without a word. The other two leave more slowly and formally. Dr. Jenkins lingers in the doorway, peering down into the dusk and listening. At last, just as a cloud erases one of four visible stars, he hears a faint cough from down among the alders. He lowers the canvas and pegs it down, and puts the phonograph and records, and then the books too, into a hole above the bunk and seals them in. After changing his blankets around so that he will lie facing the door, and putting more fuel on the fire, he stands watching the canvas again. Still only the wind, which has at last come down to earth, moves it. He prays and gets under his blankets, where, "On the inside of the bed, next the wall, he could feel, with his hand, the comfortable piece of lead pipe."

Even so brief a retelling, when we remember that the story first appeared in the fall of 1941, suggests fully enough all we need to know about the apprehension which was the source of the idea. It also brings us at once to the crux of the writing problem, for it was just the very universality of that apprehension which placed the severest strictures upon the design of the story, and so compelled me, in the first stage, to formulate the guiding principles already mentioned.

Clearly I could justify the use of such a theme only by bringing that universal apprehension into sharp focus, by so heightening the reader's reaction to what he already knew and feared as to make the vaguely possible into the concretely probable. Gradually it became evident that the means to such a concentration and heightening must be three. First, if I were to avoid the flavor of Wellsian prophecy, the great apprehension itself must be touched upon lightly and indirectly, must be little more than a taken-for-granted backdrop. Secondly, the incident played against that backdrop, and the characters engaged in it, had to be highly credible, not in terms of their situation, but in terms of an everyday American life. In short, it didn't seem to me that the desired tone could be achieved in the key of either the incident or the scene alone, but that it must arise out of the dissonant juxtaposition of the two. And finally, the manner of the story had to convey the same contrast, had to be fiddle light on the surface and bass viol deep beneath, which is to say, it had to be satirical. One cannot afford to speak seriously of the end of the world. All of these necessities, the minor and credible activity, presented against a background of doom, in a manner calculated to sustain the dissonance, added up, of course, to a very short story. One does not strain a joke about the end of the world, either.

I didn't, naturally, start with a notion of saying something about the finality of modern war, and out of that melancholy fog evolve a set of rules, and out of them a story. The process was not that orderly. First, I just began to write. I can't remember exactly what set me off. Probably it was some intensifying item of the day's news, stirring me when I had time to sit and brood on it until I had to get rid of the emotion it built up, and the first, suggestive images began to appear. Almost always, whatever may have been working up to it in my mind, recognized and unrecognized, it is some image suddenly coming alive and suggesting more to follow, or to precede, that makes me reach for a pencil. In this case it was the prairie, the vast, desolated backdrop of the dugout, which first appeared, accompanied by a feeling that such a scene implied in itself all that one could afford to say directly about a final war. In short, the critical process began with the creative, and by the time I had completed the introductory description (a slow procedure, involving much cutting, rewriting, and rearranging) the controlling principles, more or less as I have stated them, were already in full operation, the cast had appeared and been approved, and the incident had arisen out of their gathering. The story was finished, except for putting it down, which meant little more than keeping an ear open for that desirable dissonance.

The prairie first appeared blackened by old fires, full of shell craters, deeply scored everywhere by the tracks of enormous tank battles and the vestiges of hopeless entrenchment, and devoid of all present signs of human life. There were no houses, or even shells of houses, no barns, no windmills, no fences, no recognizable fields or even stubs of groves or orchards. It was bare as the moon. It suggested a warfare of almost cosmic proportions (since Hiroshima, we can delete the "almost") which was what I wanted, and it suggested, also, that a good deal of time had passed since the battle. That hint of time softening the edges of all detail, but unable to restore anything, made the destruction even more final, and sufficiently indicated, it seemed to me, that the survivors necessary to the story must be so few, and so far set back, as to be without hope or use. But then I saw that the mooniness was too complete, and could just as well mean a region that had always been desert as it could the ruin of a productive region. Yet it seemed wrong to name the place, and I still didn't want any skeletons of building against the sky. I preferred that tundralike emptiness stretching away to the western horizon. (I was looking west, perhaps because Americans have that habit, perhaps because the war we most dreaded was raging in Europe, and so, in the story time, would have gone across America westward, but probably just because the scene had first appeared in an end-of-day light, and one would naturally be looking toward the sunset.) So there appeared the broken remnants of a highway as unobtrusive tokens of the past. Clearer signs of time elapsed since the fighting were also needed, yet signs which would not too much relieve the sterility of the earth, so there grew up the sparse lines of willows and alders in the trenches and creek beds, and the stunted, new trees in the craters.

Sometime during this first viewing, though I avoided the narrowing effect of a name (the nature of the land, and the fact that the four men were unquestionably American, seemed enough in the way of location) the region became definitely the American Middle West, because it spread the devastation over the whole world to show the heart of the most isolated major power swept over, and the grain lands gone in a warfare which concentrated on cities. It made the place not only a field of the final war, but the final field as well.

Late autumn became the necessary time of year, the last season before the complete death and the somehow healing secrecy of winter, just as sunset, the last hour of vision before the secrecy of night, was the proper time of day. To begin with, the sky had been cloudless, the sunset one of those infinitely penetrable, green-gold fadings that come with cold, but now such a horizon seemed too peaceful, and even suggestive of hope. There had to be some motion in that inert landscape, some threat in the sky. So the clouds formed, moving in a wintry wind, and the sunset turned red, and then, although that came as an afterthought, in part because the professor had to hear that last faint cough down in the alders, the unmoving lower air settled in. The chief intent was that the dissonance of the two regions of air should furnish a physical lead into the moral dissonance of the action, and also that it should reinforce the threat of the black clouds across the sunset, suggest apprehension by ear and skin as well as by eye. Finally, for by now the story was fully in view, some touch of conscious life was needed, by which to move from the backdrop into the play. Hence, as also maintaining the mood, the far-off yapping of the wolf, unheard in those parts for generations, and the brief, almost invisible passage of the geese, unconcerned with the land except as a distance to get over.

The action of the story, prepared all during the arranging and rearranging of this backdrop, moved forward so swiftly, almost automatically, in its details, as to be now largely beyond recall. I do remember the vital factors of the preparation, however. I remember that the cast first appeared to me as three in number, the three who became the professor, the writer, and the musician; that they were all men because even one woman might imply a future; and that they became men of highly mental pasts because that rendered them more nearly helpless, increased their recession, and made it more likely that they would retain the necessary surface of polite conduct. I remember also that the three men first came together in the open, around a wood fire down by the creek, but that somehow nothing would happen among them there. The size and finality of the setting shrank them and paralyzed them with futility. I could not even seem to discover any reason for their bothering to get together, save an animal loneliness which had no dramatic potential except through a much longer development than I could afford. When at last it became clear that it was the scene which rendered them so unusable, the dugout, as in keeping with the tank tracks and the barbed wire, appeared in the bank behind me, and we moved into it. That was all it took. The men not only came alive, but swelled to more than life-size, filling the little cave enormously, assuming the importance for me that they had for each other, and setting the lifeless prairie away into its proper backdrop perspective. The vestigial touches of home-making effort became possible: the few and battered utensils, kept in a niche, like a saint; the peat fire and the earthen bunk, hinting of a nearly woodless world; the Army blankets and the canvas. Also, the home made necessary the host, and the professor, as likely to be the most provident and the most chairmanly, at once assumed that role, and with it his manner and his more numerous years. Indeed it was only then that he certainly became a professor, a kind of epitome of civilized man in his most familiar form, suggesting thereby a great deal through his mere presence in a cave.

When the fragments of possible conversation among the three men, the professor, the writer, and a third who was for a time alternately a painter and a musician, began to occur in the midst of the backdrop details, I shortly felt the need of a fourth man, not only because I sensed that the musician-painter was going to be nearly inarticulate, and, for the sake of variety and interplay, three speakers were preferable to two, but also because the trio was a bit too patly symbolic, and so likely to resist the individualization without which they couldn't convince. (The writer was first seen as a sculptor—which has something to do with the physical characteristics he retained—but changed his profession, partly for the same reason, to break up the rigid one-two-three alignment by drawing nearer to the professor's interests, making a one-two grouping, and partly because it better suited the intent of the tale that he should be thwarted by an absence of that so-common commodity, paper. Of clay there would still be aplenty.) So the fourth man joined the group, the man with the unknown past, the representative of the great, departed audience whose need had produced the specialists. He was a real help, for not only did he relieve the stiffness of the allegory, but he also furnished a contrasting attitude, a second psychological level, being a trifle deferential in the presence of the more specific abilities of the others, but also more resigned because his individual needs were less acute. He was, in short, different in kind, whereas the other three, all upon one level of bolder individuality, were different only in particulars: the harsh cynicism of the frustrated writer; the advanced tuberculosis which makes time so important to the musician; the grave, reluctant, orderly air of the professor. Furthermore, I believed that I had found in him another sufficiently concealed means to irony, for his deference was, of course, wholly pointless in that place and time, a mere hangover from an irrecoverable social pattern, and yet it was just that trace of deference, that touch of the conciliatory, that held together, by its remnant of drawing-room conduct, a group that otherwise would almost certainly have broken into an undesirable violence.

Once we were in the dugout, and the anonymous fourth had entered, there seemed to be only one thing lacking, that precipitating agent which would settle the whole narrative out in visible form, the reason for the gathering. I cannot remember how many reasons I fleetingly considered off the top of my mind while I completed the backdrop and caught unusable but suggestive glimpses of the civilized pasts of the men. (The professor, for instance, had taught English in a Midwestern college, specializing in Victorian Literature, but had a wide range of interests beyond that. He had lived in a small, white, frame house, with vines on the front porch, and a dark, somewhat stuffy study in it, with heavy rugs, too much furniture, and the walls lined with books, mostly old and worn, but here and there in bright, new bindings or dust jackets. He had two children, but both were grown and away from home, and he was rather lonely, because he had retired just a couple of years before the war, and his wife, a plump, bespectacled woman, although a fine mother and housekeeper, did not share any of his intellectual interests.) I remember very clearly, however, that the happiest moment of the whole preliminary came with the discovery of the portable phonograph. Beyond question it was the very object, the key symbol, for which I'd been hunting ever since my first dusky glimpse of the prairie. It was portable, which was important. It would seem valuable enough to such a man as the professor, to be worth carrying off in a crisis. It was a universally familiar object, and so would derive its dramatic virtue entirely from its present rarity. In its combined material inconsequence—for certainly it was one of the lesser gadgets of our abundantly gadgeted civilization—and spiritual consequence, as the only remaining vehicle of perhaps the highest achievement of mind and emotion of that same civilization, it became the very centerpiece of the desired dissonance, the touchstone for action and language. The title arrived with it, of course. In its presence, the relationships of the cast were rapidly established. It became evident that the small, suppressed element of conflict that was needed must spring from it and from the music it produced. As a result, the musician at once assumed the brief future that would make him desperate, and became certainly a musician rather than a painter, and also the newcomer, the stranger in the group, the man in whom the restraint of association would play the smallest part and the hunger for music the greatest. At once, also, the professor, as the owner of the treasure, became the antagonist. To all intents the story was complete.

There remained only to discover a valid and contributory means of prolonging, though backwards, into the hours before the tale opens, a meeting which would otherwise be incredibly brief, and which could not, obviously, be extended by eating and drinking. Books were beyond question the means, and certainly, in this context, the reasons for selecting the four the professor had brought with him are equally clear, at least by the time the writer has spoken of *Moby Dick* as something they can all understand now (he might usefully have dropped a word about Ishmael's coffin-boat) and added that Shelley had too much soul, and was "no earthly good." Nor is there any mystery about his selecting *The Tempest* for the reading, once we realize that Caliban and Ariel are at it again over the portable phonograph. The act of reading and the reverence accorded the books serve also as a kind of induction to the high sacrament of the music, in which the professor becomes the priest of a doomed faith and the visitors literally assume kneeling positions around the phonograph.

It is intended that the conclusion should leave with the reader a sense of unity, of the opening dissonance resolved, though not into peace, but rather by means, gently, gently, of almost entirely reducing the professor to the cave man, blending him, as it were, into the terrible landscape. As he stands suspiciously in the doorway, after the guests have departed, he sees, at the very instant he hears the coughing down in the alders, one of four bright stars suddenly hidden by a cloud. It is a sufficient sign to the primitive credulity revived in him, and indirectly, we hope, in the reader. Then also, as he stands watching the canvas he had pegged down, it is moved by "the first gusts of a lowering wind." The opening dissonance between the wuthering upper air and the still ground air is also resolved, and again, as in the case of the human dissonance, by suggesting an end, by bringing winter to the door. Yet, in the last line, as the professor lies on the earth bench, facing the billowing canvas, "On the inside of the bed, next the wall, he could feel with his hand, the comfortable piece of lead pipe." His weapon still comes from that lost world of gadgets. He cannot bring even violence to the level of the new—the very old—world in which he now lives. And of course futility, in any but the meanest and most temporary sense, attends the defense for which he is prepared.

It seemed to me that sentence plucked the proper closing note, one that might linger for a time with a tenuous but moving reminder of the whole intention. If so, it was so, happily, by means of the very last phrase, and particularly by means of the one word "comfortable." Nothing in the phrase was considered, not "comfortable" any more than the rest, but even as it came, that "comfortable" tickled me, not so much because of its immediate implication, in which the paradox was clear enough, as for some more remote, redoubling connotation which I could not, at the moment, catch hold of. Then, a few seconds after I had poked home the final period, it came to me. I had done a bit of lucky thieving from Bill of Avon. (Perhaps the professor's volume of Shakespeare had put it out handy for the borrowing.) Remember how Juliet, waking in the tomb, and not yet aware that Romeo is dead, murmurs drowsily to the gentle Friar Lawrence, "Oh, comfortable Friar—"? Oh, poor professor, with only his lead pipe. And I was sure that at least the ghost of that old, warm, trusting "comfortable" would lurk to trouble the reader as it had troubled me. Nor could I feel, considering the grim little twist I had given it, that Bill would begrudge me his word. After all, he was no mean shakes of a borrower himself.

III

The Short Story
and the Reader

*Books are to be called for and supplied on the assumption that
the process of reading is not a half-sleep, but in the highest sense
an exercise, a gymnastic struggle; that the reader is to do something for himself.*

—WALT WHITMAN

We must grant the artist his subject, his donnée: *our criticism is
applied only to what he makes of it.*

—HENRY JAMES

*To read a book well, one should read it as if one were writing it.
Begin not by sitting on the bench among the judges but by standing in the dock with the criminal. Be his fellow worker, become
his accomplice. . . . But now, when the book is finished, the
reader must leave the dock and mount the bench. He must cease
to be the friend; he must become the judge. . . . Every book
. . . has the right to be judged by the best of its kind.*

—VIRGINIA WOOLF

*Art lives upon discussion, upon experiment, upon curiosity, upon
variety of attempt, upon the exchange of views and the comparison of standpoints; and there is a presumption that those times
when no one has anything particular to say about it, and has no
reason to give for practice or preference, though they may be times
of honor, are not times of development—are times, possibly
even, a little of dullness.*

—HENRY JAMES

BILLY BUDD

HERMAN MELVILLE (1819–1891)

> ## BILLY BUDD
> ## SAILOR
>
> (An inside narrative.)
>
> What befell him
> in the year of the
> Great Mutiny
> etc.
>
> Dedicated to
> Jack Chase, Englishman,
>
> wherever that great heart may now be, here on earth
> or harboured in paradise. Captain of the maintop in
> the year 1843 in the U. S. Frigate *United States.*

Title and dedication as given in Melville's manuscript.

EDITORS' NOTE

Melville's novel—originally entitled *Billy Budd: Foretopman*—was edited by Raymond Weaver and published posthumously in 1924 as volume thirteen of *The Works* (London: Constable, 1922–1924). Until 1948 all subsequent editions reprinted Weaver's text, including the errors in his text. In 1948 F. Barron Freeman re-edited *Billy Budd* from the manuscript; he corrected some of the textual errors in Weaver's imprint, but he himself committed a great many other errors. To correct that situation Miss Elizabeth Treeman, an assistant editor of Harvard University Press, collated all previous editions with the original manuscript in the Houghton Library of Harvard University and thus completed a new and authoritative text.

There are two versions of the Treeman text: One is in *The American Tradition in Literature,* edited by S. Bradley, R. C. Beatty, and E. H. Long (New York: Norton, 1956, rev. ed. 1962). The other is in the Everyman paperback edition of *Typee and Billy Budd,* edited by Milton R. Stern (1958). Working with both the new Treeman text and the Melville manuscript, Professor Stern regularized the punctuation and spelling and—where there was doubt—chose the most probable reading as dictated by the manuscript.

Preface

The year 1797, the year of this narrative, belongs to a period which, as every thinker now feels, involved a crisis for Christendom not exceeded in its undetermined momentousness at the time by any other era whereof there is record. The opening proposition made by the Spirit of that Age involved rectification of the Old World's hereditary wrongs. In France, to some extent, this was bloodily effected. But what then? Straightway the Revolution itself became a wrongdoer, one more oppressive than the kings. Under Napoleon it enthroned upstart kings, and initiated that prolonged agony of continual war whose final throe was Waterloo. During those years not the wisest could have foreseen that the outcome of all would be what to some thinkers apparently it has since turned out to be—a political advance along nearly the whole line for Europeans.

Now, as elsewhere hinted, it was something caught from the Revolutionary Spirit that at Spithead emboldened the man-of-war's men to rise against real abuses, long-standing ones, and afterwards at the Nore to make inordinate and aggressive demands —successful resistance to which was confirmed only when the ringleaders were hung for an admonitory spectacle to the anchored fleet. Yet in a way analogous to the operation of the Revolution at large—the Great Mutiny, though by Englishmen naturally deemed monstrous at the time, doubtless gave the first latent prompting to most important reforms in the British navy.

[1]

In the time before steamships, or then more frequently than now, a stroller along the docks of any considerable sea-port would occasionally have his attention arrested by a group of bronzed mariners, man-of-war's men or merchant-sailors in holiday attire ashore on liberty. In certain instances they would flank, or, like a bodyguard quite surround some superior figure of their own class, moving along with them like Aldebaran among the lesser lights of his constellation. That signal object was the "Handsome Sailor" of the less prosaic time alike of the military and merchant navies. With no perceptible trace of the vainglorious about him, rather with the off-hand unaffectedness of natural regality, he seemed to accept the spontaneous homage of his shipmates. A somewhat remarkable instance recurs to me. In Liverpool, now half a century ago, I saw under the shadow of the great dingy street-wall of Prince's Dock (an obstruction long since removed) a common sailor, so intensely black that he must needs have been a native African of the unadulterate blood of Ham. A symmetric figure much above the average height. The two ends of a gay silk handkerchief thrown loose about the neck danced upon the displayed ebony of his chest; in his ears were big hoops of gold, and a Scotch Highland bonnet with a tartan band set off his shapely head.

It was a hot noon in July; and his face, lustrous with perspiration, beamed with barbaric good humor. In jovial sallies right and left, his white teeth flashing into view, he rollicked along, the centre of a company of his shipmates. These were made up of such an assortment of tribes and complexions as would have well fitted them to be marched up by Anacharsis Cloots before the bar of the first French Assembly as Representatives of the Human Race. At each spontaneous tribute rendered by the way-farers to this black pagod of a fellow—the tribute of a pause and stare, and less frequent an exclamation,—the motley retinue showed that they took that sort of pride

in the evoker of it which the Assyrian priests doubtless showed for their grand sculptured Bull when the faithful prostrated themselves.

To return.

If in some cases a bit of a nautical Murat in setting forth his person ashore, the
handsome sailor of the period in question evinced nothing of the dandified Billy-be·
Damn, an amusing character all but extinct now, but occasionally to be encountered,
and in a form yet more amusing than the original, at the tiller of the boats on the
tempestuous Erie Canal or, more likely, vaporing in the groggeries along the tow-
path. Invariably a proficient in his perilous calling, he was also more or less of a
mighty boxer or wrestler. It was strength and beauty. Tales of his prowess were
recited. Ashore he was the champion; afloat the spokesman; on every suitable occasion always foremost. Close-reefing topsails in a gale, there he was, astride the
weather yard-arm-end, foot in the Flemish horse as "stirrup," both hands tugging at
the "earring" as at a bridle, in very much the attitude of young Alexander curbing the
fiery Bucephalus. A superb figure, tossed up as by the horns of Taurus against the
thunderous sky, cheerily hallooing to the strenuous file along the spar.

The moral nature was seldom out of keeping with the physical make. Indeed, except as toned by the former, the comeliness and power, always attractive in masculine
conjunction, hardly could have drawn the sort of honest homage the Handsome Sailor
in some examples received from his less gifted associates.

Such a cynosure, at least in aspect, and something such too in nature, though with
important variations made apparent as the story proceeds, was welkin-eyed Billy Budd,
or Baby Budd, as more familiarly under circumstances hereafter to be given he at last
came to be called, aged twenty-one, a foretopman of the British fleet toward the close
of the last decade of the eighteenth century. It was not very long prior to the time
of the narration that follows that he had entered the King's Service, having been impressed on the Narrow Seas from a homeward-bound English merchantman into a
seventy-four outward-bound, H.M.S. *Indomitable;* which ship, as was not unusual in
those hurried days, having been obliged to put to sea short of her proper complement
of men. Plump upon Billy at first sight in the gangway the boarding officer Lieutenant
Ratcliffe pounced, even before the merchantman's crew was formally mustered on the
quarter-deck for his deliberate inspection. And him only he elected. For whether it
was because the other men when ranged before him showed to ill advantage after
Billy, or whether he had some scruples in view of the merchantman being rather short-
handed, however it might be, the officer contented himself with his first spontaneous
choice. To the surprise of the ship's company, though much to the Lieutenant's satisfaction, Billy made no demur. But, indeed, any demur would have been as idle as the
protest of a goldfinch popped into a cage.

Noting this uncomplaining acquiescence, all but cheerful one might say, the shipmates turned a surprised glance of silent reproach at the sailor. The shipmaster was
one of those worthy mortals found in every vocation, even the humbler ones—the sort
of person whom everybody agrees in calling "a respectable man." And—nor so
strange to report as it may appear to be—though a ploughman of the troubled waters,
life-long contending with the intractable elements, there was nothing this honest soul
at heart loved better than simple peace and quiet. For the rest, he was fifty or thereabouts, a little inclined to corpulence, a prepossessing face, unwhiskered, and of an
agreeable color—a rather full face, humanely intelligent in expression. On a fair day
with a fair wind and all going well, a certain musical chime in his voice seemed to be
the veritable unobstructed outcome of the innermost man. He had much prudence,

much conscientiousness, and there were occasions when these virtues were the cause of overmuch disquietude in him. On a passage, so long as his craft was in any proximity to land, no sleep for Captain Graveling. He took to heart those serious responsibilities not so heavily borne by some shipmasters.

Now while Billy Budd was down in the forecastle getting his kit together, the *Indomitable's* lieutenant, burly and bluff, nowise disconcerted by Captain Graveling's omitting to proffer the customary hospitalities on an occasion so unwelcome to him, an omission simply caused by preoccupation of thought, unceremoniously invited himself into the cabin, and also to a flask from the spirit-locker, a receptacle which his experienced eye instantly discovered. In fact he was one of those sea-dogs in whom all the hardship and peril of naval life in the great prolonged wars of his time never impaired the natural instinct for sensuous enjoyment. His duty he always faithfully did; but duty is sometimes a dry obligation, and he was for irrigating its aridity, whensoever possible, with a fertilizing decoction of strong waters. For the cabin's proprietor there was nothing left but to play the part of the enforced host with whatever grace and alacrity were practicable. As necessary adjuncts to the flask, he silently placed tumbler and water-jug before the irrepressible guest. But excusing himself from partaking just then, he dismally watched the unembarrassed officer deliberately diluting his grog a little, then tossing it off in three swallows, pushing the empty tumbler away, yet not so far as to be beyond easy reach, at the same time settling himself in his seat and smacking his lips with high satisfaction, looking straight at the host.

These proceedings over, the Master broke the silence; and there lurked a rueful reproach in the tone of his voice; "Lieutenant, you are going to take my best man from me, the jewel of 'em."

"Yes, I know" rejoined the other, immediately drawing back the tumbler preliminary to a replenishing; "Yes, I know. Sorry."

"Beg pardon, but you don't understand, Lieutenant. See here now. Before I shipped that young fellow, my forecastle was a rat-pit of quarrels. It was black times, I tell you, aboard the *'Rights'* here. I was worried to that degree my pipe had no comfort for me. But Billy came; and it was like a Catholic priest striking peace in an Irish shindy. Not that he preached to them or said or did anything in particular; but a virtue went out of him, sugaring the sour ones. They took to him like hornets to treacle; all but the buffer of the gang, the big shaggy chap with the fire-red whiskers. He indeed out of envy, perhaps, of the newcomer, and thinking such a 'sweet and pleasant fellow,' as he mockingly designated him to the others, could hardly have the spirit of a game-cock, must needs bestir himself in trying to get up an ugly row with him. Billy forebore with him and reasoned with him in a pleasant way—he is something like myself, lieutenant, to whom aught like a quarrel is hateful—but nothing served. So, in the second dog-watch one day the Red Whiskers in presence of the others, under pretence of showing Billy just whence a sirloin steak was cut—for the fellow had once been a butcher—insultingly gave him a dig under the ribs. Quick as lightning Billy let fly his arm. I dare say he never meant to do quite as much as he did, but anyhow he gave the burly fool a terrible drubbing. It took about half a minute, I should think. And, lord bless you, the lubber was astonished at the celerity. And will you believe it, Lieutenant, the Red Whiskers now really loves Billy—loves him, or is the biggest hypocrite that ever I heard of. But they all love him. Some of 'em do his washing, darn his old trousers for him; the carpenter is at odd times making a pretty little chest of drawers for him. Anybody will do anything for Billy Budd; and it's the happy family here. But now,

Lieutenant, if that young fellow goes—I know how it will be aboard the *'Rights.'* Not again very soon shall I, coming up from dinner, lean over the capstan smoking a quiet pipe—no, not very soon again, I think. Ay, Lieutenant, you are going to take away the jewel of 'em; you are going to take away my peacemaker!" And with that the good soul had really some ado in checking a rising sob.

"Well," said the officer who had listened with amused interest to all this, and now waxing merry with his tipple; "Well, blessed are the peacemakers especially the fighting peacemakers! And such are the seventy-four beauties some of which you see poking their noses out of the port-holes of yonder war-ship lying-to for me," pointing thro' the cabin window at the *Indomitable*. "But courage! don't look so downhearted, man. Why, I pledge you in advance the royal approbation. Rest assured that His Majesty will be delighted to know that in a time when his hard tack is not sought for by sailors with such avidity as should be; a time also when some shipmasters privily resent the borrowing from them a tar or two for the service; His Majesty, I say, will be delighted to learn that *one* shipmaster at least cheerfully surrenders to the King, the flower of his flock, a sailor who with equal loyalty makes no dissent.—But where's my beauty? Ah," looking through the cabin's open door, "Here he comes; and, by Jove—lugging along his chest—Apollo with his portmanteau!—My man," stepping out to him, "you can't take that big box aboard a warship. The boxes there are mostly shot-boxes. Put your duds in a bag, lad. Boot and saddle for the cavalryman, bag and hammock for the man-of-war's man."

The transfer from chest to bag was made. And, after seeing his man into the cutter and then following him down, the lieutenant pushed off from the *Rights-of-Man*. That was the merchant-ship's name; tho' by her master and crew abbreviated in sailor fashion into *The Rights*. The hard-headed Dundee owner was a staunch admirer of Thomas Paine whose book in rejoinder to Burke's arraignment of the French Revolution had then been published for some time and had gone everywhere. In christening his vessel after the title of Paine's volume, the man of Dundee was something like his contemporary shipowner, Stephen Girard of Philadelphia, whose sympathies, alike with his native land and its liberal philosophers, he evinced by naming his ships after Voltaire, Diderot, and so forth.

But now, when the boat swept under the merchant-man's stern, and officer and oarsmen were noting—some bitterly and others with a grin,—the name emblazoned there; just then it was that the new recruit jumped up from the bow where the coxswain had directed him to sit, and waving his hat to his silent shipmates sorrowfully looking over at him from the taffrail, bade the lads a genial good-bye. Then, making a salutation as to the ship herself, "And good-bye to you too, old *Rights of Man.*"

"Down, Sir!" roared the lieutenant, instantly assuming all the rigor of his rank, though with difficulty repressing a smile.

To be sure, Billy's action was a terrible breach of naval decorum. But in that decorum he had never been instructed; in consideration of which the lieutenant would hardly have been so energetic in reproof but for the concluding farewell to the ship. This he rather took as meant to convey a covert sally on the new recruit's part, a sly slur at impressment in general, and that of himself in especial. And yet, more likely, if satire it was in effect, it was hardly so by intention, for Billy tho' happily endowed with the gayety of high health, youth, and a free heart, was yet by no means of a satirical turn. The will to it and the sinister dexterity were alike wanting. To deal in double meanings and insinuations of any sort was quite foreign to his nature.

As to his enforced enlistment, that he seemed to take pretty much as he was wont to take any vicissitude of weather. Like the animals, though no philosopher, he was, without knowing it, practically a fatalist. And, it may be, that he rather liked this adventurous turn in his affairs, which promised an opening into novel scenes and martial excitements.

Aboard the *Indomitable* our merchant-sailor was forthwith rated as an able-seaman and assigned to the starboard watch of the fore-top. He was soon at home in the service, not at all disliked for his unpretentious good looks and a sort of genial happy-go-lucky air. No merrier man in his mess: in marked contrast to certain other individuals included like himself among the impressed portion of the ship's company; for these when not actively employed were sometimes, and more particularly in the last dog-watch when the drawing near of twilight induced revery, apt to fall into a saddish mood which in some partook of sullenness. But they were not so young as our fore-topman, and no few of them must have known a hearth of some sort; others may have had wives and children left, too probably, in uncertain circumstances, and hardly any but must have had acknowledged kith and kin, while for Billy, as will shortly be seen, his entire family was practically invested in himself.

[2]

Though our new-made foretopman was well received in the top and on the gun-decks, hardly here was he that cynosure he had previously been among those minor ship's companies of the merchant marine, with which companies only had he hitherto consorted.

He was young; and despite his all but fully developed frame, in aspect looked even younger than he really was, owing to a lingering adolescent expression in the as yet smooth face, all but feminine in purity of natural complexion, but where, thanks to his seagoing, the lily was quite suppressed and the rose had some ado visibly to flush through the tan.

To one essentially such a novice in the complexities of factitious life, the abrupt transition from his former and simpler sphere to the ampler and more knowing world of a great warship; this might well have abashed him had there been any conceit or vanity in his composition. Among her miscellaneous multitude, the *Indomitable* mustered several individuals who, however inferior in grade, were of no common natural stamp, sailors more signally susceptive of that air which continuous martial discipline and repeated presence in battle can in some degree impart even to the average man. As the *handsome sailor,* Billy Budd's position aboard the seventy-four was something analogous to that of a rustic beauty transplanted from the provinces and brought into competition with the highborn dames of the court. But this change of circumstances he scarce noted. As little did he observe that something about him provoked an ambiguous smile in one or two harder faces among the blue-jackets. Nor less unaware was he of the peculiar favorable effect his person and demeanor had upon the more intelligent gentlemen of the quarter-deck. Nor could this well have been otherwise. Cast in a mould peculiar to the finest physical examples of those Englishmen in whom the Saxon strain would seem not at all to partake of any Norman or other admixture, he showed in face that humane look of reposeful good nature which the Greek sculptor in some instances gave to his heroic strong man, Hercules. But this again was subtly modified by another and pervasive quality. The ear, small and shapely, the arch of the foot, the curve in mouth and nostril, even the indurated hand dyed to the orange-tawny of the toucan's bill, a hand telling alike of the halyards and tar-bucket; but, above all, something in the mobile expression, and every chance attitude and movement, something suggestive of a mother eminently favored by Love and the Graces; all this strangely indicated a lineage in direct contradiction to his lot. The mysteriousness here, became less mysterious through a matter-of-fact elicited when Billy, at the capstan, was being formally mustered into the service. Asked by the officer, a small brisk little gentleman as it chanced among other questions, his place of birth, he replied, "Please, Sir, I don't know."

"Don't know where you were born?—Who was your father?"

"God knows, Sir."

Struck by the straightforward simplicity of these replies, the officer next asked, "Do you know anything about your beginning?"

"No, Sir. But I have heard that I was found in a pretty silk-lined basket hanging one morning from the knocker of a good man's door in Bristol."

"*Found* say you? Well," throwing back his head and looking up and down the new recruit; "Well, it turns out to have been a pretty good find. Hope they'll find some more like you, my man; the fleet sadly needs them."

Yes, Billy Budd was a foundling, a presumable by-blow, and, evidently, no ignoble one. Noble descent was as evident in him as in a blood horse.

For the rest, with little or no sharpness of faculty or any trace of the wisdom of the serpent, nor yet quite a dove, he possessed that kind and degree of intelligence going along with the unconventional rectitude of a sound human creature, one to whom not yet has been proffered the questionable apple of knowledge. He was illiterate; he could not read, but he could sing, and like the illiterate nightingale was sometimes the composer of his own song.

Of self-consciousness he seemed to have little or none, or about as much as we may reasonably impute to a dog of Saint Bernard's breed.

Habitually living with the elements and knowing little more of the land than as a beach, or, rather, that portion of the terraqueous globe providentially set apart for dance-houses, doxies and tapsters, in short what sailors call a "fiddlers' green," his simple nature remained unsophisticated by those moral obliquities which are not in every case incompatible with that manufacturable thing known as respectability. But are sailors, frequenters of "fiddlers'-greens," without vices? No; but less often than with landsmen do their vices, so called, partake of crookedness of heart, seeming less to proceed from viciousness than exuberance of vitality after long constraint; frank manifestations in accordance with natural law. By his original constitution aided by the cooperating influences of his lot, Billy in many respects was little more than a sort of upright barbarian, much such perhaps as Adam presumably might have been ere the urbane Serpent wriggled himself into his company.

And here be it submitted that apparently going to corroborate the doctrine of man's fall, a doctrine now popularly ignored, it is observable that where certain virtues pristine and unadulterate peculiarly characterize anybody in the external uniform of civilization, they will upon scrutiny seem not to be derived from custom or convention, but rather to be out of keeping with these, as if indeed exceptionally transmitted from a period prior to Cain's city and citified man. The character marked by such qualities has to an unvitiated taste an untampered-with flavor like that of berries, while the man thoroughly civilized, even in a fair specimen of the breed, has to the same moral palate a questionable smack as of a compounded wine. To any stray inheritor of these primitive qualities found, like Caspar Hauser, wandering dazed in any Christian capital of our time, the good-natured poet's famous invocation, near two thousand years ago, of the good rustic out of his latitude in the Rome of the Cesars, still appropriately holds:—

> "Honest and poor, faithful in word and thought
> What has thee, Fabian, to the city brought."

Though our Handsome Sailor had as much of masculine beauty as one can expect anywhere to see; nevertheless, like the beautiful woman in one of Hawthorne's minor tales, there was just one thing amiss in him. No visible blemish indeed, as with the lady; no, but an occasional liability to a vocal defect. Though in the hour of elemental uproar or peril, he was everything that a sailor should be, yet under sudden provocation of strong heart-feeling, his voice otherwise singularly musical, as if expressive of the harmony within, was apt to develop an organic hesitancy, in fact more or less of a stutter or even worse. In this particular Billy was a striking instance that the arch interferer, the envious marplot of Eden, still has more or less to do with every human consignment to this planet of earth. In every case, one way or another he is sure to slip in his little card, as much as to remind us—I too have a hand here.

The avowal of such an imperfection in the Handsome Sailor should be evidence not alone that he is not presented as a conventional hero, but also that the story in which he is the main figure is no romance.

[3]

At the time of Billy Budd's arbitrary enlistment into the *Indomitable* that ship was on her way to join the Mediterranean fleet. No long time elapsed before the junction was effected. As one of that fleet the seventy-four participated in its movements, tho' at times on account of her superior sailing qualities, in the absence of frigates, despatched on separate duty as a scout and at times on less temporary service. But with all this the story has little concernment, restricted as it is to the inner life of one particular ship and the career of an individual sailor.

It was the summer of 1797. In the April of that year had occurred the commotion at Spithead followed in May by a second and yet more serious outbreak in the fleet at the Nore. The latter is known, and without exaggeration in the epithet, as the Great Mutiny. It was indeed a demonstration more menacing to England than the contemporary manifestoes and conquering and proselyting armies of the French Directory.

To the British Empire the Nore Mutiny was what a strike in the fire-brigade would be to London threatened by general arson. In a crisis when the kingdom might well have anticipated the famous signal that some years later published along the naval line of battle what it was that upon occasion England expected of Englishmen; *that* was the time when at the mast-heads of the three-deckers and seventy-fours moored in her own roadstead—a fleet, the right arm of a Power then all but the sole free conservative one of the Old World, the blue-jackets, to be numbered by thousands, ran up with huzzas the British colors with the union and cross wiped out; by that cancellation transmuting the flag of founded law and freedom defined, into the enemy's red meteor of unbridled and unbounded revolt. Reasonable discontent growing out of practical grievances in the fleet had been ignited into irrational combustion, as by live cinders blown across the Channel from France in flames.

The event converted into irony for a time those spirited strains of Dibdin—as a

song-writer no mean auxiliary to the English Government at the European conjuncture
—strains celebrating, among other things, the patriotic devotion of the British tar:

"And as for my life, 'tis the King's!"

Such an episode in the Island's grand naval story her naval historians naturally
abridge; one of them (G. P. R. James) candidly acknowledging that fain would he
pass it over did not "impartiality forbid fastidiousness." And yet his mention is less
a narration than a reference, having to do hardly at all with details. Nor are these
readily to be found in the libraries. Like some other events in every age befalling
states everywhere, including America, the Great Mutiny was of such character that
national pride along with views of policy would fain shade it off into the historical
background. Such events can not be ignored, but there is a considerate way of his-
torically treating them. If a well-constituted individual refrains from blazoning aught
amiss or calamitous in his family, a nation in the like circumstance may without reproach be equally discreet.

Though after parleyings between Government and the ring-leaders, and concessions
by the former as to some glaring abuses, the first uprising—that at Spithead—with
difficulty was put down, or matters for the time pacified; yet at the Nore the unforeseen renewal of insurrection on a yet larger scale, and emphasized in the conferences
that ensued by demands deemed by the authorities not only inadmissible but aggres-
sively insolent, indicated—if the Red Flag did not sufficiently do so—what was the
spirit animating the men. Final suppression, however, there was; but only made possible perhaps by the unswerving loyalty of the marine corps and a voluntary resump-
tion of loyalty among influential sections of the crews.

To some extent the Nore Mutiny may be regarded as analogous to the distempering
irruption of contagious fever in a frame constitutionally sound, and which anon throws
it off.

At all events, of these thousands of mutineers were some of the tars who not so
very long afterwards—whether wholly prompted thereto by patriotism, or pugnacious
instinct, or by both,—helped to win a coronet for Nelson at the Nile, and the naval
crown of crowns for him at Trafalgar. To the mutineers those battles, and especially
Trafalgar, were a plenary absolution and a grand one: For all that goes to make up
scenic naval display, heroic magnificence in arms, those battles, especially Trafalgar,
stand unmatched in human annals.

[4]

Concerning "The greatest sailor since our world began."
                —Tennyson

In this matter of writing, resolve as one way to keep to the main road, some by-
paths have an enticement not readily to be withstood. I am going to err into such a
by-path. If the reader will keep me company I shall be glad. At the least we can
promise ourselves that pleasure which is wickedly said to be in sinning, for a literary
sin the divergence will be.

Very likely it is no new remark, that the inventions of our time have at last brought
about a change in sea-warfare in degree corresponding to the revolution in all warfare
effected by the original introduction from China into Europe of gunpowder. The first
European fire-arm, a clumsy contrivance, was, as is well known, scouted by no few of
the knights as a base implement, good enough peradventure for weavers too craven

to stand up crossing steel with steel in frank fight. But as ashore knightly valor, tho' shorn of its blazonry, did not cease with the knights, neither on the seas, though nowadays in encounters there a certain kind of displayed gallantry be fallen out of date as hardly applicable under changed circumstances, did the nobler qualities of such naval magnates as Don John of Austria, Doria, Van Tromp, Jean Bart, the long line of British Admirals and the American Decaturs of 1812 become obsolete with their wooden walls.

Nevertheless, to anybody who can hold the Present at its worth without being inappreciative of the Past, it may be forgiven, if to such an one the solitary old hulk at Portsmouth, Nelson's *Victory*, seems to float there, not alone as the decaying monument of a fame incorruptible, but also as a poetic reproach, softened by its picturesqueness, to the *Monitors* and yet mightier hulls of the European ironclads. And this not altogether because such craft are unsightly, unavoidably lacking the symmetry and grand lines of the old battle-ships, but equally for other reasons.

There are some, perhaps, who while not altogether inaccessible to that poetic reproach just alluded to, may yet on behalf of the new order, be disposed to parry it; and this to the extent of iconoclasm, if need be. For example, prompted by the sight of the star inserted in the *Victory*'s quarter-deck designating the spot where the Great Sailor fell, these martial utilitarians may suggest considerations implying that Nelson's ornate publication of his person in battle was not only unnecessary, but not military, nay, savored of foolhardiness and vanity. They may add, too, that at Trafalgar it was in effect nothing less than a challenge to death; and death came; and that but for his bravado the victorious Admiral might possibly have survived the battle; and so, instead of having his sagacious dying injunctions overruled by his immediate successor in command, he himself, when the contest was decided, might have brought his shattered fleet to anchor, a proceeding which might have averted the deplorable loss of life by shipwreck in the elemental tempest that followed the martial one.

Well, should we set aside the more disputable point whether for various reasons it was possible to anchor the fleet, then plausibly enough the Benthamites of war may urge the above.

But the *might-have-been* is but boggy ground to build on. And, certainly, in foresight as to the larger issue of an encounter, and anxious preparations for it—buoying the deadly way and mapping it out, as at Copenhagen—few commanders have been so painstakingly circumspect as this same reckless declarer of his person in fight.

Personal prudence even when dictated by quite other than selfish considerations surely is no special virtue in a military man; while an excessive love of glory, impassioning a less burning impulse, the honest sense of duty, is the first. If the name *Wellington* is not so much of a trumpet to the blood as the simpler name *Nelson*, the reason for this may perhaps be inferred from the above. Alfred in his funeral ode on the victor of Waterloo ventures not to call him the greatest soldier of all time, tho' in the same ode he invokes Nelson as "the greatest sailor since the world began."

At Trafalgar Nelson, on the brink of opening the fight, sat down and wrote his last brief will and testament. If under the presentiment of the most magnificent of all victories to be crowned by his own glorious death, a sort of priestly motive led him to dress his person in the jewelled vouchers of his own shining deeds; if thus to have adorned himself for the altar and the sacrifice were indeed vainglory, then affectation and fustian is each more heroic line in the great epics and dramas, since in such lines the poet but embodies in verse those exaltations of sentiment that a nature like Nelson, the opportunity being given, vitalizes into acts.

[5]

Yes, the outbreak at the Nore was put down. But not every grievance was redressed. If the contractors, for example, were no longer permitted to ply some practices peculiar to their tribe everywhere, such as providing shoddy cloth, rations not sound, or false in the measure, not the less impressment, for one thing, went on. By custom sanctioned for centuries, and judicially maintained by a Lord Chancellor as late as Mansfield, that mode of manning the fleet, a mode now fallen into a sort of abeyance but never formally renounced, it was not practicable to give up in those years. Its abrogation would have crippled the indispensable fleet, one wholly under canvas, no steam-power, its innumerable sails and thousands of cannon, everything in short, worked by muscle alone; a fleet the more insatiate in demand for men, because then multiplying its ships of all grades against contingencies present and to come of the convulsed Continent.

Discontent foreran the Two Mutinies, and more or less it lurkingly survived them. Hence it was not unreasonable to apprehend some return of trouble sporadic or general. One instance of such apprehensions: In the same year with this story, Nelson, then Vice Admiral Sir Horatio, being with the fleet off the Spanish coast, was directed by the Admiral in command to shift his pennant from the *Captain* to the *Theseus;* and for this reason: that the latter ship having newly arrived on the station from home where it had taken part in the Great Mutiny, danger was apprehended from the temper of the men; and it was thought that an officer like Nelson was the one, not indeed to terrorize the crew into base subjection, but to win them, by force of his mere presence, back to an allegiance if not as enthusiastic as his own, yet as true. So it was that for a time on more than one quarter-deck anxiety did exist. At sea precautionary vigilance was strained against relapse. At short notice an engagement might come on. When it did, the lieutenants assigned to batteries felt it incumbent on them, in some instances, to stand with drawn swords behind the men working the guns.

[6]

But on board the seventy-four in which Billy now swung his hammock, very little in the manner of the men and nothing obvious in the demeanor of the officers would have suggested to an ordinary observer that the Great Mutiny was a recent event. In their general bearing and conduct the commissioned officers of a war-ship naturally take their tone from the commander, that is if he have that ascendancy of character that ought to be his.

Captain the Honorable Edward Fairfax Vere, to give his full title, was a bachelor of forty or thereabouts, a sailor of distinction even in a time prolific of renowned seamen. Though allied to the higher nobility, his advancement had not been altogether owing to influences connected with that circumstance. He had seen much service, been in various engagements, always acquitting himself as an officer mindful of the welfare of his men, but never tolerating an infraction of discipline; thoroughly versed in the science of his profession, and intrepid to the verge of temerity, though never injudiciously so. For his gallantry in the West Indian waters as flag-lieutenant under Rodney in that Admiral's crowning victory over De Grasse, he was made a post-captain.

Ashore in the garb of a civilian, scarce anyone would have taken him for a sailor, more especially that he never garnished unprofessional talk with nautical terms, and grave in his bearing, evinced little appreciation of mere humor. It was not out of keeping with these traits that on a passage when nothing demanded his paramount action, he was the most undemonstrative of men. Any landsman observing this gentleman, not conspicuous by his stature and wearing no pronounced insignia, emerging from his cabin to the open deck, and noting the silent deference of the officers retiring to leeward, might have taken him for the King's guest, a civilian aboard the King's-ship, some highly honorable discreet envoy on his way to an important post. But in fact this unobtrusiveness of demeanor may have proceeded from a certain unaffected modesty of manhood sometimes accompanying a resolute nature, a modesty evinced at all times not calling for pronounced action, and which shown in any rank of life suggests a virtue aristocratic in kind.

As with some others engaged in various departments of the world's more heroic activities, Captain Vere though practical enough upon occasion would at times betray a certain dreaminess of mood. Standing alone on the weatherside of the quarter deck, one hand holding by the rigging, he would absently gaze off at the blank sea. At the presentation to him then of some minor matter interrupting the current of his thoughts he would show more or less irascibility; but instantly he would control it.

In the navy he was popularly known by the appellation—Starry Vere. How such a designation happened to fall upon one who, whatever his sturdy qualities, was without any brilliant ones was in this wise: A favorite kinsman, Lord Denton, a free-hearted fellow, had been the first to meet and congratulate him upon his return to England from his West Indian cruise; and but the day previous turning over a copy of Andrew Marvell's poems, had lighted, not for the first time however, upon the lines entitled *Appleton House,* the name of one of the seats of their common ancestor, a hero in the German wars of the seventeenth century, in which poem occur the lines,

"This 'tis to have been from the first
In a domestic heaven nursed,
Under the discipline severe
Of Fairfax and the starry Vere."

And so, upon embracing his cousin fresh from Rodney's great victory wherein he had played so gallant a part, brimming over with just family pride in the sailor of their house, he exuberantly exclaimed, "Give ye joy, Ed; give ye joy, my starry Vere!" This got currency, and the novel prefix serving in familiar parlance readily to distinguish the *Indomitable's* Captain from another Vere his senior, a distant relative, an officer of like rank in the navy, it remained permanently attached to the surname.

[7]

In view of the part that the commander of the *Indomitable* plays in scenes shortly to follow, it may be well to fill out that sketch of his outlined in the previous chapter.

Aside from his qualities as a sea-officer, Captain Vere was an exceptional character. Unlike no few of England's renowned sailors, long and arduous service with signal devotion to it, had not resulted in absorbing and *salting* the entire man. He had a marked leaning toward everything intellectual. He loved books, never going to sea without a newly replenished library, compact but of the best. The isolated leisure, in some cases so wearisome, falling at intervals to commanders even during a war-cruise, never was tedious to Captain Vere. With nothing of that literary taste which less heeds the thing conveyed than the vehicle, his bias was towards those books to which every serious mind of superior order occupying any active post of authority in the world, naturally inclines: books treating of actual men and events no matter of who

era—history, biography and unconventional writers, who, free from cant and convention, like Montaigne, honestly and in the spirit of common sense philosophize upon
realities.

In this line of reading he found confirmation of his own more reasoned thoughts—
confirmation which he had vainly sought in social converse, so that as touching most
fundamental topics, there had got to be established in him some positive convictions,
which he forefelt would abide in him essentially unmodified so long as his intelligent
part remained unimpaired. In view of the troubled period in which his lot was cast
this was well for him. His settled convictions were as a dyke against those invading
waters of novel opinion, social, political and otherwise, which carried away as in a
torrent no few minds in those days, minds by nature not inferior to his own. While
other members of that aristocracy to which by birth he belonged were incensed at the
innovators mainly because their theories were inimical to the privileged classes, not
alone Captain Vere disinterestedly opposed them because they seemed to him incapable of embodiment in lasting institutions, but at war with the peace of the world and
the true welfare of mankind.

With minds less stored than his and less earnest, some officers of his rank, with
whom at times he would necessarily consort, found him lacking in the companionable
quality, a dry and bookish gentleman as they deemed. Upon any chance withdrawal
from their company one would be apt to say to another, something like this: "Vere
is a noble fellow, Starry Vere. Spite the gazettes, Sir Horatio," meaning him with
the Lord title, "is at bottom scarce a better seaman or fighter. But between you and
me now, don't you think there is a queer streak of the pedantic running thro' him?
Yes, like the King's yarn in a coil of navy-rope?"

Some apparent ground there was for this sort of confidential criticism; since not only
did the Captain's discourse never fall into the jocosely familiar, but in illustrating of
any point touching the stirring personages and events of the time he would be as apt
to cite some historic character or incident of antiquity as that he would cite from the
moderns. He seemed unmindful of the circumstance that to his bluff company such
remote allusions, however pertinent they might really be, were altogether alien to men
whose reading was mainly confined to the journals. But considerateness in such matters is not easy to natures constituted like Captain Vere's. Their honesty prescribes to
them directness, sometimes far-reaching like that of a migratory fowl that in its flight
never heeds when it crosses a frontier.

[8]

The lieutenants and other commissioned gentlemen forming Captain Vere's staff it
is not necessary here to particularize, nor needs it to make any mention of any of the
warrant-officers. But among the petty-officers was one who having much to do with the
story, may as well be forthwith introduced. His portrait I essay, but shall never hit it.
This was John Claggart, the Master-at-arms. But that sea-title may to landsmen seem
somewhat equivocal. Originally doubtless that petty-officer's function was the instruction of the men in the use of arms, sword or cutlas. But very long ago, owing to the
advance in gunnery making hand-to-hand encounters less frequent and giving to nitre
and sulphur the preeminence over steel, that function ceased; the master-at-arms of a
great war-ship becoming a sort of Chief of Police, charged among other matters with
the duty of preserving order on the populous lower gun-decks.

Claggart was a man about five and thirty, somewhat spare and tall, yet of no ill
figure upon the whole. His hand was too small and shapely to have been accustomed

to hard toil. The face was a notable one; the features all except the chin cleanly cut
as those on a Greek medallion; yet the chin, beardless as Tecumseh's, had something
of strange protuberant heaviness in its make that recalled the prints of the Rev. Dr.
Titus Oates, the historic deponent with the clerical drawl in the time of Charles II
and the fraud of the alleged Popish Plot. It served Claggart in his office that his eye
could cast a tutoring glance. His brow was of the sort phrenologically associated with
more than average intellect; silken jet curls partly clustering over it, making a foil to
the pallor below, a pallor tinged with a faint shade of amber akin to the hue of time-
tinted marbles of old. This complexion, singularly contrasting with the red or deeply
bronzed visages of the sailors, and in part the result of his official seclusion from the
sunlight, tho' it was not exactly displeasing, nevertheless seemed to hint of something
defective or abnormal in the constitution and blood. But his general aspect and manner were so suggestive of an education and career incongruous with his naval function
that when not actively engaged in it he looked like a man of high quality, social and
moral, who for reasons of his own was keeping incog. Nothing was known of his
former life. It might be that he was an Englishman; and yet there lurked a bit of
accent in his speech suggesting that possibly he was not such by birth, but through
naturalization in early childhood. Among certain grizzled sea-gossips of the gun-decks
and forecastle went a rumor perdue that the master-at-arms was a *chevalier* who had
volunteered into the King's navy by way of compounding for some mysterious swindle
whereof he had been arraigned at the King's Bench. The fact that nobody could substantiate this report was, of course, nothing against its secret currency. Such a rumor
once started on the gun-decks in reference to almost anyone below the rank of a
commissioned officer would, during the period assigned to this narrative, have seemed
not altogether wanting in credibility to the tarry old wiseacres of a man-of-war crew.
And indeed a man of Claggart's accomplishments, without prior nautical experience,
entering the navy at mature life, as he did, and necessarily allotted at the start to the
lowest grade in it; a man too who never made allusion to his previous life ashore;
these were circumstances which in the dearth of exact knowledge as to his true antecedents opened to the invidious a vague field for unfavorable surmise.

But the sailors' dog-watch gossip concerning him derived a vague plausibility from
the fact that now for some period the British Navy could so little afford to be squeamish in the matter of keeping up the muster-rolls, that not only were press-gangs notoriously abroad both afloat and ashore, but there was little or no secret about another
matter, namely that the London police were at liberty to capture any able-bodied
suspect, any questionable fellow at large and summarily ship him to dockyard or fleet.
Furthermore, even among voluntary enlistments there were instances where the motive
thereto partook neither of patriotic impulse nor yet of a random desire to experience
a bit of sea-life and martial adventure. Insolvent debtors of minor grade, together
with the promiscuous lame ducks of morality found in the Navy a convenient and
secure refuge. Secure, because once enlisted aboard a King's-Ship, they were as much
in sanctuary, as the transgressor of the Middle Ages harboring himself under the
shadow of the altar. Such sanctioned irregularities, which for obvious reasons the
Government would hardly think to parade at the time, and which consequently, and
as affecting the least influential class of mankind, have all but dropped into oblivion,
lend color to something for the truth whereof I do not vouch, and hence have some
scruple in stating; something I remember having seen in print though the book I
can not recall; but the same thing was personally communicated to me now more than
forty years ago by an old pensioner in a cocked hat with whom I had a most interesting

talk on the terrace at Greenwich, a Baltimore negro, a Trafalgar man. It was to this effect: In the case of a warship short of hands whose speedy sailing was imperative, the deficient quota in lack of any other way of making it good, would be eked out by draughts culled direct from the jails. For reasons previously suggested it would not perhaps be easy at the present day directly to prove or disprove the allegation. But allowed as a verity, how significant would it be of England's straits at the time, confronted by those wars which like a flight of harpies rose shrieking from the din and dust of the fallen Bastille. That era appears measurably clear to us who look back at it, and but read of it. But to the grandfathers of us graybeards, the more thoughtful of them, the genius of it presented an aspect like that of Camoen's Spirit of the Cape, an eclipsing menace mysterious and prodigious. Not America was exempt from apprehension. At the height of Napoleon's unexampled conquests, there were Americans who had fought at Bunker Hill who looked forward to the possibility that the Atlantic might prove no barrier against the ultimate schemes of this French upstart from the revolutionary chaos who seemed in act of fulfilling judgment prefigured in the Apocalypse.

But the less credence was to be given to the gun-deck talk touching Claggart, seeing that no man holding his office in a man-of-war can ever hope to be popular with the crew. Besides, in derogatory comments upon anyone against whom they have a grudge, or for any reason or no reason mislike, sailors are much like landsmen; they are apt to exaggerate or romance it.

About as much was really known to the *Indomitable's* tars of the master-at-arms' career before entering the service as an astronomer knows about a comet's travels prior to its first observable appearance in the sky. The verdict of the sea quidnuncs has been cited only by way of showing what sort of moral impression the man made upon rude uncultivated natures whose conceptions of human wickedness were necessarily of the narrowest, limited to ideas of vulgar rascality,—a thief among the swinging hammocks during a night-watch, or the man-brokers and land-sharks of the sea-ports.

It was no gossip, however, but fact, that though, as before hinted, Claggart upon his entrance into the navy was, as a novice, assigned to the least honorable section of a man-of-war's crew, embracing the drudgery, he did not long remain there.

The superior capacity he immediately evinced, his constitutional sobriety, ingratiating deference to superiors, together with a peculiar ferreting genius manifested on a singular occasion, all this capped by a certain austere patriotism abruptly advanced him to the position of master-at-arms.

Of this maritime Chief of Police the ship's-corporals, so called, were the immediate subordinates, and compliant ones; and this, as is to be noted in some business departments ashore, almost to a degree inconsistent with entire moral volition. His place put various converging wires of underground influence under the Chief's control, capable when astutely worked thro' his understrappers, of operating to the mysterious discomfort, if nothing worse, of any of the sea-commonalty.

[9]

Life in the fore-top well agreed with Billy Budd. There, when not actually engaged on the yards yet higher aloft, the topmen, who as such had been picked out for youth and activity, constituted an aerial club lounging at ease against the smaller stun'sails rolled up into cushions, spinning yarns like the lazy gods, and frequently amused with what was going on in the busy world of the decks below. No wonder then that a young fellow of Billy's disposition was well content in such society. Giving no cause of offence to anybody, he was always alert at a call. So in the merchant service it had been with him. But now such a punctiliousness in duty was shown that his topmates would sometimes good-naturedly laugh at him for it. This heightened alacrity had its cause, namely, the impression made upon him by the first formal gangwaypunishment he had ever witnessed, which befell the day following his impressment. It had been incurred by a little fellow, young, a novice, an after-guardsman absent from his assigned post when the ship was being put about; a dereliction resulting in a rather serious hitch to that manœuvre, one demanding instantaneous promptitude in letting go and making fast. When Billy saw the culprit's naked back under the scourge gridironed with red welts, and worse; when he marked the dire expression on the liberated man's face as with his woolen shirt flung over him by the executioner he rushed forward from the spot to bury himself in the crowd, Billy was horrified. He resolved that never through remissness would he make himself liable to such a visitation or do or omit aught that might merit even verbal reproof. What then was his surprise and concern when ultimately he found himself getting into petty trouble occasionally about such matters as the stowage of his bag or something amiss in his hammock, matters under the police oversight of the ship's-corporals of the lower decks, and which brought down on him a vague threat from one of them.

So heedful in all things as he was, how could this be? He could not understand it, and it more than vexed him. When he spoke to his young topmates about it they were either lightly incredulous or found something comical in his unconcealed anxiety. "Is it your bag, Billy?" said one. "Well, sew yourself up in it, bully boy, and then you'll be sure to know if anybody meddles with it."

Now there was a veteran aboard who because his years began to disqualify him for more active work had been recently assigned duty as main-mast-man in his watch, looking to the gear belayed at the rail roundabout that great spar near the deck. At off-times the foretopman had picked up some acquaintance with him, and now in his trouble it occurred to him that he might be the sort of person to go to for wise counsel. He was an old Dansker long anglicized in the service, of few words, many wrinkles and some honorable scars. His wizened face, time-tinted and weather-stained to the complexion of an antique parchment, was here and there peppered blue by the chance explosion of a gun-cartridge in action. He was an *Agamemnon*-man; some two years prior to the time of this story having served under Nelson, when but Sir Horatio, in that ship immortal in naval memory, and which, dismantled and in part broken up to her bare ribs, is seen a grand skeleton in Haydon's etching. As one of a boardingparty from the *Agamemnon* he had received a cut slantwise along one temple and cheek, leaving a long pale scar like a streak of dawn's light falling athwart the dark visage. It was on account of that scar and the affair in which it was known that he had received it, as well as from his blue-peppered complexion, that the Dansker went among the *Indomitable's* crew by the name of "Board-her-in-the-smoke."

Now the first time that his small weazel-eyes happened to light on Billy Budd, a certain grim internal merriment set all his ancient wrinkles into antic play. Was it that his eccentric unsentimental old sapience, primitive in its kind, saw or thought it saw something which, in contrast with the war-ship's environment, looked oddly incongruous in the handsome sailor? But after slyly studying him at intervals, the old

Merlin's equivocal merriment was modified; for now when the twain would meet, it would start in his face a quizzing sort of look, but it would be but momentary and sometimes replaced by an expression of speculative query as to what might eventually befall a nature like that, dropped into a world not without some man-traps and against whose subtleties simple courage, lacking experience and address and without any touch of defensive ugliness, is of little avail; and where such innocence as man is capable of does yet in a moral emergency not always sharpen the faculties or enlighten the will.

However it was, the Dansker in his ascetic way rather took to Billy. Nor was this only because of a certain philosophic interest in such a character. There was another cause. While the old man's eccentricities, sometimes bordering on the ursine, repelled the juniors, Billy, undeterred thereby, revering him as a salt hero, would make advances, never passing the old Agamemnon-man without a salutation marked by that respect which is seldom lost on the aged however crabbed at times or whatever their station in life.

There was a vein of dry humor, or what not, in the mast-man; and, whether in freak of patriarchal irony touching Billy's youth and athletic frame, or for some other and more recondite reason, from the first in addressing him he always substituted Baby for Billy. The Dansker in fact being the originator of the name by which the foretopman eventually became known aboard ship.

Well then, in his mysterious little difficulty, going in quest of the wrinkled one, Billy found him off duty in a dog-watch ruminating by himself, seated on a shot-box of the upper gun-deck, now and then surveying with a somewhat cynical regard certain of the more swaggering promenaders there. Billy recounted his trouble, again wondering how it all happened. The salt seer attentively listened, accompanying the foretopman's recital with queer twitchings of his wrinkles and problematical little sparkles of his small ferret eyes. Making an end of his story, the foretopman asked, "And now, Dansker, do tell me what you think of it."

The old man, shoving up the front of his tarpaulin and deliberately rubbing the long slant scar at the point where it entered the thin hair, laconically said, "Baby Budd, *Jemmy Legs*" (meaning the master-at-arms) "is down on you."

"*Jemmy Legs!*" ejaculated Billy, his welkin eyes expanding; "what for? Why he calls me *the sweet and pleasant young fellow,* they tell me."

"Does he so?" grinned the grizzled one; then said, "Ay, Baby Lad, a sweet voice has *Jemmy Legs*."

"No, not always. But to me he has. I seldom pass him but there comes a pleasant word."

"And that's because he's down upon you, Baby Budd."

Such reiteration along with the manner of it, incomprehensible to a novice, disturbed Billy almost as much as the mystery for which he had sought explanation. Something less unpleasingly oracular he tried to extract; but the old sea-Chiron, thinking perhaps that for the nonce he had sufficiently instructed his young Achilles, pursed his lips, gathered all his wrinkles together and would commit himself to nothing further.

Years, and those experiences which befall certain shrewder men subordinated lifelong to the will of superiors, all this had developed in the Dansker the pithy guarded cynicism that was his leading characteristic.

[10]

The next day an incident served to confirm Billy Budd in his incredulity as to the Dansker's strange summing up of the case submitted. The ship at noon, going large before the wind, was rolling on her course, and he below at dinner and engaged in some sportful talk with the members of his mess, chanced in a sudden lurch to spill the entire contents of his soup-pan upon the new scrubbed deck. Claggart, the Master-at-arms, official rattan in hand, happened to be passing along the battery in a bay of which the mess was lodged, and the greasy liquid streamed just across his path. Stepping over it, he was proceeding on his way without comment, since the matter was nothing to take notice of under the circumstances, when he happened to observe who it was that had done the spilling. His countenance changed. Pausing, he was about to ejaculate something hasty at the sailor, but checked himself, and pointing down to the streaming soup, playfully tapped him from behind with his rattan, saying in a low musical voice peculiar to him at times "Handsomely done, my lad! And hand-some is as handsome did it too!" And with that passed on. Not noted by Billy, as not coming within his view, was the involuntary smile, or rather grimace, that ac-companied Claggart's equivocal words. Aridly it drew down the thin corners of his shapely mouth. But everybody taking his remark as meant for humorous, and at which therefore as coming from a superior they were bound to laugh, "with counterfeited glee" acted accordingly; and Billy tickled, it may be, by the allusion to his being the handsome sailor, merrily joined in; then addressing his messmates exclaimed "There now, who says that Jemmy Legs is down on me!" "And who said he was, Beauty?" demanded one Donald with some surprise. Whereat the foretopman looked a little foolish, recalling that it was only one person, Board-her-in-the-smoke, who had sug-gested what to him was the smoky idea that this master-at-arms was in any peculiar way hostile to him. Meantime that functionary, resuming his path, must have mo-mentarily worn some expression less guarded than that of the bitter smile, and usurping the face from the heart, some distorting expression perhaps; for a drummer-boy heed-lessly frolicking along from the opposite direction, and chancing to come into light collision with his person, was strangely disconcerted by his aspect. Nor was the im-pression lessened when the official, impulsively giving him a sharp cut with the rattan, vehemently exclaimed, "Look where you go!"

[11]

What was the matter with the master-at-arms? And, be the matter what it might, how could it have direct relation to Billy Budd with whom, prior to the affair of the spilled soup, he had never come into any special contact official or otherwise? What indeed could the trouble have to do with one so little inclined to give offence as the merchant-ship's *peacemaker,* even him who in Claggart's own phrase was "the sweet and pleasant young fellow?" Yes, why should *Jemmy Legs,* to borrow the Dansker's expression, be *down* on the Handsome Sailor? But, at heart and not for nothing, as the late chance encounter may indicate to the discerning, down on him, secretly down on him, he assuredly was.

Now to invent something touching the more private career of Claggart, something involving Billy Budd, of which something the latter should be wholly ignorant, some romantic incident implying that Claggart's knowledge of the young blue-jacket began at some period anterior to catching sight of him on board the seventy-four—all this, not so difficult to do, might avail in a way more or less interesting to account for whatever of enigma may appear to lurk in the case. But in fact there was nothing of the sort. And yet the cause, necessarily to be assumed as the sole one assignable, is in its very realism as much charged with that prime element of Radcliffian romance, *the mysterious,* as any that the ingenuity of the author of the *Mysteries of Udolpho* could advise. For what can more partake of the mysterious than an antipathy spontaneous and profound, such as is evoked in certain exceptional mortals by the mere aspect of some other mortal, however harmless he may be, if not called forth by this very harmlessness itself?

Now there can exist no irritating juxtaposition of dissimilar personalities comparable to that which is possible aboard a great war-ship fully manned and at sea There, every day among all ranks almost every man comes into more or less of contact with almost every other man. Wholly there to avoid even the sight of an aggravating object one must needs give it Jonah's toss or jump overboard himself. Imagine how all this might eventually operate on some peculiar human creature the direct reverse of a saint?

But for the adequate comprehending of Claggart by a normal nature, these hints are insufficient. To pass from a normal nature to him one must cross "the deadly space between." And this is best done by indirection.

Long ago an honest scholar my senior, said to me in reference to one who like himself is now no more, a man so unimpeachably respectable that against him nothing was ever openly said tho' among the few something was whispered, "Yes, X—— is a nut not to be cracked by the tap of a lady's fan. You are aware that I am the adherent of no organized religion much less of any philosophy built into a system. Well, for all that, I think that to try and get into X——, enter his labyrinth and get out again, without a clue derived from some source other than what is known as *knowledge of the world*—that were hardly possible, at least for me."

"Why," said I, "X——, however singular a study to some, is yet human, and knowledge of the world assuredly implies the knowledge of human nature, and in most of its varieties."

"Yes, but a superficial knowledge of it, serving ordinary purposes. But for anything deeper, I am not certain whether to know the world and to know human nature be not two distinct branches of knowledge, which while they may coexist in the same heart, yet either may exist with little or nothing of the other. Nay, in an average man of the world, his constant rubbing with it blunts that fine spiritual insight indispensable to the understanding of the essential in certain exceptional characters, whether evil ones or good. In a matter of some importance I have seen a girl wind an old lawyer about her little finger. Nor was it the dotage of senile love. Nothing of the sort. But he knew law better than he knew the girl's heart. Coke and Blackstone hardly shed so much light into obscure spiritual places as the Hebrew prophets. And who were they? Mostly recluses."

At the time my inexperience was such that I did not quite see the drift of all this. It may be that I see it now. And, indeed, if that lexicon which is based on Holy Writ were any longer popular, one might with less difficulty define and denominate certain phenomenal men. As it is, one must turn to some authority not liable to the charge of being tinctured with the Biblical element.

In a list of definitions included in the authentic translation of Plato, a list attributed to him, occurs this: "Natural Depravity: a depravity according to nature." A definition which tho' savoring of Calvinism, by no means involves Calvin's dogmas as to total mankind. Evidently its intent makes it applicable but to individuals. Not many are the examples of this depravity which the gallows and jail supply. At any rate for notable instances, since these have no vulgar alloy of the brute in them, but invariably are dominated by intellectuality, one must go elsewhere. Civilization, especially if of the austerer sort, is auspicious to it. It folds itself in the mantle of respectability. It has its certain negative virtues serving as silent auxiliaries. It never allows wine to get within its guard. It is not going too far to say that it is without vices or small sins. There is a phenomenal pride in it that excludes them from anything mercenary or avaricious. In short the depravity here meant partakes nothing of the sordid or sensual. It is serious, but free from acerbity. Though no flatterer of mankind it never speaks ill of it.

But the thing which in eminent instances signalizes so exceptional a nature is this: though the man's even temper and discreet bearing would seem to intimate a mind peculiarly subject to the law of reason, not the less in his heart he would seem to riot in complete exemption from that law, having apparently little to do with reason further than to employ it as an ambidexter implement for effecting the irrational. That is to say: Toward the accomplishment of an aim which in wantonness of malignity would seem to partake of the insane, he will direct a cool judgment sagacious and sound.

These men are true madmen, and of the most dangerous sort, for their lunacy is not continuous but occasional, evoked by some special object; it is probably secretive, which is as much to say it is self-contained, so that when moreover, most active, it is to the average mind not distinguishable from sanity, and for the reason above suggested that whatever its aims may be, and the aim is never declared—the method and the outward proceeding are always perfectly rational.

Now something such an one was Claggart, in whom was the mania of an evil nature, not engendered by vicious training or corrupting books or licentious living, but born with him and innate, in short "a depravity according to nature."

[12]

Lawyers, Experts, Clergy
An Episode

By the way, can it be the phenomenon, disowned or at least concealed, that in some criminal cases puzzles the courts? For this cause have our juries at times not only to endure the prolonged contentions of lawyers with their fees, but also the yet more perplexing strife of the medical experts with theirs?—But why leave it to them? why not subpoena as well the clerical proficients? Their vocation bringing them into peculiar contact with so many human beings, and sometimes in their least guarded hour, in interviews very much more confidential than those of physician and patient; this would seem to qualify them to know something about those intricacies involved in the question of moral responsibility; whether in a given case, say, the crime proceeded from mania in the brain or rabies of the heart. As to any differences among themselves these clerical proficients might develop on the stand, these could hardly be greater than the direct contradictions exchanged between the remunerated medical experts.

Dark sayings are these, some will say. But why? Is it because they somewhat savor of Holy Writ in its phrase "mysteries of iniquity"? If they do, such savor was far from being intended, for little will it commend these pages to many a reader of to-day.

The point of the present story turning on the hidden nature of the master-at-arms has necessitated this chapter. With an added hint or two in connection with the incident at the mess, the resumed narrative must be left to vindicate, as it may, its own credibility.

[13]

Pale ire, envy and despair

That Claggart's figure was not amiss, and his face, save the chin, well moulded, has already been said. Of these favorable points he seemed not insensible, for he was not only neat but careful in his dress. But the form of Billy Budd was heroic; and if his face was without the intellectual look of the pallid Claggart's, not the less was it lit, like his, from within, though from a different source. The bonfire in his heart made luminous the rose-tan in his cheek.

In view of the marked contrast between the persons of the twain, it is more than probable that when the master-at-arms in the scene last given applied to the sailor the proverb *Handsome is as handsome does;* he there let escape an ironic inkling, not caught by the young sailors who heard it, as to what it was that had first moved him against Billy, namely, his significant personal beauty.

Now envy and antipathy, passions irreconcilable in reason, nevertheless in fact may spring conjoined like Chang and Eng in one birth. Is Envy then such a monster? Well, though many an arraigned mortal has in hopes of mitigated penalty pleaded guilty to horrible actions, did ever anybody seriously confess to envy? Something there is in it universally felt to be more shameful than even felonious crime. And not only does everybody disown it, but the better sort are inclined to incredulity when it is in earnest imputed to an intelligent man. But since its lodgement is in the heart not the brain, no degree of intellect supplies a guarantee against it. But Claggart's was no vulgar form of the passion. Nor, as directed toward Billy Budd did it partake of that streak of apprehensive jealousy that marred Saul's visage perturbedly brooding on the comely young David. Claggart's envy struck deeper. If askance he eyed the good looks, cheery health and frank enjoyment of young life in Billy Budd, it was because these went along with a nature that, as Claggart magnetically felt, had in its simplicity never willed malice or experienced the reactionary bite of that serpent. To him, the spirit lodged within Billy, and looking out from his welkin eyes as from windows, that ineffability it was which made the dimple in his dyed cheek, suppled his joints, and dancing in his yellow curls made him preeminently the Handsome Sailor. One person excepted, the master-at-arms was perhaps the only man in the ship intellectually capable of adequately appreciating the moral phenomenon presented in Billy Budd. And the insight but intensified his passion, which assuming various secret forms within him, at times assumed that of cynic disdain—disdain of innocence. To be nothing more than innocent! Yet in an æsthetic way he saw the charm of it, the courageous free-and-easy temper of it, and fain would have shared it, but he despaired of it.

With no power to annul the elemental evil in him, tho' readily enough he could hide it; apprehending the good, but powerless to be it; a nature like Claggart's surcharged with energy as such natures almost invariably are, what recourse is left to it but to recoil upon itself and like the scorpion for which the Creator alone is responsible, act out to the end the part allotted it.

Passion, and passion in its profoundest, is not a thing demanding a palatial stage whereon to play its part. Down among the groundlings, among the beggars and rakers of the garbage, profound passion is enacted. And the circumstances that provoke it, however trivial or mean, are no measure of its power. In the present instance the stage is a scrubbed gun-deck, and one of the external provocations a man-of-war's-man's spilled soup.

Now when the Master-at-arms noticed whence came that greasy fluid streaming before his feet, he must have taken it—to some extent wilfully, perhaps—not for the mere accident it assuredly was, but for the sly escape of a spontaneous feeling on Billy's part more or less answering to the antipathy on his own. In effect a foolish demonstration he must have thought, and very harmless, like the futile kick of a heifer, which yet were the heifer a shod stallion, would not be so harmless. Even so was it that into the gall of Claggart's envy he infused the vitriol of his contempt. But the incident confirmed to him certain tell-tale reports purveyed to his ear by *Squeak,* one of his more cunning Corporals, a grizzled little man, so nicknamed by the sailors on account of his squeaky voice, and sharp visage ferreting about the dark corners of the lower decks after interlopers, satirically suggesting to them the idea of a rat in a cellar.

From his Chief's employing him as an implicit tool in laying little traps for the worriment of the Foretopman—for it was from the Master-at-arms that the petty persecutions heretofore adverted to had proceeded—the corporal having naturally enough concluded that his master could have no love for the sailor, made it his busines, faithful understrapper that he was, to foment the ill blood by perverting to his Chief certain innocent frolics of the good natured Foretopman, besides inventing for his mouth sundry contumelious epithets he claimed to have overheard him let fall. The Master-at-arms never suspected the veracity of these reports, more especially as to the epithets, for he well knew how secretly unpopular may become a master-at-arms, at least a master-at-arms of those days zealous in his function, and how the blue-jackets shoot at him in private their raillery and wit; the nickname by which he goes among them (*Jemmy Legs*) implying under the form of merriment their cherished disrespect and dislike.

But in view of the greediness of hate for patrolmen, it hardly needed a purveyor to feed Claggart's passion. An uncommon prudence is habitual with the subtler depravity, for it has everything to hide. And in case of an injury but suspected, its secretiveness voluntarily cuts it off from enlightenment or disillusion; and, not unreluctantly, action is taken upon surmise as upon certainty. And the retaliation is apt to be in monstrous disproportion to the supposed offence; for when in anybody was revenge in its exactions aught else but an inordinate usurer? But how with Claggart's conscience? For though consciences are unlike as foreheads, every intelligence, not excluding the Scriptural devils who "believe and tremble," has one. But Claggart's conscience being but the lawyer to his will, made ogres of trifles, probably arguing that the motive imputed to Billy in spilling the soup just when he did, together with the epithets alleged, these, if nothing more, made a strong case against him; nay, justified animosity into a sort of retributive righteousness. The Pharisee is the Guy Fawkes prowling in the hid chambers underlying the Claggarts. And they can really form no conception of an unreciprocated malice. Probably, the master-at-arms' clandestine persecution of Billy was started to try the temper of the man; but it had not developed any quality in him that enmity could make official use of or even pervert into plausible self-justification; so that the occurrence at the mess, petty if it were, was a welcome one to that peculiar conscience assigned to be the private mentor of Claggart. And, for the rest, not improbably it put him upon new experiments.

[15]

Not many days after the last incident narrated, something befell Billy Budd that more gravelled him than aught that had previously occurred.

It was a warm night for the latitude; and the Foretopman, whose watch at the time was properly below, was dozing on the uppermost deck whither he had ascended from his hot hammock, one of hundreds suspended so closely wedged together over a lower gun-deck that there was little or no swing to them. He lay as in the shadow of a hill-side, stretched under the lee of the booms, a piled ridge of spare spars amidships between foremast and mainmast and among which the ship's largest boat, the launch, was stowed. Alongside of three other slumberers from below, he lay near that end of the booms which approaches the foremast; his station aloft on duty as a foretopman being just over the deck-station of the forecastlemen, entitling him according to usage to make himself more or less at home in that neighborhood.

Presently he was stirred into semi-consciousnes by somebody, who must have previously sounded the sleep of the others, touching his shoulder, and then as the Foretopman raised his head, breathing into his ear in a quick whisper, "Slip into the lee forechains, Billy; there is something in the wind. Don't speak. Quick, I will meet you there;" and disappeared.

Now Billy like sundry other essentially good-natured ones had some of the weaknesses inseparable from essential good nature; and among these was a reluctance, almost an incapacity of plumply saying *no* to an abrupt proposition not obviously absurd, on the face of it, nor obviously unfriendly, nor iniquitous. And being of warm blood he had not the phlegm tacitly to negative any proposition by unresponsive inaction. Like his sense of fear, his apprehension as to aught outside of the honest and natural was seldom very quick. Besides, upon the present occasion, the drowse from his sleep still hung upon him.

However it was, he mechanically rose, and sleepily wondering what could be in the wind, betook himself to the designated place, a narrow platform, one of six, outside of the high bulwarks and screened by the great dead-eyes and multiple columned lanyards of the shrouds and backstays; and, in a great war-ship of that time, of dimensions commensurate with the hull's magnitude; a tarry balcony in short overhanging the sea, and so secluded that one mariner of the *Indomitable,* a non-conformist old tar of a serious turn, made it even in daytime his private oratory.

In this retired nook the stranger soon joined Billy Budd. There was no moon as yet; a haze obscured the star-light. He could not distinctly see the stranger's face. Yet from something in the outline and carriage, Billy took him to be, and correctly, for one of the afterguard.

"Hist! Billy," said the man in the same quick cautionary whisper as before; "You were impressed, weren't you? Well, so was I;" and he paused, as to mark the effect. But Billy not knowing exactly what to make of this said nothing. Then the other: "We are not the only impressed ones, Billy. There's a gang of us.—Couldn't you—help—at a pinch?"

"What do you mean?" demanded Billy, here thoroughly shaking off his drowse.

"Hist, hist!" the hurried whisper now growing husky, "see here;" and the man held up two small objects faintly twinkling in the nightlight; "see, they are yours, Billy, if you'll only—"

But Billy broke in, and in his resentful eagerness to deliver himself his vocal infirmity somewhat intruded: "D-D-Damme, I don't know what you are d-d-driving at, or what you mean, but you had better g-g-go where you belong!" For the moment the fellow, as confounded, did not stir; and Billy springing to his feet, said, "If you d-don't start I'll t-t-toss you back over the r-rail!" There was no mistaking this and the mysterious emissary decamped disappearing in the direction of the mainmast in the shadow of the booms.

"Hallo, what's the matter?" here came growling from a forecastleman awakened from his deck-doze by Billy's raised voice. And as the foretopman reappeared and was recognized by him; "Ah, *Beauty,* is it you? Well, something must have been the matter for you st-st-stuttered."

"O," rejoined Billy, now mastering the impediment; "I found an afterguardsman in our part of the ship here and I bid him be off where he belongs."

"And is that all you did about it, foretopman?" gruffly demanded another, an irascible old fellow of brick-colored visage and hair, and who was known to his associate forecastlemen as *Red Pepper;* "Such sneaks I should like to marry to the gunner's daughter!" by that expression meaning that he would like to subject them to disciplinary castigation over a gun.

However, Billy's rendering of the matter satisfactorily accounted to these inquirers for the brief commotion, since of all the sections of a ship's company, the forecastlemen, veterans for the most part and bigoted in their sea-prejudices, are the most jealous in resenting territorial encroachments, especially on the part of any of the afterguard, of whom they have but a sorry opinion, chiefly landsmen, never going aloft except to reef or furl the mainsail, and in no wise competent to handle a marlinspike or turn in a *dead-eye,* say.

[16]

This incident sorely puzzled Billy Budd. It was an entirely new experience; the first time in his life that he had ever been personally approached in underhand intriguing fashion. Prior to this encounter he had known nothing of the afterguardsman, the two men being stationed wide apart, one forward and aloft during his watch, the other on deck and aft.

What could it mean? And could they really be guineas, those two glittering objects the interloper had held up to his eyes? [1] Where could the fellow get guineas? Why even spare buttons are not so plentiful at sea.[2] The more he turned the matter over, the more he was non-plussed, and made uneasy and discomforted. In his disgustful recoil from an overture which tho' he but ill comprehended he instinctively knew must involve evil of some sort, Billy Budd was like a young horse fresh from the pasture suddenly inhaling a vile whiff from some chemical factory, and by repeated snortings tries to get it out of his nostrils and lungs. This frame of mind

---

[1] The manuscript reads ". . . had held up to his (Billy's) eyes?" The intended cancellation of "(Billy's)" seems indicated. Indeed, in context the antecedent of "his" is perfectly clear without the awkward insertion of the parenthetical word.

[2] The manuscript reads, "Why even buttons spare buttons are not so plentiful at sea," with the indication Melville intended to cancel the first "buttons" rather than to intensify it rhetorically. [Notes by Milton R. Stern]

barred all desire of holding further parley with the fellow, even were it but for the purpose of gaining some enlightenment as to his design in approaching him. And yet he was not without natural curiosity to see how such a visitor in the dark would look in broad day.

He espied him the following afternoon, in his first dogwatch, below: one of the smokers on that forward part of the upper gun deck allotted to the pipe. He recognized him by his general cut and build, more than by his round freckled face and glassy eyes of pale blue, veiled with lashes all but white. And yet Billy was a bit uncertain whether indeed it were he—yonder chap about his own age chatting and laughing in free-hearted way, leaning against a gun; a genial young fellow enough to look at, and something of a rattle-brain, to all appearance. Rather chubby too for a sailor, even an afterguardsman. In short the last man in the world, one would think, to be overburthened with thoughts, especially those perilous thoughts that must needs belong to a conspirator in any serious project, or even to the underling of such a conspirator.

Altho' Billy was not aware of it, the fellow, with a sidelong watchful gaze had perceived Billy first, and then noting that Billy was looking at him, thereupon nodded a familiar sort of friendly recognition as to an old acquaintance, without interrupting the talk he was engaged in with the group of smokers. A day or two afterwards, chancing in the evening promenade on a gun deck, to pass Billy, he offered a flying word of good-fellowship as it were, which by its unexpectedness, and equivocalness under the circumstances so embarrassed Billy that he knew not how to respond to it, and let it go unnoticed.

Billy was now left more at a loss than before. The ineffectual speculation into which he was led was so disturbingly alien to him that he did his best to smother it. It never entered his mind that here was a matter which from its extreme questionableness, it was his duty as a loyal blue-jacket to report in the proper quarter. And, probably, had such a step been suggested to him, he would have been deterred from taking it by the thought, one of novice-magnanimity, that it would savor overmuch of the dirty work of a tell-tale. He kept the thing to himself. Yet upon one occasion, he could not forbear a little disburthening himself to the old Dansker, tempted thereto perhaps by the influence of a balmy night when the ship lay becalmed; the twain, silent for the most part, sitting together on deck, their heads propped against the bulwarks. But it was only a partial and anonymous account that Billy gave, the unfounded scruples above referred to preventing full disclosure to anybody. Upon hearing Billy's version, the sage Dansker seemed to divine more than he was told; and after a little meditation during which his wrinkles were pursed as into a point, quite effacing for the time that quizzing expression his face sometimes wore,—"Didn't I say so, Baby Budd?"

"Say what?" demanded Billy.

"Why, *Jemmy Legs* is *down* on you."

"And what," rejoined Billy in amazement, "has *Jemmy Legs* to do with that cracked afterguardsman?"

"Ho, it was an afterguardsman then. A cat's-paw, a cat's-paw!" And with that exclamation, which, whether it had reference to a light puff of air just then coming over the calm sea, or subtler relation to the afterguardsman, there is no telling, the old Merlin gave a twisting wrench with his black teeth at his plug of tobacco, vouchsafing no reply to Billy's impetuous question, tho' now repeated, for it was his wont to relapse into grim silence when interrogated in skeptical sort as to any of his sententious oracles, not always very clear ones, rather partaking of that obscurity which invests most Delphic deliverances from any quarter.

Long experience had very likely brought this old man to that bitter prudence which never interferes in aught and never gives advice.

[17]

Yes, despite the Dansker's pithy insistence as to the master-at-arms being at the bottom of these strange experiences of Billy on board the *Indomitable,* the young sailor was ready to ascribe them to almost anybody but the man who, to use Billy's own expression, "always had a pleasant word for him." This is to be wondered at. Yet not so much to be wondered at. In certain matters, some sailors even in mature life remain unsophisticated enough. But a young seafarer of the disposition of our athletic Foretopman, is much of a child-man. And yet a child's utter innocence is but its blank ignorance, and the innocence more or less wanes as intelligence waxes. But in Billy Budd intelligence, such as it was, had advanced, while yet his simple mindedness remained for the most part unaffected. Experience is a teacher indeed; yet did Billy's years make his experience small. Besides, he had none of that intuitive knowledge of the bad which in natures not good or incompletely so foreruns experience, and therefore may pertain, as in some instances it too clearly does pertain, even to youth.

And what could Billy know of man except of man as a mere sailor? And the old-fashioned sailor, the veritable man-before-the-mast, the sailor from boyhood up, he, tho' indeed of the same species as a landsman, is in some respects singularly distinct from him. The sailor is frankness, the landsman is finesse. Life is not a game with the sailor, demanding the long head; no intricate game of chess where few moves are made in straightforwardness, and ends are attained by indirection; an oblique, tedious, barren game hardly worth that poor candle burnt out in playing it.

Yes, as a class, sailors are in character a juvenile race. Even their deviations are marked by juvenility. And this more especially holding true with the sailors of Billy's time. Then, too, certain things which apply to all sailors, do more pointedly operate here and there, upon the junior one. Every sailor, too, is accustomed to obey orders without debating them; his life afloat is externally ruled for him; he is not brought into that promiscuous commerce with mankind where unobstructed free agency on equal terms—equal superficially, at least—soon teaches one that unless upon occasion he exercise a distrust keen in proportion to the fairness of the appearance, some foul turn may be served him. A ruled undemonstrative distrustfulness is so habitual, not with business-men so much, as with men who know their kind in less shallow relations than business, namely, certain men-of-the-world, that they come at last to employ it all but unconsciously; and some of them would very likely feel real surprise at being charged with it as one of their general characteristics.

[18]

But after the little matter at the mess Billy Budd no more found himself in strange trouble at times about his hammock or his clothesbag or what not. While, as to that smile that occasionally sunned him, and the pleasant passing word, these were if not more frequent, yet if anything more pronounced than before.

But for all that, there were certain other demonstrations now. When Claggart's unobserved glance happened to light on belted Billy rolling along the upper gun-deck in the leisure of the second dog-watch, exchanging passing broadsides of fun with other young promenaders in the crowd; that glance would follow the cheerful sea-Hyperion with a settled meditative and melancholy expression, his eyes strangely suffused with incipient feverish tears. Then would Claggart look like the man of sorrows. Yes, and sometimes the melancholy expression would have in it a touch of soft yearning, as if Claggart could even have loved Billy but for fate and ban. But this was an evanescence, and quickly repented of, as it were, by an immitigable look, pinching and shrivelling the visage into the momentary semblance of a wrinkled walnut. But sometimes catching sight in advance of the foretopman coming in his direction, he would, upon their nearing, step aside a little to let him pass, dwelling upon Billy for the moment with the glittering dental satire of a Guise. But upon any abrupt unforeseen encounter a red light would forth from his eye like a spark from an anvil in a dusk smithy. That quick fierce light was a strange one, darted from orbs which in repose were of a color nearest approaching a deeper violet, the softest of shades.

Tho' some of these caprices of the pit could not but be observed by their object, yet were they beyond the construing of such a nature. And the *thews* of Billy were hardly compatible with that sort of sensitive spiritual organisation which in some cases instinctively conveys to ignorant innocence an admonition of the proximity of the malign. He thought the Master-at-arms acted in a manner rather queer at times. That was all. But the occasional frank air and pleasant word went for what they purported to be, the young sailor never having heard as yet of the "too fair-spoken man."

Had the foretopman been conscious of having done or said anything to provoke the ill will of the official, it would have been different with him, and his sight might have been purged if not sharpened. As it was, innocence was his blinder.

So was it with him in yet another matter. Two minor officers—the Armorer and Captain of the Hold, with whom he had never exchanged a word, his position in the ship not bringing him into contact with them; these men now for the first began to cast upon Billy when they chanced to encounter him, that peculiar glance which evidences that the man from whom it comes has been some way tampered with and to the prejudice of him upon whom the glance lights. Never did it occur to Billy as a thing to be noted or a thing suspicious, tho' he well knew the fact, that the Armorer and Captain of the Hold, with the ship's-yeoman, apothecary, and others of that grade, were by naval usage, mess-mates of the master-at-arms, men with ears convenient to his confidential tongue.

But the general popularity that our *Handsome Sailor's* manly forwardness upon occasion, and irresistible good nature, indicating no mental superiority tending to excite an invidious feeling; this good will on the part of most of his shipmates made him the less to concern himself about such mute aspects toward him as those whereto allusion has just been made, aspects he could not fathom as to infer their whole import.

As to the afterguardsman, tho' Billy for reasons already given necessarily saw little of him, yet when the two did happen to meet, invariably came the fellow's off-hand cheerful recognition, sometimes accompanied by a passing pleasant word or two. Whatever that equivocal young person's original design may really have been, or the design of which he might have been the deputy, certain it was from his manner upon these occasions, that he had wholly dropped it.

It was as if his precocity of crookedness (and every vulgar villain is precocious) had for once deceived him, and the man he had sought to entrap as a simpleton had, through his very simplicity ignorantly baffled him.

But shrewd ones may opine that it was hardly possible for Billy to refrain from going up to the afterguardsman and bluntly demanding to know his purpose in the initial interview, so abruptly closed in the fore-chains. Shrewd ones may also think it but natural in Billy to set about sounding some of the other impressed men of the ship in order to discover what basis, if any, there was for the emissary's obscure suggestions as to plotting disaffection aboard. Yes, the shrewd may so think. But something more, or rather, something else than mere shrewdness is perhaps needful for the due understanding of such a character as Billy Budd's.

As to Claggart, the monomania in the man—if that indeed it were—as involuntarily disclosed by starts in the manifestations detailed, yet in general covered over by his self-contained and rational demeanor; this, like a subterranean fire was eating its way deeper and deeper in him. Something decisive must come of it.

[19]

After the mysterious interview in the fore-chains, the one so abruptly ended there by Billy, nothing especially germane to the story occurred until the events now about to be narrated.

Elsewhere it has been said that in the lack of frigates (of course better sailers than line-of-battle ships) in the English squadron up the Straits at that period, the *Indomitable* was occasionally employed not only as an available substitute for a scout, but at times on detached service of more important kind. This was not alone because of her sailing qualities, not common in a ship of her rate, but quite as much, probably, that the character of her commander, it was thought, specially adapted him for any duty where under unforeseen difficulties a prompt initiative might have to be taken in some matter demanding knowledge and ability in addition to those qualities implied in good seamanship. It was on an expedition of the latter sort, a somewhat distant one, and when the *Indomitable* was almost at her furthest remove from the fleet, that in the latter part of an afternoon-watch she unexpectedly came in sight of a ship of the enemy. It proved to be a frigate. The latter perceiving thro' the glass that the weight of men and metal would be heavily against her, invoking her light heels, crowded sail to get away. After a chase urged almost against hope and lasting until about the middle of the first dog-watch, she signally succeeded in effecting her escape.

Not long after the pursuit had been given up, and ere the excitement incident thereto had altogether waned away, the Master-at-Arms, ascending from his cavernous sphere, made his appearance cap in hand by the mainmast, respectfully waiting the notice of Captain Vere then solitary walking the weather-side of the quarter-deck, doubtless somewhat chafed at the failure of the pursuit. The spot where Claggart stood was the place allotted to men of lesser grades seeking some more particular interview either with the officer-of-the-deck or the Captain himself. But from the latter it was not often that a sailor or petty-officer of those days would seek a hearing; only some exceptional cause, would, according to established custom, have warranted that.

Presently, just as the Commander absorbed in his reflections was on the point of turning aft in his promenade, he became sensible of Claggart's presence, and saw the doffed cap held in deferential expectancy. Here be it said that Captain Vere's personal knowledge of this petty-officer had only begun at the time of the ship's last sailing from home. Claggart then for the first, in transfer from a ship detained for repairs, supplying on board the *Indomitable* the place of a previous master-at-arms disabled and ashore.

No sooner did the Commander observe who it was that now deferentially stood awaiting his notice, than a peculiar expression came over him. It was not unlike that which uncontrollably will flit across the countenance of one at unawares encountering a person who, though known to him indeed, has hardly been long enough known for thorough knowledge, but something in whose aspect nevertheless now for the first provokes a vaguely repellent distaste. But coming to a stand, and resuming much of his wonted official manner, save that a sort of impatience lurked in the intonation of the opening word, he said, "Well? what is it, Master-at-Arms?"

With the air of a subordinate grieved at the necessity of being a messenger of ill tidings, and while conscientiously determined to be frank, yet equally resolved upon shunning overstatement, Claggart at this invitation or rather summons to disburthen, spoke up. What he said, conveyed in the language of no uneducated man, was to the effect following, if not altogether in these words, namely, that during the chase and preparations for the possible encounter he had seen enough to convince him that at least one sailor aboard was a dangerous character in a ship mustering some who not only had taken a guilty part in the late serious troubles, but others also who, like the man in question, had entered His Majesty's service under another form than enlistment.

At this point Captain Vere with some impatience, interrupted him: "Be direct, man; say impressed men."

Claggart made a gesture of subservience, and proceeded.

Quite lately he (Claggart) had begun to suspect that on the gun-decks some sort of movement prompted by the sailor in question was covertly going on, but he had not thought himself warranted in reporting the suspicion so long as it remained indistinct. But from what he had that afternoon observed in the man referred to, the suspicion of something clandestine going on had advanced to a point less removed from certainty. He deeply felt, he added, the serious responsibility assumed in making a report involving such possible consequences to the individual mainly concerned, besides tending to augment those natural anxieties which every naval commander must feel in view of extraordinary outbreaks so recent as those which, he sorrowfully said it, it needed not to name.

Now at the first broaching of the matter Captain Vere, taken by surprise, could not wholly dissemble his disquietude. But as Claggart went on, the former's aspect changed into restiveness under something in the witness' manner in giving his testimony. However, he refrained from interrupting him. And Claggart, continuing, concluded with this:

"God forbid, your honor, that the *Indomitable's* should be the experience of the—"

"Never mind that!" here peremptorily broke in the superior, his face altering with anger, instinctively divining the ship that the other was about to name, one in which the Nore Mutiny had assumed a singularly tragical character that for a time jeopardized the life of its commander. Under the circumstances he was indignant at the purposed allusion. When the commissioned officers themselves were on all occasions very heedful how they referred to the recent events, for a petty-officer unnecessarily to allude to them in the presence of his Captain, this struck him as a most immodest presumption. Besides, to his quick sense of self-respect, it even looked under the circumstances something like an attempt to alarm him. Nor at first was he without some surprise that one who so far as he had hitherto come under his notice had shown considerable tact in his function should in this particular evince such lack of it.

But these thoughts and kindred dubious ones flitting across his mind were suddenly replaced by an intuitional surmise which, though as yet obscure in form, served practically to affect his reception of the ill tidings. Certain it is, that long versed in everything pertaining to the complicated gun-deck life, which like every other form of life, has its secret mines and dubious side, the side popularly disclaimed, Captain Vere did not permit himself to be unduly disturbed by the general tenor of his subordinate's report. Furthermore, if in view of recent events prompt action should be taken at the first palpable sign of recurring insubordination, for all that, not judicious would it be, he thought, to keep the idea of lingering disaffection alive by undue forwardness in crediting an informer, even if his own subordinate, and charged among other things with police surveillance of the crew. This feeling would not perhaps have so prevailed with him were it not that upon a prior occasion the patriotic zeal officially evinced by Claggart had somewhat irritated him as appearing rather supersensible and strained. Furthermore, something even in the official's self-possessed and somewhat ostentatious manner in making his specifications strangely reminded him of a bandsman, a perjurous witness in a capital case before a court-martial ashore of which when a lieutenant he, Captain Vere, had been a member.

Now the peremptory check given to Claggart in the matter of the arrested allusion was quickly followed up by this: "You say that there is at least one dangerous man aboard. Name him."

"William Budd. A foretopman, your honor—"

"William Budd," repeated Captain Vere with unfeigned astonishment; "and mean you the man that Lieutenant Ratcliffe took from the merchantman not very long ago—the young fellow who seems to be so popular with the men—Billy, the Handsome Sailor, as they call him?"

"The same, your honor; but for all his youth and good looks, a deep one. Not for nothing does he insinuate himself into the good will of his shipmates, since at the least all hands will at a pinch say a good word for him at all hazards. Did Lieutenant Ratcliffe happen to tell your honor of that adroit fling of Budd's, jumping up in the cutter's bow under the merchantman's stern when he was being taken off? It is even masqued by that sort of good humored air that at heart he resents his impressment. You have but noted his fair cheek. A man-trap may be under his ruddy-tipped daisies."

Now the *Handsome Sailor,* as a signal figure among the crew, had naturally enough attracted the Captain's attention from the first. Tho' in general not very demonstrative to his officers, he had congratulated Lieutenant Ratcliffe upon his good fortune in lighting on such a fine specimen of the genus homo, who in the nude might have posed for a statue of young Adam before the Fall.

As to Billy's adieu to the ship *Rights-of-Man,* which the boarding lieutenant had indeed reported to him but in a deferential way more as a good story than aught else, Captain Vere, tho' mistakenly understanding it as a satiric sally, had but thought so much the better of the impressed man for it; as a military sailor, admiring the spirit that could take an arbitrary enlistment so merrily and sensibly. The foretopman's conduct, too, so far as it had fallen under the Captain's notice, had confirmed the first happy augury, while the new recruit's qualities as a *sailor-man* seemed to be such that he had thought of recommending him to the executive officer for promotion to a place that would more frequently bring him under his own observation, namely, the captaincy of the mizzen-top, replacing there in the starboard watch a man not so young whom partly for that reason he deemed less fitted for the post. Be it parenthesized here that since the mizzen-top-men having not to handle such breadths of heavy canvas as the lower sails on the main-mast and the fore-mast, a young man if of the right stuff not only seems best adapted to duty there, but in fact is generally selected for the captaincy of that top, and the company under him are light hands and often but striplings. In sum, Captain Vere had from the beginning deemed Billy Budd to be what in the naval parlance of the time was called a *"King's bargain,"* that is to say, for His Britannic Majesty's navy a capital investment at small outlay or none at all.

After a brief pause during which the reminiscences above mentioned passed vividly through his mind and he weighed the import of Claggart's last suggestion conveyed in the phrase "man-trap under the daisies," and the more he weighed it the less reliance he felt in the informer's good faith. Suddenly he turned upon him and in a low voice: "Do you come to me, master-at-arms, with so foggy a tale? As to Budd, cite me an act or spoken word of his confirmatory of what you in general charge against him. Stay," drawing nearer to him, "heed what you speak. Just now, and in a case like this, there is a yard-arm-end for the false-witness."

"Ah, your honor!" sighed Claggart mildly shaking his shapely head as in sad deprecation of such unmerited severity of tone. Then, bridling—erecting himself as in virtuous self-assertion, he circumstantially alleged certain words and acts, which collectively, if credited, led to presumptions mortally inculpating Budd. And for some of these averments, he added, substantiating proof was not far.

With gray eyes impatient and distrustful essaying to fathom to the bottom Claggart's calm violet ones, Captain Vere again heard him out; then for the moment stood ruminating. The mood he evinced, Claggart—himself for the time liberated from the other's scrutiny—steadily regarded with a look difficult to render,—a look curious of the operation of his tactics, a look such as might have been that of the spokesman of the envious children of Jacob deceptively imposing upon the troubled patriarch the blood-dyed coat of young Joseph.

Though something exceptional in the moral quality of Captain Vere made him, in earnest encounter with a fellow-man, a veritable touch-stone of that man's essential nature, yet now as to Claggart and what was really going on in him, his feeling partook less of intuitional conviction than of strong suspicion clogged by strange dubieties. The perplexity he evinced proceeded less from aught touching the man informed against—as Claggart doubtless opined—than from considerations how best to act in regard to the informer. At first indeed he was naturally for summoning that substantiation of his allegations which Claggart said was at hand. But such a proceeding would result in the matter at once getting abroad, which in the present stage of it, he thought, might undesirably affect the ship's company. If Claggart was a false witness,—that closed the affair. And therefore before trying the accusation, he would first practically test the accuser; and he thought this could be done in a quiet undemonstrative way.

The measure he determined upon involved a shifting of the scene, a transfer to a place less exposed to observation than the broad quarter-deck. For although the few gunroom officers there at the time had, in due observance of naval etiquette, withdrawn to leeward the moment Captain Vere had begun his promenade on the deck's weather-side; and tho' during the colloquy with Claggart they of course ventured not to diminish the distance; and though throughout the interview Captain Vere's voice was far from high, and Claggart's silvery and low; and the wind in the cordage and the wash of the sea helped the more to put them beyond earshot; nevertheless, the interview's continuance already had attracted observation from some topmen aloft and other sailors in the waist or further forward.

Having determined upon his measures, Captain Vere forthwith took action. Abruptly turning to Claggart he asked, "Master-at-arms, is it now Budd's watch aloft?"

"No, your honor." Whereupon, "Mr. Wilkes!" summoning the nearest midshipman, "tell Albert to come to me." Albert was the Captain's hammock-boy, a sort of sea-valet in whose discretion and fidelity his master had much confidence. The lad appeared. "You know Budd the foretopman?"

"I do, Sir."

"Go find him. It is his watch off. Manage to tell him out of earshot that he is wanted aft. Contrive it that he speaks to nobody. Keep him in talk yourself. And not till you get well aft here, not till then let him know that the place where he is wanted is my cabin. You understand. Go.—Master-at-Arms, show yourself on the decks below, and when you think it time for Albert to be coming with his man, stand by quietly to follow the sailor in."

[20]

Now when the foretopman found himself closeted there, as it were, in the cabin with the Captain and Claggart, he was surprised enough. But it was a surprise unaccompanied by apprehension or distrust. To an immature nature essentially honest and humane, forewarning intimations of subtler danger from one's kind come tardily if at all. The only thing that took shape in the young sailor's mind was this: Yes, the Captain, I have always thought, looks kindly upon me. Wonder if he's going to make me his coxswain. I should like that. And maybe now he is going to ask the master-at-arms about me.

"Shut the door there, sentry," said the commander; "stand without, and let nobody come in.—Now, master-at-arms, tell this man to his face what you told of him to me;" and stood prepared to scrutinize the mutually confronting visages.

With the measured step and calm collected air of an asylum-physician approaching in the public hall some patient beginning to show indications of a coming paroxysm, Claggart deliberately advanced within short range of Billy, and mesmerically looking him in the eye, briefly recapitulated the accusation.

Not at first did Billy take it in. When he did, the rose-tan of his cheek looked struck as by white leprosy. He stood like one impaled and gagged. Meanwhile the accuser's eyes removing not as yet from the blue dilated ones, underwent a phenomenal change, their wonted rich violet color blurring into a muddy purple. Those lights of human intelligence losing human expression, gelidly protruding like the alien eyes of certain uncatalogued creatures of the deep. The first mesmeric glance was one of serpent fascination; the last was as the hungry lurch of the torpedo-fish.

"Speak, man!" said Captain Vere to the transfixed one struck by his aspect even more than by Claggart's, "Speak! defend yourself." Which appeal caused but a strange dumb gesturing and gurgling in Billy; amazement at such an accusation so suddenly sprung on inexperienced nonage; this, and, it may be horror of the accuser, serving to bring out his lurking defect and in this instance for the time intensifying it into a convulsed tongue-tie; while the intent head and entire form straining forward in an agony of ineffectual eagerness to obey the injunction to speak and defend himself, gave an expression to the face like that of a condemned Vestal priestess in the moment of being buried alive, and in the first struggle against suffocation.

Though at the time Captain Vere was quite ignorant of Billy's liability to vocal impediment, he now immediately divined it, since vividly Billy's aspect recalled to him that of a bright young schoolmate of his whom he had once seen struck by much the same startling impotence in the act of eagerly rising in the class to be foremost in response to a testing question put to it by the master. Going close up to the young sailor, and laying a soothing hand on his shoulder, he said, "There is no hurry, my boy. Take your time, take your time." Contrary to the effect intended, these words so fatherly in tone, doubtless touching Billy's heart to the quick, prompted yet more violent efforts at utterance—efforts soon ending for the time in confirming the paralysis, and bringing to his face an expression which was as a crucifixion to behold. The next instant, quick as the flame from a discharged cannon at night, his right arm shot out, and Claggart dropped to the deck. Whether intentionally or but owing to the young athlete's superior height, the blow had taken effect full upon the forehead, so shapely and intellectual-looking a feature in the master-at-arms; so that the body fell over lengthwise, like a heavy plank tilted from erectness. A gasp or two, and he lay motionless.

"Fated boy," breathed Captain Vere in tone so low as to be almost a whisper, "what have you done! But here, help me."

The twain raised the felled one from the loins up into a sitting position. The spare form flexibly acquiesced, but inertly. It was like handling a dead snake. They lowered it back. Regaining erectness Captain Vere with one hand covering his face stood to all appearance as impassive as the object at his feet. Was he absorbed in taking in all the bearings of the event and what was best not only now at once to be done, but also in the sequel? Slowly he uncovered his face; and the effect was as if the moon emerging from eclipse should reappear with quite another aspect than that which had gone into hiding. The father in him, manifested towards Billy thus far in the scene, was replaced by the military disciplinarian. In his official tone he bade the foretopman retire to a state-room aft (pointing it out), and there remain till thence summoned. This order Billy in silence mechanically obeyed. Then going to the cabin-door where it opened on the quarter-deck, Captain Vere said to the sentry without, "Tell somebody to send Albert here." When the lad appeared his master so contrived it that he should not catch sight of the prone one. "Albert," he said to him, "tell the Surgeon I wish to see him. You need not come back till called." When the Surgeon entered—a self-poised character of that grave sense and experience that hardly anything could take him aback,—Captain Vere advanced to meet him, thus unconsciously intercepting his view of Claggart, and interrupting the other's wonted ceremonious salutation, said, "Nay, tell me how it is with yonder man," directing his attention to the prostrate one.

The Surgeon looked, and for all his self-command, somewhat started at the abrupt revelation. On Claggart's always pallid complexion, thick black blood was now oozing from nostril and ear. To the gazer's professional eye it was unmistakably no living man that he saw.

"Is it so then?" said Captain Vere intently watching him. "I thought it. But verify it." Whereupon the customary tests confirmed the Surgeon's first glance, who now looking up in unfeigned concern, cast a look of intense inquisitiveness upon his superior. But Captain Vere, with one hand to his brow, was standing motionless. Suddenly, catching the Surgeon's arm convulsively, he exclaimed, pointing down to the body—"It is the divine judgment on Ananias! Look!"

Disturbed by the excited manner he had never before observed in the *Indomitable's* Captain, and as yet wholly ignorant of the affair, the prudent Surgeon nevertheless held his peace, only again looking in earnest interrogation as to what it was that had resulted in such a tragedy.

But Captain Vere was now again motionless standing absorbed in thought. But again starting, he vehemently exclaimed—"Struck dead by an angel of God! Yet the angel must hang!"

At these passionate interjections, mere incoherences to the listener as yet unapprised of the antecedents, the Surgeon was profoundly discomposed. But now as recollecting himself, Captain Vere in less harsh tone briefly related the circumstances leading up to the event.

"But come; we must despatch," he added. "Help me to remove him (meaning the body) to yonder compartment," designating one opposite that where the foretopman remained immured. Anew disturbed by a request that as implying a desire for secrecy, seemed unaccountably strange to him, there was nothing for the subordinate to do but comply.

"Go now," said Captain Vere with something of his wonted manner—"Go now. I shall presently call a drum-head court. Tell the lieutenants what has happened, and tell Mr. Mordant," meaning the captain of marines, "and charge them to keep the matter to themselves."

[21]

Full of disquietude and misgiving the Surgeon left the cabin. Was Captain Vere suddenly affected in his mind, or was it but a transient excitement, brought about by so strange and extraordinary a happening? As to the drum-head court, it struck the Surgeon as impolitic, if nothing more. The thing to do, he thought, was to place Billy Budd in confinement and in a way dictated by usage, and postpone further action in so extraordinary a case, to such time as they should rejoin the squadron, and then refer it to the Admiral. He recalled the unwonted agitation of Captain Vere and his excited exclamations so at variance with his normal manner. Was he unhinged? But assuming that he is, it is not so susceptible of proof. What then can he do? No more trying situation is conceivable than that of an officer subordinate under a Captain whom as suspects to be, not mad indeed, but yet not quite unaffected in his intellect. To argue his order to him would be insolence. To resist him would be mutiny.

In obedience to Captain Vere he communicated what had happened to the lieutenants & captain of marines; saying nothing as to the Captain's state. They fully shared his own surprise and concern. Like him too they seemed to think that such a matter should be referred to the Admiral.

[22]

Who in the rainbow can draw the line where the violet tint ends and the orange tint begins? Distinctly we see the difference of the colors, but where exactly does the one first blendingly enter into the other? So with sanity and insanity. In pronounced cases there is no question about them. But in some supposed cases, in various degrees supposedly less pronounced, to draw the exact line of demarkation few will undertake tho' for a fee some professional experts will. There is nothing namable but that some men will undertake to do it for pay.

Whether Captain Vere, as the Surgeon professionally and privately surmised, was really the sudden victim of any degree of aberration, one must determine for himself by such light as this narrative may afford.

That the unhappy event which has been narrated could not have happened at a worse juncture was but too true. For it was close on the heel of the suppressed insurrections, an aftertime very critical to naval authority, demanding from every English sea-commander two qualities not readily interfusable—prudence and rigor. Moreover there was something crucial in the case.

In the jugglery of circumstances preceding and attending the event on board the *Indomitable,* and in the light of that martial code whereby it was formally to be judged, innocence and guilt personified in Claggart and Budd in effect changed places. In a legal view the apparent victim of the tragedy was he who had sought to victimize a man blameless; and the indisputable deed of the latter, navally regarded, constituted the most heinous of military crimes. Yet more. The essential right and wrong involved in the matter, the clearer that might be, so much the worse for the responsibility of a loyal sea-commander inasmuch as he was not authorized to determine the matter on that primitive basis.

Small wonder then that the *Indomitable's* Captain, though in general a man of rapid decision, felt that circumspectness not less than promptitude was necessary. Until he could decide upon his course, and in each detail; and not only so, but until the concluding measure was upon the point of being enacted, he deemed it advisable, in view of all the circumstances to guard as much as possible against publicity. Here he may or may not have erred. Certain it is however that subsequently in the confidential talk of more than one or two gun-rooms and cabins he was not a little criticized by some officers, a fact imputed by his friends, and vehemently by his cousin Jack Denton, to professional jealousy of *Starry Vere*. Some imaginative ground for invidious comment there was. The maintenance of secrecy in the matter, the confining all knowledge of it for a time to the place where the homicide occurred, the quarter-deck cabin; in these particulars lurked some resemblance to the policy adopted in those tragedies of the palace which have occurred more than once in the capital founded by Peter the Barbarian.

The case indeed was such that fain would the *Indomitable's* captain have deferred taking any action whatever respecting it further than to keep the foretopman a close prisoner till the ship rejoined the squadron, and then submitting the matter to the judgment of his Admiral.

But a true military officer is in one particular like a true monk. Not with more of self-abnegation will the latter keep his vows of monastic obedience than the former his vows of allegiance to martial duty.

Feeling that unless quick action was taken on it, the deed of the foretopman, so soon as it should be known on the gun-decks, would tend to awaken any slumbering embers of the Nore among the crew, a sense of the urgency of the case overruled in Captain Vere every other consideration. But tho' a conscientious disciplinarian, he was no lover of authority for mere authority's sake. Very far was he from embracing opportunities for monopolizing to himself the perils of moral responsibility, none at least that could properly be referred to an official superior, or shared with him by his official equals or even subordinates. So thinking, he was glad it would not be at variance with usage to turn the matter over to a summary court of his own officers, reserving to himself as the one on whom the ultimate accountability would rest, the right of maintaining a supervision of it, or formally or informally interposing at need. Accordingly a drum-head court was summarily convened, he electing the individuals composing it, the First Lieutenant, the Captain of marines, and the Sailing Master.

In associating an officer of marines with the sea-lieutenants in a case having to do with a sailor, the Commander perhaps deviated from general custom. He was prompted thereto by the circumstance that he took that soldier to be a judicious person, thoughtful, and not altogether incapable of grappling with a difficult case unprecedented in his prior experience. Yet even as to him he was not without some latent misgiving, for withal he was an extremely good-natured man, an enjoyer of his dinner, a sound sleeper, and inclined to obesity, a man who tho' he would always maintain his manhood in battle might not prove altogether reliable in a moral dilemma involving aught of the tragic. As to the First Lieutenant and the Sailing Master, Captain Vere could not but be aware that though honest natures, of approved gallantry upon occasion, their intelligence was mostly confined to the matter of active seamanship and the fighting demands of their profession. The court was held in the same cabin where the unfortunate affair had taken place. This cabin, the Commander's, embraced the entire area under the poop-deck. Aft, and on either side, was a small state-room; the one room temporarily a jail & the other a dead-house, and a yet smaller compartment leaving a space between, expanding forward into a goodly oblong of length coinciding with the ship's beam. A skylight of moderate dimension was overhead and at each end of the oblong space were two sashed port-hole windows easily convertible back into embrasures for short carronades.

All being quickly in readiness, Billy Budd was arraigned, Captain Vere necessarily appearing as the sole witness in the case, and as such, temporarily sinking his rank, though singularly maintaining it in a matter apparently trivial, namely, that he testified from the ship's weather-side, with that object having caused the court to sit on the lee-side. Concisely he narrated all that had led up to the catastrophe, omitting nothing in Claggart's accusation and deposing as to the manner in which the prisoner had received it. At this testimony the three officers glanced with no little surprise at Billy Budd, the last man they would have suspected either of the mutinous design alleged by Claggart or the undeniable deed he himself had done.

The First Lieutenant, taking judicial primacy and turning toward the prisoner, said, "Captain Vere has spoken. Is it or is it not as Captain Vere says?" In response came syllables not so much impeded in the utterance as might have been anticipated. They were these: "Captain Vere tells the truth. It is just as Captain Vere says, but it is not as the Master-at-Arms said. I have eaten the King's bread and I am true to the King."

"I believe you, my man," said the witness, his voice indicating a suppressed emotion not otherwise betrayed.

"God will bless you for that, Your Honor!" not without stammering said Billy, and all but broke down. But immediately was recalled to self-control by another question, to which with the same emotional difficulty of utterance he said, "No, there was no malice between us. I never bore malice against the Master-at-arms. I am sorry that he is dead. I did not mean to kill him. Could I have used my tongue I would not have struck him. But he foully lied to my face and in presence of my Captain, and I had to say something, and I could only say it with a blow, God help me!"

In the impulsive above-board manner of the frank one, the court saw confirmed all that was implied in words that just previously had perplexed them, coming as they did from the testifier to the tragedy and promptly following Billy's impassioned disclaimer of mutinous intent—Captain Vere's words, "I believe you, my man."

Next it was asked of him whether he knew of or suspected aught savoring of incipient trouble (meaning mutiny, tho' the explicit term was avoided) going on in any section of the ship's company.

The reply lingered. This was naturally imputed by the court to the same vocal embarrassment which had retarded or obstructed previous answers. But in main it was otherwise here; the question immediately recalling to Billy's mind the interview with the afterguardsman in the fore-chains. But an innate repugnance to playing a part at all approaching that of an informer against one's own shipmates—the same erring sense of uninstructed honor which had stood in the way of his reporting the matter at the time though as a loyal man-of-war-man it was incumbent on him, and failure so to do if charged against him and proven, would have subjected him to the heaviest of penalties; this, with the blind feeling now his, that nothing really was being hatched, prevailed with him. When the answer came it was a negative.

"One question more," said the officer of marines now first speaking and with a troubled earnestness. "You tell us that what the Master-at-arms said against you was a lie. Now why should he have so lied, so maliciously lied, since you declare there was no malice between you?"

At that question unintentionally touching on a spiritual sphere wholly obscure to Billy's thoughts, he was nonplussed, evincing a confusion indeed that some observers, such as can readily be imagined, would have construed into involuntary evidence of hidden guilt. Nevertheless he strove some way to answer, but all at once relinquished the vain endeavor, at the same time turning an appealing glance towards Captain Vere as deeming him his best helper and friend. Captain Vere who had been seated for a time rose to his feet, addressing the interrogator. "The question you put to him comes naturally enough. But how can he rightly answer it? or anybody else? unless indeed it be he who lies within there," designating the compartment where lay the corpse. "But the prone one there will not rise to our summons. In effect, tho', as it seems to me, the point you make is hardly material. Quite aside from any conceivable motive actuating the Master-at-arms, and irrespective of the provocation to the blow, a martial court must needs in the present case confine its attention to the blow's consequence, which consequence justly is to be deemed not otherwise than as the striker's deed."

This utterance, the full significance of which it was not at all likely that Billy took in, nevertheless caused him to turn a wistful interrogative look toward the speaker, a look in its dumb expressiveness not unlike that which a dog of generous breed might turn upon his master seeking in his face some elucidation of a previous gesture ambiguous to the canine intelligence. Nor was the same utterance without marked effect upon the three officers, more especially the soldier. Couched in it seemed to them a meaning unanticipated, involving a prejudgement on the speaker's part. It served to augment a mental disturbance previously evident enough.

The soldier once more spoke; in a tone of suggestive dubiety addressing at once his associates and Captain Vere: "Nobody is present—none of the ship's company, I mean, who might shed lateral light, if any is to be had, upon what remains mysterious in this matter."

"That is thoughtfully put," said Captain Vere; "I see your drift. Ay, there is a mystery; but, to use a Scriptural phrase, it is 'a mystery of iniquity,' a matter for psychologic theologians to discuss. But what has a military court to do with it? Not to add that for us any possible investigation of it is cut off by the lasting tongue-tie of—him—in yonder," again designating the mortuary state-room. "The prisoner's deed,—with that alone we have to do."

To this, and particularly the closing reiteration, the marine soldier knowing not how aptly to reply, sadly abstained from saying aught. The First Lieutenant who at the outset had not unnaturally assumed primacy in the court, now overrulingly instructed by a glance from Captain Vere, a glance more effective than words, resumed that primacy. Turning to the prisoner, "Budd," he said, and scarce in equable tones, "Budd, if you have aught further to say for yourself, say it now."

Upon this the young sailor turned another quick glance towards Captain Vere; then, as taking a hint from that aspect, a hint confirming his own instinct that silence was now best, replied to the Lieutenant, "I have said all, Sir."

The marine—the same who had been the sentinel without the cabin-door at the time that the foretopman followed by the master-at-arms, entered it—he, standing by the sailor throughout these judicial proceedings, was now directed to take him back to the after compartment originally assigned to the prisoner and his custodian. As the twain disappeared from view, the three officers as partially liberated from some inward constraint associated with Billy's mere presence, simultaneously stirred in their seats. They exchanged looks of troubled indecision, yet feeling that decide they must and without long delay. As for Captain Vere, he for the time stood unconsciously with his back towards them, apparently in one of his absent fits, gazing out from a sashed port-hole to windward upon the monotonous blank of the twilight sea. But the court's silence continuing, broken only at moments by brief consultations in low earnest tones, this seemed to arm him and energize him. Turning, he to-and-fro paced the cabin athwart; in the returning ascent to windward, climbing the slant deck in the ship's lee roll; without knowing it symbolizing thus in his action a mind resolute to surmount difficulties even if against primitive instincts strong as the wind and the sea. Presently he came to a stand before the three. After scanning their faces he stood less as mustering his thoughts for expression, than as one inly deliberating how best to put them to well-meaning men not intellectually mature, men with whom it was necessary to demonstrate certain principles that were axioms to himself. Similar impatience as to talking is perhaps one reason that deters some minds from addressing any popular assemblies.

When speak he did, something both in the substance of what he said and his manner of saying it, showed the influence of unshared studies modifying and tempering the practical training of an active career. This, along with his phraseology now and then was suggestive of the grounds whereon rested that imputation of a certain pedantry socially alleged against him by certain naval men of wholly practical cast, captains who nevertheless would frankly concede that His Majesty's navy mustered no more efficient officer of their grade than *Starry Vere*.

What he said was to this effect: "Hitherto I have been but the witness, little more; and I should hardly think now to take another tone, that of your coadjutor, for the time, did I not perceive in you,—at the crisis too—a troubled hesitancy, proceeding, I doubt not from the clash of military duty with moral scruple—scruple vitalized by compassion. For the compassion, how can I otherwise than share it? But, mindful of paramount obligations I strive against scruples that may tend to enervate decision. Not, gentlemen, that I hide from myself that the case is an exceptional one. Speculatively regarded, it well might be referred to a jury of casuists. But for us here acting not as casuists or moralists, it is a case practical, and under martial law practically to be dealt with.

"But your scruples: do they move as in a dusk? Challenge them. Make them advance and declare themselves. Come now: do they import something like this: If, mindless of palliating circumstances, we are bound to regard the death of the Master-at-arms as the prisoner's deed, then does that deed constitute a capital crime whereof the penalty is a mortal one? But in natural justice is nothing but the prisoner's overt act to be considered? How can we adjudge to summary and shameful death a fellow-creature innocent before God, and whom we feel to be so?—Does that state it aright? You sign sad assent. Well, I too feel that, the full force of that. It is Nature. But do these buttons that we wear attest that our allegiance is to Nature? No, to the King. Though the ocean, which is inviolate Nature primeval, tho' this be the element where we move and have our being as sailors, yet as the King's officers lies our duty in a sphere correspondingly natural? So little is that true, that in receiving our commissions we in the most important regards ceased to be natural free-agents. When war is declared are we the commissioned fighters previously consulted? We fight at command. If our judgements approve the war, that is but coincidence. So in other particulars. So now. For suppose condemnation to follow these present proceedings. Would it be so much we ourselves that would condemn as it would be martial law operating through us? For that law and the rigour of it, we are not responsible. Our vowed responsibility is in this: That however pitilessly that law may operate, we nevertheless adhere to it and administer it.

"But the exceptional in the matter moves the hearts within you. Even so too is mine moved. But let not warm hearts betray heads that should be cool. Ashore in a criminal case will an upright judge allow himself off the bench to be waylaid by some tender kinswoman of the accused seeking to touch him with her tearful plea? Well the heart here denotes the feminine in man is as that piteous woman, and hard tho' it be, she must here be ruled out."

He paused, earnestly studying them for a moment; then resumed.

"But something in your aspect seems to urge that it is not solely the heart that moves in you, but also the conscience, the private conscience. But tell me whether or not, occupying the position we do, private conscience should not yield to that imperial one formulated in the code under which alone we officially proceed?"

Here the three men moved in their seats, less convinced than agitated by the course of an argument troubling but the more the spontaneous conflict within.

Perceiving which, the speaker paused for a moment; then abruptly changing his tone, went on.

"To steady us a bit, let us recur to the facts.—In wartime at sea a man-of-war's-man strikes his superior in grade, and the blow kills. Apart from its effect the blow itself is, according to the Articles of War, a capital crime. Furthermore—"

"Ay, Sir," emotionally broke in the officer of marines, "in one sense it was. But surely Budd purposed neither mutiny nor homicide."

"Surely not, my good man. And before a court less arbitrary and more merciful than a martial one, that plea would largely extenuate. At the Last Assizes it shall acquit. But how here? We proceed under the law of the Mutiny Act. In feature no child can resemble his father more than that Act resembles in spirit the thing from which it derives—War. In His Majesty's service—in this ship indeed—there are Englishmen forced to fight for the King against their will. Against their conscience, for aught we know. Tho' as their fellow-creatures some of us may appreciate their position, yet as navy officers, what reck we of it? Still less recks the enemy. Our impressed men he would fain cut down in the same swath with our volunteers. As regards the enemy's naval conscripts, some of whom may even share our own abhorrence of the regicidal French Directory, it is the same on our side. War looks but to the frontage, the appearance. And the Mutiny Act, War's child, takes after the father. Budd's intent or non-intent is nothing to the purpose.

"But while, put to it by those anxieties in you which I can not but respect, I only repeat myself—while thus strangely we prolong proceedings that should be summary —the enemy may be sighted and an engagement result. We must do; and one of two things must we do—condemn or let go."

"Can we not convict and yet mitigate the penalty?" asked the junior Lieutenant here speaking, and falteringly, for the first.

"Lieutenant, were that clearly lawful for us under the circumstances consider the consequences of such clemency. The people" (meaning the ship's company) "have native-sense; most of them are familiar with our naval usage and tradition; and how would they take it? Even could you explain to them—which our official position forbids—they, long moulded by arbitrary discipline have not that kind of intelligent responsivenes that might qualify them to comprehend and discriminate. No, to the people the foretopman's deed however it be worded in the announcement will be plain homicide committed in a flagrant act of mutiny. What penalty for that should follow, they know. But it does not follow. *Why?* they will ruminate. You know what sailors are. Will they not revert to the recent outbreak at the Nore? Ay. They know the well-founded alarm—the panic it struck throughout England. Your clement sentence they would account pusillanimous. They would think that we flinch, that we are afraid of them—afraid of practising a lawful rigor singularly demanded at this juncture lest it should provoke new troubles. What shame to us such a conjecture on their part, and how deadly to discipline. You see then, whither prompted by duty and the law I steadfastly drive. But I beseech you, my friends, do not take me amiss. I feel as you do for this unfortunate boy. But did he know our hearts, I take him to be of that generous nature that he would feel even for us on whom in this military necessity so heavy a compulsion is laid."

With that, crossing the deck he resumed his place by the sashed port-hole, tacitly leaving the three to come to a decision. On the cabin's opposite side the troubled court sat silent. Loyal lieges, plain and practical, though at bottom they dissented from some points Captain Vere had put to them, they were without the faculty, hardly had the inclination, to gainsay one whom they felt to be an earnest man, one too not less their superior in mind than in naval rank. But it is not improbable that even such of his words as were not without influence over them, less came home to them than his closing appeal to their instinct as sea-officers in the forethought he threw out as to the practical consequences to discipline, considering the unconfirmed tone of the fleet at the time, should a man-of-war's-man's violent killing at sea of a superior in grade be allowed to pass for aught else than a capital crime demanding prompt infliction of the penalty.

Not unlikely they were brought to something more or less akin to that harassed frame of mind which in the year 1842 actuated the commander of the U.S. brig-of-war *Somers* to resolve, under the so-called Articles of War, Articles modelled upon the English Mutiny Act, to resolve upon the execution at sea of a midshipman and two petty-officers as mutineers designing the seizure of the brig. Which resolution was carried out though in a time of peace and within not many days sail of home. An act vindicated by a naval court of inquiry subsequently convened ashore. History, and here cited without comment. True, the circumstances on board the *Somers* were different from those on board the *Indomitable*. But the urgency felt, well-warranted or otherwise, was much the same.

Says a writer whom few know, "Forty years after a battle it is easy for a noncombatant to reason about how it ought to have been fought. It is another thing personally and under fire to direct the fighting while involved in the obscuring smoke of it. Much so with respect to other emergencies involving considerations both practical and moral, and when it is imperative promptly to act. The greater the fog the more it imperils the steamer, and speed is put on tho' at the hazard of running somebody down. Little ween the snug card-players in the cabin of the responsibilities of the sleepless man on the bridge."

In brief, Billy Budd was formally convicted and sentenced to be hung at the yardarm in the early morning-watch, it being now night. Otherwise, as is customary in such cases, the sentence would forthwith have been carried out. In war-time on the field or in the fleet, a mortal punishment decreed by a drum-head court—on the field sometimes decreed by but a nod from the General—follows without delay on the heel of conviction without appeal.

[23]

It was Captain Vere himself who of his own motion communicated the finding of the court to the prisoner; for that purpose going to the compartment where he was in custody and bidding the marine there to withdraw for the time.

Beyond the communication of the sentence what took place at this interview was never known. But in view of the character of the twain briefly closeted in that stateroom, each radically sharing in the rarer qualities of our nature—so rare indeed as to be all but incredible to average minds however much cultivated—some conjectures may be ventured.

It would have been in consonance with the spirit of Captain Vere should he on this occasion have concealed nothing from the condemned one—should he indeed have frankly disclosed to him the part he himself had played in bringing about the decision, at the same time revealing his actuating motives. On Billy's side it is not improbable that such a confession would have been received in much the same spirit that prompted it. Not without a sort of joy indeed he might have appreciated the brave opinion of him implied in his Captain's making such a confidant of him. Nor, as to the sentence itself could he have been insensible that it was imparted to him as to one not afraid to die. Even more may have been. Captain Vere in the end may have developed the passion sometimes latent under an exterior stoical or indifferent. He was old enough to have been Billy's father. The austere devotee of military duty, letting himself melt back into what remains primeval in our formalized humanity, may in the end have caught Billy to his heart even as Abraham may have caught young Isaac on the brink of resolutely offering him up in obedience to the exacting behest. But there is no telling the sacrament, seldom if in any case revealed to the gadding world, wherever under circumstances at all akin to those here attempted to be set forth, two of great Nature's nobler order embrace. There is privacy at the time, inviolable to the survivor, and holy oblivion, the sequel to each diviner magnanimity, providentially covers all at last.

The first to encounter Captain Vere in act of leaving the compartment was the senior Lieutenant. The face he beheld, for the moment one expressive of the agony of the strong, was to that officer, tho' a man of fifty, a startling revelation. That the condemned one suffered less than he who mainly had effected the condemnation was apparently indicated by the former's exclamation in the scene soon perforce to be touched upon.

[24]

Of a series of incidents within a brief term rapidly following each other, the adequate narration may take up a term less brief, especially if explanation or comment here and there seem requisite to the better understanding of such incidents. Between the entrance into the cabin of him who never left it alive, and him who when he did leave it left it as one condemned to die; between this and the closeted interview just given less than an hour and a half had elapsed. It was an interval long enough however to awaken speculations among no few of the ship's company as to what it was that could be detaining in the cabin the master-at-arms and the sailor; for a rumor that both of them had been seen to enter it and neither of them had been seen to emerge, this rumor had got abroad upon the gun-decks and in the tops; the people of a great warship being in one respect like villagers taking microscopic note of every outward movement or non-movement going on. When therefore in weather not at all tempestuous all hands were called in the second dog-watch, a summons under such circumstances not usual in those hours, the crew were not wholly unprepared for some announcement extraordinary, one having connection too with the continued absence of the two men from their wonted haunts.

There was a moderate sea at the time; and the moon, newly risen and near to being at its full, silvered the white spar-deck wherever not blotted by the clear-cut shadows horizontally thrown of fixtures and moving men. On either side of the quarter-deck, the marine guard under arms was drawn up; and Captain Vere standing in his place surrounded by all the ward-room officers, addressed his men. In so doing his manner showed neither more nor less than that properly pertaining to his supreme position aboard his own ship. In clear terms and concise he told them what had taken place in the cabin; that the master-at-arms was dead; that he who had killed him had been already tried by a summary court and condemned to death; and that the execution would take place in the early morning watch. The word *mutiny* was not named in what he said. He refrained too from making the occasion an opportunity for any preachment as to the maintenance of discipline, thinking perhaps that under existing circumstances in the navy the consequence of violating discipline should be made to speak for itself.

The captain's announcement was listened to by the throng of standing sailors in a dumbness like that of a seated congregation of believers in hell listening to the clergyman's announcement of his Calvinistic text.

At the close, however, a confused murmur went up. It began to wax. All but instantly, then, at a sign, it was pierced and suppressed by shrill whistles of the Boatswain and his Mates piping down one watch.

To be prepared for burial Claggart's body was delivered to certain petty-officers of his mess. And here, not to clog the sequel with lateral matters, it may be added that at a suitable hour, the Master-at-arms was committed to the sea with every funeral honor properly belonging to his naval grade.

In this proceeding as in every public one growing out of the tragedy, strict adherence to usage was observed. Nor in any point could it have been at all deviated from, either with respect to Claggart or Billy Budd, without begetting undesirable speculations in the ship's company, sailors, and more particularly men-of-war's-men, being of all men the greatest sticklers for usage.

For similar cause, all communication between Captain Vere and the condemned one ended with the closeted interview already given, the latter being now surrendered to the ordinary routine preliminary to the end. This transfer under guard from the Captain's quarters was effected without unusual precautions—at least no visible ones.

If possible, not to let the men so much as surmise that their officers anticipate aught amiss from them is the tacit rule in a military ship. And the more that some sort of trouble should really be apprehended the more do the officers keep that apprehension to themselves; tho' not the less unostentatious vigilance may be augmented.

In the present instance the sentry placed over the prisoner had strict orders to let no one have communication with him but the Chaplain. And certain unobtrusive measures were taken absolutely to insure this point.

[25]

In a seventy-four of the old order the deck known as the upper gun-deck was the one covered over by the spar-deck which last though not without its armament was for the most part exposed to the weather. In general it was at all hours free from hammocks; those of the crew swinging on the lower gun-deck, and berth-deck, the latter being not only a dormitory but also the place for the stowing of the sailors' bags, and on both sides lined with the large chests or movable pantries of the many messes of the men.

On the starboard side of the *Indomitable*'s upper gun-deck, behold Billy Budd under sentry, lying prone in irons, in one of the bays formed by the regular spacing of the guns comprising the batteries on either side. All these pieces were of the heavier calibre of that period. Mounted on lumbering wooden carriages they were hampered with cumbersome harness of breeching and strong side-tackles for running them out. Guns and carriages, together with the long rammers and shorter lintstocks lodged in loops overhead—all these, as customary, were painted black; and the heavy hempen breechings, tarred to the same tint, wore the like livery of the undertakers. In contrast with the funereal hue of these surroundings the prone sailor's exterior apparel, white *jumper* and white duck trousers, each more or less soiled, dimly glimmered in the obscure light of the bay like a patch of discolored snow in early April lingering at some upland cave's black mouth. In effect he is already in his shroud or the garments that shall serve him in lieu of one. Over him, but scarce illuminating him, two battle-lanterns swing from two massive beams of the deck above. Fed with the oil supplied by the war-contractors (whose gains, honest or otherwise, are in every land an anticipated portion of the harvest of death), with flickering splashes of dirty yellow light they pollute the pale moonshine all but ineffectually struggling in obstructed flecks thro' the open ports from which the tompioned cannon protrude. Other lanterns at intervals serve but to bring out somewhat the obscurer bays which, like small confessionals or side-chapels in a cathedral, branch from the long dim-vistaed broad aisle between the two batteries of that covered tier.

Such was the deck where now lay the Handsome Sailor. Through the rose-tan of his complexion, no pallor could have shown. It would have taken days of sequestra·

tion from the winds and the sun to have brought about the effacement of that. But the skeleton in the cheekbone at the point of its angle was just beginning delicately to be defined under the warm-tinted skin. In fervid hearts self-contained, some brief experiences devour our human tissue as secret fire in a ship's hold consumes cotton in the bale.

But now lying between the two guns, as nipped in the vice of fate, Billy's agony, mainly proceeding from a generous young heart's virgin experience of the diabolical incarnate and effective in some men—the tension of that agony was over now. It survived not the something healing in the closeted interview with Captain Vere. Without movement, he lay as in a trance. That adolescent expression previously noted as his, taking on something akin to the look of a slumbering child in the cradle when the warm hearth-glow of the still chamber at night plays on the dimples that at whiles mysteriously form in the cheek, silently coming and going there. For now and then in the gyved one's trance a serene happy light born of some wandering reminiscence or dream would diffuse itself over his face, and then wane away only anew to return.

The Chaplain coming to see him and finding him thus, and perceiving no sign that he was conscious of his presence, attentively regarded him for a space, then slipping aside, withdrew for the time, peradventure feeling that even he the minister of Christ, tho' receiving his stipend from Mars, had no consolation to proffer which could result in a peace transcending that which he beheld. But in the small hours he came again. And the prisoner, now awake to his surroundings, noticed his approach, and civilly, all but cheerfully, welcomed him. But it was to little purpose that in the interview following the good man sought to bring Billy Budd to some godly understanding that he must die, and at dawn. True, Billy himself freely referred to his death as a thing close at hand; but it was something in the way that children will refer to death in general, who yet among their other sports will play a funeral with hearse and mourners.

Not that like children Billy was incapable of conceiving what death really is. No, but he was wholly without irrational fear of it, a fear more prevalent in highly civilized communities than those so-called barbarous ones which in all respects stand nearer to unadulterate Nature. And, as elsewhere said, a barbarian Billy radically was; as much so, for all the costume, as his countrymen the British captives, living trophies, made to march in the Roman triumph of Germanicus. Quite as much so as those later barbarians, young men probably, and picked specimens among the earlier British converts to Christianity, at least nominally such and taken to Rome (as today converts from lesser isles of the sea may be taken to London) of whom the Pope of that time, admiring the strangeness of their personal beauty so unlike the Italian stamp, their clear ruddy complexion and curled flaxen locks, exclaimed, "Angles" (meaning *English* the modern derivative) "Angles do you call them? And is it because they look so like angels?" Had it been later in time one would think that the Pope had in mind Fra Angelico's seraphs some of whom, plucking apples in gardens of the Hesperides have the faint rose-bud complexion of the more beautiful English girls.

If in vain the good Chaplain sought to impress the young barbarian with ideas of death akin to those conveyed in the skull, dial, and cross-bones on old tombstones; equally futile to all appearance were his efforts to bring home to him the thought of salvation and a Saviour. Billy listened, but less out of awe or reverence perhaps than from a certain natural politeness; doubtless at bottom regarding all that in much the same way that most mariners of his class take any discourse abstract or out of the common tone of the work-a-day world. And this sailor-way of taking clerical discourse is not wholly unlike the way in which the pioneer of Christianity full of transcendent miracles was received long ago on tropic isles by any superior *savage* so called—a Tahitian say of Captain Cook's time or shortly after that time. Out of natural courtesy he received, but did not appropriate. It was like a gift placed in the palm of an out-reached hand upon which the fingers do not close.

But the *Indomitable's* Chaplain was a discreet man possessing the good sense of a good heart. So he insisted not in his vocation here. At the instance of Captain Vere, a lieutenant had apprised him of pretty much everything as to Billy; and since he felt that innocence was even a better thing than religion wherewith to go to Judgement, he reluctantly withdrew; but in his emotion not without first performing an act strange enough in an Englishman, and under the circumstances yet more so in any regular priest. Stooping over, he kissed on the fair cheek his fellow-man, a felon in martial law, one who though on the confines of death he felt he could never convert to a dogma; nor for all that did he fear for his future.

Marvel not that having been made acquainted with the young sailor's essential innocence (an irruption of heretic thought hard to suppress) the worthy man lifted not a finger to avert the doom of such a martyr to martial discipline. So to do would not only have been as idle as invoking the desert, but would also have been an auda-cious transgression of the bounds of his function, one as exactly prescribed to him by military law as that of the boatswain or any other naval officer. Bluntly put, a chaplain is the minister of the Prince of Peace serving in the host of the God of War—Mars. As such, he is as incongruous as a musket would be on the altar at Christmas.[1] Why then is he there? Because he indirectly subserves the purpose attested by the cannon; because too he lends the sanction of the religion of the meek to that which practically is the abrogation of everything but brute Force.

[26]

The night, so luminous on the spar-deck, but otherwise on the cavernous ones be-low, levels so like the tiered galleries in a coal-mine—the luminous night passed away. But, like the prophet in the chariot disappearing in heaven and dropping his mantle to Elisha, the withdrawing night transferred its pale robe to the breaking day. A meek shy light appeared in the East, where stretched a diaphanous fleece of white furrowed vapor. That light slowly waxed. Suddenly *eight bells* was struck aft, responded to by one louder metallic stroke from forward. It was four o'clock in the morning. In-stantly the silver whistles were heard summoning all hands to witness punishment. Up through the great hatchways rimmed with racks of heavy shot, the watch below came pouring, overspreading with the watch already on deck the space between the mainmast and foremast including that occupied by the capacious *launch* and the black booms tiered on either side of it, boat and booms making a summit of observation for the powder-boys and younger tars. A different group comprising one watch of topmen leaned over the rail of that sea-balcony, no small one in a seventy-four, looking down on the crowd below. Man or boy, none spake but in whisper, and few spake at all. Captain Vere—as before, the central figure among the assembled commissioned officers —stood nigh the break of the poop-deck facing forward. Just below him on the quarter-deck the marines in full equipment were drawn up much as at the scene of the promulgated sentence.

At sea in the old time, the execution by halter of a military sailor was generally

[1] See Notes and Questions, p. 370.

from the fore-yard. In the present instance, for special reasons the main-yard was
assigned. Under an (weather or lee) arm of that yard the prisoner was presently
brought up, the Chaplain attending him.[1] It was noted at the time and remarked upon
afterwards, that in this final scene the good man evinced little or nothing of the per-
functory. Brief speech indeed he had with the condemned one, but the genuine Gospel
was less on his tongue than in his aspect and manner towards him. The final preparations personal to the latter being speedily brought to an end by two boatswain's-
mates, the consummation impended. Billy stood facing aft. At the penultimate moment, his words, his only ones, words wholly unobstructed in the utterance were these
—"God bless Captain Vere!" Syllables so unanticipated coming from one with the
ignominious hemp about his neck—a conventional felon's benediction directed aft
towards the quarters of honor; syllables too delivered in the clear melody of a sing-
ing-bird on the point of launching from the twig, had a phenomenal effect, not un-
enhanced by the rare personal beauty of the young sailor spiritualized now thro' late
experiences so poignantly profound.

Without volition as it were, as if indeed the ship's populace were but the vehicles
of some vocal current electric, with one voice from alow and aloft came a resonant
sympathetic echo—"God bless Captain Vere!" And yet at that instant Billy alone must
have been in their hearts, even as he was in their eyes.

At the pronounced words and the spontaneous echo that voluminously rebounded
them, Captain Vere, either thro' stoic self-control or a sort of momentary paralysis induced by emotional shock, stood erectly rigid as a musket in the ship-armorer's rack.

The hull deliberately recovering from the periodic roll to leeward was just regaining
an even keel, when the last signal, a preconcerted dumb one, was given. At the same
moment it chanced that the vapory fleece hanging low in the East, was shot thro' with
a soft glory as of the fleece of the Lamb of God seen in mystical vision, and simultaneously therewith, watched by the wedged mass of upturned faces, Billy ascended;
and, ascending, took the full rose of the dawn.

In the pinioned figure, arrived at the yard-end, to the wonder of all no motion was
apparent, none save that created by the ship's motion, in moderate weather so majestic
in a great ship ponderously cannoned.

[27]

A digression

When some days afterward in reference to the singularity just mentioned, the
Purser, a rather ruddy rotund person more accurate as an accountant than profound
as a philosopher, said at mess to the Surgeon, "What testimony to the force lodged
in will-power," the latter—saturnine spare and tall, one in whom a discreet causticity
went along with a manner less genial than polite, replied, "Your pardon, Mr. Purser.
In a hanging scientifically conducted—and under special orders I myself directed how
Budd's was to be effected—any movement following the completed suspension and
originating in the body suspended, such movement indicates mechanical spasm in the
muscular system. Hence the absence of that is no more attributable to will-power as
you call it than to horse-power—begging your pardon."

[1] Manuscript has the insertion "weather or lee" above "arm." The choice can not be
made for Melville, for there is no way to know whether he wished to utilize the ideas of
windward and leeward into the kind of significance he gave them in the court-martial
scene, when Captain Vere paced the cabin. [Note by Milton R. Stern]

"But this muscular spasm you speak of, is not that in a degree more or less invariable in these cases?"

"Assuredly so, Mr. Purser."

"How then, my good sir, do you account for its absence in this instance?"

"Mr. Purser, it is clear that your sense of the singularity in this matter equals not mine. You account for it by what you call will-power, a term not yet included in the lexicon of science. For me I do not, with my present knowledge pretend to account for it at all. Even should we assume the hypothesis that at the first touch of the halyards the action of Budd's heart, intensified by extraordinary emotion at its climax, abruptly stopt—much like a watch when in carelessly winding it up you strain at the finish, thus snapping the chain—even under that hypothesis, how account for the phenomenon that followed?"

"You admit then that the absence of spasmodic movement was phenomenal."

"It was phenomenal, Mr. Purser, in the sense that it was an appearance the cause of which is not immediately to be assigned."

"But tell me, my dear Sir," pertinaciously continued the other, "was the man's death effected by the halter, or was it a species of euthanasia?"

"*Euthanasia,* Mr. Purser, is something like your *will-power:* I doubt its authenticity as a scientific term—begging your pardon again. It is at once imaginative and metaphysical,—in short, Greek. But," abruptly changing his tone, "there is a case in the sick-bay that I do not care to leave to my assistants. Beg your pardon, but excuse me." And rising from the mess he formally withdrew.

[28]

The silence at the moment of execution and for a moment or two continuing thereafter, a silence but emphasized by the regular wash of the sea against the hull or the flutter of a sail caused by the helmsman's eyes being tempted astray, this emphasized silence was gradually disturbed by a sound not easily to be verbally rendered. Whoever has heard the freshet-wave of a torrent suddenly swelled by pouring showers in tropical mountains, showers not shared by the plain; whoever has heard the first muffled murmur of its sloping advance through precipitous woods, may form some conception of the sound now heard. The seeming remoteness of its source was because of its murmurous indistinctness since it came from close-by, even from the men massed on the ship's open deck. Being inarticulate, it was dubious in significance further than it seemed to indicate some capricious revulsion of thought or feeling such as mobs ashore are liable to, in the present instance possibly implying a sullen revocation on the men's part of their involuntary echoing of Billy's benediction. But ere the murmur had time to wax into clamor it was met by a strategic command, the more telling that it came with abrupt unexpectedness.

"Pipe down the starboard watch Boatswain, and see that they go."

Shrill as the shriek of the sea-hawk the whistles of the Boatswain and his Mates pierced that ominous low sound, dissipating it; and yielding to the mechanism of discipline, the throng was thinned by one half. For the remainder most of them were set to temporary employments connected with trimming the yards and so forth, business readily to be got up to serve occasion by any officer-of-the-deck.

Now each proceeding that follows a mortal sentence pronounced at sea by a drumhead court is characterised by promptitude not perceptibly merging into hurry, tho' bordering that. The hammock, the one which had been Billy's bed when alive, having already been ballasted with shot and otherwise prepared to serve for his canvas coffin, the last offices of the sea-undertakers, the Sail-Maker's Mates, were now speedily completed. When everything was in readiness a second call for all hands made necessary by the strategic movement before mentioned was sounded and now to witness burial.

The details of this closing formality it needs not to give. But when the tilted plank let slide its freight into the sea, a second strange human murmur was heard, blended now with another inarticulate sound proceeding from certain larger sea-fowl, whose attention having been attracted by the peculiar commotion in the water resulting from the heavy sloped dive of the shotted hamomck into the sea, flew screaming to the spot. So near the hull did they come, that the stridor or bony creak of their gaunt double-jointed pinions was audible. As the ship under light airs passed on, leaving the burial-spot astern, they still kept circling it low down with the moving shadow of their outstretched wings and the croaked requiem of their cries.

Upon sailors as superstitious as those of the age preceding ours, men-of-war's-men too who had just beheld the prodigy of repose in the form suspended in air and now foundering in the deeps; to such mariners the action of the sea-fowl, tho' dictated by mere animal greed for prey, was big with no prosaic significance. An uncertain movement began among them, in which some encroachment was made. It was tolerated but for a moment. For suddenly the drum beat to quarters, which familiar sound happening at least twice every day, had upon the present occasion a signal peremptoriness in it. True martial discipline long continued superinduces in average man a sort of impulse of docility whose operation at the official sound of command much resembles in its promptitude the effect of an instinct.

The drum-beat dissolved the multitude, distributing most of them along the batteries of the two covered gun-decks. There, as wont, the guns' crews stood by their respective cannon erect and silent. In due course the First Officer, sword under arm and standing in his place on the quarter-deck, formally received the successive reports of the sworded Lieutenants commanding the sections of batteries below; the last of which reports being made, the summed report he delivered with the customary salute to the Commander. All this occupied time, which in the present case, was the object of beating to quarters at an hour prior to the customary one. That such variance from usage was authorized by an officer like Captain Vere, a martinet as some deemed him, was evidence of the necessity for unusual action implied in what he deemed to be temporarily the mood of his men. "With mankind," he would say, "forms, measured forms are everything; and that is the import couched in the story of Orpheus with his lyre spell-binding the wild denizens of the wood." And this he once applied to the disruption of forms going on across the Channel and the consequences thereof.

At this unwonted muster at quarters, all proceeded as at the regular hour. The band on the quarter-deck played a sacred air. After which the Chaplain went thro' the customary morning service. That done, the drum beat the retreat, and toned by music and religious rites subserving the discipline & purpose of war, the men in their wonted orderly manner, dispersed to the places allotted them when not at the guns.

And now it was full day. The fleece of low-hanging vapor had vanished, licked up by the sun that late had so glorified it. And the circumambient air in the clearness of its serenity was like smooth white marble in the polished block not yet removed from the marble-dealer's yard.

[29]

The symmetry of form attainable in pure fiction can not so readily be achieved in a narration essentially having less to do with fable than with fact. Truth uncompromisingly told will always have its ragged edges; hence the conclusion of such a narration is apt to be less finished than an architectural finial.

How it fared with the Handsome Sailor during the year of the Great Mutiny has been faithfully given. But tho' properly the story ends with his life, something in way of sequel will not be amiss. Three brief chapters will suffice.

In the general re-christening under the Directory of the craft originally forming the navy of the French monarchy, the *St. Louis* line-of-battle ship was named the *Athéiste.* Such a name, like some other substituted ones in the Revolutionary fleet, while proclaiming the infidel audacity of the ruling power was yet, tho' not so intended to be, the aptest name, if one consider it, ever given to a warship; far more so indeed than the *Devastation,* the *Erebus* (the *Hell*) and similar names bestowed upon fighting-ships.

On the return-passage to the English fleet from the detached cruise during which occurred the events already recorded, the *Indomitable* fell in with the *Athéiste.* An engagement ensued; during which Captain Vere, in the act of putting his ship alongside the enemy with a view of throwing his boarders across her bulwarks, was hit by a musket-ball from a port-hole of the enemy's main cabin. More than disabled he dropped to the deck and was carried below to the same cock-pit where some of his men already lay. The senior Lieutenant took command. Under him the enemy was finally captured and though much crippled was by rare good fortune successfully taken into Gibraltar, an English port not very distant from the scene of the fight. There, Captain Vere with the rest of the wounded was put ashore. He lingered for some days, but the end came. Unhappily he was cut off too early for the Nile and Trafalgar. The spirit that spite its philosophic austerity may yet have indulged in the most secret of all passions, ambition, never attained to the fulness of fame.

Not long before death, while lying under the influence of that magical drug which soothing the physical frame mysteriously operates on the subtler element in man, he was heard to murmur words inexplicable to his attendant—"Billy Budd, Billy Budd." That these were not the accents of remorse, would seem clear from what the attendant said to the *Indomitable's* senior officer of marines who, as the most reluctant to condemn of the members of the drum-head court, too well knew, tho' here he kept the knowledge to himself, who Billy Budd was.

[30]

Some few weeks after the execution, among other matters under the head of *News from the Mediterranean,* there appeared in a naval chronicle of the time, an authorized weekly publication, an account of the affair. It was doubtless for the most part written in good faith, tho' the medium, partly rumor, through which the facts must have reached the writer, served to deflect and in part falsify them. The account was as follows:—

"On the tenth of the last month a deplorable occurrence took place on board H.M.S.

Indomitable. John Claggart, the ship's master-at-arms, discovering that some sort of plot was incipient among an inferior section of the ship's company, and that the ringleader was one William Budd; he, Claggart, in the act of arraigning the man before the Captain was vindictively stabbed to the heart by the suddenly drawn sheath-knife of Budd.

"The deed and the implement employed, sufficiently suggest that tho' mustered into the service under an English name, the assassin was no Englishman, but one of those aliens adopting English cognomens whom the present extraordinary necessities of the Service have caused to be admitted into it in considerable numbers.

"The enormity of the crime and the extreme depravity of the criminal, appear the greater in view of the character of the victim, a middle-aged man respectable and discreet, belonging to that minor official grade, the petty-officers, upon whom, as none know better than the commissioned gentlemen, the efficiency of His Majesty's navy so largely depends. His function was a responsible one; at once onerous & thankless and his fidelity in it the greater because of his strong patriotic impulse. In this instance as in so many other instances in these days, the character of this unfortunate man signally refutes, if refutation were needed, that peevish saying attributed to the late Dr. Johnson, that patriotism is the last refuge of a scoundrel.

"The criminal paid the penalty of his crime. The promptitude of the punishment has proved salutary. Nothing amiss is now apprehended aboard H.M.S. *Indomitable.*"

The above, appearing in a publication now long ago superannuated and forgotten, is all that hitherto has stood in human record to attest what manner of men respectively were John Claggart and Billy Budd.

[31]

Everything is for a term remarkable in navies. Any tangible object associated with some striking incident of the service is converted into a monument. The spar from which the Foretopman was suspended, was for some few years kept trace of by the blue-jackets. Their knowledge followed it from ship to dock-yard and again from dockyard to ship, still pursuing it even when at last reduced to a mere dock-yard boom. To them a chip of it was as a piece of the Cross. Ignorant tho' they were of the secret facts of the tragedy, and not thinking but that the penalty was somehow unavoidably inflicted from the naval point of view, for all that they instinctively felt that Billy was a sort of man as incapable of mutiny as of wilful murder. They recalled the fresh young image of the Handsome Sailor, that face never deformed by a sneer or subtler vile freak of the heart within. Their impression of him was doubtless deepened by the fact that he was gone, and in a measure mysteriously gone. At the time, on the gun-decks of the *Indomitable,* the general estimate of his nature and its unconscious simplicity eventually found rude utterance from another foretopman, one of his own watch, gifted, as some sailors are, with an artless poetic temperament; the tarry hands made some lines which after circulating among the shipboard crew for a while, finally got rudely printed at Portsmouth as a ballad. The title given to it was the sailor's.

BILLY IN THE DARBIES

Good of the Chaplain to enter Lone Bay
And down on his marrow-bones here and pray
For the likes just o' me, Billy Budd.—But look:

Through the port comes the moon-shine astray!
It tips the guard's cutlas and silvers this nook;
But 'twill die in the dawning of Billy's last day.
A jewel-block they'll make of me tomorrow,
Pendant pearl from the yard-arm end
Like the ear-drop I gave to Bristol Molly—
O, 'tis me, not the sentence they'll suspend.
Ay, Ay, all is up; and I must up too
Early in the morning, aloft from alow.
On an empty stomach, now, never it would do.
They'll give me a nibble—bit o' biscuit ere I go.
Sure, a messmate will reach me the last parting cup;
But, turning heads away from the hoist and the belay,
Heaven knows who will have the running of me up!
No pipe to those halyards.—But aren't it all sham?
A blur's in my eyes; it is dreaming that I am.
A hatchet to my hawser? all adrift to go?
The drum roll to grog, and Billy never know?
But Donald he has promised to stand by the plank:
So I'll shake a friendly hand ere I sink.
But—no! It is dead then I'll be, come to think.—
I remember Taff the Welshman when he sank.
And his cheek it was like the budding pink.
But me they'll lash me in hammock, drop me deep.
Fathoms down, fathoms down, how I'll dream fast asleep.
I feel it stealing now. Sentry, are you there?
Just ease this darbies at the wrist, and roll me over fair,
I am sleepy, and the oozy weeds about me twist.

END OF BOOK

April 19th 1891

BILLY BUDD: TESTAMENT OF RESISTANCE

PHIL WITHIM (1922–   )

When E. L. G. Watson wrote his famous article, "Melville's Testament of Acceptance," he made no attempt to prove his view. All he attempted, all he achieved, was to suggest a way of looking at the story. "Melville," said Watson, "is no longer a rebel." He has come to accept the presence of evil, and he has ceased to blame God for its existence. Other critics began to write on *Billy Budd* in the same vein. Their positions varied somewhat, but the tenor, the direction of the viewpoint was always the same: Melville had mellowed, he was resigned, as Freeman says, to the recognition of necessity.[1] In F. O. Matthiessen's words, "He has come to respect necessity. . . . Melville could now face incongruity; he could accept the existence of both good and evil. . . ." Or as Willard Thorp remarks, "In the end Melville called the truce."

There was, however, some dissent; both Alfred Kazin and Richard Chase indicated dissatisfaction with the "testament of acceptance" theory. In 1950 Joseph Schiffman, in an article which reviewed all these interpretations as well as those of Mumford, Weir, and Sedgwick, put forth a suggestion, which he credited to Gay Wilson Allen, "that *Billy Budd* might best be understood as a work of irony." Since this article appeared, a number of other critics have also objected to the "testament of acceptance" theory or have supported an ironic interpretation; sometimes they have done both.

This paper is another step in this same direction. It accepts the point of view that *Billy Budd* was written in a basically ironic style: it will attempt to establish a thesis in harmony with all of the parts of the story and to demonstrate that the "testament of acceptance" theory is essentially self-contradictory.

The body of the story is concerned with the relationships of three men: Billy Budd, John Claggart, and Captain Vere. Whatever arguments may rage concerning other elements of the story, there is general agreement as to the character and significance of Billy Budd and John Claggart. Billy Budd is the Handsome Sailor uniting "strength and beauty," whose moral nature is not "out of keeping with the physical make" (see page 255). Claggart is Billy's reverse. He is pale and unhealthy looking; his visage seems to hint of something defective or abnormal in the constitution and blood. This contrasts with the conjunction in Billy of beauty and goodness. Claggart had an "evil nature, not engendered by vicious training or corrupting books or licentious living, but born with him and innate, in short 'a depravity according to nature'" (see page 272).

Melville is explicit about his desire to have Billy and Claggart taken as types of good and bad, and this, I think, is the chief argument against those who, like Matthiessen and Freeman, consider homosexualism an aspect of the problem. For if Melville

---

[1] F. Barron Freeman, ed., *Melville's Billy Budd* (Cambridge, 1948), p. 115.
The small variations occasionally found in the punctuation and wording of quoted passages may be accounted for by the fact that Professor Withim used the Freeman edition rather than the Stern one. His page numbers have been changed to refer to those in this present volume. [Editors' note]

had desired to hint at homosexualism, he would not have denied its possibility; when speaking of Claggart's peculiar nature, he says, "In short the depravity here meant partakes nothing of the sordid or sensual" (see page 272). And speaking of Billy, he says he was "preëminently the Handsome Sailor" (see page 273) who, as Melville has told us in the opening pages on the book, typifies strength united to beauty. In those descriptions of Billy emphasizing his delicate color and the fine detail of his features, the point is to impress us with his purity, his aristocratic heritage, not his femininity. Melville takes care to remind the reader that Billy had thrashed the bully, Red Whiskers (see page 256).

But it is around the third figure, Captain Vere, that the greatest disagreement has arisen. This suggests that a detailed examination of his character and function is essential to any understanding of the novel. He is described as apparently the best type of British naval man:

> always acquitting himself as an officer mindful of the welfare of his men, but never tolerating an infraction of discipline; thoroughly versed in the science of his profession, and intrepid to the verge of temerity, though never injudiciously so. (see page 263)

He loves to read, particularly those books "treating of actual men and events no matter of what era—history, biography and unconventional writers, who, free from cant and convention, like Montaigne, honestly, and in the spirit of common sense philosophize upon realities" (see pages 264–65). In the reading he found

> confirmation of his own more reserved thoughts—confirmation which he had vainly sought in social converse, so that as touching most fundamental topics, there had got to be established in him some positive convictions which he forefelt would abide in him essentially unmodified so long as his intelligent part remained unimpaired. (see page 265)

This particular sentence creates a question as to Melville's meaning. Does he suggest here that the only result of Vere's reading is that his mind becomes more and more firmly fixed on his earliest opinions, that no author can ever modify them, either because he will not let their ideas penetrate or because he never reads books that do not agree with him; or does Melville imply that Vere's opinions are instinctively right and that all the books in Vere's library, "compact, but of the best" (see page 264) agree with him unfailingly? But it is as yet too early to decide. Melville continues to describe Vere as one whose "settled convictions were as a dyke against those invading waters of novel opinion social political and otherwise" (see page 265) and as one who opposed these novel opinions because they seemed to him not only "incapable of embodiment in lasting institutions, but at war with the peace of the world and the true welfare of mankind" (see page 265). This last phrase sounds suspiciously like cant, like sarcasm. Vere's reasons here are such terribly stock arguments that it is hard to accept them at face value.

The possibility arises that the reader is expected to understand that Vere's reasoning is presented without comment because it is simply and transparently a rationalization of an uninformed and bigoted man who reads only those authors who reinforce his views. But if this possibility is to be accepted as fact, the reader must find other implied criticism of Vere, and, indeed, it does not take much searching. Melville, for example, goes to the trouble of devoting several pages to Nelson, the greatest of English captains,[2] pointing out with approval that Nelson challenged death by his brilliant apparel.

> Personal prudence even when dictated by quite other than selfish consideration is surely no special virtue in a military man; while an excessive love of glory, impassioning a less burning impulse the honest sense of duty, is the first. (see page 262)

Nelson, of course, dies a soldier's death, while Vere dies drugged and ashore before ever reaching fame. Nelson is a fighter in direct contact with the enemy; but Vere, in the encounter described in *Billy Budd,* does not have an opportunity to catch the opposing ship. Vere is frequently used for diplomatic missions, the very opposite of a captain's usual job; Vere, says Melville, though a man of "sturdy qualities was without brilliant ones" (see page 264). Nelson is asked to take command of a ship recently involved in the Great Mutiny, for "it was thought that an officer like Nelson was the one, *not indeed to terrorize the crew into base subjection,* but to win them, by force of his mere presence back to an allegiance if not as enthusiastic as his own, yet as true" (see page 263; italics mine). Vere, in a similar situation, hangs Billy, "thinking perhaps that under existing circumstances in the navy the consequence of violating discipline should be made to speak for itself" (see page 263).

It is clear that this comparison is not favorable to Captain Vere, and if we look back to earlier descriptions, we find that they apparently contain an implied criticism: "ever mindful of the welfare of his men, but never tolerating an infraction of discipline"; "intrepid to the verge of temerity, though never injudiciously so." The second half of each statement could merely qualify the virtue mentioned in the first half, or it could cancel the virtue completely.[3]

[2] Wendell Glick, in his article "Expediency and Absolute Morality in *Billy Budd*," *PMLA*, LXVIII (153), 103–10, devotes much attention to the Nelson episode, equating Nelson not with Vere but with Billy, and discovers both to be heroic. This may be true, although the differences in station, occasion, and motivation seem to be unsurmountable obstacles to such an interpretation. On the other hand, it seems natural to compare Nelson with Vere: both are captains of ships in time of war, both are asked to deal with mutiny. An additional difficulty with Glick's article lies in the fact that his defense is built on the following unsupported statement: "[Melville] agreed with the Captain that justice to the individual is not the ultimate loyalty in a complex culture; the stability of the culture has the higher claim, and when the two conflict, justice to the individual must be abrogated to keep the order of society intact" (p. 104). Since this is exactly the point in question, so far as any interpretation of the meaning of *Billy Budd* is concerned, it seems facile to present it as axiomatic.

[3] Cf. James E. Miller, Jr., *"Billy Budd:* The Catastrophe of Innocence," *MLN,* LXXIII (1958), 168–76. Miller uses the quotations I have just cited to demonstrate the opposite of my point, namely, that Vere, as opposed to both Billy (all heart) and Claggart (all mind), "is the man of moderation with heart and intellect in ideal balance," who recognizes the "wide and necessary separation of heavenly wisdom and earthly wisdom and the 'impossibility' of the application of the one in the province of the other." In this interpretation Vere becomes a "Hero of Humanity" who shields society from the cataclysmic consequences of Billy's "nakedly spontaneous and raw innocence."

Apparently Miller does not take the quotations in question ironically, whereas I do. But how does one know when to read any line ironically? The answer, I suppose, must be: when such a reading is suggested by and found to be consistent with the total context. In this article, I have tried to submit my own reading to such a test, but I do not find that Miller has. Rather, pretty much abandoning *Billy Budd,* he retreats to *Pierre,* to the Plinlimmon pamphlet, to its famous distinction between heavenly and earthly truth and to its call for a 'virtuous expediency." Unfortunately, this pamphlet is not the clearest of Melville's work, and in Willard Thorp's words, "the critics will argue its significance perpetually."

After Claggart accuses Billy of projected mutiny, Vere decides to confront the two men with each other in his cabin. There Billy, infuriated by the charge, confused and frustrated by his stammer, strikes Claggart dead. Apparently Vere's purpose in bringing them together is to find out the truth.[4] But how does he expect the interview to accomplish this? Claggart would have accused, and Billy would have denied. There seems to be no relevant reason for Vere's decision. Claggart had suggested that there was substantiating evidence not far away, but Vere had not sent for it, since he wished to keep the affair secret because he was afraid of the crew. In short, Vere's decision is based on the single element of prudence, and he ignores all other elements inherent in the situation. Now Claggart is dead. As Vere looks on, he cries, " 'Struck dead by an angel of God. Yet the Angel must hang' " (see page 286). Vere must have acute perception, indeed, to see so quickly to the heart of so complex a situation. He realizes instantly that there is no alternative to Billy's death.

Vere calls a court-martial, reserving, however, "to himself as the one on whom the ultimate accountability would rest, the right of maintaining a supervision of it, or formally or informally interposing at need" (see page 288). During the trial the members of the court seem reluctant to hang Billy, and the Captain has to talk them into it. But it is hard to understand why Vere called the court at all. What purpose does it serve? Was it called to guide him to a right decision? But Vere had already made his decision. In any case the court did not guide him; he guided the court. Perhaps he thought the court would overrule him and free the boy. But Vere had reserved for himself the right of supervising and interfering at need. Apparently all Vere wants is to have on record a trial agreeing with his decision.

Vere begins his argument (see pages 290-292) by saying that he would not interfere with their deliberations, but that he sees them at a crisis proceeding " 'from the clashing of military duty with moral scruple.' " He advises them to " 'strive against scruples that may tend to enervate decision.' " When the men look startled, he explains thus:

> "How can we adjudge to summary and shameful death a fellow-creature innocent before God, and whom we feel to be so?—Does that state it aright? You sign sad assent. Well, I too feel that, the full force of that. It is Nature. But do these buttons that we wear attest that our allegiance is to Nature? No, to the King."

This is the main basis of his argument: we do not serve nature but the king.

> "We fight at command. If our judgments approve the war, that is but coincidence. So in other particulars. . . . Would it be so much we ourselves that would condemn as it would be martial law operating through us? For that law and the rigor of it, we are not responsible. Our vowed responsibility is in this: That however pitilessly that law may operate, we nevertheless adhere to it and administer it."

The officer of marines points out that Budd "proposed neither mutiny nor homicide." Vere agrees with him, saying that, after all, " 'At the Last Assizes it shall acquit,' "

It would seem, therefore, an invalid critical procedure to attempt to explain the uncertain meanings of *Billy Budd* by an appeal to the uncertain meanings of *Pierre*. Even if Melville's intentions, ironic or otherwise, in *Pierre* were crystal clear, which they are not, there is no guarantee that *Billy Budd* embodies them, forty years later.

[4] This point is taken from Lawrance Thompson's *Melville's Quarrel with God* (Princeton, 1952), a book which has been widely and deservedly criticized as totaling somewhat less than the sum of its parts: yet many of those parts are valuable for their detailed analyses and suggestive insights.

but not now. " 'War looks but to the frontage, the appearance. And the Mutiny Act, War's child, takes after the father. Budd's intent or non-intent is nothing to the purpose.' "

No one at any time questions his argument. No one suggests that the king's law should be in harmony with nature's law, or that if there is disagreement between them, the allegiance must be to the higher and the more universal law of nature. No one asks Vere to support his peculiar thesis; it is merely slipped in, so to speak, with the analogy of the buttons: because the men wear the king's buttons, they are to violate natural laws. Even though Vere has admitted that the Mutiny Act looks only to frontage, to the appearance, no one suggests that the point of justice is to see through appearance to reality. But the reason that no one questions Vere's arguments is that no one understands them. "Loyal lieges, plain and practical . . . they were without the faculty, hardly had the inclination to gainsay one whom they felt to be an earnest man, one too not less their superior in mind than in naval rank" (see page 292).

Vere, however, soon gives them an argument they can understand, for when the junior lieutenant asks why, if they must convict, they cannot mitigate the sentence, Vere replies that they cannot because the crew " 'will ruminate. You know what sailors are. Will they not revert to the recent outbreak at the Nore. . . . Your clement sentence they would account pusillanimous. They would think that we flinch, that we are afraid of them.' " And this is the only argument the court really understands, for, as Melville says, "it is not improbable that even such of his words as were not without influence over them, less came home to them than his closing appeal to their instincts as sea-officers. . . ." So for all the finely spun thought, the issue is decided by fear. When subtle arguments fail, Vere calls on, not a rational argument, but an emotional one: an appeal to fear.

Another clue to Vere's thinking comes after Billy has been hanged. The men are put to work at various tasks; they are swept into the routine as fast as possible. Melville writes of this:

> "With mankind" he would say "forms, measured forms are everything; and that is the import couched in the story of Orpheus with his lyre spellbinding the wild denizens of the woods." And this [Vere] once applied to the disruption of forms going on across the Channel and the consequences thereof. (see page 300)

Stripped of verbiage, Vere is saying that men cannot think for themselves, that form and habit can control men as if they were no more than beasts. Vere, in an earlier passage, had thought to himself that Billy was a " '*King's bargain*,' that is to say, for His Britannic Majesty's navy a capital investment at small outlay or none at all" (see page 283). In this light, Vere, far from being a wise man, balanced in his judgments and fair in his attitudes, is discovered to be narrow, literal, prejudiced, completely circumscribed by the needs of the navy, less compassionate than his officers, and lastly, guilty of that worst of naval sins, over-prudence.

The core of Vere's argument is that we must bow to necessity; " 'For that law and the rigor of it, we are not responsible. Our vowed responsibility is in this: That however pitilessly that law may operate, we nevertheless adhere to it and administer it' " (see page 291). A logical extension of this argument is that man should abdicate responsibility for unjust law and enforce it mechanically. Man should not try to change that which is wrong, but merely accept injustice and tyranny and lie supinely beneath them; man is to stand by and watch the innocent as indiscriminately ground under the heel of unresisted law as are the evil.

Melville makes his opposition to this view clear by dedicating the book to Jack Chase, his companion years before on the frigate *United States*. It was this voyage that became the story of *White-Jacket,* the novel that cried out so eloquently against impressment, flogging, the captain's tyranny. Jack Chase is here mentioned by name and is referred to as "a stickler for the Rights of Man and the liberties of the world." It would be ironic indeed to dedicate *Billy Budd* to such a man if the novel was devoted to submission. However, the preface (see page 254) helps to make clear the direction of the book. In it, Melville speaks of the French Revolution as an expression of "the Spirit of that Age [which] involved the rectification of the Old World's hereditary wrongs." He points out that, although the revolution had in its turn become an oppressor, the outcome was "a political advance along nearly the whole line for Europeans," and he concludes by saying,

> in a way analogous to the operation of the Revolution at large the Great Mutiny, though by Englishmen naturally deemed monstrous at the time, doubtless gave the first latent prompting to most important reforms in the British Navy.

In short, tyranny can be successfully resisted.

We can now be sure of the direction of the theme of *Billy Budd*. In local context it suggests that it is wrong to submit to unjust law. Those in power, such as Vere, should do all they can to resist the evil inherent in any institution or government. All men are flawed, but not all men are depraved; and we must not let those institutions designed to control the evil destroy the good. In a larger context, man should not resign himself to the presence of evil but must always strive against it. It is possible to check the validity of this view by making sure that the various incidents, descriptions, and points reinforce it, and that they also contradict the "testament of acceptance" theory.

Observe that Vere dies drugged and on shore before he has "attained to the fullness of fame" (see page 301). In other words, Vere's end is suitable to one who did not deserve such renown as the daring and imprudent Nelson, a man capable, as Vere is not, of inspiring his men to loyalty, of substituting persuasion for coercion.

Observe that Claggart is characterized as civilized and intellectual:

> the man's even temper and discreet bearing would seem to intimate a mind peculiarly subject to the law of reason, not the less in his heart he would seem to riot in complete exemption from that law having apparently little to do with reason further than to employ it as an ambidexter implement for effecting the irrational. (see page 272)

But such men, continues Melville,

> are true madmen, and of the most dangerous sort, for their lunacy is not continuous but occasional evoked by some special object; it is probably secretive which is as much to say it is self contained, so that when moreover, most active it is to the average mind not distinguishable from sanity. . . . (see page 272)

This material comes into sharper focus when considered in relationship to Vere.

He, like Claggart, is civilized; he, like Claggart, is intellectual; and he, like Claggart, uses reason to a bad end. Melville had suggested that Claggart was mad, and yet in Chapter 21, the surgeon, after seeing Claggart's body and hearing Vere say that the boy must hang, cannot banish this treasonable thought: "Was Captain Vere suddenly affected in his mind . . . ? Was he unhinged?" (see page 286). The surgeon reports, as instructed by Vere, to the lieutenants and the captain of the marines. "They fully stared at him in surprise and concern. Like him they seemed to think that such a matter should be reported to the Admiral" (see page 286). Melville pushes further; in the next chapter he says,

> Who in the rainbow can draw the line where the violet tint ends and the orange tint begins? . . . So with sanity and insanity. . . . Whether Captain Vere, as the Surgeon professionally and primarily surmised, was really the sudden victim of any degree of aberration, one must determine for himself by such light as this narrative can afford. (see pages 286–287)

Observe that Billy was removed from a ship called the *Rights of Man* by a lieutenant named Ratcliffe.

Observe that, although Vere was "solicitous of his men's welfare," yet the day after Billy was impressed, the captain flogged "a little fellow, young, a novice an afterguardsman absent from his assigned post when the ship was being put about . . . ." (see page 268). It is useful to remember here that, when Melville was a novice, he was almost flogged for the same reason, but was saved by the interference of Jack Chase.

Observe that white is not used to portray innocence, as Matthiessen suggests; on the contrary, it is used as Melville had used it in *Moby-Dick:* to imply terror and possibly evil. For example, Claggart is described as pale in visage; Billy, when accused of treachery, appears "struck as by white leprosy" (see page 284); the young man who tries to persuade Billy to join a mutiny had "glassy eyes of pale blue, veiled with lashes all but white" (see page 277); Claggart's voice is silvery and low; the whistles used to pipe the men to witness the punishment of Billy are silver whistles; the moon that shines at midnight as Vere tells the men about Billy's sentence silvers the white spar-deck (see page 294) as, in the ballad also, it silvers the bay where Billy lies shackled, awaiting death. In this light the whiteness of Billy's clothes may not be a sign of his purity but of the evil which is successfully destroying him; and the "circumambient air of the clearness of its serenity . . . like smooth white marble" (see page 300), which surrounds him as he hangs from the yardarm, may be more concerned with all-conquering evil than with submissive purity.

Observe that Vere appears at the court-martial as the sole witness, "and as such temporarily sinking his rank, though singularly maintaining it in a matter apparently trivial, namely, that he testified from the ship's weather-side with that object having caused the court to sit on the lee-side" (see page 288). Vere thus chooses the side which puts him literally and metaphorically above the court and gives him, in the slang meaning of the term, the advantage.

Vere, when preparing to address the court, that is, to persuade it to his opinion, paces the cabin,

> in the returning ascent to windward, climbing the slant deck in the ship's lee roll; without knowing it symbolizing thus in his action a mind resolute to surmount difficulties even if against primitive instincts strong as the wind and the sea. (see page 290)

But Melville has suggested already that the instincts of the untutored barbarian are sounder than the civilized intellect.

Observe that this is corroborated in the very next paragraph. "When speak he did, something both in the substance of what he said and his manner of saying it, showed the influence of unshared studies modifying and tempering the practical training of an active career" (see page 290). But practicality is exactly what is called for. Vere never refers to these qualities, preferring instead to weave a complex skein of thought which none of his court, though thoroughly competent, can follow.

Even the governing circumstance of the entire story, namely, the recent mutinies and the consequent peril hovering over the fleet, does not go unchallenged by Melville. For at the conclusion of Vere's speech, just after his appeal to the fear of a new revolt, Melville describes the court's frame of mind as akin to that

> which in the year 1842 actuated the commander of the U.S. brig-of-war *Somers* to resolve, under the so-called Articles of War, Articles modelled upon the English Mutiny Act, to resolve upon the execution at sea of a midshipman and two petty-officers as mutineers designing the seizure of the brig. Which resolution was carried out though in a time of peace and within not many days sail of home. An act vindicated by a naval court of inquiry subsequently convened ashore. History, and here cited without comment. True, the circumstances on board the *Somers* were different from those on board the *Indomitable.* But the urgency felt, well-warranted or otherwise, was much the same. (see pages 292–293)

Thus, Melville introduces a case whose justice had been considered extremely dubious and which, after forty years, was still being debated in the papers. Melville does not stop here; the last two sentences state that the circumstances are not the same, and that perhaps the need for swift action on the *Indomitable* is urgent and perhaps it is not. Thus even the circumstance responsible for Vere's basic motive is undermined.

It should be pointed out that the adherents of the "testament of acceptance" theory have to deal not only with the unsuitability of Captain Vere as a spokesman for Melville, but they also have to explain away the presence of a number of contradictions which arise in the story solely as a result of their position. For example, if the story concerns the acceptance of necessary evil, then why does Melville continue beyond the death of Billy, where, and only where, an emotional equilibrium favorable to such an acceptance is attained? Vere's untimely death would be a poor reward for so faithful a servant and in the "acceptance" context would be meaningless, for the point is made and the tale ended with Billy's death. Only an ironical reversing of the point would justify continuation of the story.

It is even possible to bring into question the tone of the hanging scene. Joseph Schiffman, B. R. McElderry, and Harry Campbell have each noted contradictions in this scene that arise only if the story is interpreted as an "acceptance." Schiffman points out that, even though the crew echoes Billy's cry, "God bless Captain Vere," they are not thinking of the captain, for, in Melville's words, "yet at that instant Billy alone must have been in their hearts, even as he was in their eyes" (see page 298).

B. R. McElderry demonstrates that Billy's cry is not unprecedented in the literature of the sea; he cites two plays and a novel by Marryat which have similar scenes. Thus Billy's cry is

> what Melville said it was: "a conventional felon's benediction directed aft towards the quarters of honor . . . ." It is the traditional ritual of the condemned man forgiving the official who is duty bound to order his death.

If this episode is taken ironically, then it fits the rest of the story as so far interpreted and acquires tremendous power. For Billy is willing to die as Isaac or as Christ was willing; he accepts all the captain's arguments, but it is Billy alone who is noble. The captain suffers and wishes he could avoid his duty, but he has no nobility and above all no trust in man. Yet Billy's very acceptance of his role is the evidence that proves man can be trusted, that man can rise above the need for forms.

Harry Campbell has analyzed the hanging scene and perceives therein an attempt on Melville's part to strike a balance between the sacrificial religious aspect and the aspect of the scene as sheer injustice, as an execution. For example, Melville says that Billy ascended; and ascending, took the full rose of the dawn." But he ascends only to the yardarm, where he remains a pinioned figure. Campbell also notes that the reading of the early *Baby Budd, Sailor* * for "rosy dawn" was the powerful religious term "shekinah" and that the "silence accompanying the ascension" later becomes "The silence at the moment of execution." This last change, particularly, suggests that Melville wants us to realize that Billy's death, though noble, is still unjust. If Vere had had such nobility and strength, Billy need not have died. As Kark Zink has said, "The lesson is not that Billy learns to accept the necessary harshness of the forms, but that in their high impersonality there is a dangerous lack of discrimination—dangerous to the individual and to the social structure itself."

Another contradiction inherent in the "acceptance" theory lies in Melville's argument that barbarians with their instincts and warm hearts have sounder values than civilized men with their intricate intellects and their rabied hearts. Would it not be contradictory for Melville to suggest this not once, but twice, and then have Vere, Melville's foremost spokesman, weave a complex intellectual argument? Would it not be contradictory for Melville to have Billy die bravely, crying "God bless Captain Vere," and then have Vere say directly that mankind is a denizen of the forest and must be controlled by form and routine?

Would it not be contradictory, in the "testament of acceptance" framework, for Melville to use for the captain's name a word which at first glance suggests *veritas* "truth," but on second glance can as easily suggest *veritus* "fear," or on third glance, *vir* "man"?

Would it not be contradictory for him to use as symbols of evil flogging, impressment, arbitrary hanging, when these evils had been corrected by the time that he wrote this story, partly through his own writing?

Would it not be contradictory for Melville to use Vere as a symbol of the proper recognition of necessary evil: a man who had opposed the French Revolution and all its new social and political doctrines which since have changed the globe and reduced tyranny, injustice, poverty, and disease? Might it not be argued that, since Vere was wrong in his judgment of these attempts to change existing evils, he might also be wrong about the case in hand?

Would it not be contradictory for Melville to have a captain who is intelligent and widely read in both the ancients and the moderns, who does not apply this breadth of experience, who sees no larger context than the immediate needs of the navy?

Again, would it not be contradictory for Melville to represent Billy as inarticulate,

* This short story is included in F. Barron Freeman's *Melville's Billy Budd*. [Editors' note]

nonthinking, naïve, emotionally adolescent, and morally undeveloped, and then expect the reader to accept his cry, "God bless Captain Vere," as indicative of full understanding, instinctive or otherwise.

And finally, is not the "acceptance" theory contradictory to all that Melville stood for and fought for throughout his entire life? He had been a seaman and had witnessed at first hand the floggings and the tyrannies of the captains. He had never approved of such practices, and in *White-Jacket* he thundered against them from every angle.

> No matter, then, what may be the consequences of its abolition; no matter if we have to dismantle our fleets, and our unprotected commerce should fall a prey to the spoiler, the awful admonitions of justice and humanity demand that abolition without procrastination; in a voice that is not to be mistaken, demand that abolition to-day. It is not a dollar-and-cent question of expediency; it is a matter of *right and wrong*. And if any man can lay his hand on his heart, and solemnly say that this scourging is right, let that man but once feel the lash on his own back, and in his agony you will hear the apostate call the seventh heavens to witness that it is *wrong*. And, in the name of immortal manhood, would to God that every man who upholds this thing were scourged at the gangway till he recanted.

Melville was a fighter, he was stubborn, he never accepted the easy way out. Would it not then be contradictory for him, after a lifetime of resisting practical evil in the world at large and metaphysical evil in his novels, at the very end to discover that he had been wrong all along and that his duty had always been to lie down and accept evil as unavoidable?

It is now possible to review the story swiftly. It begins with a cue from a narrator; a rebellion, like the French Revolution or the Spithead Mutiny, may result in good, although in the beginning it may not seem so. Thus, rebellion is justified in the first pages, the implication being that evil can and perhaps should be resisted. We have seen how the various characteristics of the three main actors are clues to the working out of this theme. Claggart is evil through and through; he possesses the perverted intelligence of a serpent, an intelligence used for irrational purposes. Billy Budd, on the contrary, is pure innocence, acting and judging on instinct alone. When Vere is introduced, his central characteristic is his intellection, by means of which he can justify or rationalize an over-prudence that leads to injustice. The chapter on Nelson reminds us that Vere's kind of caution and Vere's way of preventing possible mutiny are not admirable.

It may be argued that, while both Vere and Claggart possess intelligence, Vere uses his wisely and justly. But this argument collapses when it is perceived that Vere does not do what reason would suggest in so dubious a case, i.e., jail Billy until they reach land. The real point is, of course, that Vere does not act on reason and intelligence at all, but on fear; his intelligence, instead of being a guide, is a perverted instrument. Such scenes as the confusion of the officers and the doubt of the surgeon concerning Vere's sanity make sense only when regarded as putting into issue Vere's stature and ability.

It may also be argued that such episodes are intended to demonstrate that Vere and only Vere has the intelligence and insight to perceive the deeper issues. But this explanation falls to the ground when it is realized that Vere's whole argument is irrational and that his final appeal is to brute force. The ballad at the end becomes particularly rich in this context. Billy is to be sacrificed, but unjustly and unnecessarily so. The ballad, written by one of his comrades who does not understand the issues but who feels obscurely the truth of the matter in spite of a calumnious official report, speaks of Billy as unafraid but sad. Billy, being innocence personified, does not fear death; but as an unjust sacrifice, he is pictured as alone and unhappy. He longs for companionship and affection and thinks wistfully of his friends; in the end he contemplates with a melancholy resignation his death:

> Fathoms down, fathoms down, how I'll dream fast asleep.
> I feel it stealing now. Sentry are you there?
> Just ease these darbies at the wrist,
> And roll me over fair.
> I am sleepy, and the oozy weeds about me twist.
>   (see page 303)

Thus, Billy's cry, "God bless Captain Vere," is the crowning irony and really the climax of the story, for he was hanged unjustly. Melville says here that a harsh truth of this harsh world is that good folk can be misled, that they can be abused by the evil simply because they are trusting. Thus Melville reminds us that we must keep up the good fight: evil must not remain uncontested. And he does so not by a call to arms but by demonstrating the consequences of unresisting acquiescence.

THE DAUGHTERS OF THE LATE COLONEL

KATHERINE MANSFIELD (1888–1923)

I

The week after was one of the busiest weeks of their lives. Even when they went to bed it was only their bodies that lay down and rested; their minds went on, thinking things out, talking things over, wondering, deciding, trying to remember where . . .

Constantia lay like a statue, her hands by her sides, her feet just overlapping each other, the sheet up to her chin. She stared at the ceiling.

"Do you think that father would mind if we gave his top-hat to the porter?"

"The porter?" snapped Josephine. "Why ever the porter? What a very extraordinary idea!"

"Because," said Constantia slowly, "he must often have to go to funerals. And

I noticed at—at the cemetery that he only had a bowler." She paused. "I thought then how very much he'd appreciate a top-hat. We ought to give him a present, too. He was always very nice to father."

"But," cried Josephine, flouncing on her pillow and staring across the dark at Constantia, "father's head!" And suddenly, for one awful moment, she nearly giggled. Not, of course, that she felt in the least like giggling. It must have been habit. Years ago, when they had stayed awake at night talking, their beds had simply heaved. And now the porter's head, disappearing, popped out, like a candle, under father's hat. . . . The giggle mounted, mounted; she clenched her hands; she fought it down; she frowned fiercely at the dark and said, "Remember" terribly sternly.

"We can decide tomorrow," she sighed.

Constantia had noticed nothing; she sighed.

"Do you think we ought to have our dressing-gowns dyed as well?"

"Black?" almost shrieked Josephine.

"Well, what else?" said Constantia. "I was thinking—it doesn't seem quite sincere, in a way, to wear black out of doors when we're fully dressed, and then when we're at home——"

"But nobody sees us," said Josephine. She gave the bedclothes such a twitch that both her feet became uncovered, and she had to creep up the pillows to get them well under again.

"Kate does," said Constantia. "And the postman very well might."

Josephine thought of her dark-red slippers, which matched her dressing-gown, and of Constantia's favorite indefinite green ones which went with hers. Black! Two black dressing-gowns and two pairs of black woolly slippers, creeping off to the bathroom like black cats.

"I don't think it's absolutely necessary," said she.

Silence. Then Constantia said, "We shall have to post the papers with the notice in them tomorrow to catch the Ceylon mail. . . . How many letters have we had up till now?"

"Twenty-three."

Josephine had replied to them all, and twenty-three times when she came to "We miss our dear father so much," she had broken down and had to use her handkerchief, and on some of them even to soak up a very light-blue tear with an edge of blotting-paper. Strange! She couldn't have put it on—but twenty-three times. Even now, though, when she said over to herself sadly, "We miss our dear father *so* much" she could have cried if she'd wanted to.

"Have you got enough stamps?" came from Constantia.

"Oh, how could I tell?" said Josephine crossly. "What's the good of asking me that now?"

"I was just wondering," said Constantia mildly.

Silence again. There came a little rustle, a scurry, a hop.

"A mouse," said Constantia.

"It can't be a mouse because there aren't any crumbs," said Josephine.

"But it doesn't know there aren't," said Constantia.

A spasm of pity squeezed her heart. Poor little thing! She wished she'd left a tiny piece of biscuit on the dressing-table. It was awful to think of it not finding anything. What would it do?

"I can't think of how they manage to live at all," she said slowly.

"Who?" demanded Josephine.

And Constantia said more loudly than she meant to, "Mice."

Josephine was furious. "Oh, what nonsense, Con!" she said. "What have mice got to do with it? You're asleep."

"I don't think I am," said Constantia. She shut her eyes to make sure. She was.

Josephine arched her spine, pulled up her knees, folded her arms so that her fists came under her ears, and pressed her cheek hard against the pillow.

II

Another thing that complicated matters was they had Nurse Andrews staying on with them that week. It was their own fault; they had asked her. It was Josephine's idea. On the morning—well, on the last morning, when the doctor had gone, Josephine had said to Constantia, "Don't you think it would be rather nice if we asked Nurse Andrews to stay on for a week as our guest?"

"Very nice," said Constantia.

"I thought," went on Josephine quickly, "I should just say this afternoon, after we've paid her, 'My sister and I would be very pleased, after all you've done for us, Nurse Andrews, if you would stay on for a week as our guest.' I'd have to put that in about being our guest in case—"

"Oh, but she could hardly expect to be paid!" cried Constantia.

"One never knows," said Josephine sagely.

Nurse Andrews had, of course, jumped at the idea. But it was a bother. It meant they had to have regular sit-down meals at the proper times, whereas if they'd been alone they could have just asked Kate if she wouldn't have minded bringing them a tray wherever they were. And meal-times now that the strain was over were rather a trial.

Nurse Andrews was simply fearful about butter. Really they couldn't help feeling that about butter, at least, she took advantage of their kindness. And she had that maddening habit of asking for just an inch more bread to finish what she had on her plate, and then, at the last mouthful, absentmindedly—of course it wasn't absentmindedly—taking another helping. Josephine got very red when this happened, and she fastened her small, bead-like eyes on the table-cloth as if she saw a minute strange insect creeping through the web of it. But Constantia's long, pale face lengthened and set, and she gazed away—away—far over the desert to where that line of camels unwound like a thread of wool.

"When I was with Lady Tukes," said Nurse Andrews, "she had such a dainty little contrayvance for the buttah. It was a silvah Cupid balanced on the—on the bordah of a glass dish, holding a tayny fork. And when you wanted some buttah you simply pressed his foot and he bent down and speared you a piece. It was quite a gayme."

Josephine could hardly bear that. But "I think those things are very extravagant," was all she said.

"But whey?" asked Nurse Andrews, beaming through her eye-glasses. "No one, surely, would take more buttah than one wanted—would one?"

"Ring, Con," cried Josephine. She couldn't trust herself to reply.

And proud young Kate, the enchanted princess, came in to see what the old tabbies wanted now. She snatched away their plates of mock something or other and slapped down a white, terrified blanc-mange.

"Jam, please, Kate," said Josephine kindly.

Kate knelt and burst open the side-board, lifted the lid of the jam-pot, saw it was empty, put it on the table, and stalked off.

"I'm afraid," said Nurse Andrews a moment later, "there isn't any."

"Oh, what a bother!" said Josephine. She bit her lip. "What had we better do?"

Constantia looked dubious. "We can't disturb Kate again," she said softly.

Nurse Andrews waited, smiling at them both. Her eyes wandered, spying at every-thing behind her eye-glasses. Constantia in despair went back to her camels. Josephine frowned heavily—concentrated. If it hadn't been for this idiotic woman she and Con would, of course, have eaten their blanc-mange without. Suddenly the idea came.

"I know," she said. "Marmalade. There's some marmalade in the side-board. Get it, Con."

"I hope," laughed Nurse Andrews, and her laugh was like a spoon tinkling against a medicine-glass—"I hope it's not very bittah marmalayde."

III

But, after all, it was not long now, and then she'd be gone for good. And there was no getting away from the fact that she had been very kind to father. She had nursed him day and night at the end. Indeed, both Constantia and Josephine felt privately that she had rather overdone the not leaving him at the very last. For when they had gone in to say good-bye Nurse Andrews had sat beside his bed the whole time, holding his wrist and pretending to look at her watch. It couldn't have been necessary. It was so tactless, too. Supposing father had wanted to say something—something private to them. Not that he had. Oh, far from it! He lay there, purple, a dark, angry purple in the face, and never even looked at them when they came in. Then, as they were standing there, wondering what to do, he had suddenly opened one eye. Oh, what a difference it would have made, what a difference to their memory of him, how much easier to tell people about it, if he had only opened both! But no—one eye only. It glared at them a moment and then . . . went out.

IV

It had made it very awkward for them when Mr. Farolles, of St. John's, called the same afternoon.

"The end was quite peaceful, I trust?" were the first words he said as he glided towards them through the dark drawing-room.

"Quite," said Josephine faintly. They both hung their heads. Both of them felt certain that eye wasn't at all a peaceful eye.

"Won't you sit down?" said Josephine.

"Thank you, Miss Pinner," said Mr. Farolles gratefully. He folded his coat-tails and began to lower himself into father's armchair, but just as he touched it he almost sprang up and slid into the next chair instead.

He coughed. Josephine clasped her hands; Constantia looked vague.

"I want you to feel, Miss Pinner," said Mr. Farolles, "and you, Miss Constantia, that I'm trying to be helpful. I want to be helpful to you both, if you will let me.

These are the times," said Mr. Farolles, very simply and earnestly, "when God means us to be helpful to one another."

"Thank you very much, Mr. Farolles," said Josephine and Constantia.

"Not at all," said Mr. Farolles gently. He drew his kid gloves through his fingers and leaned a little forward. "And if either of you would like a little Communion. either or both of you, here *and* now, you have only to tell me. A little Communion is often very helpful—a great comfort," he added tenderly.

But the idea of a little Communion terrified them. What! In the drawing-room by themselves—with no—no altar or anything! The piano would be much too high, thought Constantia, and Mr. Farolles could not possibly lean over it with the chalice. And Kate would be sure to come bursting in and interrupt them, thought Josephine. And supposing the bell rang in the middle? It might be somebody important—about their mourning. Would they get up reverently and go out, or would they have to wait . . . in torture?

"Perhaps you will send round a note by your good Kate if you would care for it later," said Mr. Farolles.

"Oh, yes, thank you very much!" they both said.

Mr. Farolles got up and took his black straw hat from the round table.

"And about the funeral," he said softly. "I may arrange that—as your dear father's old friend and yours, Miss Pinner—and Miss Constantia?"

Josephine and Constantia got up too.

"I should like it to be quite simple," said Josephine firmly, "and not too expensive. At the same time, I should like—"

"A good one that will last," thought dreamy Constantia, as if Josephine were buying a night-gown. But of course Josephine didn't say that. "One suitable to our father's position." She was very nervous.

"I'll run round to our good friend Mr. Knight," said Mr. Farolles soothingly. "I will ask him to come and see you. I am sure you will find him very helpful indeed."

V

Well, at any rate, all that part of it was over, though neither of them could possibly believe that father was never coming back. Josephine had had a moment of absolute terror at the cemetery, while the coffin was lowered, to think that she and Constantia had done this thing without asking his permission. What would father say when he found out? For he was bound to find out sooner or later. He always did. "Buried. You two girls had me *buried!*" She heard his stick thumping. Oh, what would they say? What possible excuse could they make? It sounded such an appallingly heartless thing to do. Such a wicked advantage to take of a person because he happened to be helpless at the moment. The other people seemed to treat it all as a matter of course. They were strangers; they couldn't be expected to understand that father was the very last person for such a thing to happen to. No, the entire blame for it all would fall on her and Constantia. And the expense, she thought, stepping into the tight-buttoned cab. When she had to show him the bills. What would he say then?

She heard him absolutely roaring, "And do you expect me to pay for this gimcrack excursion of yours?"

"Oh," groaned poor Josephine aloud, "we shouldn't have done it, Con!"

And Constantia, pale as a lemon in all that blackness, said in a frightened whisper, "Done what, Jug?"

"Let them bu-bury father like that," said Josephine, breaking down and crying into her new, queer-smelling mourning handkerchief.

"But what else could we have done?" asked Constantia wonderingly. "We couldn't have kept him, Jug—we couldn't have kept him unburied. At any rate, not in a flat that size."

Josephine blew her nose; the cab was dreadfully stuffy.

"I don't know," she said forlornly. "It is all so dreadful. I feel we ought to have tried to, just for a time at least. To make perfectly sure. One thing's certain"—and her tears sprang out again—"father will never forgive us for this—never!"

VI

Father would never forgive them. That was what they felt more than ever when, two mornings later, they went into his room to go through his things. They had discussed it quite calmly. It was even down on Josephine's list of things to be done. *Go through father's things and settle about them.* But that was a very different matter from saying after breakfast:

"Well, are you ready, Con?"

"Yes, Jug—when you are."

"Then I think we'd better get it over."

It was dark in the hall. It had been a rule for years never to disturb father in the morning, whatever happened. And now they were going to open the door without knocking even. . . . Constantia's eyes were enormous at the idea; Josephine felt weak in the knees.

"You—you go first," she gasped, pushing Constantia.

But Constantia said, as she always had said on those occasions. "No, Jug, that's not fair. You're eldest."

Josephine was going to say—what at other times she wouldn't have owned to for the world—what she kept for her very last weapon, "But you're tallest," when they noticed that the kitchen door was open, and there stood Kate. . . .

"Very stiff," said Josephine, grasping the door-handle and doing her best to turn it. As if anything ever deceived Kate.

It couldn't be helped. That girl was . . . Then the door was shut behind them, but—but they weren't in father's room at all. They might have suddenly walked through the wall by mistake into a different flat altogether. Was the door just behind them? They were too frightened to look. Josephine knew that if it was it was holding itself tight shut; Constantia felt that, like the doors in dreams, it hadn't any handle at all. It was the coldness which made it so awful. Or the whiteness—which? Everything was covered. The blinds were down, a cloth hung over the mirror, a sheet hid the bed; a huge fan of white paper filled the fireplace. Constantia timidly put out her hand; she almost expected a snowflake to fall. Josephine felt a queer tingling in her nose, as if her nose was freezing. Then a cab klop-klopped over the cobbles below, and the quiet seemed to shake into little pieces.

"I had better pull up a blind," said Josephine bravely.

"Yes, it might be a good idea," whispered Constantia.

They only gave the blind a touch, but it flew up and the cord flew after, rolling round the blind-stick, and the little tassel tapped as if trying to get free. That was too much for Constantia.

"Don't you think—don't you think we might put it off for another day?" she whispered.

"Why?" snapped Josephine, feeling, as usual, much better now that she knew for certain that Constantia was terrified. "It's got to be done. But I do wish you wouldn't whisper, Con."

"I didn't know I was whispering," whispered Constantia.

"And why do you keep staring at the bed?" said Josephine, raising her voice almost defiantly. "There's nothing *on* the bed."

"Oh, Jug, don't say so!" said poor Connie. "At any rate, not so loudly."

Josephine felt herself that she had gone too far. She took a wide swerve over to the chest of drawers, put out her hand, but quickly drew it back again.

"Connie!" she gasped, and she wheeled round and leaned with her back against the chest of drawers.

"Oh, Jug—What?"

Josephine could only glare. She had the most extraordinary feeling that she had just escaped something awful. But how could she explain to Constantia that father was in the chest of drawers? He was in the top drawer with his handkerchiefs and neckties, or in the next with his shirts and pajamas, or in the lowest of all with his suits. He was watching there, hidden away—just behind the door-handle—ready to spring.

She pulled a funny old-fashioned face at Constantia, just as she used to in the old days when she was going to cry.

"I can't open," she nearly wailed.

"No, don't, Jug," whispered Constantia, earnestly. "It's much better not to. Don't let's open anything. At any rate, not for a long time."

"But—but it seems so weak," said Josephine, breaking down.

"But why not be weak for once, Jug?" argued Constantia, whispering quite fiercely. "If it is weak." And her pale stare flew from the locked writing-table—so safe—to the huge glittering wardrobe, and she began to breathe in a queer, panting way. "Why shouldn't we be weak for once in our lives, Jug? It's quite excusable. Let's be weak—be weak, Jug. It's much nicer to be weak than to be strong."

And then she did one of those amazingly bold things that she'd done about twice before in their lives; she marched over to the wardrobe, turned the key, and took it out of the lock. Took it out of the lock and held it up to Josephine, showing Josephine by her extraordinary smile that she knew what she'd done, she'd risked deliberately father being in there among his overcoats.

If the huge wardrobe had lurched forward, had crashed down on Constantia, Josephine wouldn't have been surprised. On the contrary, she would have thought it the only suitable thing to happen. But nothing happened. Only the room seemed quieter than ever, and bigger flakes of cold air fell on Josephine's shoulders and knees. She began to shiver.

"Come, Jug," said Constantia, still with that awful callous smile, and Josephine followed just as she had that last time, when Constantia had pushed Benny into the round pond.

VII

But the strain told on them when they were back in the dining-room. They sat down, very shaky, and looked at each other.

"I don't feel I can settle to anything," said Josephine, "until I've had something. Do you think we could ask Kate for two cups of hot water?"

"I really don't see why we shouldn't," said Constantia carefully. She was quite normal again. "I won't ring. I'll go to the kitchen door and ask her."

"Yes, do," said Josephine, sinking down into a chair. "Tell her, just two cups, Con, nothing else—on a tray."

"She needn't even put the jug on, need she?" said Constantia, as though Kate might very well complain if the jug had been there.

"Oh, no, certainly not! The jug's not at all necessary. She can pour it direct out of the kettle," cried Josephine, feeling that would be a labour-saving indeed.

Their cold lips quivered at the greenish brims. Josephine curved her small red hands round the cup; Constantia sat up and blew on the wavy steam, making it flutter from one side to the other.

"Speaking of Benny," said Josephine.

And though Benny hadn't been mentioned Constantia immediately looked as though he had.

"He'll expect us to send him something of father's, of course. But it's so difficult to know what to send to Ceylon."

"You mean things get unstuck so on the voyage," murmured Constantia.

"No, lost," said Josephine sharply. "You know there's no post. Only runners."

Both paused to watch a black man in white linen drawers running through the pale fields for dear life, with a large brown-paper parcel in his hands. Josephine's black man was tiny; he scurried along glistening like an ant. But there was something blind and tireless about Constantia's tall, thin fellow which made him, she decided, a very unpleasant person indeed . . . On the veranda, dressed all in white and wearing a cork helmet, stood Benny. His right hand shook up and down, as father's did when he was impatient. And behind him, not in the least interested, sat Hilda, the unknown sister-in-law. She swung in a cane rocker and flicked over the leaves of the *Tatler*.

"I think his watch would be the most suitable present," said Josephine.

Constantia looked up; she seemed surprised.

"Oh, would you trust a gold watch to a native?"

"But of course I'd disguise it," said Josephine. "No one would know it was a watch." She liked the idea of having to make a parcel such a curious shape that no one could possibly guess what it was. She even thought for a moment of hiding the watch in a narrow cardboard corset-box that she'd kept by her for a long time, waiting for it to come in for something. It was such a beautiful firm cardboard. But, no, it wouldn't be appropriate for this occasion. It had lettering on it: *Medium Women's 28. Extra Firm Busks*. It would be almost too much of a surprise for Benny to open that and find father's watch inside.

"And of course it isn't as though it would be going—ticking, I mean," said Constantia, who was still thinking of the native love of jewellery. "At least," she added, "it would be very strange if after all that time it was."

VIII

Josephine made no reply. She had flown off on one of her tangents. She had suddenly thought of Cyril. Wasn't it more usual for the only grandson to have the watch? And then dear Cyril was so appreciative, and a gold watch meant so much to a young man. Benny, in all probability, had quite got out of the habit of watches; men so seldom wore waistcoats in those hot climates. Whereas Cyril in London wore them from year's end to year's end. And it would be so nice for her and Constantia, when he came to tea, to know it was there. "I see you've got on grandfather's watch, Cyril." It would be somehow so satisfactory.

Dear boy! What a blow his sweet, sympathetic little note had been. Of course they quite understood; but it was most unfortunate.

"It would have been such a point, having him," said Josephine.

"And he would have enjoyed it so," said Constantia, not thinking what she was saying.

However, as soon as he got back he was coming to tea with his aunties. Cyril to tea was one of their rare treats.

"Now, Cyril, you mustn't be frightened of our cakes. Your Auntie Con and I bought them at Buzzard's this morning. We know what a man's appetite is. So don't be ashamed of making a good tea."

Josephine cut recklessly into the rich dark cake that stood for her winter gloves or the soling and heeling of Constantia's only respectable shoes. But Cyril was most unmanlike in appetite.

"I say, Aunt Josephine, I simply can't. I've only just had lunch, you know."

"Oh, Cyril, that can't be true! It's after four," cried Josephine. Constantia sat with her knife poised over the chocolate-roll.

"It is, all the same," said Cyril. "I had to meet a man at Victoria, and he kept me hanging about till . . . there was only time to get lunch and to come on here. And he gave me—phew"—Cyril put his hand to his forehead—"a terrific blowout," he said.

It was disappointing—today of all days. But still he couldn't be expected to know.

"But you'll have a meringue, won't you, Cyril?" said Aunt Josephine. "These meringues were bought specially for you. Your dear father was so fond of them. We were sure you are, too."

"I *am*, Aunt Josephine," cried Cyril ardently. "Do you mind if I take half to begin with?"

"Not at all, dear boy; but we mustn't let you off with that."

"Is your dear father still so fond of meringues?" asked Auntie Con gently. She winced faintly as she broke through the shell of hers.

"Well, I don't quite know, Auntie Con," said Cyril breezily.

At that they both looked up.

"Don't know?" almost snapped Josephine. "Don't know a thing like that about your own father, Cyril?"

"Surely," said Auntie Con softly.

Cyril tried to laugh it off. "Oh, well," he said, "it's such a long time since—" He faltered. He stopped. Their faces were too much for him.

"Even *so*," said Josephine.

And Auntie Con looked.

Cyril put down his teacup. "Wait a bit," he cried. "Wait a bit, Aunt Josephine. What am I thinking of?"

He looked up. They were beginning to brighten. Cyril slapped his knee.

"Of course," he said, "it was meringues. How could I have forgotten? Yes, Aunt Josephine, you're perfectly right. Father's most frightfully keen on meringues."

They didn't only beam. Aunt Josephine went scarlet with pleasure; Auntie Con gave a deep, deep sigh.

"And now, Cyril, you must come and see father," said Josephine. "He knows you were coming today."

"Right," said Cyril, very firmly and heartily. He got up from his chair; suddenly he glanced at the clock.

"I say, Auntie Con, isn't your clock a bit slow? I've got to meet a man at—at Paddington just after five. I'm afraid I shan't be able to stay very long with grandfather."

"Oh he won't expect you to say *very* long!" said Aunt Josephine.

Constantia was still gazing at the clock. She couldn't make up her mind if it was fast or slow. It was one or the other, she felt almost certain of that. At any rate, it had been.

Cyril still lingered. "Aren't you coming along, Auntie Con?"

"Of course," said Josephine, "we shall all go. Come on, Con."

IX

They knocked at the door, and Cyril followed his aunts into grandfather's hot, sweetish room.

"Come on," said Grandfather Pinner. "Don't hang about. What is it? What've you been up to?"

He was sitting in front of a roaring fire, clasping his stick. He had a thick rug over his knees. On his lap there lay a beautiful pale yellow silk handkerchief.

"It's Cyril, father," said Josephine shyly. And she took Cyril's hand and led him forward.

"Good afternoon, grandfather," said Cyril, trying to take his hand out of Aunt Josephine's. Grandfather Pinner shot his eyes at Cyril in the way he was famous for. Where was Auntie Con? She stood on the other side of Aunt Josephine; her long arms hung down in front of her; her hands were clasped. She never took her eyes off grandfather.

"Well," said Grandfather Pinner, beginning to thump, "what have you got to tell me?"

What had he, what had he got to tell him? Cyril felt himself smiling like a perfect imbecile. The room was stifling, too.

But Aunt Josephine came to his rescue. She cried brightly, "Cyril says his father is still very fond of meringues, father dear."

"Eh?" said Grandfather Pinner, curving his hand like a purple meringue-shell over one ear.

Josephine repeated, "Cyril says his father is still very fond of meringues."

"Can't hear," said old Colonel Pinner. And he waved Josephine away with his stick, then pointed to Cyril. "Tell me what she's trying to say," he said.

(My God!) "Must I?" said Cyril, blushing and staring at Aunt Josephine.

"Do, dear," she smiled. "It will please him so much."

"Come on, out with it!" cried Colonel Pinner testily, beginning to thump again.

And Cyril leaned forward and yelled, "Father's still very fond of meringues."

At that Grandfather Pinner jumped as though he had been shot.

"Don't shout!" he cried. "What's the matter with the boy? *Meringues!* What about 'em?"

"Oh, Aunt Josephine, must we go on?" groaned Cyril desperately.

"It's quite all right, dear boy," said Aunt Josephine, as though he and she were at the dentist's together. "He'll understand in a minute." And she whispered to Cyril, "He's getting a bit deaf, you know." Then she leaned forward and really bawled at Grandfather Pinner, "Cyril only wanted to tell you, father dear, that *his* father is still very fond of meringues."

Colonel Pinner heard that time, heard and brooded, looking Cyril up and down.

"What an esstraordinary thing!" said old Grandfather Pinner. "What an esstraordinary thing to come all this way here to tell me!"

And Cyril felt it *was*.

"Yes, I shall send Cyril the watch," said Josephine.

"That would be very nice," said Constantia. "I seem to remember last time he came here there was some little trouble about the time."

x

They were interrupted by Kate bursting through the door in her usual fashion, as though she had discovered some secret panel in the wall.

"Fried or boiled?" asked the bold voice.

Fried or boiled? Josephine and Constantia were quite bewildered for the moment. They could hardly take it in.

"Fried or boiled what, Kate?" asked Josephine, trying to begin to concentrate.

Kate gave a loud sniff. "Fish."

"Well, why didn't you say so immediately?" Josephine reproached her gently. "How could you expect us to understand? There are a great many things in this world, you know, which are fried or boiled." And after such a display of courage, she said quite brightly to Constantia, "Which do you prefer, Con?"

"I think it might be nice to have it fried," said Constantia. "On the other hand, of course boiled fish is very nice. I think I prefer both equally well. . . . Unless you . . . In that case—"

"I shall fry it," said Kate, and she bounced back, leaving their door open and slamming the door of her kitchen.

Josephine gazed at Constantia; she raised her pale eyebrows until they rippled away into her pale hair. She got up. She said in a very lofty, imposing way, "Do you mind following me into the drawing-room, Constantia? I've something of great importance to discuss with you."

For it was always to the drawing-room they retired when they wanted to talk over Kate.

Josephine closed the door meaningly. "Sit down, Constantia," she said, still very grand. She might have been receiving Constantia for the first time. And Con looked round vaguely for a chair, as though she felt indeed quite a stranger.

"Now, the question is," said Josephine, bending forward, "whether we shall keep her or not."

"That is the question," agreed Constantia.

"And this time," said Josephine firmly, "we must come to a definite decision."

Constantia looked for a moment as though she might begin going over all the other times, but she pulled herself together and said, "Yes, Jug."

"You see, Con," explained Josephine, "everything is so changed now." Constantia looked up quickly. "I mean," went on Josephine, "we're not dependent on Kate as we were." And she blushed faintly. "There's not father to cook for."

"That is perfectly true," agreed Constantia. "Father certainly doesn't want any cooking now, whatever else—"

Josephine broke in sharply, "You're not sleepy, are you, Con?"

"Sleepy, Jug?" Constantia was wide-eyed.

"Well, concentrate more," said Josephine sharply, and she returned to the subject. "What it comes to is, if we did"—and this she barely breathed, glancing at the door—"give Kate notice"—she raised her voice again—"we could manage our own food."

"Why not?" cried Constantia. She couldn't help smiling. The idea was so exciting. She clasped her hands. "What should we live on, Jug?"

"Oh, eggs in various forms!" said Jug, lofty again. "And besides, there are all the cooked foods."

"But I've always heard," said Constantia, "they are considered so very expensive."

"Not if one buys them in moderation," said Josephine. But she tore herself away from the fascinating bypath and dragged Constantia after her.

"What we've got to decide now, however, is whether we really do trust Kate or not."

Constantia leaned back. Her flat little laugh flew from her lips.

"Isn't it curious, Jug," said she, "that just on this one subject I've never been able to quite make up my mind."

XI

She never had. The whole difficulty was to prove anything. How did one prove things, how could one? Suppose Kate had stood in front of her and deliberately made a face. Mightn't she very well have been in pain? Wasn't it impossible, at any rate, to ask Kate if she was making a face at her? If Kate answered "No"—and of course she would say "No"—what a position! How undignified! Then again Constantia suspected, she was almost certain, that Kate went to her chest of drawers when she and Josephine were out, not to take things but to spy. Many times she had come back to find her amethyst cross in the most unlikely places, under her lace ties or on top of her evening Bertha. More than once she had laid a trap for Kate. She had arranged things in a special order and then called Josephine to witness.

"You see, Jug?"

"Quite, Con."

"Now we shall be able to tell."

But, oh, dear, when she did go to look, she was as far off from proof as ever! If anything was displaced, it might so very well have happened as she closed the drawer; a jolt might have done it so easily.

"You come, Jug, and decide. I really can't. It's too difficult."

But after a long pause and a long glare Josephine would sigh, "Now you've put the doubt into my mind, Con, I'm sure I can't tell myself."

"Well, we can't postpone it again," said Josephine. "If we postpone it this time—"

XII

But at that moment in the street below a barrel-organ struck up. Josephine and Constantia sprang to their feet together.

"Run, Con," said Josephine. "Run quickly. There's six-pence on the—"

Then they remembered. It didn't matter. They would never have to stop the organ-grinder again. Never again would she and Constantia be told to make that monkey take his noise somewhere else. Never would sound that loud, strange bellow when father thought they were not hurrying enough. The organ-grinder might play there all day and the stick would not thump.

It never will thump again,
It never will thump again,

played the barrel-organ.

What was Constantia thinking? She had such a strange smile; she looked different. She couldn't be going to cry.

"Jug, Jug," said Constantia softly, pressing her hands together. "Do you know what day it is? It's Saturday. It's a week today, a whole week."

A week since father died,
A week since father died,

cried the barrel-organ. And Josephine, too, forgot to be practical and sensible; she smiled faintly, strangely. On the Indian carpet there fell a square of sunlight, pale red; it came and went and came—and stayed, deepened—until it shone almost golden.

"The sun's out," said Josephine, as though it really mattered.

A perfect fountain of bubbling notes shook from the barrel-organ, round, bright notes, carelessly scattered.

Constantia lifted her big, cold hands as if to catch them, and then her hands fell again. She walked over to the mantel-piece to her favourite Buddha. And the stone and gilt image, whose smile always gave her such a queer feeling, almost a pain and yet a pleasant pain, seemed today to be more than smiling. He knew something; he had a secret. "I know something you don't know," said her Buddha. Oh, what was it, what could it be? And yet she had always felt there was . . . something.

The sunlight pressed through the windows, thieved its way in, flashed its light over the furniture and the photographs. Josephine watched it. When it came to mother's photograph, the enlargement over the piano, it lingered as though puzzled to find so little remained of mother, except the earrings shaped like tiny pagodas and a black feather boa. Why did the photographs of dead people always fade so? wondered Josephine. As soon as a person was dead her photograph died too. But, of course, this one of mother was very old. It was thirty-five years old. Josephine remembered standing on a chair and pointing out that feather boa to Constantia and telling her that it was a snake that had killed their mother in Ceylon. . . . Would everything have been different if mother hadn't died? She didn't see why. Aunt Florence had lived with them until they had left school, and they had moved three times and had their yearly holiday and . . . and there'd been changes of servants, of course.

Some little sparrows, young sparrows they sounded, chirped on the window-ledge. *Yeep-eyeep-yeep.* But Josephine felt they were not sparrows, not on the window-ledge. It was inside her, that queer little crying noise. *Yeep-eyeep-yeep.* Ah, what was it crying, so weak and forlorn?

If mother had lived, might they have married? But there had been nobody for them to marry. There had been father's Anglo-Indian friends before he quarrelled with them. But after that she and Constantia never met a single man except clergymen. How did one meet men? Or even if they'd met them, how could they have got to know men well enough to be more than strangers? One read of people having adventures, being followed, and so on. But nobody had ever followed Constantia and her. Oh, yes, there had been one year at Eastbourne a mysterious man at their boarding-house who had put a note on the jug of hot water outside their bedroom door! But by the time Connie had found it the steam had made the writing too faint to read; they couldn't even make out to which of them it was addressed. And he had left the next day. And that was all. The rest had been looking after father, and at the same time keeping out of father's way. But now? But now? The thieving sun touched Josephine gently. She lifted her face. She was drawn over to the window by gentle beams . . .

Until the barrel-organ stopped playing Constantia stayed before the Buddha, wondering, but not as usual, not vaguely. This time her wonder was like longing. She remembered the times she had come in here, crept out of bed in her nightgown when the moon was full, and lain on the floor with her arms outstretched, as though she was crucified. Why? The big, pale moon had made her do it. The horrible dancing figures on the carved screen had leered at her and she hadn't minded. She remembered too how, whenever they were at the seaside, she had gone off by herself and got as close to the sea as she could, and sung something, something she had made up, while she gazed all over that restless water. There had been this other life, running out, bringing things home in bags, getting things on approval, discussing them with Jug, taking them back to get more things on approval, and arranging father's trays and trying not to annoy father. But it all seemed to have happened in a kind of tunnel. It wasn't real. It was only when she came out of the tunnel into the moonlight or by the sea or into a thunderstorm that she really felt herself. What did it mean? What did it all lead to? Now? Now?

She turned away from the Buddha with one of her vague gestures. She went over to where Josephine was standing. She wanted to say something to Josephine, something frightfully important, about—about the future and what . . .

"Don't you think perhaps—" she began.

But Josephine interrupted her. "I was wondering if now—" she murmured. They stopped; they waited for each other.

"Go on, Con," said Josephine.

"No, no, Jug; after you," said Constantia.

"No, say what you were going to say. You began," said Josephine.

"I . . . I'd rather hear what you were going to say first," said Constantia.

"Don't be absurd, Con."

"Really, Jug."

"Connie!"

"Oh, *Jug!*"

A pause. Then Constantia said faintly, "I can't say what I was going to say, Jug, because I've forgotten what it was . . . that I was going to say."

Josephine was silent for a moment. She stared at a big cloud where the sun had been. Then she replied shortly, "I've forgotten too."

KATHERINE MANSFIELD: ARTIST IN MINIATURE
(Student Analysis)

ARTHUR NELSON (1922–1945) *

. . . The main characters of "The Daughters of the Late Colonel" are two spinsters, Constantia and Josephine, daughters of a retired colonel of the British foreign service; the effect of his death upon them is the immediate theme of the story. Comedy and tragedy are co-existent in them: their childlike helplessness is comic, providing the constant which is carried by the tone straight through the story. Comic also is the contrast between them: Constantia is vague and absent-minded, Josephine practical and efficient. But the *reason* for their common weakness is tragic: the narrow confinement of their lives due to environmental circumstances, and to their domination by, and utter dependence upon, their aged father. Similarly tragic is the reason for the contrast between them: Constantia has accepted her weakness in an escape from life, while Josephine has tried, unsuccessfully, to overcome hers. But the author never tells us this in so many words; she allows us to deduce it from her presentation of them in comic terms.

In the last episode, Constantia sums up her life by reflecting that "it had all taken place in a kind of tunnel." The word "tunnel" here denotes darkness, fear, confinement, monotony and purposelessness. To provide sufficient cause for the use of this word, the author must in the previous episodes have brought out, without destroying her humor, these five qualities, and must have made it clear that they have been characteristic of the *entire* lives of her characters. She must also have created a high enough tension to prevent bathos when it is finally resolved in the blank despair of this word. These two things are accomplished primarily by means of structure, setting and detail.

Her structure, . . . by its use of episode and retrospection simulates the action of memory, and gives a sense of extension in time. In this story, there are twelve episodes which seem at first to have no particular reason for their order, to be merely glimpses selected at random from the week following the Colonel's death. A second reading, however, shows their sequence to have a definite part in bringing out the implications which cause the tension.

The first six episodes reveal the sisters' pitiful plight as primarily the result of their father's domination; the last six show it in relation to the isolation of their past environment. Both groups of six form units in themselves, Episode 6 acting as a climax to the first group (in the sense that it is a focal point of the irony), Episode 12 to the second and to the whole story. Each group revolves around one of the only two episodes, 3 and 9, in which the Colonel actually appears, thus keeping the fact of his influence central throughout.

* Arthur Nelson wrote this essay while a first-year student of literature at Yale University. His essay was first published in the *Yale Literary Magazine* in April, 1941. It was reprinted in *The Art of Modern Fiction*. by Ray B. West Jr. and R. W Stallman (Rinehart, 1949).

Episode 1 contains in embryo all the elements of the story; it describes four trivial incidents, each one of which defines the two characters in both their similarity and their contrast. Their "thinking things out, talking things over, wondering, deciding, trying to remember where" in the first paragraph characterizes not just their present occupation, but that of their entire lives (monotony, lack of purpose). And Josephine's hysterical weeping at the same place twenty-three times in replying to their letters of condolence is, apart from its surface humor, an indication of the emotional release effected in her subconscious by the ironic words, "We miss our dear father so much." He has been at once the cause of their misery and their only reason for living: they miss him, but not as a father.

The second, third and fourth episodes begin the themes of loneliness and fear, emphasizing the irony of the death and its aftermath, as evidenced in the sisters' pathetic inability to understand reality or to cope with little emergencies. Episode 2 is taken up with the annoying personality of Nurse Andrews, whose laugh is "like a spoon tinkling against a medicine-glass"; Episode 4, with the equally objectionable minister, Mr. Farolles, bent on giving them a "little Communion" in the drawing-room. These are the only two people to enter the house in the week following the Colonel's death, making them symbolic of the meager contacts that have made up the social lives of Constantia and Josephine (as comes out in the last episode when Josephine reflects that she "had never met a single man except clergymen"). Episode 3, a brief paragraph squeezed in between 2 and 4, recounts the anticlimax of the death-scene: all father did when they came in was to open one eye which, after glaring at them a moment, simply "—went out." The brevity of this episode and its position between two longer ones give exactly the impression of a sharp, painful recollection, refusing to allow itself to be hidden among other less painful ones.

The fifth and sixth episodes, taking place respectively in a cab after the funeral and in father's vacated room, continue the fear theme begun in the third; they depict in vivid terms the hypnotic effect he continues to exercise over them even after death. In the sixth, the central tragedy of the story is summed up indirectly by Constantia when she says, exhorting Josephine not to open father's bureau, "Why shouldn't we be weak for once in our lives" and performs the "amazingly bold act" of removing the key. The irony here is that she is really exhorting Josephine to be weak not "for once," but as they have always been so; and her removal of the key is "bold" only in that it is an acceptance of her weakness.

We have now a half-idea of the reason beneath the superficial comedy, the next three episodes—seven, eight and nine—give us, retrospectively, the other half, heretofore barely suggested—the loneliness of their position as women in the man's world of the British colonial system. The separation of the family appears through their naïve conjectures about their brother Benny, away for years in Ceylon; their pitiful need for an object of affection, in the reënactment of one of their rare treats, "Cyril to tea." (Cyril is their nephew.) Episode 9 unites both the influential factors—father and environment—in one scene, wholly occupied with the attempts of Cyril and his aunts to explain to the deaf Colonel that his son Benny is still fond of meringues. It also repeats the anticlimax of Episode 3 in the ridiculous appearance of the old man who has inspired so much fear.

The several associations of the "tunnel" towards which the author has been working are by this time fairly evident; a last one, lack of purpose, now comes to the surface in two episodes which deal with the pettiness of the relation between the sisters and Kate, their servant. This acquires poignancy in the light of what we already know of their loneliness. Indecision and doubt dominate in these two episodes, preparing for the last one, in which all the implications of the previous eleven are drawn together into one persistent question: "What now?" Past and future merge with present as the tension resolves in the image of the tunnel, and the author, having built up step by step the walls behind and around her characters, now abandons them, with no sign of any opening in the endless darkness ahead.

It is, of course, through her use of suggestive detail that she links all these episodes together and creates the tension from which the emotional impact of the last episode is derived. Having in mind the general structure of the story, we are now in a position to see it as it should be seen—as an organic whole, and to analyze the function of detail in that whole. This function is, again, comparable to that in a painting: each individual sense-impression acts not only in the setting of the particular episode in which it occurs, but also in the pattern of which the episodes are parts. The episodic structure is merely a frame for this organization of detail. Similarly, every descriptive detail applied to the physical appearance of a character applies with equal aptness to her personality and even to her past experience.

Thus, when Constantia is described in the first episode as lying "like a statue," the image tells us, first of her physical position at the moment, then of her personality (stoical, apathetic), and finally of her life (bleak, cold, unvaried). This is reënforced by a passage in Episode 7, in which she is seen picturing to herself a native runner in Ceylon: "but there was something blind and tireless about Constantia's tall, thin fellow"; and again in the last episode, when she lifts her "big, cold hands" to catch the notes of the barrel-organ.

A very important detail is, in Episode 3, the dying Colonel's single glaring eye, which is a concentration into one image of the entire father-daughter relationship. It expresses, in addition to an old man's petulance, precisely the *hypnotic* influence he has had, and still has, over them, and lends a sharpness to the irony of his death.

This episode is linked with the other one (9) in which he appears by a deft use of detail. In Episode 3 his face is described as an angry purple in color. In 9, when they are trying to tell him about his son and meringues, he curves his hand over one ear "like a purple meringue-shell." The simile, drawn from the context, adds immediacy to the image—"shell" suggesting dryness, "purple," high blood-pressure—and fuses it with the memory of his death.

The fifth and sixth episodes are those in which fear is most stressed. The sense of confinement predominant in both of them (one in a "tight-buttoned cab," the other in the dead man's room) prepares for the tunnel-image; and the emotion is further intensified by the sharp contrast in color between them—one pitch black, the other cold white. The fear-suggesting properties of black are increased when, in the cab, Constantia is called "pale as a lemon in all that blackness." A lemon being the most commonplace of objects, it works here toward conveying, humorously, the negative quality of her personality, modifying the conception we had formed from the statue simile.

The ninth episode is, as we have seen, intensely ironic when we find that the Colonel is after all nothing more than a deaf old gentleman. But there is one suggestion—faint, easily overlooked—of something else: on his lap there lies "a beautiful pale yellow silk handkerchief." This one detail colors the whole episode, the whole story; for the pale handkerchief with its many associations of past youth, beauty and grandeur, here transforms the particular into the universal human tragedy of old age and faded glory.

But it is in the last episode that the greatest use of the symbolic associations of objects in the setting is made. Here the barrel-organ, providing the impulse that sends the sisters' minds back over the years, becomes, as Constantia lifts her hands to catch its "fountain of round, bright notes," identified with all the bright, sparkling world outside the confining wall of their experience. As they sit listening, a beam of sunlight enters the room, and we realize that this is its first appearance—that sunlight, in fact, has until now been absent altogether. This makes it here an extremely effective symbol of their first uncertain glimmer of hope; the way it has to *press, thieve* its way in makes the darkness, of which we had been only half aware, seem suddenly tangible, oppressive. The beam (their hope) now falls on a faded photograph, symbolic of decay and futility, reawakening their dead memories, and impressing upon them the unreality of their hope. When finally, in the last line, the sun disappears behind a cloud, returning them to darkness, it is actually the faded photograph which has made it disappear.

Such use of symbolic detail and insight comparison is the most important element of that elusive thing known as Katherine Mansfield's "style." The latter term includes, in fact, all the other separate elements—tension, structure, setting—and can be understood only after an analysis of these. Its effectiveness has been found to lie in its power of conveying an emotional experience all at once, in its entirety. As one critic has said, one gets the impression that her life has consisted of a continuous bombardment of "moments"; moments in which sounds, colors and smells unite to produce a single, sharp sensation. The words themselves, by following the broken, sporadic rhythm of thought-language, do not merely describe, but *are* the sensation. The way this happens can be illustrated by a single passage taken from the sixth episode of "The Daughters" (Kate has just caught them hesitating fearfully at the door—quickly they go in) :

> It couldn't be helped. That girl was . . . Then the door was shut behind them, but—but they weren't in father's room at all. They might have suddenly walked through the wall by mistake into a different flat together. Was the door just behind them? They were too frightened to look. Josephine knew that if it was it was holding itself tight shut; Constantia felt that, like the doors in dreams, it hadn't any handle at all. It was the coldness which made it so awful. Or the whiteness—which? Everything was covered. The blinds were down, a cloth hung over the mirror, a sheet hid the bed; a huge fan of white paper filled the fireplace. Constantia timidly put out her hand; she almost expected a snowflake to fall. Josephine felt a queer tingling in her nose, as if her nose was freezing. Then a cab klop-klopped over the cobbles below, and the quiet seemed to shake into little pieces.

This passage shows, first, how the words simulate thoughts to convey the emotion: "but—but they weren't in father's room at all." Then a quick insight comparison: "They might have suddenly walked through the wall by mistake . . ." to reenforce the emotion. The idea of the door as a malignant entity, holding itself shut, or without a handle, makes much more vivid the sense of confinement than objective description could have done. The coldness and whiteness, after a quick inventory of the specific white objects in the room to particularize the picture, now fuse into their logical product—snow, providing the excuse for Josephine's "tingling" nose, equally suggestive of fear and coldness. By this time the imagery has created what might be a peaceful winter scene, but for the confinement and other-worldliness of the first lines. The inter-reaction of the two—soft, soundless snow, against panic—captures so perfectly the silent blankness of a room in which some one has recently died that the quiet literally *does* "shake into little pieces," so great is the relief when a sound breaks the spell.

This last phrase is a typical device of Katherine Mansfield's: she has simply taken the ordinary expression, "the silence was broken," and revivified it by endowing it with a force commensurate to the emotion. No better instance could be found of the essential "secret" of her work; what she has done to a cliché here, she has done on a larger scale to the clichés of life.

A HUNGER-ARTIST *

FRANZ KAFKA (1883–1924)

In recent decades there has been a distinct falling-off in the interest shown in hunger-artists. Whereas in earlier times one could stage such exhibitions at one's own expense and be quite sure of success, today such a thing is utterly impossible. Those were other times. In those days the entire city occupied itself with the hunger-artist; the interest in him grew from fast day to fast day; every one wanted to see the hunger-artist at least once a day, and in the latter stages there were regular subscribers who sat before the small latticed cage for days on end. Performances were given at night too, in order to heighten the effect by torchlight. On sunny days the cage was carried out into the open, and on these occasions it was especially the children to whom the hunger-artist was exhibited. But whereas for the adults he was often no more than a source of amusement, of which they partook only because it was the stylish thing to do, the children would gaze upon him open-mouthed, holding one another by the hand for safety's sake, as he sat there on his straw, scorning even so much as a chair, deathly pale, dressed in black tights, his ribs protruding powerfully, sometimes nodding politely and answering questions with a forced smile, even thrusting his arm through the bars to let them feel his emaciation, then lapsing once more into complete self-absorption and paying attention to no one, ignoring even the striking of the clock which was the cage's sole decoration, looking straight before him with eyes almost closed, and sipping occasionally from a tiny glass of water to wet his lips.

Besides the spectators who merely came and went, there were also regular guards chosen by the public—usually butchers, for some remarkable reason, and always by threes—to whom was assigned the task of watching the hunger-artist day and night, lest he might succeed after all in surreptitiously partaking of nourishment. But that was no more than a formality, introduced to satisfy the masses, because the initiated were well aware that the hunger-artist would never under any circumstances, not even under compulsion, partake of any nourishment during the period of fasting. His

* Translation by M. L. Nielsen.

honor as an artist forbade such a thing. Of course not every guard could comprehend this. Sometimes there were groups of watchers who were very lax in their guard duty, who would purposely sit down together in a distant corner and absorb themselves in a game of cards with the obvious intention of allowing the hunger-artist a little refreshment which they seemed to believe he could produce from some secret supply. To the hunger-artist nothing was more painful than such guards; they filled him with unspeakable sadness; they made fasting terribly difficult for him. Sometimes he would overcome his weakness and sing during such a watch as this, sing as long as his strength held out, just to show the people how unjust were their suspicions. But it availed him little; in such cases they would simply marvel at the cleverness which enabled him to eat even while singing. Much more to his liking were the guards who sat down close to the cage, and not satisfied with the gloomy illumination of the hall, turned upon him the pocket torches with which they had been provided by the impresario. The bright light bothered him not at all. Sleep was impossible in any case, and he could always drowse a little, under any illumination and at any hour, even when the hall was noisy and overcrowded. He was only too willing to pass the night with such watchers entirely without sleep; he would put himself out to joke with them, to tell them tales of his wanderings or on the other hand to listen to their stories: anything to stay awake, to be able to show them again and again that he had nothing edible in his cage and that he was fasting as none of them could possibly do. But his happiest moment was when morning came and a sumptuous breakfast was brought to them at his expense, and he saw them fall upon it with the appetite of healthy men who had spent a tiresome night in wakeful watching. To be sure there were people who pretended to see in this breakfast an unseemly attempt to influence the guards, but that was going too far, and when they were asked whether they would be willing to take upon themselves the task of watching through the night for the sake of the thing itself and without the breakfast, they made a wry face, though they continued to harbor their suspicions just the same.

After all, this was simply one of the suspicions unavoidably connected with fasting. Obviously no one was in a position to spend every day and night as a watchman at the side of the hunger-artist, and no one could be sure from his own observation that the fasting was really uninterrupted and complete; only the hunger-artist himself could know that, and so only he who was the faster could be at the same time a completely satisfied spectator of his fasting. And yet for another reason he never was satisfied. Perhaps it wasn't fasting at all which made him so emaciated that some people to their great regret had to stay away because they couldn't bear the sight of him; perhaps his emaciation came solely from his dissatisfaction with himself. For the fact was that only he and no one else, not even the initiated, knew how easy a thing it was to fast. It was the easiest thing in the world. He didn't keep it a secret either, but no one would believe him. At best people said he was modest, but usually he was accused of being a publicity hound or even an out-and-out fraud for whom fasting was easy because he knew how to make it easy, and who had the cheek on top of that practically to admit as much. All this he was forced to accept; he had become accustomed to it in the course of years; but inside him was the constant gnawing of dissatisfaction.

And yet never, never once at the end of any hunger period—this all were forced to admit—had he left his cage willingly. The impresario had set forty days as the maximum period for fasting, beyond that he would never let the fasting go, not even in the great world centers—and for a very good reason. Experience had shown that for about forty days, through the use of gradually intensified publicity, the interest of a city could be brought to an ever higher pitch, but that at the end of that time public enthusiasm began to wane and a marked decrease in patronage became apparent. There were of course minor differences in this respect from city to city and country to country, but the rule was that forty days was the maximum time. And so on the fortieth day the door of the flower-bedecked cage was opened, an enthusiastic audience filled the amphitheater, a military band played, two doctors entered the cage to carry out the necessary measurements on the body of the hunger-artist, the results were announced to the hall through a megaphone, and finally there came two young ladies, happy in the knowledge that they and no one else had been chosen for the task, whose duty it was to lead the hunger-artist from his cage and down a few steps at the bottom of which stood a tiny table set with a carefully-chosen invalid's repast. And at this moment the hunger-artist invariably rebelled. He was willing enough to place his bony arms into the helping hands which the young ladies extended as they bent over him, but he didn't want to stand up. Why stop just now, at the end of forty days? He could have borne it much longer, immeasurably longer; why stop just now, at the point when his fasting was at its best—no, not even yet at its best. Why did they want to rob him of the honor of fasting on, of becoming not only the greatest hunger-artist of all time, which he probably was already, but of surpassing himself beyond measure, for he sensed that there was no limit to his capacity for fasting. Why did this throng, which pretended to marvel so at his feat, have so little patience with him? If he could bear to go on fasting, why could they not bear with him? Besides he was weary, his seat in the straw was comfortable, and now they wanted him to rouse himself, stand up, and go to the meal, the very thought of which induced in him a nausea which he was barely able to suppress out of respect for the women. And he looked into the eyes of the women who appeared so friendly but were in reality so cruel and wearily shook the head which was so much too heavy for the fragile neck. But now there happened the thing which always happened at this point. The impresario would come, and silently—for the music rendered speech impossible—he would raise his arms over the hunger-artist as if inviting heaven to look down upon its work here upon the straw, this pitiful martyr—and martyr the hunger-artist was, to be sure, though in an entirely different sense. Then he would grasp the hunger-artist about his frail waist, trying as he did to make it obvious by his exaggerated caution with what a fragile object he was dealing, and, after surreptitiously shaking him a little and causing his legs to wobble and his body to sway uncontrollably, would turn him over to the ladies, who had meanwhile turned as pale as death. Now the hunger-artist offered no further resistance. His head lay on his chest, as if it had rolled there and somehow inexplicably stuck fast; his torso was cavernous; his legs, impelled by the urge to self-preservation, were pressed tightly together at the knees, and yet his feet scraped the earth as if it were not real, as if they were seeking the real one. And the entire weight of his body, light though it was, rested upon one of the ladies, who, breathless and looking about imploringly for help (she had not pictured this post of honor thus), first tried to avoid contact with the hunger-artist by stretching her neck as far as possible, and then—since this availed her nothing and her more fortunate companion did nothing to help her, but simply contented herself with carrying the hand of the hunger-artist, a mere bundle of bones, in her own trembling hand—she broke into tears to the accompaniment of delighted laughter from the audience, and had to be relieved at her post by an attendant who had long been held in readiness. Then came the meal, a little of which the impresario managed to force down the half-unconscious hunger-artist, the while he chattered amiably to divert attention from his condition; then a toast was spoken to the public, which the impresario pretended had been whispered to him by the hunger-artist; the orchestra provided a mighty climax with a flourish of trumpets; the crowd broke up, and no one had the right to be dissatisfied with what he had seen, no one but the hunger-artist, always only he.

And so it went on for many years, with only brief intervals of recuperation. He lived in apparent glory, honored by the world, but for the most part filled with a gloomy melancholy which was deepened by the fact that no one understood it. And indeed what comfort could one offer him? What else could he wish for? And when sometimes a good-natured person appeared who felt sorry for him and tried to explain to him that his sadness was caused by the lack of food, it was quite likely—especially if the fasting period was far advanced—that the hunger-artist would answer by flying into a rage and terrifying all those around him by shaking the bars of his cage like a wild animal. But for such outbreaks the impresario had a method of punishment which he was very fond of employing. He would apologize to the assembled public on behalf of the hunger-artist and admit that his conduct could be pardoned only by understanding the irritability caused by fasting, an irritability which would be less easy to understand in a well-fed person; then he would lead logically to the hunger-artist's claim—also to be explained by his over-wrought state—that he could fast much longer, and would praise the lofty endeavor, worthy determination and great self-denial which were evidenced by this claim. But then he would attempt to refute this claim simply by passing around photographs—which at the same time were offered for sale—in which one could see the hunger-artist on the fortieth day of fasting, lying in bed and so weak that he was on the point of expiring. This perversion of the truth, so well known to the hunger-artist, and yet so unnerving when applied, was more than he could bear. That which was the effect of the premature ending of the fasting was here being set forth as its cause! Against this lack of understanding, this universal lack of understanding, it was impossible to fight. Each time he would stand at the bars and listen eagerly to what the impresario was saying, but always when the photographs were brought forth he would relax his hold on the bars and sink back onto the straw, and once more the reassured public could come near and view him undisturbed.

When the witnesses of such scenes thought back on them a few years later, they found it hard to understand themselves. For meanwhile the aforementioned transformation had taken place. Perhaps there were deep-lying reasons for it; but who was interested in seeking them out? At any rate, the pampered hunger-artist one day found himself abandoned by the pleasure-seeking multitude, which preferred to flock to other spectacles. Once again the impresario raced through half of Europe with him to see whether the old interest would not here and there manifest itself. But in vain; as if by some secret agreement a genuine dislike for fasting exhibitions had everywhere developed. In reality of course it couldn't have come as suddenly as all that, and now one tardily remembered certain warning signs which at the time, in the intoxication of success, had not been sufficiently heeded or sufficiently combatted—but it was too late now to do anything about it. To be sure it was certain that one day the time for fasting would come again, but for the living that was no comfort. What was the hunger-artist to do now?—He whom thousands had acclaimed couldn't put himself on display in the exhibition booths at small annual fairs, and as for going into some other profession he was not only too old but above all too fanatically devoted to fasting. And so he dismissed the impresario, the companion of a brilliant career, and hired himself out to a great circus. In order to spare his feelings, he did not even examine the terms of his contract.

A great circus with its huge throng of contrasting yet complementary men and animals and its masses of equipment can always find a place for another attraction, even a hunger-artist—that is, if his claims are modest enough. But in this case it was not only the hunger-artist who was engaged, but also his old and well-known name itself. Indeed it wasn't even possible to say, in view of the peculiar nature of this art which showed no flagging with increasing age, that a superannuated artist no longer at the height of his powers had taken refuge in a quiet position with a circus. On the contrary: the hunger-artist gave assurance that he could fast as well as he ever could—a thoroughly credible claim—indeed, he even maintained that, if allowed to go his own way (a privilege immediately granted to him), he would only now for the first time set the world in justifiable astonishment, a claim which, in view of the temper of times, forgotten by the hunger-artist in his zeal, evinced no more than a smile from those who were in the know.

Actually, however, even the hunger-artist did not lose sight of the true state of affairs, and he was not at all surprised when he saw that his cage was stationed not in the middle of the circus as a feature attraction but out in the vicinity of the menagerie, a place which in its own way certainly was accessible enough. Large, gaily-colored signs surrounded the cage and proclaimed what was to be seen there. During the intermissions in the performances, when the crowds thronged to see the animals fed, it was almost unavoidable that they should pass by the hunger-artist and pause there for a little. Perhaps they would have stayed there longer had it not been for the fact that the people who were pushing impatiently from the rear in the narrow alley way, not understanding the reason for the delay on the way to the eagerly-awaited stalls, made a longer and more leisurely view impossible. This explained too why the hunger-artist, though longing impatiently for these visits, which he naturally saw as his reason for existence, couldn't help feeling at the same time a certain apprehension. At first he could scarcely wait for the intermissions; he would note the approach of the throng with charmed anticipation; but only too soon he became convinced of the fact that again and again, without exception, they were on their way to the animals, and his experience in this matter overcame even the most stubborn, almost conscious self-deception. And this view of the throng from a distance continued to be the most agreeable one. For once they had reached his cage, he was immediately submerged in a sea of shouting, cursing people who formed ever-changing groups, one made up of those who wanted to view him at their leisure—not because they had any understanding for him, but simply impelled by a whim or out of sheer willfulness (and these soon became for the hunger-artist the more unpleasant)—and the other consisting of those who were bent on getting immediately to the stalls. Once the great crowd had passed by, there would come the stragglers, and these of course, for whom there was no obstacle to stopping had they only felt the desire, strode by with hurried steps in order not to be late at the stalls. And it was no more than a fortunate but infrequent stroke of luck when the father of a family would come by with his children, point to the hunger-artist, and explain in detail what it was all about; and he would tell about earlier times when he had been present at similar but incomparably finer exhibitions. But naturally the children, on account of inadequate preparation in the schools and in life, always remained without any understanding. What did fasting mean to them? And yet in the sparkling of their penetrating eyes they gave a hint of new and more merciful days to come. Perhaps, the hunger-artist would say to himself on such occasions, everything would be better if his station were not quite so close to the animals. It made the choice too easy for the people, to say nothing of the fact that the evil odors from the stalls, the restlessness of the animals at night, the sight of pieces of raw meat for the beasts of prey being carried by, and the screams of the animals at feeding time offended him and kept him in a constant state of depression. But he didn't venture to complain to the management; after all he owed to the animals the fact that he had so many visitors, among whom there might be now and then one destined for him. And who knew to what spot they might banish him if he reminded them of his existence, and of the fact that, when seen aright, he served only as a hindrance on the way to the animals.

A minor hindrance, to be sure, and one that was constantly growing smaller. People came to take for granted the novelty of having anyone demand attention for a hunger-artist in modern times, and this taking-for-granted spelled his doom. Let him fast with all the skill of which he was capable—and he did—but nothing could save him now, people simply passed him by. Just try to explain the art of fasting to some one! He who has no feeling for it simply cannot comprehend it. The beautiful signs grew dirty and illegible; they were torn down, and it occurred to no one to replace them. The little board showing the number of days of fasting achieved, which at first had been conscientiously changed, had remained the same for weeks on end, for the attendants had grown weary even of this little task. And so the hunger-artist fasted on without hindrance, as he had once dreamed of doing, and was able to do it without difficulty, just as he had once predicted, but no one counted the days; no one, not even the hunger-artist himself, knew how great his achievement actually was, and his heart grew heavy. And if on occasion some idler stopped, ridiculed the old numbers on the board, and spoke of fraud, it was the most stupid lie which indifference and inborn malice could possibly invent, because it was not the hunger-artist who was cheating; he was doing his duty honorably, but the world was cheating him of his reward.

And yet more days passed, but that too had its end. Once one of the managers happened to notice the cage, and he asked the attendants why such a good serviceable cage with its putrid straw should be left standing unused. No one could say, until one of them, with the help of the numbered board, remembered the hunger-artist. The straw was probed with poles, and inside they found the hunger-artist. "You're still fasting?" asked the manager. "When in heaven's name will you be done?" "Forgive me, all of you," whispered the hunger-artist. "Certainly," said the manager, and he pointed to his head with his finger to indicate the hunger-artist's condition to the attendants, "we forgive you." "I always wanted you to admire my fasting," said the hunger-artist. "And we do admire it," replied the manager obligingly. "But you shouldn't admire it," said the hunger-artist. "Well, then, we don't admire it," said the manager, "but why shouldn't we admire it?" "Because I have to fast, I can't help myself," said the hunger-artist. "Just listen to that," said the manager; "and why can't you help yourself?" "Because," said the hunger-artist, and he lifted his dainty head a little, and, thrusting his lips forward as if for a kiss, spoke directly into the manager's ear so that no word would be lost, "because I could find no food to my liking. If I had found it, believe me, I should have caused no stir, I should have eaten my fill just as you do, and all others." Those were his last words, but in his glazed eyes there remained the firm, though no longer proud, conviction that he was still fasting.

"Well, now clean things up!" said the manager, and they buried the hunger-artist together with the straw. And into the cage they put a young panther. It was perceptibly refreshing even to the dullest temperament to see this wild animal hurl itself about in this cage which so long had been desolate. He lacked for nothing. Without any delay, the keepers brought him just the kind of food he craved. And he appeared not even to miss his freedom. This noble body, healthy to the point of bursting, seemed in fact to carry its own freedom around with it (a freedom which appeared to reside somewhere in the region of its teeth) ; and its joy in living issued forth from its throat with such fierceness that it wasn't easy for those who watched it to stand firm. But they overcame their hesitation, crowded about the cage, and just couldn't tear themselves away.

AN INTERPRETATION OF FRANZ KAFKA'S
"A HUNGER-ARTIST"

R. W. STALLMAN (1911–   )

"A Hunger-Artist" is an allegory, but Kafka's method is quite different from that of such an allegorist as Bunyan. In *Pilgrim's Progress* each character represents the trait, virtue, or vice which his name signifies—Christian, Faithful, Envy, Lord Hategood, and so on. Bunyan manipulates these characters through a story whose every element has a direct meaning in his moral parable. Further, these meanings are constant throughout the story: Faithful is always faithful, Envy is always envious, Appolion is always the epitome of evil, the town of Vanity Fair is so called because *"all* that is there sold, or that cometh thither, is vanity." In the allegories of the quite different but equally familiar *Gulliver's Travels* the same constancy of image is found. The rope-skipping Lilliputians satirize political preferment; the dispute between the Big-Endians and the Little-Endians satirizes theological controversy. Both sets of terms are equally fantastic, but the one having to do with egg-breaking has no connection with the one having to do with rope-jumping. There is no overlap of meaning from one unit into the next.

Kafka's method is very different. He employs symbols rather than allegorical images. He assigns mutiple meanings to his realistic or fantastic details; their significance is therefore not constant, nor can they be paraphrased back into point-by-point equivalents. As D. H. Lawrence puts it, "An allegorical image has a *meaning.* Mr. Facing-both-ways has a meaning. But I defy you to lay your finger on the full meaning of Janus, who is a symbol." Kafka employs continuous symbolization. Therefore we find his images meaning different things not only at different times but *at the same time.* There is a constant interweaving of symbolical meanings, an overlapping of allegorical patterns. As we shall see, it is possible to read the allegory of "A Hunger-Artist" on at least three different levels; there is never a time when we can say that any of its elements means *precisely and exactly this.*

The same thing is true of the story pattern. Bunyan and Swift employ narratives that proceed in logical order from their assumptions. Bunyan assumes that Christian will make a journey through a land which never existed to a City not of this life;

Swift assumes the tiny world of Lilliput and the gigantic one of Brobdingnag. Having postulated these, however, they stick to their facts; the frame of reference is always constant. It is no accident that *Pilgrim's Progress* and *Gulliver's Travels* have been read as adventure stories by generations of children happily ignorant of allegory and satire.

Kafka is no more bound by precision in his narrative than in his symbols. He has a fantastic genius for imparting a sense of everyday reality while completely ignoring everyday logic. His symbolic objects do not conform to the nature of objects in the actual world; they are subject not to the determinate laws of nature, but rather to the laws of that unique world in which they have their special function. The hunger-artist hires himself out to a great circus, an enormous, complex, and efficient machine which nevertheless contrives to forget his existence so completely that he is finally discovered only by probing into the "putrid straw" of his "empty" cage. Obviously this is a circus of fantasy; like the rest of Kafka's "facts," it is an imaginary phenomenon that belongs to a dream world. In "A Hunger-Artist" the laws of physics and biology are defied, the facts of human existence distorted. Though all the details are apparently simple and commonplace, they become, on closer examination, elusive, charged with multiple significance. It is impossible to keep Kafka's facts as facts or to suppress or minimize their metaphorical character. As a starting point for this analysis of "A Hunger-Artist," here is a matter-of-fact account of the story stripped of interpretation:

The story is about a once-popular spectacle staged for the entertainment of a pleasure-seeking public: the exhibition of a professional "hunger-artist" performing in a cage of straw his stunt of "fasting." His cage's sole decoration is a clock. His spectators see him as a trickster and common circus-freak and therefore they expect him to cheat, to break fast on the sly. But fasting is his sole reason for existing, his life purpose; not even under compulsion would he partake of food. For him, to fast is the easiest thing he can do; and so he says, but no one believes in him. Because the public distrusts him, he is guarded—usually by three butchers —and prevented from fasting beyond a forty-day period, not for humane reasons, but only because patronage stops after that time. His guards tempt him with food and sometimes mistreat him; yet they breakfast on food supplied at his expense! A great public festival celebrates his achievement, and thus he is "honored by the world." But when he is removed from his cage he collapses in a rage, not from hunger, but from having been cheated of the honor of fasting on and on and on and of becoming thus "the greatest hunger-artist of all time." Though emaciated almost to the point of death, he quickly recovers and after brief intervals of recuperation performs again and again.

Nowadays, however, he has been abandoned for other spectacles. People visit his cage in the circus tent, but only because it is next to the menagerie. His spectators are fascinated by the animals. All's changed: there is, apparently, no clock, and the once beautiful signs to announce the purpose of his act have been torn down. Now no tally is kept of the number of fasting days achieved. There are no guards. "And so the hunger-artist fasted on without hindrance, as he had once dreamed of doing . . . just as he had once predicted, but no one counted the days; no one, not even the hunger-artist himself, knew how great his achievement was and his heart grew heavy." Thus the world robs him of his reward. Indifference replaces admiration and on this note he expires. He is buried with the straw of his cage and replaced by a panther, who devours fiercely the food he naturally craves. The people crowd about his cage.

We notice that the facts in this "matter-of-fact" account are not in themselves complete or sufficient, and that our attempt to take them at their matter-of-fact or literal level is quite impossible. They seem to compete with each other and to thrust us beyond their literal properties into the plane of their allegorical significance. That clock seems to be simply a clock; it does not apparently represent anything else. And yet no literal meaning can be ascribed to that bizarre clock. It strikes the hour just like a real clock, but, so to speak, it does not appear to tick. The life of this hunger-artist is unclocked. He exists outside time, and periodically he survives starvation sieges no ordinary man could endure. (Actually, a calendar would be the logical means for reckoning the artist's fasting days.) As for the other facts, these objects likewise suggest symbolic significance. It is impossible to reduce Kafka's facts to a single self-consistent system of meaning. The trouble is that his meanings emerge at several planes at once, and the planes are inter-connected. No complete paraphrase is possible.

We cannot confine Kafka's meaning to a single circle of thought. The plight of the hunger-artist in his cage represents the plight of the artist in the modern world: his dissociation from the society in which he lives. By this reading of the story, "A Hunger-Artist" is a sociological allegory. But we can also interpret the hunger-artist to represent a mystic, a holy man, or a priest. By this reading the story allegorizes in historical perspective the plight of religion. A third possible interpretation projects us into a metaphysical allegory: the hunger-artist represents spirit, man as a spiritual being; the panther, in contrast, represents matter, the animal nature of man. If the story is translated into metaphysical terms, the division is between the spiritual and the physical; into religious terms, between the divine and the human, the soul and the body; into sociological terms, between the artist and his society. Kafka's blueprint—the groundplan of ideas upon which he has built this structure of parables—is tool-marked with these three different systems of thought.

Consider first the story as an allegory of the dilemma of the artist. He is set in contrast to the multitude. The people who attend his exhibitions of fasting cannot comprehend his art. "Just try to explain the art of fasting to some one! He who has no feeling for it simply cannot comprehend it." The artist starves himself for the sake of his vision. He has faith in his vision, faith in himself, and integrity of aesthetic conscience. As the initiated alone understood, "the hunger-artist would never under any circumstances, not even under compulsion, partake of any nourishment during the period of fasting. His honor as an artist forbade such a thing." It is his vision, solely this, which nourishes him. Of course the artist can "fast" as no one else can do. It's not everyone who is an artist. We concede, "in view of the peculiar nature of this art which showed no flagging with increasing age," the claim he makes of limitless capacity for creating works of art. But if his public is devoid of any sympathetic understanding of the artist and of his art, if his public has no faith in him, how then can he cling to this faith in himself? It is because his public is an unbeliever that the artist is in a cage (the cage symbolizes his isolation). Society and the artist—each disbelieves in the other. And so the artist comes to disbelieve, finally, in himself; he cannot survive in isolation.

The hunger-artist is emaciated because of the disunity within himself, which is the result of his dissociation of soul from body, and because of the disjunction between himself and his society. It is his denial of the world of materiality that is the source of his gnawing doubt and "constant state of depression." He repudiates half of life, and the multitude repudiate him. The public reject the emaciated body of the artist for the healthy body of the panther—they reject art for life itself. These two occupants of the cage, the purely spiritual and the purely bestial, represent, then, the dual nature of man. The people outside the cage, with whom he is also contrasted, crave the same food as the panther. For them, as for the beast, their joy in living issues from their throat—and from their belly. These human and bestial beings represent the sensuous physical realm of matter. They are all-flesh, whereas the hunger-artist is no-flesh. In the one we have pure matter; in the other, pure spirit. But the hunger-artist, as pure soul, is a failure. Though he is apparently free from those gnawing dissatisfactions which our purely physical appetites create in us again and again, nevertheless he is not entirely free from the claims of the body, from the claims of matter, from the claims of the world in which he lives. At the same time that he denies the evil natural social world he longs for some recognition of his fasting from the public; he wants the people to crowd around his cage. Finally, "though longing impatiently for these visits [of the people on their way to the eagerly-awaited stalls], which he naturally saw as his reason for existence, [he] couldn't help feeling at the same time a certain apprehension." He apprehends the truth that he who is the faster cannot be "at the same time a completely satisfied spectator of his fasting." He sees that an existence of pure spirituality is impossible to man. He sees that this insatiable hunger with which he, as artist or as mystic, is possessed is at bottom only the sign of his maladjusted, and therefore imperfect, soul.

Compete detachment from physical reality is spiritual death. This statement sums up the meaning of "A Hunger-Artist" in so far as the story is an allegory about the nature of man. What is man, matter or spirit? The story might be described as a kind of critique of this philosophical problem. Spirit and matter—each is needed to fulfill the other. At the moment of his death the hunger-artist recognizes his failure as an artist or creator. For this super-annuated artist there is no possibility of resurrection because in our present-day world not spirit but matter is recognized. The fact that matter has today triumphed over spirit is recognized by the dying hunger-artist as he confesses his secret. I had to fast, he admits, because I could find no food to my liking. Fasting, you see, was my destiny. But " 'If I had found it [e.g., food to my liking], believe me, I should have caused no stir, I should have eaten my fill just as you do, and all the others.' Those were his last words, but in his glazed eyes there remained the firm, though no longer proud, conviction that he was still fasting." Here, then, is the key to his enigma. Cut off from the multitude, the artist performing his creative act (his fasting) has to die daily and be daily reborn. This is a martyrdom, but for what purpose? The creative artist cannot also be his own public; he dies when no one cares that he and his art should live. Devotion to an aesthetic or spiritual vision cannot be an end in itself. Pure creativeness is impossible, even as absolute spirituality is impossible. The creative imagination must feed upon all reality. For art is but a vision of reality. The artist, no less than the mystic-faster, must live in the world of mundane life. Art requires the material conditions of life, and these conditions nourish it. Life is at once the subject of art and its wellspring.

It is the clock in the hunger-artist's cage that triumphs over the artist. It is time that triumphs over the very one who denies the flux of time, which is our present reality. The clock in his cage is a mockery of the artist's faith in the immortality of his creative act or vision, a mockery of his faith in his art as an artifice of eternity. The tragedy of Kafka's hunger-artist is not that he dies, but that he fails to die into life. As he dies he seeks recognition from those whom he has all his life repudiated: " 'I always wanted you to admire my fasting,' said the hunger-artist." It is his confession that spirit has no absolute sovereignty over matter, soul has no absolute sovereignty over body, and art has no absolute sovereignty over life. Throughout the story the author laments the passing of our hunger-artists, their decline and extinction in our present-day civilization. But nonetheless throughout the story all the logic is weighted against this hunger-artist's efforts at autarchy. In his last words we are given his confession that the artist must come to terms with life, with the civilization in which he lives, the world of total reality. "Forgive me, all of you," he whispers to the circus manager, as though in a confessional before some priest. And they forgive him. They forgive him for his blasphemy against nature.

In the same way that Kafka's sets of facts can be translated into allegorical terms at the philosophical and aesthetic levels of meaning, so too in terms of the religious allegory the multiple meanings of the facts overlap. Our post-Renaissance world has discarded the philosopher, the artist, and the mystic. The hunger-artist as mystic-faster is dead. Call him priest or artist, he has been rejected by the "pleasure-seeking multitude" and replaced by other amusements; for instance, by the exhibition of a live panther. It was different in times past. For example, in the Middle Ages and in the Renaissance he "lived in apparent glory, honored by the world." Then he had his patron. (The patron of the artist was the impresario.) He had his critics, the butchers who guarded him out of the public distrust of his creative act. And he had his historians, the attendants who recorded his creative act or kept count of his remarkable performances. In those times he was at least admired for his achievements as an imitator of life. In his cage he imitated a panther: ". . . deathly pale, dressed in black tights, his ribs protruding powerfully, sometimes nodding politely and answering questions with a forced smile, even thrusting his arm through the bars to let them feel his emaciation . . . and paying attention to no one . . . looking straight before him with eyes almost closed. . . ." But what a poor imitation of real life he presented! In those times he was at least celebrated (albeit, not without hypocrisy), honored by rituals conscientiously enacted upon appointed fast days. Consider this hunger-artist as mystic-faster or priest. At one time, everyone attended his services daily. Regular subscribers sat, as in church pews, "before the small latticed cage for days on end." Everyone pretended to marvel at his holy fast. Actually, however, not one worshiper had faith. Nevertheless, despite this sham of faith in him, he submitted again and again to crucifixion by these pretenders to faith. He was a martyr for his divine cause. The multitude, because "it was the stylish thing to do," attended his "small latticed cage"—they attended it as they might a confessional box. But the multitude, since it does not understand what Faith is, has no sin to confess. The hunger-priest hears no confession. (Ironically it is he who, in dying, confesses.) In short, all mankind—apart from a few acolytes to his cult, disbelieves this Christ who many times died for man's sake. And when he dies, see how these disbelievers exploit the drama of his death. Here is Kafka's parody on the drama of the Virgin mourning the loss of her Son.

> But now there happened the thing which always happened at this point. The impresario would come, and silently—for the music rendered speech impossible— he would raise his arms over the hunger-artist as if inviting heaven to look down upon its work here upon the straw, this pitiful martyr—and martyr the hunger-artist was, to be sure, though in an entirely different sense. Then he would grasp the hunger-artist about his frail waist, trying as he did to make it obvious by his exaggerated caution with what a fragile object he was dealing, and after surreptitiously shaking him a little and causing his legs to wobble and his body to sway uncontrollably, would turn him over to the ladies, who had meanwhile turned as pale as death.

The ladies who so cruelly sentimentalize over his martyrdom represent sympathy without understanding; a sympathy which is devoid of understanding is mere self-sentiment. One of the ladies weeps—but not for him. She breaks into tears only in shame for having touched him.

> And the entire weight of his body, light though it was, rested upon one of the ladies, who, breathless and looking imploringly for help (she had not pictured this post of honor thus), first tried to avoid contact with the hunger-artist by stretching her neck as far as possible, and then . . . she broke into tears to the accompaniment of delighted laughter from the audience . . .

It is a mock lamentation that these two Marys perform.

NOTES AND QUESTIONS

I: The Short Story

3. THE CATBIRD SEAT
JAMES THURBER

What weapon does Mr. Martin have to "rub out" Mrs. Barrows when he calls at her apartment? He considers using the metal paper knife but on trying its point he finds: "It was *blunt*. It wouldn't do." Comment on the word *blunt*—what does it suggest about Mr. Martin? And about Mrs. Barrows? Why is Mrs. Barrows' first name "Ulgine"? Explain the title of the story, "The Catbird Seat." What is suggested by the name "Martin"? What prepares us to know that Mr. Martin's little scheme is bound to succeed? And why should Mr. Fitweiler discredit Mrs. Barrows' story? In what sense is the ending of the story a surprise ending? Does it involve a situation that is reversed, a turnabout?

8. A TRIP TO CZARDIS
EDWIN GRANBERRY

10.40, Okeechobee: A large shallow lake in Florida.

This story is told from a sharply limited point of view—that of the boy Jim. Can you suggest any reason why Granberry preferred to use the third person pronoun rather than the first person? Notice that the story communicates on two levels—the level of the boys and the level of the reader who sees and understands more than they do. Is the style of the story appropriate to both levels?

What are the differences between Jim and Dan'l? Why is it right that the author tells us nothing of the crime for which the father is to be executed? Do we learn all that is necessary about the mother? Why is the opening effective? Does it parallel the later psychological "awakening" that is part of the theme of the story? Is there any symbolism in the story, or any meaning beyond the obvious tragic one? For instance, should the pomegranate tree be interpreted symbolically?

13. TWO FRIENDS
GUY DE MAUPASSANT

Are the descriptions of spring mornings and autumn afternoons, near the beginning of the story, necessary? Is the brief political discussion between the two friends significant? In what way does Mount Valerien serve as a symbol? What is the character of the Prussian officer? How is he like Mount Valerien? Is there any difference in the character of the two friends? Is there any similarity intended between war and fishing? Is the irony of M. Sauvage's pleasantry about offering fried fish made too obvious? How does Maupassant avoid sentimentality?

17. A LITTLE CLOUD
JAMES JOYCE

Whereas in "Two Friends" character was revealed through similarity and the description of external events, in "A Little Cloud" the revelation comes chiefly through contrast and the description of internal workings of a mind. Are there other differences in method? What is the "Cloud" of the title? What is the significance of all the diminutives in the story—"little cloud," "Little Chandler," "a little man," "childish white teeth," "an infant hope," "little house," etc.? Is Chandler psychologically mature? Why is his admiration for Gallaher phrased in clichés—"fearless accent," "unspoiled by success," "heart was in the right place," "deserved to win," "he had lived, he had seen the world," etc.? Could Chandler ever become a poet? (Compare this portrait of a would-be poet with what is indicated by the selections in the part of this book entitled "The Poem and the Creative Process.") What is significant in his liking the particular poem by Byron that is quoted in the story? Point out the stereotyped responses in Little Chandler's attitude toward his environment and toward his supposed ambition.

What is symbolic of immaturity during his walk to Corless's? Is his rebelliousness against life much less inchoate and childish than that of his wailing baby son? Now consider the contrasting Gallaher. Is he deserving of anyone's admiration? What do you think of his "talent" as evidenced in the remark about his "considering cap" that so impresses Little Chandler? What do we learn about Gallaher's standards of value from his remarks about Paris, from his observations of life in Berlin and elsewhere? Is Gallaher adolescent in his own way? Define the similarities and differences between the two men.

26. THE GLOVES
COLETTE AUDRY

In this brief story the characters of three persons are skilfully revealed through the tensions that develop among them, tensions that are frequently indicated by references to hands, eyes, etc. Define the tensions between the detective and the manager, the manager and the woman, the woman and the detective. There are also internal conflicts—between the woman and her gloved, strangely detached hands, "which presumed to have a life of their own"; between the manager and his voice—"he seemed to be listening to his own voice." Is there anything similar in the detective? Why does the manager conceal the theft of the gloves by the detective? Why is it significant that he "felt his hands grow wet"? What is significant in the fact that towards the end the woman is able to hold the detective "under her stare"? Why does the woman steal the ashtray? Why does the detective steal the gloves? Why does the manager tear up the filing card?

31. THE BLACK GODMOTHER
JOHN GALSWORTHY

32.1, Osmunda: A species of fern found in bogs and marshy woods in Britain.

34.13, Death of Procris: A painting by Piero di Cosimo (1462–1521), Florentine artist. Procris, the wife of Cephalus, was accidentally and unknowingly killed by her husband during a hunt in mistake for an animal. According to one version of the myth the name of the dog silently watching her die was Lelops. In the painting there is a satyr at her head, Lelops at her feet, and several other dogs in the background, indifferent to the event.

This brief story could be called an anec-

dote or parable. What are the characteristics of these types? Note the statement of the theme at the beginning. Is there any suspense in "The Black Godmother"? What is the significance of the title? Why is a narrator used? What is his character? What kind of persons are his listeners? Why is the setting left indefinite? What would the story lose if there was no black retriever sitting beside the narrator? Is the ending effective? Why? In what way does this story have wider implications than a simple tale about a particular dog?

34. AMY FOSTER
JOSEPH CONRAD

Although there are striking similarities in theme and incident between this story (published 1901) and "The Black Godmother" (published 1912), the differences are much more important. Both stories concern a fear-motivated cruelty toward a misunderstood victim, but "Amy Foster" includes in its theme many more aspects of human behavior than does the other story. Both of the victims are in a sense castaways, both suffer beatings by a succession of persons who misinterpret actions of a victim who is unable to communicate, both are forcibly "captured," both utter strange cries, both (after an interval of kindness from one person) die wretchedly and alone and unmourned. Moreover, both stories are told to friends by narrators who took it upon themselves to find out the complete stories, and both stories are in a sense told to illustrate an abstract truth or "moral." On the other hand, the differences though less easy to enumerate are nevertheless all important: they are responsible for the fact that Conrad's story is a piece of great literature whereas Galsworthy's, though interesting, is less important. The differences are to be looked for in the vividness of setting, the complexity of theme and characterization, the emotional power, the closely integrated structure, and the overtones and general symbolic implications of Conrad's story.

Close study of the two stories will be well repaid with a better appreciation of the characteristics of great literary art. Many writers could produce a "Black Godmother," but only a master could create "Amy Foster."

Consider first the way Conrad presents his narrative. The story of Amy and Yanko has happened quite a long time previously.

It was told to a friend by Dr. Kennedy, and is being retold to the reader by this friend as author-narrator. What are some of the possible reasons for this deliberate indirection? On the practical level, it is at once clear that neither Amy nor Yanko could tell their own stories, since both are inarticulate victims of forces they not only cannot control but cannot even define. Kennedy as a narrator has many advantages: he is intelligent and interested, while being possessed of some scientific detachment; he is too busy for active participation, but as a doctor he would be called in at moments of great crisis; he seeks understanding but is not omniscient, and therefore some mysteries can convincingly remain unexplained; etc. But, at the same time, Kennedy is himself an actor in the main story; he is involved in the fate of Yanko; he has even a certain responsibility for it, along with the residents of the district. On the other hand, the author-narrator, Kennedy's friend, is a visitor, capable of including Kennedy in the same perspective as the others. Now, why are the two lapses of time desirable—the lapse between the events and Kennedy's telling them to his friend, and the lapse between the friend's hearing the story and telling it as author?

Does not the deliberate indirection in the presentation of the story correspond to one of the themes of the story? This theme is the desire for and simultaneously the difficulty of understanding human nature and communicating between human beings—coupled with the fact that not one but many persons are involved in understanding the life of every man. Notice, for instance, how we constantly see Yanko in at least two simultaneous ways—through the unfriendly eyes of the fear-ridden country folk and through the sympathetic eyes of the indignant doctor. As a matter of fact, one should probably add to this double vision the view of the author-narrator and even of the readers, since all participate in the imaginative comprehension of Yanko. In this connection one might ask what Conrad considered to be the role of imagination in life—at least as seen in this story.

What is the character of Dr. Kennedy? How does he differ from his friend to whom he tells the story? What is gained by introducing Kennedy's story as Conrad does—first giving the setting, then the meeting with Amy on the doctor's rounds without the friend knowing anything about her, followed by the description of Yanko (without his being named or his connection with Amy stated) as a remembered contrast to the plodding workman, the later resuming of the story in the doctor's study, and so on?

Consider the setting itself—the opening description, the drive, the doctor's study with its wide casement, etc. What is gained by such shifts of place? What is the significance of the description (by the friend, notice, not by Kennedy) of the sunset's glow upon the horses and wagon, a description which comes just after the meeting with Amy and the doctor's friend's listless designation of her as "a dull creature"? What is the significance of the next description of the "joyous and sombre aspect" of the grasslands, which is followed by the first description of Yanko as he passes along the road in vibrant contrast to the stolid villagers? In what way are references to the sea used in the story (apart from the shipwreck scenes)? What other examples are there of Conrad's use of nature and of physical details to comment on or influence or objectify human behavior?

Conrad adroitly uses parallel events to create the sense of inevitability and to enrich the emotional texture of the story. For instance, Amy's treatment of the parrot parallels her later treatment of Yanko; her fearful flight through the night with her child parallels that of Yanko after the shipwreck; Yanko's dying in the rain and the dark, face down in a puddle of water, parallels his near-dying in the shipwreck; Yanko on his straw pallet covered with horse blankets parallels Little Yanko in his cot at the end of the story. Are there other similar parallels? Notice the different occasions on which Kennedy uses the comparison of "a bird caught in a snare."

Why was Amy attracted to Yanko? Why was she unmoved by criticism of him before marriage, but affected afterwards? Why were the villagers opposed to him? Answering "fear of the Incomprehensible" or some equivalent is inadequate, since the "why" is merely pushed farther back: *Why* are men afraid of the incomprehensible? Is Kennedy satisfied that he understands these questions? Is the author?

Perhaps the story is really one on the fundamental mystery of life, the mystery of human relationships of love and hate, pity and fear. The story may also have autobiographical significance, since Conrad himself, as a Pole who spoke no English until he was a mature man, was, at one stage in his life, like Yanko, a man isolated by language and customs from the people among whom his lot was cast. Taking a larger perspective, one might ask if the story could symbolically represent the life of every individual, dangerously arriving at birth into an incomprehensible world of violence and strangeness, a world including some pity and love but more cruelty and indifference? Could it be the story of Mankind emerging out of mystery and a dim past into an incomprehensible world with which it is forced to make terms as best it can—"cast out mysteriously by the sea to perish in the supreme disaster of loneliness and despair"—a picture of man's fate not too far removed from that advanced by some thinkers of the past half century?

The end of the story—suggesting resurrection of the parent in the child—is worth noting. How does it serve to extend the dimensions of the story?

52. THE SECOND DEATH
GRAHAM GREENE

The Gospel of St. Luke (7:11–15) describes a miracle by Jesus: "And it came to pass the day after, that he went into a city called Nain, and many of his disciples went with him, and much people. Now when he came nigh to the gate of the city, behold, there was a dead man carried out, the only son of his mother, and she was a widow. . . . And when the Lord saw her, he had compassion on her, and said unto her, 'Weep not.' And he came and touched the bier: and they that bare him stood still. And he said, 'Young man, I say unto thee, Arise.' And he that was dead sat up, and began to speak. And he delivered him to his mother."

Is it significant that not only the narrator in Greene's story, but also the mother and son, remain nameless? Is this a story mainly about the son or about the narrator? Explain. Do the early references to the keen eyesight of the narrator sufficiently prepare for the ending of the story? Why does Greene depict all three principal characters as far from admirable persons, a feature without parallel in the Biblical story?

Compare this story with "The Demon Lover" (p. 55). Are the two stories best described as psychological or supernatural in substance?

55. THE DEMON LOVER
ELIZABETH BOWEN

This story, like "The Second Death" (p. 52) and "Ligeia" (p. 105), involves mysterious and/or supernatural events. How important is the setting—the city damaged by bombing, the abandoned street, the silence, etc.? Although we are told that "no human eye watched Mrs. Drover's return," what subsequent details subtly imply that she is not "alone"? Through what stages does the author achieve a rising sense of tension?

In what way is it significant that "under no conditions" could Mrs. Drover remember her lover's face? The letter is signed "K" and addressed to "Kathleen." What may be suggested by this identity of initials? Could Mrs. Drover be viewed as a mentally disturbed person imagining unreal terrors? What aspects of the story can be regarded as symbolic?

59. THE UPTURNED FACE
STEPHEN CRANE

59.6, Spitzbergen infantry: Though "The Upturned Face" was inspired by Crane's experience in the Spanish American War, the action and setting belong to no particular war. The "Spitzbergen infantry" and the "Rostina sharpshooters" are entirely imaginary.

Would this story be significantly altered if no bullets were flying overhead? What is the difference between the two officers? Why does the adjutant cry, "let us say something—while he can hear us"? Have the opening words of the prayer any connection with the reluctance to cover the upturned face? Why does Lean become angry at the end? Compare this story with the poem by Owen on p. 772.

62. A CLEAN, WELL-LIGHTED PLACE
ERNEST HEMINGWAY

64.30, bodegas: wine-cellars. **41, nada y pues nada:** nothing, and . . . well . . . nothing. **49, Otro loco mas:** another crazy one. **65.6, copita:** little cup.

What are the main "scenes" that constitute the structure of this story? How is contrast used as the method of developing both characters and theme? Why is the contrast between youth and age not fundamental? In the brief dialogue—"He was in despair." "What about?" "Nothing."—which waiter answers "Nothing"? Defend your opinion. How do these speeches foreshadow the whole later development of the story? Why is the emphasis placed on "a clean, well-lighted place" rather than on an entertaining or lively place? Would amusement cure the despair that arises from the loss of faith in a meaningful world? What, then, is symbolized by "a clean, well-lighted place," which both the old man and the old waiter value so highly? What is indicated by the fact that although the old man drinks brandy, the old waiter drinks coffee in a "bright and pleasant" coffee bar? Is the difference in drinks or the similarity in surroundings the essential? Are the values by which the younger waiter lives very admirable ones? What is the effect achieved by the author in using such a spare and simple style to deal with a rather large philosophical theme? Would the story be more effective if the theme were stated more directly? Why, or why not?

65. PASTE

HENRY JAMES

Henry James, in his Preface to *The Author of Beltraffio . . . And Other Tales* (London: Macmillan Co., 1922), wrote as follows:

The origin of "Paste" . . . was to consist but of the ingenious thought of transposing the terms of one of Guy de Maupassant's admirable *contes*. In "La Parure" ["The Necklace"] a poor young woman, under "social" stress, the need of making an appearance on an important occasion, borrows from an old school friend, now much richer than herself, a pearl necklace which she has the appalling misfortune to lose by some mischance never afterwards cleared up. Her life and her pride, as well as her husband's with them, become subject, from the hour of the awful accident, to the redemption of their debt; which, effort by effort, sacrifice by sacrifice, franc by franc, with specious pretexts, excuses, a rage of desperate explanation of their failure to restore the missing object, they finally obliterate—all to find that their whole consciousness and life have been convulsed and deformed in vain, that the pearls were but highly artful "imitation" and that their passionate penance has ruined them for nothing. It seemed harmless sport simply to turn the situation round—to shift, in other words, the ground of the horrid mistake, making this a matter not of

a false treasure supposed to be true and precious, but of a real treasure supposed to be false and hollow: though a new little "drama," a new setting for *my* pearls—and as different as possible from the other—had of course withal to be found.

For a person who has not read de Maupassant's story, James's summary of the plot might be supplemented by making clearer one important point. Not very long after the loss of the necklace, the young woman and her husband, by selling and pawning their possessions and borrowing a huge sum of money, were able to get a jeweller to produce a copy or imitation of the lost necklace—in real pearls, of course, such as they thought the lost necklace had consisted of. This they returned to the original owner who thereafter for years wore a necklace of real pearls thinking them to be paste. Not until a lifetime of grinding penury had at last repaid all the borrowed money did the woman who lost the pearls tell the owner the truth. The story ends with the revelation to the reader, as well as to the poor woman, that the real or original necklace was imitation. And only then does the owner learn that the necklace she thought was her original paste or imitation one was in fact real.

Does James's story depend for its effect on a "surprise twist" at the end? Is his main concern (a) with the truth about the necklace or (b) with the truth about the characters involved? From the summary of de Maupassant's story, would you conclude that his concern is with human morality or with an "irony of fate"? What about James's story?

How important is Mrs. Guy in the story? Define the several moral issues in the story —and the different standards of morality revealed by the several characters.

75. AN OCCURRENCE AT OWL CREEK BRIDGE

AMBROSE BIERCE

Obviously, the psychological facts at the moment of death—the possibility of such a vision as Farquhar's—cannot be truly known. Is the value of the story thereby affected? Though the story is narrated in the third person, the point of view throughout is that of Farquhar. His character, therefore, is the keystone of the story. What observations and thoughts show him to have some knowledge of military procedures? On the other hand, what is the evidence that, emotionally, he is a romantic caught up in a world of stark reality? What is indicated by such phrases as "chafed under the inglorious restraint," "the larger life of a soldier," "no service too humble . . . no adventure too dangerous"? Why is he unsuspicious of the passing soldier's gray uniform? Is the impersonal word "Occurrence" in the title of the story a commentary on Farquhar's romanticism, on his "wishful thinking"?

How does the ticking of the watch prepare us for the later lengthy vision? How well do the details of the vision parallel the probable physical facts of the hanging? What is indicated by the details in the vision gradually becoming less "realistic"—the trees come to seem like "giant garden plants," the forest seems "interminable," the road "wide and straight as a city street," the carpeting of turf, etc.? Is the theme of the story an indictment of war, an ironic revelation that military efficiency does not yield to the wishful thinking of romantic amateurs, or something else?

81. MR. ARCULARIS
CONRAD AIKEN

81.6, Cavalleria Rusticana: A one-act opera by Pietro Mascagni (first performed in 1890) in which Turiddu, a young Sicilian peasant, returns from war to find his sweetheart, Lola, married to Alfio, the well-to-do village carter. For consolation Turiddu woos and wins, but not honorably, Santuzza, who loves him as ardently as he has loved the fickle Lola. Her jealousy aroused, Lola exerts her coquetry and regains Turiddu, betraying her husband. Learning of the perfidy of his wife from Santuzza, Alfio challenges Turiddu and kills him. Among the opera's best-known melodies are Turiddu's drinking song "Hail the ruby wine"; his prelude-song in praise of Lola, sung before the curtain rises, "O Lola fair as flowers in beauty smiling"; the Easter chorus in the church and village square; and the famous intermezzo for the orchestra, occurring just before Turiddu and his mistress Lola leave the church service.

82.32, Ain't it grand: Possibly a tag from the chorus of a London music-hall song.

83.1, But let there be no moaning: An echo from Tennyson's "Crossing the Bar." The exact words are: "And may there be no moaning of the bar, / When I put out

to sea." There is a pun, of course, on the word "bar" in Aiken's story.

83.43, Melozzo da Forli: An Italian painter (c. 1438–1494), first master of the so-called Roman school which later included such figures as Raphael and Michelangelo. Melozzo anticipated Correggio in representing celestial events as they would appear to a person looking up from below.

84.7, déjà vu: already seen; seen before.

89.27, sea . . . multitudinously incarnadined: An echo from Shakespeare's *Macbeth,* Act II, Sc. ii, ll. 61-63.

90.5, Tomorrow and tomorrow and tomorrow: Also from *Macbeth,* Act V, Sc. v, l. 19. The entire speech of Macbeth is relevant.

Tomorrow, and tomorrow, and tomorrow,
Creeps in this petty pace from day to day
To the last syllable of recorded time;
And all our yesterdays have lighted fools
The way to dusty death. Out, out, brief candle!
Life's but a walking shadow, a poor player
That struts and frets his hour upon the stage
And then is heard no more. It is a tale
Told by an idiot, full of sound and fury,
Signifying nothing.

90.26, When I was a tadpole and you were a fish: An echo from a poem entitled "Evolution" (1895), by Langdon Smith.

90.27, Battle of Teutoburg Forest: In the years 9 and 15 A.D., Arminius, the German national hero, decisively defeated two Roman forces led by Varus and Germanicus in battles in Teutoburg Forest.

92.22, On such a night as this—: An echo from Shakespeare's *The Merchant of Venice,* Act V, Sc. i, ll. 1-24, where the two lovers, Lorenzo and Jessica, vie with each other in recalling the actions of other lovers on similar occasions. The phrase repeated in Shakespeare's play, however, is *"In* such a night as this."

Like "An Occurrence at Owl Creek Bridge," this story presents as a sequence of actual events what in the end proves to be a stream of mental images passing through the mind of a dying man. Compare the two stories in the degree of "realism" obtained in the imaginative stream. What events, images, and symbols in both stories help prepare the reader for the discovery that the events are those in fantasy?

In "Mr. Arcularis," what is symbolized by the coldness? By the ship and the sea voyage? By the journey into space? What is suggested by the discontinuity of the story at several points? What is the significance of the touches of humor, the word play, and the occasional use of literary quotations? What is the significance of the recurrence of the melody from *Cavalleria Rusticana?*

Comment on the references to Mr. Arcularis's feeling like a child (wanting to cry; *etc.*), and the references to his mother, his father, and his father's home. Explain how the steward's reference to the coffin in the hold and Mr. Arcularis's observation of the circumambulating people prepare for the sleepwalking and the stellar flights. Define the relationship between Clarice Dean and Mr. Arcularis—noting, for instance, the similarity of the names *Clarice* and *Arcularis.* Does it matter that we never learn what Mr. Arcularis presumably feels "worried" or "guilty" about—as both the parson and the doctor guess that he does? Would the story be improved if it began, as well as ended, in the hospital's operating room? Justify your opinion.

This story has been dramatized for both stage and radio. In both versions a possibly important glimpse is provided into Mr. Arcularis's past. As a child, he spied upon a morning meeting between his very pretty mother and his high-spirited uncle—a younger brother of the boy's father. The uncle's favorite tune was the melody which now haunts Mr. Arcularis. The mother and the uncle go off together in a cabin boat, a storm comes up, they do not return. Next morning the child discovers the boat sunk among reeds, with the pair inside the cabin. By implication, they had been lovers.

Try to explain why this glimpse seemed to be necessary in a drama but not in a short story. *Could* it have been included in the story? If so, explain how. Does the omission give the story a more universal significance?

93. MY KINSMAN, MAJOR MOLINEUX
Nathaniel Hawthorne

93.10, Hutchinson: Thomas Hutchinson (1711–1780), author of *The History of the*

Colony of Massachusetts Bay, from 1628 . . . to . . . 1750, 2 vols. (1764, 1767).

97.9, philosopher seeking an honest man: The supposed hopeless search of Diogenes (412–323, B.C.), Greek philosopher, often shown with a lantern in his hand.

98.17, Moonshine of Pyramus and Thisbe: See Shakespeare's *A Midsummer Night's Dream,* Act III, Sc. i; Act V, Sc. i.

Hawthorne here demonstrates, in one of his earliest stories (first published 1832), that he had already mastered the creation of atmosphere, the invention of meaningful incidents, and, above all, the introduction of characteristic symbolic overtones through the adroit treatment of details. If this story is read on the "realistic" level only, the response is likely to be an acknowledgment of a certain pictorial vividness and perhaps psychological insights into the behavior of a youth under environmental influences; but, at the same time, such a reader is likely to feel that the story lacks "point," that the "build up" leads only to a "breakdown" at the end. However, the story can be read on a level other than the realistic. In fact, a number of symbolic meanings are possible —indicating in Hawthorne not artistic confusion but, on the contrary, a positive richness of imagination.

For instance, the story can be read as a parable of the growth of American independence from Britain, as Q. D. Leavis contends in *The Sewanee Review,* 59:198–205 (Spring, 1951). In this reading, Robin is young America, who is at first desirous of advancing himself through the aid of his kinsman (the mother country), who is then bewildered by insurrectionary currents, but who finally joins in with the noisy mob, led by "war personified," in repudiating dependency and ejecting the representatives of foreign rule. As the gentleman tells Robin at the end: "You are a shrewd youth, you may rise in the world without the help of your kinsman." But it is possible also to read the story with psychological rather than political connotations—that a youth looks for assistance and guidance from his elders, as represented not merely by the uncle but by the various older men whom Robin accosts, but all fail him, either ridiculing, misleading, or deliberately bewildering him, until the youth eventually comes to learn for himself the distinctions between the true and false, the dream and the reality. Or the story can be read as a kind of moral parable of human life—the characters and "institutions" encountered on an individual's journey through life. In this reading, the barber shop, tavern, brothel, mansion, church—for instance—become symbolic of such abstractions as vanity, intemperance, unchastity, social rank, religion. Finally, if the reader at the beginning of the story should be struck by the parallel between Robin's paying the ferryman the last of his money and the crossing of the river Styx in Greek mythology, with Charon demanding his fare, then the story unfolds in an entirely different fashion. And there are perhaps other possibilities more cogent than those suggested here. Certainly we know enough about Hawthorne to recognize that he spoke the literal truth when he once said of himself that he had "an inveterate love of allegory."

Could the initial paragraph of "My Kinsman, Major Molineux" be dropped without serious loss? Why, or why not? Examine the successive descriptions of the kinds of streets or districts in the town traversed by Robin in his search, and the successive persons he questions. Are they significantly varied? Are the recurrent outbursts of laughter significant? How do they contribute to both the theme and the atmosphere of the story? What is indicated by the contrast between the moonlight falling on the Bible in the empty church in town and the "golden light" of the sun on the Bible read in family gatherings at Robin's country home? What is suggested by the fact that in Robin's dream of home he finds himself barred from entering? What is the significance of such remarks as these: "Am I here, or there?"; ". . . his mind kept vibrating between fancy and reality"; "May not a man have several voices, Robin, as well as two complexions?"

105. LIGEIA
EDGAR ALLAN POE

This story was first published in September, 1838. The poem "The Conqueror Worm" was first published in 1843 and not united with the story until the story was reprinted in the *Broadway Journal* in 1845 —seven years after the first version had appeared. Some adjustment of the sentences before and after the poem was made necessary by the insertion.

105.5, Joseph Glanvill: An English philosopher (1636–1680). The supposed quotation has not been found in Glanvill's extant writings, and is presumably Poe's own invention.

105.26, Ashtophet: The reference seems to be to Ashtoreth, or Ashtaroth, an oriental name for Astarte, goddess of fertility and reproduction, creatress of life, representing the feminine principle.

105.36, daughters of Delos: On the island of Delos, Greek maidens brought offerings to the temple of Artemis, with whom Ashtoreth was at least partly identified.

105.39, Bacon: Francis Bacon, Baron Verulam (1561–1626), in his essay "Of Beauty" actually wrote: "There is no excellent beauty that hath not some strangeness in the proportion."

106.7–8, gentle prominence of the regions above the temples: Poe's interest in phrenology is reflected in his description of Ligeia. The characteristic here mentioned supposedly denotes "Love of Life" and is thus a foreshadowing of the dénouement of the story. See Edward Hungerford: "Poe and Phrenology," *American Literature,* II, 209-231 (1930).

106.21, Cleomenes: Cleomenes, the son of Apollodorus, was the sculptor of the Venus of Medici. Poe attributes his inspiration to a dream sent by Apollo.

106.26, Nourjahad: An allusion to the exotic setting of a novel by Frances Sheridan (1724–1766), *The History of Nourjahad* (1767).

106.39, Democritus: A Greek philosopher, of the fifth century, B.C., who said that truth lies in a deep well.

106.41, twin stars of Leda: Leda and Zeus had twin sons, Castor and Pollux, whose names were given to the two brightest stars in the constellation Gemini. See the poem by W. B. Yeats, "Leda and the Swan," p. 692.

107.49, wisdom too divinely precious: See *Genesis* 2:16–17.

108.11, Azrael: The angel of death, in Jewish and Mohammedan religions, who separates the soul from the body.

"Ligeia" is a story in the Gothic tradition, a literary movement that arose in the eighteenth century and is still far from dead. A Gothic story was designed to produce an effect of horror through the use of sensational material, supernatural or otherwise mysterious events, an atmosphere of gloom and foreboding, romantically "decayed" architecture, and so on—"haunted rooms to match haunted minds," in short. Even a modern example of the Gothic tradition—such as Faulkner's "A Rose for Emily" (p. 114)—reveals many of the same features.

Central to understanding "Ligeia" is the question of how we should regard the narrator. Is he a rational and more or less ordinary man who is truthfully reporting his experiences with a woman possessed of such tremendous will-power that she makes a supernatural conquest of death? Or is he, on the other hand, a mentally disturbed person whom we must consider an "unreliable narrator" in that he reports as "fact" what are really his own fevered desires or hallucinations?

The whole story is narrated in the past tense, but we are not told how much time has elapsed since the events described. Notice in the fourth paragraph from the end the parenthetical phrase "(what marvel that I shudder as I write?)." The story ends apparently with the return to life and motion of Ligeia *in her own physical person,* yet in the opening paragraph the narrator has referred to her as one "who is no more." If this is a rational narrative about a supernatural event, should what we are told in the first and last paragraphs be reconciled or explained in some way?

Philip Pendleton Cooke, a contemporary of Poe, protested what he called "a violation of the ghostly proprieties . . . how the Lady Ligeia—a wandering essence—could, in quickening *the body of the Lady Rowena* (such is the idea) become suddenly the visible, bodily Ligeia." In reply, Poe wrote:

. . . it was necessary, since "Morella" was written, to modify "Ligeia." I was forced to be content with a sudden half-consciousness, on the part of the narrator, that Ligeia stood before him. One point I have not fully carried out —I should have intimated that the *will* did not perfect its intention— there should have been a relapse—a final one—and Ligeia (who had only succeeded in so much as to convey an idea of the truth to the narrator) should be at length entombed as Rowena—the bodily alterations having gradually faded away.

Poe frequently revised his writings for later printings, but despite this apparent admission of a fault in the story he considered to be his best he never changed the ending of the story. Does the phrase "who is no more" in the first paragraph sufficiently indicate the point Poe says he didn't "fully" carry out? What would the story gain or lose if Poe had added a concluding paragraph which would have met Cooke's objection?

What significance is to be attached to the "immense learning" of Ligeia? Is the theme of the poem "The Conqueror Worm," written by Ligeia only a few days before her death, consistent with the idea in the "Glanvill" quotation? Who is the more impressed by this quotation, Ligeia or the narrator? Notice in the fourth paragraph the narrator's association between Glanvill's words and Ligeia's eyes.

What is suggested by the narrator's increasing use of opium? By the recurrence, "as if in the dotage of grief," of a taste he had had "even in childhood" for a mixture of "regal magnificence" and decayed grandeur—as represented by the abbey and its furnishings? Why is no explanation offered of why he married the Lady Rowena? Why is she described so very briefly, whereas Ligeia had been pictured for the reader in minute detail? Consider the things about Ligeia which the narrator, at the beginning of the story, says he either "cannot remember" or has "never known"—particularly about her family. Could the narrator's scorn of the "thirst for gold" in Rowena's family be partly an attempt to portion off some of the responsibility for her unhappy fate? Of Rowena the narrator says: "I loathed her with a hatred belonging more to demon than to man." Do his actions and thoughts during her illnesses reflect this extreme revulsion?

Just before Rowena drinks the wine the narrator reports flatly that he "had felt" something pass by him and that he "saw" a shadow on the carpet, but he changes the form of his expression when he describes the "ruby-drops"; here he says "I saw, or may have dreamed I saw." What significance may be found in this change—and in the reasons he gives for not preventing Rowena from swallowing the wine?

If we regard Ligeia as the central character, a woman with superhuman strength of will, can we regard the strange thoughts and behavior of her husband after her death—including his cruel treatment of the innocent Rowena—as controlled by Ligeia from the grave? That is, does Ligeia cause him to prepare the place and provide the person (Rowena) for her resurrection? Is there, in the first half of the story, sufficient preparation for interpreting Ligeia as a ruthless woman who would commit murder in order to have her will?

Compare the effect of horror produced by this story with that produced by Faulkner's "A Rose for Emily." Each story ends with a kind of surprise twist which impells the reader to reconsider the whole story in a new light. In what way is this kind of ending particularly suitable to a "Gothic" story? Is the ending of Poe's poem "The Raven" (p. 853) another example of such a twist?

114. A ROSE FOR EMILY
William Faulkner

Faulkner's story, like Poe's "Ligeia," contains such "Gothic" materials as mystery, death, sensationalism, and abnormal psychology. In Emily's decaying mansion there is even a bridal chamber as macabre in effect (if not in furnishings) as the one in Poe's story. Both stories involve characters who refuse to accept human mortality and the ravages of time with, as Faulkner says, "its mathematical progression." Although one story ends with a resurrected spouse and the other with a dead one, the thrill of horror evoked in the reader is clearly comparable. Moreover, in both stories the characteristics of the narrator are of prime importance.

In "A Rose for Emily" the narrator is a kind of plural personality; he is less an individual than a representative of the townspeople of Jefferson, for his attitude towards Emily is complex and his knowledge spans decades of her life. The sequence of events in Poe's story is completely straightforward even though the lapse of time is indefinite; but Faulkner's narrator deliberately rejects chronological sequence while being apparently scrupulous about the lapses of time. Instead, he uses what might be called an "association of ideas" pattern of narration, as seen in the sentence: "So she vanquished them [about taxes] . . . just as she had vanquished their fathers thirty years before about the smell." What differences in effect are achieved in the two stories by these differences in method? Similarly, what differences in theme and credibility are produced by having one story told by a uniquely individual narrator and the other by a spokesman for the town? Could Faulkner's narrator, like Poe's, be considered as a possibly "unreliable" witness?

Can "A Rose for Emily" be interpreted as a story about a staunch individualist living in a town enamored of a pattern of "accepted" behavior derived from a past that has vanished? Does Emily herself both embody and exploit such a past—while flouting its code? Is she, like Ligeia, to be considered as a woman of extraordinary willpower and force of personality who refuses to acknowledge the limitations or restrictions upon ordinary mortals? What is signified by the fact that at different times she resists acknowledging that her father, Colonel Sartoris, and her lover are each dead? What connection exists between such refusals and her inflexibility towards the tax officials, postal officials, the druggist from whom she buys the arsenic, the Baptist minister, and the public gossips discussing her carriage rides with Homer Barron?

At one point the narrator describes Emily as "dear, inescapable, impervious, tranquil, and perverse." What incidents or remarks supply illustrations of each of these separate adjectives?

What exactly is the attitude of the town and the different generations of townsfolk towards Emily? towards her relatives? towards Homer Barron? Does Emily in any degree symbolize the South in its clinging to a dead but unburied past? When Emily insists that her father is still alive the narrator excuses her by saying: "We remembered all the young men her father had driven away, and we knew that with nothing left, she would have to cling to that which had robbed her, as people will." Is there psychological validity in this statement? Is there sociological validity in the latter part of the sentence as applied to the townspeople's nostalgic worship of an irrecoverable past? What is the significance of the title of the story?

In the early part of the story what allusions and imagery redolent of death and decay prepare the reader for the final revelation? What stages in Emily's life are indicated by her changing appearance as described through the story? Contrast Emily's behavior, as the daughter of a dominant father, with that of the two sisters in "The Daughters of the Late Colonel" (p. 314). What details in Faulkner's story (apart from the ending) create the atmosphere of grim horror and suspense in contrast with the tone of pathetic humor created in the Mansfield story?

120. THE BEAR
William Faulkner

121.24, old Priam: Priam was king of Troy, married first to Arisbe, then to

Hecuba. According to Homer, Priam fathered 50 sons and 12 daughters.

128.46, the five stanzas: See "Ode on a Grecian Urn," by John Keats, p. 694.

Like Hawthorne's "My Kinsman, Major Molineux," Faulkner's story, on the realistic level, seems to be a rather inconclusive account of a series of vivid experiences. But as a symbolic story, "The Bear" emerges as a masterly treatment of a boy's discovery of himself and of a system of values. As in all good symbolic stories, the symbols in "The Bear" open perspectives rather than close them; in other words, the reader should not ask for point-to-point correspondences between the symbols and any one set of abstractions. In the story, the father "explains" the meaning of the boy's experience by reading him a poem which presents its "truth" through another set of symbols, opening other perspectives. The clear implication is that abstractions such as "truth" and "meaning" exist as a pattern of relationships among concrete objects or experiences, and that without the concrete terms—that is, the symbols—the relationship is not apparent, is perhaps even non-existent. When the boy says of the poet, "He's talking about a girl," the father replies, "He had to talk about something. He was talking about truth." The same remark applies to Faulkner's story as well. Faulkner is talking about a bear and a boy because he had to talk about something— but Faulkner is also talking about truth and honor and a number of other abstractions that can only be talked about in a meaningful way by talking apparently about something else.

At what point in the story does it become evident that this is more than a hunting story? What is suggested by "the wilderness"? Is it merely a geographical area or something metaphysical, such as might be indicated (but of course not defined) in such a phrase as "the mystery of the unknown in the universe and in human life"? In what way does the bear epitomize this "wilderness"? What is suggested by the references to the bear's "immortality"? What qualities are illustrated by the bear, in its actions and also in its attitude towards the boy? At what stages in his initiation does the boy acquire some or all of the abstract values listed by the father towards the end of the story? What is meant by the boy's leaving behind "the three lifeless mechanicals with which . . . he had fended the wilderness off"? What qualities are represented by Sam Fathers? By the fyce?

130. THE HORSE DEALER'S DAUGHTER
D. H. LAWRENCE

What motivated Mabel to attempt suicide, what drew her into the pond of "dead water"? What is symbolized by that pond? And what is symbolized by land? Is it a way of life that enslaves or disappoints them all, even the doctor? Define Mabel's attitude toward her mother.

Mabel is saved and restored to life, symbolically as well as literally. Is the fact that Fergusson is a doctor rather than something else—say, a priest—*symbolically* significant?

Comment on the following passages: "It was as if she had the life of his body in her hands, and he could not extricate himself." "Then, as it were suddenly, he smelt the horrid stagnant smell of the water." "He never intended to love her. But now it was over. He had crossed over the gulf to her, and all that he had left behind had shrivelled and become void." "His own watch had stopped."

About Joe we are told that "He felt he was done for now. . . . He would marry and go into harness. His life was over, he would be a subject animal now." Do these words apply also to Fergusson, or is there a difference between his plight and Joe's? If so, what constitutes that difference? Does Mabel's future promise to be similar or different?

141. SIXTEEN
JESSAMYN WEST

142.3, As Blake observed: The poet, William Blake (1757–1827). The allusion is to the opening line of his "Auguries of Innocence," but subsequent lines also have relevance to the story:

To see a World in a grain of sand
And a Heaven in a wild flower,
Hold Infinity in the palm of your hand,
And Eternity in an hour.

How the living behave in the presence of death provides the substance of innumerable stories, for the fact of death is the most poignant of all universals, an event to which everyone responds in a self-revealing way. In this story and the one that follows two young girls confront death for the first time. These stories are followed by two others ("The Lament" and "The Fly") in each of which a father is confronted with the death of an only son. The differences in response are largely individual, but age and relationship are also factors.

In "Sixteen" Cress Delahanty knows that "she, of course, would never grow old." Death was something that happens only to other people, to the old—just as living is for the young. "What had death to do with her?" Her going home because her grandfather is dying is, she protests to Edwin, "just a convention." Do her parents so regard it? "She ought to be here," says her father. "It's the only thing to do." Is Edwin's different attitude accounted for? What attitude is held by the girls in the dorm? Why can Cress "see far more sense" in helping care for her grandfather physically than in "any talking or being talked to"? Is she right?

This story is presented in five separate scenes. Is each equally necessary? Explain. How would you account for the split which the parents feel has developed between them and their daughter, or between the daughter as she used to be and as she now appears to be? What is appropriate in the unseasonal necessity to keep the smudge pots burning? Is it significant that the violets are provided by Edith rather than by Edwin or Cress herself? The grandfather is described as "holding the bouquet against his face, letting the wilted blossoms spray across one cheek like a pulled-up sheet of flowering earth." Is this effective writing? Why?

What exactly was Cress's "great discovery"?

145. THE FIRST DEATH OF HER LIFE
Elizabeth Taylor

This brief story is built upon contrasts of many kinds, beginning with the different wording of the two imagined letters to Lucy's employer (why are they different?) and ending unlike a film, with no musical finale but only the noise of her father's clumsy run across the wet gravel. What are some other contrasts and what effects are achieved by each?

Brief though the story is we actually learn from it a surprising amount not only about Lucy but about her mother and father and even something about their neighbors.

What is suggested about Lucy by such phrases as the following: "her mind was always composing letters," "little scenes she selected to prove . . . ," "ready to be on her best behavior," "felt she had met this happening halfway," and "thought it was like the end of a film"? What does the champagne mean to Lucy? To her mother? To her father?

Twice the mother is described as "staring"—at the "dreary street" and at the "white lilac," and twice the adjective "bruised" appears, modifying Lucy's knees and her mother's face. The word "wounded" also occurs twice: the "wounded look" in the mother's eyes as she looks at the street, and Lucy "looking wounded and aloof" as she walks down the hospital corridor. Explain the implications in these repetitions.

Why is the title of the story a good one?

147. THE LAMENT
Anton Chekhov

In this story, as in "The Fly" (p. 150), a father is trying to cope with the fact of a son's death. Both fathers reveal a desire for some kind of ceremonial occasion or form for expressing or yielding to their grief, although their motives differ. Is this desire for a befitting ritual the psychological base of funeral services and mourning customs? Explain.

In "The Lament" Iona has two kinds of grief. The first, of course, is a result of his son's death, but the second, which is almost as great, is provoked by his inability to find anyone to listen to the whole story ("Is it nothing he has to tell?"). Is it this second grief to which he "abandons himself" after the hall porter rejects him, for are we not told later, at the stables, that he "dares not think of his son" or "picture him to himself" when he is alone?

Yet Iona "can speak about him to anyone." Why? Is it because verbal expression of feelings is a well-known kind of ritualistic behavior—as when we urge people in trouble to "talk out" their sorrow? Is it because in a sense he does not experience or "know" his grief fully until he expresses it in words? Is it because he wants others to acknowledge the importance of what has happened? Or, finally, is it because in telling the story *about* his son's death he can for a little while evade full realization of the *fact* that his son is indeed dead and buried? What is suggested by his thought that it is "better" to talk to women, because, even though they are "stupid," "two words are enough to make them sob"?

Four times Iona deliberately seeks a human listener, descending the social scale from an officer to a fellow cabman. Is social status reflected in their responses? Is it plausible that of the three "gay young gentlemen" the humpback should be the worst-mannered? Why does Iona "smile" as he starts to tell the officer of his son's death, and, even while enduring jibes and blows, "laugh" and "giggle" in trying to open the subject with the young men? What is the role of the jostling, swearing, or indifferent crowds in the streets or on the sidewalks?

The story opens with Iona and his horse isolated amidst noisy throngs and closes with Iona and his horse isolated in the stable. Point out the places through the story at which Chekhov lightly "humanizes" the little horse and so prepares us for the final scene of Iona turning to an animal for human comfort. How does Chekhov avoid sentimentalizing his material?

Contrast the function of the horse in this story with the fly in the following story.

150. THE FLY
KATHERINE MANSFIELD

Woodifield brings back the memory of the lost son when he remarks about the boy's grave, and the Boss arranges himself for a little session of memorial to his son: "He wanted, he intended, he had arranged to weep. . . ." Is the story intending a criticism of the Boss because he no longer possesses the capacity to feel? Notice that in the incident of the pot of jam as retold by Woodifield there is the phrase "trading on our feelings." How does this apply to the Boss? Notice also that the Boss constantly uses clichés—such as "sacrilege to tamper," "a terrible shock," "time . . . could make no difference," "a broken man with his life in ruins," "Never say die," etc., etc. Clichés are the common coin of stock responses, and that the Boss speaks and thinks in stock phrases is surely illuminating.

Although the Boss had declared that having a son had alone given meaning and and value to both his life and his business, what reveals that he has in fact acted as if nothing had been changed by the son's death? Has he simply closed his mind to the finality of death, or was his declaration

insincere? After he rescues the fly from its accidental fall into the inkwell which could have been its grave, the Boss becomes absorbed in the fly's successful return to life —indeed, its refusal to die pleases him so much that he wishes to witness again and again this victory over death. Why? The Boss does not deliberately "kill" the fly, but does he recognize his responsibility in having subjected it to tests of performance beyond its ability? Had he also demanded too much of his son? Why has the Boss never gone to see his son's grave, and visualizes him only as unchanged and asleep? Now that he has seen a rather messy death on the blotter before his eyes, does the reality and irrevocableness of death overwhelm him?

The attitude of Woodifield's family towards "Reggie" parallels that of the Boss towards his son, and yet it diverges from it too. Woodifield cannot remember what he had in mind when he started out in the morning. There is also significant similarity between the Boss's agreeing with Woodifield, though "he hadn't the least idea" what he was agreeing with, and his inability at the end of the story to understand what caused the "grinding feeling of wretchedness" and to remember what he had been thinking about before. What other parallelisms do you find in the story? In what sense is Woodifield like a fly to the Boss? In what sense is the Boss himself like a fly? Why is the Boss without a name?

154. A STILL MOMENT
EUDORA WELTY

154.1, Lorenzo Dow: Dow (1777–1834) was an evangelist and itinerant preacher, who during the most active years of his life traveled through many of the Southern states, visiting Indians, preaching many sermons a week, carrying his own brand of Protestantism wherever he felt called to go. He made at least one visit to Ireland, in answer to a divine call to preach to the Roman Catholics there. He married Peggy Holcomb (1780–1820) in 1804, with the understanding that she was not to restrict his roamings. The day after the marriage he left for a trip to the lower Mississippi region. He kept a journal or diary of his dreams and adventures.

154.1, Natchez Trace: An early road from Natchez on the Mississippi to Nashville, Tennessee. By treaties with the Indians, a right of way was obtained in

1801, and in 1806 Congress authorized a certain amount of construction. For several decades the Trace was rather dangerous for travel because of the prevalence of men like Murrell.

155.30, white hat: An allusion to the mitre, a liturgical head-dress usually made of white silk, worn by bishops and some other dignitaries of the Roman Catholic Church.

156.4, James Murrell: A famous outlaw of the Old Southwest, who terrorized the region for decades before being finally captured in 1834. At first he operated alone, but gradually gathered about him a large and murderous gang whose violence and cruelty were notorious. He was reputed to be planning a great Negro insurrection, the "Mystic Rebellion"—needless to say, not for any benefit to the Negroes. After his capture he served a ten-year term for Negro-stealing, and died of tuberculosis a few years afterwards.

157.15, Audubon: John James Audubon (1785–1851), artist and naturalist. Numerous legends gathered about his name and origins, but he was born in Santo Domingo of a French father and Creole mother. He was taken to France as a child, studied for a time under the French painter Jacques Louis David (1748–1825), but returned to America in 1804. Between 1810 and about 1819 he was engaged in rather unsuccessful business ventures in Kentucky, preferring to spend his time on extended trips about the country following his interests as a naturalist and drawing his pictures of birds. His later career, arranging for the publication of his drawings and journals, need not concern us here.

In this story the three protagonists are historical figures, but they are also very complex symbols. The author draws upon biographical facts, and in a sense her representations are true-to-life portraits (though not, of course, photographic), but quite obviously her interest lies less in the "real" persons she uses than in what they can serve to signify. On the most obvious level we meet the man of God, the man of the Devil, and the man of Knowledge and Beauty—the good man, the bad man, and the amoral man. But each of these "simple" types, after examination, unfolds as highly complex. In other words, this is a story that is very rich in its symbolic pattern; the questions which follow barely begin to reveal the manifold implications. Close study of the details of this brief masterpiece will be repaid by a fuller appreciation of the art of the short story.

What is Lorenzo's attitude towards Time? Does he live in and for the Past, Present, or Future? What is suggested in the phrase "Destroy the present," which we are told "must have been the first thing that was whispered in Murrell's heart"? What is Audubon's attitude toward Past, Present, and Future? Explain the full significance of the title of the story. What is similar in the way in which Lorenzo and Murrell see their surroundings? How does Audubon differ? How is it fitting that Audubon is on foot, whereas the others ride? Both Lorenzo and Murrell believe themselves to be, in their opposite ways, instruments in the hands of larger powers (God and Devil). Is Audubon of a similar opinion about himself? What might be said to be the principal ambition of each of the three? Does Audubon typify the creative artist or the scientist—or both? Explain why and how.

What does the heron symbolize? What does each of the three see in the heron? What does each "learn" from the experience? How is what each observer sees and learns consistent with his own character? What is suggested by this diversity of response or interpretation? Is this diversity of interpretation comparable to the different interpretations, by different readers, of symbolic stories—such as this one?

161. STRANGE COMFORT AFFORDED BY THE PROFESSION
MALCOLM LOWRY

161.1, Sigbjorn: Norwegian name signifying "bear-conqueror."

161.4, Il poeta inglese . . . : The English equivalent is given below the lyre.

162.15, Trelawny: Edward John Trelawny (1792–1881) met Shelley and Byron in Pisa early in 1822 and was their frequent companion until Shelley was drowned on July 8th while sailing in his sloop with two others. The bodies were recovered some weeks later, but local quarantine regulations prohibited the removal of the bodies from the beach. Trelawny superintended the cremation of the remains with fitting Greek rites, snatching Shelley's heart from the flames for later burial. In Shelley's pocket was a volume of Keats's poems.

162.36, drowned Phoenician sailor: Probably an allusion to line 47 of *The Waste Land* by T. S. Eliot, where the same phrase occurs, and is a reference to a card in the Tarot pack used by a fortune teller to predict the future.

162.40, In Memoriam: A poem by Alfred Tennyson commemorating the death at an early age of his friend Arthur Henry Hallam (1811–1833).

162.40, All Quiet on the Western Front: A German novel of the First World War (1914–18) by Erich Maria Remarque. When translated into English in 1933 it became a best-seller.

162.41, Green Light: Although various 20th century books have borne this title, the reference is probably to the best-selling novel by Lloyd C. Douglas, published in 1935.

162.41, Field Book of Western Birds: Numerous "Field Books" have appeared in this century, not only for birds but for mushrooms, insects, flowers, etc. The reference here may be to Roger Tory Peterson's *A Field Guide to Western Birds,* published in Boston, 1941.

163.1, Severn: Joseph Severn (1793–1879) was a painter who accompanied Keats on his journey to Italy in his desperate bid for life. Severn spent much of his later life in Italy, and his body was placed in a grave adjoining that of Keats in the English Cemetery in Rome.

163.20, Brown: Charles Armitage Brown (1786–1842), one of the circle of Keats's friends who helped supply the money for Keats's trip to Italy.

164.2, Proust: Marcel Proust (1871–1922), a French novelist.

164.3, Ariel's song: See *The Tempest,* Act I, Scene 2, line 398 (p. 601). The next three lines of this song (ll. 399–401) are inscribed on Shelley's tombstone. The line "Those are pearls that were his eyes" is incorporated into the line of Eliot's *The Waste Land* which immediately follows the reference to the "drowned Phoenician sailor."

164.15, MAMERTINE PRISON: The medieval name for the Tullianum, originally a cistern but later used as a dungeon into which prisoners were lowered through a hole in the stone floor of a vaulted room built above it. This hole in Roman times was the only access, but stairs have since been built. Sigbjørn's notebook entry contains some errors of spelling and fact, presumably deliberate on Lowry's part for

satiric effect. Besides "Tullianus" for "Tullianum," there is "Martinianus" for "Martinian," "Abondius" for "Abundius," and "Sanniti" for "Samniti" (*i.e.,* Samnites).

164.21, Processus and Martinian: Roman martyrs. Their connection with Peter and Paul in the Tullianum is merely legendary.

164.21, Victims: politicians: The principal "politicians" put to death in the Tullianum were Lentulus and other followers of Catiline involved in the "Conspiracy of Catiline" denounced by Cicero. Catiline himself was killed in battle in 62 B.C.

164.22, Pontius: Gavius Pontius was a Samnite general, beheaded in 290 B.C. at the end of the Third Samnite War. The Samnites were a warlike Appenine people who resisted the growing power of Rome in Italy.

164.22, Jugurtha: By a complicated and violent series of intrigues and warfare Jugurtha nearly succeeded in creating a nation-state of Numidia. He was eventually defeated by Gaius Marius and betrayed by his father-in-law Bocchus. After being paraded in chains in Marius's triumph in Rome (104 B.C.), he was, according to the *Oxford Classical Dictionary,* "strangled" (not starved) in the Tullianum.

164.22, Aristobulus: A Jewish ruler who lost his throne when Pompey seized Jerusalem in 63 B.C. He was taken prisoner, paraded in chains in Pompey's triumph in 61 B.C., and then executed.

164.23, Vercingetorix: Chief of the Averni, he was perhaps Julius Caesar's most formidable opponent in the Gallic wars. Finally forced to surrender in 52 B.C., he was exhibited in chains in Caesar's triumph in 46 B.C. (*not* 49 B.C.) and then executed.

164.24, Abondius (i.e., Abundius): Christian martyr, drowned in the public sewers (about 258 A.D.) during the persecutions under Valerian. At one time the Tullianum was connected with a branch of the main sewer (*Cloaca Maxima*) in Rome.

164.25, Gogol: Nikolai Gogol (1809–1852), Russian novelist, whose first works were romantic but who later turned to realism. After living in Italy he became increasingly interested in mysticism and asceticism. His practices in asceticism reduced his health seriously.

164.25, Vielgorsky: a Russian prince dying of tuberculosis in Rome when Gogol met him. During May, 1839, Gogol spent many hours at his young friend's bedside.

164.26, They do not heed me . . . :
These sentences appear in Gogol's *Memoirs of a Madman,* published in 1835; they are quoted by his biographer Nabokov.

164.29, Nabokov: Vladimir Nabokov (1899–   ), Russian-born novelist, whose biography of Gogol was published in 1944. The phrases describing Gogol's death while being given medical attention are quoted (with slight changes) from the opening pages of this book.

164.31, Henrik Ibsen: Norwegian poet and dramatist (1828–1906), who struggled against poverty and public indifference until he was nearly forty. He lived in Rome from about 1864 to 1868.

164.31–2, Thomas Mann, German novelist (1875–1955), who received the Nobel prize in 1929, opposed the Nazi régime of Hitler, and eventually became an American citizen in 1940.

164.32, ditto brother: Heinrich Mann (1871–1950), brother of Thomas and also himself a novelist and playwright. Like his brother, he went into exile because of the Nazis, first in France and then in the United States.

164.32, Buddenbrooks: Thomas Mann's earliest success was a novel published in 1901 about a Buddenbrook family (based on the Mann family). The novel was partly written in Italy, where Thomas lived for a year with his brother Heinrich.

164.32, Pippo Spano: Another name for Filippo Scolari (1369–1426), general, diplomat, and statesman. Born near Florence, Scolari rose high in the service of Sigismund (1368–1437), the Roman emperor and king of Bohemia and Hungary.

164.33, Prosper Mérimée: French novelist and essayist (1803–1870), famed as a stylist and (perhaps undeservedly) as cynic, with an interest in the voluptuous and horrible.

164.35, Schiller: Johann Christoph Friedrich von Schiller (1759–1805), German poet, dramatist, and philosopher. After an uncongenial training in a military school, where he wrote his earliest poetry and completed his first drama, he was appointed in 1780 to an ill-paid position as regimental doctor in Stuttgart. The Duke of Wurttemberg was unsympathetic to Schiller's literary ambitions, and Schiller fled the principality to Mannheim, where he lived precariously for some years while writing energetically. The last fifteen years of his life were shadowed by illness which, however, did not seem to affect either the amount or quality of his writing. There are, perhaps, some parallels in the facts of Schiller's life and those of Edgar Allan Poe.

164.35–6, Fitzgerald in Forum: The reference is probably to the American novelist F. Scott Fitzgerald (1896–1940). With his wife Zelda, Fitzgerald lived in Rome during the winter of 1924–25, when they spent much time with members of the film company making *Ben Hur.* The company had built, according to Fitzgerald, "bigger and grander papier-maché arenas than the real ones" (*The Crack-Up*). Traces of these experiences appear in Fitzgerald's novel *Tender is the Night* (1934); "along the Appian Way . . . they came to a huge set of the forum, larger than the forum itself."

164.36, Eliot in Colosseum: Probably refers to the poet Thomas Stearns Eliot (1888–   ) who has spent various periods in Rome, where he has also lectured and participated in conferences. In December, 1947, during the second of his Rome conferences he discussed Poe's reputation in Europe. One of Poe's well-known poems is entitled "The Coliseum," part of an uncompleted Roman drama.

164.40, Maxim Gorky: Russian novelist, dramatist, and critic (1868–1936). The name is a pseudonym, "Gorki" meaning "the bitter one." Orphaned at an early age (like Poe), Gorky received little formal education and followed various trades before publishing his first sketch in 1892 under his pseudonym. His real name was Aleksei Maksimovich Peshkov. A supporter of the Communist revolution, Gorky nevertheless lived in Italy from 1921–32.

164.40, Volga Boatsman: A Russian folk-song made widely known in this century through being included in the repertoire of the Russian operatic bass Feodor Ivanovich Chaliapin (1873–1938). Chaliapin sang for many seasons in both Europe and America until shortly before his death. The connection of the song with Gorky is presumably the common nationality.

164.41, saintly Fisherman: Probably a whimsical reference to T. S. Eliot, in whose poem, *The Waste Land,* appear these lines:
> I sat upon the shore
Fishing, with the arid plain behind me.
For Eliot, water was an important symbol, and *The Waste Land* employs allusions and imagery concerning a "Fisher King" drawn from Jessie L. Weston's book on the Grail legend, *From Ritual to Romance* (1920). The fish was also an early Christian symbol for Christ. Eliot was interested (unlike

Gorky) in revivifying Christian traditions in the modern world. He also once described himself as "Anglo-Catholic in religion, royalist in politics, and classicist in literature." Hence an encounter between Eliot and Gorky, who was probably an atheist and certainly a Communist, would conceivably have had interesting if not "funny" results!

165.33, Poe's Helen: Jane Stith Stanard, mother of a Richmond schoolmate of Poe, in whose home he received an affectionate welcome about 1823. She was apparently as beautiful as she was kind, but tragedy struck when she became insane and died in April 1824. For the poem Poe later wrote to her memory, including the phrase "agate lamp," see p. 727.

165.37, did Poe really live here: Poe's home in Richmond was with his foster-father John Allan, with whom he had several misunderstandings and quarrels beginning about 1826. In March, 1827, after a particularly violent quarrel, Poe left the Allan home and lived for a few days in a tavern—but this was, of course, some years after Mrs. Stanard's death.

165.40, Talking Horse: [not identified]

165.42, Patrick Henry: The Virginia statesman (1736–1799) in a speech on March 23, 1775 to the Virginia Convention closed with the words. "Is life so dear or peace so sweet as to be purchased at the price of chains and slavery? Forbid it, Almighty God! I know not what course others may take, but as for me, give me liberty or give me death!" The famous words obviously did not apply to the slaves Henry himself owned, for although he decried slavery (along with Washington, Jefferson, and others), and admitted he could not justify owning slaves, he excused himself by citing "the general inconvenience of living without them."

166.34, letter by Poe: In the two extracts from this letter, the word "that" is omitted after "feel" and the comma after "day" should be a dash.

167.15, Poe's astrolabe: Beginning with his early poem *Al Aaraaf,* Poe's poetry shows a continuing interest in stars and other celestial bodies. An astrolabe was an instrument for observing the positions of heavenly bodies, now superseded by the sextant. That Poe ever owned an astrolabe is most doubtful.

167.15, Keats's tankard: Keats was very fond of claret, but although he writes lyrically of drinking this wine from glasses and goblets, the "tankard" is as hypothetical as Poe's astrolabe. In the chapter "Keats and Claret" in his biography of the poet, John Middleton Murry suggests that it was the cavalier drinking of "bumpers" of claret that explains the line "beaded bubbles winking at the brim" in "Ode to a Nightingale" (p. 702). As Murry says of the English 18th century practice: "You brimmed your glass and you tossed it down . . . even the thought of it now makes the wine-lover wince."

167.15–16, Shelley's "Useful Knots . . .": As an ardent amateur yachtsman, Shelley must have learned and used the standard seaman's knots; hypothetically, some such book may well have been his. (As a onetime seaman himself, Malcolm Lowry might also have studied such a book.)

167.21, I am perishing . . . : This is the conclusion of Poe's last known letter to his foster-father, John Allan, who died eleven months later—apparently without answering this letter. At the time, Poe was experiencing extreme poverty and discouragement, and had, he said, received no assistance from Allan for "more than two years." In copying Poe's words, Sigbjørn omits "nor addicted to any vice—" after "idle—" and also omits a comma after "pity me."

167.44, Hyperion: A long but unfinished poem by Keats, published in 1820.

167.45, philosophic achievement: A reference to Poe's *Eureka,* a prose work published in 1848, in which Poe sets forth a theory of the universe, harmoniously ordered, with implications in literary criticism and ethics.

167.46, negative capability: A phrase used by Keats in a letter to his brothers written December 21st, 1817. The phrase and the meaning Keats attached to it have occasioned much critical comment. Keats wrote: "several things dove-tailed in my mind, and at once it struck me what quality went to form a Man of Achievement, especially in Literature, and which Shakespeare possessed so enormously—I mean *Negative Capability,* that is, when a man is capable of being in uncertainties, mysteries, doubts, without any irritable reaching after fact and reason. . . ."

168.1, Conrad: Joseph Conrad, the novelist (1857–1924). The sea provides the setting for most of his works, and one of them—*Typhoon* (1902)—presents an unforgettable picture of a ship caught in a violent storm.

168.6, Baudelaire: Charles Baudelaire (1821–1867), the French poet, who was much influenced by Poe. His translations of Poe's short stories in 1856 and 1857 and general enthusiasm for the American author account in large degree for Poe's high reputation in France.

168.8, And they are gone: See the last stanza of "The Eve of St. Agnes" (p. 877).

168.13–14, "Ulalume" . . . "To a Nightingale": The first poem is by Poe (see p. 685), the second by Keats (p. 702).

168.18, Flaubert: Gustave Flaubert (1821–1880), French novelist. His quoted remark literally means "They are in the truth" but could be paraphrased as "They are living a truer life."

168.18, Kafka: Franz Kafka (1883–1924) was born in Prague. Most of his work, including his three novels, was published after his death by tuberculosis.

168.23, George Orwell: English novelist and essayist (1903–1950), author of the novel *1984* (1949) a bitter prediction of what our life and thinking might become under dictatorship.

169.17, Lo, death hath reared himself . . . : See Poe's "The City in the Sea" (p. 682).

169.27, No, no, go not to . . . : See Keats's "Ode on Melancholy" (p. 910). Virginia Dare is the brand name of an American wine.

169.35, Buchmanite tendencies: The reference is to Frank Buchman, founder of the Oxford Group Movement, well-known in the 1930's, and later of the Moral Rearmament organization.

"Strange Comfort . . ." is, among other things, a rich amalgam of literary and biographical allusions. Close to the heart of its meaning are the lines of Ariel's song in *The Tempest* (p. 601):

Of his bones are coral made . . .
Nothing of him that doth fade
But doth suffer a sea-change
Into something rich and strange.

In the moving sea of Sigbjørn's thoughts, the relics of dead writers (both physical and literary) do indeed suffer change into something rich and strange—including perhaps the strange comfort afforded a living and struggling author by discovering contrasts and parallels with his predecessors.

The narrative is built out of accidental juxtapositions, shifts of scene, associations of ideas, literary echoes, and fragmentary recollections; yet an effect of unity is achieved. How? The story seems largely concerned with death, poverty, despairing aspirations, but can its tone or atmosphere be described as gloomy or morbid? Explain.

The character Sigbjørn Wilderness appears elsewhere in Lowry's fiction based on his own experiences,* and is perhaps to be regarded as a kind of *alter ego*. For instance, the Seattle episode in "Strange Comfort . . ." reflects Lowry's own situation in Vancouver in 1938–1939. Does Lowry maintain an objective attitude towards Sigbjørn? Is Sigbjørn to be regarded as a comic, a pathetic, a tragic, an eccentric, or a commonplace figure?

An experience has "little reality" for him (p. 163), Sigbjørn admits, unless he writes it down. (Compare also the phrase "the special reality of Sigbjørn's notebook" [p. 168].) Does this characteristic relate to his belief that ordinary people resent the poet's "magical monopoly, his possession of words" (p. 168)? Who live "the true life" (*dans le vrai*)—humanity at large or poets and artists? Explain. What attitude towards art is suggested by public preference for poets who look "just like folks"? How does "the great glass case of art" make a private life "more public" than even the museum exposure of private correspondence?

In this ebullient *jeu d'esprit* occur many satiric thrusts: at the persons who establish and equip historic shrines and at the tourists who visit them; at the modern poets who fuse unique personal experience and echoes of their reading into esoteric symbolic utterance whose import is not wholly comprehensible even by themselves (note the context of the phrase "jotted down as if he imagined he were writing a species of poem"); at harassed academic scholars desperate for publications ("compare in what sense, Keats, with what, in what sense, with Poe," etc.); at his own *alter ego*, Wilderness ("For now, damn it, he wouldn't be able to use it" and "perhaps he would remember enough of it").

And many others!

Is "Strange Comfort . . .", then, to be classified as primarily a satire?

What function in the story is played by repetition? By Sigbjørn's drinking? In what way is the place in which he drinks (whose name he didn't stop to "copy down"!) particularly appropriate? Is the ending of the story effective?

* See his posthumous volume of stories, *Hear Us O Lord From Heaven Thy Dwelling Place* (New York: Lippincott, 1961).

II: The Short Story and the Creative Process

173. ETHAN BRAND
NATHANIEL HAWTHORNE

173.20, as we have seen: This is one of several phrases in the story referring to nonexistent earlier chapters. When Hawthorne first published the story he used as a kind of subtitle the phrase. "A Chapter from an Abortive Romance." But if other chapters were projected and written, they do not now exist, and there seems to be little reason why they ever should have existed, since the story as published is complete in itself.

173.32, Delectable Mountains: The mountains in Bunyan's *Pilgrim's Progress* from which Christian first sees the Celestial City.

178.40, Esther of our tale: See the first note above.

179.37, Jew of Nuremberg: Note the change from the notebook entry.

"My father," said Julian Hawthorne, "was two men, one sympathetic and intuitional, the other critical and logical; together they formed a combination which could not be thrown off its feet." In Nathaniel's fiction this doubleness of character transposes into themes of engagement with life versus withdrawal from man and God, dramas of open spaces where secret guilt is disclosed and locked rooms where the heart remains unopened. Hawthorne's symbols disclose the author himself, and the unresolved conflicts in the man are reflected in the moral ambivalence of his themes and symbols. Ambiguity is his artistic creed. No darkness is absolute, no sunlight is pure; light manifests shadow, and darkness shines."

Nature, for instance, is frequently used by Hawthorne to comment upon the human plight. How does his description of the sunlit surroundings on the morning after Brand's death-by-fire hint at the meaning of Brand's death? Is Nature, as Joe thinks, rejoicing at Brand's extinction; or is Nature rejoicing at his final redemption? What are the implications of such a sentence as "Stepping from one to another of the clouds that rested on the hills, and thence to the loftier brotherhood that sailed in air, it seemed almost as if a mortal man might thus ascend into the heavenly regions" [p.

182]? Compare this morning scene with that of the preceding evening and night, the one lighted by the sun, the other by burning marble.

Just before leaping into the kiln, Ethan had bent over to watch the blue flames which "danced madly, as within a magic circle." The figure of a circle applies to a great many of the objects and actions in the story—and indeed the very structure of the story itself is circular. On its literal level, a man starts a search at a particular time and place, pursues it round the world, and ends where he began. He seeks the Unpardonable Sin by ranging widely among mankind, but finds it in the innermost circle of his own heart. And at the end of the story we are told that within a circle of snow-white lime lie the bones of Ethan Brand—and within the circle of bones themselves there remains "the shape of a human heart."

What does the failure of Bartram to understand the moral import of the phenomenon he discovers reveal of Bartram's own character? What is indicated by his final remark? Is Bartram or Ethan Brand the more selfish, smug, and hard of the two? "Was the fellow's heart made of marble?" How would you answer Bartram's question? Does Bartram display here his own unpardonable sin?

Notice the part played earlier in the story by the circle of curious onlookers who come first to look at Ethan Brand and then at the Jew's showbox. What is signified by the physical deformities of Lawyer Giles? Is he also deformed psychologically or morally? How is the doctor similar to Ethan Brand? Does the dog chasing his tail provide too obvious an anology with Ethan Brand's life? Are there parallels with Ethan in the search by Old Humphrey for his daughter, and in the endless travels of the Jew of Nuremberg—the legendary Wandering Jew? Just as Ethan locates the Unpardonable Sin in the kiln of his own heart, so the showman finds the Unpardonable Sin a heavy burden in his showbox—as he whispers to Ethan Brand. What is the literal and symbolic function in the story of Old Humphrey's daughter?

What is suggested by likening the showman's hairy hand manipulating the scenes in the showbox to "the Hand of Destiny"? Does the implied contrast between the real (the "hairy hand") and the illusion (the "Hand of Destiny") carry over into other elements in the story? When viewed through the "magnifying-glasses," little Joe's face to some of the spectators was that of a Titanic child filled with merriment; but when Ethan applies his eyes to the magnifying lens, the child's face alters radically. Later, in his solitary vigil, Ethan looks into another kind of showbox—the fiery kiln—and what he sees there is also a horror. On the other hand, what Bartram sees when he looks is very different. Does the story suggest that what is found is in the eye of the beholder?

What part in the story is played by laughter, not only that of Ethan—which reverberates throughout the story from the roar which heralds his appearance to the final peal which rolls through the dreams of the lime-burner and his little son—but that of others in the story? Compare the use of laughter in this story with that in "My Kinsman, Major Molineux," p. 93.

183. SOURCE MATERIAL FOR "ETHAN BRAND"
Nathaniel Hawthorne

Although most of the excerpts given here are taken from Hawthorne's notebooks—particularly the record of events of a holiday excursion to North Adams, Mass., July 26 to Sept. 9, 1838—a few passages from short stories written prior to "Ethan Brand" are included to indicate the earlier existence of ideas which undoubtedly contributed to the creation of Ethan's character and situation. Notice that the "source materials" cover a time span of fifteen years, since "Ethan Brand" was first published in January, 1850.

Although for purposes of convenience these passages have been gathered together in series here, the student should remember that for Hawthorne himself they were written with a great deal of intervening matter which he rejected as useless for this particular story.

183.4, Wakefield: These sentences form the concluding "moral" of one of Hawthorne's earliest published tales—"Wakefield." This tale is about a man who left his home for a whim, stayed away many years, and found himself unable to resume his former life when he at last wished to do so.

183.8, the portrait painter: This passage comes from "The Prophetic Pictures," a short story dealing with a character-type of frequent occurrence in Hawthorne's fiction.

188.21, Rappaccini: The scientist in the story "Rappaccini's Daughter." In studying the effect of poisons on living organisms, Rappaccini raised his daughter along with the poisonous plants in his garden until she too became deadly to all forms of natural life.

188.26, Unpardonable Sin: Hawthorne's view of this sin reminds every reader of the many examples in his fiction of characters who separated the intellect from the heart, who substituted intellectual analysis for sympathetic brotherhood. Beside Ethan Brand one would place Rappaccini, Chillingworth, Hollingsworth, Holgrave, Kenyon, and others. Some were saved in time, some not. It was a sin or state of existence which Hawthorne felt might all too easily develop in himself.

188.34, Julian: Hawthorne's son, about three years old at this time. This item may represent the many passages in the notebooks in which Hawthorne recorded the doings, sayings, and characteristics of his children, Una and Julian—from whom he derived hints and even direct examples of child behavior that he used in his fiction.

What characteristics of Hawthorne may be inferred from the kind of material he includes in his notebooks? How does the style of the notebook entries differ from that of the stories?

189. A LODGING FOR THE NIGHT
Robert Louis Stevenson

190.40, medlar: A European fruit resembling a crabapple, unfit to eat until it begins to decay from over-ripeness. Villon is making a grim jest about the decaying corpses on the public gallows.:

191.7, Elias: i.e., Elijah. See II Kings, 2:11.

191.8, Hominibus impossible: Part of a Latin phrase which means "Impossible to men but possible to God."

197.4, Seigneur de Brisetout: a fictitious nobleman.

199.28, Cui Deus foeminam tradit: To whom God gives woman.

Does the impression of Villon gained from the story (first published in October, 1877) differ from that gained from the essay, published two months earlier? Does Stevenson, in both essay and story, give equal weight to the dual aspects of Villon's character: the poet of imagination, sensitivity, and intelligence; and the petty criminal, sensuous, dishonest, and craven? What details in the story illustrate each of these aspects of Villon?

In this story, published years before the invention of moving pictures, Stevenson introduces his narrative in a way subsequently used in many films: a panoramic "shot" of a city at night, with the "camera-eye" gradually narrowing down to a specific area (the cemetery), then to a house, and then into the house to a particular room, with a sweeping "shot" of the room before we finally focus upon the "hero" of the tale. How effective is this type of introduction?

Among the details invented by Stevenson for his piece of fiction about Villon, three of the more important are Thevenin's "red curls," the dead prostitute, and the lord of Brisetout. Are the inventions successful? Are there details in the biographical sketch that would serve as well? In presenting the argument between Villon and Brisetout, is Stevenson completely objective? Is he more objective than in the biographical sketch?

Compare the endings of the essay and the short story. What is similar and what is different in the impression left on the reader? Is each equally effective in its respective place? Though Stevenson had already published several reviews and essays, "A Lodging for the Night" was his first short story to be published. Can you detect any signs of a beginner's hand?

201. FRANÇOIS VILLON
ROBERT LOUIS STEVENSON

202.44, Jehan Frollo: A character in Victor Hugo's novel *Notre Dame de Paris* (1831), a romance of the reign of Louis XI, king of France (1461–1483).

205.29, Marina, Boult: Characters in Shakespeare's *Pericles.* See Act IV, Sc. vi, ll. 169-170. Marina has been sold by her captors to a brothel. Boult is a pimp.

205.35, Murger: Henry Murger (1822–1861), a French writer whose *Scènes de la vie de Bohême* (1848) was afterwards the basis of Puccini's opera, *La Bohéme* (1898).

206.38, Idle Apprentice: One of a series of twelve prints, entitled "Industry and Idleness," by William Hogarth (1697–1764), the great English pictorial satirist.

206.48, Clerks: i.e., clerics. Used chiefly of students proceeding towards a degree.

207.4–5, benefit of clergy: The privilege, claimed by the medieval Church, of demanding trial before an ecclesiastical court for one of the clergy when accused of crime before a temporal tribunal. A smattering of Latin was sometimes sufficient to enable a man to claim "benefit of clergy." He did not have to be an actual member of a religious order to be designated a "cleric." Ecclesiastical courts were generally more lenient except in crimes against the Church.

211.3, Nathan's parable: See *II Samuel,* 12:1-7.

211.18, La pluye nous a debuez, etc.: Richard Aldington's translation of this stanza from Villon's "Epitaph: in ballade form" is as follows:

The rain doth weaken all our strength and lave
Us, the sun blackens us again and dries;
Our eyes the ravens hollow like a grave.
Our beards and eyebrows are plucked off by pies [*i.e.,* magpies]
Never rest comes to us in any wise;
Now here, now there, as the wind sways, sway we,
Swung at the wind's high pleasure ceaselessly,
More pecked by birds than hazel-nuts that ripen.
Be ye not then of our fraternity,
But pray to God that all we be forgiven.

214.43, mauvais pauvre: a seedy rascal.
215.18–19, Ballade . . . best known: Dante Gabriel Rossetti has an excellent English translation of this poem under the title "The Ballad of Dead Ladies."

In the two selections from Stevenson we have an author dealing with the same material for nearly the same purpose (character portrayal), but using two different forms: a biographical essay and a short story.

As in most fiction, the organization of the story is perfectly chronological. How does this differ from the organization of Stevenson's essay? Would Stevenson's *essay* have been improved if it were organized even less chronologically—that is if, for instance, it had logically followed the "points" set forth in the subtitle of the essay: "Student, Poet, and Housebreaker"? Why, or why not?

Stevenson's essay on Villon was first published in August 1877. Five years later, when he republished it in a volume with a number of other biographical pieces collected from magazines, he wrote a special Preface to the collection. In this Preface he confessed that in order "to condense in a few pages the events of a whole lifetime" and to present his subjects from the striking "point of view" demanded in magazine publication, he was forced to omit "all the more neutral circumstances from the lives of his subjects." That kind of omission, he declared, by "negative exaggeration . . . lends to the matter in hand a certain false and specious glitter." Of the Villon essay, in particular, Stevenson wrote:

> I am tempted to regret that I ever wrote on this subject, not merely because the paper strikes me as too picturesque by half, but because I regarded Villon as a bad fellow. Others still think well of him, and can find beautiful and human traits where I saw nothing but artistic evil; and by the principle of the art, those should have written of the man, and not I. Where you see no good, silence is the best. Though this penitence comes too late, it may be well, at least, to give it expression.
>
> . . . Villon . . . still gives us the most vivid and shocking impression of reality. Even if that were not worth doing at all, it would be worth doing as well as he does it; for the pleasure we take in the author's skill repays us, or at least reconciles us to the baseness of his attitude.

Can Stevenson's be called a factual essay? Comment on its objectivity, organization, kinds of evidence, etc. What qualities of style—diction, figures of speech, use of allusions, etc.—are shown in the essay?

216. THE OPEN BOAT
STEPHEN CRANE

Trace the contrasts indicated within the story between life on land and life on the sea. Are any allegorical implications present? What does the "wind-tower" in Section VII symbolize? Are there other symbols in the story? What qualities in nature are emphasized? Is the theme of "the brotherhood of men" mentioned at the start of Section III an important one throughout the story? Explain. What is the function of the verse about the dying Legionnaire in Section VI? What is the purpose of the humor encountered at several points in the story? What characteristics of Crane's style are illustrated in such phrases as "These waves were most wrongfully and barbarously abrupt and tall" (p. 216), "cold, comfortable sea-water" (p. 227), "There is a certain immovable quality to a shore" (p. 230), "Striking the sand with each particular part of his body" (p. 231)?

Show how the death of the oiler is prepared for in the course of the story—especially in Section I. Is there a contradiction here between Crane's art—which depicts a meaningful pattern leading to the oiler's death (though not "causing" it)—and his naturalistic philosophy which regards the death as pure chance (any of the others might equally have been drowned instead)? What was the correspondent's attitude towards the sea at the start of the story? Is it the same throughout the story, and at the end?

Trace the land imagery impinging upon the plight of the men at sea. What purpose or effect has this land imagery?

What are the most important ways in which the story differs from the newspaper reports of the same incident—subject, theme, tone, etc.?

232. NEWSPAPER ACCOUNTS OF THE WRECK OF THE *COMMODORE*

In these four news reports of the sinking of the *Commodore* and the open boat voyage of four men we have fairly characteristic pieces of journalism, including "eyewitness" accounts and an article by a special correspondent. They are reproduced here for the contrast they offer to the imaginative use of the same material in the masterly short story "The Open Boat".

Do you think the language attributed to the "survivor" and the "cook" in the first news report is accurately reproduced? Contrast such phrases as "their cries were heartrending" and "he never quailed when he . . . saw the foaming and raging billows" with the dialogue given by Crane in his short story. Which is the more "true-to-life," the factual or the fictional? Is the language attributed to Captain Murphy in the third report more probable? Consider such remarks as "but to our chagrin the water gained upon us," "go whither the elements carried her," and "one of nature's noblemen." Why is the fourth report, by Crane himself, better than the accounts of the other reporters and eyewitnesses? Captain Murphy and Crane in their factual accounts both mention the furiously undressing man on the shore who finally helps them land; compare the descriptions here with the account of the same episode in the short story.

From other contemporary records Cyrus Day discovers discrepancies between the facts and the fictional voyage of the dinghy in Crane's "The Open Boat." He points out also some errors in Crane's seamanship. ("Stephen Crane and the Ten-foot Dinghy," *Boston University Studies in English,* III [Winter 1957], 193-213.) What Day's essay makes clear is that Crane's story is not as faithful to the facts as previously assumed.

Studies of "The Open Boat" are listed in "Selected Checklist With an Index to Studies of Separate Works" in the Stephen Crane Special Number of *Modern Fiction Studies,* 5 (Autumn 1959). This issue also presents an important collection of essays on Crane's works—including "The Open Boat."

241. THE PORTABLE PHONO-GRAPH

WALTER VAN TILBURG CLARK

What effect is achieved by combining natural and mechanical details in the opening paragraphs? Comment on such phrases as "cloud strips like threats," "little islands of an old oil pavement," "falling meteors," "rakish remnants of fence . . . one portion of tangled and multiple barbed wire," "expeditionary talk," "like the mouth of a mine tunnel"? Why is the setting not geographically identified? Why is the season autumn

rather than one of the other seasons? What does the portable phonograph symbolize? How do the attitudes of the four men toward it differ? In what respect are their attitudes similar? What is symbolized by the cave? By the four flying stars mentioned near the end of the story? What are some of the other symbolic objects and actions in the story? Does this story (first published in 1941) depend too much on topical events of our times? What is suggested by the Doctor's fear at the end of the story?

Compare this story with Hawthorne's "Ethan Brand" (p. 173) and Kafka's "A Hunger-Artist" (p. 332)—both of which are also allegorical stories replete with symbolism.

Clark's own account of the writing of the story, in "The Ghost of an Apprehension," reveals the origin of the story to be a mood or upsurging of emotion, followed by the "coming alive" in his mind of the physical setting which fitted the mood, and then the discovering and inventing of fictional actions or "plot" to dramatize and communicate the initiating intention. Do you think this to be a common creative pattern? Insofar as one can deduce from the evidence, do the processes followed by Hawthorne, Crane, and Stevenson, as revealed in this section, seem similar to Clark's? Is Clark equally successful in all three aspects of the story: mood or atmosphere, setting, and plot?

III: The Short Story and the Reader

254. BILLY BUDD

HERMAN MELVILLE

254.25, Aldebaran: A star in the constellation of Taurus, and one of the twenty brightest stars in the sky.

254.33, Ham: The second son of Noah, who aroused his father's displeasure and was cursed. See *Genesis* 9:20-27. Noah prophesied at the time: "A servant of servants shall he be unto his brethren." Ham, whose name in Hebrew means *brown,* was frequently asserted to be the forefather of the Negro peoples.

254.41, Anarcharsis Cloots: Baptised Jean Baptiste, he was born into a wealthy family of the Prussian nobility. At the age of 20 he adopted the revolutionary republicanism and rationalistic philosophy of his times,

and started traveling the continent preaching liberty, equality, fraternity, and rationalism. In 1790 he led a delegation of 36 alleged foreigners, supposed to represent many different nationalities, before the bar of the French Assembly, and in the name of this "Embassy of the Human Race" he demanded that the whole world subscribe to the doctrines of the Rights of Man and of the Citizen. He dropped his title of baron and assumed the name Anarcharsis from a contemporary philosophical romance by J. J. Barthélemy: *The Travels of the Young Anarcharsis in Greece Towards the Middle of the 4th Century B.C.* He eventually lost favor with Robespierre, and was guillotined in 1794, at the age of 39.

255.4, Murat: Joachim Murat (1767–1815) was an innkeeper's son who rose with

Napoleon and became King of Naples. Reputed to be the most dashing cavalry leader of his times, he was immensely popular with his troops.

255.15, Bucephalus: Favorite war horse of Alexander the Great.

255.15, Taurus: A constellation of stars, fabled by the Greeks to be the bull which after tossing Europa across his back carried her across the seas to Crete. Taurus was afterwards raised to the sky by Jupiter as a constellation.

257.4, peacemaker: Cf. *Matthew* 5.9: "Blessed are the peacemakers: for they shall be called the children of God."

257.26, Paine: Thomas Paine (1737–1809), a very influential propagandist during the American Revolution, later returned to England where in 1791 he published *The Rights of Man,* eloquently upholding the libertarian principles of the French Revolution in answer to Edmund Burke's *Reflections on the Revolution in France.*

257.30–31, Voltaire, Diderot: Two French writers of the pre-Revolutionary period whose writings helped clarify the issues and create the intellectual atmosphere leading to the reform demands of 1789.

259.45, Cain: See *Genesis* 4. Cain, the eldest son of Adam and Eve, killed his brother Abel, thereby becoming the first murderer.

260.1, Caspar Hauser: A German youth famous in the 19th Century because of an apparent mystery about his birth and antecedents. In May 1828, at about the age of 16, he appeared in Nuremberg, wandering in bewilderment about the streets. He had letters on him stating that he had been kept in close confinement since infancy by a peasant guardian, who had, however, taught him reading, writing, and Christianity. He died in 1833 as the result of a wound—whether inflicted by himself or by others is not known.

260.5, "Honest and poor . . .": See *Epigrams,* Book IV, 5, by Martial (43–102? A.D.) a Roman writer.

260.8, "one of Hawthorne's minor tales": See Hawthorne's story "The Birthmark."

260.32–33, French Directory: After the fall of Robespierre (in 1794), the French Convention set up a Directory of five members, assisted by two legislative bodies. The Directory controlled France until overthrown by Napoleon's coup d'état in 1799.

260.36, famous signal: Lord Nelson's famous exhortation to his men before the battle of Trafalgar: "England expects every man to do his duty."

260.46, Dibdin: Charles Dibdin (1745–1814), prolific English composer of operatic dramas, martial ballads, sea songs and street songs. His output numbered about 1400 songs of various kinds. His ballad "Poor Jack" contains the line "As for my life, 'tis the king's"—quoted by Melville.

261.5, G. P. R. James: Melville here erroneously uses the name of a contemporary English popular novelist for that of the British naval historian William James, author of the six-volume *Naval History of Great Britain* (London, 1860).

261.29, Nelson: Horatio Nelson, British naval hero. When war broke out with revolutionary France, Nelson was appointed captain of the *Agamemnon* (1794), and served chiefly in the Mediterranean until he was disabled by the loss of an arm in 1797. He was victorious over the French fleet at the Nile (1798), as well as over the Spanish fleet in 1797 in the great battle off Cape St. Vincent. In 1801, during the battle of Copenhagen against the Danish fleet, occurred the famous incident of his putting his telescope to his blind eye when informed that his commanding officer had signalled for retreat. When the war reopened after the collapse of the Peace of Amiens, Nelson as Commander-in-Chief led his ships to victory at Trafalgar in 1805, though it cost him his life—he was struck by a bullet from a sharpshooter firing from an enemy ship, the *Redoutable.* He died aboard his flagship, the *Victory.*

261.34, "The greatest sailor. . . .": Quoted from Alfred Tennyson's "Ode on the Death of the Duke of Wellington" (1852). Wellington was the British military hero of the Napoleonic wars, his career culminating in the defeat of Napoleon at Waterloo in 1815.

262.5–6, Don John, Doria, Van Tromp, Jean Bart, Decatur: All famous naval commanders—respectively Austrian, Genoese, Dutch, French, and American.

262.29, Benthamites: Believers in the doctrines of Jeremy Bentham (1748–1832), who held that "the greatest happiness of the greatest number is the foundation of morals. . . ."

263.39–40, Rodney . . . de Grasse: George Rodney (1718–1792), British Admiral, whose crowning victory over the comte de Grasse took place off Dominica in 1782.

265.2, Montaigne: Michel de Montaigne (1533–1592), famous French essayist.

266.2, Tecumseh: Famous Shawnee chief, organizer of an Indian confederacy; he fought with the British in the War of 1812.

266.4, Dr. Titus Oates: Titus Oates (1649–1705) was an English conspirator who, to serve his own ambitions, posed as a Roman Catholic to help uncover alleged Catholic plots against the British crown. He forged evidence of various kinds and as a result of the hysteria he helped foment, many Jesuits and other Roman Catholics were accused of treason.

267.10, Camoen's: Luis de Camoëns (1524–1580), greatest of Portuguese lyric and epic poets, wrote *The Lusiad,* a magnificent account of the voyage of Vasco da Gama, discoverer of the sea route to India around the Cape of Good Hope in 1497.

267.16, Apocalypse: The final book of the New Testament, "The Revelation of St. John the Divine."

268.37, Haydon: Benjamin Robert Haydon (1786–1846), British painter and a friend of John Keats.

269.1, Merlin: A 5th Century magician and prophet, in medieval romance.

269.41, Chiron: In Greek myth, a centaur famous for his wisdom and knowledge of healing. He was the teacher of Achilles, the hero of Homer's *Iliad.*

270.18, "counterfeited glee": See *The Deserted Village* by Oliver Goldsmith, l. 201, relating to a severe schoolmaster.

271.5, Radcliffe: Ann Radcliffe (1764–1823), famous author of "Gothic" romances, published *The Mysteries of Udolpho* in 1794.

271.40, Coke and Blackstone: English lawyers, whose law textbooks exerted great authority for many decades.

272.1, "Calvin's dogma": The doctrine of total depravity—that all human beings at birth are depraved in sin because of Adam's fall.

272.44, "mysteries of iniquity": See *II Thessalonians* ii, 7 ff.

273.6, "Pale ire . . .": Cf. Milton, *Paradise Lost,* IV, l. 115. Satan, approaching Eden, resolves "Evil, be thou my Good." In the turmoil of his thoughts, "his face/ Thrice changed with pale—ire, envy, and despair."

273.19, Chang and Eng: The original "Siamese twins." Two men of Chinese extraction, born in Siam in 1811, were brought to America in 1829 and widely exhibited, and died in North Carolina in 1874.

273.27–28, Saul . . . David: See *I Samuel* 18.6-16.

274.43, Guy Fawkes: Guy Fawkes (1570–1606), the English conspirator, was con-

verted to Roman Catholicism in his early manhood and became involved in plots against the English government. The famed Gunpowder Plot was an attempt to blow up the House of Lords. Fawkes was found lurking among the hidden casks of gunpowder and was arrested.

279.2, Hyperion: In Greek myth, a Titan and father of Helios, the sun-god. Hyperion was famed for his beauty.

279.3, "man of sorrows": *Isaiah* 53.3. Various phrases in this 53rd chapter of *Isaiah* may have been in Melville's mind during the conception of Claggart—*e.g.,* "Smitten of God, and afflicted . . . the Lord hath laid on him the iniquity of us all"; "He was taken from prison and from judgment: and who shall declare his generation?" But in other ways the "man of sorrows" sketched by Isaiah differs radically from the character of Claggart.

279.10, "dental satire of a Guise": Probably a reference to Charles of Guise (1524–1574), Cardinal of Lorraine—a man whose insincerity and treachery were matched only by his intrigues and cruelties. He was a member of a very powerful family of nobility in 16th Century France.

283.32, "envious children of Jacob": See *Genesis* 37.31-32.

286.5, Ananias: There are two men of this name mentioned in *The Acts of the Apostles:* (1) a priest by whose order St. Paul was struck in the mouth; (2) a liar struck dead for telling a falsehood to Peter. In the generic sense, Ananias means any liar. The Ananias Melville intended is the one associated with Peter, struck dead for lying (*Acts* 5, 1-5)—just as Claggart is struck dead.

287.34, Peter the Barbarian: Peter I, Czar of Russia (1682–1725), also called Peter the Great. He founded St. Petersburg as the new Russian capital in 1703.

291.44, last Assizes: Judgement Day.

293.40, Abraham . . . Isaac: See *Genesis* 22.1-13.

296.32, Germanicus: Germanicus Caesar (15 B.C.–19 A.D.), a Roman general, nephew of Mark Antony.

296.40, Fra Angelico: Giovanni da Fiesole (1387–1455), an Italian painter.

296.40, gardens of the Hesperides: The gardens in which grew the golden apples of Greek mythology. The Hesperides were the maidens entrusted with guarding the apples.

297.3, Captain Cook: James Cook (1728–1779), the English naval explorer, visited Tahiti in 1769.

297.22, at Christmas: Professor Stern explained his rendering of this sentence from the manuscript as follows: "The manuscript originally read: '. . . as incongruous as a musket would be on the altar at Christmas.' The words 'would be on the altar' are canceled, 'that' is written above 'a musket,' and what *might* be 'Blücher etc.' is written above 'would be on the altar.' The name Blücher (an ally of Wellington at Waterloo) is problematical at best. Melville never got to write out whatever he intended by this enigmatic note to himself." Professor Stern goes on to say that he has restored the original manuscript version since what Melville intended cannot now be known and since the original version makes more sense than the mere note of intention.

297.28, "prophet in the chariot . . . Elisha": The prophet Elijah ascended by "a whirlwind into heaven" in "a chariot of fire." As Elijah rose upward in the presence of his young follower Elisha, the prophet's mantle fell from him; Elisha took it up and wrought miracles. See *II Kings* 2.7-15.

300.35, Orpheus: In Greek myth, Orpheus was given a lyre by Apollo and the Muses taught him to use it so well that he charmed not only the beasts but the trees and stones.

302.17, Dr. Johnson: Samuel Johnson (1709-1784), a great man of letters in 18th Century England.

302.42, Darbies: manacles or shackling irons.

What is there in the beginning of the story that foreshadows Billy Budd's tragic death? What, for instance, is accomplished by the incident between Billy and Red Whiskers, in the first chapter? Even before that, in Melville's dedication of his book to Jack Chase, we encounter the words: "Wherever that great heart may now be. . . ." How do these words function in the story itself? What is *in* the story that harks back to these words as motif or theme? How does the incident of the spilled soup, in Chapter 10, look forward to what follows?

Melville opens Chapter 29 by writing: "The symmetry of form attainable in pure fiction cannot so readily be achieved in a narration essentially having less to do with fable than with fact." Explain what Melville means by asserting his novel has "less to do with fable than with fact." Do you agree with Melville about his book? To what extent does Melville seem to have reconstructed facts into fable? Did Melville compose this sentence because he felt the need to forestall the criticism that his own novel lacked "symmetry of form"—especially in the concluding sections of the narrative? Do these sections—from Chapter 30 to the end—represent, in your opinion, a spoiling of the architectonics of the whole story, a lapse from a "symmetry of form"?

What does the death of Captain Vere contribute, *as pattern,* to what precedes Chapter 29? What does Chapter 30, particularly the account of the Budd-Claggart affair quoted from the naval chronicle, contribute to the *theme* or *motif* of the entire narrative? Again, what purpose is served by the discussion of Billy's manner of dying—a discussion called "A Digression" (Chapter 27)? And earlier in the story, is the inclusion of descriptions of the Spithead and Nore mutinies fully justified? Explain.

On hearing Claggart's accusation, Billy, we are told, "stood like one impaled and gagged." At the moment of his death, a vapory fleece hanging low in the East "was shot thro' with a soft glory as of the fleece of the Lamb of God seen in mystical vision. . . ." As Billy dies, he ascends; "and, ascending, took the full rose of the dawn." And after his death he is remembered reverently by the crew, and even the spar used in the hanging "was for some years kept trace of by the bluejackets. . . . To them a chip of it was as a piece of the Cross." By these and similar details what seems to be implied about the manner and the meaning of Billy's death?

Melville was a man who knew the Bible thoroughly, reading it frequently and writing marginal comments (sometimes critical ones) on passages that particularly struck him. The Biblical allusions scattered throughout the novel will repay study.

What does Melville achieve by the use of color symbolism in the story? Note the recurrence of the color rose in connection with Billy—the "rose-tan" of his cheek as well as the color of the morning sky when he dies. What is the meaning of the phrase used to describe Billy at the moment of Claggart's accusation—"the rose-tan of his cheek looked struck as by white leprosy"? How account for the seeming inaccuracy in "*white* leprosy"? Elsewhere in the story, what does white versus black signify?

About Billy we are told in Chapter 8 that "Nothing was known of his former life." (Is anything much known about Claggart's former life?) When Billy is questioned by an officer as to his place of birth (Chapter 2), he confesses ignorance; all he knows is that he is a foundling: "I was found in a pretty silk-lined basket hanging one morning from the knocker of a good man's door in Bristol." (What is the key word in this passage—"silk-lined" or "good"? Melville's manuscript shows that he had first written "in a basket of oakum"; comment on the alteration.) When the officer asks Billy "Who was your father?" Billy replies, "God knows, Sir." Then in Chapter 23 (p. 293), Captain Vere is said to be "old enough to have been Billy's father" and there is the allusion to Abraham and his son Isaac. Are we intended to conjecture an *actual* parental connection?

Define the relationship, in terms of myth, between Billy and Vere, and in the light of this relationship comment on Billy's last words: "God bless Captain Vere!" And also on Vere's last words: "Billy Budd, Billy Budd." Is there any connection between Vere's last words and Melville's inscription to Jack Chase in the dedication at the beginning of the novel?

Is Billy's character depicted more accurately in the ballad sung by his shipmates than in the naval chronicle account? Do the words attributed to Billy by the balladist—the grim humour and wry puns, for instance—fit the character of Billy presented earlier?

The moral and philosophical implications of *Billy Budd* are numerous and inviting. Consider, for instance, some of the antitheses treated: depravity versus innocence, intuition versus "knowledge of the world," the earthly versus the heavenly, head versus heart, military duty versus private conscience, war versus religion, landsmen versus seamen, the society versus the individual, and many others—all raised here.

304. BILLY BUDD: TESTAMENT OF RESISTANCE
PHIL WITHIM

As suggested by the references to other commentators in his essay, Withim is attempting to refute a widely held interpretation of Melville's novel, one in which Vere is considered an admirable figure. Does Withim support his point of view with fairly-chosen references to the text of *Billy Budd?* Does he neglect the religious implications of the story, the apparent parallel-

ism between Billy and Christ, between Vere and Abraham or God—or do such implications merely reinforce Withim's argument?

Compare Captain Vere, as Withim sees him, with the character Creon in Sophocles' *Antigone.* Both men are formalists preaching obedience to the established social order whether or not it conflicts with a higher law. Does Melville present Vere too sympathetically—at least in the light of how Creon is portrayed in one or both of the translations given in this book (pp. 375–445)?

A convenient collection of essays and comments on Melville's novel is *Melville's Billy Budd and the Critics,* ed. by William T. Stafford (San Francisco, Wadsworth, 1961).

314. THE DAUGHTERS OF THE LATE COLONEL
KATHERINE MANSFIELD

Although the focus here is upon the characters of the "daughters," nevertheless the five other characters in the story emerge clearly. For instance, what does the phrase "proud young Kate, the enchanted princess" reveal of the maid's character? What phrases in the opening paragraph of the story summarize the whole lives of the two sisters? How do the sisters differ? What are some examples of their lack of a sense of proportion, their confusing the trivial with the important? Arrange the events of the twelve episodes in chronological order. How does the episodic form of the story parallel and reveal the characters of the sisters? Why does the author mix together events from the remembered past and imagined future with the present thoughts and experiences of Jug and Con?

Explain the symbolic use in the story of the watches and clocks, slow time and fast time, etc. How is the sisters' reluctance to decide anything, to accept finality in anything, related to these time symbols? Do the imaginary flights indulged in by the sisters suggest that only in this way could they escape their father's domination, escape into their own timeless realm? Why is the tone of the story deliberately made a humorous one? Select words and phrases that contribute to this tone. Point out some resemblances between this story of continuing immaturity and Joyce's "A Little Cloud." Point out differences in narrative technique and "atmosphere."

Compare the tone and theme of this

Mansfield story with that of Faulkner's "A Rose for Emily" (p. 114)—a "Gothic" story about a daughter who outlives a dominating father.

Does Mr. Nelson in his analysis place too much emphasis on the "tunnel" image —or does he support his contention with adequate evidence?

332. A HUNGER-ARTIST
FRANZ KAFKA

Compare this story with Hawthorne's "My Kinsman, Major Molineux." Both are stories that can be read as realistic narratives, though as such both seem eventually unsatisfactory. Despite their apparent realism, both are actually stories of symbolism, even though the symbols cannot perhaps be mechanically equated with static abstractions. Both stories invite their readers to venture on voyages of imaginative discovery in an ambiguous world. (The very ambiguity, of course, might be termed the "realism" of the stories, since life's experiences are themselves ambiguous, with meanings far to seek and difficult to find.) According to one view, the hunger-artist symbolizes the plight of the creative artist in an increasingly shoddy and materialistic world. According to another, the artist is representative of religion in a period of shift from spiritual to physical values. According to a third, the artist is the moral man who tries to live for and by his ideal in a world of the skeptical and indifferent. Some of the details in the narrative seem difficult to reconcile with one or another of these views; perhaps all views are to be held at once.

Part Two

DRAMA

I

The Play

ANTIGONE

SOPHOCLES (496?–406 B.C.)

Translation by Dudley Fitts and Robert Fitzgerald

CHARACTERS

ANTIGONE	CREON	A SENTRY
ISMENE	HAIMON	A MESSENGER
EURYDICE	TEIRESIAS	CHORUS (*with a leader or* CHORAGOS)

Because of the curse that their father had laid upon them, ETEOCLES *and* POLYNEICES *quarreled about the royal power, and* POLYNEICES *was finally driven from Thebes. He took refuge in Argos and married the daughter of* KING ADRASTOS; *then, as one of seven captains whose commander was* ADRASTOS, *he marched upon Thebes to recover his throne. In the assault,* ETEOCLES *and* POLYNEICES *met at the Seventh Gate and killed each other in combat.* CREON *became king, and his first official act was to forbid, on pain of death, the burial of* POLYNEICES.

SCENE: *Before the palace of* CREON, *King of Thebes. A central double door, and two lateral doors. A platform extends the length of the façade, and from this platform three steps lead down into the orchestra, or chorus-ground. Time: dawn of the day after the repulse of the Argive army from the assault on Thebes.*

PROLOGUE

ANTIGONE *and* ISMENE *enter from the central door of the Palace.*

ANTIGONE.   Ismene, dear sister,
You would think that we had already suffered enough
For the curse on Oedipus:
I cannot imagine any grief
That you and I have not gone through. And now—
Have they told you the new decree of our King Creon?

ISMENE.   I have heard nothing: I know
That two sisters lost two brothers, a double death
In a single hour; and I know that the Argive army
Fled in the night; but beyond this, nothing.

ANTIGONE.   I thought so. And that is why I wanted you
To come out here with me. There is something we must do.

ISMENE.   Why do you speak so strangely?

ANTIGONE.   Listen, Ismene:
             Creon buried our brother Eteocles
             With military honours, gave him a soldier's funeral,
             And it was right that he should; but Polyneices,
             Who fought as bravely and died as miserably,—
             They say that Creon has sworn
             No one shall bury him, no one mourn for him,   20
             But his body must lie in the fields, a sweet treasure
             For carrion birds to find as they search for food.
             That is what they say, and our good Creon is coming here
             To announce it publicly; and the penalty—
             Stoning to death in the public square!
                                                 There it is,
             And now you can prove what you are:
             A true sister, or a traitor to your family.

ISMENE.   Antigone, you are mad! What could I possibly do?

ANTIGONE.   You must decide whether you will help me or not.

ISMENE.   I do not understand you. Help you in what?   30

ANTIGONE.   Ismene, I am going to bury him. Will you come?

ISMENE.   Bury him! You have just said the new law forbids it.

ANTIGONE.   He is my brother. And he is your brother, too.

ISMENE.   But think of the danger! Think what Creon will do!

ANTIGONE.   Creon is not strong enough to stand in my way.

ISMENE.   Ah sister!
             Oedipus died, everyone hating him
             For what his own search brought to light, his eyes
             Ripped out by his own hand; and Iocaste died,
             His mother and wife at once: she twisted the cords   40
             That strangled her life; and our two brothers died,
             Each killed by the other's sword. And we are left:
             But oh, Antigone,
             Think how much more terrible than these
             Our own death would be if we should go against Creon
             And do what he has forbidden! We are only women,
             We cannot fight with men, Antigone!
             The law is strong, we must give in to the law
             In this thing, and in worse. I beg the Dead
             To forgive me, but I am helpless: I must yield   50
             To those in authority. And I think it is dangerous business
             To be always meddling.

ANTIGONE.   If that is what you think,
             I should not want you, even if you asked to come.

You have made your choice, you can be what you want to be.
But I will bury him; and if I must die,
I say that this crime is holy: I shall lie down
With him in death, and I shall be as dear
To him as he to me.
                    It is the dead,
Not the living, who make the longest demands:
We die for ever . . .
                    You may do as you like,   50
Since apparently the laws of the gods mean nothing to you.

ISMENE.   They mean a great deal to me; but I have no strength
            To break laws that were made for the public good.

ANTIGONE.   That must be your excuse, I suppose. But as for me,
            I will bury the brother I love.

ISMENE.   Antigone,
            I am so afraid for you!

ANTIGONE.   You need not be:
            You have yourself to consider, after all.

ISMENE.   But no one must hear of this, you must tell no one!
            I will keep it a secret, I promise!

ANTIGONE.   Oh tell it! Tell everyone!
            Think how they'll hate you when it all comes out   70
            If they learn that you knew about it all the time!

ISMENE.   So fiery! You should be cold with fear.

ANTIGONE.   Perhaps. But I am doing only what I must.

ISMENE.   But can you do it? I say that you cannot.

ANTIGONE.   Very well: when my strength gives out, I shall do no more.

ISMENE.   Impossible things should not be tried at all.

ANTIGONE.   Go away, Ismene:
            I shall be hating you soon, and the dead will too,
            For your words are hateful. Leave me my foolish plan:
            I am not afraid of the danger; if it means death,   80
            It will not be the worst of deaths—death without honour.

ISMENE.   Go then, if you feel that you must.
            You are unwise,
            But a loyal friend indeed to those who love you.

(*Exit into the Palace.* ANTIGONE *goes off, Left. Enters the* CHORUS.)

PARODOS

CHORUS.	Now the long blade of the sun, lying	[STROPHE 1

                     Level east to west, touches with glory
                     Thebes of the Seven Gates. Open, unlidded
                     Eye of the golden day! O marching light
                     Across the eddy and rush of Dirce's stream,
                     Striking the white shields of the enemy
                     Thrown headlong backward from the blaze of morning'

CHORAGOS.   Polyneices their commander
                     Roused them with windy phrases,
                     He the wild eagle screaming   10
                     Insults above our land,
                     His wings their shields of snow,
                     His crest their marshalled helms.

CHORUS.   Against our seven gates in a yawning ring   [ANTISTROPHE 1
                     The famished spears came onward in the night;
                     But before his jaws were sated with our blood,
                     Or pinefire took the garland of our towers,
                     He was thrown back; and as he turned, great Thebes—
                     No tender victim for his noisy power—
                     Rose like a dragon behind him, shouting war.   20

CHORAGOS.   For God hates utterly
                     The bray of bragging tongues;
                     And when he beheld their smiling,
                     Their swagger of golden helms,
                     The frown of his thunder blasted
                     Their first man from our walls.

CHORUS.   We heard his shout of triumph high in the air   [STROPHE 2
                     Turn to a scream; far out in a flaming arc
                     He fell with his windy torch, and the earth struck him.
                     And others storming in fury no less than his   30
                     Found shock of death in the dusty joy of battle.

CHORAGOS.   Seven captains at seven gates
                     Yielded their clanging arms to the god
                     That bends the battle-line and breaks it.
                     These two only, brothers in blood,
                     Face to face in matchless rage,
                     Mirroring each the other's death,
                     Clashed in long combat.

CHORUS.   But now in the beautiful morning of victory   [ANTISTROPHE 2
                     Let Thebes of the many chariots sing for joy!   40
                     With hearts for dancing we'll take leave of war:
                     Our temples shall be sweet with hymns of praise,
                     And the long night shall echo with our chorus.

SCENE I

CHORAGOS. But now at last our new King is coming:
Creon of Thebes, Menoiceus' son.
In this auspicious dawn of his reign
What are the new complexities
That shifting Fate has woven for him?
What is his counsel? Why has he summoned
The old men to hear him?

(Enter CREON *from the Palace. He addresses the* CHORUS *from the top step.)*

CREON. Gentlemen: I have the honour to inform you that our Ship of State,
which recent storms have threatened to destroy, has come safely to harbour at last, guided by the merciful wisdom of Heaven. I have   10
summoned you here this morning because I know that I can depend
upon you: your devotion to King Laïos was absolute; you never hesitated in your duty to our late ruler Oedipus; and when Oedipus died,
your loyalty was transferred to his children. Unfortunately, as you
know, his two sons, the princes Eteocles and Polyneices, have killed
each other in battle; and I, as the next in blood, have succeeded to the
full power of the throne.

I am aware, of course, that no Ruler can expect complete loyalty from
his subjects until he has been tested in office. Nevertheless, I say to you
at the very outset that I have nothing but contempt for the kind of   20
Governor who is afraid, for whatever reason, to follow the course that
he knows is best for the State; and as for the man who sets private
friendship above the public welfare,—I have no use for him, either. I
call God to witness that if I saw my country headed for ruin, I should
not be afraid to speak out plainly; and I need hardly remind you that
I would never have any dealings with an enemy of the people. No one
values friendship more highly than I; but we must remember that
friends made at the risk of wrecking our Ship are not real friends
at all.

These are my principles, at any rate, and that is why I have made   30
the following decision concerning the sons of Oedipus: Eteocles, who
died as a man should die, fighting for his country, is to be buried with
full military honours, with all the ceremony that is usual when the
greatest heroes die; but his brother Polyneices, who broke his exile to
come back with fire and sword against his native city and the shrines of
his father's gods, whose one idea was to spill the blood of his blood
and sell his own people into slavery—Polyneices, I say, is to have no
burial: no man is to touch him or say the least prayer for him; he shall
lie on the plain, unburied; and the birds and the scavenging dogs can
do with him whatever they like.   40

This is my command, and you can see the wisdom behind it. As long
as I am King, no traitor is going to be honoured with the loyal man.

But whoever shows by word and deed that he is on the side of the State,
—he shall have my respect while he is living, and my reverence when
he is dead.

CHORAGOS.   If that is your will, Creon son of Menoiceus,
              You have the right to enforce it: we are yours.

CREON.   That is my will. Take care that you do your part.

CHORAGOS.   We are old men: let the younger ones carry it out.

CREON.   I do not mean that: the sentries have been appointed.   50

CHORAGOS.   Then what is it that you would have us do?

CREON.   You will give no support to whoever breaks this law.

CHORAGOS.   Only a crazy man is in love with death!

CREON.   And death it is; yet money talks, and the wisest
              Have sometimes been known to count a few coins too many.

(*Enter* SENTRY.)

SENTRY.   I'll not say that I'm out of breath from running, King, because every
              time I stopped to think about what I have to tell you, I felt like going
              back. And all the time a voice kept saying, 'You fool, don't you know
              you're walking straight into trouble?'; and then another voice: 'Yes,
              but if you let somebody else get the news to Creon first, it will be   60
              even worse than that for you!' But good sense won out, at least I hope
              it was good sense, and here I am with a story that makes no sense at all;
              but I'll tell it anyhow, because, as they say, what's going to happen's
              going to happen, and—

CREON.   Come to the point. What have you to say?

SENTRY.   I did not do it. I did not see who did it. You must not punish me for
              what someone else has done.

CREON.   A comprehensive defense! More effective, perhaps,
              If I knew its purpose. Come: what is it?

SENTRY.   A dreadful thing . . . I don't know how to put it—   70

CREON.   Out with it!

SENTRY.   Well, then;
              The dead man—
                          Polyneices—

(*Pause. The* SENTRY *is overcome, fumbles for words.* CREON *waits impassively.*)

                          out there—
                                    someone,—
              New dust on the slimy flesh!

(*Pause. No sign from* CREON.)

> Someone has given it burial that way, and
> Gone . . .

(*Long pause.* CREON *finally speaks with deadly control.*)

CREON.   And the man who dared do this?

SENTRY.   I swear I
> Do not know! You must believe me!
>   Listen:
> The ground was dry, not a sign of digging, no,
> Not a wheel track in the dust, no trace of anyone.
> It was when they relieved us this morning: and one of them,   80
> The corporal, pointed to it.
>   There it was,
> The strangest—
>   Look:
> The body, just mounted over with light dust: you see?
> Not buried really, but as if they'd covered it
> Just enough for the ghost's peace. And no sign
> Of dogs or any wild animal that had been there.
>
> And then what a scene there was! Every man of us
> Accusing the other: we all proved the other man did it,
> We all had proof that we could not have done it.
> We were ready to take hot iron in our hands,   90
> Walk through fire, swear by all the gods,
> *It was not I!*
> *I do not know who it was, but it was not I!*

(CREON'S *rage has been mounting steadily, but the* SENTRY *is too intent upon his story
to notice it.*)

> And then, when this came to nothing, someone said
> A thing that silenced us and made us stare
> Down at the ground: you had to be told the news,
> And one of us had to do it! We threw the dice,
> And the bad luck fell to me. So here I am,
> No happier to be here than you are to have me:
> Nobody likes the man who brings bad news.   100

CHORAGOS.   I have been wondering, King: can it be that the gods have done this?

CREON.   (*furiously*) Stop!
> Must you doddering wrecks
> Go out of your heads entirely? 'The gods!'
> Intolerable!
> The gods favour this corpse? Why? How had he served them?
> Tried to loot their temples, burn their images,

Yes, and the whole State, and its laws with it!
Is it your senile opinion that the gods love to honour bad men?
A pious thought!—
               No, from the very beginning   110
There have been those who have whispered together,
Stiff-necked anarchists, putting their heads together,
Scheming against me in alleys. These are the men,
And they have bribed my own guard to do this thing.
(*sententiously*) Money!
There's nothing in the world so demoralising as money.
Down go your cities,
Homes gone, men gone, honest hearts corrupted,
Crookedness of all kinds, and all for money!
               (*to* SENTRY) But you—!
I swear by God and by the throne of God,   120
The man who has done this thing shall pay for it!
Find that man, bring him here to me, or your death
Will be the least of your problems: I'll string you up
Alive, and there will be certain ways to make you
Discover your employer before you die;
And the process may teach you a lesson you seem to have missed·
The dearest profit is sometimes all too dear.
That depends on the source. Do you understand me?
A fortune won is often misfortune.

SENTRY.   King, may I speak?

CREON.   Your very voice distresses me.   130

SENTRY.   Are you sure that it is my voice, and not your conscience?

CREON.   By God, he wants to analyse me now!

SENTRY.   It is not what I say, but what has been done, that hurts you.

CREON.   You talk too much.

SENTRY.   Maybe; but I've done nothing.

CREON.   Sold your soul for some silver: that's all you've done.

SENTRY.   How dreadful it is when the right judge judges wrong!

CREON.   Your figures of speech
May entertain you now; but unless you bring me the man,
You will get little profit from them in the end.

                              (*Exit* CREON *into the Palace*)

SENTRY.   'Bring me the man'—!   140
I'd like nothing better than bringing him the man!

But bring him or not, you have seen the last of me here.
At any rate, I am safe!

(Exit SENTRY)

ODE I

CHORUS.   Numberless are the world's wonders, but none   [STROPHE 1
More wonderful than man; the stormgrey sea
Yields to his prows, the huge crests bear him high;
Earth, holy and inexhaustible, is graven
With shining furrows where his plows have gone
Year after year, the timeless labour of stallions.

The lightboned birds and beasts that cling to cover,   [ANTISTROPHE 1
The lithe fish lighting their reaches of dim water,
All are taken, tamed in the net of his mind;
The lion on the hill, the wild horse windy-maned,   10
Resign to him; and his blunt yoke has broken
The sultry shoulders of the mountain bull.

Words also, and thought as rapid as air,   [STROPHE 2
He fashions to his good use; statecraft is his,
And his the skill that deflects the arrows of snow,
The spears of winter rain: from every wind
He has made himself secure—from all but one:
In the late wind of death he cannot stand.

O clear intelligence, force beyond all measure!   [ANTISTROPHE 2
O fate of man, working both good and evil!   20
When the laws are kept, how proudly his city stands!
When the laws are broken, what of his city then?
Never may the anarchic man find rest at my hearth,
Never be it said that my thoughts are his thoughts.

SCENE II

Re-enter SENTRY *leading* ANTIGONE.

CHORAGOS.   What does this mean? Surely this captive woman
Is the Princess, Antigone. Why should she be taken?

SENTRY.   Here is the one who did it! We caught her
In the very act of burying him.—Where is Creon?

CHORAGOS.   Just coming from the house.

(Enter CREON, *Center.)*

CREON.   What has happened?
Why have you come back so soon?

SENTRY.   (*expansively*)   O King,
A man should never be too sure of anything:
I would have sworn
That you'd not see me here again: your anger
Frightened me so, and the things you threatened me with;   10
But how could I tell then
That I'd be able to solve the case so soon?

No dice-throwing this time: I was only too glad to come!

Here is this woman. She is the guilty one:
We found her trying to bury him.

Take her, then; question her; judge her as you will.
I am through with the whole thing now, and glad of it.

CREON.   But this is Antigone! Why have you brought her here?

SENTRY.   She was burying him, I tell you!

CREON.   (*severely*)   Is this the truth?

SENTRY.   I saw her with my own eyes. Can I say more?   20

CREON.   _   The details: come, tell me quickly!

SENTRY.   It was like this:
After those terrible threats of yours, King,
We went back and brushed the dust away from the body.
The flesh was soft by now, and stinking,
So we sat on a hill to windward and kept guard.
No napping this time! We kept each other awake.
But nothing happened until the white round sun
Whirled in the centre of the round sky over us:
Then, suddenly,
A storm of dust roared up from the earth, and the sky   30
Went out, the plain vanished with all its trees
In the stinging dark. We closed our eyes and endured it.
The whirlwind lasted a long time, but it passed;
And then we looked, and there was Antigone!
I have seen
A mother bird come back to a stripped nest, heard
Her crying bitterly a broken note or two
For the young ones stolen. Just so, when this girl
Found the bare corpse, and all her love's work wasted,
She wept, and cried on heaven to damn the hands   40
That had done this thing
                                   And then she brought more dust
And sprinkled wine three times for her brother's ghost.

We ran and took her at once. She was not afraid,
Not even when we charged her with what she had done.

She denied nothing.
     And this was a comfort to me,
And some uneasiness: for it is a good thing
To escape from death, but it is no great pleasure
To bring death to a friend.
       Yet I always say
There is nothing so comfortable as your own safe skin!

CREON.   (*slowly, dangerously*) And you, Antigone,   50
You with your head hanging,—do you confess this thing?

ANTIGONE, I do. I deny nothing.

CREON.   (*to* SENTRY) You may go.

                (*Exit* SENTRY)

(*to* ANTIGONE) Tell me, tell me briefly:
Had you heard my proclamation touching this matter?

ANTIGONE. It was public. Could I help hearing it?

CREON. And yet you dared defy the law.

ANTIGONE.   I dared.
It was not God's proclamation. That final Justice
That rules the world below makes no such laws.

Your edict, King, was strong,
But all your strength is weakness itself against   60
The immortal unrecorded laws of God.
They are not merely now: they were, and shall be,
Operative for ever, beyond man utterly.

I knew I must die, even without your decree:
I am only mortal. And if I must die
Now, before it is my time to die,
Surely this is no hardship: can anyone
Living, as I live, with evil all about me,
Think Death less than a friend? This death of mine
Is of no importance; but if I had left my brother   70
Lying in death unburied, I should have suffered.
Now I do not.
     You smile at me. Ah Creon,
Think me a fool, if you like; but it may well be
That a fool convicts me of folly.

CHORAGOS. Like father, like daughter: both headstrong, deaf to reason!
She has never learned to yield.

CREON.   She has much to learn.
The inflexible heart breaks first, the toughest iron
Cracks first, and the wildest horses bend their necks

At the pull of the smallest curb.
Pride? In a slave?
This girl is guilty of a double insolence,   80
Breaking the given laws and boasting of it.
Who is the man here,
She or I, if this crime goes unpunished?
Sister's child, or more than sister's child,
Or closer yet in blood—she and her sister
Win bitter death for this!
(*to servants*)   Go, some of you,
Arrest Ismene. I accuse her equally.
Bring her: you will find her sniffling in the house there.

Her mind's a traitor: crimes kept in the dark
Cry for light, and the guardian brain shudders;   90
But how much worse than this
Is brazen boasting of barefaced anarchy!

ANTIGONE.   Creon, what more do you want than my death?

CREON.
Nothing.
That gives me everything.

ANTIGONE.
Then I beg you: kill me.
This talking is a great weariness: your words
Are distasteful to me, and I am sure that mine
Seem so to you. And yet they should not seem so:
I should have praise and honour for what I have done.
All these men here would praise me
Were their lips not frozen shut with fear of you.   100

(*bitterly*) Ah the good fortune of kings,
Licensed to say and do whatever they please!

CREON.   You are alone here in that opinion.

ANTIGONE.   No, they are with me. But they keep their tongues in leash.

CREON.   Maybe. But you are guilty, and they are not.

ANTIGONE.   There is no guilt in reverence for the dead.

CREON.   But Eteocles—was he not your brother too?

ANTIGONE.   My brother too.

CREON.   And you insult his memory?

ANTIGONE.   (*softly*) The dead man would not say that I insult it.

CREON.   He would; for you honour a traitor as much as him.   110

ANTIGONE.   His own brother, traitor or not, and equal in blood.

CREON.   He made war on his country. Eteocles defended it.

ANTIGONE.   Nevertheless, there are honours due all the dead.

CREON.   But not the same for the wicked as for the just.

ANTIGONE.   Ah Creon, Creon,
              Which of us can say what the gods hold wicked?

CREON.   An enemy is an enemy, even dead.

ANTIGONE.   It is my nature to join in love, not hate.

CREON.   (*finally losing patience*) Go join them, then; if you must have your
                  love,
              Find it in hell!   120

CHORAGOS.   But see, Ismene comes:

(*Enter* ISMENE, *guarded.*)

              Those tears are sisterly, the cloud
              That shadows her eyes rains down gentle sorrow.

CREON.   You too, Ismene,
              Snake in my ordered house, sucking my blood
              Stealthily—and all the time I never knew
              That these two sisters were aiming at my throne! Ismene,
              Do you confess your share in this crime, or deny it?
              Answer me.

ISMENE.   Yes, if she will let me say so. I am guilty.   130

ANTIGONE.   (*coldly*) No, Ismene. You have no right to say so.
              You would not help me, and I will not have you help me.

ISMENE.   But now I know what you meant; and I am here
              To join you, to take my share of punishment.

ANTIGONE.   The dead man and the gods who rule the dead
              Know whose act this was. Words are not friends.

ISMENE.   Do you refuse me, Antigone? I want to die with you:
              I too have a duty that I must discharge to the dead.

ANTIGONE.   You shall not lessen my death by sharing it.

ISMENE.   What do I care for life when you are dead?   140

ANTIGONE.   Ask Creon. You're always hanging on his opinions.

ISMENE.   You are laughing at me. Why, Antigone?

ANTIGONE.   It's a joyless laughter, Ismene.

ISMENE.	But can I do nothing?

ANTIGONE.   Yes. Save yourself. I shall not envy you.
There are those who will praise you; I shall have honour, too.

ISMENE.   But we are equally guilty!

ANTIGONE.   No, more, Ismene.
You are alive, but I belong to Death.

CREON.   (*to the* CHORUS) Gentlemen, I beg you to observe these girls:
One has just now lost her mind; the other
It seems, has never had a mind at all.   150

ISMENE.   Grief teaches the steadiest minds to waver, King.

CREON.   Yours certainly did, when you assumed guilt with the guilty!

ISMENE.   But how could I go on living without her?

CREON.   You are.
She is already dead.

ISMENE.   But your own son's bride!

CREON.   There are places enough for him to push his plow.
I want no wicked women for my sons!

ISMENE.   O dearest Haimon, how your father wrongs you!

CREON.   I've had enough of your childish talk of marriage!

CHORAGOS.   Do you really intend to steal this girl from your son?

CREON.   No; Death will do that for me.

CHORAGOS.   Then she must die?   160

CREON.   You dazzle me.
           —But enough of this talk!
(*to* GUARDS) You, there, take them away and guard them well:
For they are but women, and even brave men run
When they see Death coming.

                   (*Exeunt* ISMENE, ANTIGONE, *and* GUARDS)

ODE II

                                      [STROPHE 1

CHORUS.   Fortunate is the man who has never tasted God's vengeance!
Where once the anger of heaven has struck, that house is shaken
For ever: damnation rises behind each child
Like a wave cresting out of the black northeast,

When the long darkness under sea roars up
And bursts drumming death upon the windwhipped sand.

[ANTISTROPHE I

I have seen this gathering sorrow from time long past
Loom upon Oedipus' children: generation from generation
Takes the compulsive rage of the enemy god.
So lately this last flower of Oedipus' line   10
Drank the sunlight! but now a passionate word
And a handful of dust have closed up all its beauty.

    What mortal arrogance   [STROPHE 2
    Transcends the wrath of Zeus?
Sleep cannot lull him, nor the effortless long months
Of the timeless gods: but he is young for ever,
And his house is the shining day of high Olympos.
    All that is and shall be,
    And all the past, is his.
No pride on earth is free of the curse of heaven.   20

    The straying dreams of men   [ANTISTROPHE 2
    May bring them ghosts of joy:
But as they drowse, the waking embers burn them;
Or they walk with fixed eyes, as blind men walk.
But the ancient wisdom speaks for our own time:
    Fate works most for woe
    With Folly's fairest show.
Man's little pleasure is the spring of sorrow.

SCENE III

CHORAGOS.   But here is Haimon, King, the last of all your sons.
Is it grief for Antigone that brings him here,
And bitterness at being robbed of his bride?

(*Enter* HAIMON.)

CREON.   We shall soon see, and no need of diviners.
                      —Son,
You have heard my final judgment on that girl:
Have you come here hating me, or have you come
With deference and with love, whatever I do?

HAIMON.   I am your son, father. You are my guide.
You make things clear for me, and I obey you.
No marriage means more to me than your continuing wisdom.   10

CREON.   Good. That is the way to behave: subordinate
Everything else, my son, to your father's will.
This is what a man prays for, that he may get
Sons attentive and dutiful in his house,

Each one hating his father's enemies,
Honouring his father's friends. But if his sons
Fail him, if they turn out unprofitably,
What has he fathered but trouble for himself
And amusement for the malicious?
                                    So you are right
Not to lose your head over this woman.   20
Your pleasure with her would soon grow cold, Haimon,
And then you'd have a hellcat in bed and elsewhere.
Let her find her husband in Hell!
Of all the people in this city, only she
Has had contempt for my law and broken it.

Do you want me to show myself weak before the people?
Or to break my sworn word? No, and I will not.
The woman dies.
I suppose she'll plead 'family ties.' Well, let her.
If I permit my own family to rebel,   30
How shall I earn the world's obedience?
Show me the man who keep his house in hand,
He's fit for public authority.
                                    I'll have no dealings
With law-breakers, critics of the government:
Whoever is chosen to govern should be obeyed—
Must be obeyed, in all things, great and small,
Just and unjust! O Haimon,
The man who knows how to obey, and that man only,
Knows how to give commands when the time comes.
You can depend on him, no matter how fast   40
The spears come: he's a good soldier, he'll stick it out.

Anarchy, anarchy! Show me a greater evil!
This is why cities tumble and the great houses rain down,
This is what scatters armies!

No, no: good lives are made so by discipline.
We keep the laws then, and the lawmakers,
And no woman shall seduce us. If we must lose,
Let's lose to a man, at least! Is a woman stronger than we?

CHORAGOS.   Unless time has rusted my wits,
             What you say, King, is said with point and dignity.   50

HAIMON.   (*boyishly earnest*) Father:
             Reason is God's crowning gift to man, and you are right
             To warn me against losing mine. I cannot say—
             I hope that I shall never want to say!—that you
             Have reasoned badly. Yet there are other men
             Who can reason, too; and their opinions might be helpful.
             You are not in a position to know everything

That people say or do, or what they feel:
Your temper terrifies them—everyone
Will tell you only what you like to hear.   60
But I, at any rate, can listen; and I have heard them
Muttering and whispering in the dark about this girl.
They say no woman has ever, so unreasonably,
Died so shameful a death for a generous act:
'She covered her brother's body. Is this indecent?
'She kept him from dogs and vultures. Is this a crime?
'Death?—She should have all the honour that we can give her!'

This is the way they talk out there in the city.

You must believe me:
Nothing is closer to me than your happiness.   70
What could be closer? Must not any son
Value his father's fortune as his father does his?
I beg you, do not be unchangeable:
Do not believe that you alone can be right.
The man who thinks that,
The man who maintains that only he has the power
To reason correctly, the gift to speak, the soul—
A man like that, when you know him, turns out empty.

It is not reason never to yield to reason!

In flood time you can see how some trees bend,   80
And because they bend, even their twigs are safe,
While stubborn trees are torn up, roots and all.
And the same thing happens in sailing:
Make your sheet fast, never slacken,—and over you go,
Head over heels and under: and there's your voyage.
Forget you are angry! Let yourself be moved!
I know I am young; but please let me say this:
The ideal condition
Would be, I admit, that men should be right by instinct;
But since we are all too likely to go astray,   90
The reasonable thing is to learn from those who can teach.

CHORAGOS.   You will do well to listen to him, King,
If what he says is sensible. And you, Haimon,
Must listen to your father.—Both speak well.

CREON.   You consider it right for a man of my years and experience
To go to school to a boy?

HAIMON.   It is not right
If I am wrong. But if I am young, and right,
What does my age matter?

CREON.   You think it right to stand up for an anarchist?

| HAIMON. | Not at all. I pay no respect to criminals. | 100 |

CREON.   Then she is not a criminal?

HAIMON.   The City would deny it, to a man.

CREON.   And the City proposes to teach me how to rule?

HAIMON.   Ah. Who is it that's talking like a boy now?

CREON.   My voice is the one voice giving orders in this City!

HAIMON.   It is no City if it takes orders from one voice.

CREON.   The State is the King!

HAIMON.   Yes, if the State is a desert.

(*Pause.*)

CREON.   This boy, it seems, has sold out to a woman.

HAIMON.   If you are a woman: my concern is only for you.

CREON.   So? Your 'concern'! In a public brawl with your father!   110

HAIMON.   How about you, in a public brawl with justice?

CREON.   With justice, when all that I do is within my rights?

HAIMON.   You have no right to trample on God's right.

CREON.   (*completely out of control*) Fool, adolescent fool! Taken in by a
           woman!

HAIMON.   You'll never see me taken in by anything vile.

CREON.   Every word you say is for her!

HAIMON.   (*quietly, darkly*)   And for you.
           And for me. And for the gods under the earth.

CREON.   You'll never marry her while she lives.

HAIMON.   Then she must die.—But her death will cause another.

CREON.   Another?   120
           Have you lost your senses? Is this an open threat?

HAIMON.   There is no threat in speaking to emptiness.

CREON.   I swear you'll regret this superior tone of yours!
           You are the empty one!

HAIMON.   If you were not my father,
           I'd say you were perverse.

CREON.   You girlstruck fool, don't play at words with me!

HAIMON.   I am sorry. You prefer silence.

CREON.   Now, by God—!
I swear, by all the gods in heaven above us,
You'll watch it, I swear you shall!
                    (*to the* SERVANTS) Bring her out!
Bring the woman out! Let her die before his eyes,   130
Here, this instant, with her bridegroom beside her!

HAIMON.   Not here, no; she will not die here, King.
And you will never see my face again.
Go on raving as long as you've a friend to endure you.

                                        (*Exit* HAIMON)

CHORAGOS.   Gone, gone.
Creon, a young man in a rage is dangerous!

CREON.   Let him do, or dream to do, more than a man can.
He shall not save these girls from death.

CHORAGOS.   These girls?
You have sentenced them both?

CREON.   No, you are right.
I will not kill the one whose hands are clean.   140

CHORAGOS.   But Antigone?

CREON.   (*sombrely*) I will carry her far away
Out there in the wilderness, and lock her
Living in a vault of stone. She shall have food,
As the custom is, to absolve the State of her death.
And there let her pray to the gods of Hell:
They are her only gods:
Perhaps they will show her an escape from death,
Or she may learn,
                though late,
That piety shown the dead is pity in vain.

                                        (*Exit* CREON)

ODE III

CHORUS.   Love, unconquerable   [STROPHE
Waster of rich men, keeper
Of warm lights and all-night vigil
In the soft face of a girl:
Sea-wanderer, forest-visitor!
Even the pure Immortals cannot escape you,

And mortal man, in his one day's dusk,
Trembles before your glory.

Surely you swerve upon ruin   [ANTISTROPHE
The just man's consenting heart,   10
As here you have made bright anger
Strike between father and son—
And none has conquered but Love!
A girl's glance working the will of heaven:
Pleasure to her alone who mocks us,
Merciless Aphrodite.

SCENE IV

CHORAGOS.   (*as* ANTIGONE *enters guarded*) But I can no longer stand in awe of
                  this,
              Nor, seeing what I see, keep back my tears.
              Here is Antigone, passing to that chamber
              Where all find sleep at last.

ANTIGONE.   Look upon me, friends, and pity me   [STROPHE 1
              Turning back at the night's edge to say
              Good-bye to the sun that shines for me no longer;
              Now sleepy Death
              Summons me down to Acheron, that cold shore:
              There is no bridesong there, nor any music.   10

CHORUS.   Yet not unpraised, not without a kind of honour,
              You walk at last into the underworld;
              Untouched by sickness, broken by no sword.
              What woman has ever found your way to death?

ANTIGONE.   How often I have heard the story of Niobe,   [ANTISTROPHE 1
              Tantalos' wretched daughter, how the stone
              Clung fast about her, ivy-close: and they say
              The rain falls endlessly
              And sifting soft snow; her tears are never done.
              I feel the loneliness of her death in mine.   20

CHORUS.   But she was born of heaven, and you
              Are woman, woman-born. If her death is yours,
              A mortal woman's, is this not for you
              Glory in our world and in the world beyond?

ANTIGONE.   You laugh at me. Ah, friends, friends,   [STROPHE 2
              Can you not wait until I am dead? O Thebes,
              O men many-charioted, in love with Fortune,
              Dear springs of Dirce, sacred Theban grove,
              Be witnesses for me, denied all pity,
              Unjustly judged! and think a word of love   30

For her whose path turns
Under dark earth, where there are no more tears.

CHORUS. You have passed beyond human daring and come at last
Into a place of stone where Justice sits.
I cannot tell
What shape of your father's guilt appears in this.

ANTIGONE. You have touched it at last: that bridal bed   [ANTISTROPHE 2
Unspeakable, horror of son and mother mingling:
Their crime, infection of all our family!
O Oedipus, father and brother!   40
Your marriage strikes from the grave to murder mine.
I have been a stranger here in my own land:
All my life
The blasphemy of my birth has followed me.

CHORUS. Reverence is a virtue, but strength
Lives in established law: that must prevail.
You have made your choice,
Your death is the doing of your conscious hand.

ANTIGONE. Then let me go, since all your words are bitter,   [EPODE
And the very light of the sun is cold to me.   50
Lead me to my vigil, where I must have
Neither love nor lamentation; no song, but silence.

(CREON *interrupts impatiently*.)

CREON. If dirges and planned lamentations could put off death,
Men would be singing for ever.
              (*to the* SERVANTS) Take her, go!
You know your orders: take her to the vault
And leave her alone there. And if she lives or dies,
That's her affair, not ours: our hands are clean.

ANTIGONE. O tomb, vaulted bride-bed in eternal rock,
Soon I shall be with my own again
Where Persephone welcomes the thin ghosts underground: 60
And I shall see my father again, and you, mother,
And dearest Polyneices—
                    dearest indeed
To me, since it was my hand
That washed him clean and poured the ritual wine:
And my reward is death before my time!

And yet, as men's hearts know, I have done no wrong,
I have not sinned before God. Or if I have,
I shall know the truth in death. But if the guilt
Lies upon Creon who judged me, then, I pray,
May his punishment equal my own.

CHORAGOS.   O passionate heart,   70
          Unyielding, tormented still by the same winds!

CREON.   Her guards shall have good cause to regret their delaying.

ANTIGONE. Ah! That voice is like the voice of death!

CREON.   I can give you no reason to think you are mistaken.

ANTIGONE. Thebes, and you my fathers' gods,
          And rulers of Thebes, you see me now, the last
          Unhappy daughter of a line of kings,
          Your kings, led away to death. You will remember
          What things I suffer, and at what men's hands,
          Because I would not transgress the laws of heaven.   80
          (*to the* GUARDS, *simply*) Come: let us wait no longer.

                                      (*Exit* ANTIGONE, *Left, guarded*)

ODE IV

CHORUS.   All Danae's beauty was locked away   [STROPHE 1
          In a brazen cell where the sunlight could not come:
          A small room, still as any grave, enclosed her.
          Yet she was a princess too,
          And Zeus in a rain of gold poured love upon her.
          O child, child,
          No power in wealth or war
          Or tough sea-blackened ships
          Can prevail against untiring Destiny!

          And Dryas' son also, that furious king,   10   [ANTISTROPHE 1
          Bore the god's prisoning anger for his pride:
          Sealed up by Dionysos in deaf stone,
          His madness died among echoes.
          So at the last he learned what dreadful power
          His tongue had mocked:
          For he had profaned the revels,
          And fired the wrath of the nine
          Implacable Sisters that love the sound of the flute.

          And old men tell a half-remembered tale   [STROPHE 2
          Of horror done where a dark ledge splits the sea   20
          And a double surf beats on the grey shores:
          How a king's new woman, sick
          With hatred for the queen he had imprisoned,
          Ripped out his two sons' eyes with her bloody hands
          While grinning Ares watched the shuttle plunge
          Four times: four blind wounds crying for revenge,

          Crying, tears and blood mingled.—Piteously born,   [ANTISTROPHE 2
          Those sons whose mother was of heavenly birth!

Her father was the god of the North Wind
And she was cradled by gales,   30
She raced with young colts on the glittering hills
And walked untrammeled in the open light:
But in her marriage deathless Fate found means
To build a tomb like yours for all her joy.

SCENE V

(*Enter blind* TEIRESIAS, *led by a boy. The opening speeches of* TEIRESIAS *should be in singsong contrast to the realistic lines of* CREON.)

TEIRESIAS. This is the way the blind man comes, Princes, Princes,
Lock-step, two heads lit by the eyes of one.

CREON. What new thing have you to tell us, old Teiresias?

TEIRESIAS. I have much to tell you: listen to the prophet, Creon.

CREON. I am not aware that I have ever failed to listen.

TEIRESIAS. Then you have done wisely, King, and ruled well.

CREON. I admit my debt to you. But what have you to say?

TEIRESIAS. This, Creon: you stand once more on the edge of fate.

CREON. What do you mean? Your words are a kind of dread.   10

TEIRESIAS. Listen, Creon:
I was sitting in my chair of augury, at the place
Where the birds gather about me. They were all a-chatter,
As is their habit, when suddenly I heard
A strange note in their jangling, a scream, a
Whirring fury; I knew that they were fighting,
Tearing each other, dying
In a whirlwind of wings clashing. And I was afraid.
I began the rites of burnt-offering at the altar,
But Hephaistos failed me: instead of bright flame,   20
There was only the sputtering slime of the fat thigh-flesh
Melting: the entrails dissolved in grey smoke,
The bare bone burst from the welter. And no blaze!

This was a sign from heaven. My boy described it,
Seeing for me as I see for others.

I tell you, Creon, you yourself have brought
This new calamity upon us. Our hearths and altars
Are stained with the corruption of dogs and carrion birds
That glut themselves on the corpse of Oedipus' son.
The gods are deaf when we pray to them, their fire   30
Recoils from our offering, their birds of omen

Have no cry of comfort, for they are gorged
With the thick blood of the dead.
                                    O my son,
These are no trifles! Think: all men make mistakes,
But a good man yields when he knows his course is wrong,
And repairs the evil. The only crime is pride.

Give in to the dead man, then: do not fight with a corpse—
What glory is it to kill a man who is dead?
Think, I beg you:
It is for your own good that I speak as I do.   40
You should be able to yield for your own good.

CREON.   It seems that prophets have made me their especial province.
All my life long
I have been a kind of butt for the dull arrows
Of doddering fortune-tellers!
                                    No, Teiresias:
If your birds—if the great eagles of God himself
Should carry him stinking bit by bit to heaven,
I would not yield. I am not afraid of pollution:
No man can defile the gods.
                                    Do what you will,
Go into business, make money, speculate   50
In India gold or that synthetic gold from Sardis,
Get rich otherwise than by my consent to bury him.
Teiresias, it is a sorry thing when a wise man
Sells his wisdom, lets out his words for hire!

TEIRESIAS.   Ah Creon! Is there no man left in the world—

CREON.   To do what?—Come, let's have the aphorism!

TEIRESIAS.   No man who knows that wisdom outweighs any wealth?

CREON.   As surely as bribes are baser than any baseness.

TEIRESIAS.   You are sick, Creon! You are deathly sick!

CREON.   As you say: it is not my place to challenge a prophet.   60

TEIRESIAS.   Yet you have said my prophecy is for sale.

CREON.   The generation of prophets has always loved gold.

TEIRESIAS.   The generation of kings has always loved brass.

CREON.   You forget yourself! You are speaking to your King.

TEIRESIAS.   I know it. You are a king because of me.

CREON.   You have a certain skill; but you have sold out.

TEIRESIAS.   King, you will drive me to words that—

CREON.   Say them, say them!
               Only remember: I will not pay you for them.

TEIRESIAS.   No, you will find them too costly.

CREON.   No doubt. Speak:
               Whatever you say, you will not change my will.   70

TEIRESIAS.   Then take this, and take it to heart!
               The time is not far off when you shall pay back
               Corpse for corpse, flesh of your own flesh.
               You have thrust the child of this world into living night,
               You have kept from the gods below the child that is theirs:
               The one in a grave before her death, the other,
               Dead, denied the grave. This is your crime:
               And the Furies and the dark gods of Hell
               Are swift with terrible punishment for you.

               Do you want to buy me now, Creon?

                                            Not many days,   80
               And your house will be full of men and women weeping,
               And curses will be hurled at you from far
               Cities grieving for sons unburied, left to rot before the walls
                    of Thebes.

               These are my arrows, Creon: they are all for you.

               (*to* BOY) But come, child: lead me home.
               Let him waste his fine anger upon younger men.
               Maybe he will learn at last
               To control a wiser tongue in a better head.

                                                        (*Exit* TEIRESIAS)

CHORAGOS.   The old man has gone, King, but his words
               Remain to plague us. I am old, too,   90
               But I can not remember that he was ever false.

CREON.   That is true. . . . It troubles me.
               Oh it is hard to give in! but it is worse
               To risk everything for stubborn pride.

CHORAGOS.   Creon: take my advice.

CREON.   What shall I do?

CHORAGOS.   Go quickly: free Antigone from her vault
               And build a tomb for the body of Polyneices.

CREON.   You would have me do this?

CHORAGOS.   Creon, yes!
And it must be done at once: God moves
Swiftly to cancel the folly of stubborn men.   100

CREON.   It is hard to deny the heart! But I
Will do it: I will not fight with destiny.

CHORAGOS.   You must go yourself, you cannot leave it to others.

CREON.   I will go.
              —Bring axes, servants:
Come with me to the tomb. I buried her, I
Will set her free.
              Oh quickly!
My mind misgives—
The laws of the gods are mighty, and a man must serve them
To the last day of his life!

                                              (*Exit* CREON)

PÆAN

CHORAGOS.   God of many names   [STROPHE 1

CHORUS.   O Iacchos
                              son
of Cadmeian Semele
                    O born of the Thunder!
Guardian of the West
                    Regent
of Eleusis' plain
                    O Prince of mænad Thebes
and the Dragon Field by rippling Ismenos:

CHORAGOS.   God of many names   [ANTISTROPHE 1

CHORUS.   the flame of torches
flares on our hills
                    the nymphs of Iacchos

dance at the spring of Castalia:

from the vine-close mountain
                              come ah come in ivy:
Evohé evohé! sings through the streets of Thebes   10

CHORAGOS.   God of many names   [STROPHE 2

CHORUS.   Iacchos of Thebes
heavenly child
                    Semele bride of the Thunderer!

The shadow of plague is upon us:
                    come
with clement feet
                    oh come from Parnasos
down the long slopes
                    across the lamenting water

CHORAGOS.   Iô Fire! Chorister of the throbbing stars!   [ANTISTROPHE 2
            O purest among the voices of the night!
            Thou son of God, blaze for us!

CHORUS.   Come with choric rapture of circling Mænads
            Who cry *Iô Iacche!*

                    God of many names!   20

EXODOS

Enter MESSENGER.

MESSENGER. Men of the line of Cadmos, you who live
            Near Amphion's citadel:
                            I cannot say
            Of any condition of human life 'This is fixed,
            This is clearly good, or bad.' Fate raises up,
            And Fate casts down the happy and unhappy alike:
            No man can foretell his Fate.
                            Take the case of Creon:
            Creon was happy once, as I count happiness:
            Victorious in battle, sole governor of the land,
            Fortunate father of children nobly born.
            And now it has all gone from him! Who can say   10
            That a man is still alive when his life's joy fails?
            He is a walking dead man. Grant him rich,
            Let him live like a king in his great house:
            If his pleasure is gone, I would not give
            So much as the shadow of smoke for all he owns.

CHORAGOS.   Your words hint at sorrow: what is your news for us?

MESSENGER. They are dead. The living are guilty of their death.

CHORAGOS.   Who is guilty? Who is dead? Speak!

MESSENGER.   Haimon.
            Haimon is dead; and the hand that killed him
            Is his own hand.

CHORAGOS.   His father's? or his own?   20

MESSENGER. His own, driven mad by the murder his father had done.

CHORAGOS. Teiresias, Teiresias, how clearly you saw it all!

MESSENGER. This is my news: you must draw what conclusions you can from it.

CHORAGOS. But look: Eurydice, our Queen:
Has she overheard us?

(Enter EURYDICE from the Palace, Center.)

EURYDICE. I have heard something, friends:
As I was unlocking the gate of Pallas' shrine,
For I needed her help today, I heard a voice
Telling of some new sorrow. And I fainted
There at the temple with all my maidens about me.   30
But speak again: whatever it is, I can bear it:
Grief and I are no strangers.

MESSENGER.   Dearest Lady,
I will tell you plainly all that I have seen.
I shall not try to comfort you: what is the use,
Since comfort could lie only in what is not true?
The truth is always best.
                              I went with Creon
To the outer plain where Polyneices was lying,
No friend to pity him, his body shredded by dogs.
We made our prayers in that place to Hecate
And Pluto, that they would be merciful. And we bathed   40
The corpse with holy water, and we brought
Fresh-broken branches to burn what was left of it,
And upon the urn we heaped up a towering barrow
Of the earth of his own land.
                              When we were done, we ran
To the vault where Antigone lay on her couch of stone.
One of the servants had gone ahead,
And while he was yet far off he heard a voice
Grieving within the chamber, and he came back
And told Creon. And as the King went closer,
The air was full of wailing, the words lost,   50
And he begged us to make all haste. 'Am I a prophet?'
He said, weeping, 'And must I walk this road,
'The saddest of all that I have gone before?
'My son's voice calls me on. Oh quickly, quickly!
'Look through the crevice there, and tell me
'If it is Haimon, or some deception of the gods!'

We obeyed; and in the cavern's farthest corner
We saw her lying:
She had made a noose of her fine linen veil
And hanged herself. Haimon lay beside her,   60
His arms about her waist, lamenting her,

His love lost under ground, crying out
That his father had stolen her away from him.
When Creon saw him the tears rushed to his eyes
And he called to him: 'What have you done, child? Speak to me.
'What are you thinking that makes your eyes so strange?
'O my son, my son, I come to you on my knees!'
But Haimon spat in his face. He said not a word,
Staring—
                    And suddenly drew his sword
And lunged. Creon shrank back, the blade missed; and the boy,   70
Desperate against himself, drove it half its length
Into his own side, and fell. And as he died
He gathered Antigone close in his arms again,
Choking, his blood bright red on her white cheek.
And now he lies dead with the dead, and she is his
At last, his bride in the houses of the dead.

                                        (*Exit* EURYDICE *into the Palace*)

CHORAGOS.   She has left us without a word. What can this mean?

MESSENGER.   It troubles me, too; yet she knows what is best,
             Her grief is too great for public lamentation,
             And doubtless she has gone to her chamber to weep   80
             For her dead son, leading her maidens in his dirge.

CHORAGOS.   It may be so: but I fear this deep silence.

(*Pause.*)

MESSENGER.   I will see what she is doing. I will go in.

                                        (*Exit* MESSENGER *into the Palace*)

(*Enter* CREON *with attendants, bearing* HAIMON'S *body.*)

CHORAGOS.   But here is the King himself: oh look at him,
             Bearing his own damnation in his arms.

CREON.   Nothing you say can touch me any more.
             My own blind heart has brought me
             From darkness to final darkness. Here you see
             The father murdering, the murdered son—
             And all my civic wisdom!   90
             Haimon my son, so young, so young to die,
             I was the fool, not you; and you died for me.

CHORAGOS.   That is the truth; but you were late in learning it.

CREON.   This truth is hard to bear. Surely a god
             Has crushed me beneath the hugest weight of heaven,

And driven me headlong a barbaric way
To trample out the thing I held most dear.

The pains that men will take to come to pain!

(*Enter* MESSENGER *from the Palace.*)

MESSENGER. The burden you carry in your hands is heavy,
But it is not all: you will find more in your house.   100

CREON. What burden worse than this shall I find there?

MESSENGER. The Queen is dead.

CREON. O port of death, deaf world,
Is there no pity for me? And you, Angel of evil,
I was dead, and your words are death again.
Is it true, boy? Can it be true?
Is my wife dead? Has death bred death?

MESSENGER. You can see for yourself.

(*The doors are opened, and the body of* EURYDICE *disclosed within.*)

CREON. Oh pity!
All true, all true, and more than I can bear!   110
O my wife, my son!

MESSENGER. She stood before the altar, and her heart
Welcomed the knife her own hand guided,
And a great cry burst from her lips for Megareus dead,
And for Haimon dead, her sons; and her last breath
Was a curse for their father, the murderer of her sons.
And she fell, and the dark flowed in through her closing eyes

CREON. O God, I am sick with fear.
Are there no swords here? Has no one a blow for me?

MESSENGER. Her curse is upon you for the deaths of both.   120

CREON. It is right that it should be. I alone am guilty.
I know it, and I say it. Lead me in,
Quickly, friends.
I have neither life nor substance. Lead me in.

CHORAGOS. You are right, if there can be right in so much wrong.
The briefest way is best in a world of sorrow.

CREON. Let it come,
Let death come quickly, and be kind to me.
I would not ever see the sun again.

CHORAGOS.   All that will come when it will; but we, meanwhile,   130
             Have much to do. Leave the future to itself.

CREON.   All my heart was in that prayer!

CHORAGOS.   Then do not pray any more: the sky is deaf.

CREON.   Lead me away. I have been rash and foolish.
             I have killed my son and my wife.
             I look for comfort; my comfort lies here dead.
             Whatever my hands have touched has come to nothing.
             Fate has brought all my pride to a thought of dust.

(As CREON *is being led into the house, the* CHORAGOS *advances and speaks directly
    to the audience.*)

CHORAGOS.   There is no happiness where there is no wisdom;
             No wisdom but in submission to the gods.   140
             Big words are always punished,
             And proud men in old age learn to be wise.

ANTIGONE

JEAN ANOUILH (1910–   )

Adapted and Translated by Lewis Galantiere

THE SETTING

A gray cloth cyclorama, semi-circular, hangs at the back of the set. At the bottom of the cyclorama, a stair, of three steps, sweeps in a semi-circle. Downstage, right and left, two archways. The curtains part in the center for entrance and exit.

A table stands left of center-stage, with matching chairs set at either end. A small stool is placed right of the chair at the right of the table.

ANTIGONE, *her hands clasped round her knees, sits on the top step. The* THREE GUARDS *sit on the steps, in a small group, playing cards. The* CHORUS *stands up on the top step.* EURYDICE *sits on the top step, just left of center, knitting. The* NURSE *sits on the second step, left of* EURYDICE. ISMENE *stands in front of arch, left, facing* HAEMON, *who stands left of her.* CREON *sits in the chair at right end of the table, his arm over the shoulder of his* PAGE, *who sits on the stool beside his chair. The* MESSENGER *is leaning against the downstage portal of the right arch.*

(*The curtain rises slowly; then the* CHORUS *turns and moves downstage.*)

CHORUS. Well, here we are.

These people that you see here are about to act out for you the story of Antigone.

That thin little creature sitting by herself, staring straight ahead, seeing nothing, is Antigone. She is thinking. She is thinking that the instant I finish telling you who's who and what's what in this play, she will burst forth as the tense, sallow, wilful girl who would never listen to reason and who is about to rise up alone against Creon, her uncle, the King.

Another thing that she is thinking is this: she is going to die. Antigone is only twenty years old. She would much rather live than die. But there is no help for it. When you are on the side of the gods against the tyrant, of Man against the State, of purity against corruption—when, in short, your name is Antigone, there is only one part you can play; and she will have to play hers through to the end.

Mind you, Antigone doesn't know all these things about herself. I know them because it is my business to know them. That's what a Greek Chorus is for. All that she knows is that Creon will not allow her dead brother to be buried; and that in spite of Creon, she must bury him. Antigone doesn't think, she acts; she doesn't reason, she feels. And from the moment the curtain went up, she began to feel that inhuman forces were whirling her out of this world, snatching her away from her sister, Ismene, whom you see smiling and chatting with that young man, making her an instrument of the gods in a way she cannot fathom but that she will faithfully pursue.

You have never seen inhuman forces at work? You will, tonight.

(CHORUS *turns and indicates* HAEMON.)

The young man talking to Ismene—to the pliant and reasonable Ismene—is Haemon. He is the King's son, Creon's son. Antigone and he are engaged to be married. You wouldn't have thought she was his type. He likes dancing, sports, competition; he likes women, too. Now look at Ismene again. She is certainly more beautiful than Antigone. She is the girl you'd think he'd go for. Well . . . There was a ball one night. Ismene wore a new evening dress. She was radiant. Haemon danced every dance with her; he wouldn't look at any other girl. And yet, that same night, before the dance was over, suddenly he went in search of Antigone, found her sitting alone—like that, with her arms clasped round her knees—and asked her to marry him. It didn't seem to surprise Antigone in the least. She looked up at him out of those solemn eyes of hers, then smiled sort of sadly; and she said "yes." That was all. Well, here is Haemon expecting to marry Antigone. He won't, of course. He didn't know, when he asked her, that the earth wasn't made to hold a husband of Antigone, and that this princely distinction was to earn him no more than the right to die sooner than he might otherwise have done.

(CHORUS *turns toward* CREON.)

That gray-haired, powerfully built man sitting lost in thought, with his little page at his side, is Creon, the King. His face is lined. He is tired. He practices the difficult art of a leader of men. When he was younger, when Oedipus was King and Creon was no more than the King's brother-in-law, he was different. He loved music, bought rare manuscripts, was a kind of art patron. He used to while away whole afternoons in the antique shops of this city of Thebes. But Oedipus died. Oedipus' sons died. Creon's moment had come. He took over the kingdom.

(CHORUS *moves downstage. Reflects a moment.*)

I'll tell you something about Creon. He has a tendency to fool himself. This leader of men, this brilliant debater and logician, likes to believe that if it were not for his sense of responsibility, he would step down from the throne and go back to collecting manuscripts. But the fact is, he loves being King. He's an artist who has always believed that he could govern just as well as any man of action could; and he's quite sure that no god nor any man can tell him anything about what is best for the common people.

Creon has a wife, a Queen. Her name is Eurydice. There she sits, the gentle old lady with the knitting, next to the Nurse who brought up the two girls. She will go on knitting all through the play, till the time comes for her to go to her room and die. She is a good woman, a worthy, loving soul. But she is no help to her husband. Creon has to face the music alone. Alone with his Page, who is too young to be of any help.

The others? Well, let's see.

(*He points toward the* MESSENGER.)

That pale young man leaning against the wall is the Messenger. Later on, he will come running in to announce that Haemon is dead. He has a premonition of catastrophe. That's what he is brooding over. That's why he won't mingle with the others.

As for those three pasty-faced card players—they are the guards, members of

Creon's police force. They chew tobacco; one smells of garlic, another of beer; but they're not a bad lot. They have wives they are afraid of, kids who are afraid of them; they're bothered by the little day-to-day worries that beset us all. At the same time—they are policemen: eternally innocent, no matter what crimes are committed; eternally indifferent, for nothing that happens can matter to them. They are quite prepared to arrest anybody at all, including Creon himself, should the order be given by a new leader.

That's the lot. Now for the play.

Oedipus, who was the father of the two girls, Antigone and Ismene, had also two sons, Eteocles and Polynices. After Oedipus died, it was agreed that the two sons should share his throne, each to reign over Thebes in alternate years.

(*Gradually, the lights on the stage have been dimmed.*)

But when Eteocles, the elder son, had reigned a full year, and time had come for him to step down, he refused to yield up the throne to his younger brother. There was civil war. Polynices brought up allies—six foreign princes; and in the course of the war he and his foreigners were defeated, each in front of one of the seven gates of the city. The two brothers fought, and they killed one another in single combat just outside the city walls. Now Creon is King.

(CHORUS *is leaning, at this point, against the left proscenium arch. By now the stage is dark, with only the cyclorama bathed in dark blue. A single spot lights up the face of* CHORUS.)

Creon has issued a solemn edict that Eteocles, with whom he had sided, is to be buried with pomp and honors, and that Polynices is to be left to rot. The vultures and the dogs are to bloat themselves on his carcass. Nobody is to go into mourning for him. No gravestone is to be set up in his memory. And above all, any person who attempts to give him religious burial will himself be put to death.

It is against this blasphemy that Antigone rebels. What is for Creon merely the climax of a political purge, is for her an outrage against her dead brother which swells and grows until she perceives that it is an offense against God and against all men.

(*The light on* CHORUS *vanishes and* CHORUS *disappears through the left arch. It is dawn, gray and ashen, in a house asleep.* ANTIGONE *steals in from out-of-doors, through the arch right. She is carrying her sandals in her hand. She pauses, looking off through the arch, taut, listening, then turns and moves across downstage. As she reaches the table, she sees the* NURSE *approaching through the arch left. She runs quickly towards the exit. As she reaches the steps, the* NURSE *enters through arch and stands still when she sees* ANTIGONE.)

NURSE. Where have you been?

ANTIGONE. Nowhere. It was beautiful. The whole world was gray when I went out. And now—you wouldn't recognize it. It's like a post card: all pink, and green and yellow. You'll have to get up earlier, Nurse, if you want to see a world without color.

NURSE. It was still pitch black when I got up. I went to your room, for I thought you might have flung off your blanket in the night. You weren't there.

ANTIGONE (*comes down the steps*). The garden was lovely. It was still asleep.

NURSE. You hadn't slept in your bed. I couldn't find you. I went to the back door. You'd left it half open.

ANTIGONE. The fields were wet. They were waiting for something to happen. The whole world was breathless, waiting. I can't tell you what a roaring noise I seemed to make as I went up the road. I took off my sandals and slipped into a field.

(*She moves down to the stool and sits.*)

NURSE (*kneels at* ANTIGONE'S *feet to chafe them and put on the sandals*). You'll do well to wash your feet before you go back to bed, Miss.

ANTIGONE. I'm not going back to bed.

NURSE. Don't be a fool! You get some sleep! And me, getting up to see if she hasn't flung off her blanket; and I find her bed cold and nobody in it!

ANTIGONE. Do you think that if a person got up every morning like this, it would be just as thrilling every morning to be the first girl out-of-doors?

(NURSE *puts* ANTIGONE'S *left foot down, lifts her other foot and chafes it.*)

NURSE. Morning my grandmother! It was night. It still is. And now, my girl, you'll stop trying to squirm out of this and tell me what you were up to. Where've you been?

ANTIGONE. That's true. It was still night. There wasn't a soul out-of-doors but me who thought that it was morning.

NURSE. Oh, my little flibberty-gibbet! Just can't imagine what I'm talking about, can she? Go on with you! I know that game. Where have you been, wicked girl?

ANTIGONE (*soberly*). No. Not wicked.

NURSE. You went out to meet someone, didn't you? Deny it if you can.

ANTIGONE. Yes. I went out to meet someone.

NURSE. A lover?

ANTIGONE. Yes, Nurse. Yes, the poor dear. I have a lover.

NURSE (*stands up; bursting out*). Ah, that's very nice now, isn't it? Such goings-on! You, the daughter of a king, running out to meet lovers. And we work our fingers to the bone for you, we slave to bring you up like young ladies! (*She sits on chair right of table.*) You're all alike, all of you. Even you—who never used to stop to primp in front of a looking-glass, or smear your mouth with rouge, or dindle and dandle to make the boys ogle you, and you ogle back. How many times I'd say to myself, "Now that one, now: I wish she was a little more of a coquette—always wearing the same dress, her hair tumbling round her face. One thing's sure," I'd say to myself, "none of the boys will look at her while Ismene's around, all curled and cute and tidy and trim. I'll have this one on my hands the rest of my life." And now, you see? Just like your sister, after all. Only worse: a hypocrite. Who is the lad? Some little scamp, eh? Somebody you can't bring home and show to your family, and say, "Well, this is him, and I mean to marry him and no other." That's how it is, is it? Answer me!

ANTIGONE (*smiling faintly*). That's how it is. Yes, Nurse.

NURSE. Yes, says she! God save us! I took her when she wasn't that high. I promised her poor mother I'd make a lady of her. And look at her! But don't you go thinking this is the end of this, my young 'un. I'm only your nurse and you can play deaf and dumb with me; I don't count. But your uncle Creon will hear of this! That, I promise you.

ANTIGONE (*a little weary*). Yes, Creon will hear of this.

NURSE. And we'll hear what he has to say when he finds out that you go wandering alone o' nights. Not to mention Haemon. For the girl's engaged! Going to be married! Going to be married, and she hops out of bed at four in the morning to meet somebody else in a field.

ANTIGONE. Please, Nurse, I want to be alone.

NURSE. And if you so much as speak of it, she says she wants to be alone!

ANTIGONE. Nanny, you shouldn't scold, dear. This isn't a day when you should be losing your temper.

NURSE. Not scold, indeed! Along with the rest of it, I'm to like it. Didn't I promise your mother? What would she say if she was here? "Old Stupid!" That's what she'd call me. "Old Stupid. Not to know how to keep my little girl pure! Spend your life making them behave, watching over them like a mother hen, running after them with mufflers and sweaters to keep them warm and eggnogs to make them strong; and then at four o'clock in the morning snoring in your bed and letting them slip out into the bushes." That's what she'd say, your mother. And I'd stand there, dying of shame if I wasn't dead already. And all I could do would be not to dare look her in the face; and "That's true," I'd say. "That's all true what you say, Your Majesty."

ANTIGONE. Nanny, dear. Dear Nanny. Don't cry. You'll be able to look Mamma in the face when it's your time to see her. And she'll say, "Good morning, Nanny. Thank you for my little Antigone. You did look after her so well." She knows why I went out this morning.

NURSE. Not to meet a lover?

ANTIGONE. No. Not to meet a lover.

NURSE. Well, you've a queer way of teasing me, I must say! Not to know when she's teasing me! (*Rises to stand behind* ANTIGONE.) I must be getting awfully old, that's what it is. But if you loved me, you'd tell me the truth. You'd tell me why your bed was empty when I went along to tuck you in. Wouldn't you?

ANTIGONE. Please, Nanny, don't cry any more. (ANTIGONE *turns partly towards* NURSE, *puts an arm up to* NURSE'S *shoulder. With her other hand,* ANTIGONE *caresses* NURSE'S *face.*) There, now, my sweet red apple. Do you remember how I used to rub your cheeks to make them shine? My dear, wrinkled red apple! I didn't do anything tonight that was worth sending tears down the little gullies of your dear face. I am pure, and I swear that I have no other lover than Haemon. If you like, I'll swear that I shall never have any other lover than Haemon. Save your tears, Nanny, save them, Nanny dear; you may still need them. When you cry like that, I become a little girl again; and I mustn't be a little girl today.

(ANTIGONE *rises and moves upstage.* ISMENE *enters through arch left. She pauses in front of arch.*)

ISMENE. Antigone! What are you doing up at this hour? I've just been to your room.

NURSE. The two of you, now! You're both going mad, to be up before the kitchen fire has been started. Do you like running about without a mouthful of breakfast? Do you think it's decent for the daughters of a king? (*She turns to* ISMENE.) And look at you with no wraps on, and the sun not up! I'll have you both on my hands with colds before I know it.

ANTIGONE. Nanny dear, go away now. It's not chilly, really. Summer's here. Go make us some coffee. Please, Nanny, I'd love some coffee. It would do me so much good.

NURSE. My poor baby! Her head's swimming, what with nothing on her stomach, and I stand here like an idiot when I could be getting her something hot to drink.

(NURSE *exits. A pause.*)

ISMENE. Aren't you well?

ANTIGONE. Of course I am. Just a little tired. I got up too early.

(ANTIGONE *sits on chair, suddenly tired.*)

ISMENE. I couldn't sleep, either.

ANTIGONE. Ismene, you ought not to go without your beauty sleep.

ISMENE. Don't make fun of me.

ANTIGONE. I'm not, Ismene, truly. This particular morning, seeing how beautiful you are makes everything easier for me. Wasn't I a miserable little beast when we were small? I used to fling mud at you, and put worms down your neck. I remember tying you to a tree and cutting off your hair. Your beautiful hair! How easy it must be never to be unreasonable with all that smooth silken hair so beautifully set round your head.

ISMENE (*abruptly*). Why do you insist upon talking about other things?

ANTIGONE (*gently*). I am not talking about other things.

ISMENE. Antigone, I've thought about it a lot.

ANTIGONE. Have you?

ISMENE. I thought about it all night long. Antigone, you're mad.

ANTIGONE. Am I?

ISMENE. We cannot do it.

ANTIGONE. Why not?

ISMENE. Creon will have us put to death.

ANTIGONE. Of course he will. That's what he's here for. He will do what he has to do, and we will do what we have to do. He is bound to put us to death. We are bound to go out and bury our brother. That's the way it is. What do you think we can do to change it?

ISMENE (*releases* ANTIGONE's *hand; draws back a step*). I don't want to die.

ANTIGONE. I'd prefer not to die, myself.

ISMENE. Listen to me, Antigone. I thought about it all night. I always think things over, and you don't. You are impulsive. You get a notion in your head and you jump up and do the thing straight off. And if it's silly, well, so much the worse for you. Whereas, *I* think things out.

ANTIGONE. Sometimes it is better not to think too much.

ISMENE. I don't agree with you! (ANTIGONE *looks at* ISMENE, *then turns and moves to chair behind table.* ISMENE *leans on end of table top, toward* ANTIGONE.) Oh, I know it's horrible. And I pity Polynices just as much as you do. But all the same, I sort of see what Uncle Creon means.

ANTIGONE. I don't want to "sort of see" anything.

ISMENE. Uncle Creon is the king. He has to set an example!

ANTIGONE. Example! Do you call that edict an example? Polynices is cheated out of his rights. He makes war. Creon sides against him, and he is killed. After which Creon insists that Polynices must rot and putrefy and be mangled by dogs and birds, with no priest to bury him. And you talk to me of examples!

ISMENE. Oh, Antigone, you don't understand!

ANTIGONE. What in God's name is there to understand? Except that a man's body lies rotting, unburied. And that he is my brother. And that I must bury him.

ISMENE. But Creon won't let us bury him. And he is stronger than we are. He has made himself king.

ANTIGONE (*sits on chair*). I am not listening to you.

ISMENE (*kneels on stool, facing* ANTIGONE). You must! You know how Creon organizes things. His mob will come running, howling as it runs. A thousand arms will seize our arms. A thousand breaths will breathe into our faces. Like one single pair of eyes, a thousand eyes will stare at us. We'll be driven in a tumbrel through their hatred, through the smell of them and their cruel roaring laughter. We'll be dragged to the scaffold for torture, surrounded by guards with their idiot faces all bloated, their animal hands clean-washed for the sacrifice, their beefy eyes squinting as they stare at us. And we'll know that no shrieking and no begging will make them understand that we want to live. And we shall suffer, we shall feel pain rising in us until it becomes so unbearable that we *know* it must stop. But it won't stop; it will go on rising and rising, like a screaming voice. Oh, I can't, I can't, Antigone! (*A pause.*)

ANTIGONE. How well you have thought it all out.

ISMENE. I thought of it all night long. Didn't you?

ANTIGONE. Oh, yes.

ISMENE. I'm an awful coward, Antigone.

ANTIGONE. So am I. But what has that to do with it?

ISMENE. But, Antigone! Don't you want to go on living?

ANTIGONE. Go on living! Who was it that was always the first out of bed because she loved the touch of the cold morning air on her bare skin? Who was always the last to bed because nothing less than infinite weariness could wean her from the lingering night?

ISMENE (*clasps* ANTIGONE'S *hands, in a sudden rush of tenderness*). Antigone! Darling little sister!

ANTIGONE (*repulsing her*). No! For heaven's sake! Don't paw me! And stop sniveling! You say you've thought it all out. The howling mob—the torture—the fear of death . . . They've made up your mind for you. Is that it?

ISMENE. Yes.

ANTIGONE. All right. They're as good excuses as any.

ISMENE (*turns to* ANTIGONE). Antigone, be sensible. It's all very well for men to believe in ideas and die for them. But you are a girl!

ANTIGONE. Don't I know I'm a girl? Haven't I spent my life cursing the fact that I was a girl?

ISMENE (*with spirit*). Antigone! You have everything in the world to make you happy. All you have to do is reach out for it. You are going to be married; you are young; you are beautiful . . .

ANTIGONE. I am not beautiful.

ISMENE. Yes, you are! Not the way other girls are. But it's always you that the little tough boys turn to look back at when they pass us in the street. And when you go by, the little girls stop talking. They stare and stare at you, until we've turned a corner.

ANTIGONE (*a faint smile*). "Little tough boys—little girls."

ISMENE (*challengingly*). And what about Haemon? (*A pause.*)

ANTIGONE. I shall see Haemon this morning. I'll take care of Haemon. Go back to bed now, Ismene. The sun is coming up, and, as you can see, there is nothing I can do today. Our brother Polynices is as well guarded as if he had won the war and were sitting on his throne.

ISMENE. What are you going to do?

NURSE (*calls from off-stage*). Come along, my dove. Come to breakfast.

ANTIGONE. I don't feel like going to bed. However, if you like, I'll promise not to leave the house till you wake up.

ISMENE. And you will listen to reason, won't you? You'll let me talk to you about this again? Promise?

ANTIGONE. I promise. I'll let you talk. I'll let all of you talk. Go to bed, now. You're white with weariness.

(ISMENE *goes to arch and exits.* NURSE *enters through arch, speaking as she enters.*)

NURSE. Come along, my dove. I've made you some coffee and toast and jam.

(*She turns toward arch as if to exit.*)

ANTIGONE. I'm not really hungry, Nurse.

(NURSE *stops, looks at* ANTIGONE, *then moves behind her.*)

NURSE (*very tenderly*). Where is your pain?

ANTIGONE. Nowhere, Nanny dear. But you must keep me warm and safe, the way you used to do when I was little. Nanny! Stronger than all fever, stronger than any nightmare, stronger than the shadow of the cupboard that used to turn into a dragon on the bedroom wall. Give me your hand, Nanny, as if I were ill in bed, and you sitting beside me.

NURSE. My sparrow, my lamb! What is it that's eating your heart out?

ANTIGONE. Oh, it's just that I'm a little young still for what I have to go through. But nobody but you must know that.

NURSE (*places her other arm around* ANTIGONE's *shoulder*). A little young for what, my kitten?

ANTIGONE. Nothing in particular, Nanny. Just—all this. Oh, it's so good that you are here. I can hold your callused hand, your hand that is so prompt to ward off evil. You are very powerful, Nanny.

NURSE. What is it you want me to do for you, my baby?

ANTIGONE. There isn't anything to do, except put your hand like this against my cheek. (*She places the* NURSE's *hand against her cheek. A pause, then, as* ANTIGONE *leans back, her eyes shut.*) There! I'm not afraid any more. Not afraid of the wicked ogre, nor of the sandman, nor of the dwarf who steals little children. (*A pause.* ANTIGONE *resumes on another note.*) Nanny . . .

NURSE. Yes?

ANTIGONE. My dog, Puff . . .

NURSE (*straightens up, draws her hand away*). Well?

ANTIGONE. Promise me that you will never scold her again.

NURSE. Dogs that dirty up a house with their filthy paws deserve to be scolded.

ANTIGONE. And promise me that you will talk to her. That you will talk to her often

NURSE (*turns and looks at* ANTIGONE). Me, talk to a dog!

ANTIGONE. Yes. But mind you: you are not to talk to her the way people usually talk to dogs. You're to talk to her the way I talk to her.

NURSE. I don't see why the both of us have to make fools of ourselves. So long as you're here, one ought to be enough.

ANTIGONE. But if there was a reason why I couldn't go on talking to her . . .

NURSE (*interrupting*). Couldn't go on talking to her? And why couldn't you go on talking to her? What kind of poppy-cock . . . ?

ANTIGONE. And if she got too unhappy, if she moaned and moaned, waiting for me with her nose under the door the way she does when I'm out all day, then the best thing, Nanny, might be to have her mercifully put to sleep.

NURSE. Now what *has* got into you this morning? (HAEMON *enters through arch.*) Running round in the darkness, won't sleep, won't eat— (ANTIGONE *sees* HAEMON.) and now it's her dog she wants killed. I never . . .

ANTIGONE (*interrupting*). Nanny! Haemon is here. Go inside, please. And don't forget that you've promised me. (NURSE *goes to arch and exits.* ANTIGONE *rises.*) Haemon, Haemon! Forgive me for quarreling with you last night. (*She crosses quickly to* HAEMON *and they embrace.*) Forgive me for everything. It was all my fault. I beg you to forgive me.

HAEMON. You know that I've forgiven you. You had hardly slammed the door, your perfume still hung in the room, when I had already forgiven you. (*He holds her in his arms and smiles at her. Then draws slightly back.*) You stole that perfume. From whom?

ANTIGONE. Ismene.

HAEMON. And the rouge? and the face powder? and the dress? Whom did you steal them from?

ANTIGONE. Ismene.

HAEMON. And in whose honor did you get yourself up so elegantly?

ANTIGONE. I'll tell you everything. (*She draws him closer.*) Oh, darling, what a fool I was! To waste a whole evening! A whole, beautiful evening!

HAEMON. We'll have other evenings, my sweet.

ANTIGONE. Perhaps we won't.

HAEMON. And other quarrels, too. A happy love is full of quarrels, you know.

ANTIGONE. A happy love, yes. Haemon, listen to me.

HAEMON. Yes?

ANTIGONE. Don't laugh at me this morning. Be serious.

HAEMON. I am serious.

ANTIGONE. And hold me tight. Tighter than you have ever held me. I want all your strength to flow into me.

HAEMON. There! With all my strength. (*A pause.*)

ANTIGONE (*breathless*). That's good. (*They stand for a moment, silent and motionless.*) Haemon! I wanted to tell you. You know—the little boy we were going to have when we were married?

HAEMON. Yes?

ANTIGONE. I'd have protected him against everything in the world.

HAEMON. Yes, dearest.

ANTIGONE. Oh, you don't know how I should have held him in my arms and given him my strength. He wouldn't have been afraid of anything. Our little boy, Haemon! His mother wouldn't have been very imposing: her hair wouldn't always have been brushed; but she would have been strong where he was concerned, so much stronger than all those real mothers with their real bosoms and their aprons round their middle. You believe that, don't you, Haemon?

HAEMON (*soothingly*). Yes, yes, my darling.

ANTIGONE. And you believe me when I say that you would have had a real wife?

HAEMON. Darling, you are my real wife.

ANTIGONE (*pressing against him and crying out*). Haemon, you loved me! You did love me that night, didn't you? You're sure of it!

HAEMON (*rocking her gently*). What night, my sweet?

ANTIGONE. And you are very sure, aren't you, that that night, at the dance, when you came to the corner where I was sitting, there was no mistake? It was me you were looking for? It wasn't another girl? And you're sure that never, not in your most secret heart of hearts, have you said to yourself that it was Ismene you ought to have asked to marry you?

HAEMON (*reproachfully*). Antigone, you are idiotic. You might give me credit for knowing my own mind. It's you I love, and no one else.

ANTIGONE. But you love me as a woman—as a woman wants to be loved, don't you? Your arms around me aren't lying, are they? Your hands, so warm against my back—they're not lying? This warmth, this confidence, this sense that I am safe, secure, that flows through me as I stand here with my cheek in the hollow of your shoulder: they are not lies, are they?

HAEMON. Antigone, darling, I love you exactly as you love me. With all of myself.

(*They kiss.*)

ANTIGONE. I'm sallow, and I'm scrawny. Ismene is pink and golden. She's like a fruit.

HAEMON. Look here, Antigone . . .

ANTIGONE. Ah, dearest, I am ashamed of myself. But this morning, this special morning, I must know. Tell me the truth! I beg you to tell me the truth! When you think about me, when it strikes you suddenly that I am going to belong to you— do you have the feeling that—that a great empty space is being hollowed out inside you, that there is something inside you that is just—dying?

HAEMON. Yes, I do, I do. (*A pause.*)

ANTIGONE. That's the way I feel. And another thing. I wanted you to know that I should have been very proud to be your wife—the woman whose shoulder you would put your hand on as you sat down to table, absent-mindedly, as upon a thing that belonged to you. (*After a moment, draws away from him. Her tone changes.*) There! Now I have two things more to tell you. And when I have told them to you, you must go away instantly, without asking any questions. However strange they may seem to you. However much they may hurt you. Swear that you will!

HAEMON (*beginning to be troubled*). What are these things that you are going to tell me?

ANTIGONE. Swear, first, that you will go away without one word. Without so much as looking at me. (*She looks at him, wretchedness in her face.*) You hear me, Haemon. Swear it, please. This is the last mad wish that you will ever have to grant me. (*A pause.*)

HAEMON. I swear it, since you insist. But I must tell you that I don't like this at all.

ANTIGONE. Please, Haemon. It's very serious. You must listen to me and do as I ask. First, about last night, when I came to your house. You asked me a moment ago why I wore Ismene's dress and rouge. It was because I was stupid. I wasn't very sure that you loved me as a woman; and I did it—because I wanted you to take me. I wanted to be your wife before . . .

HAEMON. Oh, my darling . . .

ANTIGONE (*shuts him off*). You swore you wouldn't ask any questions. You swore, Haemon. (*Turns her face away and goes on in a hard voice.*) As a matter of fact, I'll tell you why. I wanted to be your wife last night because I love you that way very—very strongly. And also because— Oh, my darling, my darling, forgive me; I'm going to cause you quite a lot of pain. (*She draws away from him.*) I wanted it also because I shall never, never be able to marry you, never! (HAEMON *is stupefied and mute; then he moves a step toward her.*) Haemon! You took a solemn oath! You swore! Leave me quickly. Tomorrow—tomorrow the whole thing will be clear to you. Even before tomorrow: this afternoon. If you please, Haemon, go now. It is the only thing left that you can do for me if you still love me. (*A pause as* HAEMON *stares at her. Then he turns and goes out through the arch.* ANTIGONE *stands motionless, then moves to chair at end of table and lets herself gently down on it. In a mild voice, as of calm after storm.*) Well, it's over for Haemon, Antigone.

(ISMENE *enters through arch, pauses for a moment in front of it when she sees* ANTIGONE, *then crosses behind table.*)

ISMENE. I can't sleep. I'm terrified. I'm so afraid that even though it is daylight, you'll still try to bury Polynices. Antigone, you remember what Polynices was like. He was our brother, of course. But he's dead; and he never loved us. He was a bad brother. He was like an enemy in this house. He never thought of you. Why should you think of him? What if he does have to lie rotting in a field? It's Creon's doing, not ours. Don't try to change things. You can't bury Polynices. I'm older than you are and I won't let you!

ANTIGONE. You are too late, Ismene. When you first saw me this morning, I had just come in from burying him.

(ANTIGONE *exits through arch. The lighting, which by this time has reached a point of early morning sun, is quickly dimmed out, leaving the stage bathed in a light-blue color.* ISMENE *runs out after* ANTIGONE. *On* ISMENE'S *exit the lights are brought up suddenly to suggest a later period of the day.* CREON *and* PAGE *enter through curtain upstage.* CREON *stands on the top step; his* PAGE *stands at his right side.*)

CREON. A private of the guards, you say? One of those standing watch over the body? Show him in.

(*The* PAGE *crosses to arch and exits.* CREON *moves down to end of table.* PAGE *re-enters, preceded by the* FIRST GUARD, *livid with fear.* PAGE *remains on up-stage side of arch.* GUARD *salutes.*)

GUARD. Private Jonas, Second Battalion.

CREON. What are you doing here?

GUARD. It's like this, chief. Soon as it happened, we said: "Got to tell the chief about this before anybody else spills it. He'll want to know right away." So we tossed a coin to see which one would come up and tell you about it. You see, chief, we thought only one man better come because, after all, you don't want to leave the body without a guard. Right? I mean, there's three of us on duty, guarding the body.

CREON. What's wrong about the body?

GUARD. Chief, I've been seventeen years in the service. Volunteer. Wounded three times. Two citations. My record's clean. I know my business and I know my place. I carry out orders. Sir, ask any officer in the battalion; they'll tell you. "Leave it to Jonas. Give him an order; he'll carry it out." That's what they'll tell you, chief. Jonas, that's me—that's my name.

CREON. What's the matter with you, man? What are you shaking for?

GUARD. By rights it's the corporal's job, chief. I've been recommended for a corporal but they haven't put it through yet. June, it was supposed to go through.

CREON (*interrupts*). Stop chattering and tell me why you are here. If anything has gone wrong I'll break all three of you.

GUARD. Nobody can say we didn't keep our eye on that body. We had the two o'clock watch—the tough one. You know how it is, chief. It's nearly the end of the night. Your eyes are like lead. You've got a crick in the back of your neck. There's shadows, and the fog is beginning to roll in. A fine watch they give us! And me, seventeen years in the service. But we was doing our duty, all right. On our feet, all of us. Anybody says we were sleeping is a liar. First place, it was too cold. Second place . . . (CREON *makes a gesture of impatience.*) Yes, chief. Well, I turned round and looked at the body. We wasn't only ten feet away from it, but that's how I am. I was keeping my eye on it. (*Shouts.*) Listen, chief, I was the first man to see it! Me! They'll tell you. I was the one let out that yell!

CREON. What for? What was the matter?

GUARD. Chief, the body! Somebody had been there and buried it. (CREON *comes down a step on the stair. The* GUARD *becomes more frightened.*) It wasn't much, you understand. With us three there, it couldn't have been. Just covered over with a little dirt, that's all. But enough to hide it from the buzzards.

CREON. By God, I'll . . . ! (*He looks intently at the* GUARD.) You are sure that it couldn't have been a dog, scratching up the earth?

GUARD. Not a chance, chief. That's kind of what we hoped it was. But the earth was scattered over the body just like the priests tell you you should do it. Whoever did that job knew what he was doing, all right.

CREON. Who could have dared? (*He turns and looks at the* GUARD.) Was there anything to indicate who might have done it?

GUARD. Not a thing, chief. Maybe we heard a footstep—I can't swear to it. Of course we started right in to search, and the corporal found a shovel, a kid's shovel no bigger than that, all rusty and everything. Corporal's got the shovel for you. We thought maybe a kid did it.

CREON (*to himself*). A kid! (*He looks away from the* GUARD.) I broke the back of the rebellion; but like a snake, it is coming together again. Polynices' friends, with their gold, blocked by my orders in the banks of Thebes. The leaders of the mob allied to envious princes. And the temple priests, always ready for a bit of fishing in troubled waters. A kid! I can imagine what he is like, their kid: a baby-faced killer, creeping in the night with a toy shovel under his jacket. (*He looks at his* PAGE.) Though why shouldn't they have corrupted a real child? There is something, now, to soften the hearts and weaken the minds of the populace! Very touching! Very useful to them, an innocent child. A martyr. A real white-faced baby of fourteen who will spit with contempt at the guards who kill him. A free gift to their cause: the precious, innocent blood of a child on my hands. (*He turns to the* GUARD.) They must have accomplices in the Guard itself. Look here, you. Who knows about this?

GUARD. Only us three, chief. We flipped a coin, and I came right over.

CREON. Right. Listen, now. You will continue on duty. When the relief squad comes up, you will tell them to return to barracks. You will uncover the body. If another attempt is made to bury it, I shall expect you to make an arrest and bring the person straight to me. And you will keep your mouths shut. Not one word of this to a human soul. You are all guilty of neglect of duty, and you will be punished; but if the rumor spreads through Thebes that the body received burial, you will be shot—all three of you.

GUARD (*excitedly*). Chief, we never told nobody, I swear we didn't! Anyhow, I've been up here. Suppose my pals spilled it to the relief; I couldn't have been with them and here, too. That wouldn't be my fault if they talked. Chief, I've got two kids. You're my witness, chief, it couldn't have been me. I was here with you. I've got a witness! If anybody talked, it couldn't have been me! I was . . .

CREON (*interrupting*). Clear out! If the story doesn't get round, you won't be shot. (*The* GUARD *salutes, turns, and exits on the run.* CREON *turns and paces upstage, then comes down to the end of the table.*) A child! (*He looks at* PAGE.) Come here, my lad. (PAGE *crosses to side of* CREON. CREON *puts his hand on* PAGE's *shoulder.*) Would you defy me with your little shovel? (PAGE *looks up at*

CREON.) Of course you would. You would do it, too. (*A pause.* CREON *looks away from* PAGE *and murmurs.*) A child!

(CREON *and* PAGE *go slowly upstage center to top step.* PAGE *draws aside the curtain, through which* CREON *exits with* PAGE *behind him. As soon as* CREON *and* PAGE *have disappeared,* CHORUS *enters and leans against the upstage portal of arch, left. The lighting is brought up to its brightest point to suggest mid-afternoon.* CHORUS *allows a pause to indicate that a crucial moment has been reached in the play, then moves slowly downstage center. He stands for a moment silent, reflecting, and then smiles faintly.*)

CHORUS. The spring is wound up tight. It will uncoil of itself. That is what is so convenient in tragedy. The least little turn of the wrist will do the job. Anything will set it going: a glance at a girl who happens to be lifting her arms to her hair as you go by; a feeling when you wake up on a fine morning that you'd like a little respect paid to you today, as if it were as easy to order as a second cup of coffee; one question too many, idly thrown out over a friendly drink—and the tragedy is on.

The rest is automatic. You don't need to lift a finger. The machine is in perfect order; it has been oiled ever since time began, and it runs without friction. Death, treason, and sorrow are on the march; and they move in the wake of storm, of tears, of stillness. Every kind of stillness. The hush when the executioner's axe goes up at the end of the last act. The unbreathable silence when, at the beginning of the play, the two lovers, their hearts bared, their bodies naked, stand for the first time face to face in the darkened room, afraid to stir. The silence inside you when the roaring crowd acclaims the winner—so that you think of a film without a soundtrack, mouths agape and no sound coming out of them, a clamor that is no more than a picture; and you, the victor, already vanquished, alone in the desert of your silence. That is tragedy.

Tragedy is clean, it is firm, it is flawless. It has nothing to do with melodrama—with wicked villains, persecuted maidens, avengers, sudden revelations and eleventh-hour repentances. Death, in a melodrama, is really horrible because it is never inevitable. The dear old father might so easily have been saved; the honest young man might so easily have brought in the police five minutes earlier.

In a tragedy, nothing is in doubt and everyone's destiny is known. That makes for tranquillity. There is a sort of fellow-feeling among characters in a tragedy: he who kills is as innocent as he who gets killed: it's all a matter of what part you are playing. Tragedy is restful; and the reason is that hope, that foul, deceitful thing, has no part in it. There isn't any hope. You're trapped. The whole sky has fallen on you, and all you can do about it is to shout.

Don't mistake me: I said "shout": I did not say groan, whimper, complain. That, you cannot do. But you can shout aloud; you can get all those things said that you never thought you'd be able to say—or never even knew you had it in you to say. And you don't say these things because it will do any good to say them: you know better than that. You say them for their own sake; you say them because you learn a lot from them.

In melodrama, you argue and struggle in the hope of escape. That is vulgar; it's practical. But in tragedy, where there is no temptation to try to escape, argument is gratuitous: it's kingly. (*Voices of the* GUARDS *and scuffling sounds heard through the archway.* CHORUS *looks in that direction, then in a changed tone.*) The play is on. Antigone has been caught. For the first time in her life, little Antigone is going to be able to be herself.

(CHORUS *exits through arch. A pause, while the off-stage voices rise in volume, then the* FIRST GUARD *enters, followed by* SECOND *and* THIRD GUARDS, *holding the arms of* ANTIGONE *and dragging her along. The* FIRST GUARD, *speaking as he enters, crosses swiftly to end of the table. The* TWO GUARDS *and* ANTIGONE *stop downstage.*)

FIRST GUARD (*recovered from his fright*). Come on, now, Miss, give it a rest. The chief will be here in a minute and you can tell him about it. All I know is my orders. I don't want to know what you were doing there. People always have excuses; but I can't afford to listen to them, see. Say, if we had to listen to all the people who want to tell us what's the matter with this country, we'd never get our work done. (*To the* GUARDS.) You keep hold of her and I'll see that she keeps her face shut.

ANTIGONE. They are hurting me. Tell them to take their dirty hands off me.

FIRST GUARD. Dirty hands, eh? The least you can do is try to be polite, Miss. Look at me: I'm polite.

ANTIGONE. Tell them to let me go. I shan't run away. My father was King Oedipus. I am Antigone.

FIRST GUARD. King Oedipus' little girl! What do you know about that! Listen, Miss, the night watch never picks up a lady, but she says, you better be careful; I'm sleeping with the police commissioner. (*The* GUARDS *laugh.*)

ANTIGONE. I don't mind being killed, but I don't want them to touch me.

FIRST GUARD. Yeah? And what about stiffs, and dirt, and such like? You wasn't afraid to touch them, was you? "Their dirty hands!" Take a look at your own hands. (ANTIGONE, *handcuffed, smiles despite herself as she looks down at her hands. They are grubby.*) Guess you must have lost your shovel, didn't you? Had to go at it with your fingernails the second time, I guess. By God, I never saw such nerve! I turn my back for about five seconds; I ask a pal for a chew; I say "thanks"; I get the tobacco stowed away in my cheek—the whole thing don't take ten seconds; and there she is, clawing away like a hyena. Right out in broad daylight! And boy! did she scratch and kick when I grabbed her! Straight for my eyes with them nails she went. And yelling something fierce about, "I ain't finished yet; let me finish!" She ain't got all her marbles!

SECOND GUARD. I pinched a nut like that the other day. Right on the main square, she was, histin' up her skirts and showing her behind to anybody wanted to take a look.

FIRST GUARD. Listen, we're going to get a bonus out of this. What do you say we throw a party, the three of us?

SECOND GUARD. At the old woman's? Behind Market Street?

THIRD GUARD. Suits me. Sunday would be a good day. We're off duty Sunday. What do you say we bring our wives?

FIRST GUARD. Nix. Let's have some fun this time. Bring your wife, there's always something goes wrong. First place, what do you do with the kids? Bring them, they always want to go to the can just when you're right in the middle of a game of cards or something. Say, listen. Who would have thought an hour ago that us three would be talking about throwing a party right now? The way I felt when the old man was interrogatin' me, we'd be lucky if we got off with being docked a month's pay. I want to tell you, I was scared.

SECOND GUARD. You sure we're going to get a bonus?

FIRST GUARD. Yeah. Something tells me this is big stuff.

THIRD GUARD (*to* SECOND GUARD). What's-his-name, you know—in the Third Battalion? He got an extra month's pay for catching a fire-bug.

SECOND GUARD. If we get an extra month's pay, I vote we throw the party at the Arabian's.

FIRST GUARD. You're crazy! He charges twice as much for liquor as anybody else in town. Unless you want to go upstairs, of course. Can't do that at the old woman's.

THIRD GUARD. Say, we can't keep this from our wives, no matter how you figure it. You get an extra month's pay, and what happens? Everybody in the battalion knows it, and your wife knows it too. They might even line up the battalion and give it to you in front of everybody, so how could you keep your wife from finding out?

FIRST GUARD. Well, we'll see about that. If they do the job out in the barracks-yard —of course that means women, kids, everything.

ANTIGONE. I should like to sit down, if you please.

(*A pause, as the* FIRST GUARD *thinks it over.*)

FIRST GUARD. Let her sit down. But keep hold of her. (*The two* GUARDS *start to lead her towards the chair at end of table. The curtain upstage opens, and* CREON *enters, followed by his* PAGE. FIRST GUARD *turns and moves upstage a few steps, sees* CREON.) 'Tenshun!

(*The three* GUARDS *salute.* CREON, *seeing* ANTIGONE *handcuffed to* THIRD GUARD, *stops on the top step, astonished.*)

CREON. Antigone! (*To the* FIRST GUARD.) Take off those handcuffs! (FIRST GUARD *crosses above table to left of* ANTIGONE.) What is this?

(CREON *and his* PAGE *come down off the steps.* FIRST GUARD *takes key from his pocket and unlocks the cuff on* ANTIGONE'S *hand.* ANTIGONE *rubs her wrist as she crosses below table toward chair at end of table.* SECOND *and* THIRD GUARDS *step back to front of arch.* FIRST GUARD *turns upstage toward* CREON.)

FIRST GUARD. The watch, chief. We all came this time.

CREON. Who is guarding the body?

FIRST GUARD. We sent for the relief. (CREON *comes down.*)

CREON. But I gave orders that the relief was to go back to barracks and stay there! (ANTIGONE *sits on chair at left of table.*) I told you not to open your mouth about this!

FIRST GUARD. Nobody's said anything, chief. We made this arrest, and brought the party in, the way you said we should.

CREON (*to* ANTIGONE). Where did these men find you?

FIRST GUARD. Right by the body.

CREON. What were you doing near your brother's body? You knew what my orders were.

FIRST GUARD. What was she doing? Chief, that's why we brought her in. She was digging up the dirt with her nails. She was trying to cover up the body all over again.

CREON. Do you realize what you are saying?

FIRST GUARD. Chief, ask these men here. After I reported to you, I went back, and first thing we did, we uncovered the body. The sun was coming up and it was beginning to smell, so we moved it up on a little rise to get him in the wind. Of course you wouldn't expect any trouble in broad daylight. But just the same, we decided one of us better keep his eye peeled all the time. About noon, what with the sun and the smell, being the wind dropped, and I wasn't feeling none too good, I went over to my pal to get a chew. I just had time to say "thanks" and stick it in my mouth, when I turned round and there she was, clawing away at the dirt with both hands. Right out in broad daylight! Wouldn't you think when she saw me come running, she'd quit and beat it out of there? Not her! She went right on digging as fast as she could, as if I wasn't there at all. And when I grabbed her, she scratched and bit and yelled to leave her alone, she hadn't finished yet, the body wasn't all covered yet, and the like of that.

CREON (*to* ANTIGONE). Is this true?

ANTIGONE. Yes, it is true.

FIRST GUARD. We scraped the dirt off as fast as we could, then we sent for the relief and we posted them. But we didn't tell them a thing, chief. And we brought in the party so's you could see her. And that's the truth, so help me God.

CREON (*to* ANTIGONE). And was it you who covered the body the first time? In the night?

ANTIGONE. Yes, it was. With a toy shovel we used to take to the seashore when we were children. It was Polynices' own shovel; he had cut his name in the handle. That was why I left it with him. But these men took it away; so the next time, I had to do it with my hands.

FIRST GUARD. Chief, she was clawing away like a wild animal. Matter of fact, first minute we saw her, what with the heat haze and everything, my pal says, "That must be a dog," he says. "Dog!" I says, "That's a girl, that is!" And it was.

CREON. Very well. (*Turns to the* PAGE.) Show these men to the ante-room. (*The* PAGE *crosses to the arch, stands there, waiting.* CREON *moves behind the table. To the* FIRST GUARD.) You three men will wait outside. I may want a report from you later.

FIRST GUARD. Do I put the cuffs back on her, chief?

CREON. No. (*The three* GUARDS *salute, do an about-face and exit through arch right.* PAGE *follows them out. A pause.*) Had you told anybody what you meant to do?

ANTIGONE. No.

CREON. Did you meet anyone on your way—coming or going?

ANTIGONE. No, nobody.

CREON. Sure of that, are you?

ANTIGONE. Perfectly sure.

CREON. Very well. Now listen to me. You will go straight to your room. When you get there, you will go to bed. You will say that you are not well and that you have not been out since yesterday. Your nurse will tell the same story. (*He looks toward arch, through which the* GUARDS *have exited.*) And I'll dispose of those three men.

ANTIGONE. Uncle Creon, you are going to a lot of trouble for no good reason. You must know that I'll do it all over again tonight.

(*A pause. They look one another in the eye.*)

CREON. Why did you try to bury your brother?

ANTIGONE. I owed it to him.

CREON. I had forbidden it.

ANTIGONE. I owed it to him. Those who are not buried wander eternally and find no rest. Everybody knows that. I owe it to my brother to unlock the house of the dead in which my father and my mother are waiting to welcome him. Polynices has earned his rest.

CREON. Polynices was a rebel and a traitor, and you know it.

ANTIGONE. He was my brother, and he was a human being. Who, except you, wants my brother's body to rot in a field? Does God want that? Do the people want it?

CREON. God and the people of Thebes are not concerned in this. You heard my edict. It was proclaimed throughout Thebes. You read my edict. It was posted up on the city walls.

ANTIGONE. Of course I did.

CREON. You knew the punishment I decreed for any person who attempted to give him burial.

ANTIGONE. Yes, I knew the punishment.

CREON. Did you by any chance act on the assumption that a daughter of Oedipus, a daughter of Oedipus' stubborn pride, was above the law?

ANTIGONE. No, I did not act on that assumption.

CREON. Because if you had acted on that assumption, Antigone, you would have been deeply wrong. Nobody has a more sacred obligation to obey the law than those who make the law. You are a daughter of lawmakers, a daughter of kings, Antigone. You must observe the law.

ANTIGONE. Had I been a scullery maid washing my dishes when that law was read aloud to me, I should have scrubbed the greasy water from my arms and gone out in my apron to bury my brother.

CREON. What nonsense! If you had been a scullery maid, there would have been no doubt in your mind about the seriousness of that edict. You would have known that it meant death; and you would have been satisfied to weep for your brother in your kitchen. But you! You thought that because you come of the royal line, because you were my niece and were going to marry my son, I shouldn't dare have you killed.

ANTIGONE. You are mistaken. Quite the contrary. I never doubted for an instant that you would have me put to death.

(*A pause, as* CREON *stares fixedly at her.*)

CREON. The pride of Oedipus! Oedipus and his headstrong pride all over again. I can see your father in you—and I believe you. Of course you thought that I should have you killed! Proud as you are, it seemed to you a natural climax in your existence. Your father was like that. For him as for you human happiness was meaningless; and mere human misery was not enough to satisfy his passion for torment. (*He sits on stool behind the table.*) You come of people for whom the human vestment is a kind of strait-jacket: it cracks at the seams. You spend your lives wriggling to get out of it. Nothing less than a cosy tea-party with death and destiny will quench your thirst. The happiest hour of your father's life came when he listened greedily to the story of how, unknown to himself, he had killed his own father and dishonored the bed of his own mother. Drop by drop, word by word, he drank in the dark story that the gods had destined him, first to live and then to hear. How avidly men and women drink the brew of such a tale when their names are Oedipus—and Antigone! And it is so simple, afterwards, to do what your father did, to put out one's eyes and take one's daughter begging on the highways.

Let me tell you, Antigone: those days are over for Thebes. Thebes has a right to a king without a past. My name, thank God, is only Creon. I stand here with both feet firm on the ground; with both hands in my pockets; and I have decided that so long as I am king—being less ambitious than your father was—I shall merely devote myself to introducing a little order into this absurd kingdom; if that is possible.

Don't think that being a king seems to me romantic. It is my trade; a trade a man has to work at every day; and like every other trade, it isn't all beer and skittles. But since it is my trade, I take it seriously. And if, tomorrow, some wild and bearded messenger walks in from some wild and distant valley—which is what happened to your dad—and tells me that he's not quite sure who my parents were, but thinks that my wife Eurydice is actually my mother, I shall ask him to do me the kindness to go back where he came from; and I shan't let a little matter like that persuade me to order my wife to take a blood test and the police to let me know whether or not my birth certificate was forged. Kings, my girl, have other things to do than to surrender themselves to their private feelings. (*He looks at her and smiles.*) Hand *you* over to be killed! (*He rises, moves to end of table and sits on the top of table.*) I have other plans for you. You're going to marry Haemon; and I want you to fatten up a bit so that you can give him a sturdy boy. Let me assure you that Thebes needs that boy a good deal more than it needs your death. You will go to your room, now, and do as you have been told; and you won't say a word about this to anybody. Don't fret about the guards; I'll see that their mouths are shut. And don't annihilate me with those eyes. I know that you think I am a brute, and I'm sure you must consider me very prosaic. But the fact is, I have always been fond of you, stubborn though you always were. Don't forget that the first doll you ever had came from me. (*A pause.* ANTIGONE *says nothing, rises and crosses slowly below the table toward the arch.* CREON *turns and watches her; then.*) Where are you going?

ANTIGONE (*stops downstage. Without any show of rebellion*). You know very well where I am going.

CREON (*after a pause*). What sort of game are you playing?

ANTIGONE. I am not playing games.

CREON. Antigone, do you realize that if, apart from those three guards, a single soul finds out what you have tried to do, it will be impossible for me to avoid putting you to death? There is still a chance that I can save you; but only if you keep this to yourself and give up your crazy purpose. Five minutes more, and it will be too late. You understand that?

ANTIGONE. I must go bury my brother. Those men uncovered him.

CREON. What good will it do? You know that there are other men standing guard over Polynices. And even if you did cover him over with earth again, the earth would again be removed.

ANTIGONE. I know all that. I know it. But that much, at least, I can do. And what a person can do, a person should do. (*Pause.*)

CREON. Tell me, Antigone, do you believe all that flummery about religious burial? Do you really believe that a so-called shade of your brother is condemned to wander forever homeless if a little earth is not flung on his corpse to the accompaniment of some priestly abracadabra? Have you ever listened to the priests of Thebes when they were mumbling their formula? Have you ever watched their dreary sullen faces while they were preparing the dead for burial—skipping half the gestures required by the ritual, swallowing half their words, hustling the dead into their graves out of fear that they might be late for lunch?

ANTIGONE. Yes, I have seen all that.

CREON. And did you never say to yourself as you watched them, that if someone you really loved lay dead under the shuffling, mumbling ministrations of the priests, you would scream aloud and beg the priests to leave the dead in peace?

ANTIGONE. No, Creon. There is God and there are His priests. They are not the same things. You are not free to do with men as you wish—not even when they are dead.

CREON. And you are going to stop me, are you?

ANTIGONE. Yes, I am going to stop you.

(*A pause as they stand looking at one another.*)

CREON. You must want very much to die. You look like a trapped animal.

ANTIGONE. Stop feeling sorry for me. Do as I do. Do your job. But if you are a human being, do it quickly.

CREON (*takes a step toward her*). I want to save you, Antigone.

ANTIGONE. You are the King, and you are all-powerful. But that you cannot do.

CREON. You think not?

ANTIGONE. Neither save me nor stop me.

CREON. Prideful Antigone!

ANTIGONE. Only this can you do: have me put to death.

CREON. Have you tortured, perhaps?

ANTIGONE. Why would you do that? To see me cry? To hear me beg for mercy? Or swear whatever you wish, and then begin over again? (*A pause.*)

CREON. You listen to me. You have cast me for the villain in this little play of yours, and yourself for the heroine. And you know it, you damned little mischief-maker! But don't you drive me too far! If I were one of your preposterous little tyrants that Greece is full of, you would be lying in a ditch this minute with your tongue pulled out and your body drawn and quartered. But you can see something in my face that makes me hesitate to send for the guards and turn you over to them. Instead, I let you go on arguing; and you taunt me, you take the offensive. (*He grasps her left wrist.*) What are you driving at, you she-devil?

ANTIGONE. Let me go. You are hurting my arm.

CREON (*gripping her tighter*). I will not let you go.

ANTIGONE (*moans*). Oh!

CREON. I was a fool to waste words. I should have done this from the beginning. (*He looks at her.*) I may be your uncle; but we are not a particularly affectionate family. Are we, eh? (*Through his teeth as he twists.*) Are we? (CREON *propels* ANTIGONE *round below him to his side.*) What fun for you, eh? To be able to spit in the face of a King who has all the power in the world; a man who has done his own killing in his day; who has killed people just as pitiable as you are— and who is still soft enough to go to all this trouble in order to keep you from being killed.

(*A pause.*)

ANTIGONE. Now you are squeezing my arm too tightly. It doesn't hurt any more.

(CREON *stares at her, then drops her arm.*)

CREON. I shall save you yet. (*He goes below the table to the chair at end of table, takes off his coat and places it on the chair.*) God knows, I have things enough to do today without wasting my time on an insect like you. But urgent things can wait. I am not going to let politics be the cause of your death. For it is a fact that this whole business is nothing but politics: the mournful shade of Polynices, the decomposing corpse, the sentimental weeping and the hysteria that you mistake for heroism, nothing but politics.

Look here. I may not be soft, but I'm fastidious. I like things clean, ship-shape, well scrubbed. Don't think that I am not just as offended as you are by the thought of that meat rotting in the sun. In the evening, when the breeze comes in off the sea, you can smell it in the palace, and it nauseates me. But I refuse even to shut my window. The people of Thebes have got to have their noses rubbed into it a little longer. My God! If it was up to me, I should have had them bury your brother long ago as a mere matter of public hygiene. I admit that what I am doing is childish. But it is by childish tricks like this that men are governed. And if the feather-headed rabble I govern are to understand what's what, that stench has got to fill the town for a month!

ANTIGONE (*turns to him*). You are a loathsome man!

CREON. I agree. My trade forces me to be. We could argue whether I ought or ought not to follow my trade; but once I take on the job, I must do it properly.

ANTIGONE. Why do you do it at all?

CREON. My dear, I woke up one morning and found myself King of Thebes. God knows, there were other things I loved in life more than power.

ANTIGONE. Then you should have said no.

CREON. Yes, I could have done that. Only, I felt that it would have been cowardly. I should have been like a workman who turns down a job that has to be done. So I said yes.

ANTIGONE. So much the worse for you, then. I didn't say yes. I can say no to anything I think vile, and I don't have to count the cost. But because you said yes to your lust for power, all that you can do, for all of your crown, your trappings, and your guards—all that you can do is to have me killed.

CREON. Listen to me.

ANTIGONE. If I want to. I don't have to listen to you if I don't want to. There is nothing you can tell me that I don't know. Whereas, I can tell you a thousand things that you don't know. You stand there, drinking in my words. (*She moves behind chair.*) Why is it that you don't call your guards? I'll tell you why. You want to hear me out to the end; that's why.

CREON. You amuse me.

ANTIGONE. Oh, no, I don't. I frighten you. That is why you talk about saving me. Everything would be so much easier if you had a docile, tongue-tied little Antigone living in the palace. But you are going to have to bury Polynices or put me to death today—one of the two—and you know it. And that's what frightens you.

CREON. Very well. I am afraid, then. Does that satisfy you? I am afraid that if you insist upon it, I shall have to have you killed. And I don't want to.

ANTIGONE. I don't have to do things that I think are wrong. If it comes to that, you didn't really want to leave my brother's body unburied, did you? Say it! Admit that you didn't.

CREON. I have said it already.

ANTIGONE. But you did it just the same. And now, though you don't want to do it, you are going to have me killed. And you call that being a king!

CREON. Yes, I call that being a king.

ANTIGONE. Poor Creon! My nails are broken, my fingers are bleeding, my arms are covered with the welts left by the paws of your guards—but I am a queen!

CREON. Then why not have pity on me, and live? Isn't your brother's corpse, rotting under my windows, payment enough for peace and order in Thebes?

ANTIGONE. What have I to do with your slave's peace and your barbarian's order? No, Creon! You said yes, and made yourself king. Now you will never stop paying.

CREON. But God in Heaven! Won't you try to understand me! I'm trying hard enough to understand you! There had to be one man who said yes. Somebody had to agree to captain the ship. She had sprung a hundred leaks; she was loaded to the waterline with crime, ignorance, poverty. The wheel was swinging with the wind. The crew refused to work and were looting the cargo. The officers were building a raft, ready to slip overboard and desert the ship. The mast was splitting, the sails were beginning to rip. Every man-jack on board was about to drown—and only because the only thing they thought of was their own skins and their cheap little day-to-day traffic. Was that a time, do you think, for playing with words like yes and no? You grab the wheel, you right the ship in the face of a mountain of water. You shout an order, and if one man refuses to obey, you shoot straight into the mob. Into the mob, I say! The beast as nameless as the wave that crashes down upon your deck; as nameless as the whipping wind. The thing that drops when you shoot may be someone who poured you a drink the night before; but it has no name. And you, braced at the wheel, you have no name, either. Nothing has a name—except the ship, and the storm. (*A pause as he looks at her.*) Now do you understand?

ANTIGONE. I am not here to understand. Not what you call understand. I am here to say no to you, and bury Polynices.

CREON. It is easy to say no.

ANTIGONE. Not always.

CREON. It is easy to say no. To say yes, you have to sweat and roll up your sleeves and plunge both hands into life up to the elbows. It is easy to say no, even if saying no means death. All you have to do is to sit still and wait. Wait to go on living; wait to be killed. That is the coward's part. *No* is one of your man-made words. Can you imagine a world in which trees say *no* to the sap? In which beasts say *no* to hunger or to propagation? Animals are good, simple, tough. They move in droves, nudging one another onwards, all traveling the same road. Some of them keel over; but the rest go on; and no matter how many may fall by the wayside, there are always those few left who go on bringing their young into the world, traveling the same road with the same obstinate will, unchanged from those who went before.

ANTIGONE. Animals, eh, Creon! What a king you could be if only men were animals!

(*A pause.* CREON *turns and looks at her.*)

CREON. You despise me, don't you? (ANTIGONE *is silent.* CREON *goes on, as if to himself.*) Strange. Again and again, I have imagined myself holding this conversation with a pale young man I have never seen in the flesh. He would have come to assassinate me, and would have failed. I would be trying to find out from him why he wanted to kill me. But with all my logic and all my powers of debate, the only thing I could get out of him would be that he despised me. Who would have thought that that white-faced boy would turn out to be you? And that the debate would arise out of something so meaningless as the burial of your brother?

ANTIGONE (*repeats contemptuously*). Meaningless!

CREON (*earnestly, almost desperately*). And yet, you must hear me out. My part is not a heroic one, but I shall play my part. I shall have you put to death. Only before I do, I want to make one last appeal. I want to be sure that you know what you are doing as well as I know what I am doing. Antigone, do you know what you are dying for? Do you know the sordid story to which you are going to sign your name in blood, for all time to come?

ANTIGONE. What story?

CREON. The story of Eteocles and Polynices, the story of your brothers. You think you know it, but you don't. Nobody in Thebes knows that story but me. And it seems to me, this afternoon, that you have a right to know it, too. (*A pause as* ANTIGONE *moves to chair and sits.*) It's not a pretty story. (*He turns, gets stool from behind the table and places it between the table and the chair.*) You'll see. (*He looks at her for a moment.*) Tell me, first. What do you remember about your brothers? They were older than you, so they must have looked down on you. And I imagine that they tormented you—pulled your pigtails, broke your dolls, whispered secrets to each other to put you in a rage.

ANTIGONE. They were big and I was little.

CREON. And later on, when they came home wearing evening clothes, smoking cigarettes, they would have nothing to do with you; and you thought they were wonderful.

ANTIGONE. They were boys and I was a girl.

CREON. You didn't know why, exactly, but you knew that they were making your mother unhappy. You saw her in tears over them; and your father would fly into a rage because of them. You heard them come in, slamming doors, laughing noisily in the corridors—insolent, spineless, unruly, smelling of drink.

ANTIGONE (*staring outward*). Once, it was very early and we had just got up. I saw them coming home, and hid behind a door. Polynices was very pale and his eyes were shining. He was so handsome in his evening clothes. He saw me, and said: "Here, this is for you"; and he gave me a big paper flower that he had brought home from his night out.

CREON. And of course you still have that flower. Last night, before you crept out, you opened a drawer and looked at it for a time, to give yourself courage.

ANTIGONE. Who told you so?

CREON. Poor Antigone! With her nightclub flower. Do you know what your brother was?

ANTIGONE. Whatever he was, I know that you will say vile things about him.

CREON. A cheap, idiotic bounder, that is what he was. A cruel, vicious little voluptuary. A little beast with just wit enough to drive a car faster and throw more money away than any of his pals. I was with your father one day when Polynices, having lost a lot of money gambling, asked him to settle the debt; and when your father refused, the boy raised his hand against him and called him a vile name.

ANTIGONE. That's a lie!

CREON. He struck your father in the face with his fist. It was pitiful. Your father sat at his desk with his head in his hands. His nose was bleeding. He was weeping with anguish. And in a corner of your father's study, Polynices stood sneering and lighting a cigarette.

ANTIGONE. That's a lie. (*A pause.*)

CREON. When did you last see Polynices alive? When you were twelve years old. *That's* true, isn't it?

ANTIGONE. Yes, that's true.

CREON. Now you know why. Oedipus was too chicken-hearted to have the boy locked up. Polynices was allowed to go off and join the Argive army. And as soon as he reached Argos, the attempts upon your father's life began—upon the life of an old man who couldn't make up his mind to die, couldn't bear to be parted from his kingship. One after another, men slipped into Thebes from Argos for the purpose of assassinating him, and every killer that we caught always ended by confessing who had put him up to it, who had paid him to try it. And it wasn't only Polynices. That is really what I am trying to tell you. I want you to know what went on in the back room, in the kitchen of politics; I want you to know what took place in the wings of this drama in which you are burning to play a part.

Yesterday, I gave Eteocles a State funeral, with pomp and honors. Today, Eteocles is a saint and a hero in the eyes of all Thebes. The whole city turned out to bury him. The schoolchildren emptied their piggy-banks to buy wreaths for him. Old men, orating in quavering, hypocritical voices, glorified the virtues of the great-hearted brother, the devoted son, the loyal prince. I made a speech myself; and every temple priest was present with an appropriate show of sorrow and solemnity in his stupid face. And military honors were accorded the dead here.

Well, what else could I have done? People had taken sides in the civil war. Both sides couldn't be wrong; that would be too much. I couldn't have made them swallow the truth. Two gangsters were more of a luxury than I could afford. (*He pauses for a moment.*) And this is the whole point of my story. Eteocles, that virtuous brother, was just as rotten as Polynices. That great-hearted son had done his best, too, to procure the assassination of his father. That loyal prince had also offered to sell out Thebes to the highest bidder.

Funny, isn't it? Polynices lies rotting in the sun while Eteocles is given a hero's funeral and will be housed in a marble vault. Yet I have absolute proof that everything that Polynices did, Eteocles had plotted to do. They were a pair of blackguards—both engaged in selling out Thebes, and both engaged in selling out each other; and they died like the cheap gangsters they were, over a division of the spoils.

But, as I told you a moment ago, I had to make a martyr of one of them. I sent out to the holocaust for their bodies; they were found clasped in one another's arms—for the first time in their lives, I imagine. Each had been spitted on the other's sword, and the Argive cavalry had trampled them down. They were mashed to a pulp, Antigone. I had the prettier of the two carcasses brought in, and gave it a State funeral; and I left the other to rot. I didn't know which was which. And I assure you, I didn't care.

(*Long silence, neither looking at the other.*)

ANTIGONE (*in a mild voice*). Why do you tell me all this? (*Another pause.*)

CREON (*relaxed in the belief that he has defeated her, speaks with pompous self-satisfaction*). You hold a treasure in your hands, Antigone—life, I mean. (*He picks up his coat from the chair, puts it on.*) And you were about to throw it away. Would it have been better to let you die a victim to that obscene story? Don't think me fatuous if I say that I understand you; and that at your age I should have done the same thing. A moment ago, when we were quarreling, you said I was drinking in your words. I was. But it wasn't you I was listening to; it was a lad named Creon who lived here in Thebes many years ago. He was thin and pale, as you are. His mind, too, was filled with thoughts of self-sacrifice. Go find Haemon. And get married quickly, Antigone. Be happy. Life is not what you think it is.

Life is a child playing round your feet, a tool you hold firmly in your grip, a bench you sit down upon in the evening, in your garden. People will tell you that that's not life, that life is something else. They will tell you this because they need your strength and your fire, and they will want to make use of you. Don't listen to them. Believe me, the only poor consolation that we have in our old age is to discover that what I have just said to you is true. Life is nothing more than the happiness that you get out of it.

ANTIGONE (*murmurs, lost in thought*). Happiness . . .

CREON (*suddenly a little self-conscious*). Not much of a word, is it?

ANTIGONE (*quietly*). What kind of happiness do you foresee for me? Paint me the picture of your happy Antigone. What are the unimportant little sins that I shall have to commit before I am allowed to sink my teeth into life and tear happiness from it? Tell me: to whom shall I have to lie? Upon whom shall I have to fawn? To whom must I sell myself? Whom do you want me to leave dying, while I turn away my eyes?

CREON. Antigone, be quiet.

ANTIGONE. Why do you tell me to be quiet when all I want to know is what I have to do to be happy? You tell me that life is so wonderful. I want to know what I have to do in order to be able to say that myself.

CREON. Do you love Haemon?

ANTIGONE. Yes, I love Haemon. The Haemon I love is hard and young, faithful and difficult to satisfy, the way I am. But if what I love in Haemon is to be worn away like a stone step by the tread of the thing you call life, the thing you call happiness; if Haemon reaches the point where he stops growing pale with fear when I grow pale, stops thinking that I must have been killed in an accident when I am five minutes late, stops feeling that he is alone on earth when I laugh and he doesn't know why—if he too has to learn to say yes to everything—why, no, then, no! I do not love Haemon!

CREON. You don't know what you are talking about!

ANTIGONE. I do know what I am talking about! It is you who have lost your way and don't know what to say. I am too far away from you now, talking to you from a kingdom you can't get into, with your quick tongue and your hollow heart. (*Laughs.*) I laugh, Creon, because I see suddenly what a transparent hypocrite you are. Creon, the family man! Creon, the contented sitter on benches, in the evening, in his garden! Creon, desecrating the dead while he tries to fob me off with platitudes about happiness!

CREON. It is your happiness, too, Antigone!

ANTIGONE. I spit on your happiness! I spit on your idea of life—that life that must go on, come what may. You are all like dogs that lick everything they smell. You with your promise of a humdrum happiness—provided a person doesn't ask too much of life. I want everything of life, I do; and I want it now! I want it total, complete: otherwise I reject it! If life must be a thing of fear and lying and compromise; if life cannot be free, gallant, incorruptible—then, Creon, I choose death!

CREON. Scream on, daughter of Oedipus! Scream on, in your father's own voice!

ANTIGONE. In my father's own voice, yes! The voice of a king who died to purify his people, whereas you live to make them vile. You've told me that you'd like to bury Polynices, but that there are political reasons why—what was that horrible thing you said?—why that stench has got to fill the town for a month. I have nothing to do with your politics. Tell me why I can't bury him.

CREON. Because it's my order.

ANTIGONE. The order of a coward King who makes war upon the dead!

CREON. Be quiet, I say!

ANTIGONE. Why do you want me to be quiet? Because you know that I am right? Do you think I can't tell from your face that what I'm saying is true? Of course, it's true. But no, you can't admit it; because you have to growl and defend the bone that you call politics.

CREON (*grasps her by her arms*). Shut up! If you could see how ugly you are, shrieking those words!

ANTIGONE. Yes, I am ugly! Father was ugly, too. (CREON *releases her arms, turns and moves away. Stands with his back to* ANTIGONE.) But father became beautiful. And do you know when? (*She follows him to behind the table.*) At the very end. When all his questions had been answered. When he could no longer doubt that he *had* killed his own father; that he *had* gone to bed with his own mother. When he was absolutely certain that he had to die if the plague was to be lifted from his people. Then he was at peace; then he could smile, almost; then he became beautiful . . . Whereas you! Look at yourself, Creon! That never-extinguished glint of fear and suspicion in the corner of your eye—that ever-present crease in the corner of your power-loving mouth. Creon, you spoke the word a moment ago: the smelly kitchen of politics. That's where you were fathered and pupped—in a filthy kitchen!

CREON (*turns to her*). I order you to shut up! Do you hear me!

ANTIGONE. *You* order me? Cook! Do you really believe that you can give me orders?

CREON. Antigone! The ante-room is full of people! Do you want them to hear you?

ANTIGONE. Open the doors! Let us make sure that they can hear me!

CREON. By God! You shut up, I tell you!

(ISMENE *enters through arch.*)

ISMENE (*distraught*). Antigone!

ANTIGONE (*turns to* ISMENE). You, too? What do you want?

ISMENE. Oh, forgive me, Antigone. I've come back. I'll go with you now.

ANTIGONE. Where will you go with me?

ISMENE (*to* CREON). Creon! If you kill her, you'll have to kill me, too. I was with her. I helped her bury Polynices.

ANTIGONE. Oh, no, Ismene! You had your chance to come with me in the black night, creeping on your hands and knees. You had your chance to claw up the earth with your nails, as I did; to get yourself caught like a thief, as I did. And you refused it.

ISMENE. Not any more. If you die, I don't want to live. I'll do it alone tonight.

ANTIGONE. You hear that, Creon? (*She turns round toward* CREON.) The thing is catching! Who knows but that lots of people will catch the disease from me! What are you waiting for? Call in your guards! Come on, Creon! Show a little courage! It only hurts for a minute! Come on, cook!

CREON (*turns toward arch and calls*). Guards! (GUARDS *enter through arch.*)

ANTIGONE (*in a great cry of relief*). At last, Creon!

(CHORUS *enters through left arch.*)

CREON (*to the* GUARDS). Take her away! (CREON *goes up onto top step.* GUARDS *grasp* ANTIGONE *by her arms, turn and hustle her towards the arch right and exit.* ISMENE *mimes horror, backs away towards the arch left, then turns and runs out through the arch. A long pause, as* CREON *moves slowly downstage.*)

CHORUS (*behind* CREON. *Speaks in a deliberate voice*). You are out of your mind, Creon. What have you done?

CREON (*his back to* CHORUS). She had to die.

CHORUS. You must not let Antigone die. We shall carry the scar of her death for centuries.

CREON. She insisted. No man on earth was strong enough to dissuade her. Polynices was a mere pretext. When she had to give up that pretext, she found another one—that life and happiness were tawdry things and not worth possessing. She was bent upon only one thing: to reject life and to die.

CHORUS. You say so, Creon. But it is not the truth.

CREON. What do you want me to do for her? Condemn her to live?

HAEMON (*calls from off-stage*). Father!

(HAEMON *enters through arch right.* CREON *turns toward him.*)

CREON. Haemon, forget Antigone. Forget her, my dearest boy.

HAEMON. How can you talk like that?

CREON (*grasps* HAEMON *by the hands*). I did everything I could to save her, Haemon. I used every argument. I swear I did. The girl doesn't love you. She could have gone on living for you; but she refused. She wanted it this way; she wanted to die.

HAEMON. Father! The Guards are dragging Antigone away! You've got to stop them! (*He breaks away from* CREON.)

CREON (*looks away from* HAEMON). I can't stop them. It's too late. Antigone has spoken. The story is all over Thebes. I cannot save her now.

CHORUS. Creon, you must find a way to keep Antigone from being put to death.

CREON. I cannot.

CHORUS. You must recall your edict. You must order the burial of Polynices.

CREON. Too late. The law must be obeyed. I can do nothing.

HAEMON. But, Father, you are master in Thebes!

CREON. I am master under the law. Not above the law.

HAEMON. But you made that law yourself. What you ordained, you can repeal. You cannot let Antigone be taken from me.

CREON. I cannot do anything else, my poor boy. She must die and you must live.

HAEMON. Live, you say! Live a life without Antigone? A life in which I am to go on admiring you as you busy yourself about your kingdom; go on admiring you as you make your persuasive speeches and strike your attitudes? Not without Antigone. I love Antigone. She never struck a pose and waited for me to admire her. Mirrors meant nothing to her. She never looked at herself. She looked at me, and expected me to be somebody. And I was—when I was with her. Do you think I am not going after her? I will not live without Antigone!

CREON. Haemon—you will have to resign yourself to life without Antigone. (*He moves to left of* HAEMON.) Sooner or later there comes a day of sorrow in each man's life when he must cease to be a child and take up the burden of being a man. That day has come for you.

HAEMON (*backs away a step*). That giant strength, that courage. That massive god who used to pick me up in his arms and shelter me from shadows and monsters —was that you, Father? Was it of you I stood in awe? Was that man you?

CREON. Yes, Haemon, that was me.

HAEMON. Then you are not that man today. For if you were, you'd know that your enemies are abroad in every street. You'd know that the people are stirring and murmuring against you. You cannot put Antigone to death. She will not have been dead an hour before shame will sit on every Theban doorstep and horror will fill every Theban heart. Already the people are full of fear and anger because you have not buried Polynices. If you kill Antigone, they will hate you!

CREON. Silence! That edict stands!

HAEMON (*stares at* CREON *for a moment*). I tell you again that I will not live without Antigone.

(*Turns and goes quickly out through arch.*)

CHORUS. Creon, the gods have a way of punishing injustice.

CREON (*contemptuously*). The gods!

CHORUS. Creon, that boy is wounded to death.

CREON. We are all wounded to death.

(FIRST GUARD *enters through arch right, followed by* SECOND *and* THIRD GUARDS *pulling* ANTIGONE *along with them.*)

FIRST GUARD. Chief, the people are crowding into the palace!

ANTIGONE. Creon, you are going to kill me; let that be enough. I want to be alone until it is over.

CREON. Empty the palace! Guards at the gates!

(CREON *quickly crosses toward the arch and exits. Two* GUARDS *release* ANTIGONE *and exit behind* CREON. CHORUS *goes out through arch left. The lighting dims so that only the area about the table is lighted. The cyclorama is covered with a dark blue color. The scene is intended to suggest a prison cell, filled with shadows and dimly lit.* ANTIGONE *moves to stool and sits. The* FIRST GUARD *stands upstage. He watches* ANTIGONE, *and as she sits, he begins pacing slowly downstage, then upstage. A pause.*)

ANTIGONE (*turns and looks at the* GUARD). It's you, is it?

GUARD. What do you mean, me?

ANTIGONE. The last human face that I shall see. (*A pause as they look at one another; then* GUARD *paces upstage; turns and crosses behind table.*) Was it you that arrested me this morning?

GUARD. Yes, that was me.

ANTIGONE. You hurt me. There was no need for you to hurt me. Did I act as if I was trying to escape?

GUARD. Come on now, Miss. It was my business to bring you in. I did it.

(*A pause. He paces to and fro upstage. Only the sound of his boots is heard.*)

ANTIGONE. How old are you?

GUARD. Thirty-nine.

ANTIGONE. Have you any children?

GUARD. Yeah. Two.

ANTIGONE. Do you love your children?

GUARD. What's that got to do with you?

(*A pause. He paces upstage and downstage.*)

ANTIGONE. How long have you been in the Guards?

GUARD. Since the war. I was in the army. Sergeant. Then I joined the Guards.

ANTIGONE. Does one have to have been an army sergeant to get into the Guards?

GUARD. Supposed to be. Either that or on special detail. But when they make you a guard, you lose your stripes.

ANTIGONE (*murmurs*). I see.

GUARD. Yes. Of course, if you're a guard, everybody knows you're something special; they know you're an old non-com. Take pay, for instance. When you're a guard you get your pay, and on top of that you get six months' extra pay, to make sure you don't lose anything by not being a sergeant any more.

ANTIGONE (*barely audible*). I see.

GUARD. That's what I'm telling you. That's why sergeants, now, they don't like guards. Maybe you noticed they try to make out they're better than us? Promotion, that's what it is. In the army, anybody can get promoted. All you need is good conduct. Now in the Guards, it's slow, and you have to know your business—like how to make out a report and the like of that. But when you're a non-com in the Guards, you've got something that even a sergeant-major ain't got. For instance . . .

ANTIGONE (*breaking him off*). Listen.

GUARD. Yes, Miss.

ANTIGONE. I'm going to die soon.

(*The GUARD looks at her a moment, then turns and moves away.*)

GUARD. For instance, people have a lot of respect for guards, they have. A guard may be a soldier, but he's kind of in the civil service, too.

ANTIGONE. Do you think it hurts to die?

GUARD. How would I know? Of course, if somebody sticks a sabre in your gut and turns it round, it hurts.

ANTIGONE. How are they going to put me to death?

GUARD. Well, I'll tell you. I heard the proclamation, all right. There isn't much that gets away from me. It seems that they don't want to dirty up . . . Wait a minute. How did that go now? (*He stares into space and recites from memory.*) "In order that our fair city shall not be pol-luted with her sinful blood, she shall be im-mured—im-mured." That means, they shove you in a cave and wall up the cave.

ANTIGONE. Alive?

GUARD. Yes . . .

(*He moves away a few steps.*)

ANTIGONE (*murmurs*). O tomb! O bridal bed! Alone!

(ANTIGONE *sits there, a tiny figure in the middle of the stage. You would say she felt a little chilly. She wraps her arms around herself.*)

GUARD. Yep! Outside the southeast gate of the town. In the Cave of Hades. In broad daylight. Some detail, eh, for them that's on the job! First they thought maybe it was a job for the army. Now it looks like it's going to be the Guards. There's an outfit for you! Nothing the Guards can't do. No wonder the army's jealous.

ANTIGONE. A pair of animals.

GUARD. What do you mean, a pair of animals?

ANTIGONE. When the winds blow cold, all they need do is to press close against one another. I am all alone.

GUARD. Say, is there anything you want? I can send out for it, you know.

ANTIGONE. You are very kind. (*A pause.* ANTIGONE *looks up at the* GUARD.) Yes, there is something I want. I want you to give someone a letter from me, when I am dead.

GUARD. How's that again? A letter?

ANTIGONE. Yes, I want to write a letter; and I want you to give it to someone for me.

GUARD (*straightens up*). Hey, wait a minute. Take it easy. It's as much as my job is worth to go handing out letters from prisoners.

ANTIGONE (*removes a ring from her finger and holds it out toward him*). I'll give you this ring if you will do it.

GUARD. Is it gold?

(*He takes the ring from her.*)

ANTIGONE. Yes, it is gold.

GUARD (*shakes his head*). Uh-uh. No can do. Suppose they go through my pockets. I might get six months for a thing like that. (*He stares at the ring, then glances off right to make sure that he is not being watched.*) Listen, tell you what I'll do. You tell me what you want to say, and I'll write it down in my book. Then afterwards, I'll tear out the pages and give them to the party, see? If it's in my handwriting, it's all right.

ANTIGONE (*winces*). In your handwriting? (*She shudders slightly.*) No. That would be awful. The poor darling! In your handwriting.

GUARD (*offers back the ring*). O.K. It's no skin off my nose.

ANTIGONE (*quickly*). Of course, of course. No, keep the ring. But hurry. Time is getting short. Where is your notebook? (*The GUARD pockets the ring, takes his notebook and pencil from his pocket, puts his foot up on chair, and rests the notebook on his knee, licks his pencil.*) Ready? (*He nods.*) Write, now. "My darling . . ."

GUARD (*writes as he mutters*). The boy friend, eh?

ANTIGONE. "My darling. I had to die, and perhaps you will not love me any more . . ."

GUARD (*mutters as he writes*). ". . . will not love me any more."

ANTIGONE. "Perhaps it would have been simple to accept life . . ."

GUARD (*repeats as he writes*). ". . . to accept life . . ."

ANTIGONE. "But it was not for myself. And now, it's so dreadful here alone. I am afraid . . . (*She glances wildly about.*) And these shadows . . ."

GUARD (*looks at her*). Wait a minute! How fast do you think I can write?

ANTIGONE (*takes hold of herself*). Where are you?

GUARD (*reads from his notebook*). ". . . dreadful here alone. I am afraid . . ."

ANTIGONE. No. Scratch that out. Nobody must know that. They have no right to know. It's as if they saw me naked and touched me, after I was dead. Scratch it all out. Just write: "Forgive me."

GUARD (*looks at* ANTIGONE). I cut out everything you said there at the end, and I put down, "Forgive me"?

ANTIGONE. Yes. "Forgive me, my darling. But it wasn't for myself. I love you." (*She murmurs, as* GUARD *writes.*) No, it wasn't for myself.

GUARD (*finishes the letter*). ". . . I love you." (*He looks at her.*) Is that all?

ANTIGONE. That's all.

GUARD (*straightens up, looks at notebook*). Damn funny letter.

ANTIGONE. I know.

GUARD (*looks at her*). Who is it to? (*A sudden roll of drums begins and continues until after* ANTIGONE *exits. The* FIRST GUARD *pockets the notebook and shouts at* ANTIGONE.) O.K. That's enough out of you! Come on!

(*At the sound of the drum roll,* SECOND *and* THIRD GUARDS *enter through the right arch.* ANTIGONE *rises.* GUARDS *seize her and exit with her. The lighting moves up to suggest late afternoon.* CHORUS *enters.*)

CHORUS. And now it is Creon's turn.

(MESSENGER *runs through the arch right.*)

MESSENGER. The Queen . . . the Queen! Where is the Queen?

CHORUS. What do you want with the Queen? What have you to tell the Queen?

MESSENGER. News to break her heart. Antigone had just been thrust into the cave. They hadn't finished heaving the last blocks of stone into place when Creon and the rest heard a sudden moaning from the tomb. A hush fell over us all, for it was not the voice of Antigone. It was Haemon's voice that came forth from the tomb. Everybody looked at Creon; and he howled like a man demented: "Take away the stones! Take away the stones!" The slaves leaped at the wall of stones, and Creon worked with them, sweating and tearing at the blocks with his bleeding hands. Finally a narrow opening was forced, and into it slipped the smallest guard.

Antigone had hanged herself by the cord of her robe, by the red and golden twisted cord of her robe. The cord was round her neck like a child's collar. Haemon was on his knees, holding her in his arms and moaning, his face buried in her robe. More stones were removed, and Creon went into the tomb. He tried to raise Haemon to his feet. I could hear him begging Haemon to rise to his feet. Haemon was deaf to his father's voice, till suddenly he stood up of his own accord, his eyes dark and burning. Anguish was in his face, but it was the face of a little boy. He stared at his father. Then suddenly he struck him—hard; and he drew his sword. Creon leapt out of range. Haemon went on staring at him, his eyes full of contempt—a glance that was like a knife, and that Creon couldn't escape. The King stood trembling in the far corner of the tomb, and Haemon went on staring. Then, without a word, he stabbed himself and lay down beside Antigone, embracing her in a great pool of blood.

(*A pause as* CREON *and* PAGE *enter through arch on the* MESSENGER'S *last words.* CHORUS *and the* MESSENGER *both turn to look at* CREON, *then the* MESSENGER *exits through curtain.*)

CREON. I have had them laid out side by side. They are together at last, and at peace. Two lovers on the morrow of their bridal. Their work is done.

CHORUS. But not yours, Creon. You have still one thing to learn. Eurydice, the Queen, your wife . . .

CREON. A good woman. Always busy with her garden, her preserves, her sweaters— those sweaters she never stopped knitting for the poor. Strange, how the poor never stop needing sweaters. One would almost think that was all they needed.

CHORUS. The poor in Thebes are going to be cold this winter, Creon. When the Queen was told of her son's death, she waited carefully until she had finished her row, then put down her knitting calmly—as she did everything. She went up to her room, her lavender-scented room, with its embroidered doilies and its pictures framed in plush; and there, Creon, she cut her throat. She is laid out now in one of those two old-fashioned twin beds, exactly where you went to her one night when she was still a maiden. Her smile is still the same, scarcely a shade more melancholy. And if it were not for that great red blot on the bed linen by her neck, one might think she was asleep.

CREON (*in a dull voice*). She, too. They are all asleep. (*Pause.*) It must be good to sleep.

CHORUS. Tomorrow they will sleep sweetly in the ground, Creon. You will bury them tomorrow. You who would not bury Polynices today will bury Eurydice and Haemon tomorrow. And Antigone, too . (*Pause.*) The gods take a hand in every game, Creon. Even politics.

CREON (*nodding soberly*). The gods!

CHORUS. And now you are alone, Creon.

CREON. Yes, all alone. (*He remains lost in thought as the hour strikes. To* PAGE.) What time was that?

PAGE. Five o'clock, Sir.

CREON. What have we on at five o'clock?

PAGE. Cabinet meeting, Sir.

CREON. Cabinet meeting. Well, we might as well go along to it.

(CREON *and* PAGE *exit slowly through arch left and* CHORUS *moves downstage.*)

CHORUS. And there we are. All those who were meant to die have died. Those who believed one thing, those who believed the contrary thing, and even those who believed nothing at all, yet were caught up in the web without knowing why. All dead: stiff, useless, rotting.

Creon was the most rational, the most plausible of tyrants. But like all tyrants, he refused to distinguish between the things that are Caesar's and the things that are God's. Now and again, in the three thousand years since the first Antigone was heard of, someone has had to come forward to remind men of this distinction. And whether we say that the result is Christianity, or popular revolution, or underground resistance, the cause is always the same—a passionate belief that moral law exists, and a passionate regard for the sanctity of human personality.

Well, Antigone is calm tonight. She has played her part.

(*Three* GUARDS *enter, resume their places on steps as at the rise of the curtain, and begin to play cards.*)

A great melancholy wave of unrest now settles down upon Thebes, upon the empty palace, upon Creon, who can now begin to long for his own death.

Only the guards are left, and none of this matters to them. It's no skin off their noses. They go on playing cards.

(CHORUS *walks toward the arch left as*)

THE CURTAIN FALLS

THE WILD DUCK

HENRIK IBSEN (1828–1906)

CHARACTERS

WERLE, *a merchant, manufacturer, etc.*
GREGERS WERLE, *his son.*
OLD EKDAL.
HIALMAR EKDAL, *his son, a photographer.*
GINA EKDAL, *Hialmar's wife.*
HEDVIG, *their daughter, a girl of fourteen.*
MRS. SÖRBY, *Werle's housekeeper.*
RELLING, *a doctor.*
MOLVIK, *student of theology.*

GRÅBERG, *Werle's bookkeeper.*
PETTERSEN, *Werle's servant.*
JENSEN, *a hired waiter.*
A FLABBY GENTLEMAN.
A THIN-HAIRED GENTLEMAN.
A SHORT-SIGHTED GENTLEMAN.
SIX OTHER GENTLEMEN, *guests at Werle's dinner-party.*
SEVERAL HIRED WAITERS.

The first act passes in WERLE'S *house, the remaining acts at* HIALMAR EKDAL'S.

Pronunciation of Names: GREGERS WERLE = *Grayghers Verlë;* HIALMAR EKDAL = *Yalmar Aykdal;* GINA = *Cheena;* GRÅBERG = *Groberg;* JENSEN = *Yensen.*

ACT I

At WERLE'S *house. A richly and comfortably furnished study; bookcases and upholstered furniture; a writing-table, with papers and documents, in the centre of the room; lighted lamps with green shades, giving a subdued light. At the back, open folding-doors with curtains drawn back. Within is seen a large and handsome room, brilliantly lighted with lamps and branching candlesticks. In front, on the right (in the study), a small baize door leads into* WERLE'S *office. On the left, in front, a fireplace with a glowing coal fire, and farther back a double door leading into the dining-room.*

WERLE'S *servant,* PETTERSEN, *in livery, and* JENSEN, *the hired waiter, in black, are putting the study in order. In the large room, two or three other hired waiters are moving about, arranging things and lighting more candles. From the dining-room, the hum of conversation and laughter of many voices are heard; a glass is tapped with a knife; silence follows, and a toast is proposed; shouts of "Bravo!" and then again a buzz of conversation.*

PETTERSEN *(lights a lamp on the chimney-place and places a shade over it).* Hark to them, Jensen! now the old man's on his legs holding a long palaver about Mrs. Sörby.

JENSEN *(pushing forward an armchair).* Is it true, what folks say, that they're—very good friends, eh?

446

PETTERSEN. Lord knows.

JENSEN. I've heard tell as he's been a lively customer in his day.

PETTERSEN. May be.

JENSEN. And he's giving this spread in honour of his son, they say.

PETTERSEN. Yes. His son came home yesterday.

JENSEN. This is the first time I ever heard as Mr. Werle had a son.

PETTERSEN. Oh, yes, he has a son, right enough. But he's a fixture, as you might say, up at the Höidal works. He's never once come to town all the years I've been in service here.

A WAITER (*in the doorway of the other room*). Pettersen, here's an old fellow wanting . . .

PETTERSEN (*mutters*). The devil—who's this now?

(OLD EKDAL *appears from the right, in the inner room. He is dressed in a threadbare overcoat with a high collar; he wears woollen mittens and carries in his hand a stick and a fur cap. Under his arm, a brown paper parcel. Dirty red-brown wig and small grey moustache.*)

PETTERSEN (*goes towards him*). Good Lord—what do you want here?

EKDAL (*in the doorway*). Must get into the office, Pettersen.

PETTERSEN. The office was closed an hour ago, and . . .

EKDAL. So they told me at the front door. But Gråberg's in there still. Let me slip in this way, Pettersen; there's a good fellow. (*Points towards the baize door*) It's not the first time I've come this way.

PETTERSEN. Well, you may pass. (*Opens the door*) But mind you go out again the proper way, for we've got company.

EKDAL. I know, I know—h'm! Thanks, Pettersen, good old friend! Thanks! (*Mutters softly*) Ass!

(*He goes into the office;* PETTERSEN *shuts the door after him.*)

JENSEN. Is he one of the office people?

PETTERSEN. No, he's only an outside hand that does odd jobs of copying. But he's been a tip-topper in his day, has old Ekdal.

JENSEN. You can see he's been through a lot.

PETTERSEN. Yes; he was an army officer, you know.

JENSEN. You don't say so?

PETTERSEN. No mistake about it. But then he went into the timber trade or something of the sort. They say he once played Mr. Werle a very nasty trick. They were partners in the Höidal works at the time. Oh, I know old Ekdal well, I do. Many a nip of bitters and bottle of ale we two have drunk at Madam Eriksen's.

JENSEN. He don't look as if he'd much to stand treat with.

PETTERSEN. Why, bless you, Jensen, it's me that stands treat. I always think there's no harm in being a bit civil to folks that have seen better days.

JENSEN. Did he go bankrupt, then?

PETTERSEN. Worse than that. He went to prison.

JENSEN. To prison!

PETTERSEN. Or perhaps it was the Penitentiary. (*Listens*) Sh! They're leaving the table.

(*The dining-room door is thrown open from within by a couple of waiters.* MRS. SÖRBY *comes out conversing with two gentlemen. Gradually the whole company follows, amongst them* WERLE. *Last come* HIALMAR EKDAL *and* GREGERS WERLE.)

MRS. SÖRBY (*in passing, to the servant*). Tell them to serve the coffee in the music-room, Pettersen.

PETTERSEN. Very well, Madam.

(*She goes with the two gentlemen into the inner room and thence out to the right.* PETTERSEN *and* JENSEN *go out the same way.*)

A FLABBY GENTLEMAN (*to a* THIN-HAIRED GENTLEMAN). Whew! What a dinner!— It was no joke to do it justice!

THE THIN-HAIRED GENTLEMAN. Oh, with a little good-will one can get through a lot in three hours.

THE FLABBY GENTLEMAN. Yes, but afterwards, afterwards, my dear Chamberlain!

A THIRD GENTLEMAN. I hear the coffee and maraschino are to be served in the music-room.

THE FLABBY GENTLEMAN. Bravo! Then perhaps Mrs. Sörby will play us something.

THE THIN-HAIRED GENTLEMAN (*in a low voice*). I hope Mrs. Sörby mayn't play us a tune we don't like, one of these days!

THE FLABBY GENTLEMAN. Oh, no, not she! Bertha will never turn against her old friends.

(*They laugh and pass into the inner room.*)

WERLE (*in a low voice, dejectedly*). I don't think anybody noticed it, Gregers.

GREGERS (*looks at him*). Noticed what?

WERLE. Did you not notice it either?

GREGERS. What do you mean?

WERLE. We were thirteen at table.

GREGERS. Indeed? Were there thirteen of us?

WERLE (*glances towards* HIALMAR EKDAL). Our usual party is twelve. (*To the others*) This way, gentlemen!

(WERLE *and the others, all except* HIALMAR *and* GREGERS, *go out by the back, to the right.*)

HIALMAR (*who has overheard the conversation*). You ought not to have invited me, Gregers.

GREGERS. What! Not ask my best and only friend to a party supposed to be in my honour . . . ?

HIALMAR. But I don't think your father likes it. You see I am quite outside his circle.

GREGERS. So I hear. But I wanted to see you and have a talk with you, and I certainly shan't be staying long.—Ah, we two old schoolfellows have drifted far apart from each other. It must be sixteen or seventeen years since we met.

HIALMAR. Is it so long?

GREGERS. It is indeed. Well, how goes it with you? You look well. You have put on flesh and grown almost stout.

HIALMAR. Well, "stout" is scarcely the word; but I daresay I look a little more of a man than I used to.

GREGERS. Yes, you do; your outer man is in first-rate condition.

HIALMAR (*in a tone of gloom*). Ah, but the inner man! That is a very different matter, I can tell you! Of course you know of the terrible catastrophe that has befallen me and mine since last we met.

GREGERS (*more softly*). How are things going with your father now?

HIALMAR. Don't let us talk of it, old fellow. Of course my poor unhappy father lives with me. He hasn't another soul in the world to care for him. But you can understand that this is a miserable subject for me.—Tell me, rather, how you have been getting on up at the works.

GREGERS. I have had a delightfully lonely time of it—plenty of leisure to think and think about things. Come over here; we may as well make ourselves comfortable.

(*He seats himself in an armchair by the fire and draws* HIALMAR *down into another alongside of it.*)

HIALMAR (*sentimentally*). After all, Gregers, I thank you for inviting me to your father's table; for I take it as a sign that you have got over your feeling against me.

GREGERS (*surprised*). How could you imagine I had any feeling against you?

HIALMAR. You had at first, you know.

GREGERS. How at first?

HIALMAR. After the great misfortune. It was natural enough that you should. Your father was within an ace of being drawn into that—well, that terrible business.

GREGERS. Why should that give me any feeling against you? Who can have put that into your head?

HIALMAR. I know it did, Gregers; your father told me so himself.

GREGERS (*starts*). My father! Oh, indeed. H'm.—Was that why you never let me hear from you?—not a single word.

HIALMAR. Yes.

GREGERS. Not even when you made up your mind to become a photographer?

HIALMAR. Your father said I had better not write to you at all, about anything.

GREGERS (*looking straight before him*). Well, well, perhaps he was right.—But tell me now, Hialmar: are you pretty well satisfied with your present position?

HIALMAR (*with a little sigh*). Oh, yes, I am; I have really no cause to complain. At first, as you may guess, I felt it a little strange. It was such a totally new state of things for me. But of course my whole circumstances were totally changed. Father's utter, irretrievable ruin,—the shame and disgrace of it, Gregers . . .

GREGERS (*affected*). Yes, yes; I understand.

HIALMAR. I couldn't think of remaining at college; there wasn't a shilling to spare; on the contrary, there were debts—mainly to your father, I believe . . .

GREGERS. H'm . . .

HIALMAR. In short, I thought it best to break, once for all, with my old surroundings and associations. It was your father that specially urged me to it; and since he interested himself so much in me . . .

GREGERS. My father did?

HIALMAR. Yes, you surely knew that, didn't you? Where do you suppose I found the money to learn photography, and to furnish a studio and make a start? All that cost a pretty penny, I can tell you.

GREGERS. And my father provided the money?

HIALMAR. Yes, my dear fellow, didn't you know? I understood him to say he had written to you about it.

GREGERS. Not a word about his part in the business. He must have forgotten it. Our correspondence has always been purely a business one. So it was my father that . . . !

HIALMAR. Yes, certainly. He didn't wish it to be generally known; but he it was. And of course it was he, too, that put me in a position to marry. Don't you— don't you know about that either?

GREGERS. No, I haven't heard a word of it. (*Shakes him by the arm*) But, my dear Hialmar, I can't tell you what pleasure all this gives me—pleasure, and self-reproach. I have perhaps done my father injustice after all—in some things. This proves that he has a heart. It shows a sort of compunction . . .

HIALMAR. Compunction . . . ?

GREGERS. Yes, yes—whatever you like to call it. Oh, I can't tell you how glad I am to hear this of father.—So you are a married man, Hialmar! That is further than I shall ever get. Well, I hope you are happy in your married life?

HIALMAR. Yes, thoroughly happy. She is as good and capable a wife as any man could wish for. And she is by no means without culture.

GREGERS (*rather surprised*). No, of course not.

HIALMAR. You see, life is itself an education. Her daily intercourse with me . . . And then we know one or two rather remarkable men, who come a good deal about us. I assure you, you would hardly know Gina again.

GREGERS. Gina?

HIALMAR. Yes; had you forgotten that her name was Gina?

GREGERS. Whose name? I haven't the slightest idea . . .

HIALMAR. Don't you remember that she used to be in service here?

GREGERS (*looks at him*). Is it Gina Hansen . . . ?

HIALMAR. Yes, of course it is Gina Hansen.

GREGERS. . . . who kept house for us during the last year of my mother's illness?

HIALMAR. Yes, exactly. But, my dear friend, I'm quite sure your father told you that I was married.

GREGERS (*who has risen*). Oh, yes, he mentioned it; but not that . . . (*Walking about the room*) Stay—perhaps he did—now that I think of it. My father always writes such short letters. (*Half seats himself on the arm of the chair*) Now tell me, Hialmar—this is interesting—how did you come to know Gina —your wife?

HIALMAR. The simplest thing in the world. You know Gina did not stay here long; everything was so much upset at that time, owing to your mother's illness and so forth, that Gina was not equal to it all; so she gave notice and left. That was the year before your mother died—or it may have been the same year.

GREGERS. It was the same year. I was up at the works then. But afterwards . . . ?

HIALMAR. Well, Gina lived at home with her mother, Madam Hansen, an excellent hard-working woman, who kept a little eating-house. She had a room to let, too; a very nice comfortable room.

GREGERS. And I suppose you were lucky enough to secure it?

HIALMAR. Yes; in fact, it was your father that recommended it to me. So it was there, you see, that I really came to know Gina.

GREGERS. And then you got engaged?

HIALMAR. Yes. It doesn't take young people long to fall in love . . . ; h'm . . .

GREGERS (*rises and moves about a little*). Tell me: was it after your engagement—was it then that my father—I mean was it then that you began to take up photography?

HIALMAR. Yes, precisely. I wanted to make a start and to set up house as soon as possible; and your father and I agreed that this photography business was the readiest way. Gina thought so, too. Oh, and there was another thing in its favour, by-the-bye; it happened, luckily, that Gina had learnt to retouch.

GREGER. That chimed in marvellously.

HIALMAR (*pleased, rises*). Yes, didn't it? Don't you think it was a marvellous piece of luck?

GREGERS. Oh, unquestionably. My father seems to have been almost a kind of providence for you.

HIALMAR (*with emotion*). He did not forsake his old friend's son in the hour of his need. For he has a heart, you see.

MRS. SÖRBY (*enters, arm-in-arm with* WERLE). Nonsense, my dear Mr. Werle; you mustn't stop there any longer staring at all the lights. It's very bad for you.

WERLE (*lets go her arm and passes his hand over his eyes*). I daresay you are right.

(PETTERSEN *and* JENSEN *carry round refreshment trays.*)

MRS. SÖRBY (*to the guests in the other room*). This way, if you please, gentlemen. Whoever wants a glass of punch must be so good as to come in here.

THE FLABBY GENTLEMAN (*comes up to* MRS. SÖRBY). Surely, it isn't possible that you have suspended our cherished right to smoke?

MRS. SÖRBY. Yes. No smoking here, in Mr. Werle's sanctum, Chamberlain.

THE THIN-HAIRED GENTLEMAN. When did you enact these stringent amendments on the cigar law, Mrs. Sörby?

MRS. SÖRBY. After the last dinner, Chamberlain, when certain persons permitted themselves to overstep the mark.

THE THIN-HAIRED GENTLEMAN. And may one never overstep the mark a little bit, Madame Bertha? Not the least little bit?

MRS. SÖRBY. Not in any respect whatsoever, Mr. Balle.

(*Most of the guests have assembled in the study; servants hand round glasses of punch.*)

WERLE (*to* HIALMAR, *who is standing beside a table*). What are you studying so intensely, Ekdal?

HIALMAR. Only an album, Mr. Werle.

THE THIN-HAIRED GENTLEMAN (*who is wandering about*). Ah, photographs! They are quite in your line, of course.

THE FLABBY GENTLEMAN (*in an armchair*). Haven't you brought any of your own with you?

HIALMAR. No, I haven't.

THE FLABBY GENTLEMAN. You ought to have; it's very good for the digestion to sit and look at pictures.

THE THIN-HAIRED GENTLEMAN. And it contributes to the entertainment, you know.

THE SHORT-SIGHTED GENTLEMAN. And all contributions are thankfully received.

MRS. SÖRBY. The Chamberlains think that when one is invited out to dinner, one ought to exert oneself a little in return, Mr. Ekdal.

THE FLABBY GENTLEMAN. Where one dines so well, that duty becomes a pleasure.

THE THIN-HAIRED GENTLEMAN. And when it's a case of the struggle for existence, you know . . .

MRS. SÖRBY. I quite agree with you!

(*They continue the conversation, with laughter and joking.*)

GREGERS (*softly*). You must join in, Hialmar.

HIALMAR (*writhing*). What am I to talk about?

THE FLABBY GENTLEMAN. Don't you think, Mr. Werle, that Tokay may be con-sidered one of the more wholesome sorts of wine?

WERLE (*by the fire*). I can answer for the Tokay you had today, at any rate; it's one of the very finest seasons. Of course you would notice that.

THE FLABBY GENTLEMAN. Yes, it had a remarkably delicate flavour.

HIALMAR (*shyly*). Is there any difference between the seasons?

THE FLABBY GENTLEMAN (*laughs*). Come! That's good!

WERLE (*smiles*). It really doesn't pay to set fine wine before you.

THE THIN-HAIRED GENTLEMAN. Tokay is like photographs, Mr. Ekdal: they both need sunshine. Am I right?

HIALMAR. Yes, light is important no doubt.

MRS. SÖRBY. And it's exactly the same with Chamberlains—they, too, depend very much on sunshine,* as the saying is.

THE THIN-HAIRED GENTLEMAN. Oh, fie! That's a very threadbare sarcasm!

THE SHORT-SIGHTED GENTLEMAN. Mrs. Sörby is coming out . . .

THE FLABBY GENTLEMAN. . . . and at our expense, too. (*Holds up his finger reprovingly*) Oh, Madame Bertha, Madame Bertha!

MRS. SÖRBY. Yes, and there's not the least doubt that the seasons differ greatly. The old vintages are the finest.

THE SHORT-SIGHTED GENTLEMAN. Do you reckon me among the old vintages?

MRS. SÖRBY. Oh, far from it.

THE THIN-HAIRED GENTLEMAN. There now! But me, dear Mrs. Sörby . . . ?

THE FLABBY GENTLEMAN. Yes, and me? What vintage should you say that we belong to?

MRS. SÖRBY. Why, to the sweet vintage, gentlemen.

(*She sips a glass of punch. The gentlemen laugh and flirt with her.*)

WERLE. Mrs. Sörby can always find a loop-hole—when she wants to. Fill your glasses, gentlemen! Pettersen, will you see to it . . . ! Gregers, suppose we have a glass together. (GREGERS *does not move*) Won't you join us, Ekdal? I found no opportunity of drinking with you at table.

(GRÅBERG, *the bookkeeper, looks in at the baize door.*)

GRÅBERG. Excuse me, sir, but I can't get out.

WERLE. Have you been locked in again?

GRÅBERG. Yes, and Flakstad has carried off the keys.

* The "sunshine" of court favour.

WERLE. Well, you can pass out this way.

GRÅBERG. But there's some one else . . .

WERLE. All right; come through, both of you. Don't be afraid.

(GRÅBERG *and* OLD EKDAL *come out of the office.*)

WERLE (*involuntarily*). Ugh!

(*The laughter and talk among the guests cease.* HIALMAR *starts at the sight of his father, puts down his glass and turns towards the fireplace.*)

EKDAL (*does not look up, but makes little bows to both sides as he passes, murmuring*). Beg pardon, come the wrong way. Door locked—door locked. Beg pardon.

(*He and* GRÅBERG *go out by the back, to the right.*)

WERLE (*between his teeth*). That idiot Gråberg.

GREGERS (*open-mouthed and staring, to* HIALMAR). Why surely that wasn't . . . !

THE FLABBY GENTLEMAN. What's the matter? Who was it?

GREGERS. Oh, nobody, only the bookkeeper and some one with him.

THE SHORT-SIGHTED GENTLEMAN (*to* HIALMAR). Did you know that man?

HIALMAR. I don't know—I didn't notice . . .

THE FLABBY GENTLEMAN. What the deuce has come over every one?

(*He joins another group who are talking softly.*)

MRS. SÖRBY (*whispers to the servant*). Give him something to take with him;—something good, mind.

PETTERSEN (*nods*). I'll see to it. (*Goes out.*)

GREGERS (*softly and with emotion, to* HIALMAR). So that was really he!

HIALMAR. Yes.

GREGERS. And you could stand there and deny that you knew him!

HIALMAR (*whispers vehemently*). But how could I . . . !

GREGERS. . . . acknowledge your own father?

HIALMAR (*with pain*). Oh, if you were in my place . . .

(*The conversation amongst the guests, which has been carried on in a low tone, now swells into constrained joviality.*)

THE THIN-HAIRED GENTLEMAN (*approaching* HIALMAR *and* GREGERS *in a friendly manner*). Aha! Reviving old college memories, eh? Don't you smoke, Mr. Ekdal? May I give you a light? Oh, by-the-bye, we mustn't . . .

HIALMAR. No, thank you, I won't . . .

THE FLABBY GENTLEMAN. Haven't you a nice little poem you could recite to us, Mr. Ekdal? You used to recite so charmingly.

HIALMAR. I am sorry I can't remember anything.

THE FLABBY GENTLEMAN. Oh, that's a pity. Well, what shall we do, Balle?

(*Both gentlemen move away and pass into the other room.*)

HIALMAR (*gloomily*). Gregers—I am going! When a man has felt the crushing hand of Fate, you see . . . Say good-bye to your father for me.

GREGERS. Yes, yes. Are you going straight home?

HIALMAR. Yes. Why?

GREGERS. Oh, because I may perhaps look in on you later.

HIALMAR. No, you mustn't do that. You must not come to my home. Mine is a melancholy abode, Gregers; especially after a splendid banquet like this. We can always arrange to meet somewhere in the town.

MRS. SÖRBY (*who has quietly approached*). Are you going, Ekdal?

HIALMAR. Yes.

MRS. SÖRBY. Remember me to Gina.

HIALMAR. Thanks.

MRS. SÖRBY. And say I am coming up to see her one of these days.

HIALMAR. Yes, thank you. (*To* GREGERS) Stay here; I will slip out unobserved.

(*He saunters away, then into the other room, and so out to the right.*)

MRS. SÖRBY (*softly to the servant, who has come back*). Well, did you give the old man something?

PETTERSEN. Yes; I sent him off with a bottle of cognac.

MRS. SÖRBY. Oh, you might have thought of something better than that.

PETTERSEN. Oh, no, Mrs. Sörby; cognac is what he likes best in the world.

THE FLABBY GENTLEMAN (*in the doorway with a sheet of music in his hand*). Shall we play a duet, Mrs. Sörby?

MRS. SÖRBY. Yes, suppose we do.

THE GUESTS. Bravo, bravo!

(She goes with all the guests through the back room, out to the right. GREGERS *remains standing by the fire.* WERLE *is looking for something on the writing-table and appears to wish that* GREGERS *would go; as* GREGERS *does not move,* WERLE *goes towards the door.)*

GREGERS. Father, won't you stay a moment?

WERLE *(stops).* What is it?

GREGERS. I must have a word with you.

WERLE. Can it not wait till we are alone?

GREGERS. No, it cannot; for perhaps we shall never be alone together.

WERLE *(drawing nearer).* What do you mean by that?

(During what follows, the pianoforte is faintly heard from the distant music-room.)

GREGERS. How has that family been allowed to go so miserably to the wall?

WERLE. You mean the Ekdals, I suppose.

GREGERS. Yes, I mean the Ekdals. Lieutenant Ekdal was once so closely associated with you.

WERLE. Much too closely; I have felt that to my cost for many a year. It is thanks to him that I—yes I—have had a kind of slur cast upon my reputation.

GREGERS *(softly).* Are you sure that he alone was to blame?

WERLE. Who else do you suppose . . . ?

GREGERS. You and he acted together in that affair of the forests . . .

WERLE. But was it not Ekdal that drew the map of the tracts we had bought—that fraudulent map! It was he who felled all that timber illegally on Government ground. In fact, the whole management was in his hands. I was quite in the dark as to what Lieutenant Ekdal was doing.

GREGERS. Lieutenant Ekdal himself seems to have been very much in the dark as to what he was doing.

WERLE. That may be. But the fact remains that he was found guilty and I acquitted.

GREGERS. Yes, I know that nothing was proved against you.

WERLE. Acquittal is acquittal. Why do you rake up these old miseries that turned my hair grey before its time? Is that the sort of thing you have been brooding over up there, all these years? I can assure you, Gregers, here in the town the whole story has been forgotten long ago—so far as *I* am concerned.

GREGERS. But that unhappy Ekdal family . . .

WERLE. What would you have had me do for the people? When Ekdal came out of prison he was a broken-down being, past all help. There are people in the world who dive to the bottom the moment they get a couple of slugs in their body and never come to the surface again. You may take my word for it, Gregers, I have done all I could without positively laying myself open to all sorts of suspicion and gossip . . .

GREGERS. Suspicion . . . ? Oh, I see.

WERLE. I have given Ekdal copying to do for the office, and I pay him far, far more for it than his work is worth . . .

GREGERS (*without looking at him*). H'm; that I don't doubt.

WERLE. You laugh? Do you think I am not telling you the truth? Well, I certainly can't refer you to my books, for I never enter payments of that sort.

GREGERS (*smiles coldly*). No, there are certain payments it is best to keep no account of.

WERLE (*taken aback*). What do you mean by that?

GREGERS (*mustering up courage*). Have you entered what it cost you to have Hialmar Ekdal taught photography?

WERLE. I? How "entered" it?

GREGERS. I have learnt that it was you who paid for his training. And I have learnt, too, that it was you who enabled him to set up house so comfortably.

WERLE. Well, and yet you talk as though I had done nothing for the Ekdals! I can assure you these people have cost me enough in all conscience.

GREGERS. Have you entered any of these expenses in your books?

WERLE. Why do you ask?

GREGERS. Oh, I have my reasons. Now tell me: when you interested yourself so warmly in your old friend's son—it was just before his marriage, was it not?

WERLE. Why, deuce take it—after all these years, how can I . . . ?

GREGERS. You wrote me a letter about that time—a business letter, of course; and in a postscript you mentioned—quite briefly—that Hialmar Ekdal had married a Miss Hansen.

WERLE. Yes, that was quite right. That was her name.

GREGERS. But you did not mention that this Miss Hansen was Gina Hansen—our former housekeeper.

WERLE (*with a forced laugh of derision*). No; to tell the truth, it didn't occur to me that you were so particularly interested in our former housekeeper.

GREGERS. No more I was. But (*lowers his voice*) there were others in this house who were particularly interested in her.

WERLE. What do you mean by that? (*Flaring up*) You are not alluding to me, I hope?

GREGERS (*softly but firmly*). Yes, I am alluding to you.

WERLE. And you dare . . . ! You presume to . . . ! How can that ungrateful hound—that photographer fellow—how dare he go making such insinuations!

GREGERS. Hialmar has never breathed a word about this. I don't believe he has the faintest suspicion of such a thing.

WERLE. Then where have you got it from? Who can have put such notions in your head?

GREGERS. My poor unhappy mother told me; and that the very last time I saw her.

WERLE. Your mother! I might have known as much! You and she—you always held together. It was she who turned you against me, from the first.

GREGERS. No, it was all that she had to suffer and submit to, until she broke down and came to such a pitiful end.

WERLE. Oh, she had nothing to suffer or submit to; not more than most people, at all events. But there's no getting on with morbid, overstrained creatures—that I have learnt to my cost.—And you could go on nursing such a suspicion—burrowing into all sorts of old rumours and slanders against your own father! I must say, Gregers, I really think that at your age you might find something more useful to do.

GREGERS. Yes, it is high time.

WERLE. Then perhaps your mind would be easier than it seems to be now. What can be your object in remaining up at the works, year out and year in, drudging away like a common clerk, and not drawing a farthing more than the ordinary monthly wage? It is downright folly.

GREGERS. Ah, if I were only sure of that.

WERLE. I understand you well enough. You want to be independent; you won't be beholden to me for anything. Well, now there happens to be an opportunity for you to become independent, your own master in everything.

GREGERS. Indeed? In what way . . . ?

WERLE. When I wrote you insisting on your coming to town at once—h'm . . .

GREGERS. Yes, what is it you really want of me? I have been waiting all day to know.

WERLE. I want to propose that you should enter the firm, as partner.

GREGERS. I! Join your firm? As partner?

WERLE. Yes. It would not involve our being constantly together. You could take over the business here in town, and I should move up to the works.

GREGERS. You would?

WERLE. The fact is, I am not so fit for work as I once was. I am obliged to spare my eyes, Gregers; they have begun to trouble me.

GREGERS. They have always been weak.

WERLE. Not as they are now. And besides, circumstances might possibly make it desirable for me to live up there—for a time, at any rate.

GREGERS. That is certainly quite a new idea to me.

WERLE. Listen, Gregers: there are many things that stand between us; but we are father and son after all. We ought surely to be able to come to some sort of understanding with each other.

GREGERS. Outwardly, you mean, of course?

WERLE. Well, even that would be something. Think it over, Gregers. Don't you think it ought to be possible? Eh?

GREGERS (*looking at him coldly*). There is something behind all this.

WERLE. How so?

GREGERS. You want to make use of me in some way.

WERLE. In such a close relationship as ours, the one can always be useful to the other.

GREGERS. Yes, so people say.

WERLE. I want very much to have you at home with me for a time. I am a lonely man, Gregers; I have always felt lonely, all my life through; but most of all now that I am getting up in years. I feel the need of some one about me . . .

GREGERS. You have Mrs. Sörby.

WERLE. Yes, I have her; and she has become, I may say, almost indispensable to me. She is lively and even-tempered; she brightens up the house; and that is a very great thing for me.

GREGERS. Well, then, you have everything just as you wish it.

WERLE. Yes, but I am afraid it can't last. A woman so situated may easily find herself in a false position, in the eyes of the world. For that matter it does a man no good, either.

GREGERS. Oh, when a man gives such dinners as you give, he can risk a great deal.

WERLE. Yes, but how about the woman, Gregers? I fear she won't accept the situation much longer; and even if she did—even if, out of attachment to me, she were to take her chance of gossip and scandal and all that . . . ? Do you think, Gregers —you with your strong sense of justice . . .

GREGERS (*interrupts him*). Tell me in one word: are you thinking of marrying her?

WERLE. Suppose I were thinking of it? What then?

GREGERS. That's what I say: what then?

WERLE. Should you be inflexibly opposed to it?

GREGERS. Not at all. Not by any means.

WERLE. I was not sure whether your devotion to your mother's memory . . .

GREGERS. I am not overstrained.

WERLE. Well, whatever you may or may not be, at all events you have lifted a great weight from my mind. I am extremely pleased that I can reckon on your concurrence in this matter.

GREGERS (*looking intently at him*). Now I see the use you want to put me to.

WERLE. Use to put you to? What an expression!

GREGERS. Oh, don't let us be nice in our choice of words—not when we are alone together, at any rate. (*With a short laugh*) Well, well! So this is what made it absolutely essential that I should come to town in person. For the sake of Mrs. Sörby, we are to get up a pretence at family life in the house—a tableau of filial affection! That will be something new indeed.

WERLE. How dare you speak in that tone!

GREGERS. Was there ever any family life here? Never since I can remember. But now, forsooth, your plans demand something of the sort. No doubt it will have an excellent effect when it is reported that the son has hastened home, on the wings of filial piety, to the grey-haired father's wedding-feast. What will then remain of all the rumours as to the wrongs the poor dead mother had to submit to? Not a vestige. Her son annihilates them at one stroke.

WERLE. Gregers—I believe there is no one in the world you detest as you do me.

GREGERS (*softly*). I have seen you at too close quarters.

WERLE. You have seen me with your mother's eyes. (*Lowers his voice a little*) But you should remember that her eyes were—clouded now and then.

GREGERS (*quivering*). I see what you are hinting at. But who was to blame for mother's unfortunate weakness? Why you, and all those . . . ! The last of them was this woman that you palmed off upon Hialmar Ekdal, when you were . . . Ugh!

WERLE (*shrugs his shoulders*). Word for word as if it were your mother speaking!

GREGERS (*without heeding*). And there he is now, with his great, confiding, child-like mind, compassed about with all this treachery—living under the same roof with such a creature and never dreaming that what he calls his home is built upon a lie! (*Comes a step nearer*) When I look back upon your past, I seem to see a battle-field with shattered lives on every hand.

WERLE. I begin to think the chasm that divides us is too wide.

GREGERS (*bowing, with self-command*). So I have observed; and therefore I take my hat and go.

WERLE. You are going! Out of the house?

GREGERS. Yes. For at last I see my mission in life.

WERLE. What mission?

GREGERS. You would only laugh if I told you.

WERLE. A lonely man doesn't laugh so easily, Gregers.

GREGERS (*pointing towards the background*). Look, father,—the Chamberlains are playing blind-man's-buff with Mrs. Sörby.—Good-night and good-bye.

(*He goes out by the back to the right. Sounds of laughter and merriment from the company, who are now visible in the outer room.*)

WERLE (*muttering contemptuously after* GREGERS). Ha . . . ! Poor wretch—and he says he is not overstrained!

(*The Curtain Falls.*)

ACT II

HIALMAR EKDAL'S *studio, a good-sized room, evidently in the top story of the building. On the right, a sloping roof of large panes of glass, half-covered by a blue curtain. In the right-hand corner, at the back, the entrance door; farther forward, on the same side, a door leading to the sitting-room. Two doors on the opposite side, and between them an iron stove. At the back, a wide double sliding-door. The studio is plainly but comfortably fitted up and furnished. Between the doors on the right, standing out a little from the wall, a sofa with a table and some chairs; on the table a lighted lamp with a shade; beside the stove an old arm-chair. Photographic instruments and apparatus of different kinds lying about the room. Against the back wall, to the left of the double door, stands a bookcase containing a few books, boxes, and bottles of chemicals, instruments, tools, and other objects. Photographs and small articles, such as camel's-hair pencils, paper, and so forth, lie on the table.*

GINA EKDAL *sits on a chair by the table, sewing.* HEDVIG *is sitting on the sofa, with her hands shading her eyes and her thumbs in her ears, reading a book.*

GINA (*glances once or twice at* HEDVIG, *as if with secret anxiety; then says*). Hedvig!

(HEDVIG *does not hear.*)

GINA (*repeats more loudly*). Hedvig!

HEDVIG (*takes away her hands and looks up*). Yes, mother?

GINA. Hedvig dear, you mustn't sit reading any longer now.

HEDVIG. Oh, mother, mayn't I read a little more? Just a little bit?

GINA. No, no, you must put away your book now. Father doesn't like it; he never reads hisself in the evening.

HEDVIG (*shuts the book*). No, father doesn't care much about reading.

GINA (*puts aside her sewing and takes up a lead pencil and a little account-book from the table*). Can you remember how much we paid for the butter today?

HEDVIG. It was one crown sixty-five.

GINA. That's right. (*Puts it down*) It's terrible what a lot of butter we get through in this house. Then there was the smoked sausage, and the cheese—let me see— (*Writes*)—and the ham—(*Adds up*) Yes, that makes just . . .

HEDVIG. And then the beer.

GINA. Yes, to be sure. (*Writes*) How it do mount up! But we can't manage with no less.

HEDVIG. And then you and I didn't need anything hot for dinner, as father was out.

GINA. No; that was so much to the good. And then I took eight crowns fifty for the photographs.

HEDVIG. Really! So much as that?

GINA. Exactly eight crowns fifty.

(*Silence.* GINA *takes up her sewing again,* HEDVIG *takes paper and pencil and begins to draw, shading her eyes with her left hand.*)

HEDVIG. Isn't it jolly to think that father is at Mr. Werle's big dinner-party?

GINA. You know he's not really Mr. Werle's guest. It was the son invited him. (*After a pause*) We have nothing to do with that Mr. Werle.

HEDVIG. I'm longing for father to come home. He promised to ask Mrs. Sörby for something nice for me.

GINA. Yes, there's plenty of good things going in that house, I can teïl you.

HEDVIG (*goes on drawing*). And I believe I'm a little hungry, too.

(OLD EKDAL, *with the paper parcel under his arm and another parcel in his coat pocket, comes in by the entrance door.*)

GINA. How late you are today, grandfather!

EKDAL. They had locked the office door. Had to wait in Gråberg's room. And then they let me through—h'm.

HEDVIG. Did you get some more copying to do, grandfather?

EKDAL. This whole packet. Just look

GINA. That's capital.

HEDVIG. And you have another parcel in your pocket.

EKDAL. Eh? Oh, never mind, that's nothing. (*Puts his stick away in a corner*) This work will keep me going a long time, Gina. (*Opens one of the sliding-doors in the back wall a little*) Hush! (*Peeps into the room for a moment, then pushes the door carefully to again*) Hee-hee! They're fast asleep, all the lot of them. And she's gone into the basket herself. Hee-hee!

HEDVIG. Are you sure she isn't cold in that basket, grandfather?

EKDAL. Not a bit of it! Cold? With all that straw? (*Goes towards the farther door on the left*) There are matches in here, I suppose.

GINA. The matches is on the drawers.

(EKDAL *goes into his room.*)

HEDVIG. It's nice that grandfather has got all that copying.

GINA. Yes, poor old father; it means a bit of pocket-money for him.

HEDVIG. And he won't be able to sit the whole forenoon down at that horrid Madam Eriksen's.

GINA. No more he won't. (*Short silence.*)

HEDVIG. Do you suppose they are still at the dinner-table?

GINA. Goodness knows; as like as not.

HEDVIG. Think of all the delicious things father is having to eat! I'm certain he'll be in splendid spirits when he comes. Don't you think so, mother?

GINA. Yes; and if only we could tell him we'd got the room let . . .

HEDVIG. But we don't need that this evening.

GINA. Oh, we'd be none the worse of it, I can tell you. It's no use to us as it is.

HEDVIG. I mean we don't need it this evening, for father will be in a good humour at any rate. It is best to keep the letting of the room for another time.

GINA (*looks across at her*). You like having some good news to tell father when he comes home in the evening?

HEDVIG. Yes; for then things are pleasanter somehow.

GINA (*thinking to herself*). Yes, yes, there's something in that.

(OLD EKDAL *comes in again and is going out by the foremost door to the left.*)

GINA (*half turning in her chair*). Do you want something out of the kitchen, grandfather?

EKDAL. Yes, yes, I do. Don't you trouble. (*Goes out.*)

GINA. He's not poking away at the fire, is he? (*Waits a moment*) Hedvig, go and see what he's about.

(EKDAL *comes in again with a small jug of steaming hot water.*)

HEDVIG. Have you been getting some hot water, grandfather?

EKDAL. Yes, hot water. Want it for something. Want to write, and the ink has got as thick as porridge—h'm.

GINA. But you'd best have your supper first, grandfather. It's laid in there.

EKDAL. Can't be bothered with supper, Gina. Very busy, I tell you. No one's to come to my room. No one—h'm.

(*He goes into his room;* GINA *and* HEDVIG *look at each other.*)

GINA (*softly*). Can you imagine where he's got money from?

HEDWIG. From Gråberg, perhaps.

GINA. Not a bit of it. Gråberg always sends the money to me.

HEDVIG. Then he must have got a bottle on credit somewhere.

GINA. Poor grandfather, who'd give him credit?

(HIALMAR EKDAL, *in an overcoat and grey felt hat, comes in from the right.*)

GINA (*throws down her sewing and rises*). Why, Ekdal, is that you already?

HEDVIG (*at the same time jumping up*). Fancy your coming so soon, father!

HIALMAR (*taking off his hat*). Yes, most of the people were coming away.

HEDVIG. So early?

HIALMAR. Yes, it was a dinner-party, you know. (*Is taking off his overcoat.*)

GINA. Let me help you.

HEDVIG. Me, too.

(*They draw off his coat;* GINA *hangs it up on the back wall.*)

HEDVIG. Were there many people there, father?

HIALMAR. Oh, no, not many. We were about twelve or fourteen at table.

GINA. And you had some talk with them all?

HIALMAR. Oh, yes, a little; but Gregers took me up most of the time.

GINA. Is Gregers as ugly as ever?

HIALMAR. Well, he's not very much to look at. Hasn't the old man come home?

HEDVIG. Yes, grandfather is in his room, writing.

HIALMAR. Did he say anything?

GINA. No, what should he say?

HIALMAR. Didn't he say anything about . . . ? I heard something about his having been with Gråberg. I'll go in and see him for a moment.

GINA. No, no, better not.

HIALMAR. Why not? Did he say he didn't want me to go in?

GINA. I don't think he wants to see nobody this evening . . .

HEDVIG (*making signs*). H'm—h'm!

GINA (*not noticing*). . . . he has been in to fetch hot water . . .

HIALMAR. Aha! Then he's . . .

GINA. Yes, I suppose so.

HIALMAR. Oh, God! my poor old white-haired father! . . . Well, well; there let him sit and get all the enjoyment he can.

(OLD EKDAL, *in an indoor coat and with a lighted pipe, comes from his room.*)

EKDAL. Got home? Thought it was you I heard talking.

HIALMAR. Yes, I have just come.

EKDAL. You didn't see me, did you?

HIALMAR. No, but they told me you had passed through—so I thought I would follow you.

EKDAL. H'm, good of you, Hialmar.—Who were they, all those fellows?

HIALMAR. Oh, all sorts of people. There was Chamberlain Flor, and Chamberlain Balle, and Chamberlain Kaspersen and Chamberlain—this, that, and the other— I don't know who all . . .

EKDAL (*nodding*). Hear that, Gina! Chamberlains every one of them!

GINA. Yes, I hear as they're terrible genteel in that house nowadays.

HEDVIG. Did the Chamberlains sing, father? Or did they read aloud?

HIALMAR. No, they only talked nonsense. They wanted me to recite something for them; but I knew better than that.

EKDAL. You weren't to be persuaded, eh?

GINA. Oh, you might have done it.

HIALMAR. No; one mustn't be at everybody's beck and call. (*Walks about the room*) That's not my way, at any rate.

EKDAL. No, no; Hialmar's not to be had for the asking, he isn't.

HIALMAR. I don't see why *I* should bother myself to entertain people on the rare occasions when I go into society. Let the others exert themselves. These fellows go from one great dinner-table to the next and gorge and guzzle day out and day in. It's for them to bestir themselves and do something in return for all the good feeding they get.

GINA. But you didn't say that?

HIALMAR (*humming*). Ho-ho-ho . . . ; faith, I gave them a bit of my mind.

EKDAL. Not the Chamberlains?

HIALMAR. Oh, why not? (*Lightly*) After that, we had a little discussion about Tokay.

EKDAL. Tokay! There's a fine wine for you!

HIALMAR (*comes to a standstill*). It may be a fine wine. But of course you know the vintages differ; it all depends on how much sunshine the grapes have had.

GINA. Why, you know everything, Ekdal.

EKDAL. And did they dispute that?

HIALMAR. They tried to; but they were requested to observe that it was just the same with Chamberlains—that with them, too, different batches were of different qualities.

GINA. What things you do think of!

EKDAL. Hee-hee! So they got that in their pipes, too?

HIALMAR. Right in their teeth.

EKDAL. Do you hear that, Gina? He said it right in the very teeth of all the Chamberlains.

GINA. Fancy . . . ! Right in their teeth!

HIALMAR. Yes, but I don't want it talked about. One doesn't speak of such things. The whole affair passed off quite amicably of course. They were nice, genial fellows; I didn't want to wound them—not I!

EKDAL. Right in their teeth, though . . . !

HEDVIG (*caressingly*). How nice it is to see you in a dress-coat! It suits you so well, father.

HIALMAR. Yes, don't you think so? And this one really fits to perfection. It fits almost as if it had been made for me;—a little tight in the arm-holes perhaps;—help me, Hedwig (*takes off the coat*). I think I'll put on my jacket. Where is my jacket, Gina?

GINA. Here it is. (*Brings the jacket and helps him.*)

HIALMAR. That's it! Don't forget to send the coat back to Molvik first thing tomorrow morning.

GINA (*laying it away*). I'll be sure and see to it.

HIALMAR (*stretching himself*). After all, there's a more homely feeling about this. A free-and-easy indoor costume suits my whole personality better. Don't you think so, Hedvig?

HEDVIG. Yes, father.

HIALMAR. When I loosen my necktie into a pair of flowing ends—like this—eh?

HEDVIG. Yes, that goes so well with your moustache and the sweep of your curls,

HIALMAR. I should not call them curls exactly; I should rather say locks.

HEDVIG. Yes, they are too big for curls.

HIALMAR. Locks describes them better.

HEDVIG (*after a pause, twitching his jacket*). Father.

HIALMAR. Well, what is it?

HEDVIG. Oh, you know very well.

HIALMAR. No, really I don't . . .

HEDVIG (*half laughing, half whimpering*). Oh, yes, father; now don't tease me any longer!

HIALMAR. Why, what do you mean?

HEDVIG (*shaking him*). Oh, what nonsense; come, where are they, father? All the good things you promised me, you know?

HIALMAR. Oh—if I haven't forgotten all about them!

HEDVIG. Now you're only teasing me, father! Oh, it's too bad of you! Where have you put them?

HIALMAR. No, I positively forgot to get anything. But wait a little! I have something else for you, Hedvig. (*Goes and searches in the pockets of the coat.*)

HEDVIG (*skipping and clapping her hands*). Oh, mother, mother!

GINA. There, you see; if you only give him time . . .

HIALMAR (*with a paper*). Look, here it is.

HEDVIG. That? Why, that's only a paper.

HIALMAR. That is the bill of fare, my dear; the whole bill of fare. Here you see: "Menu"—that means bill of fare.

HEDVIG. Haven't you anything else?

HIALMAR. I forgot the other things, I tell you. But you may take my word for it, these dainties are very unsatisfying. Sit down at the table and read the bill of fare, and then I'll describe to you how the dishes taste. Here you are, Hedvig.

HEDVIG (*gulping down her tears*). Thank you. (*She seats herself, but does not read;* GINA *makes signs to her;* HIALMAR *notices it.*)

HIALMAR (*pacing up and down the room*). It's monstrous what absurd things the father of a family is expected to think of; and if he forgets the smallest trifle, he is treated to sour faces at once. Well, well, one gets used to that, too. (*Stops near the stove, by the old man's chair*) Have you peeped in there this evening, father?

EKDAL. Yes, to be sure I have. She's gone into the basket.

HIALMAR. Ah, she has gone into the basket. Then she's beginning to get used to it.

EKDAL. Yes; just as I prophesied. But you know there are still a few little things . . .

HIALMAR. A few improvements, yes.

EKDAL. They've got to be made, you know.

HIALMAR. Yes, let us have a talk about the improvements, father. Come, let us sit on the sofa.

EKDAL. All right. H'm—think I'll just fill my pipe first. Must clean it out, too. H'm. (*He goes into his room.*)

GINA (*smiling to* HIALMAR). His pipe!

HIALMAR. Oh, yes, yes, Gina; let him alone—the poor, shipwrecked old man.—Yes, these improvements—we had better get them out of hand tomorrow.

GINA. You'll hardly have time tomorrow, Ekdal.

HEDVIG (*interposing*). Oh, yes he will, mother!

GINA. . . . for remember them prints that has to be retouched; they've sent for them time after time.

HIALMAR. There now! those prints again! I shall get them finished all right! Have any new orders come in?

GINA. No, worse luck; tomorrow I have nothing but those two sittings, you know.

HIALMAR. Nothing else? Oh, no, if people won't set about things with a will . . .

GINA. But what more can I do? Don't I advertise in the papers as much as we can afford?

HIALMAR. Yes, the papers, the papers; you see how much good they do. And I suppose no one has been to look at the room either?

GINA. No, not yet.

HIALMAR. That was only to be expected. If people won't keep their eyes open. . . . Nothing can be done without a real effort, Gina!

HEDVIG (*going towards him*). Shall I fetch you the flute, father?

HIALMAR. No; no flute for me; *I* want no pleasures in this world. (*Pacing about*) Yes, indeed I will work tomorrow; you shall see if I don't. You may be sure I shall work as long as my strength holds out.

GINA. But my dear, good Ekdal, I didn't mean it in that way.

HEDVIG. Father, mayn't I bring in a bottle of beer?

HIALMAR. No, certainly not. I require nothing, nothing . . . (*Comes to a standstill*) Beer? Was it beer you were talking about?

HEDVIG (*cheerfully*). Yes, father; beautiful, fresh beer.

HIALMAR. Well—since you insist upon it, you may bring in a bottle.

GINA. Yes, do; and we'll be nice and cosy.

(HEDVIG *runs towards the kitchen door.*)

HIALMAR (*by the stove, stops her, looks at her, puts his arm round her neck and presses her to him*). Hedvig, Hedvig!

HEDVIG (*with tears of joy*). My dear, kind father!

HIALMAR. No, don't call me that. Here have I been feasting at the rich man's table,— battening at the groaning board . . . ! And I couldn't even . . . !

GINA (*sitting at the table*). Oh, nonsense, nonsense, Ekdal.

HIALMAR. It's not nonsense! And yet you mustn't be too hard upon me. You know that I love you for all that.

HEDVIG (*throwing her arms round him*). And we love you, oh so dearly, father!

HIALMAR. And if I am unreasonable once in a while,—why then—you must remember that I am a man beset by a host of cares. There, there! (*Dries his eyes*) No beer at such a moment as this. Give me the flute.

(HEDVIG *runs to the bookcase and fetches it.*)

HIALMAR. Thanks! That's right. With my flute in my hand and you two at my side . . . ah . . . !

(HEDVIG *seats herself at the table near* GINA; HIALMAR *paces backwards and forwards, pipes up vigorously and plays a Bohemian peasant dance, but in a slow plaintive tempo, and with sentimental expression.*)

HIALMAR (*breaking off the melody, holds out his left hand to* GINA *and says with emotion*). Our roof may be poor and humble, Gina; but it is home. And with all my heart I say: here dwells my happiness.

(*He begins to play again; almost immediately after, a knocking is heard at the entrance door.*)

GINA (*rising*). Hush, Ekdal,—I think there's some one at the door.

HIALMAR (*laying the flute on the bookcase*). There! Again!

(GINA *goes and opens the door.*)

GREGERS WERLE (*in the passage*). Excuse me . . .

GINA (*starting back slightly*). Oh!

GREGERS. . . . does not Mr. Ekdal, the photographer, live here?

GINA. Yes, he does.

HIALMAR (*going towards the door*). Gregers! You here after all? Well, come in then.

GREGERS (*coming in*). I told you I would come and look you up.

HIALMAR. But this evening . . . ? Have you left the party?

GREGERS. I have left both the party and my father's house.—Good evening, Mrs Ekdal. I don't know whether you recognize me?

GINA. Oh, yes; it's not difficult to know young Mr. Werle again.

GREGERS. No, I am like my mother; and no doubt you remember her.

HIALMAR. Left your father's house, did you say?

GREGERS. Yes, I have gone to a hotel.

HIALMAR. Indeed. Well, since you're here, take off your coat and sit down.

GREGERS. Thanks.

(*He takes off his overcoat. He is now dressed in a plain grey suit of a countrified cut.*)

HIALMAR. Here, on the sofa. Make yourself comfortable.

(GREGERS *seats himself on the sofa;* HIALMAR *takes a chair at the table.*)

GREGERS (*looking around him*). So these are your quarters, Hialmar—this is your home.

HIALMAR. This is the studio, as you see . . .

GINA. But it's the largest of our rooms, so we generally sit here.

HIALMAR. We used to live in a better place; but this flat has one great advantage: there are such capital outer rooms . . .

GINA. And we have a room on the other side of the passage that we can let.

GREGERS (*to* HIALMAR). Ah—so you have lodgers, too?

HIALMAR. No, not yet. They're not so easy to find, you see; you have to keep your eyes open. (*To* HEDVIG) What about the beer, eh?

(HEDVIG *nods and goes out into the kitchen.*)

GREGERS. So that is your daughter?

HIALMAR. Yes, that is Hedvig.

GREGERS. And she is your only child?

HIALMAR. Yes, the only one. She is the joy of our lives, and—(*lowering his voice*)— at the same time our deepest sorrow, Gregers.

GREGERS. What do you mean?

HIALMAR. She is in serious danger of losing her eyesight.

GREGERS. Becoming blind?

HIALMAR. Yes. Only the first symptoms have appeared as yet, and she may not feel it much for some time. But the doctor has warned us. It is coming, inexorably.

GREGERS. What a terrible misfortune! How do you account for it?

HIALMAR (*sighs*). Hereditary, no doubt.

GREGERS (*starting*). Hereditary?

GINA. Ekdal's mother had weak eyes.

HIALMAR. Yes, so my father says; I can't remember.

GREGERS. Poor child! And how does she take it?

HIALMAR. Oh, you can imagine we haven't the heart to tell her of it. She dreams of no danger. Gay and careless and chirping like a little bird, she flutters onward into a life of endless night. (*Overcome*) Oh, it is cruelly hard on me, Gregers.

(HEDVIG *brings a tray with beer and glasses, which she sets upon the table.*)

HIALMAR (*stroking her hair*). Thanks, thanks, Hedvig.

(HEDVIG *puts her arm around his neck and whispers in his ear.*)

HIALMAR. No, no bread and butter just now. (*Looks up*) But perhaps you would like some, Gregers.

GREGERS (*with a gesture of refusal*). No, no thank you.

HIALMAR (*still melancholy*). Well, you can bring in a little all the same. If you have a crust, that is all I want. And plenty of butter on it, mind.

(HEDVIG *nods gaily and goes out into the kitchen again.*)

GREGERS (*who has been following her with his eyes*). She seems quite strong and healthy otherwise.

GINA. Yes. In other ways there's nothing amiss with her, thank goodness.

GREGERS. She promises to be very like you, Mrs. Ekdal. How old is she now?

GINA. Hedvig is close on fourteen; her birthday is the day after tomorrow.

GREGERS. She is pretty tall for her age, then.

GINA. Yes, she's shot up wonderful this last year.

GREGERS. It makes one realize one's own age to see these young people growing up.— How long is it now since you were married?

GINA. We've been married—let me see—just on fifteen years.

GREGERS. Is it so long as that?

GINA (*becomes attentive; looks at him*). Yes, it is indeed.

HIALMAR. Yes, so it is. Fifteen years all but a few months. (*Changing his tone*) They must have been long years for you, up at the works, Gregers.

GREGERS. They seemed long while I was living them; now they are over, I hardly know how the time has gone.

(OLD EKDAL *comes from his room without his pipe, but with his old-fashioned uni-*
form cap on his head; his gait is somewhat unsteady.)

EKDAL. Come now, Hialmar. let's sit down and have a good talk about this—h'm—
what was it again?

HIALMAR (*going towards him*). Father, we have a visitor here—Gregers Werle.—I
don't know if you remember him.

EKDAL (*looking at* GREGERS, *who has risen*). Werle? Is that the son? What does
he want with me?

HIALMAR. Nothing; it's me he has come to see.

EKDAL. Oh! Then there's nothing wrong?

HIALMAR. No, no, of course not.

EKDAL (*with a large gesture*). Not that I'm afraid, you know, but . . .

GREGERS (*goes over to him*). I bring you a greeting from your old hunting-grounds,
Lieutenant Ekdal.

EKDAL. Hunting-grounds?

GREGERS. Yes, up in Höidal, about the works, you know.

EKDAL. Oh, up there. Yes, I knew all those places well in the old days.

GREGERS. You were a great sportsman then.

EKDAL. So I was, I don't deny it. You're looking at my uniform cap. I don't ask
anybody's leave to wear it in the house. So long as I don't go out in the streets
with it. . . .

(HEDVIG *brings a plate of bread and butter, which she puts upon the table.*)

HIALMAR. Sit down, father, and have a glass of beer. Help yourself, Gregers.

(EKDAL *mutters and stumbles over to the sofa.* GREGERS *seats himself on the chair*
nearest to him, HIALMAR *on the other side of* GREGERS. GINA *sits a little way*
from the table, sewing; HEDVIG *stands beside her father.*)

GREGERS. Can you remember, Lieutenant Ekdal, how Hialmar and I used to come
up and visit you in the summer and at Christmas?

EKDAL. Did you? No, no, no; I don't remember it. But sure enough I've been a
tidy bit of a sportsman in my day. I've shot bears, too. I've shot nine of 'em,
no less.

GREGERS (*looking sympathetically at him*). And now you never get any shooting?

EKDAL. Can't just say that, sir. Get a shot now and then perhaps. Of course not in
the old way. For the woods you see—the woods, the woods . . . ! (*Drinks*)
Are the woods fine up there now?

GREGERS. Not so fine as in your time. They have been thinned a good deal.

EKDAL. Thinned? (*More softly, and as if afraid*) It's dangerous work that. Bad things come of it. The woods revenge themselves.

HIALMAR (*filling up his glass*). Come—a little more, father.

GREGERS. How can a man like you—such a man for the open air—live in the midst of a stuffy town, boxed within four walls?

EKDAL (*laughs quietly and glances at* HIALMAR). Oh, it's not bad here. Not at all so bad.

GREGERS. But don't you miss all the things that used to be a part of your very being— the cool sweeping breezes, the free life in the woods and on the uplands, among beasts and birds . . . ?

EKDAL (*smiling*). Hialmar, shall we let him see it?

HIALMAR (*hastily and a little embarrassed*). Oh, no, no, father; not this evening.

GREGERS. What does he want to show me?

HIALMAR. Oh, it's only something—you can see it another time.

GREGERS (*continues, to the old man*). You see, I have been thinking, Lieutenant Ekdal, that you should come up with me to the works; I am sure to be going back soon. No doubt you could get some copying there, too. And here, you have nothing on earth to interest you—nothing to liven you up.

EKDAL (*stares in astonishment at him*). Have I nothing on earth to . . . !

GREGERS. Of course you have Hialmar; but then he has his own family. And a man like you, who has always had such a passion for what is free and wild . . .

EKDAL (*thumps the table*). Hialmar, he shall see it!

HIALMAR. Oh, do you think it's worth while, father? It's all dark.

EKDAL. Nonsense; it's moonlight. (*Rises*) He shall see it, I tell you. Let me pass! Come and help me, Hialmar.

HEDVIG. Oh, yes, do, father!

HIALMAR (*rising*). Very well then.

GREGERS (*to* GINA). What is it?

GINA. Oh, nothing so very wonderful, after all.

(EKDAL *and* HIALMAR *have gone to the back wall and are each pushing back a side of the sliding door;* HEDVIG *helps the old man;* GREGERS *remains standing by the sofa;* GINA *sits still and sews. Through the open doorway a large, deep, irregular garret is seen with odd nooks and corners; a couple of stove-pipes running through it, from rooms below. There are skylights through which clear moon-beams shine in on some parts of the great room; others lie in deep shadow.)*

EKDAL (*to* GREGERS). You may come close up if you like.

GREGERS (*going over to them*). Why, what is it?

EKDAL. Look for yourself. H'm.

HIALMAR (*somewhat embarrassed*). This belongs to father, you understand.

GREGERS (*at the door, looks into the garret*). Why, you keep poultry, Lieutenant Ekdal.

EKDAL. Should think we did keep poultry. They've gone to roost now. But you should just see our fowls by daylight, sir!

HEDVIG. And there's a . . .

EKDAL. Sh—sh! don't say anything about it yet.

GREGERS. And you have pigeons, too, I see.

EKDAL. Oh, yes, haven't we just got pigeons! They have their nest-boxes up there under the roof-tree; for pigeons like to roost high, you see.

HIALMAR. They aren't all common pigeons.

EKDAL. Common! Should think not indeed! We have tumblers and a pair of pouters, too. But come here! Can you see that hutch down there by the wall?

GREGERS. Yes; what do you use it for?

EKDAL. That's where the rabbits sleep, sir.

GREGERS. Dear me; so you have rabbits, too?

EDKAL. Yes, you may take my word for it, we have rabbits! He wants to know if we have rabbits, Hialmar! H'm! But now comes the thing, let me tell you! Here we have it! Move away, Hedvig. Stand here; that's right,—and now look down there.—Don't you see a basket with straw in it?

GREGERS. Yes. And I can see a fowl lying in the basket.

EKDAL. H'm—"a fowl" . . .

GREGERS. Isn't it a duck?

EKDAL (*hurt*). Why, of course it's a duck.

HIALMAR. But what kind of duck, do you think?

HEDVIG. It's not just a common duck . . .

EKDAL. Sh!

GREGERS. And it's not a Muscovy duck either.

EKDAL. No, Mr.—Werle; it's not a Muscovy duck; for it's a wild duck!

GREGERS. Is it really? A wild duck?

EKDAL. Yes, that's what it is. That "fowl" as you call it—is the wild duck. It's our wild duck, sir.

HEDVIG. My wild duck. It belongs to me.

GREGERS. And can it live up here in the garret? Does it thrive?

EKDAL. Of course it has a trough of water to splash about in, you know.

HIALMAR. Fresh water every other day.

GINA (*turning towards* HIALMAR). But my dear Ekdal, it's getting icy cold here.

EKDAL. H'm, we had better shut up then. It's as well not to disturb their night's rest, too. Close up, Hedvig.

(HIALMAR *and* HEDVIG *push the garret doors together.*)

EKDAL. Another time you shall see her properly. (*Seats himself in the armchair by the stove*) Oh, they're curious things, these wild ducks. I can tell you.

GREGERS. How did you manage to catch it, Lieutenant Ekdal?

EKDAL. *I* didn't catch it. There's a certain man in this town whom we have to thank for it.

GREGERS (*starts slightly*). That man was not my father, was he?

EKDAL. You've hit it. Your father and no one else. H'm.

HIALMAR. Strange that you should guess that, Gregers.

GREGERS. You were telling me that you owed so many things to my father; and so I thought perhaps . . .

GINA. But we didn't get the duck from Mr. Werle himself . . .

EKDAL. Its Håkon Werle we have to thank for her, all the same, Gina. (*To* GREGERS) He was shooting from a boat, you see, and he brought her down. But your father's sight is not very good now. H'm; she was only wounded.

GREGERS. Ah! She got a couple of slugs in her body, I suppose.

HIALMAR. Yes, two or three.

HEDVIG. She was hit under the wing, so that she couldn't fly.

GREGERS. And I suppose she dived to the bottom, eh?

EKDAL (*sleepily, in a thick voice*). Of course. Always do that, wild ducks do. They shoot to the bottom as deep as they can get, sir—and bite themselves fast in the tangle and seaweed—and all the devil's own mess that grows down there. And they never come up again.

GREGERS. But your wild duck came up again, Lieutenant Ekdal.

EKDAL. He had such an amazingly clever dog, your father had. And that dog—he dived in after the duck and fetched her up again.

GREGERS (*who has turned to* HIALMAR). And then she was sent to you here?

HIALMAR. Not at once; at first your father took her home. But she wouldn't thrive there; so Pettersen was told to put an end to her . . .

EKDAL (*half asleep*). H'm—yes—Pettersen—that ass . . .

HIALMAR (*speaking more softly*). That was how we got her, you see; for father knows Pettersen a little; and when he heard about the wild duck he got him to hand her over to us.

GREGERS. And now she thrives as well as possible in the garret there?

HIALMAR. Yes, wonderfully well. She has got fat. You see, she has lived in there so long now that she has forgotten her natural wild life; and it all depends on that.

GREGERS. You are right there, Hialmar. Be sure you never let her get a glimpse of the sky and the sea. . . . But I mustn't stay any longer; I think your father is asleep.

HIALMAR. Oh, as for that . . .

GREGERS. But, by-the-bye—you said you had a room to let—a spare room?

HIALMAR. Yes; what then? Do you know of anybody . . . ?

GREGERS. Can I have that room?

HIALMAR. You?

GINA. Oh, no, Mr. Werle, you . . .

GREGERS. May I have the room? If so, I'll take possession first thing tomorrow morning.

HIALMAR. Yes, with the greatest pleasure . . .

GINA. But, Mr. Werle, I'm sure it's not at all the sort of room for you.

HIALMAR. Why, Gina! how can you say that?

GINA. Why, because the room's neither large enough nor light enough, and . . .

GREGERS. That really doesn't matter, Mrs. Ekdal.

HIALMAR. I call it quite a nice room, and not at all badly furnished either.

GINA. But remember the pair of them underneath.

GREGERS. What pair?

GINA. Well, there's one as has been a tutor . . .

HIALMAR. That's Molvik—Mr. Molvik, B.A.

GINA. And then there's a doctor, by the name of Relling.

GREGERS. Relling? I know him a little; he practised for a time up in Höidal.

GINA. They're a regular rackety pair, they are. As often as not, they're out on the loose in the evenings; and then they come home at all hours, and they're not always just . . .

GREGERS. One soon gets used to that sort of thing. I daresay I shall be like the wild duck . . .

GINA. H'm; I think you ought to sleep upon it first, anyway.

GREGERS. You seem very unwilling to have me in the house, Mrs. Ekdal.

GINA. Oh, no! What makes you think that?

HIALMAR. Well, you really behave strangely about it, Gina. (*To* GREGERS) Then I suppose you intend to remain in the town for the present?

GREGERS (*putting on his overcoat*). Yes, now I intend to remain here.

HIALMAR. And yet not at your father's? What do you propose to do, then?

GREGERS. Ah, if I only knew that, Hialmar, I shouldn't be so badly off! But when one has the misfortune to be called Gregers—! "Gregers"—and then "Werle" after it; did you ever hear anything so hideous?

HIALMAR. Oh, I don't think so at all.

GREGERS. Ugh! Bah! I feel I should like to spit upon the fellow that answers to such a name. But when a man is once for all doomed to be Gregers—Werle in this world, as I am . . .

HIALMAR (*laughs*). Ha, ha! If you weren't Gregers Werle, what would you like to be?

GREGERS. If I should choose, I should like best to be a clever dog.

GINA. A dog!

HEDVIG (*involuntarily*). Oh, no!

GREGERS. Yes, an amazingly clever dog; one that goes to the bottom after wild ducks when they dive and bite themselves fast in tangle and seaweed, down among the ooze.

HIALMAR. Upon my word now, Gregers—I don't in the least know what you're driving at.

GREGERS. Oh, well, you might not be much the wiser if you did. It's understood, then, that I move in early tomorrow morning. (*To* GINA) I won't give you any trouble: I do everything for myself. (*To* HIALMAR) We can talk about the rest tomorrow —Good-night, Mrs. Ekdal. (*Nods to* HEDVIG) Good-night.

GINA. Good-night, Mr. Werle.

HEDVIG. Good-night.

HIALMAR (*who has lighted a candle*). Wait a moment; I must show you a light; the stairs are sure to be dark.

(GREGERS *and* HIALMAR *go out by the passage door.*)

GINA (*looking straight before her, with her sewing in her lap*). Wasn't that queer-like talk about wanting to be a dog?

HEDVIG. Do you know, mother—I believe he meant something quite different by that.

GINA. Why, what should he mean?

HEDVIG. Oh, I don't know; but it seemed to me he meant something different from what he said—all the time.

GINA. Do you think so? Yes, it was sort of queer.

HIALMAR (*comes back*). The lamp was still burning. (*Puts out the candle and sets it down*) Ah, now one can get a mouthful of food at last. (*Begins to eat the bread and butter*) Well, you see, Gina—if only you keep your eyes open . . .

GINA. How, keep your eyes open . . . ?

HIALMAR. Why, haven't we at last had the luck to get the room let? And just think— to a person like Gregers—a good old friend.

GINA. Well, I don't know what to say about it.

HEDVIG. Oh, mother, you'll see; it'll be such fun!

HIALMAR. You're very strange. You were so bent upon getting the room let before; and now you don't like it.

GINA. Yes, I do, Ekdal; if it had only been to some one else . . . But what do you suppose Mr. Werle will say?

HIALMAR. Old Werle? It doesn't concern him.

GINA. But surely you can see that there's something amiss between them again, or the young man wouldn't be leaving home. You know very well those two can't get on with each other.

HIALMAR. Very likely not, but . . .

GINA. And now Mr. Werle may fancy it's you that has egged him on . . .

HIALMAR. Let him fancy so, then! Mr. Werle has done a great deal for me; far be it from me to deny it. But that doesn't make me everlastingly dependent upon him.

GINA. But, my dear Ekdal, maybe grandfather'll suffer for it. He may lose the little bit of work he gets from Gråberg.

HIALMAR. I could almost say: so much the better! Is it not humiliating for a man like me to see his grey-haired father treated as a pariah? But now I believe the fulness of time is at hand. (*Takes a fresh piece of bread and butter*) As sure as I have a mission in life, I mean to fulfil it now!

HEDVIG. Oh, yes, father, do!

GINA. Hush! Don't wake him!

HIALMAR (*more softly*). I will fulfil it, I say. The day shall come when . . . And that is why I say it's a good thing we have let the room; for that makes me more independent. The man who has a mission in life must be independent. (*By the armchair, with emotion*) Poor old white-haired father! Rely on your Hialmar. He has broad shoulders—strong shoulders, at any rate. You shall yet wake up some fine day and . . . (*To* GINA) Do you not believe it?

GINA (*rising*). Yes, of course I do; but in the meantime suppose we see about getting him to bed.

HIALMAR. Yes, come.

(*They take hold of the old man carefully.*)

(*The Curtain Falls.*)

ACT III

HIALMAR EKDAL'S *studio. It is morning: the daylight shines through the large window in the slanting roof; the curtain is drawn back.*
HIALMAR *is sitting at the table, busy retouching a photograph; several others lie before him. Presently* GINA, *wearing her hat and cloak, enters by the passage door; she has a covered basket on her arm.*

HIALMAR. Back already, Gina?

GINA. Oh, yes, one can't let the grass grow under one's feet. (*Sets her basket on a chair and takes off her things.*)

HIALMAR. Did you look in at Gregers' room?

GINA. Yes, that I did. It's a rare sight, I can tell you; he's made a pretty mess to start off with.

HIALMAR. How so?

GINA. He was determined to do everything for himself, he said; so he sets to **work** to light the stove, and what must he do but screw down the damper till the whole room is full of smoke. Ugh! There was a smell fit to . . .

HIALMAR. Well, really!

GINA. But that's not the worst of it; for then he thinks he'll put out the fire, and goes and empties his water-jug into the stove and so makes the whole floor one filthy puddle.

HIALMAR. How annoying!

GINA. I've got the porter's wife to clear up after him, pig that he is! But the room won't be fit to live in till the afternoon.

HIALMAR. What's he doing with himself in the meantime?

GINA. He said he was going out for a little while.

HIALMAR. I looked in upon him, too, for a moment—after you had gone.

GINA. So I heard. You've asked him to lunch.

HIALMAR. Just to a little bit of early lunch, you know. It's his first day—we can hardly do less. You've got something in the house, I suppose?

GINA. I shall have to find something or other.

HIALMAR. And don't cut it too fine, for I fancy Relling and Molvik are coming up, too. I just happened to meet Relling on the stairs, you see; so I had to . . .

GINA. Oh, are we to have those two as well?

HIALMAR. Good Lord—a couple more or less can't make any difference.

OLD EKDAL (*opens his door and looks in*). I say, Hialmar . . . (*Sees* GINA) Oh!

GINA. Do you want anything, grandfather?

EKDAL. Oh, no, it doesn't matter. H'm! (*Retires again.*)

GINA (*takes up the basket*). Be sure you see that he doesn't go out.

HIALMAR. All right, all right. And, Gina, a little herring-salad wouldn't be a bad idea; Relling and Molvik were out on the loose again last night.

GINA. If only they don't come before I'm ready for them . . .

HIALMAR. No, of course they won't; take your own time.

GINA. Very well; and meanwhile you can be working a bit.

HIALMAR. Well, I am working! I am working as hard as I can!

GINA. Then you'll have that job off your hands, you see.

(*She goes out to the kitchen with her basket.* HIALMAR *sits for a time pencilling away at the photograph, in an indolent and listless manner.*)

EKDAL (*peeps in, looks round the studio and says softly*). Are you busy?

HIALMAR. Yes, I'm toiling at these wretched pictures . . .

EKDAL. Well, well, never mind,—since you're so busy—h'm. (*He goes out again; the door stands open.*)

HIALMAR (*continues for some time in silence; then he lays down his brush and goes over to the door*). Are you busy, father?

EKDAL (*in a grumbling tone, within*). If you're busy, I'm busy, too. H'm!

HIALMAR. Oh, very well, then. (*Goes to his work again.*)

EKDAL (*presently, coming to the door again*). H'm; I say, Hialmar, I'm not so very busy, you know.

HIALMAR. I thought you were writing.

EKDAL. Oh, the devil take it! can't Gråberg wait a day or two? After all, it's not a matter of life and death.

HIALMAR. No; and you're not his slave either.

EKDAL. And about that other business in there . . .

HIALMAR. Just what I was thinking of. Do you want to go in? Shall I open the door for you?

EKDAL. Well, it wouldn't be a bad notion.

HIALMAR (*rises*). Then we'd have that off our hands.

EKDAL. Yes, exactly. It's got to be ready first thing tomorrow. It is tomorrow, isn't it? H'm?

HIALMAR. Yes, of course it's tomorrow.

(HIALMAR *and* EKDAL *push aside each his half of the sliding door. The morning sun is shining in through the skylights; some doves are flying about; others sit cooing, upon the perches; the hens are heard clucking now and then, further back in the garret.*)

HIALMAR. There; now you can get to work, father.

EKDAL (*goes in*). Aren't you coming, too?

HIALMAR. Well, really, do you know . . .; I almost think . . . (*Sees* GINA *at the kitchen door*) I? No; I haven't time; I must work.—But now for our new con-trivance . . .

(*He pulls a cord, a curtain slips down inside, the lower part consisting of a piece of old sailcloth, the upper part of a stretched fishing net. The floor of the garret is thus no longer visible.*)

HIALMAR (*goes to the table*). So! Now, perhaps I can sit in peace for a little while.

GINA. Is he rampaging in there again?

HIALMAR. Would you rather have had him slip down to Madam Eriksen's? (*Seats himself*) Do you want anything? You know you said . . .

GINA. I only wanted to ask if you think we can lay the table for lunch here?

HIALMAR. Yes; we have no early appointment, I suppose?

GINA. No, I expect no one today except those two sweethearts that are to be taken together.

HIALMAR. Why the deuce couldn't they be taken together another day!

GINA. Don't you know, I told them to come in the afternoon, when you are having your nap.

HIALMAR. Oh, that's capital. Very well, let us have lunch here then.

GINA. All right; but there's no hurry about laying the cloth; you can have the table for a good while yet.

HIALMAR. Do you think I am not sticking at my work? I'm at it as hard as I can!

GINA. Then you'll be free later on, you know. (*Goes out into the kitchen again. Short pause.*)

EKDAL (*in the garret doorway, behind the net*). Hialmar!

HIALMAR. Well?

EKDAL. Afraid we shall have to move the water-trough, after all.

HIALMAR. What else have I been saying all along?

EKDAL. H'm—h'm—h'm. (*Goes away from the door again.* HIALMAR *goes on working a little; glances towards the garret and half rises.* HEDVIG *comes in from the kitchen.*)

HIALMAR (*sits down again hurriedly*). What do you want?

HEDVIG. I only wanted to come in beside you, father.

HIALMAR (*after a pause*). What makes you go prying around like that? Perhaps you are told off to watch me?

HEDVIG. No, no.

HIALMAR. What is your mother doing out there?

HEDVIG. Oh, mother's in the middle of making the herring-salad. (*Goes to the table*) Isn't there any little thing I could help you with, father?

HIALMAR. Oh, no. It is right that I should bear the whole burden—so long as my strength holds out. Set your mind at rest, Hedvig; if only your father keeps his health . . .

HEDVIG. Oh, no, father! You mustn't talk in that horrid way.

(*She wanders about a little, stops by the doorway and looks into the garret.*)

HIALMAR. Tell me, what is he doing?

HEDVIG. I think he's making a new path to the water-trough.

HIALMAR. He can never manage that by himself! And here am I doomed to sit . . . !

HEDVIG (*goes to him*). Let me take the brush, father; I can do it, quite well.

HIALMAR. Oh, nonsense; you will only hurt your eyes.

HEDVIG. Not a bit. Give me the brush.

HIALMAR (*rising*). Well, it won't take more than a minute or two.

HEDVIG. Pooh, what harm can it do then? (*Takes the brush*) There! (*Seats herself*) I can begin upon this one.

HIALMAR. But mind you don't hurt your eyes! Do you hear? *I* won't be answerable; you do it on your own responsibility—understand that.

HEDVIG (*retouching*). Yes, yes, I understand.

HIALMAR. You are quite clever at it, Hedvig. Only a minute or two, you know.

(*He slips through by the edge of the curtain into the garret.* HEDVIG *sits at her work.* HIALMAR *and* EKDAL *are heard disputing inside.*)

HIALMAR (*appears behind the net*). I say, Hedvig—give me those pincers that are lying on the shelf. And the chisel. (*Turns away inside*) Now you shall see, father. Just let me show you first what I mean!

(HEDVIG *has fetched the required tools from the shelf and hands them to him through the net.*)

HIALMAR. Ah, thanks. I didn't come a moment too soon. (*Goes back from the curtain again; they are heard carpentering and talking inside.* HEDVIG *stands looking in at them. A moment later there is a knock at the passage door; she does not notice it.*)

GREGERS WERLE (*bareheaded, in indoor dress, enters and stops near the door*). H'm . . . !

HEDVIG (*turns and goes towards him*). Good morning. Please come in.

GREGERS. Thank you. (*Looking towards the garret*) You seem to have workpeople in the house.

HEDVIG. No, it is only father and grandfather. I'll tell them you are here.

GREGERS. No, no, don't do that; I would rather wait a little. (*Seats himself on the sofa.*)

HEDVIG. It looks so untidy here . . . (*Begins to clear away the photographs.*)

GREGERS. Oh, don't take them away. Are those prints that have to be finished off?

HEDVIG. Yes, they are a few I was helping father with.

GREGERS. Please don't let me disturb you.

HEDVIG. Oh, no.

(*She gathers the things to her and sits down to work;* GREGERS *looks at her, meanwhile, in silence.*)

GREGERS. Did the wild duck sleep well last night?

HEDVIG. Yes, I think so, thanks.

GREGERS (*turning towards the garret*). It looks quite different by day from what it did last night in the moonlight.

HEDVIG. Yes, it changes ever so much. It looks different in the morning and in the afternoon; and it's different on rainy days from what it is in fine weather.

GREGERS. Have you noticed that?

HEDVIG. Yes, how could I help it?

GREGERS. Are you, too, fond of being in there with the wild duck?

HEDVIG. Yes, when I can manage it . . .

GREGERS. But I suppose you haven't much spare time; you go to school, no doubt.

HEDVIG. No, not now; father is afraid of my hurting my eyes.

GREGERS. Oh; then he reads with you himself?

HEDVIG. Father has promised to read with me; but he has never had time yet.

GREGERS. Then is there nobody else to give you a little help?

HEDVIG. Yes, there is Mr. Molvik; but he is not always exactly—quite . . .

GREGERS. Sober?

HEDVIG. Yes, I suppose that's it:

GREGERS. Why, then you must have any amount of time on your hands. And in there I suppose it is a sort of world by itself?

HEDVIG. Oh, yes, quite. And there are such lots of wonderful things.

GREGERS. Indeed?

HEDVIG. Yes, there are big cupboards full of books; and a great many of the books have pictures in them.

GREGERS. Aha!

HEDVIG. And there's an old bureau with drawers and flaps, and a big clock with figures that go out and in. But the clock isn't going now.

GREGERS. So time has come to a standstill in there—in the wild duck's domain.

HEDVIG. Yes. And then there's an old paint-box and things of that sort; and all the books.

GREGERS. And you read the books, I suppose?

HEDVIG. Oh, yes, when I get the chance. Most of them are English though, and I don't understand English. But then I look at the pictures.—There is one great big book called "Harrison's History of London." * It must be a hundred years old; and there are such heaps of pictures in it. At the beginning there is Death with an hour-glass and a woman. I think that is horrid. But then there are all the other pictures of churches and castles and streets and great ships sailing on the sea.

GREGERS. But tell me, where did all those wonderful things come from?

HEDVIG. Oh, an old sea captain once lived here, and he brought them home with him. They used to call him "The Flying Dutchman." That was curious, because he wasn't a Dutchman at all.

GREGERS. Was he not?

HEDVIG. No. But at last he was drowned at sea; and so he left all those things behind him.

GREGERS. Tell me now—when you are sitting in there looking at the pictures, don't you wish you could travel and see the real world for yourself?

HEDVIG. Oh, no! I mean always to stay at home and help father and mother.

GREGERS. To retouch photographs?

HEDVIG. No, not only that. I should love above everything to learn to engrave pictures like those in the English books.

GREGERS. H'm. What does your father say to that?

* A *New and Universal History of the Cities of London and Westminster,* by Walter Harrison, London, 1775, folio.

HEDVIG. I don't think father likes it; father is strange about such things. Only think, he talks of my learning basket-making and straw-plaiting! But I don't think that would be much good.

GREGERS. Oh, no, I don't think so either.

HEDVIG. But father was right in saying that if I had learnt basket-making I could have made the new basket for the wild duck.

GREGERS. So you could; and it was you that ought to have done it, wasn't it?

HEDVIG. Yes, for it's my wild duck.

GREGERS. Of course it is.

HEDVIG. Yes, it belongs to me. But I lend it to father and grandfather as often as they please.

GREGERS. Indeed? What do they do with it?

HEDVIG. Oh, they look after it, and build places for it, and so on.

GREGERS. I see; for no doubt the wild duck is by far the most distinguished inhabitant of the garret?

HEDVIG. Yes, indeed she is; for she is a real wild fowl, you know. And then she is so much to be pitied; she has no one to care for, poor thing.

GREGERS. She has no family, as the rabbits have . . .

HEDVIG. No. The hens, too, many of them, were chickens together; but she has been taken right away from all her friends. And then there is so much that is strange about the wild duck. Nobody knows her, and nobody knows where she came from either.

GREGERS. And she has been down in the depths of the sea.

HEDVIG (*with a quick glance at him, represses a smile and asks*). Why do you say "the depths of the sea"?

GREGERS. What else should I say?

HEDVIG. You could say "the bottom of the sea." *

GREGERS. Oh, mayn't I just as well say the depths of the sea?

HEDVIG. Yes; but it sounds so strange to me when other people speak of the depths of the sea.

GREGERS. Why so? Tell me why?

HEDVIG. No, I won't; it's so stupid.

* Gregers here uses the old-fashioned expression "havsens bund," while Hedvig would have him use the more commonplace "havets bund" or "havbunden."

GREGERS. Oh, no, I am sure it's not. Do tell me why you smiled.

HEDVIG. Well, this is the reason: whenever I come to realize suddenly—in a flash—what is in there, it always seems to me that the whole room and everything in it should be called "the depths of the sea."—But that is so stupid.

GREGERS. You mustn't say that.

HEDVIG. Oh, yes, for you know it is only a garret.

GREGERS (*looks fixedly at her*). Are you so sure of that?

HEDVIG (*astonished*). That it's a garret?

GREGERS. Are you quite certain of it?

(HEDVIG *is silent, and looks at him open-mouthed.* GINA *comes in from the kitchen with the table things.*)

GREGERS (*rising*). I have come in upon you too early.

GINA. Oh, you must be somewhere; and we're nearly ready now, anyway. Clear the table, Hedvig.

(HEDVIG *clears away her things; she and* GINA *lay the cloth during what follows.* GREGERS *seats himself in the armchair and turns over an album.*)

GREGERS. I hear you can retouch, Mrs. Ekdal.

GINA (*with a side glance*). Yes, I can.

GREGERS. That was exceedingly lucky.

GINA. How—lucky?

GREGERS. Since Ekdal took to photography, I mean.

HEDVIG. Mother can take photographs, too.

GINA. Oh, yes; I was bound to learn that.

GREGERS. So it is really you that carry on the business, I suppose?

GINA. Yes, when Ekdal hasn't time himself . . .

GREGERS. He is a great deal taken up with his old father, I daresay.

GINA. Yes; and then you can't expect a man like Ekdal to do nothing but take car-de-visits of Dick, Tom and Harry.

GREGERS. I quite agree with you; but having once gone in for the thing . . .

GINA. You can surely understand, Mr. Werle, that Ekdal's not like one of your common photographers.

GREGERS. Of course not; but still . . .

(*A shot is fired within the garret.*)

GREGERS (*starting up*). What's that?

GINA. Ugh! now they're firing again!

GREGERS. Have they firearms in there?

HEDVIG. They are out shooting.

GREGERS. What! (*At the door of the garret*) Are you shooting, Hialmar?

HIALMAR (*inside the net*). Are you there? I didn't know; I was so taken up . . .
(*To* HEDVIG) Why did you not let us know? (*Comes into the studio.*)

GREGERS. Do you go shooting in the garret?

HIALMAR (*showing a double-barrelled pistol*). Oh, only with this thing.

GINA. Yes, you and grandfather will do yourselves a mischief some day with that
there pigstol.

HIALMAR (*with irritation*). I believe I have told you that this kind of firearm is called
a pistol.

GINA. Oh, that doesn't make it much better, that I can see.

GREGERS. So you have become a sportsman, too, Hialmar?

HIALMAR. Only a little rabbit-shooting now and then. Mostly to please father, you
understand.

GINA. Men are strange beings; they must always have something to pervert theirselves
with.

HIALMAR (*snappishly*). Just so; we must always have something to divert ourselves
with.

GINA. Yes, that's just what I say.

HIALMAR. H'm. (*To* GREGERS) You see the garret is fortunately so situated that no
one can hear us shooting. (*Lays the pistol on the top shelf of the bookcase*)
Don't touch the pistol, Hedvig! One of the barrels is loaded; remember that.

GREGERS (*looking through the net*). You have a fowling-piece, too, I see.

HIALMAR. That is father's old gun. It's of no use now; something has gone wrong
with the lock. But it's fun to have it all the same; for we can take it to pieces
now and then, and clean and grease it, and screw it together again.—Of course,
it's mostly father that fiddle-faddles with all that sort of thing.

HEDVIG (*beside* GREGERS). Now you can see the wild duck properly.

GREGERS. I was just looking at her. One of her wings seems to me to droop a bit.

HEDVIG. Well, no wonder; her wing was broken, you know.

GREGERS. And she trails one foot a little. Isn't that so?

HIALMAR. Perhaps a very little bit.

HEDVIG. Yes, it was by that foot the dog took hold of her.

HIALMAR. But otherwise she hasn't the least thing the matter with her; and that is simply marvellous for a creature that has a charge of shot in her body and has been between a dog's teeth . . .

GREGERS (*with a glance at* HEDVIG) . . . and that has lain in the depths of the sea— so long.

HEDVIG (*smiling*). Yes.

GINA (*laying the table*). That blessed wild duck! What a lot of fuss you do make over her.

HIALMAR. H'm;—will lunch soon be ready?

GINA. Yes, directly. Hedvig, you must come and help me now.

(GINA *and* HEDVIG *go out into the kitchen.*)

HIALMAR (*in a low voice*). I think you had better not stand there looking in at father; he doesn't like it. (GREGERS *moves away from the garret door.*) Besides, I may as well shut up before the others come. (*Claps his hands to drive the fowls back*) Shh-shh, in with you! (*Draws up the curtain and pulls the doors together*) All the contrivances are my own invention. It's really quite amusing to have things of this sort to potter with and to put to rights when they get out of order. And it's absolutely necessary, too; for Gina objects to having rabbits and fowls in the studio.

GREGERS. To be sure; and I suppose the studio is your wife's special department?

HIALMAR. As a rule, I leave the everyday details of business to her; for then I can take refuge in the parlour and give my mind to more important things.

GREGERS. What things may they be, Hialmar?

HIALMAR. I wonder you have not asked that question sooner. But perhaps you haven't heard of the invention?

GREGERS. The invention? No.

HIALMAR. Really? Have you not? Oh, no, out there in the wilds . . .

GREGERS. So you have invented something, have you?

HIALMAR. It is not quite completed yet; but I am working at it. You can easily imagine that when I resolved to devote myself to photography, it wasn't simply with the idea of taking likenesses of all sorts of commonplace people.

GREGERS. No; your wife was saying the same thing just now.

HIALMAR. I swore that if I consecrated my powers to this handicraft, I would so exalt it that it should become both an art and a science. And to that end I determined to make this great invention.

GREGERS. And what is the nature of the invention? What purpose does it serve?

HIALMAR. Oh, my dear fellow, you mustn't ask for details yet. It takes time, you see. And you must not think that my motive is vanity. It is not for my own sake that I am working. Oh, no; it is my life's mission that stands before me night and day.

GREGERS. What is your life's mission?

HIALMAR. Do you forget the old man with the silver hair?

GREGERS. Your poor father? Well, but what can you do for him?

HIALMAR. I can raise up his self-respect from the dead, by restoring the name of Ekdal to honour and dignity.

GREGERS. Then that is your life's mission?

HIALMAR. Yes. I will rescue the shipwrecked man. For shipwrecked he was, by the very first blast of the storm. Even while those terrible investigations were going on, he was no longer himself. That pistol there—the one we use to shoot rabbits with—has played its part in the tragedy of the house of Ekdal.

GREGERS. The pistol? Indeed?

HIALMAR. When the sentence of imprisonment was passed—he had the pistol in his hand . . .

GREGERS. Had he . . . ?

HIALMAR. Yes; but he dared not use it. His courage failed him. So broken, so demoralized was he even then! Oh, can you understand it? He, a soldier; he, who had shot nine bears, and who was descended from two lieutenant-colonels—one after the other, of course. Can you understand it, Gregers?

GREGERS. Yes, I understand it well enough.

HIALMAR. I cannot. And once more the pistol played a part in the history of our house. When he had put on the grey clothes and was under lock and key—oh, that was a terrible time for me, I can tell you. I kept the blinds drawn down over both my windows. When I peeped out, I saw the sun shining as if nothing had happened. I could not understand it. I saw people going along the street, laughing and talking about indifferent things. I could not understand it. It seemed to me that the whole of existence must be at a standstill—as if under an eclipse.

GREGERS. I felt that, too, when my mother died.

HIALMAR. It was in such an hour that Hialmar Ekdal pointed the pistol at his own breast.

GREGERS. You, too, thought of . . . !

HIALMAR. Yes.

GREGERS. But you did not fire?

HIALMAR. No. At the decisive moment I won the victory over myself. I remained in life. But I can assure you it takes some courage to choose life under circumstances like those.

GREGERS. Well, that depends on how you look at it.

HIALMAR. Yes, indeed, it takes courage. But I am glad I was firm; for now I shall soon perfect my invention; and Dr. Relling thinks, as I do myself, that father may be allowed to wear his uniform again. I will demand that as my sole reward.

GREGERS. So that is what he meant about his uniform . . . ?

HIALMAR. Yes, that is what he most yearns for. You can't think how my heart bleeds for him. Every time we celebrate any little family festival—Gina's and my wedding-day, or whatever it may be—in comes the old man in the lieutenant's uniform of happier days. But if he only hears a knock at the door—for he daren't show himself to strangers, you know—he hurries back to his room again as fast as his old legs can carry him. Oh, it's heart-rending for a son to see such things!

GREGERS. How long do you think it will take you to finish your invention?

HIALMAR. Come now, you mustn't expect me to enter into particulars like that. An invention is not a thing completely under one's own control. It depends largely on inspiration—on intuition—and it is almost impossible to predict when the inspiration may come.

GREGERS. But it's advancing?

HIALMAR. Yes, certainly, it is advancing. I turn it over in my mind every day; I am full of it. Every afternoon, when I have had my dinner, I shut myself up in the parlour, where I can ponder undisturbed. But I can't be goaded to it; it's not a bit of good; Relling says so, too.

GREGERS. And you don't think that all that business in the garret draws you off and distracts you too much?

HIALMAR. No, no, no; quite the contrary. You mustn't say that. I cannot be everlastingly absorbed in the same laborious train of thought. I must have something alongside of it to fill up the time of waiting. The inspiration, the intuition, you see—when it comes, it comes, and there's an end of it.

GREGERS. My dear Hialmar, I almost think you have something of the wild duck in you.

HIALMAR. Something of the wild duck? How do you mean?

GREGERS. You have dived down and bitten yourself fast in the undergrowth.

HIALMAR. Are you alluding to the well-nigh fatal shot that has broken my father's wing—and mine, too?

GREGERS. Not exactly to that. I don't say that your wing has been broken; but you have strayed into a poisonous marsh, Hialmar; an insidious disease has taken hold of you, and you have sunk down to die in the dark.

HIALMAR. I? To die in the dark? Look here, Gregers, you must really leave off talking such nonsense.

GREGERS. Don't be afraid; I shall find a way to help you up again. I, too, have a mission in life now; I found it yesterday.

HIALMAR. That's all very well; but you will please leave me out of it. I can assure you that—apart from my very natural melancholy, of course—I am as contented as any one can wish to be.

GREGERS. Your contentment is an effect of the marsh poison.

HIALMAR. Now, my dear Gregers, pray do not go on about disease and poison; I am not used to that sort of talk. In my house nobody ever speaks to me about unpleasant things.

GREGERS. Ah, that I can easily believe.

HIALMAR. It's not good for me, you see. And there are no marsh poisons here, as you express it. The poor photographer's roof is lowly, I know—and my circumstances are narrow. But I am an inventor, and I am the breadwinner of a family. That exalts me above my mean surroundings.—Ah, here comes lunch!

(GINA *and* HEDVIG *bring bottles of ale, a decanter of brandy, glasses, etc. At the same time,* RELLING *and* MOLVIK *enter from the passage; they are both without hat or overcoat.* MOLVIK *is dressed in black.*)

GINA (*placing the things upon the table*). Ah, you two have come in the nick of time.

RELLING. Molvik got it into his head that he could smell herring-salad, and then there was no holding him.—Good morning again, Ekdal.

HIALMAR. Gregers, let me introduce you to Mr. Molvik. Doctor . . . Oh, you know Relling, don't you?

GREGERS. Yes, slightly.

RELLING. Oh, Mr. Werle, junior! Yes, we two have had one or two little skirmishes up at the Höidal works. You've just moved in?

GREGERS. I moved in this morning.

RELLING. Molvik and I live right under you; so you haven't far to go for the doctor and the clergyman, if you should need anything in that line

GREGERS. Thanks, it's not quite unlikely; for yesterday we were thirteen at table.

HIALMAR. Oh, come now, don't let us get upon unpleasant subjects again!

RELLING. You may make your mind easy, Ekdal; I'll be hanged if the finger of fate points to you.

HIALMAR. I should hope not, for the sake of my family. But let us sit down now. and eat and drink and be merry.

GREGERS. Shall we not wait for your father?

HIALMAR. No, his lunch will be taken in to him later. Come along!

(*The men seat themselves at table, and eat and drink.* GINA *and* HEDVIG *go in and out and wait upon them.*)

RELLING. Molvik was frightfully stewed yesterday, Mrs. Ekdal.

GINA. Really? Yesterday again?

RELLING. Didn't you hear him when I brought him home last night?

GINA. No, I can't say I did.

RELLING. That was a good thing, for Molvik was disgusting last night.

GINA. Is that true, Molvik?

MOLVIK. Let us draw a veil over last night's proceedings. That sort of thing is totally foreign to my better self.

RELLING (*to* GREGERS). It comes over him like a sort of possession, and then I have to go out on the loose with him. Mr. Molvik is dæmonic, you see.

GREGERS. Dæmonic?

RELLING. Molvik is dæmonic, yes.

GREGERS. H'm.

RELLING. And dæmonic natures are not made to walk straight through the world; they must meander a little now and then.—Well, so you still stick up there at those horrible grimy works?

GREGERS. I have stuck there until now.

RELLING. And did you ever manage to collect that claim you went about presenting?

GREGERS. Claim? (*Understands him*) Ah, I see.

HIALMAR. Have you been presenting claims, Gregers?

GREGERS. Oh, nonsense.

RELLING. Faith, but he has, though! He went around to all the cotters' cabins presenting something he called "the claim of the ideal."

GREGERS. I was young then.

RELLING. You're right; you were very young. And as for the claim of the ideal—you never got it honoured while *I* was up there.

GREGERS. Nor since either.

RELLING. Ah, then you've learnt to knock a little discount off, I expect.

GREGERS. Never, when I have a true man to deal with.

HIALMAR. No, I should think, indeed. A little butter, Gina.

RELLING. And a slice of bacon for Molvik.

MOLVIK. Ugh, not bacon! (*A knock at the garret door.*)

HIALMAR. Open the door, Hedvig; father wants to come out.

(HEDVIG *goes and opens the door a little way;* EKDAL *enters with a fresh rabbit-skin; she closes the door after him.*)

EKDAL. Good morning, gentlemen! Good sport today. Shot a big one.

HIALMAR. And you've gone and skinned it without waiting for me . . . !

EKDAL. Salted it, too. It's good tender meat, is rabbit; it's sweet; it tastes like sugar. Good appetite to you gentlemen. (*Goes into his room.*)

MOLVIK (*rising*). Excuse me . . . ; I can't . . . ; I must get downstairs immediately . . .

RELLING. Drink some soda water, man!

MOLVIK (*hurrying away*). Ugh—ugh! (*Goes out by the passage door.*)

RELLING (*to* HIALMAR). Let us drain a glass to the old hunter.

HIALMAR (*clinks glasses with him*). To the undaunted sportsman who has looked death in the face!

RELLING. To the grey-haired . . . (*Drinks*) By-the-bye, is his hair grey or white?

HIALMAR. Something between the two, I fancy; for that matter, he has very few hairs left of any colour.

RELLING. Well, well, one can get through the world with a wig. After all, you are a happy man, Ekdal; you have your noble mission to labour for . . .

HIALMAR. And I do labour, I can tell you.

RELLING. And then you have your excellent wife, shuffling quietly in and out in her felt slippers, and that see-saw walk of hers, and making everything cosy and comfortable about you.

HIALMAR. Yes, Gina—(*nods to her*)—you are a good helpmate on the path of life.

GINA. Oh, don't sit there cricketizing me.

RELLING. And your Hedvig, too, Ekdal!

HIALMAR (*affected*). The child, yes! The child before everything! Hedvig, come here to me. (*Strokes her hair*) What day is it tomorrow, eh?

HEDVIG (*shaking him*). Oh, no, you're not to say anything, father.

HIALMAR. It cuts me to the heart when I think what a poor affair it will be; only a little festivity in the garret . . .

HEDVIG. Oh, but that's just what I like!

RELLING. Just you wait till the wonderful invention sees the light, Hedvig!

HIALMAR. Yes, indeed—then you shall see . . . ! Hedvig, I have resolved to make your future secure. You shall live in comfort all your days. I will demand—something or other—on your behalf. That shall be the poor inventor's sole reward.

HEDVIG (*whispering, with her arms round his neck*). Oh, you dear, kind father!

RELLING (*to* GREGERS). Come now, don't you find it pleasant, for once in a way, to sit at a well-spread table in a happy family circle?

HIALMAR. Ah, yes, I really prize these social hours.

GREGERS. For my part, I don't thrive in marsh vapours.

RELLING. Marsh vapours?

HIALMAR. Oh, don't begin with that stuff again!

GINA. Goodness knows there's no marsh vapours in this house, Mr. Werle; I give the place a good airing every blessed day.

GREGERS (*leaves the table*). No airing you can give will drive out the taint I mean.

HIALMAR. Taint!

GINA. Yes, what do you say to that, Ekdal!

RELLING. Excuse me—may it not be you yourself that have brought the taint from those mines up there?

GREGERS. It is like you to call what I bring into this house a taint.

RELLING (*goes up to him*). Look here, Mr. Werle, junior: I have a strong suspicion that you are still carrying about that "claim of the ideal," large as life, in your coat-tail pocket.

GREGERS. I carry it in my breast.

RELLING. Well, wherever you carry it, I advise you not to come dunning us with it, so long as *I* am on the premises.

GREGERS. And if I do so nonetheless?

RELLING. Then you'll go head-foremost down the stairs; now I've warned you.

HIALMAR (*rising*). Oh, but Relling . . . !

GREGERS. Yes, you may turn me out . . .

GINA (*interposing between them*). We can't have that, Relling. But I must say, Mr. Werle, it ill becomes you to talk about vapours and taints, after all the mess you made with your stove. (*A knock at the passage door.*)

HEDVIG. Mother, there's somebody knocking.

HIALMAR. There now, we're going to have a whole lot of people!

GINA. I'll go . . . (*Goes over and opens the door, starts, and draws back*) Oh-oh, dear!

(WERLE, *in a fur coat, advances one step into the room.*)

WERLE. Excuse me; but I think my son is staying here.

GINA (*with a gulp*). Yes.

HIALMAR (*approaching him*). Won't you do us the honour to . . . ?

WERLE. Thank you, I merely wish to speak to my son.

GREGERS. What is it? Here I am.

WERLE. I want a few words with you, in your room.

GREGERS. In my room? Very well . . . (*About to go.*)

GINA. No, no, your room's not in a fit state . . .

WERLE. Well then, out in the passage here; I want to have a few words with you alone.

HIALMAR. You can have them here, sir. Come into the parlour, Relling.

(HIALMAR *and* RELLING *go off to the right.* GINA *takes* HEDVIG *with her into the kitchen.*)

GREGERS (*after a short pause*). Well, now we are alone.

WERLE. From something you let fall last evening, and from your coming to lodge with the Ekdals, I can't help inferring that you intend to make yourself unpleasant to me, in one way or another.

GREGERS. I intend to open Hialmar Ekdal's eyes. He shall see his position as it really is—that is all.

WERLE. Is that the mission in life you spoke of yesterday?

GREGERS. Yes. You have left me no other.

WERLE. Is it I, then, that crippled your mind, Gregers?

GREGERS. You have crippled my whole life. I am not thinking of all that about mother . . . But it's thanks to you that I am continually haunted and harassed by a guilty conscience.

WERLE. Indeed! It is your conscience that troubles you, is it?

GREGERS. I ought to have taken a stand against you when the trap was set for Lieutenant Ekdal. I ought to have cautioned him; for I had a misgiving as to what was in the wind.

WERLE. Yes, that was the time to have spoken.

GREGERS. I did not dare to, I was so cowed and spiritless. I was mortally afraid of you—not only then, but long afterwards.

WERLE. You have got over that fear now, it appears.

GREGERS. Yes, fortunately. The wrong done to old Ekdal, both by me and by—others, can never be undone; but Hialmar I can rescue from all the falsehood and deception that are bringing him to ruin.

WERLE. Do you think that will be doing him a kindness?

GREGERS. I have not the least doubt of it.

WERLE. You think our worthy photographer is the sort of man to appreciate such friendly offices?

GREGERS. Yes, I do.

WERLE. H'm—we shall see.

GREGERS. Besides, if I am to go on living, I must try to find some cure for my sick conscience.

WERLE. It will never be sound. Your conscience has been sickly from childhood. That is a legacy from your mother, Gregers—the only one she left you.

GREGERS (*with a scornful half-smile*). Have you not yet forgiven her for the mistake you made in supposing she would bring you a fortune?

WERLE. Don't let us wander from the point.—Then you hold to your purpose of setting young Ekdal upon what you imagine to be the right scent?

GREGERS. Yes, that is my fixed resolve.

WERLE. Well, in that case I might have spared myself this visit; for, of course, it **is** useless to ask whether you will return home with me?

GREGERS. Quite useless.

WERLE. And I suppose you won't enter the firm either?

GREGERS. No.

WERLE. Very good. But as I am thinking of marrying again, your share in the property will fall to you at once.*

GREGERS (*quickly*). No, I do not want that.

WERLE. You don't want it?

GREGERS. No, I dare not take it, for conscience' sake.

WERLE (*after a pause*). Are you going up to the works again?

GREGERS. No; I consider myself released from your service.

WERLE. But what are you going to do?

GREGERS. Only to fulfill my mission; nothing more.

WERLE. Well, but afterwards? What are you going to live upon?

GREGERS. I have laid by a little out of my salary.

WERLE. How long will that last?

GREGERS. I think it will last my time.

WERLE. What do you mean?

GREGERS. I shall answer no more questions.

WERLE. Good-bye then, Gregers.

GREGERS. Good-bye. (WERLE *goes.*)

HIALMAR (*peeping in*). He's gone, isn't he?

GREGERS. Yes.

(HIALMAR *and* RELLING *enter; also* GINA *and* HEDVIG *from the kitchen.*)

RELLING. That luncheon-party was a failure.

GREGERS. Put on your coat, Hialmar; I want you to come for a long walk with me.

HIALMAR. With pleasure. What was it your father wanted? Had it anything to do with me?

GREGERS. Come along. We must have a talk. I'll go and put on my overcoat. (*Goes out by the passage door.*)

* By Norwegian law, before a widower can marry again, a certain proportion of his property must be settled on his children by his former marriage.

GINA. You shouldn't go out with him, Ekdal.

RELLING. No, don't you do it. Stay where you are.

HIALMAR (*gets his hat and overcoat*). Oh, nonsense! When a friend of my youth feels impelled to open his mind to me in private . . .

RELLING. But devil take it—don't you see that the fellow's mad, cracked, demented!

GINA. There, what did I tell you! His mother before him had crazy fits like that sometimes.

HIALMAR. The more need for a friend's watchful eye. (*To* GINA) Be sure you have dinner ready in good time. Good-bye for the present. (*Goes out by the passage door.*)

RELLING. It's a thousand pities the fellow didn't go to hell through one of the Höidal mines.

GINA. Good Lord! what makes you say that?

RELLING (*muttering*). Oh, I have my own reasons.

GINA. Do you think young Werle is really mad?

RELLING. No, worse luck; he's no madder than most other people. But one disease he has certainly got in his system.

GINA. What is it that's the matter with him?

RELLING. Well, I'll tell you, Mrs. Ekdal. He is suffering from an acute attack of integrity.

GINA. Integrity?

HEDVIG. Is that a kind of disease?

RELLING. Yes, it's a national disease; but it only appears sporadically. (*Nods to* GINA) Thanks for your hospitality. (*He goes out by the passage door.*)

GINA (*moving restlessly to and fro*). Ugh, that Gregers Werle—he was always a wretched creature.

HEDVIG (*standing by the table and looking searchingly at her*). I think all this is very strange.

(*The Curtain Falls.*)

ACT IV

HIALMAR EKDAL'S *studio. A photograph has just been taken; a camera with the cloth over it, a pedestal, two chairs, a folding table, etc., are standing out in the room. Afternoon light; the sun is going down; a little later it begins to grow dusk.*

GINA *stands in the passage doorway, with a little box and a wet glass plate in her hand, and is speaking to somebody outside.*

GINA. Yes, certainly. When I make a promise I keep it. The first dozen shall be ready on Monday. Good afternoon.

(*Someone is heard going downstairs.* GINA *shuts the door, slips the plate into the box and puts it into the covered camera.*)

HEDVIG (*comes in from the kitchen*). Are they gone?

GINA (*tidying up*). Yes, thank goodness, I've got rid of them at last.

HEDVIG. But can you imagine why father hasn't come home yet?

GINA. Are you sure he's not down in Relling's room?

HEDVIG. No, he's not; I ran down the kitchen stair just now and asked.

GINA. And his dinner standing and getting cold, too.

HEDVIG. Yes, I can't understand it. Father's always so careful to be home to dinner!

GINA. Oh, he'll be here directly, you'll see.

HEDVIG. I wish he would come; everything seems so queer today.

GINA (*calls out*). There he is!

(HIALMAR EKDAL *comes in at the passage door.*)

HEDVIG (*going to him*). Father! Oh, what a time we've been waiting for you!

GINA (*glancing sidelong at him*). You've been out a long time, Ekdal.

HIALMAR (*without looking at her*). Rather long, yes.

(*He takes off his overcoat;* GINA *and* HEDVIG *go to help him; he motions them away.*)

GINA. Perhaps you've had dinner with Werle?

HIALMAR (*hanging up his coat*). No.

GINA (*going towards the kitchen door*). Then I'll bring some in for you.

HIALMAR. No; let the dinner alone. I want nothing to eat.

HEDVIG (*going nearer to him*). Are you not well, father?

HIALMAR. Well? Oh, yes, well enough. We have had a tiring walk, Gregers and I.

GINA. You didn't ought to have gone so far, Ekdal; you're not used to it.

HIALMAR. H'm; there's many a thing a man must get used to in this world. (*Wanders about the room*) Has any one been here whilst I was out?

GINA. Nobody but the two sweethearts.

HIALMAR. No new orders?

GINA. No, not today.

HEDVIG. There will be some tomorrow, father, you'll see.

HIALMAR. I hope there will; for tomorrow I am going to set to work in real earnest.

HEDVIG. Tomorrow! Don't you remember what day it is tomorrow?

HIALMAR. Oh, yes, by-the-bye. . . . Well, the day after, then. Henceforth I mean to do everything myself; I shall take all the work into my own hands.

GINA. Why, what can be the good of that, Ekdal? It'll only make your life a burden to you. I can manage the photography all right; and you can go on working at your invention.

HEDVIG. And think of the wild duck, father,—and all the hens and rabbits and . . . !

HIALMAR. Don't talk to me of all that trash! From tomorrow I will never set foot in the garret again.

HEDVIG. Oh, but father, you promised that we should have a little party . . .

HIALMAR. H'm, true. Well, then, from the day after tomorrow. I should almost like to wring that cursed wild duck's neck!

HEDVIG (*shrieks*). The wild duck!

GINA. Well, I never!

HEDVIG (*shaking him*). Oh, no, father; you know it's my wild duck!

HIALMAR. That is why I don't do it. I haven't the heart to—for your sake, Hedvig. But in my inmost soul I feel that I ought to do it. I ought not to tolerate under my roof a creature that has been through those hands.

GINA. Why, good gracious, even if grandfather did get it from that poor creature, Pettersen . . .

HIALMAR (*wandering about*). There are certain claims—what shall I call them?—let me say claims of the ideal—certain obligations, which a man cannot disregard without injury to his soul.

HEDVIG (*going after him*). But think of the wild duck,—the poor wild duck!

HIALMAR (*stops*). I tell you I will spare it—for your sake. Not a hair of its head shall be—I mean, it shall be spared. There are greater problems than that to be dealt with. But you should go out a little now, Hedvig, as usual; it is getting dusk enough for you now.

HEDVIG. No, I don't care about going out now.

HIALMAR. Yes, do; it seems to me your eyes are blinking a great deal; all these vapours in here are bad for you. The air is heavy under this roof.

HEDVIG. Very well, then, I'll run down the kitchen stair and go for a little walk. My cloak and hat?—oh, they're in my own room. Father—be sure you don't do the wild duck any harm whilst I'm out.

HIALMAR. Not a feather of its head shall be touched. (*Draws her to him*) You and I, Hedvig—we two . . . ! Well, go along.

(HEDVIG *nods to her parents and goes out through the kitchen.*)

HIALMAR (*walks about without looking up*). Gina.

GINA. Yes?

HIALMAR. From tomorrow—or, say, from the day after tomorrow—I should like to keep the household account-book myself.

GINA. Do you want to keep the accounts, too, now?

HIALMAR. Yes; or to check the receipts at any rate.

GINA. Lord help us! that's soon done.

HIALMAR. One would hardly think so; at any rate, you seem to make the money go a very long way. (*Stops and looks at her*) How do you manage it?

GINA. It's because me and Hedvig, we need so little.

HIALMAR. Is it the case that father is very liberally paid for the copying he does for Mr. Werle?

GINA. I don't know as he gets anything out of the way. I don't know the rates for that sort of work.

HIALMAR. Well, what does he get, about? Let me hear!

GINA. Oh, it varies; I daresay it'll come to about as much as he costs us, with a little pocket-money over.

HIALMAR. As much as he costs us! And you have never told me this before!

GINA. No. How could I tell you? It pleased you so much to think he got everything from you.

HIALMAR. And he gets it from Mr. Werle.

GINA. Oh, well, he has plenty and to spare, he has.

HIALMAR. Light the lamp for me, please!

GINA (*lighting the lamp*). And, of course, we don't know as it's Mr. Werle himself, it may be Gråberg . . .

HIALMAR. Why attempt such an evasion?

GINA. I don't know; I only thought . . .

HIALMAR. H'm.

GINA. It wasn't me that got grandfather that copying. It was Bertha, when she used to come about us.

HIALMAR. It seems to me your voice is trembling.

GINA (*putting the lamp-shade on*). Is it?

HIALMAR. And your hands are shaking, are they not?

GINA (*firmly*). Come right out with it, Ekdal. What has he been saying about me?

HIALMAR. Is it true—can it be true that—that there was an—an understanding between you and Mr. Werle, while you were in service there?

GINA. That's not true. Not at that time. Mr. Werle did come after me, that's a fact. And his wife thought there was something in it, and then she made such a hocus-pocus and hurly-burly, and she hustled me and bustled me about so, that I left her service.

HIALMAR. But afterwards, then?

GINA. Well, then I went home. And mother—well, she wasn't the woman you took her for, Ekdal; she kept on worrying and worrying at me about one thing and another—for Mr. Werle was a widower by that time.

HIALMAR. Well, and then?

GINA. I suppose you've got to know it. He gave me no peace until he'd had his way.

HIALMAR (*striking his hands together*). And this is the mother of my child! How could you hide this from me?

GINA. Yes, it was wrong of me; I ought certainly to have told you long ago.

HIALMAR. You should have told me at the very first;—then I should have known the sort of woman you were.

GINA. But would you have married me all the same?

HIALMAR. How can you dream that I would?

GINA. That's just why I didn't dare tell you anything, then. For I'd come to care for you so much, you see; and I couldn't go and make myself utterly miserable . . .

HIALMAR (*walks about*). And this is my Hedvig's mother. And to know that all I see before me—(*kicks a chair*)—all that I call my home—I owe to a favoured predecessor! Oh, that scoundrel Werle!

GINA. Do you repent of the fourteen—the fifteen years we've lived together?

HIALMAR (*placing himself in front of her*). Have you not every day, every hour, repented of the spider's-web of deceit you have spun around me? Answer me that! How could you help writhing with penitence and remorse?

GINA. Oh, my dear Ekdal, I've had all I could do to look after the house and get through the day's work . . .

HIALMAR. Then you never think of reviewing your past?

GINA. No; Heaven knows I'd almost forgotten those old stories.

HIALMAR. Oh, this dull, callous contentment! To me there is something revolting about it. Think of it—never so much as a twinge of remorse!

GINA. But tell me, Ekdal—what would have become of you if you hadn't had a wife like me?

HIALMAR. Like you . . . !

GINA. Yes; for you know I've always been a bit more practical and wide-awake than you. Of course I'm a year or two older.

HIALMAR. What would have become of me!

GINA. You'd got into all sorts of bad ways when first you met me; that you can't deny.

HIALMAR. "Bad ways" do you call them? Little do you know what a man goes through when he is in grief and despair—especially a man of my fiery temperament.

GINA. Well, well, that may be so. And I've no reason to crow over you, neither; for you turned a moral of a husband, that you did, as soon as ever you had a house and home of your own.—And now we'd got everything so nice and cosy about us; and me and Hedvig was just thinking we'd soon be able to let ourselves go a bit, in the way of both food and clothes.

HIALMAR. In the swamp of deceit, yes.

GINA. I wish to goodness that detestable thing had never set his foot inside our doors!

HIALMAR. And I, too, thought my home such a pleasant one. That was a delusion. Where shall I now find the elasticity of spirit to bring my invention into the world of reality? Perhaps it will die with me; and then it will be your past, Gina, that will have killed it.

GINA (*nearly crying*). You mustn't say such things, Ekdal. Me, that has only wanted to do the best I could for you, all my days!

HIALMAR. I ask you, what becomes of the breadwinner's dream? When I used to lie in there on the sofa and brood over my invention, I had a clear enough presentiment that it would sap my vitality to the last drop. I felt even then that the day when I held the patent in my hand—that day—would bring my—release. And then it was my dream that you should live on after me, the dead inventor's well-to-do widow.

GINA (*drying her tears*). No, you mustn't talk like that, Ekdal. May the Lord never let me see the day I am left a widow!

HIALMAR. Oh, the whole dream has vanished. It is all over now. All over!

(GREGERS WERLE *opens the passage door cautiously and looks in.*)

GREGERS. May I come in?

HIALMAR. Yes, come in.

GREGERS (*comes forward, his face beaming with satisfaction, and holds out both his hands to them*). Well, dear friends . . . ! (*Looks from one to the other and whispers to* HIALMAR) Have you not done it yet?

HIALMAR (*aloud*). It is done.

GREGERS. It is?

HIALMAR. I have passed through the bitterest moments of my life.

GREGERS. But also, I trust, the most ennobling.

HIALMAR. Well, at any rate, we have got through it for the present.

GINA. God forgive you, Mr. Werle.

GREGERS (*in great surprise*). But I don't understand this.

HIALMAR. What don't you understand?

GREGERS. After so great a crisis—a crisis that is to be the starting-point of an entirely new life—of a communion founded on truth and free from all taint of deception . . .

HIALMAR. Yes, yes, I know; I know that quite well.

GREGERS. I confidently expected, when I entered the room, to find the light of transfiguration shining upon me from both husband and wife. And now I see nothing but dullness, oppression, gloom . . .

GINA. Oh, is that it? (*Takes off the lamp-shade.*)

GREGERS. You will not understand me, Mrs. Ekdal. Ah, well, you, I suppose, need time to. . . . But you, Hialmar? Surely you feel a new consecration after the great crisis.

HIALMAR. Yes, of course I do. That is—in a sort of way.

GREGERS. For surely nothing in the world can compare with the joy of forgiving one who has erred and raising her up to oneself in love.

HIALMAR. Do you think a man can so easily throw off the bitter cup I have drained?

GREGERS. No, not a common man, perhaps. But a man like you . . . !

HIALMAR. Good God! I know that well enough. But you must keep me up to it, Gregers. It takes time, you know.

GREGERS. You have much of the wild duck in you, Hialmar. (RELLING *has come in at the passage door.*)

RELLING. Oho! is the wild duck to the fore again?

HIALMAR. Yes; Mr. Werle's wing-broken victim.

RELLING. Mr. Werle's . . . ? So it's him you are talking about?

HIALMAR. Him and—ourselves.

RELLING (*in an undertone to* GREGERS). May the devil fly away with you!

HIALMAR. What is that you are saying?

RELLING. Only uttering a heartfelt wish that this quack-salver would take himself off. If he stays here, he is quite equal to making an utter mess of life, for both of you.

GREGERS. These two will not make a mess of life, Mr. Relling. Of course I won't speak of Hialmar—him we know. But she, too, in her innermost heart, has certainly something loyal and sincere . . .

GINA (*almost crying*). You might have let me alone for what I was, then.

RELLING (*to* GREGERS). Is it rude to ask what you really want in this house?

GREGERS. To lay the foundations of a true marriage.

RELLING. So you don't think Ekdal's marriage is good enough as it is?

GREGERS. No doubt it is as good a marriage as most others, worse luck. But a true marriage it has yet to become.

HIALMAR. You have never had eyes for the claims of the ideal, Relling.

RELLING. Rubbish, my boy!—but excuse me, Mr. Werle: how many—in round numbers—how many true marriages have you seen in the course of your life?

GREGERS. Scarcely a single one.

RELLING. Nor I either.

GREGERS. But I have seen innumerable marriages of the opposite kind. And it has been my fate to see at close quarters what ruin such a marriage can work in two human souls.

HIALMAR. A man's whole moral basis may give way beneath his feet; that is the terrible part of it.

RELLING. Well, I can't say I've ever been exactly married, so I don't pretend to speak with authority. But this I know, that the child enters into the marriage problem. And you must leave the child in peace.

HIALMAR. Oh—Hedvig! my poor Hedvig!

RELLING. Yes, you must be good enough to keep Hedvig outside of all this. You two are grown-up people; you are free, in God's name, to make what mess and muddle you please of your life. But you must deal cautiously with Hedvig, I tell you; else you may do her a great injury.

HIALMAR. An injury!

RELLING. Yes, or she may do herself an injury—and perhaps others, too.

GINA. How can you know that, Relling?

HIALMAR. Her sight is in no immediate danger, is it?

RELLING. I am not talking about her sight. Hedvig is at a critical age. She may be getting all sorts of mischief into her head.

GINA. That's true—I've noticed it already! She's taken to carrying on with the fire, out in the kitchen. She calls it playing at house-on-fire. I'm often scared for fear she really sets fire to the house.

RELLING. You see; I thought as much.

GREGERS (*to* RELLING). But how do you account for that?

RELLING (*sullenly*). Her constitution's changing, sir.

HIALMAR. So long as the child has me . . . ! So long as *I* am above ground . . . ! (*A knock at the door.*)

GINA. Hush, Ekdal; there's some one in the passage. (*Calls out*) Come in!

(MRS. SÖRBY, *in walking dress, comes in.*)

MRS. SÖRBY. Good evening.

GINA (*going towards her*). Is it really you, Bertha?

MRS. SÖRBY. Yes, of course it is. But I'm disturbing you, I'm afraid?

HIALMAR. No, not at all; an emissary from that house . . .

MRS. SÖRBY (*to* GINA). To tell the truth, I hoped your men-folk would be out at this time. I just ran up to have a little chat with you, and to say good-bye.

GINA. Good-bye? Are you going away, then?

MRS. SÖRBY. Yes, tomorrow morning,—up to Höidal. Mr. Werle started this afternoon. (*Lightly to* GREGERS) He asked me to say good-bye for him.

GINA. Only fancy . . . !

HIALMAR. So Mr. Werle has gone? And now you are going after him?

MRS. SÖRBY. Yes, what do you say to that, Ekdal?

HIALMAR. I say: beware!

GREGERS. I must explain the situation. My father and Mrs. Sörby are going to be married.

HIALMAR. Going to be married!

GINA. Oh, Bertha! So it's come to that at last!

RELLING (*his voice quivering a little*). This is surely not true?

MRS. SÖRBY. Yes, my dear Relling, it's true enough.

RELLING. You are going to marry again?

MRS. SÖRBY. Yes, it looks like it. Werle has got a special license, and we are going to be married quite quietly, up at the works.

GREGERS. Then I must wish you all happiness, like a dutiful stepson.

MRS. SÖRBY. Thank you very much—if you mean what you say. I certainly hope it will lead to happiness, both for Werle and for me.

RELLING. You have every reason to hope that. Mr. Werle never gets drunk—so far as I know; and I don't suppose he's in the habit of thrashing his wives, like the late lamented horse-doctor.

MRS. SÖRBY. Come now, let Sörby rest in peace. He had his good points, too.

RELLING. Mr. Werle has better ones, I have no doubt.

MRS. SÖRBY. He hasn't frittered away all that was good in him, at any rate. The man who does that must take the consequences.

RELLING. I shall go out with Molvik this evening.

MRS. SÖRBY. You mustn't do that, Relling. Don't do it—for my sake.

RELLING. There's nothing else for it. (*To* HIALMAR) If you're going with us, come along.

GINA. No, thank you. Ekdal doesn't go in for that sort of dissertation.

HIALMAR (*half aloud, in vexation*). Oh, do hold your tongue!

RELLING. Good-bye, Mrs.—Werle. (*Goes out through the passage door.*)

GREGERS (*to* MRS. SÖRBY). You seem to know Dr. Relling pretty intimately.

MRS. SÖRBY. Yes, we have known each other for many years. At one time it seemed as if things might have gone further between us.

GREGERS. It was surely lucky for you that they did not.

MRS. SÖRBY. You may well say that. But I have always been wary of acting on impulse. A woman can't afford absolutely to throw herself away.

GREGERS. Are you not in the least afraid that I may let my father know about this old friendship?

MRS. SÖRBY. Why, of course, I have told him all about it myself.

GREGERS. Indeed?

MRS. SÖRBY. Your father knows every single thing that can, with any truth, be said about me. I have told him all; it was the first thing I did when I saw what was in his mind.

GREGERS. Then you have been franker than most people, I think.

MRS. SÖRBY. I have always been frank. We women find that the best policy.

HIALMAR. What do you say to that, Gina?

GINA. Oh, we're not all alike, us women aren't. Some are made one way, some another.

MRS. SÖRBY. Well, for my part, Gina, I believe it's wisest to do as I've done. And Werle has no secrets either, on his side. That's really the great bond between us, you see. Now he can talk to me as openly as a child. He has never had the chance to do that before. Fancy a man like him, full of health and vigour, passing his whole youth and the best years of his life in listening to nothing but penitential sermons! And very often the sermons had for their text the most imaginary offenses—at least so I understand.

GINA. That's true enough.

GREGERS. If you ladies are going to follow up this topic, I had better withdraw.

MRS. SÖRBY. You can stay as far as that's concerned. I shan't say a word more. But I wanted you to know that I had done nothing secretly or in an underhand way. I may seem to have come in for a great piece of luck; and so I have, in a sense. But after all, I don't think I am getting any more than I am giving. I shall stand by him always, and I can tend and care for him as no one else can, now that he is getting helpless.

HIALMAR. Getting helpless?

GREGERS (to MRS. SÖRBY). Hush, don't speak of that here.

MRS. SÖRBY. There is no disguising it any longer, however much he would like to. He is going blind.

HIALMAR (*starts*). Going blind? That's strange. He, too, going blind!

GINA. Lots of people do.

MRS. SÖRBY. And you can imagine what that means to a business man. Well, I shall try as well as I can to make my eyes take the place of his. But I mustn't stay any longer; I have such heaps of things to do.—Oh, by-the-bye, Ekdal, I was to tell you that if there is anything Werle can do for you, you must just apply to Gråberg.

GREGERS. That offer I am sure Hialmar Ekdal will decline with thanks.

MRS. SÖRBY. Indeed? I don't think he used to be so . . .

GINA. No, Bertha, Ekdal doesn't need anything from Mr. Werle now.

HIALMAR (*slowly, and with emphasis*). Will you present my compliments to your future husband and say that I intend very shortly to call upon Mr. Gråberg . . .

GREGERS. What! You don't really mean that?

HIALMAR. To call upon Mr. Gråberg, I say, and obtain an account of the sum I owe his principal. I will pay that debt of honour—ha ha ha! a debt of honour, let us call it! In any case, I will pay the whole with five per cent. interest.

GINA. But, my dear Ekdal, God knows we haven't got the money to do it.

HIALMAR. Be good enough to tell your future husband that I am working assiduously at my invention. Please tell him that what sustains me in this laborious task is the wish to free myself from a torturing burden of debt. That is my reason for proceeding with the invention. The entire profits shall be devoted to releasing me from my pecuniary obligations to your future husband.

MRS. SÖRBY. Something has happened here.

HIALMAR. Yes, you are right.

MRS. SÖRBY. Well, good-bye. I had something else to speak to you about, Gina; but it must keep till another time. Good-bye.

(HIALMAR *and* GREGERS *bow silently.* GINA *follows* MRS. SÖRBY *to the door.*)

HIALMAR. Not beyond the threshold, Gina!

(MRS. SÖRBY *goes;* GINA *shuts the door after her.*)

HIALMAR. There now, Gregers, I have got that burden of debt off my mind.

GREGERS. You soon will, at all events.

HIALMAR. I think my attitude may be called correct.

GREGERS. You are the man I have always taken you for.

HIALMAR. In certain cases, it is impossible to disregard the claim of the ideal. Yet, as the breadwinner of a family, I cannot but writhe and groan under it. I can tell you it is no joke for a man without capital to attempt the repayment of a long-standing obligation, over which, so to speak, the dust of oblivion had gathered. But it cannot be helped: the Man in me demands his rights.

GREGERS (*laying his hand on* HIALMAR'S *shoulder*). My dear Hialmar—was it not a good thing I came?

HIALMAR. Yes.

GREGERS. Are you not glad to have had your true position made clear to you?

HIALMAR (*somewhat impatiently*). Yes, of course I am. But there is one thing that is revolting to my sense of justice.

GREGERS. And what is that?

HIALMAR. It is that—but I don't know whether I ought to express myself so unreservedly about your father.

GREGERS. Say what you please, so far as I am concerned.

HIALMAR. Well, then, is it not exasperating to think that it is not I, but he, who will realize the true marriage?

GREGERS. How can you say such a thing?

HIALMAR. Because it is clearly the case. Isn't the marriage between your father and Mrs. Sörby founded upon complete confidence, upon entire and unreserved candour on both sides? They hide nothing from each other, they keep no secrets in the background; their relation is based, if I may put it so, on mutual confession and absolution.

GREGERS. Well, what then?

HIALMAR. Well, is not that the whole thing? Did you not yourself say that this was precisely the difficulty that had to be overcome in order to found a true marriage?

GREGERS. But this is a totally different matter, Hialmar. You surely don't compare either yourself or your wife with those two . . . ? Oh, you understand me well enough.

HIALMAR. Say what you like, there is something in all this that hurts and offends my sense of justice. It really looks as if there were no just providence to rule the world.

GINA. Oh, no, Ekdal; for God's sake don't say such things.

GREGERS. H'm; don't let us get upon those questions.

HIALMAR. And yet, after all, I cannot but recognize the guiding finger of fate. He is going blind.

GINA. Oh, you can't be sure of that.

HIALMAR. There is no doubt about it. At all events there ought not to be; for in that very fact lies the righteous retribution. He has hoodwinked a confiding fellow creature in days gone by . . .

GREGERS. I fear he has hoodwinked many.

HIALMAR. And now comes inexorable, mysterious Fate and demands Werle's own eyes.

GINA. Oh, how dare you say such dreadful things! You make me quite scared.

HIALMAR. It is profitable, now and then, to plunge deep into the night side of existence.

(HEDVIG, *in her hat and cloak, comes in by the passage door. She is pleasurably excited and out of breath.*)

GINA. Are you back already?

HEDVIG. Yes, I didn't care to go any farther. It was a good thing, too; for I've just met some one at the door.

HIALMAR. It must have been that Mrs. Sörby.

HEDVIG. Yes.

HIALMAR (*walks up and down*). I hope you have seen her for the last time.

(*Silence.* HEDVIG, *discouraged, looks first at one and then at the other, trying to divine their frame of mind.*)

HEDVIG (*approaching, coaxingly*). Father.

HIALMAR. Well—what is it, Hedvig?

HEDVIG. Mrs. Sörby had something with her for me.

HIALMAR (*stops*). For you?

HEDVIG. Yes, something for tomorrow.

GINA. Bertha has always given you some little thing on your birthday.

HIALMAR. What is it?

HEDVIG. Oh, you mustn't see it now. Mother is to give it to me tomorrow morning before I'm up.

HIALMAR. What is all this hocus-pocus that I am to be in the dark about!

HEDVIG (*quickly*). Oh, no, you may see it if you like. It's a big letter. (*Takes the letter out of her cloak pocket.*)

HIALMAR. A letter, too?

HEDVIG. Yes, it is only a letter. The rest will come afterwards, I suppose. But fancy—a letter! I've never had a letter before. And there's "Miss" written upon it. (*Reads*) "Miss Hedvig Ekdal." Only fancy—that's me!

HIALMAR. Let me see that letter.

HEDVIG (*hands it to him*). There it is.

HIALMAR. That is Mr. Werle's hand.

GINA. Are you sure of that, Ekdal?

HIALMAR. Look for yourself.

GINA. Oh, what do *I* know about such-like things?

HIALMAR. Hedvig, may I open the letter—and read it?

HEDVIG. Yes, of course you may, if you want to.

GINA. No, not tonight, Ekdal; it's to be kept till tomorrow.

HEDVIG (*softly*). Oh can't you let him read it! It's sure to be something good; and then father will be glad, and everything will be nice again.

HIALMAR. I may open it, then?

HEDVIG. Yes, do, father. I'm so anxious to know what it is.

HIALMAR. Well and good. (*Opens the letter, takes out a paper, reads it through and appears bewildered*) What is this . . . !

GINA. What does it say?

HEDVIG. Oh, yes, father—tell us!

HIALMAR. Be quiet. (*Reads it through again; he has turned pale, but says with self-control:*) It is a deed of gift, Hedvig.

HEDVIG. Is it? What sort of gift am I to have?

HIALMAR. Read for yourself.

(HEDVIG *goes over and reads for a time by the lamp.*)

HIALMAR (*half-aloud, clenching his hands*). The eyes! The eyes—and then that letter!

HEDVIG (*leaves off reading*). Yes, but it seems to me that it's grandfather that's to have it.

HIALMAR (*takes letter from her*). Gina—can you understand this?

GINA. I know nothing whatever about it; tell me what's the matter.

HIALMAR. Mr. Werle writes to Hedvig that her old grandfather need not trouble himself any longer with the copying, but that he can henceforth draw on the office for a hundred crowns a month . . .

GREGERS. Aha!

HEDVIG. A hundred crowns, mother! I read that.

GINA. What a good thing for grandfather!

HIALMAR. . . . a hundred crowns a month so long as he needs it—that means, of course, so long as he lives.

GINA. Well, so he's provided for, poor dear.

HIALMAR. But there is more to come. You didn't read that, Hedvig. Afterwards this gift is to pass on to you.

HEDVIG. To me! The whole of it?

HIALMAR. He says that the same amount is assured to you for the whole of your life. Do you hear that, Gina?

GINA. Yes, I hear.

HEDVIG. Fancy—all that money for me! (*Shakes him*) Father, father, aren't you glad . . . ?

HIALMAR (*eluding her*). Glad! (*Walks about*) Oh, what vistas—what perspectives open up before me! It is Hedvig, Hedvig that he showers these benefactions upon!

GINA. Yes, because it's Hedvig's birthday . . .

HEDVIG. And you'll get it all the same, father! You know quite well I shall give all the money to you and mother.

HIALMAR. To mother, yes! There we have it.

GREGERS. Hialmar, this is a trap he is setting for you.

HIALMAR. Do you think it's another trap?

GREGERS. When he was here this morning he said: Hialmar Ekdal is not the man you imagine him to be.

HIALMAR. Not the man . . . !

GREGERS. That you shall see, he said.

HIALMAR. He meant you should see that I would let myself be bought off . . . . !

HEDVIG. Oh, mother, what does all this mean?

GINA. Go and take off your things.

(HEDVIG *goes out by the kitchen door, half-crying.*)

GREGERS. Yes, Hialmar—now is the time to show who was right, he or I.

HIALMAR (*slowly tears the paper across, lays both pieces on the table and says*). Here is my answer.

GREGERS. Just what I expected.

HIALMAR (*goes over to* GINA, *who stands by the stove, and says in a low voice*). Now please make a clean breast of it. If the connection between you and him was quite over when you—came to care for me, as you call it—why did he place us in a position to marry?

GINA. I suppose he thought as he could come and go in our house.

HIALMAR. Only that? Was not he afraid of a possible contingency?

GINA. I don't know what you mean.

HIALMAR. I want to know whether—your child has the right to live under my roof.

GINA (*draws herself up; her eyes flash*). You ask that!

HIALMAR. You shall answer me this one question: Does Hedvig belong to me— or . . . ? Well!

GINA (*looking at him with cold defiance*). I don't know.

HIALMAR (*quivering a little*). You don't know!

GINA. How should *I* know. A creature like me . . .

HIALMAR (*quietly turning away from her*). Then I have nothing more to do in this house.

GREGERS. Take care, Hialmar! Think what you are doing!

HIALMAR (*puts on his overcoat*). In this case, there is nothing for a man like me to think twice about.

GREGERS. Yes, indeed, there are endless things to be considered. You three must be together if you are to attain the true frame of mind for self-sacrifice and for-giveness.

HIALMAR. I don't want to attain it. Never, never! My hat! (*Takes his hat*) My home has fallen in ruins about me. (*Bursts into tears*) Gregers, I have no child!

HEDVIG (*who has opened the kitchen door*). What is that you're saying? (*Coming to him*) Father, father!

GINA. There, you see!

HIALMAR. Don't come near me, Hedvig! Keep far away. I cannot bear to see you. Oh! those eyes . . . ! Good-bye. (*Makes for the door.*)

HEDVIG (*clinging close to him and screaming loudly*). No! no! Don't leave me!

GINA (*cries out*). Look at the child, Ekdal! Look at the child!

HIALMAR. I will not! I cannot! I must get out—away from all this!

(*He tears himself away from* HEDVIG *and goes out by the passage door.*)

HEDVIG (*with despairing eyes*). He is going away from us, mother! He is going away from us! He will never come back again!

GINA. Don't cry, Hedvig. Father's sure to come back again.

HEDVIG (*throws herself sobbing on the sofa*). No, no, he'll never come home to us any more.

GREGERS. Do you believe I meant all for the best, Mrs. Ekdal?

GINA. Yes, I daresay you did; but God forgive you, all the same.

HEDVIG (*lying on the sofa*). Oh, this will kill me! What have I done to him? Mother, you must fetch him home again!

GINA. Yes, yes, yes; only be quiet, and I'll go out and look for him. (*Puts on her outdoor things*) Perhaps he's gone in to Relling's. But you mustn't lie there and cry. Promise me!

HEDVIG (*weeping convulsively*). Yes, I'll stop, I'll stop; if only father comes back!

GREGERS (*to* GINA, *who is going*). After all, had you not better leave him to fight out his bitter fight to the end?

GINA. Oh, he can do that afterwards. First of all, we must get the child quieted. (*Goes out by the passage door.*)

HEDVIG (*sits up and dries her tears*). Now you must tell me what all this means. Why doesn't father want me any more?

GREGERS. You mustn't ask that till you are a big girl—quite grown-up.

HEDVIG (*sobs*). But I can't go on being as miserable as this till I'm grown-up.—I think I know what it is.—Perhaps I'm not really father's child.

GREGERS (*uneasily*). How could that be?

HEDVIG. Mother might have found me. And perhaps father has just got to know it; I've read of such things.

GREGERS. Well, but if it were so . . .

HEDVIG. I think he might be just as fond of me for all that. Yes, fonder almost. We got the wild duck in a present, you know, and I love it so dearly all the same.

GREGERS (*turning the conversation*). Ah, the wild duck, by-the-bye! Let us talk about the wild duck a little, Hedvig.

HEDVIG. The poor wild duck! He doesn't want to see it any more either. Only think, he wanted to wring its neck!

GREGERS. Oh, he won't do that.

HEDVIG. No; but he said he would like to. And I think it was horrid of father to say it; for I pray for the wild duck every night and ask that it may be preserved from death and all that is evil.

GREGERS (*looking at her*). Do you say your prayers every night?

HEDVIG. Yes.

GREGERS. Who taught you to do that?

HEDVIG. I myself; one time when father was very ill, and had leeches on his neck and said that death was staring him in the face.

GREGERS. Well?

HEDVIG. Then I prayed for him as I lay in bed; and since then I have always kept it up.

GREGERS. And now you pray for the wild duck, too?

HEDVIG. I thought it was best to bring in the wild duck; for she was so weakly at first.

GREGERS. Do you pray in the morning, too?

HEDVIG. No, of course not.

GREGERS. Why not in the morning as well?

HEDVIG. In the morning it's light, you know, and there's nothing in particular to be afraid of.

GREGERS. And your father was going to wring the neck of the wild duck that you love so dearly?

HEDVIG. No; he said he ought to wring its neck, but he would spare it for my sake; and that was kind of father.

GREGERS (*coming a little nearer*). But suppose you were to sacrifice the wild duck of your own free will for his sake.

HEDVIG (*rising*). The wild duck!

GREGERS. Suppose you were to make a free-will offering for his sake, of the dearest treasure you have in the world!

HEDVIG. Do you think that would do any good?

GREGERS. Try it, Hedvig.

HEDVIG (*softly, with flashing eyes*). Yes, I will try it.

GREGERS. Have you really the courage for it, do you think?

HEDVIG. I'll ask grandfather to shoot the wild duck for me.

GREGERS. Yes, do. But not a word to your mother about it.

HEDVIG. Why not?

GREGERS. She doesn't understand us.

HEDVIG. The wild duck! I'll try it tomorrow morning.

(GINA *comes in by the passage door.*)

HEDVIG (*going towards her*). Did you find him, mother?

GINA. No, but I heard as he had called and taken Relling with him.

GREGERS. Are you sure of that?

GINA. Yes, the porter's wife said so. Molvik went with them, too, she said.

GREGERS. This evening, when his mind so sorely needs to wrestle in solitude . . . !

GINA (*takes off her things*). Yes, men are strange creatures, so they are. The Lord only knows where Relling has dragged him to! I ran over to Madam Eriksen's, but they weren't there.

HEDVIG (*struggling to keep back her tears*). Oh, if he should never come home any more!

GREGERS. He will come home again. I shall have news to give him tomorrow; and then you shall see how he comes home. You may rely upon that, Hedvig, and sleep in peace. Good-night.

(*He goes out by the passage door.*)

HEDVIG (*throws herself sobbing on* GINA'S *neck*). Mother, mother!

GINA (*pats her shoulder and sighs*). Ah, yes; Relling was right, he was. That's what comes of it when crazy creatures go about presenting the claims of the—what-you-may-call-it.

(*The Curtain Falls.*)

ACT V

HIALMAR EKDAL'S *studio. Cold, grey morning light. Wet snow lies upon the large panes of the sloping roof-windows.*

GINA *comes from the kitchen with an apron and bib on, and carrying a dusting-brush and a duster; she goes towards the sitting-room door. At the same moment* HEDVIG *comes hurriedly in from the passage.*

GINA (*stops*). Well?

HEDVIG. Oh, mother, I almost think he's down at Relling's . . .

GINA. There, you see!

HEDVIG. . . . because the porter's wife says she could hear that Relling had two people with him when he came home last night.

GINA. That's just what I thought.

HEDVIG. But it's no use his being there, if he won't come up to us.

GINA. I'll go down and speak to him at all events.

(OLD EKDAL, *in dressing-gown and slippers, and with a lighted pipe, appears at the door of his room.*)

EKDAL. Hialmar . . . Isn't Hialmar at home?

GINA. No, he's gone out.

EKDAL. So early? And in such a tearing snowstorm? Well, well; just as he pleases; I can take my morning walk alone.

(*He slides the garret door aside;* HEDVIG *helps him; he goes in; she closes it after him.*)

HEDVIG (*in an undertone*). Only think, mother, when poor grandfather hears that father is going to leave us.

GINA. Oh, nonsense; grandfather mustn't hear anything about it. It was a heaven's mercy he wasn't at home yesterday in all that hurly-burly.

HEDVIG. Yes, but . . .

(GREGERS *comes in by the passage door.*)

GREGERS. Well, have you any news of him?

GINA. They say he's down at Relling's.

GREGERS. At Relling's! Has he really been out with those creatures?

GINA. Yes, like enough.

GREGERS. When he ought to have been yearning for solitude, to collect and clear his thoughts . . .

GINA. Yes, you may well say so.

(RELLING *enters from the passage.*)

HEDVIG (*going to him*). Is father in your room?

GINA (*at the same time*). Is he there?

RELLING. Yes, to be sure he is.

HEDVIG. And you never let us know!

RELLING. Yes, I'm a brute. But in the first place I had to look after the other brute; I mean our dæmonic friend, of course; and then I fell so dead asleep that . . .

GINA. What does Ekdal say today?

RELLING. He says nothing whatever.

HEDVIG. Doesn't he speak?

RELLING. Not a blessed word.

GREGERS. No, no; I can understand that very well.

GINA. But what's he doing then?

RELLING. He's lying on the sofa, snoring.

GINA. Oh, is he? Yes, Ekdal's a rare one to snore.

HEDVIG. Asleep? Can he sleep?

RELLING. Well it certainly looks like it.

GREGERS. No wonder, after the spiritual conflict that has rent him . . .

GINA. And then he's never been used to gadding about out of doors at night.

HEDVIG. Perhaps it's a good thing that he's getting sleep, mother.

GINA. Of course it is; and we must take care we don't wake him up too early. Thank you, Relling. I must get the house cleaned up a bit now, and then . . . Come and help me, Hedvig.

(GINA *and* HEDVIG *go into the sitting-room.*)

GREGERS (*turning to* RELLING). What is your explanation of the spiritual tumult that is now going on in Hialmar Ekdal?

RELLING. Devil a bit of a spiritual tumult have *I* noticed in him.

GREGERS. What! Not at such a crisis, when his whole life has been placed on a new foundation . . . ? How can you think that such an individuality as Hialmar's . . . ?

RELLING. Oh, individuality—he! If he ever had any tendency to the abnormal developments you call individuality, I can assure you it was rooted out of him while he was still in his teens.

GREGERS. That would be strange indeed,—considering the loving care with which he was brought up.

RELLING. By those two high-flown, hysterical maiden aunts, you mean?

GREGERS. Let me tell you that they were women who never forgot the claim of the ideal—but of course you will only jeer at me again.

RELLING. No, I'm in no humour for that. I know all about those ladies; for he has ladled out no end of rhetoric on the subject of his "two soul-mothers." But I don't think he has much to thank them for. Ekdal's misfortune is that in his own circle he has always been looked upon as a shining light . . .

GREGERS. Not without reason, surely. Look at the depth of his mind!

RELLING. *I* have never discovered it. That his father believed in it I don't so much wonder; the old lieutenant has been an ass all his days.

GREGERS. He has had a child-like mind all his days; that is what you cannot understand.

RELLING. Well, so be it. But then, when our dear, sweet Hialmar went to college, he at once passed for the great light of the future amongst his comrades, too! He was handsome, the rascal—red and white—a shop-girl's dream of manly beauty; and with his superficially emotional temperament, and his sympathetic voice and his talent for declaiming other people's verses and other people's thoughts . . .

GREGERS (*indignantly*). Is it Hialmar Ekdal you are talking about in this strain?

RELLING. Yes, with your permission; I am simply giving you an inside view of the idol you are grovelling before.

GREGERS. I should hardly have thought I was quite stone blind.

RELLING. Yes, you are—or not far from it. You are a sick man, too, you see.

GREGERS. You are right there.

RELLING. Yes. Yours is a complicated case. First of all there is that plaguy integrity-fever; and then—what's worse—you are always in a delirium of hero-worship; you must always have something to adore, outside yourself.

GREGERS. Yes, I must certainly seek it outside myself.

RELLING. But you make such shocking mistakes about every new phœnix you think you have discovered. Here again you have come to a cotter's cabin with your claim of the ideal; and the people of the house are insolvent.

GREGERS. If you don't think better than that of Hialmar Ekdal, what pleasure can you find in being everlastingly with him?

RELLING. Well, you see, I'm supposed to be a sort of a doctor—save the mark! I can't but give a hand to the poor sick folk who live under the same roof with me.

GREGERS. Oh, indeed! Hialmar Ekdal is sick, too, is he!

RELLING. Most people are, worse luck.

GREGERS. And what remedy are you applying in Hialmar's case?

RELLING. My usual one. I am cultivating the life-illusion * in him.

GREGERS. Life—illusion? I didn't catch what you said.

RELLING. Yes, I said illusion. For illusion, you know, is the stimulating principle.

GREGERS. May I ask with what illusion Hialmar is inoculated?

RELLING. No, thank you; I don't betray professional secrets to quack-salvers. You
would probably go and muddle his case still more than you have already. But my
method is infallible. I have applied it to Molvik as well. I have made him
"dæmonic." That's the blister I have to put on his neck.

GREGERS. Is he not really dæmonic, then?

RELLING. What the devil do you mean by dæmonic! It's only a piece of gibberish I've
invented to keep up a spark of life in him. But for that, the poor harmless
creature would have succumbed to self-contempt and despair many a long year
ago. And then the old lieutenant! But he has hit upon his own cure, you see.

GREGERS. Lieutenant Ekdal? What of him?

RELLING. Just think of the old bear-hunter shutting himself up in that dark garret to
shoot rabbits! I tell you there is not a happier sportsman in the world than that
old man pottering about in there among all that rubbish. The four or five
withered Christmas trees he has saved up are the same to him as the whole great
fresh Höidal forest; the cock and the hens are big game-birds in the fir-tops; and
the rabbits that flop about the garret floor are the bears he has to battle with—the
mighty hunter of the mountains!

GREGERS. Poor unfortunate old man! Yes; he has indeed had to narrow the ideals
of his youth.

RELLING. While I think of it, Mr. Werle, junior—don't use that foreign word: ideals.
We have the excellent native word: lies.

GREGERS. Do you think the two things are related?

RELLING. Yes, just about as closely as typhus and putrid fever.

GREGERS. Dr. Relling, I shall not give up the struggle until I have rescued Hialmar
from your clutches!

RELLING. So much the worse for him. Rob the average man of his life-illusion, and
you rob him of his happiness at the same stroke. (*To* HEDVIG, *who comes in from
the sitting-room*) Well, little wild-duck-mother, I'm just going down to see
whether papa is still lying meditating upon that wonderful invention of his.
(*Goes out by passage door.*)

  * "Livslögnen," literally "the life-lie."

GREGERS (*approaches* HEDVIG). I can see by your face that you have not yet done it.

HEDVIG. What? Oh, that about the wild duck! No.

GREGERS. I suppose your courage failed when the time came.

HEDVIG. No, that wasn't it. But when I awoke this morning and remembered what we had been talking about, it seemed so strange.

GREGERS. Strange?

HEDVIG. Yes, I don't know . . . Yesterday evening, at the moment, I thought there was something so delightful about it; but since I have slept and thought of it again, it somehow doesn't seem worth while.

GREGERS. Ah, I thought you could not have grown up quite unharmed in this house.

HEDVIG. I don't care about that, if only father would come up . . .

GREGERS. Oh, if only your eyes had been open to that which gives life its value—if you possessed the true, joyous, fearless spirit of sacrifice, you would soon see how he would come up to you.—But I believe in you still, Hedvig.

(*He goes out by the passage door.* HEDVIG *wanders about the room for a time; she is on the point of going into the kitchen when a knock is heard at the garret door.* HEDVIG *goes over and opens it a little; old* EKDAL *comes out; she pushes the door to again.*)

EKDAL. H'm, it's not much fun to take one's morning walk alone.

HEDVIG. Wouldn't you like to go shooting, grandfather?

EKDAL. It's not the weather for it today. It's so dark there, you can scarcely see where you're going.

HEDVIG. Do you never want to shoot anything besides the rabbits?

EKDAL. Do you think the rabbits aren't good enough?

HEDVIG. Yes, but what about the wild duck?

EKDAL. Ho-ho! are you afraid I shall shoot your wild duck? Never in the world. Never.

HEDVIG. No, I suppose you couldn't; they say it's very difficult to shoot wild ducks.

EKDAL. Couldn't! Should rather think I could.

HEDVIG. How would you set about it, grandfather?—I don't mean with my wild duck, but with others?

EKDAL. I should take care to shoot them in the breast, you know; that's the surest place. And then you must shoot against the feathers, you see—not the way of the feathers.

HEDVIG. Do they die then, grandfather?

EKDAL. Yes, they die right enough—when you shoot properly. Well, I must go and brush up a bit. H'm—understand—h'm (*Goes into his room.*)

(HEDVIG *waits a little, glances towards the sitting-room door, goes over to the bookcase, stands on tip-toe, takes the double-barrelled pistol down from the shelf and looks at it.* GINA, *with brush and duster, comes from the sitting-room.* HEDVIG *hastily lays down the pistol, unobserved.*)

GINA. Don't stand raking amongst father's things, Hedvig.

HEDVIG (*goes away from the bookcase*). I was only going to tidy up a little.

GINA. You'd better go into the kitchen and see if the coffee's keeping hot; I'll take his breakfast on a tray, when I go down to him.

(HEDVIG *goes out.* GINA *begins to sweep and clean up the studio. Presently the passage door is opened with hesitation, and* HIALMAR EKDAL *looks in. He has on his overcoat, but not his hat; he is unwashed, and his hair is dishevelled and unkempt. His eyes are dull and heavy.*)

GINA (*standing with the brush in her hand and looking at him*). Oh, there now, Ekdal—so you've come after all!

HIALMAR (*comes in and answers in a toneless voice*). I come—only to depart again immediately.

GINA. Yes, yes, I suppose so. But, Lord help us! what a sight you are!

HIALMAR. A sight?

GINA. And your nice winter coat, too! Well, that's done for.

HEDVIG (*at the kitchen door*). Mother, hadn't I better . . . ? (*Sees* HIALMAR, *gives a loud scream of joy and runs to him.*) Oh, father, father!

HIALMAR (*turns away and makes a gesture of repulsion*). Away, away, away! (*To* GINA) Keep her away from me, I say!

GINA (*in a low tone*). Go into the sitting-room, Hedvig.

(HEDVIG *does so without a word.*)

HIALMAR (*fussily pulls out the table-drawer*). I must have my books with me. Where are my books?

GINA. Which books?

HIALMAR. My scientific books, of course; the technical magazines I require for my invention.

GINA (*searches in the bookcase*). Is it these here paper-covered ones?

HIALMAR. Yes, of course.

GINA (*lays a heap of magazines on the table*). Shan't I get Hedvig to cut them for you?

HIALMAR. I don't require to have them cut for me. (*Short silence.*)

GINA. Then you're still set on leaving us, Ekdal?

HIALMAR (*rummaging amongst the books*). Yes, that is a matter of course, I should think.

GINA. Well, well.

HIALMAR (*vehemently*). How can I live here, to be stabbed to the heart every hour of the day?

GINA. God forgive you for thinking such vile things of me.

HIALMAR. Prove . . . !

GINA. I think it's you as has got to prove.

HIALMAR. After a past like yours? There are certain claims—I may almost call them claims of the ideal . . .

GINA. But what about grandfather? What's to become of him, poor dear!

HIALMAR. I know my duty; my helpless father will come with me. I am going out into the town to make arrangements . . . H'm—(*hesitatingly*)—has any one found my hat on the stairs?

GINA. No. Have you lost your hat?

HIALMAR. Of course I had it on when I came in last night; there's no doubt about that; but I couldn't find it this morning.

GINA. Lord help us! where have you been to with those two ne'er-do-wells?

HIALMAR. Oh, don't bother me about trifles. Do you suppose I am in the mood to remember details?

GINA. If only you haven't caught cold, Ekdal . . . (*Goes out into the kitchen.*)

HIALMAR (*talks to himself in a low tone of irritation, whilst he empties the table-drawer*). You're a scoundrel, Relling!—You're a low fellow!—Ah, you shameless tempter!—I wish I could get some one to stick a knife into you!

(*He lays some old letters on one side, finds the torn document of yesterday, takes it up and looks at the pieces; puts it down hurriedly as* GINA *enters.*)

GINA (*sets a tray with coffee, etc., on the table*). Here's a drop of something hot, if you'd fancy it. And there's some bread and butter and a snack of salt meat.

HIALMAR (*glancing at the tray*). Salt meat? Never under this roof! It's true I have not had a mouthful of solid food for nearly twenty-four hours; but no matter.—

My memoranda! The commencement of my autobiography! What has become of my diary, and all my important papers? (*Opens the sitting-room door but draws back*) She is there, too!

GINA. Good Lord! the child must be somewhere!

HIALMAR. Come out.

(*He makes room; HEDVIG comes, scared, into the studio.*)

HIALMAR (*with his hand upon the door-handle, says to GINA*). In these, the last moments I spend in my former home, I wish to be spared from interlopers . . . (*Goes into the room.*)

HEDVIG (*with a bound towards her mother, asks softly, trembling*). Does that mean me?

GINA. Stay out in the kitchen, Hedvig; or, no—you'd best go into your own room. (*Speaks to HIALMAR as she goes in to him*) Wait a bit, Ekdal; don't rummage so in the drawers; *I* know where everything is.

HEDVIG (*stands a moment immovable, in terror and perplexity, biting her lips to keep back the tears; then she clenches her hands convulsively and says softly*). The wild duck.

(*She steals over and takes the pistol from the shelf, opens the garret door a little way, creeps in and draws the door to after her. HIALMAR and GINA can be heard disputing in the sitting-room.*)

HIALMAR (*comes in with some manuscript books and old loose papers, which he lays upon the table*). That portmanteau is of no use! There are a thousand and one things I must drag with me.

GINA (*following with the portmanteau*). Why not leave all the rest for the present and only take a shirt and a pair of woollen drawers with you?

HIALMAR. Whew!—all these exhausting preparations . . . ! (*Pulls off his overcoat and throws it upon the sofa.*)

GINA. And there's the coffee getting cold.

HIALMAR. H'm. (*Drinks a mouthful without thinking of it and then another.*)

GINA (*dusting the backs of the chairs*). A nice job you'll have to find such another big garret for the rabbits.

HIALMAR. What! Am I to drag all those rabbits with me, too?

GINA. You don't suppose grandfather can get on without his rabbits.

HIALMAR. He must just get used to doing without them. Have not *I* to sacrifice very much greater things than rabbits!

GINA (*dusting the bookcase*). Shall I put the flute in the portmanteau for you?

HIALMAR. No. No flute for me. But give me the pistol!

GINA. Do you want to take the pistol with you?

HIALMAR. Yes. My loaded pistol.

GINA (*searching for it*). It's gone. He must have taken it in with him.

HIALMAR. Is he in the garret?

GINA. Yes, of course he's in the garret.

HIALMAR. H'm—poor lonely old man.

(*He takes a piece of bread and butter, eats it, and finishes his cup of coffee.*)

GINA. If we hadn't have let that room, you could have moved in there.

HIALMAR. And continued to live under the same roof with . . . ! Never,—never!

GINA. But couldn't you put up with the sitting-room for a day or two? You could have it all to yourself.

HIALMAR. Never within these walls!

GINA. Well, then, down with Relling and Molvik.

HIALMAR. Don't mention those wretches' names to me! The very thought of them almost takes away my appetite.—Oh, no, I must go out into the storm and the snow-drift,—go from house to house and seek shelter for my father and myself.

GINA. But you've got no hat, Ekdal! You've been and lost your hat, you know.

HIALMAR. Oh, those two brutes, those slaves of all the vices! A hat must be procured. (*Takes another piece of bread and butter*) Some arrangements must be made. For I have no mind to throw away my life, either. (*Looks for something on the tray.*)

GINA. What are you looking for?

HIALMAR. Butter.

GINA. I'll get some at once. (*Goes into the kitchen.*)

HIALMAR (*calls after her*). Oh, it doesn't matter; dry bread is good enough for me.

GINA (*brings a dish of butter*). Look here; this is fresh churned.

(*She pours out another cup of coffee for him; he seats himself on the sofa, spreads more butter on the already buttered bread, and eats and drinks a while in silence.*)

HIALMAR. Could I, without being subject to intrusion—intrusion of any sort—could I live in the sitting-room there for a day or two?

GINA. Yes, to be sure you could, if you only would.

HIALMAR. For I see no possibility of getting all father's things out in such a hurry.

GINA. And, besides, you've surely got to tell him first as you don't mean to live with us others no more.

HIALMAR (*pushes away his coffee cup*). Yes, there is that, too; I shall have to lay bare the whole tangled story to him . . . I must turn matters over; I must have breathing-time; I cannot take all these burdens on my shoulders in a single day.

GINA. No, especially in such horrible weather as it is outside.

HIALMAR (*touching* WERLE'S *letter*). I see that paper is still lying about here.

GINA. Yes, *I* haven't touched it.

HIALMAR. So far as I am concerned it is mere waste paper . . .

GINA. Well, *I* have certainly no notion of making any use of it.

HIALMAR. . . . but we had better not let it get lost all the same;—in all the upset when I move, it might easily . . .

GINA. I'll take good care of it, Ekdal.

HAILMAR. The donation is in the first instance made to father, and it rests with him to accept or decline it.

GINA (*sighs*). Yes, poor old father . . .

HIALMAR. To make quite safe . . . Where shall I find some gum?

GINA (*goes to the bookcase*). Here's the gum-pot.

HIALMAR. And a brush?

GINA. The brush is here, too. (*Brings him the things.*)

HIALMAR (*takes a pair of scissors*). Just a strip of paper at the back . . . (*Clips and gums*) Far be it from me to lay hands upon what is not my own—and least of all upon what belongs to a destitute old man—and to—the other as well.—There now. Let it lie there for a time; and when it is dry, take it away. I wish never to see that document again. Never!

(GREGERS WERLE *enters from the passage*.)

GREGERS (*somewhat surprised*). What,—are you sitting here, Hialmar?

HIALMAR (*rises hurriedly*). I had sunk down from fatigue.

GREGERS. You have been having breakfast, I see.

HIALMAR. The body sometimes makes its claims felt, too.

GREGERS. What have you decided to do?

HIALMAR. For a man like me, there is only one course possible. I am just putting my most important things together. But it takes time, you know.

GINA (*with a touch of impatience*). Am I to get the room ready for you, or am I to pack your portmanteau?

HIALMAR (*after a glance of annoyance at* GREGERS). Pack—and get the room ready!

GINA (*takes the portmanteau*). Very well; then I'll put in the shirt and the other things. (*Goes into the sitting-room and draws the door to after her.*)

GREGERS (*after a short silence*). I never dreamed that this would be the end of it. Do you really feel it a necessity to leave house and home?

HIALMAR (*wanders about restlessly*). What would you have me do?—I am not fitted to bear unhappiness, Gregers. I must feel secure and at peace in my surroundings.

GREGERS. But can you not feel that here? Just try it. I should have thought you had firm ground to build upon now—if only you start afresh. And remember, you have your invention to live for.

HIALMAR. Oh, don't talk about my invention. It's perhaps still in the dim distance.

GREGERS. Indeed!

HIALMAR. Why, great heavens, what would you have me invent? Other people have invented almost everything already. It becomes more and more difficult every day . . .

GREGERS. And you have devoted so much labour to it.

HIALMAR. It was that blackguard Relling that urged me to it.

GREGERS. Relling?

HIALMAR. Yes, it was he that first made me realize my aptitude for making some notable discovery in photography.

GREGERS. Aha—it was Relling!

HIALMAR. Oh, I have been so truly happy over it! Not so much for the sake of the invention itself, as because Hedvig believed in it—believed in it with a child's whole eagerness of faith.—At least, I have been fool enough to go and imagine that she believed in it.

GREGERS. Can you really think Hedvig has been false to you?

HIALMAR. I can think anything now. It is Hedvig that stands in my way. She will blot out the sunlight from my whole life.

GREGERS. Hedvig! Is it Hedvig you are talking of? How should she blot out your sunlight?

HIALMAR (*without answering*). How unutterably I have loved that child! How unutterably happy I have felt every time I came home to my humble room, and she flew to meet me, with her sweet little blinking eyes. Oh, confiding fool that I have been! I love her unutterably;—and I yielded myself up to the dream, the delusion, that she loved me unutterably in return.

GREGERS. Do you call that a delusion?

HIALMAR. How should I know? I can get nothing out of Gina; and besides, she is totally blind to the ideal side of these complications. But to you I feel impelled to open my mind, Gregers. I cannot shake off this frightful doubt—perhaps Hedvig has never really and honestly loved me.

GREGERS. What would you say if she were to give you a proof of her love? (*Listens*) What's that? I thought I heard the wild duck . . . ?

HIALMAR. It's the wild duck quacking. Father's in the garret.

GREGERS. Is he? (*His face lights up with joy*) I say, you may yet have proof that your poor misunderstood Hedvig loves you!

HIALMAR. Oh, what proof can she give me? I dare not believe in any assurance from that quarter.

GREGERS. Hedvig does not know what deceit means.

HIALMAR. Oh, Gregers, that is just what I cannot be sure of. Who knows what Gina and that Mrs. Sörby may many a time have sat here whispering and tattling about? And Hedvig usually has her ears open, I can tell you. Perhaps the deed of gift was not such a surprise to her, after all. In fact, I'm not sure but that I noticed something of the sort.

GREGERS. What spirit is this that has taken possession of you?

HIALMAR. I have had my eyes opened. Just you notice;—you'll see, the deed of gift is only a beginning. Mrs. Sörby has always been a good deal taken up with Hedvig; and now she has the power to do whatever she likes for the child. They can take her from me whenever they please.

GREGERS. Hedvig will never, never leave you.

HIALMAR. Don't be so sure of that. If only they beckon to her and throw out a golden bait . . . ! And, oh! I have loved her so unspeakably! I would have counted it my highest happiness to take her tenderly by the hand and lead her, as one leads a timid child through a great dark empty room!—I am cruelly certain now that the poor photographer in his humble attic has never really and truly been anything to her. She has only cunningly contrived to keep on a good footing with him until the time came.

GREGERS. You don't believe that yourself, Hialmar.

HIALMAR. That is just the terrible part of it—I don't know what to believe,—I never can know it. But can you really doubt that it must be as I say? Ho-ho, you have far too much faith in the claim of the ideal, my good Gregers! If those others came, with the glamour of wealth about them, and called to the child:—"Leave him: come to us: here life awaits you . . . !"

GREGERS (*quickly*). Well, what then?

HIALMAR. If I then asked her: Hedvig, are you willing to renounce that life for me? (*Laughs scornfully*) No, thank you! You would soon hear what answer I should get. (*A pistol shot is heard from within the garret.*)

GREGERS (*loudly and joyfully*). Hialmar!

HIALMAR. There now; he must needs go shooting, too.

GINA (*comes in*). Oh, Ekdal, I can hear grandfather blazing away in the garret by hisself.

HIALMAR. I'll look in . . .

GREGERS (*eagerly, with emotion*). Wait a moment! Do you know what that was?

HIALMAR. Yes, of course I know.

GREGERS. No, you don't know. But *I* do. That was the proof!

HIALMAR. What proof?

GREGERS. It was a child's free-will offering. She has got your father to shoot the wild duck.

HIALMAR. To shoot the wild duck!

GINA. Oh, think of that . . . !

HIALMAR. What was that for?

GREGERS. She wanted to sacrifice to you her most cherished possession; for then she thought you would surely come to love her again.

HIALMAR (*tenderly, with emotion*). Oh, poor child!

GINA. What things she does think of!

GREGERS. She only wanted your love again, Hialmar. She could not live without it.

GINA (*struggling with her tears*). There, you can see for yourself, Ekdal.

HIALMAR. Gina, where is she?

GINA (*sniffs*). Poor dear, she's sitting out in the kitchen, I dare say.

HIALMAR (*goes over, tears open the kitchen door and says*). Hedvig, come, come in to me! (*Looks around*) No, she's not here.

GINA. Then she must be in her own little room.

HIALMAR (*without*). No, she's not here either. (*Comes in*) She must have gone out.

GINA. Yes, you wouldn't have her anywheres in the house.

HIALMAR. Oh, if she would only come home quickly, so that I can tell her . . . Every-thing will come right now, Gregers; now I believe we can begin life afresh.

GREGERS (*quietly*). I knew it: I knew the child would make amends.

(OLD EKDAL *appears at the door of his room; he is in full uniform and is busy buck-ling on his sword.*)

HIALMAR (*astonished*). Father! Are you there?

GINA. Have you been firing in your room?

EKDAL (*resentfully, approaching*). So you go shooting alone, do you, Hialmar?

HIALMAR (*excited and confused*). Then it wasn't you that fired that shot in the garret?

EKDAL. Me that fired? H'm.

GREGERS (*calls out to* HIALMAR). She has shot the wild duck herself!

HIALMAR. What can it mean? (*Hastens to the garret door, tears it aside, looks in and calls loudly*). Hedvig!

GINA (*runs to the door*). Good God, what's that!

HIALMAR (*goes in*). She's lying on the floor!

GREGERS. Hedvig! lying on the floor! (*Goes in to* HIALMAR)

GINA (*at the same time*). Hedvig! (*Inside the garret*) No, no, no!

EKDAL. Ho-ho! does she go shooting, too, now?

(HIALMAR, GINA *and* GREGERS *carry* HEDVIG *into the studio; in her dangling right hand she holds the pistol fast clasped in her fingers.*)

HIALMAR (*distracted*). The pistol has gone off. She has wounded herself. Call for help! Help!

GINA (*runs into the passage and calls down*). Relling! Relling! Doctor Relling; come up as quick as you can!

(HIALMAR *and* GREGERS *lay* HEDVIG *down on the sofa.*)

EKDAL (*quietly*). The woods avenge themselves.

HIALMAR (*on his knees beside* HEDVIG). She'll soon come to now. She's coming to . . . ; yes, yes, yes.

GINA (*who has come in again*). Where has she hurt herself? I can't see anything . . .

(RELLING *comes hurriedly, and immediately after him* MOLVIK; *the latter without his waistcoat and necktie, and with his coat open.*)

RELLING. What's the matter here?

GINA. They say Hedvig has shot herself.

HIALMAR. Come and help us!

RELLING. Shot herself!

(*He pushes the table aside and begins to examine her.*)

HIALMAR (*kneeling and looking anxiously up at him*). It can't be dangerous? Speak, Reeling! She is scarcely bleeding at all. It can't be dangerous?

RELLING. How did it happen?

HIALMAR. Oh, we don't know . . .

GINA. She wanted to shoot the wild duck.

RELLING. The wild duck?

HIALMAR. The pistol must have gone off.

RELLING. H'm. Indeed.

EKDAL. The woods avenge themselves. But I'm not afraid, all the same. (*Goes into the garret and closes the door after him.*)

HIALMAR. Well, Relling,—why don't you say something?

RELLING. The ball has entered the breast.

HIALMAR. Yes, but she's coming to!

RELLING. Surely you can see that Hedvig is dead.

GINA (*bursts into tears*). Oh, my child, my child . . .

GREGERS (*huskily*). In the depths of the sea . . .

HIALMAR (*jumps up*). No, no, she must live! Oh, for God's sake, Relling—only a moment—only just till I can tell her how unspeakably I loved her all the time!

RELLING. The bullet has gone through her heart. Internal hemorrhage. Death must have been instantaneous.

HIALMAR. And I! I hunted her from me like an animal! And she crept terrified into the garret and died for love of me! (*Sobbing*) I can never atone to her! I can never tell her . . . ! (*Clenches his hands and cries, upwards*) O thou above . . . ! If thou be indeed! Why hast thou done this thing to me?

GINA. Hush, hush, you mustn't go on that awful way. We had no right to keep her, I suppose.

MOLVIK. The child is not dead, but sleepeth.

RELLING. Bosh!

HIALMAR (*becomes calm, goes over to the sofa, folds his arms and looks at* HEDVIG). There she lies so stiff and still.

RELLING (*tries to loosen the pistol*). She's holding it so tight, so tight.

GINA. No, no, Relling, don't break her fingers; let the pistol be.

HIALMAR. She shall take it with her.

GINA. Yes, let her. But the child mustn't lie here for a show. She shall go to her own room, so she shall. Help me, Ekdal. (HIALMAR *and* GINA *take* HEDVIG *between them.*)

HIALMAR (*as they are carrying her*). Oh, Gina, Gina, can you survive this!

GINA. We must help each other to bear it. For now at least she belongs to both of us.

MOLVIK (*stretches out his arms and mumbles*). Blessed be the Lord; to earth thou shalt return; to earth thou shalt return . . .

RELLING (*whispers*). Hold your tongue, you fool; you're drunk.

(HIALMAR *and* GINA *carry the body out through the kitchen door.* RELLING *shuts it after them.* MOLVIK *slinks out into the passage.*)

RELLING (*goes over to* GREGERS *and says*). No one shall ever convince me that the pistol went off by accident.

GREGERS (*who has stood terrified with convulsive twitchings*). Who can say how the dreadful thing happened?

RELLING. The powder has burnt the body of her dress. She must have pressed the pistol right against her breast and fired.

GREGERS. Hedvig has not died in vain. Did you not see how sorrow set free what is noble in him?

RELLING. Most people are ennobled by the actual presence of death. But how long do you suppose this nobility will last in him?

GREGERS. Why should it not endure and increase throughout his life?

RELLING. Before a year is over, little Hedvig will be nothing to him but a pretty theme for declamation.

GREGERS. How dare you say that of Hialmar Ekdal?

RELLING. We will talk of this again, when the grass has first withered on her grave. Then you'll hear him spouting about "the child too early torn from her father's heart"; then you'll see him steep himself in a syrup of sentiment and self-admiration and self-pity. Just you wait!

GREGERS. If you are right and I am wrong, then life is not worth living.

RELLING. Oh, life would be quite tolerable, after all, if only we could be rid of the confounded duns that keep on pestering us, in our poverty, with the claim of the ideal.

GREGERS (*looking straight before him*). In that case, I am glad that my destiny is what it is.

RELLING. May I inquire,—what is your destiny?

GREGERS (*going*). To be the thirteenth at table.

RELLING. The devil it is.

(*The Curtain Falls.*)

BILLY BUDD

LOUIS O. COXE (1918–   ) and ROBERT CHAPMAN (1919–   )

CHARACTERS

JENKINS, *Captain of the Maintop*
THE DANSKER, *Mainmast Man*
JACKSON, *Maintopman*
JOHN CLAGGART, *Master-at-Arms*
TALBOT, *Maintopman*
BUTLER, *Maintopman*
KINCAID, *Maintopman*
PAYNE, *Maintopman*
O'DANIEL, *Maintopman*
MESSBOY
SQUEAK, *Master-at-Arms' Man*
DUNCAN, *Mate of the Main Deck*

SURGEON
GARDINER, *a Midshipman*
BILLY BUDD, *Foretopman*
EDWARD FAIRFAX VERE, *Captain, Royal Navy*
HALLAM, *a Marine*
REA, *a Midshipman*
PHILIP MICHAEL SEYMOUR, *First Officer*
JOHN RATCLIFFE, *First Lieutenant*
BORDMAN WYATT, *Sailing Master*
STOLL, *Helmsman*
BYREN, *Relief Helmsman*
DRUMMER

The entire action takes place aboard H.M.S. Indomitable *at sea, August, 1798, the year following the Naval mutinies at Spithead and the Nore.*

ACT I

SCENE I

Although outside it is a fine morning in early August, the between-decks compartment of the crew's quarters assigned to the maintopmen is dark and shadowy except for the light spilling down the companionway from above and, through the open gun-ports, the flicker of sunlight reflected on the water. The smoking lamp burns feebly over a wooden mess table and two benches lowered for use.

JENKINS *sits at the table mending a piece of clothing. In the shadow the* DANSKER *sits motionless on a low sea chest, smoking a pipe. Neither man speaks for a long minute.*

Then JACKSON *appears on deck at the top of the companionway and lurches down into the compartment. He is doubled up in pain.*

CLAGGART (*off*). You there! Jackson!

JACKSON. Oh Christ, he's followed me!

JENKINS. Who?

JACKSON. Master-at-Arms. He'll send me aloft again sure, and I can't hang on . . .

JENKINS. What the devil's wrong with you, jack? Here, sit down.

CLAGGART (*entering down the companionway*). Why have you come down off the mainmast, Jackson? Your watch over?

538

JACKSON. Sick, Mister Claggart, I'm bloody sick, so I'm shaking up there on the yard till I near fell off.

JENKINS. Grab an arm, mate, I'll take you along to sick-bay.

CLAGGART. Stand away from him, Jenkins. (*To* JACKSON) Just where does this sick ness strike you, in the guts, or limbs? Or in the head? Does it exist at all?

JENKINS. You can see he's sick as a puking cat, plain as your stick.

CLAGGART. The role of Good Samaritan hardly fits you, Jenkins. (*To* JACKSON) Now up, man. Turn topside.

JACKSON. I can't, I can't, I'm deathly sick, God help me, sir!

CLAGGART. That's hard. But this ship needs all hands. We're undermanned. The aches and pains of landsmen have their cures, but ours have none. You'll have to get aloft. Now move!

JACKSON. I ain't bluffing, sir, swear I'm not! Please, Mister Claggart . . . I got Cooper's leave, he says all right, I can come down.

CLAGGART. You have not got my leave. Cooper is captain of the maintop and ought to know better. Four men to every spar, and no replacements. Now up. Back where you belong.

JACKSON (*starts up the ladder*). God, sir, I can't, I can't stand it! It'll be my death, sure!

CLAGGART. No more talk, man! Up you get! Start! (JACKSON *goes painfully up the ladder and out of sight on deck.* CLAGGART *starts out after him*)

JENKINS (*mutters*). God damn your bloody heart!

CLAGGART. Did you say something, Jenkins? (JENKINS *does not answer.* CLAGGART *goes out, calling after* JACKSON) Now Jackson, get along. Up! Up!

JENKINS. I'll stick him one day before long! I will, if I hang for it.

(*Laughter and talk in the next compartment followed by entrance of* BUTLER, TALBOT *and* KINCAID.)

BUTLER. Messboy!

TALBOT. Haul in the slops!

KINCAID. Suppose we'll get the new man? The jack they 'pressed this morning off that merchantman? I see 'em come alongside just now.

TALBOT. I pity that poor bastard, so I do. I hear they get good pay on merchant ships. Eat good, too, and them treated like the God-damn Prince of Wales. (MESSBOY *enters with an iron pot of food and spits on the deck*) Spit in it, damn you. Can't taste no worse.

MESSBOY. Ain't nobody making you eat it, mate. You can wash your feet in it if you like.

(O'DANIEL *and* PAYNE *enter.*)

TALBOT. What's eating you, Jenkins? Ain't you going to join the banquet?

JENKINS. By God, I seen a thing just now I won't stand for! I'm sitting here off watch, and I seen it all. That blacksnake Claggart kicked Jackson back aloft, and him sick as a pinkass baby in a cradle, as any fool could see.

PAYNE. He's the Master-at-Arms, ain't he?

JENKINS. Cooper sent him down. Who's captain of the starboard watch, him or Claggart? Cooper could have found him a relief. Plain murder, by God!

TALBOT. You think Claggart can get away with what he does without Captain Starry Vere knows what's going on? Him and that red snapper Seymour, and them other bloody officers!

JENKINS. Jackson'll fall. By God, no man can hang to a spar sick like that. He'll fall sure.

O'DANIEL. Tush, man, nobody falls in His Majesty's Navy. We lose our footing. 'Tis flying we do, to be sure.

TALBOT. I tell you it's Vere that's the cause of it! Our glorious fine Captain Vere, with a league of braid around his arm and a ramrod up his bum.

O'DANIEL. Vere, is it. As captains go, mate, let me tell you, he's an angel with a harp alongside of the skipper on the *Royal George*. Every day that one flogged a dozen men. Picked 'em by lottery, by God. Never took the gratings down till they was rusty with blood. Ho! This Vere's a saint in heaven after him.

JENKINS. Ram the *Royal George* and everybody in her! Claggart's the man we want, and the sooner the better, say I!

O'DANIEL. Ah, we'd had him puking his blood at Spithead, the devil rot his wick.

BUTLER. You was there, O'Daniel? At Spithead?

O'DANIEL. Aye. I was. Wherever do you find Englishmen doing a smart thing, you'll find an Irishman is at the bottom of it. Oho, fine it was, every day of it, with the officers quaking in their cabins, spitting green, and the whole English government wetting their breeches from the fear of us! Ah, lovely it was, lovely!

TALBOT. Belay your Irish noise, you fat-mouthed mackerel-snatcher. I'll tell you this, we need men on here is not afraid to use their knives if it come to that. And you can be bloody sure it will come to that, mind my word, Mickey Cork.

JENKINS. What did you ever use your knife for, Talbot, but to scratch your lice? Ah, you're a dancing daredevil, you are for sure.

TALBOT. I'll be happy to show you, if you like.

JENKINS. Trouble will be hunting you out, mate, if you're not careful.

TALBOT. Trouble! You whoreson cockney cullion! There's not a man aboard don't know you for a coward, you whining bitch-boy!

JENKINS Get out.

TALBOT. Damn your seed, I'm not afraid of you, or your sniveling hangbys, either!

JENKINS. Move! Get out of it, or by God I'll run my knife to the hilts in you!

TALBOT. You son of a whore! Pigsticker!

(*They attack one another with drawn knives,* JENKINS *reaching suddenly across the table to seize* TALBOT. *Silently they thrash around the compartment upsetting benches and food while the others look on unmoved.*)

O'DANIEL. Ah, I do love to see two Englishmen fighting each other. It's fonder they are of killing themselves than fighting their proper enemies. (*Laughs hoarsely*)

PAYNE. Tomorrow's rum on Jenkins. Any bets?

KINCAID. He's never lost one yet.

(JENKINS *throws* TALBOT *on the deck and holds the knife at his throat for a moment before letting him up, first taking his knife. He holds out his hand.*)

JENKINS. I'm leading seaman in this compartment, mind that. (TALBOT *hits* JENKINS' *hand and goes off angrily*)

KINCAID. You're captain, that's all right by me.

O'DANIEL. Eyes in the boat, lads. Here comes *pfft*-face.

(SQUEAK, BILLY *and* GARDINER *appear on deck and start down the companionway.*)

GARDINER. Hang it, step lively, boy! Your ship is . . . Doff your hat to officers when they speak to you! By God, I'll teach you to touch your hat to a midshipman's coat, if it's only stuck on a broomstick to dry!

BILLY. Aye, sir.

(*The men react to* GARDINER *with yawns and gestures behind his back.*)

GARDINER. Very well. Your ship is *H.M.S. Indomitable* now, and we sail her tautly, and we tolerate no nonsense. Is that clear?

BILLY. Aye, sir.

GARDINER (*to* SQUEAK). See this new man is assigned to a watch, and get him squared away. (*To* BILLY) You're green, of course, I can see that. But I expect we'll ripen you. (*He trips going up the ladder and* SQUEAK *tries to help him*) Carry on.
                                                                        (GARDINER *exits*)

SQUEAK. My name's Squeak. I'm the Master-at-Arms' man. Have you met the Master-at-Arms yet, Mister Claggart? (BILLY *shakes his head*) Oh, you'll like him. He's a nice fellow. (O'DANIEL *chokes on his pipe smoke and the other men react similarly*) Stow your gear along in there. This here's the larboard section of the maintop. Captain of the watch is Jenkins. Him, there. Report to him. (*He pats* BILLY *on the chest and grins before starting up the ladder*)

JENKINS. What's a green hand dumped in here for?

SQUEAK. Complaining, Jenkins?

JENKINS. I'm asking. What's wrong with that?

SQUEAK. Mister Claggart wants him here, that's why. Maybe he wants for Billy Boy to set you pigs an example. Refer any more complaints to the Master-at-Arms!

(*Exits.* BILLY *grins at the men, who return his look.*)

BILLY. My name is Budd. Billy, if you like.

KINCAID. I'm Kincaid. This is where you swing your hammock. That's O'Daniel, this here's Payne, and Butler. This is Jenkins, captain of the watch, and that old jack's called the Dansker. Don't know why, unless maybe he's Danish. You ever had a real name, Dansker?

DANSKER. Not for many years.

BUTLER. You'd be the new impressed man?

BILLY. Aye, so I am. I just came off the *Rights of Man* this morning.

DANSKER. Forget about the *Rights of Man* now, lad.

JENKINS. How long you been going to sea, baby?

BILLY. About ten years, but in the merchant service.

O'DANIEL. Merchant service! Whissht! (*Laughs hoarsely*)

BILLY. I know I'm new at Navy work, and probably there'll be some things I'll need help with.

JENKINS. No doubt, little boy.

BILLY. I'll learn fast, never fear. But she's a big old girl, this ship. I never was in a ship-of-the-line before. I'd have got lost trying to find the mess by myself. Maybe fallen in the magazine!

O'DANIEL. Ah, you get used to it. She's big, is this tub, but she's not so big you can get lost in her.

PAYNE. Sometimes I wish to God you could. Maybe we could lose O'Daniel.

(BILLY *laughs and the others join.*)

BILLY. You're Irish, aren't you? I like the Irish. There was an Irishman on the *Rights of Man*, with big red whiskers . . . when I came away, he gave me a silver knife. This is it.

O'DANIEL. It's a beauty. Mind you keep an eye on it.

BUTLER. What's the matter, boy?

BILLY. I was just thinking, maybe I won't ever see my friends again.

O'DANIEL. If they was Irish, don't you worry at all. The Irish is liable to turn up almost anywheres, excepting England and the fires of hell, which is much the same.

PAYNE. Danny, if it wasn't for the harps, the devil wouldn't have nothing to do. What was potato-eaters doing on a merchant ship?

BILLY. Just sailors, like me. Most of us had no other home, even the skipper. He was a kind old bloke. Looked fierce, but he always had a kind word. Used to keep a bird in a cage in his cabin. The skipper let me feed the bird sometimes. Worms right out of the ship's biscuit. That was mostly all the meat we got.

O'DANIEL. The bargemen is in Navy biscuit would eat the bird.

KINCAID. Sit down here, Bill. Maggots or not, this is what we get. You hungry?

BILLY. I'm always hungry.

KINCAID. Try your first sample of His Majesty's bounty. We don't know what it is, but we been eating it for a long time.

BUTLER. Here, eat mine. Tastes like it's been eat before, anyhow.

JENKINS. Give him more lobscouse, Butler. We got to keep the roses in his cheeks, ain't we, boy?

BILLY (*laughing*). I could eat anything right now. Even this.

O'DANIEL. Help you to forget about home and mother, lad.

JENKINS. Tell us about home and mother, Baby Budd.

BILLY. There's not much to tell. I've got no home, and never had a family to remember.

JENKINS. Ain't that too bad.

BILLY. Oh, I'd feel a lot worse if I'd been 'pressed with a wife and children.

KINCAID. That's the truth.

O'DANIEL. We're all patriotic volunteers.

KINCAID. Guano! Wait till my hitch is up, you won't see no more of me.

BUTLER. Three weeks drunk in Portsmouth, then back in the ruddy fleet.

DANSKER. Men like us got no other home.

O'DANIEL. No other home, is it? Ah 'tis so thick the sweet thoughts is in here, I can scarce breathe.

PAYNE. Then you can strangle or get out.

JENKINS. Aye, get along, you lousy harp, give us some fresh air.

O'DANIEL. If you begged me to stay itself, I'd be off to where there's smarter lads. Boy, let you pay no heed to these white mice, mind what I say. And be hanged, the lot of yous! (*He starts up the ladder*)

KINCAID. You'll catch it, Danny, if Captain holds an inspection.

O'DANIEL (*returning*). Ah whissht, I was forgetting that. And I do think that me figure shows up better here below than it does in the broad daylight.

BILLY. Inspection today?

PAYNE. Ah, the Old Man crawls over the ship from arsehole to appetite any time he ain't got nothing else to do. You never know when till you see him.

KINCAID. What the devil he wants to inspect this hooker for, I can't figure. He's seen it before.

BUTLER. He ain't seen Billy.

BILLY. What's the Captain like? On the *Rights of Man*, the captain . . .

JENKINS. You going to jaw some more about that rocking horse? I suppose *you* was at Spithead, too?

BILLY. Spithead? Where is that?

JENKINS. A little party the Navy had a year ago. A mutiny, Baby, a mutiny. Know what that is?

BILLY. Why did they mutiny?

O'DANIEL. Arra, it's easy to see you're new to the Navy.

JENKINS. Jimmy-Legs is ten good God-damn reasons for it, himself.

BILLY. Who's Jimmy-Legs?

KINCAID. Master-at-Arms. We call him Jimmy-Legs.

BUTLER. Watch out for that one, Billy.

PAYNE. He's the devil himself between decks.

O'DANIEL. What d'you expect, the saints of heaven? Not in an English tub.

BILLY. Why don't you like the Master-at-Arms?

JENKINS. You'll find out soon enough, Baby.

BUTLER. Watch him, boy. Jenkins can tell you. He's had a time or two with Claggart.

JENKINS. Aye, and I'll have another one day before too long.

BUTLER. Sure, Jenkins. You look after Bill.

JENKINS. How old are you, kid? Sixteen?

BILLY. I don't know, maybe . . . twenty.

JENKINS. He don't even know how old he is! My guess is, too young to know what his parts are for.

O'DANIEL. Is it anybody is that young?

KINCAID. Stow it, Jenkins. Come on, don't pay no attention to him. He's feeling ugly today.

JENKINS. Well now, ain't you getting holier than a bloody bishop. Let him talk up for himself, if he don't like it.

KINCAID. Stow it, I say. You got no reason to crawl over Bill. Let him be.

BILLY. That's all right, Tom. I don't mind a joke. Black's the white of me eye, mates!

(*All laugh except* JENKINS.)

JENKINS. Mama taught you pretty manners, huh? Oh! Ain't got no mama, you say? Well now, think what that makes you! (*Laughs*)

BILLY. Tell me what you mean, Mister Jenkins.

PAYNE. What's gnawing your arse, Jenkins? Can't you see the boy's trying to be friendly?

JENKINS. You forgetting who's leading seaman here? Come on, Baby, talk back, why don't you? Scared?

BILLY. N-no. Why do you think I'd be scared, M-M-Mister Jenkins?

JENKINS. He stammers! What do you know! The little bastard's so scared he's stammering.

BILLY. Don't call me that again.

JENKINS. Sounds good, ha? Sounds fine. I like the way it rolls out your mouth. Bastard Baby Budd . . .

(BILLY *strikes him.* JENKINS *staggers and falls, pulls a knife and gets up, lunging at* BILLY. PAYNE, BUTLER *and* KINCAID *get up and stand close to* BILLY, *silently protecting him.*)

JENKINS. Get away, God damn you! He's got to find out who gives orders here.

KINCAID. Not this time, Jenkins. Lay off.

O'DANIEL. Belay it. You're wearing me out, the pair of yous.

BUTLER. Put away the knife.

(JENKINS *sees their determination and relaxes a little, uncertain what to do.*)

BILLY. Will you shake hands? Or would you rather fight?

JENKINS. You little bas . . . (*Lunges forward.* BILLY *catches his arm and bends it, holding* JENKINS *cursing and powerless*)

BILLY. That's enough, mate. Pipe down and let us be.

O'DANIEL. Good lad! Save the great strength is in you, Jenkins, for fighting the devil is after your soul.

JENKINS. All right, all right. You can let me go now.

O'DANIEL. Leave him go, lad. I won't hurt him at all.

BILLY. You're like Red Whiskers on the *Rights*, he liked to fight too. (*Freeing him*) Will you shake hands, mate?

JENKINS (*momentarily uncertain what to do*). Shake hands, is it? . . . Well, you beat me fair. You got guts, which is more than I give you credit for. (*They shake hands*)

KINCAID. You're a hell of a peacemaker, Bill.

PAYNE. That's the only time I ever hear Jenkins eating his own words.

O'DANIEL. Ah, that's a terrible diet, would make any man puke.

JENKINS. Don't you be getting any wrong ideas. I'm still a match for you!

KINCAID. Better belay your mess gear, Bill.

JENKINS. Where you come from, Baby?

PAYNE. Stow it! Jimmy-Legs!

(BILLY *goes on talking as* CLAGGART *enters.*)

BILLY. I don't know, I guess from Portsmouth. I never lived ashore, that I can remember. Where do you come from? (*Drops a pot on deck.* CLAGGART *stands over him*)

CLAGGART. Handsomely done, young fellow, handsomely done. And handsome is as handsome did it, too. You can wipe that up, Jenkins. (*To* BILLY) What is your name?

BILLY. Budd, sir. William Budd, ship *Rights of Man.*

CLAGGART. Your ship is *H.M.S. Indomitable* now.

BILLY. Aye, sir.

CLAGGART. You look sturdy. What was your station aboard the merchantman?

BILLY. M-m-mizzentopman, sir.

CLAGGART. You like that station?

BILLY. Aye, sir, well enough.

CLAGGART. How long have you been at sea?

BILLY. Ten years, sir, near as I can tell.

CLAGGART. Education?

BILLY. None, sir.

CLAGGART. So. You come aboard with nothing but your face to recommend you. Well, while beauty is always welcome, that alone may not avail us much against the French. There are other requirements in the service.

BILLY. I'll learn quickly, sir.

CLAGGART. The sea's a taskmaster, young fellow. It salts the sweetness out of boyish faces. You cannot tell what motion lies asleep in that flat water. Down where the manta drifts, and the shark and ray, storms wait for a wind while all the surface dazzles.

BILLY. I am a seaman, sir. I love the sea. I've hardly lived ashore.

CLAGGART. Then let the wind and sea have license to plunder at their will. As of today, a new maintopman swings between sky and water. (*He turns toward the ladder and notices the mess on deck*) I thought I asked you to wipe that up, Jenkins.

JENKINS. That's the messboy's job.

CLAGGART. Clean up, Jenkins. (JENKINS *hesitates.*) That is an order. Turn to.

BILLY. I'll give you a hand, Jenkins. Come on.

CLAGGART. Ah, there. See how helpful Billy is. Why can't you take a leaf from this innocent young David's book, Jenkins? (*Turns away.* JENKINS *accidentally brushes against him and receives a savage cut from* CLAGGART'S *rattan across his face*) Watch what you're doing, man!

JENKINS. I swear . . . !

CLAGGART. Yes, what is it that you swear? Well, speak. Nothing at all to say? Then hear me: I have my methods with unruly tempers.

(*On deck there is a loud crescendo scream and a crash. Running footsteps, shouts, voice calling for the* SURGEON. *The men surge toward the ladder.*)

CLAGGART. Stand fast! (SQUEAK *enters down the hatchway, whispers to* CLAGGART.) All right, I know. (SQUEAK *comes down into the compartment and runs off*)

JENKINS. It's Jackson! I knew it, by God, I told you so!

(*Men turn to stare at* CLAGGART *as several sailors enter down the companionway, bearing the body of* JACKSON, *inert and shattered. They carry him through the compartment and off to sick-bay.*)

SURGEON (*as he moves through the compartment*). Clear the way, you men. Take him into the sick-bay, through here. Carry him gently. Easy, now. Easy. (*Exit*)

JENKINS (*pointing to* CLAGGART). He sent him back aloft. Killed him, he did!

O'DANIEL. Might as well have knifed him.

CLAGGART. Stand fast. Stop where you are. Your man Jackson is looked after.

O'DANIEL (*in a low voice*). Then he's a dead man surely.

CLAGGART. Who spoke?

JENKINS. We'll have a showdown now! After him, mates! Cut into him!

(*The men move toward* CLAGGART *in a rush, drawing knives and cursing him, as* CAPTAIN VERE *appears in the companion hatchway.*)

VERE. Stand fast! Hold where you are. Master-at-Arms, what is the matter here?

(*The men stop in their tracks and stare at* VERE, *who comes part way down the ladder.*)

CLAGGART. These dogs are out of temper, sir.

VERE (*to men*). You will come to attention when I address you! Let me remind you that this ship is at war. This is a wartime cruise, and this vessel sails under the Articles of War. Volunteer or 'pressed man, veteran seaman or recruit, you are no longer citizens, but sailors: a crew that I shall work into a weapon. One lawless act, one spurt of rebel temper from any man in this ship, high or low, I will pay out in coin you know of. You have but two duties: to fight and to obey, and I will bend each contumacious spirit, each stiff-necked prideful soul of you, or crush the spirit in you if I must. Abide by the Articles of War and my commands, or they will cut you down. Now: choose. (*The men are silent*) Very well. Master-at-Arms, this accident on deck, the sailor fallen from the yardarm. Do you know how it occurred?

CLAGGART. I do not, sir.

VERE. You are his messmates. Does any man of you know how this occurred? (*To* BUTLER) You?

BUTLER. No, sir.

VERE. Jenkins, do you?

JENKINS (*hesitates a moment.* CLAGGART *moves slightly, tapping his hand with the rattan*). No, sir.

VERE (*notices the cut on* JENKIN'S *face*). What's this, what's this? Speak up, man. I want no random bloodshed aboard this ship.

JENKINS. I . . . fell, Captain. Fell, and . . . and cut my cheek.

VERE. I see. You fell. Master-at-Arms, you will excuse this man from duty till the Surgeon tends him.

CLAGGART. Aye, aye, sir.

VERE. We must not wound ourselves, draining the blood from enterprise that takes a whole man. (*He turns to go up the ladder and sees* BILLY) Well. This is a new face. Who are you, boy?

CLAGGART. Maintopman 'pressed from the *Rights of Man* this morning, sir. William Budd.

VERE. Let him speak for himself. (BILLY *tries to speak but can only stammer incoherently.*) That's all right, boy, take your time. No need to be nervous.

BILLY. I saw a man go aloft, sir, as I came on board just a while ago. He looked sick, sir, he did. This officer was there, too, he can tell you. (*To* CLAGGART) Don't you remember, sir?

VERE. Did you send a sick man, aloft, Master-at-Arms?

CLAGGART. I did not, sir.

VERE. Very well. (*To* BILLY) Well, Budd. I hope you take to Navy life and duty without too much regret. We go to fight the French and shall need wits and hearts about us equal to the task.

BILLY. I'll do my best, sir.

VERE. I'm sure you will. We are all here to do our several duties, and though they may seem petty from one aspect, still they must all be done. The Admiral himself looks small and idle to the man like you who can see him from the maintop, threading his pattern on the quarterdeck. The Navy's only life.

(SURGEON *enters.*)

SURGEON. Captain—Jackson, the man who fell just now—he's dead, sir.

VERE (*after a pause*). Carry on, Master-at-Arms.

(*He goes out up the companionway.* SURGEON *exits.*)

CLAGGART. You've made a good impression on the Captain, Billy Budd. You have a pleasant way with you. If you wish to make a good impression on me, you will need to curb your tongue. Jenkins, I thought you were ordered to sick-bay. Jump to it. And I suggest you change that shirt. See how fouled it is with a peculiar stain. Why can't you keep clean like Billy here? (*He strikes* JENKINS *viciously on the arm with his rattan, smiles at him, and exits up the ladder*)

JENKINS. God damn his flaming soul! I can't stand it no more!

BILLY. I don't see what you can do, mate. He didn't mean it when he hurt you then.

JENKINS. Listen, boy, I know Jimmy-Legs. He lives on hurting people. Stay away from him, and keep your mouth shut, if you don't want trouble.

O'DANIEL. Did you hear the lad speak up to the skipper?

PAYNE. Aye, you watch your tongue, Bill. Claggart will be after you for talking up like that.

KINCAID. He's a cool one, Billy is. None of us got the nerve.

BUTLER. It's nerve gets a man in trouble in this tub.

DANSKER. Jimmy-Legs is down on you already, Billy.

BILLY. Down on me? Why he's friendly to me.

JENKINS. Claggart don't make no friends.

O'DANIEL. You seen Jackson when they brought him below. That's how friendly he gets. (*Bosun's pipe off.*)

DUNCAN (*off*). Relieve the watch!

KINCAID. First watch on the *Indomitable*, Bill. Better lay up to the mainmast and report. (*Exit*)

BUTLER. Don't slip off the yardarm.

PAYNE. Watch your step.

BILLY. Not me. You watch for me. Got to find the mainmast, and I'm in a hurry.

O'DANIEL. You'll never find your way in this old tub. I'll come along and show you. If anybody comes calling for O'Daniel while I'm out, take the message.

PAYNE. O'Daniel couldn't find his breeches if they wasn't buttoned on. You come with me. (BILLY *and* PAYNE *go off*)

JENKINS. Poor bastard. I pity him, I do.

BUTLER. He's dead, ain't he? Better off than us.

JENKINS. Not Jackson. I mean the baby here. Billy.

BUTLER. We could have fared worse for a messmate.

JENKINS. Aye. He can take care of himself. Heave up the table.

SCENE II

In the early evening of the same day, the off-duty sections of the crew are mustered aft on the maindeck for JACKSON'S *funeral. Above them* CAPTAIN VERE *stands uncovered at the forward break of the quarterdeck, reading the Committal Prayer. The westward sky is bright yellow and red, but fades into darkness as the scene progresses.*

The men are uncovered and stand at attention.

VERE. Unto Almighty God we commend the soul of our brother departed and we commit his body to the deep, in sure and certain hope of the resurrection unto Eternal Life, through our Lord Jesus Christ, at whose coming in glorious majesty to judge the world, the sea shall give up her dead, and the corruptible bodies of those who sleep in Him shall be changed and made like unto His glorious body according to the mighty working whereby He is able to subdue all things unto Himself. Amen.

MEN. Amen.

(*Short drum-roll followed by a muffled splash as* JACKSON'S *body slips over the side. Then the bosun's pipe. Officers cover and march off.*)

CLAGGART. Ship's company: Cover! Petty officers, dismiss your divisions.

VOICE (*off*). Carpenters and gunners: Dismiss!

VOICE (*off*). Afterguardsmen: Dismiss!

VOICE (*off*). Fore, main, and mizzentopmen: Dismiss!

(*The men break formation and go off, excepting* BUTLER, JENKINS, PAYNE, KINCAID *and* BILLY, *who gather near the ratlines, at the rail.*)

BUTLER. I suppose in this clear water you could see him go down for quite a way.

BILLY. We're moving slow in this calm.

JENKINS. There'll be wind enough before dawn.

BUTLER. And that's the end of Enoch Jackson. Over the side he goes, and his mates forget him.

JENKINS Whatever's happened to Jackson, he ain't worried none. He's got a hundred fathoms over him to keep him warm and cosy.

BILLY. I'd rather be buried at sea than on the beach, when I come to die. Will you stand by the plank, Tom, so I'll shake a friendly hand before I sink? Oh! But it's dead I'll be then, come to think! (*All laugh*)

PAYNE. Don't you worry none. By that time, you won't give a sailmaker's damn.

KINCAID. It's only living makes sense to me, anyhow.

BILLY. Aye, I like to live. Even when it seems bad, there's a lot that's good in it.

JENKINS. Maybe for you, Bill. You wouldn't know trouble if it come up and spit in your eye.

BILLY. Don't you try now, mate! You might miss, and I got a clean jumper on!

PAYNE. That's the way to be, if you ask me. There's always trouble, if you know where to look for it.

BUTLER. You don't have to see nothing if you close your eyes.

KINCAID. When I close my eyes I sleep sound as a drunk marine.

BILLY. Aye, after I roll in my hammock, it's one, two, three, and I'm deep down under.

JENKINS. Well it's down under for me right now. Let's lay below.

KINCAID. Aye, we'll be on watch before long. Coming, Bill?

BILLY. I think I'll stay and watch the water for a while. I like to watch the sea at night.

JENKINS. Aye. It's deep and silent, and it can drown a man before he knows it.

BILLY. Sleep sound, mates. (*All but* JENKINS *go down the companion hatchway.*)

JENKINS. Billy: stay clear of Jimmy-Legs.

(JENKINS *exits down the hatchway.* BILLY *is left alone staring over the side until* CLAGGART *enters. He does not see* BILLY, *but stops near the quarterdeck ladder and gazes fixedly seaward.*)

BILLY. Good evening, sir.

CLAGGART (*startled, then subtly sarcastic*). Good evening.

BILLY. Will it be all right if I stay topside a bit to watch the water?

CLAGGART. I suppose the Handsome Sailor may do many things forbidden to his messmates.

BILLY. Yes, sir. The sea's calm tonight, isn't it? Calm and peaceful.

CLAGGART. The sea's deceitful, boy: calm above, and underneath, a world of gliding monsters preying on their fellows. Murderers, all of them. Only the sharpest teeth survive.

BILLY. I'd like to know about such things, as you do, sir.

CLAGGART. You're an ingenuous sailor, Billy Budd. Is there, behind that youthful face, the wisdom pretty virtue has need of? Even the gods must know their rivals, boy; and Christ had first to recognize the ills before he cured 'em.

BILLY. What, sir?

CLAGGART. Never mind. But tell me this: how have you stomach to stand here and talk to me? Are you so innocent and ignorant of what I am? You know my reputation. Jenkins and the rest are witnesses, and certainly you've heard them talking to me. Half of them would knife me in the back some night and do it gladly; Jenkins is thinking of it. Doubtless he'll try one day. How do you dare, then? Have you not intelligence enough to be afraid of me? To hate me as all the others do?

BILLY. Why should I be afraid of you, sir? You speak to me friendly when we meet. I know some of the men . . . are fearful of you, sir, but I can't believe they're right about it.

CLAGGART. You're a fool, fellow. In time, you'll learn to fear me like the rest. Young you are, and scarcely used to the fit of your man's flesh.

BILLY. I know they're wrong, sir. You aren't like they say. Nobody could be so.

CLAGGART. So . . . ? So what, boy? Vicious, did you mean to say, or brutal? But they aren't wrong, and you would see it, but for those blue eyes that light so kindly on your fellow men.

BILLY. Oh, I've got no education, I know that. There must be a lot of things a man misses when he's ignorant. But learning's hard. Must be sort of lonely, too.

CLAGGART. What are you prating of, half-man, half-child? Your messmates crowd around, admire your yellow hair and your blue eyes, do tricks and favors for you out of love, and you talk about loneliness!

BILLY. I just noticed the way you were looking off to leeward as I came up, sir. Kind of sad, you were looking.

CLAGGART. Not sadness, boy. Another feeling, more like . . . pleasure. That's it. I can feel it now, looking at you. A certain . . . pleasure.

BILLY (flattered). Thank you, sir.

CLAGGART (annoyed at BILLY's incomprehension). Pah.

BILLY. Just talking with you, sir, I can tell they're wrong about you. They're ignorant, like me.

CLAGGART. Compliment for compliment, eh, boy? Have you no heart for terror, fellow? You've seen this stick in use. Have you not got sense and spleen and liver to be scared, even to be cowardly?

BILLY. No, sir, I guess not. I like talking to you, sir. But please, sir, tell me something.

CLAGGART. I wonder if I can. Well, ask it.

BILLY. Why do you want us to believe you're cruel, and not really like everybody else?

CLAGGART. I think you are the only child alive who wouldn't understand if I explained; or else you'd not believe it

BILLY. Oh, I'd believe you, sir. There's much I could learn from you: I never knew a man like you before.

CLAGGART (*slowly*). Do you—like me, Billy Budd?

BILLY. You've always been most pleasant with me, sir.

CLAGGART. Have I?

BILLY. Yes, sir. In the mess, the day I came aboard? And almost every day you have a pleasant word.

CLAGGART. And what I have said tonight, are these pleasant words?

BILLY. Yes, sir. I was wondering . . . could I talk to you between watches, when you've nothing else to do?

CLAGGART. You're a plausible boy, Billy. Aye, the nights are long, and talking serves to pass them.

BILLY. Thank you, sir. That would mean a lot to me.

CLAGGART. Perhaps to me as well. (*Drops his rattan.* BILLY *picks it up and hands it back to him.* CLAGGART *stares at it a moment, then at* BILLY) No. No! Charm me, too, would you! Get away!

BILLY (*surprised and puzzled*). Aye, sir.

(*He exits down the hatchway. After a pause in which* CLAGGART *recovers his self-control* SQUEAK *appears.*)

CLAGGART (*without turning*). Come here. I thought I told you to put that new seaman Budd on report. Why was it not done?

SQUEAK. I tried, Mister Claggart, sir. I couldn't find nothing out of place. Gear all stowed perfect.

CLAGGART. Then disarrange it. You know the practice. I want him on report.

SQUEAK. Two of his messmates is once nearly caught me at it before.

CLAGGART. Then be more careful. Now get along and see you make out something.

(SQUEAK *scurries off below decks as* VERE *comes into sight on the quarterdeck.*)

VERE. Master-at-Arms. What is that man doing above decks?

CLAGGART. Ship's corporal, sir. A routine report.

VERE. There is nothing in this ship of so routine a nature that I do not concern myself in it. Remember that.

CLAGGART. Aye, aye, sir. With your permission, sir. (*Exit*)

(VERE *walks along the deck and scans the sails as* SEYMOUR *enters.*)

SEYMOUR. Fine evening, sir.

VERE. Yes, a fine evening, Seymour. How is the glass?

SEYMOUR. Falling, I believe, sir. I think we'll toss a little before morning. Well, I suppose I should be in my cabin inspecting the deck logs.

VERE. Stay for a moment, Seymour. In the days and nights to come, you and I will not often have an opportunity to stand easy and talk.

SEYMOUR. Aye, sir. I expect the French will put us to our stations any hour now.

VERE. Are you impressed by omens, Seymour? This seaman we've just buried: I think of him as an omen of some sort, a melancholy prologue to this voyage.

SEYMOUR. Aye, sir. Hard on the sailor, certainly, but that's the service. But we've been lucky in other ways. An accident, now, that's unavoidable.

VERE. It was more than an accident, Seymour.

SEYMOUR. This maintop sailor? How do you mean, sir?

VERE. The man was sent aloft sick, by the Master-at-Arms, contrary to my standing order. Budd, the new seaman, implied as much, and the maintop watch confirmed it. The Master-at-Arms lied to me.

SEYMOUR. What are you going to do, sir? What action can you take? He's a valuable man, one we can hardly do without as things are now.

VERE. I shall do nothing at present, only wait and observe him. No court-martial could do more than strip him of his rank for such misconduct. I will let him have his head until some act puts him squarely counter to the law, then let the law consume him.

SEYMOUR. Why trouble the natural order to no purpose? Shouldn't we let it be?

VERE. Must a man always shrug, let things alone and drift? Would to God I could take this power of mine and break him now, smash all the laws to powder and be a man again.

SEYMOUR. We must serve the law, sir, or give up the right and privilege of service. It's how we live.

VERE. Live? Oh, you're right. Below this deck are men who at a call skip on the hurling spars against the wind, at Beat-to-quarters run as if they willed it. Yet each of us steps alone within this pattern, this formal movement centered on itself. Men live and die, taken by pattern, born to it, knowing nothing. No man can defy the code we live by and not be broken by it.

SEYMOUR. You are the Captain, sir. You maintain that code.

VERE. Keep an order we cannot understand. That's true. The world demands it: demands that at the back of every peacemaker there be the gun, the gallows and the gaol. I talk of justice, and would turn the law gentle for those who serve here; but a Claggart stands in my shadow, for I need him. So the world goes, wanting not justice, but order . . . to be let alone to hug its own iniquities. Let a man work to windward of that law and he'll be hove down. No hope for him, none.

(*Enter* WYATT.)

WYATT. Eight o'clock report, sir. Ship inspected and all in order.

SEYMOUR. Very well, carry on. (WYATT *goes off*) By your leave, sir. Good night.
(*Exit*)

(VERE *remains, crosses to the hatch and looks down, then slowly upward at the set of the sails.*)

SCENE III

The maindeck several nights later.

Four bells is struck offstage. A sailor climbs wearily down the ratlines, drops to the deck and goes below. CLAGGART *stands by the larboard rail.*

As BILLY *enters from below decks, he sees the Master-at-Arms.*

BILLY. Hello, sir. (CLAGGART *looks at him without answering, then turns and goes off forward. The* DANSKER *follows* BILLY *up onto the deck*) Well, that's all there is to tell, Dansker. I always lash my hammock just so, and stow my gear same as all the others. They don't get in trouble.

DANSKER. Mister Claggart is down upon you, Billy.

BILLY. Jimmy-Legs? Why he calls me the sweet and pleasant fellow, they tell me.

DANSKER. Does he so, Baby lad? Aye, a sweet voice has Mister Claggart.

BILLY. For me he has. I seldom pass him but there comes a pleasant word.

DANSKER. And that's because he's down upon you.

BILLY. But he's my friend. I know he talks a little strange, but he's my friend.

DANSKER. Nobody's friend is Jimmy-Legs. Yours least of all, maybe. Lay aloft, Baby. You'll be late to relieve your watch.

BILLY. Aye, Dansker.

(*He climbs up the ratlines out of sight. The* DANSKER *watches him go.* CLAGGART *appears, but the* DANSKER *ignores him and goes off aft. As* JENKINS *comes into view climbing down the ratlines,* CLAGGART *gestures off and fades into a shadowy corner of the deck near the quarterdeck ladder.* SQUEAK *enters as* JENKINS *drops to the deck, and intercepts him as he starts down the companionway.*)

SQUEAK. It's all right, mate, slack off and stay a bit.

JENKINS. What do you want? I pick my own company.

SQUEAK. So does I, mate, so does I. And if I may make so bold to say it, you'll be smarter to pick your company more careful.

JENKINS. If you got something to say to me, talk up, else I'll get below.

SQUEAK. Don't be hasty, now, mate, don't be in a sweat. It's haste gets good men into trouble. What d'you think of our new hand here, Billy Boy? Mister Claggart's taken with him, too. Fine young fellow, ha?

JENKINS. Talk plain. What d'you mean?

SQUEAK. I overheard him talking just this day. Would maybe surprise you some, what he had to say about yourself and a few other lads.

JENKINS. What?

SQUEAK. Aoh, bit of talk about his messmates. He don't fancy us! Not like his feather boys aboard the merchantman.

JENKINS. You lying cut-throat, try something else! Billy's in my mess; since he come on board he's rare been out of my sight. You're lying, you bloody nark! I know you too well. You'll need to try some other way to get Bill into trouble. Get away, and don't come lying to me no more.

SQUEAK. Aoh, so it's that friendly you are! Well, now, ain't that sweet! You're not smart, Jenkins. Remember, man: I tried to help you out. When you're feeling the cat between your shoulders . . .

JENKINS (seizing him). Damn your lies! Get back to Jimmy-Legs and kiss his butt. And stay out of my way! (Throws SQUEAK down and exits.)

(SQUEAK watches him go. CLAGGART steps out of the shadows.)

CLAGGART. I heard your little talk. You lack subtlety; but I'm the greater fool to use you in these matters. You're inept.

SQUEAK. Aoh! Why don't you do it yourself, if you don't need me!

CLAGGART. I need nobody, least of all a rum-soaked footpad from the Old Bailey. If you wish to have free rein with your distasteful habits, mind your cockney manners! I stand between you and the flogging whip. Improve your style, or you stand tomorrow forenoon at the gratings!

SQUEAK. I only meant as you could do it better, Mister Claggart, I wouldn't say nothing to . . .

CLAGGART (cuts him on the arm with his rattan). Don't touch me!—Keep Budd in petty troubles, that you can do. Unlash his hammock. Keep him on report. In time I'll let you know what plans I have for him. Get aft! (SQUEAK, eager to get away, scuttles aft as the DANSKER enters.) Well, old man. Moon's in and out tonight. There's weather somewhere. (The DANSKER turns down the night lamp over the cabin door and starts off.) Stay and have a pipe.

DANSKER. I have the watch.

CLAGGART. You take your duties as seriously as ever.

DANSKER. Aye. They are all of life for an old seaman like me. (*Turns to go*)

CLAGGART. You move away from me as though I were some kind of stalking beast. You avoid me, too.

DANSKER. Your word, John, "too."

CLAGGART. You know what I mean. The hands detest me. You are a hand, older than most, and older in your hatred, I have no doubt. But why, man? You at least should see me as I am, a man who knows how the world's made: made as I am.

DANSKER. How can I know what goes on in your head?

CLAGGART. The enigmatic Dansker. Come, it's dark, we can drop disguises when night serves to hold the disclosing soul apart.

DANSKER. You know who you remind me of . . . maintopman: Billy Budd.

CLAGGART. More enigmas! That sunny, smiling infant with no spleen nor knowledge in his head?

DANSKER. I'll leave you now.

CLAGGART. No, stay a while. This is a night for secrets and disclosures.

DANSKER. You have half the truth and Billy Budd the other. He can't see there's evil in the world, and you won't see the good.

CLAGGART. So. And I take it you come in between.

DANSKER. I keep outside. I am too old to stand between sky and water.

CLAGGART. And yet you hate me, too.

DANSKER. I hate an incomplete man.

CLAGGART. Damn all this talk. Hate me and have done. Let it alone, I say. Whatever else it is, this thing is Man, still!

DANSKER. I'll be off.

CLAGGART. Don't go. The moon's gone under. Let us talk this out. You are a wise man in your senile way.

DANSKER. Then take this for all my wisdom. You recognize the hatred of your shipmates as an honor paid to a soul they cannot understand. Your fine contempt for human love is nothing but regret.

CLAGGART. Stop there. I know the rest by heart. Nothing you say to me but clatters in my belly, watch on watch. Aye: when this arm moves out in gesture of love, it mocks me with a blow. Who lifts this arm? What officer commands this hireling flesh? Somewhere below the farthest marks and deeps, God anchors hearts, and his sea rusts mine hollow. The flukes break in the bottom, and I slack and stand, go in and out forever at God's humor. Look at this sea: for all her easy swell, who knows what bones, ribs and decay are fathomed at her base and move in her motion, so that on the flattest water, the very stricture of the dead can kill that beauty with a dance of death?—Here is a man. He holds, past fathom curves, drowned fleets of human agonies that gesture when the long tide pulls.

DANSKER. Aye, John. But you must know that other men are moved so. Look up some evening at the quarterdeck for another poor thoughtful devil like you, like me, pacing all night between his doubts.

CLAGGART. What, Vere? That fine-drawn manner doesn't deceive me. There's a whited sepulchre, like all soft-spoken charmers of this world.

DANSKER. You don't believe in anything besides yourself, eh John?

CLAGGART. I've said what I have said. I know myself, and look to that. You should try it. Go to your post, old man, and your ever-lasting duties. (CLAGGART *turns away.* BILLY *scrambles into view down the ratlines and calls out excitedly.*)

BILLY. Quarterdeck ho!

RATCLIFFE (*coming forward to the forward break of the quarterdeck*). Sound off!

BILLY. Strange sail one mile off the larboard beam!

CLAGGART (*to* DANSKER). A Frenchman! Get to your station.

RATCLIFFE (*on the quarterdeck ladder*). Mister Duncan! Sound Beat-to-quarters! Clear for action!

DUNCAN (*offstage*). Aye aye, sir!

RATCLIFFE. Gardiner! (*Enter* GARDINER.)

GARDINER. Sir?

RATCLIFFE. Report to the Captain, strange sail on the larboard beam. Then send Payne to the wheel. (*Exit* GARDINER.) Master-at-Arms, send a man to the mast to relay lookout's reports. Inspect battle stations and report to me when they are fully manned.

CLAGGART. Aye aye, sir. (*Exit*)

VOICE (*off*). She's a French frigate! Steering east by south! (*Enter* VERE *and* SEYMOUR.)

VERE. Prepare to make chase. Have your quartermaster steer small.

RATCLIFFE. Aye aye, sir.

(*Enter the* DRUMMER *and sound Beat-to-quarters. Men run on, to gun stations, rigging, crossing stage and off.*)

SEYMOUR. She's too fast for us, sir. We'll never come up with her.

VERE. We are bound to try, though we were sure to fail. And we may smell powder before this chase is over.

CLAGGART (*re-entering*). Battle stations fully manned, sir!

SEYMOUR. May we try a shot at her now?

VERE. She's drawing south. Yes, commence firing, Mr. Seymour.

SEYMOUR. Larboard battery, fire one!

DUNCAN. Fire! (*Fire one gun.*)

VERE. Fire at will!

SEYMOUR. Fire at will!

(*Guns fire dissynchronously.*)

ACT II

SCENE I

*The quarterdeck and part of the maindeck a few minutes before 0800. A high wind.
On the quarterdeck are Lieutenant* WYATT, *Midshipman* REA *and the helmsman,*
STOLL.

REA. I'm glad this watch is over. I'm tired.

WYATT. Make your entry in the log before your relief comes up. Bring it out here
and I'll sign it.

REA. Aye, sir. What was our last position, do you remember?

WYATT. Thirteen ten west, forty-three forty north.

REA. And an easterly breeze.

WYATT. Aye, make it so. That'll make Ratcliffe happy. Last time he had an east wind,
she blew his hat over the side. And put down "Running ground swell."

REA. Aye aye, sir.   (*Exit*)

WYATT. Helmsman, keep her close-hauled.

STOLL. I can't, sir. Too much cloth in the wind.

WYATT. Well hold her close as you can, and let the next watch reef sail if they like.

STOLL. Aye aye, sir. (*Enter* RATCLIFFE.)

WYATT. Morning, Johnny! You're on time!

RATCLIFFE. What's the course?

WYATT. Steady south. Wind's easterly. Glass is dropping.

RATCLIFFE. East wind? Damn it. (*Enter* BYREN, *the relief helmsman.*) By the way,
you forgot to sign the order book.

WYATT. All right. Thanks.

STOLL. I've been relieved, sir. Byren has the helm.

WYATT. Very well. (*Exit* STOLL.) Who's mate of your watch?

RATCLIFFE. The Admiralty midshipman. That lobcock Gardiner, hang him. (*Eight bells.*)

WYATT. Where the devil is he? It's eight. (*Enter* REA *and* GARDINER *separately, meeting.*)

RATCLIFFE. There he comes. He looks happy. That means trouble for some poor devil. (GARDINER *snatches the log out of* REA'S *hands and bounds up to the quarterdeck.*)

REA. I've been relieved, sir. Horatio, Lord Gardiner has the watch.

WYATT. Ah, Midshipman Gardiner. The backbone of the British Navy.

RATCLIFFE. The backside, if you ask me.

WYATT. All right, Rea. You can turn in.   (REA *exits*)

RATCLIFFE. Pity we lost that Frenchman last night. A little action would season the monotony of these interminable watches.

WYATT. Did you ever hear of a ship-of-the-line running down a frigate, even with the wind? Ah, it's a magnificent morning! Thickening overcast, heavy ground swell, a fresh levanter breeze, and you, Johnny, are the Pride of the Morning!

RATCLIFFE. Mmmm. Has the skipper been on deck yet?

WYATT. Not since sunrise. He came up then and paced the deck and stared off east like a sleepwalker. Then went below again without a word.

RATCLIFFE. He thinks too much.

WYATT. Well if you ever make captain, your crew won't have that to complain of, anyway. Am I relieved?

RATCLIFFE. Yes, I relieve you. (*Tosses his cap to* WYATT) Here. Take this below, will you?

WYATT. What? You'll be out of uniform, man. Mister Gardiner wouldn't approve of your standing watch without a hat, would you, Midshipman Gardiner?

GARDINER. Sir, the Articles state that officers on watch . . .

RATCLIFFE. Well hang it, I lost twelve shillings the last time my hat went over the rail, and this is the only other one I've got. To hell with the Articles.

WYATT. Mind your language! It's downright mutinous. Well, don't expect me to stand your watches if you catch your death of cold. Good morning.   (*Exit*)

GARDINER. Midshipman Rea, sir, I don't like to say it, but his log entries are impossible.

RATCLIFFE. Then enter yourself, Mister Gardiner. So are you.

GARDINER. Yes, sir. But I do think he ought to be told . . .

RATCLIFFE. Go find the Captain and report to him the wind's abeam. Respectfully suggest we ought to take in topsails.

GARDINER. Aye aye, sir. (*Goes down stairs.*)

RATCLIFFE. And don't forget to tell him I haven't got a hat.

GARDINER. What's that, sir?

RATCLIFFE. Nothing, sir! You got my order. Dump your ballast and shove off.

GARDINER. I thought you spoke to me, sir.

RATCLIFFE. I avoid that whenever possible. Move!

GARDINER. Yes, sir.

RATCLIFFE. Ye gods, what a brat. Nothing off, helmsman. She's well enough thus.

BYREN. Nothing off, sir.

GARDINER (*nearly bumping into* VERE *as he emerges from cabin, followed by* SEYMOUR *and* HALLAM). Atten-tion!

RATCLIFFE. Good morning, sir.

VERE. Morning, Mister Ratcliffe.

GARDINER (*starting after* VERE, *bumps into* HALLAM). Damn it, man, watch what you're doing!

VERE. Midshipman Gardiner.

GARDINER. Sir?

VERE. How long, pray, have you been in this ship, or any ship?

GARDINER. This is my first cruise, sir.

VERE. Your first cruise. A wartime cruise as well. And you are a midshipman. A midshipman, Mister Gardiner, let me tell you, is neither fish, flesh, nor fowl, and certainly no seaman. You're a saltwater hermaphrodite, Mister Gardiner. And unless you have a mind to be generally known as Spit-kit Gardiner, I recommend more tolerance toward the men. Now, is that clear?

GARDINER. Aye aye, sir!

VERE. Very well, you may carry on.

RATCLIFFE. We've a weather helm, sir, and bow seas.

VERE. Take in topsails, if you please, Mister Ratcliffe.

RATCLIFFE. Aye aye, sir. Mister Duncan!

DUNCAN (*enters*). Aye, sir?

RATCLIFFE. Douse your topsails and topgallants. Haul in the weather braces.

DUNCAN. Aye aye, sir. (*Exit*) Away aloft! Hands by topgallant sheets and halyards!

GARDINER. Aloft there! Keep fast the weather sheets till the yards are down, da . . if you please!

RATCLIFFE. Get aloft yourself, Mister Gardiner, see they do it right, since you're not satisfied.

GARDINER. Sir, the Articles state that . . .

RATCLIFFE. Did you hear me?

GARDINER. Aye aye, sir.   (*Exits up ratlines*)

DUNCAN (*off*). Haul tort!

VERE. You disapprove of Gardiner, Mister Ratcliffe?

RATCLIFFE. He seems to think he's the only midshipman aboard capable of doing anything properly. He's always looking at you as if your hat weren't squared.

VERE. That is an unfortunate simile under the present circumstances.

RATCLIFFE (*caught*). Oh, I—er— Keep her close to the wind, helmsman. Don't fall away!

DUNCAN (*off*). Let go topgallant bowlines!

VERE. I think Gardiner has had enough correction for one day. Call him down to our level, Mister Ratcliffe.

RATCLIFFE. Aye, sir. Mister Gardiner! You may come off your perch now! (BILLY *descends rigging and starts offstage.*) What do you think of our new man Budd, Captain?

SEYMOUR. That boy did a smart piece of work for us last night, sir. He's the nimblest man on the tops I've ever watched. Wyatt wants him for captain of the foretop.

VERE. Very well, let Budd take the post. He certainly deserves it for his actions last night during the chase. I'll speak to him myself.

SEYMOUR. He'll like hearing it from you, sir.

VERE. Hallam, go call Budd, the lad moving forward there. (*Exit* HALLAM. GARDINER *appears, looking sick.*) Well done, Gardiner. You may lay below and draw an extra tot of rum. You look . . . chilly.

GARDINER. Thank you, sir.   (*Exit*)

SEYMOUR. By the way, sir, Budd has been on the Master-at-Arms' report once or twice for some petty misdemeanor. Nothing serious. (*Steps aside with* RATCLIFFE. BILLY *enters, followed by* HALLAM.)

BILLY. You sent for me, sir?

VERE. Yes, Budd. Your division officer recommends you for a post of more responsibility. He thinks you can perform duties of a higher station, and so do I, after last night. So I've agreed that you shall have Williams' place on the foretop.

BILLY. But—Williams is captain of the foretop, sir.

VERE. The station calls for a younger man. Lieutenant Wyatt asked for you, and the spirit you showed last night warrants it. That is a real honor for a man so new on board.

BILLY. The Navy's new to me, Captain, but I hardly know anything else but the sea and ships.

VERE. And how do you like us, now that the awesomeness has worn away a bit?

BILLY. The Navy's a bustling world, sir. Bigger than the *Rights of Man*, and I get lost sometimes. But my mates lend me a hand. Why even Jimmy-Legs—beg pardon, sir, the Master-at-Arms, I mean—he's good to me, too

VERE. The sea and the Navy exact a discipline, but it need not be a harsh one. In some ways I envy the man who dances across the tops and seems to rule the ship and sea below. Up there is a pleach of ropes for you to make a world of. Though winds have their way with tackle of your world, you live at ease against your strength and the round bole of the mast in your back. You are a king up there, while the water curds and frolics at the forefoot. I envy you that stance.

BILLY. You can trust me, Captain.

VERE. I do, boy. Very well, that's all.

BILLY. Aye aye, sir. Thank you, sir, thank you!   (*Runs off*)

VERE. Hallam, find the Master-at-Arms and bid him report to me.

HALLAM. Aye aye, sir.   (*Exit.* SEYMOUR *joins* VERE)

VERE. If I had a son, I'd hope for one like Budd.

SEYMOUR. Aye, sir. Fine boy. He's a force for order in this ship, certainly. I hope his charm's contagious.

VERE. One such is enough. Men cannot stand very much perfection. It's a disease that we stamp out at its first rash showing. (*Enter* CLAGGART. SEYMOUR *withdraws*.) Master-at-Arms, I want to make a change on the Watch, Quarter and Station Bill. I needn't have troubled you about it until later, but I am especially interested in this change.

CLAGGART. The time of day is indifferent to me, sir.

VERE. Williams, present captain of the foretop, is assigned to the afterguard. I am replacing him with Budd.

CLAGGART. William Budd, sir? You do not mean the so-called Handsome Sailor?

VERE Aye, William Budd, the new seaman from the *Rights of Man*.

CLAGGART. I know him, sir.

VERE. Do you find anything unusual in this replacement?

CLAGGART. You must be aware, sir, that he is . . .

VERE. Well? That he is what? I know he's an able seaman.

CLAGGART. Nothing, sir. But I wondered if he were entirely trustworthy. He has been aboard such a brief time.

VERE. Long enough to prove himself to me, and to his shipmates.

CLAGGART. Very good, sir.

VERE. He is captain of the foretop. That is all.

CLAGGART. With your permission, sir. Will there not be some dissatisfaction among the foretopmen who have been aboard much longer than Budd?

VERE. Master-at-Arms: I concern myself with these matters. They are none of your function. Until such time as the senior topmen formally object to Budd for incapacity, he is captain of the foretop. Make it so on the Bill.   (*Exit*)

RATCLIFFE. What are you waiting for, man? Light to dawn? Promotion? You got the order.

CLAGGART. With your permission, sir.

(*As* CLAGGART *goes off,* RATCLIFFE *spits over the rail.*)

SCENE II

Forward part of the deck. Night. Eight bells. A man descends the rigging and goes off. CLAGGART *enters, stands by the hatch for a moment, then exits forward.* BILLY *comes down off watch, drops to the deck and remains in shadow, leaning over the rail, looking seaward.* JENKINS *stealthily and silently comes up from below deck.*

BILLY. Jenkins! What you doing topside . . . (JENKINS *puts his hand over* BILLY'S *mouth.*)

JENKINS. (*in a whisper*). Stow the noise! (*Releases* BILLY.)

BILLY. You're after Mister Claggart, like you said you would!

JENKINS. Well? What about it? You try and stop me?

BILLY. He knows, Jenkins! I tell you, he knows! He's ready for you!

JENKINS. Then by God, I'll oblige him! I been waiting up here every night, waiting for him to come by when it's dark. Now get away and let me do it!

BILLY. No! I won't let you hang yourself!

JENKINS. I don't give a fiddler's damn what happens to me! Move out of my way, mate!

BILLY. No! Give me the knife.

JENKINS. The knife's for Claggart. You're a nice boy, Bill, but I ain't playing with you. You get away below, quick. This game ain't for boys.

BILLY. Damme, no, Jenkins! You'll hang yourself!

JENKINS. Take your hands off! The moon's under, I can do it now! Oh, sweet mother of God, leave me go!

BILLY. No!

JENKINS. Yes, by God!

(JENKINS *strikes* BILLY; *struggle, in which* BILLY *wrests knife from* JENKINS, *and it falls on deck.* BILLY *knocks* JENKINS *down.*)

CLAGGART (*offstage*). What's that noise? Stand where you are! (*Entering*) You again! Well? Explain this pageant.

BILLY. He . . . I had to hit him, sir. He struck at me.

CLAGGART. Mm. And drew that knife on you, too, no doubt.

BILLY. Yes, sir.

CLAGGART. I have been waiting, forward there, for Jenkins. You intercepted him, I take it.

BILLY. I didn't know you were looking for him, sir.

CLAGGART. You shouldn't meddle, my fine young friend, in matters that don't concern you! I was expecting him. (*Enter* DANSKER.) There, help the body up. I do not thank you, boy, for cheating me of the pleasure of his punishment.

WYATT (*offstage*). What's the disturbance there? You, forward on the spardeck!

CLAGGART. Master-at-Arms reports all in order, sir!

WYATT (*offstage*). Stand where you are.

CLAGGART. The sweet and pleasant fellow saved you, Jenkins. But I reserve you still for my own justice in due time. Say nothing to this officer. (*Enter* WYATT.)

WYATT. What's the matter, Master-at-Arms? It's an odd hour for stargazing.

CLAGGART. A slight matter, sir. I found these two men together here on deck, contrary to the Captain's orders. I was sending them below when you called out.

WYATT. Oh, is that all. Carry on, then.

CLAGGART. Aye aye, sir. Now then, get below, both of you. (*Enter* VERE *followed by* HALLAM. *The* DANSKER *goes off.*) Atten-tion!

VERE. Wyatt, what's this mean?

WYATT. Two men on deck without permission, sir.

VERE. Is there no more to this? The story's lame, man. What occurred? (*Silence*) Very well, then. Go along, both of you.

BILLY. Aye aye, sir. Come along, mate.   (*Exits with* JENKINS)

VERE. Your knife, Master-at-Arms?

CLAGGART. William Budd's, sir, I believe.

VERE. Return it to him.   (*Exits with* HALLAM *and* WYATT)

(CLAGGART *raps rail with rattan.* SQUEAK *approaches warily.*)

CLAGGART. Listen carefully; you may make up for your late mistake if you do this smartly. Give Budd just time enough to get to sleep. At four bells wake him. Bring him to the lee forechains. You understand?

SQUEAK. Mister Claggart, sir .   . we done enough to him. He's a good lad, Mister Claggart. Couldn't it be somebody else? Jenkins, maybe?

CLAGGART. So. He's softened your heart too, eh? Do as you're ordered, man, or I'll see your back laid raw with a flogging whip! Remember: I will be watching you. Bring him to the lee forechains. And when you're there . . .

SQUEAK. Dansker. Moving forward.

CLAGGART. Step back, you fool. Wait for me.

(*Exit* SQUEAK. *The* DANSKER *enters.*)

DANSKER. Baby saved you, eh? And you are angry.

CLAGGART. Saved me, you say? From what? I've tried to tempt Jenkins to this blow, so as to break his toplofty spirit with his neck; and I am "saved" by that guileless idiot! He'd turn the other cheek to me, in Christian kindness! Well, there's a second pleasure in striking that same face twice. I can destroy him, too, if I choose to do it!

DANSKER. Crazy, crazy.

CLAGGART. All right, old man, call it madness then. Whatever its name, it will plunder the sweetness from that face, or it will kill us both.

DANSKER. You are afraid of him.

CLAGGART. Afraid? Of Budd? What nonsense is that?

DANSKER. He usurps the crew; they turn from hating you to loving him, and leave you impotent.

CLAGGART. That bastard innocent frighten me! That witless kindness that spills from him has neither force nor aim. Stand out from between us, or you founder together, sink in five hundred fathoms with him, if I want it so!

DANSKER. Aye, then, if you take that tack, let it be both of us. You expect me to sit by and watch your deliberate arm seize him and force him under?

CLAGGART. Why not? You have always done that. I thought your practice was to stay outside. What breeds the saintly knight errant in you?

DANSKER. I am old, but I have some manhood left.

CLAGGART. What can you do? You've drifted with the tide too long, old one. You are as involved as I am now.

DANSKER. So you may say. In this ship a man lives as he can, and finds a way to make life tolerable for himself. I did so. That was a fault. But no longer.

CLAGGART. Stand clear. You haven't courage to cross me.

DANSKER. Eh, I'm not afraid of you; I see your scheme.

CLAGGART. Damn your feeble, ineffectual eyes! (*Striking him; the* DANSKER *falls*) You can see only what I let you see!

DANSKER. Say what you like. I see your scheme; so will Captain if need be.

CLAGGART (*pulling him to his feet*). Take a warning for yourself, old man. And keep away! You are on watch, eh? Well, go back to sleep again, or I'll report you.

(DANSKER *exits.* CLAGGART *watches him go, then violently breaks his rattan and throws the pieces over the side.*)

SCENE II

Forward part of the main deck. Four bells. CLAGGART *stands with one hand on the rail, waiting. After a short pause, hearing a sound, he fades into shadow.* SQUEAK *enters, bending over and running.*

SQUEAK. Hssssssssssst! (BILLY, *sleepy and rubbing his eyes, enters.*)

BILLY. You brought me all the way up here, out of my hammock. Now what do you want?

SQUEAK. I heard you're captain of the foretop, Bill. That right?

BILLY. Aye. What's that to do with you?

SQUEAK. Ah, now you can be more use to your shipmates then ever you was before.

BILLY. What?

SQUEAK. You was impressed, now, weren't you? Well, so was I. We're not the only impressed ones, Billy. There's a gang of us. Could you help . . . at a pinch?

BILLY. What do you mean?

SQUEAK. See here . . . (*Holds up two coins*) Here's two gold guineas for you, Bill. Put in with us. Most of the men aboard are only waiting for a word, and they'll follow you. There's more for you where these come from. What d'you say? If you join us, Bill, there's not a man aboard won't come along! Are you with us? The ship'll be ours when we're ready to take it!

BILLY. Damme, I don't know what you're driving at, but you had better go where you belong! (SQUEAK, *surprised, does not move.* BILLY *springs up*) If you don't start, I'll toss you back over the rail! (SQUEAK *decamps.* BILLY *watches him and starts off himself.* DANSKER, *offstage, calls out.*)

DANSKER. Hallo, what's the matter? (*Enters*) Ah, Beauty, is it you again? Something must have been the matter, for you stammered. (CLAGGART *appears and comes forward.*)

CLAGGART. You seem to favor the maindeck, Billy Budd. What brings you topside at this hour, man, against my orders and the Captain's?

BILLY. I . . . found an afterguardsman in our part of the ship here, and I bid him be off where he belongs.

DANSKER. And is that all you did about it, boy?

BILLY. Aye, Dansker, nothing more.

CLAGGART. A strange sort of hour to police the deck. Name the afterguardsman.

BILLY. I . . . can't say, Mister Claggart. I couldn't see him clear enough.

DANSKER. Don't be a fool, speak up, accuse him.

CLAGGART. Well?

BILLY. I can't say, sir.

CLAGGART. You refuse? Then get below, and stay where you belong.

BILLY. Aye aye, sir. Good night, sir. Good night, Dansker. *(Exit)*

CLAGGART. I'm glad you saw this mutinous behavior.

DANSKER. Your crazy brain squeezes out false conclusions. He has done nothing except find you out, though he's too innocent to know it.

CLAGGART. I am not hoodwinked by his weak excuse. What else would he be doing at this hour, but fanning rebel tempers like his own?

DANSKER. I stood in the shadows forward when your pander Squeak slipped by me, running from this place. You set him on, on purpose to trap Billy.

CLAGGART. And I will do that, old man. But you will say nothing about it; see you don't. *(Enter* VERE *followed by* HALLAM.*)*

VERE. Well, Master-at-Arms? You stand long watches.

CLAGGART. Sir. May I take the liberty of reserving my explanation for your private ear. I believe your interest in this matter would incline you to prefer some privacy.

VERE *(to* DANSKER *and* HALLAM*)*. Leave us. Hallam, stand within hail. *(*DANSKER *and* HALLAM *go off)* Well? What is it you wish to say, Master-at-Arms?

CLAGGART. During my rounds this night, I have seen enough to convince me that one man aboard, at least, is dangerous; especially in a ship which musters some who took a guilty part in the late serious uprisings . . .

VERE. You may spare a reference to that.

CLAGGART. Your pardon, sir. Quite lately I have begun to notice signs of some sort of movement secretly afoot, and prompted by the man in question. I thought myself not warranted, so long as this suspicion was only indistinct, in reporting it. But recently . . .

VERE. Come to the point, man.

CLAGGART. Sir, I deeply feel the cruel responsibility of making a report involving such serious consequences to the sailor mainly concerned. But God forbid, sir, that this ship should suffer the experience of the Nore.

VERE. Never mind that! You say there is one dangerous man. Name him.

CLAGGART. William Budd, the . . captain of the foretop.

VERE. William Budd?

CLAGGART. The same, sir. But for all his youth and appealing manners, a secret, vicious lad.

VERE. How, vicious?

CLAGGART. He insinuates himself into the good will of his mates so that they will at least say a word for him, perhaps even take action with him, should it come to that. With your pardon, sir; you note but his fair face; under that there lies a man-trap.

VERE (*after a pause*). Master-at-Arms, I intend to test your accusation here and now. Hallam! (*Enter* HALLAM.)

HALLAM. Aye, sir.

VERE. Find Budd, the foretopman. Manage to tell him out of earshot that he is wanted here. Keep him in talk yourself. Go along.

HALLAM. Aye aye, sir. (*Exit*)

VERE (*angry and perturbed*). Do you come to me with such a foggy tale, Master-at-Arms? As to William Budd, cite me an act, or spoken word of his, confirming what you here in general charge against him. Wait; weigh what you speak. Just now, and in this case, there is the yardarm end for false witness.

CLAGGART. I understand, sir. Tonight, when on my rounds, discovering Budd's hammock was unused, I combed the ship, and found him in conclave with several growlers; men, who, like himself, spread unrest and rebellion in the crew. They were collected here, near the lee forechains, and when I ordered them below, young Budd and others threatened me, and swore they'd drop me, and some officers they hate, overboard, some misty night. Should you, sir, desire substantial proof, it is not far.

(*Enter* HALLAM, *followed by* BILLY.)

VERE. Hallam, stand apart and see that we are not disturbed. (HALLAM *exits.*) And now, Master-at-Arms, tell this man to his face what you told me of him.

CLAGGART (*moving near to* BILLY, *and looking directly at him*). Certainly, sir. I said this man, this William Budd, acting so out of angry resentment against impressment and his officers, against this ship, this Service, and the King, breeds in the crew a spirit of rebellion against the officers, the mates, and me, urging some outrage like the late revolt. I myself have seen and heard him speak with manifest malingerers and men who growl of mistreatment, harshness, unfair pay and similar complaints. I say this man threatened his officers with murder, and was bent tonight on urging other men to act concertedly in mutiny. I have nothing further to say, sir.

(BILLY *tries to speak, but can make only incoherent sounds. He seems to be in pain from the contortions of his face and the gurgling which is all he can effect for speech.*)

VERE. Speak, man, speak! Defend yourself! (*Remembering* BILLY'S *impediment, goes to him and puts a hand on his shoulder reassuringly.*) There is no hurry, boy. Take your time, take your time.

(After agonized dumb gesturing and stammering, increased by VERE'S *kindness,* BILLY'S *arm hits out at* CLAGGART. CLAGGART *staggers, falls, lies still.)*

VERE. Stand back, man! It was a lie, then! (BILLY, *shaking, only stares at the body.* VERE *raises the body to a sitting position. Since* CLAGGART *remains inert,* VERE *lowers him again slowly, then rises.* BILLY *tries again to speak, without success; he is crying and badly frightened.)* No need to speak now, Billy. Hallam! (*Enter* HALLAM.) Tell the Surgeon I wish to see him here at once. And bid Mister Seymour report to my cabin without delay. (*To* BILLY) Retire to the stateroom aft. Remain there till I summon you. (BILLY *exits.* VERE *waits, turning once to stare at* CLAGGART'S *body. Enter the* SURGEON.) Surgeon, tell me how it is with him. (SURGEON *bends over* CLAGGART *briefly, then looks up in surprise.*) Come, we must dispatch. Go now. I shall presently call a drumhead court to try the man who out of God's own instinct dropped him there. Tell the lieutenants that a foretopman has, in an accidental fury, killed this man. Inform the Captain of Marines as well, and charge them to keep the matter to themselves. (SURGEON *exits.*) The divine judgment of Ananias! Struck dead by the Angel of God . . . and I must judge the Angel. Can I save him? Have I that choice?

ACT III

SCENE I

CAPTAIN VERE'S *cabin, a quarter of an hour later.* VERE *and* SEYMOUR.

SEYMOUR. Budd beat a man to death! What had he done?

VERE. Lied again: lied to Budd's face, hoping to kill him by it. Oh, the boy was tempted to it past endurance.

SEYMOUR. False witness has its penalty, sir. Budd has set our justice right.

VERE. Aye, too right. This natural, right act, done in an instinct's fever of recognition, was late and fatal.

SEYMOUR. What are you going to do, Captain? Isn't this last lie of the Master-at-Arms the very act you were waiting for, so as to let the law destroy him, as you said? He should have suffered at the yardarm if Billy hadn't killed him.

VERE. Yes. He should. But by fair process of authority. Budd has prevented that, and turned the law against himself.

SEYMOUR. You can't condemn the boy for answering with his arm for lack of words! The motive was clearly justified.

VERE. Aye, but was the act? For God's sake try, try to convince me I am wrong!

SEYMOUR. This Master-at-Arms, you knew him for a liar, a vicious dog.

VERE. A dog's obeyed in office. Claggart was authority.

SEYMOUR. Then authority's an evil!

VERE. It often is. But it commands, and no man is its equal, not Billy, nor you, nor I. It will strike us down, and rightly, if we resist it.

SEYMOUR. Rightly! What power gives evil its authority? We should thank God the man's dead, and the world well rid of that particular devil.

VERE. Our life has ways to hedge its evil in. No one must go above them; even innocents. Laws of one kind or other shape our course from birth to death. These are the laws pronouncing Billy's guilt; Admiralty codes are merely shadows of them.

SEYMOUR. That's tyranny, not law, forcing conformity to wrongs, giving the victory to the devil himself!

VERE. I thought so once. But without this lawful tyranny, what should we have but worse tyranny of anarchy and chaos? So aboard this man-of-war. Oh, if I were a man alone, manhood would declare for Billy.

SEYMOUR. Then do it. Put your strength and your authority behind Budd, and let him go.

VERE. When I think I could have watched him grow in comely wholesomeness of manhood . . . all lost now. What could have been, quenched in evil, swept out by that undertow.

SEYMOUR. It's more than anyone can have to answer for, Captain; to his peers, or to his God. Let him go free and try on mortal flesh! Will you urge a noose for him, marked like a common felon, and that devil still to have his wish, killing the boy at last?

VERE. Can I do otherwise? I'd give my life to save his, if I could.

SEYMOUR. It's in your hands, Captain. Only you can help him now.

VERE. Billy, Billy. What have we done to you? (*Knock*) Yes, come in. (*Enter* HALLAM.)

HALLAM. Lieutenants Ratcliffe and Wyatt, sir.

VERE. Let them come in. (*Enter* RATCLIFFE *and* WYATT.)

SEYMOUR. You both know why you've been summoned hither?

WYATT. Yes, sir.

RATCLIFFE. Aye, sir, in a general sort of way.

SEYMOUR. Then take your chairs. Ratcliffe. You here, Wyatt. You are appointed members of a court-martial convened under extraordinary circumstances by Captain Vere. I am Senior Member, and I declare this court open. (WYATT, RATCLIFFE, *and* SEYMOUR *sit*. VERE *remains standing, apart*.) Sentry, bring the prisoner in. (HALLAM *salutes and exits*.) As you know, the Master-at-Arms has been killed by the foretopman, Budd. Whether by accident or by design, and whether the act shall carry the penalty of death or no, you are to decide. There is only one witness, Captain Vere. I shall call upon him to give his deposition as soon as the sentry brings in the prisoner. (*An uneasy silence*.)

WYATT. Budd wouldn't kill a minnow without good reason.

RATCLIFFE. What did the . . .

SEYMOUR. I had rather you did not express an opinion until after you have heard the evidence. (*Another awkward silence.* HALLAM *finally enters with* BILLY.) Sentry, stand outside. (*Exit* HALLAM.) You may sit down.

BILLY. Th-th-thank you, sir.

SEYMOUR. Captain: will you be good enough to give us your account?

VERE (*turning toward them*). I speak not as your Captain, but as witness before this court. The Master-at-Arms early this morning detailed to me an account of mutinous sentiments expressed by Budd, and in particular, spoke of overhearing a specific conversation last night on the mid-watch. He alleged that Budd offered him violence and threatened further violence against the officers.

WYATT. Budd a mutineer! That's absurd, he's the best-liked man . . .

RATCLIFFE. Did the Master-at-Arms specify who the other malcontents were, sir?

VERE. He did not. He said merely that he was in possession of substantial proof of his accusation.

SEYMOUR. With your permission, sir . . . Budd, did you speak with anyone in the Master-at-Arms' hearing last night?

BILLY. I . . . spoke a little . . . with the Dansker, sir.

WYATT. Who is the Dansker?

BILLY. He's just called the Dansker, sir. He's always called so.

RATCLIFFE. I know him. A mainmast sailor.

SEYMOUR. Sentry. (*Enter* HALLAM.)

HALLAM. Sir.

SEYMOUR. Do you know a mainmast sailor referred to as "the Dansker"?

HALLAM. Aye, sir.

SEYMOUR. Go on deck and find him. Let him know apart that he is wanted here, and arrange it so that none of the other people notice his withdrawing. See you do it tactfully. I want no curiosity aroused among the men.

HALLAM. Aye aye, sir.   (*Exit*)

SEYMOUR. Please go on.

VERE. I sent at once for Budd. I ordered the Master-at-Arms to be present at this interview, to make his accusation to Budd's face.

RATCLIFFE. May I ask what was the prisoner's reaction on being confronted by the Master-at-Arms?

VERE. I perceived no sign of uneasiness in his demeanor. I believe he smiled.

RATCLIFFE. And for the Master-at-Arms?

VERE. When I directed him to repeat his accusation, he faced Budd and did so.

WYATT. Did Budd reply?

VERE. He tried to speak, but could not frame his words.

SEYMOUR. And then, sir?

VERE. He answered with blows, and his accuser fell. . . . It was apparent at once that the attack was fatal, but I summoned the Surgeon to verify the fact. (*Turns away.*)

SEYMOUR (*to* BILLY). You have heard Captain Vere's account. Is it, or is it not, as he says?

BILLY. Captain Vere tells the truth. It is just as Captain Vere says, but it is not as the Master-at-Arms said. I have eaten the King's bread, and I am true to the King.

VERE. I believe you, boy.

BILLY. God knows . . . I . . . thank you, sir.

SEYMOUR. Was there any malice between you and the Master-at-Arms?

BILLY. I bore no malice against the Master-at-Arms. I'm sorry he is dead. I did not mean to kill him. If I'd found my tongue, I would not have struck him. But he lied foully to my face, and I . . . had to say . . . something . . . and I could only say it . . . with a blow. God help me.

SEYMOUR. One question more—you tell us that what the Master-at-Arms said against you was a lie. Now, why should he have lied with such obvious malice, when you have declared that there was no malice between you? (BILLY *looks appealingly at* VERE.) Did you hear my question?

BILLY. I . . . I . . .

VERE. The question you put to him comes naturally enough. But can he rightly answer it? Or anyone else, unless, indeed, it be he who lies within there. (*Knock and enter immediately* HALLAM.)

HALLAM. The mainmast man, sir.

SEYMOUR. Send him in. (HALLAM *nods off and the* DANSKER *enters.* HALLAM *withdraws, closing door.*) State your name and station.

DANSKER. I have no name. I'm called the Dansker, that's all I know. Mainmast man.

SEYMOUR. You have been summoned in secrecy to appear as a witness before this court, of which I am Senior Member. I may not at this time disclose to you the nature of the offense being tried. However, the offender is William Budd, foretopman. (*Pause*) Do you consent to give this court your testimony, though ignorant of the case at trial, and further, to keep in strictest confidence all that passes here?

DANSKER. Aye.

SEYMOUR (*pushes forward a Bible*). Do you so swear?

DANSKER (*touching the Bible*). I do.

SEYMOUR. Then this is my question. In your opinion, is there malice between Budd and the Master-at-Arms?

DANSKER. Aye.

VERE (*wheeling around*). How!

SEYMOUR. Explain your statement.

DANSKER. How should he not have hated him?

SEYMOUR. Be plain, man. We do not deal in riddles here.

DANSKER. Master-at-Arms bore malice towards a grace he could not have. There was no reason for it.

RATCLIFFE. In other words, this malice was one-sided?

DANSKER. Aye.

RATCLIFFE. And you cannot explain how it arose?

DANSKER. Master-at-Arms hated Billy . . .

SEYMOUR. One moment. I notice that you have been using the past tense in your testimony. Why?

DANSKER. I look around and sense finality here.

WYATT. You cannot explain further the cause of Claggart's hate for Budd?

DANSKER. Master-at-Arms made his world in his own image. Pride was his demon, and he kept it strong by others' fear of him. Billy could not imagine such a nature, saw nothing but a lonely man, strange, but a man still, nothing to be feared. So Claggart, lest his world be proven false, planned Billy's death. The final reason is beyond my thinking.

VERE. Aye, that is thoughtfully put. There is a mystery in iniquity. But it seems to me, Seymour, that the point we seek here is hardly material.

SEYMOUR. Aye, sir. Very well, you may go.

DANSKER. One thing more. Since this Master-at-Arms first came on board from God knows where, I have seen his shadow lengthen along the deck, and being under it, I was afraid. Whatever happened here, I am in part to blame—more than this lad. (*To* BILLY) I am an old man, Billy. You—try to—forgive me.   (*Exit*)

SEYMOUR. Have you any further questions to put to the accused?

RATCLIFFE. No.

WYATT. None.

SEYMOUR. William Budd, if you have anything further to say for yourself, say it now.

BILLY (*after glance at* VERE). I have said all, sir.

SEYMOUR. Sentry. (*Enter* HALLAM.) Remove the prisoner to the after compartment. (HALLAM *and* BILLY *exit. A long pause*) Have you anything to say, Ratcliffe?

RATCLIFFE. Yes, sir. Claggart was killed because Budd couldn't speak. In that sense, that he stammers, he's a cripple. You don't hang a man for that, for speaking the only way he could.

WYATT. If you condemn him, it's the same thing as condoning the apparent lie the Master-at-Arms clearly told. I'd have struck him, too. The boy is clearly innocent, struck him in self-defense.

RATCLIFFE. Aye. I'm ready to acquit him now.

SEYMOUR. Good. Then we can reach a verdict at once.

VERE. Hitherto I have been a witness at this trial, no more. And I hesitate to interfere, except that at this clear crisis you ignore one fact we cannot close our eyes to.

SEYMOUR. With your pardon, sir, as Senior Member of this court, I must ask if you speak now as our commanding officer or as a private man.

VERE. As convening authority, Seymour. I summoned this court, and I must review its findings and approve them before passing them on to the Admiralty.

SEYMOUR. Aye, sir, that is your right.

VERE. No right. Which of us here has rights? Is is my duty, and I must perform it. Budd has killed a man—his superior officer.

SEYMOUR. We have found a verdict, sir.

VERE. I know that, Seymour. Your verdict sets him free, and so would I wish to do. But are we free to choose as we would do if we were private citizens? The Admiralty has its code. Do you suppose it cares who Budd is? Who you and I are?

SEYMOUR. We don't forget that, sir. But surely Claggart's tales were simply lies. We've established that.

VERE. Aye. But the Nore and Spithead were brute facts, and must not come again. The men were starved out before, but if they should think we are afraid . . .

RATCLIFFE. Captain, how could they? They certainly know Budd is no mutineer.

WYATT. Of course not. Since he came on board, he's done more to keep the crew in hand than any of us.

SEYMOUR. That's true. The men took naturally to him.

VERE. As officers we are concerned to keep this ship effective as a weapon. And the law says what we must do in such a case as this. Come now, you know the facts, and the Mutiny Act's provisions. At sea, in time of war, an impressed man strikes his superior officer, and the blow is fatal. The mere blow alone would hang him, at least according to the Act. Well then, the men on board know that as well as you and I. And we acquit him. They have sense, they know the proper penalty to follow, and yet it does not follow.

SEYMOUR. But they know Budd, sir, and Claggart too, I daresay. Would they not applaud the decision that frees Budd? They would thank us.

WYATT. String him to a yard, and they'll turn round and rescue him, and string us up instead!

RATCLIFFE. Aye, that's a point. It's twice as dangerous to hang the boy as it would be to let him go. If there's a mutinous temper in the crew, condemning Budd would surely set it off.

VERE. That is possible. Whatever step we take, the risk is great; but it is ours. That is what makes us officers. Yet if in fear of what our office demands we shirk our duty, we only play at war, at being men. If by our lawful rigor mutiny comes, there is no blame for us. But if in fear, miscalled a kind of mercy, we pardon Budd against specific order, and then the crew revolts, how culpable and weak our verdict would appear! The men on board know what our case is, how we are haunted by the Spithead risings. Have they forgotten how the panic spread through England? No. Your clemency would be accounted fear, and they would say we flinch from practising a lawful rigor lest new outbreaks be provoked. What a shame to us! And what a deadly blow to discipline!

RATCLIFFE. I concede that, sir. But this case is exceptional, and pity, if we are men, is bound to move us, Captain.

VERE. So am I moved. Yet we cannot have warm hearts betraying heads that should be cool. In such a case ashore, an upright judge does not allow the pleading tears of women to touch his nature. Here at sea, the heart, the female in a man, weeps like a woman. She must be ruled out, hard though it be. (*Pause*) Still silent? Very well, I see that something in all your downcast faces seems to urge that not alone the heart moves hesitancy. Conscience, perhaps. The private conscience moves you.

WYATT. Aye, that's it, sir. How can we condemn this man and live at peace again within ourselves? We have our standards; ethics, if you like.

VERE. Challenge your scruples! They move as in a dusk. Come, do they import something like this: if we are bound to judge, regardless of palliating circumstances, the death of Claggart as the prisoner's deed, then does that deed appear a capital crime whereof the penalty is mortal? But can we adjudge to summary and shameful death a fellow creature innocent before God, and whom we feel to be so? Does that state the case rightly?

SEYMOUR. That is my feeling, sir.

VERE. You all feel, I am sure, that the boy in effect is innocent; that what he did was from an unhappy stricture of speech that made him speak with blows. And I believe that, too; believe as you do, that he struck his man down, tempted beyond endurance. Acquit him, then, you say, as innocent?

RATCLIFFE. Exactly! Oh, I know the Articles prescribe death for what Budd has done, but that . . .

WYATT. Oh, stow the Articles! They don't account for such a case as this. You yourself say Budd is innocent.

VERE. In intent, Wyatt, in intent.

WYATT. Does that count for nothing? His whole attitude, his motive, count for nothing? If his intent . . .

VERE. The intent or non-intent of Budd is nothing to the purpose. In a court more merciful than martial it would extenuate, and shall, at the last Assizes, set him free. But here we have these alternatives only: condemn or let go.

SEYMOUR. But it seems to me we've got to consider the problem as a moral one, sir, despite the fact that we're not moralists. When Claggart told you his lie, the case immediately went beyond the scope of military justice.

VERE. I, too, feel that. But do these gold stripes across our arms attest that our allegiance is to Nature?

RATCLIFFE. To our country, sir.

VERE. Aye, Ratcliffe; to the King. And though the sea, which is inviolate Nature primeval, though it be the element whereon we move and have our being as sailors, is our official duty hence to Nature? No. So little is that true that we resign our freedom when we put this on. And when war is declared, are we, the fighters commissioned to destroy, consulted first?

WYATT. Does that deny us the right to act like men? We're not trying a murderer, a dockside cut-throat!

VERE. The gold we wear shows that we serve the King, the Law. What does it matter that our acts are fatal to our manhood, if we serve as we are forced to serve? What bitter salt leagues move between our code and God's own judgments! We are conscripts, every one, upright in this uniform of flesh. There is no truce to war born in the womb. We fight at command.

WYATT. All I know is that I can't sit by and see Budd hanged!

VERE. I say we fight by order, by command of our superiors. And if our judgments approve the war, it is only coincidence. And so it is with all our acts. So now, would it be so much we ourselves who speak as judges here, as it would be martial law operating through us? For that law, and for its rigor, we are not responsible. Our duty lies in this: that we are servants only.

RATCLIFFE. The Admiralty doesn't want service like that. What good would it do? Who'd profit by Budd's death?

WYATT. You want to make us murderers!

SEYMOUR. Wyatt! Control yourself!

VERE. What is this vessel that you serve in, Wyatt, an ark of peace? Go count her guns; then tell your conscience to lie quiet, if you can.

RATCLIFFE. But that is war. This would be downright killing!

SEYMOUR. It's all war, Ratcliffe; war to the death, for all of us.

VERE. You see that, Seymour? That this war began before our time?

SEYMOUR. And will end long after it.

VERE. Here we have the Mutiny Act for justice. No child can own a closer tie to parent than can that Act to what it stems from: War. This is a wartime cruise and in this ship are Englishmen who fight against their wills, perhaps against their conscience, 'pressed by war into the service of the King. Though we as fellow creatures understand their lot, what does it matter to the officer, or to the enemy? The French will cut down conscripts in the same swath with volunteers, and we will do as much for them. War has no business with anything but surfaces. War's child, the Mutiny Act, is featured like the father.

RATCLIFFE. Couldn't we mitigate the penalty if we convict him?

VERE. No, Ratcliffe. The penalty is prescribed.

RATCLIFFE. I'd like to think it over, Captain. I'm not sure.

VERE. I repeat, then, that while we ponder and you hesitate over anxieties I confess to sharing, the enemy comes nearer. We must act, and quickly. The French close in on us; the crew will find out shortly what has happened. Our consciences are private matters, Ratcliffe. But we are public men, controlling life and death within this world at sea. Tell me whether or not in our positions we dare let our consciences take precedence of the code that makes us officers and calls this case to trial.

RATCLIFFE (after a pause; quietly). No, sir.

WYATT. Can you stand Budd's murder on your conscience?

SEYMOUR. Wyatt! Hold your tongue!

WYATT (jumping up). I say let him go!

SEYMOUR. Sit down, sir!

VERE. Let him speak.

WYATT. I won't bear a hand to hang a man I know is innocent! My blood's not cold enough. I can't give the kind of judgment you want to force on us! I ask to be excused from sitting upon this court.

SEYMOUR. Do you know what you're saying? Sit down and hold your tongue, man!

VERE. The kind of judgment I ask of you is only this, Wyatt: that you recognize your function in this ship. I believe you know it quite as well as we, yet you rebel. Can't you see that you must first strip off the uniform you wear, and after that your flesh, before you can escape the case at issue here? Decide you must, Wyatt. Oh, you may be excused and wash your hands of it, but someone must decide. We are the law; law orders us to act, and shows us how. Do you imagine Seymour, or Ratcliffe here, or I, would not save this boy if we could see a way consistent with our duties? Acquit Budd if you can. God knows I wish I could. If in your mind as well as in your heart, you can say freely that his life is not forfeit to the law we serve, reason with us! Show us how to save him without putting aside our function. Or if you can't do that, teach us to put by our responsibility and not betray ourselves. Can you do this? Speak, man, speak! Show us how! Save him, Wyatt, and you save us all. (WYATT slowly sits down.) You recognize the logic of the choice I force upon you. But do not think me pitiless in thus demanding sentence on a luckless boy. I feel as you do for him. But even more, I think there is a grace of soul within him that shall forgive the law we bind him with, and pity us, stretched on the cross of choice. (*Turns away.*)

SEYMOUR. Well, gentlemen. Will you decide. (*Officers write their verdicts on paper before them, and hand them to* SEYMOUR, *who rises, draws his dirk and places it on the table, pointing forward*) He is condemned, sir. Shall we appoint the dawn?

SCENE II

CAPTAIN VERE'S *cabin, 0400. Ship's bell strikes offstage.* VERE *sitting alone at his desk. Knock at the door.*

VERE. Come in. (*Enter* SEYMOUR.) Oh, it's Seymour.

SEYMOUR. It's eight bells, Captain.

VERE. What's the hour of sunrise?

SEYMOUR. Four fifty-two, sir.

VERE. Eight bells. And one bell at four-thirty. Odd and even numbers caught between two hands. Budd shall not live to hear the odd made even or wrong made right. —Call all hands to quarters at four-thirty.

SEYMOUR. Aye aye, Captain. (*Turns irresolutely.*)

VERE. The wind has slackened, I think. How is the glass?

SEYMOUR. It's risen slightly. Sea has flattened out.

VERE. Fair weather after foul . . . it's all nature, nature and law. How exigent are these Mediterranean climates of the heart, and temperate zones of mind!

SEYMOUR. Have you been here all night, sir?

VERE. All night, Seymour . . . all my life moving between dark and dark. It has been a long night, but day will be quick and deadly on the mainyard. D'you think, Seymour, a man can forgive a wrong done of the heart's own election?

SEYMOUR. Most people are decent enough. You can forgive them trespasses.

VERE. No, by God. There's wickedness alive. It's dead now in one man, but it's alive to feel and smell at night . . . Seymour, go below. Get Budd and bring him here.

SEYMOUR. But Captain . . .

VERE. Do as you're told. Get Budd and bring him here. (SEYMOUR *exits.* VERE *sits motionless for a few moments, then rises and goes to the cabin door*) Sentry.

HALLAM. Yes, sir?

VERE. Who has the deck this watch?

HALLAM. Mister Ratcliffe, Captain.

VERE. Very well. (*Pause*) Sentry!

HALLAM. Sir?

VERE. When Mister Seymour has returned, admit him right way.

HALLAM. Aye aye, Captain.

VERE. The wind's still sharp. You must be cold there, Hallam. Go to the leeward side. I'll be responsible.

HALLAM. Thank you, sir. This is the coldest hour now, just before sunrise.

VERE (*closes door, returns slowly to his desk*). The lamp holds steady when the vessel heels. Does the law hang straight in crooked lives? It burns, and shapes nothing but shadows here, plumb in the twisting cabin of the mind. (*Footsteps, voices.* VERE *turns to door. Enter* SEYMOUR, BILLY *and* HALLAM.) Take off the manacles. (HALLAM *frees* BILLY.)

SEYMOUR (*to* HALLAM). Outside, man. Bear a hand   (*Exits wtih* HALLAM)

VERE. Sit down. No, it's better that I stand.

BILLY. I was thinking, locked up below there . . . the Captain knows the rights of this. He'll save me if it's right. Then you sent for me. Is there hope for me, Captain?

VERE. Billy, what hope is there?

BILLY. Tell me why. I only want to understand.

VERE. How young you still are, Billy! Oh, I can tell you this: nothing is lost of anything that happens. I have given you the judgment of the world . . . deadly constraint . . . a length of hemp and a yardarm. I have done this to you, no one else.

BILLY. I can't get the rights of all that's happened.

VERE. There's not much right, Billy. Only necessity. You and Claggart broke man's compromise with good and evil, and both of you must pay the penalty.

BILLY. Penalty? What for? Would anyone make laws just to be broken by fellows like me?

VERE. Aye, boy. You have learned this late. Most of us find out early and trim to a middle course.

BILLY. Do you mean . . . it's better to be like that?

VERE. Better as this world goes. When a man is born, he takes a guilt upon him, I can't say how or why. And life takes its revenge on those who hurt its pride with innocence.

BILLY. Do you think Claggart knew it would come to this?

VERE. He knew he would kill you, and he died to gain that end. But if you trust me, he'll not win entirely.

BILLY. How could he hate me like that?

VERE. The world we breathe is love and hatred both, but hatred must not win the victory.

BILLY. Claggart is dead. Now I'm to hang. Doesn't that show the law is wrong, when it can't choose between him and me?

VERE. Yes, it's all wrong, all wrong.

BILLY. I don't know, Captain. I never was a hand to wonder about things, but now I think that maybe there's a kind of cruelty in people that's just as much a part of them as kindness, say, or honesty, or m-m-m . . . I can't find words, I guess, Captain.

VERE. There are no words. We are all prisoners of deadly forms that are made to break us to their measure. Nothing has power to overcome them, except forgiveness. . . . Can you forgive what I have done?

BILLY. I *can* trust you, can't I? *Can* you show me it's all right, my being . . .

VERE (*turns away; a long pause*). It's nearly dawn, lad. In the Spanish villages they're lighting fires.

BILLY. I'm not afraid, sir. (*Steps toward* VERE) It's getting light.

VERE. There's no time for either of us left. Go, take the morning. God knows you have the right to it. And when you are on the mainyard, think of me, and pray for those who must make choices. Hallam. (*Enter* HALLAM *in doorway.*) Take Budd into your charge. (BILLY *and* HALLAM *go out.*) Time has run out.

SCENE III

Main deck aft. Drum-to-formation. Crew forming up. WYATT, *Midshipmen* GARDINER *and* REA.

WYATT. Bear a hand. Form the men up in ranks.

GARDINER. Aye, sir. All right, you! Close ranks! Move up, Stoll. That's better. Talbot, square your hat. Form up straight there, damn it! (*Drum. Men come to attention.*)

WYATT. Division commanders report!

VOICE (*off*). Carpenters and gunners, present or accounted for, sir!

VOICE (*off*). Marine Detachment, present or accounted for, sir!

VOICE (*off*). Afterguard, present or accounted for, sir!

GARDINER. Fore, main and mizzentopmen . . . one absentee!

WYATT. All hands will stand by to witness punishment! Stand easy.

VOICES (*off*). Stand easy! (WYATT *walks away from men. Murmur in ranks.*)

KINCAID. Where the devil is Billy? He wasn't in his hammock when they piped us up.

O'DANIEL. He'll be getting himself in trouble if he don't fall in.

KINCAID. Who the hell they punishing, and what for?

JENKINS. It's got to be flogging, or they wouldn't have us all up here.

KINCAID. Vere never flogs anybody. And there ain't no gratings up.

DANSKER. They flog men at noon. The early morning's for hanging.

KINCAID. Hanging! (*The word travels back.*) Who? What for?

O'DANIEL. The skipper, he don't confide in me no more.

KINCAID. I thought they waited till they got ashore before they hanged a man.

DANSKER. Not in wartime.

JENKINS. He goes up them ratlines, out on the yard, they slips a noose around his neck, and then he jumps and hangs himself.

O'DANIEL. They'd have the devil's work getting O'Daniel to jump.

KINCAID. It's jump, or get pushed.

JENKINS. Where's Claggart? God, you don't suppose it's Claggart! Oh, Judas, let it be that fishblooded nark!

KINCAID. Not him. He's too smart, he is.

JENKINS. Where is he, then? He ain't here.

DANSKER. He is here.

KINCAID. Where? I don't see him.

DANSKER. He is here.

KINCAID. Ah . . . you're balmy, old man.

(*Enter* VERE, SEYMOUR, RATCLIFFE *and the* SURGEON. *Drum sounds Attention.*)

WYATT (*to* SEYMOUR). Ship's company present to witness execution, sir.

SEYMOUR. Very well. (*To* VERE) Ship's company present to witness execution, sir. (VERE *nods.*)

SEYMOUR (*to* WYATT). Lieutenant Wyatt, have the prisoner brought forward.

WYATT. Aye, aye, sir. (*Marches to wing*) Sentries, bring forward the prisoner. (*Marches back to his post.*)

(*Enter* BILLY *with two sentries. Astonished murmur through the crew, who momentarily break ranks.*)

WYATT. No talking in ranks! (*Continued restless movement and murmuring*) Form up!

GARDINER. You men are at attention!

WYATT (*over subdued muttering*). You hear me? Silence in ranks!

(Silence. Sentries lead BILLY *to the foot of the ropes.* SEYMOUR *looks at* VERE, *who nods.* SEYMOUR *steps forward and reads.)*

SEYMOUR. Proceedings of the court-martial held aboard *H.M.S. Indomitable* on the eighth August, 1798. Convened under the authority of Edward Fairfax Vere, Senior Captain, Royal Navy, and composed of the First Officer, the Sailing Master, and the First Lieutenant of said vessel. In the case of William Budd, foretopman, Royal Navy. While attached and so serving in the aforesaid vessel, he did, on the eighth day of August, 1798, strike and kill his superior officer, one John Claggart, Master-at-Arms, Royal Navy.

(Crew breaks out uneasily, astonished, talking excitedly.)

JENKINS. Billy! Did you, boy? ⎤
VOICE. Good lad!   ⎥   *All*
VOICE. Serves him proper!   ⎥ *together*
KINCAID. Hi, Billy! Hurrah!   ⎦

WYATT. Quiet! Silence, you men! Form up!

GARDINER. Stand at attention, hang you! Silence in the ranks!

WYATT. Do you hear? *(Excited muttering, low voices.)*

SEYMOUR. You will be silent and remain at strict attention until dismissed. *(Silence)* . . . Master-at-Arms, Royal Navy. Therefore, the court sentences the afore-mentioned William Budd, foretopman, Royal Navy, to die by hanging on the first watch of the day following these proceedings. By authority of his Gracious Majesty George Rex and Alan Napier, Viscount Kelsey, First Sea Lord. Signed, Philip Seymour, Senior Member.

(During the last phrases of the reading, the crew, upon hearing the sentence, breaks out again, some stepping forward, shouting; they are in an ugly temper.)

VOICES. No he don't!   ⎤
   Not if I know it!   ⎥
   Hang the jemmies instead, I say! ⎥
   You ain't hanging Billy,   ⎥   *All*
   Not Billy, you bloody swineheads! ⎥ *together*
   Not him, by Christ! damn your eyes! ⎥
   Let them dance on a rope's end!   ⎦

WYATT. Stand back! Sentries, guard your prisoner, if you have to fire!

GARDINER. Stand back, you damned clods! Keep back!

SEYMOUR *(steps forward)*. Silence there! You will resume discipline instantly! Be warned. *(Waits a silent moment. Men stop in disordered formation.)* Stand back into ranks.

GARDINER. Form up again, quick about it now! *(There is a surly movement into irregular lines.)*

SEYMOUR (*warily resuming procedure*). Prisoner, have you anything to say? (BILLY *shakes his head.*) If you have nothing to say, when the drum roll is sounded, you will proceed to carry out the sentence of this court. (*Signals to* WYATT.)

WYATT. Sound off!

(*Drums roll.* BILLY *turns and starts up the ropes.*)

VOICES. Get him! Now!
  Bill! Stay where you are, boy, don't do it!
  Wait, Billy! Wait!   *All*
  Rush the deck, mates! Don't let them do it!   *together*
  We're here, Bill, don't you worry!

BILLY (*stops, turns forward, looks at* VERE, *and shouts out loud and clear, without trace of stammer*). God bless Captain Vere!

(*A second's pause;* VERE *is profoundly shaken;* BILLY *goes quickly up the ropes and out of sight. The crew moves back a step, is silent; officers and men in deep breathless quiet watch him out of sight and are staring overhead as the curtain falls.*)

II

The Play and the Creative Process

All the world's a stage,
And all the men and women merely players:
They have their exits and their entrances,
And one man in his time plays many parts,
His acts being seven ages.
—WILLIAM SHAKESPEARE

The arts are fragments of the time and place which produced
them and cannot be comprehended either conceptually or imagi-
natively, outwardly or inwardly, without a knowledge and im-
aginative understanding of their context.
—ERIC BENTLEY

. . . a real drama . . . needs a masterly structure. It needs to be
shaped and fashioned and laid together, and this process makes
a demand upon an artist's rarest gifts. He must combine and ar-
range, interpolate and eliminate, play the joiner with the most
attentive skill; and yet at the end effectually bury his tools and
his sawdust, and invest his elaborate skeleton with the smoothest
and most polished integument. . . .
To work successfully beneath a few grave, rigid laws, is always
a strong man's highest ideal of success. . . .
In a play, certainly, the subject is of more importance than in any
other work of art. Infelicity, triviality, vagueness of subject, may
be outweighed in a poem, a novel, or a picture, by charm of
manner, by ingenuity of execution; but in a drama the subject is
of the essence of the work—it is the work. If it is feeble, the
work can have no force; if it is shapeless, the work must be
amorphous.
—HENRY JAMES

THE TEMPEST

WILLIAM SHAKESPEARE (1564–1616)

Edited and Annotated by Hardin Craig

DRAMATIS PERSONAE

ALONSO, *King of Naples.*
SEBASTIAN, *his brother.*
PROSPERO, *the right Duke of Milan.*
ANTONIO, *his brother, the usurping Duke of Milan.*
FERDINAND, *son to the King of Naples.*
GONZALO, *an honest old Counsellor.*
ADRIAN,
FRANCISCO, } *Lords.*
CALIBAN, *a savage and deformed Slave.*

TRINCULO, *a Jester.*
STEPHANO, *a drunken Butler.*
MASTER OF A SHIP.
BOATSWAIN.
MARINERS.
MIRANDA, *daughter to Prospero.*
ARIEL, *an airy Spirit.*
IRIS,
CERES,
JUNO, } *presented by Spirits.*
NYMPHS,
REAPERS,
OTHER SPIRITS *attending on Prospero.*

SCENE—*A ship at Sea: an island.*

ACT I

SCENE I. *On a ship at sea: a tempestuous noise of thunder and lightning heard.*

Enter a SHIP-MASTER *and a* BOATSWAIN.

MASTER.   Boatswain!

BOATSWAIN.   Here, master: what cheer?

MASTER.   Good, speak to the mariners: fall to 't, yarely or we run ourselves aground: bestir, bestir.   (*Exit*)

(*Enter* MARINERS.)

BOATSWAIN.   Heigh, my hearts! cheerly, cheerly, my hearts! yare, yare! Take in the topsail. Tend to the master's whistle. Blow, till thou burst thy wind, if room enough!

(*Enter* ALONSO, SEBASTIAN, ANTONIO, FERDINAND, GONZALO, *and others.*)

ALONSO.   Good boatswain, have care. Where 's the master? Play the men.

BOATSWAIN.   I pray now, keep below.

ACT I. SCENE I.   **1. Boatswain:** under-officer in a ship, having to do with sails and rigging and the supervision of the crew at work. **3. Good:** probably, good friend. **fall . . . yarely:** set to work nimbly. **6. Tend:** attend. **Blow,** etc.: addressed to the storm. **8. Play the**

587

ALONSO.   Where is the master, boatswain?

BOATSWAIN.   Do you not hear him? You mar our labour: keep your cabins: you do assist the storm.

GONZALO.   Nay, good, be patient.

BOATSWAIN.   When the sea is. Hence! What cares these roarers for the name of king? To cabin: silence! trouble us not.

GONZALO.   Good, yet remember whom thou hast aboard.

BOATSWAIN.   None that I more love than myself. You are a counsellor; if you can command these elements to silence, and work the peace of the present, we will not hand a rope more; use your authority: if you cannot, give thanks you have lived so long, and make yourself ready in your 20 cabin for the mischance of the hour, if it so hap. Cheerly, good hearts! Out of our way, I say.   (*Exit*)

GONZALO.   I have great comfort from this fellow: methinks he hath no drowning mark upon him; his complexion is perfect gallows. Stand fast, good Fate, to his hanging: make the rope of his destiny our cable, for our own doth little advantage. If he be not born to be hanged, our case is miserable.   (*Exeunt*)

(*Re-enter* BOATSWAIN.)

BOATSWAIN.   Down with the topmast! yare! lower, lower! Bring her to try with main-course. (*A cry within.*) A plague upon this howling! they are louder than the weather or our office.   30

(*Re-enter* SEBASTIAN, ANTONIO, *and* GONZALO.)

                Yet again! what do you here? Shall we give o'er and drown? Have you a mind to sink?

SEBASTIAN.   A pox o' your throat, you bawling, blasphemous, incharitable dog!

BOATSWAIN.   Work you then.

ANTONIO.   Hang, cur! hang, you whoreson, insolent noisemaker! We are less afraid to be drowned than thou art.

GONZALO.   I'll warrant him for drowning; though the ship were no stronger than a nutshell and as leaky as an unstanched wench.

BOATSWAIN.   Lay her a-hold! set her two courses off to sea again; lay her off.

men: New Cambridge editors define as "pipe all hands." **14. cares:** described as a singular verb used with a plural subject on account of haste; also as an old northern plural of the verb in *s*. **roarers:** waves or winds, or both; allusion to *roarer* meaning "bully," "blusterer." **18. work . . . present:** calm the storm. **19. hand:** handle. **24. complexion . . . gallows:** appearance shows he was born to be hanged. **26. doth little advantage,** is of little benefit. **28-29. Bring . . . course:** sail her close to the wind by means of the mainsail. **29-30. they . . . office:** the passengers make more noise than the winds or than we do at work. **37. warrant him for drowning:** guarantee that he will never be drowned. **39. a-hold:** close to the wind. **courses:** probably, sails; i.e., they would set her foresail as well as her mainsail.

(*Enter* MARINERS *wet.*)

MARINERS.　All lost! to prayers, to prayers! all lost!　　　　　**40**

BOATSWAIN.　What, must our mouths be cold?

GONZALO.　The king and prince at prayers! let's assist them,
　　　　　For our case is as theirs.

SEBASTIAN.　　　　　　　　　I'm out of patience.

ANTONIO.　We are merely cheated of our lives by drunkards:
　　　　　This wide-chapp'd rascal—would thou mightst lie drowning
　　　　　The washing of ten tides!

GONZALO.　　　　　　　He'll be hang'd yet,
　　　　　Though every drop of water swear against it
　　　　　And gape at widest to glut him.

(A CONFUSED NOISE WITHIN: 'Mercy on us!'—
　　　　　'We split, we split!'—'Farewell my wife and children!'　　**50**
　　　　　'Farewell, brother!'—'We split, we split, we split!')

ANTONIO.　Let 's all sink with the king.

SEBASTIAN.　Let 's take leave of him.　　　　　(*Exeunt* ANTONIO *and* SEBASTIAN)

GONZALO.　Now would I give a thousand furlongs of sea for an acre of barren
　　　　　ground, long heath, brown furze, any thing. The wills above be done!
　　　　　but I would fain die a dry death.　　　　　(*Exeunt*)

SCENE II. *The island. Before* PROSPERO'S *cell.*

Enter PROSPERO *and* MIRANDA.

MIRANDA.　If by your art, my dearest father, you have
　　　　　Put the wild waters in this roar, allay them.
　　　　　The sky, it seems, would pour down stinking pitch,
　　　　　But that the sea, mounting to the welkin's cheek,
　　　　　Dashes the fire out. O, I have suffer'd
　　　　　With those that I saw suffer: a brave vessel,
　　　　　Who had, no doubt, some noble creature in her,
　　　　　Dash'd all to pieces. O, the cry did knock
　　　　　Against my very heart. Poor souls, they perish'd.
　　　　　Had I been any god of power, I would　　　　　**10**
　　　　　Have sunk the sea within the earth or ere
　　　　　It should the good ship so have swallow'd and
　　　　　The fraughting souls within her.

41. **must . . . cold:** let us heat up our mouths with liquor. **44. merely:** absolutely, entirely.
45. wide-chapp'd: with mouth wide open. **45-46. lie . . . tides.** Pirates were hanged on the
shore and left until three tides had come in. **48. glut,** swallow. **50. split,** i.e., on the rocks.
55. long heath, defined as "open barren ground"; also as "heather." **furze,** broom,
or gorse (a prickly shrub); F: firrs, taken to mean "firs" (New Cambridge).
　　SCENE II. **3. stinking pitch,** suggestion of heat. **4. But that,** were it not that. **13.**
fraughting, forming the cargo.

PROSPERO.   Be collected:
No more amazement: tell your piteous heart
There's no harm done.

MIRANDA.   O, woe the day!

PROSPERO.   No harm.
I have done nothing but in care of thee,
Of thee, my dear one, thee, my daughter, who
Art ignorant of what thou art, nought knowing
Of whence I am, nor that I am more better
Than Prospero, master of a full poor cell,   20
And thy no greater father.

MIRANDA.   More to know
Did never meddle with my thoughts.

PROSPERO.   'Tis time
I should inform thee farther. Lend thy hand,
And pluck my magic garment from me. So: (*Lays down his mantle*)
Lie there, my art. Wipe thou thine eyes; have comfort.
The direful spectacle of the wreck, which touch'd
The very virtue of compassion in thee,
I have with such provision in mine art
So safely ordered that there is no soul—
No, not so much perdition as an hair   30
Betid to any creature in the vessel
Which thou heard'st cry, which thou saw'st sink. Sit down;
For thou must now know farther.

MIRANDA.   You have often
Begun to tell me what I am, but stopp'd
And left me to a bootless inquisition,
Concluding 'Stay: not yet.'

PROSPERO.   The hour 's now come;
The very minute bids thee ope thine ear;
Obey and be attentive. Canst thou remember
A time before we came unto this cell?
I do not think thou canst, for then thou wast not   40
Out three years old.

MIRANDA.   Certainly, sir, I can.

PROSPERO.   By what? by any other house or person?
Of any thing the image tell me that
Hath kept with thy remembrance.

MIRANDA.   'Tis far off
And rather like a dream than an assurance

---

14. amazement, astonishment, bewilderment. piteous, pitiful. 19. more better, double comparative, as often. 20. full, very, exceedingly. 22. meddle, mingle. 24. So, used with a gesture, meaning "good," "very well." 28. provision, foresight. 29. no soul, i.e., lost; many emendations. 30. perdition, loss. 31. Betid, happened. 35. bootless inquisition, profitless inquiry. 41. Out, fully. 45-46. assurance . . .

That my remembrance warrants. Had I not
Four or five women once that tended me?

PROSPERO. Thou hadst, and more, Miranda. But how is it
That this lives in thy mind? What seest thou else
In the dark backward and abysm of time?   50
If thou remember'st aught ere thou camest here,
How thou camest here thou mayst.

MIRANDA.   But that I do not.

PROSPERO. Twelve year since, Miranda, twelve year since,
Thy father was the Duke of Milan and
A prince of power.

MIRANDA.   Sir, are not you my father?

PROSPERO. Thy mother was a piece of virtue, and
She said thou wast my daughter; and thy father
Was Duke of Milan; and thou his only heir
And princess no worse issued.

MIRANDA.   O the heavens!
What foul play had we, that we came from thence?   60
Or blessed was 't we did?

PROSPERO.   Both, both, my girl:
By foul play, as thou say'st, were we heaved thence,
But blessedly holp hither.

MIRANDA.   O, my heart bleeds
To think o' the teen that I have turn'd you to,
Which is from my remembrance! Please you, farther.

PROSPERO. My brother and thy uncle, call'd Antonio—
I pray thee, mark me—that a brother should
Be so perfidious!—he whom next thyself
Of all the world I loved and to him put
The manage of my state; as at that time   70
Through all the signories it was the first
And Prospero the prime duke, being so reputed
In dignity, and for the liberal arts
Without a parallel; those being all my study,
The government I cast upon my brother
And to my state grew stranger, being transported
And rapt in secret studies. Thy false uncle—
Dost thou attend me?

MIRANDA.   Sir, most heedfully.

warrants, certainty that my memory guarantees. **56. piece,** masterpiece. **59. issued,**
born. **64. teen . . . to,** trouble I have brought you into. **65. from,** i.e., has no place
in. **70. manage,** management. **71. signories,** states of northern Italy. **73. liberal arts,**
allusion to the learned studies of the Middle Ages. **76. state,** position as ruler.
77. Secret studies, magic, the occult.

PROSPERO.	Being once perfected how to grant suits,
	How to deny them, who to advance and who	80
	To trash for over-topping, new created
	The creatures that were mine, I say, or changed 'em,
	Or else new form'd 'em; having both the key
	Of officer and office, set all hearts i' the state
	To what tune pleased his ear; that now he was
	The ivy which had hid my princely trunk,
	And suck'd my verdure out on 't. Thou attend'st not.

MIRANDA.   O, good sir, I do.

PROSPERO.   I pray thee, mark me.
I, thus neglecting worldly ends, all dedicated
To closeness and the bettering of my mind   90
With that which, but by being so retired,
O'er-prized all popular rate, in my false brother
Awaked an evil nature; and my trust,
Like a good parent, did beget of him
A falsehood in its contrary as great
As my trust was; which had indeed no limit,
A confidence sans bound. He being thus lorded,
Not only with what my revenue yielded,
But what my power might else exact, like one
Who having into truth, by telling of it,   100
Made such a sinner of his memory,
To credit his own lie, he did believe
He was indeed the duke; out o' the substitution,
And executing the outward face of royalty,
With all prerogative: hence his ambition growing—
Dost thou hear?

MIRANDA.   Your tale, sir, would cure deafness.

PROSPERO.   To have no screen between this part he play'd
And him he play'd it for, he needs will be
Absolute Milan. Me, poor man, my library
Was dukedom large enough: of temporal royalties   110
He thinks me now incapable; confederates—

79. **perfected,** informed completely. 81. **trash,** check a hound by tying a weight to its neck. **over-topping,** running too far ahead of the pack. 83. **key,** tool for tuning stringed instruments, with suggestion of the usual meaning.

90. **closeness,** retirement, seclusion. 91-92. **but . . . rate,** except that it was done in retirement, (would have) surpassed in value all popular estimate. 93. **Awaked.** *I* in line 89 is the subject. 95. **in its contrary,** of an opposite kind. 97. **lorded,** raised to lordship. 100-102. **Who . . . lie,** a difficult passage; the meaning is: He had lied so long that he believed his own lies. New Cambridge editors read *minted* for *into,* interpreting the passage as a figure from coining of baser metals, so that *telling* means "counting," *substitution* means "the substituting of baser metals for gold," and *executing . . . royalty* means "stamping the coins." 109. **Absolute Milan,** actual duke of Milan. 110. **royalties,** prerogatives and rights of a sovereign. 111. **confederates,** conspires.

So dry he was for sway—wi' the King of Naples
To give him annual tribute, do him homage,
Subject his coronet to his crown and bend
The dukedom yet unbow'd—alas, poor Milan!—
To most ignoble stooping.

MIRANDA.   O the heavens!

PROSPERO.   Mark his condition and the event; then tell me
If this might be a brother.

MIRANDA.   I should sin
To think but nobly of my grandmother:
Good wombs have borne bad sons.

PROSPERO.   Now the condition.   120
This King of Naples, being an enemy
To me inveterate, hearkens my brother's suit;
Which was, that he, in lieu o' the premises
Of homage and I know not how much tribute,
Should presently extirpate me and mine
Out of the dukedom and confer fair Milan
With all the honours on my brother: whereon,
A treacherous army levied, one midnight
Fated to the purpose did Antonio open
The gates of Milan, and, i' the dead of darkness,   130
The ministers for the purpose hurried thence
Me and thy crying self.

MIRANDA.   Alack, for pity!
I, not remembering how I cried out then,
Will cry it o'er again: it is a hint
That wrings mine eyes to 't.

PROSPERO.   Hear a little further
And then I'll bring thee to the present business
Which now 's upon 's; without the which this story
Were most impertinent.

MIRANDA.   Wherefore did they not
That hour destroy us?

PROSPERO.   Well demanded, wench:
My tale provokes that question. Dear, they durst not,   140
So dear the love my people bore me, nor set
A mark so bloody on the business, but
With colours fairer painted their foul ends.

---

112. **dry,** thirsty, eager. 123. **in . . . premises,** in return for the stipulations. 125. **presently,** at once, immediately. 131. **ministers,** those employed to serve Antonio. 134. **hint,** occasion. 135. **wrings . . . to,** forces. 138. **impertinent,** irrelevant. 139. **wench,** used as a term of affectionate address. 143. **colours,** pretexts, excuses.

In few, they hurried us aboard a bark,
Bore us some leagues to sea; where they prepared
A rotten carcass of a boat, not rigg'd,
Nor tackle, sail, nor mast; the very rats
Instinctively have quit it: there they hoist us,
To cry to the sea that roar'd to us, to sigh
To the winds whose pity, sighing back again,   150
Did us but loving wrong.

MIRANDA.   Alack, what trouble
Was I then to you!

PROSPERO.   O, a cherubin
Thou wast that did preserve me. Thou didst smile,
Infused with a fortitude from heaven.
When I have deck'd the sea with drops full salt,
Under my burthen groan'd; which raised in me
An undergoing stomach, to bear up
Against what should ensue.

MIRANDA.   How came we ashore?

PROSPERO.   By Providence divine.
Some food we had and some fresh water that   160
A noble Neapolitan, Gonzalo,
Out of his charity, who being then appointed
Master of this design, did give us, with
Rich garments, linens, stuffs and necessaries,
Which since have steaded much; so, of his gentleness,
Knowing I loved my books, he furnish'd me
From mine own library with volumes that
I prize above my dukedom.

MIRANDA.   Would I might
But ever see that man!

PROSPERO.   Now I arise: (*Resumes his mantle*)
Sit still, and hear the last of our sea-sorrow.   170
Here in this island we arrived; and here
Have I, thy schoolmaster, made thee more profit
Than other princesses can that have more time
For vainer hours and tutors not so careful.

MIRANDA.   Heavens thank you for 't! And now, I pray you, sir,
For still 'tis beating in my mind, your reason
For raising this sea-storm?

144. few, few words. 146. boat, F: *butt*, which might be retained with the meaning "tub" (for boat). 148. hoist, heaved, lifted. 151. loving wrong, figure of speech called oxymoron, in which, to emphasize a contrast, contradictory terms are associated; the *wrong* done by sea and winds was wrought by seeming sympathy. 152. cherubin, plural used as singular; applied to an angelic woman. 155. deck'd. New Cambridge editors read *eked*, increased. 156. which, i.e., the smile. 157. undergoing stomach, courage to undergo. 165. steaded, been useful.

PROSPERO.   Know thus far forth.
              By accident most strange, bountiful Fortune,
              Now my dear lady, hath mine enemies
              Brought to this shore; and by my prescience   180
              I find my zenith doth depend upon
              A most auspicious star, whose influence
              If now I court not but omit, my fortunes
              Will ever after droop. Here cease more questions:
              Thou art inclined to sleep; 'tis a good dulness,
              And give it way: I know thou canst not choose. (*Miranda sleeps*)
              Come away, servant, come. I am ready now.
              Approach, my Ariel, come.

(*Enter* ARIEL.)

ARIEL.   All hail, great master! grave sir, hail! I come
              To answer thy best pleasure; be 't to fly,   190
              To swim, to dive into the fire, to ride
              On the curl'd clouds, to thy strong bidding task
              Ariel and all his quality.

PROSPERO.   Hast thou, spirit,
              Perform'd to point the tempest that I bade thee?

ARIEL.   To every article.
              I boarded the king's ship; now on the beak,
              Now in the waist, the deck, in every cabin,
              I flamed amazement: sometime I 'ld divide,
              And burn in many places; on the topmast,
              The yards and bowsprit, would I flame distinctly,   200
              Then meet and join. Jove's lightnings, the precursors
              O' the dreadful thunder-claps, more momentary
              And sight-outrunning were not; the fire and cracks
              Of sulphurous roaring the most mighty Neptune
              Seem to besiege and make his bold waves tremble,
              Yea, his dread trident shake.

PROSPERO.   My brave spirit!
              Who was so firm, so constant, that this coil
              Would not infect his reason?

ARIEL.   Not a soul
              But felt a fever of the mad and play'd
              Some tricks of desperation. All but mariners   210
              Plunged in the foaming brine and quit the vessel,
              Then all afire with me: the king's son, Ferdinand,

181. zenith, height of fortune; astrological term. 185. dulness, drowsiness. 187. Come
away, come. 192. task, make demands upon. 194. point, i.e., to the smallest detail. 196.
beak, prow. 197. waist, midship. deck, poopdeck at the stern. 198. flamed amazement,
caused amazement by flame. 200. distinctly, separately. 202. momentary, instantaneous.
207. coil, turmoil. 209. fever of the mad, i.e., such as madmen feel. Some editors follow
Dryden in reading *mind*.

With hair up-staring,—then like reeds, not hair,—
Was the first man that leap'd; cried, 'Hell is empty,
And all the devils are here.'

PROSPERO.   Why, that 's my spirit!
But was not this nigh shore?

ARIEL.   Close by, my master.

PROSPERO.   But are they, Ariel, safe?

ARIEL.   Not a hair perish'd;
On their sustaining garments not a blemish,
But fresher than before: and, as thou badest me,
In troops I have dispersed them 'bout the isle.   220
The king's son have I landed by himself;
Whom I left cooling of the air with sighs
In an odd angle of the isle and sitting,
His arms in this sad knot.

PROSPERO.   Of the king's ship
The mariners say how thou hast disposed
And all the rest o' the fleet.

ARIEL.   Safely in harbour
Is the king's ship; in the deep nook, where once
Thou call'dst me up at midnight to fetch dew
From the still-vex'd Bermoothes, there she 's hid:
The mariners all under hatches stow'd;   230
Who, with a charm join'd to their suffer'd labour,
I have left asleep: and for the rest o' the fleet
Which I dispersed, they all have met again
And are upon the Mediterranean flote,
Bound sadly home for Naples,
Supposing that they saw the king's ship wreck'd
And his great person perish.

PROSPERO.   Ariel, thy charge
Exactly is perform'd: but there 's more work.
What is the time o' the day?

ARIEL.   Past the mid season.

PROSPERO.   At least two glasses. The time 'twixt six and now   240
Must by us both be spent most preciously.

213. up-staring, standing on end. 218. sustaining garments, probably, garments that sustained them in the sea. 223. angle, corner. 227. nook, bay. 228. fetch dew, for some incantation. 229. Bermoothes, Bermudas; a possible reference to *A Discovery of the Bermudas* (1610), one of the sources of the play. 234. flote, sea, or possibly, flotilla, i.e., making for the Mediterranean flotilla (New Cambridge). 240. glasses, i.e., hourglasses.

ARIEL.   Is there more toil? Since thou dost give me pains,
                Let me remember thee what thou hast promised,
                Which is not yet perform'd me.

PROSPERO.   How now? moody?
                What is 't thou canst demand?

ARIEL.   My liberty.

PROSPERO.   Before the time be out? no more!

ARIEL.   I prithee,
                Remember I have done thee worthy service;
                Told thee no lies, made thee no mistakings, served
                Without or grudge or grumblings: thou didst promise
                To bate me a full year.

PROSPERO.   Dost thou forget   250
                From what a torment I did free thee?

ARIEL.   No.

PROSPERO.   Thou dost, and think'st it much to tread the ooze
                Of the salt deep,
                To run upon the sharp wind of the north,
                To do me business in the veins o' the earth
                When it is baked with frost.

ARIEL.   I do not, sir.

PROSPERO.   Thou liest, malignant thing! Hast thou forgot
                The foul witch Sycorax, who with age and envy
                Was grown into a hoop? hast thou forgot her?

ARIEL.   No, sir.

PROSPERO.   Thou hast. Where was she born? speak; tell me.   260

ARIEL.   Sir, in Argier.

PROSPERO.   O, was she so? I must
                Once in a month recount what thou hast been,
                Which thou forget'st. This damn'd witch Sycorax,
                For mischiefs manifold and sorceries terrible
                To enter human hearing, from Argier,
                Thou know'st, was banish'd: for one thing she did
                They would not take her life. Is not this true?

243. remember, remind.
248. mistakings, errors. 250. bate . . . year, remit me a year of service. Ariel, as a
spirit, longs for freedom; as a spirit, he is also incapable of affection or gratitude as entertained by human beings. 249. grudge, reluctance, grumbling. 258. Sycorax, name of
unknown origin; according to one conjecture made up of σῦς, a sow, and κόραξ, a raven.
261. Argier, Algiers. 266. one thing she did, allusion not explained; taken by New Cambridge editors as evidence of a cut in the play. Lamb suggested that Shakespeare was
thinking of the witch who saved Algiers from Charles V in 1541 by raising a storm that

ARIEL.	Ay, sir.

PROSPERO.   This blue-eyed hag was hither brought with child
                And here was left by the sailors. Thou, my slave,   270
                As thou report'st thyself, wast then her servant;
                And, for thou wast a spirit too delicate
                To act her earthy and abhorr'd commands,
                Refusing her grand hests, she did confine thee,
                By help of her more potent ministers
                And in her most unmitigable rage,
                Into a cloven pine; within which rift
                Imprison'd thou didst painfully remain
                A dozen years; within which space she died
                And left thee there; where thou did'st vent thy groans   280
                As fast as mill-wheels strike. Then was this island—
                Save for the son that she did litter here,
                A freckled whelp hag-born—not honour'd with
                A human shape.

ARIEL.   Yes, Caliban her son.

PROSPERO.   Dull thing, I say so; he, that Caliban
                Whom now I keep in service. Thou best know'st
                What torment I did find thee in; thy groans
                Did make wolves howl and penetrate the breasts
                Of ever angry bears: it was a torment
                To lay upon the damn'd, which Sycorax   290
                Could not again undo: it was mine art,
                When I arrived and heard thee, that made gape
                The pine and let thee out.

ARIEL.   I thank thee, master.

PROSPERO.   If thou more murmur'st, I will rend an oak
                And peg thee in his knotty entrails till
                Thou hast howl'd away twelve winters.

ARIEL.   Pardon, master;
                I will be correspondent to command
                And do my spiriting gently.

PROSPERO.   Do so, and after two days
                I will discharge thee.

ARIEL.   That 's my noble master!
                What shall I do? say what; what shall I do?   300

PROSPERO.   Go make thyself like a nymph o' the sea: be subject
                To no sight but thine and mine, invisible
                To every eyeball else. Go take this shape

dispersed his fleet. The allusion may be to the pregnancy of Sycorax. **269. blue-eyed**, usually interpreted as referring to dark circles under the eyes. Staunton suggested *blear-eyed*. **274. hests**, commands. **275. ministers**, serving spirits. **283. freckled**, spotted. **297. correspondent**, responsive, submissive. **298. gently**, in cheerful and proper fashion.

And hither come in 't: go, hence with diligence!   (*Exit* ARIEL)
Awake, dear heart, awake! thou hast slept well;
Awake!

MIRANDA.   The strangeness of your story put
Heaviness in me.

PROSPERO.   Shake it off. Come on;
We'll visit Caliban my slave, who never
Yields us kind answer.

MIRANDA.   'Tis a villain, sir,
I do not love to look on.

PROSPERO.   But, as 'tis,   310
We cannot miss him: he does make our fire,
Fetch in our wood and serves in offices
That profit us. What, ho! slave! Caliban!
Thou earth, thou! speak.

CALIBAN.   (*within*) There 's wood enough within.

PROSPERO.   Come forth, I say! there 's other business for thee:
Come, thou tortoise! when?

(*Re-enter* ARIEL *like a water-nymph.*)

Fine apparition! My quaint Ariel,
Hark in thine ear.

ARIEL.   My lord, it shall be done.   (*Exit*)

PROSPERO.   Thou poisonous slave, got by the devil himself
Upon thy wicked dam, come forth!   320

(*Enter* CALIBAN.)

CALIBAN.   As wicked dew as e'er my mother brush'd
With raven's feather from unwholesome fen
Drop on you both! a south-west blow on ye
And blister you all o'er!

PROSPERO.   For this, be sure, to-night thou shalt have cramps,
Side-stitches that shall pen thy breath up; urchins
Shall, for that vast of night that they may work,
All exercise on thee; thou shalt be pinch'd
As thick as honeycomb, each pinch more stinging
Than bees that made 'em.

CALIBAN.   I must eat my dinner.   330
This island 's mine, by Sycorax my mother,

---

311. miss, do without. **312. offices**, probably domestic services. **317. quaint**, dainty or clever. **321. wicked**, mischievous, harmful. **323. south-west**, i.e., wind (bringing disease). **326. urchins**, hedgehogs; here, suggesting goblins. **327. vast**, long hours. **328. exercise**, practice, work.

Which thou takest from me. When thou camest first,
Thou strokedst me and madest much of me, wouldst give me
Water with berries in 't, and teach me how
To name the bigger light, and how the less,
That burn by day and night: and then I loved thee
And show'd thee all the qualities o' the isle,
The fresh springs, brine-pits, barren place and fertile:
Cursed be I that did so! All the charms
Of Sycorax, toads, beetles, bats, light on you!   340
For I am all the subjects that you have,
Which first was mine own king: and here you sty me
In this hard rock, whiles you do keep from me
The rest o' the island.

PROSPERO.   Thou most lying slave,
Whom stripes may move, not kindness! I have used thee,
Filth as thou art, with human care, and lodged thee
In mine own cell, till thou didst seek to violate
The honour of my child.

CALIBAN.   O ho, O ho! would 't had been done!
Thou didst prevent me; I had peopled else   350
This isle with Calibans.

PROSPERO.   Abhorred slave,
Which any print of goodness wilt not take,
Being capable of all ill! I pitied thee,
Took pains to make thee speak, taught thee each hour
One thing or other: when thou didst not, savage,
Know thine own meaning, but wouldst gabble like
A thing most brutish, I endow'd thy purposes
With words that made them known. But thy vile race,
Though thou didst learn, had that in 't which good natures
Could not abide to be with; therefore wast thou   360
Deservedly confined into this rock,
Who hadst deserved more than a prison.

CALIBAN.   You taught me language; and my profit on 't
Is, I know how to curse. The red plague rid you
For learning me your language!

PROSPERO.   Hag-seed, hence!
Fetch us in fuel; and be quick, thou 'rt best,
To answer other business. Shrug'st thou, malice?
If thou neglect'st or dost unwillingly

---

334. berries. Strachey's *Repertory,* one of the sources, says that the Bermudas were full of thickets of "goodly Cedar . . . the Berries whereof, our men seething, straining, and letting stand some three or foure daies, made a kind of pleasant drinke." **338. brine-pits,** salt springs. **342. sty,** put in sty. **346. human,** humane. **351-362. Abhorred . . . prison.** F. assigns this speech to Miranda. This may be correct, since Prospero seems to break in suddenly in line 365. **357-358 endow'd . . . known,** enabled you to make known what was going on in your mind. **358. race,** natural disposition. **364. red plague,** bubonic plague. **rid,** destroy, with play on *red.* **365. Hag-seed,** hag's offspring.

What I command, I'll rack thee with old cramps,
Fill all thy bones with aches, make thee roar   370
That beasts shall tremble at thy din.

CALIBAN.   No, pray thee.
(*aside*) I must obey: his art is of such power,
It would control my dam's god, Setebos,
And make a vassal of him.

PROSPERO.   So, slave; hence!   (*Exit* CALIBAN)

(*Re-enter* ARIEL, *invisible, playing and singing;* FERDINAND *following.*)

ARIEL'S *song.*

Come unto these yellow sands,
    And then take hands:
Courtsied when you have and kiss'd
    The wild waves whist,
Foot it featly here and there;   380
And sweet sprites, the burthen bear.
Burthen (*dispersedly*). Hark, hark!
            Bow-wow.
    The watch-dogs bark:
            Bow-wow.
ARIEL.   Hark, hark! I hear
        The strain of strutting chanticleer
        Cry, Cock-a-diddle-dow.

FERDINAND.   Where should this music be? i' the air or the earth?
        It sounds no more: and, sure, it waits upon
        Some god o' the island. Sitting on a bank,
        Weeping again the king my father's wreck,   390
        This music crept by me upon the waters,
        Allaying both their fury and my passion
        With its sweet air: thence I have follow'd it,
        Or it hath drawn me rather. But 'tis gone.
        No, it begins again.

ARIEL (*sings*).

Full fathom five thy father lies;
    Of his bones are coral made;
Those are pearls that were his eyes:
    Nothing of him that doth fade
But doth suffer a sea-change   400
Into something rich and strange.
Sea-nymphs hourly ring his knell:

Burthen. Ding-dong.

370. aches, pronounced "aitches." **373. Setebos,** mentioned in Eden's *History of Travel*
(1577) as a deity, or devil, of the Patagonians. **376-378. Come . . . kiss'd,** three motions before the dance—take hands, curtsy, kiss (New Cambridge). **379. whist,** silent. **380. featly,**
neatly. **381.** *burthen,* refrain. **399-400 Nothing . . . sea-change,** his fading or decaying parts

ARIEL.   Hark! now I hear them,—Ding-dong, bell.

FERDINAND.   The ditty does remember my drown'd father.
              This is no mortal business, nor no sound
              That the earth owes. I hear it now above me.

PROSPERO.   The fringed curtains of thine eye advance
              And say what thou seest yond.

MIRANDA.   What is 't? a spirit?
              Lord, how it looks about! Believe me, sir,   410
              It carries a brave form. But 'tis a spirit.

PROSPERO.   No, wench; it eats and sleeps and hath such senses
              As we have, such. This gallant which thou seest
              Was in the wreck; and, but he 's something stain'd
              With grief that 's beauty's canker, thou mightst call him
              A goodly person: he hath lost his fellows
              And strays about to find 'em.

MIRANDA.   I might call him
              A thing divine, for nothing natural
              I ever saw so noble.

PROSPERO.   (aside) It goes on, I see,
              As my soul prompts it. Spirit, fine spirit! I'll free thee   420
              Within two days for this.

FERDINAND.   Most sure, the goddess
              On whom these airs attend! Vouchsafe my prayer
              May know if you remain upon this island;
              And that you will some good instruction give
              How I may bear me here: my prime request,
              Which I do last pronounce is, O you wonder!
              If you be maid or no?

MIRANDA.   No wonder, sir;
              But certainly a maid.

FERDINAND.   My language! heavens!
              I am the best of them that speak this speech,
              Were I but where 'tis spoken.

PROSPERO.   How? the best?   430
              What wert thou, if the King of Naples heard thee?

FERDINAND.   A single thing, as I am now, that wonders
              To hear thee speak of Naples. He does hear me;
              And that he does I weep: myself am Naples,

merely undergo a change by the sea. **405. remember,** commemorate. **414. something,**
somewhat. **415 canker,** cankerworm (feeding on buds and leaves). **419. It goes on,** my
charm works. **422. airs,** Ariel's music. **423. remain,** dwell. **429. best,** i.e., in birth. **432.
single,** solitary, with a suggestion of feebleness.

Who with mine eyes, never since at ebb, beheld
The king my father wreck'd.

MIRANDA.   Alack, for mercy!

FERDINAND.   Yes, faith, and all his lords; the Duke of Milan
And his brave son being twain.

PROSPERO.   (aside) The Duke of Milan
And his more braver daughter could control thee,
If now 'twere fit to do 't. At the first sight   440
They have changed eyes. Delicate Ariel,
I'll set thee free for this. (To FERDINAND) A word, good sir;
I fear you have done yourself some wrong: a word.

MIRANDA.   Why speaks my father so ungently? This
Is the third man that e'er I saw, the first
That e'er I sigh'd for: pity move my father
To be inclined my way!

FERDINAND.   O, if a virgin,
And your affection not gone forth, I'll make you
The queen of Naples.

PROSPERO.   Soft, sir! one word more.
(aside) They are both in either's powers; but this swift business   450
I must uneasy make, lest too light winning
Make the prize light. (To FERDINAND) One word more; I charge thee
That thou attend me: thou dost here usurp
The name thou owest not; and hast put thyself
Upon this island as a spy, to win it
From me, the lord on 't.

FERDINAND.   No, as I am a man.

MIRANDA.   There 's nothing ill can dwell in such a temple:
If the ill spirit have so fair a house,
Good things will strive to dwell with 't.

PROSPERO.   Follow me.
Speak not you for him; he 's a traitor. Come;   460
I'll manacle thy neck and feet together:
Sea-water shalt thou drink; thy food shall be
The fresh-brook mussels, wither'd roots and husks
Wherein the acorn cradled. Follow.

FERDINAND.   No;
I will resist such entertainment till
Mine enemy has more power.
(*Draws, and is charmed from moving.*)

439. control, confute. **441. changed eyes**, exchanged amorous glances, with suggestion
of the eye as the origin of the passion of love. **443. done . . . wrong**, are mistaken. **451.
uneasy**, difficult. **451, 452. light, light**, easy, cheap. **454. owest**, ownest. **463. husks**, chaff
(of grain). **465. entertainment**, treatment.

MIRANDA.   O dear father,
Make not too rash a trial of him, for
He 's gentle and not fearful.

PROSPERO.   What? I say,
My foot my tutor? Put thy sword up, traitor;
Who makest a show but darest not strike, thy conscience   470
Is so possess'd with guilt: come from thy ward,
For I can here disarm thee with this stick
And make thy weapon drop.

MIRANDA.   Beseech you, father.
PROSPERO.   Hence! hang not on my garments.

MIRANDA.   Sir, have pity;
I'll be his surety.

PROSPERO.   Silence! one word more
Shall make me chide thee, if not hate thee. What!
An advocate for an impostor! hush!
Thou think'st there is no more such shapes as he,
Having seen but him and Caliban: foolish wench!
To the most of men this is a Caliban   480
And they to him are angels.

MIRANDA.   My affections
Are then most humble; I have no ambition
To see a goodlier man.

PROSPERO.   Come on; obey:
Thy nerves are in their infancy again
And have no vigour in them.

FERDINAND.   So they are;
My spirits, as in a dream, are all bound up.
My father's loss, the weakness which I feel,
The wreck of all my friends, nor this man's threats,
To whom I am subdued, are but light to me,
Might I but through my prison once a day   490
Behold this maid: all corners else o' the earth
Let liberty make use of; space enough
Have I in such a prison.

PROSPERO.   (*aside*) It works. (*To* FERDINAND) Come on.
Thou hast done well, fine Ariel! (*To* FERDINAND) Follow me.
(*To* ARIEL) Hark what thou else shalt do me.

468. gentle, well-born, high-spirited. not fearful, not dangerous (because incapable
of treachery). 469. foot, subordinate. Miranda (the foot) presumes to instruct Prospero
(the head). 471. come . . . ward. New Cambridge editors read comma after *come,* with
the meaning, "Come, off thy guard." 484. nerves, sinews. 491-492. all . . . of, those who
are free may have all the rest of the world.

MIRANDA.	Be of comfort;

My father 's of a better nature, sir,
Than he appears by speech: this is unwonted
Which now came from him.

PROSPERO.   Thou shalt be as free
As mountain winds: but then exactly do
All points of my command.

ARIEL.   To the syllable.   500

PROSPERO.   Come, follow. Speak not for him.   (*Exeunt*)

ACT II

SCENE I. *Another part of the island.*

Enter ALONSO, SEBASTIAN, ANTONIO, GONZALO, ADRIAN, FRANCISCO, *and others.*

GONZALO.   Beseech you, sir, be merry; you have cause,
So have we all, of joy; for our escape
Is much beyond our loss. Our hint of woe
Is common; every day some sailor's wife,
The masters of some merchant and the merchant
Have just our theme of woe; but for the miracle,
I mean our preservation, few in millions
Can speak like us: then wisely, good sir, weigh
Our sorrow with our comfort.

ALONSO.   Prithee, peace.

SEBASTIAN.   He receives comfort like cold porridge.   10

ANTONIO.   The visitor will not give him o'er so.

SEBASTIAN.   Look, he 's winding up the watch of his wit; by and by it will strike.

GONZALO.   Sir,—

SEBASTIAN.   One: tell.

GONZALO.   When every grief is entertain'd that 's offer'd,
Comes to the entertainer—

SEBASTIAN.   A dollar.

GONZALO.   Dolour comes to him, indeed: you have spoken truer than you purposed.

SEBASTIAN.   You have taken it wiselier than I meant you should.

GONZALO.   Therefore, my lord,—   20

ANTONIO.   Fie, what a spendthrift is he of his tongue!

ACT II. SCENE I.   5. merchant, merchant, merchant vessel, merchant.   11. visitor, one taking nourishment to the sick.   16. entertainer, one who entertains a feeling; Sebastian takes the word to mean "one who provides entertainment."   17. dollar, widely circulated coin, the Ger-

ALONSO.	I prithee, spare.
GONZALO.	Well, I have done: but yet,—
SEBASTIAN.	He will be talking.
ANTONIO.	Which, of he or Adrian, for a good wager, first begins to crow?
SEBASTIAN.	The old cock.
ANTONIO.	The cockerel.
SEBASTIAN.	Done. The wager?
ANTONIO.	A laughter.
SEBASTIAN.	A match!
ADRIAN.	Though this island seem to be desert,—
SEBASTIAN.	Ha, ha, ha! So, you 're paid.
ADRIAN.	Uninhabitable and almost inaccessible,—
SEBASTIAN.	Yet,—
ADRIAN.	Yet,—
ANTONIO.	He could not miss 't.
ADRIAN.	It must needs be of subtle, tender and delicate temperance.
ANTONIO.	Temperance was a delicate wench.
SEBASTIAN.	Ay, and a subtle; as he most learnedly delivered.
ADRIAN.	The air breathes upon us here most sweetly.
SEBASTIAN.	As if it had lungs and rotten ones.
ANTONIO.	Or as 'twere perfumed by a fen.
GONZALO.	Here is every thing advantageous to life.
ANTONIO.	True; save means to live.
SEBASTIAN.	Of that there 's none, or little.
GONZALO.	How lush and lusty the grass looks! how green!
ANTONIO.	The ground indeed is tawny.
SEBASTIAN.	With an eye of green in 't.
ANTONIO.	He misses not much.

30

40

man *Thaler* and the Spanish *piece of eight;* with pun on *Dolour* in the next line. **29. laughter,** sitting of eggs. When Adrian (*the cockerel*) begins to speak (l. 31), Sebastian loses the bet and pays with a *laugh* (Ha, ha, ha! l. 32) for a *laughter.* **30. A match,** a bargain; agreed. **36. He . . . miss 't,** i.e., even if it is uninhabitable and inaccessible, he could not refrain from talking about it. **37. temperance,** temperature. **38. Temperance,** a Puritan name for women, thought also to refer to Temperance, a character in Chapman's *May Day* (1611). **47. tawny,** dull brown. **48. eye,** tinge.

SEBASTIAN.	No; he doth but mistake the truth totally.	50
GONZALO.	But the rarity of it is,—which is indeed almost beyond credit,—	
SEBASTIAN.	As many vouched rarities are.	
GONZALO.	That our garments, being, as they were, drenched in the sea, hold notwithstanding their freshness and glosses, being rather new-dyed than stained with salt water.	
ANTONIO.	If but one of his pockets could speak, would it not say he lies?	
SEBASTIAN.	Ay, or very falsely pocket up his report.	
GONZALO.	Methinks our garments are now as fresh as when we put them on first in Afric, at the marriage of the king's fair daughter Claribel to the King of Tunis.	60
SEBASTIAN.	'Twas a sweet marriage, and we prosper well in our return.	
ADRIAN.	Tunis was never graced before with such a paragon to their queen.	
GONZALO.	Not since widow Dido's time.	
ANTONIO.	Widow! a pox o' that! How came that widow in? widow Dido!	
SEBASTIAN.	What if he had said 'widower Æneas' too? Good Lord, how you take it!	
ADRIAN.	'Widow Dido' said you? you make me study of that: she was of Carthage, not of Tunis.	
GONZALO.	This Tunis, sir, was Carthage.	
ADRIAN.	Carthage?	
GONZALO.	I assure you, Carthage.	70
SEBASTIAN.	His word is more than the miraculous harp; he hath raised the wall and houses too.	
ANTONIO.	What impossible matter will he make easy next?	
SEBASTIAN.	I think he will carry this island home in his pocket and give it his son for an apple.	
ANTONIO.	And, sowing the kernels of it in the sea, bring forth more islands.	
GONZALO.	Ay.	
ANTONIO.	Why, in good time.	
GONZALO.	Sir, we were talking that our garments seem now as fresh as when we were at Tunis at the marriage of your daughter, who is now queen.	80

54. glosses, New Cambridge: *gloss.* **56. pockets.** Some editors suppose that reference is made to mud in the pockets. There is, at any rate, some peculiarity in Gonzalo's appearance. **63. widow Dido,** queen of Carthage deserted by Aeneas; possible topical reference to Chapman's *Widow's Tears,* or some other play. **71. miraculous harp,** allusion to Amphion's harp with which he raised the walls of Thebes. **78, in good time,** vague expression of agreement or approbation.

ANTONIO.   And the rarest that e'er came there.

SEBASTIAN.   Bate, I beseech you, widow Dido.

ANTONIO.   O, widow Dido! ay, widow Dido.

GONZALO.   Is not, sir, my doublet as fresh as the first day I wore it? I mean, in a
                sort.

ANTONIO.   That sort was well fished for.

GONZALO.   When I wore it at your daughter's marriage?

ALONSO.   You cram these words into mine ears against
                The stomach of my sense. Would I had never
                Married my daughter there! for, coming thence,   90
                My son is lost and, in my rate, she too,
                Who is so far from Italy removed
                I ne'er again shall see her. O thou mine heir
                Of Naples and of Milan, what strange fish
                Hath made his meal on thee?

FRANCISCO.   Sir, he may live:
                I saw him beat the surges under him,
                And ride upon their backs; he trod the water,
                Whose enmity he flung aside, and breasted
                The surge most swoln that met him; his bold head
                'Bove the contentious waves he kept, and oar'd   100
                Himself with his good arms in lusty stroke
                To the shore, that o'er his wave-worn basis bow'd,
                As stooping to relieve him: I not doubt
                He came alive to land.

ALONSO.   No, no, he 's gone.

SEBASTIAN.   Sir, you may thank yourself for this great loss,
                That would not bless our Europe with your daughter,
                But rather loose her to an African;
                Where she at least is banish'd from your eye,
                Who hath cause to wet the grief on 't.

ALONSO.   Prithee, peace.

SEBASTIAN.   You were kneel'd to and importuned otherwise   110
                By all of us, and the fair soul herself
                Weigh'd between loathness and obedience, at
                Which end o' the beam should bow. We have lost your son,
                I fear, for ever: Milan and Naples have

  82. Bate, leave out. 86 sort, lucky catch after much angling; probable suggestion of the
age of the garment, with a play on *sort* in line 85. 95-104. Sir . . . land, *Francisco's* only
speech. New Cambridge editors think the speech belongs to Gonzalo, and see in its assignment to Francisco a relic of an older version. 102. basis, foot, base. 107. loose, so F;
Globe: *lose.*
  109. Who, which (eye). 111-113. the fair . . . bow, the fair soul herself was poised
uncertain between unwillingness and obedience as to which end of the scale should sink.

Moe widows in them of this business' making
Than we bring men to comfort them:
The fault 's your own.

ALONSO.   So is the dear'st o' the loss.

GONZALO.   My lord Sebastian.
The truth you speak doth lack some gentleness
And time to speak it in: you rub the sore,   120
When you should bring the plaster.

SEBASTIAN.   Very well.

ANTONIO.   And most chirurgeonly.

GONZALO.   It is foul weather in us all, good sir,
When you are cloudy.

SEBASTIAN.   Foul weather?

ANTONIO.   Very foul.

GONZALO.   Had I plantation of this isle, my lord,—

ANTONIO.   He 'ld sow 't with nettle-seed.

SEBASTIAN.   Or docks, or mallows.

GONZALO.   And were the king on 't, what would I do?

SEBASTIAN.   'Scape being drunk for want of wine.

GONZALO.   I' the commonwealth I would by contraries
Execute all things; for no kind of traffic   130
Would I admit; no name of magistrate;
Letters should not be known; riches, poverty,
And use of service, none; contract, succession,
Bourn, bound of land, tilth, vineyard, none;
No use of metal, corn, or wine, or oil;
No occupation; all men idle, all;
And women too, but innocent and pure;
No sovereignty;—

SEBASTIAN.   Yet he would be king on 't.

ANTONIO.   The latter end of his commonwealth forgets the beginning.

GONZALO.   All things in common nature should produce   140
Without sweat or endeavour: treason, felony,

115. Moe, more. 122. chirurgeonly, like a skilled surgeon. 123. foul. The pun on this word is not clear. New Cambridge edition suggests that there was something suggestive of a bird in Gonzalo's appearance. 125. plantation, colonization; subsequent play on the literal meaning. 129-138. I' the . . . sovereignty. This passage on man in his primitive state is based on Montaigne, Essays, I, xxx, and derived from Florio's translation (1603). [For the passage cited, see below, p. 628.—Editors' note.]
132. Letters, learning. 133. use of service, custom of employing servants. succession, holding of property by right of inheritance. 134. Bourn, boundaries. bound of land,

Sword, pike, knife, gun, or need of any engine,
Would I not have; but nature should bring forth,
Of it own kind, all foison, all abundance,
To feed my innocent people.

SEBASTIAN.   No marrying 'mong his subjects?

ANTONIO.   None, man; all idle; whores and knaves.

GONZALO.   I would with such perfection govern, sir,
To excel the golden age.

SEBASTIAN.   God save his majesty!

ANTONIO.   Long live Gonzalo!

GONZALO.   And,—do you mark me, sir?   150

ALONSO.   Prithee, no more: thou dost talk nothing to me.

GONZALO.   I do well believe your highness; and did it to minister occasion to these
gentlemen, who are of such sensible and nimble lungs that they always
use to laugh at nothing.

ANTONIO.   'Twas you we laughed at.

GONZALO.   Who in this kind of merry fooling am nothing to you: so you may
continue and laugh at nothing still.

ANTONIO.   What a blow was there given!

SEBASTIAN.   An it had not fallen flat-long.

GONZALO.   You are gentlemen of brave mettle; you would lift the moon out of
her sphere, if she would continue in it five weeks without changing. 160

(*Enter* ARIEL, *invisible, playing solemn music.*)

SEBASTIAN.   We would so, and then go a bat-fowling.

ANTONIO.   Nay, good my lord, be not angry.

GONZALO.   No, I warrant you; I will not adventure my discretion so weakly. Will
you laugh me asleep, for I am very heavy?

ANTONIO.   Go sleep, and hear us.

(*All sleep except* ALONSO, SEBASTIAN, *and* ANTONIO.)

landmarks. **tilth,** tillage of soil. **142. engine,** instrument of warfare. **144. it,** its. **foison,**
plenty. **149. God.** Omitted in F in deference to the statute forbidding profanity on the
stage. **151. talk,** talk of. **153. sensible,** sensitive. **nimble,** easily excited. **158. flat-long,**
with the flat of the sword. **159. mettle,** temper, nature. **159–160. lift . . . sphere.** As a
planet in the old astronomy, the moon had a crystal sphere in which she moved. Gonzalo
means that they would lift the moon out of her sphere if she remained steady in it.
161. bat-fowling, hunting birds at night with lantern and stick; also, gulling a simpleton.
Gonzalo is the simpleton (or fowl), and Sebastian will use the moon as his lantern.
163. adventure, risk. **165. Go . . . us,** let our laughing send you to sleep, or, go to sleep

ALONSO.   What, all so soon asleep! I wish mine eyes
                Would, with themselves, shut up my thoughts: I find
                They are inclined to do so.

SEBASTIAN.   Please you, sir,
                Do not omit the heavy offer of it: 170
                It seldom visits sorrow; when it doth,
                It is a comforter.

ANTONIO.   We two, my lord,
                Will guard your person while you take your rest,
                And watch your safety.

ALONSO.   Thank you. Wondrous heavy

(ALONSO *sleeps. Exit* ARIEL.)

SEBASTIAN.   What a strange drowsiness possesses them!

ANTONIO.   It is the quality o' the climate.

SEBASTIAN.   Why
                Doth it not then our eyelids sink? I find not
                Myself disposed to sleep.

ANTONIO.   Nor I; my spirits are nimble.
                They fell together all, as by consent;
                They dropp'd, as by a thunder-stroke. What might,   180
                Worthy Sebastian? O, what might?—No more:—
                And yet methinks I see it in thy face,
                What thou shouldst be: the occasion speaks thee, and
                My strong imagination sees a crown
                Dropping upon thy head.

SEBASTIAN.   What, art thou waking?

ANTONIO.   Do you not hear me speak?

SEBASTIAN.   I do; and surely
                It is a sleepy language and thou speak'st
                Out of thy sleep. What is it thou didst say?
                This is a strange repose, to be asleep
                With eyes wide open; standing, speaking, moving,   190
                And yet so fast asleep.

ANTONIO.   Noble Sebastian,
                Thou let'st thy fortune sleep—die, rather; wink'st
                Whiles thou art waking.

SEBASTIAN.   Thou dost snore distinctly;
                There 's meaning in thy snores.

and hear us laugh at you. **170. omit,** neglect. **heavy,** drowsy. **179. consent,** agreement
as to a course of action. **183. speaks,** calls upon, proclaims (thee) king. **192. wink'st,**
closest thine eyes. **193. distinctly,** with separate and individual sounds.

ANTONIO.   I am more serious than my custom: you
              Must be so too, if heed me; which to do
              Trebles thee o'er.

SEBASTIAN.   Well, I am standing water.

ANTONIO.   I'll teach you how to flow.

SEBASTIAN.   Do so: to ebb
              Hereditary sloth instructs me.

ANTONIO.   O,
              If you but knew how you the purpose cherish   200
              Whiles thus you mock it! how, in stripping it,
              You more invest it! Ebbing men, indeed,
              Most often do so near the bottom run
              By their own fear or sloth.

SEBASTIAN.   Prithee, say on:
              The setting of thine eye and cheek proclaim
              A matter from thee, and a birth indeed
              Which throes thee much to yield.

ANTONIO.   Thus, sir:
              Although this lord of weak remembrance, this,
              Who shall be of as little memory
              When he is earth'd, hath here almost persuaded,—   210
              For he 's a spirit of persuasion, only
              Professes to persuade,—the king his son's alive,
              'Tis as impossible that he 's undrown'd
              As he that sleeps here swims.

SEBASTIAN.   I have no hope
              That he 's undrown'd.

ANTONIO.   O, out of that 'no hope'
              What great hope have you! no hope that way is
              Another way so high a hope that even
              Ambition cannot pierce a wink beyond,
              But doubt discovery there. Will you grant with me
              That Ferdinand is drown'd?

SEBASTIAN.   He 's gone.

197. **Trebles.** New Cambridge editors read *Troubles* in view of *standing water.* Onions defines as "makes thee three times as great." **standing water,** water which neither flows nor ebbs.

200. **purpose,** i.e., of being king. 201. **stripping it,** stripping off all pretense, revealing it. 202. **invest,** array, adorn. **Ebbing men,** men whose fortunes ebb, leaving them stranded. 205. **setting,** set expression. 206. **matter,** matter of importance. 207. **throes,** pains. 208. **this lord,** Gonzalo. **remembrance,** power of remembering. 210. **earth'd,** buried. 212. **Professes to persuade,** he was a privy councilor. 216. **that way,** i.e., in regard to Ferdinand's being saved. 218–219. **Ambition . . . there,** ambition itself cannot see any further than that hope (of the crown) without doubting the reality of the objects it sees. Furness, following Nicholson's conjecture of *dout* (extinguish) for *doubt,* interprets, "when

ANTONIO.   Then, tell me,   220
Who's the next heir of Naples?

SEBASTIAN.   Claribel.

ANTONIO.   She that is queen of Tunis; she that dwells
Ten leagues beyond man's life; she that from Naples
Can have no note, unless the sun were post—
The man i' the moon 's too slow—till new-born chins
Be rough and razorable; she that—from whom?
We all were sea-swallow'd, though some cast again,
And by that destiny to perform an act
Whereof what 's past is prologue, what to come
In yours and my discharge.

SEBASTIAN.   What stuff is this! how say you?   230
'Tis true, my brother's daughter 's queen of Tunis;
So is she heir of Naples; 'twixt which regions
There is some space.

ANTONIO.   A space whose every cubit
Seems to cry out, 'How shall that Claribel
Measure us back to Naples? Keep in Tunis,
And let Sebastian wake.' Say, this were death
That now hath seized them; why, they were no worse
Than now they are. There be that can rule Naples
As well as he that sleeps; lords that can prate
As amply and unnecessarily   240
As this Gonzalo; I myself could make
A chough of as deep chat. O, that you bore
The mind that I do! what a sleep were this
For your advancement! Do you understand me?

SEBASTIAN.   Methinks I do.

ANTONIO.   And how does your content
Tender your own good fortune?

SEBASTIAN.   I remember
You did supplant your brother Prospero.

ANTONIO.   True:
And look how well my garments sit upon me;
Much feater than before; my brother's servants
Were then my fellows; now they are my men.   250

ambition pierces to its furthest wink there discovery ceases, and the crown is found."
223. Ten . . . life, it would take more than a lifetime to get there. **224. note,** intimation.
226. she . . . whom, broken and difficult construction. **from whom?** Probably, from whom
will she learn? **227. cast,** were disgorged, with pun on *casting* (of parts for a play).
230. discharge, performance, i.e., to get done. **235. Measure us,** find (her) way. **235-236.
Keep . . . wake,** let her stay in Tunis, and let Sebastian wake (to his good fortune).
241-242. I . . . chat, I could teach a jackdaw to talk as wisely. **245. content,** desire contentment. **246. Tender,** provide for. **249. feater,** more becomingly.

SEBASTIAN.   But, for your conscience?

ANTONIO.   Ay, sir; where lies that? if 'twere a kibe,
              'Twould put me to my slipper: but I feel not
              This deity in my bosom: twenty consciences,
              That stand 'twixt me and Milan, candied be they
              And melt ere they molest! Here lies your brother,
              No better than the earth he lies upon,
              If he were that which now he 's like, that 's dead;
              Whom I, with this obedient steel, three inches of it,
              Can lay to bed for ever; whiles you, doing thus,   260
              To the perpetual wink for aye might put
              This ancient morsel, this Sir Prudence, who
              Should not upbraid our course. For all the rest,
              They'll take suggestion as a cat laps milk;
              They'll tell the clock to any business that
              We say befits the hour.

SEBASTIAN.   Thy case, dear friend,
              Shall be my precedent; as thou got'st Milan,
              I'll come by Naples. Draw thy sword: one stroke
              Shall free thee from the tribute which thou payest;
              And I the king shall love thee.

ANTONIO.   Draw together;   270
              And when I rear my hand, do you the like,
              To fall it on Gonzalo.

SEBASTIAN.   O, but one word.

(They talk apart.)

(Re-enter ARIEL, *invisible.)*

ARIEL.   My master through his art foresees the danger
              That you, his friend, are in; and sends me forth—
              For else his project dies—to keep them living.
              (Sings in GONZALO'S *ear)*
                        While you here do snoring lie,
                        Open-eyed conspiracy
                            His time doth take.
                        If of life you keep a care,
                        Shake off slumber, and beware: 280
                            Awake, awake!

ANTONIO.   Then let us both be sudden.

GONZALO.   Now, good angels
              Preserve the king.

(They wake.)

252. kibe, sore on the heel. 253. put . . . slipper, compel me to wear my slipper. 255. candied, frozen, congealed. 261. wink, sleep. 262. ancient morsel, Gonzalo. 265. tell the clock, count the strokes as we do, i.e., be subservient to us. 272. fall it, let it fall. 278. time, opportunity. 282. sudden, swift in action.

ALONSO.   Why, how now? ho, awake! Why are you drawn?
           Wherefore this ghastly looking?

GONZALO.   What 's the matter?

SEBASTIAN. Whiles we stood here securing your repose,
           Even now, we heard a hollow burst of bellowing
           Like bulls, or rather lions: did 't not wake you?
           It struck mine ear most terribly.

ALONSO.   I heard nothing.

ANTONIO.   O, 'twas a din to fright a monster's ear,   296
           To make an earthquake! sure, it was the roar
           Of a whole herd of lions.

ALONSO.   Heard you this, Gonzalo?

GONZALO.   Upon mine honour, sir, I heard a humming,
           And that a strange one too, which did awake me:
           I shaked you, sir, and cried: as mine eyes open'd,
           I saw their weapons drawn: there was a noise,
           That 's verily. 'Tis best we stand upon our guard,
           Or that we quit this place: let 's draw our weapons.

ALONSO.   Lead off this ground; and let 's make further search
           For my poor son.   300

GONZALO.   Heavens keep him from these beasts!
           For he is, sure, i' the island.

ALONSO.   Lead away.

ARIEL.   Prospero my lord shall know what I have done:
           So, king, go safely on to seek thy son.   (*Exeunt*)

SCENE II. *Another part of the island.*

Enter CALIBAN *with a burden of wood. A noise of thunder heard.*

CALIBAN.   All the infections that the sun sucks up
           From bogs, fens, flats, on Prosper fall and make him
           By inch-meal a disease! His spirits hear me
           And yet I needs must curse. But they'll nor pinch,
           Fright me with urchin-shows, pitch me i' the mire,
           Nor lead me, like a firebrand, in the dark
           Out of my way, unless he bid 'em; but
           For every trifle are they set upon me;
           Sometime like apes that mow and chatter at me
           And after bite me, then like hedgehogs which   10
           Lie tumbling in my barefoot way and mount

293. humming, i.e., Ariel's song. 297. verily, true.
   SCENE II. 3. inch-meal, little by little. 5. urchin-shows, appearances as goblins. 9. mow,
make faces.

Their pricks at my footfall; sometime am I
All wound with adders who with cloven tongues
Do hiss me into madness.
          (*Enter* TRINCULO.) Lo, now, lo!
Here comes a spirit of his, and to torment me
For bringing wood in slowly. I'll fall flat;
Perchance he will not mind me.

TRINCULO.   Here 's neither bush nor shrub, to bear off any weather at all, and
              another storm brewing; I hear it sing i' the wind: yond same black
              cloud, yond huge one, looks like a foul bombard that would shed   20
              his liquor. If it should thunder as it did before, I know not where to
              hide my head: yond same cloud cannot choose but fall by pailfuls. What
              have we here? a man or a fish? dead or alive? A fish: he smells like a
              fish; a very ancient and fish-like smell; a kind of not of the newest
              Poor-John. A strange fish! Were I in England now, as once I was, and
              had but this fish painted, not a holiday fool there but would give a
              piece of silver: there would this monster make a man; any strange beast
              there makes a man: when they will not give a doit to relieve a lame
              beggar, they will lay out ten to see a dead Indian. Legged like a man!
              and his fins like arms! Warm o' my troth! I do now let loose my   30
              opinion; hold it no longer: this is no fish, but an islander, that hath
              lately suffered by a thunderbolt. (*Thunder.*) Alas, the storm is come
              again! my best way is to creep under his gaberdine; there is no other
              shelter hereabout: misery acquaints a man with strange bed-fellows. I
              will here shroud till the dregs of the storm be past.

(*Enter* STEPHANO, *singing: a bottle in his hand.*)

STEPHANO.   I shall no more to sea, to sea,
                                  Here shall I die ashore—
              This is a very scurvy tune to sing at a man 's funeral: well, here 's my
              comfort. (*Drinks*)
              (*Sings*)   The master, the swabber, the boatswain and I,   40
                                  The gunner and his mate
                            Loved Mall, Meg and Marian and Margery,
                                  But none of us cared for Kate;
                                  For she had a tongue with a tang,
                                  Would cry to a sailor, Go hang!
                            She loved not the savour of tar nor of pitch,
                            Yet a tailor might scratch her where'er she did itch:
                                  Then to sea, boys, and let her go hang!
              This is a scurvy tune too: but here 's my comfort. (*Drinks*)

CALIBAN.   Do not torment me: Oh!   50

18. **bear off**, keep off. 20. **foul bombard**, dirty leathern bottle. 25. **Poor-John**, salted
hake, type of poor fare. **fish**. Malone cites a license issued by the Master of the
Revels (1632) "to shew a strange fish for half a yeare." 26. **painted**, i.e., on a board to
be hung up outside a booth. 27. **make a man**, i.e., make his fortune. 33. **gaberdine**, cloak,
loose upper garment. 35. **shroud**, take shelter. **dregs**, last remains.

STEPHANO. What 's the matter? Have we devils here? Do you put tricks upon 's with savages and men of Ind, ha? I have not 'scaped drowning to be afeard now of your four legs; for it hath been said, As proper a man as ever went on four legs cannot make him give ground; and it shall be said so again while Stephano breathes at nostrils.

CALIBAN. The spirit torments me; Oh!

STEPHANO. This is some monster of the isle with four legs, who hath got, as I take it, an ague. Where the devil should he learn our language? I will give him some relief, if it be but for that. If I can recover him and keep him tame and get to Naples with him, he 's a present for any emperor 60 that ever trod on neat's-leather.

CALIBAN. Do not torment me, prithee; I'll bring my wood home faster.

STEPHANO. He's in his fit now and does not talk after the wisest. He shall taste of my bottle: if he have never drunk wine afore, it will go near to remove his fit. If I can recover him and keep him tame, I will not take too much for him; he shall pay for him that hath him, and that soundly.

CALIBAN. Thou dost me yet but little hurt; thou wilt anon, I know it by thy trembling: now Prosper works upon thee.

STEPHANO. Come on your ways; open your mouth; here is that which will give language to you, cat: open your mouth; this will shake your shak- 70 ing, I can tell you, and that soundly: you cannot tell who 's your friend: open your chaps again.

TRINCULO. I should know that voice: it should be—but he is drowned; and these are devils: O defend me!

STEPHANO. Four legs and two voices: a most delicate monster! His forward voice now is to speak well of his friend; his backward voice is to utter foul speeches and to detract. If all the wine in my bottle will recover him, I will help his ague. Come. Amen! I will pour some in thy other mouth.

TRINCULO. Stephano! 80

STEPHANO. Doth thy other mouth call me? Mercy, mercy! This is a devil, and no monster: I will leave him; I have no long spoon.

TRINCULO. Stephano! If thou beest Stephano, touch me and speak to me; for I am Trinculo—be not afeard—thy good friend Trinculo.

STEPHANO. If thou beest Trinculo, come forth: I'll pull thee by the lesser legs: if any be Trinculo's legs, these are they. Thou art very Trinculo indeed!

---

52. Ind, India, or vaguely, the East. **59. recover,** restore. **61. neat's-leather,** leather from the skin of an animal of the ox kind. **65-66. take too much,** ironical, meaning: He will take as much as he can get. **68. trembling,** suggestion of demonic possession. **70. cat . . . mouth,** allusion to the proverb, "Good liquor will make a cat speak." **82. long spoon,** allusion to the proverb, "He that sups with the devil has need of a long spoon."

How camest thou to be the siege of this moon-calf? can he vent Trinculos?

TRINCULO. I took him to be killed with a thunder-stroke. But art thou not drowned, Stephano? I hope now thou art not drowned. Is the storm overblown? I hid me under the dead moon-calf's gaberdine for fear of the   90 storm. And art thou living, Stephano? O Stephano, two Neapolitans 'scaped!

STEPHANO. Prithee, do not turn me about; my stomach is not constant.

CALIBAN. (aside) These be fine things, an if they be not sprites.
That 's a brave god and bears celestial liquor.
I will kneel to him.

STEPHANO. How didst thou 'scape? How camest thou hither? swear by this bottle how thou camest hither. I escaped upon a butt of sack which the sailors heaved o'erboard, by this bottle! which I made of the bark of a tree with mine own hands since I was cast ashore.   100

CALIBAN. I'll swear upon that bottle to be thy true subject; for the liquor is not earthly.

STEPHANO. Here; swear then how thou escapedst.

TRINCULO. Swum ashore, man, like a duck: I can swim like a duck, I'll be sworn.

STEPHANO. Here, kiss the book. Though thou canst swim like a duck, thou art made like a goose.

TRINCULO. O Stephano, hast any more of this?

STEPHANO. The whole butt, man: my cellar is in a rock by the sea-side where my wine is hid. How now, moon-calf! how does thine ague?

CALIBAN. Hast thou not dropp'd from heaven?   110

STEPHANO. Out o' the moon, I do assure thee: I was the man i' the moon when time was.

CALIBAN. I have seen thee in her and I do adore thee:
My mistress show'd me thee and thy dog and thy bush.

STEPHANO. Come, swear to that; kiss the book: I will furnish it anon with new contents: swear.

TRINCULO. By this good light, this is a very shallow monster! I afeard of him! A very weak monster! The man i' the moon! A most poor credulous monster! Well drawn, monster, in good sooth!

86. moon-calf, monster, abortion (supposed to be caused by the influence of the moon).
93. not constant, unsteady. 98. butt of sack, barrel of Canary wine. 105. kiss the book. He gives him the bottle instead of the Bible on which to make his oath. 111-112. when time was, once upon a time. 114. dog . . . bush. See *A Midsummer-Night's Dream*, V, i, 136. 119. Well drawn. Caliban takes a good draft of the wine.

CALIBAN.	I'll show thee every fertile inch o' th' island; 120 And I will kiss thy foot: I prithee, be my god.
TRINCULO.	By this light, a most perfidious and drunken monster! when 's god 's asleep, he'll rob his bottle.
CALIBAN.	I'll kiss thy foot; I'll swear myself thy subject.
STEPHANO.	Come on then; down, and swear.
TRINCULO.	I shall laugh myself to death at this puppy-headed monster. A most scurvy monster! I could find in my heart to beat him,—
STEPHANO.	Come, kiss.
TRINCULO.	But that the poor monster 's in drink: an abominable monster!
CALIBAN.	I'll show thee the best springs; I'll pluck thee berries; 130 I'll fish for thee and get thee wood enough. A plague upon the tyrant that I serve! I'll bear him no more sticks, but follow thee, Thou wondrous man.
TRINCULO.	A most ridiculous monster, to make a wonder of a poor drunkard!
CALIBAN.	I prithee, let me bring thee where crabs grow; And I with my long nails will dig thee pig-nuts; Show thee a jay's nest and instruct thee how To snare the nimble marmoset; I'll bring thee To clustering filberts and sometimes I'll get thee 140 Young scamels from the rock. Wilt thou go with me?
STEPHANO.	I prithee now, lead the way without any more talking. Trinculo, the king and all our company else being drowned, we will inherit here: here; bear my bottle: fellow Trinculo, we'll fill him by and by again.
CALIBAN.	(*Sings drunkenly*) Farewell, master; farewell, farewell!
TRINCULO.	A howling monster; a drunken monster!

CALIBAN.	No more dams I'll make for fish;
	              Nor fetch in firing
	              At requiring;
	Nor scrape trencher, nor wash dish: 150
	              'Ban, 'Ban, Cacaliban
	              Has a new master: get a new man.
	        Freedom, hey-day! hey-day, freedom! freedom, hey-day, freedom!

STEPHANO.	O brave monster! Lead the way. (*Exeunt*)

122. perfidious, faithless, pagan. 137. pig-nuts, roundish tubers of *bunium flexuosum;*
earth-chestnuts. 139. marmoset, small monkey. 141. scamels, not explained. Keightley
conjectured *seamels* (seagulls), Theobald: *stannels* (kestrels); New Cambridge editors call
attention to the fact that "seamews" occurs in Strachey's letter. 143. inherit, take possession

ACT III

SCENE I. *Before* PROSPERO'S *cell.*

Enter FERDINAND, *bearing a log.*

FERDINAND.   There be some sports are painful, and their labour
Delight in them sets off: some kinds of baseness
Are nobly undergone and most poor matters
Point to rich ends. This my mean task
Would be as heavy to me as odious, but
The mistress which I serve quickens what 's dead
And makes my labours pleasures: O, she is
Ten times more gentle than her father 's crabbed,
And he 's composed of harshness. I must remove
Some thousands of these logs and pile them up,   **10**
Upon a sore injunction: my sweet mistress
Weeps when she sees me work, and says, such baseness
Had never like executor. I forget:
But these sweet thoughts do even refresh my labours,
Most busy lest, when I do it.

(*Enter* MIRANDA; *and* PROSPERO *at a distance, unseen.*)

MIRANDA.   Alas, now, pray you,
Work not so hard: I would the lightning had
Burnt up those logs that you are enjoin'd to pile!
Pray, set it down and rest you: when this burns,
'Twill weep for having wearied you. My father
Is hard at study; pray now, rest yourself;   **20**
He 's safe for these three hours.

FERDINAND.   O most dear mistress,
The sun will set before I shall discharge
What I must strive to do.

MIRANDA.   If you'll sit down,
I'll bear your logs the while: pray, give me that;
I'll carry it to the pile.

FERDINAND.   No, precious creature;
I had rather crack my sinews, break my back,
Than you should such dishonour undergo,
While I sit lazy by.

MIRANDA.   It would become me
As well as it does you: and I should do it
With much more ease; for my good will is to it,   **30**
And yours it is against.

ACT III. SCENE I. **11. sore**, grievous, severe. **13. executor**, performer. **15. Most . . . lest,** unexplained; Spedding suggests *Most busiest when idlest*; New Cambridge editors suggest *busy-idlest,* employed in trifles.

PROSPERO.   Poor worm, thou art infected!
This visitation shows it.

MIRANDA.   You look wearily.

FERDINAND.   No, noble mistress; 'tis fresh morning with me
When you are by at night. I do beseech you—
Chiefly that I might set it in my prayers—
What is your name?

MIRANDA.   Miranda.—O my father,
I have broke your hest to say so!

FERDINAND.   .   Admired Miranda!
Indeed the top of admiration! worth
What 's dearest to the world! Full many a lady
I have eyed with best regard and many a time   40
The harmony of their tongues hath into bondage
Brought my too diligent ear: for several virtues
Have I liked several women; never any
With so full soul, but some defect in her
Did quarrel with the noblest grace she owed
And put it to the foil: but you, O you,
So perfect and so peerless, are created
Of every creature's best!

MIRANDA.   I do not know
One of my sex; no woman's face remember,
Save, from my glass, mine own; nor have I seen   50
More that I may call men than you, good friend,
And my dear father: how features are abroad,
I am skilless of; but, by my modesty,
The jewel in my dower, I would not wish
Any companion in the world but you,
Nor can imagination form a shape,
Besides yourself, to like of. But I prattle
Something too wildly and my father's precepts
I therein do forget.

FERDINAND.   I am in my condition
A prince, Miranda; I do think, a king;   60
I would, not so!—and would no more endure
This wooden slavery than to suffer
The flesh-fly blow my mouth. Hear my soul speak:
The very instant that I saw you, did
My heart fly to your service; there resides,
To make me slave to it; and for your sake
Am I this patient log-man.

MIRANDA.   Do you love me?

32. **visitation**, affliction.   37. **Admired Miranda**, the two words have the same meaning.
45. **owed**, possessed.   46. **put . . . foil**, disgraced it; a wrestling phrase.   53. **skilless**, ignorant.

FERDINAND. O heaven, O earth, bear witness to this sound
            And crown what I profess with kind event
            If I speak true! if hollowly, invert   70
            What best is boded me to mischief! I
            Beyond all limit of what else i' the world
            Do love, prize, honour you.

MIRANDA.   I am a fool
            To weep at what I am glad of.

PROSPERO.   Fair encounter
            Of two most rare affections! Heavens rain grace
            On that which breeds between 'em!

FERDINAND.   Wherefore weep you?

MIRANDA.   At mine unworthiness that dare not offer
            What I desire to give, and much less take
            What I shall die to want. But this is trifling;
            And all the more it seeks to hide itself,   80
            The bigger bulk it shows. Hence, bashful cunning!
            And prompt me, plain and holy innocence!
            I am your wife, if you will marry me;
            If not, I'll die your maid: to be your fellow
            You may deny me; but I'll be your servant,
            Whether you will or no.

FERDINAND.   My mistress, dearest;
            And I thus humble ever.

MIRANDA.   My husband, then?

FERDINAND. Ay, with a heart as willing
            As bondage e'er of freedom: here 's my hand.

MIRANDA.   And mine, with my heart in 't: and now farewell   90
            Till half an hour hence.

FERDINAND.   A thousand thousand!
                    (*Exeunt* FERDINAND *and* MIRANDA *severally*)

PROSPERO.   So glad of this as they I cannot be,
            Who are surprised withal; but my rejoicing
            At nothing can be more. I'll to my book,
            For yet ere supper-time must I perform
            Much business appertaining.   (*Exit*)

70. hollowly, insincerely, falsely. 79. to want, through wanting. 84. fellow, equal. 91. thousand thousand, i.e., farewells. 94. book, book of magic. 96. appertaining, incumbent upon me.

SCENE II. *Another part of the island.*

Enter CALIBAN, STEPHANO, *and* TRINCULO.

STEPHANO.   Tell not me; when the butt is out, we will drink water; not a drop
             before: therefore bear up, and board 'em. Servant-monster, drink to me.

TRINCULO.   Servant-monster! the folly of this island! They say there 's but five upon
             this isle: we are three of them; if th' other two be brained like us, the
             state totters.

STEPHANO.   Drink, servant-monster, when I bid thee: thy eyes are almost set in thy
             head.

TRINCULO.   Where should they be set else? he were a brave monster indeed, if they
             were set in his tail.

STEPHANO.   My man-monster hath drown'd his tongue in sack: for my part,   10
             the sea cannot drown me; I swam, ere I could recover the shore, five and
             thirty leagues off and on. By this light, thou shalt be my lieutenant,
             monster, or my standard.

TRINCULO.   Your lieutenant, if you list; he 's no standard.

STEPHANO.   We'll not run, Monsieur Monster.

TRINCULO.   Nor go neither; but you'll lie like dogs and yet say nothing neither

STEPHANO.   Moon-calf, speak once in thy life, if thou beest a good moon-calf.

CALIBAN.   How does thy honour? Let me lick thy shoe.
             I'll not serve him; he is not valiant.

TRINCULO.   Thou liest, most ignorant monster: I am in case to justle a con-   20
             stable. Why, thou deboshed fish, thou, was there ever man a coward
             that hath drunk so much sack as I to-day? Wilt thou tell a monstrous
             lie, being but half a fish and half a monster?

CALIBAN.   Lo, how he mocks me! wilt thou let him, my lord?

TRINCULO.   'Lord' quoth he. That a monster should be such a natural!

CALIBAN.   Lo, lo, again! bite him to death, I prithee.

STEPHANO.   Trinculo, keep a good tongue in your head; if you prove a mutineer,—
             the next tree! The poor monster 's my subject and he shall not suffer
             indignity.

CALIBAN.   I thank my noble lord. Wilt thou be pleased to hearken once again   30
             to the suit I made to thee?

SCENE II. **2. bear up,** put the helm up so as to bring the ship into the wind. **board 'em,**
climb aboard: both phrases refer to drinking. **4. brained,** endowed with brains. **6. thy
eyes . . . head,** current description of drunkenness meaning that the eyes are fixed in a
stare, or dimmed by drink. **13. standard,** standard-bearer. **14. standard,** something that
stands up. **16. go,** walk. **20. case,** condition. **justle,** jostle. **21. deboshed,** debauched.
25. natural, idiot.

STEPHANO.   Marry, will I: kneel and repeat *it*; I will stand, and so shall Trinculo.

(*Enter* ARIEL, *invisible.*)

CALIBAN.   As I told thee before, I am subject to a tyrant, a sorcerer, that by his cunning hath cheated me of the island.

ARIEL.   Thou liest.

CALIBAN.   Thou liest, thou jesting monkey, thou: I would my valiant master would destroy thee! I do not lie.

STEPHANO.   Trinculo, if you trouble him any more in 's tale, by this hand, I will supplant some of your teeth.

TRINCULO.   Why, I said nothing.   40

STEPHANO.   Mum, then, and no more. Proceed.

CALIBAN.   I say, by sorcery he got this isle;
From me he got it. If thy greatness will
Revenge it on him,—for I know thou darest,
But this thing dare not,—

STEPHANO.   That 's most certain.

CALIBAN.   Thou shalt be lord of it and I'll serve thee.

STEPHANO.   How now shall this be compassed?
Canst thou bring me to the party?

CALIBAN.   Yea, yea, my lord: I'll yield him thee asleep,   50
Where thou mayst knock a nail into his head.

ARIEL.   Thou liest; thou canst not.

CALIBAN.   What a pied ninny 's this! Thou scurvy patch!
I do beseech thy greatness, give him blows
And take his bottle from him: when that 's gone
He shall drink nought but brine; for I'll not show him
Where the quick freshes are.

STEPHANO.   Trinculo, run into no further danger: interrupt the monster one word further, and, by this hand, I'll turn my mercy out o' doors and make a stock-fish of thee.

TRINCULO.   Why, what did I? I did nothing. I'll go farther off.   60

STEPHANO.   Didst thou not say he lied?

ARIEL.   Thou liest.

STEPHANO.   Do I so? take thou that. (*Beats* TRINCULO) As you like this, give me the lie another time.

39. **supplant**, displace. 49. **party**, the one concerned in this affair. 53. **pied ninny**, fool in motley. **patch**, common word for *fool*. 57. **quick freshes**, running springs. 59. **stock-fish**, dried cod beaten before boiling.

TRINCULO.   I did not give the lie. Out o' your wits and hearing too? A pox o'
             your bottle! this ran sack and drinking do. A murrain on your monster,
             and the devil take your fingers!

CALIBAN.   Ha, ha, ha!

STEPHANO.   Now, forward with your tale. Prithee, stand farther off.

CALIBAN.   Beat him enough: after a little time   70
             I'll beat him too.

STEPHANO.   Stand farther. Come, proceed.

CALIBAN.   Why, as I told thee, 'tis a custom with him,
             I' th' afternoon to sleep: there thou mayst brain him,
             Having first seized his books, or with a log
             Batter his skull, or paunch him with a stake,
             Or cut his wezand with thy knife. Remember
             First to possess his books; for without them
             He 's but a sot, as I am, nor hath not
             One spirit to command: they all do hate him   80
             As rootedly as I. Burn but his books.
             He has brave utensils,—for so he calls them,—
             Which, when he has a house, he'll deck withal.
             And that most deeply to consider is
             The beauty of his daughter; he himself
             Calls her a nonpareil: I never saw a woman,
             But only Sycorax my dam and she;
             But she as far surpasseth Sycorax
             As great'st does least.

STEPHANO.   Is it so brave a lass?

CALIBAN.   Ay, lord; she will become thy bed, I warrant.   90
             And bring thee forth brave brood.

STEPHANO.   Monster, I will kill this man: his daughter and I will be king and
             queen,—save our graces!—and Trinculo and thyself shall be viceroys.
             Dost thou like the plot, Trinculo?

TRINCULO.   Excellent.

STEPHANO.   Give me thy hand: I am sorry I beat thee; but, while thou livest, keep a
             good tongue in thy head.

CALIBAN.   Within this half hour will he be asleep:
             Wilt thou destroy him then?

STEPHANO.   Ay, on mine honour.

ARIEL.   This will I tell my master.   100

---

66. murrain, plague. 75. paunch, stab in the belly. 76, wezand, windpipe. 79. sot, fool.
82. utensils, household goods. 83. deck, adorn. 86. nonpareil, one having no equal.

CALIBAN.   Thou makest me merry; I am full of pleasure:
              Let us be jocund: will you troll the catch
              You taught me but while-ere?

STEPHANO.   At thy request, monster, I will do reason, any reason. Come on, Trin-
              culo, let us sing. (*Sings*)
                        Flout 'em and scout 'em
                        And scout 'em and flout 'em;
                        Thought is free.

CALIBAN.   That's not the tune.

(ARIEL *plays the tune on a tabor and pipe.*)

STEPHANO.   What is this same?   110

TRINCULO.   This is the tune of our catch, played by the picture of Nobody.

STEPHANO.   If thou beest a man, show thyself in thy likeness: if thou beest a devil,
              take 't as thou list.

TRINCULO.   O, forgive me my sins!

STEPHANO.   He that dies pays all debts: I defy thee. Mercy upon us!

CALIBAN.   Art thou afeard?

STEPHANO.   No, monster, not I.

CALIBAN.   Be not afeard; the isle is full of noises,
              Sounds and sweet airs, that give delight and hurt not.
              Sometimes a thousand twangling instruments   120
              Will hum about mine ears, and sometime voices
              That, if I then had waked after long sleep,
              Will make me sleep again: and then, in dreaming,
              The clouds methought would open and show riches
              Ready to drop upon me, that, when I waked,
              I cried to dream again.

STEPHANO.   This will prove a brave kingdom to me, where I shall have my music
              for nothing.

CALIBAN.   When Prospero is destroyed.

STEPHANO.   That shall be by and by: I remember the story.   130

TRINCULO.   The sound is going away; let's follow it, and after do our work.

STEPHANO.   Lead, monster; we'll follow. I would I could see this taborer; he lays
              it on.

TRINCULO.   Wilt come? I'll follow, Stephano.   (*Exeunt*)

102. **troll the catch**, sing the song. 103. **while-ere**, a while since. 107. **scout**, deride
(Onions). New Cambridge editors emend. *cout* (befool). 109. **Stage Direction: tabor,**
small drum. 111. **picture of Nobody**, an unexplained topical allusion. New Cambridge
editors suggest a reference to the sign of "Nobody" used by John Trundle, bookseller and
printer. 132. **taborer**, drummer.

SCENE III. *Another part of the island.*

Enter ALONSO, SEBASTIAN, ANTONIO, GONZALO, ADRIAN, FRANCISCO, *and others.*

GONZALO. By 'r lakin, I can go no further, sir;
My old bones ache: here 's a maze trod indeed
Through forth-rights and meanders! By your patience,
I needs must rest me.

ALONSO.   Old lord, I cannot blame thee,
Who am myself attach'd with weariness,
To the dulling of my spirits: sit down, and rest.
Even here I will put off my hope and keep it
No longer for my flatterer: he is drown'd
Whom thus we stray to find, and the sea mocks
Our frustrate search on land. Well, let him go.   10

ANTONIO. (*aside to* SEBASTIAN) I am right glad that he 's so out of hope
Do not, for one repulse, forego the purpose
That you resolved to effect.

SEBASTIAN. (*aside to* ANTONIO) The next advantage
Will we take throughly.

ANTONIO. (*aside to* SEBASTIAN) Let it be to-night;
For, now they are oppress'd with travel, they
Will not, nor cannot, use such vigilance
As when they are fresh.

SEBASTIAN. (*aside to* ANTONIO) I say, to-night: no more.

(*Solemn and strange music.*)

ALONSO. What harmony is this? My good friends, hark!

GONZALO. Marvellous sweet music!

(*Enter* PROSPERO *above, invisible. Enter several strange Shapes, bringing in a banquet; they dance about it with gentle actions of salutation; and, inviting the King, &c. to eat, they depart.*)

ALONSO. Give us kind keepers, heavens! What were these?   20

SEBASTIAN. A living drollery. Now I will believe
That there are unicorns, that in Arabia
There is one tree, the phœnix' throne, one phœnix
At this hour reigning there.

ANTONIO.   I'll believe both;
And what does else want credit, come to me,
And I'll be sworn 'tis true: travellers ne'er did lie,
Though fools at home condemn 'em.

SCENE III. 1. **By 'r lakin,** by our Lady. 3. **forth-rights and meanders,** paths straight and crooked. 5. **attach'd,** seized. 14. **throughly,** thoroughly, completely. 20. **keepers,** guardian angels. 21. **drollery,** puppet show.

GONZALO.   If in Naples
I should report this now, would they believe me?
If I should say, I saw such islanders—
For, certes, these are people of the island—   30
Who, though they are of monstrous shape, yet, note,
Their manners are more gentle-kind than of
Our human generation you shall find
Many, nay, almost any.

PROSPERO.   (*aside*) Honest lord,
Thou hast said well; for some of you there present
Are worse than devils.

ALONSO.   I cannot too much muse
Such shapes, such gesture and such sound, expressing,
Although they want the use of tongue, a kind
Of excellent dumb discourse.

PROSPERO.   (*aside*) Praise in departing.

FRANCISCO.   They vanish'd strangely.

SEBASTIAN.   No matter, since   40
They have left their viands behind; for we have stomachs.
Will 't please you taste of what is here?

ALONSO.   Not I.

GONZALO.   Faith, sir, you need not fear. When we were boys,
Who would believe that there were mountaineers
Dew-lapp'd like bulls, whose throats had hanging at 'em
Wallets of flesh? or that there were such men
Whose heads stood in their breasts? which now we find
Each putter-out of five for one will bring us
Good warrant of.

ALONSO.   I will stand to and feed,
Although my last: no matter, since I feel   50
The best is past. Brother, my lord the duke,
Stand to and do as we.

(*Thunder and lighting. Enter* ARIEL, *like a harpy; claps his wings upon the table;
and, with a quaint device, the banquet vanishes.*)

ARIEL.   You are three men of sin, whom Destiny,
That hath to instrument this lower world

30. certes, certainly. 36. muse, wonder at.
   39. Praise in departing, proverbial expression meaning, "Praise comes at the end." Yale
editor interprets as "Save your praise until the end of the performance." 45. Dew-lapp'd,
having a dewlap, or fold of skin hanging from the neck, as cattle; often supposed to
refer to people afflicted with goiter. 47. heads . . . breasts. Furness quotes Grey's reference
to Pliny, who so describes the Blemmyi; other late accounts; cf. *Othello,* I, iii, 145. 48.
putter-out . . . one, one who invests money, or gambles on the risks of travel on the
condition that, if he returns safely, he is to receive five times the amount deposited. 52.
Stage Direction: harpy, a fabulous monster with a woman's face and vulture's body

And what is in 't, the never-surfeited sea
Hath caused to belch up you; and on this island
Where man doth not inhabit; you 'mongst men
Being most unfit to live, I have made you mad;
And even with such-like valour men hang and drown
Their proper selves.   (ALONSO, SEBASTIAN, &c. *draw their swords*.)
              You fools! I and my fellows   60
Are ministers of Fate: the elements,
Of whom your swords are temper'd, may as well
Wound the loud winds, or with bemock'd-at stabs
Kill the still-closing waters, as diminish
One dowle that 's in my plume: my fellow-ministers
Are like invulnerable. If you could hurt,
Your swords are now too massy for your strengths
And will not be uplifted. But remember—
For that 's my business to you—that you three
From Milan did supplant good Prospero;   70
Exposed unto the sea, which hath requit it,
Him and his innocent child: for which foul deed
The powers, delaying, not forgetting, have
Incensed the seas and shores, yea, all the creatures,
Against your peace. Thee of thy son, Alonso,
They have bereft; and do pronounce by me
Lingering perdition, worse than any death
Can be at once, shall step by step attend
You and your ways; whose wraths to guard you from—
Which here, in this most desolate isle, else falls   80
Upon your heads—is nothing but heart-sorrow
And a clear life ensuing.

(*He vanishes in thunder; then, to soft music, enter the Shapes again, and dance, with mocks and mows, and carrying out the table.*)

PROSPERO.   Bravely the figure of this harpy hast thou
               Perform'd, my Ariel; a grace it had, devouring:
               Of my instruction hast thou nothing bated
               In what thou hadst to say: so, with good life
               And observation strange, my meaner ministers
               Their several kinds have done. My high charms work
               And these mine enemies are all knit up
               In their distractions; they now are in my power;   90
               And in these fits I leave them, while I visit

supposed to be a minister of divine vengeance. **quaint device,** ingenious stage contrivance; perhaps harpies seemed to swallow the food. **54-55. That . . . in 't,** that uses this lower world and what is in it as instruments (for its purposes). **65. dowle,** soft, fine feather. **plume,** plumage (?) (Onions). **66. like,** likewise, similarly. **71. requit,** requited, avenged. **82. clear,** unspotted, innocent. **84. devouring.** New Cambridge editors conjecture *devoiring* (serving, waiting at table). **86. so . . . life,** with faithful reproduction. **87. observation**

Young Ferdinand, whom they suppose is drown'd,
And his and mine loved darling.   (*Exit above*)

GONZALO.   I' the name of something holy, sir, why stand you
In this strange stare?

ALONSO.   O, it is monstrous, monstrous!
Methought the billows spoke and told me of it;
The winds did sing it to me, and the thunder,
That deep and dreadful organ-pipe, pronounced
The name of Prosper: it did bass my trespass.
Therefore my son i' the ooze is bedded, and   100
I'll seek him deeper than e'er plummet sounded
And with him there lie mudded.   (*Exit*)

SEBASTIAN.   But one fiend at a time,
I'll fight their legions o'er.

ANTONIO.   I'll be thy second.
                              (*Exeunt* SEBASTIAN *and* ANTONIO)

GONZALO.   All three of them are desperate: their great guilt,
Like poison given to work a great time after,
Now 'gins to bite the spirits. I do beseech you
That are of suppler joints, follow them swiftly
And hinder them from what this ecstasy
May now provoke them to.

ADRIAN.   Follow, I pray you.   (*Exeunt*)

ACT IV

SCENE I. *Before* PROSPERO'S *cell.*

Enter PROSPERO, FERDINAND, *and* MIRANDA.

PROSPERO.   If I have too austerely punish'd you,
Your compensation makes amends, for I
Have given you here a thrid of mine own life,
Or that for which I live; who once again
I tender to thy hand: all thy vexations
Were but my trials of thy love, and thou
Hast strangely stood the test: here, afore Heaven,
I ratify this my rich gift. O Ferdinand,
Do not smile at me that I boast her off,
For thou shalt find she will outstrip all praise   10
And make it halt behind her.

strange, rare attention to detail. **99. bass my trespass**, proclaimed my trespass like a bass
note in music. **106. bite the spirits**, i.e., conscience troubles them.
    ACT IV. SCENE I. **3. thrid**, defined as "thread," "narrative"; F: *third*, which is probably
correct—the other thirds were Prospero himself and his wife. **7. strangely**, extraordinarily.
9. off, to best advantage (W. J. Craig).

FERDINAND.   I do believe it
    Against an oracle.

PROSPERO.   Then, as my gift and thine own acquisition
    Worthily purchased, take my daughter: but
    If thou dost break her virgin-knot before
    All sanctimonious ceremonies may
    With full and holy rite be minister'd,
    No sweet aspersion shall the heavens let fall
    To make this contract grow; but barren hate,
    Sour-eyed disdain and discord shall bestrew   20
    The union of your bed with weeds so loathly
    That you shall hate it both: therefore take heed,
    As Hymen's lamps shall light you.

FERDINAND.   As I hope
    For quiet days, fair issue and long life,
    With such love as 'tis now, the murkiest den,
    The most opportune place, the strong'st suggestion
    Our worser genius can, shall never melt
    Mine honour into lust, to take away
    The edge of that day's celebration
    When I shall think, or Phœbus' steeds are founder'd,   30
    Or Night kept chain'd below.

PROSPERO.   Fairly spoke.
    Sit then and talk with her; she is thine own.
    What, Ariel! my industrious servant, Ariel!

(*Enter* ARIEL.)

ARIEL.   What would my potent master? here I am.

PROSPERO.   Thou and thy meaner fellows your last service
    Did worthily perform; and I must use you
    In such another trick. Go bring the rabble,
    O'er whom I give thee power, here to this place:
    Incite them to quick motion; for I must
    Bestow upon the eyes of this young couple   40
    Some vanity of mine art: it is my promise,
    And they expect it from me.

ARIEL.   Presently?

PROSPERO.   Ay, with a twink.

ARIEL.   Before you can say 'come' and 'go,'
    And breathe twice and cry 'so, so,'

---

16. **sanctimonious**, sacred. 18. **aspersion**, dew, shower.
  23. **Hymen's**. Hymen was the Greek and Roman god of marriage. 27. **genius,**
evil genius, or evil attendant spirit. **can**, is able to offer. 29. **edge**, enjoyment. 30.
founder'd, broken down, made lame. 35. **meaner fellows**, Ariel's subordinate assistants.
37. **rabble**, band. 41. **vanity**, illusion. 43. **with a twink**, in the twinkling of an eye.

Each one, tripping on his toe,
Will be here with mop and mow.
Do you love me, master? no?

PROSPERO.   Dearly, my delicate Ariel. Do not approach
Till thou does hear me call.

ARIEL.   Well, I conceive.   (*Exit*)   50

PROSPERO.   Look thou be true; do not give dalliance
Too much the rein: the strongest oaths are straw
To the fire i' the blood: be more abstemious,
Or else, good night your vow!

FERDINAND.   I warrant you, sir;
The white cold virgin snow upon my heart
Abates the ardour of my liver.

PROSPERO.   Well.
Now come, my Ariel! bring a corollary,
Rather than want a spirit: appear, and pertly!
No tongue! all eyes! be silent.   (*Soft music*)

(*Enter* IRIS.)

IRIS   Ceres, most bounteous lady, thy rich leas   60
Of wheat, rye, barley, vetches, oats and pease;
Thy turfy mountains, where live nibbling sheep,
And flat meads thatch'd with stover, them to keep;
Thy banks with pioned and twilled brims,
Which spongy April at thy hest betrims,
To make cold nymphs chaste crowns; and thy broom-groves,
Whose shadow the dismissed bachelor loves,
Being lass-lorn; thy pole-clipt vineyard;
And thy sea-marge, sterile and rocky-hard,
Where thou thyself dost air;—the queen o' the sky,   70
Whose watery arch and messenger am I,
Bids thee leave these, and with her sovereign grace,
Here on this grass-plot, in this very place,
To come and sport: her peacocks fly amain:
Approach, rich Ceres, her to entertain.

(*Enter* CERES.)

47. **mop and mow**, grimace and made faces. 56. **liver**, as the seat of the passions. 57. **corollary**, supernumerary. 58. **pertly**, briskly. 60-138. **Ceres . . . footing.** This is the most perfect example of the masque in Shakespeare. His authorship of it has, however, sometimes been called in question. For another example of a masque in honor of betrothal see the end of *A Midsummer-Night's Dream.* 63. **stover**, fodder for cattle. 64. **pioned and twilled**, unexplained; excavated (?) or trenched (?) (Onions), ridged (New Cambridge), grown over with peonies and lilies (Hanmer). 66. **broom-groves**, groves of broom (?). 68. **pole-clipt**, hedged in with poles. 70. **dost air**, enjoy the air (?). 71. **watery arch**, rainbow. Iris was goddess of the rainbow. 74. **amain**, with full force or speed. 75. **Ceres**, part played

CERES.   Hail, many-colour'd messenger, that ne'er
          Dost disobey the wife of Jupiter;
          Who with thy saffron wings upon my flowers
          Diffusest honey-drops, refreshing showers,
          And with each end of thy blue bow dost crown   80
          My bosky acres and my unshrubb'd down,
          Rich scarf to my proud earth; why hath thy queen
          Summon'd me hither, to this short-grass'd green?

IRIS.   A contract of true love to celebrate;
          And some donation freely to estate
          On the blest lovers.

CERES.   Tell me, heavenly bow,
          If Venus or her son, as thou dost know,
          Do now attend the queen? Since they did plot
          The means that dusky Dis my daughter got,
          Her and her blind boy's scandal'd company   90
          I have forsworn.

IRIS.   Of her society
          Be not afraid: I met her deity
          Cutting the clouds towards Paphos and her son
          Dove-drawn with her. Here thought they to have done
          Some wanton charm upon this man and maid,
          Whose vows are, that no bed-right shall be paid
          Till Hymen's torch be lighted: but in vain;
          Mars's hot minion is return'd again;
          Her waspish-headed son has broke his arrows,
          Swears he will shoot no more but play with sparrows   100
          And be a boy right out.

CERES.   High'st queen of state,
          Great Juno, comes; I know her by her gait.

(*Enter* JUNO.)

JUNO.   How does my bounteous sister? Go with me
          To bless this twain, that they may prosperous be
          And honour'd in their issue.

(*They sing:*)

JUNO.   Honour, riches, marriage-blessing,
          Long continuance, and increasing,
          Hourly joys be still upon you!
          Juno sings her blessings on you.

by Ariel; see l. 167. **81. bosky,** covered with shrubs. **unshrubb'd down,** shrubless upland.
89. Dis . . . got. Pluto, god of the infernal regions, carried off Persephone, daughter of
Ceres, to be his bride in Hades. **90. scandal'd,** brought into disrepute; New Cambridge
editors suggest sandal'd. **93. Paphos,** a town in the island of Cyprus, sacred to Venus.
98. Mars's . . . minion, Venus, the beloved of Mars. **99. waspish-headed,** fiery, hot-
headed (?).

CERES.   Earth's increase, foison plenty,   110
          Barns and garners never empty,
          Vines with clustering bunches growing,
          Plants with goodly burthen bowing;

          Spring come to you at the farthest
          In the very end of harvest!
          Scarcity and want shall shun you;
          Ceres' blessing so is on you.

FERDINAND.   This is a most majestic vision, and
              Harmonious charmingly. May I be bold
              To think these spirits?

PROSPERO.   Spirits, which by mine art   120
              I have from their confines call'd to enact
              My present fancies.

FERDINAND.   Let me live here ever;
              So rare a wonder'd father and a wife
              Makes this place Paradise.

(JUNO *and* CERES *whisper, and send* IRIS *on employment.*)

PROSPERO.   Sweet, now, silence!
              Juno and Ceres whisper seriously;
              There 's something else to do: hush, and be mute,
              Or else our spell is marr'd.

IRIS.   You nymphs, call'd Naiads, of the windring brooks,
         With your sedged crowns and ever-harmless looks,
         Leave your crisp channels and on this green land   130
         Answer your summons; Juno does command:
         Come, temperate nymphs, and help to celebrate
         A contract of true love; be not too late.

(*Enter certain* NYMPHS.)

         You sunburnt sicklemen, of August weary,
         Come hither from the furrow and be merry:
         Make holiday; your rye-straw hats put on
         And these fresh nymphs encounter every one
         In country footing.

(*Enter certain* REAPERS, *properly habited: they join with the* NYMPHS *in a graceful
    dance; towards the end whereof* PROSPERO *starts suddenly, and speaks; after
    which, to a strange, hollow, and confused noise, they heavily vanish.*)

110. **foison plenty,** plentiful harvest. 119. **charmingly,** with magic charm.
123. **wonder'd,** wonder-performing. 128. **Naiads,** spirits of lakes, rivers, brooks, and fountains. **windring,** wandering (?) or winding (?). 130. **crisp,** curled, rippled. 132. **temperate,**
chaste. 134. **sicklemen,** reapers with sickles or reaping hooks. 138. **country footing,**

PROSPERO.   (*aside*) I had forgot that foul conspiracy
              Of the beast Caliban and his confederates   140
              Against my life: the minute of their plot
              Is almost come. (*To the* SPIRITS) Well done! avoid; no more!

FERDINAND.   This is strange: your father's in some passion
              That works him strongly.

MIRANDA.   Never till this day
              Saw I him touch'd with anger so distemper'd.

PROSPERO.   You do look, my son, in a moved sort,
              As if you were dismay'd: be cheerful, sir.
              Our revels now are ended. These our actors,
              As I foretold you, were all spirits and
              Are melted into air, into thin air: 150
              And, like the baseless fabric of this vision,
              The cloud-capp'd towers, the gorgeous palaces,
              The solemn temples, the great globe itself,
              Yea, all which it inherit, shall dissolve
              And, like this insubstantial pageant faded,
              Leave not a rack behind. We are such stuff
              As dreams are made on, and our little life
              Is rounded with a sleep. Sir, I am vex'd;
              Bear with my weakness; my old brain is troubled:
              Be not disturb'd with my infirmity: 160
              If you be pleased, retire into my cell
              And there repose: a turn or two I'll walk,
              To still my beating mind.

FERDINAND, MIRANDA.   We wish your peace.   (*Exeunt*)

PROSPERO.   Come with a thought. I thank thee, Ariel: come.

(*Enter* ARIEL.)

ARIEL.   Thy thoughts I cleave to. What's thy pleasure?

PROSPERO.   Spirit,
              We must prepare to meet with Caliban.

ARIEL.   Ay, my commander: when I presented Ceres,
              I thought to have told thee of it, but I fear'd
              Lest I might anger thee.

PROSPERO.   Say again, where didst thou leave these varlets?   170

ARIEL.   I told you, sir, they were red-hot with drinking;
              So full of valour that they smote the air
              For breathing in their faces; beat the ground

country-dancing. **Stage Direction: heavily,** sorrowfully. **142. avoid,** depart, withdraw.
144. works, affects. **145. distemper'd,** vexed. **146. sort,** state, condition. **154. which it
inherit,** who possess it. **156. rack,** mass of cloud driven before the wind in the upper
air (Onions). **164. with a thought,** on the instant.

For kissing of their feet; yet always bending
Towards their project. Then I beat my tabor;
At which, like unback'd colts, they prick'd their ears,
Advanced their eyelids, lifted up their noses
As they smelt music: so I charm'd their ears
That calf-like they my lowing follow'd through
Tooth'd briers, sharp furzes, pricking goss and thorns,   180
Which enter'd their frail shins: at last I left them
I' the filthy-mantled pool beyond your cell,
There dancing up to the chins, that the foul lake
O'erstunk their feet.

PROSPERO.   This was well done, my bird.
Thy shape invisible retain thou still:
The trumpery in my house, go bring it hither,
For stale to catch these thieves.

ARIEL.   I go, I go.   (*Exit*)

PROSPERO.   A devil, a born devil, on whose nature
Nurture can never stick; on whom my pains,
Humanely taken, all, all lost, quite lost;   190
And as with age his body uglier grows,
So his mind cankers. I will plague them all,
Even to roaring. (*Re-enter* ARIEL, *loaden with glistering apparel, &c.*)
Come, hang them on this line.

(PROSPERO *and* ARIEL *remain, invisible. Enter* CALIBAN, STEPHANO, *and* TRINCULO,
  all wet.)

CALIBAN.   Pray you, tread softly, that the blind mole may not
Hear a foot fall: we now are near his cell.

STEPHANO.   Monster, your fairy, which you say is a harmless fairy, has done little
better than played the Jack with us.

TRINCULO.   Monster, I do smell all horse-piss; at which my nose is in great indignation.   200

STEPHANO.   So is mine. Do you hear, monster? If I should take a displeasure
against you, look you,—

TRINCULO.   Thou wert but a lost monster.

CALIBAN.   Good my lord, give me thy favour still.
Be patient, for the prize I'll bring thee to
Shall hoodwink this mischance: therefore speak softly.
All 's hush'd as midnight yet.

176. unback'd, unbroken, unridden.
180. goss, gorse, a prickly shrub. 182. filthy-mantled, covered with vegetable coating,
slimy. 184. feet, New Cambridge conjectures: *sweat*. bird, used as a term of endearment.
187. stale, decoy. 189. Nurture, education, culture. 193. line, probably, lime tree. 198.
played the Jack, done a mean trick. *Jack* has a double meaning, "knave" and "will-o'-the-
wisp." 206. hoodwink, cover up; hawking term.

TRINCULO.   Ay, but to lose our bottles in the pool,—

STEPHANO.   There is not only disgrace and dishonour in that, monster, but an
             infinite loss.   210

TRINCULO.   That 's more to me than my wetting: yet this is your harmless fairy,
             monster.

STEPHANO.   I will fetch off my bottle, though I be o'er ears for my labour.

CALIBAN.   Prithee, my king, be quiet. See'st thou here,
             This is the mouth o' the cell: no noise, and enter.
             Do that good mischief which may make this island
             Thine own for ever, and I, thy Caliban,
             For aye thy foot-licker.

STEPHANO.   Give me thy hand. I do begin to have bloody thoughts.

TRINCULO.   O king Stephano! O peer! O worthy Stephano! look what a   220
             wardrobe here is for thee!

CALIBAN.   Let it alone, thou fool; it is but trash.

TRINCULO.   O, ho, monster! we know what belongs to a frippery. O king Stephano!

STEPHANO.   Put off that gown, Trinculo; by this hand, I'll have that gown.

TRINCULO.   Thy grace shall have it.

CALIBAN.   The dropsy drown this fool! what do you mean
             To dote thus on such luggage? Let 's alone
             And do the murder first: if he awake,
             From toe to crown he'll fill our skins with pinches,
             Make us strange stuff.   230

STEPHANO.   Be you quiet, monster. Mistress line, is not this my jerkin? Now is
             the jerkin under the line: now, jerkin, you are like to lose your hair
             and prove a bald jerkin.

TRINCULO.   Do, do: we steal by line and level, an 't like your grace.

STEPHANO.   I thank thee for that jest; here 's a garment for 't: wit shall not go
             unrewarded while I am king of this country. 'Steal by line and level'
             is an excellent pass of pate; there 's another garment for 't.

TRINCULO.   Monster, come, put some lime upon your fingers, and away with the rest.

218. foot-licker, fawning servant.
220. king Stephano, allusion to the old ballad begining, "King Stephen was a worthy peer."
223. frippery, place where cast-off clothes are sold. 227. luggage, impedimenta, heavy stuff
to be carried. 231. Mistress line, clothesline. 232. jerkin, jacket made of leather. under
the line, under the lime tree, with punning allusion, probably, to the equinoctial line.
lose your hair. The jerkin will lose all its hair when Stephano wears it. 234. by line
and level, i.e., by means of instruments, or, methodically, like dishonest carpenters and
masons. 237. pass of pate, folly of wit. 238. lime, birdlime.

CALIBAN. I will have none on 't: we shall lose our time,
And all be turn'd to barnacles, or to apes   240
With foreheads villanous low.

STEPHANO. Monster, lay to your fingers: help to bear this away where my hogshead of wine is, or I'll turn you out of my kingdom: go to, carry this.

TRINCULO. And this.

STEPHANO. Ay, and this.

(*A noise of hunters heard. Enter divers* SPIRITS, *in shape of dogs and hounds, and hunt them about,* PROSPERO *and* ARIEL *setting them on.*)

PROSPERO. Hey, Mountain, hey!

ARIEL. Silver! there it goes, Silver!

PROSPERO. Fury, Fury! there, Tyrant, there! hark! hark!

(CALIBAN, STEPHANO, *and* TRINCULO *are driven out.*)

Go charge my goblins that they grind their joints
With dry convulsions, shorten up their sinews   250
With aged cramps, and more pinch-spotted make them
Than pard or cat o' mountain.

ARIEL.   Hark, they roar!

PROSPERO. Let them be hunted soundly. At this hour
Lie at my mercy all mine enemies:
Shortly shall all my labours end, and thou
Shalt have the air at freedom: for a little
Follow, and do me service.   (*Exeunt*)

ACT V

SCENE I. *Before* PROSPERO'S *cell.*

Enter PROSPERO *in his magic robes, and* ARIEL.

PROSPERO. Now does my project gather to a head:
My charms crack not; my spirits obey; and time
Goes upright with his carriage. How 's the day?

ARIEL. On the sixth hour; at which time, my lord,
You said our work should cease.

240. barnacles, barnacle geese, formerly supposed to be hatched from seashells attached to trees and to fall thence into the water; possibly, the ordinary meaning is intended. 250. convulsions, cramps. 252. pard, panther or leopard. cat o' mountain, wildcat.
ACT. V. SCENE I. 2. crack, figure not entirely clear; possibly, since his project gathers "to a head," the reference is to an ulcer; "the breaking of magic bands" has been suggested. He may merely mean that his charms do not fail. 3. carriage, burden. How's

PROSPERO.   I did say so,
When first I raised the tempest. Say, my spirit,
How fares the king and 's followers?

ARIEL.   Confined together
In the same fashion as you gave in charge,
Just as you left them; all prisoners, sir,
In the line-grove which weather-fends your cell;   10
They cannot budge till your release. The king,
His brother and yours, abide all three distracted
And the remainder mourning over them,
Brimful of sorrow and dismay; but chiefly
Him that you term'd, sir, 'The good old lord, Gonzalo;'
His tears run down his beard, like winter's drops
From eaves of reeds. Your charm so strongly works 'em
That if you now beheld them, your affections
Would become tender.

PROSPERO.   Dost thou think so, spirit?

ARIEL.   Mine would, sir, were I human.

PROSPERO.   And mine shall.   20
Hast thou, which art but air, a touch, a feeling
Of their afflictions, and shall not myself,
One of their kind, that relish all as sharply,
Passion as they, be kindlier moved than thou art?
Though with their high wrongs I am struck to the quick,
Yet with my nobler reason 'gainst my fury
Do I take part: the rarer action is
In virtue than in vengeance: they being penitent,
The sole drift of my purpose doth extend
Not a frown further. Go release them, Ariel: 30
My charms I'll break, their senses I'll restore,
And they shall be themselves.

ARIEL.   I'll fetch them, sir.   (*Exit*)

PROSPERO.   Ye elves of hills, brooks, standing lakes and groves,
And ye that on the sands with printless foot
Do chase the ebbing Neptune and do fly him
When he comes back; you demi-puppets that
By moonshine do the green sour ringlets make,
Whereof the ewe not bites, and you whose pastime

---

the day? What time is it? **10. line-grove,** grove of lime trees. **weather-fends,** protects
from the weather. **17. eaves of reeds,** thatch. **23. all,** quite. **27. rarer,** nobler. **33-57.**
Ye . . . book. This famous passage is an embellished paraphrase of Golding's translation
of Ovid's *Metamorphoses*, vii, 197–219. [For the passage cited, see below, p. 628.—The
Editors.] Critics have often seen in Prospero's farewell to magic an analogue to Shakespeare's farewell to the stage. *The Tempest* is the next to his last complete play. After
writing it he probably retired to Stratford. **36. demi-puppets,** elves and fairies; literally,
puppets of half-size. **37. green sour ringlets,** fairy rings, circles of grass produced by

Is to make midnight mushrooms, that rejoice
To hear the solemn curfew; by whose aid, 40
Weak masters though ye be, I have bedimm'd
The noontide sun, call'd forth the mutinous winds,
And 'twixt the green sea and the azured vault
Set roaring war: to the dread rattling thunder
Have I given fire and rifted Jove's stout oak
With his own bolt; the strong-based promontory
Have I made shake and by the spurs pluck'd up
The pine and cedar: graves at my command
Have waked their sleepers, oped, and let 'em forth
By my so potent art. But this rough magic 50
I here abjure, and, when I have required
Some heavenly music, which even now I do,
To work mine end upon their senses that
This airy charm is for, I'll break my staff,
Bury it certain fathoms in the earth,
And deeper than did ever plummet sound
I'll drown my book.

(*Solemn music.*)

(*Re-enter* ARIEL *before: then* ALONSO, *with a frantic gesture, attended by* GONZALO;
SEBASTIAN *and* ANTONIO *in like manner, attended by* ADRIAN *and* FRANCISCO:
they all enter the circle which PROSPERO *had made, and there stand charmed;
which* PROSPERO *observing, speaks:*)

A solemn air and the best comforter
To an unsettled fancy cure thy brains,
Now useless, boil'd within thy skull! There stand, 60
For you are spell-stopp'd.
Holy Gonzalo, honourable man,
Mine eyes, even sociable to the show of thine,
Fall fellowly drops. The charm dissolves apace,
And as the morning steals upon the night,
Melting the darkness, so their rising senses
Begin to chase the ignorant fumes that mantle
Their clearer reason. O good Gonzalo,
My true preserver, and a loyal sir
To him thou follow'st! I will pay thy graces 70
Home both in word and deed. Most cruelly
Didst thou, Alonso, use me and my daughter:
Thy brother was a furtherer in the act.
Thou art pinch'd for 't now, Sebastian. Flesh and blood,

fungus within the soil. **40. curfew.** The curfew, which sent people to bed, would send the spirits on their rounds. **44-45. to . . . fire,** the dread rattling thunderbolt I have discharged. **47. spurs,** roots. **50. rough magic.** Prospero will cease the practice of compulsive physical magic in favor of the magic of goodness and wisdom. **60. boil'd,** made hot with humors. **63. sociable,** sympathetic. **show,** appearance. **64. Fall,** let fall. **67. ignorant fumes.** The fumes which rose up into the brain to produce sleep brought with them unconsciousness. **74. pinch'd.** The references to pinching here and in line

You, brother mine, that entertain'd ambition,
Expell'd remorse and nature; who, with Sebastian,
Whose inward pinches therefore are most strong,
Would here have kill'd your king; I do forgive thee,
Unnatural though thou art. Their understanding
Begins to swell, and the approaching tide   80
Will shortly fill the reasonable shore
That now lies foul and muddy. Not one of them
That yet looks on me, or would know me: Ariel,
Fetch me the hat and rapier in my cell:
I will discase me, and myself present
As I was sometime Milan: quickly, spirit;
Thou shalt ere long be free.

(ARIEL *sings and helps to attire him.*)

ARIEL'S *song.*

    Where the bee sucks, there suck I:
    In a cowslip's bell I lie;
    There I couch when owls do cry.   90
    On the bat's back I do fly
    After summer merrily.
Merrily, merrily shall I live now
Under the blossom that hangs on the bough.

PROSPERO. Why, that 's my dainty Ariel! I shall miss thee;
But yet thou shalt have freedom: so, so, so.
To the king's ship, invisible as thou art:
There shalt thou find the mariners asleep
Under the hatches; the master and the boatswain
Being awake, enforce them to this place,   100
And presently, I prithee.

ARIEL. I drink the air before me, and return
Or ere your pulse twice beat.   (*Exit*)

GONZALO. All torment, trouble, wonder and amazement
Inhabits here: some heavenly power guide us
Out of this fearful country!

PROSPERO.   Behold, sir king.
The wronged Duke of Milan, Prospero:
For more assurance that a living prince
Does now speak to thee, I embrace thy body;
And to thee and thy company I bid   110
A hearty welcome.

77 suggest physical pain and hardship, also pangs of conscience. **85. discase,** undress.
90. couch, to lie down as on a couch, or, more probably lie hidden. 96. so, so, so,
that will do very well.

ALONSO.   Whether thou be'st he or no,
Or some enchanted trifle to abuse me,
As late I have been, I not know: thy pulse
Beats as of flesh and blood; and, since I saw thee,
The affliction of my mind amends, with which,
I fear, a madness held me: this must crave,
An if this be at all, a most strange story.
Thy dukedom I resign and do entreat
Thou pardon me my wrongs. But how should Prospero
Be living and be here?

PROSPERO.   First, noble friend,   120
Let me embrace thine age, whose honour cannot
Be measured or confined.

GONZALO.   Whether this be
Or be not, I'll not swear.

PROSPERO.   You do yet taste
Some subtilties o' the isle, that will not let you
Believe things certain. Welcome, my friends all!
(*aside to* SEBASTIAN *and* ANTONIO:)
But you, my brace of lords, were I so minded,
I here could pluck his highness' frown upon you
And justify you traitors: at this time
I will tell no tales.

SEBASTIAN.   (*aside*) The devil speaks in him.

PROSPERO.   No.
For you, most wicked sir, whom to call brother   130
Would even infect my mouth, I do forgive
Thy rankest fault; all of them; and require
My dukedom of thee, which perforce, I know,
Thou must restore.

ALONSO.   If thou be'st Prospero,
Give us particulars of thy preservation;
How thou hast met us here, who three hours since
Were wreck'd upon this shore; where I have lost—
How sharp the point of this remembrance is!—
My dear son Ferdinand.

PROSPERO.   I am woe for 't, sir.

ALONSO.   Irreparable is the loss, and patience   140
Says it is past her cure.

PROSPERO.   I rather think
You have not sought her help, of whose soft grace

---

112. **trifle,** trick of magic. **abuse,** deceive. 124. **subtilties,** illusions.
128. **justify you,** prove you to be. 139. **woe,** sorry.

For the like loss I have her sovereign aid
And rest myself content.

ALONSO.   You the like loss!

PROSPERO.   As great to me as late; and, supportable
To make the dear loss, have I means much weaker
Than you may call to comfort you, for I
Have lost my daughter.

ALONSO.   A daughter?
O heavens, that they were living both in Naples,
The king and queen there! that they were, I wish   150
Myself were mudded in that oozy bed
Where my son lies. When did you lose your daughter?

PROSPERO.   In this last tempest. I perceive, these lords
At this encounter do so much admire
That they devour their reason and scarce think
Their eyes do offices of truth, their words
Are natural breath: but, howsoe'er you have
Been justled from your senses, know for certain
That I am Prospero and that very duke
Which was thrust forth of Milan, who most strangely   160
Upon this shore, where you were wreck'd, was landed,
To be the lord on 't. No more yet of this;
For 'tis a chronicle of day by day,
Not a relation for a breakfast nor
Befitting this first meeting. Welcome, sir;
This cell 's my court: here have I few attendants
And subjects none abroad: pray you, look in.
My dukedom since you have given me again,
I will requite you with as good a thing;
At least bring forth a wonder, to content ye   170
As much as me my dukedom.

(*Here* PROSPERO *discovers* FERDINAND *and* MIRANDA, *playing at chess.*)

MIRANDA.   Sweet lord, you play me false.

FERDINAND.   No, my dear'st love,
I would not for the world.

MIRANDA.   Yes, for a score of kingdoms you should wrangle,
And I would call it fair play.

ALONSO.   If this prove
A vision of the island, one dear son
Shall I twice lose.

145. late, i.e., as great to me as it is recent. **155. devour,** render null, destroy. **174. score,** double meaning: game or wager in which the score is reckoned by kingdoms, and also twenty kingdoms. **wrangle,** meaning (1) contend in a game or wager, and (2) argue or contend in words.

SEBASTIAN.   A most high miracle!

FERDINAND.   Though the seas threaten, they are merciful;
I have cursed them without cause. (*Kneels.*)

ALONSO.   Now all the blessings
Of a glad father compass thee about!   180
Arise, and say how thou camest here.

MIRANDA.   O, wonder!
How many goodly creatures are there here!
How beauteous mankind is! O brave new world,
That has such people in 't!

PROSPERO.   'Tis new to thee.

ALONSO.   What is this maid with whom thou wast at play?
Your eld'st acquaintance cannot be three hours:
Is she the goddess that hath sever'd us,
And brought us thus together?

FERDINAND.   Sir, she is mortal;
But by immortal Providence she 's mine:
I chose her when I could not ask my father   190
For his advice, nor thought I had one. She
Is daughter to this famous Duke of Milan,
Of whom so often I have heard renown,
But never saw before; of whom I have
Received a second life; and second father
This lady makes him to me.

ALONSO.   I am hers:
But, O, how oddly will it sound that I
Must ask my child forgiveness!

PROSPERO.   There, sir, stop:
Let us not burthen our remembrance with
A heaviness that 's gone.

GONZALO.   I have inly wept   200
Or should have spoke ere this. Look down, you gods,
And on this couple drop a blessed crown!
For it is you that have chalk'd forth the way
Which brought us hither.

ALONSO.   I say, Amen, Gonzalo!

GONZALO.   Was Milan thrust from Milan, that his issue
Should become kings of Naples? O, rejoice
Beyond a common joy, and set it down
With gold on lasting pillars: In one voyage

186. eld'st, earliest. 193. renown, report, fame. 203. chalk'd, traced out the way as with chalk.

Did Claribel her husband find at Tunis
And Ferdinand, her brother, found a wife   210
Where he himself was lost, Prospero his dukedom
In a poor isle and all of us ourselves
When no man was his own.

ALONSO.   (*To* FERDINAND *and* MIRANDA) Give me your hands:
Let grief and sorrow still embrace his heart
That doth not wish you joy!

GONZALO.   Be it so! Amen!

(*Re-enter* ARIEL, *with the* MASTER *and* BOATSWAIN *amazedly following.*)

O, look, sir, look, sir! here is more of us:
I prophesied, if a gallows were on land,
This fellow could not drown. Now, blasphemy,
That swear'st grace o'erboard, not an oath on shore?
Hast thou no mouth by land? What is the news?   220

BOATSWAIN.   The best news is, that we have safely found
Our king and company; the next, our ship—
Which, but three glasses since, we gave out split—
Is tight and yare and bravely rigg'd as when
We first put out to sea.

ARIEL.   (*aside to* PROSPERO) Sir, all this service
Have I done since I went.

PROSPERO.   (*aside to* ARIEL) My tricksy spirit!

ALONSO.   These are not natural events; they strengthen
From strange to stranger. Say, how came you hither?

BOATSWAIN.   If I did think, sir, I were well awake,
I 'ld strive to tell you. We were dead of sleep,   230
And—how we know not—all clapp'd under hatches;
Where but even now with strange and several noises
Of roaring, shrieking, howling, jingling chains,
And moe diversity of sounds, all horrible,
We were awaked; straightway, at liberty;
Where we, in all her trim, freshly beheld
Our royal, good and gallant ship, our master
Capering to eye her: on a trice, so please you,
Even in a dream, were we divided from them
And were brought moping hither.

ARIEL.   (*aside to* PROSPERO) Was 't well done?   240

PROSPERO.   (*aside to* ARIEL) Bravely, my diligence. Thou shalt be free.

---

213. own, i.e., master of his senses. **223. glasses,** hourglasses, hours. **split,** i.e., wrecked on a rock. **224. yare,** ready. **236. freshly beheld,** beheld her fresh; transferred epithet. **238. Capering,** dancing for joy. **240. moping,** moving in a state of bewilderment.

ALONSO.   This is as strange a maze as e'er men trod;
And there is in this business more than nature
Was ever conduct of: some oracle
Must rectify our knowledge.

PROSPERO.   Sir, my liege,
Do not infest your mind with beating on
The strangeness of this business; at pick'd leisure
Which shall be shortly, single I'll resolve you,
Which to you shall seem probable, of every
These happen'd accidents; till when, be cheerful   250
And think of each thing well. (*Aside to* ARIEL) Come hither, spirit:
Set Caliban and his companions free;
Untie the spell. How fares my gracious sir?   (*Exit* ARIEL)
There are yet missing of your company
Some few odd lads that you remember not.

(*Re-enter* ARIEL, *driving in* CALIBAN, STEPHANO *and* TRINCULO, *in their stolen apparel.*)

STEPHANO.   Every man shift for all the rest, and let no man take care for himself;
for all is but fortune. Coragio, bully-monster, coragio!

TRINCULO.   If these be true spies which I wear in my head, here 's a goodly sight.

CALIBAN.   O Setebos, these be brave spirits indeed!
How fine my master is! I am afraid   260
He will chastise me.

SEBASTIAN.   Ha, ha!
What things are these, my lord Antonio?
Will money buy 'em?

ANTONIO.   Very like; one of them
Is a plain fish, and, no doubt, marketable.

PROSPERO.   Mark but the badges of these men, my lords,
Then say if they be true. This mis-shapen knave,
His mother was a witch, and one so strong
That could control the moon, make flows and ebbs,
And deal in her command without her power.
These three have robb'd me; and this demi-devil—   270
For he 's a bastard one—had plotted with them
To take my life. Two of these fellows you
Must know and own; this thing of darkness I
Acknowledge mine.

244. **conduct,** guide, leader.
246. **infest,** harass, disturb. **beating on,** pondering or hammering as on an anvil.
247. **pick'd,** chosen. 248. **single,** i.e., when we are alone together. F has no comma after
shortly, in which reading *single* means "unbroken," "absolute." 257. **Coragio,** courage.
bully-monster, gallant monster. 258. **spies,** observers. 265. **badges,** emblems of cloth or
silver worn on the arms of retainers. 269. **deal . . . power,** wield the moon's power, either

CALIBAN.	I shall be pinch'd to death.
ALONSO.	Is not this Stephano, my drunken butler?
SEBASTIAN.	He is drunk now: where had he wine?
ALONSO.	And Trinculo is reeling ripe: where should they
	Find this grand liquor that hath gilded 'em?
	How camest thou in this pickle?
TRINCULO.	I have been in such a pickle since I saw you last that, I fear me, 280
	will never out of my bones: I shall not fear fly-blowing.
SEBASTIAN.	Why, how now, Stephano!
STEPHANO.	O, touch me not; I am not Stephano, but a cramp.
PROSPERO.	You 'ld be king o' the isle, sirrah?
STEPHANO.	I should have been a sore one then.
ALONSO.	This is a strange thing as e'er I look'd on. (*Pointing to* CALIBAN)
PROSPERO.	He is as disproportion'd in his manners
	As in his shape. Go, sirrah, to my cell;
	Take with you your companions; as you look
	To have my pardon, trim it handsomely. 290
CALIBAN.	Ay, that I will; and I'll be wise hereafter
	And seek for grace. What a thrice-double ass
	Was I, to take this drunkard for a god
	And worship this dull fool!
PROSPERO.	Go to; away!
ALONSO.	Hence, and bestow your luggage where you found it.
SEBASTIAN.	Or stole it, rather. (*Exeunt* CALIBAN, STEPHANO, *and* TRINCULO)
PROSPERO.	Sir, I invite your highness and your train
	To my poor cell, where you shall take your rest
	For this one night; which, part of it, I'll waste
	With such discourse as, I not doubt, shall make it 300
	Go quick away; the story of my life
	And the particular accidents gone by
	Since I came to this isle: and in the morn
	I'll bring you to your ship and so to **Naples,**
	Where I have hope to see the nuptial
	Of these our dear-beloved solemnized;
	And thence retire me to my Milan, where
	Every third thought shall be my grave.

without her authority, or beyond her influence. The line is ambiguous. **277. ripe,** drunk. **278. gilded,** flushed, made drunk. **281. fly-blowing.** They are pickled with drink and the slime of the pond, and pickling prevents *fly-blowing*. **292–294. What . . . fool.** Caliban is superior in intelligence to his companions. **302. accidents,** occurrences, events.

ALONSO.   I long
To hear the story of your life, which must
Take the ear strangely.

PROSPERO.   I'll deliver all;   310
And promise you calm seas, auspicious gales
And sail so expeditious that shall catch
Your royal fleet far off. (*Aside to* ARIEL) My Ariel, chick,
That is thy charge: then to the elements
Be free, and fare thou well! Please you, draw near.   (*Exeunt*)

EPILOGUE

Spoken by PROSPERO.

Now my charms are all o'erthrown,
And what strength I have 's mine own,
Which is most faint: now, 'tis true,
I must be here confined by you,
Or sent to Naples. Let me not,
Since I have my dukedom got
And pardon'd the deceiver, dwell
In this bare island by your spell;
But release me from my bands
With the help of your good hands: 10
Gentle breath of yours my sails
Must fill, or else my project fails,
Which was to please. Now I want
Spirits to enforce, art to enchant,
And my ending is despair,
Unless I be relieved by prayer,
Which pierces so that it assaults
Mercy itself and frees all faults.
As you from crimes would pardon'd be,
Let your indulgence set me free.   20

310. **Take,** take effect upon. **deliver,** declare, relate.
EPILOGUE. 10. **hands,** applause.

From INTRODUCTION TO *THE TEMPEST* *

HARDIN CRAIG (1875-   )

The Tempest is written in Shakespeare's most mature style and seems to have been composed late in 1610 or early in 1611. . . . The story dramatized in *The Tempest* was of a romantic nature and appears in several analogous versions. The poet William Collins (1721–1759), who was a scholarly man, told Thomas Warton, the first great historian of English literature, that he had read the actual source of *The Tempest* in an Italian short story, now lost. The reference he gave Warton was wrong, but some confirmation of his statement has come from various sources. The parallel to *The Tempest* longest known is a comedy by the Nuremberg dramatist Jakob Ayrer (1543–1605), *Die schöne Sidea,* and the resemblance is unmistakable. Another analogue is found in a Spanish collection of novels, *Noches de Invierno,* by Antonio de Eslava, published in 1609 or 1610, and, finally, Sir Edmund Chambers in his account of *The Tempest* in *William Shakespeare: A Study of Facts and Problems* (1930, I, 490–494) lays stress on various scenarios for *commedie dell' arte* contained in a manuscript in Rome and published by Neri. These scenarios deal with shipwrecks, islands, sailors, and native maidens, as also with a magician and with various kinds of gods and devils. In Eslava there are suggestions of a Bulgarian origin for the main plot, and this clue was followed by M. Henri Grégoire in an article entitled "The Bulgarian Origin of Shakespeare's *The Tempest*" (*Studies in Philology,* XXXVIII, 1940, 236–256). Grégoire does not find an immediate source for Shakespeare's play, but he does show that the story is based on events in Bulgarian and Byzantine history of the tenth and eleventh centuries. He shows also that the narrative made its way into Italy and appears in *Il regno degli Slavi* (1601) of the Italian Abbé Mauro Orbini and perhaps elsewhere in Italian literature, whence it would almost certainly have been excerpted and used as a *novella* or short story. . . .

The process of fitting parts together to form a unified complex of events was always, and particularly in the later stages of his work, characteristic of Shakespeare's procedure as a dramatist. . . . *The Tempest* also possesses this feature. To be sure, the main structure, that of the wronged prince and magician who gets his enemy in his power and makes peace with him by arranging a marriage between his own daughter and a good son of his enemy, is itself a large block from one quarry, large but not all that was needed. In the process of his amplification of this plot Shakespeare shows the tendency to gather beautiful or significant bits from various sources, which add facility or richness to his theme.

Specifically, Shakespeare brought to his story a body of material of great current interest, namely, exploration of strange lands. He borrowed from Sylvester Jourdan's *A Discovery of the Bermudas* (1610) and from William Strachey's *A true Repertory of the wrack and redemption of Sir Thomas Gates, Knight, upon and from the ilands of the Bermudas,* a letter dated July 15, 1610, and probably seen in manuscript.[1] With

---

* From *An Introduction to Shakespeare,* edited by Hardin Craig. Copyright, 1952, by Scott, Foresman and Company. By permission of Scott, Foresman and Company.

[1] Excerpts from these accounts by Jourdan and Strachey may be found on pp. 651 and 652. [*Editors' note*]

his usual thoroughness Shakespeare seems also to have read an anonymous pamphlet, also published in 1610, called *A True Declaration of the estate of the Colonie of Virginia.* From these works Shakespeare cannot be said to have derived much that was tangible or important. He never becomes definite geographically, but he did get atmosphere and perhaps minor incident from these accounts of colonization and shipwreck. Capell discovered that Shakespeare had made a definite and somewhat extensive borrowing from Montaigne's essay *Des Cannibales* [2] in *The Tempest,* Act II, scene i, lines 129–145. Steevens pointed out that Prospero's famous speech about the disappearance of the vision (IV, i, 146–163) is taken in idea at least from Sir William Alexander's *Tragedie of Darius* (1603).[3] There are other minor borrowings that increase the beauty and significance of the play. The one thing we lack is a better background for the magic of the play. We need to know more about how Shakespeare conceived of both Ariel and Caliban. They are both elemental spirits, and Ariel seems quite definitely to belong to air and fire. Caliban, on the other hand, suggests earth and water, lower and more evil elements. But the nature of Caliban is not clear, and his pedigree suggests that he may be a cross between the rosicrucian spirits of earth and water and the savages of the western world.

Particularly, these borrowings and this magic look to the exaltation of Prospero, and this was no doubt Shakespeare's intention. Nowhere, unless in Hamlet, has Shakespeare been at such pains to endow a character with such virtues and accomplishments. Prospero is both generous and just, clever and simple-hearted. He has mastered his own experience and with it the experience of the world. He is wise, and his wisdom, like all true wisdom, is the way in which he bears and applies his vast learning. It is natural enough to admire him. Prospero's eloquence alone would win the admiration of the world. But critics and producers have made of *The Tempest* merely a portrait of Prospero. A great school of them, headed by Edward Dowden, have thought that in depicting Prospero, Shakespeare was painting a portrait of himself. When Prospero broke his staff and buried it certain fathoms deep in the earth and drowned his book deeper than ever did plummet sound, they saw the image of William Shakespeare leaving the theater and returning to Stratford to end his days. This is innocent enough and not without interest and fitness, but to exalt Prospero and neglect the rest of the play is certainly to forget the romance and to spoil *The Tempest* as a drama on the stage.

This overexaltation of Prospero serves as a key and a caution both in the reading and the playing of *The Tempest.* If one can put one's attention on other things and other people in the drama besides Prospero, one can get a far better impression of the dramatic power of the play. It was no small thing in the Renaissance to lose a dukedom, and the persons to whom Prospero lost his, himself innocent, were base and deserving of great punishment. Prospero's duty as a prince and an upright man called upon him to demand retribution and recall. The story of Ferdinand and Miranda has an almost unequaled beauty and simplicity. The plot of Sebastian and Antonio against the life of Alonso is dangerous. "King" Stephano and Trinculo are associated with Caliban to produce most excellent low comedy. Shakespeare's study of the cool elemental spirit Ariel, master of song and device, is perfect, and Caliban, played by some of the greatest of Shakespearean actors, is a mysterious triumph in character depiction. But the play must be studied as Shakespeare conceived it, that is, as a whole. Great as Prospero is, he tends to be static. There is no struggle. Prospero can do everything, and there is little drama in omnipotence. There are other elements of dramatic and

---

[2] See p. 654. [Editors' note]   [3] See p. 655. [Editors' note.]

poetic interest in the play, and one asks if it would do injury even to Prospero to associate him with normal characters and events. There is, for example, something memorable in old Gonzalo, one of those wise and faithful aged counselors, like Menenius Agrippa in *Coriolanus,* who appear frequently in Shakespeare's later plays. Indeed, it is obvious that Prospero would be more interestingly realized by a fuller recognition of his humanity. One would like to see *The Tempest* played and read with a fairer, broader emphasis on all parts of the play.

As a stage play, *The Tempest* has actually suffered from the greatness of its spectacular possibilities. The stage has tended to formalize, if not vulgarize, the play, and the noble reaches of poetic suggestiveness and symbolic beauty have been caught by readers and not by theater-goers. With readers, thinkers, poets, and students *The Tempest* has been a great favorite, whereas in theaters its finer significances have tended to be lost in mere magic, scenic beauty, and spectacular effects. Dryden and D'Avenant rewrote Shakespeare's play in 1667 as *The Tempest or the Enchanted Island,* and that operatic version, which does frightful violence to almost everything we prize in Shakespeare's play, banished *The Tempest* from the stage for generations. It affected adversely the performances of David Garrick, John Philip Kemble, and even William Macready. Samuel Phelps played Shakespeare's play at Sadler's Wells in 1847, as did Charles Kean in a famous spectacular performance in 1857. Sir Herbert Beerbohm Tree's much admired presentation of *The Tempest* in 1904 was, like most other modern renditions, at the limit of scenic magnificence. The stage history of *The Tempest* is disappointing, but as a great piece of literature it stands secure. It may be that ultimately our dramatic public will be able to grasp the beauty and subtlety of one of Shakespeare's greatest works.

SOME SOURCE MATERIALS OF *THE TEMPEST*

I. *From* A DISCOVERY OF THE BERMUDAS, OTHERWISE CALLED THE ISLE OF DEVILS . . . (1610)
Sylvester Jourdan

[After three days and nights, the crew of *The Sea-Venture,* wearied with pumping] were even resolved, without any hope of their lives, to shut up the hatches and to have committed themselves to the mercy of the sea. . . . So that some of them having some good and comfortable waters [liquor] in the ship, fetched them, and drunk one to the other, taking their last leave one of the other. . . . [But suddenly Sir George Somers, in command of the expedition, descried land, and encouraged them to work at the pumps. They complied, though so weary] that for the most part they were fallen asleep in corners. [Fortunately, the ship] fell in between two rocks, where she was fast lodged and locked, for further budging. [One hundred and fifty men got safely ashore, and saved some part of their provisions and supplies, which later enabled them to fit out another vessel to carry them to Virginia.]

But our delivery was not more strange in falling so opportunely and happily upon the land, as [than] our feeding and provision was, beyond our hopes, and all men's expectations, most admirable; for the Islands of the Bermudas, as every man knoweth that hath heard or read of them, were never inhabited by any Christian or heathen people, but ever esteemed and reputed a most prodigious and enchanted place, affording nothing but gusts, storms, and foul weather; which made every navigator and mariner to avoid them as Scylla and Charybdis, or as they would shun the Devil himself; and no man was ever heard to make for this place, but as, against their wills, they have, by storms and dangerousness of the rocks lying seven leagues into the sea, suffered shipwreck. Yet did we find there the air so temperate and the country so aboundingly fruitful of all fit necessaries for the sustentation and preservation of man's life, that, most in a manner of all our provision of bread, beer, and victuals, being quite spoiled in lying long drowned in salt water, notwithstanding we were there for the space of nine months (few days over or under) we were not only well refreshed, comforted, and with good satiety contented, but out of the abundance thereof provided us some reasonable quantity and proportion of provision to carry us for Virginia, and to maintain ourselves and that company we found there;—wherefore my opinion sincerely of this island is that whereas it hath been, and is still accounted the most dangerous, unfortunate, and forlorn place of the world, it is in truth the richest, healthfulest, and pleasing land, (the quantity and bigness thereof considered,) and merely natural, as ever man set foot upon.

[There was a great abundance of fish], very fat and sweet, and of that proportion and bigness that three of them will conveniently [burden] two men: those we called rock-fish. . . .

There is fowl in great abundance in the islands, where they breed, that there hath been taken in two or three hours a thousand at the least, being of the bigness of a good pigeon.

Another sea-fowl there is that lieth in little holes in the ground, like unto a cony-hole, and are in great numbers; exceeding good meat, very fat and sweet (those we had in the winter) and their eggs are white and of that bigness that they are not to be known from hen-eggs. . . .

II. *From* A TRUE REPERTORY OF THE WRECK AND REDEMPTION. . . .

William Strachey

[Starting from Plymouth on June 2, 1609, the expedition encountered no difficulties until] on St. James's Day, July 24, being Monday (preparing for no less all the black night before) the clouds gathering thick upon us, and the winds singing, and whistling most unusually . . . a dreadful storm and hideous began to blow from out the Northeast, which swelling, and roaring as it were by fits, some hours with more violence than others, at length did beat all light from heaven; which like a hell of darkness turned black upon us, so much the more fuller of horror, as in such cases horror and fear use to overrun the troubled, and overmastered senses of all, which (taken up with amazement) the ears lay so sensible to the terrible cries, and murmurs of the winds, and distraction of our company, as who was most armed, and best prepared, was not a little shaken. . . . Sometimes [the storm] strikes in our ship amongst women, and passengers, not used to such hurly and discomforts, made us look one upon the other with troubled hearts, and panting bosoms: our clamours drowned in the winds, and the winds in thunder. Prayers might well be in the heart and lips, but drowned in the outcries of the Officers. . . . The sea swelled above the clouds, and gave battle unto heaven. . . . there was not a moment in which the sudden splitting or instant oversetting of the ship was not expected. . . .

During all this time, the heavens looked so black upon us, that it was not possible the elevation of the Pole [star] might be observed. . . . Only upon the Thursday night Sir George Somers being upon the watch, had an apparition of a little round light, like a faint star, trembling, and streaming along with a sparkling blaze, half the height upon the main mast, and shooting sometimes from shroud to shroud, tempting to settle as it were upon any of the four shrouds: and for three or four hours together, or rather more, half the night it kept with us, running sometimes along the mainyard to the very end, and then returning. At which, Sir George Somers called divers [persons] about him, and showed them the same, who observed it with much wonder and carefulness: but upon a sudden, towards the morning watch, they lost sight of it, and knew not what way it made. The superstitious seamen make many constructions of this sea-fire, which nevertheless is usual in storms: the same (it may be) which the Grecians were wont to call *Castor* and *Pollux*. . . . The Italians call it (a *sacred body*) *Corpo Sancto*: the Spaniards call it *St. Elmo*. . . .

[We] threw overboard much luggage . . . and staved many a butt of beer, hogsheads of oil, cider, wine and vinegar. . . . It being now Friday, the fourth morning, it wanted little, to have shut up the hatches, and commending our sinful souls to God, committed the ship to the mercy of the sea . . . but see the goodness and sweet introduction of better hope, by our merciful God given unto us. Sir George Somers, when no man dreamed of such happiness, had discovered, and cried Land. . . . Having no hope to save [the ship] by coming to an anchor . . . we were forced to run her ashore, as near the land as we could. . . . And by the mercy of God . . . all our men, women, and children, about the number of one hundred and fifty [we brought] safe into the island.

We found it to be the dangerous and dreaded island, or rather islands, of the Bermuda . . . [which] be so terrible to all that ever touched on them, and such tempests, thunders, and other fearful objects are seen and heard about them, that they be called commonly the Devil's Islands, and are feared and avoided of all sea travelers alive, above any other place in the world. . . . It being counted of most, that they can be no habitation for men, but rather given over to devils and wicked spirits. . . .

There is not through the whole islands, either [plains], valleys, or fresh rivers. They are full of [groves] of goodly cedar . . . the berries whereof, our men seething, straining, and letting stand some three or four days, made a kind of pleasant drink. . . .

Sure it is, that there are no rivers nor running springs of fresh water to be found upon any of [the islands]: when we came first we digged and found certain gushings and soft bubblings . . . fed with rain water, which soon . . . vanisheth away. . . .

The shore and bays . . . afforded great store of fish . . . . A kind of web-footed fowl there is, of the bigness of an English green plover, or sea-mew . . . these gather themselves together and breed in those islands which are high . . . there in the ground they have their burrows, like conies in a warren . . . they were a good and well relished fowl, fat and full as a partridge. . . . There are . . . two or three islands full of their burrows. . . . [These birds] for their blindness (for they see weakly in the day) and for their cry and hooting, we called the sea-owl; they will bite cruelly with their crooked bills. . . .

We had knowledge that there were wild hogs upon the island, at first by our own swine preserved from the wreck and brought to shore: for they straying into the woods, an huge wild boar followed down to our quarter, which at night was watched and taken in this sort. One of Sir George Somers' men went and lay among the swine, when the boar being come and groveled by the sows, he put over his hand and rubbed the side gently of the boar, which then lay still, by which means he fastened a rope with a sliding knot to the hinder leg and so took him. . . .

Sure it was happy for us . . . that we . . . had our Governor with us . . . els:, I am persuaded, we had most of us finished our days there, so willing were the major part of the common sort (especially when they found such a plenty of victuals) to settle a foundation of ever inhabiting there. . . . Some dangerous and secret discontents nourished amongst us had like to have been the parents of bloody issues and mischiefs; . . . what hath a more adamantine power to draw unto it the con ent and attraction of the idle, untoward, and wretched number of the many, than liberty, and fullness of sensuality? . . . [There were three mutinous conspiracies; at least ne conspirator was executed and a couple of others were left behind as outlaws when ie rest of the company finally finished building the pinnace which took them on to Virginia.]

III. *From* Michel de Montaigne's Essay "OF THE CANNIBALS"

Translation by John Florio (*1603*)

It is a nation . . . that hath no kind of traffic, no knowledge of letters, no intelligence of numbers, no name of magistrate, nor of politic superiority; no use of service, of richness or of poverty; no contracts, no successions, no partitions, no occupation but idle; no respect of kindred, but common; no apparel but natural; no manuring of lands, no use of wine, corn, or metal. The very words that import lying, falsehood, treason, dissimulations, covetousness, envie, detraction, and pardon were never heard of amongst them. . . .

These leave this full possession of goods in common, and without division to their heirs, without other claim or title but that which Nature doth plainly impart unto all creatures, even as she brings them into the world.

[See *The Tempest*, Act II, Sc. I, ll. 129–145.]

IV. *From* Ovid's METAMORPHOSES, BOOK VII, LINES 197–206

Translation by Arthur Golding (*1567*)

Ye airs and winds: ye elves of hills, of brooks, of woods alone,
Of standing lakes, and of the night; approach ye every one
Through help of whom (the crooked banks much wondering at the thing)
I have compelled streams to run clean backward to their spring.
By charms I make the calm seas rough, and make the rough seas plain,
And cover all the sky with clouds and chase them thence again.
By charms I raise and lay the winds, and burst the viper's jaw.
And from the bowels of the earth both stones and trees do draw.
Whole woods and forests I remove: I make the mountains shake,
And even the earth itself to groan and fearfully to quake.
I call up dead men from their graves, and thee, O lightsome Moon
I darken oft, though beaten brass abate thy peril soon.
Our sorcery dims the morning fair, and darks the sun at noon.

[See *The Tempest*, Act V, Sc. I, ll. 33–50.]

V. *From* THE TRAGEDY OF DARIUS (1603)

William Alexander

Let greatness of her glassy scepters vaunt;
Not scepters, no, but reeds, soon bruised soon broken:
   And let this worldly pomp our wits enchant.
All fades, and scarcely leaves behind a token.
   Those golden palaces, those gorgeous halls,
With furniture superfluously fair:
   Those stately courts, those sky-encountering walls
Evanish all like vapours in the air.

   [See *The Tempest,* Act IV, Sc. I, ll. 151–156.]

III

The Play and the Reader

. . . The purpose of playing, whose end, both at the first and now, was and is, to hold, as 't were, the mirror up to nature; to show virtue her own feature, scorn her own image, and the very age and body of the time his form and pressure. Now this over-done, or come tardy off, though it makes the unskilful laugh, cannot but make the judicious grieve; the censure of the which one must, in your allowance, o'erweigh a whole theatre of others.
—WILLIAM SHAKESPEARE

The critic occupies the same relation to the work of art that he criticizes as the artist does to the visible world of form and colour, or the unseen world of passion and thought. . . . I would call criticism a creation within a creation. For just as the great artists, from Homer and Aeschylus, down to Shakespeare and Keats, did not go directly to life for their subject-matter, but sought for it in myth, and legend, and ancient tale, so the critic deals with materials that others have, as it were, purified for him, and to which imaginative form and colour have been added.
—OSCAR WILDE

To criticize is to appreciate, to appropriate, to take intellectual possession, to establish in fine a relation with the criticized thing and make it one's own.
—HENRY JAMES

What I like in a good author is not what he says, but what he whispers.
—LOGAN PEARSALL SMITH

There is no luck in literary reputation. They who make up the final verdict upon every book are not the partial and noisy read-ers of the hour when it appears; but a court as of angels, a public not to be bribed, not to be entreated, and not to be overawed, decides upon every man's title to fame.
—RALPH WALDO EMERSON

III

The Play and the Reader

THE MEANING OF *THE TEMPEST*

HAROLD C. GODDARD (1878–1950)

. . . *The Tempest* has an unrivaled power to inspire in almost all sensitive readers a belief that it contains a secret meaning. Even those who make no attempt to search it out retain the feeling that it is there and that if it could only be found it would lead close not merely to the heart of Shakespeare's convictions about life but close to the heart of life itself. Naturally I have no reference here to the many minute and elaborate allegorical interpretations of the play that have been offered, which, even if they were convincing within their own limits, could have only a historical, biographical, or other subpoetical interest. What I have in mind rather are more modest attempts to connect and elucidate the main themes and symbols around which the poem is obviously built and which seem to have in peculiar degree the power, in Keats's words, to "tease us out of thought as doth eternity." To set out to interpret *The Tempest* (which I do not intend to do) is one thing; to point out certain aspects of its symbolism and thematic structure with which any satisfactory interpretation must come to terms as a sort of minimum requirement is another and much less ambitious undertaking.

To begin with, this play is centrally concerned with the three things that Shakespeare had perhaps come to value most highly in life: liberty, love, and wonder—the identical trinity, by the way, that Hafiz, long before Shakespeare, had also chosen. Concerned with realities rather than with names, the poet not only gives examples of these things but, to make clear what they are in their purity, shows us what they are in their perversions: license is set over against liberty; lust against love; banality, but more particularly "wonders," against wonder.

And the play has also what might be called a biological theme. As has often been pointed out, the characters are arranged in a sort of evolutionary hierarchy from Caliban, who is a kind of demi-creature of water and earth, up through human strata of various stages of development to Ariel, who is all fire and air—though it is made clear that where human nature becomes degenerate it seems to sink to a level lower than that of Caliban.

Closely allied to this, yet distinct from it, is a psychological interest. The play is fairly saturated with references to sleep and waking—and to various states of consciousness and unconsciousness between the two, drowsiness, daydreaming, dreaming, trance, hallucination, and other hypnagogic conditions. Likewise *The Tempest* is filled from end to end with noises and music—from the thunder and roaring of the storm itself, the howling of beasts, through the sounds and sweet airs of the Enchanted Isle that could charm even Caliban, through every variety of human utterance from the cries and coarse ballads of drunkards to the voices of lovers, up finally to the songs of Ariel. And Shakespeare seems interested not only in these two things, sleep and music, but even more in the relation between them—in the relation, to put it more pedantically, between music and the unconscious mind. The voices of the isle could induce such sleep in Caliban that when he waked he cried to dream again. Miranda falls asleep on the entrance of Ariel and awakens on his exit. The same is true in some degree of the other good characters, but not of the baser ones, who become victims on at least one occasion of an evil form of waking hallucination. All these reactions turn on the receptivity of the unconscious mind.

These various themes and symbols are inextricably interwoven, and, seen from a slightly different angle, give us Shakespeare's final word on a subject that had engaged his attention from the beginning: the different kinds of power that men possess and are possessed by. Here the political and religious aspects of the story merge as we are carried all the way from the demonic tyranny of the witch Sycorax to the reign of pure goodness in old Gonzalo's ideal commonwealth. More specifically, we have within the main action of the play: the political and military power of Alonso and Antonio, the magical power of Prospero, the alcoholic power of Stephano, the unveiling power of love in Ferdinand and Miranda, and the musical power of Ariel. (Nor am I omitting, though I may seem to be, the religious power of forgiveness.)

The play culminates in three emancipations—of Caliban from the enthralment of the drunken Stephano, of Prospero from his magic, and of Ariel from the service of Prospero in the cause of that magic (not to mention the emancipation from moral bondage of Alonso and his companions). What might be called, grotesquely, the biography of Ariel gives at least an intimation of what these interrelated emancipations mean, though we must beware here not to fetter the play within any rigid allegory. For twelve years—"years" doubtless comparable to the "days" of creation in Genesis—Ariel was imprisoned in a cloven pine by the witch Sycorax because he was

> a spirit too delicate
> To act her earthy and abhorr'd commands.

This imprisonment, once imposed, Sycorax is powerless to undo and Prospero with his art must come to the rescue. What does this signify? Might it not mean that when imagination is enslaved by the senses superstition usurps its function—and the senses become powerless to release it? It must be set free by knowledge and reason. But that is not the end of the story. Out from under the domination of the senses, imagination now becomes the slave of the very intellect that rescued it. Prospero is now master and the delicate spirit he has set free from Sycorax is impressed into the service of his magic—even at one point at the threat of a second imprisonment, in a cloven oak, of like duration as the first, if he complains. Here, again, is a Prospero remote enough from anything we associate with Shakespeare.

What is the character of Prospero's magic? If it is not black art, it certainly is not "white" in the sense of being dedicated unreservedly to noble ends. Prospero was indeed the victim of injustice. But his main miracle, the raising of the tempest, appears to have been undertaken primarily to get his enemies within his power for purposes of revenge. Moreover, his magic banquets and charmed swords have an element of mere display about them that is reminiscent of the "wonders" of the common conjurer. The higher the nature of the miracle sought, the more Prospero seems to intrust its execution to Ariel's improvisation, as in the saving of Gonzalo and most of all the falling in love of Ferdinand and Miranda. Prospero willed this love affair, but the bringing of it into being was plainly Ariel's work, and his success so delights Prospero that he promises his servant his freedom as a reward:

PROSPERO.   It goes on, I see,
        As my soul prompts it.

(Not, notice, "as I ordered" but "as my soul prompts"!)

> Spirit, fine spirit! I'll free thee
> Within two days for this.

And as if he would not have us miss the point, the poet repeats it a moment later:

> At the first sight
> They have chang'd eyes. Delicate Ariel,
> I'll set thee free for this!

He sees that this is Ariel's accomplishment—nothing of his own magic at all. (From Prospero's command to his servant to summon his "rabble" of spirits and "incite them to quick motion" we seem entitled to think that even the wedding masque is mainly the latter's doing.) As in the case of Lear and his Fool, the servant has become the master of the master, a fact that comes out emphatically when Prospero has his enemies at his mercy. He is then in the same position as was the banished Coriolanus, except that the force at his command is knowledge and magic rather than the sword.

> Now does my project gather to a head,

he cries triumphantly in the first line of the last act. His foes, along with some innocent ones entangled with them, are powerless to budge, and we feel that he is now about to get even for the injustices they formerly inflicted on him. And then, like Virgilia with her kiss, Ariel speaks:

> ARIEL. Him that you term'd, sir, "the good old lord, Gonzalo,"
> His tears run down his beard like winter's drops
> From eaves of reeds. Your charm so strongly works them
> That if you now beheld them, your affections
> Would become tender.
> PROSPERO.   Dost thou think so, spirit?
> ARIEL. Mine would, sir, were I human.
> PROSPERO.   And mine shall.
> Hast thou, which art but air, a touch, a feeling
> Of their afflictions, and shall not myself,
> One of their kind, that relish all as sharply
> Passion as they, be kindlier mov'd than thou art?
> Though with their high wrongs I am struck to the quick,
> Yet with my nobler reason 'gainst my fury
> Do I take part. The rarer action is
> In virtue than in vengeance. They being penitent,
> The sole drift of my purpose doth extend
> Not a frown further. Go release them, Ariel.
> My charms I'll break, their senses I'll restore,
> And they shall be themselves.

Prospero thinks it is his reason that overcomes his fury. But what has just happened contradicts him. It was his angel that whispered the suggestion in his ear. And a man's angel or genius is not to be confused with the man himself.[1] Indeed this very

---

[1] "Thy demon—that's thy spirit which keeps thee" (*Antony and Cleopatra*, II, iii, 19). [All footnotes in the essay are Professor Goddard's.]

one of Prospero's is a spirit whose independence he is about to declare. Crying, "My charms I'll break," he invokes the elves and demi-puppets—"weak masters" who have helped him to do only such trifles as to bedim the sun and call forth winds—and bids farewell forever to them and magic. Ariel, his strong master, enters on the instant, with music, to displace them. And forthwith follows a wonder that genuinely deserves the name—the forgiveness and reconciliation that Prospero has just resolved on. Here is a divine right of kings to which even the strictest equalitarian could not object—the intervention of one of those angels in whom Richard II, because he was unworthy, trusted in vain. Here is the counterpart and antithesis of Macbeth's surrender to the Witches. As they tempted him to crime and death, so Ariel tempts Prospero to forgiveness and life.

How all this illuminates what has gone before! The stages in Ariel's estate now stand out unmistakable. While he was subjected to Sycorax, he was imprisoned and powerless. While he obeys Prospero, he performs material wonders—though even then, if the initiative is left to him, he goes beyond them. Finally, when it is he who whispers the hint in Prospero's ear and Prospero obeys *him,* the wonder of a spiritual miracle occurs. Music replaces magic; Ariel's songs achieve what is beyond the scope of Prospero's wand.

Those who, once powerful, suffer defeat, are restored to power, and then might take revenge but do not—they hold the keys of peace. That is what the end of *The Tempest* seems to say, as Shakespeare himself said it in the 94th sonnet:

> They that have power to hurt and will do none . . .
> They rightly do inherit heaven's graces.

It is an old truth—no discovery of Shakespeare's. But crowning as it does the last act of what was probably the last full play he ever wrote, backed up by hundreds, we might almost say thousands, of minute particulars from his previous works, and embodied in his own practice of understanding rather than judging all humanity from saint to sinner, it acquires the character of a revelation.

> Be cheerful
> And think of each thing well.

By itself, that could sound commonplace or even banal. But against the inferno of the Tragedies, it is no silly philosophy of smiling evil out of existence.

II

> Where the bee sucks, there suck I,

sings Ariel when Prospero tells him the moment of his release is near,

> Where the bee sucks, there suck I.
> In a cowslip's bell I lie;
> There I couch when owls do cry.
> On the bat's back I do fly
> After summer merrily.
> Merrily, merrily shall I live now
> Under the blossom that hangs on the bough.

This angel will not use his freedom to fly away to some distant heaven: he will hide under the nearest flower. The world of spirit, in other words, is not Another World after all. It is this world rightly seen and heard. From end to end *The Tempest* reiterates this. To innocent senses the isle itself is pure loveliness; to corrupted ones it is no better than a swamp.

> ADRIAN. The air breathes upon us here most sweetly.
> SEBASTIAN. As if it had lungs, and rotten ones.
> ANTONIO. Or as 'twere perfumed by a fen.
> GONZALO. Here is everything advantageous to life.
> ANTONIO. True; save means to live.

Even in Caliban an Ariel slumbers. He loves the voices of the isle, and his moral awakening at the end—

> What a thrice-double ass
> Was I, to take this drunkard for a god
> And worship this dull fool!

—though passed over swiftly is as hopeful a note as is struck in the entire play. Prospero was wrong in thinking that Caliban was impervious to education.

But it is Miranda of course, of the human inhabitants of the isle, who gives supreme expression to the way the world looks to uncontaminated senses and imagination:

> O, wonder!
> How many goodly creatures are there here!
> How beauteous mankind is! O brave new world
> That has such people in 't!

Imagination, as dreams show, is something that awakens in most of us only when the senses are put to sleep. It is only when *they* awaken refreshed at sunrise that we occasionally see the world for a moment as God intended us to. But really, Shakespeare is telling us in *The Tempest,* sense and spirit are as much made for each other as lovers are. It is appetite and intellect that have put an abyss between them. That is what Prospero the Magician learned from Ariel and his own child. Miranda did not need to read *King Lear.* But unless we have a child or angel to teach us, we do. We must go to Shakespeare and the other poets—for poetry, as Shelley said, "lifts the veil from the hidden beauty of the world and makes familiar things as if they were not familiar."

But whatever may be true of the rest of us, why does a poet need poetry? It is easy to see why a young poet does. But why should an old one?

We have noted how Shakespeare's need for drama in the narrower sense yielded to his need for poetry. Was his need for poetry now yielding to his need for life? It was the moment after Prospero listened to his spirit that he decided to break his staff and drown his book. Perhaps Shakespeare at last perceived that dramatic compositions, even poetic ones, are only airy charms. Perhaps he said to himself,

> . . . this rough magic
> I here abjure:

I will return from the necromancy of art to the wonder of life itself. Whatever he said or didn't say, he must have come to realize what creative minds in the end are almost bound to see: that the arts are to men only what toys are to children, a means for the

rehearsal of life. And so, paradoxically, the object of art is to get rid of the arts.
When they mature, the art of life will be substituted for them—as children outgrow
their toys.

> Merrily, merrily shall I live now
> Under the blossom that hangs on the bough.

Perhaps Shakespeare had himself in mind when he wrote those lines of Ariel's. I
picture him retired to Stratford lying under a plum tree in May doing "nothing."
"Had I a little son," said Charles Lamb, "I would christen him Nothing-to-Do; he
should do nothing." Shakespeare would have understood. "Nothing brings me all
things."

III

Shakespeare could have bidden farewell to the theater in no better way than through
Ariel, for no figure he ever created more utterly transcends the stage. How shall Ariel
be acted? The most graceful girl to be found for the part, the most charming boy,
will instantly blur or erase the Shakespearean conception. Which, indeed, should play
the role, if it is to be played, boy or girl? And what pronoun should be resorted to in
referring to this spirit of music and the dance? The paucity of language compels us,
as in the case of the angels, to use either the masculine or the feminine. But neither
will do. Ariel is above sex. In that respect this ultimate creation of the poet's genius
seems like the culmination of something he had been seeking all his life. From Adonis
and the Young Man of the Sonnets, through Rosalind and Hamlet, Desdemona and
Cordelia, on to Imogen, Florizel and Cadwal, Ferdinand and Miranda (remember her
willingness to carry logs!), Shakespeare is bent on finding men and women who, without losing the virtues and integrity of their own sex, have also the virtues of the other.
If Shakespeare had no admiration for the womanly woman in the sense of the clinging vine, neither had he any for the manly man as embodied in what our generation
refers to as the "he-man" or the "red-blooded man." He scorned the gentleman, but
all his best men are gentle men. Whatever else he may be, Ariel is a symbol of this
union of the masculine and feminine elements of the soul.

But what makes Ariel even more akin, if possible, to the spirit of his maker is the
capacity to assume any form or shape, to perform any function, to be at home in any
element. By universal consent this is close to Shakespeare's supreme gift. And there
is no better example of it than his creation (along with Caliban) of this very Ariel—
a creature so unique that he seems to have sprung full-blown from the head of his
maker. But even Ariel has been prepared for. From Puck with his flower juice
squeezed in lovers' eyes, to the Fool with his wise folly whispered in Lear's ear, Ariel
has seldom been far away in Shakespeare wherever spiritual force from without comes
to the rescue of weak or foolish or proud humanity. Who shall say that Ariel was not
there when the God Hercules left Antony and music was heard in the air, or when
Cleopatra herself turned to fire and air?

IV

Of the many universal symbols on which *The Tempest* is erected that of the island
is fundamental. An island is a bit of a higher element rising out of a lower—like a
fragment of consciousness thrusting up out of the ocean of unconsciousness. Like a

clearing in the wilderness or a walled city, like a temple or a monastery, it is a piece of cosmos set over against chaos and ready to defend itself if chaos, as it will be bound to do, tries to bring it back under its old domination. It is a magic circle, a small area of perfection shutting out all the rest of infinite space. What wonder that an island has come to be a symbol of birth and of rebirth, or that from the fabled Atlantis and that earthly island, the Garden of Eden, to the latest Utopia, an island, literal or metaphorical, is more often than any other the spot the human imagination chooses for a fresh experiment in life! [2]

Like Ariel himself, this island play, *The Tempest,* is so *sui generis* that we do not easily see how naturally it emerges from the rest of Shakespeare. In its emphasis on parent and child and the theme of reconciliation, its kinship with the others in the group of plays that begins with *Pericles,* it is true, is a commonplace. But its roots go deeper than that.

Prospero, Duke of Milan, deprived of his dukedom and exiled on an island, is restored at the end to his former place, a man so altered by his experience that henceforth, he declares, every third thought shall be his grave. Obviously, this is the pattern of *As You Like It* with the Forest of Arden in place of the Enchanted Isle and with the difference that the Senior Duke is in no need of regeneration. But, less obviously, this theme of the King, Prince, Duke, or other person of high estate losing his place or inheritance only to recover it or its spiritual equivalent, after exile or suffering, in a sense in which he never possessed it before, is repeated by Shakespeare over and over. All stemming in a way from that early and under-valued study of King Henry VI, *Measure for Measure, King Lear, Timon of Athens, Coriolanus, Antony and Cleopatra,* and parts of *Pericles, Cymbeline* and *The Winter's Tale* are built on this situation. They all, in one way or another, contrast with and supplement *Hamlet,* whose hero propounds the same problem, wavers on the edge of a fresh solution, only to offer in the end the old erroneous answer. They all, in various keys, reiterate the theme of Timon: "Nothing brings me all things."

But it is not just those who have lost worldly kingdoms in a literal sense who come to realize this truth. Shakespeare uses the same idea metaphorically. Over and over in his plays when the object valued or the person loved is taken away, an imaginative object or person, more than compensating for the loss, appears in its place.

Friar Francis in *Much Ado about Nothing* formulates the psychology of it. Hero, accused at the marriage altar by Claudio of unfaithfulness, falls unconscious—dead, it is thought at first. Give it out that she is dead, advises Friar Francis later, and you will perceive a miracle: the real Hero will be reborn in Claudio's soul.

> So will it fare with Claudio.
> When he shall hear she died upon his words,
> The idea of her life shall sweetly creep
> Into his study of imagination,
> And every lovely organ of her life
> Shall come apparell'd in more precious habit,
> More moving-delicate and full of life,
> Into the eye and prospect of his soul,
> Than when she liv'd indeed.

[2] A rarely beautiful and subtle example is Green Island in Sarah Orne Jewett's *The Country of the Pointed Firs.*

And so it proves, when the supposedly dead Hero, posing as her own cousin, is produced, and Claudio, seeing now with his imagination, superimposes his purified memory on the new bride and cries, "Another Hero!" Another Hero indeed, and yet the same. Beatrice and Benedick, too, are toppled out of their pride and disdain by a variation of the same psychology. Listening to "lies" about each other and themselves that are nearer the truth than the counterfeit personalities their wit has created, and shaken into sincerity by Claudio's mistreatment of Hero, they bid farewell to contempt and confess their love. And as if fascinated by the situation, Shakespeare relies on it yet again in *All's Well That Ends Well,* when Bertram resees the "dead" Helena at the end. In the light comedy of these over-theatrical plays, however, Claudio and Bertram have acted so outrageously that their conversions are to many modern readers or spectators unconvincing. Some will suspect the poet himself of skepticism or irony in these happy endings.

But the moment we pass to tragedy we accept this psychology without question. Romeo falls in love with Juliet at first sight but he loves her utterly only when she lies "dead" at his feet. Hamlet [3] realizes what Ophelia is to him only when he has driven her to madness and death and is literally with her in her grave. Othello recognizes the divinity of Desdemona only after he has killed her. Lear "sees" Cordelia fully only when she is dead in his arms. Antony becomes conqueror of himself only when he believes that Cleopatra has committed suicide, and Cleopatra is translated into fire and air only when her Emperor has proved his faith by taking his own life. The number of repetitions of this theme or situation in the Tragedies is startling and it is continued in modified form in the last group of plays. Posthumus discards his Italian weeds and his shame only when he believes he has murdered Imogen. Leontes falls truly in love with the "dead" wife he has wronged only when she is transformed into a statue. Symbolically this last instance might stand for all. The "illusion" of loss permits the senses to see life as if it were a work of art. In how many cases imagination is the child of death: in tragedy generally of death itself, in comedy often of a false report of death—death being the supreme "nothing" that brings "all things." In the dramatic romances especially Shakespeare seems to be asking whether some great shock short of death cannot awaken the imagination as death itself does in the Tragedies. In banishment, exile, or separation Shakespeare finds such shocks, but even these understudies of death, as they might be called, are rather the necessary condition than the cause of the awakening. Prospero on his island is not enough. There must be a Miranda too. And in all the plays where this theme of exile is conspicuous, of which *The Tempest* is the typical and terminal one, we never fail to find childhood or a childlike innocence preserved into maturity as seed for the soil that has been plowed by adversity. It is not chance that in these last plays there are so many children, unspotted maidens (and young men) together with older women and old men who have attained the wisdom of a renewed childhood: young Mamillius, Cadwal and Polydore, Perdita and Florizel, Marina, Imogen, Ferdinand and Miranda, Hermione, Paulina, Belarius, the Old Shepherd and Prospero himself. (The innocent Desdemona is in a sense the tragic mother of them all.) One of the certainties about the later Shakespeare is his conviction of the reciprocal necessity of childhood to age and of age to childhood. Confirming *King Lear* these plays assert that where the older generation has sinned it must seek pardon of the younger generation:

> ALONSO. But O! how oddly will it sound that I
> Must ask my child forgiveness!

[3] This case, it is admitted, is debatable.

but where it has kept virtuous, as Belarius did, its function is to help keep the younger generation uncontaminated by the world—uncontaminated by it, be it noted, not unacquainted with it. For Shakespeare is the last one to advocate the closing of eyes to fact. Only he keeps faith in the power of imagination to subdue fact to its own shape. *The Tempest* seems like the summation and consummation of what he has been saying on that subject all his life. Prospero, when expelled from his dukedom, is a narrow and partial man. Thanks to his child, the island, and Ariel, he gives promise of coming back to it something like a whole one. But an integrated man is only another name for an imaginative man. And so the marriage of Ferdinand and Miranda is not the only union this play celebrates, nor is the island the only symbol of wholeness. On this isle we have all found ourselves, Gonzalo proclaims in the end, "when no man was his own." In this location of spiritual treasure within the self ("The Kingdom of Heaven is within you") as well as in its emphasis on childhood and forgiveness, together with the note of humility and the appeal for mercy on which its epilogue ends, *The Tempest* is a profoundly Christian play.

V

When we consider out of what this poem is woven, is it any wonder it produces the effect it does? Its action takes place on an enchanted island. Its main human character is a magician. Its most celestial figure is the very spirit of metamorphosis. Its most earthy one undergoes a seemingly impossible transformation—an extreme example of the moral regeneration that comes to a number of others in the play. Its atmosphere throughout is as insubstantial as a rainbow. (Iris herself actually appears at one point.) The best-remembered sentence from its best-remembered speech is

> We are such stuff
> As dreams are made on.

Shakespeare must have known what would happen within the minds of readers and auditors to such a diaphanous and ethereal thing. Life, as he had long since discovered, reveals as much of herself to any man as he brings to her—and no two bring the same. Bright or dark, the world seems contrived to confirm whatever idea of it we conceive it under. A poem, in proportion as it is like life, like that world, will do the same. What else than this is the ultimate meaning of the Shakespearean firmament at which we have been gazing—this human universe we have been passing in review —wherein hundreds of stars, though they inhabit the same sky, differ in glory each from each? A single universal symbol invites projection as surely as a mirror does reflection. *The Tempest* is crowded with such symbols from end to end. How inevitable that it should tempt the sensitive reader, as the stories of Belarius did Cadwal, to "strike life" into it and "show much more his own conceiving"! So long as we reverence and do not neglect its text, what *The Tempest* means, then, is what it means to you or to me. And it will never mean when we are in one mood precisely what it does when we are in another, or mean tomorrow precisely what it does today. And so, as in the case of *Hamlet,* and in due degree of the other plays, each age will find its own interpretation of *The Tempest,* and, miraculously, it will seem to have been written for each age. A main thing it says to our age ought to be plain. Its great opposed symbols are the tempest of Prospero, which Ariel made as Prospero's slave, and Ariel's music, which Ariel made of his own free will. The former is the result of necromantic science or theurgy. The latter is a spontaneous overflow of joy in life. The one creates an opportunity for revenge. The other resolves the situation thus created. What that says to a generation that has used its own science to make an atomic bomb is as illuminating as a flash of lightning by night.

VI

If lovers of Shakespeare were asked to select a single passage from his works best representative of both his poetry and his philosophy of life, there would probably be nearly unanimous agreement in choosing Prospero's lines beginning,

> Our revels now are ended. . . .

through

> We are such stuff
> As dreams are made on, and our little life
> Is rounded with a sleep.

In their context, as Prospero utters them, they are susceptible of a profoundly sad, not to say pessimistic, interpretation. But as Shakespeare's words the world has on the whole refused to take them so, finding in them rather a supreme expression of the mystery and wonder of life. "Rounded with a sleep" can mean several other things than ended with a sleep, and when did a dream ever exist without a dreamer?

There is one little word here, of only two letters, that makes all the difference. Most commentators explain that "We are such stuff as dreams are made on" means according to Elizabethan usage, as indeed it may, "We are such stuff as dreams are made of." But it may also mean just what it says to the unlearned modern mind. Whether we are such stuff as dreams are made of is at best a matter of opinion or conviction, even though Shakespeare's authority is supposed to support the assertion. But that we are such stuff as dreams are made on is a matter of fact. It is indeed the one datum of consciousness—more nearly ultimate even than Descartes's *Cogito, ergo sum.* The science of our age seeks to explain the constitution of matter. But perhaps the final secret and definition of matter will turn out to be not some mathematical formula but simply this: Matter is that stuff on which dreams can be imprinted, that substance, in other words, on which creative energy can be projected. How else could things as frail as dreams have survived the tempest and chaos of material evolution?

> How with this rage shall beauty hold a plea,
> Whose action is no stronger than a flower?

A question that contains its own answer.

NOTES AND QUESTIONS

I: The Play

375. ANTIGONE

SOPHOCLES

Translation by Dudley Fitts
and Robert Fitzgerald

From a commentary by the translators:

"We have made cuts only when it seemed absolutely necessary. The most notable example is that of a passage of sixteen lines . . . which has been bracketed as spurious, either in whole or part, by the best critics. . . . In a like manner we have not hesitated to use free paraphrase when a literal rendering of the Greek would result in obscurity . . . [as when] Sophocles' audience would be certain to recognize the allusions [to unnamed mythological characters] . . . forgotten now. . . .

"The Chorus is composed, says the Scholiast, of "certain old men of Thebes: leading citizens ("O men many-charioted, in love with Fortune") to whom Creon addresses his fatal decree, and from whom he later takes advice. Sophocles' Chorus probably numbered fifteen, including the Choragos, or Leader; its function was to chant the Odes and, in the person of the Choragos, to participate in the action. . . ."

406. ANTIGONE

JEAN ANOUILH

Adapted and translated by
Lewis Galantiere

In this play Jean Anouilh (pronounced Ahn-oo-ee) in no sense offers a "translation" of Sophocles' play. He freely changes incidents and characters, and pays very little attention to the religious bases of the original, yet he adheres to the main structure of the plot and even to the theatrical form of the Greek original.

When Anouilh's play was first staged in February, 1944, Paris was occupied by the Nazis, whose permission had to be obtained before any play was performed. The pragmatic reasonableness of Creon in his ele-vation of the State above the individual may have seemed good sense to the Nazi officials, but during the play's run the sympathy of the French audiences was overwhelmingly with Antigone. So was Anouilh's, whose actress wife played the rôle. To the French, Antigone represented the spirit of the Resistance Underground—to resist to the death, if necessary, to say "No" out of unflinching and unreasoning faith in some higher principle, even if practical common sense (and self-preservation) seemed to be ranged on the opposite side.

Anouilh's play contains such anachronisms as references to cars and cigarettes. What are some others? What effect is produced by this historical inaccuracy? Do the *ideas* of this play (or of Sophocles' original) seem anachronistic? Explain.

What are the "inhuman forces" which Anouilh's Chorus speaks of as driving Antigone? Why "inhuman"? Does what the Chorus tells us about the coming fate of the various characters spoil the suspense? Why, or why not?

How does the opening conversation between the Nurse and Antigone seem to foreshadow the future? What type of person does the Nurse represent? What is revealed of Creon in his confident assumption, at first, that the attempt to cover Polynices' body was the work of "Polynices' friends, with their gold"?

"In a tragedy," says the Chorus (p. 421), "nothing is in doubt and everyone's destiny is known. That makes for tranquility." Discuss this statement, and also the distinction made between tragedy and melodrama.

What purpose is served by the discussion among the three Guards about their reward for capturing Antigone?

Creon admits that his insistence on Polynices' body remaining unburied ("meat rotting in the sun") is "childish. But it is by childish tricks that men are governed." Do you agree?

Antigone says "I can say no to anything I think vile, and I don't have to count the cost," whereas Creon was of the opinion that if he had refused to govern he would "have been like a workman who turns down a job that has to be done." From other parts of the play, show how Antigone and Creon act in accordance with the principles stated here.

Is Antigone unreasonable in being unswerved by the disclosure that both Polynices and Eteocles were, in Creon's words, "a pair of blackguards"? Why is Creon wrong when he later says that Antigone shifted to another "pretext"—the pretext that "life and happiness were tawdry things" —after he told her about her brothers?

Is Creon unreasonable in demanding obedience to his "childish" decree? Raised here is a question of the kind and extent of the obedience or respect due to properly constituted authority, whether king or state. Creon talks much about the importance of order, law, and government; but does he ever come to grips with the *purpose* or *end* towards which law and government are presumably directed?

*   *   *

What are the more important differences between Sophocles' Creon and that of Anouilh? Between the other pairs of characters? Explain the various ways in which the endings of the two plays differ.

What differences exist in the tone and substance of what the Chorus utters in the two plays? What is lost (or gained) by Anouilh's reduction of the Chorus to one speaker instead of many? The dust-storm in Sophocles' play that hides Antigone's second visit to the body of Polynices is not mentioned by Anouilh. What implication resides in the storm that Anouilh apparently wished to leave out of his play?

In the Greek original, then, the central theme seems to be the question of whether or not a decree of the State or ruler should override a divine obligation. Is this also the central question of Anouilh's play? Explain.

In his *Sophocles, a Study of Heroic Humanism* (Cambridge, Harvard University Press, 1951, p. 85), Cedric H. Whitman writes as follows:

"If any conceptual contrast fits the *Antigone,* it is the contrast between true and false authority, between the ideal citizen and the lawless ruler.

"Antigone's nature has done much damage to her, even as Creon's specious talk has done much to give him dignity, in the eyes of readers. Given a situation in which a high-minded young girl buries her brother in defiance of a royal decree, it would have been easy for Sophocles to make her pathetic. But Antigone is not pathetic. Sharp-tongued, contemptuous, almost ferocious in her declarations of her right, she fights fire with fire. She is at war from the minute the play opens until her death. Such a challenging piece of ungentle womanhood may have been more immediately intelligible to antiquity in the context of an heroic past; to modern minds it has presented a puzzle. Antigone is a woman in serious danger, and yet she talks like an empress. She must be wrong, or at least improper. She ought to have realized her place and urged the tender weakness of her sex; instead, she calls King Creon a fool to his face. Her very harshness has tended to throw some sympathy on Creon's side and raise the presumption that the king had a right to decree what he would regarding the burial of traitors. If Antigone denied that right, Creon at least was the king, not she, and he must enforce obedience. But at once we are plunged into the question of the justice of the law, the legality of authority. It is Antigone's claim that a higher law delimits the temporal authority of a king, and that if there is conflict, the king's law must yield. . . ."

446. THE WILD DUCK
HENRIK IBSEN

In what sense does the entire action of Act I represent, in terms of the whole play, a "front" or mask? What is the party at Werle's house *masking?*

Mrs. Sörby, Werle's housekeeper, engages with the guests at Werle's party in a game of Blind Man's Bluff. What is signified? Just previous to this incident, with which Act I ends, Werle tells his son that his eyes have begun to trouble him, and Gregers replies: "They have always been weak." He intends a double meaning, and Ibsen is here using a symbolic device. In Act IV, Mrs. Sörby says that Werle is going blind, to which Gina replies: "Lots of people do." To how many persons in the play does this apply? Who is *not* blind, symbolically speaking, and what are all the others blind to? Though Werle is losing his eyesight, is Gregers correct in his implied accusation that always his father's eyesight has been at fault? Does Gregers himself possess *good* "eyesight"? From the point of view of Relling, what is not good about Gregers' "eyesight"? In Shakespeare's *The Tragedy of King Lear,* Kent admonishes Lear, the self-deposed king: "See better, Lear." In what sense might Relling speak the same words to Gregers?

Werle, as Hialmar sees him, has "hoodwinked a confiding fellow creature in days gone by." Who else in the play "hookwinks a confiding fellow creature"? What part would Relling take in hoodwinking others? Gina hoodwinks her husband, but Gregers hoodwinks himself. Gregers believes that he can "rescue" Hialmar "from all the falsehood and deception that are bringing him to ruin" (Act II). But Hialmar is not rescued, and Gregers himself sinks under his own lie and deception. Define that self-delusion which blinds Gregers. He compares himself with "an amazingly clever dog; one that goes to the bottom after wild ducks when they dive and bite themselves fast in tangle and sea-weed, down among the ooze" (Act II). Explain the symbolism here. Hedwig says, about Gregers's wanting to be like a dog, "I believe he meant something quite different by that." What *did* Gregers mean?

How does this metaphor of the wild duck "rescued" by the dog apply to the relationship between Gregers and his father? Between Gregers and Hialmar? Between Gregers and Hedwig? In the relationship between Gregers and Relling, however, the dog who "rescues" the wild duck is not Gregers. Explain how and why Ibsen has inverted the metaphoric situation, as well as the literal one from which the metaphor springs. What purpose is served by this inverted symbol? What theme or meaning emerges? (For another instance of inversion of symbol see Katherine Mansfield's short story "The Fly." Pages 150–154.)

The literal wild duck fetched up from the bottom of the pond by Werle's "clever dog" survives in the garret now, in an alien environment, and splashes about in a trough there filled with fresh water every day. She didn't thrive at Werle's house, but she thrives now under Ekdal's care in the garret at Hialmar's house. Why should this be the case? As Hialmar says: "You see, she has lived in there so long now that she has forgotten her natural wild life; and all depends on that." And Gregers

replies: "Be sure you never let her get a glimpse of the sky and the sea. . . ." Explain the meaning of this passage. In what sense is Ekdal a "wild duck"? And Hialmar? Hedwig claims the wild duck as her very own: "It belongs to me" (Act II). Gregers persuades Hedwig to "sacrifice the wild duck" for the sake of her father, as a "free-will offering, for his sake, of the dearest treasure you have in the world!" To wring the neck of the wild duck *means* what? And why does Gregers persuade Hedwig to wring the neck of the wild duck? Does she do it? Hedwig's "blindness" is said to be "hereditary" (Act II). It is also symbolical. In what sense do we all share Hedwig's "blindness"? Does Hedwig finally attain to a moment of insight and recognition of the truth?

Why has Ibsen designated Hialmar as a "photographer"? Hedwig, like Werle, is in danger of losing her eyesight, but nevertheless Hialmar lets her work at his photography, *tinting* the pictures. What is the symbolic import and purpose here? Hialmar's photography is one form of retreat from life, and Ekdal's garret with the wild duck is another. What others are there? Does the "claim of the ideal" provide another example? How so? The trouble with Hialmar, according to Relling, is that "in his own circle he has always been looked upon as a shining light—" (Act V). It's that very light that has blinded him from seeing himself and from seeing the world for what it is. Old Ekdal supplies the parallel to Hialmar. What they have feared is the dark places where truth lies concealed. The wild duck "looks quite different by day from what it did last night in the moonlight" (Act III), and Hedwig in the night prays for the duck—*not* in the morning, because "In the morning it's light, you know, and there's nothing in particular to be afraid of" (Act IV). What meaning attaches to *light* and *darkness*? Hialmar's photographs are made in the light but developed in darkness, and they are tinted under lamplight.

When Gregers enters Hialmar's apartment (Act IV), he complains about the gloom there, and Gina takes off the lampshade. Why does Ibsen inject this particular action at this particular moment? Just previous to Gregers's visit Hialmar asks Gina to light the lamp for him, and Gina does so and then puts on the lampshade. Why does this action occur where it does, and what does it signify in terms of the context of the conversation between Gina and Hialmar? Why does Gina shade the light from Hialmar? In what other ways does Gina shade the "light" from her husband? Does Mrs. Sörby shade the truth from Werle?

Does the "claim of the ideal" equate as meaning with "light" or with "darkness"? Does truth exist at the Hoidal Works or in Ekdal's garret? What wisdom has the person who is a "wild duck," and what wisdom has the person who is the dog retrieving the duck from dark places? What validity emerges from the play, considering it from the author's point of view, for quests for the truth, cure-alls prescribed against illusions, the "delirium of hero-worship," or the claim of the "conscience"? Locate instances of expressions of noble sentiments throughout the play and show how these are exploded by contradictory facts. What does this device of contrasted moods tell about the author's own philosophy of life or attitude toward it?

538. BILLY BUDD
Louis O. Coxe and
Robert Chapman

What occurrence in Chapter 15 of the novel, *Billy Budd,* has been changed in this dramatization? What does the play gain or lose by this changed portion? What other changes do you notice throughout the play? What themes or motifs in the novel are not incorporated into the play? Is the play more than a translation or dramatic reproduction of Melville's novel?

Have the playwrights succeeded in translating into dramatic terms the characteristic Melville defines as "natural depravity"? Explain. Are the changes made in the rôle of the Dansker necessary? What is lost by the play's omission of Captain Vere's death?

How does the play differ from the novel in terms of religious symbolism?

Part Three

POETRY

I

The Poem

A poet is, before anything else, a person who is passionately in love with language. Whether this love is a sign of his poetic gift or the gift itself—for falling in love is given not chosen—I don't know, but it is certainly the sign by which one recognizes whether a young man is potentially a poet or not.

—W. H. Auden

The poet . . . does not take a truth and write a poem about it. What happens is that, in the process of writing (if the poem is successful), some unguessed or dimly perceived truth grows clearer to him

—C. Day Lewis

[A poet's] power of making words express what he feels is indistinguishable from his awareness of what he feels. . . . He is a poet because his interest in his experience is not separable from his interest in words; because, that is, of his habit of seeking by the evocative use of words to sharpen his awareness of his ways of feeling, so making these communicable.

—F. R. Leavis

What Beethoven meant by his symphony, or Turner by his picture, was not something which you can name, but the picture and the symphony. Meaning they have, but what *meaning can be said in no language but their own: and we know this, though some strange delusion makes us think the meaning has less worth because we cannot put it into words. Well, it is just the same with poetry. But because poetry* is *words, we vainly fancy that some other words than its own will express its meaning. And they will do so no more . . . than words will express the meaning of the Dresden Madonna.*

—A. C. Bradley

i. The Poem as Picture

The poems in this section render in poetic medium a portrait or a landscape; and some of them are related to particular paintings or sculptures. They are all predominantly imagistic and pictorial, recreating by concrete sensual imagery a scene, object, or person. Some of them are landscape poems presenting a perspective from some special point of view, not unlike that employed in landscape paintings. All these poems have subject and theme, some of them are dramatic, and they might also be classified accordingly under the one category or the other, but the category under which they are now grouped serves best to point up the primary attribute of these poems as pictures.

"I HEAR AN ARMY CHARGING . . ."

JAMES JOYCE (1882–1941)

I hear an army charging upon the land,
    And the thunder of horses plunging, foam about their knees:
Arrogant, in black armour, behind them stand,
    Disdaining the reins, with fluttering whips, the charioteers.

They cry unto the night their battle-name:
    I moan in sleep when I hear afar their whirling laughter.
They cleave the gloom of dreams, a blinding flame,
    Clanging, clanging upon the heart as upon an anvil.

They come shaking in triumph their long, green hair:
    They come out of the sea and run shouting by the shore.   10
My heart, have you no wisdom thus to despair?
    My love, my love, my love, why have you left me alone?

THE TIDE RISES, THE TIDE FALLS

HENRY WADSWORTH LONGFELLOW (1807–1882)

The tide rises, the tide falls,
The twilight darkens, the curlew calls;
Along the sea-sands damp and brown
The traveller hastens toward the town,
    And the tide rises, the tide falls.

Darkness settles on roofs and walls,
But the sea, the sea in the darkness calls;
The little waves, with their soft, white
    hands,
Efface the footprints in the sands,
    And the tide rises, the tide falls.   10

The morning breaks, the steeds in their
    stalls
Stamp and neigh, as the hostler calls;
The day returns, but nevermore
Returns the traveller to the shore,
    And the tide rises, the tide falls.

"LOVELIEST OF TREES . . ."

A. E. HOUSMAN (1859–1936)

Loveliest of trees, the cherry now
Is hung with bloom along the bough,
And stands about the woodland ride
Wearing white for Eastertide.

Now, of my threescore years and ten,
Twenty will not come again,

And take from seventy springs a score,
It only leaves me fifty more.

And since to look at things in bloom
Fifty springs are little room,   10
About the woodlands I will go
To see the cherry hung with snow.

COME IN

ROBERT FROST (1874–1963)

As I came to the edge of the woods,
Thrush music—hark!
Now if it was dusk outside,
Inside it was dark.

Too dark in the woods for a bird
By sleight of wing
To better its perch for the night,
Though it still could sing.

The last of the light of the sun
That had died in the west   10

Still lived for one song more
In a thrush's breast.

Far in the pillared dark
Thrush music went—
Almost like a call to come in
To the dark and lament.

But no, I was out for stars:
I would not come in.
I meant not even if asked,
And I hadn't been.   20

THE DARKLING THRUSH

THOMAS HARDY (1840–1928)

I leaned upon a coppice gate
    When Frost was specter-gray,
And Winter's dregs made desolate
    The weakening eye of day.
The tangled bine-stems scored the sky
    Like strings from broken lyres,
And all mankind that haunted nigh
    Had sought their household fires.

The land's sharp features seemed to be
    The Century's corpse outleant;   10
His crypt the cloudy canopy,
    The wind his death-lament.
The ancient pulse of germ and birth
    Was shrunken hard and dry,
And every spirit upon earth
    Seemed fervorless as I.

At once a voice burst forth among
  The bleak twigs overhead
In a full-hearted evensong
  Of joy illimited;   20
An aged thrust, frail, gaunt and small,
  In blast-beruffled plume,
Had chosen thus to fling his soul
  Upon the growing gloom.

So little cause for carolings
  Of such ecstatic sound
Was written on terrestrial things
  Afar or nigh around,
That I could think there trembled through
  His happy good-night air   30
Some blessed hope, whereof he knew
  And I was unaware.

Dec. 31, 1900

NEUTRAL TONES

THOMAS HARDY (1840–1928)

We stood by a pond that winter day,
And the sun was white, as though chidden of God,
And a few leaves lay on the starving sod,
  —They had fallen from an ash, and were gray.

Your eyes on me were as eyes that rove
Over tedious riddles solved years ago;
And some words played between us to and fro
  On which lost the more by our love.

The smile on your mouth was the deadest thing   10
Alive enough to have strength to die;
And a grin of bitterness swept thereby
  Like an ominous bird a-wing. . . .

Since then, keen lessons that love deceives,
And wrings with wrong, have shaped to me
Your face, and the God-curst sun, and a tree,
  And a pond edged with grayish leaves.

HEAT

ARCHIBALD LAMPMAN (1861–1899)

From plains that reel to southward, dim,
  The road runs by me white and bare;
Up the steep hill it seems to swim
  Beyond, and melt into the glare.
Upward half-way, or it may be
  Nearer the summit, slowly steals
A hay-cart, moving dustily
  With idly clacking wheels.

By his cart's side the wagoner
  Is slouching slowly at his ease,   10
Half-hidden in the windless blur
  Of white dust puffing to his knees.
This wagon on the height above,
  From sky to sky on either hand,
Is the sole thing that seems to move
  In all the heat-held land.

Beyond me in the fields the sun
  Soaks in the grass and hath his will;
I count the marguerites one by one;
  Even the buttercups are still.   20
On the brook yonder not a breath
  Disturbs the spider or the midge.
The water-bugs draw close beneath
  The cool gloom of the bridge.

Where the far elm-tree shadows flood
  Dark patches in the burning grass,
The cows, each with her peaceful cud,
  Lie waiting for the heat to pass.
From somewhere on the slope near by
  Into the pale depth of the noon   30
A wandering thrush slides leisurely
  His thin revolving tune.

In intervals of dreams I hear
  The cricket from the droughty ground;
The grasshoppers spin into mine ear
  A small innumerable sound.
I lift mine eyes sometimes to gaze:
  The burning sky-line blinds my sight:
The woods far off are blue with haze:
  The hills are drenched in light.   40

And yet to me not this or that
  Is always sharp or always sweet;
In the sloped shadow of my hat
  I lean at rest, and drain the heat;
Nay more, I think some blessed power
  Hath brought me wandering idly here:
In the full furnace of this hour
  My thoughts grow keen and clear.

THE WOODSPURGE

DANTE GABRIEL ROSSETTI (1828–1882)

The wind flapped loose, the wind was
    still,
Shaken out dead from tree and hill:
I had walked on at the wind's will,—
I sat now, for the wind was still.

Between my knees my forehead was,—
My lips, drawn in, said not Alas!
My hair was over in the grass,
My naked ears heard the day pass.

My eyes, wide open, had the run
Of some ten weeds to fix upon;   10
Among those few, out of the sun,
The woodspurge flowered, three cups in
    one.

From perfect grief there need not be
Wisdom or even memory:
One thing then learnt remains to me,—
The woodspurge has a cup of three.

THIS AMBER SUNSTREAM

MARK VAN DOREN (1894–   )

This amber sunstream, with an hour to live,
Flows carelessly, and does not save itself;
Nor recognizes any entered room—
This room; nor hears the clock upon a shelf,
Declaring the lone hour; for where it goes
All space in a great silence ever flows.

No living man may know it till this hour,
When the clear sunstream, thickening to amber,
Moves like a sea, and the sunk hulls of houses

Let it come slowly through, as divers clamber,
Feeling for gold. So now into this room
Peer the large eyes, unopen to their doom.

Another hour and nothing will be here.
Even upon themselves the eyes will close.
Nor will this bulk, withdrawing, die outdoors
In night, that from another silence flows.
No living man in any western room
But sits at amber sunset round a tomb.

COMPOSED UPON WESTMINSTER BRIDGE SEPT. 3, 1802

WILLIAM WORDSWORTH (1770–1850)

Earth has not anything to show more fair:
Dull would he be of soul who could pass by
A sight so touching in its majesty:
This City now doth, like a garment, wear
The beauty of the morning; silent, bare,
Ships, towers, domes, theatres, and temples lie
Open unto the fields, and to the sky;
All bright and glittering in the smokeless air.
Never did sun more beautifully steep
In his first splendour, valley, rock, or hill;   10
Ne'er saw I, never felt, a calm so deep!
The river glideth at his own sweet will:
Dear God! the very houses seem asleep;
And all that mighty heart is lying still!

THE CITY IN THE SEA

EDGAR ALLAN POE (1809–1849)

Lo! Death has reared himself a throne
In a strange city lying alone
Far down within the dim West,
Where the good and the bad and the
        worst and the best
Have gone to their eternal rest.
There shrines and palaces and towers
(Time-eaten towers that tremble not)
Resemble nothing that is ours.
Around, by lifting winds forgot,
Resignedly beneath the sky   10
The melancholy waters lie.

No rays from the holy heaven come down
On the long night-time of that town;
But light from out the lurid sea
Streams up the turrets silently,
Gleams up the pinnacles far and free:
Up domes, up spires, up kingly halls,
Up fanes, up Babylon-like walls,
Up shadowy long-forgotten bowers
Of sculptured ivy and stone flowers,   20
Up many and many a marvelous shrine
Whose wreathèd friezes intertwine
The viol, the violet, and the vine.

Resignedly beneath the sky
The melancholy waters lie.
So blend the turrets and shadows there
That all seem pendulous in air,
While from a proud tower in the town
Death looks gigantically down.

There open fanes and gaping graves   30
Yawn level with the luminous waves;
But not the riches there that lie
In each idol's diamond eye,—
Not the gayly-jeweled dead,
Tempt the waters from their bed;
For no ripples curl, alas,
Along that wilderness of glass;
No swellings tell that winds may be

Upon some far-off happier sea;
No heavings hint that winds have been
On seas less hideously serene!   41

But lo, a stir is in the air!
The wave—there is a movement there!
As if the towers had thrust aside,
In slightly sinking, the dull tide;
As if their tops had feebly given
A void within the filmy Heaven!
The waves have now a redder glow,
The hours are breathing faint and low;
And when, amid no earthly moans,   50
Down, down that town shall settle hence,
Hell, rising from a thousand thrones,
Shall do it reverence.

ODE TO THE WEST WIND

PERCY BYSSHE SHELLEY (1792–1822)

I

O wild West Wind, thou breath of Autumn's being,
Thou, from whose unseen presence the leaves dead
Are driven, like ghosts from an enchanter fleeing,

Yellow, and black, and pale, and hectic red,
Pestilence-stricken multitudes: O thou,
Who chariotest to their dark wintry bed

The wingèd seeds, where they lie cold and low,
Each like a corpse within its grave, until
Thine azure sister of the Spring shall blow

Her clarion o'er the dreaming earth, and fill   10
(Driving sweet buds like flocks to feed in air)
With living hues and odours plain and hill:

Wild Spirit, which art moving everywhere;
Destroyer and preserver; hear, oh, hear!

II

Thou on whose stream, mid the steep sky's commotion,
Loose clouds like earth's decaying leaves are shed,
Shook from the tangled boughs of Heaven and Ocean,

Angels of rain and lightning: there are spread
On the blue surface of thine aëry surge,
Like the bright hair uplifted from the head   20

Of some fierce Maenad, even from the dim verge
Of the horizon to the zenith's height,
The locks of the approaching storm. Thou dirge

Of the dying year, to which this closing night
Will be the dome of a vast sepulchre,
Vaulted with all thy congregated might

Of vapours, from whose solid atmosphere
Black rain, and fire, and hail will burst: oh, hear!

III
Thou who didst waken from his summer dreams
The blue Mediterranean, where he lay,   30
Lulled by the coil of his crystálline streams,

Beside a pumice isle in Baiae's bay,
And saw in sleep old palaces and towers
Quivering within the wave's intenser day,

All overgrown with azure moss and flowers
So sweet, the sense faints picturing them! Thou
For whose path the Atlantic's level powers

Cleave themselves into chasms, while far below
The sea-blooms and the oozy woods which wear
The sapless foliage of the ocean, know   40

Thy voice, and suddenly grow gray with fear,
And tremble and despoil themselves: oh, hear!

IV
If I were a dead leaf thou mightest bear;
If I were a swift cloud to fly with thee;
A wave to pant beneath thy power, and share

The impulse of thy strength, only less free
Than thou, O uncontrollable! If even
I were as in my boyhood, and could be

The comrade of thy wanderings over Heaven,
As then, when to outstrip thy skiey speed   50
Scarce seemed a vision; I would ne'er have striven

As thus with thee in prayer in my sore need.
Oh, lift me as a wave, a leaf, a cloud!
I fall upon the thorns of life! I bleed!

A heavy weight of hours has chained and bowed
One too like thee: tameless, and swift, and proud.

V

Make me thy lyre, even as the forest is;
What if my leaves are falling like its own!
The tumult of thy mighty harmonies

Will take from both a deep, autumnal tone,   60
Sweet though in sadness. Be thou, Spirit fierce,
My spirit! Be thou me, impetuous one!

Drive my dead thoughts over the universe
Like withered leaves to quicken a new birth!
And, by the incantation of this verse,

Scatter, as from an unextinguished hearth
Ashes and sparks, my words among mankind!
Be through my lips to unawakened earth

The trumpet of a prophecy! O, Wind,
If Winter comes, can Spring be far behind?   70

YOU, ANDREW MARVELL

ARCHIBALD MacLEISH (1892–   )

And here face down beneath the sun
And here upon earth's noonward height
To feel the always coming on
The always rising of the night

To feel creep up the curving east
The earthly chill of dusk and slow
Upon those under lands the vast
And ever climbing shadow grow

And strange at Ecbatan the trees
Take leaf by leaf the evening strange   10
The flooding dark about their knees
The mountains over Persia change

And now at Kermanshah the gate
Dark empty and the withered grass
And through the twilight now the late
Few travellers in the westward pass

And Baghdad darken and the bridge
Across the silent river gone

And through Arabia the edge
Of evening widen and steal on   20

And deepen on Palmyra's street
The wheel rut in the ruined stone
And Lebanon fade out and Crete
High through the clouds and overblown

And over Sicily the air
Still flashing with the landward gulls
And loom and slowly disappear
The sails above the shadowy hulls

And Spain go under and the shore
Of Africa the gilded sand   30
And evening vanish and no more
The low pale light across that land

Nor now the long light on the sea
And here face downward in the sun
To feel how swift how secretly
The shadow of the night comes on . . .

THE EAGLE

ALFRED, LORD TENNYSON (1809–1892)

He clasps the crag with crooked hands;
Close to the sun in lonely lands,
Ringed with the azure world, he stands.

The wrinkled sea beneath him crawls;
He watches from his mountain walls,
And like a thunderbolt he falls.

GOD'S GRANDEUR

GERARD MANLEY HOPKINS (1844–1898)

The world is charged with the grandeur of God.
    It will flame out, like shining from shook foil;
    It gathers to a greatness, like the ooze of oil
Crushed. Why do men then now not reck his rod?
Generations have trod, have trod, have trod;
    And all is seared with trade; bleared, smeared with toil;
    And wears man's smudge and shares man's smell; the soil
Is bare now, nor can foot feel, being shod.

And for all this, nature is never spent;
    There lives the dearest freshness deep down things;
And though the last lights off the black West went
    Oh, morning, at the brown brink eastward, springs—
Because the Holy Ghost over the bent
    World broods with warm breast and with ah! bright wings.

10

LUCIFER IN STARLIGHT

GEORGE MEREDITH (1828–1909)

On a starred night Prince Lucifer uprose.
Tired of his dark dominion swung the fiend
Above the rolling ball in cloud part screened,
Where sinners hugged their specter of repose.
Poor prey to his hot fit of pride were those.
And now upon his western wing he leaned,
Now his huge bulk o'er Afric's sands careened,
Now the black planet shadowed Arctic snows.
Soaring through wider zones that pricked his scars
With memory of the old revolt from Awe,

10

He reached a middle height, and at the stars,
Which are the brain of heaven, he looked, and sank.
Around the ancient track marched, rank on rank,
The army of unalterable law.

THE BLESSED DAMOZEL

DANTE GABRIEL ROSSETTI (1828–1882)

The blessed damozel leaned out
  From the gold bar of Heaven;
Her eyes were deeper than the depth
  Of waters stilled at even;
She had three lilies in her hand,
  And the stars in her hair were seven.

Her robe, ungirt from clasp to hem,
  No wrought flowers did adorn,
But a white rose of Mary's gift,
  For service meetly worn;   10
Her hair that lay along her back
  Was yellow like ripe corn.

Herseemed she scarce had been a day
  One of God's choristers;
The wonder was not yet quite gone
  From that still look of hers;
Albeit, to them she left, her day
  Had counted as ten years.

(To one, it is ten years of years.
  . . . Yet now, and in this place,   20
Surely she leaned o'er me—her hair
  Fell all about my face. . . .
Nothing: the autumn-fall of leaves.
  The whole year sets apace.)

It was the rampart of God's house
  That she was standing on;
By God built over the sheer depth
  The which is Space begun;
So high, that looking downward thence
  She scarce could see the sun.   30

It lies in Heaven, across the flood
  Of ether, as a bridge.
Beneath, the tides of day and night
  With flame and darkness ridge
The void, as low as where this earth
  Spins like a fretful midge.

Around her, lovers, newly met
  'Mid deathless love's acclaims,
Spoke evermore among themselves
  Their heart-remembered names;   40
And the souls mounting up to God
  Went by her like thin flames.

And still she bowed herself and stooped
  Out of the circling charm;
Until her bosom must have made
  The bar she leaned on warm,
And the lilies lay as if asleep
  Along her bended arm.

From the fixed place of Heaven she saw
  Time like a pulse shake fierce   50
Through all the world. Her gaze still strove
  Within the gulf to pierce
Its path; and now she spoke as when
  The stars sang in their spheres.

The sun was gone now; the curled moon
  Was like a little feather
Fluttering far down the gulf; and now
  She spoke through the still weather.
Her voice was like the voice the stars
  Had when they sang together.   60

(Ah sweet! Even now, in that bird's song,
  Strove not her accents there,
Fain to be hearkened? When those bells
  Possessed the mid-day air,
Strove not her steps to reach my side
  Down all the echoing stair?)

"I wish that he were come to me,
  For he will come," she said.
"Have I not prayed in Heaven?—on earth,
  Lord, Lord, has he not prayed?   70
Are not two prayers a perfect strength?
  And shall I feel afraid?

"When round his head the aureole clings,
  And he is clothed in white,
I'll take his hand and go with him
  To the deep wells of light;
As unto a stream we will step down,
  And bathe there in God's sight.

"We two will stand beside that shrine,
  Occult, withheld, untrod,   80
Whose lamps are stirred continually
  With prayer sent up to God;
And see our old prayers, granted, melt
  Each like a little cloud.

"We two will lie i' the shadow of
  That living mystic tree
Within whose secret growth the Dove
  Is sometimes felt to be,
While every leaf that His plumes touch
  Saith His Name audibly.   90

"And I myself will teach to him,
  I myself, lying so,
The songs I sing here; which his voice
  Shall pause in, hushed and slow,
And find some knowledge at each pause,
  Or some new thing to know."

(Alas! We two, we two, thou say'st!
  Yea, one wast thou with me,
That once of old. But shall God lift
  To endless unity   100
The soul whose likeness with thy soul
  Was but its love for thee?)

"We two," she said, "will seek the groves
  Where the lady Mary is,
With her five handmaidens, whose names
  Are five sweet symphonies,
Cecily, Gertrude, Magdalen,
  Margaret and Rosalys.

"Circlewise sit they, with bound locks
  And foreheads garlanded;   110
Into the fine cloth white like flame
  Weaving the golden thread,
To fashion the birth-robes for them
  Who are just born, being dead.

"He shall fear, haply, and be dumb:
  Then will I lay my cheek
To his, and tell about our love,
  Not once abashed or weak:
And the dear Mother will approve
  My pride, and let me speak.   120

"Herself shall bring us, hand in hand,
  To him round whom all souls
Kneel, the clear-ranged unnumbered heads
  Bowed with their aureoles:
And angels meeting us shall sing
  To their citherns and citoles.

"There will I ask of Christ the Lord
  Thus much for him and me:—
Only to live as once on earth
  With Love,—only to be,   130
As then awhile, for ever now
  Together, I and he."

She gazed and listened and then said,
  Less sad of speech than mild,—
"All this is when he comes." She ceased.
  The light thrilled towards her, filled
With angels in strong level flight.
  Her eyes prayed, and she smiled.

(I saw her smile.) But soon their path
  Was vague in distant spheres: 140
And then she cast her arms along
  The golden barriers,
And laid her face between her hands,
  And wept. (I heard her tears.)

ULALUME

EDGAR ALLAN POE (1809–1849)

The skies they were ashen and sober;
  The leaves they were crispèd and sere—
  The leaves they were withering and
    sere:

It was night in the lonesome October
  Of my most immemorial year:
It was hard by the dim lake of Auber,
  In the misty mid region of Weir—

It was down by the dank tarn of Auber,
In the ghoul-haunted woodland of
Weir.

Here once, through an alley Titanic,   10
Of cypress, I roamed with my Soul—
Of cypress, with Psyche, my Soul.
These were days when my heart was
volcanic
As the scoriac rivers that roll—
As the lavas that restless roll
Their sulphurous currents down Yaanek
In the ultimate climes of the Pole—
That groan as they roll down Mount
Yaanek
In the realms of the Boreal Pole.

Our talk had been serious and sober   20
But our thoughts they were palsied and
sere—
Our memories were treacherous and
sere;
For we knew not the month was October,
And we marked not the night of the
year
(Ah, night of all nights in the year!)—
We noted not the dim lake of Auber
(Though once we had journeyed down
here)—
We remembered not the dank tarn of
Auber,
Nor the ghoul-haunted woodland of
Weir.

And now, as the night was senescent   30
And star-dials pointed to morn—
As the star-dials hinted of morn—
At the end of our path a liquescent
And nebulous lustre was born,
Out of which a miraculous crescent
Arose with a duplicate horn—
Astarte's bediamonded crescent
Distinct with its duplicate horn.

And I said: "She is warmer than Dian;
She rolls through an ether of sighs—
She revels in a region of sighs.   41
She has seen that the tears are not dry on
These cheeks, where the worm never
dies,
And has come past the stars of the Lion,

To point us the path to the skies—
To the Lethean peace of the skies—
Come up, in despite of the Lion,
To shine on us with her bright eyes—
Come up through the lair of the Lion,
With love in her luminous eyes."   50

But Psyche, uplifting her finger,
Said: "Sadly this star I mistrust—
Her parlor I strangely mistrust:
Ah, hasten!—ah, let us not linger!
Ah, fly!—let us fly!—for we must."
In terror she spoke, letting sink her
Wings till they trailed in the dust—
In agony sobbed, letting sink her
Plumes till they trailed in the dust—
Till they sorrowfully trailed in the dust.

I replied: "This is nothing but dreaming:
Let us on by this tremulous light!   62
Let us bathe in this crystalline light!
Its Sibyllic splendor is beaming
With Hope and in Beauty to-night:—
See!—it flickers up the sky through the
night!
Ah, we safely may trust to its gleaming,
And be sure it will lead us aright—
We surely may trust to a gleaming,
That cannot but guide us aright,   70
Since it flickers up to Heaven through
the night."

Thus I pacified Psyche and kissed her,
And tempted her out of her gloom—
And conquered her scruples and gloom;
And we passed to the end of the vista,
But were stopped by the door of a
tomb—
By the door of a legended tomb;
And I said: "What is written, sweet sister,
On the door of this legended tomb?"
She replied: "Ulalume—Ulalume!—
'Tis the vault of thy lost Ulalume!"   81

Then my heart it grew ashen and sober
As the leaves that were crispèd and
sere—
As the leaves that were withering and
sere;
And I cried: "It was surely October
On *this* very night of last year

That I journeyed—I journeyed down
    here!—
That I brought a dread burden down
    here—
On this night of all nights in the year,
Ah, what demon hath tempted me here?
Well I know, now, this dim lake of
    Auber—   91
    This misty mid region of Weir—
Well I know, now, this dank tarn of
    Auber,
    This ghoul-haunted woodland of
    Weir."

Said we, then—the two, then: "Ah, can it
    Have been that the woodlandish
      ghouls—
    The pitiful, the merciful ghouls—
To bar up our way and to ban it
    From the secret that lies in these
      wolds—
    From the thing that lies hidden in these
      wolds—   100
Have drawn up the spectre of a planet
    From the limbo of lunary souls—
This sinfully scintillant planet
    From the Hell of the planetary souls?"

MY AUNT

OLIVER WENDELL HOLMES (1809–1894)

My aunt! my dear unmarried aunt!
    Long years have o'er her flown;
Yet still she strains the aching clasp
    That binds her virgin zone;
I know it hurts her,—though she looks
    As cheerful as she can;
Her waist is ampler than her life,
    For life is but a span.

My aunt! my poor deluded aunt!
    Her hair is almost gray;   10
Why will she train that winter curl
    In such a spring-like way?
How can she lay her glasses down,
    And say she reads as well,
When through a double convex lens
    She just makes out to spell?

Her father,—grandpapa! forgive
    This erring lip its smiles,—
Vowed she should make the finest girl
    Within a hundred miles;   20
He sent her to a stylish school;
    'Twas in her thirteenth June;
And with her, as the rules required,
    "Two towels and a spoon."

They braced my aunt against a board,
    To make her straight and tall;
They laced her up, they starved her down,
    To make her light and small;
They pinched her feet, they singed her
    hair,
    They screwed it up with pins;—   30
O never mortal suffered more
    In penance for her sins.

So, when my precious aunt was done,
    My grandsire brought her back;
(By daylight, lest some rabid youth
    Might follow on the track;)
"Ah!" said my grandsire, as he shook
    Some powder in his pan,
"What could this lovely creature do
    Against a desperate man!"   40

Alas! nor chariot, nor barouche,
    Nor bandit cavalcade,
Tore from the trembling father's arms
    His all-accomplished maid.
For her how happy had it been!
    And Heaven had spared to me
To see one sad, ungathered rose
    On my ancestral tree.

AUNT HELEN

T. S. ELIOT (1888–   )

Miss Helen Slingsby was my maiden aunt,
And lived in a small house near a fashionable square
Cared for by servants to the number of four.
Now when she died there was silence in heaven
And silence at her end of the street.
The shutters were drawn and the undertaker wiped his feet—
He was aware that this sort of thing had occurred before.
The dogs were handsomely provided for,
But shortly afterwards the parrot died too.
The Dresden clock continued ticking on the mantelpiece,   10
And the footman sat upon the dining-table
Holding the second housemaid on his knees—
Who had always been so careful while her mistress lived.

AN EPITAPH

WALTER DE LA MARE (1873–1956)

Here lies a most beautiful lady:
Light of step and heart was she;
I think she was the most beautiful lady
That ever was in the West Country.
But beauty vanishes; beauty passes;
However rare—rare it be;
And when I crumble, who will remember
This lady of the West Country?

HERE LIES A LADY

JOHN CROWE RANSOM (1888–   )

Here lies a lady of beauty and high degree.
Of chills and fever she died, of fever and chills,
The delight of her husband, her aunts, an infant of three,
And of medicos marveling sweetly on her ills.

For either she burned, and her confident eyes would blaze,
And her fingers fly in a manner to puzzle their heads—
What was she making? Why, nothing; she sat in a maze
Of old scraps of laces, snipped into curious shreds—

Or this would pass, and the light of her fire decline
Till she lay discouraged and cold as a thin stalk white and blown   10

And would not open her eyes, to kisses, to wine.
The sixth of these states was her last; the cold settled down.

Sweet ladies, long may ye bloom, and toughly I hope ye may thole,
But was she not lucky? In flowers and lace and mourning,
In love and great honor we bade God rest her soul
After six little spaces of chill, and six of burning.

FOR A DEAD LADY

EDWIN ARLINGTON ROBINSON (1869–1935)

No more with overflowing light
Shall fill the eyes that now are faded,
Nor shall another's fringe with night
Their woman-hidden world as they did.
No more shall quiver down the days
The flowing wonder of her ways,
Whereof no language may requite
The shifting and the many-shaded.

The grace, divine, definitive,
Clings only as a faint forestalling;   10
The laugh that love could not forgive
Is hushed, and answers to no calling;

The forehead and the little ears
Have gone where Saturn keeps the years;
The breast where roses could not live
Has done with rising and with falling.

The beauty, shattered by the laws
That have creation in their keeping,
No longer trembles at applause,
Or over children that are sleeping;   20
And we who delve in beauty's lore
Know all that we have known before
Of what inexorable cause
Makes Time so vicious in his reaping.

FROM THE HAZEL BOUGH

EARLE BIRNEY (1904–   )

He met a lady
    on a lazy street
hazel eyes
    and little plush feet

her legs swam by
    like lovely trout
eyes were trees
    where boys leant out

hands in the dark and
    a river side   10
round breasts rising
    with the finger's tide

she was plump as a finch
    and live as a salmon
gay as silk and
    proud as a Brahmin

they winked when they met
    and laughed when they parted
never took time
    to be brokenhearted   20

but no man sees
    where the trout lie now
or what leans out
    from the hazel bough

MUSÉE DES BEAUX ARTS

W. H. AUDEN (1907–   )

About suffering they were never wrong,
The Old Masters: how well they understood
Its human position; how it takes place
While someone else is eating or opening a window or just walking dully along;
How, when the aged are reverently, passionately waiting
For the miraculous birth, there always must be
Children who did not specially want it to happen, skating
On a pond at the edge of the wood:
They never forgot
That even the dreadful martyrdom must run its course   10
Anyhow in a corner, some untidy spot
Where the dogs go on with their doggy life and the torturer's horse
Scratches its innocent behind on a tree.

In Brueghel's *Icarus,* for instance: how everything turns away
Quite leisurely from the disaster; the ploughman may
Have heard the splash, the forsaken cry,
But for him it was not an important failure; the sun shone
As it had to on the white legs disappearing into the green
Water; and the expensive delicate ship that must have seen
Something amazing, a boy falling out of the sky,   20
Had somewhere to get to and sailed calmly on.

HUNTERS IN THE SNOW: BRUEGHEL

JOSEPH LANGLAND (1917–   )

Quail and rabbit hunters with tawny hounds,
Shadowless, out of late afternoon
Trudge toward the neutral evening of indeterminate form.
Done with their blood-annunciated day
Public dogs and all the passionless mongrels
Through deep snow
Trail their deliberate masters
Descending from the upper village home in lovering light.
Sooty lamps
Glow in the stone-carved kitchens.   10

This is the fabulous hour of shape and form
When Flemish children are gray-black-olive
And green-dark-brown
Scattered and skating informal figures
On the mill ice pond.

Moving in stillness
A hunched dame struggles with her bundled sticks,
Letting her evening's comfort cudgel her
While she, like jug or wheel, like a wagon cart
Walked by lazy oxen along the old snowlanes,   20
Creeps and crunches down the dusky street.
High in the fire-red dooryard
Half unhitched the sign of the Inn
Hangs in wind
Tipped to the pitch of the roof.
Near it anonymous parents and peasant girl,
Living like proverbs carved in the alehouse walls,
Gather the country evening into their arms
And lean to the glowing flames.

Now in the dimming distance fades   30
The other village; across the valley
Imperturbable Flemish cliffs and crags
Vaguely advance, close in, loom
Lost in nearness. Now
The night-black raven perched in branching boughs
Opens its early wing and slipping out
Above the gray-green valley
Weaves a net of slumber over the snow-capped homes.
And now the church, and then the walls and roofs
Of all the little houses are become   40
Close kin to shadow with small lantern eyes.
And now the bird of evening
With shadows streaming down from its gliding wings
Circles the neighboring hills
Of Hertogenbosch, Brabant.

Darkness stalks the hunters,
Slowly sliding down,
Falling in beating rings and soft diagonals.
Lodged in the vague vast valley the village sleeps.

WINTER LANDSCAPE

JOHN BERRYMAN (1914–   )

The three men coming down the winter hill
In brown, with tall poles and a pack of hounds
At heel, through the arrangement of the trees,
Past the five figures at the burning straw,
Returning cold and silent to their town,

Returning to the drifted snow, the rink
Lively with children, to the older men,
The long companions they can never reach,
The blue light, men with ladders, by the church
The sledge and shadow in the twilit street,   10

Are not aware that in the sandy time
To come, the evil waste of history
Outstretched, they will be seen upon the brow
Of that same hill: when all their company
Will have been irrecoverably lost,

These men, this particular three in brown
Witnessed by birds will keep the scene and say
By their configuration with the trees,
The small bridge, the red houses and the fire,
What place, what time, what morning occasion   20

Sent them into the wood, a pack of hounds
At heel and the tall poles upon their shoulders,
Thence to return as now we see them and
Ankle-deep in snow down the winter hill
Descend, while three birds watch and the fourth flies.

LEDA AND THE SWAN

WILLIAM BUTLER YEATS (1865–1939)

A sudden blow: the great wings beating still
Above the staggering girl, her thighs caressed
By the dark webs, her nape caught in his bill,
He holds her helpless breast upon his breast.

How can those terrified vague fingers push
The feathered glory from her loosening thighs?
And how can body, laid in that white rush,
But feel the strange heart beating where it lies?

A shudder in the loins engenders there
The broken wall, the burning roof and tower   10
And Agememnon dead.
                              Being so caught up,
So mastered by the brute blood of the air,
Did she put on his knowledge with his power
Before the indifferent beak could let her drop?

SOLDIERS BATHING

F. T. PRINCE (1912–   )

The sea at evening moves across the sand.
Under a reddening sky I watch the freedom of a band
Of soldiers who belong to me. Stripped bare
For bathing in the sea, they shout and run in the warm air;
Their flesh, worn by the trade of war, revives
And my mind towards the meaning of it strives.

All's pathos now. The body that was gross,
Rank, ravening, disgusting in the act or in repose,
All fever, filth and sweat, its bestial strength
And bestial decay, by pain and labor grows at length   10
Fragile and luminous. Poor bare forked animal,
Conscious of his desires and needs and flesh that rise and fall,
Stands in the soft air, tasting after toil
The sweetness of his nakedness: letting the sea-waves coil
Their frothy tongues about his feet, forgets
His hatred of the war, its terrible pressure that begets
That machinery of death and slavery,
Each being a slave and making slaves of others; finds that he
Remembers his proud freedom in a game,
Mocking himself; and comically mimics fear and shame.   20

He plays with death and animality.
And, reading in the shadows of his pallid flesh, I see
The idea of Michelangelo's cartoon
Of soldiers bathing, breaking off before they were half done
At some sortie of the enemy, an episode
Of the Pisan wars with Florence. I remember how he showed
Their muscular limbs that clamber from the water
And heads that turn across the shoulder, eager for the slaughter,
Forgetful of their bodies that are bare
And hot to buckle on and use the weapons lying there.   30
—And I think too of the theme another found
When, shadowing men's bodies on a sinister red ground—
Was it Ucello or Pollaiuolo?—
Painted a naked battle: warriors, straddled, hacked the foe,
Dug their bare toes into the soil and slew
The brother-naked man who lay between their feet and drew
His lips back from his teeth in a grimace.

They were Italians who knew war's sorrow and disgrace
And showed the thing suspended, stripped. A theme
Born out of the experience of that horrible extreme   40
Of war beneath a sky where the air flows
With *Lachrimae Christi*. For that rage, that bitterness, those blows

That hatred of the slain, what could it be
But indirectly or directly a commentary
On the Crucifixion? and the picture burns
With indignation and pity and despair by turns
Because it is the obverse of the scene
Where Christ hangs murdered, stripped, upon the Cross.
I mean,
That is the explanation of its rage.

And we too have our bitterness and pity that engage   50
Blood, spirit in this war. But night begins,
Night of the mind: who nowadays is conscious of our sins?
Though every human deed concerns our blood,
And even we must know what nobody has understood,
That some great love is over all we do
And that is what has driven us to fury, for so few
Can suffer all the terror of that love:
The terror of that love has set us spinning in this groove
Greasy with our blood.
           These dry themselves and dress,
Resume their shirts, forget the fright and shame of nakedness.   60
Because to love is terrible we prefer
The freedom of our crimes; yet, as I drink the dusky air,
I feel a strange delight that fills me full,
Strange gratitude, as if evil itself were beautiful,
And kiss the wound in thought, while in the west
I watch a streak of red that might have issued from Christ's breast.

ODE ON A GRECIAN URN

JOHN KEATS (1795–1821)

Thou still unravished bride of quietness,
   Thou foster-child of Silence and slow Time,
Sylvan historian, who canst thus express
   A flowery tale more sweetly than our rhyme:
What leaf-fringed legend haunts about thy shape
    Of deities or mortals, or of both,
      In Tempe or the dales of Arcady?
   What men or gods are these? What maidens loth?
What mad pursuit? What struggle to escape?
      What pipes and timbrels? What wild ecstasy?   10

Heard melodies are sweet, but those unheard
   Are sweeter; therefore, ye soft pipes, play on;
Not to the sensual ear, but, more endeared,
   Pipe to the spirit ditties of no tone:

Fair youth, beneath the trees, thou canst not leave
   Thy song, nor ever can those trees be bare;
      Bold Lover, never, never canst thou kiss,
Though winning near the goal—yet, do not grieve;
      She cannot fade, though thou hast not thy bliss,
   Forever wilt thou love, and she be fair!   20

Ah, happy, happy boughs! that cannot shed
   Your leaves, nor ever bid the Spring adieu;
And, happy melodist, unweariéd,
   Forever piping songs forever new.
More happy love! more happy, happy love!
   Forever warm and still to be enjoyed,
      Forever panting, and forever young;
All breathing human passion far above,
   That leaves a heart high-sorrowful and cloyed,
      A burning forehead, and a parching tongue.   30

Who are these coming to the sacrifice?
   To what green altar, O mysterious priest,
Lead'st thou that heifer lowing at the skies,
   And all her silken flanks with garlands dressed?
What little town by river or seashore,
   Or mountain-built with peaceful citadel,
      Is emptied of this folk, this pious morn?
And, little town, thy streets forevermore
   Will silent be; and not a soul to tell
      Why thou art desolate, can e'er return.   40

O Attic shape! Fair attitude! with brede
   Of marble men and maidens overwrought,
With forest branches and the trodden weed;
   Thou, silent form, dost tease us out of thought
As doth eternity: Cold Pastoral!
   When old age shall this generation waste,
      Thou shalt remain, in midst of other woe
Than ours, a friend to man, to whom thou say'st,
   "Beauty is truth, truth beauty,"—that is all
      Ye know on earth, and all ye need to know.   50

ii. The Poem as Subject and Theme

ARS POETICA

ARCHIBALD MacLEISH (1892–   )

A poem should be palpable and mute
As a globed fruit

Dumb
As old medallions to the thumb

Silent as the sleeve-worn stone
Of casement ledges where the moss has grown—

A poem should be wordless
As the flight of birds

A poem should be motionless in time
As the moon climbs   10

Leaving, as the moon releases
Twig by twig the night-entangled trees,

Leaving, as the moon behind the winter leaves,
Memory by memory the mind—

A poem should be motionless in time
As the moon climbs

A poem should be equal to:
Not true

For all the history of grief
An empty doorway and a maple leaf   20

For love
The leaning grasses and two lights above the sea—

A poem should not mean
But be.

TO HOLD IN A POEM

A. J. M. SMITH (1902–   )

I would take words
As crisp and as white
As our snow; as our birds
Swift and sure in their flight;

As clear and as cold
As our ice; as strong as a jack pine;
As young as a trillium, and old
As Laurentia's long undulant line;

Sweet-smelling and bright
As new rain; as hard   10

And as smooth and as white
As a brook pebble cold and unmarred;

To hold in a poem of words
Like water in colorless glass
The spirit of mountains like birds,
Of forests as pointed as grass;

To hold in a verse as austere
As the spirit of prairie and river,
Lonely, unbuyable, dear,
The North, as a deed, and forever.   20

THE POET AT NIGHT-FALL

GLENWAY WESCOTT (1901–   )

I see no equivalents
For that which I see,
Among words.

And sounds are nowhere repeated,
Vowel for vocal wind
Or shaking leaf.

Ah me, beauty does not enclose life,
But blows through it—
Like that idea, the wind,

Which is unseen and useless,   10

Even superseded upon
The scarred sea;

Which goes and comes
Altering every aspect—
The poplar, the splashing crest—

Altering all, in that moment
When it is not
Because we see it not.

But who would hang
Like a wind-bell   20
On a porch where no wind ever blows?

"POET"

WILLIAM JAY SMITH (1918–   )

After, each, word, he, places, a, comma,
A, remarkable, effect, indeed,
It, gives, you, jitters, when, you, look,
It, gives, you, hiccoughs, when, you, read.

POETRY

MARIANNE MOORE (1887–   )

I, too, dislike it: there are things that are important beyond all this fiddle.
   Reading it, however, with a perfect contempt for it, one discovers in
   it after all, a place for the genuine.
      Hands that can grasp, eyes
      that can dilate, hair that can rise
         if it must, these things are important not because a

high-sounding interpretation can be put upon them but because they are
   useful. When they become so derivative as to become unintelligible,
   the same thing may be said for all of us, that we
      do not admire what   10
      we cannot understand: the bat
         holding on upside down or in quest of something to

eat, elephants pushing, a wild horse taking a roll, a tireless wolf under
   a tree, the immovable critic twitching his skin like a horse that feels a flea, the baseball fan, the statistician—
      nor is it valid
         to discriminate against 'business documents and

school-books'; all these phenomena are important. One must make a distinction
   however: when dragged into prominence by half poets, the result is not poetry,
   nor till the poets among us can be   20
      'literalists of
      the imagination'—above
         insolence and triviality and can present

for inspection, 'imaginary gardens with real toads in them', shall we have
   it. In the meantime, if you demand on the one hand,
   the raw material of poetry in
      all its rawness and
      that which is on the other hand
         genuine, you are interested in poetry.

A NOISELESS PATIENT SPIDER

WALT WHITMAN (1819–1892)

A noiseless patient spider,
I mark'd where on a little promontory it stood isolated,
Mark'd how to explore the vacant vast surrounding,
It launch'd forth filament, filament, filament, out of itself,
Ever unreeling them, ever tirelessly speeding them.

And you O my soul where you stand,
Surrounded, detached, in measureless oceans of space,
Ceaselessly musing, venturing, throwing, seeking the spheres to connect them,
Till the bridge you will need be form'd, till the ductile anchor hold,
Till the gossamer thread you fling catch somewhere, O my soul.   10

THE SPIDER HOLDS A SILVER BALL

EMILY DICKINSON (1830–1886)

The spider holds a silver ball
In unperceivèd hands
And dancing softly to himself
His yarn of pearl unwinds.

He plies from naught to naught
In unsubstantial trade,
Supplants our tapestries with his
In half the period—

An hour to rear supreme
His theories of light,   10
Then dangle from the housewife's broom,
His sophistries forgot.

THE SNAKE

EMILY DICKINSON (1830–1886)

A narrow fellow in the grass
Occasionally rides;
You may have met him,—did you not?
His notice sudden is.

The grass divides as with a comb,
A spotted shaft is seen;
And then it closes at your feet
And opens further on.

He likes a boggy acre,
A floor too cool for corn.   10
Yet when a child, and barefoot,
I more than once, at morn,

Have passed, I thought, a whiplash
Unbraiding in the sun,—
When, stooping to secure it,
It wrinkled, and was gone.

Several of nature's people
I know, and they know me;
I feel for them a transport
Of cordiality;   20

But never met this fellow,
Attended or alone,
Without a tighter breathing,
And zero at the bone.

SNAKE

D. H. LAWRENCE (1885–1930)

A snake came to my water-trough
On a hot, hot day, and I in pyjamas for the heat,
To drink there.

In the deep, strange-scented shade of the great dark carob-tree
I came down the steps with my pitcher
And must wait, must stand and wait, for there he was at the trough before me.

He reached down from a fissure in the earth-wall in the gloom
And trailed his yellow-brown slackness soft-bellied down, over the edge of the stone
    trough
And rested his throat upon the stone bottom,
And where the water had dripped from the tap, in a small clearness,   10
He sipped with his straight mouth,
Softly drank through his straight gums, into his slack long body,
Silently.

Someone was before me at my water-trough,
And I, like a second comer, waiting.

He lifted his head from his drinking, as cattle do,
And looked at me vaguely, as drinking cattle do,
And flickered his two-forked tongue from his lips, and mused a moment,
And stooped and drank a little more,
Being earth brown, earth golden from the burning burning bowels of the earth   20
On the day of Sicilian July, with Etna smoking.

The voice of my education said to me
He must be killed,
For in Sicily the black, black snakes are innocent, the gold are venomous.

And voices in me said, If you were a man
You would take a stick and break him now, and finish him off.

But I must confess how I liked him,
How glad I was he had come like a guest in quiet, to drink at my water-trough
And depart peaceful, pacified, and thankless,
Into the burning bowels of this earth.   30

Was it cowardice, that I dared not kill him?
Was it perversity, that I longed to talk to him?
Was it humility, to feel so honoured?
I felt so honoured.

And yet those voices:
If you were not afraid, you would kill him!

And truly I was afraid, I was most afraid,
But even so, honoured still more
That he should seek my hospitality
From out the dark door of the secret earth.   40

He drank enough
And lifted his head, dreamily, as one who has drunken,
And flickered his tongue like a forked night on the air, so black,
Seeming to lick his lips,
And looked around like a god, unseeing, into the air,
And slowly turned his head,
And slowly, very slowly, as if thrice adream,
Proceeded to draw his slow length curving round
And climb again the broken bank of my wall-face.

And as he put his head into that dreadful hole,   50
And as he slowly drew up, snake-easing his shoulders, and entered farther,
A sort of horror, a sort of protest against his withdrawing, into that horrid black hole,
Deliberately going into the blackness, and slowly drawing himself after,
Overcame me now his back was turned.

I looked round, I put down my pitcher,
I picked up a clumsy log
And threw it at the water-trough with a clatter.

I think it did not hit him,
But suddenly that part of him that was left behind convulsed in undignified haste,
Writhed like lightning, and was gone   60
Into the black hole, the earth-lipped fissure in the wall-front,
At which, in the intense still noon, I stared with fascination.

And immediately I regretted it.
I thought how paltry, how vulgar, what a mean act!
I despised myself and the voices of my accursed human education.

And I thought of the albatross,
And I wished he would come back, my snake.

For he seemed to me again like a king,
Like a king in exile, uncrowned in the underworld,
Now due to be crowned again.   70

And so, I missed my chance with one of the lords
Of life.
And I have something to expiate;
A pettiness.

ODE TO A NIGHTINGALE

JOHN KEATS (1795–1821)

My heart aches, and a drowsy numbness pains
  My sense, as though of hemlock I had drunk,
Or emptied some dull opiate to the drains
  One minute past, and Lethe-wards had sunk:
'Tis not through envy of thy happy lot,
  But being too happy in thine happiness,—
    That thou, light-wingèd Dryad of the trees,
      In some melodious plot
  Of beechen green, and shadows numberless,
    Singest of summer in full-throated ease.   10

O, for a draught of vintage! that hath been
  Cool'd a long age in the deep-delved earth,
Tasting of Flora and the country green,
  Dance, and Provençal song, and sunburnt mirth!
O for a beaker full of the warm South,
  Full of the true, the blushful Hippocrene,
    With beaded bubbles winking at the brim,
      And purple-stainèd mouth;
  That I might drink, and leave the world unseen,
    And with thee fade away into the forest dim: 20

Fade far away, dissolve, and quite forget
  What thou among the leaves hast never known,
The weariness, the fever, and the fret
  Here, where men sit and hear each other groan;
Where palsy shakes a few, sad, last gray hairs,
  Where youth grows pale, and spectre-thin, and dies;
    Where but to think is to be full of sorrow
      And leaden-eyed despairs,
  Where Beauty cannot keep her lustrous eyes,
    Or new Love pine at them beyond tomorrow.   30

Away! away! for I will fly to thee,
  Not charioted by Bacchus and his pards,
But on the viewless wings of Poesy,
  Though the dull brain perplexes and retards:
Already with thee! tender is the night,

And haply the Queen-Moon is on her throne,
  Cluster'd around by all her starry Fays;
    But here there is no light,
Save what from heaven is with the breezes blown
  Through verdurous glooms and winding mossy ways.   40

I cannot see what flowers are at my feet,
  Nor what soft incense hangs upon the boughs,
But, in embalmèd darkness, guess each sweet
  Wherewith the seasonable month endows
The grass, the thicket, and the fruit-tree wild;
  White hawthorn, and the pastoral eglantine;
    Fast fading violets cover'd up in leaves;
      And mid-May's eldest child,
The coming musk-rose, full of dewy wine,
  The murmurous haunt of flies on summer eves.   50

Darkling I listen; and, for many a time
I have been half in love with easeful Death,
Call'd him soft names in many a musèd rhyme,
  To take into the air my quiet breath;
Now more than ever seems it rich to die,
  To cease upon the midnight with no pain,
    While thou art pouring forth thy soul abroad
      In such an ecstasy!
Still wouldst thou sing, and I have ears in vain—
  To thy high requiem become a sod.   60

Thou wast not born for death, immortal Bird!
  No hungry generations tread thee down;
The voice I hear this passing night was heard
  In ancient days by emperor and clown:
Perhaps the self-same song that found a path
  Through the sad heart of Ruth, when, sick for home,
    She stood in tears amid the alien corn;
      The same that oft-times hath
Charm'd magic casements, opening on the foam
  Of perilous seas, in faery lands forlorn.   70

Forlorn! the very word is like a bell
  To toll me back from thee to my sole self!
Adieu! the fancy cannot cheat so well
  As she is fam'd to do, deceiving elf.
Adieu! adieu! thy plaintive anthem fades
  Past the near meadows, over the still stream,
    Up the hill-side; and now 'tis buried deep
      In the next valley-glades:
Was it a vision, or a waking dream?
  Fled is that music:—Do I wake or sleep?   80

PHILOMELA

MATTHEW ARNOLD (1822–1888)

Hark! ah the nightingale—
The tawny-throated!
Hark, from that moonlit cedar what a burst!
What triumph! hark!—what pain!
O wanderer from a Grecian shore,
Still, after many years, in distant lands,
Still nourishing in thy bewildered brain
That wild, unquenched, deep-sunken, old-world pain—
    Say, will it never heal?
And can this fragrant lawn   10
With its cool trees, and night,
And the sweet, tranquil Thames,
And moonshine, and the dew,
To thy racked heart and brain
    Afford no balm?

    Dost thou to-night behold
Here, through the moonlight on this English grass,
The unfriendly palace in the Thracian wild?
    Dost thou again peruse
With hot cheeks and seared eyes   20
The too clear web, and thy dumb sister's shame?

    Dost thou once more assay
Thy flight, and feel come over thee,
Poor fugitive, the feathery change
Once more, and once more seem to make resound
With love and hate, triumph and agony,
Lone Daulis, and the high Cephissian vale?
    Listen, Eugenia—
How thick the bursts come crowding through the leaves!
    Again—thou hearest?   30
Eternal passion!
Eternal pain!

PHILOMELA

JOHN CROWE RANSOM (1888–   )

Procne, Philomela, and Itylus,
Your names are liquid, your improbable tale
Is recited in the classic numbers of the nightingale.
Ah, but our numbers are not felicitous,
It goes not liquidly for us.

Perched on a Roman ilex, and duly apostrophized,
The nightingale descanted unto Ovid;
She has even appeared to the Teutons, the swilled and gravid;
At Fontainebleau it may be the bird was gallicized;
Never was she baptized.   10

To England came Philomela with her pain,
Fleeing the hawk her husband; querulous ghost,
She wanders when he sits heavy on his roost,
Utters herself in the original again,
The untranslatable refrain.

Not to these shores she came! this other Thrace,
Environ barbarous to the royal Attic;
How could her delicate dirge run democratic,
Delivered in a cloudless boundless public place
To an inordinate race?   20

I pernoctated with the Oxford students once,
And in the quadrangles, in the cloisters, on the Cher,
Precociously knocked at antique doors ajar,
Fatuously touched the hems of the hierophants,
Sick of my dissonance.

I went out to Bagley Wood, I climbed the hill;
Even the moon had slanted off in a twinkling,
I heard the sepulchral owl and a few bells tinkling,
There was no more villainous day to unfulfil,
The diuturnity was still.   30

Up from the darkest wood where Philomela sat,
Her fairy numbers issued. What then ailed me?
My ears are called capacious but they failed me,
Her classics registered a little flat!
I rose, and venomously spat.

Philomela, Philomela, lover of song,
I am in despair if we may make us worthy,
A bantering breed sophistical and swarthy;
Unto more beautiful, persistently more young
Thy fabulous provinces belong.   40

"WHEN TO THE SESSIONS OF SWEET SILENT THOUGHT"

WILLIAM SHAKESPEARE (1564–1616)

When to the sessions of sweet silent thought
I summon up remembrance of things past,
I sigh the lack of many a thing I sought,
And with old woes new wail my dear time's waste:
Then can I drown an eye, unused to flow,

For precious friends hid in death's dateless night,
And weep afresh love's long since cancelled woe,
And moan the expense of many a vanished sight:
Then can I grieve at grievances foregone,
And heavily from woe to woe tell o'er   10
The sad account of fore-bemoanèd moan,
Which I new pay as if not paid before.
But if the while I think on thee, dear friend,
All losses are restored and sorrows end.

MY LOST YOUTH

HENRY WADSWORTH LONGFELLOW (1807–1882)

Often I think of the beautiful town
  That is seated by the sea;
Often in thought go up and down
The pleasant streets of that dear old town,
  And my youth comes back to me.
    And a verse of a Lapland song
    Is haunting my memory still:
    "A boy's will is the wind's will,
And the thoughts of youth are long, long
    thoughts."

I can see the shadowy lines of its trees, 10
  And catch, in sudden gleams,
The sheen of the far-surrounding seas,
And islands that were the Hesperides
  Of all my boyish dreams.
    And the burden of that old song,
    It murmurs and whispers still:
    "A boy's will is the wind's will,
And the thoughts of youth are long, long
    thoughts."

I remember the black wharves and the slips,
  And the sea-tides tossing free;   20
And Spanish sailors with bearded lips,
And the beauty and mystery of the ships,
  And the magic of the sea.
    And the voice of that wayward song
    Is singing and saying still:
    "A boy's will is the wind's will,
And the thoughts of youth are long, long
    thoughts."

I remember the bulwarks by the shore,
  And the fort upon the hill;
The sunrise gun, with its hollow roar, 30
The drumbeat repeated o'er and o'er,
  And the bugle wild and shrill.
    And the music of that old song
    Throbs in my memory still:
    "A boy's will is the wind's will,
And the thoughts of youth are long, long
    thoughts."

I remember the sea-fight far away,
  How it thundered o'er the tide!
And the dead captains, as they lay
In their graves, o'erlooking the tranquil
    bay   40
  Where they in battle died.
    And the sound of that mournful song
    Goes through me with a thrill:
    "A boy's will is the wind's will,
And the thoughts of youth are long, long
    thoughts."

I can see the breezy dome of groves,
  The shadows of Deering's Woods;
And the friendships old and the early loves
Come back with a Sabbath sound, as of
    doves
  In quiet neighborhoods.   50
    And the verse of that sweet old song,
    It flutters and murmurs still:
    "A boy's will is the wind's will,
And the thoughts of youth are long, long
    thoughts."

I remember the gleams and glooms that
dart
Across the schoolboy's brain;
The song and the silence in the heart,
That in part are prophecies, and in part
Are longings wild and vain.
And the voice of that fitful song 60
Sings on, and is never still:
"A boy's will is the wind's will,
And the thoughts of youth are long, long
thoughts."

There are things of which I may not
speak;
There are dreams that cannot die;
There are thoughts that make the strong
heart weak,
And bring a pallor into the cheek,
And a mist before the eye.
And the words of that fatal song
Come over me like a chill: 70
"A boy's will is the wind's will,
And the thoughts of youth are long, long
thoughts."

Strange to me now are the forms I meet,
When I visit the dear old town;
But the native air is pure and sweet,
And the trees that o'ershadow each well-
known street,
As they balance up and down,
Are singing the beautiful song,
Are sighing and whispering still:
"A boy's will is the wind's will, 80
And the thoughts of youth are long, long
thoughts."

And Deering's Woods are fresh and fair,
And with joy that is almost pain
My heart goes back to wander there,
And among the dreams of the days that
were,
I find my lost youth again.
And the strange and beautiful song,
Sings on, and is never still:
"A boy's will is the wind's will,
And the thoughts of youth are long, long
thoughts." 90

FERN HILL

DYLAN THOMAS (1914–1953)

Now as I was young and easy under the apple boughs
About the lilting house and happy as the grass was green,
The night above the dingle starry,
Time let me hail and climb
Golden in the heydays of his eyes,
And honoured among wagons I was prince of the apple towns
And once below a time I lordly had the trees and leaves
Trail with daisies and barley
Down the rivers of the windfall light.

And as I was green and carefree, famous among the barns   10
About the happy yard and singing as the farm was home,
In the sun that is young once only,
Time let me play and be
Golden in the mercy of his means,
And green and golden I was huntsman and herdsman, the calves
Sang to my horn, the foxes on the hills barked clear and cold,
And the sabbath rang slowly
In the pebbles of the holy streams.

All the sun long it was running, it was lovely, the hay-
Fields high as the house, the tunes from the chimneys, it was air   20
                And playing, lovely and watery
                    And fire green as grass.
            And nightly under the simple stars
As I rode to sleep the owls were bearing the farm away,
All the moon long I heard, blessed among stables, the nightjars
                Flying with the ricks, and the horses
                    Flashing into the dark.

And then to awake, and the farm, like a wanderer white
With the dew, come back, the cock on his shoulder: it was all
                Shining, it was Adam and maiden,   30
                    The sky gathered again
                And the sun grew round that very day.
So it must have been after the birth of the simple light
In the first, spinning place, the spellbound horses walking warm
                Out of the whinnying green stable
                    On to the fields of praise.

And honoured among foxes and pheasants by the gay house
Under the new made clouds and happy as the heart was long
                In the sun born over and over,
                    I ran my heedless ways,   40
                My wishes raced through the house-high hay
And nothing I cared, at my sky blue trades, that time allows
In all his tuneful turning so few and such morning songs
                Before the children green and golden
                    Follow him out of grace,

Nothing I cared, in the lamb white days, that time would take me
Up to the swallow thronged loft by the shadow of my hand,
                In the moon that is always rising,
                    Nor that riding to sleep
                I should hear him fly with the high fields   56
And wake to the farm forever fled from the childless land.
Oh as I was young and easy in the mercy of his means,
                Time held me green and dying
                Though I sang in my chains like the sea.

PIANO

D. H. LAWRENCE (1885–1930)

Softly, in the dusk, a woman is singing to me;
Taking me back down the vista of years, till I see
A child sitting under the piano, in the boom of the tingling strings
And pressing the small, poised feet of a mother who smiles as she sings.

In spite of myself, the insidious mastery of song
Betrays me back, till the heart of me weeps to belong
To the old Sunday evenings at home, with winter outside
And hymns in the cozy parlor, the tinkling piano our guide.

So now it is vain for the singer to burst into clamor
With the great black piano appassionato. The glamour   10
Of childish days is upon me, my manhood is cast
Down in the flood of remembrance, I weep like a child for the past.

THE DEATH OF LINCOLN

WILLIAM CULLEN BRYANT (1794–1878)

Oh, slow to smite and swift to spare,
    Gentle and merciful and just!
Who, in the fear of God, didst bear
    The sword of power, a nation's trust!

In sorrow by thy bier we stand,
    Amid the awe that hushes all,
And speak the anguish of a land
    That shook with horror at thy fall.

Thy task is done; the bond are free:
    We bear thee to an honored grave,   10
Whose proudest monument shall be
    The broken fetters of the slave.

Pure was thy life; its bloody close
    Hath placed thee with the sons of light,
Among the noble host of those
    Who perished in the cause of Right.

O CAPTAIN! MY CAPTAIN!

WALT WHITMAN (1819–1892)

O Captain! my Captain! our fearful trip is done,
The ship has weather'd every rack, the prize we sought is won,
The port is near, the bells I hear, the people all exulting,
While follow eyes the steady keel, the vessel grim and daring;
    But O heart! heart! heart!
      O the bleeding drops of red,
        Where on the deck my Captain lies,
        Fallen cold and dead.

O Captain! my Captain! rise up and hear the bells;
Rise up—for you the flag is flung—for you the bugle trills,   10
For you bouquets and ribbon'd wreaths—for you the shores a-crowding,
For you they call, the swaying mass, their eager faces turning;
    Here Captain! dear father!
      The arm beneath your head!
        It is some dream that on the deck,
        You've fallen cold and dead.

My Captain does not answer, his lips are pale and still,
My father does not feel my arm, he has no pulse nor will,
The ship is anchor'd safe and sound, its voyage closed and done,
From fearful trip the victor ship comes in with object won: 20
  Exult O shores, and ring O bells!
   But I with mournful tread,
    Walk the deck my Captain lies,
    Fallen cold and dead.

WHEN LILACS LAST IN THE DOORWAY BLOOM'D

WALT WHITMAN (1819–1892)

1

When lilacs last in the dooryard bloom'd,
And the great star early droop'd in the western sky in the night,
I mourn'd, and yet shall mourn with ever-returning spring.

Ever-returning spring, trinity sure to me you bring,
Lilac blooming perennial and drooping star in the west,
And thought of him I love.

2

O powerful western fallen star!
O shades of night—O moody, tearful night!
O great star disappear'd—O the black murk that hides the star!
O cruel hands that hold me powerless—O helpless soul of me!   10
O harsh surrounding cloud that will not free my soul.

3

In the dooryard fronting an old farm-house near the whitewash'd palings,
Stands the lilac-bush tall-growing with heart-shaped leaves of rich green,
With many a pointed blossom rising delicate, with the perfume strong I love,
With every leaf a miracle—and from this bush in the dooryard,
With delicate-color'd blossoms and heart-shaped leaves of rich green,
A sprig with its flower I break.

4

In the swamp in secluded recesses,
A shy and hidden bird is warbling a song.

Solitary the thrush,   20
The hermit withdrawn to himself, avoiding the settlements,
Sings by himself a song.

Song of the bleeding throat,
Death's outlet song of life, (for well dear brother I know,
If thou wast not granted to sing thou would'st surely die.)

5

Over the breast of the spring, the land, amid cities,
Amid lanes and through old woods, where lately the violets peep'd from the ground,
     spotting the gray debris,
Amid the grass in the fields each side of the lanes, passing the endless grass,
Passing the yellow-spear'd wheat, every grain from its shroud in the dark-blown fields
     uprisen,
Passing the apple-tree blows of white and pink in the orchards,   30
Carrying a corpse to where it shall rest in the grave,
Night and day journeys a coffin.

6

Coffin that passes through lanes and streets,
Through day and night with the great cloud darkening the land,
With the pomp of the inloop'd flags with the cities draped in black,
With the show of the States themselves as of crape-veil'd women standing,
With processions long and winding and the flambeaus of the night,
With the countless torches lit, with the silent sea of faces and the unbared heads,
With the waiting depot, the arriving coffin, and the sombre faces,
With dirges through the night, with the thousand voices rising strong and solemn,   40
With all the mournful voices of the dirges pour'd around the coffin,
The dim-lit churches and the shuddering organs—where amid these you journey,
With the tolling bells' perpetual clang,
Here, coffin that slowly passes,
I gave you my sprig of lilac.

7

(Nor for you, for one alone,
Blossoms and branches green to coffins all I bring,
For fresh as the morning, thus would I chant a song for you O sane and sacred death.

All over bouquets of roses,
O death, I cover you over with roses and early lilies,   50
But mostly and now the lilac that blooms the first,
Copious I break, I break the sprigs from the bushes,
With loaded arms I come, pouring for you,
For you and the coffins all of you O death.)

8

O western orb sailing the heaven,
Now I know what you must have meant as a month since I walk'd,
As I walk'd in silence the transparent shadowy night,
As I saw you had something to tell as you bent to me night after night,
As you droop'd from the sky low down as if to my side, (while the other stars all
     look'd on,)
As we wander'd together the solemn night, (for something I know not what kept me
     from sleep,)   60
As the night advanced, and I saw on the rim of the west how full you were of woe.

As I stood on the rising ground in the breeze in the cool transparent **night**,
As I watch'd where you pass'd and was lost in the netherward black of the night,
As my soul in its trouble dissatisfied sank, as where you sad orb,
Concluded, dropt in the night, and was gone.

9

Sing on there in the swamp,
O singer bashful and tender, I hear your notes, I hear your call,
I hear, I come presently, I understand you,
But a moment I linger, for the lustrous star has detain'd me,
The star my departing comrade holds and detains me.   70

10

O how shall I warble myself for the dead one there I loved?
And how shall I deck my song for the large sweet soul that has gone?
And what shall my perfume be for the grave of him I love?

Sea-winds blown from east and west,
Blown from the Eastern sea and blown from the Western sea, till there on the prairies meeting,
These and with these and the breath of my chant,
I'll perfume the grave of him I love.

11

O what shall I hang on the chamber walls?
And what shall the pictures be that I hang on the walls,
To adorn the burial-house of him I love?   80

Pictures of growing spring and farms and homes,
With the Fourth-month eve at sundown, and the gray smoke lucid and bright,
With floods of the yellow gold of the gorgeous, indolent, sinking sun, burning, expanding the air,
With the fresh sweet herbage under foot, and the pale green leaves of the trees prolific,
In the distance the flowing glaze, the breast of the river, with a wind-dapple here and there,
With ranging hills on the banks, with many a line against the sky, and shadows,
And the city at hand with dwellings so dense, and stacks of chimneys,
And all the scenes of life and the workshops, and the workmen homeward returning.

12

Lo, body and soul—this land,
My own Manhattan with spires, and the sparkling and hurrying tides, and the ships,
The varied and ample land, the South and the North in the light, Ohio's shores and flashing Missouri,   91
And ever the far-spreading prairies cover'd with grass and corn.

Lo, the most excellent sun so calm and haughty,
The violet and purple morn with just-felt breezes,

The gentle soft-born measureless light,
The miracle spreading bathing all, the fulfill'd moon,
The coming eve delicious, the welcome night and the stars,
Over my cities shining all, enveloping man and land.

13

Sing on, sing on you gray-brown bird,
Sing from the swamps, the recesses, pour your chant from the bushes,   100
Limitless out of the dusk, out of the cedars and pines.

Sing on dearest brother, warble your reedy song,
Loud human song, with voice of uttermost woe.

O liquid and free and tender!
O wild and loose to my soul—O wondrous singer!
You only I hear—yet the star holds me, (but will soon depart,)
Yet the lilac with mastering odor holds me.

14

Now while I sat in the day and look'd forth,
In the close of the day with its light and the fields of spring, and the farmers preparing
    their crops,
In the large unconscious scenery of my land with its lakes and forests,   110
In the heavenly aerial beauty, (after the perturb'd winds and the storms,)
Under the arching heavens of the afternoon swift passing, and the voices of children
    and women,
The many-moving sea-tides, and I saw the ships how they sail'd,
And the summer approaching with richness, and the fields all busy with labor,
And the infinite separate houses, how they all went on, each with its meals and minutia
    of daily usages,
And the streets how their throbbings throbb'd, and the cities pent—lo, then and there,
Falling upon them all and among them all, enveloping me with the rest,
Appear'd the cloud, appear'd the long black trail,
And I knew death, its thought, and the sacred knowledge of death.

Then with the knowledge of death as walking one side of me,   120
And the thought of death close-walking the other side of me,
And I in the middle as with companions, and as holding the hands of companions,
I fled forth into the hiding receiving night that talks not,
Down to the shores of the water, the path by the swamp in the dimness,
To the solemn shadowy cedars and ghostly pines so still.

And the singer so shy to the rest receiv'd me,
The gray-brown bird I know receiv'd us comrades three,
And he sang the carol of death, and a verse for him I love.

From deep secluded recesses,
From the fragrant cedars and the ghostly pines so still,   130
Came the carol of the bird.

And the charm of the carol rapt me,
As I held as if by their hands my comrades in the night,
And the voice of my spirit tallied the song of the bird.

Come lovely and soothing death,
Undulate round the world, serenely arriving, arriving,
In the day, in the night, to all, to each,
Sooner or later delicate death.

Prais'd be the fathomless universe,
For life and joy, and for objects and knowledge curious, 140
And for love, sweet love—but praise! praise! praise!
For the sure-enwinding arms of cool-enfolding death.

Dark mother always gliding near with soft feet,
Have none chanted for thee a chant of fullest welcome?
Then I chant it for thee, I glorify thee above all,
I bring thee a song that when thou must indeed come, come unfalteringly.

Approach strong deliveress,
When it is so, when thou hast taken them I joyously sing the dead,
Lost in the loving floating ocean of thee,
Laved in the flood of thy bliss O death. 150

From me to thee glad serenades,
Dances for thee I propose saluting thee, adornments and feastings for thee,
And the sights of the open landscape and the high-spread sky are fitting,
And life and the fields, and the huge and thoughtful night.

The night in silence under many a star,
The ocean shore and the husky whispering wave whose voice I know,
And the soul turning to thee O vast and well-veil'd death,
And the body gratefully nestling close to thee.

Over the tree-tops I float thee a song,
Over the rising and sinking waves, over the myriad fields and the prairies wide, 160
Over the dense-pack'd cities all and the teeming wharves and ways,
I float this carol with joy, with joy to thee O death.

15

To the tally of my soul,
Loud and strong kept up the gray-brown bird,
With pure deliberate notes spreading filling the night.

Loud in the pines and cedars dim,
Clear in the freshness moist and the swamp-perfume,
And I with my comrades there in the night.

While my sight that was bound in my eyes unclosed,
As to long panoramas of visions.   170

And I saw askant the armies,
I saw as in noiseless dreams hundreds of battle-flags,
Borne through the smoke of the battles and pierc'd with missiles I saw them,
And carried hither and yon through the smoke, and torn and bloody,
And at last but a few shreds left on the staffs, (and all in silence,)
And the staffs all splinter'd and broken.

I saw battle-corpses, myriads of them,
And the white skeletons of young men, I saw them,
I saw the debris and debris of all the slain soldiers of the war,
But I saw they were not as was thought,   180
They themselves were fully at rest, they suffer'd not,
The living remain'd and suffer'd, the mother suffer'd,
And the wife and the child and the musing comrade suffer'd,
And the armies that remain'd suffer'd.

16

Passing the visions, passing the night,
Passing, unloosing the hold of my comrades' hands,
Passing the song of the hermit bird and the tallying song of my soul,
Victorious song, death's outlet song, yet varying ever-altering song,
As low and wailing, yet clear the notes, rising and falling, flooding the night,
Sadly sinking and fainting, as warning and warning, and yet again bursting with joy.
Covering the earth and filling the spread of the heaven,   191
As that powerful psalm in the night I heard from recesses,
Passing, I leave thee lilac with heart-shaped leaves,
I leave thee there in the dooryard, blooming, returning with spring.

I cease from my song for thee,
From my gaze on thee in the west, fronting the west, communing with thee,
O comrade lustrous with silver face in the night.

Yet each to keep and all, retrievements out of the night,
The song, the wondrous chant of the gray-brown bird,
And the tallying chant, the echo arous'd in my soul,   200
With the lustrous and drooping star with the countenance full of woe,
With the holders holding my hand nearing the call of the bird,
Comrades mine and I in the midst, and their memory ever to keep, for the dead I
     loved so well,
For the sweetest, wisest soul of all my days and lands—and this for his dear sake,
Lilac and star and bird twined with the chant of my soul,
There in the fragrant pines and the cedars dusk and dim.

SUNBURNED ULYSSES

FREDERICK PROKOSCH (1908–   )

Sunburned Ulysses, when he leaned over the water
And heard through the lapping of the waves
That calculating music, heard more than the noise of wind or the noise of water:
As he strained his ears, he heard the monotonous profound
Music of lost mariners moving landward through the water,
He heard, rising from graves of sand, sea-pitted and sea-pillared graves,
The sobbing and interminable voices of the drowned.

Scarcely to be grasped as anything other than music,
Being almost wholly woven into the sound of waves, he heard
Emerging from the crested, sun-dipped lethargy of the afternoon,   10
Distinct and terrifying words. Yet not a word
Could he recall—or at least, he never told, being in love
With no one; hard and isolated, in love with change alone.
With a bird's yearning to move seasonally and the sharp, mean eyes of a bird.

O blacker and deeper than the depths off Portugal,
Some of us have glimpsed that rock, that goddess rising from the sea,
And as we labour to find for what we were intended,
Slowly, as the spirit is sharpened, the senses are vilified.
Even the sly faces and the weatherbeaten faces all, all
Are caught and brought to punishment. Though they have not died,   20
Their eyes are those of a dead man, or a dead animal.

Black-eyed Ulysses, being an astute and eagle-hearted man,
A heavily loined, lumbering man with a bird's eye and a bird's unrest,
As he listened and heard through the lapping of the waves
That loud, heart-breaking music, understood. Sweat poured from his brown chest.
Loving the unattainable and forbidden, in love with change alone,
He recognized the frightful necessity in the song of the sirens: for he likewise possessed
Flesh fanned easily into fire, and a heart as hard as a stone.

ULYSSES

ROBERT GRAVES (1895–   )

To this much-tossed Ulysses, never done
    With woman whether gowned as wife or whore,

Penelope and Circe seemed as one:
She like a whore made his lewd fancies run,
   And wifely she a hero to him bore.

Their counter-changings terrified his way:
   They were the clashing rocks, Symplegades,
Scylla and Charybdis too were they;
Now they were storms frosting the sea with spray
   And now the lotus orchard's filthy ease.   10

They multiplied into the Sirens' throng,
   Forewarned by fear of whom he stood bound fast,
   Hand and foot helpless at the vessel's mast,
Yet would not stop his ears: daring their song
   He groaned and sweated till that shore was past.

One, two and many: flesh had made him blind,
   Flesh had one pleasure only in the act,
Flesh set one purpose only in the mind—
Triumph of flesh and afterwards to find
   Still those same terrors wherewith flesh was racked.   20

His wiles were witty and his fame far known,
Every king's daughter sought him for her own,
   Yet he was nothing to be won or lost.
   All lands to him were Ithaca: love-tossed
He loathed the fraud, yet would not bed alone.

STEAMBOATS, VIADUCTS, AND RAILWAYS

WILLIAM WORDSWORTH (1770–1850)

Motions and Means, on land and sea at war
With old poetic feeling, not for this,
Shall ye, by Poets even, be judged amiss!
Nor shall your presence, howsoe'er it mar
The loveliness of Nature, prove a bar
To the Mind's gaining that prophetic sense
Of future change, that point of vision, whence
May be discovered what in soul ye are.
In spite of all that beauty may disown

In your harsh features, Nature doth embrace   10
Her lawful offspring in Man's art; and Time,
Pleased with your triumphs o'er his brother Space,
Accepts from your bold hands the proffered crown
Of hope, and smiles on you with cheer sublime.

THE LOCOMOTIVE

EMILY DICKINSON (1830–1886)

I like to see it lap the miles,
And lick the valleys up,
And stop to feed itself at tanks;
And then, prodigious, step

Around a pile of mountains,
And, supercilious, peer
In shanties by the sides of roads;
And then a quarry pare

To fit its sides, and crawl between,
Complaining all the while   10
In horrid, hooting stanza;
Then chase itself down hill

And neigh like Boanerges;
Then, punctual as a star,
Stop—docile and omnipotent—
At its own stable door.

TO A LOCOMOTIVE IN WINTER

WALT WHITMAN (1819–1892)

Thee for my recitative,
Thee in the driving storm even as now, the snow, the winter-day declining,
Thee in thy panoply, thy measur'd dual throbbing and thy beat convulsive,
Thy black cylindric body, golden brass and silvery steel,
Thy ponderous side-bars, parallel and connecting rods, gyrating, shuttling at thy sides,
Thy metrical, now swelling pant and roar, now tapering in the distance,
Thy great protruding head-light fix'd in front,
Thy long, pale, floating vapor-pennants, tinged with delicate purple,
The dense and murky clouds out-belching from thy smoke-stack,
Thy knitted frame, thy springs and valves, the tremulous twinkle of thy wheels,   10
Thy train of cars behind, obedient, merrily following,
Through gale or calm, now swift, now slack, yet steadily careering;
Type of the modern—emblem of motion and power—pulse of the continent,
For once come serve the Muse and merge in verse, even as here I see thee,
With storm and buffeting gusts of wind and falling snow,

By day thy warning ringing bell to sound its notes,
By night thy silent signal lamps to swing.

Fierce-throated beauty!
Roll through my chant with all thy lawless music, thy swinging lamps at night,
Thy madly-whistled laughter, echoing, rumbling like an earthquake, rousing all,   20
Law of thyself complete, thine own track firmly holding,
(No sweetness debonair of tearful harp or glib piano thine,)
Thy trills of shrieks by rocks and hills return'd,
Launch'd o'er the prairies wide, across the lakes,
To the free skies unpent and glad and strong.

THE EXPRESS

STEPHEN SPENDER (1909–   )

After the first powerful plain manifesto
The black statement of pistons, without more fuss
But gliding like a queen, she leaves the station.
Without bowing and with restrained unconcern
She passes the houses which humbly crowd outside,
The gasworks and at last the heavy page
Of death, printed by gravestones in the cemetery.
Beyond the town there lies the open country
Where, gathering speed, she acquires mystery,
The luminous self-possession of ships on ocean.   10
It is now she begins to sing—at first quite low
Then loud, and at last with a jazzy madness—
The song of her whistle screaming at curves,
Of deafening tunnels, brakes, innumerable bolts.
And always light, aerial, underneath
Goes the elate metre of her wheels.
Steaming through metal landscape on her lines
She plunges new eras of wild happiness
Where speed throws up strange shapes, broad curves
And parallels clean like the steel of guns.   20
At last, further than Edinburgh or Rome,
Beyond the crest of the world, she reaches night
Where only a low streamline brightness
Of phosphorus on the tossing hills is white.
Ah, like a comet through flame she moves entranced
Wrapt in her music no bird song, no, nor bough
Breaking with honey buds, shall ever equal.

AN IRISH AIRMAN FORESEES HIS DEATH

WILLIAM BUTLER YEATS (1865–1939)

I know that I shall meet my fate
Somewhere among the clouds above;
Those that I fight I do not hate,
Those that I guard I do not love;
My country is Kiltartan Cross,
My countrymen Kiltartan's poor,
No likely end could bring them loss
Or leave them happier than before.
Nor law, nor duty bade me fight,
Nor public men, nor cheering crowds,   10
A lonely impulse of delight
Drove to this tumult in the clouds;
I balanced all, brought all to mind,
The years to come seemed waste of breath,
A waste of breath the years behind
In balance with this life, this death.

HIGH FLIGHT

JOHN GILLESPIE MAGEE (1922–1941)

Oh, I have slipped the surly bonds of earth
And danced the skies on laughter-silvered wings;
Sunward I've climbed and joined the tumbling mirth
Of sun-split clouds—and done a hundred things
You have not dreamed of—wheeled and soared and swung
High in the sunlit silence. Hov'ring there,
I've chased the shouting wind along and flung
My eager craft through footless halls of air.
Up, up the long delirious, burning blue
I've topped the wind-swept heights with easy grace,   10
Where never lark, or even eagle, flew;
And, while with silent, lifting mind I've trod
The high untrespassed sanctity of space,
Put out my hand and touched the face of God.

THE LANDSCAPE NEAR AN AERODROME

STEPHEN SPENDER (1909–   )

More beautiful and soft than any moth
With burring furred antennae feeling its huge path
Through dusk, the air-liner with shut-off engines
Glides over suburbs and the sleeves set trailing tall
To point the wind. Gently, broadly, she falls,
Scarcely disturbing charted currents of air.

Lulled by descent, the travelers across sea
And across feminine land indulging its easy limbs
In miles of softness, now let their eyes trained by watching
Penetrate through dusk the outskirts of this town   10
Here where industry shows a fraying edge.
Here they may see what is being done.

Beyond the winking masthead light
And the landing-ground, they observe the outposts
Of work: chimneys like lank black fingers
Or figures frightening and mad: and squat buildings
With their strange air behind trees, like women's faces
Shattered by grief. Here where few houses
Moan with faint light behind their blinds
They remark the unhomely sense of complaint, like a dog   20
Shut out and shivering at the foreign moon.

In the last sweep of love, they pass over fields
Behind the aerodrome, where boys play all day
Hacking dead grass: whose cries, like wild birds,
Settle upon the nearest roofs
But soon are hid under the loud city.

Then, as they land, they hear the tolling bell
Reaching across the landscape of hysteria
To where, larger than all the charcoaled batteries
And imaged towers against that dying sky,   30
Religion stands, the church blocking the sun.

NEXT PLEASE

PHILIP LARKIN (1922–   )

Always too eager for the future, we
Pick up bad habits of expectancy.
Something is always approaching; every day
Till then we say,

Watching from a bluff the tiny, clear
Sparkling armada of promises draw near.
How slow they are! And how much time they waste,
Refusing to make haste!

Yet still they leave us holding wretched stalks
Of disappointment, for, though nothing balks   10
Each big approach, leaning with brasswork prinked,
Each rope distinct,

Flagged, and the figurehead with golden tits
Arching our way, it never anchors; it's
No sooner present than it turns to past.
Right to the last

We think each one will heave to and unload
All good into our lives, all we are owed
For waiting so devoutly and so long.
But we are wrong: 20

Only one ship is seeking us, a black-
Sailed unfamiliar, towing at her back
A huge and birdless silence. In her wake
No waters breed or break.

THE FIGUREHEAD

R. W. STALLMAN (1911–   )

Stepping on air in slippered toes,
Arms slanting back where bowsprit rose
When seafoam flaked her chiseled hair,
Suspended thus, leaning on air,

Uprears against the museum-wall
As though a sudden wind had caught her;
And yet where no wind is at all,
Where no sea is she sails ghost-water,
Swan-breasting seas that are not there.
The rage that's in her painted stare   **10**
Remembers yet what seas she drew,
What waiting port, what unreached shore:

All's past and done with—ship and crew
Drowned in that past we voyage for.
As backward race the waves, so we
Plunge on and backwards go instead—

The relics of our history
Widowed like this figurehead.

iii. The Poem as Comparison

The poems in this section create their meanings by comparisons between one thing and another, as in Spenser's "My love is like to ice, and I to fire." The comparison in the poem is not concealed; on the contrary, it is clearly stated. The whole poem, in terms of structure, is neither more nor less than an analogy. All poetry is of course made of comparisons—"simple or complex, open or concealed. The richness of poetry," to quote Mr. J. Isaacs, "is obtained by mixing or interweaving or juxtaposing these comparisons. . . . In prose all comparisons are simple and uncompounded. In poetry all metaphors are mixed metaphors."

THREE SONNETS

WILLIAM SHAKESPEARE (1564–1616)

SONNET 18

Shall I compare thee to a summer's day?
Thou art more lovely and more temperate:
Rough winds do shake the darling buds of May,
And summer's lease hath all too short a date:
Sometimes too hot the eye of heaven shines,
And often is his gold complexion dimm'd;
And every fair from fair sometime declines,
By chance, or nature's changing course, untrimm'd;
But thy eternal summer shall not fade,
Nor lose possession of that fair thou owest;   10
Nor shall Death brag thou wander'st in his shade,
When in eternal lines to time thou growest:
So long as men can breathe, or eyes can see,
So long lives this, and this gives life to thee.

SONNET 33

Full many a glorious morning have I seen
Flatter the mountain-tops with sovereign eye,
Kissing with golden face the meadows green,
Gilding pale streams with heavenly alchemy;
Anon permit the basest clouds to ride
With ugly rack on his celestial face,

And from the forlorn world his visage hide,
Stealing unseen to west with this disgrace:
Even so my sun one early morn did shine
With all-triumphant splendour on my brow;   10
But, out, alack! he was but one hour mine,
The region cloud hath masked him from me now.
Yet him for this my love no whit disdaineth;
Suns of the world may stain when heaven's sun staineth.

SONNET 73

That time of year thou may'st in me behold
When yellow leaves, or none, or few, do hang
Upon those boughs which shake against the cold,
Bare ruined choirs, where late the sweet birds sang.
In me thou see'st the twilight of such day
As after sunset fadeth in the west;
Which by and by black night doth take away,
Death's second self, that seals up all in rest.
In me thou see'st the glowing of such fire,
That on the ashes of his youth doth lie,   10
As the death-bed whereon it must expire,
Consumed with that which it was nourished by.
This thou perceivest, which makes thy love more strong.
To love that well which thou must leave ere long.

"MY LOVE IS LIKE TO ICE . . ."

(From AMORETTI)

EDMUND SPENSER (1552–1599)

My Love is like to ice, and I to fire:
How comes it then that this her cold so great
Is not dissolved through my so hot desire,
But harder grows the more I her entreat?
Or how comes it that my exceeding heat
Is not allayed by her heart-frozen cold,
But that I burn much more in boiling sweat,
And feel my flames augmented manifold?
What more miraculous thing may be told,
That fire, which all things melts, should harden ice,   10
And ice, which is congeal'd with senseless cold,
Should kindle fire by wonderful device?
    Such is the power of love in gentle mind,
    That it can alter all the course of kind.

A VALEDICTION: FORBIDDING MOURNING

JOHN DONNE (1573–1631)

As virtuous men pass mildly away,
  And whisper to their souls to go,
Whilst some of their sad friends do say,
  "The breath goes now," and some say,
    "No,"

So let us melt and make no noise,
  No tear-floods nor sigh-tempests move;
'Twere profanation of our joys
  To tell the laity our love.

Moving of th' earth brings harms and
    fears;
  Men reckon what it did and meant; 10
But trepidation of the spheres,
  Though greater far, is innocent.

Dull sublunary lovers' love,
  Whose soul is sense, cannot admit
Absence, because it doth remove
  Those things which elemented it.

But we by a love so much refin'd
  That ourselves know not what it is,

Interassurèd of the mind,   19
  Care less eyes, lips, and hands to miss.

Our two souls, therefore, which are one,
  Though I must go, endure not yet
A breach, but an expansion,
  Like gold to airy thinness beat.

If they be two, they are two so
  As stiff twin compasses are two;
Thy soul, the fix'd foot, makes no show
  To move, but doth if th' other do.

And though it in the center sit,
  Yet when the other far doth roam, 30
It leans and hearkens after it,
  And grows erect as that comes home.

Such wilt thou be to me, who must,
  Like th' other foot, obliquely run;
Thy firmness makes my circle just,
  And makes me end where I begun.

THE DEFINITION OF LOVE

ANDREW MARVELL (1621–1678)

My Love is of a birth as rare
As 'tis, for object, strange and high:
It was begotten by Despair
Upon Impossibility.

Magnanimous Despair alone
Could show me so divine a thing,
Where feeble Hope could ne'er have flown
But vainly flapped its tinsel wing.

And yet I quickly might arrive
Where my extended soul is fixt, 10
But Fate does iron wedges drive,
And always crowds itself betwixt.

For Fate with jealous eye does see
Two perfect loves; nor lets them close:
Their union would her ruin be,
And her tyrannic power depose.

And therefore her decrees of steel
Us as the distant poles have placed,
(Though love's whole world on us doth
    wheel)
Not by themselves to be embraced. 20

Unless the giddy heaven fall,
And earth some new convulsion tear;
And, us to join, the world should all
Be cramped into a planisphere.

As lines, so loves oblique may well
Themselves in every angle greet:
But ours, so truly parallel,
Though infinite, can never meet.

Therefore the love which us doth bind,
But Fate so enviously debars,　　　30
Is the conjunction of the mind,
And opposition of the stars.

"THERE IS A GARDEN IN HER FACE"

THOMAS CAMPION (1567–1620)

There is a garden in her face
Where roses and white lilies grow;
A heavenly paradise is that place
Wherein all pleasant fruits do flow.
　　There cherries grow which none may
　　　buy,
　　Till "Cherry ripe" themselves do cry.

Those cherries fairly do enclose
Of orient pearl a double row,
Which when her lovely laughter shows, 9

They look like rose-buds filled with snow,
　Yet them nor peer nor prince can buy,
　Till "Cherry ripe" themselves do cry.

Her eyes like angels watch them still,
Her brows like bended bows do stand,
Threatening with piercing frowns to kill
All that attempt, with eye or hand,
　Those sacred cherries to come nigh
　Till "Cherry ripe" themselves do cry.

TO THE VIRGINS, TO MAKE MUCH OF TIME

ROBERT HERRICK (1591–1674)

Gather ye rose-buds while ye may,
　Old Time is still a-flying:
And this same flower that smiles to-day,
　To-morrow will be dying.

The glorious lamp of Heaven, the sun,
　The higher he's a-getting;
The sooner will his race be run,
　And nearer he's to setting.

That age is best, which is the first,
　When youth and blood are warmer; 10
But being spent, the worse, and worst
　Times, still succeed the former.

Then be not coy, but use your time;
　And while ye may, go marry:
For having lost but once your prime,
　You may for ever tarry.

TO HELEN

EDGAR ALLAN POE (1809–1849)

Helen, thy beauty is to me
　Like those Nicæan barks of yore
That gently, o'er a perfumed sea,
　The weary, wayworn wanderer bore
　To his own native shore.

On desperate seas long wont to roam,
　Thy hyacinth hair, thy classic face,

Thy Naiad airs, have brought me home
　To the glory that was Greece
　And the grandeur that was Rome. 10

Lo! in yon brilliant window-niche
How statue-like I see thee stand,
The agate lamp within thy hand!
　Ah, Psyche, from the regions which
　Are Holy Land!

"HOW DO I LOVE THEE. . . ."

(*From SONNETS FROM THE PORTUGUESE*)

ELIZABETH BARRETT BROWNING (1806–1861)

SONNET 43

How do I love thee? Let me count the ways.
I love thee to the depth and breadth and height
My soul can reach, when feeling out of sight
For the ends of Being and ideal Grace.
I love thee to the level of everyday's
Most quiet need, by sun and candle-light.
I love thee freely, as men strive for Right;
I love thee purely, as they turn from Praise.
I love thee with the passion put to use
In my old griefs, and with my childhood's faith.   10
I love thee with a love I seemed to lose
With my lost saints,—I love thee with the breath,
Smiles, tears, of all my life!—and, if God choose,
I shall but love thee better after death.

"THUS PITEOUSLY LOVE CLOSED. . . ."

(*From MODERN LOVE*)

GEORGE MEREDITH (1828–1909)

Thus piteously Love closed what he begat:
The union of this ever-diverse pair!
These two were rapid falcons in a snare,
Condemned to do the flitting of the bat.
Lovers beneath the singing sky of May,
They wandered once; clear as the dew on flowers:
But they fed not on the advancing hours:
Their hearts held cravings for the buried day.
Then each applied to each that fatal knife,
Deep questioning, which probes to endless dole.   10
Ah, what a dusty answer gets the soul
When hot for certainties in this our life!—
In tragic hints here see what evermore
Moves dark as yonder midnight ocean's force,
Thundering like ramping hosts of warrior horse,
To throw that faint thin line upon the shore!

AUTUMNUS

JOSHUA SYLVESTER (1563–1618)

When the leaves in autumn wither,
  With a tawny tannèd face,
  Warped and wrinkled-up together,
The year's late beauty to disgrace:

There thy life's glass may'st thou find thee,
  Green now, gray now, gone anon;
  Leaving (worldling) of thine own,
Neither fruit, nor leaf behind thee.

VIRTUE

GEORGE HERBERT (1593–1633)

Sweet day, so cool, so calm, so bright,
The bridal of the earth and sky;
The dew shall weep thy fall tonight,
    For thou must die.

Sweet spring, full of sweet days and roses,
A box where sweets compacted lie;   10
My music shows ye have your closes,
    And all must die.

Sweet rose, whose hue angry and brave
Bids the rash gazer wipe his eye;
Thy root is ever in its grave,
    And thou must die.

Only a sweet and virtuous soul,
Like seasoned timber, never gives;
But though the whole world turn to coal,
    Then chiefly lives.

TO DAFFODILS

ROBERT HERRICK (1591–1674)

Fair daffodils, we weep to see
  You haste away so soon;
As yet the early-rising sun
  Has not attain'd his noon.
    Stay, stay,
  Until the hasting day
    Has run
  But to the even-song;
And, having pray'd together, we
  Will go with you along.   10

We have short time to stay, as you.
  We have as short a Spring;
As quick a growth to meet decay,
  As you, or any thing.
    We die,
  As your hours do, and dry
    Away,
  Like to the Summer's rain;
Or as the pearls of morning's dew
  Ne'er to be found again.   20

THE WILD HONEYSUCKLE

PHILIP FRENEAU (1752–1832)

Fair flower, that dost so comely grow,
  Hid in this silent, dull retreat,
Untouched thy honeyed blossoms blow,
  Unseen thy little branches greet:
    No roving foot shall crush thee here,
    No busy hand provoke a tear.

By Nature's self in white arrayed,
  She bade thee shun the vulgar eye,
And planted here the guardian shade,
  And sent soft waters murmuring by;   10
    Thus quietly thy summer goes,
    Thy days declining to repose.

Smit with those charms that must decay,
  I grieve to see your future doom;
They died—nor were those flowers more
    gay,
    The flowers that did in Eden bloom;
      Unpitying frosts and autumn's power
      Shall leave no vestige of this flower.

From morning suns and evening dews
  At first thy little being came: 20
If nothing once, you nothing lose,
  For when you die you are the same;
    The space between is but an hour,
    The frail duration of a flower.

THE RETURN

EDNA ST. VINCENT MILLAY (1892–1950)

Earth does not understand her child,
  Who from the loud gregarious town
Returns, depleted and defiled,
  To the still woods, to fling him down.

Earth can not count the sons she bore:
  The wounded lynx, the wounded man
Come trailing blood unto her door;
  She shelters both as best she can.

But she is early up and out,
  To trim the year or strip its bones; 10

She has no time to stand about
  Talking of him in undertones

Who has no aim but to forget,
  Be left in peace, be lying thus
For days, for years, for centuries yet,
  Unshaven and anonymous;

Who, marked for failure, dulled by grief,
  Has traded in his wife and friend
For this warm ledge, this alder leaf:
  Comfort that does not comprehend. 20

DAYS

RALPH WALDO EMERSON (1803–1882)

Daughters of Time, the hypocritic Days,
Muffled and dumb like barefoot dervishes,
And marching single in an endless file,
Bring diadems and fagots in their hands.
To each they offer gifts after his will,
Bread, kingdoms, stars, and sky that holds
    them all.

I, in my pleachéd garden, watched the
    pomp,
Forgot my morning wishes, hastily
Took a few herbs and apples, and the
    Day
Turned and departed silent. I, too late,
Under her solemn fillet saw the scorn. 11

DIRGE IN WOODS

GEORGE MEREDITH (1828–1909)

A wind sways the pines,
    And below
Not a breath of wild air;
Still as the mosses that glow
On the flooring and over the lines
Of the roots here and there.
The pine-tree drops its dead;
They are quiet, as under the sea.

Overhead, overhead
Rushes life in a race,   10
As the clouds the clouds chase;
    And we go,
And we drop like the fruits of the tree,
    Even we,
    Even so.

BIRCHES

ROBERT FROST (1874–1963)

When I see birches bend to left and right
Across the lines of straighter darker trees,
I like to think some boy's been swinging them.
But swinging doesn't bend them down to stay.
Ice-storms do that. Often you must have seen them
Loaded with ice a sunny winter morning
After a rain. They click upon themselves
As the breeze rises, and turn many-colored
As the stir cracks and crazes their enamel.
Soon the sun's warmth makes them shed crystal shells 10
Shattering and avalanching on the snow-crust—
Such heaps of broken glass to sweep away
You'd think the inner dome of heaven had fallen.
They are dragged to the withered bracken by the load,
And they seem not to break; though once they are bowed
So low for long, they never right themselves:
You may see their trunks arching in the woods
Years afterwards, trailing their leaves on the ground
Like girls on hands and knees that throw their hair
Before them over their heads to dry in the sun. 20
But I was going to say when Truth broke in
With all her matter-of-fact about the ice-storm
I should prefer to have some boy bend them
As he went out and in to fetch the cows—
Some boy too far from town to learn baseball,
Whose only play was what he found himself,
Summer or winter, and could play alone.
One by one he subdued his father's trees
By riding them down over and over again
Until he took the stiffness out of them, 30
And not one but hung limp, not one was left
For him to conquer. He learned all there was
To learn about not launching out too soon
And so not carrying the tree away
Clear to the ground. He always kept his poise
To the top branches, climbing carefully
With the same pains you use to fill a cup
Up to the brim, and even above the brim.
Then he flung outward, feet first, with a swish,
Kicking his way down through the air to the ground. 40
So was I once myself a swinger of birches.
And so I dream of going back to be.
It's when I'm weary of considerations,
And life is too much like a pathless wood
Where your face burns and tickles with the cobwebs

Broken across it, and one eye is weeping
From a twig's having lashed across it open.
I'd like to get away from earth awhile
And then come back to it and begin over.
May no fate willfully misunderstand me   50
And half grant what I wish and snatch me away
Not to return. Earth's the right place for love:
I don't know where it's likely to go better.
I'd like to go by climbing a birch tree,
And climb black branches up a snow-white trunk
Toward heaven, till the tree could bear no more,
But dipped its top and set me down again.
That would be good both going and coming back.
One could do worse than be a swinger of birches.

TREE AT MY WINDOW

ROBERT FROST (1874–1963)

Tree at my window, window tree,
My sash is lowered when night comes on;
But let there never be curtain drawn
Between you and me.

Vague dream-head lifted out of the
          ground,
And thing next most diffuse to cloud,
Not all your light tongues talking aloud
Could be profound.

But tree, I have seen you taken and tossed,
And if you have seen me when I slept,   10
You have seen me when I was taken and
          swept
And all but lost.

That day she put our heads together,
Fate had her imagination about her,
Your head so much concerned with outer,
Mine with inner, weather.

MENDING WALL

ROBERT FROST (1874–1963)

Something there is that doesn't love a wall,
That sends the frozen-ground-swell under it,
And spills the upper bowlders in the sun;
And makes gaps even two can pass abreast.
The work of hunters is another thing:
I have come after them and made repair
Where they have left not one stone on a stone,
But they would have the rabbit out of hiding,
To please the yelping dogs. The gaps I mean,
No one has seen them made or heard them made,   10
But at spring mending-time we find them there.
I let my neighbor know beyond the hill;

And on a day we meet to walk the line
And set the wall between us once again.
We keep the wall between us as we go.
To each the bowlders that have fallen to each.
And some are loaves and some so nearly balls
We have to use a spell to make them balance:
"Stay where you are until our backs are turned!"
We wear our fingers rough with handling them.   20
Oh, just another kind of outdoor game,
One on a side. It comes to little more:
There where it is we do not need the wall:
He is all pine and I am apple-orchard.
My apple trees will never get across
And eat the cones under his pines, I tell him.
He only says, "Good fences make good neighbors."
Spring is the mischief in me, and I wonder
If I could put a notion in his head:
"*Why* do they make good neighbors? Isn't it   30
Where there are cows? But here there are no cows.
Before I build a wall I'd ask to know
What I was walling in or walling out,
And to whom I was like to give offense.
Something there is that doesn't love a wall,
That wants it down!" I could say "elves" to him,
But it's not elves exactly, and I'd rather
He said it for himself. I see him there,
Bringing a stone grasped firmly by the top
In each hand, like an old-stone savage armed.   40
He moves in darkness, as it seems to me,
Not of woods only and the shade of trees.
He will not go behind his father's saying,
And he likes having thought of it so well
He says again, "Good fences make good neighbors."

DOMINATION OF BLACK

WALLACE STEVENS (1879–1955)

At night, by the fire,
The colors of the bushes
And of the fallen leaves,
Repeating themselves,
Turned in the room,
Like the leaves themselves
Turning in the wind.
Yes: but the color of the heavy hemlocks

Came striding.
And I remembered the cry of the peacocks.   10

The colors of their tails
Were like the leaves themselves
Turning in the wind,
In the twilight wind.
They swept over the room,
Just as they flew from the boughs of the hemlocks
Down to the ground.
I heard them cry—the peacocks.
Was it a cry against the twilight
Or against the leaves themselves   20
Turning in the wind,
Turning as the flames
Turned in the fire,
Turning as the tails of the peacocks
Turned in the loud fire,
Loud as the hemlocks
Full of the cry of the peacocks?
Or was it a cry against the hemlocks?

Out of the window,
I saw how the planets gathered   30
Like the leaves themselves
Turning in the wind.
I saw how the night came,
Came striding like the color of the heavy hemlocks.
I felt afraid.
And I remembered the cry of the peacocks.

MINE NO. 6

MALCOLM COWLEY (1898–   )

They scoured the hill with steel and living brooms
of fire, that none else living might persist;
here crouch their cabins, here the tipple looms
uncompromising, black against the mist.

All day their wagons lumber past, the wide
squat wheels hub deep, the horses strained and still;
a headlong rain pours down all day to hide
the blackened stumps, the ulcerated hill.

Beauty, perfection, I have loved you fiercely
—even in this windy slum, where fear
drips from the eaves with April rain, and scarcely
a leaf sprouts, and a wilderness of pain
brings forth its stillborn children—even here
. . . your long white cruel fingers at my brain.

10

DESERT PLACES

ROBERT FROST (1874–1963)

Snow falling and night falling fast, oh, fast
In a field I looked into going past,
And the ground almost covered smooth in snow,
But a few weeds and stubble showing last.

The woods around it have it—it is theirs.
All animals are smothered in their lairs.
I am too absent-spirited to count:
The loneliness includes me unawares.

And lonely as it is, that loneliness
Will be more lonely ere it will be less,
A blanker whiteness of benighted snow,
With no expression—nothing to express.

10

They cannot scare me with their empty spaces
Between stars—on stars void of human races.
I have it in me so much nearer home
To scare myself with my own desert places.

MIRAGE

R. P. BLACKMUR (1904–   )

The wind was in another country, and
the day had gathered to its heart of noon
the sum of silence, heat, and stricken time.
Not a ripple spread. The sea mirrored
perfectly all the nothing in the sky.
We had to walk about to keep our eyes
from seeing nothing, and our hearts from
    stopping
at nothing. Then most suddenly we saw
horizon on horizon lifting up
out of the sea's edge a shining mountain
sun-yellow and sea-green; against it surf
flung spray and spume into the miles of
    sky.
Somebody said mirage, and it was gone,
but there I have been living ever since.

9

JUGGLER

RICHARD WILBUR (1921–   )

A ball will bounce, but less and less. It's not
A light-hearted thing, resents its own resilience.
Falling is what it loves, and the earth falls
So in our hearts from brilliance,
Settles and is forgot.
It takes a skyblue juggler with five red balls
To shake our gravity up. Whee, in the air
The balls roll round, wheel on his wheeling hands,
Learning the ways of lightness, alter to spheres
Grazing his finger ends,   10
Cling to their courses there,
Swinging a small heaven about his ears.

But a heaven is easier made of nothing at all
Than the earth regained, and still and sole within
The spin of worlds, with a gesture sure and noble
He reels that heaven in,
Landing it ball by ball,
And trades it all for a broom, a plate, a table.

Oh, on his toe the table is turning, the broom's
Balancing up on his nose, and the plate whirls   20
On the tip of the broom! Damn, what a show, we cry:
The boys stamp, and the girls
Shriek, and the drum booms
And all comes down, and he bows and says goodbye.

If the juggler is tired now, if the broom stands
In the dust again, if the table starts to drop
Through the daily dark again, and though the plate
Lies flat on the table top,
For him we batter our hands
Who has won for once over the world's weight.   30

CARGOES

JOHN MASEFIELD (1878–   )

Quinquireme of Nineveh from distant Ophir,
Rowing home to haven in sunny Palestine,
With a cargo of ivory,
And apes and peacocks,
Sandalwood, cedarwood, and sweet white wine.

Stately Spanish galleon coming from the Isthmus,
Dipping through the Tropics by the palm-green shores,
With a cargo of diamonds,
Emeralds, amethysts,
Topazes, and cinnamon, and gold moidores.   10

Dirty British coaster with a salt-caked smoke-stack
Butting through the channel in the mad March days,
With a cargo of Tyne coal,
Road-rails, pig-lead,
Firewood, iron-ware, and cheap tin trays.

iv. The Poem as Narrative

Early narrative poems were frequently ballads, short narratives told lyrically. This restricted meaning of the term "ballad" is rather recent, that is, since the 18th century. The two main types of ballads are the folk ballad, traditional English and Scottish songs that were handed down orally, and the literary ballad. The ballad is a later form of poetry than primitive song; the ballad is dramatic in form.

The traditional ballad measure is the quatrain with alternating 4 and 3 beats per line. This regularized stanza is frequently used in the imitative literary ballad, as in Coleridge's "The Rime of the Ancient Mariner." Keats' "La Belle Dame Sans Merci" provides an innovation on the standard form. See also A. E. Housman's "Is My Team Ploughing," p. 772.

THE THREE RAVENS

ANONYMOUS

There were three ravens sat on a tree,
  Downe a downe, hay downe, hay downe
There were three ravens sat on a tree,
  With a downe
There were three ravens sat on a tree,
They were as blacke as they might be.
  With a downe derrie, derrie, derrie,
    downe, downe.

The one of them said to his mate,
"Where shall we our breakfast take?"

"Downe in yonder greene field,   10
There lies a knight slain under his shield.

"His hounds they lie downe at his feete,
So well they can their master keepe.

"His haukes they flie so eagerly,
There's no fowle dare him come nie."

Downe there comes a fallow doe,
As great with yong as she might goe.

She lift up his bloudy hed,
And kist his wounds that were so red.

She got him up upon her backe,   20
And carried him to earthen lake.

She buried him before the prime,
She was dead herselfe ere even-song time.

God send every gentleman,
Such haukes, such hounds, and such a
    leman.

16, fallow doe: the reference is to the knight's wife or lover. 25, leman: (archaic) —sweetheart.

THE TWA CORBIES

ANONYMOUS

As I was walking all alane,
I heard twa corbies making a mane;
The tane unto the t'other say,
"Where sall we gang and dine today?"

"In behint yon auld fail dyke,
I wot there lies a new slain knight;
And naebody kens that he lies there
But his hawk, his hound, and lady fair.

"His hound is to the hunting gane,
His hawk to fetch the wild-fowl hame, 10

His lady's ta'en another mate,
So we may mak our dinner sweet.

"Ye'll sit on his white hause-bane,
And I'll pike out his bonny blue een;
Wi ae lock o his gowden hair
We'll theek our nest when it grows bare.

"Mony a one for him makes mane,
But nane sall ken where he is gane;
Oer his white banes, when they are bare,
The wind sall blaw for evermair." 20

2, twa corbies: (Scottish dialect)—two crows or ravens. **2, mane:** moan, lament. **3, tane:** one. **4, gang:** go. **5, fail dyke:** turf wall. **6, wot:** know. **10, hame:** home. **13, hause-bane:** neck-bone. **14, een:** eyes. **16, theek:** thatch.

SIR PATRICK SPENS

ANONYMOUS

The king sits in Dumferling toune,
  Drinking the blude-reid wine:
"O whar will I get guid sailor,
  To sail this schip of mine?"

Up and spak an eldern knicht,
  Sat at the kings richt kne:
"Sir Patrick Spens is the best sailor,
  That sails upon the se."

The king has written a braid letter,
  And signed it wi his hand, 10
And sent it to Sir Patrick Spens,
  Was walking on the sand.

The first line that Sir Patrick red,
  A loud lauch laughéd he;
The next line that Sir Patrick red,
  The teir blinded his ee.

"O wha is this has don this deid,
  This ill deid don to me,
To send me out this time o' the yeir,
  To sail upon the se! 20

"Mak hast, mak hast, my mirry men all,
  Our guid schip sails the morne:"

"O say na sae, my master deir,
  For I feir a deadlie storme.

"Late, late yestreen I saw the new moone,
  Wi the auld moone in hir arme,
And I feir, I feir, my deir master,
  That we will cum to harme."

O our Scots nobles wer richt laith
  To weet their cork-heild schoone; 30
Bot lang owre a' the play wer playd,
  Thair hats they swam aboone.

O lang, lang may their ladies sit,
  Wi thair fans into their hand,
Or eir they se Sir Patrick Spens
  Cum sailing to the land.

O lang, lang may the ladies stand,
  Wi thair gold kems in their hair,
Waiting for thair ain deir lords,
  For they'll se thame na mair. 40

Haf owre, haf owre to Aberdour,
  It's fiftie fadom deip,
And thair lies guid Sir Patrick Spens,
  Wi the Scot lords at his feit.

9, braid: full, long. **14, lauch:** laugh. **16, ee:** eye. **29, laith:** loath. **30, weet their cork-heild schoone:** wet their cork-heeled shoes. **31, lang owre a' the play . . . :** long before the whole play. . . . **32, aboone:** above. **38, kems:** combs. **41, haf owre:** half [the way] over.

THE WIFE OF USHER'S WELL

ANONYMOUS

There lived a wife at Usher's Well,
  And a wealthy wife was she;
She had three stout and stalwart sons,
  And sent them o'er the sea.

They hadna been a week from her,
  A week but barely ane,
Whan word came to the carline wife,
  That her three sons were gane.

They hadna been a week from her,
  A week but barely three,   10
Whan word came to the carline wife,
  That her sons she'd never see.

"I wish the wind may never cease,
  Nor fashes in the flood,
Till my three sons come hame to me,
  In earthly flesh and blood."

It fell about the Martinmass,
  When nights are lang and mirk,
The carline wife's three sons came hame,
  And their hats were o' the birk.   20

It neither grew in syke nor ditch,
  Nor yet in ony sheugh;
But at the gates o' Paradise,
  That birk grew fair eneugh.

"Blow up the fire, my maidens;
  Bring water from the well!
For a' my house shall feast this night,
  Since my three sons are well."

And she has made to them a bed,
  She's made it large and wide;   30
And she's ta'en her mantle her about,
  Sat down at the bed-side.

Up then crew the red, red cock,
  And up and crew the gray;
The eldest to the youngest said,
  " 'Tis time we were away."

The cock he hadna craw'd but once,
  And clapp'd his wings at a',
When the youngest to the eldest said,
  "Brother, we must awa.   40

"The cock doth craw, the day doth daw,
  The channerin' worm doth chide:
Gin we be mist out o' our place,
  A sair pain we maun bide.

"Fare ye weel, my mother dear!
  Fareweel to barn and byre!
And fare ye weel, the bonny lass,
  That kindles my mother's fire."

7, **carline:** old woman. 14, **fashes:** storms, troubles. 17, **Martinmass:** November 11. 18, **mirk:** dark. 20, **birk:** birch. 21, **syke:** trench. 22, **sheugh:** furrow. 36, **'Tis time** . . . : it was believed that at cockcrow the dead must all return to their graves. 42, **channerin':** fretting. 43, **Gin:** If. 46, **byre:** cowshed.

THE UNQUIET GRAVE

ANONYMOUS

"The wind doth blow today, my love,
  And a few small drops of rain;
I never had but one true-love,
  In cold grave she was lain.

"I'll do as much for my true-love
  As any young man may;
I'll sit and mourn all at her grave
  For a twelvemonth and a day."

The twelvemonth and a day being up,
  The dead began to speak: 10

"Oh, who sits weeping on my grave,
  And will not let me sleep?"

" 'Tis I, my love, sits on your grave,
  And will not let you sleep;
For I crave one kiss of your clay-cold lips,
  And that is all I seek."

"You crave one kiss of my clay-cold lips;
  But my breath smells earthy strong;
If you have one kiss of my clay-cold lips,
  Your time will not be long.   20

" 'Tis down in yonder garden green,
    Love, where we used to walk,
The finest flower that ere was seen
    Is withered to a stalk.

"The stalk is withered dry, my love,
    So will our hearts decay;
So make yourself content, my love,
    Till God calls you away."

BONNY BARBARA ALLAN
ANONYMOUS

It was in and about the Martinmas time,
    When the green leaves were a falling,
That Sir John Graeme, in the West Country,
    Fell in love with Barbara Allan.

He sent his man down through the town,
    To the place where she was dwelling:
"O haste and come to my master dear,
    Gin ye be Barbara Allan."

O hooly, hooly rose she up,
    To the place where he was lying,   10
And when she drew the curtain by,
    "Young man, I think you're dying."

"O it's I'm sick, and very, very sick,
    And 't is a' for Barbara Allan:"
"O the better for me ye's never be,
    Tho your heart's blood were a spilling.

"O dinna ye mind, young man," said she,
    "When ye was in the tavern a drinking,
That ye made the healths gae round and
    round,
    And slighted Barbara Allan?"   20

He turned his face unto the wall,
    And death was with him dealing:
"Adieu, adieu, my dear friends all,
    And be kind to Barbara Allan."

And slowly, slowly raise she up,
    And slowly, slowly left him,
And sighing said, she could not stay,
    Since death of life had reft him.

She had not gane a mile but twa,
    When she heard the dead-bell ringing,
And every jow that the dead-bell geid,   31
    It cry'd, Woe to Barbara Allan!

"O mother, mother, make my bed!
    O make it saft and narrow!
Since my love died for me to-day,
    I'll die for him to-morrow."

1, Martinmas: November 11. 8, Gin: If.
9, hooly: softly, slowly. 15, ye's: ye shall.
17, dinna ye mind: do ye not remember?
31, jow: stroke; geid: gave.

BARBARA ALLEN'S CRUELTY
ANONYMOUS

In Scarlet town, where I was born,
    There was a fair maid dwellin',
Made every youth cry *Well-a-way!*
    Her name was Barbara Allen.

All in the merry month of May,
    When green buds they were swellin',
Young Jemmy Grove on his death-bed lay,
    For love of Barbara Allen.

He sent his man in to her then,
    To the town where she was dwellin';   10
"O haste and come to my master dear,
    If your name be Barbara Allen."

So slowly, slowly rase she up,
    And slowly she came nigh him,
And when she drew the curtain by,
    "Young man, I think you're dyin'."

"O it's I am sick and very very sick,
    And it's all for Barbara Allen."
"O the better for me ye'se never be,   19
    Tho' your heart's blood were a-spillin'!

"O dinna ye mind, young man," says she,
    "When the red wine ye were fillin',
That ye made the healths go round and
    round,
    And slighted Barbara Allen?"

He turned his face unto the wall,
    And death was with him dealin':
"Adieu, adieu, my dear friends all,
    And be kind to Barbara Allen!"

As she was walking o'er the fields,
    She heard the dead-bell knellin';   30
And every jow the dead-bell gave
    Cried "Woe to Barbara Allen."

"O mother, mother, make my bed,
    O make it saft and narrow:
My love has died for me to-day,
    I'll die for him to-morrow.

"Farewell," she said, "ye virgins all,
    And shun the fault I fell in:
Henceforth take warning by the fall
    Of cruel Barbara Allen."   40

EDWARD

ANONYMOUS

"Why dois your brand sae drap wi bluid,
    Edward, Edward,
Why dois your brand sae drap wi bluid,
    And why sae sad gang yee O?"
"O I hae killed my hauke sae guid,
    Mither, mither,
O I hae killed my hauke sae guid,
    And I had nae mair bot hee O."

"Your haukis bluid was nevir sae reid,
    Edward, Edward,   10
Your haukis bluid was nevir sae reid,
    My deir son I tell thee O."
"O I hae killed my reid-roan steid,
    Mither, mither,
O I hae killed my reid-roan steid,
    That erst was sae fair and frie O."

"Your steid was auld, and ye hae got mair,
    Edward, Edward,
Your steid was auld, and ye hae got mair,
    Sum other dule ye drie O"   20
"O I hae killed my fadir deir,
    Mither, mither.
O I hae killed my fadir deir,
    Alas, and wae is mee O!"

"And whatten penance wul ye drie for that,
    Edward, Edward,
And whatten penance will ye drie for
    that?
My deir son, now tell me O."
"Ile set my feit in yonder boat,
    Mither, mither,   30
Ile set my feit in yonder boat,
    And Ile fare ovir the sea O."

"And what wul ye doe wi your towirs and
    your ha,
    Edward, Edward?
And what wul you doe wi your towirs and
    your ha,
    That were sae fair to see O?"
"Ile let thame stand tul they doun fa,
    Mither, mither,
Ile let thame stand tul they doun fa,
    For here nevir mair maun I bee O."   40

"And what wul ye leive to your bairns and
    your wife,
    Edward, Edward?
And what wul ye leive to your bairns and
    your wife,
    Whan ye gang ovir the sea O?"
"The warldis room, late them beg thrae
    life,
    Mither, mither,
The warldis room, late them beg thrae
    life,
    For thame nevir mair wul I see O."

"Ana what wul ye leive to your ain mither
    deir,
    Edward, Edward?   50
And what wul ye leive to your ain mither
    deir?
    My deir son, now tell me O."
"The curse of hell frae me sall ye beir,
    Mither, mither,
The curse of hell frae me sall ye beir,
    Sic counseils ye gave to me O."

1, **dois:** does; **brand:** sword, knife. 4,
gang: go, walk. 8, **bot:** but. 16, **erst:**
formerly; **frie:** good, fine. 20, **dule ye
drie:** grief ye suffer.

33, **ha:** hall. 37, **tul:** till; **fa:** fall. 40,
maun: must. 41, **bairns:** children. 45,
warldis: world's; **late:** let; **thrae:** through.
56, **Sic:** Such.

LORD RANDAL

ANONYMOUS

"O where hae ye been, Lord Randal, my son?
O where hae ye been, my handsome young man?"
"I hae been to the wild wood; mother, make my bed soon,
For I'm weary wi' hunting, and fain wald lie down."

"Where gat ye your dinner, Lord Randal, my son?
Where gat ye your dinner, my handsome young man?"
"I dined wi' my true-love; mother, make my bed soon,
For I'm weary wi' hunting, and fain wald lie down."

"What gat ye to your dinner, Lord Randal, my son?
What gat ye to your dinner, my handsome young man?"   10
"I gat eels boil'd in broo; mother, make my bed soon,
For I'm weary wi' hunting, and fain wald lie down."

"What became of your bloodhounds, Lord Randal, my son?
What became of your bloodhounds my handsome young man?"
"O they swell'd and they died; mother, make my bed soon,
For I'm weary wi' hunting, and fain wald lie down."

"O I fear ye are poison'd, Lord Randal, my son!
O I fear ye are poison'd, my handsome young man!"
"O yes! I am poison'd; mother, make my bed soon,
For I'm sick at the heart, and I fain wald lie down."   20

4, **wald:** would. 11, **broo:** brew, broth.

LA BELLE DAME SANS MERCI

JOHN KEATS (1795–1821)

O what can ail thee, knight-at-arms!
    Alone and palely loitering!
The sedge has withered from the lake,
    And no birds sing.

O what can ail thee, knight-at-arms!
    So haggard and so woe-begone?
The squirrel's granary is full,
    And the harvest's done.

I see a lily on thy brow
    With anguish moist and fever dew,   10
And on thy cheeks a fading rose
    Fast withereth too.

I met a lady in the meads,
    Full beautiful—a faery's child,
Her hair was long, her foot was light,
    And her eyes were wild.

I made a garland for her head,
    And bracelets too, and fragrant zone;
She looked at me as she did love,
    And made sweet moan.   20

I set her on my pacing steed,
    And nothing else saw all day long.
For sidelong would she bend, and sing
    A faery's song.

She found me roots of relish sweet,
  And honey wild, and manna dew,
And sure in language strange she said—
  'I love thee true.'

She took me to her elfin grot,
  And there she wept, and sighed full
    sore,   30
And there I shut her wild wild eyes
  With kisses four.

And there she lullèd me asleep,
  And there I dreamed—Ah! woe betide!
The latest dream I ever dreamed
  On the cold hill's side.

I saw pale kings and princes too,
  Pale warriors, death-pale were they all;
They cried—'La Belle Dame sans Merci
  Hath thee in thrall!'   40

I saw their starved lips in the gloam,
  With horrid warning gapèd wide,
And I awoke and found me here,
  On the cold hill's side.

And this is why I sojourn here,
  Alone and palely loitering,
Though the sedge is withered from the
    lake
  And no birds sing.

LA BELLE DAME SANS MERCI

ROLFE HUMPHRIES (1894–   )

Three of us walking, and two of us were tall,
  Walking, in this dream,
On a down-hill path, in a grove of laurel and pine,
  On our way to a pleasant stream.

  —*Who is the third who always walks beside you?*

And the third was not so tall, but her eyes were clear,
  And her look so sweet and mild
That rather than wife and mother, she seemed to be
  An innocent-hearted child.

  —*Who is the third who always walks beside you?*   10

We paused on the path, through the green and lovely wood,
  For a moment, in the dream;
We had plenty of time, we felt no wise compelled
  To rush to reach the stream.

And all of a sudden she raised her ringless hand
  And pointed straight at me,
And cried, "How ugly and horrible he is!
  Look for yourself, and see!"

"Look for yourself, and see!" she cried aloud,
  In rage and fright, and you,   20
Obedient to her voice and gesture, turned,
  Looked, and saw it was true.

I was no more I, but a lewd and evil shape,
    Coarse-grained and dead as stone,
And the sight of the utter stark and staring truth
    Numbed you in every bone.

And she held the pose, and she looked at you, and smiled,
    Turned over her hand, and screamed,
Screamed, and vanished: and you awoke, alone,
    To face what you had dreamed.   30

—Who is the third who always walks beside you?

THE RIME OF THE ANCIENT MARINER

IN SEVEN PARTS

SAMUEL TAYLOR COLERIDGE (1772–1834)

ARGUMENT

How a ship having passed the Line was driven by storms to the cold country toward the south pole, and how from thence she made her course to the tropical latitude of the great Pacific Ocean; and of the strange things that befell; and in what manner the ancient Mariner came back to his own country.

PART I

An ancient Mariner meeteth three Gallants bidden to a wedding-feast, and detaineth one.

It is an ancient Mariner,
And he stoppeth one of three.
"By thy long gray beard and glittering eye,
Now wherefore stopp'st thou me?

The Bridegroom's doors are opened wide,
And I am next of kin;
The guests are met, the feast is set:
May'st hear the merry din."

He holds him with his skinny hand,
"There was a ship," quoth he.   10
"Hold off! unhand me, gray-beard loon!"
Eftsoons his hand dropt he.

The Wedding-Guest is spell-bound by the eye of the old sea-faring man, and constrained to hear his tale.

He holds him with his glittering eye—
The Wedding-Guest stood still,
And listens like a three years' child:
The Mariner hath his will.

The Wedding-Guest sat on a stone:
He cannot choose but hear;
And thus spake on that ancient man,
The bright-eyed Mariner.

"The ship was cheered, the harbor cleared,
Merrily did we drop
Below the kirk, below the hill,
Below the lighthouse top.

The Mariner tells how
the ship sailed southward
with a good wind and fair
weather, till it reached the
Line.

The sun came up upon the left,
Out of the sea came he!
And he shone bright, and on the right
Went down into the sea.

Higher and higher every day,
Till over the mast at noon—"   30
The Wedding-Guest here beat his breast,
For he heard the loud bassoon.

The Wedding-Guest
heareth the bridal music;
but the Mariner continueth
his tale.

The bride hath paced into the hall,
Red as a rose is she;
Nodding their heads before her goes
The merry minstrelsy.

The Wedding-Guest he beat his breast,
Yet he cannot choose but hear;
And thus spake on that ancient man,
The bright-eyed Mariner.   40

The ship driven by a
storm toward the south
pole.

"And now the storm-blast came, and he
Was tyrannous and strong:
He struck with his o'ertaking wings,
And chased us south along.

With sloping masts and dipping prow,
As who pursued with yell and blow
Still treads the shadow of his foe,
And forward bends his head,
The ship drove fast, loud roared the blast,
And southward aye we fled.   50

And now there came both mist and snow,
And it grew wondrous cold:
And ice, mast-high, came floating by,
As green as emerald.

The land of ice, and of
fearful sounds where no
living thing was to be
seen.

And through the drifts the snowy clifts
Did send a dismal sheen:
Nor shapes of men nor beasts we ken—
The ice was all between.

The ice was here, the ice was there,
The ice was all around: 60

It cracked and growled, and roared and howled,
Like noises in a swound!

At length did cross an Albatross,
Thorough the fog it came;
As if it had been a Christian soul,
We hailed it in God's name.

It ate the food it ne'er had eat,
And round and round it flew.
The ice did split with a thunder-fit;
The helmsman steered us through! 70

And a good south wind sprung up behind;
The Albatross did follow,
And every day, for food or play,
Came to the mariners' hollo!

In mist or cloud, on mast or shroud,
It perched for vespers nine;
Whiles all the night, through fog-smoke white,
Glimmered the white moon-shine."

"God save thee, ancient Mariner!
From the fiends, that plague thee thus!—
Why look'st thou so?"—"With my cross-bow
I shot the Albatross. 80

PART II

"The Sun now rose upon the right:
Out of the sea came he,
Still hid in mist, and on the left
Went down into the sea.

And the good south wind still blew behind,
But no sweet bird did follow,
Nor any day for food or play
Came to the mariners' hollo! 90

And I had done a hellish thing,
And it would work 'em woe:
For all averred, I had killed the bird
That made the breeze to blow.
'Ah wretch!' said they, 'the bird to slay,
That made the breeze to blow!'

Nor dim nor red, like God's own head,
The glorious Sun uprist:
Then all averred, I had killed the bird

That brought the fog and mist.   100
' 'Twas right,' said they, 'such birds to slay,
That bring the fog and mist.'

The fair breeze continues; the ship enters the Pacific Ocean, and sails northward, even till it reaches the Line.

The fair breeze blew, the white foam flew,
The furrow followed free;
We were the first that ever burst
Into that silent sea.

The ship hath been suddenly becalmed.

Down dropt the breeze, the sails dropt down,
'Twas sad as sad could be;
And we did speak only to break
The silence of the sea!   110

All in a hot and copper sky,
The bloody Sun, at noon,
Right up above the mast did stand,
No bigger than the Moon.

Day after day, day after day,
We stuck, nor breath nor motion;
As idle as a painted ship
Upon a painted ocean.

And the Albatross begins to be avenged.

Water, water, everywhere,
And all the boards did shrink;   120
Water, water, everywhere
Nor any drop to drink.

The very deep did rot: O Christ!
That ever this should be!
Yea, slimy things did crawl with legs
Upon the slimy sea.

About, about, in reel and rout
The death-fires danced at night;
The water, like a witch's oils,
Burnt green, and blue, and white.   130

A Spirit had followed them; one of the invisible inhabitants of this planet, neither departed souls nor angels; concerning whom the learned Jew, Josephus, and the Platonic Constantinopolitan, Michael Psellus, may be consulted. They are very numerous, and there is no climate or element without one or more.

And some in dreams assured were
Of the Spirit that plagued us so:
Nine fathom deep he had followed us
From the land of mist and snow.

And every tongue, through utter drought,
Was withered at the root;
We could not speak, no more than if
We had been choked with soot.

The ship-mates, in their sore distress, would fain throw the whole guilt on the ancient Mariner: in sign whereof they hang the dead sea-bird round his neck.

Ah! well a-day! what evil looks
Had I from old and young!
Instead of the cross, the Albatross
About my neck was hung.

140

PART III

The ancient Mariner beholdeth a sign in the element afar off.

"There passed a weary time. Each throat
Was parched, and glazed each eye.
A weary time! a weary time!
How glazed each weary eye,
When looking westward, I beheld
A something in the sky.

At first it seemed a little speck,
And then it seemed a mist;
It moved and moved, and took at last
A certain shape, I wist.

150

A speck, a mist, a shape, I wist!
And still it neared and neared:
As if it dodged a water-sprite,
It plunged and tacked and veered.

At its nearer approach, it seemeth him to be a ship; and at a dear ransom he freeth his speech from the bonds of thirst.

With throats unslaked, with black lips baked,
We could nor laugh nor wail;
Through utter drought all dumb we stood!
I bit my arm, I sucked the blood,
And cried, 'A sail! a sail!'

160

A flash of joy;

With throats unslaked, with black lips baked,
Agape they heard me call;
Gramercy! they for joy did grin,
And all at once their breath drew in,
As they were drinking all.

And horror follows. For can it be a ship that comes onward without wind or tide?

'See! see! (I cried) she tacks no more!
Hither to work us weal;
Without a breeze, without a tide,
She steadies with upright keel!'

170

The western wave was all a-flame;
The day was well nigh done!
Almost upon the western wave
Rested the broad bright Sun;
When that strange shape drove suddenly
Betwixt us and the Sun.

It seemeth him but the
skeleton of a ship.

And straight the Sun was flecked with bars,
(Heaven's Mother send us grace!)
As if through a dungeon-grate he peered
With broad and burning face.   180

Alas! (thought I, and my heart beat loud)
How fast she nears and nears!
Are those her sails that glance in the Sun,
Like restless gossameres?

And its ribs are seen as
bars on the face of the
setting Sun. The Spectre-
Woman and her Death-
mate, and no other on
board the skeleton-ship.
Like vessel, like crew!

Are those her ribs through which the Sun
Did peer, as through a grate?
And is that Woman all her crew?
Is that a Death? and are there two?
Is Death that woman's mate?

Her lips were red, her looks were free,   190
Her locks were yellow as gold:
Her skin was as white as leprosy,
The nightmare Life-in-Death was she,
Who thicks man's blood with cold.

Death and Life-in-Death
have diced for the ship's
crew, and she (the latter)
winneth the ancient
Mariner.

The naked hulk alongside came,
And the twain were casting dice;
'The game is done! I've won! I've won!'
Quoth she, and whistles thrice.

No twilight within the
courts of the Sun.

The Sun's rim dips; the stars rush out:
At one stride comes the dark;   200
With far-heard whisper, o'er the sea,
Off shot the spectre-bark.

At the rising of the Moon,

We listened and looked sideways up!
Fear at my heart, as at a cup,
My life-blood seemed to sip!
The stars were dim, and thick the night,
The steersman's face by his lamp gleamed white;
From the sails the dew did drip—
Till clomb above the eastern bar
The horned Moon, with one bright star   210
Within the nether tip.

One after another,

One after one, by the star-dogged Moon,
Too quick for groan or sigh,
Each turned his face with a ghastly pang,
And cursed me with his eye.

His shipmates drop down
dead.

Four times fifty living men,
(And I heard nor sigh nor groan)

With heavy thump, a lifeless lump,
They dropped down one by one.

But Life-in-Death begins her work on the ancient Mariner.

The souls did from their bodies fly,— 220
They fled to bliss or woe!
And every soul, it passed me by,
Like the whizz of my cross-bow!"

PART IV

The Wedding-Guest feareth that a Spirit is talking to him;

"I fear thee, ancient Mariner!
I fear thy skinny hand!
And thou art long, and lank, and brown,
As is the ribbed sea-sand.

But the ancient Mariner assureth him of his bodily life, and proceedeth to relate his horrible penance.

I fear thee and thy glittering eye,
And thy skinny hand, so brown."—
"Fear not, fear not, thou Wedding-Guest! 230
This body dropt not down.

Alone, alone, all, all alone,
Alone on a wide, wide sea!
And never a saint took pity on
My soul in agony.

He despiseth the creatures of the calm.

The many men, so beautiful!
And they all dead did lie:
And a thousand thousand slimy things
Lived on; and so did I.

And envieth that they should live, and so many lie dead.

I looked upon the rotting sea, 240
And drew my eyes away;
I looked upon the rotting deck,
And there the dead men lay.

I looked to heaven, and tried to pray;
But or ever a prayer had gusht,
A wicked whisper came, and made
My heart as dry as dust.

I closed my lids, and kept them close,
And the balls like pulses beat;
For the sky and the sea, and the sea and the sky 250
Lay like a load on my weary eye,
And the dead were at my feet.

But the curse liveth for him in the eye of the dead men.

The cold sweat melted from their limbs,
Nor rot nor reek did they:
The look with which they looked on me
Had never passed away.

An orphan's curse would drag to hell
A spirit from on high;
But oh! more horrible than that
Is the curse in a dead man's eye!   260
Seven days, seven nights, I saw that curse,
And yet I could not die.

In his loneliness and fixed-ness he yearneth toward the journeying Moon, and the stars that still sojourn, yet still move onward; and everywhere the blue sky belongs to them, and is their appointed rest, and their native country and their own natural homes, which they enter un-announced, as lords that are certainly expected and yet there is a silent joy at their arrival.

The moving Moon went up the sky,
And nowhere did abide:
Softly she was going up,
And a star or two beside—

Her beams bemocked the sultry main,
Like April hoar-frost spread;
But where the ship's huge shadow lay,
The charmèd water burnt alway   270
A still and awful red.

By the light of the Moon he beholdeth God's creatures of the great calm.

Beyond the shadow of the ship,
I watched the water-snakes:
They moved in tracks of shining white,
And when they reared, the elfish light
Fell off in hoary flakes.

Within the shadow of the ship
I watched their rich attire:
Blue, glossy green, and velvet black,
They coiled and swam; and every track   280
Was a flash of golden fire.

Their beauty and their happiness.

O happy living things! no tongue
Their beauty might declare:
A spring of love gushed from my heart,

He blesseth them in his heart.

And I blessed them unaware:
Sure my kind saint took pity on me,
And I blessed them unaware.

The spell begins to break.

The selfsame moment I could pray;
And from my neck so free
The Albatross fell off, and sank   290
Like lead into the sea.

PART V

"Oh sleep! it is a gentle thing,
Beloved from pole to pole!
To Mary Queen the praise be given!
She sent the gentle sleep from Heaven,
That slid into my soul.

By grace of the holy
Mother, the ancient
Mariner is refreshed with
rain.

The silly buckets on the deck,
That had so long remained,
I dreamt that they were filled with dew;
And when I awoke, it rained.   300

My lips were wet, my throat was cold,
My garments all were dank;
Sure I had drunken in my dreams,
And still my body drank.

I moved, and could not feel my limbs;
I was so light—almost
I thought that I had died in sleep,
And was a blessed ghost.

He heareth sounds and
seeth strange sights and
commotions in the sky and
the element.

And soon I heard a roaring wind:
It did not come anear;   310
But with its sound it shook the sails,
That were so thin and sere.

The upper air burst into life!
And a hundred fire-flags sheen,
To and fro they were hurried about!
And to and fro, and in and out,
The wan stars danced between.

And the coming wind did roar more loud,
And the sails did sigh like sedge;
And the rain poured down from one black cloud;   320
The Moon was at its edge.

The thick black cloud was cleft, and still
The Moon was at its side:
Like waters shot from some high crag,
The lightning fell with never a jag,
A river steep and wide.

The loud wind never reached the ship,
Yet now the ship moved on!
Beneath the lightning and the Moon
The dead men gave a groan.   330

The bodies of the ship's
crew are inspired, and the
ship moves on;

They groaned, they stirred, they all uprose,
Nor spake, nor moved their eyes;
It had been strange, even in a dream,
To have seen those dead men rise.

The helmsman steered, the ship moved on;
Yet never a breeze up blew;
The mariners all 'gan work the ropes,

Where they were wont to do;
They raised their limbs like lifeless tools—
We were a ghastly crew.   340

The body of my brother's son
Stood by me, knee to knee:
The body and I pulled at one rope
But he said nought to me."

"I fear thee, ancient Mariner!"
"Be calm, thou Wedding-Guest!
'Twas not those souls that fled in pain,
Which to their corses came again,
But a troop of spirits blest:

For when it dawned—they dropped their arms,   350
And clustered round the mast;
Sweet sounds rose slowly through their mouths,
And from their bodies passed.

Around, around, flew each sweet sound,
Then darted to the Sun;
Slowly the sounds came back again,
Now mixed, now one by one.

Sometimes a-dropping from the sky
I heard the sky-lark sing;
Sometimes all little birds that are,   360
How they seemed to fill the sea and air
With their sweet jargoning!

And now 'twas like all instruments,
Now like a lonely flute;
And now it is an angel's song,
That makes the heavens be mute.

It ceased; yet still the sails made on
A pleasant noise till noon,
A noise like of a hidden brook
In the leafy month of June,   370
That to the sleeping woods all night
Singeth a quiet tune.

Till noon we quietly sailed on,
Yet never a breeze did breathe:
Slowly and smoothly went the ship,
Moved onward from beneath.

The lonesome Spirit from the south pole carries on the ship as far as the Line, in obedience to the angelic troop, but still requireth vengeance.

Under the keel nine fathom deep,
From the land of mist and snow,
The Spirit slid: and it was he
That made the ship to go.
The sails at noon left off their tune,
And the ship stood still also.

380

The Sun, right up above the mast,
Had fixed her to the ocean:
But in a minute she 'gan stir,
With a short uneasy motion—
Backwards and forwards half her length
With a short uneasy motion.

Then like a pawing horse let go,
She made a sudden bound:
It flung the blood into my head,
And I fell down in a swound.

390

The Polar Spirit's fellow-daemons, the invisible inhabitants of the element, take part in his wrong; and two of them relate, one to the other, that penance long and heavy for the ancient Mariner hath been accorded to the Polar Spirit, who returneth southward.

How long in that same fit I lay,
I have not to declare;
But ere my living life returned,
I heard and in my soul discerned
Two voices in the air.

'Is it he?' quoth one, 'Is this the man?
By Him who died on cross,
With his cruel bow he laid full low
The harmless Albatross.

400

The Spirit who bideth by himself
In the land of mist and snow,
He loved the bird that loved the man
Who shot him with his bow.'

The other was a softer voice,
As soft as honey-dew:
Quoth he, 'The man hath penance done,
And penance more will do.'

PART VI

First Voice

" 'But tell me, tell me! speak again,
Thy soft response renewing—
What makes that ship drive on so fast?
What is the ocean doing?'

416

Second Voice

'Still as a slave before his lord,
The ocean hath no blast;
His great bright eye most silently
Up to the moon is cast—

If he may know which way to go;
For she guides him smooth or grim.
See, brother, see! how graciously   420
She looketh down on him.'

First Voice

'But why drives on that ship so fast,
Without or wave or wind?'

Second Voice

'The air is cut away before,
And closes from behind.

Fly, brother, fly! more high, more high!
Or we shall be belated:
For slow and slow that ship will go,
When the Mariner's trance is abated.'

I woke, and we were sailing on   430
As in a gentle weather:
'Twas night, calm night, the moon was high,
The dead men stood together.

All stood together on the deck,
For a charnel-dungeon fitter:
All fixed on me their stony eyes,
That in the Moon did glitter.

The pang, the curse, with which they died,
Had never passed away:
I could not draw my eyes from theirs,   440
Nor turn them up to pray.

And now this spell was snapt: once more
I viewed the ocean green,
And looked far forth, yet little saw
Of what had else been seen—

Like one, that on a lonesome road
Doth walk in fear and dread,
And having once turned round walks on,
And turns no more his head;
Because he knows a frightful fiend   450
Doth close behind him tread.

Side notes:

The Mariner hath been cast into a trance; for the angelic power causeth the vessel to drive northward faster than human life could endure.

The supernatural motion is retarded; the Mariner awakes, and his penance begins anew.

The curse is finally expiated.

But soon there breathed a wind on me,
Nor sound nor motion made:
Its path was not upon the sea,
In ripple or in shade.

It raised my hair, it fanned my cheek
Like a meadow-gale of spring—
It mingled strangely with my fears,
Yet it felt like a welcoming.

Swiftly, swiftly flew the ship,   460
Yet she sailed softly too:
Sweetly, sweetly blew the breeze—
On me alone it blew.

And the ancient Mariner beholdeth his native country

Oh! dream of joy! is this indeed
The light-house top I see?
Is this the hill? is this the kirk?
Is this mine own countree?

We drifted o'er the harbor-bar,
And I with sobs did pray—
O let me be awake, my God!   470
Or let me sleep alway.

The harbor-bay was clear as glass,
So smoothly it was strewn!
And on the bay the moonlight lay,
And the shadow of the Moon.

The rock shone bright, the kirk no less,
That stands above the rock:
The moonlight steeped in silentness
The steady weathercock.

And the bay was white with silent light   480
Till rising from the same,
Full many shapes, that shadows were,
In crimson colors came.

The angelic spirits leave the dead bodies,

A little distance from the prow
Those crimson shadows were:
I turned my eyes upon the deck—
Oh, Christ! what saw I there!

And appear in their own forms of light.

Each corse lay flat, lifeless and flat,
And, by the holy rood!
A man all light, a seraph-man,   490
On every corse there stood.

This seraph-band, each waved his hand;
It was a heavenly sight!
They stood as signals to the land,
Each one a lovely light;

This seraph-band, each waved his hand,
No voice did they impart—
No voice; but oh! the silence sank
Like music on my heart.

But soon I heard the dash of oars,   500
I heard the Pilot's cheer;
My head was turned perforce away,
And I saw a boat appear.

The Pilot and the Pilot's boy,
I heard them coming fast:
Dear Lord in Heaven! it was a joy
The dead men could not blast.

I saw a third—I heard his voice:
It is the Hermit good!
He singeth loud his godly hymns   510
That he makes in the wood.
He'll shrieve my soul; he'll wash away
The Albatross's blood.

PART VII

The Hermit of the Wood

"This Hermit good lives in that wood
Which slopes down to the sea.
How loudly his sweet voice he rears!
He loves to talk with marineres
That come from a far countree.

He kneels at morn, and noon, and eve—
He hath a cushion plump: 520
It is the moss that wholly hides
The rotted old oak-stump.

The skiff-boat neared: I heard them talk,
'Why, this is strange, I trow!
Where are those lights so many and fair,
That signal made but now?'

Approacheth the ship with
wonder.

'Strange, by my faith!' the Hermit said—
'And they answered not our cheer!
The planks look warped! and see those sails,
How thin they are and sere!   530
I never saw aught like to them,
Unless perchance it were

Brown skeletons of leaves that lag
My forest-brook along;
When the ivy-tod is heavy with snow,
And the owlet whoops to the wolf below,
That eats the she-wolf's young.'

'Dear Lord! it hath a fiendish look—
(The Pilot made reply)
I am a-feared'—'Push on, push on!' 540
Said the Hermit cheerily.

The boat came closer to the ship,
But I nor spake nor stirred;
The boat came close beneath the ship,
And straight a sound was heard.

The ship suddenly sinketh. Under the water it rumbled on,
Still louder and more dread:
It reached the ship, it split the bay;
The ship went down like lead.

The ancient Mariner is Stunned by that loud and dreadful sound, 550
saved in the Pilot's boat. Which sky and ocean smote,
Like one that hath been seven days drowned
My body lay afloat;
But swift as dreams, myself I found
Within the Pilot's boat.

Upon the whirl, where sank the ship,
The boat spun round and round;
And all was still, save that the hill
Was telling of the sound.

I moved my lips—the Pilot shrieked 560
And fell down in a fit;
The holy Hermit raised his eyes,
And prayed where he did sit.

I took the oars: the Pilot's boy,
Who now doth crazy go,
Laughed loud and long, and all the while
His eyes went to and fro.
'Ha! ha!' quoth he, 'full plain I see,
The Devil knows how to row.'

And now, all in my own countree, 570
I stood on the firm land!
The Hermit stepped forth from the boat,
And scarcely he could stand.

The ancient Mariner
earnestly entreateth the
Hermit to shrieve him;
and the penance of life
falls on him.

O shrieve me, shrieve me, holy man!'
The Hermit crossed his brow.
'Say quick,' quoth he, 'I bid thee say—
What manner of man art thou?'

Forthwith this frame of mine was wrenched
With a woful agony,
Which forced me to begin my tale;   580
And then it left me free.

And ever and anon
throughout his future life
an agony constraineth him
to travel from land to
land,

Since then, at an uncertain hour,
That agony returns:
And till my ghastly tale is told,
This heart within me burns.

I pass, like night, from land to land;
I have strange power of speech;
That moment that his face I see,
I know the man that must hear me:
To him my tale I teach.   590

What loud uproar bursts from that door!
The wedding-guests are there:
But in the garden-bower the bride
And bride-maids singing are:
And hark the little vesper bell
Which biddeth me to prayer!

O Wedding-Guest! this soul hath been
Alone on a wide, wide sea;
So lonely 'twas, that God himself
Scarce seemèd there to be.   600

O sweeter than the marriage-feast,
'Tis sweeter far to me,
To walk together to the kirk
With a goodly company!—

To walk together to the kirk,
And all together pray,
While each to his great Father bends,
Old men, and babes, and loving friends,
And youths and maidens gay!

And to teach, by his own
example, love and
reverence to all things
that God made and loveth.

Farewell, farewell! but this I tell   610
To thee, thou Wedding-Guest!
He prayeth well, who loveth well
Both man and bird and beast.

He prayeth best, who loveth best
All things both great and small;

For the dear God who loveth us,
He made and loveth all."

The Mariner, whose eye is bright,
Whose beard with age is hoar,
Is gone: and now the Wedding-Guest   620
Turned from the Bridegroom's door.

He went like one that hath been stunned,
And is of sense forlorn:
A sadder and a wiser man,
He rose the morrow morn.

THE HAYSTACK IN THE FLOODS

WILLIAM MORRIS (1834–1896)

Had she come all the way for this,
To part at last without a kiss?
Yea, had she borne the dirt and rain
That her own eyes might see him slain
Beside the haystack in the floods?

Along the dripping leafless woods,
The stirrup touching either shoe,
She rode astride as troopers do;
With kirtle kilted to her knee,
To which the mud splashed wretchedly;   10
And the wet dripped from every tree
Upon her head and heavy hair,
And on her eyelids broad and fair;
The tears and rain ran down her face.

By fits and starts they rode apace,
And very often was his place
Far off from her; he had to ride
Ahead, to see what might betide
When the roads crossed; and sometimes, when
There rose a murmuring from his men,   20
Had to turn back with promises;
Ah me! she had but little ease;
And often for pure doubt and dread
She sobbed, made giddy in the head
By the swift riding; while, for cold,
Her slender fingers scarce could hold
The wet reins; yea, and scarcely, too,
She felt the foot within her shoe
Against the stirrip: all for this,
To part at last without a kiss   30
Beside the haystack in the floods.

For when they neared that old soaked hay,
They saw across the only way
That Judas, Godmar, and the three
Red running lions dismally
Grinned from his pennon, under which
In one straight line along the ditch,
They counted thirty heads.

　　　　　　So then,
While Robert turned round to his men,
She saw at once the wretched end,   40
And, stooping down, tried hard to rend
Her coif the wrong way from her head,
And hid her eyes; while Robert said:
"Nay, love, 'tis scarcely two to one;
At Poictiers where we made them run
So fast—why, sweet my love, good cheer,
The Gascon frontier is so near,
Nought after us."

　　　　　　But, "O," she said,
"My God! my God! I have to tread
The long way back without you; then   50
The court at Paris; those six men;
The gratings of the Chatelet;
The swift Seine on some rainy day
Like this, and people standing by,
And laughing, while my weak hands try
To recollect how strong men swim.
All this, or else a life with him,
For which I should be damned at last;
Would God that this next hour were past!"

He answered not, but cried his cry,   60
"St. George for Marny!" cheerily;
And laid his hand upon her rein.
Alas! no man of all his train
Gave back that cheery cry again;
And, while for rage his thumb beat fast
Upon his sword-hilt, some one cast
About his neck a kerchief long,
And bound him.

　　　　　　Then they went along
To Godmar; who said: "Now, Jehane,
Your lover's life is on the wane   70
So fast, that, if this very hour
You yield not as my paramour,

He will not see the rain leave off—
Nay, keep your tongue from gibe and scoff,
Sir Robert, or I slay you now."

She laid her hand upon her brow,
Then gazed upon the palm, as though
She thought her forehead bled, and—"No,"
She said, and turned her head away,
As there were nothing else to say,
And everything were settled: red
Grew Godmar's face from chin to head:
"Jehane, on yonder hill there stands
My castle, guarding well my lands:
What hinders me from taking you,
And doing that I list to do
To your fair wilful body, while
Your knight lies dead?"

             A wicked smile
Wrinkled her face, her lips grew thin,
A long way out she thrust her chin:
"You know that I should strangle you
While you were sleeping; or bite through
Your throat, by God's help—ah!" she said,
"Lord Jesus, pity your poor maid!
For in such wise they hem me in,
I cannot choose but sin and sin,
Whatever happens: yet I think
They could not make me eat or drink,
And so should I just reach my rest."
"Nay, if you do not my behest,
O Jehane! though I love you well,"
Said Godmar, "would I fail to tell
All that I know?" "Foul lies," she said.
"Eh! lies, my Jehane? by God's head,
At Paris folks would deem them true!
Do you know, Jehane, they cry for you:
'Jehane the brown! Jehane the brown!
Give us Jehane to burn or drown!'—
Eh—gag me Robert!—sweet my friend,
This were indeed a piteous end
For those long fingers, and long feet,
And long neck, and smooth shoulders sweet;
An end that few men would forget
That saw it—So, an hour yet:
Consider, Jehane, which to take
Of life or death!"

80

90

100

110

So, scarce awake,
Dismounting, did she leave that place,
And totter some yards: with her face
Turned upward to the sky she lay,
Her head on a wet heap of hay,   120
And fell asleep: and while she slept,
And did not dream, the minutes crept
Round to the twelve again; but she,
Being waked at last, sighed quietly,
And strangely childlike came, and said:
"I will not." Straightway Godmar's head,
As though it hung on strong wires, turned
Most sharply round, and his face burned.
For Robert—both his eyes were dry,
He could not weep, but gloomily   130
He seemed to watch the rain; yea, too,
His lips were firm; he tried once more
To touch her lips; she reached out, sore
And vain desire so tortured them,
The poor gray lips, and now the hem
Of his sleeve brushed them.

                                    With a start
Up Godmar rose, thrust them apart;
From Robert's throat he loosed the bands
Of silk and mail; with empty hands
Held out, she stood and gazed, and saw   140
The long bright blade without a flaw
Glide out from Godmar's sheath, his hand
In Robert's hair; she saw him bend
Back Robert's head; she saw him send
The thin steel down; the blow told well,
Right backward the knight Robert fell,
And moaned as dogs do, being half dead,
Unwitting, as I deem: so then
Godmar turned grinning to his men,
Who ran, some five or six and beat   150
His head to pieces at their feet.
Then Godmar turned again and said:
"So, Jehane, the first fitte is read!
Take not, my lady, that your way
Lies backward to the Chatelet!"
She shook her head and gazed awhile
At her cold hands with a rueful smile,
As though this thing had made her mad.

This was the parting that they had
Beside the haystack in the floods.

DAVID

EARLE BIRNEY (1904–   )

I

David and I that summer cut trails on the Survey,
All week in the valley for wages, in air that was steeped
In the wail of mosquitoes, but over the sunalive weekends
We climbed, to get from the ruck of the camp, the surly

Poker, the wrangling, the snoring under the fetid
Tents, and because we had joy in our lengthening coltish
Muscles, and mountains for David were made to see over,
Stairs from the valleys and steps to the sun's retreats.

II

Our first was Mount Gleam. We hiked in the long afternoon
To a curling lake and lost the lure of the faceted   10
Cone in the swell of its sprawling shoulders. Past
The inlet we grilled our bacon, the strips festooned

On a poplar prong, in the hurrying slant of the sunset.
Then the two of us rolled in the blanket while round us the cold
Pines thrust at the stars. The dawn was a floating
Of mists till we reached to the slopes above timber, and won

To snow like fire in the sunlight. The peak was upthrust
Like a fist in a frozen ocean of rock that swirled
Into valleys the moon could be rolled in. Remotely unfurling
Eastward the alien prairie glittered. Down through the dusty   20

Skree on the west we descended, and David showed me
How to use the give of shale for giant incredible
Strides. I remember, before the larches' edge,
That I jumped a long green surf of juniper flowing

Away from the wind, and landed in gentian and saxifrage
Spilled on the moss. Then the darkening firs
And the sudden whirring of water that knifed down a fern-hidden
Cliff and splashed unseen into mist in the shadows.

III

One Sunday on Rampart's arête a rainsquall caught us,
And passed, and we clung by our blueing fingers and bootnails   30

An endless hour in the sun, not daring to move
Till the ice had steamed from the slate. And David taught me

How time on a knife-edge can pass with the guessing of fragments
Remembered from poets, the naming of strata beside one,
And matching of stories from schooldays. . . . We crawled astride
The peak to feast on the marching ranges flagged

By the fading shreds of the shattered stormcloud. Lingering
There it was David who spied to the south, remote,
And unmapped, a sunlit spire on Sawback, an overhang
Crooked like a talon. David named it the Finger.   40

That day we chanced on the skull and the splayed white ribs
Of a mountain goat underneath a cliff, caught tight
On a rock. Around were the silken feathers of kites.
And that was the first I knew that a goat could slip.

                                    IV

And then Inglismaldie. Now I remember only
The long ascent of the lonely valley, the live
Pine spirally scarred by lightning, the slicing pipe
Of invisible pika, and great prints, by the lowest

Snow, of a grizzly. There it was too that David
Taught me to read the scroll of coral in limestone   50
And the beetle-seal in the shale of ghostly trilobites,
Letters delivered to man from the Cambrian waves.

                                    V

On Sundance we tried from the col and the going was hard.
The air howled from our feet to the smudged rocks
And the papery lake below. At an outthrust we balked
Till David clung with his left to a dint in the scarp,

Lobbed the iceaxe over the rocky lip,
Slipped from his holds and hung by the quivering pick,
Twisted his long legs up into space and kicked
To the crest. Then grinning, he reached with his freckled wrist   60

And drew me up after. We set a new time for that climb.
That day returning we found a robin gyrating
In grass, wing-broken. I caught it to tame but David
Took and killed it, and said, "Could you teach it to fly?"

VI

In August, the second attempt, we ascended The Fortress.
By the forks of the Spray we caught five trout and fried them
Over a balsam fire. The woods were alive
With the vaulting of mule-deer and drenched with clouds all the morning,

Till we burst at noon to the flashing and floating round
Of the peaks. Coming down we picked in our hats the bright
And sunhot raspberries, eating them under a mighty
Spruce, while a marten moving like quicksilver scouted us.

70

VII

But always we talked of the Finger on Sawback, unknown
And hooked, till the first afternoon in September we slogged
Through the musky woods, past a swamp that quivered with frog-song
And camped by a bottle-green lake. But under the cold

Breath of the glacier sleep would not come, the moonlight
Etching the Finger. We rose and trod past the feathery
Larch, while the stars went out, and the quiet heather
Flushed, and the skyline pulsed with the surging bloom

80

Of incredible dawn in the Rockies. David spotted
Bighorns across the moraine and sent them leaping
With yodels the ramparts redoubled and rolled to the peaks
And the peaks to the sun. The ice in the morning thaw

Was a gurgling world of crystal and cold blue chasms,
And seracs that shone like frozen saltgreen waves.
At the base of the Finger we tried once and failed. Then David
Edged to the west and discovered the chimney; the last

Hundred feet we fought the rock and shouldered and kneed
Our way for an hour and made it. Unroping we formed
A cairn on the rotting tip. Then I turned to look north
At the glistening wedge of giant Assiniboine, heedless

90

Of handhold. And one foot gave. I swayed and shouted.
David turned sharp and reached out his arm and steadied me
Turning again with a grin and his lips ready
To jest. But the strain crumbled his foothold. Without

A gasp he was gone. I froze to the sound of grating
Edge-nails and fingers, the slither of stones, the lone
Second of silence, the nightmare thud. Then only
The wind and the muted beat of unknowing cascades.

100

VIII

Somehow I worked down the fifty impossible feet
To the ledge, calling and getting no answer but echoes
Released in the cirque, and trying not to reflect
What an answer would mean. He lay still, with his lean

Young face upturned and strangely unmarred, but his legs
Splayed beneath him, beside the final drop,
Six hundred feet sheer to the ice. My throat stopped
When I reached him, for he was alive. He opened his gray

Straight eyes and brokenly murmured "over . . . over."
And I, feeling beneath him a cruel fang   110
Of the ledge thrust in his back, but not understanding,
Mumbled stupidly, "Best not to move," and spoke

Of his pain. But he said, "I can't move. . . . If only I felt
Some pain." Then my shame stung the tears to my eyes
As I crouched, and I cursed myself, but he cried,
Louder, "No, Bobbie! Don't ever blame yourself.

I didn't test my foothold." He shut the lids
Of his eyes to the stare of the sky, while I moistened his lips
From our water flask and tearing my shirt into strips
I swabbed the shredded hands. But the blood slid   120

From his side and stained the stone and the thirsting lichens,
And yet I dared not lift him up from the gore
Of the rock. Then he whispered, "Bob, I want to go over!"
This time I knew what he meant and I grasped for a lie

And said, "I'll be back here by midnight with ropes
And men from the camp and we'll cradle you out." But I knew
That the day and the night must pass and the cold dews
Of another morning before such men unknowing

The ways of mountains could win to the chimney's top.
And then, how long? And he knew . . . and the hell of hours   130
After that, if he lived till we came, roping him out.
But I curled beside him and whispered, "The bleeding will stop.

You can last." He said only, "Perhaps. . . . For what? A wheelchair,
Bob?" His eyes brightening with fever upbraided me.
I could not look at him more and said, "Then I'll stay
With you." But he did not speak, for the clouding fever.

I lay dazed and stared at the long valley,
The glistening hair of a creek on the rug stretched

By the firs, while the sun leaned round and flooded the ledge,
The moss, and David still as a broken doll. 140

I hunched to my knees to leave, but he called and his voice
Now was sharpened with fear. "For Christ's sake push me over!
If I could move . . . Or die . . ." The sweat ran from his forehead,
But only his eyes moved. A kite was buoying

Blackly its wings over the wrinkled ice.
The purr of a waterfall rose and sank with the wind.
Above us climbed the last joint of the Finger
Beckoning bleakly the wide indifferent sky.

Even then in the sun it grew cold lying there . . . And I knew
He had tested his holds. It was I who had not . . . I looked 150
At the blood on the ledge, and the far valley. I looked
At last in his eyes. He breathed, "I'd do it for you, Bob."

IX

I will not remember how nor why I could twist
Up the wind-devilled peak, and down through the chimney's empty
Horror, and over the traverse alone. I remember
Only the pounding fear I would stumble on It

When I came to the grave-cold maw of the bergschrund . . . reeling
Over the sun-cankered snowbridge, shying the caves
In the névé . . . the fear, and the need to make sure It was there
On the ice, the running and falling and running, leaping 160

Of gaping greenthroated crevasses, alone and pursued
By the Finger's lengthening shadow. At last through the fanged
And blinding seracs I slid to the milky wrangling
Falls at the glacier's snout, through the rocks piled huge

On the humped moraine, and into the spectral larches,
Alone. By the glooming lake I sank and chilled
My mouth but I could not rest and stumbled still
To the valley, losing my way in the ragged marsh.

I was glad of the mire that covered the stains, on my ripped
Boots, of his blood, but panic was on me, the reek 170
Of the bog, the purple glimmer of toadstools obscene
In the twilight. I staggered clear to a firewaste, tripped

And fell with a shriek on my shoulder. It somehow eased
My heart to know I was hurt, but I did not faint
And I could not stop while over me hung the range
Of the Sawback. In blackness I searched for the trail by the creek

And found it. . . . My feet squelched a slug and horror
Rose again in my nostrils. I hurled myself
Down the path. In the woods behind some animal yelped.
Then I saw the glimmer of tents and babbled my story.

I said that he fell straight to the ice where they found him,
And none but the sun and incurious clouds have lingered
Around the marks of that day on the ledge of the Finger,
That day, the last of my youth, on the last of our mountains.

180

v. The Poem as Drama

Poems may be described as "dramatic" when they present scenes as in a drama or, again, when they stage an intrigue or plot. The epithet "dramatic" applies also to poems in which the narrator addresses himself to a second person, a listener whose attitude is expressed (as in the dialogue poem of A. E. Housman: "Is My Team Ploughing") or merely implied. An example of this last kind, with a silent listener, is Robert Browning's "My Last Duchess." The narrator's speech in Alfred Tennyson's "Ulysses" is public speech; in John Donne's "The Good-Morrow" it is private song. The woman addressed in Andrew Marvell's "To His Coy Mistress" does not reply, but we know her mind. In Robinson's "Mr. Flood's Party" and T. S. Eliot's "The Love Song of J. Alfred Prufrock" (see pp. 785, 935) the listeners are the self-same persons who speak the poems.

The poems of Donne and Eliot are dramatic, however, not merely because a listener is implied. They are dramatic in several senses of the poem as drama. The primary definition of "dramatic" is found in poems whose meaning is discovered through a dramatic process. Such poems (Donne's and Eliot's, for example) convey the impression of our going through the process of a mind thinking, arguing a point or proposition, arriving by skilful chess procedure at every next move. A dramatic poem is any poem that creates an "illusion of thought in action." It is the poem that forces us to participate in the shifting thought-processes of the speaker or narrator.

THE PIPER

WILLIAM BLAKE (1757–1827)

Piping down the valleys wild,
　Piping songs of pleasant glee,
On a cloud I saw a child,
　And he laughing said to me:

"Pipe a song about a Lamb!"
　So I piped with merry cheer.
"Piper, pipe that song again;"
　So I piped: he wept to hear.

"Drop thy pipe, thy happy pipe;
　Sing thy songs of happy cheer:"　10

So I sang the same again,
　While he wept with joy to hear.

"Piper, sit thee down and write
　In a book, that all may read."
So he vanished from my sight,
　And I plucked a hollow reed,

And I made a rural pen,
　And I stained the water clear,
And I wrote my happy songs
　Every child may joy to hear.　20

"I DIED FOR BEAUTY"

EMILY DICKINSON (1830–1886)

I died for beauty, but was scarce
Adjusted in the tomb,
When one who died for truth was lain
In an adjoining room.

He questioned softly why I failed?
"For beauty," I replied.

"And I for truth,—the two are one;
We brethren are," he said.

And so, as kinsmen met a night,
We talked between the rooms,   10
Until the moss had reached our lips,
And covered up our names.

FUTILITY

WILFRED OWEN (1893–1918)

Move him in the sun—
Gently its touch awoke him once,
At home, whispering of fields unsown.
Always it woke him, even in France
Until this morning and this snow.
If anything might rouse him now
The kind old sun will know.

Think how it wakes the seeds,—
Woke, once, the clays of a cold star.
Are limbs, so dear-achieved, are sides, 10
Full-nerved—still warm—too hard to stir?
Was it for this the clay grew tall?
—O what made fatuous sunbeams toil
To break earth's sleep at all?

"IS MY TEAM PLOUGHING"

A. E. HOUSMAN (1859–1936)

"Is my team ploughing,
  That I was used to drive
And hear the harness jingle
  When I was man alive?"

Aye, the horses trample,
  The harness jingles now;
No change though you lie under
  The land you used to plough.

"Is football playing
  Along the river shore,   10
With lads to chase the leather,
  Now I stand up no more?"

Aye, the ball is flying,
  The lads play heart and soul;
The goal stands up, the keeper
  Stands up to keep the goal.

"Is my girl happy,
  That I thought hard to leave,
And has she tired of weeping
  As she lies down at eve?"   20

Aye, she lies down lightly,
  She lies not down to weep:
Your girl is well contented.
  Be still, my lad, and sleep.

"Is my friend hearty,
  Now I am thin and pine;
And has he found to sleep in
  A better bed than mine?"

Aye, lad, I lie easy,
  I lie as lads would choose;   30
I cheer a dead man's sweetheart.
  Never ask me whose.

TO AN ATHLETE DYING YOUNG

A. E. HOUSMAN (1859–1936)

The time you won your town the race
We chaired you through the market-place;
Man and boy stood cheering by,
And home we brought you shoulder-high.

Today, the road all runners come,
Shoulder-high we bring you home,
And set you at your threshold down,
Townsman of a stiller town.

Smart lad, to slip betimes away
From fields where glory does not stay,   10
And early though the laurel grows
It withers quicker than the rose.

Eyes the shady night has shut
Cannot see the record cut,

And silence sounds no worse than cheers
After earth has stopped the ears.

Now you will not swell the rout
Of lads that wore their honors out,
Runners whom renown outran
And the name died before the man.   20

So set, before its echoes fade,
The fleet foot on the sill of shade,
And hold to the low lintel up
The still-defended challenge cup.

And round that early-laurelled head
Will flock to gaze the strengthless dead,
And find unwithered on its curls
The garland briefer than a girl's.

THE FUNERAL

JOHN DONNE (1573–1631)

Who ever comes to shroud me, do not harm,
　　Nor question much
That subtle wreath of hair, which crowns my arm;
The mystery, the sign you must not touch,
　　For 'tis my outward Soul,
Viceroy to that, which then to heaven being gone,
　　Will leave this to control,
And keep these limbs, her provinces, from dissolution.

For if the sinewy thread my brain lets fall
　　Through every part,   10
Can tie those parts, and make me one of all,
These hairs, which upward grew, and strength and art
　　Have from a better brain,
Can better do it. Except she meant that I
　　By this should know my pain,
As prisoners then are manacled, when they're condemn'd to die.

Whate'er she meant by it, bury it with me,
　　For since I am
Love's martyr, it might breed idolatry
If into others' hands these reliques came.   20

As 'twas humility
To afford to it all that a Soul can do,
    So, 'tis some bravery,
That, since you would save none of me, I bury some of you.

THE CANONIZATION

JOHN DONNE (1573–1631)

For God's sake hold your tongue, and let me love,
    Or chide my palsy, or my gout,
    My five gray hairs, or ruined fortune flout;
With wealth your state, your mind with arts improve,
        Take you a course, get you a place,
        Observe this honor, or his grace;
    Or the king's real, or his stampèd face
        Contemplate; what you will, approve,
        So you will let me love.

Alas! alas! who's injured by my love?   10
    What merchant's ships have my sighs drowned?
    Who says my tears have overflowed his ground?
When did my colds a forward spring remove?
        When did the heats which my veins fill
        Add one more to the plaguy bill?
    Soldiers find wars, and lawyers find out still
        Litigious men, which quarrels move,
        Though she and I do love.

Call's what you will, we are made such by love;
    Call her one, me another fly;   20
    We're tapers too, and at our own cost die,
And we in us find th'eagle and the dove.
        The phoenix riddle hath more wit
        By us; we two being one, are it;
    So, to one neutral thing both sexes fit.
        We die and rise the same, and prove
        Mysterious by this love.

We can die by it, if not live by love,
    And if unfit for tomb or hearse
    Our legend be, it will be fit for verse;   30
And if no piece of chronicle we prove,
        We'll build in sonnets pretty rooms;
        As well a well-wrought urn becomes
The greatest ashes, as half-acre tombs,

And by these hymns all shall approve
Us canonized for love;

And thus invoke us: "You, whom reverend love
  Made one another's hermitage;
   You, to whom love was peace, that now is rage;
Who did the whole world's soul contract, and drove   40
    Into the glasses of your eyes
      (So made such mirrors, and such spies,
That they did all to you epitomize)
   Countries, towns, courts, beg from above
   A pattern of your love."

PIAZZA PIECE

JOHN CROWE RANSOM (1888–   )

—I am a gentleman in a dustcoat trying
To make you hear. Your ears are soft and small
And listen to an old man not at all;
They want the young men's whispering and sighing.
But see the roses on your trellis dying
And hear the spectral singing of the moon—
For I must have my lovely lady soon.
I am a gentleman in a dustcoat trying.
—I am a lady young in beauty waiting
Until my true love comes, and then we kiss.   10
But what gray man among the vines is this
Whose words are dry and faint as in a dream?
Back from my trellis, sir, before I scream!
I am a lady young in beauty waiting.

"SINCE THERE'S NO HELP . . ."

MICHAEL DRAYTON (1563–1631)

Since there's no help, come, let us kiss and part.
Nay, I have done, you get no more of me.
And I am glad, yea, glad with all my heart,
That thus so cleanly I myself can free;
Shake hands for ever, cancel all our vows,
And when we meet at any time again,
Be it not seen in either of our brows
That we one jot of former love retain.
Now at the last gasp of Love's latest breath,
When, his pulse failing, Passion speechless lies,   10
When Faith is kneeling by his bed of death,
And Innocence is closing up his eyes—
  Now, if thou wouldst, when all have given him over,
  From death to life thou might'st him yet recover.

"I WILL NOT LET THEE GO"

ROBERT BRIDGES (1844–1930)

I will not let thee go.
Ends all our month-long love in this?
　　Can it be summed up so,
　　Quit in a single kiss?
I will not let thee go.

I will not let thee go.
If thy words' breath could scare thy deeds,
　　As the soft south can blow
　　And toss the feathered seeds,
Then might I let thee go.　　　　　　10

I will not let thee go.
Had not the great sun seen, I might;
　　Or were he reckoned slow
　　To bring the false to light,
Then might I let thee go.

I will not let thee go.
The stars that crowd the summer skies
　　Have watched us so below
　　With all their million eyes,
I dare not let thee go.　　　　　　20

I will not let thee go.
Have we not chid the changeful moon,
　　Now rising late, and now
　　Because she set too soon,
And shall I let thee go?

I will not let thee go.
Have not the young flowers been content,
　　Plucked ere their buds could blow,
　　To seal our sacrament?
I cannot let thee go.　　　　　　30

I will not let thee go.
I hold thee by too many bands:
　　Thou sayest farewell, and lo!
　　I have thee by the hands,
And will not let thee go.

SONG ("SWEETEST LOVE . . .")

JOHN DONNE (1573–1631)

Sweetest love, I do not go
For weariness of thee,
Nor in hope the world can show
A fitter love for me;
　　But since that I
Must die at last, 'tis best
Thus to use myself in jest
By feigned deaths to die.

Yesternight the Sun went hence
And yet is here today,　　　　　　10
He hath no desire nor sense,
Nor half so short a way;
　　Then fear not me,
But believe that I shall make
Speedier journeys, since I take
More wings and spurs than he.

O how feeble is man's power,
That if good fortune fall,
Cannot add another hour,
Nor a lost hour recall!　　　　　　20
　　But come bad chance,
And we join to't our strength,
And we teach it art and length,
Itself o'er us t' advance.

When thou sigh'st, thou sigh'st not wind,
But sigh'st my soul away;
When thou weep'st, unkindly kind,
My life's blood doth decay.
　　It cannot be
That thou lov'st me, as thou say'st;　　30
If in thine my life thou waste,
That art the best of me.

Let not thy divining heart
Forethink me any ill,
Destiny may take thy part
And may thy fears fulfil;

But think that we
Are but turn'd aside to sleep.
They who one another keep
Alive, ne'er parted be.   40

THE GOOD-MORROW

JOHN DONNE (1573–1631)

I wonder by my troth what thou and I
Did till we loved? were we not weaned till then?
But sucked on country pleasures childishly?
Or snorted we in the seven sleepers' den?
'Twas so; but this, all pleasures fancies be.
If ever any beauty I did see,
Which I desired and got, 'twas but a dream of thee.

And now good morrow to our waking souls,
Which watch not one another out of fear;
For love all love of other sights controls,   10
And makes one little room an everywhere.
Let sea-discoverers to new worlds have gone,
Let maps to other, worlds on worlds have shown,
Let us possess one world, each hath one, and is one.

My face in thine eye, thine in mine appears,
And true plain hearts do in the faces rest;
Where can we find two better hemispheres
Without sharp North, without declining West?
Whatever dies was not mixt equally;
If our two loves be one, or thou and I   20
Love so alike that none do slacken, none can die.

"WESTERN WIND, WHEN WILT THOU BLOW"

ANONYMOUS (16TH CENTURY)

Western wind, when wilt thou blow,
   The small rain down can rain?
Christ, if my love were in my arms
   And I in my bed again!

TO HIS COY MISTRESS

ANDREW MARVELL (1621–1678)

Had we but world enough, and time,
This coyness, lady, were no crime.
We would sit down and think which way
To walk, and pass our long love's day;
Thou by the Indian Ganges' side
Shouldst rubies find; I by the tide
Of Humber would complain. I would
Love you ten years before the Flood;
And you should, if you please, refuse
Till the conversion of the Jews.   10
My vegetable love should grow
Vaster than empires, and more slow.
An hundred years should go to praise
Thine eyes, and on thy forehead gaze;
Two hundred to adore each breast,
But thirty thousand to the rest;
An age at least to every part,
And the last age should show your heart.
For, lady, you deserve this state,
Nor would I love at lower rate.   20

But at my back I always hear
Time's wingèd chariot hurrying near;
And yonder all before us lie

Deserts of vast eternity.
Thy beauty shall no more be found,
Nor in thy marble vault shall sound
My echoing song; then worms shall try
That long preserved virginity,
And your quaint honor turn to dust,
And into ashes all my lust.   30
The grave's a fine and private place,
But none, I think, do there embrace.

Now therefore, while the youthful hue
Sits on thy skin like morning dew,
And while thy willing soul transpires
At every pore with instant fires,
Now let us sport us while we may;
And now, like am'rous birds of prey,
Rather at once our time devour,
Than languish in his slow-chapped power.
Let us roll all our strength, and all   41
Our sweetness, up into one ball;
And tear our pleasures with rough strife
Through the iron gates of life.
Thus, though we cannot make our sun
Stand still, yet we will make him run.

THE CONSTANT LOVER

SIR JOHN SUCKLING (1609–1642)

Out upon it, I have loved
  Three whole days together!
And am like to love three more,
  If it prove fair weather.

Time shall moult away his wings,
  Ere he shall discover
In the whole wide world again
  Such a constant lover.

But the spite on't is, no praise
  Is due at all to me: 10
Love with me had made no stays,
  Had it any been but she.

Had it any been but she,
  And that very face,
There had been at least ere this
  A dozen dozen in her place.

PORPHYRIA'S LOVER

ROBERT BROWNING (1812–1889)

The rain set early in to-night,
  The sullen wind was soon awake,
It tore the elm-tops down for spite,

And did its worst to vex the lake,
I listened with heart fit to break.
When glided in Porphyria; straight

She shut the cold out and the storm,
And kneeled and made the cheerless grate
  Blaze up, and all the cottage warm;
Which done, she rose, and from her form
Withdrew the dripping cloak and shawl,
  And laid her soiled gloves by, untied
Her hat and let the damp hair fall,   13
  And, last, she sat down by my side
And called me. When no voice replied,
She put my arm about her waist,
  And made her smooth white shoulder
    bare,
And all her yellow hair displaced,
  And, stooping, made my cheek lie there,
And spread o'er all her yellow hair,
Murmuring how she loved me—she   21
  Too weak, for all her heart's endeavour,
To set its struggling passion free
  From pride, and vainer ties dissever,
And give herself to me for ever.
But passion sometimes would prevail,
  Nor could to-night's gay feast restrain
A sudden thought of one so pale
  For love of her, and all in vain;
So, she was come through wind and rain.
Be sure I looked up at her eyes   31
  Happy and proud; at last I knew

Porphyria worshipped me; surprise
  Made my heart swell, and still it grew
While I debated what to do.
That moment she was mine, mine, fair,
  Perfectly pure and good: I found
A thing to do, and all her hair
  In one long yellow string I wound
Three times her little throat around,   40
  And strangled her. No pain felt she;
I am quite sure she felt no pain.
As a shut bud that holds a bee,
  I warily oped her lids; again
Laughed the blue eyes without a stain.
And I untightened next the tress
  About her neck; her cheek once more
Blushed bright beneath my burning kiss:
  I propped her head up as before,
Only, this time *my* shoulder bore   50
Her head, which droops upon it still:
  The smiling rosy little head,
So glad it has its utmost will,
  That all it scorned at once is fled,
And I, its love, am gained instead!
Porphyria's love; she guessed not how
  Her darling one wish would be heard.
And thus we sit together now,
  And all night long we have not stirred,
And yet God has not said a word!   60

MY LAST DUCHESS

ROBERT BROWNING (1812–1889)

SCENE: FERRARA

That's my last Duchess painted on the wall,
Looking as if she were alive. I call
That piece a wonder, now: Frà Pandolf's hands
Worked busily a day, and there she stands.
Will 't please you sit and look at her? I said
"Frà Pandolf" by design, for never read
Strangers like you that pictured countenance,
The depth and passion of its earnest glance,
But to myself they turned (since none puts by
The curtain I have drawn for you, but I)   10
And seemed as they would ask me, if they durst,
How such a glance came there; so, not the first
Are you to turn and ask thus. Sir, 'twas not
Her husband's presence only, called that spot
Of joy into the Duchess' cheek; perhaps
Frà Pandolf chanced to say, "Her mantle laps

Over my lady's wrist too much," or "Paint
Must never hope to reproduce the faint
Half-flush that dies along her throat:" such stuff
Was courtesy, she thought, and cause enough   20
For calling up that spot of joy. She had
A heart—how shall I say?—too soon made glad,
Too easily impressed; she liked whate'er
She looked on, and her looks went everywhere.
Sir, 'twas all one! My favour at her breast,
The dropping of the daylight in the West,
The bough of cherries some officious fool
Broke in the orchard for her, the white mule
She rode with round the terrace—all and each
Would draw from her alike the approving speech,   30
Or blush, at least. She thanked men,—good! but thanked
Somehow—I know not how—as if she ranked
My gift of a nine-hundred-years-old name
With anybody's gift. Who'd stoop to blame
This sort of trifling? Even had you skill
In speech—(which I have not)—to make your will
Quite clear to such an one, and say, "Just this
Or that in you disgusts me; here you miss,
Or there exceed the mark"—and if she let
Herself be lessoned so, nor plainly set   40
Her wits to yours, forsooth, and made excuse,
—E'en then would be some stooping; and I choose
Never to stoop. Oh sir, she smiled, no doubt,
Whene'er I passed her; but who passed without
Much the same smile? This grew; I gave commands;
Then all smiles stopped together. There she stands
As if alive. Will 't please you rise? We'll meet
The company below, then. I repeat,
The Count your master's known munificence
Is ample warrant that no just pretence   50
Of mine for dowry will be disallowed;
Though his fair daughter's self, as I avowed
At starting, is my object. Nay, we'll go
Together down, sir. Notice Neptune, though,
Taming a sea-horse, thought a rarity,
Which Claus of Innsbruck cast in bronze for me!

ULYSSES

ALFRED, LORD TENNYSON (1809–1892)

It little profits that an idle king,
By this still hearth, among these barren crags,
Match'd with an aged wife, I mete and dole
Unequal laws unto a savage race,

That hoard, and sleep, and feed, and know not me.
I cannot rest from travel: I will drink
Life to the lees: all times I have enjoy'd
Greatly, have suffer'd greatly, both with those
That loved me, and alone; on shore, and when
Thro' scudding drifts the rainy Hyades   10
Vext the dim sea: I am become a name;
For always roaming with a hungry heart
Much have I seen and known; cities of men
And manners, climates, councils, governments,
Myself not least, but honour'd of them all;
And drunk delight of battle with my peers,
Far on the ringing plains of windy Troy.
I am a part of all that I have met;
Yet all experience is an arch wherethro'
Gleams that untravell'd world, whose margin fades   20
For ever and for ever when I move.
How dull it is to pause, to make an end,
To rust unburnish'd, not to shine in use!
As tho' to breathe were life. Life piled on life
Were all too little, and of one to me
Little remains: but every hour is saved
From that eternal silence, something more,
A bringer of new things; and vile it were
For some three suns to store and hoard myself,
And this gray spirit yearning in desire   30
To follow knowledge like a sinking star,
Beyond the utmost bound of human thought.
    This is my son, mine own Telemachus,
To whom I leave the sceptre and the isle—
Well-loved of me, discerning to fulfil
This labour, by slow prudence to make mild
A rugged people, and thro' soft degrees
Subdue them to the useful and the good.
Most blameless is he, centred in the sphere
Of common duties, decent not to fail   40
In offices of tenderness, and pay
Meet adoration to my household gods,
When I am gone. He works his work, I mine.
    There lies the port; the vessel puffs her sail:
There gloom the dark broad seas. My mariners,
Souls that have toil'd, and wrought, and thought with me—
That ever with a frolic welcome took
The thunder and the sunshine, and opposed
Free hearts, free foreheads—you and I are old;
Old age hath yet his honour and his toil;   50
Death closes all: but something ere the end,
Some work of noble note, may yet be done,
Not unbecoming men that strove with Gods.

The lights begin to twinkle from the rocks:
The long day wanes: the slow moon climbs: the deep
Moans round with many voices. Come, my friends,
'Tis not too late to seek a newer world.
Push off, and sitting well in order smite
The sounding furrows; for my purpose holds
To sail beyond the sunset, and the baths   60
Of all the western stars, until I die.
It may be that the gulfs will wash us down:
It may be we shall touch the Happy Isles,
And see the great Achilles, whom we knew.
Tho' much is taken, much abides; and tho'
We are not now that strength which in old days
Moved earth and heaven; that which we are, we are;
One equal temper of heroic hearts,
Made weak by time and fate, but strong in will
To strive, to seek, to find, and not to yield.   70

SPRING AND FALL: TO A YOUNG CHILD

GERARD MANLEY HOPKINS (1844–1889)

Márgarét, are you grieving
Over Goldengrove unleaving?
Leáves, líke the things of man, you
With your fresh thoughts care for, can
    you?
Ah! ás the heart grows older
It will come to such sights colder
By and by, nor spare a sigh

Though worlds of wanwood leafmeal lie;
And yet you wíll weep and know why.
Now no matter, child, the name: 10
Sórrow's spríngs áre the same.
Nor mouth had, no nor mind, expressed
What heart heard of, ghost guessed:
It ís the blight man was born for,
It is Margaret you mourn for.

THE LISTENERS

WALTER DE LA MARE (1873–1956)

"Is there anybody there?" said the Traveler,
    Knocking on the moonlit door;
And his horse in the silence champed the
    grasses
Of the forest's ferny floor.
And a bird flew up out of the turret,
    Above the Traveler's head:
And he smote upon the door again a sec-
    ond time;
    "Is there anybody there?" he said.
But no one descended to the Traveler;
    No head from the leaf-fringed sill   10
Leaned over and looked into his gray eyes,
    Where he stood perplexed and still.

But only a host of phantom listeners
    That dwelt in the lone house then
Stood listening in the quiet of the moon-
    light
    To that voice from the world of men:
Stood thronging the faint moonbeams on
    the dark stair
    That goes down to the empty hall,
Hearkening in an air stirred and shaken
    By the lonely Traveler's call.   20
And he felt in his heart their strangeness,
    Their stillness answering his cry,
While his horse moved, cropping the dark
    turf,

'Neath the starred and leafy sky;
For he suddenly smote on the door, even
  Louder, and lifted his head:—
"Tell them I came, and no one answered,
  That I kept my word," he said.
Never the least stir made the listeners,
  Though every word he spake   30

Fell echoing through the shadowiness of
    the still house
From the one man left awake:
Aye, they heard his foot upon the stirrup,
  And the sound of iron on stone,
And how the silence surged softly back-
    ward,
  When the plunging hoofs were gone.

NEW YEAR'S EVE

THOMAS HARDY (1840–1928)

"I have finished another year," said God,
  "In grey, green, white, and brown;
I have strewn the leaf upon the sod,
Sealed up the worm within the clod,
  And let the last sun down."

"And what's the good of it?" I said,
  "What reasons made you call
From formless void this earth we tread,
When nine-and-ninety can be read
  Why nought should be at all?   10

"Yea, Sire; why shaped you us, 'who in
  This tabernacle groan'—
If ever a joy he found herein,
Such joy no man had wished to win
  If he had never known!"

Then he: "My labours—logicless—
  You may explain; not I:
Sense-sealed I have wrought, without a
    guess
That I evolved a Consciousness
  To ask for reasons why.   20

"Strange that ephemeral creatures who
  By my own ordering are,
Should see the shortness of my view,
Use ethic tests I never knew,
  Or made provision for!"

He sank to raptness as of yore,
  And opening New Year's Day
Wove it by rote as theretofore,
And went on working evermore
  In his unweeting way.   30

PATTERNS

AMY LOWELL (1874–1925)

I walk down the garden paths,
And all the daffodils
Are blowing, and the bright blue squills.
I walk down the patterned garden-paths
In my stiff, brocaded gown.
With my powdered hair and jeweled fan,
I too am a rare
Pattern. As I wander down
The garden paths.
My dress is richly figured,   10
And the train
Makes a pink and silver stain

On the gravel, and the thrift
Of the borders.
Just a plate of current fashion,
Tripping by in high-heeled, ribboned
    shoes.
Not a softness anywhere about me,
Only whalebone and brocade.
And I sink on a seat in the shade
Of a lime tree. For my passion   20
Wars against the stiff brocade.
The daffodils and squills
Flutter in the breeze

As they please.
And I weep;
For the lime-tree is in blossom
And one small flower has dropped upon
my bosom.

And the plashing of waterdrops
In the marble fountain
Comes down the garden-paths.   30
The dripping never stops.
Underneath my stiffened gown
Is the softness of a woman bathing in a
marble basin,
A basin in the midst of hedges grown
So thick, she cannot see her lover hiding,
But she guesses he is near,
And the sliding of the water
Seems the stroking of a dear
Hand upon her.   39
What is Summer in a fine brocaded gown!
I should like to see it lying in a heap upon
the ground.
All the pink and silver crumpled up on
the ground.

I would be the pink and silver as I ran
along the paths,
And he would stumble after,
Bewildered by my laughter.
I should see the sun flashing from his
sword-hilt and the buckles on his
shoes.
I would choose
To lead him in a maze along the patterned
paths,
A bright and laughing maze for my heavy-
booted lover.
Till he caught me in the shade,   50
And the buttons of his waistcoat bruised
my body as he clasped me,
Aching, melting, unafraid.
With the shadows of the leaves and the
sundrops,
And the plopping of the waterdrops,
All about us in the open afternoon—
I am very like to swoon
With my weight of this brocade,
For the sun sifts through the shade.

Underneath the fallen blossom
In my bosom   60
Is a letter I have hid.
It was brought to me this morning by a
rider from the Duke.
"Madam, we regret to inform you that
Lord Hartwell
Died in action Thursday se'nnight."
As I read it in the white, morning sun-
light,
The letters squirmed like snakes.
"Any answer, Madam?" said my footman.
"No," I told him.
"See that the messenger takes some re-
freshment.
"No, no answer."   70
And I walked into the garden,
Up and down the patterned paths,
In my stiff, correct brocade.
The blue and yellow flowers stood up
proudly in the sun,
Each one.
I stood upright too,
Held rigid to the pattern
By the stiffness of my gown;
Up and down I walked,
Up and down.   80

In a month he would have been my hus-
band.
In a month, here, underneath this lime,
We would have broke the pattern;
He for me, and I for him,
He as Colonel, I as Lady,
On this shady seat.
He had a whim
That sunlight carried blessing.
And I answered, "It shall be as you have
said."
Now he is dead.   90

In Summer and in Winter I shall walk
Up and down
The patterned garden-paths
In my stiff, brocaded gown.
The squills and daffodils
Will give place to pillared roses, and to
asters, and to snow.

I shall go
Up and down
In my gown.
Gorgeously arrayed,   100
Boned and stayed.
And the softness of my body will be
    guarded from embrace

By each button, hook, and lace.
For the man who should loose me is dead,
Fighting with the Duke in Flanders,
In a pattern called a war.
Christ! What are patterns for?

MR. FLOOD'S PARTY

EDWIN ARLINGTON ROBINSON (1869–1935)

Old Eben Flood, climbing alone one night
Over the hill between the town below
And the forsaken upland hermitage
That held as much as he should ever know
On earth again of home, paused warily.
The road was his with not a native near;
And Eben, having leisure, said aloud,
For no man else in Tilbury Town to hear:

"Well, Mr. Flood, we have the harvest
    moon
Again, and we may not have many more;
The bird is on the wing, the poet says, 11
And you and I have said it here before.
Drink to the bird." He raised up to the
    light
The jug that he had gone so far to fill,
And answered huskily: "Well, Mr. Flood,
Since you propose it, I believe I will."

Alone, as if enduring to the end
A valiant armor of scarred hopes outworn,
He stood there in the middle of the road
Like Roland's ghost winding a silent
    horn.
Below him, in the town among the trees,
Where friends of other days had honored
    him,
A phantom salutation of the dead
Rang thinly till old Eben's eyes were dim.

Then, as a mother lays her sleeping child
Down tenderly, fearing it may awake,
He set the jug down slowly at his feet
With trembling care, knowing that most
    things break.
And only when assured that on firm earth
It stood, as the uncertain lives of men 30

Assuredly did not, he paced away,
And with his hand extended paused again:

"Well, Mr. Flood, we have not met like
    this
In a long time; and many a change has
    come
To both of us, I fear, since last it was
We had a drop together. Welcome home!"
Convivially returning with himself,
Again he raised the jug up to the light;
And with an acquiescent quaver said: 39
"Well, Mr. Flood, if you insist, I might.

"Only a very little, Mr. Flood—
For auld lang syne. No more, sir; that
    will do."
So, for the time, apparently it did,
And Eben evidently thought so too;
For soon amid the silver loneliness
Of night he lifted up his voice and sang,
Secure, with only two moons listening,
Until the whole harmonious landscape
    rang—

"For auld lang syne." The weary throat
    gave out,
The last word wavered; and the song
    being done,   50
He raised again the jug regretfully
And shook his head, and was again alone.
There was not much that was ahead of
    him,
And there was nothing in the town be-
    low—
Where strangers would have shut the
    many doors
That many friends had opened long ago.

MY PAPA'S WALTZ

THEODORE ROETHKE (1908–   )

The whisky on your breath
Could make a small boy dizzy;
But I hung on like death:
Such waltzing was not easy.

We romped until the pans
Slid from the kitchen shelf;
My mother's countenance
Could not unfrown itself.

The hand that held my wrist
Was battered on one knuckle;   10
At every step you missed
My right ear scraped a buckle.

You beat time on my head
With a palm caked hard by dirt,
Then waltzed me off to bed
Still clinging to your shirt.

vi. The Poem as Satire and Parody

"MY MISTRESS' EYES ARE NOTHING LIKE THE SUN"

WILLIAM SHAKESPEARE (1564–1616)

SONNET 130

My mistress' eyes are nothing like the sun;
Coral is far more red than her lips' red:
If snow be white, why then her breasts are dun;
If hairs be wires, black wires grow on her head.
I have seen roses damasked, red and white,
But no such roses see I in her cheeks;
And in some perfumes is there more delight
Than in the breath that from my mistress reeks.
I love to hear her speak, yet well I know
That music hath a far more pleasing sound: 10
I grant I never saw a goddess go,—
My mistress, when she walks, treads on the ground:
    And yet, by heaven, I think my love as rare
    As any she belied with false compare.

[BELINDA PREPARES FOR DAY]

(*From THE RAPE OF THE LOCK*)

ALEXANDER POPE (1688–1744)

Sol through white curtains shot a timorous ray,
And oped those eyes that must eclipse the day:
Now lap-dogs give themselves the rousing shake,
And sleepless lovers, just at twelve, awake:
Thrice rung the bell, the slipper knocked the ground,
And the pressed watch returned a silver sound.
Belinda still her downy pillow prest,
Her guardian SYLPH prolonged the balmy rest: . . .
Seemed to her ear his winning lips to lay,
And thus in whispers said, or seemed to say: 10
   "Fairest of mortals, thou distinguished care
Of thousand bright Inhabitants of Air! . . .
Hear and believe! thy own importance know,

Nor bound thy narrow views to things below.
Some secret truths, from learnèd pride concealed,
To Maids alone and Children are revealed:
What though no credit doubting Wits may give?
The Fair and Innocent shall still believe.
Know, then, unnumbered Spirits round thee fly,
The light Militia of the lower sky: 20
These, though unseen, are ever on the wing,
Hang o'er the Box, and hover round the Ring.
Think what an equipage thou hast in Air,
And view with scorn two Pages and a Chair. . . .
   "Oft, when the world imagine women stray,
The Sylphs through mystic mazes guide their way;
Through all the giddy circle they pursue,
And old impertinence expel by new.
What tender maid but must a victim fall
To one man's treat, but for another's ball?   30
When Florio speaks what virgin could withstand,
If gentle Damon did not squeeze her hand?
With varying vanities, from every part,
They shift the moving Toyshop of their heart;
Where wigs with wigs, with sword-knots sword-knots strive,
Beaux banish beaux, and coaches coaches drive.
This erring mortals Levity may call;
Oh blind to truth! the Sylphs contrive it all.
   "Of these am I, who thy protection claim,
A watchful sprite, and Ariel is my name.   40
Late, as I ranged the crystal wilds of air,
In the clear Mirror of thy ruling Star
I saw, alas! some dread event impend,
Ere to the main this morning sun descend,
But heaven reveals not what, or how, or where:
Warned by the Sylph, oh pious maid, beware!
This to disclose is all thy guardian can:
Beware of all, but most beware of man!"
   He said; when Shock, who thought she slept too long,
Leaped up, and waked his mistress with his tongue. . . .   50
   And now, unveiled, the Toilet stands displayed,
Each silver Vase in mystic order laid.
First, robed in white, the Nymph intent adores,
With head uncovered, the Cosmetic powers.
A heavenly image in the glass appears,
To that she bends, to that her eyes she rears;
Th' inferior Priestess, at her altar's side,
Trembling begins the sacred rites of Pride.
Unnumbered treasures ope at once, and here
The various offerings of the world appear;   60
From each she nicely culls with curious toil,
And decks the Goddess with the glittering spoil.

This casket India's glowing gems unlocks,
And all Arabia breathes from yonder box.
The Tortoise here and Elephant unite,
Transformed to combs, the speckled, and the white.
Here files of pins extend their shining rows,
Puffs, Powders, Patches, Bibles, Billet-doux.
Now awful beauty puts on all its arms;
The fair each moment rises in her charms,   70
Repairs her smiles, awakens every grace,
And calls forth all the wonders of her face;
Sees by degrees a purer blush arise,
And keener lightnings quicken in her eyes.
The busy Sylphs surround their darling care,
These set the head, and those divide the hair,
Some fold the sleeve, whilst others plait the gown;
And Betty's praised for labours not her own.

POEM, OR BEAUTY HURTS MR. VINAL

E. E. CUMMINGS (1894–1962)

take it from me kiddo
believe me
my country, 'tis of

you, land of the Cluett
Shirt Boston Garter and Spearmint
Girl With The Wrigley Eyes (of you
land of the Arrow Ide
and Earl &
Wilson
Collars) of you i   10
sing: land of Abraham Lincoln and Lydia E. Pinkham,
land above all of Just Add Hot Water And Serve—
from every B.V.D.

let freedom ring

amen. i do however protest, anent the un
-spontaneous and otherwise scented merde which
greets one (Everywhere Why) as divine poesy per
that and this radically defunct periodical. i would

suggest that certain ideas gestures
rhymes, like Gillette Razor Blades   20
having been used and reused
to the mystical moment of duilness emphatically are
Not To Be Resharpened. (Case in point

if we are to believe these gently O sweetly
melancholy trillers amid the thrillers
these crepuscular violinists among my and your
skyscrapers—Helen & Cleopatra were Just Too Lovely,
The Snail's On The Thorn enter Morn and God's
In His andsoforth

do you get me?) according   30
to such supposedly indigenous
throstles Art is O World O Life
a formula: example, Turn Your Shirttails Into
Drawers and If It Isn't An Eastman It Isn't A
Kodak therefore my friends let
us now sing each and all fortissimo A-
mer
i

ca, I
love,   40
You. And there're a
hun-dred-mil-lion-oth-ers, like
all of you successfully if
delicately gelded (or spaded)
gentlemen(and ladies)—pretty

littleliverpill-
hearted-Nujolneeding-There's-A-Reason
americans (who tensetendoned and with
upward vacant eyes, painfully
perpetually crouched, quivering, upon the   50
sternly allotted sandpile
—how silently
emit a tiny violetflavored nuisance: Odor?

ono.
comes out like a ribbon lies flat on the brush

THE UNKNOWN CITIZEN

(To JS /07/M/378
This Marble Monument
Is Erected by the State)

W. H. AUDEN (1907-   )

He was found by the Bureau of Statistics to be
One against whom there was no official complaint,
And all the reports on his conduct agree
That, in the modern sense of an old-fashioned word, he was a saint,

For in everything he did he served the Greater Community.
Except for the War till the day he retired
He worked in a factory and never got fired,
But satisfied his employers, Fudge Motors Inc.
Yet he wasn't a scab or odd in his views,
For his Union reports that he paid his dues,   10
(Our report on his Union shows it was sound)
And our Social Psychology workers found
That he was popular with his mates and liked a drink.
The Press are convinced that he bought a paper every day
And that his reactions to advertisements were normal in every way.
Policies taken out in his name prove that he was fully insured,
And his Health-card shows he was once in hospital but left it cured.
Both Producers Research and High-Grade Living declare
He was fully sensible to the advantages of the Instalment Plan
And had everything necessary to the Modern Man,   20
A phonograph, a radio, a car and a frigidaire.
Our researchers into Public Opinion are content
That he held the proper opinions for the time of year;
When there was peace, he was for peace; when there was war, he went.
He was married and added five children to the population,
Which our Eugenist says was the right number for a parent of his generation,
And our teachers report that he never interfered with their education.
Was he free? Was he happy? The question is absurd:
Had anything been wrong, we should certainly have heard.

DIRGE

KENNETH FEARING (1902–1961)

1-2-3 was the number he played but today the number came 3-2-1;
   bought his Carbide at 30 and it went to 29; had the favorite at Bowie but the track
   was slow—

O, executive type, would you like to drive a floating power, knee-action, silk-upholstered
   six? Wed a Hollywood star? Shoot the course in 58? Draw to the ace, king, jack?
   O, fellow with a will who won't take no, watch out for three cigarettes on the same,
   single match; O democratic voter born in August under Mars, beware of liquidated
   rails—

Dénouement to dénouement, he took a personal pride in the certain, certain way he
   lived his own, private life,   10
   but nevertheless, they shut off his gas; nevertheless, the bank foreclosed; nevertheless, the landlord called; nevertheless, the radio broke,

And twelve o'clock arrived just once too often,
   just the same he wore one grey tweed suit, bought one straw hat, drank one straight
   Scotch, walked one short step, took one long look, drew one deep breath,
   just one too many,

And wow he died as wow he lived,
  going whop to the office and blooie home to sleep and biff got married and bam had
    children and oof got fired,
  zowie did he live and zowie did he die,

With who the hell are you at the corner of his casket, and where the hell we going on
    the right hand silver knob, and who the hell cares walking second from the end
    with an American Beauty wreath from why the hell not.

Very much missed by the circulation staff of the New York Evening Post; deeply,
  deeply mourned by the B.M.T.,

Wham, Mr. Roosevelt; pow, Sears Roebuck; awk, big dipper; bop, summer rain;
  bong, Mr., bong, Mr., bong, Mr., bong.

MINIVER CHEEVY

EDWIN ARLINGTON ROBINSON (1869–1935)

Miniver Cheevy, child of scorn,
  Grew lean while he assailed the seasons;
He wept that he was ever born,
  And he had reasons.

Miniver loved the days of old
  When swords were bright and steeds
    were prancing;
The vision of a warrior bold
  Would set him dancing.

Miniver sighed for what was not,
  And dreamed, and rested from his
    labors;   10
He dreamed of Thebes and Camelot,
  And Priam's neighbors.

Miniver mourned the ripe renown
  That made so many a name so fragrant;
He mourned Romance, now on the town,
  And Art, a vagrant.

Miniver loved the Medici,
  Albeit he had never seen one;
He would have sinned incessantly
  Could he have been one.   20

Miniver cursed the commonplace
  And eyed a khaki suit with loathing;
He missed the medieval grace
  Of iron clothing.

Miniver scorned the gold he sought,
  But sore annoyed was he without it;
Miniver thought, and thought, and
    thought,
  And thought about it.

Miniver Cheevy, born too late,
  Scratched his head and kept on thinking;
Miniver coughed, and called it fate,   31
  And kept on drinking.

NEWSREEL

C. DAY LEWIS (1904–   )

Enter the dream-house, brothers and sisters, leaving
  Your debts asleep, your history at the door:

This is the home for heroes, and this loving
Darkness a fur you can afford.

Fish in their tank electrically heated
Nose without envy the glass wall: for them
Clerk, spy, nurse, killer, prince, the great and the defeated,
Move in a mute day-dream.

Bathed in this common source, you gape incurious
At what your active hours have willed—   10
Sleep-walking on that silver wall, the furious
Sick shapes and pregnant fancies in your world.

There is the mayor opening the oyster season:
A society wedding: the autumn hats look swell:
An old crock's race, and a politician
In fishing-waders to prove that all is well.

Oh, look at the warplanes! Screaming hysteric treble
In the long power-dive, like gannets they fall steep.
But what are they to trouble—
These silver shadows to trouble your watery, womb-deep sleep?   20

See the big guns, rising, groping, erected
To plant death in your world's soft womb.
Fire-bud, smoke-blossom, iron steel projected—
Are these exotics? They will grow nearer home:

Grow nearer home—and out of the dream-house stumbling
One night into a strangling air and the flung
Rags of children and thunder of stone niagaras tumbling,
You'll know you slept too long.

TO A SINISTER POTATO

PETER VIERECK (1916–   )

O vast earth-apple, waiting to be fried,
Of all life's starers the most many-eyed,
What furtive purpose hatched you long ago
In Indiana or in Idaho?

In Indiana and in Idaho
Snug underground, the great potatoes
      grow,
Puffed up with secret paranoias unguessed
By all the duped and starch-fed Middle
      West.

Like coiled-up springs or like a will-to-
      power,   9
The fat and earthy lurkers bide their hour,
The silent watchers of our raucous show
In Indiana or in Idaho.

"They think us dull, a food and not a
      flower.
Wait! We'll outshine all roses in our
      hour.

Not wholesomeness but mania swells us so
In Indiana and in Idaho.

"In each Kiwanis Club on every plate,
So bland and health-exuding do we wait
That Indiana never, never knows
How much we envy stars and hate the
    rose."   20

Some doom will strike (as all potatoes
    know)
When—once too often mashed in
    Idaho—
From its cocoon the drabbest of earth's
    powers
Rises and is a star.
And shines.
And lours.

ON THE VANITY OF EARTHLY GREATNESS

ARTHUR GUITERMAN (1871–1943)

The tusks that clashed in mighty brawls
Of mastodons, are billiard balls.

The sword of Charlemagne the Just
Is ferric oxide, known as rust.

The grizzly bear whose potent hug
Was feared by all, is now a rug.

Great Cæsar's bust is on the shelf,
And I don't feel so well myself!

"NEXT TO OF COURSE GOD . . ."

E. E. CUMMINGS (1894–1962)

"next to of course god america i
love you land of the pilgrims' and so forth oh
say can you see by the dawn's early my
country 'tis of centuries come and go
and are no more what of it we should worry
in every language even deafanddumb
thy sons acclaim your glorious name by gorry
by jingo by gee by gosh by gum
why talk of beauty what could be more beautiful than these heroic happy dead   10
who rushed like lions to the roaring slaughter
they did not stop to think they died instead
then shall the voice of liberty be mute?"

He spoke. And drank rapidly a glass of water.

WHITE CHRISTMAS

W. R. RODGERS (1911–   )

Punctually at Christmas the soft plush
Of sentiment snows down, embosoms all
The sharp and pointed shapes of venom, shawls
The hills and hides the shocking holes of this

Uneven world of want and wealth, cushions
With cosy wish like cotton-wool the cool
Arm's-length interstices of caste and class,
And into obese folds subtracts from sight
All truculent acts, bleeding the world white.

Punctually that glib pair, Peace and Good-will,   10
Emerges royally to take the air,
Collect the bows, assimilate the smiles,
Of waiting men. It is a genial time;
Angels, like stalactites, descend from heaven;
Bishops distribute their own weight in words,
Congratulate the poor on Christlike lack;
And the member for the constituency
Feeds the five thousand, and has plenty back.

Punctually, to-night, in old stone circles
Of set reunion, families stiffly sit   20
And listen: this is the night and this the happy time
When the tinned milk of human kindness is
Upheld and holed by radio-appeal:
Hushed are hurrying heels on hard roads,
And every parlour's a pink pond of light
To the cold and travelling man going by
In the dark, without a bark or a bite.

But punctually to-morrow you will see
All this silent and dissembling world
Of stilted sentiment suddenly melt   30
Into mush and watery welter of words
Beneath the warm and moving traffic of
Feet and actual fact. Over the stark plain
The silted mill-chimneys once again spread
Their sackcloth and ashes, a flowing mane
Of repentance for the false day that's fled.

THE LATEST DECALOGUE

ARTHUR HUGH CLOUGH (1819–1861)

Thou shalt have one God only; who
Would be at the expense of two?
No graven images may be
Worshipped, except the currency:
Swear not at all; for, for thy curse
Thine enemy is none the worse:

At church on Sunday to attend
Will serve to keep the world thy friend:
Honour thy parents; that is, all
From whom advancement may befall: 10
Thou shalt not kill; but needst not strive
Officiously to keep alive:

Do not adultery commit;　　　　　Thou shalt not covet; but tradition
Advantage rarely comes of it:　　　Approves all forms of competition.　20
Thou shalt not steal; an empty feat,　The sum of all is, thou shalt love,
When it's so lucrative to cheat:　　If any body, God above:
Bear not false witness; let the lie　At any rate shall never labour
Have time on its own wings to fly:　*More* than thyself to love thy neighbor.

"NEARING AGAIN THE LEGENDARY ISLE"

C. DAY LEWIS (1904–　　)

Nearing again the legendary isle
Where sirens sang and mariners were skinned,
We wonder now what was there to beguile
That such stout fellows left their bones behind.

Those chorus-girls are surely past their prime,
Voices grow shrill and paint is wearing thin,
Lips that sealed up the sense from gnawing time
Now beg the favor with a graveyard grin.

We have no flesh to spare and they can't bite,
Hunger and sweat have stripped us to the bone;　　10
A skeleton crew we toil upon the tide
And mock the theme-song meant to lure us on:

No need to stop the ears, avert the eyes
From purple rhetoric of evening skies.

THE SIRENS

JOHN MANIFOLD (1915–　　)

Odysseus heard the sirens; they were singing
Music by Wolf and Weinberger and Morley
About a region where the swans go winging,
Vines are in colour, girls are growing surely

Into nubility, and pylons bringing
Leisure and power to farms that live securely
Without a landlord. Still, his eyes were stinging
With salt and seablink, and the ropes hurt sorely.

Odysseus saw the sirens; they were charming,
Blonde, with snub breasts and little neat posteriors,　10
But could not take his mind off the alarming

Weather report, his mutineers in irons,
The radio failing; it was bloody serious.
In twenty minutes he forgot the sirens.

CUCKOO SONG

ANONYMOUS (ABOUT 1250 A.D.)

Sumer is icumen in,
  Lhude sing cuccu!
Groweth sed, and bloweth med,
  And springth the wode nu—
      Sing cuccu!

Awe bleteth after lomb,
  Lhouth after calve cu;

Bulluc sterteth, bucke verteth,
  Murie sing cuccu!

Cuccu, cuccu, well singes thu, cuccu:
  Ne swike thu naver nu;   10
Sing cuccu, nu, sing cuccu,
  Sing cuccu, sing cuccu, nu!

ANCIENT MUSIC

EZRA POUND (1885–   )

Winter is icummen in,
Lhude sing Goddamm,
Raineth drop and staineth slop,
And how the wind doth ramm!
      Sing: Goddamm.
Skiddeth bus and sloppeth us,
An ague hath my ham.
Freezeth river, turneth liver,
      Damn you, sing: Goddamm.
Goddamm, Goddamm, 'tis why I am, Goddamm,   10
      So 'gainst the winter's balm.
Sing goddamm, damm, sing Goddamm,
Sing goddamm, sing goddamm, DAMM.

THE PASSIONATE SHEPHERD TO HIS LOVE

CHRISTOPHER MARLOWE (1564–1593)

Come live with me and be my love,
And we will all the pleasures prove
That valleys, groves, hills, and fields,
Woods, or steepy mountains yields.

And we will sit upon the rocks
Seeing the shepherds feed their flocks,
By shallow rivers, to whose falls
Melodious birds sing madrigals.

And I will make thee beds of roses
And a thousand fragrant posies,   10
A cap of flowers, and a kirtle
Embroidered all with leaves of myrtle;

A gown made of the finest wool,
Which from our pretty lambs we pull;
Fair lined slippers for the cold,
With buckles of the purest gold;

A belt of straw and ivy-buds
With coral clasps and amber studs:
And if these pleasures may thee move,
Come live with me and be my love.   20

The shepherd swains shall dance and sing
For thy delight each May morning:
If these delights thy mind may move,
Then live with me and be my love.

"COME LIVE WITH ME AND BE MY LOVE"

C. DAY LEWIS (1904–   )

Come, live with me and be my love,
And we will all the pleasures prove
Of peace and plenty, bed and board,
That chance employment may afford.

I'll handle dainties on the docks
And thou shalt read of summer frocks:
At evening by the sour canals
We'll hope to hear some madrigals.

Care on thy maiden brow shall put
A wreath of wrinkles, and thy foot   10
Be shod with pain: not silken dress
But toil shall tire thy loveliness.

Hunger shall make thy modest zone
And cheat fond death of all but bone—
If these delights thy mind may move,
Then live with me and be my love.

from IN MEMORIAM

ALFRED, LORD TENNYSON (1809–1892)

54

Oh yet we trust that somehow good
    Will be the final goal of ill,
    To pangs of nature, sins of will,
Defects of doubt, and taints of blood;

That nothing walks with aimless feet;
    That not one life shall be destroyed,
    Or cast as rubbish to the void,
When God hath made the pile complete;

That not a worm is cloven in vain;
    That not a moth with vain desire   10

Is shrivelled in a fruitless fire,
Or but subserves another's gain.

Behold, we know not anything;
    I can but trust that good shall fall
    At last—far off—at last, to all,
And every winter change to spring.

So runs my dream: but what am I?
    An infant crying in the night:
    An infant crying for the light:
And with no language but a cry.   20

HEAVEN
RUPERT BROOKE (1887–1915)

Fish (fly-replete, in depth of June,
Dawdling away their wat'ry noon)
Ponder deep wisdom, dark or clear,
Each secret fishy hope or fear.
Fish say, they have their Stream and Pond;
But is there anything Beyond?
This life cannot be All, they swear,
For how unpleasant, if it were!
One may not doubt that, somehow, Good
Shall come of Water and of Mud;   10
And sure, the reverent eye must see
A purpose in Liquidity.
We darkly know, by Faith we cry,
The future is not Wholly Dry.
Mud unto mud!—Death eddies near—
Not here the appointed End, not here!
But somewhere, beyond Space and Time,
Is wetter water, slimier slime!
And there (they trust) there swimmeth
    One
Who swam ere rivers were begun,   20
Immense, of fishy form and mind,
Squamous, omnipotent, and kind;
And under that Almighty Fin,
The littlest fish may enter in.
Oh! never fly conceals a hook,
Fish say, in the Eternal Brook,
But more than mundane weeds are there,
And mud, celestially fair;
Fat caterpillars drift around,
And Paradisal grubs are found;   30
Unfading moths, immortal flies,
And the worm that never dies.
And in that Heaven of all their wish,
There shall be no more land, say fish.

---

from A SHROPSHIRE LAD
A. E. HOUSMAN (1859–1936)

XLIV

Shot? so quick, so clean an ending?
    Oh that was right, lad, that was brave:
Yours was not an ill for mending,
    'Twas best to take it to the grave.

Oh you had forethought, you could reason,
    And saw your road and where it led,
And early wise and brave in season
    Put the pistol to your head.

Oh soon, and better so than later
    After long disgrace and scorn,   10
You shot dead the household traitor,
    The soul that should not have been born.

Right you guessed the rising morrow
    And scorned to tread the mire you must:
Dust's your wages, son of sorrow,
    But men may come to worse than dust.

Souls undone, undoing others,—
    Long time since the tale began.
You would not live to wrong your
    brothers:
Oh lad, you died as fits a man.   20

"WHAT, STILL ALIVE AT TWENTY-TWO . . ."
HUGH KINGSMILL (1889–1949)

What, still alive at twenty-two,
A clean, upstanding chap like you?
Sure, if your throat 'tis hard to slit,
Slit your girl's, and swing for it.

Like enough, you won't be glad,
When they come to hang you, lad:
But bacon's not the only thing
That's cured by hanging from a string.

So, when the spilt ink of the night
Spreads o'er the blotting-pad of light,
Lads whose job is still to do
Shall whet their knives, and think of you.

SEA-FEVER

JOHN MASEFIELD (1878–   )

I must go down to the seas again, to the lonely sea and the sky,
And all I ask is a tall ship and a star to steer her by,
And the wheel's kick and the wind's song and the white sail's shaking,
And a grey mist on the sea's face and a grey dawn breaking.

I must go down to the seas again, for the call of the running tide
Is a wild call and a clear call that may not be denied;
And all I ask is a windy day with the white clouds flying,
And the flung spray and the blown spume, and the sea-gulls crying.

I must go down to the seas again to the vagrant gypsy life,   9
To the gull's way and the whale's way where the wind's like a whetted knife;
And all I ask is a merry yarn from a laughing fellow-rover,
And quiet sleep and a sweet dream when the long trick's over.

SEA-CHILL

ARTHUR GUITERMAN (1871–1943)

When Mrs. John Masefield and her husband, the author of "I Must Go Down to the Seas Again," arrived here on a liner, she said to a reporter, "It was too uppy-downy, and Mr. Masefield was ill."—News item.

I must go down to the seas again, where the billows romp and reel,
So all I ask is a large ship that rides on an even keel,
And a mild breeze and a broad deck with a slight list to leeward,
And a clean chair in a snug nook and a nice, kind steward.

I must go down to the seas again, the sport of wind and tide,
As the gray wave and the green wave play leapfrog over the side.
And all I want is a glassy calm with a bone-dry scupper,
A good book and a warm rug and a light, plain supper.

I must go down to the seas again, though there I'm a total loss,
And can't say which is worst, the pitch, the plunge, the roll, the toss.   10
But all I ask is a safe retreat in a bar well tended,
And a soft berth and a smooth course till the long trip's ended.

vii. The Poem as Translation

It is indeed impossible to translate poetry, in the sense of finding a precise equivalent to poetical language. But it is none the less possible to be inspired to write fine native verse by the inspiration of fine foreign verse.

—G. K. Chesterton

. . . in true poetry it is, in strictness, impossible to express the meaning in any but its own words, or to change the words without changing the meaning. A translation of such poetry is not really the old meaning in a new dress; it is a new product, something like the poem, though, if one chooses to say so, more like it in the aspect of meaning than in the aspect of form.

—A. C. Bradley

[THE WYF OF BATHE]

GEOFFREY CHAUCER (1340?–1400)
(from The Prologue to *The Canterbury Tales*)

A good *Wyf* was ther of bisyde *Bathe;*
But she was som-del deef, and that was scathe.
Of clooth-making she hadde swiche an haunt,
She passed hem of Ypres and of Gaunt.
In al the parisshe wyf ne was ther noon
That to th' offring bifore hir sholde goon;
And if ther dide, certeyn, so wrooth was she,
That she was out of alle charitee.
Hir coverchiefs ful fyne were of ground;
I dorste swere they weyeden ten pound   10
That on a Sonday were upon hir heed.
Hir hosen weren of fyn scarlet reed,
Ful streite y-teyd, and shoos ful moiste and newe.
Bold was hir face, and fair, and reed of hewe.
She was a worthy womman al hir lyve,
Housbondes at chirche-dore she hadde fyve,
Withouten other companye in youthe—
But therof nedeth nat to speke as nouthe.
And thryes hadde she been at Jerusalem;
She hadde passed many a straunge streem;   20
At Rome she hadde been, and at Boloigne,
In Galice at Seint Jame, and at Coloigne.

She coude muche of wandring by the weye:
Gat-tothed was she, soothly for to seye.
Up-on an amblere esily she sat,
Y-wimpled wel, and on hir heed an hat
As brood as is a bokeler or a targe:
A foot-mantel aboute hir hipes large,
And on hir feet a paire of spores sharpe.
In felawschip wel coude she laughe and carpe.   30
Of remedyes of love she knew per-chaunce,
For she coude of that art the olde daunce.

[THE WIFE OF BATH]

GEOFFREY CHAUCER (1340?–1400)
(*translation by R. M. Lumiansky*)

There was a good *Wife* from near Bath, but she was somewhat deaf, which was a
shame. She had such skill in clothmaking that she surpassed the weavers of Ypres and
Ghent. In all her parish there was no woman who could go before her to the offertory;
and if someone did, the Wife of Bath was certainly so angry that she lost all charitable
feeling. Her kerchiefs were of fine texture; those she wore upon her head on Sunday
weighed, I swear, ten pounds. Her fine scarlet hose were carefully tied, and her shoes
were uncracked and new. Her face was bold and fair and red. All of her life she had
been an estimable woman: she had had five husbands, not to mention other company
in her youth—but of that we need not speak now. And three times she had been to
Jerusalem; she had crossed many a foreign river; she had been to Rome, to Bologna,
to St. James' shrine in Galicia, and to Cologne. About journeying through the country
she knew a great deal. To tell the truth she was gap-toothed. She sat her gentle horse
easily, and wore a fine headdress with a hat as broad as a buckler or a shield, a riding
skirt about her large hips, and a pair of sharp spurs on her heels. She knew how to
laugh and joke in company, and all the remedies of love, for her skill was great in
that old game.

[THE WIFE OF BATH]

GEOFFREY CHAUCER (1340?–1400)
(*translation by Theodore Morrison*)

A worthy woman there was from near the city
Of Bath, but somewhat deaf, and more's the pity.
For weaving she possessed so great a bent
She outdid the people of Ypres and of Ghent.
No other woman dreamed of such a thing
As to precede her at the offering,
Or if any did, she fell in such a wrath

She dried up all the charity in Bath.
She wore fine kerchiefs of old-fashioned air,
And on a Sunday morning, I could swear,   10
She had ten pounds of linen on her head.
Her stockings were of finest scarlet-red,
Laced tightly, and her shoes were soft and new.
Bold was her face, and fair, and red in hue.
She had been an excellent woman all her life.
Five men in turn had taken her to wife,
Omitting other youthful company—
But let that pass for now! Over the sea
She had traveled freely; many a distant stream
She crossed, and visited Jerusalem   20
Three times. She had been at Rome and at Boulogne,
At the shrine of Compostella, and at Cologne.
She had wandered by the way through many a scene.
Her teeth were set with little gaps between.
Easily on her ambling horse she sat.
She was well wimpled, and she wore a hat
As wide in circuit as a shield or targe.
A skirt swathed up her hips, and they were large.
Upon her feet she wore sharp-roweled spurs.
She was a good fellow; a ready tongue was hers.   30
All remedies of love she knew by name,
For she had all the tricks of that old game.

EIN FICHTENBAUM STEHT EINSAM

HEINRICH HEINE (1797–1856)

Ein Fichtenbaum steht einsam
Im Norden auf kahler Höh'.
Ihn schläfert; mit weisser Decke
Umhüllen ihn Eis und Schnee.

Er träumt von einer Palme,
Die fern im Morgenland
Einsam und schweigend trauert
Auf brennender Felsenwand.

A PINE TREE TOWERS LONELY

HEINRICH HEINE (1797–1856)
(translation by Aaron Kramer)

A pine tree towers lonely
In the north, on a barren height.
He's drowsy; ice and snowdrift
Quilt him in covers of white.

He dreams about a palm tree
That, far in the East alone,
Looks down in silent sorrow
From her cliff of blazing stone.

A PINE TREE STANDS SO LONELY

HEINRICH HEINE (1797–1856)
(translation by Louis Untermeyer)

A pine tree stands so lonely
  In the North where the high winds
    blow,
He sleeps; and the whitest blanket
  Wraps him in ice and snow.

He dreams—dreams of a palm-tree
  That far in an Orient land,
Languishes, lonely and drooping,
  Upon the burning sand.

THERE STANDS A LONELY FIR-TREE

HEINRICH HEINE (1797–1856)
(translation by Charles Godfrey Leland)

There stands a lonely fir-tree
  Far north on a naked height;
He slumbers—the ice and snowdrifts
  Enfold him in mantle white.

He is dreaming of a palm-tree
  That far in the Eastern land
Grieves lonely and uncomplaining
  On a waste of scorching sand.

DIE BOTSCHAFT

HEINRICH HEINE (1797–1856)

Mein Knecht! steh auf und sattle schnell
Und wirf dich auf dein Ross,
Und jage rasch durch Wald und Feld
Nach König Duncans Schloss.

Dort schleiche in den Stall, und wart,
Bis dich der Stallbub' schaut.
Den forsch' mir aus: ,,Sprich, welche ist
Von Duncans Töchtern Braut?''

Und spricht der Bub': ,,Die Braune ist's'',
So bring mir schnell die Mär'.
Doch spricht der Bub': ,,Die Blonde ist's'',
So eilt das nicht so sehr.

Dann geh zum Meister Seiler hin,
Und kauf mir einen Strick,
Und reite langsam, sprich kein Wort,
Und bring' mir den zurück.

10

THE MESSENGER

HEINRICH HEINE (1797–1856)
(translation by Charles Godfrey Leland)

Arise, my page-boy, saddle quick,
  Leap on thy courser bold;
Gallop amain o'er hill and plain
  To royal Duncan's hold.

Hie to the stables there and wait
  Till thee the groom has spied,
Then ask, "Of Duncan's daughters which,
  I prithee, is the bride?"

If the knave says, "The dark-eyed maid,"
  Spur back and bring the news.   10
If the knave says, "The blue-eyed maid,"
  Then lesser speed may'st use.

Then to the nearest rope-walk go,
  And buy me there a cord;
And slowly ride and bring it me,
  But never speak a word.

THE MESSAGE

HEINRICH HEINE (1797–1856)
(translation by Louis Untermeyer)

My page! arise and quickly mount
  The horse of swiftest stride;
And breathlessly, through wood and field,
  To Duncan's palace ride.

Wait softly in the stable there
  Until you are espied;
Then ask, "Which one of Duncan's girls
  Is going to be a bride?"

And if they say "The dark-haired one"
  Then rush home like the blast.   10
But if they say "The light-haired one"
  You need not ride so fast.

But in the village buy a rope,
  A rope with toughened strands.
Then ride back slowly, speak no word,
  And place it in my hands.

THE MESSAGE

BY HEINRICH HEINE (1797–1856)
(translation by Kate Freiligrath Kroeker)

Up, boy! arise, and saddle quick,
And mount your swiftest steed,
And to King Duncan's castle ride
O'er bush and brake with speed.

There slip into the stable soft,
Till one shall see you hide,
Then ask him: Which of Duncan's girls
Is she that is a bride?

And if he says, The dark-haired one,
  Then give your mare the spur;   10
But if he say, The fair-haired one,
  You need not hurry here.

You only need, if that's the case,
  Buy me a hempen cord,
Ride slowly back and give it me,
  But never speak a word.

CHANSON DE LA PLUS HAUTE TOUR

ARTHUR RIMBAUD (1854–1891)

Qu'il vienne, qui'il vienne,
Le temps dont on s'éprenne.

J'ai tant fait patience
Qu'à jamais j'oublie.
Craintes et souffrances
Aux cieux sont parties.
Et la soif malsaine
Obscurcit mes veines.

Qu'il vienne, qu'il vienne,

Le temps dont on s'éprenne.   10

Telle la prairie
A l'oubli livrée,
Grandie et fleurie
D'encens et d'ivraies,
Au bourdon farouche
De très sales mouches.

Qu'il vienne, qu'il vienne,
Le temps dont on s'éprenne.

SONG OF THE HIGHEST TOWER

ARTHUR RIMBAUD (1854–1891)
(translation by Louise Varèse)

O may it come, the time of love,
The time we'd be enamoured of.

I've been patient too long,
My memory is dead,
All fears and all wrongs
To the heavens have fled.
While all my veins burst
With a sickly thirst.

O may it come, the time of love,

The time we'd be enamoured of.   10

Like the meadow that is dreaming
Forgetful of cares,
Flourishing and flowering
With incense and tares,
Where fierce buzzings rise
Of the very dirty flies.

O may it come, the time of love,
The time we'd be enamoured of.

SONG OF THE TOPMOST TOWER

ARTHUR RIMBAUD (1854–1891)
(translation by Edgell Rickword)

May they come, may they come,
The days which enchant us.

I have been so long resigned
That I forgot it all.
Fears and sufferings
To the skies are gone,
And the unclean thirst
Darkens my veins.

May they come may they come,

The days which enchant us.   10

Like the meadows
Left to ruin,
Spreading and overgrown
With flowers and weeds,
In the angry humming
Of filthy flies.

May they come, may they come
The days which enchant us.

SONG FROM THE HIGHEST TOWER

ARTHUR RIMBAUD (1854–1891)
(*translation by Maxwell Singer*)

May it come nigher and nigher,
The day we so greatly desire.

I have borne so much
That my mind from it flies.
My fears and suffering
Have fled to the skies,
And an unhealthy thirst
Clogs my veins till they burst.

May it come nigher and nigher,

The day we so greatly desire.   10

Like a meadow
Completely forgotten,
With wildings and weeds
Grown over and rotten,
To the droning replies
Of the filthiest flies.

May it come nigher and nigher,
The day we so greatly desire.

CHANSON D'AUTOMNE

PAUL VERLAINE (1844–1896)

Les sanglots longs
Des violons
  De l'automne
Blessent mon coeur
D'un langueur
  Monotone.

Tout suffocant
Et blême, quand
  Sonne l'heure,

Je me souviens   10
Des jours anciens
  Et je pleure.

Et je m'en vais
Au vent mauvais
  Qui m'emporte
Deçà, delà,
Pareil à la
  Feuille morte.

CHANSON D'AUTOMNE

PAUL VERLAINE (1844–1896)
(*translation by Arthur Symons*)

When a sighing begins
In the violins
Of the autumn-song,
My heart is drowned
In the slow sound
Languorous and long.

Pale as with pain,
Breath fails me when
The hour tolls deep.

My thoughts recover   10
The days that are over,
And I weep.

And I go
Where the winds know,
Broken and brief,
To and fro,
As the winds blow
A dead leaf.

SONG OF AUTUMN

PAUL VERLAINE (1844–1896)

(translation by Roland Gant and Claude Archer)

The slow sobbing
Of the violins
  Of autumn
Wounds my heart
With a monotonous
  Languor.

Breathless
And pale, when
  The hour sounds,

I recall to mind   10
The days of old
  And I weep.

And I go
With the evil wind
  Which carries me
To and fro,
Just like
  A dead leaf.

HARMONIE DU SOIR

CHARLES BAUDELAIRE (1821–1867)

Voici venir les temps où vibrant sur sa tige
Chaque fleur s'évapore ainsi qu'un encensoir;
Les sons et les parfums tournent dans l'air du soir;
Valse mélancolique et langoureux vertige!

Chaque fleur s'évapore ainsi qu'un encensoir;
Le violon frémit comme un coeur qu'on afflige;
Valse mélancolique et langoureux vertige!
Le ciel est triste et beau comme un grand reposoir.

Le violon frémit comme un coeur qu'on afflige,
Un coeur tendre, qui hait le néant vaste et noir!   10
Le ciel est triste et beau comme un grand reposoir;
Le soleil s'est noyé dans son sang qui se fige.

Un coeur tendre qui hait le néant vaste et noir,
Du passé lumineux recueille tout vestige!
Le soleil s'est noyé dans son sang qui se fige . . .
Ton souvenir en moi luit comme un ostensoir!

HARMONIE DU SOIR

CHARLES BAUDELAIRE (1821–1867)
(translation by Lord Alfred Douglas)

Now is the hour when, swinging in the breeze,
Each flower, like a censer, sheds its sweet.

The air is full of scents and melodies,
O languorous waltz! O swoon of dancing feet!

Each flower, like a censer, sheds its sweet,
The violins are like sad souls that cry,
O languorous waltz! O swoon of dancing feet!
A shrine of Death and Beauty is the sky.

The violins are like sad souls that cry,
Poor souls that hate the vast black night of Death;   10
A shrine of Death and Beauty is the sky.
Drowned in red blood, the Sun gives up his breath.

This soul that hates the vast black night of Death
Takes all the luminous past back tenderly,
Drowned in red blood, the Sun gives up his breath.
Thine image like a monstrance shines in me.

EVENING HARMONY

CHARLES BAUDELAIRE (1821–1867)
(*translation by Dorothy Martin*)

Now comes the hour when, in the quivering light,
Each flower to heaven exhales, a censer fair;
Perfumes and sounds wheel in the evening air,
A mournful waltz, a languorous, whirling flight!

Each flower to heaven exhales, a censer fair;
The violin sobs, a soul in sorrowing plight,
A mournful waltz, a languorous, whirling flight!
The sky, sad, lovely tomb, knows not of care.

The violin sobs, a soul in sorrowing plight,
A heart too tender for the void's dark lair.   10
The sky, sad, lovely tomb, knows not of care;
The sun sinks, drowned in his own blood, from sight.

A heart too tender for the void's dark lair
Gathers each memory of all past delight.
The sun sinks, drowned in his own blood, from sight;
And in my soul you shine, a monstrance rare!

II

The Poem and the Creative Process

Any reaction to stimulus may be causally explained; but the creative act, which is the absolute antithesis of mere reaction, will for ever elude the human understanding.
—CARL GUSTAV JUNG

What is this borderland of dream and logic, of fantasy and reason, where the roots and tentacles of mind and personality float and drift into the sudden shaping of a flash resulting in a scheme, a form, a design, an invention, a machine, an image, a song, a symphony, a drama, a poem? There are those who believe they know—and those who hope they may yet know.
—CARL SANDBURG

A man may be born a poet, but he has to make himself an artist as well. He must master the instrument. . . . Without clarified construction and technical control, no poetical communication can be effective.
—SIEGFRIED SASSOON

What a poem means is as much what it means to others as what it means to the author; and indeed, in the course of time, a poet may become merely a reader in respect to his own works, forgetting his original meaning—or without forgetting, merely changing.
—T. S. ELIOT

i. The Origins of Poetry

WHAT IS A POET?

(From the Preface to *Lyrical Ballads*)

WILLIAM WORDSWORTH (1770–1850)

What is a Poet? . . . He is a man speaking to men: a man, it is true, endowed with more lively sensibility, more enthusiasm and tenderness, who has a greater knowledge of human nature, and a more comprehensive soul, than are supposed to be common among mankind; a man pleased with his own passions and volitions, and who rejoices more than other men in the spirit of life that is in him; delighting to contemplate similar volitions and passions as manifested in the goings-on of the Universe, and habitually impelled to create them where he does not find them. To these qualities he has added a disposition to be affected more than other men by absent things as if they were present; an ability of conjuring up in himself passions, which are indeed far from being the same as those produced by real events, yet (especially in those parts of the general sympathy which are pleasing and delightful) do more nearly resemble the passions produced by real events than anything which, from the motions of their own minds merely, other men are accustomed to feel in themselves;—whence, and from practice, he has acquired a greater readiness and power in expressing what he thinks and feels, and especially those thoughts and feelings which, by his own choice, or from the structure of his own mind, arise in him without immediate external excitement. . . .

The Poet writes under one restriction only, namely, that of the necessity of giving immediate pleasure to a human Being possessed of that information which may be expected from him, not as a lawyer, a physician, a mariner, an astronomer, or a natural philosopher, but as a Man. Except this one restriction, there is no object standing between the Poet and the image of things; between this, and the Biographer and Historian, there are a thousand.

Nor let this necessity of producing immediate pleasure be considered as a degradation of the Poet's art. It is far otherwise. It is an acknowledgment of the beauty of the universe, an acknowledgment the more sincere because not formal, but indirect; it is a task light and easy to him who looks at the world in the spirit of love: further, it is a homage paid to the native and naked dignity of man, to the grand elementary principle of pleasure, by which he knows, and feels, and lives, and moves.

POETRY AND THE POET

ELIZABETH DREW (1887–   )

. . . There are almost as many definitions of poetry as there are poets and critics who have written about it. The trouble with most of them is that they tend to be so abstract and nebulous. "Poetry is a spirit . . . it comes we know not whence." "Poetry is an intuition into the hidden nature of things." "Poetry is the breath and finer spirit of all knowledge." "Poetry is that which comprehends all science, and that to which all science must be referred." "Poetry is a continuous substance or energy." "Poetry is a glimpse of the divine." But whatever poetry is, it is not something else. It is not religion, or philosophy, or aesthetics, or science, or knowledge. It is poetry. And poetry, as "Q" said, is the stuff poets have written. This again, however, is the snake swallowing its own tail; it does not get us very much further. It again only reminds us that poetry is something unlike anything else, and something difficult to define. It is in the same class of definition as Emily Dickinson's—"If I read a book . . . and I feel physically as if the top of my head were taken off, I know that is poetry . . . is there any other way?"

Ultimately, perhaps, there *is* no other way of knowing. That is, poetry is a particular stimulus, which provides a certain kind of response in the right sort of reader. And the whole business of criticism is an effort to try and discover what the nature of that stimulus is, and what the nature of that response is and what makes the right sort of reader.

Abstractions do not help us: they cannot supply the answer to that immediate and practical question: what is the difference between

> Wake: the silver dusk returning
> Up the beach of darkness brims

and "Wake, the sun is rising"? Or between

> So when you or I are made
> A fable, song or fleeting shade;
> All love, all liking, all delight
> Lies drown'd with us in endless night.

and "When we die, our love will end"?

The verses and the bare statements have the same meaning; they are different ways of conveying the same sense or thought or idea. That is clear; and it is equally clear that that is all they do have in common. Beyond that, at once we feel that in the poetry we are in a different world from that of the prose statements. It is different in two ways. First, *its mode of experiencing the thought or idea or subject or material presented to it, is different*; and secondly, *the words in which the experience is communicated are different*. In those two facts lie the whole theory and practice of poetry.

The raw material of poetry is human experience: all poetry is made from that. Not only from rare and subtle and mysterious and spiritual and abstract and esoteric experiences, but from all and every form of human experience. As Wordsworth says: "it is the honorable characteristic of poetry that its materials are to be found in every subject which can interest the human mind." Poetry is made from birth and death, from childhood, youth, and old age; from love, jealousy, ambition, faith, cruelty, kindliness, rage, loyalty, laughter; from the solid commonplaces on which all living is based, and the most subtle and recondite mood and movement of the individual personality; from the ecstasy of the mystic and the rape of the lock; from the fall of man, and an idiot boy; from a rainbow and a rabbit; from *la belle dame sans merci* and the servant girl coming downstairs in the morning.

But the poet apprehends and interprets this general experience in ways which belong to him alone.

2.

On a certain October day in the year 1816, Charles Cowden Clarke told his young friend John Keats that he had been lent a copy of Chapman's translation of Homer, and he asked Keats to come and explore it with him that evening. Keats went, and the two friends read on through the night till dawn, not beginning at the beginning and working through the epics, but picking out what Cowden Clarke calls "the famousest passages," or "looking into" it, as Keats himself expressed it. Then the young medical student walked back to his own home in another part of London as the day was breaking. When Cowden Clarke came down to a late breakfast next morning at 10 o'clock he found on the table an envelope in Keats's handwriting. Inside was a sheet of paper containing a sonnet:

> Much have I travell'd in the realms of gold,
> And many goodly states and kingdoms seen;
> Round many western islands have I been
> Which bards in fealty to Apollo hold.
> Oft of one wide expanse had I been told
> That deep-brow'd Homer ruled as his demesne:
> Yet could I never judge what men might mean
> Till I heard Chapman speak out loud and bold:
> Then felt I like some watcher of the skies
> When a new planet swims into his ken;
> Or like stout Cortez, when with wond'ring eyes
> He stared at the Pacific—and all his men
> Look'd at each other with a wild surmise—
> Silent, upon a peak in Darien.

These two young men had had a common experience the night before. They had read a book together. Cowden Clarke has left a description of that evening in prose. Keats has left a poem. We should surely be able to discover something of what is vital to the nature of poetry and the poet by a contrast of the two methods of communication and an examination of the particular character of each.

3.

They have one great point of similarity. With both, the experience has become *words.* It is no longer the actual reading of a book which Charles Cowden Clarke shared with John Keats. Both the prose and the poetry are collections of words, and everything which we as readers receive from reading them, reaches us through the words the writers have chosen.

Cowden Clarke tells us the facts of the matter as they appeared to him.

> "A beautiful copy of the folio edition of Chapman's translation of Homer had been lent me. It was the property of Mr. Alsager, the gentleman who for years had contributed no small share of celebrity to the great reputation of the *Times* newspaper by the masterly manner in which he conducted the money-market department of that journal. . . .
>
> 'Well, then, we were put in possession of the Homer of Chapman, and to work we went, turning to some of the "famousest" passages, as we had scrappily known them in Pope's version. . . ."

Then follows an account of some of the passages,* and of the arrival of the sonnet next morning.

Now let us read the sonnet again and see how the matter appeared to Keats. Again we are in that world we have already visited. What *is* its peculiar quality? We have said that within it, we are always conscious of two things. First, that the way in which the poet has seen and felt the experience is different from that in which the ordinary man sees and feels experience. It is different, first of all, because instead of being a diffused and general impression of loosely related objects and events, it is a synthesis, in which whatever is significant and eternal in the experience is present, and from which whatever is insignificant and temporal has been excluded. The actual scene and the actual sequence of events in it have been excluded, but the heart and core of its emotional reality to the poet has been seized upon by some mysterious power, revealed in all its riches, and unified into a splendid isolation. And this revelation is made in a particular way. It is not achieved by analysis or argument or statement or description. It is created directly by the poetic vision, and the essence of the poetic vision is that it embodies itself always in the form of symbols. In one complete act of apprehension, Keats embodies the heart and core of that experience with Cowden Clarke into the central symbol of a voyage of discovery. He at once challenges our attention and raises the pitch of the experience which we are to share to a different level, by the first line:

Much have I travell'd in the realms of gold.

At once we are far away from Mr. Alsager and his masterly conduct of the money-market department in the London *Times*: from Cowden Clarke, too, and the very slightly patronizing way in which he pointed out the finest passages to his young friend. Reading Homer is no longer concerned with a certain copy of the book in a particular time and place. It is part of the adventures of the poet's personality in the whole world of books.

At once, too, we become conscious of the second great difference between the world of poetry and the world of statement. *The words are different.* Just as the poet has seen and felt the experience in a special way, so he uses his medium of interpreting and communicating the experience in a special way. Words are no longer merely the means of *conveying* facts. They are concerned to *suggest the quality* of those facts. They are no longer *practical*: they are *evocative*. Here they are required to communicate the quality which the poet discerns in his beloved world of books and reading, and all the richness, the rareness, the colour, the sovereign power which dwell for him in the atmosphere of that world, he incarnates in the two words he uses to suggest it, *the realms of gold*. All its associations with romance, with poetry, with the medieval flavour he loved, with Greek myth, and Apollo, the Greek God of song and sunrise,

---

* Two of the passages may be found on pp. 821–823. [*Editors' note*]

he packed into his description of the islands in those golden realms, *which bards in fealty to Apollo hold.*

And now the central symbol of the poet's voyage of discovery among books is en-larged and enriched by the creation of new images and a swelling and intensification of the emotion. The atmosphere of excited exploration is changed to that of triumphant achievement. Words loaded with atmosphere and colour give place to those clear direct monosyllables, *I heard Chapman speak out loud and bold.* And finally we are swept forward to see and feel those two marvellous symbols of the living spirit of discovery, which form the sestet of the sonnet. As we read of Cortez, too, the unity of the imagery throughout is strengthened by the echo of the "realms of gold" in the first line. For the realms of gold, besides being Keats's creation of a name for the world of reading, is the literal translation of "el dorado," the mythical land the conquistadors set out to find, and the greatest of the conquistadors was Cortez.[1]

By that act of apprehension, indeed, which the poetic vision of Keats achieved from all the materials which that experience presented to it, and by the language which gave it form, is created in fourteen lines of verse, a new world. A world in which the original experience he shared with Cowden Clarke—the actual experience of spending a night in reading a book, no longer exists. Instead of a scene in which the actors were Charles Cowden Clarke and John Keats and Mr. Alsager's copy of Chapman's Homer, there is a world, contained within the confines of an abstract shape of fourteen lines, in which romance and Eldorado and Greece, Homer and Apollo, Chapman and Cortez and the poet himself, Darien and the empyrean, all harmonize into one exquisite unity of being.

4.

How poetry comes to the poet is a mystery. The idea of the Muse is an obvious symbol of the fact which all creators have felt to be true—that inspiration is a reality. Something of what Mozart describes in one of his letters happens to every artist.

> "When I am feeling well and in good humour . . . thoughts come in swarms and with marvellous ease. . . . Once I catch my air, another comes soon to join the first, according to the requirements of the whole composition. . . . Then my mind kindles—the work grows—I keep hearing it and bring it out more and more clearly, and the composition ends by being completely executed in my mind, however long it may be."

Something, which is usually called the imagination, comes to the poet which not only sharpens and intensifies all the faculties he shares in common with his fellow men, but creates a new function of his mind which they do not possess. It is a function which enables the poet to release his imprisoned and chafing vitality in the particular form it needs to take, that is, in the poetic act. Keats describes himself, when the creative passion is upon him, as living under an everlasting restraint, never relieved except when he was composing. Wordsworth calls it a passion and a power, by which we "see into the life of things." This must be what Keats means, too, when he declares that a poet is the most unpoetical thing in existence because he has no identity, he is continually filling some other body, and thus partaking of experience in unfamiliar modes. When he is possessed by the need to write poetry, the poet only exists with

[1] See *Studies in Keats.* J. Middleton Murry.

great difficulty and distress in the actual and factual world about him. His mind is not functioning in that world: he is a stranger there. For the passion and the power generate in him "unknown modes of being." And it is this sense of unknown modes of being, this faculty for revealing things to the mind in relationships which are hidden in normal experience, which is the innermost secret of poetic genius. The poet, as Wordsworth again says, rejoices more than other men in the spirit of life which is in him, but besides the passion of perception which that joy brings him, is that particular power of synthesizing perceptions which other men lack: that power of conceiving experiences in the terms of something else; of seizing and communicating analogies; of creating symbol, image, metaphor; and of associating in this way different levels and kinds of experience (such as exploring and Homer and astronomy and reading books), so that their conjunction, by some mysterious intellectual and emotional chemistry, creates a new quality of experience, a new "mode of being" which was not there before, and which is unlike anything else.

The working of this power is a mystery. It remains a mystery even when its results have been minutely examined. For instance, it so happens that we have the actual clues to all the associations on which the creative passion of Keats seized, and on which it worked when he was composing the famous sonnet. We can guess why it was that Homer and astronomy and Cortez and Darien thronged his mind together,[2] and it is possible to work out in a small way the same process which has already been recreated so brilliantly by J. Livingston Lowes in regard to *The Ancient Mariner* and *Kubla Khan*.

As Keats walked home through the quiet streets, with the stars fading out into the dawn, he may well have had his imagination kindled to an image of "a watcher of the skies," but this may have been helped by a particular memory of the past. A few years before, when Keats had left school, he had won a prize. It was an introduction to astronomy by a man called Bonnycastle. One of the chapters is called "Of the new Planets and other discoveries." The author was fond of lightening his discourses with passages from the poets, and one of these passages was definitely one of those "famousest passages" from Homer (in Pope's translation) which Cowden Clarke mentions—the shipwreck of Ulysses in the fifth book. He said Keats gave one of his "delighted stares" as they read the description together—evidently remembering the stilted version of it quoted by Bonnycastle. And so we get the image of the poet as he discovers the "demesne" of Homer:

> like some watcher of the skies
> When a new planet swims into his ken.

We can trace, too, something of the working of Keats's mind as it found the famous simile of Cortez and Darien. It is a recollection from a passage in Robertson's *History of America*. The associations of that evening must have made Keats re-live in memory much of his school-days at Enfield. The headmaster of the school was Cowden Clarke's father; the Bonnycastle was a school prize, Keats and Cowden Clarke had made friends over poetry, and we have his direct testimony that Robertson's *History* was one of Keats's favorite books in the school library. It was a small jump, as his mind busied itself with ideas of books and discoveries, from Bonnycastle and astronomy, to Robertson and Darien. In that book he had read

[2] See *Essays and Studies of the English Association*—vol. XVI, for a much fuller account of this.

"The isthmus of Darien is not above sixty miles in breadth, but this neck of land . . . is stretched by a chain of lofty mountains . . . which render it a barrier of solidity sufficient to resist the impulses of two opposite oceans. . . .

"At length the Indians assured them, that from the top of the next mountain they should discover the ocean which was the object of their wishes. When, with infinite toil, they had climbed up the greater part of the steep ascent, Balboa commanded his men to halt, and advanced alone to the summit, that he might be the first who should enjoy a spectacle which he had so long desired. As soon as he beheld the South Sea stretching in endless prospect below him, he fell on his knees, and lifting up his hands to Heaven, returned thanks to God. . . . His followers, observing his transports of joy, rushed forward to join in his wonder, exultation and gratitude."

Why Keats confused Cortez and Balboa we do not know, but we can make a guess. It may have been that immediately before the passage in Robertson of Balboa discovering the Pacific, is a description of a Spanish expedition in which Cortez figures: or it may have been that, as we know from Leigh Hunt, Keats had seen the portrait of Cortez by Titian, and had been greatly impressed by the eyes—the "eagle eyes" which appeared in the later version of the poem.

The only other change Keats made was to alter the line *"Yet could I never judge what men could mean"* to *"Yet did I never breathe its pure serene,"* an echo from Dante which definitely links with the idea of the empyrean and the watcher of the skies.

The picture of Cortez' men owed something to *The Rape of Lucrece*:

> Enchanted Tarquin answers with surmise
> In silent wonder of still gazing eyes.

5.

Here we can catch a glimpse of the poetic process; of the unifying harmonizing power over material which the poet possesses. A poem is a synthesis of memoried impressions, which the average liver of life leaves in their original chaotic state. "Life is like a blind and limitless expanse of sky, for ever dividing into tiny drops of circumstance that rain down, thick and fast, a ceaseless, meaningless drip. Art is like the dauntless plastic force that builds up stubborn amorphous substance cell by cell into the frail geometry of a shell." Into the deep well of our subconscious memory go all the impressions and reminiscences and facts which fall upon our minds and senses and emotions. And there in general they lie, a huddled sleeping company; or they come out straggling and inchoate, the mere tricks of disconnected association. But the poet, with the fire of his imagination, remints these scraps of memorized litter into new-welded living form, pouring them into a fresh mould, and stamping them with the new bright impress of his own vitality. Poetry and life differ, just as coal and diamonds differ, though the basis of both is exactly the same substance.

The poet remains a man as other men. He is not a mixture of a prophet, a seer, a priest and a medicine man. He may be any manner of man: as moral as Tennyson, as pagan as Keats; as classic as Housman, as romantic as Swinburne; as optimistic as Browning, as pessimistic as Hardy; as mystic as Blake, as practical as Pope; as subtle as de la Mare, as simple as Herrick. The experience he uses as a starting point may be anything: a story, a mood, a moment, an incident, a character, a comment. It may be high or low, grave or gay, steady or fleeting. But whatever it is, it will begin by stirring within him that ferment of excitement, that mysterious working of the glands or the nerve centres or whatever it is which we call inspiration. The sense of inspiration itself is incommunicable. That passion of "burning with mental bliss" as a modern poet has called it, cannot be transferred, any more than a love poem can communicate the passion of love. The communicable part of the experience, the part with which criticism can concern itself, is that which can be, and is, embodied in words. *Poetry is a special use of words.*

6.

Obviously, poetry is impossible without words. A dumb poet, a mute inglorious Milton, is a contradiction in terms. We may say loosely that a sunset or a pretty woman is a perfect poem, but we mean nothing by that except that we consider the sunset or the woman a beautiful thing. We may say of someone that he or she has the mind of a poet, but all we mean is that he or she is sensitive or subtle above the average. Poetry is the communication of experience through the medium of language used in a certain way. We have already said that the poet's use of language is evocative, not practical. The poet does not find words to project the "plain sense" of the experience he wishes to express. He finds words to express the whole infinitely complicated business of its happening *to him*: the emotions it aroused, the sensations which accompanied it, the atmosphere it created, the memories it awakened. And that not vaguely, but the exact tone and shade and composition of all these things. This evocative, suggestive value of words is an essential of poetry, but it is a quality which poetry shares with a great deal of prose. When we read in Dorothy Wordsworth's journal * that the daffodils "tossed and reeled and danced and seemed as if they verily laughed in the wind," there is no distinction between the way in which she uses language to express her experience, and the way her brother uses it to express the same experience as he saw and felt it.

> I wandered lonely as a cloud
> That floats on high o'er vales and hills,
> When all at once I saw a crowd,
> A host, of golden daffodils;
> Beside the lake, beneath the trees,
> Fluttering and dancing in the breeze.

* Dorothy Wordsworth, in her journal for April 15, 1802, records the episode as follows:

"It was a threatening, misty morning, but mild. . . . The wind was furious, and we thought we must have returned. We first rested in the large boat-house, then under a furze bush opposite Mr. Clarkson's. Saw the plough going in the field. The wind seized our breath. The Lake was rough. There was a boat by itself floating in the middle of the bay below Water Millock. . . . When we were in the woods beyond Gowbarrow Park we saw a few daffodils close to the water-side. We fancied that the lake had floated the seeds ashore, and that the little colony had so sprung up. But as we went along there were more and yet more; and at last, under the boughs of the trees, we saw that there was a long belt of them along the shore, about the breadth of a country turnpike road. I never saw daffodils so beautiful. They grew among the mossy stones about and about them; some rested their heads upon these stones as on a pillow for weariness; and the rest tossed and reeled and danced, and seemed as if they verily laughed with the wind, that blew upon them over the lake; they looked so gay, ever glancing, ever changing. This wind blew directly over the lake to them. There was here and there a little knot, and a few stragglers a few yards higher up; but they were so few as not to disturb the simplicity, unity, and life of that one busy highway. . . ." [Quoted by the editors from *The Journals of Dorothy Wordsworth*, ed. by E. de Selincourt (London: Macmillan Co. 1941), I. 131-132.]

> Continuous as the stars that shine
> And twinkle on the milky way,
> They stretched in never-ending line
> Along the margin of a bay: 10
> Ten thousand saw I at a glance,
> Tossing their heads in sprightly dance.
>
> The waves beside them danced; but they
> Out-did the sparkling waves in glee:
> A poet could not but be gay,
> In such a jocund company:
> I gazed—and gazed—but little thought
> What wealth the show to me had brought:
>
> For oft, when on my couch I lie
> In vacant or in pensive mood,   20
> They flash upon that inward eye
> Which is the bliss of solitude;
> And then my heart with pleasure fills,
> And dances with the daffodils.

In the same way a great deal of the prose of Virginia Woolf is the prose of a poet. That is, the way she apprehends experience, both in its intensity and its subtlety, and in the power she has of revealing "unknown modes of being" through her creation and association of images, is the way of a poet. Her "thought" is "poetic thought": but her medium of expression is prose. There is one essential difference in the use of language which is present in Keats's sonnet and in Wordsworth's poem, which is absent from Dorothy Wordsworth and Virginia Woolf. It is the element of *sustained, unified organic rhythm*. This sounds an ugly and clumsy description, perhaps, but it is not possible to simplify it. Prose has its rhythms no less than verse, so to say that poetry is rhythmical language is not enough. It is not enough to say that poetry possesses a regular rhythm, since much free verse does not possess it, and is none the less poetry for that. It is a rhythm which only arises when experience has been conceived in a certain way, at a certain pitch and with a certain tension. Poetry is a use of words which creates a living organism, which builds up a unique harmony of being in which this rhythm—both in its larger sense of the general design, movement or flow of the poetic thought, and in its more limited sense of the sound pattern—is always an essential and intrinsic part.

[EDITORS' NOTE]

From CHAPMAN'S *HOMER*

Of the several passages cited by Clarke as having delighted Keats and himself that night, two will perhaps suffice here. The first, called by Clarke "the prodigious description of Neptune's passage to the Achive ships," shows Neptune deciding to interfere in a naval battle on behalf of the Greeks:

> [Neptune] sat aloft on th' utmost top of shady Samothrace,
> And view'd the fight. His chosen seat stood in so brave a place,
> That Priam's city, the Achive ships, all Ida, did appear
> To his full view; who from the sea was therefore seated there.

He took such ruth to see the Greeks by Troy sustain such ill,
And, mightily incens'd with Jove, stoop'd straight from that steep hill,
That shook as he flew off, so hard his parting press'd the height.
The woods, and all the great hills near, trembled beneath the weight
Of his immortal moving feet. Three steps he only took,
Before he far-off Ægas reach'd, but, with the fourth, it shook   10
With his dread entry. In the depth of those seas he did hold
His bright and glorious palace, built of never-rusting gold;
And there arriv'd, he put in coach his brazen-footed steeds,
All golden-maned, and pac'd with wings; and all in golden weeds
He cloth'd himself. The golden scourge, most elegantly done,
He took, and mounted to his seat; and then the God begun
To drive his chariot through the waves. From whirlpits ev'ry way
The whales exulted under him, and knew their king; the sea
For joy did open; and, his horse so swift and lightly flew,
The under axletree of brass no drop of water drew;   20
And thus these deathless coursers brought their king to th' Achive ships.

[Chapman's *Iliad,* Bk. XIII, ll.11-31. Edited by
Richard Hooper (London, 1865).]

Of the second passage Clarke writes: "One scene I could not fail to introduce him
to—the shipwreck of Ulysses, . . . where Ulysses is cast up on the shores of Phæacia,
and I had the reward of one of his delightful stares. . . ." Ulysses, having lost his
ship in a tempest, has been struggling in the water for two days when he at last catches
sight of "an unhop'd for shore" but one which presents such difficulties that he is
almost in despair:

A curs'd surge 'gainst a cutting rock impell'd
His naked body, which it gash'd and tore,
And had his bones broke, if but one sea more
Had cast him on it. But She prompted him,
That never fail'd, and bade him no more swim
Still off and on, but boldly force the shore,
And hug the rock that him so rudely tore;
Which he with both hands sigh'd and clasp'd, till past
The billow's rage was; when 'scap'd, back so fast
The rock repuls'd it, that it reft his hold,
Sucking him from it, and far back he rolled.
And as the polypus that (forc'd from home
Amidst the soft seas, and near rough land come
For shelter 'gainst the storms that beat on her
At open sea, as she abroad doth err)
A deal of gravel, and sharp little stones,
Needfully gathers in her hollow bones,
So he forc'd hither by the sharper ill,
Shunning the smoother, where he best hop'd, still
The worst succeeded; for the cruel friend,   20
To which he cling'd for succour, off did rend
From his broad hands the soaken flesh so sore,
That off he fell .   .

Finally he succeeds in getting ashore at the mouth of a stream:

> Then forth he came, his knees falt'ring, both
> His strong hands hanging down, and all with froth
> His cheeks and nostrils flowing, voice and breath
> Spent to all use, and down he sunk to death.
> The sea had soak'd his heart through; all his veins
> His toils had rack'd t' a labouring woman's pains.
> Dead weary was he. . . .

> [Chapman's *Odyssey*, Bk. V, ll. 561-583; 608-614. Edited
> by Richard Hooper (London, 1874).]

From POPE'S *HOMER*

The account of Ulysses' struggles as given in Alexander Pope's version, which was
the one that Keats had previously known, runs as follows:

> . . . a monstrous wave upbore
> The chief, and dash'd him on the craggy shore:
> Torn was his skin, nor had the ribs been whole,
> But instant Pallas enter'd in his soul.
> Close to the cliff with both his hands he clung,
> And stuck adherent, and suspended hung;
> Till the huge surf roll'd off: then, backward sweep
> The refluent tides, and plunge him in the deep.
> As when the polypus, from forth his cave
> Torn with full force, reluctant beats the wave,   1C
> His ragged claws are stuck with stones and sands;
> So the rough rock had shagg'd Ulysses' hands. . . .

> That moment, fainting as he touch'd the shore,
> He dropp'd his sinewy arms: his knees no more
> Perform'd their office, or his weight upheld:
> His swoln heart heaved: his bloated body swell'd:
> From mouth and nose the briny torrent ran;
> And lost in lassitude lay all the man,
> Deprived of voice, of motion, and of breath;
> The soul scarce waking in the arms of death. . . .   20

> [Pope's *Odyssey*, Home Library ed. (A. L. Burt, n.d.).]

From THE FIGURE A POEM MAKES

ROBERT FROST (1874–1963)

. . . It should be of the pleasure of a poem itself to tell how it can. The figure a
poem makes. It begins in delight and ends in wisdom. The figure is the same as for
love. No one can really hold that the ecstasy should be static and stand still in one
place. It begins in delight, it inclines to the impulse, it assumes direction with the first
line laid down, it runs a course of lucky events, and ends in a clarification of life—not

necessarily a great clarification, such as sects and cults are founded on, but in a momentary stay against confusion. It has denouement. It has an outcome that though unforeseen was predestined from the first image of the original mood—and indeed from the very mood. It is but a trick poem and no poem at all if the best of it was thought of first and saved for the last. It finds its own name as it goes and discovers the best waiting for it in some final phrase at once wise and sad—the happy-sad blend of the drinking song.

No tears in the writer, no tears in the reader. No surprise for the writer, no surprise for the reader. For me the initial delight is in the surprise of remembering something I didn't know I knew. I am in a place, a situation, as if I had materialized from cloud or risen out of the ground. There is a glad recognition of the long lost and the rest follows. Step by step the wonder of unexpected supply keeps growing. The impressions most useful to my purpose seem always those I was unaware of and so made no note of at the time when taken, and the conclusion is come to that like giants we are always hurling experience ahead of us to pave the future with against the day when we may want to strike a line of purpose across it for somewhere. The line will have the more charm for not being mechanically straight. We enjoy the straight crookedness of a good walking stick. . . .

Scholars and artists thrown together are often annoyed at the puzzle of where they differ. Both work from knowledge; but I suspect they differ most importantly in the way their knowledge is come by. Scholars get theirs with conscientious thoroughness along projected lines of logic; poets theirs cavalierly and as it happens in and out of books. They stick to nothing deliberately, but let what will stick to them like burrs where they walk in the fields. No acquirement is on assignment, or even self-assignment. Knowledge of the second kind is much more available in the wild free ways of wit and art. A schoolboy may be defined as one who can tell you what he knows in the order in which he learned it. The artist must value himself as he snatches a thing from some previous order in time and space into a new order with not so much as a ligature clinging to it of the old place where it was organic. . . .

ROBERT FROST: A TIME TO LISTEN

REGINALD L. COOK (1903–   )

What Henry James said of Ivan Turgenev is certainly true of Robert Frost. "He was the richest, the most delightful, of talkers, and his face, his person, his temper, the thoroughness with which he had been equipped for human intercourse, make in the memory of his friends, an image which is completed, but not thrown into the shade, by his literary distinction." Frost belongs with the interesting talkers. . . .

One reason why he talks so well is because his big frame is perfectly relaxed. He possesses the harmonious physical and mental co-ordination of a natural athlete whose poise is the result of relaxation. As his body relaxes, his mind flexes. Inward restraint counterpoises outer enthusiasm and inner enthusiasm counterbalances outer restraint. . . .

. . . His voice, sauntering along at an unhurried clip, expresses an amiable and sensitive personality in an idiom that is more colloquial than urbane. One night we were in the kitchen of his farmhouse in South Shaftsbury, Vermont, and he read from the little blue-bound books in which he puts his new poems. It had been a day of drizzling rain, and mist still hovered in the bottom lands. He tilted his chair against the enamel sink, the fire untended, dying, and read "The Leaf-treader," "Depart-mental," "The Vindictives," and "The White-tailed Hornet." Outside a pheasant squawked several times, and it was in this setting that I heard the rise and fall of that tone-sensitive voice. It is one of the easiest voices to listen to I ever heard.

He is also one of the easiest persons with whom to talk that I have ever known. It is true, as a friend of mine says in idiom, "he'll stay there talking until the last dog is dead." But what he says is good listening. "I have an endless resourcefulness to change my ground," he says, and it is this endless resourcefulness which animates the talk. Now he is talking about glass shirts, soon it will be water witches or dowsers, and there will be no end to the surprise topics. Much of what he is saying deserves to be remembered. . . .

In the range of his talk what he has to say about the writing of poems is memo-rable. Poetry has been one of the really important things to him. He has given all he had to give to the writing of it. Once he described to me the time when he thought he had first caught what he was after. It was in the lines from "My Butterfly":

> The gray grass is scarce dappled with the snow;
> Its two banks have not shut upon the river.

And he described the feeling he had when he knew that he had come through in those lines. "It's a funny thing," he said with intense feeling in his voice, "like tears inside."

For twenty years I have listened to Frost and from these talks gathered a kind of *ars poetica*. When I asked him once if a poem originated in an intuitive impulse, he shrugged off the word "intuitive" as apparently esoteric. He did not approve of as-cribing mystifying terms to the writing of poems. When he has a good co-ordination of body, mind, and spirit—an optimum condition certainly—he feels what he describes as "a funny sort of command" over words; "a nice kind of summons." In these moods the poem gets started and develops from "ecstasy at some surprise in the mind." He gets a "clue" and is drawn on by what he calls "a gatherer."

Once he explained the genesis of the poem "Departmental." "How did you come to write it?" I inquired.

"You mean what it *rides* on?" And, without awaiting a reply, he continued: "A *queer* feeling or mood toward something, and then fulfils it." By *it* he means, of course, the mood toward something. While he was living at Key West in the winter of 1935, the sight of an ant and a moth on a table suggested the basic idea already latent in his mind, and being in a responsive mood he started his poem and went through with it. In his manuscript copy there were crossed-out lines and interline-ations; but he had carried it through to its "triumphal intention." The greatest satis-faction comes, he feels, when you can say: "Here is a poem that is a triumphal intention, that bore right through and dismissed itself." The "triumphal intention" is the source of his delight: it is the consummation of "the pure emergence [of the poem] from the logic of the thing." But "the pure emergence" is not necessarily in a straight line; it is more like following stepping-stones across a field in a kind of straight-crookedness. What is memorable in the writing is the "resolved perplexity." There is so much more suspense in perplexity than in preconceived ends. Can he fetch it off? Can he resolve it? "Aye, there's the leverage!"

In the making of form his organic method is diametrically the opposite of Poe's method as illustrated in "The Philosophy of Composition." * He considers the prepared

* See p. 855. [*Editors' note*]

and outlined piece of art suspect. "If it is thought out first and expressed last, I dismiss it," he says with finality. He does not write with the end in mind and then attempt to make things fit it. Instead, he proceeds, in Benjamin Franklin's words, "regularly from things known to things unknown, distinctly and clearly without confusion." After the poem finds its direction in the first line, it rides on its own impulse. "Like a piece of ice on a hot stove, the poem must ride on its own melting," he says. He does not try to wrench out the significance of the experience inherent in the poetic impulse; he tries only to release it. From its origin in the mood, which committed the poet, until the final line is set down, the poem unfolds organically, like a leaf from a bud.

He does not keep a notebook; he deprecates keeping one. The tendency for the writer with a notebook is to put down his thought finished or unfinished, and there it is. Frost depends upon memory and recall. The only freedom, as he says, is the freedom of his materials, and he realizes this freedom by apt recalls from past experience. And to make sure that he does not always turn backward, he welcomes enough of the new to freshen, not to stifle, his thought. If what attracts his attention has any real significance, he believes that it will stay in his mind, and by turning to it now and then he can develop it further. Part of the pleasure of lecturing or conversing or writing is to take up one of these unfinished thoughts and unfold it a little further. It provides the elements of surprise and freshness to the audience as much as to the poet. Apparently for him to write is to finish a thought and, in the main, he prefers to keep unfolding these thoughts rather than prematurely closing them. Some have been growing since he was a very young man.

He has counseled "build soil," and I think he follows his own line of thought. He has turned thought back and back again, until the tilth of him is "sweating-full" and "drips" poetry and wisdom. The poems he writes are really produced from observed data that may go ten or twenty or more years deep in his life. He tells how Wilfred Wilson Gibson, whom he had known in England, used to search every nook and cranny for poetic materials. This has not been the way he has worked. He has not set out deliberately to write about this or that; he has not "worked up" something to write about. His sharp eyes have picked up the things which his unhurried mind has absorbed at leisure. And he has been content to wait patiently for experience to settle. In consequence his poems have not been the product of superficial retinal glances. They have been the product of the longest meditation he could give them. He has written only under a compelling and controlled impulse. Until the composing mood came, he has been well satisfied to gloat "on things of this world."

One estimates the success of Frost's organic method by the tenacity with which he clings to the coattails of his inspiration. To insure a successful outcome, there must be no letting-go but a steady holding-on. It is a dauntless and an exhilarating method and has, among other advantages, the one of suspense or surprise. Intense is the suspense as the poet follows through to a dimly perceived but ultimate fulfilment of his expression. "The best of a poem," he says, "is when you first make it, the curve that it takes, the shape, the run, the flow, and then you can come back to it."

In form a poem is a limited number of sentences. These sentences lie in the poem like a little set of boxes in a Japanese puzzle-box. The limitation in the number of sentences gives the poem an advantage over any other literary form. He prefers the compactness of integrated sentences to the diffusiveness of Walt Whitman and the free-verse writers. He remarks satirically. "We used to say that the beauty of poetry was that it helped you to remember it. Free verse is better; you can remake it." And even more sharply he says, "Writing free verse is like playing tennis with the net down."

The source of the poetic sentences consists in seeing likenesses in life which are brought together through metaphor. "Stopping by Woods on a Snowy Evening," he says, is the product of several thoughts brought together. Different lines represent different time intervals in his life. The opposite of what he really believes about metaphor comes out in the following ironical blast at the contemporary obscurantists: "It has been lately found that it is harder to make a disconnection than a connection. The universe is not a continuity; it is a discontinuity. When you write a poem, your first object ought to be to put something into it that nobody can connect with anything else. When you have done that, you have elation. You used to get your fun out of the expression of a poem. The new-fashioned way is to enjoy the theory on which it is written."

These sentences that the poet uses are very important. An effective sentence must have the quality of memorableness, for it should be "a thing caught whole by the ear as spoken." To write a poem is to go "a-sentencing," and what he likes is "the singing of the sentences into the form." The following eleven lines from "Happiness Makes Up in Height for What It Lacks in Length" illustrates what he means by a poetic sentence.

> Oh, stormy stormy world,
> The days you were not swirled
> Around with mist and cloud,
> Or wrapped as in a shroud,
> And the sun's brilliant ball
> Was not in part or all
> Obscured from mortal view—
> Were days so very few
> I can but wonder whence
> I get the lasting sense
> Of so much warmth and light.

He thinks that the worst thing you can feel about a poem is that the sentences have been stretched or squeezed, and the worst is to squeeze them. He prefers the natural, cursive quality and the easy flow in Shakespeare to the "hot, tight, and cramped" sonnets of Rossetti. He tries to find the point of balance between sluggishness where, as he says, things "creak," and glibness, where one says more than should properly be said. The poet should never squeeze or cheat or do violence to the sentence. Nor should he alter it from what it should be by nature. The trouble with the poet, like the average human being, is that he indulges a tendency to be sweet to himself. For the poet the only hope is to divest himself of the last ego. He is too frequently the victim of self-deception and likes to believe that what he does is just right. Addressing these self-deceivers, Frost says, "You've got to get the self-love out of a poem and transform the love into a bleak honesty."

Each poetic sentence does double duty. It "conveys one meaning by word and syntax, another by the tone of voice it indicates. In irony, the tone indicated contradicts the words." Thus a poem is "saying one thing and meaning another—a form of honest duplicity." Most writers have just one tone—a tone of statement. Others try to vary this tone by lengthening or shortening the poetic sentences. Frost has, however, varied this tone by using dramatic images of speech. A dramatic image of speech is simply the precise tone of voice by which the meaning in the words is communicated. He adheres to the regular metrical patterns, but he varies the regularity by the "tones of voice." These voice-tones are to be taken not as dialect but as accent. Words he calls "a kind of notation and writing-down of the voice," and he associates the origin of style with the "observing ear." It is "picked up," he says, "by the observing ear." He defines it as "the texture of the tones of the speaking voice. One has it as a visitation."

A poem is not only a set or assortment of poetic sentences; it is also a set or assortment of dramatic images of speech. For example, the following stanza from Christina Rossetti's "Uphill" contains dramatic images of speech:

> Does the road wind uphill all the way?
> Yes, to the very end.
> Will the day's journey take the whole long day?
> From morn to night, my friend.

And the following quotation from his own "Blueberries" contains a very successful dramatic image in the last sentence.

> There had been some berries—but those were all gone.
> He didn't say where they had been. He went on:
> I'm sure—I'm sure—as polite as could be.

A real intensity inheres in the dramatic expression which would vary twenty end-stop lines. When the poet succeeds in varying the tones of the phrases, the poem grows intense with dramatic expression. The height of poetry consists in the dramatic give-and-take. Drama, he believes, is the capstone of poetry. In the lyric the dramatic give-and-take is within one's self and not between two people, as in the dramatic dialogue. Because of the voice-tones in his poems, he calls them "talk-songs." And he says of himself, "I am on one of the scales between two things—intoning and talking. I bear a little more toward talking."

To my inquiry as to how he tests a new poem, he replied that, first, he must have a right kind of feeling about it—a kind of feeling that what he writes is good. He must feel "in form" like a baseball pitcher. Second, he appraises the poem critically in order to make sure that he is not being too nice to himself. He sets the poem against all he knows—against the masters, technique, experience, to make sure that it is all right. The poem must be interesting, but the poet must be careful about being too interested in himself. "We are more interesting to ourselves than we have a right to be," he explained. The two characteristics in writing that he stresses are interest and accuracy, and the latter especially in the use of words. Two qualities of a good poem are honesty and integrity; its tests are brilliance (in the sense of originality) and validity (in the sense of strong as opposed to the invalid). The height of the great poet is his performance, and in great poetry there is something of the quality of ice forming where the crystals ramify in beautiful patterns. That is to say, the performance consists in blending beautiful lines and thoughts.

Robert Frost's talk, like his poetry, is the crystallization of what in himself he essentially is—a wise, neighborly man, rooted and seasoned in New England soil and climate, who possesses the two most cherishable gifts of a writer: creative thought and a personal idiom. It will be a long time before the determined tone of his voice fades from earshot when he says: "I like clarification of idea; I like to see the issues drawn," or "I stand against arrogance of the rights of the law," or when he says in a tone of quiet certainty, "What I like to see is nobility." Like Emerson, he speaks the thought that suggests itself and, like Thoreau, he listens behind him for his wit, and thus shows new proportions to the problem and sets the inquirer thinking anew. A rare, uninhibited talker is this poet, who, like Socrates, lightens a peripatetic talk with extempore flashes of responsive wit.

KUBLA KHAN: OR A VISION IN A DREAM

SAMUEL TAYLOR COLERIDGE (1772–1834)

In Xanadu did Kubla Khan
A stately pleasure-dome decree;
Where Alph, the sacred river, ran
Through caverns measureless to man
Down to a sunless sea.

So twice five miles of fertile ground
With walls and towers were girdled
   round:
And here were gardens bright with sinu-
   ous rills,
Where blossomed many an incense-bearing
   tree;
And here were forests ancient as the hills
Enfolding sunny spots of greenery.   11

But oh! that deep romantic chasm which
   slanted
Down the green hill athwart a cedarn
   cover!
A savage place! as holy and enchanted
As e'er beneath a waning moon was
   haunted
By woman wailing for her demon-lover!
And from this chasm, with ceaseless tur-
   moil seething,
As if this earth in fast thick pants were
   breathing   18
A mighty fountain momently was forced:
Amid whose swift half-intermittent burst
Huge fragments vaulted like rebounding
   hail,
Or chaffy grain beneath the thresher's
   flail:
And 'mid these dancing rocks at once and
   ever
It flung up momently the sacred river.

Five miles meandering with a mazy motion
Through wood and dale the sacred river
   ran,
Then reached the caverns measureless to
   man,
And sank in tumult to a lifeless ocean:
And 'mid this tumult Kubla heard from
   far
Ancestral voices prophesying war!   30

The shadow of the dome of pleasure
Floated midway on the waves;
Where was heard the mingled measure
From the fountain and the caves.
It was a miracle of rare device,
A sunny pleasure-dome with caves of ice!

A damsel with a dulcimer
In a vision once I saw:
It was an Abyssinian maid,
And on her dulcimer she played,   40
Singing of Mount Abora.
Could I revive with me
Her symphony and song,
To such a deep delight 'twould win me,
That with music loud and long,
I would build that dome in air,
That sunny dome! those caves of ice!
And all who heard should see them
   there,—
And all should cry, Beware! Beware!—
His flashing eyes, his floating hair!   50
Weave a circle round him thrice,
And close your eyes with holy dread,
For he on honey-dew hath fed,
And drunk the milk of Paradise.

A NOTE ON THE ORIGIN OF "KUBLA KHAN"

When "Kubla Khan" was first published in 1816, Coleridge prefaced it with an account of its origin:

> The following fragment is here published at the request of a poet of great and deserved celebrity [Lord Byron], and, as far as the Author's own opinions are concerned, rather as a psychological curiosity, than on the ground of any supposed *poetic* merits.
>
> In the summer of the year 1797, the author, then in ill health, had retired to a lonely farmhouse between Porlock and Linton, on the Exmoor confines of Somerset and Devonshire. In consequence of a slight indisposition, an anodyne had been prescribed, from the effects of which he fell asleep in his chair at the moment that he was reading the following sentence, or words of the same substance, in *Purchas's Pilgrimage:* "Here the Khan Kubla commanded a palace to be built, and a stately garden thereunto. And thus ten miles of fertile ground were inclosed within a wall." The author continued for about three hours in a profound sleep, at least of the external senses, during which time he has the most vivid confidence, that he could not have composed less than from two to three hundred lines; if that indeed can be called composition in which all the images rose up before him as *things,* with a parallel production of the correspondent expressions; without any sensation or consciousness of effort. On awakening he appeared to himself to have a distinct recollection of the whole, and taking his pen, ink, and paper, instantly and eagerly wrote down the lines that are here preserved. At this moment he was unfortunately called out by a person on business from Porlock, and detained by him above an hour, and on his return to his room, found, to his no small surprise and mortification, that though he still retained some vague and dim recollection of the general purport of the vision, yet, with the exception of some eight or ten scattered lines and images, all the rest had passed away like the images on the surface of a stream into which a stone has been cast, but, alas! without the after restoration of the latter.

In an undated manuscript Coleridge elsewhere described his state at the time of writing the poem as "a sort of Reverie, brought on by two grains of Opium, taken to check a dysentery."

John Livingston Lowes in *The Road to Xanadu* (Boston: Houghton Mifflin Co., 1927) has tracked down, in the wide range of Coleridge's reading, the origin of nearly every image and most of the phrases used in the poem—a most fascinating journey of discovery in the land of the poetic imagination. But neither the enchantment of the poem nor its meaning can be accounted for by the simple facts that Coleridge sometimes used opium and had always been an omnivorous reader.

COLERIDGE

WINFIELD TOWNLEY SCOTT (1910–   )

Old father, blessed ghost, mariner
Of my launching, fixer of the bloody sun
Round which my condemned and lifelong voyage
Swerves and follows—follows again, ignorant

What tropic oceans, what icy straits
Hide ahead, or winds across the magnet
Shudder deeper than engines, or tides
Trouble the ways before the invisible pole
Set under that unsetting sun;
old talker   10
Glittering through my childhood—voice and eyes
Compellent to hold, to send me out to
Find home by way of Vinland, India, by
Horns of undiscovered coasts that sounded
Music undeniable till the sea
Flamed with mirage that grayed all gold;
old
Detective of death in the boy's hand in the lane—
Resolve my life again. By this invocation
Invoke me—blessed ghost, old father.
20

AUTHOR'S NOTE ON THE ORIGIN OF "COLERIDGE"

"Coleridge" is altogether an autobiographical poem of an intensely personal kind. Whatever verses I may have written as a child, it was my first encounter—as a high school sophomore—with *The Rime of the Ancient Mariner* that caught me once and for all in the trap of poetry. There is the basis of the poem—"mariner of my launching." The actual occasion of the poem is as personal. It was written in July, 1951, just after I had resigned from newspaper work in which I had been employed for twenty years. In other words, I was at last free—so to speak—to tend that trap without interruptions save those I might choose or those my inabilities might impose. Therefore, the renewed invocation.

I think the details of the poem need no comment from me except the possibly obscure reference to the "detective of death in the boy's hand in the lane." The reference is to John Keats, to his impulsive grasping of Coleridge's hand one day in a lane near Highgate, and to Coleridge's remark to his friend Joseph Henry Green "There is death in that hand." See Amy Lowell: *John Keats,* Vol. II (New York: Houghton Mifflin, 1925), pp. 210-211.

—Letter to R. W. Stallman from W. T. Scott (26 June 1961).

"CHILDE ROLAND TO THE DARK TOWER CAME" *

ROBERT BROWNING (1812–1889)

My first thought was, he lied in every word,
   That hoary cripple, with malicious eye
   Askance to watch the working of his lie

* See Edgar's Song in *Lear.* [*Browning's note*]

On mine, and mouth scarce able to afford
Suppression of the glee, that pursed and scored
   Its edge, at one more victim gained thereby.

What else should he be set for, with his staff?
   What, save to waylay with his lies, ensnare
   All travelers who might find him posted there,
And ask the road? I guessed what skull-like laugh   10
Would break, what crutch 'gin write my epitaph
   For pastime in the dusty thoroughfare,

If at his counsel I should turn aside
   Into that ominous tract which, all agree,
   Hides the Dark Tower. Yet acquiescingly
I did turn as he pointed: neither pride
Nor hope rekindling at the end descried,
   So much as gladness that some end might be.

For, what with my whole world-wide wandering,
   What with my search drawn out through years, my hope   20
   Dwindled into a ghost not fit to cope
With that obstreperous joy success would bring,
I hardly tried now to rebuke the spring
   My heart made, finding failure in its scope.

As when a sick man very near to death
   Seems dead indeed, and feels begin and end
   The tears, and takes the farewell of each friend,
And hears one bid the other go, draw breath
Freelier outside, ("since all is o'er," he saith,
   "And the blow fallen no grieving can amend;")   30

While some discuss if near the other graves
   Be room enough for this, and when a day
   Suits best for carrying the corpse away,
With care about the banners, scarves and staves:
And still the man hears all, and only craves
   He may not shame such tender love and stay.

Thus, I had so long suffered in this quest,
   Heard failure prophesied so oft, been writ
   So many times among "The Band"—to wit,
The knights who to the Dark Tower's search addressed   40
Their steps—that just to fail as they, seemed best,
   And all the doubt was now—should I be fit?

So, quiet as despair, I turned from him,
   That hateful cripple, out of his highway
   Into the path he pointed. All the day

Had been a dreary one at best, and dim
Was settling to its close, yet shot one grim
   Red leer to see the plain catch its estray.

For mark! no sooner was I fairly found
   Pledged to the plain, after a pace or two,
   Than, pausing to throw backward a last view
O'er the safe road, 'twas gone; gray plain all round:
Nothing but plain to the horizon's bound.
   I might go on; nought else remained to do.

So, on I went. I think I never saw
   Such starved ignoble nature; nothing throve:
   For flowers—as well expect a cedar grove!
But cockle, spurge, according to their law
Might propagate their kind, with none to awe,
   You'd think; a burr had been a treasure trove.

No! penury, inertness and grimace,
   In some strange sort, were the land's portion. "See
   Or shut your eyes," said Nature peevishly,
"It nothing skills: I cannot help my case:
'Tis the Last Judgment's fire must cure this place,
   Calcine its clods and set my prisoners free."

If there pushed any ragged thistle-stalk
   Above its mates, the head was chopped; the bents
   Were jealous else. What made those holes and rents
In the dock's harsh swarth leaves, bruised as to baulk
All hope of greenness? 'tis a brute must walk
   Pashing their life out, with a brute's intents.

As for the grass, it grew as scant as hair
   In leprosy; thin dry blades pricked the mud
   Which underneath looked kneaded up with blood.
One stiff blind horse, his every bone a-stare,
Stood stupefied, however he came there:
   Thrust out past service from the devil's stud!

Alive? he might be dead for aught I know,
   With that red gaunt and colloped neck astrain,
   And shut eyes underneath the rusty mane;
Seldom went such grotesqueness with such woe;
I never saw a brute I hated so;
   He must be wicked to deserve such pain.

I shut my eyes and turned them on my heart.
   As a man calls for wine before he fights,
   I asked one draught of earlier, happier sights,

50

60

70

80

Ere fitly I could hope to play my part.
Think first, fight afterwards—the soldier's art:
   One taste of the old time sets all to rights.   90

Not it! I fancied Cuthbert's reddening face
   Beneath its garniture of curly gold,
   Dear fellow, till I almost felt him fold
An arm in mine to fix me to the place,
That way he used. Alas, one night's disgrace!
   Out went my heart's new fire and left it cold.

Giles then, the soul of honor—there he stands
   Frank as ten years ago when knighted first.
   What honest man should dare (he said) he durst.
Good—but the scene shifts—faugh! what hangman hands   100
Pin to his breast a parchment? His own bands
   Read it. Poor traitor, spit upon and curst!

Better this present than a past like that;
   Back therefore to my darkening path again!
   No sound, no sight as far as eye could strain.
Will the night send a howlet or a bat?
I asked: when something on the dismal flat
   Came to arrest my thoughts and change their train.

A sudden little river crossed my path
   As unexpected as a serpent comes.   110
   No sluggish tide congenial to the glooms;
This, as it frothed by, might have been a bath
For the fiend's glowing hoof—to see the wrath
   Of its black eddy bespate with flakes and spumes.

So petty yet so spiteful! All along,
   Low scrubby alders kneeled down over it;
   Drenched willows flung them headlong in a fit
Of mute despair, a suicidal throng:
The river which had done them all the wrong,
   Whate'er that was, rolled by, deterred no whit.   120

Which, while I forded,—good saints, how I feared
   To set my foot upon a dead man's cheek,
   Each step, or feel the spear I thrust to seek
For hollows, tangled in his hair or beard!
—It may have been a water-rat I speared,
   But, ugh! it sounded like a baby's shriek.

Glad was I when I reached the other bank.
   Now for a better country. Vain presage!
   Who were the strugglers, what war did they wage,

Whose savage trample thus could pad the dank   130
Soil to a plash? Toads in a poisoned tank,
    Or wild cats in a red-hot iron cage—

The fight must so have seemed in that fell cirque.
    What penned them there, with all the plain to choose?
    No foot-print leading to that horrid mews,
None out of it. Mad brewage set to work
Their brains, no doubt, like galley-slaves the Turk
    Pits for his pastime, Christians against Jews.

And more than that—a furlong on—why, there!
    What bad use was that engine for, that wheel,   140
    Or brake, not wheel—that harrow fit to reel
Men's bodies out like silk? with all the air
Of Tophet's tool, on earth left unaware,
    Or brought to sharpen its rusty teeth of steel.

Then came a bit of stubbed ground, once a wood,
    Next a marsh, it would seem, and now mere earth
    Desperate and done with; (so a fool finds mirth,
Makes a thing and then mars it, till his mood
Changes and off he goes!) within a rood—
    Bog, clay and rubble, sand and stark black dearth.   150

Now blotches rankling, colored gay and grim,
    Now patches where some leanness of the soil's
    Broke into moss or substances like boils;
Then came some palsied oak, a cleft in him
Like a distorted mouth that splits its rim
    Gaping at death, and dies while it recoils.

And just as far as ever from the end!
    Nought in the distance but the evening, nought
    To point my footstep further! At the thought,
A great black bird, Apollyon's bosom-friend,   160
Sailed past, nor beat his wide wing dragon-penned
    That brushed my cap—perchance the guide I sought.

For, looking up, aware I somehow grew,
    'Spite of the dusk, the plain had given place
    All round to mountains—with such name to grace
Mere ugly heights and heaps now stolen in view.
How thus they had surprised me,—solve it you!
    How to get from them was no clearer case.

Yet half I seemed to recognize some trick
    Of mischief happened to me, God knows when—   170
    In a bad dream perhaps. Here ended, then,

Progress this way. When, in the very nick
Of giving up, one time more, came a click
    As when a trap shuts—you're inside the den!

Burningly it came on me all at once,
    This was the place! those two hills on the right,
    Crouched like two bulls locked horn in horn in fight;
While to the left, a tall scalped mountain . . . Dunce,
Dotard, a-dozing at the very nonce,
    After a life spent training for the sight!   180

What in the midst lay but the Tower itself?
    The round squat turret, blind as the fool's heart,
    Built of brown stone, without a counterpart
In the whole world. The tempest's mocking elf
Points to the shipman thus the unseen shelf
    He strikes on, only when the timbers start.

Not see? because of night perhaps?—why, day
    Came back again for that! before it left,
    The dying sunset kindled through a cleft:
The hills, like giants at a hunting, lay,   190
Chin upon hand, to see the game at bay,—
    "Now stab and end the creature—to the heft!"

Not hear? when noise was everywhere! it tolled
    Increasing like a bell. Names in my ears,
    Of all the lost adventurers my peers,—
How such a one was strong, and such was bold,
And such was fortunate, yet each of old
    Lost, lost! one moment knelled the woe of years.

There they stood, ranged along the hillsides, met
    To view the last of me, a living frame   200
    For one more picture! in a sheet of flame
I saw them and I knew them all. And yet
Dauntless the slug-horn to my lips I set
    And blew. *"Childe Roland to the Dark Tower came."*

SOURCES OF ROBERT BROWNING'S "CHILDE ROLAND"

Browning always insisted that his poem had its source in the song sung by Edgar,
the Fool in Shakespeare's *King Lear*:

> Childe Rowland to the dark tower came;
> His word was still—Fie, foh, and fum,
> I smell the blood of a British man. [III, iv, 171-3]

On one occasion Browning admitted that other ingredients had been "a tower which
[he] once saw in the Carrara Mountains, a painting which caught his eye years later
in Paris; and the figure of a horse in the tapestry in his own drawing-room" [Mrs. S.

Orr: *Handbook to the Works of Browning* (1886), p. 266n.]. In an article describing a visit to the poet, the Rev. J. W. Chadwick also mentions this tapestry:

> Upon the lengthwise wall of the room . . . was a long, wide band of tapestry, on which I thought I recognized the miserable horse of Childe Roland's pilgrimage;—
>
> > One stiff blind horse, his every bone a-stare,
> > Stood stupefied, however he came there:
> > Thrust out past service from the devil's stud!
>
> I asked Mr. Browning if the beast of the tapestry was the beast of the poem; and he said yes, and descanted somewhat on his lean monstrosity. But only a Browning could have evolved the stanzas of the poem from the woven image. I further asked him if he had said that he only wrote *Childe Roland* for its realistic imagery, without any moral purpose . . . and he protested he never had. . . . [Quoted in H. E. Scudder: *Complete Poetical Works of Browning* (1895), p. 1020.]

Browning, 35 years after writing the poem, gave this account of its origin:

> 'T was like this: one year . . . I had been very lazy; I resolved that I would write something every day. Well, the first day I wrote about some roses, suggested by a magnificent basket that some one had sent my wife. [This poem was "Women and Roses".] The next day [January 2, 1852] Childe Roland came upon me as a kind of dream. I had to write it, then and there, and I finished it the same day, I believe. But it was simply that I had to do it. I did not know then what I meant beyond that, and I'm sure I don't know now. But I am very fond of it. [Quoted in W. C. DeVane: *A Browning Handbook* (Crofts, 1935), p. 204.]

During his lifetime, Browning consistently disassociated himself from the various allegorical interpretations of the poem put forward by admirers. Once when he was asked if he agreed with a certain interpretation he said: "Oh, no, not at all. Understand, I don't repudiate it, either. I only mean I was conscious of no allegorical intention in writing it." [Quoted by DeVane, *loc. cit.*] On another similar occasion he described the poem as "only a fantasy," and on still another, when J. W. Chadwick asked "if constancy to an ideal—'He that endureth to the end shall be saved'—was not a sufficient understanding of the central purpose of the poem, he [Browning] said, 'Yes, just about that.' " [Quoted by Scudder, *loc. cit.*]

But in all matters concerning his poems and his personal life Browning was a consistently reticent man. (For example, see his poems "At the 'Mermaid'," "House," and "Shop.") As a result, students of Browning have not been content with Browning's own statements about the origins of "Childe Roland." The two most valuable conjectures on the subject are Harold Golder's "Browning's *Childe Roland,*" *PMLA,* 39:963–978 (Dec., 1924) and W. C. DeVane's "The Landscape of Browning's *Childe Roland,*" *PMLA,* 40:426–432 (June, 1925). Accepting Browning's statements as indicating the *conscious* sources of the poem, these scholars undertook the task of "establishing a subconscious connection between Edgar's maudlin words and the material from which Browning obviously drew," as Golder puts it; or, in DeVane's words, of finding "for the sources of *Childe Roland* materials so familiar to Browning at the impressionable time of his life as to have become a part of his mental character."

Because Browning usually composed his poems slowly and deliberately, whereas "Childe Roland" was written in one day during a powerful creative drive, the probability seems to be that some psychic experience such as a "dream" or "fantasy," to use Browning's own words, was indeed at the source. (Golder reminds us that Coleridge's "Kubla Khan" also took its origin in a fragment of reading and that it, too, displays a great richness of details and association drawn upon subconsciously from wide reading and experience.) In a dream not only would the pictorial quality be powerful and vivid but it would overwhelm logical connections between the shifting scenes. Moreover, the subconscious mind in its wide ranging would tap resources which the conscious mind might fail to recognize.

It is well known that the chief part of Browning's education and very considerable erudition came from his eager reading of books in his father's large and well-chosen library. Golder and DeVane, therefore, turned their attention to the books that Browning probably or certainly read as a child.

Golder investigated the literature of nursery tales, legends, and romances, and uncovered some remarkable parallels—without, admittedly, proving beyond cavil that Browning actually did read the particular tales—or, rather, editions of the tales— employed by Golder. The "fie, foh, fum, I smell the blood" doggerel of Edgar's song is found in such nursery tales as *Hop-o'-my-Thumb, Jack and the Bean-stalk,* and *Jack the Giant Killer* in editions with which Browning might well have been familiar, and would form associations which could lie below the conscious mature mind. The fusing of details in these stories gives such ingredients as defiance of power (*e.g.,* giants), adventurous and dangerous travel through desolate landscape, an equivocal guide, and a trumpet suspended before a gate with an inscription:

> "Whoever can this trumpet blow,
> Shall soon the giant overthrow,
> And break the black enchantment straight,
> So all shall be in happy state."

"Jack had no sooner read this inscription, but he blew the trumpet."

Other material woven into the fabric of associations probably came from chivalric legends and romances: the difficulties and failures in the search for the Grail, the guides—sometimes frauds and sometimes magicians—consulted by errant knights at cross-roads, the supernatural aspects of landscape, the fear of failure and hope of success, the horn or trumpet sounded in challenge, etc. For instance, in *The Seven Champions of Christendom* there are many enchanted towers, strange landscapes, magic horns, etc. Among the specially noteworthy episodes is one describing St. George coming to a desolate land:

> Osmond, a necromancer, wrought the destruction . . . for by his magic arts and damned charms, he raised from the earth a mighty tower, the mortar whereof he mingled with virgin's blood, wherein are such enchantments wrought, that the light of the sun and the brightness of the skies are quenched, and the earth blasted with a terrible vapour and black mist that ascended from the tower, whereby a general darkness overspread our land, the compass of twenty-four leagues, so this country is clean wasted and destroyed.

In his ride through the darkness of the enchanted valley St. George crosses a river as black as pitch, while about his head fly monstrous birds. From other episodes in *The Seven Champions* Golder quotes additional striking similarities.

On the other hand, W. C. DeVane concentrates his attention on a single book not only definitely known to have been read by Browning as a child, but one on which Browning's opinion is known. On the fly-leaf of the book—Gerard de Lairesse's *The Art of Painting in All its Branches* (London, 1778)—Browning wrote in 1874:

> I read this book more often and with greater delight when I was a child than any other: and still remember the main of it most gratefully for the good I seem to have got from the prints and wonderful text.

DeVane contends that "the young Browning's ideas of the horrible in landscape" were fashioned by a chapter in Lairesse's book entitled "Of Things Deformed and Broken, Falsely called Painter-like."

"In *Childe Roland* the landscape is everything, and through it Browning is trying to create in us an impression of horror that he himself has once experienced . . . and it was Lairesse who dictated, though sometimes in a faint and disguised speech, the landscape that the line from Lear conjured up in the poet's mind."

Lairesse's discussion of "things . . . falsely called painter-like" is given in the form of an imaginary "walk" undertaken to discover a landscape replete with ugly details:

> . . . a piece with deformed trees, widely branched and leaved, and disorderly spreading from east towards west, crooked bodied, old and rent, full of knots and hollowness; also grounds without roads or ways, sharp hills, and monstrous mountains filling the offscape, rough or ruined buildings with their parts lying up and down in confusion; likewise muddy brooks, a gloomy sky, abounding with heavy clouds; the field furnished with lean cattle and vagabonds or gypsies: such a piece, I say, is not to be called a fine landscape. Can any one, without reason, assert him to be a painter-like object, who appears as a lame and dirty beggar, cloathed in rags, splay-footed, bound about the head with a nasty clout, having a skin as yellow as a baked pudding, killing vermin; or in fine, any such paltry figure?

In his imaginary "walk" Lairesse describes coming into a country so "strange" and "desolate," "without paths or roads, that I knew not where to walk"; and after passing a ruined and shattered temple he crosses "a morass abounding with vermin" and comes upon "a small rivulet full of big and little clods of earth and pebbles." The whole region was one of "muddy water, decayed and broken stones, pieces of wood, barren shrubs and bushes, rough grounds, toads, snakes, etc." At length he comes into a region

> full of open hollows and cuts, over-run here and there, with moss and barren shrubs. On the right side was a deep morassy valley . . . and on the left appeared an inaccessible ruined building, like an heap of stone, swarming with adders, snakes and other venomous creatures. Behind me, the ground was so uneven, full of ups and downs and pathless, that I thought it impossible to get from the place.

In other regions encountered during his "walk" he finds that "everything is excessively mouldered, fouled, and over-run with wild plants and shrubs," and even oaks "which had been thunder-struck; the stem cleft from top to bottom."

After quoting these several passages, DeVane urges caution: ". . . in spite of the similarity of detail, it would be a mistake to insist too strongly upon it. . . . The background of sharp hill and scalped mountain, the little river, the starved ignoble nature, the lean cattle, the roadless land . . . —these things were never thought of as having an outside source, chiefly because they had become so much a part of Browning's imaginative experience that he thought they had always been his own. And yet . . . it is not the detail that finally convinces us, but rather the tone of such a passage as the following, taken from near the end of the 'walk':"

> It was here so lonesome and gastly, that I was seized with a cold sweat; wherefore I mended my pace, in order to get out of it; and being got to the other side, and ten or twelve paces from it, I found myself again at the lake before-mentioned; near which lay a shattered tomb, with the corpse half tumbled out. The head and one arm rested on a large root of a tree lying near it; the lid was almost slid off, and just on the totter, and a snake, from underneath, was creeping into the tomb. A sight frightful indeed.

"It is such passages as these," DeVane comments, "that must have impressed themselves indelibly upon the mind of the growing Browning."

Both Golder and DeVane are well aware that their uncovering of such material as has been quoted above does not in any way "explain" the imaginative power of the poem. There are hundreds or thousands of persons who in their impressionable years have been exposed to the same or comparable materials but who remained incapable of synthesizing the mass of details, consciously or unconsciously, into a powerful work of art. The similarities, however striking they may seem, are still less remarkable than the differences wrought by the creative processes of the poet's mind.

———

ii. The Composition of Poetry

HOW A POEM IS MADE

C. DAY LEWIS (1905–   )

Children look down upon the morning-gray
Tissue of mist that veils a valley's lap:
Their fingers itch to tear it and unwrap
The flags, the roundabouts, the gala day.
They watch the spring rise inexhaustibly—
A breathing thread out of the eddied sand,
Sufficient to their day: but half their mind
Is on the sailed and glittering estuary.
Fondly we wish their mist might never break,
Knowing it hides so much that best were hidden:
We'd chain them by the spring, lest it should broaden
For them into a quicksand and a wreck.
But they slip through our fingers like the source,
Like mist, like time that has flagged out their course.

The seed of this poem was a strong feeling I had about my own two children. It is a feeling most parents have, at one time or another—a feeling of sadness that their children must grow up, must leave their protection and go out into the dangerous and difficult world. When you are young, you sometimes resent your parents having that feeling: you *want* to grow up and be independent.

Now, if you look at the poem again, you'll see there are two themes, or subjects, in it—the original one, my *own* feeling, which comes out in the last six lines; and the *children's* feeling of impatience and expectation, which comes out in the first eight. These two themes are intended to balance and contrast with each other.

Before I actually start writing a poem, I often find a line of verse comes into my head—a line which gives me a clue to the theme and pattern which the poem will develop: a sort of key-line. When I sat down to begin this sonnet, such a line of verse at once came into my head. That line (it is the only one I didn't have to work for) was "The flags, the roundabouts, the gala day." I thought about this line, and saw that it was an image of a fête or a fair, the sort of thing a child looks forward to; obviously, it symbolized (that is, "stood for") the grown-up world which a child is so impatient to enter. The idea of *impatience* then added some more lines—the first three. Here, the early-morning mist covering the valley represents the veil which the children wish to tear away, as they would tear the tissue paper off a birthday present—the veil which shuts them off from the grown-up world. The image came out of my memory, recalled from a day several years ago when I was taking my children to school in Devonshire, and we paused at the top of a hill and saw the whole of the valley below covered with mist: I remembered thinking at the time that it looked like tissue paper, but I'd forgotten all about the incident until I began to write this poem.

Next, I wanted a second image-sequence, as a variation on the theme expressed in the first four lines. You'll find it in lines 5 to 8—the picture of a spring bubbling up out of the earth, and the children bending down to watch its "breathing thread." The word "breathing" gives you a clue to the meaning of this passage: the spring represents life near its source, *young* life; and the children are only half satisfied with it; "half their mind" is looking forward to the time when their life will have broadened out, as a stream broadens into an estuary, and become more important and exciting. The image of the spring, like that of the mist, came out of my memory: it was a particular spring, near a country house in Ireland, which used to fascinate me as a child; I remember spending hours watching it, wondering how such a tiny thread of water managed to force its way out of the earth.

Next, the other theme had to be started—the *parents'* feeling about the children going out into the world. Notice that, although this theme was the original seed of the poem, it now occupies a relatively small space (lines 9 to 12): it often happens, when you are writing a poem, that you find the poem turning out quite differently from what you expected—in other words, you don't know what a poem is going to be like till you have gone some way with the composing of it; indeed, to a certain extent, a poem *composes itself.* Lines 9–12 say, quite simply, "We grownups wish the mist of childhood might never break for our children, because, when it does, they'll see the world is not such a pleasant place as they imagined. We'd like to chain them to their childhood, to save them from being hurt ('a quicksand and a wreck') as everyone must sometimes be hurt by life when he grows up." But the poem couldn't end like that, could it? After all, a parent can't really prevent his children growing up, even if it was right for him to try and do so—which it isn't. So, in the last two lines, I describe how children grow independent of their parents, slipping away from them like mist or water ("the source") slips through one's fingers: they must fend for themselves, run their own race—and time has already "flagged out their course."

I wonder whether you have noticed something about those last six lines. Except for the quicksand and the wreck there are no new images in them. Even the phrase "flagged out their course" (which, by the way, is another memory-image of mine, derived from a two-mile steeplechase I ran in as a boy of fourteen)—even this phrase echoes "the flags" of line 4. Instead of using new images, I have repeated those of the first eight lines—mist, the spring, the estuary ("lest it should *broaden* For them into a quicksand and a wreck"), the flags. . . . [An] important part is played in poetry by repetition. It is not only words and phrases, but also images, which can be repeated. And they are repeated in this poem, so that you can see the two main themes from a number of different angles, just as you can see many different reflections of yourself if you walk down a corridor of mirrors.

Lastly, what I have told you about the sources of these particular images will help you to understand how a poem grows. The seed of this poem took root in my mind. Then, without my being aware of it, it somehow attracted to itself several experiences I had had at quite different periods of my life and forgotten about. It got hold of a Devonshire mist, an Irish spring, and a steeplechase course in Dorset; it added an estuary with yachts sailing on it (I still don't know where that last picture came from): and, when I began to write the poem, these four images rose out of my mind all ready to illustrate the theme. . . .

THE MAKING OF A POEM

STEPHEN SPENDER (1909–   )

Apology

It would be inexcusable to discuss my own way of writing poetry unless I were able to relate this to a wider view of the problems which poets attempt to solve when they sit down at a desk or table to write, or walk around composing their poems in their heads. There is a danger of my appearing to put across my own experiences as the general rule, when every poet's way of going about his work and his experience of being a poet are different, and when my own poetry may not be good enough to lend my example any authority.

Yet the writing of poetry is an activity which makes certain demands of attention on the poet and which requires that he should have certain qualifications of ear, vision, imagination, memory and so on. He should be able to think in images, he should have as great a mastery of language as a painter has over his palette, even if the range of his language be very limited. All this means that, in ordinary society, a poet has to adapt himself, more or less consciously, to the demands of his vocation, and hence the peculiarities of poets and the condition of inspiration which many people have said is near to madness. One poet's example is only his adaptation of his personality to the demands of poetry, but if it is clearly stated it may help us to understand other poets, and even something of poetry.

Today we lack very much a whole view of poetry, and have instead many one-sided views of certain aspects of poetry which have been advertised as the only aims which poets should attempt. Movements such as free verse, imagism, surrealism, expressionism, personalism and so on, tend to make people think that poetry is simply a matter of not writing in metre or rhyme, or of free association, or of thinking in images, or of a kind of drawing room madness (surrealism) which corresponds to drawing room communism. Here is a string of ideas: Night, dark, stars, immensity, blue, voluptuous, clinging, columns, clouds, moon, sickle, harvest, vast camp fire, hell. Is this poetry? A lot of strings of words almost as simple as this are set down on the backs of envelopes and posted off to editors or to poets by the vast army of amateurs who think that to be illogical is to be poetic, with that fond question. Thus I hope that this discussion of how poets work will imply a wider and completer view of poets.

Concentration

The problem of creative writing is essentially one of concentration, and the supposed eccentricities of poets are usually due to mechanical habits or rituals developed in order to concentrate. Concentration, of course, for the purpose of writing poetry, is different from the kind of concentration required for working out a sum. It is a focussing of the attention in a special way, so that the poet is aware of all the implications and possible developments of his idea, just as one might say that a plant was not concentrating on developing mechanically in one direction, but in many directions, towards the warmth and light with its leaves, and towards the water with its roots, all at the same time.

Schiller liked to have a smell of rotten apples, concealed beneath the lid of his desk, under his nose when he was composing poetry. Walter de la Mare has told me that he must smoke when writing. Auden drinks endless cups of tea. Coffee is my own addiction, besides smoking a great deal, which I hardly ever do except when I am writing. I notice also that as I attain a greater concentration, this tends to make me forget the taste of the cigarette in my mouth, and then I have a desire to smoke two or even three cigarettes at a time, in order that the sensation from the outside may penetrate through the wall of concentration which I have built round myself.

For goodness sake, though, do not think that rotten apples or cigarettes or tea have anything to do with the quality of the work of a Schiller, a de la Mare, or an Auden. They are a part of a concentration which has already been attained rather than the causes of concentration. De la Mare once said to me that he thought the desire to smoke when writing poetry arose from a need, not of a stimulus, but to canalize a distracting leak of his attention away from his writing towards the distraction which is always present in one's environment. Concentration may be disturbed by someone whistling in the street or the ticking of a clock. There is always a slight tendency of the body to sabotage the attention of the mind by providing some distraction. If this need for distraction can be directed into one channel—such as the odor of rotten apples or the taste of tobacco or tea—then other distractions outside oneself are put out of competition.

Another possible explanation is that the concentrated effort of writing poetry is a spiritual activity which makes one completely forget, for the time being, that one has a body. It is a disturbance of the balance of body and mind and for this reason one needs a kind of anchor of sensation with the physical world. Hence the craving for a scent or taste or even, sometimes, for sexual activity. Poets speak of the necessity of writing poetry rather than of a liking for doing it. It is spiritual compulsion, a strain-ing of the mind to attain heights surrounded by abysses and it cannot be entirely happy, for in the most important sense, the only reward worth having is absolutely denied: for, however confident a poet may be, he is never quite sure that all his energy is not misdirected nor that what he is writing is great poetry. At the moment when art attains its highest attainment it reaches beyond its medium of words or paints or music, and the artist finds himself realizing that these instruments are inadequate to the spirit of what he is trying to say.

Different poets concentrate in different ways. In my own mind I make a sharp dis-tinction between two types of concentration: one is immediate and complete, the other is plodding and only completed by stages. Some poets write immediately works which, when they are written, scarcely need revision. Others write their poems by stages, feeling their way from rough draft to rough draft, until finally, after many revisions, they have produced a result which may seem to have very little connection with their early sketches.

These two opposite processes are vividly illustrated in two examples drawn from music: Mozart and Beethoven. Mozart thought out symphonies, quartets, even scenes from operas, entirely in his head—often on a journey or perhaps while dealing with pressing problems—and then he transcribed them, in their completeness, onto paper. Beethoven wrote fragments of themes in notebooks which he kept beside him, working on and developing them over years. Often his first ideas were of a clumsiness which makes scholars marvel how he could, at the end, have developed from them such miraculous results.

Thus genius works in different ways to achieve its ends. But although the Mozartian type of genius is the more brilliant and dazzling, genius, unlike virtuosity, is judged by greatness of result, not by brilliance of performance. The result must be the fullest development in a created æsthetic form of an original moment of insight, and it does not matter whether genius devotes a lifetime to producing a small result if that result be immortal. The difference between two types of genius is that one type (the Mozartian) is able to plumb the greatest depths of his own experience by the tremendous effort of a moment, the other (the Beethovenian) must dig deeper and deeper into his consciousness, layer by layer. What counts in either case is the vision which sees and pursues and attains the end; the logic of the artistic purpose.

A poet may be divinely gifted with a lucid and intense and purposive intellect; he may be clumsy and slow; that does not matter, what matters is integrity of purpose and the ability to maintain the purpose without losing oneself. Myself, I am scarcely capable of immediate concentration in poetry. My mind is not clear, my will is weak, I suffer from an excess of ideas and a weak sense of form. For every poem that I begin to write, I think of at least ten which I do not write down at all. For every poem which I do write down, there are seven or eight which I never complete.

The method which I adopt therefore is to write down as many ideas as possible, in however rough a form, in notebooks (I have at least twenty of these, on a shelf beside my desk, going back over fifteen years). I then make use of some of the sketches and discard others.

The best way of explaining how I develop the rough ideas which I use, is to take an example. Here is a Notebook begun in 1944. About a hundred pages of it are covered with writing, and from this have emerged about six poems. Each idea, when it first occurs, is given a number. Sometimes the ideas do not get beyond one line. For example No. 3 (never developed) is the one line:—

A language of flesh and roses.

I shall return to this line in a few pages, when I speak of inspiration. For the moment, I turn to No. 13, because here is an idea which has been developed to its conclusion. The first sketch begins thus:—

a) There are some days when the sea lies like a harp
Stretched flat beneath the cliffs. The waves
Like wires burn with the sun's copper glow
  [all the murmuring blue
    every silent]

Between whose spaces every image
Of sky [field and] hedge and field and boat
Dwells like the huge face of the afternoon.
[Lies]

When the heat grows tired, the afternoon
Out of the land may breathe a sigh
[Across the wires like a hand. They vibrate
With]
Which moves across those wires like a soft hand
[Then the vibration]
Between whose spaces the vibration holds
Every bird-cry, dog's bark, man-shout
And creak of rollock from the land and sky
With all the music of the afternoon.

Obviously these lines are attempts to sketch out an idea which exists clearly enough on some level of the mind where it yet eludes the attempt to state it. At this stage, a poem is like a face which one seems to be able to visualize clearly in the eye of memory, but when one examines it mentally or tries to think it out, feature by feature, it seems to fade.

The idea of this poem is a vision of the sea. The faith of the poet is that if this vision is clearly stated it will be significant. The vision is of the sea stretched under a cliff. On top of the cliff there are fields, hedges, houses. Horses draw carts along lanes, dogs bark far inland, bells ring in the distance. The shore seems laden with hedges, roses, horses and men, all high above the sea, on a very fine summer day when the ocean seems to reflect and absorb the shore. Then the small strung-out glittering waves of the sea lying under the shore are like the strings of a harp which catch the sunlight. Between these strings lies the reflection of the shore. Butterflies are wafted out over the waves, which they mistake for the fields of the chalky landscape, searching them for flowers. On a day such as this, the land, reflected in the sea, appears to enter into the sea, as though it lies under it, like Atlantis. The wires of the harp are like a seen music fusing seascape and landscape.

Looking at this vision in another way, it obviously has symbolic value. The sea represents death and eternity, the land represents the brief life of the summer and of one human generation which passes into the sea of eternity. But let me here say at once that although the poet may be conscious of this aspect of his vision, it is exactly what he wants to avoid stating, or even being too concerned with. His job is to recreate his vision, and let it speak its moral for itself. The poet must distinguish clearly in his own mind between that which most definitely must be said and that which must not be said. The unsaid inner meaning is revealed in the music and the tonality of the poem, and the poet is conscious of it in his knowledge that a certain tone of voice, a certain rhythm, are necessary.

In the next twenty versions of the poem I felt my way towards the clarification of the seen picture, the music and the inner feeling. In the first version quoted above there is the phrase in the second and third lines

The waves
Like wires burn with the sun's copper glow.

This phrase fuses the image of the sea with the idea of music, and it is therefore a key-phrase, because the theme of the poem is the fusion of the land with the sea. Here, then, are several versions of these one and a quarter lines, in the order in which they were written:—

b) The waves are wires
Burning as with the secret song of fires

c) The day burns in the trembling wires
With a vast music golden in the eyes

d) The day glows on its trembling wires
Singing a golden music in the eyes

e) The day glows on its burning wires
Like waves of music golden to the eyes.

f) Afternoon burns upon its wires
Lines of music dazzling the eyes

g) Afternoon gilds its tingling wires
To a visual silent music of the eyes

In the final version, these two lines appear as in the following stanza:—

h) There are some days the happy ocean lies
Like an unfingered harp, below the land.

Afternoon gilds all the silent wires
Into a burning music of the eyes.

On mirroring paths between those fine-strung fires
The shore, laden with roses, horses, spires,
Wanders in water, imaged above ribbed sand.

Inspiration

The hard work evinced in these examples, which are only a fraction of the work put into the whole poem, may cause the reader to wonder whether there is no such thing as inspiration, or whether it is merely Stephen Spender who is uninspired. The answer is that everything in poetry is work except inspiration, whether this work is achieved at one swift stroke, as Mozart wrote his music, or whether it is a slow process of evolution from stage to stage. Here again, I have to qualify the word "work," as I qualified the word "concentration": the work on a line of poetry may take the form of putting a version aside for a few days, weeks or years, and then taking it up again, when it may be found that the line has, in the interval of time, almost rewritten itself.

Inspiration is the beginning of a poem and **it is also** its final goal. It is the first idea which drops into the poet's mind and it is the final idea which he at last achieves in words. In between this start and this winning post there is the hard race, the sweat and toil.

Paul Valéry speaks of the *"une ligne donnée"* of a poem. One line is given to the poet by God or by nature, the rest he has to discover for himself.

My own experience of inspiration is certainly that of a line or a phrase or a word or sometimes something still vague, a dim cloud of an idea which I feel must be condensed into a shower of words. The peculiarity of the key word or line is that it does not merely attract, as, say, the word "braggadocio" attracts. It occurs in what seems to be an active, male, germinal form as though it were the centre of a statement requiring a beginning and an end, and as though it had an impulse in a certain direction Here are examples:—

A language of flesh and roses

This phrase (not very satisfactory in itself) brings to my mind a whole series of experiences and the idea of a poem which I shall perhaps write some years hence. I was standing in the corridor of a train passing through the Black Country. I saw a landscape of pits and pitheads, artificial mountains, jagged yellow wounds in the earth, everything transformed as though by the toil of an enormous animal or giant tearing up the earth in search of prey or treasure. Oddly enough, a stranger next to me in the corridor echoed my inmost thought. He said: "Everything there is man-made." At this moment the line flashed into my head

A language of flesh and roses.

The sequence of my thought was as follows: the industrial landscape which seems by now a routine and act of God which enslaves both employers and workers who serve and profit by it, is actually the expression of man's will. Men willed it to be so, and the pitheads, slag-heaps and the ghastly disregard of anything but the pursuit of wealth, are a symbol of modern man's mind. In other words, the world which we create—the world of slums and telegrams and newspapers—is a kind of language of our inner wishes and thoughts. Although this is so, it is obviously a language which has got outside our control. It is a confused language, an irresponsible senile gibberish. This thought greatly distressed me, and I started thinking that if the phenomena created by humanity are really like words in a language, what kind of language do we really aspire to? All this sequence of thought flashed into my mind with the answer which came before the question: *A language of flesh and roses.*

I hope this example will give the reader some idea of what I mean by inspiration. Now the line, which I shall not repeat again, is a way of thinking imaginatively. If the line embodies some of the ideas which I have related above, these ideas must be further made clear in other lines. That is the terrifying challenge of poetry. Can I think out the logic of images? How easy it is to explain here the poem that I would have liked to write! How difficult it would be to write it. For writing it would imply living my way through the imaged experience of all these ideas, which here are mere abstractions, and such an effort of imaginative experience requires a lifetime of patience and watching.

Here is an example of a cloudy form of thought germinated by the word *cross,* which is the key word of the poem which exists formlessly in my mind. Recently my wife had a son. On the first day that I visited her after the boy's birth, I went by bus to the hospital. Passing through the streets on the top of the bus, they all seemed very clean, and the thought occurred to me that everything was prepared for our child. Past generations have toiled so that any child born today inherits, with his generation, cities, streets, organization, the most elaborate machinery for living. Everything has been provided for him by people dead long before he was born. Then, naturally enough, sadder thoughts colored this picture for me, and I reflected how he also inherited vast maladjustments, vast human wrongs. Then I thought of the child as like a pin-point of present existence, the moment incarnate, in whom the whole of the past, and all possible futures *cross.* This word *cross* somehow suggested the whole situation to me of a child born into the world and also of the form of a poem about his situation. When the word *cross* appeared in the poem, the idea of the past should give place to the idea of the future and it should be apparent that the *cross* in which present and future meet is the secret of an individual human existence. And here again, the unspoken secret which lies beyond the poem, the moral significance of other meanings of the word "cross" begins to glow with its virtue that should never be said and yet should shine through every image in the poem.

This account of inspiration is probably weak beside the accounts that other poets might give. I am writing of my own experience, and my own inspiration seems to me like the faintest flash of insight into the nature of reality beside that of other poets whom I can think of. However, it is possible that I describe here a kind of experience which, however slight it may be, is far truer to the real poetic experience than Aldous Huxley's account of how a young poet writes poetry in his novel *Time Must Have a Stop.* It is hard to imagine anything more self-conscious and unpoetic than Mr. Huxley's account.

Memory

If the art of concentrating in a particular way is the discipline necessary for poetry to reveal itself, memory exercised in a particular way is the natural gift of poetic genius. The poet, above all else, is a person who never forgets certain sense-impressions which he has experienced and which he can re-live again and again as though with all their original freshness.

All poets have this highly developed sensitive apparatus of memory, and they are usually aware of experiences which happened to them at the earliest age and which retain their pristine significance throughout life. The meeting of Dante and Beatrice when the poet was only nine years of age is the experience which became a symbol in Dante's mind around which the *Divine Comedy* crystallized. The experience of nature which forms the subject of Wordsworth's poetry was an extension of a childhood vision of "natural presences" which surrounded the boy Wordsworth. And his decision in later life to live in the Lake District was a decision to return to the scene of these childhood memories which were the most important experiences in his poetry. There is evidence for the importance of this kind of memory in all the creative arts, and the argument certainly applies to prose which is creative. Sir Osbert Sitwell has told me that his book *Before the Bombardment,* which contains an extremely civilized and satiric account of the social life of Scarborough before and during the last war, was based on his observations of life in that resort before he had reached the age of twelve.

It therefore is not surprising that although I have no memory for telephone numbers, addresses, faces and where I have put this morning's correspondence, I have a perfect memory for the sensation of certain experiences which are crystallized for me around certain associations. I could demonstrate this from my own life by the overwhelming nature of associations which, suddenly aroused, have carried me back so completely into the past, particularly into my childhood, that I have lost all sense of the present time and place. But the best proofs of this power of memory are found in the odd lines of poems written in note books fifteen years ago. A few fragments of unfinished poems enable me to enter immediately into the experiences from which they were derived, the circumstances in which they were written, and the unwritten feelings in the poem that were projected but never put into words.

> . . . Knowledge of a full sun
> That runs up his big sky, above
> The hill, then in those trees and throws
> His smiling on the turf.

That is an incomplete idea of fifteen years ago, and I remember exactly a balcony of a house facing a road, and, on the other side of the road, pine trees, beyond which lay the sea. Every morning the sun sprang up, first of all above the horizon of the sea, then it climbed to the tops of the trees and shone on my window. And this memory connects with the sun that shines through my window in London now in spring and early summer. So that the memory is not exactly a memory. It is more like one prong upon which a whole calendar of similar experiences happening throughout years collect. A memory once clearly stated ceases to be a memory, it becomes perpetually present, because every time we experience something which recalls it, the clear and lucid original experience imposes its formal beauty on the new experiences. It is thus no longer a memory but an experience lived through again and again

Turning over these old note books, my eye catches some lines, in a projected long poem, which immediately re-shape themselves into the following short portrait of a woman's face:—

> Her eyes are gleaming fish
> Caught in her nervous face, as if in a net.
> Her hair is wild and fair, haloing her cheeks
> Like a fantastic flare of Southern sun.
> There is madness in her cherishing her children.
> Sometimes, perhaps a single time in years,
> Her wandering fingers stoop to arrange some flowers—
> Then in her hands her whole life stops and weeps.

It is perhaps true to say that memory is the faculty of poetry, because the imagination itself is an exercise of memory. There is nothing we imagine which we do not already know. And our ability to imagine is our ability to remember what we have already once experienced and to apply it to some different situation. Thus the greatest poets are those with memories so great that they extend beyond their strongest experiences to their minutest observations of people and things far outside their own self-centredness (the weakness of memory is its self-centredness: hence the narcissistic nature of most poetry).

Here I can detect my own greatest weakness. My memory is defective and self-centred. I lack the confidence in using it to create situations outside myself, although I believe that, in theory, there are very few situations in life which a poet should not be able to imagine, because it is a fact that most poets have experienced almost every situation in life. I do not mean by this that a poet who writes about a Polar Expedition has actually been to the North Pole. I mean, though, that he has been cold, hungry, etc., so that it is possible for him by remembering imaginatively his own felt experiences to know what it is like to explore the North Pole. That is where I fail. I cannot write about going to the North Pole.

Faith

It is evident that a faith in their vocation, mystical in intensity, sustains poets. There are many illustrations from the lives of poets to show this, and Shakespeare's sonnets are full of expressions of his faith in the immortality of his lines.

From my experience I can clarify the nature of this faith. When I was nine, we went to the Lake District, and there my parents read me some of the poems of Wordsworth. My sense of the sacredness of the task of poetry began then, and I have always felt that a poet's was a sacred vocation, like a saint's. Since I was nine, I have wanted to be various things, for example, Prime Minister (when I was twelve). Like some other poets I am attracted by the life of power and the life of action, but I am still more repelled by them. Power involves forcing oneself upon the attention of historians by doing things and occupying offices which are, in themselves, important, so that what is truly powerful is not the soul of a so-called powerful and prominent man but the position which he fills and the things which he does. Similarly, the life of "action" which seems so very positive is, in fact, a selective, even a negative, kind of life. A man of action does one thing or several things because he does not do something else. Usually men who do very spectacular things fail completely to do the ordinary things which fill the lives of most normal people, and which would be far more heroic and spectacular, perhaps, if they did not happen to be done by many people. Thus in practice the life of action has always seemed to me an act of cutting oneself off from life.

Although it is true that poets are vain and ambitious, their vanity and ambition is of the purest kind attainable in this world, for the saint renounces ambition. They are ambitious to be accepted for what they ultimately are as revealed by their inmost experiences, their finest perceptions, their deepest feelings, their uttermost sense of truth, in their poetry. They cannot cheat about these things, because the quality of their own being is revealed not in the noble sentiments which their poetry expresses, but in sensibility, control of language, rhythm and music, things which cannot be attained by a vote of confidence from an electorate, or by the office of Poet Laureate. Of course, work is tremendously important, but, in poetry, even the greatest labor can only serve to reveal the intrinsic qualities of soul of the poet as he really is.

Since there can be no cheating, the poet, like the saint, stands in all his works before the bar of a perpetual day of judgment. His vanity of course is pleased by success, though even success may contribute to his understanding that popularity does not confer on him the favorable judgment of all the ages which he seeks. For what does it mean to be praised by one's own age, which is soaked in crimes and stupidity, except perhaps that future ages, wise where we are foolish, will see him as a typical expression of this age's crimes and stupidity? Nor is lack of success a guarantee of great poetry, though there are some who pretend that it is. Nor can the critics, at any rate beyond a certain limited point of technical judgment, be trusted.

The poet's faith is therefore, firstly, a mystique of vocation, secondly, a faith in his own truth, combined with his own devotion to a task. There can really be no greater faith than the confidence that one is doing one's utmost to fulfil one's high vocation, and it is this that has inspired all the greatest poets. At the same time this faith is coupled with a deep humility because one knows that, ultimately, judgment does not rest with oneself. All one can do is to achieve nakedness, to be what one is with all one's faculties and perceptions, strengthened by all the skill which one can acquire, and then to stand before the judgment of time.

In my notebooks, I find the following Prose Poem, which expresses these thoughts:

> Bring me peace bring me power bring me assurance. Let me reach the bright day, the high chair, the plain desk, where my hand at last controls the words, where anxiety no longer undermines me. If I don't reach these I'm thrown to the wolves, I'm a restless animal wandering from place to place, from experience to experience.
>
> Give me the humility and the judgment to live alone with the deep and rich satisfaction of my own creating: not to be thrown into doubt by a word of spite or disapproval.
>
> In the last analysis don't mind whether your work is good or bad so long as it has the completeness, the enormity of the whole world which you love.

Song

Inspiration and song are the irreducible final qualities of a poet which makes his vocation different from all others. Inspiration is an experience in which a line or an idea is given to one, and perhaps also a state of mind in which one writes one's best poetry. Song is far more difficult to define. It is the music which a poem as yet unthought of will assume, the empty womb of poetry for ever in the poet's consciousness, waiting for the fertilizing seed.

Sometimes, when I lie in a state of half-waking half-sleeping, I am conscious of a stream of words which seem to pass through my mind, without their having a meaning, but they have a sound, a sound of passion, or a sound recalling poetry that I know. Again sometimes when I am writing, the music of the words I am trying to shape takes me far beyond the words, I am aware of a rhythm, a dance, a fury, which is as yet empty of words.

In these observations, I have said little about headaches, midnight oil, pints of beer or of claret, love affairs, and so on, which are supposed to be stations on the journeys of poets through life. There is no doubt that writing poetry, when a poem appears to succeed, results in an intense physical excitement, a sense of release and ecstasy. On the other hand, I dread writing poetry, for, I suppose, the following reasons: a poem is a terrible journey, a painful effort of concentrating the imagination; words are an extremely difficult medium to use, and sometimes when one has spent days trying to say a thing clearly one finds that one has only said it dully; above all, the writing of a poem brings one face to face with one's own personality with all its familiar and clumsy limitations. In every other phase of existence, one can exercise the orthodoxy of a conventional routine: one can be polite to one's friends, one can get through the day at the office, one can pose, one can draw attention to one's position in society, one is—in a word—dealing with men. In poetry, one is wrestling with a god.

Usually, when I have completed a poem, I think "this is my best poem," and I wish to publish it at once. This is partly because I only write when I have something new to say, which seems more worth while than what I have said before, partly because optimism about my present and future makes me despise my past. A few days after I have finished a poem, I relegate it to the past of all my other wasted efforts, all the books I do not wish to open.

Perhaps the greatest pleasure I have got from poems that I have written is when I have heard some lines quoted which I have not at once recognized. And I have thought "how good and how interesting," before I have realized that they are my own.

In common with other creative writers I pretend that I am not, and I am, exceedingly affected by unsympathetic criticism, whilst praise usually makes me suspect that the reviewer does not know what he is talking about. Why are writers so sensitive to criticism? Partly, because it is their business to be sensitive, and they are sensitive about this as about other things. Partly, because every serious creative writer is really in his heart concerned with reputation and not with success (the most successful writer I have known, Sir Hugh Walpole, was far and away the most unhappy about his reputation, because the "highbrows" did not like him). Again, I suspect that every writer is secretly writing for *someone,* probably for a parent or teacher who did not believe in him in childhood. The critic who refuses to "understand" immediately becomes identified with this person, and the understanding of many admirers only adds to the writer's secret bitterness if this one refusal persists.

Gradually one realizes that there is always this someone who will not like one's work. Then, perhaps, literature becomes a humble exercise of faith in being all that one can be in one's art, of being more than oneself, expecting little, but with a faith in the mystery of poetry which gradually expands into a faith in the mysterious service of truth.

Yet what failures there are! And how much mud sticks to one; mud not thrown by other people but acquired in the course of earning one's living, answering or not answering the letters which one receives, supporting or not supporting public causes. All one can hope is that this mud is composed of little grains of sand which will produce pearls.

THE RAVEN

EDGAR ALLAN POE (1809-1849)

Once upon a midnight dreary, while I pondered, weak and weary,
Over many a quaint and curious volume of forgotten lore,
While I nodded, nearly napping, suddenly there came a tapping,
As of some one gently rapping, rapping at my chamber door.
" 'Tis some visitor," I muttered, "tapping at my chamber door—
   Only this, and nothing more."

Ah, distinctly I remember it was in the bleak December,
And each separate dying ember wrought its ghost upon the floor.
Eagerly I wished the morrow;—vainly I had sought to borrow
From my books surcease of sorrow—sorrow for the lost Lenore—   **10**
For the rare and radiant maiden whom the angels name Lenore—
   Nameless here for evermore.

And the silken, sad, uncertain rustling of each purple curtain
Thrilled me—filled me with fantastic terrors never felt before;
So that now, to still the beating of my heart, I stood repeating,
" 'Tis some visitor entreating entrance at my chamber door—
Some late visitor entreating entrance at my chamber door;—
   This it is and nothing more."

Presently my soul grew stronger; hesitating then no longer,
"Sir," said I, "or Madam, truly your forgiveness I implore;   **20**
But the fact is I was napping, and so gently you came rapping,
And so faintly you came tapping, tapping at my chamber door,
That I scarce was sure I heard you"—here I opened wide the door;—
   Darkness there, and nothing more.

Deep into that darkness peering, long I stood there wondering, fearing,
Doubting, dreaming dreams no mortal ever dared to dream before;
But the silence was unbroken, and the stillness gave no token,
And the only word there spoken was the whispered word, "Lenore!"
This I whispered, and an echo murmured back the word, "Lenore!"
   Merely this and nothing more.   **30**

Back into the chamber turning, all my soul within me burning,
Soon I heard again a tapping somewhat louder than before.
"Surely," said I, "surely that is something at my window lattice;
Let me see, then, what thereat is, and this mystery explore—
Let my heart be still a moment and this mystery explore;—
   'Tis the wind and nothing more!"

Open here I flung the shutter, when, with many a flirt and flutter,
In there stepped a stately raven of the saintly days of yore;
Not the least obeisance made he; not an instant stopped or stayed he;

But, with mien of lord or lady, perched above my chamber door—   40
Perched upon a bust of Pallas just above my chamber door—
            Perched, and sat, and nothing more.

Then this ebony bird beguiling my sad fancy into smiling,
By the grave and stern decorum of the countenance it wore,
"Though thy crest be shorn and shaven, thou," I said, "art sure no craven
Ghastly grim and ancient raven wandering from the Nightly shore—
Tell me what thy lordly name is on the Night's Plutonian shore!"
            Quoth the raven, "Nevermore."

Much I marveled this ungainly fowl to hear discourse so plainly,
Though its answer little meaning—little relevancy bore;   50
For we cannot help agreeing that no living human being
Ever yet was blessed with seeing bird above his chamber door—
Bird or beast upon the sculptured bust above his chamber door,
            With such name as "Nevermore."

But the raven, sitting lonely on the placid bust, spoke only
That one word, as if his soul in that one word he did outpour.
Nothing farther then he uttered—not a feather then he fluttered—
Till I scarcely more than muttered "Other friends have flown before—
On the morrow *he* will leave me, as my hopes have flown before."
            Then the bird said, "Nevermore."   60

Startled at the stillness broken by reply so aptly spoken,
"Doubtless," said I, "what it utters is its only stock and store
Caught from some unhappy master whom unmerciful Disaster
Followed fast and followed faster till his songs one burden bore—
Till the dirges of his Hope that melancholy burden bore
            Of 'Never—nevermore.' "

But the raven still beguiling all my sad soul into smiling,
Straight I wheeled a cushioned seat in front of bird and bust and door;
Then, upon the velvet sinking, I betook myself to linking
Fancy unto fancy, thinking what this ominous bird of yore—   70
What this grim, ungainly, ghastly, gaunt, and ominous bird of yore
            Meant in croaking "Nevermore."

This I sat engaged in guessing, but no syllable expressing
To the fowl whose fiery eyes now burned into my bosom's core;
This and more I sat divining, with my head at ease reclining
On the cushion's velvet lining that the lamplight gloated o'er,
But whose velvet violet lining with the lamplight gloating o'er,
            She shall press, ah, nevermore!

Then, methought, the air grew denser, perfumed from an unseen censer
Swung by angels whose faint foot-falls tinkled on the tufted floor.   80
"Wretch," I cried, "thy God hath lent thee—by these angels he hath sent thee

Respite—respite and nepenthe from thy memories of Lenore!
Quaff, oh quaff this kind nepenthe and forget this lost Lenore!"
    Quoth the raven, "Nevermore."

"Prophet!" said I, "thing of evil!—prophet still, if bird or devil!—
Whether Tempter sent, or whether tempest tossed thee here ashore
Desolate yet all undaunted, on this desert land enchanted—
On this home by Horror haunted—tell me truly, I implore—
Is there—*is* there balm in Gilead?—tell me—tell me, I implore!"
    Quoth the raven, "Nevermore."   **90**

"Prophet!" said I, "thing of evil- -prophet still, if bird or devil!
By that Heaven that bends above us—by that God we both adore—
Tell this soul with sorrow laden if, within the distant Aidenn,
It shall clasp a sainted maiden whom the angels name Lenore—
Clasp a rare and radiant maiden whom the angels name Lenore."
    Quoth the raven, "Nevermore."

"Be that word our sign of parting, bird or fiend!" I shrieked, upstarting—
"Get thee back into the tempest and the Night's Plutonian shore!
Leave no black plume as a token of that lie thy soul hath spoken!
Leave my loneliness unbroken!—quit the bust above my door!   **100**
Take thy beak from out my heart, and take thy form from off my door!"
    Quoth the raven, "Nevermore."

And the raven, never flitting, still is sitting, still is sitting
On the pallid bust of Pallas just above my chamber door;
And his eyes have all the seeming of a demon's that is dreaming,
And the lamplight o'er him streaming throws his shadow on the floor;
And my soul from out that shadow that lies floating on the floor
    Shall be lifted—nevermore!

THE PHILOSOPHY OF COMPOSITION

EDGAR ALLAN POE (1809–1849)

. . . Nothing is more clear than that every plot, worth the name, must be elaborated to its *dénouement* before anything be attempted with the pen. It is only with the *dénouement* constantly in view that we can give a plot its indispensable air of consequence, or causation, by making the incidents, and especially the tone at all points, tend to the development of the intention.

There is a radical error, I think, in the usual mode of constructing a story. Either history affords a thesis—or one is suggested by an incident of the day—or, at best, the author sets himself to work in the combination of striking events to form merely the basis of his narrative—designing, generally, to fill in with description, dialogue, or autorial comment, whatever crevices of fact, or action, may, from page to page, render themselves apparent.

I prefer commencing with the consideration of an *effect*. Keeping originality *always* in view—for he is false to himself who ventures to dispense with so obvious and so easily attainable a source of interest—I say to myself, in the first place,—"Of the innumerable effects, or impressions, of which the heart, the intellect, or (more generally) the soul is susceptible, what one shall I, on the present occasion, select?" Having chosen a novel, first, and secondly a vivid effect, I consider whether it can be best wrought by incident or tone—whether by ordinary incidents and peculiar tone, or the converse, or by peculiarity both of incident and tone—afterward looking about me (or rather within) for such combinations of event, or tone, as shall best aid me in the construction of the effect.

I have often thought how interesting a magazine paper might be written by any author who would—that is to say who could—detail, step by step, the processes by which any one of his compositions attained its ultimate point of completion. Why such a paper has never been given to the world, I am much at a loss to say—but, perhaps, the autorial vanity has had more to do with the omission than any one other cause. Most writers—poets in especial—prefer having it understood that they compose by a species of fine frenzy—an ecstatic intuition—and would positively shudder at letting the public take a peep behind the scenes, at the elaborate and vacillating crudities of thought—at the true purposes seized only at the last moment—at the innumerable glimpses of idea that arrived not at the maturity of full view—at the fully matured fancies discarded in despair as unmanageable—at the cautious selections and rejections —at the painful erasures and interpolations—in a word, at the wheels and pinions— the tackle for scene-shifting—the step-ladders and demon-traps—the cock's feathers, the red paint and the black patches, which, in the ninety-nine cases out of the hundred, constitute the properties of the literary *histrio*.

I am aware, on the other hand, that the case is by no means common, in which an author is at all in condition to retrace the steps by which his conclusions have been attained. In general, suggestions, having arisen pell-mell, are pursued and forgotten in a similar manner.

For my own part, I have neither sympathy with the repugnance alluded to, nor, at any time the least difficulty in recalling to mind the progressive steps of any of my compositions; and, since the interest of an analysis, or reconstruction, such as I have considered a *desideratum,* is quite independent of any real or fancied interest in the thing analyzed, it will not be regarded as a breach of decorum on my part to show the *modus operandi* by which some one of my own works was put together. I select "The Raven," as most generally known. It is my design to render it manifest that no one point in its composition is referable either to accident or intuition—that the work proceeded, step by step, to its completion with the precision and rigid consequence of a mathematical problem.

Let us dismiss, as irrelevant to the poem, *per se,* the circumstance—or say the necessity—which, in the first place, gave rise to the intention of composing *a* poem that should suit at once the popular and the critical taste.

We commence, then, with this intention.

The initial consideration was that of extent. If any literary work is too long to be read at one sitting, we must be content to dispense with the immensely important effect derivable from unity of impression—for, if two sittings be required, the affairs of the world interfere, and everything like totality is at once destroyed. But since, *ceteris paribus,* no poet can afford to dispense with *anything* that may advance his design, it but remains to be seen whether there is, in extent, any advantage to counterbalance the loss of unity which attends it. Here I say no, at once. What we term a long poem is, in fact, merely a succession of brief ones—that is to say, of brief poetical effects. It is needless to demonstrate that a poem is such, only inasmuch as it intensely excites, by elevating, the soul; and all intense excitements are, through a psychal necessity, brief. For this reason, at least one half of the "Paradise Lost" is essentially prose—a succession of poetical excitements interspersed, *inevitably,* with corresponding depressions—the whole being deprived, through the extremeness of its length, of the vastly important artistic element, totality, or unity, of effect.

It appears evident, then, that there is a distinct limit, as regards length, to all works of literary art—the limit of a single sitting—and that, although in certain classes of prose composition, such as "Robinson Crusoe" (demanding no unity), this limit may be advantageously overpassed, it can never properly be overpassed in a poem. Within this limit, the extent of a poem may be made to bear mathematical relation to its merit—in other words, to the excitement or elevation—again in other words, to the degree of the true poetical effect which it is capable of inducing; for it is clear that the brevity must be in direct ratio of the intensity of the intended effect:—this, with one proviso—that a certain degree of duration is absolutely requisite for the production of any effect at all.

Holding in view these considerations, as well as that degree of excitement which I deemed not above the popular, while not below the critical, taste, I reached at once what I conceived the proper *length* for my intended poem—a length of about one hundred lines. It is, in fact, a hundred and eight.

My next thought concerned the choice of an impression, or effect, to be conveyed: and here I may as well observe that, throughout the construction, I kept steadily in view the design of rendering the work *universally* appreciable. I should be carried too far out of my immediate topic were I to demonstrate a point upon which I have repeatedly insisted, and which, with the poetical, stands not in the slightest need of demonstration—the point, I mean, that Beauty is the sole legitimate province of the poem. A few words, however, in elucidation of my real meaning, which some of my friends have evinced a disposition to misrepresent. That pleasure which is at once the most intense, the most elevating, and the most pure, is, I believe, found in the contemplation of the beautiful. When, indeed, men speak of Beauty, they mean, precisely, not a quality, as is supposed, but an effect—they refer, in short, just to that intense and pure elevation of *soul—not* of intellect, or of heart—upon which I have commented, and which is experienced in consequence of contemplating "the beautiful." Now I designate Beauty as the province of the poem, merely because it is an obvious rule of Art that effects should be made to spring from direct causes—that objects should be attained through means best adapted for their attainment—no one as yet having been weak enough to deny that the peculiar elevation alluded to is *most readily* attained in the poem. Now the object Truth, or the satisfaction of the intellect, and the object Passion, or the excitement of the heart, are, although attainable, to a certain extent, in poetry, far more readily attainable in prose. Truth, in fact, demands a precision, and Passion a *homeliness* (the truly passionate will comprehend me) which are absolutely antagonistic to that Beauty which, I maintain, is the excitement, or pleasurable elevation, of the soul. It by no means follows from anything here said, that passion, or even truth, may not be introduced, and even profitably introduced, into a poem—for they may serve in elucidation, or aid the general effect, as do discords in music, by contrast—but the true artist will always contrive, first, to tone them into proper subservience to the predominant aim, and, secondly, to enveil them, as far as possible, in that Beauty which is the atmosphere and the essence of the poem.

Regarding, then, Beauty as my province, my next question referred to the *tone* of its highest manifestation—and all experience has shown that this tone is one of *sadness.*

Beauty of whatever kind, in its supreme development, invariably excites the sensitive soul to tears. Melancholy is thus the most legitimate of all the poetical tones.

The length, the province, and the tone, being thus determined, I betook myself to ordinary induction, with the view of obtaining some artistic piquancy which might serve me as a key-note in the construction of the poem—some pivot upon which the whole structure might turn. In carefully thinking over all the usual artistic effects— or more properly *points,* in the theatrical sense—I did not fail to perceive immediately that no one had been so universally employed as that of the *refrain.* The universality of its employment sufficed to assure me of its intrinsic value, and spared me the neces- sity of submitting it to analysis. I considered it, however, with regard to its suscepti- bility of improvement, and soon saw it to be in a primitive condition. As commonly used, the *refrain,* or burden, not only is limited to lyric verse, but depends for its impression upon the force of monotone—both in sound and thought. The pleasure is deduced solely from the sense of identity—of repetition. I resolved to diversify, and so heighten, the effect, by adhering, in general, to the monotone of sound, while I con- tinually varied that of thought: that is to say, I determined to produce continuously novel effects, by the variation *of the application* of the *refrain*—the *refrain* itself remaining, for the most part, unvaried.

These points being settled, I next bethought me of the *nature* of my *refrain.* Since its application was to be repeatedly varied, it was clear that the *refrain* itself must be brief, for there would have been an insurmountable difficulty in frequent variations of application in any sentence of length. In proportion to the brevity of the sentence, would, of course, be the facility of the variation. This led me at once to a single word as the best *refrain.*

The question now arose as to the *character* of the word. Having made up my mind to a *refrain,* the division of the poem into stanzas was, of course, a corollary: the *refrain* forming the close to each stanza. That such a close, to have force, must be sonorous and susceptible of protracted emphasis, admitted no doubt: and these considerations inevitably led me to the long *o* as the most sonorous vowel, in connection with *r* as the most producible consonant.

The sound of the *refrain* being thus determined, it became necessary to select a word embodying this sound, and at the same time in the fullest possible keeping with that melancholy which I had predetermined as the tone of the poem. In such a search it would have been absolutely impossible to overlook the word "Nevermore." In fact, it was the very first which presented itself.

The next *desideratum* was a pretext for the continuous use of the one word "never- more." In observing the difficulty which I at once found in inventing a sufficiently plausible reason for its continuous repetition, I did not fail to perceive that this diffi- culty arose solely from the pre-assumption that the word was to be so continuously or monotonously spoken by a *human* being—I did not fail to perceive, in short, that the difficulty lay in the reconciliation of this monotony with the exercise of reason on the part of the creature repeating the word. Here, then, immediately arose the idea of a *non*-reasoning creature capable of speech; and, very naturally, a parrot, in the first instance, suggested itself, but was superseded forthwith by a Raven, as equally capable of speech, and infinitely more in keeping with the intended *tone.*

I had now gone so far as the conception of a Raven—the bird of ill omen—monoto- nously repeating the one word, "Nevermore," at the conclusion of each stanza, in a poem of melancholy tone, and in length about one hundred lines. Now, never losing sight of the object *supremeness,* or perfection, at all points, I asked myself—"Of all melancholy topics, what, according to the *universal* understanding of mankind, is the *most* melancholy?" Death—was the obvious reply. "And when," I said, "is this most melancholy of topics most poetical?" From what I have already explained at some length, the answer, here also, is obvious—"When it most closely allies itself to *Beauty:* the death, then, of a beautiful woman is, unquestionably, the most poetical topic in the world—and equally is it beyond doubt that the lips best suited for such topic are those of a bereaved lover."

I had now to combine the two ideas, of a lover lamenting his deceased mistress and a Raven continuously repeating the word "Nevermore."—I had to combine these, bearing in mind my design of varying at every turn the *application* of the word repeated; but the only intelligible mode of such combination is that of imagining the Raven employing the word in answer to the queries of the lover. And here it was that I saw at once the opportunity afforded for the effect on which I had been depending—that is to say, the effect of the *variation of application.* I saw that I could make the first query propounded by the lover—the first query to which the Raven should reply "Nevermore"—that I could make this first query a commonplace one—the second less so—the third still less, and so on—until at length the lover, startled from his original *nonchalance* by the melancholy character of the word itself—by its frequent repetition —and by a consideration of the ominous reputation of the fowl that uttered it—is at length excited to superstition, and wildly propounds queries of a far different character —queries whose solution he has passionately at heart—propounds them half in superstition and half in that species of despair which delights in self-torture—propounds them not altogether because he believes in the prophetic or demoniac character of the bird (which, reason assures him, is merely repeating a lesson learned by rote) but because he experiences a frenzied pleasure in so modeling his questions as to receive from the *expected* "Nevermore" the most delicious because the most intolerable of sorrow. Perceiving the opportunity thus afforded me—or, more strictly, thus forced upon me in the progress of the construction—I first established in mind the climax, or concluding query—that query to which "Nevermore" should be in the last place an answer—that in reply to which this word "Nevermore" should involve the uttermost conceivable amount of sorrow and despair.

Here then the poem may be said to have its beginning—at the end, where all works of art should begin—for it was here, at this point of my preconsiderations, that I first put pen to paper in the composition of the stanza:

> "Prophet," said I, "thing of evil! prophet still if bird or devil!
> By that heaven that bends above us—by that God we both adore,
> Tell this soul with sorrow laden, if within the distant Aidenn,
> It shall clasp a sainted maiden whom the angels name Lenore—
> Clasp a rare and radiant maiden whom the angels name Lenore."
> Quoth the Raven "Nevermore."

I composed this stanza, at this point, first that, by establishing the climax, I might the better vary and graduate, as regards seriousness and importance, the preceding queries of the lover—and, secondly, that I might definitely settle the rhythm, the metre, and the length and general arrangement of the stanza—as well as graduate the stanzas which were to precede, so that none of them might surpass this in rhythmical effect. Had I been able, in the subsequent composition, to construct more vigorous stanzas, I should, without scruple, have purposely enfeebled them, so as not to interfere with the climacteric effect.

And here I may as well say a few words of the versification. My first object (as usual) was originality. The extent to which this has been neglected, in versification, is one of the most unaccountable things in the world. Admitting that there is little possibility of variety in mere *rhythm*, it is still clear that the possible varieties of metre and stanza are absolutely infinite—and yet, *for centuries, no man, in verse, has ever done, or ever seemed to think of doing, an original thing.* The fact is, that originality (unless in minds of very unusual force) is by no means a matter, as some suppose, of impulse or intuition. In general, to be found, it must be elaborately sought, and although a positive merit of the highest class, demands in its attainment less of invention than negation.

Of course, I pretend to no originality in either the rhythm or metre of the "Raven." The former is trochaic—the latter is octameter acatalectic, alternating with heptameter catalectic repeated in the *refrain* of the fifth verse, and terminating with tetrameter catalectic. Less pedantically—the feet employed throughout (trochees) consist of a long syllable followed by a short; the first line of the stanza consists of eight of these feet—the second of seven and a half (in effect two-thirds)—the third of eight—the fourth of seven and a half—the fifth the same—the sixth three and a half. Now, each of these lines, taken individually, has been employed before, and what originality the "Raven" has, is in their *combination into stanza;* nothing even remotely approaching this combination has ever been attempted. The effect of this originality of combination is aided by other unusual, and some altogether novel effects, arising from an extension of the application of the principles of rhyme and alliteration.

The next point to be considered was the mode of bringing together the lover and the Raven—and the first branch of this consideration was the *locale.* For this the most natural suggestion might seem to be a forest, or the fields—but it has always appeared to me that a close *circumscription of space* is absolutely necessary to the effect of insulated incident:—it has the force of a frame to a picture. It has an indisputable moral power in keeping concentrated the attention, and, of course, must not be confounded with mere unity of place.

I determined, then, to place the lover in his chamber—in a chamber rendered sacred to him by memories of her who had frequented it. The room is represented as richly furnished—this in mere pursuance of the ideas I have already explained on the subject of Beauty, as the sole true poetical thesis.

The *locale* being thus determined, I had now to introduce the bird—and the thought of introducing him through the window, was inevitable. The idea of making the lover suppose, in the first instance, that the flapping of the wings of the bird against the shutter, is a "tapping" at the door, originated in the wish to increase, by prolonging, the reader's curiosity, and in a desire to admit the incidental effect arising from the lover's throwing open the door, finding all dark, and thence adopting the half-fancy that it was the spirit of his mistress that knocked.

I made the night tempestuous, first, to account for the Raven's seeking admission, and secondly, for the effect of contrast with the (physical) serenity within the chamber.

I made the bird alight on the bust of Pallas, also for the effect of contrast between the marble and the plumage—it being understood that the bust was absolutely *suggested* by the bird—the bust of *Pallas* being chosen, first, as most in keeping with the scholarship of the lover, and, secondly, for the sonorousness of the word, Pallas, itself.

About the middle of the poem, also, I have availed myself of the force of contrast, with a view of deepening the ultimate impression. For example, an air of the fantastic —approaching as nearly to the ludicrous as was admissible—is given to the Raven's entrance. He comes in "with many a flirt and flutter."

Not the *least obeisance made he*—not a moment stopped or stayed he,
But with mien of lord or lady, perched above my chamber door.

In the two stanzas which follow, the design is more obviously carried out:—

Then this ebony bird beguiling my sad fancy into smiling
By the *grave and stern decorum of the countenance it wore,*
"Though thy *crest be shorn and shaven* thou," I said, "art sure no craven,
Ghastly grim and ancient Raven wandering from the nightly shore—
Tell me what thy lordly name is on the Night's Plutonian shore?"
Quoth the Raven "Nevermore."

Much I marvelled *this ungainly fowl* to hear discourse so plainly
Though its answer little meaning—little relevancy bore;
For we cannot help agreeing that no living human being
Ever yet was blessed with seeing bird above his chamber door—
Bird or beast upon the sculptured bust above his chamber door,
With such name as "Nevermore."

The effect of the *dénouement* being thus provided for, I immediately drop the fantastic for a tone of the most profound seriousness:—this tone commencing in the stanza directly following the one last quoted, with the line,

But the Raven, sitting lonely on that placid bust, spoke only, etc.

From this epoch the lover no longer jests—no longer sees anything even of the fantastic in the Raven's demeanor. He speaks of him as a "grim, ungainly, ghastly, gaunt, and ominous bird of yore," and feels the "fiery eyes" burning into his "bosom's core." This revolution of thought, or fancy, on the lover's part, is intended to induce a similar one on the part of the reader—to bring the mind into a proper frame for the *dénouement*—which is now brought about as rapidly and as *directly* as possible.

With the *dénouement* proper—with the Raven's reply, "Nevermore," to the lover's final demand if he shall meet his mistress in another world—the poem, in its obvious phase, that of a simple narartive, may be said to have its completion. So far, everything is within the limits of the accountable—of the real. A raven, having learned by rote the single word "Nevermore," and having escaped from the custody of its owner, is driven at midnight, through the violence of a storm, to seek admission at a window from which a light still gleams—the chamber-window of a student, occupied half in poring over a volume, half in dreaming of a beloved mistress deceased. The casement being thrown open at the fluttering of the bird's wings, the bird itself perches on the most convenient seat out of the immediate reach of the student, who, amused by the incident and the oddity of the visitor's demeanor, demands of it, in jest and without looking for a reply, its name. The raven addressed, answers with its customary word, "Nevermore"—a word which finds immediate echo in the melancholy heart of the student, who, giving utterance aloud to certain thoughts suggested by the occasion, is again startled by the fowl's repetition of "Nevermore." The student now guesses the state of the case, but is impelled, as I have before explained, by the human thirst for self-torture, and in part by superstition, to propound such queries to the bird as will bring him, the lover, the most of the luxury of sorrow, through the anticipated answer "Nevermore." With the indulgence, to the extreme, of this self-torture, the narration, in what I have termed its first or obvious phase, has a natural termination, and so far there has been no overstepping of the limits of the real.

But in subjects so handled, however skilfully, or with however vivid an array of incident, there is always a certain hardness or nakedness, which repels the artistical eye. Two things are invariably required—first, some amount of complexity, or more properly, adaptation; and, secondly, some amount of suggestiveness—some under-current, however indefinite, of meaning. It is this latter, in especial, which imparts to a work of art so much of that *richness* (to borrow from colloquy a forcible term) which we are too fond of confounding with *the ideal*. It is the *excess* of the suggested meaning— it is the rendering this the upper instead of the under current of the theme—which turns into prose (and that of the very flattest kind) the so-called poetry of the so-called transcendentalists.

Holding these opinions, I added the two concluding stanzas of the poem—their suggestiveness being thus made to pervade all the narrative which has preceded them. The under-current of meaning is rendered first apparent in the lines—

> "Take thy beak from out *my heart,* and take thy form from off my door!"
> Quoth the Raven, "Nevermore!"

It will be observed that the words, "from out my heart," involve the first metaphorical expression in the poem. They, with the answer, "Nevermore," dispose the mind to seek a moral in all that has been previously narrated. The reader begins now to regard the Raven as emblematical—but it is not until the very last line of the very last stanza, that the intention of making him emblematical of *Mournful and Never-ending Remembrance* is permitted distinctly to be seen:

> And the Raven, never flitting, still is sitting, still is sitting,
> On the pallid bust of Pallas, just above my chamber door;
> And his eyes have all the seeming of a demon's that is dreaming,
> And the lamplight o'er him streaming throws his shadow on the floor;
> And my soul *from out that shadow* that lies floating on the floor
> Shall be lifted—nevermore.

iii. The Revision of Poetry

_____

TWO VERSIONS OF A SHAKESPEARE SONNET: A STUDY IN ORIGINAL PUNCTUATION AND SPELLING

ROBERT GRAVES (1895–   )

Here are two versions of a sonnet by Shakespeare: first, the version found in *The Oxford Book of English Verse* and other popular anthologies whose editors may be assumed to have chosen this sonnet from all the rest as being particularly easy to understand; next, the version printed in the 1609 edition of the *Sonnets* and apparently copied from Shakespeare's original manuscript, though Shakespeare is most unlikely to have seen the proofs. The alterations, it will be noticed in a comparison of the two versions, are with a few exceptions chiefly in the punctuation and spelling. By showing what a great difference to the sense the juggling of punctuation marks has made in the original sonnet, we shall perhaps be able to persuade the plain reader to sympathize with what seems typographical perversity in Mr. Cummings. The modernizing of the spelling is not quite so serious a matter, though we shall see that to change a word like *blouddy* to *bloody* makes a difference not only in the atmosphere of the word but in its sound as well.

SONNET 129

I

Th' expense of Spirit in a waste of shame
Is lust in action; and till action, lust
Is perjured, murderous, bloody, full of blame,
Savage, extreme, rude, cruel, not to trust;
Enjoy'd no sooner but despisèd straight;   5
Past reason hunted; and, no sooner had,
Past reason hated, as a swallow'd bait
On purpose laid to make the taker mad:
Mad in pursuit, and in possession so;
Had, having, and in quest to have, extreme;   10
A bliss in proof, and proved, a very woe;
Before, a joy proposed; behind, a dream.
  All this the world well knows; yet none knows well
  To shun the heaven that leads men to this hell.

2

Th' expence of Spirit in a waste of shame
Is lust in action, and till action, lust
Is periurd, murdrous, blouddy full of blame,
Sauage, extreame, rude, cruell, not to trust,
Inioyd no sooner but dispised straight,   5
Past reason hunted, and no sooner had
Past reason hated as a swollowed bayt,
On purpose layd to make the taker mad.
Made In pursut and in possession so,
Had, hauing, and in quest, to haue extreame,   10
A blisse in proofe and proud and very wo,
Before a ioy proposd behind a dreame,
    All this the world well knowes yet none knowes well,
    To shun the heauen that leads men to this hell.

First, to compare the spelling. As a matter of course the *u* in *proud* and *heauen* changes to *v*; the Elizabethans had no typographical *v*. There are other words in which the change of spelling does not seem to matter. *Expence, cruell, bayt, layd, pursut, blisse, proofe, wo*—these words taken by themselves are not necessarily affected by modernization, though much of the original atmosphere of the poem is lost by changing them in the gross. Sheer facility in reading a poem is no gain when one tries to discover what the poem looked like to the poet who wrote it. But other changes designed to increase reading facility involve more than changes in spelling. *Periurd* to *perjured*, and *murdrous* to *murderous*, would have meant, to Shakespeare, the addition of another syllable. *Inioyd*, with the same number of syllables as *periurd*, is however printed *Enjoy'd*; while *swollowed*, which must have been meant as a three-syllabled word (Shakespeare used *ed* as a separate syllable very strictly and frequently allowed himself an extra syllable in his iambic foot) is printed *swallow'd*. When we come to *dispised*, we find in the modern version an accent over the last syllable. These liberties do not make the poem any easier; they only make it less accurate. The sound of the poem suffers through re-spelling as well as through alterations in the rhythm made by this use of apostrophes and accents. *Blouddy* was pronounced more like *blue-dy* than *bluddy*; the *ea* of *extreame* and *dreame* sounded like the *ea* in *great*; and *periurd* was probably pronounced more like *peryurd* than *pergeurd*.

But it is the changes in punctuation which do the most damage: not only to the atmosphere of the poem but to its meaning. In the second line a semicolon substituted for a comma after the first *action* gives a longer rest than Shakespeare gave; it also cuts the idea short at *action* instead of keeping *in action* and *till action* together as well as the two *lust*'s. A comma after *blouddy* makes this a separate characterization and thus reduces the weight of the whole phrase as rhythmic relief to the string of adjectives; it probably had the adverbial form of *blouddily*. Next, several semicolons are substituted for commas; these introduce pauses which break up the continuous interpenetration of images. If Shakespeare had intended such pauses he would have used semicolons, as he does elsewhere. Particularly serious is the interpolation of a comma after *no sooner had,* which confines the phrase to the special meaning 'lust no sooner had *past reason* is hated past reason.' Shakespeare did not write in the syntax of prose but in a sensitive poetic flow. The comma might as well have been put between *reason* and *hated;* it would have limited the meaning, but no more than has been done here. On the other hand a comma is omitted where Shakespeare was careful to put one, after *bayt*. With the comma, *On purpose layd*—though it refers to *bayt*—also looks back to the original idea of *lust;* without the comma it merely continues the figure of *bayt*. In the original there is a full stop at *mad,* closing the octave; in the emended version a colon is used, making the next line run on and causing the unpardonable change from *Made* to *Mad.* The capital 'I' of *In* shows how carefully the printer copied the manuscript. Evidently, Shakespeare first wrote the line without *Made,* and then, deciding that such an irregular line was too dramatic, added *Made* without troubling to change the capital 'I' to a small one. In any case *Made* necessarily follows from *make* of the preceding line: 'to make the taker mad, made (mad)'; but it also enlarges the mad-making bayt to the generally extreame-making lust. The change from *Made* to *Mad* limits the final *so* of this line to *Mad* and provokes a change from comma to semicolon—'Mad in pursuit and in possession so (mad)'—whereas *mad* is only vaguely echoed in this line from the preceding one. The meaning of the original line is: 'Made In pursut and in possession as follows,' and also: 'Made In pursut and in possession as has been said.'

The comma between *in quest* and *to have extreame* has been moved forward to separate *have* from *extreame.* This line originally stood for a number of interwoven meanings:

1. The taker of the bait, the man in pursuit and in possession of lust, is made mad: is so made that he experiences both extremes at once. (What these extremes are the lines following show.)

2. The *Had, having and in quest,* might well have been written in parentheses. They explain, by way of interjection, that lust comprises all the stages of lust: the afterlust period (*Had*), the actual experience of lust (*having*), and the anticipation of lust (*in quest*); and that the extremes of lust are felt in all these stages (*to have extreame* —i.e. to have in extreme degree).

3. Further, one stage in lust is like the others, is as extreme as the others. All the distinctions made in the poem between *lust in action* and *till action lust,* between lust *In pursut* and lust *in possession* are made to show that in the end there are no real distinctions. *Had, having and in quest* is the summing up of this fact.

4. *Had* and *having* double the sense of *possession* to match the double sense of *action* implied by *Th' expence of Spirit in a waste of shame;* and *in quest* naturally refers to *In pursut,* which in turn recalls *till action.*

5. Throughout the poem it must be kept in mind that words qualifying the lust-interest refer interchangeably to the man who lusts, the object of lust and lust in the abstract. This interchangeability accounts for the apparently ungrammatical effect of the line.

With the emended punctuation the line has only one narrow sense, and this not precisely Shakespeare's; the semicolon placed after *so* of the preceding line, cuts the close co-operation between them. The shifting of the comma not only removes a pause where Shakespeare put one, and thus changes the rhythm, but the line itself loses point and does not pull its weight. In this punctuation the *whole* line ought to be put into parentheses, as being a mere repetition. The *to have* linked with *in quest* is superfluous; *extreme* set off by itself is merely a descriptive adjective already used. Moreover, when the line is thus isolated between two semicolons, *Had, having,* etc., instead of effecting a harmony between the interchangeable senses, disjoints them and becomes ungrammatical. *Mad in pursuit, and in possession so* refers only to *the taker mad.* The next line, *A blisse in proofe and proud and very wo,* should explain *to have extreame;* it is not merely another parenthetical line as in the emended version. To fulfil the paradox implied in *extreame* it should mean that lust is a bliss during the proof and after the proof, and also *very wo* (truly woe) during and after the proof. The emended line, *A bliss in proof, and proved, a very woe,* which refers only to lust in the abstract, not equally to the man who lusts, means that lust is a bliss during the proof but a woe after the proof—and thus denies what Shakespeare has been at pains to show all along, that lust is all things at all times.

Once the editors began repunctuating the line they had to tamper with the words themselves. A comma after *proof* demanded a comma after *provd.* A comma after *provd* made it necessary to change *and very wo* so that it should apply to *provd* only. Another semicolon which they have put at the end of this line again breaks the continuity of the sense: the succeeding line becomes only another antithesis or rhetorical balance ('a joy in prospect, but a dream in retrospect,' to repeat the sense of 'a bliss during proof but woe after proof'), instead of carrying on the intricate and careful argument that runs without a stop through the whole sestet. The importance of the line is that it takes all the meanings in the poem one stage further. Lust in the extreme goes beyond both bliss and woe: it goes beyond reality. It is no longer lust *Had, having and in quest;* it is lust face to face with *love.* Even when consummated, lust still stands before an unconsummated joy, a proposed joy, and proposed not as a joy possible of consummation but as one only to be known through the dream by which lust leads itself on, the dream behind which this proposed joy, this love, seems to lie. This is the over-riding meaning of the line. It has other meanings, but they all defer to this. For example, it may also be read: 'Before a joy can be proposed, it must first be renounced as a real joy, it must be put behind as a dream'; or: 'Before the man in lust is a prospect of joy, yet he knows by experience that this is only a dream'; or: 'Beforehand he says that he proposed lust to be a joy, afterwards he says that it came as involuntarily as a dream'; or: 'Before (in face of) a joy proposed only as a consequence of a dream, with a dream impelling him from behind.' All these and even more readings of the line are possible and legitimate, and each reading could in turn be made to explain precisely why the taker is made mad, or how lust is *to have extreme,* or why it is both a *blisse* and *very wo.* The punctuated line in the emended version, cut off from what has gone before and from what follows, can mean only: 'In prospect, lust is a joy; in retrospect, a dream.' Though a possible contributory meaning, when made the *only* meaning it presents as the theme of the poem that lust is impossible of satisfaction, whereas the theme, as carried on by the next line, is that lust as lust *is* satisfiable but that satisfied lust is in conflict with itself.

The next line, if unpunctuated except for the comma Shakespeare put at the end, is a general statement of this conflict: the man in lust is torn between lust as he well knows it in common with the world and lust in his personal experience which crazes him to hope for more than lust from lust. The force of the second *well* is to deny the first *well:* no one really knows anything of lust except in personal experience, and only through personal experience can lust be known *well* rather than 'well-known.' But separate the second *well* from the first, as in the emended version, and the direct opposition between *world* and *none, well knowes* and *knowes well* is destroyed, as well as the word-play between *well knowes* and *knowes well;* for by the removal of the comma after the second *well,* this becomes an adverb modifying *To shun* in the following line—*well* now means merely 'successfully' in association with *To shun,* instead of 'well enough' in association with *knowes.* This repunctuation also robs *All this* of its significance, since it refers not only to all that has gone before but to the last line too: 'All this the world well knowes yet none knowes well' the moral to be drawn from the character of lust (i.e. to shun the heaven that leads men to this hell). The character and the moral of lust the whole world well knows, but no one knows the character and the moral really well unless he disregards the moral warning and engages in lust: no one knows lust well enough to shun it because, though he knows it is both heavenly and hellish, lust can never be recognized until it has proved itself lust by turning heaven into hell.

The effect of this emended punctuation has been to restrict meanings to special interpretations of special words. Shakespeare's punctuation allows the variety of meanings he actually intends; if we must choose any one meaning, then we owe it to Shakespeare to choose at least one he intended and one embracing as many meanings as possible, that is, the most difficult meaning. It is always the most difficult meaning which is the most nearly final. No prose interpretation of poetry can have complete finality, can be difficult enough. Shakespeare's editors, in trying to clarify him for the plain man, weakened and diluted his poetry and in effect deprived him of clarity. There is only one way to clarify Shakespeare: to print him as he wrote or as near as one can get to this. Making poetry easy for the reader should mean showing clearly how difficult it really is.

THE TIGER

WILLIAM BLAKE (1757–1827)

[ORIGINAL DRAFT]

1. Tyger Tyger burning bright
   In the forests of the night
   What immortal hand & eye
                  or
   ~~Could~~ frame thy fearful symmetry
   ~~Dare~~

2. ~~In what~~ distant deeps or skies
   ~~Burnt in~~
   ~~Burnt the~~ fire of thine eyes
   ~~The cruel~~
   On what wings dare he aspire
   What the hand dare sieze the fire

2. [Revised]
   ~~Burnt in distant deeps or skies~~
   ~~The cruel fire of thine eyes~~
   ~~Could heart descend or wings aspire~~
   ~~What the hand dare sieze the fire~~

3. And what shoulder & what art
   Could twist the sinews of thy heart
   And when thy heart began to beat
   What dread hand & what dread feet

[FINAL VERSION]

1. Tiger! Tiger! burning bright
   In the forests of the night,
   What immortal hand or eye
   Could frame thy fearful symmetry?

2. In what distant deeps or skies
   Burnt the fire of thine eyes?
   On what wings dare he aspire?
   What the hand dare seize the fire?

3. And what shoulder, and what art,
   Could twist the sinews of thy heart?
   And when thy heart began to beat, 11
   What dread hand? and what dread feet?

[ORIGINAL DRAFT]   [FINAL VERSION]

~~Could fetch it from the furnace deep~~
~~And in thy horrid ribs dare steep~~
~~In the well of sanguine woe~~
~~In what clay & in what mould~~
~~Were thy eyes of fury rolld~~

4. ~~What~~ the hammer ~~what~~ the chain   4. What the hammer? what the chain?
    ~~Where~~   ~~where~~   In what furnace was thy brain?
    In what furnace was thy brain   What the anvil? what dread grasp
    What the anvil What ~~the arm~~   Dare its deadly terrors clasp?
                         ~~arm~~
                         ~~grasp~~
                         ~~clasp~~
                    dread grasp
    ~~Could~~ its deadly terrors ~~clasp~~
    Dare   ~~grasp~~
                      clasp

5. And ~~did he laugh~~ his work to see   5. When the stars threw down their
        dare he ~~smile~~   spears,
                ~~laugh~~   And water'd heaven with their tears,
                                                         Did he smile his work to see?
3. ~~What the shoulder what the knee~~   Did he who made the Lamb make
            ~~ankle~~   thee?   20
    ~~Did~~ he who made the lamb make thee
    Dare
    When the stars threw down their
        spears
    And waterd heaven with their tears

6. Tyger Tyger burning bright   6. Tiger! Tiger! burning bright
    In the forests of the night   In the forests of the night,
    What immortal hand & eye   What immortal hand or eye,
    Dare ~~form~~ thy fearful symmetry   Dare frame thy fearful symmetry?
        frame

THE EVE OF ST. AGNES

JOHN KEATS (1795–1821)

I

St. Agnes' Eve—Ah, bitter chill it was!
The owl, for all his feathers, was a-cold;
The hare limped trembling through the frozen grass,
And silent was the flock in woolly fold:
Numb were the Beadsman's fingers, while he told
His rosary, and while his frosted breath,
Like pious incense from a censer old,

Seemed taking flight for heaven, without a death,
Past the sweet Virgin's picture, while his prayer he saith.

2

His prayer he saith, this patient, holy man;   10
Then takes his lamp, and riseth from his knees,
And back returneth, meagre, barefoot, wan,
Along the chapel aisle by slow degrees:
The sculptured dead, on each side, seem to freeze,
Emprisoned in black, purgatorial rails:
Knights, ladies, praying in dumb orat'ries,
He passeth by; and this weak spirit fails
To think how they may ache in icy hoods and mails.

3

Northward he turneth through a little door,
And scarce three steps, ere Music's golden tongue   20
Flattered to tears this aged man and poor;
But no—already had his deathbell rung:
The joys of all his life were said and sung:
His was harsh penance on St. Agnes' Eve:
Another way he went, and soon among
Rough ashes sat he for his soul's reprieve,
And all night kept awake, for sinners' sake to grieve.

4

That ancient Beadsman heard the prelude soft;
And so it chanced, for many a door was wide,
From hurry to and fro. Soon, up aloft,   30
The silver, snarling trumpets 'gan to chide:
The level chambers, ready with their pride,
Were glowing to receive a thousand guests:
The carvèd angels, ever eager-eyed,
Stared, where upon their heads the cornice rests,
With hair blown back, and wings put cross-wise on their breasts.

5

At length burst in the argent revelry,
With plume, tiara, and all rich array,
Numerous as shadows haunting faerily
The brain, new stuffed, in youth, with triumphs gay   40
Of old romance. These let us wish away,
And turn, sole-thoughted, to one Lady there,
Whose heart had brooded, all that wintry day,
On love, and winged St. Agnes' saintly care,
As she had heard old dames full many times declare.

6

They told her how, upon St. Agnes' Eve,
Young virgins might have visions of delight,
And soft adorings from their loves receive
Upon the honeyed middle of the night,

If ceremonies due they did aright;
As, supperless to bed they must retire,
And couch supine their beauties, lily white;
Nor look behind, nor sideways, but require
Of Heaven with upward eyes for all that they desire.

7

Full of this whim was thoughtful Madeline:
The music, yearning like a God in pain,
She scarcely heard: her maiden eyes divine,
Fixed on the floor, saw many a sweeping train
Pass by—she heeded not at all: in vain
Came many a tiptoe, amorous cavalier,
And back retired; not cooled by high disdain,
But she saw not: her heart was otherwhere:
She sighed for Agnes' dreams, the sweetest of the year.

8

She danced along with vague, regardless eyes,
Anxious her lips, her breathing quick and short:
The hallowed hour was near at hand: she sighs
Amid the timbrels, and the thronged resort
Of whisperers in anger, or in sport;
'Mid looks of love, defiance, hate, and scorn,
Hoodwinked with faery fancy; all amort,
Save to St. Agnes and her lambs unshorn,
And all the bliss to be before tomorrow morn.

9

So, purposing each moment to retire,
She lingered still. Meantime, across the moors,
Had come young Porphyro, with heart on fire
For Madeline. Beside the portal doors,
Buttressed from moonlight, stands he, and implores
All saints to give him sight of Madeline,
But for one moment in the tedious hours,
That he might gaze and worship all unseen;
Perchance speak, kneel, touch, kiss—in sooth such things have been.

10

He ventures in: let no buzzed whisper tell:
All eyes be muffled, or a hundred swords
Will storm his heart, Love's fev'rous citadel:
For him, those chambers held barbarian hordes,
Hyena foemen, and hot-blooded lords,
Whose very dogs would execrations howl
Against his lineage: not one breast affords
Him any mercy, in that mansion foul,
Save one old beldame, weak in body and in soul.

11

Ah, happy chance! the agèd creature came,
Shuffling along with ivory-headed wand,
To where he stood, hid from the torch's flame,
Behind a broad hall-pillar, far beyond
The sound of merriment and chorus bland:
He startled her; but soon she knew his face,
And grasped his fingers in her palsied hand,
Saying, "Mercy, Porphyro! hie thee from this place:
"They are all here tonight, the whole blood-thirsty race!

12

"Get hence! get hence! there's dwarfish Hildebrand;   100
He had a fever late, and in the fit
He cursèd thee and thine, both house and land:
Then there's that old Lord Maurice, not a whit
More tame for his gray hairs—Alas me! flit!
Flit like a ghost away."—"Ah, Gossip dear,
We're safe enough; here in this arm-chair sit,
And tell me how"—"Good Saints! not here, not here;
Follow me, child, or else these stones will be thy bier."

13

He followed through a lowly archèd way,
Brushing the cobwebs with his lofty plume,   110
And as she mutter'd "Well-a—well-a-day!"
He found him in a little moonlight room,
Pale, latticed, chill, and silent as a tomb.
"Now tell me where is Madeline," said he,
"O tell me, Angela, by the holy loom
Which none but secret sisterhood may see,
When they St. Agnes' wool are weaving piously."

14

"St. Agnes! Ah! it is St. Agnes' Eve—
Yet men will murder upon holy days:
Thou must hold water in a witch's sieve,   120
And be liege-lord of all the Elves and Fays,
To venture so: it fills me with amaze
To see thee, Porphyro!—St. Agnes' Eve!
God's help! my lady fair the conjuror plays
This very night: good angels her deceive!
But let me laugh awhile, I've mickle time to grieve."

15

Feebly she laugheth in the languid moon,
While Porphyro upon her face doth look,
Like puzzled urchin on an agèd crone
Who keepeth closed a wond'rous riddle-book.   130

As spectacled she sits in chimney nook.
But soon his eyes grew brilliant, when she told
His lady's purpose; and he scarce could brook
Tears, at the thought of those enchantments cold,
And Madeline asleep in lap of legends old.

16

Sudden a thought came like a full-blown rose,
Flushing his brow, and in his painèd heart
Made purple riot: then doth he propose
A stratagem, that makes the beldame start:
"A cruel man and impious thou art: 140
Sweet lady, let her pray, and sleep, and dream
Alone with her good angels, far apart
From wicked men like thee. Go, go!—I deem
Thou canst not surely be the same that thou didst seem."

17

"I will not harm her, by all saints I swear,"
Quoth Porphyro: "O may I ne'er find grace
When my weak voice shall whisper its last prayer,
If one of her soft ringlets I displace,
Or look with ruffian passion in her face:
Good Angela, believe me by these tears;   150
Or I will, even in a moment's space,
Awake, with horrid shout, my foemen's ears,
And beard them, though they be more fanged than wolves and bears."

18

"Ah! why wilt thou affright a feeble soul?
A poor, weak, palsy-stricken, churchyard thing,
Whose passing-bell may ere the midnight toll;
Whose prayers for thee, each morn and evening,
Were never missed."—Thus plaining, doth she bring
A gentler speech from burning Porphyro;
So woful, and of such deep sorrowing,   160
That Angela gives a promise she will do
Whatever he shall wish, betide her weal or woe.

19

Which was, to lead him, in close secrecy,
Even to Madeline's chamber, and there hide
Him in a closet, of such privacy
That he might see her beauty unespied,
And win perhaps that night a peerless bride,
While legioned faeries paced the coverlet,
And pale enchantment held her sleepy-eyed.
Never on such a night have lovers met,   170
Since Merlin paid his Demon all the monstrous debt.

20

"It shall be as thou wishest," said the Dame:
"All cates and dainties shall be storèd there
Quickly on this feast-night: by the tambour frame
Her own lute thou wilt see: no time to spare,
For I am slow and feeble, and scarce dare
On such a catering trust my dizzy head.
Wait here, my child, with patience; kneel in prayer
The while: Ah! thou must needs the lady wed,
Or may I never leave my grave among the dead." 180

21

So saying, she hobbled off with busy fear.
The lover's endless minutes slowly passed;
The dame returned, and whispered in his ear
To follow her; with agèd eyes aghast
From fright of dim espial. Safe at last,
Through many a dusky gallery, they gain
The maiden's chamber, silken, hushed, and chaste;
Where Porphyro took covert, pleased amain.
His poor guide hurried back with agues in her brain.

22

Her falt'ring hand upon the balustrade, 191
Old Angela was feeling for the stair,
When Madeline, St. Agnes' charmèd maid,
Rose, like a missioned spirit, unaware:
With silver taper's light, and pious care,
She turned, and down the agèd gossip led
To a safe level matting. Now prepare,
Young Porphyro, for gazing on that bed;
She comes, she comes again, like ring-dove frayed and fled.

23

Out went the taper as she hurried in;
Its little smoke, in pallid moonshine, died: 200
She closed the door, she panted, all akin
To spirits of the air, and visions wide:
No uttered syllable, or, woe betide!
But to her heart, her heart was voluble,
Paining with eloquence her balmy side;
As though a tongueless nightingale should swell
Her throat in vain, and die, heart-stifled, in her dell.

24

A casement high and triple-arched there was,
All garlanded with carven imag'ries
Of fruits, and flowers, and bunches of knot-grass, 210
And diamonded with panes of quaint device,

Innumerable of stains and splendid dyes,
As are the tiger-moth's deep-damasked wings;
And in the midst, 'mong thousand heraldries,
And twilight saints, and dim emblazonings,
A shielded scutcheon blushed with blood of queens and kings.

25

Full on this casement shone the wintry moon,
And threw warm gules on Madeline's fair breast,
As down she knelt for heaven's grace and boon;
Rose-bloom fell on her hands, together prest,   220
And on her silver cross soft amethyst,
And on her hair a glory, like a saint:
She seemed a splendid angel, newly drest,
Save wings, for heaven:—Porphyro grew faint:
She knelt, so pure a thing, so free from mortal taint.

26

Anon his heart revives: her vespers done,
Of all its wreathèd pearls her hair she frees;
Unclasps her warmèd jewels one by one;
Loosens her fragrant bodice; by degrees
Her rich attire creeps rustling to her knees: 230
Half-hidden, like a mermaid in sea-weed,
Pensive awhile she dreams awake, and sees,
In fancy, fair St. Agnes in her bed,
But dares not look behind, or all the charm is fled.

27

Soon, trembling in her soft and chilly nest,
In sort of wakeful swoon, perplexed she lay,
Until the poppied warmth of sleep oppressed
Her soothèd limbs, and soul fatigued away;
Flown, like a thought, until the morrow-day;
Blissfully havened both from joy and pain;   240
Clasped like a missal where swart Paynims pray;
Blinded alike from sunshine and from rain,
As though a rose should shut, and be a bud again.

28

Stol'n to this paradise, and so entranced,
Porphyro gazed upon her empty dress,
And listened to her breathing, if it chanced
To wake into a slumberous tenderness;
Which when he heard, that minute did he bless,
And breathed himself: then from the closet crept,
Noiseless as fear in a wide wilderness,   250
And over the hushed carpet, silent, stept,
And 'tween the curtains peeped. where, lo!—how fast she slept.

29

Then by the bed-side, where the faded moon
Made a dim, silver twilight, soft he set
A table, and, half anguished, threw thereon
A cloth of woven crimson, gold, and jet:—
O for some drowsy Morphean amulet!
The boisterous, midnight, festive clarion,
The kettle-drum, and far-heard clarinet,
Affray his ears, though but in dying tone:—   260
The hall door shuts again, and all the noise is gone.

30

And still she slept an azure-lidded sleep,
In blanchèd linen, smooth, and lavendered,
While he from forth the closet brought a heap
Of candied apple, quince, and plum, and gourd;
With jellies soother than the creamy curd,
And lucent syrups, tinct with cinnamon;
Manna and dates, in argosy transferred
From Fez; and spicèd dainties, every one,   270
From silken Samarcand to cedared Lebanon.

31

These delicates he heaped with glowing hand
On golden dishes and in baskets bright
Of wreathèd silver: sumptuous they stand
In the retired quiet of the night,
Filling the chilly room with perfume light.—
"And now, my love, my seraph fair, awake!
Thou art my heaven, and I thine eremite:
Open thine eyes, for meek St. Agnes' sake,
Or I shall drowse beside thee, so my soul doth ache."

32

Thus whispering, his warm, unnervèd arm   280
Sank in her pillow. Shaded was her dream
By the dusk curtains:—'twas a midnight charm
Impossible to melt as icèd stream:
The lustrous salvers in the moonlight gleam;
Broad golden fringe upon the carpet lies:
It seemed he never, never could redeem
From such a stedfast spell his lady's eyes;
So mused awhile, entoiled in woofèd phantasies.

33

Awakening up, he took her hollow lute,—
Tumultuous,—and, in chords that tenderest be,   290
He played an ancient ditty, long since mute,
In Provence called, "La belle dame sans merci:"

Close to her ear touching the melody;—
Wherewith disturbed, she utter'd a soft moan:
He ceased—she panted quick—and suddenly
Her blue affrayèd eyes wide open shone:
Upon his knees he sank, pale as smooth-sculptured stone.

34

Her eyes were open, but she still beheld,
Now wide awake, the vision of her sleep:
There was a painful change, that nigh expelled   300
The blisses of her dream so pure and deep
At which fair Madeline began to weep,
And moan forth witless words with many a sigh;
While still her gaze on Porphyro would keep;
Who knelt, with joinèd hands and piteous eye,
Fearing to move or speak, she looked so dreamingly.

35

"Ah, Porphyro!" said she, "but even now
Thy voice was at sweet tremble in mine ear,
Made tuneable with every sweetest vow;
And those sad eyes were spiritual and clear: 310
How changed thou art! how pallid, chill, and drear!
Give me that voice again, my Porphyro,
Those looks immortal, those complainings dear!
Oh, leave me not in this eternal woe,
For if thou diest, my Love, I know not where to go."

36

Beyond a mortal man impassioned far
At these voluptuous accents, he arose,
Ethereal, flushed, and like a throbbing star
Seen mid the sapphire heaven's deep repose;
Into her dream he melted, as the rose   320
Blendeth its odor with the violet,—
Solution sweet: meantime the frost wind blows
Like Love's alarum pattering the sharp sleet
Against the window panes; St. Agnes' moon hath set.

37

'Tis dark: quick pattereth the flaw-blown sleet.
"This is no dream, my bride, my Madeline!"
'Tis dark: the iced gusts still rave and beat:
"No dream, alas! alas! and woe is mine!
Porphyro will leave me here to fade and pine.
Cruel! what traitor could thee hither bring?   330
I curse not, for my heart is lost in thine,
Though thou forsakest a deceivèd thing;—
A dove forlorn and lost with sick unprunèd wing."

38

"My Madeline! sweet dreamer! lovely bride!
Say, may I be for aye thy vassal blest?
Thy beauty's shield, heart-shaped and vermeil-dyed?
Ah, silver shrine, here will I take my rest
After so many hours of toil and quest,
A famished pilgrim,—saved by miracle.
Though I have found, I will not rob thy nest,   340
Saving of thy sweet self; if thou think'st well
To trust, fair Madeline, to no rude infidel.

39

"Hark! 'tis an elfin-storm from faery land,
Of haggard seeming, but a boon indeed:
Arise—arise! the morning is at hand;—
The bloated wassailers will never heed;—
Let us away, my love, with happy speed;
There are no ears to hear, or eyes to see,—
Drowned all in Rhenish and the sleepy mead:
Awake! arise! my love, and fearless be,   350
For o'er the southern moors I have a home for thee."

40

She hurried at his words, beset with fears,
For there were sleeping dragons all around,
At glaring watch, perhaps, with ready spears—
Down the wide stairs a darkling way they found;
In all the house was heard no human sound.
A chain-drooped lamp was flickering by each door;
The arras, rich with horseman, hawk, and hound,
Fluttered in the besieging wind's uproar;
And the long carpets rose along the gusty floor.   360

41

They glide, like phantoms, into the wide hall;
Like phantoms, to the iron porch they glide,
Where lay the Porter, in uneasy sprawl,
With a huge empty flagon by his side:
The wakeful bloodhound rose, and shook his hide,
But his sagacious eye an inmate owns:
By one, and one, the bolts full easy slide:—
The chains lie silent on the footworn stones;
The key turns, and the door upon its hinges groans.

42

And they are gone: aye, ages long ago   370
These lovers fled away into the storm.
That night the Baron dreamt of many a woe,
And all his warrior-guests with shade and form

Of witch, and demon, and large coffin-worm,
Were long be-nightmared. Angela the old
Died palsy-twitched, with meagre face deform;
The Beadsman, after thousand aves told,
For aye unsought-for slept among his ashes cold.

FROM THE MANUSCRIPTS OF
KEATS' "THE EVE OF ST. AGNES"

There exists, in Keats' own handwriting, a manuscript which is almost certainly the first working draft of the poem, complete except for the first seven stanzas. The original work sheets of these seven stanzas have not been found, but a close friend, Richard Woodhouse Jr., made a copy of the whole poem when its first draft was completed. Some changes were made in this draft before the poem appeared in print. [For a complete and fascinating analysis of all the versions of the poem the indispensable study is M. R. Ridley's *Keats' Craftsmanship: A Study in Poetic Development* (Oxford, 1933).] It is from Woodhouse's transcript of the first draft that the following versions of stanzas 3–6 are derived:

(stanza 3)

. . . harsh penance on St. Agnes's Eve:
Another way he turn'd; and soon among
Black ashes sat he for his soul's reprieve,
And all night kept awake, for sinners' souls to grieve.

(stanza 3a—not used in final version)

But there are ears may hear sweet melodies,
And there are eyes to brighten festivals,
And there are feet for nimble minstrelsies,
And many a lip that for the red wine calls—
Follow, then follow to the illumin'd halls,
Follow me youth—and leave the Eremite—
Give him a tear—then trophied banneral
And many a brilliant tasseling of light
Shall droop from archèd ways this high Baronial night.

(stanza 4)

That ancient Beadsman heard the prelude soft,
And so it chanc'd, for many a door was wide
From hurry to and fro—and now aloft,
The silver snarling trumpets 'gan to chide;
The level chambers ready with their pride
Seem'd anxious to receive a thousand guests:
The carvèd angels ever eager-eyed
Stared, where upon their heads the cornice rests,
With hair blown back, and wings put cross-wise on their breasts.

(stanza 5)

At length step in the argent revelers
With plume, tiara, and all rich array;
Ah what are they? the idle pulse scarce stirs,
The muse should never make the spirit gay;
Away, bright dulness, laughing fools away,—
And let me tell of one sweet lady there
Whose heart had brooded all that wintry day
On love, and wing'd St. Agnes' saintly care,
As she had heard old Dames full many times declare.

(stanza 6)

. . . soft adorings of their loves receive . . .
And lay supine their beauties lily white. . . .

(stanza 6a)

For some unknown reason this stanza was omitted from the published version, even
though it was apparently written late. Woodhouse saw it for the first time on Sunday,
Sept. 12, 1819, when Keats visited him with a fair copy of the poem. Writing to his
friend John Taylor, Woodhouse goes on: "He [Keats] has made trifling alterations,
inserted an additional stanza early in the poem to make the *legend* more intelligible,
and correspondent with what afterwards takes place, particularly with respect to the
supper & the playing on the Lute. . . ." [See H. E. Rollins, ed., *The Keats Circle*
(Cambridge, Mass., 1948), p. 91.]

'Twas said her future lord would there appear
Offering as sacrifice—all in the dream—
Delicious food even to her lips brought near:
Viands and wine and fruit and sugar'd cream,
To touch her palate with the fine extreme
Or relish: then soft music heard; and then
More pleasures followed in a dizzy stream
Palpable almost: then to wake again
Warm in the virgin morn, no weeping Magdalen.

[From here on the manuscript in Keats' own handwriting is being followed. Since it
is impossible to reproduce in type a much-revised handwritten draft, some modifica-
tions have been made in the reproduction for the purpose of making the revisions
intelligible in print. Keats' hurried slips in spelling are retained.]

(stanza 8)

She danc'd along with vague uneager ~~look~~ eyes
~~Her anxious lips full pulpd with rosy thoughts~~ mouth
Anxious her lips, her breathing quick and short
The hour was near at hand—~~and~~ hallowed she sighs
Amid the Timbrels, and the throng'd ressort

Of Whisperers in anger or in sport—
'Mid Looks of Love, defiance, hate and scorn,
    Hoodwink'd   faery
~~She was hoodwink'd~~ with fancy—all a mort
Save to St. Agnes and her Lambs unshorn
And all the Bliss to be before tomorrow morn

(stanza 9)

~~So purposing each moment to retire~~
~~She lingered fearful who might~~
She lingered still—meantime across the Moors
Had come young Porphyro with heart afire
           Beside
          ~~Within~~ the Portal Doors
For Madeline. ~~Most piteous he implores~~
~~Sh~~ Buttress'd from Moonlight stands he and implores
All saints to give him sight of Madeline
But for one moment in the tedious hours
           and worship all unseen
That he might gaze—~~or speak, or kneel~~
Perchance speak,—kneel—touch—kiss—in sooth such things have been.

(stanza 22)

~~There secreted~~
Scarce had old Angela the Stair case found
                  Swan
Ere Madeline, like an affrighted ~~Bird~~
Flew past her
~~Old An~~
~~Scarce had~~
With fautling hand upon the Ballustrad
Old Angela was feeling for the Stair
When Madeline St. Agnes charmed Maid
      missioned
Rose like a spirit ~~to her~~ unaware
    With silver
~~And with her~~ taper's light and gentle care
~~Guided her~~
       down   led
She turn'd and ~~led~~ the aged gossip ~~down~~
To ~~the~~ a save level matting—now prepare
Young Porphyro a-gazing on that Bed
She comes she comes again like ring dove fray'd and fled.

(stanzas 24 and 25)

[In his discussion of stanzas 24 and 25, Professor M. R. Ridley gives invaluable guidance through the complex creative process. The following quotations are taken from *Keats' Craftsmanship* (Oxford, 1933), pp. 149 ff.]

"For showing Keats the pure craftsman delighting in his mastery of his craft these next two stanzas are unequalled in the poem. There is no emotional stress to distract, no excitement of action to hurry him. He is quietly setting his stage for the climax, and he can take his time over making it as richly perfect as it can be made."

(stanza 24)

A Casement ~~ach'd~~ tripple archd and diamonded
  With many coloured glass fronted the Moon
      whereof
In midst ~~of which~~ a shilded scutcheon shed
  High blushing gules: ~~upon she kneeled saintly~~ down
  And inly prayed for grace and heavenly boon
  The blood red gules fell on her silver cross
  And ~~her~~ white(est) hands devout
here was
  A Casement tipple archd and high
  All garlanded with carven imageries
Of fruits & ~~trailing~~ flowers and sunny corn
                              ears parchd

A Casement high and tripple archd there was
All gardneded with carven imageries
Of fruits and flowers and bunches of knot grass;
  And diamonded with panes of quaint device
  Innumerable of stains and splendid dies
                    sunset
  As is the tiger moths ~~rich~~ deep ~~damasked~~ wings
  ~~As is the wing of evening tiger moths;~~
            whereoft   thousand
  ~~And~~ in ~~the~~ midst 'mong ~~man~~ heraldries
  And ~~dim twilight~~ twilight saints and dim emblasonings
A shielded scutcheon blushd with Blood of Queens & Kings

(stanza 25)

Full on this Casement shone the wintry moon
      ~~warm~~ rich   breast
  And threw ~~red~~ gules on Madelines fair ~~face~~
As down she kneel'd for heavens grace and boon
                        fell
~~And~~ rose ~~with red~~ bloom on her hands together
  ~~Tinging her pious~~ hands ~~together~~ prest
      on her
And silver cross soft Amethyst
And on her hair a glory like a Saint's
Shee seem'd ~~like an immortal agel drest~~
            silvery angel newly drest,
                  Lionel
  Save wings, for heaven— ~~Porphyro~~ grew faint
She knelt too pure a thing, too free from motal taint

"He remembers [Professor Ridley goes on] the arched windows and the stained glass from Mrs. Radcliffe and possibly the *deux escharboncles* from Blanchefleur's chamber; * and he starts with a kind of fluent rough sketch.

A Casement ach'd

But let us make it bigger (? for more light and a better display of glass) and also more defined in outline; so

A Casement tripple archd and diamonded

(we notice that instinct for line, always strong in Keats, which gives first the outline of the window and then fills it with the intersecting tracery of the leading)

With many coloured glass fronted the Moon
In midst ~~of which~~ wereof a shilded scutcheon shed
High blushing gules, upon

But, before the gules is shed on her, Madeline, who was left at the door, must be brought forward; so *upon* is deleted and a colon goes in after gules; and pictures from Mrs. Radcliffe come back to him; in one of which he remembers somewhere a silver cross which will catch the light:

High blushing gules: she kneeled saintly down
And inly prayed for grace and heavenly boon;
The blood red gules fell on her silver cross
And her white hands devout

(with, I think, an experimental change of *her white* into *whitest*).

"Well, there at least is some of the material in the rough; but it will not do as it stands, if only for the purely technical reason that *down* will only rhyme with *moon* and *boon* if one is Burns. And apart from that there is a fumbling of touch in the repetition of *gules*. But most of the material is much too good to let go. So Keats takes it all to pieces, like a man making the stained-glass window of which he is talking, and begins to put the fragments together in a different design. And first he decides that Madeline had better be postponed till the next stanza. He will indulge himself with the luxury of a piece of pure description and give himself ample room for the development of the window and the moonlight. He starts by elaborating the window:

A Casement tipple archd and high

presumably going to end *there was* but he concludes that this had better come at the beginning, and we get

There was
A Casement tipple archd and high
All garlanded with carven imageries
Of fruits & trailing flowers and sunny corn

which is excellent except that it does not rhyme; so *trailing* goes out and the line is completed with *ears parchd* ready to rhyme with the first line when the latter was transposed. But the transposition is not made, because there suddenly recurs to him a

* The references are to Mrs. Ann Radcliffe's *The Mysteries of Udolpho* (1794) and a French translation of Giovanni Boccaccio's *Il Filocolo*. The presumption is that Keats was drawing upon his memories of scenes in these stories. [*Editors' note*]

word ('knot-grass') from a passage which he had marked in *A Midsummer Night's Dream* [1] that will rhyme with the first line as he first had it in mind. So he starts all over again.

> A Casement high and tripple archd there was
> All gardneded [*he is in a hurry now*] with carven imageries
> Of fruits and flowers and bunches of knot grass;
> And diamonded with panes of quaint device
> Innumerable of stains and splendid dies
> As is the wing of evening tiger moths;
> And in the midst 'mong ~~man~~ thousand heraldries
> And dim twilight

At this point he sees how to give emphasis to both *dim* and *twilight* by separating them, and so cancels them to write

> And twilight saints and dim emblasonings
> A shielded scutcheon blushd with Blood of Queens and Kings

But now the sixth line is left hanging unrhymed. He makes a minor alteration in the seventh line, so that it starts *In midst whereoft;* then he feels that the line about the stains and dies, even though he is half-conscious that it is a reminiscence, is a fine line in itself, and that the line which follows, even apart from the easily secured rhyme, will not at present take the weight of its predecessor. So for the final touch for his stanza he begins the operation which makes of the tiger moths and their wings one of the richest of even his opulent lines. He first deletes it altogether and starts

> As is the tiger moths rich [2]

no, let us have both a more significant word and an alliteration

> deep damasked wings

and then the force of association is too much for him; the splendid and innumerable dies when he first met them were the hues of sunset, and he acknowledges his debt by writing *sunset* for *damasked,* and so for the moment left the stanza, for once, we may hope, well satisfied. In the second draft he diminished the over-emphatic *s*'s of the third line by writing *fruit,* went back to the simpler *And in the midst,* and, surely rightly, reinstated *damasked.*

"Keats is now ready to work into his design the other pieces that are left over, and, as he is no longer trying to compress into one stanza the material of two, he has space to develop the second part of his picture, the moonlight and Madeline. The impression of cold can be maintained by the moon being *wintry,* and the picture of Madeline complete instead of a sketch.

> Full on this Casement shone the wintry moon
> And threw red gules on Madelines fair face

---

[1] See Act III, Sc. ii, 329.
[2] *rich* is the accepted reading, but I am not happy about it: the initial letter is not like Keats' initial *r*, and the two that follow are more like *ci* than *ic* (though that is not unlike Keats in a hurry).

Red is redundant and becomes first *warm* and then *rich* (carried over from the deletion in the last stanza); *face* suffers from all possible disabilities; it suggests no feasible
rhyme except *grace* which cannot be deferred till the fourth line; it is feebly Leigh
Huntian; and in any case we do not want the heroine red in the face, even though by
the operation of lunar cosmetics; so alter it to *breast,* and we have:

> Full on this Casement shone the wintry moon
> And threw rich gules on Madelines fair breast
> As down she kneel d for heavens grace and boon
> Tinging her pious hands together prest
> And silver cross

But the fourth line is not satisfactory, and also it occurs to him that the window of
innumerable stains seems incapable of transmitting anything but gules, which is both
illogical and dull; so he gets to work on the fourth line, and after a deal of experi-
mentation, of which the stages are obscure, we arrive, with a dubious rhyme, at the
end of the fifth line

> Rose bloom fell on her hands together prest [3]
> And on her silver cross soft Amethyst
> And on her hair a glory like a Saint's—
> She seem'd ~~like an immortal agel drest~~
>   silvery angel newly drest,
> Save wings for heaven—Porphyro grew faint
> She knelt too pure a thing, too free from motal taint—

And the stanza is tidied up by the deletion of the final *s* of *Saint's.* In the second draft
Keats reverted to the much happier first thought of *warm,* and changed the rather
inhuman and metallic silver angel to *a splendid angel.*"

[3] What exactly happened with this line is hard to determine. What we find in the
draft, as nearly as print can represent it, is the following:

> ~~And~~ rose ~~with red~~ bloom fell on her hands together
>   ~~Tinging her pious~~ hands ~~together~~ prest

The results of the first alteration were meant I think to be

> Tinging with red her hands together prest

the second

> And rose bloom on her hands together prest

the third

> Rose bloom fell on her hands together prest

but this does not at all account for the firm deletion of the first *together* and I cannot
make any combination of the words before us that will make a line with *together* omitted.
And one cannot help wondering, though it would upset the idea that Keats was wanting
more varied colour, whether *rose* did not start life as a verb, in contrast to *down she
kneeld.*

There is one interesting small point, which indicates the rapidity with which Keats
wrote when composing. In line 7 as altered there is clearly an *a* wanted before silvery.
And Keats omitted it because he thought it was there. The *d* of *seem'd* is not only badly
made, but widely spaced from the rest of the word, and Keats' eye was caught by it as
he re-wrote the line and took it for the *a* that was needed.

(stanza 26)

But soon his heart revives—her prayers said
  She ~~lays aside her veil~~   pearled
      strips her hair of all its wreath~~ed pearl~~
~~Unclasps her bosom jewels~~
~~And twists it in one knot upon her head~~

                  ~~soon~~
But soon his heart revives—her prayers(ing) done,
  ~~Sh~~ Of all ~~her~~ its wreathed pearl she strips her hair
Unclasps her warmed jewels one by one
      ~~her bursting~~
  Loosens ~~her boddice from her~~
      ~~her Boddice lace~~ string
      ~~her Boddice and her bosom bare~~
      her
  Loosens her fragrant ~~boddice~~ and doth bare
  Her

26

Anon
~~But soon~~ his heart revives—her praying done
                   frees
  Of all its wreathéd pearl her hair she ~~strips~~
Unclasps her warmed jewels one by one
             by degrees
      ~~to her knees~~
  Loosens her fragrant boddice: ~~and down slips~~
  Her sweet attire ~~falls light~~ ~~creeps down by~~
      creeps rusteling to her knees
      Mermaid   in sea weed
  Half hidden like a ~~Syren of the Sea~~
  ~~And more melodious~~   dreaming
      She stands awhile in thought, and sees
  In fancy fair Saint Agnes in her bed
But dares not look behind or all the charm is ~~fled~~ dead

[Professor Ridley continues:]

    "But soon his heart revives—her prayers said

And now Keats addresses himself to the delicate business of getting Madeline undressed. He probably, as Mr. W. T. Arnold pointed out, called to his aid a passage in
Browne's *Britannia's Pastorals:*

      And as a lovely maiden, pure and chaste,
      With naked ivory neck, a gown unlaced,
      Within her chamber, when the day is fled,
      Makes poor her garments to enrich her bed:
      First she puts off her lily-silken gown,
      That shrinks for sorrow as she lays it down;
      Her breasts all bare, her kirtle slipping down,

    .   .   .   .

      Prepares for sweetest rest.

though I am not clear that there is anything very specific there by way of parallel except the *unlaced* and the *slipping down* and the latter could at least as well have been derived from a visual as from a literary memory. However, with whatever memories, Keats begins:

> She lays aside her veil

But this is the first that we have heard of a veil, and anyway it is not important, so cut it out and try

> She strips her hair of all its wreathed pearl

and then try this the other way round,

> its pearled wreath

and go on

> Unclasps her bosom jewels

but this (apart from the awkwardness of *bosom* as an adjective) is going too fast and leaves the hair unfinished, so delete it and write

> And twists it in one knot upon her head

But Keats now knows that he is getting well out of his depth, so the whole thing disappears and he starts again, having made up his mind we may suppose that in this unfamiliar region the only thing for it is rigorous compression:

> But soon his heart revives—her prayers done

(changed first, to avoid the awkward dissyllable, into *her prayers soon done* and then into *her praying done*)

> ~~Sh~~ Of all ~~her~~ its wreathed pearl she strips her hair
> Unclasps her warmed jewels one by one

So far so good; but now comes a desperate moment which can only be indicated by an attempt to represent the agitations of the draft:

> ~~her bursting~~
> Loosens ~~her boddice from her~~
>   ~~her Boddice lace~~ string
>   ~~her Boddice and her bosom bare~~
> her

One can almost see Keats arriving, at the fourth attempt and with clenched teeth, at the end of the line and a rhyme for *hair,* even though grammar has been sacrificed to get there; and hear the sigh with which he writes the final and undeleted *her* but refuses to write *Boddice* for the fourth time. At this point he turns the page and tries the line again, this time with happier success:

> Loosens her fragrant boddice and doth bare
> Her

But by now it is time for a new attempt, and after an idle moment of recuperation, in which he goes back and counts the stanzas he has written, he numbers [4] this one (the first he has numbered since he started) and advances to the attack once more.

> Anon
> But soon his heart revives—her praying done
> Of all its wreathèd pearl her hair she strips
> Unclasps her warmed jewels one by one
> Loosens her fragrant boddice: and down slips
> Her sweet attire

At any rate we are once for all done with the boddice; but Keats finds himself stuck in the middle of a line when he wants to be at the end of it; so he alters *and down slips* to *to her knees,* which allows him to hold the verb up as long as he wishes, makes the consequential alteration of *frees* for *strips* in the second line, and takes up line 5 again. First he tries

> Her sweet attire falls light

and then

> creeps down by

which was presumably to continue

> slow degrees

when it occurs to him to put the degrees earlier and the knees here, and he arrives at

> Loosens her fragrant boddice: by degrees
> Her sweet attire creeps rusteling to her knees
> Half hidden like a Syren of the Sea
> And more melodious

But he finds that associations have run away with him, since there is no point in Madeline being either more or less melodious than a Syren (unless he had for the moment intentions of making her rather than Porphyro sing like Mrs. Radcliffe's damsels); so

> Half hidden like a Mermaid in sea weed
> She stands awhile in thought; and sees

the line being then completed by the insertion of *dreaming* before *thought,*

> In fancy fair Saint Agnes in her bed
> But dares not look behind or all the charm is ~~fled~~ dead

In the second draft the *praying* is specified as *vespers,* the attire becomes *rich* instead of *sweet,* the seventh line opens

> Pensive awhile she dreams awake

and *fled* comes in again for *dead.*

---

[4] The numbering of this stanza (26) and of the only other which he numbered (33), coinciding as it does with that of the printed text, indicates that Keats had cut out the 'additional' stanza between III and IV more or less as soon as it was written.

"There at last, after all the difficulties, is Madeline rather summarily undressed, and she is left shivering in the midst of her discarded raiment with no hint of Mother Bunch's clean shift or any other shift.* But all the King's horses and men will not drag Keats back over this stricken field again, and, nightdress or no nightdress, Madeline must be got safely into bed as rapidly as may be."

(stanza 27)

~~Then stepping forth she slips~~
~~The charm fled not—she did not look behind~~
~~But~~ Soon trembling in her soft and chilly nest
~~She lay and had not seen her~~
~~She lay; and as and till the poppied warmth of sleep~~
She lay, in sort of wakeful swoon perplext
Util the poppied warmth of sleep opprest
Her soothed Limbs, and Soul fatigued away;
Flown like a thought until the morrow day,
Blissfully havend both from joy and pain
Clasped   ~~shut clasped~~
~~Shut~~ like a Missal where swart paynims pray—
~~Dead to~~ Blinded alike from Sunshine and from rain
                         ~~close~~ shut
As though a rose should ~~shut~~ and be a bud again

[Professor Ridley continues:]

"Then stepping forth she slips

deleted at once,

The charm fled not—she did not look behind;
Soon trembling in her soft and chilly nest

('chilly'; no wonder).
At this point it seems better to give up the first line altogether, so it is cancelled and we start with the second, and go on

She lay and had not seen her

also cancelled;

She lay ~~and as~~ and till the poppied warmth of sleep

also cancelled; but it has contained an idea which is retained:

She lay, in sort of wakeful swoon perplext

and this only requires transposition to serve

In sort of wakeful swoon perplext she lay
Util the poppied warmth of sleep opprest
Her soothed Limbs, and Soul fatigued away;

* In a previous passage Professor Ridley has suggested that Keats might have used a chapbook entitled *Mother Bunches Closet newly broke open* as a source for some of the details regarding the observances prescribed for girls who followed the St. Agnes' Eve ritual. In this chapbook occurs this passage: "at night before thou goest to bed put on the best shift thou hast. . . ." [Editors' note.]

Flown like a thought until the morrow day;
Blissfully havend both from joy and pain
Shut like a Missal where swart paynims pray—

Several alternatives are tried, *Like a shut Missal, Like a clasp'd Missal,* and finally

Clasp'd like a Missal where swart paynims pray—
~~Dead to~~ Blinded alike from Sunshine and from rain
As though a rose should ~~shut close~~ shut and be a bud again.'

(stanza 28)

~~Her slumbrous breathing~~
  ~~The listning Porphyro her breathing heard~~
  ~~And when~~
    ~~The entranced Porphyro stol'n to Paradise~~
  Stol'n to this Paradize and so entranc'd
      Porphyro
  ~~Porphyro~~ gazed upon her empty dress
And listen to her breathing, if it chanc'd
  To wake into a slumbrous tenderness
  Which when he heard ~~he breath'd himself~~
                            that minute did he bless
  And breath'd himself: then from the closet crept
      Silent
      Noiseless   ~~amid~~   in a ~~wild~~ wide
  ~~Silent~~ as Fear, ~~and   ?   not with~~ a wildeness
                      hush'd
  And ~~o'er~~ over the ~~silent~~ carpet ~~hushing~~ silent stept
And 'tween the Curtains peep'd, and lo¹ how fast she slept

(stanza 29)

Then ~~on~~ by the bed side where the fading Moon
  Made an illumed twilight soft he set
              and with anguish   spread
A Table, ~~light, and stilly threw~~ theron
  A Cloth of woven crimson gold and jet—
  O for some drowy morphean amulet:
                festive \   ~~Ball~~
  The boisterous midnight ̧Clarioņ of the ~~feast~~
  ~~Sounded though faint and far away~~
  ~~Came Sound in his ears~~
  And kettle drums and far heard clarinet
  ~~Reach'd his scar'd ears~~
                    in
  Affray'd his ears though but ~~with~~ faintest tone ̧
  The Hall door shut_s again and all the noise ~~was~~ is gone.

(stanza 30)

    ~~But~~
  ~~And still she slept:~~
  And still she slept an azure-lidded sleep
    In blanched linen smooth and lavender'd,
  While he from frorth the closet brought a heap

~~fruits~~

Of candied ~~sweets~~ ~~sweets with~~ and plumb and gourd

    apple Quince

                    creamed

With jellies soother than the ~~dairy~~ curd

           tinct   cinnamon

And lucent syrups ~~smooth~~ with ~~crannamon~~ [?]

~~And sugar'd dates from that o'er Euphrates fard~~

              ~~in Brigantine transferrd~~

                      ~~transferrd~~

    Manna and daites in Bragine ~~wild~~ ~~transferrd~~

             ~~and Manna~~

~~And Manna wild and~~   ~~Bragantine~~

             ~~sugar'd~~ dates transferrd

argosy

~~In Brigantine from Fez~~

From fez—and spiced danties every one

    ~~glutted~~

From ~~wealthy~~ Samarchand to cedard lebanon

    silken

(stanzas 35–37)

Keats' first draft of these stanzas and his subsequent alterations of them displeased some of his friends—particularly Richard Woodhouse. In his letter to John Taylor, already quoted in part on page 879, Woodhouse wrote:

> There was another alteration, which I abused for "a full hour by the *Temple* clock." You know if a thing has a decent side, I generally look no further—As the Poem was orig'y written, *we* innocent ones (ladies & myself) might very well have supposed that Porphyro, when acquainted with Madeline's love for him, & when "he arose, Etherial flush'd &c. &c (turn to it) set himself at once to persuade her to go off with him, & succeeded & went over the "Dartmoor black" (now changed for some other place) to be married, in right honest and sober wise. But, as it is now altered, as soon as M. has confessed her love, P. winds by degrees his arm round her, presses breast to breast, and acts all the acts of a bonâ fide husband, while she fancies she is only playing the part of a Wife in a dream. This alteration is of about three stanzas; and tho' there are no improper expressions but all is left to inference, and tho' profanely speaking, the Interest on the reader's imagination is greatly heightened, yet I do apprehend it will render the poem unfit for ladies, & indeed scarcely to be mentioned to them among the "things that are."—He says he does not want ladies to read his poetry: that he writes for men, & that if in the former poem there was an opening for a doubt what took place, it was his fault for not writing clearly and comprehensively— that he sh'd despise a man who would be such an eunuch in sentiment as to leave a maid, with that Character about her, in such a situation: & sho'd despise himself to write about it &c &c &c—and all this sort of Keats-like rhodomontade. [Rollins, *op. cit.*, p. 92.]

Woodhouse seems to imply that Keats had written some other and more explicit stanzas at this point in the poem; but, if so, the objectors triumphed over the poet, for no such stanzas now exist.

STOPPING BY WOODS ON A SNOWY EVENING
ROBERT FROST (1874–1963)

Whose woods these are I think I know.
His house is in the village though;
He will not see me stopping here
To watch his woods fill up with snow.

My little horse must think it queer
To stop without a farmhouse near
Between the woods and frozen lake
The darkest evening of the year.

He gives his harness bells a shake
To ask if there is some mistake.   10
The only other sound's the sweep
Of easy wind and downy flake.

The woods are lovely, dark and deep.
But I have promises to keep,
And miles to go before I sleep,
And miles to go before I sleep.

ON FROST'S "STOPPING BY WOODS . . ." *

JOHN HOLMES (1904–1962)

This facsimile [1] is a reproduction of the last three stanzas of "Stopping by Woods on a Snowy Evening" as Robert Frost worked it out. We know from the poet that he had just written the long poem, "New Hampshire," in one all-night unbroken stretch of composition, and that he then turned a page of his workbook and wrote this short poem without stopping. This fact has interesting implications. "New Hampshire" is a discourse in the idiomatic blank verse that is so peculiarly Frost's own style—the rhythms of natural speech matched to the strict but inconspicuous iambic pentameter, the beat always discernible but never formal. It is reasonable to suppose that after the hours spent in writing the long poem, in its loosened but never loose manner, he was ready, unconsciously, for a poem in strict pattern. He had also obviously had in his head for some time the incident on which the short poem was to be based, as well as the use he wished to make of it. He committed himself, as he has said, to the four-stress iambic line and to the *aaba* rime-scheme, in the first stanza, which he wrote rapidly and did not revise. He knew what he had seen, and he knew how he wanted to write it.

> Whose woods these are I think I know.
> His house is in the village though;
> He will not see me stopping here
> To watch his woods fill up with snow.

"That went off so easily I was tempted into the added difficulty of picking up my 3 for my 1-2-4 to go on with in the second stanza. I was amused and scared at what that got me into," Frost says. The facsimile shows what it got him into, how he got out of it, and how he achieved the poem as it meant itself to be written.

It began with what was the actual experience of stopping at night by some dark woods in winter, and the fact that there were two horses. He remembered what he saw then. "The steaming horses think it queer." But the poem needs truth more than fact, and he cancels the line, and begins again, "The horse begins to think it queer," but doesn't like the word "begins," needing in the allowed space a word that will particularize the horse, so writes "The little horse must think it queer." Now he runs into a grammatical difficulty, which must somehow be solved before he gets on into the poem he already feels sure of. "I launched into the construction 'My little horse must think it queer that we should stop.' I didn't like omitting the 'that' and I had no room for 'should.' I had the luck to get out of it with the infinitive." This groping and warming-up has a kind of impatience, an urgency to get on with the poem, but not until all the parts are right. At this point the poet knew and did not know how the poem would end. He knew the feel, and the sense, and almost everything about the form—certainly enough to know when he got off the track.

Whether he revised the third line here or later we cannot know. But we can see in several places in this poem his changes toward particularization. The line "Between a

---

* See also the essay by Earl Daniels on p. 932.
[1] On p. 891.

forest and a lake" is a notation, and "Between the woods and frozen lake" is a finished line of poetry. "A forest" is too big, too vague, but "the woods" is definite, and bounded; you get lost in a forest, but you can walk through and out of the woods, and probably you know who owns it—Vermonters do, as he has said in the first stanza. "A lake" has not the specific condition or picture of "frozen lake." This sort of revision, or what Frost calls, "touching up," is what makes a poem—this, plus the first inspiration. Either one, without the other, is unlikely to make a good poem.

The next stanza comes easier, because the rime-scheme has been determined, and one unexpected obstacle has been overcome. But once more there is a delay, as the poet makes a decision as to the "he" or "she"—and the more important and more interesting one about the falling snow. In writing "downy flake" for "fall of flake" the gain is great not only for accuracy of feeling and fact, but also for the music of the lines. The simple alliteration in "fall of flake" is canceled in favor of the word, one word, "downy," which blends with the vowel-chords a poet half-consciously makes and modulates as he goes. In this instance, it half-chimes with "sounds" and adds a rounder, fuller, and yet quieter tone.

Now the carry-over rime is "sweep," a fortunate one, really, and important to the final solution of the rime-scheme. It is not too much to assume, knowing all we know about the circumstances of the writing of this poem—the all-night composition of "New Hampshire," and the sudden urge to catch and shape still another saved idea— that the darker, more confident, more rapid strokes of the pen show the poet's growing excitement. The end is in sight. The thing he believed could happen will happen, surely now, and he must hurry to get it onto the page. This is the real moment of power, and any poet's greatest satisfaction.

"The woods are lovely dark and deep / But I have promises to keep." The first two lines of the last stanza come fast, and flow beautifully, the crest of the poem's emotion and its music. We cannot know whether he had held them in his head, or had swept up to and into them as he felt the destined pattern fulfilling itself.

Then, with success in sight, there comes an awkward and unexpected stumble. He writes, "That bid me give the reins a shake," which may have been the fact and the action. But the rime is wrong. Not only has the rime been used in the previous stanza, but so has the image of the horse shaking his head and reins. Things are moving fast now, no doubt impatiently, but certainly with determination, shown in the heavy black lines of abrupt cancellation. He strikes out "me give the reins a shake," and writes above it, so the line will read, "That bid me on, and there are miles," and then the whole thing comes through! Of course! "Miles to go . . ."

That's what it was supposed to be—the feeling of silence and dark, almost overpowering the man, but the necessity of going on. "And miles to go before I sleep." Then the triumph in the whole thing, the only right and perfect last line, solving the problem of the carried-over rime, keeping the half-tranced state, and the dark, and the solitude, and man's great effort to be responsible man . . . the repetition of that line.

"Stopping by Woods on a Snowy Evening" can be studied as perfected structure, with the photostat manuscript to show that art is not, though it must always appear to be, effortless. It can be thought of as a picture: the whites, grays, and blacks of the masses and areas of lake, field, and woods, with the tiny figure of the man in the sleigh, and the horse. And it can be thought of as a statement of man's everlasting responsibility to man; though the dark and nothingness tempt him to surrender, he will not give in. It is interesting to compare this poem with two later pieces of Frost's, in which he uses the same image, "Desert Places," * and "Come In," * none like, all on the

---

* For these poems, see pages 735, 676. [*Editors' note*]

first level of his poetry, and all three built on the image of the pull of wildness and lawlessness against man's conscious will and the promises he has made to be kept.

A NOTE BY THE EDITORS

In a letter to Charles Madison, dated February 26, 1950, Frost confesses "the trade secret" about the writing of the last stanza of "Stopping by Woods." The poet says that he wrote the third line of the stanza "in such a way as to call for another stanza when I didn't want another stanza and didn't have another stanza in me, but with great presence of mind and a sense of what a good boy I was I instantly struck the line out and made my exit with a repeat end." [See Cleanth Brooks and Robert Penn Warren: *Understanding Poetry* (Holt, rev. ed., 1950).]

The first "And miles to go before I sleep" was therefore originally written as the fourth line of the stanza—with the crossed-out line, ending first in "shake" and then in "miles," the one that called for another stanza. Repeating the line "And miles to go before I sleep" not only solved for Frost a technical problem but gave him a sense of triumphant satisfaction at a "resolved perplexity" and "pure emergence from the logic of the thing"—to use his own words. See "Robert Frost: A Time to Listen," by Reginald L. Cook, pp. 824–829.

THE LATER YEATS

HERBERT READ (1893–   )

There is no doubt that Yeats was influenced, and influenced for the good, by the technique of some of his juniors, notably by Ezra Pound.

The change can best be examined in an early poem which Yeats actually rewrote in his later manner. "The Sorrow of Love" was originally published in 1893; as late as the 1912 edition of the *Poems* and perhaps later, it read as follows:

> The quarrel of the sparrows in the eaves,
> The full round moon and the star-laden sky,
> And the loud song of the ever-singing leaves,
> Had hid away earth's old and weary cry.
>
> And then you came with those red mournful lips
> And with you came the whole of the world's tears
> And all the trouble of her labouring ships,
> And all the trouble of her myriad years.
>
> And now the sparrows warring in the eaves
> The curd-pale moon, the white stars in the sky,
> And the loud chaunting of the unquiet leaves,
> Are shaken with earth's old and weary cry.

In the 1933 edition of the *Collected Poems* this poem has been rewritten and reads as follows:

> The brawling of a sparrow in the eaves
> The brilliant moon and all the milky sky,
> And all that famous harmony of leaves,
> Had blotted out man's image and his cry.
>
> A girl arose that had red mournful lips
> And seemed the greatness of the world in tears,
> Doomed like Odysseus and the labouring ships
> And proud as Priam murdered with his peers;
>
> Arose, and on the instant clamorous eaves,
> A climbing moon upon an empty sky,
> And all that lamentation of the leaves,
> Could but compose man's image and his cry.

The change, it will be seen, is very drastic, but is it altogether a change for the good? It is, let us observe, in the first place, a change of diction and not of structure; and that is true of all the changes that occurred in Yeats's verse. "All the revisions I have made," Yeats once said to me, "have been in the direction of making my poems less poetic." His aim, therefore, has been very much the same as Wordsworth's—to get rid of "the inane and gaudy phraseology" of an outworn poetic tradition. The suggestion I wish to put forward is that diction and structure are so closely related in the generation of a poem, that you cannot fundamentally change the one without changing the other. But before elaborating that suggestion, let us look at the actual changes which Yeats made in the poem quoted.

Line 1.—*Brawling* is substituted for *quarrel*. In itself I do not think the word is any improvement, but the change is necessitated by a change in line 2; *quarrel* would not go well with *brilliant*, whereas *brawling* provides a good alliterative and assonantal match. *Sparrows* becomes singular—a gain in precision.

Line 2.—*full round* was perhaps felt to be a commonplace epithet, but is *brilliant* any better? It is rather vaguer. But this change is perhaps in its turn dictated by the change from *star-laden* to *milky*. *Star-laden* is a very early-Yeatsian, Celtic twilight epithet of just the kind the poet presumably wanted to get rid of; and since a brilliant moon will cancel out the stars, *milky* becomes a more expressive (incidentally a metaphorical) epithet.

Line 3.—*ever-singing* was probably felt to be a cliché, and *loud* is not very exact for the sound of leaves. But *famous harmony* seems to me to be a vaguer and weaker substitute; it is a dead phrase, without any inherent poetic tone. In fact, it is prose.

Line 4.—A completely new image is substituted. *Earth's old and weary cry* was probably felt to be a false and indefinite metaphor. *Blotted* is a gain in sound value, and links alliteratively with *brawling* and *brilliant;* it has an onomatopœic value, and provides a much-needed acceleration of the rhythm.

Line 5.—A definite image of *a girl* is substituted for the vague *you; arose* gives alliteration with *red.*

Line 6.—*the whole of the world's tears* was perhaps felt to be rather a ridiculous image; the new image is more precise, but still difficult to visualize.

Lines 7 and 8.—A completely new image is substituted. The repetition of *And all the trouble of her* was probably felt to be banal, and *myriad years* to be a cliché. The introduction of well-known classical allusions is a gain in precision and in the emotional surplus attaching to legendary names.

Line 9.—The refrain motive of the sparrows in the eaves is dropped—it is a romantic device, and two such devices in one quatrain were felt to be a little too much. The introduction of a time element, *on the instant,* adds dramatic force to the poem. *Clamorous* is a good sonorous word, if a little too emphatic for the noise made by a single sparrow; but it provides alliteration with *climbing, lamentation, leaves, could, compose* and *cry.*

Line 10.—The fresh and effective *curd-pale* had to be dropped, since the moon had become brilliant in the first verse; for the same reason the white stars had to be excluded. *Climbing,* though it sounds well enough, is rather commonplace, and *empty* is banal.

Line 11.—*Loud* must be dropped to agree with the first verse; *chaunting* is an artificial metaphor. The new line has a forceful alliterative movement. But I doubt if a "modern" poet would use a word like *lamentation* in connection with *leaves;* it is almost a cliché.

Line 12.—The changes are largely dictated by the new form of line 4, and by the desire for alliteration. But *compose* involves a process difficult to visualize, and the line as a whole does not bring the poem to such a definite and inevitable conclusion as in the first version.

These are analytical notes, and perhaps on a reckoning the plus and minus of it all cancels out. It is necessary, in the end, to compare the synthetic feeling of the two versions, and here one can only state a personal reaction. My own is definitely in favour of the earlier version. In spite of the romantic diction against which Yeats rightly reacted, I feel that it produces a unity of effect which, romantic as it is, is superior in force to the more definite, more classical diction of the later version. For the truth is, that the poem in essence and inception is irradicably romantic, and had better retain its romantic diction and imagery. As it is, the new version has a patchy effect. The old suit may have been shabby, but it was of a good cut and an even tone; the patches of new classical cloth are too obvious and too disjointed.

This image, with a little stretching, will serve for my objection to Yeats's later verse (but naturally it is only an objection on the highest plane of technical criticism—the kind of criticism that poets exchange between themselves, and which is not meant for laymen). Though he makes his poems out of the latest suitings, all of good classical (or which comes to the same thing) modernist cloth, the cut is still romantic.

> I dreamed as in my bed I lay,
> All night's fathomless wisdom come,
> That I had shorn my locks away
> And laid them on Love's lettered tomb:
> But something bore them out of sight
> In a great tumult of the air,
> And after nailed upon the night
> Berenice's burning hair.

The gesture here, in spite of its precision, is still romantic; and such poems stand out, luxuriant in the pruned orchard of the later verse. The pruning has produced a larger fruit, a clearer thought: but the effect is rather bleak, the prose of scientific culture rather than the poetry of natural growth. A complete change of spirit requires a change of form; of structure as well as of diction. And though one or two poems, such as "Byzantium," seem to promise the necessary developments, Yeats remained to the end faithful to the spirit of another age.

III

The Poem and the Reader

Every reader is necessarily a critic, good or bad; to neglect careful technical criticism is to deny the poem a fair hearing; hasty decision often produces sentimental judgment, and sometimes the hasty reader even accuses the poet of sentimentality, whereas the fault lies in his own inadequate response. The fullest appreciation of poetry or of any art may require as much training and effort as the appreciation of mathematics, and the effort is justified by the additional delight.

—MICHAEL ROBERTS

The chief use of the "meaning" of a poem, in the ordinary sense, may be . . . to satisfy one habit of the reader, to keep his mind diverted and quiet, while the poem does its work upon him; much as the imaginary burglar is always provided with a bit of nice meat for the house-dog.

—T. S. ELIOT

Poetry should please by a fine excess and not by singularity. It should strike the reader as a wording of his own highest thoughts, and appear almost as a remembrance.

—JOHN KEATS

The ideal reader must be sensitive to words over their whole poetic range, and respond to poetry musically, emotionally, imaginatively, and in other ways besides.

—KATHERINE M. WILSON

HOW TO CRITICIZE A POEM

(*In the Manner of Certain Contemporary Critics*)

THEODORE SPENCER (1902–1949)

1

I propose to examine the following poem:

> Thirty days hath September,
> April, June and November:
> All the rest have thirty-one,
> Excepting February alone,
> Which has only eight and a score
> Till leap-year gives it one day more.

2

The previous critics who have studied this poem, Coleridge among them, have failed to explain what we may describe as its fundamental *dynamic*. This I now propose to do. The first thing to observe is the order in which the names (or verbal constructs) of the months are presented. According to the prose meaning—what I shall henceforth call the prose-*demand*—"September" should not precede, it should follow "April," as a glance at the calendar will show. Indeed "September" should follow not only "April," it should also follow "June" if the prose-demand is to be properly satisfied. The prose order of the first two lines should therefore read: "Thirty days hath April, June, September and November." That is the only sequence consonant with prose logic.

3

Why then, we ask ourselves, did the poet violate what educated readers know to be the facts? Was he ignorant of the calendar, believing that September preceded April in the progress of the seasons? It is difficult to imagine that such was the case. We must find another explanation. It is here that the principle of dynamic analysis comes to our aid.

4

Dynamic analysis proves that the most successful poetry achieves its effect by producing an *expectation* in the reader's mind before his sensibility is fully prepared to receive the full impact of the poem. The reader makes a *proto-response* which preconditions him to the total response toward which his fully equilibrized organs of apperception subconsciously tend. It is this proto-response which the poet has here so sensitively manipulated. The ordinary reader, trained only to prose-demands, expects the usual order of the months. But the poet's sensibility knows that poetic truth is more immediately effective than the truth of literal chronology. He does not *state* the inevitable sequence; he *prepares* us for it. In his profound analysis of the two varieties of mensual time, he puts the *gentlest* month first. (Notice how the harsh sound of "pt" in "September" is softened by the "e" sound on either side of it.) It is the month in which vegetation first begins to fade, but which does not as yet give us a sense of tragic fatality.

5

Hence the poet prepares us, dynamically, for what is to follow. By beginning his list of the months *in medias res,* he is enabled to return later to the beginning of the series of contrasts which is the subject of his poem. The analogy to the "Oedipus Rex" of Euripides and the "Iliad" of Dante at once becomes clear. Recent criticism has only too often failed to observe that these works also illustrate the dynamic method by beginning in the middle of things. It is a striking fact, hitherto (I believe) unnoticed, that a Latin poem called the "Aeneid" does much the same thing. We expect the author of that poem to begin with the departure of his hero from Troy, just as we expect the author of our poem to begin with "April." But in neither case is our expectation fulfilled. Cato, the author of the "Aeneid," creates dynamic suspense by beginning with Aeneas in Carthage; our anonymous poet treats his readers' sensibilities in a similar fashion by beginning with "September," and then *going back* to "April" and "June."

6

But the sensibility of the poet does not stop at this point. Having described what is true of *four* months, he disposes of *seven* more with masterly economy. In a series of pungent constructs his sensibility sums up their inexorable limitations: they *All* (the capitalization should be noted) "have thirty-one." The poet's sensibility communicates a feeling to the sensibility of the reader so that the sensibility of both, with reference to their previous but independent sensibilities, is fused into that momentary communion of sensibility which is the final sensibility that poetry can give both to the sensibility of the poet and the sensibility of the reader. The texture and structure of the poem have erupted into a major reaction. The ambiguity of equilibrium is achieved.

7

Against these two groups of spatial, temporal and numerical measurements—one consisting of four months, the other of seven—the tragic individual, the sole exception, "February," is dramatically placed. February is "alone," is cut off from communion with his fellows. The tragic note is struck the moment "February" is mentioned. For the initial sound of the word "excepting" is "X," and as that sound strikes the sensibility of the reader's ear a number of associations subconsciously accumulate. We think of the spot, the murderous and lonely spot, which "X" has so frequently marked; we remember the examinations of our childhood where the wrong answers were implacably signaled with "X"; we think of ex-kings and exile, of lonely crossroads and executions, of the inexorable anonymity of those who cannot sign their names. . . .

8

And yet the poet gives us one ray of hope, though it eventually proves to be illusory. The lonely "February" (notice how the "alone" in line four is echoed by the "only" in line five), the solitary and maladjusted individual who is obviously the hero and crucial figure of the poem, is not condemned to the routine which his fellows, in their different ways, must forever obey. Like Hamlet, he has a capacity for change. He is a symbol of individualism, and the rhythm of the lines which are devoted to him signalize a gayety, however desperate, which immediately wins our sympathy and reverberates profoundly in our sensibility.

9

But (and this is the illusion to which I have previously referred) in spite of all his variety, his capacity for change, "February" cannot quite accomplish (and in this his tragedy consists) the *quantitative* value of the society in which circumstances have put him. No matter how often he may alternate from twenty-eight to twenty-nine (the poet, with his exquisite sensibility, does not actually *mention* those humiliating numbers), he can never achieve the bourgeois, if anonymous, security of "thirty-one," nor equal the more modest and aristocratic assurance of "thirty." Decade after decade, century after century, millennium after millennium, he is eternally frustrated. The only symbol of change in a changeless society, he is continually beaten down. Once every four years he tries to rise, to achieve the high, if delusive, level of his dreams. But he fails. He is always one day short, and the three years before the recurrence of his next effort are a sad interval in which the remembrance of previous disappointment melts into the futility of hope, only to sink back once more into the frustration of despair. Like Tantalus he is forever stretched upon a wheel.

10

So far I have been concerned chiefly with the dynamic *analysis* of the poem. Further study should reveal the *synthesis* which can be made on the basis of the analysis which my thesis has tentatively attempted to bring to an emphasis. This, perhaps, the reader with a proper sensibility can achieve for himself.

HUMPTY DUMPTY AND SYMBOLISM

BERNARD M. KNIEGER (1922–   )

> Humpty Dumpty sat on a wall,
> Humpty Dumpty had a great fall:
> All the king's horses and all the king's men
> Cannot put Humpty Dumpty together again.

When is an egg not an egg? When the egg is Humpty Dumpty—that is, primarily a literary symbol, might be one answer. Certainly, nothing in the poem specifically identifies Humpty Dumpty as an egg, as a member of the anti-egg faction of my sophomore literature class immediately pointed out. Furthermore, Humpty Dumpty's behavior is most unegglike. "How can an egg sit on a wall?" added a supporting dissident. "It might just as well be a glass jar." But through a thoroughgoing analysis of "Humpty Dumpty," even an anti-eggian may come to see that the reader must bring cultural knowledge to the reading of a literary work (particularly of a poem), that a work may be powerful to the degree that it departs from realism, that the meanings of a symbol cannot be exhausted, that a poem may be enjoyed for many reasons—its sound, organization, dramatic situation, humor, ethical content, and use of symbolism. . . .

How do the pro-eggians know that Humpty Dumpty is an egg? Of course, they've seen illustrations from Mother Goose. "But can't the portrait," asks an anti-eggian, "represent an artist's mistaken interpretation of the nursery rhyme?" "Be that as it may, and how could that question ever be answered?" is the reply. "Humpty Dumpty is a traditional figure in our culture, always identified as an egg. So Humpty Dumpty's eggness cannot be disputed; the question is, rather, of what is Humpty Dumpty a symbol, and how successfully?"

First, however, the pro-eggian must concede that Humpty Dumpty's behavior is truly most unegglike: eggs do not sit on walls. Moreover, no monarch would be so foolish as to try to put a broken egg together again, or rather expect his horses and men to achieve this goal. In other words, "Humpty Dumpty" is a fantasy in which—surprisingly enough to both anti- and pro-eggian students, weaned on realism, they think —the effectiveness of the communication of the theme is in direct relationship to the fantasy of the dramatic situation. The poem's fantasy achieves two results: the poem is funny; attention is focused on the theme.

An egg sitting on a wall is an amusing concept to the child, and perhaps to the adult. Expecting fierce, warlike horses (source of the king's power) and an army of men to put together the fragile, broken egg is an even more amusing visual image. But how better dramatize the universal desire to undo what has been done? Thus, the poet brings home through this picturesque example based on homely experience —we've all broken eggs and wanted to put them together again—the futility of trying to undo certain actions.

Not only the concluding couplet, but also the poem as a whole dramatizes the limits of temporal power: certain actions cannot be done; others should not be. Thus eggs which sit on walls risk almost certain destruction. As an egg, Humpty Dumpty is a symbol of fragility; as an egg sitting on a wall, he is a symbol of aspiring pride. Pride, however, is a human trait; so Humpty Dumpty emerges as a symbol of sinful man.

"Humpty Dumpty," in its fullest implications, is definitely a religious poem, an example of how folk wisdom, if you will, justifies the ways of God to man in four lines. Eggs have a seemingly hard exterior but a ridiculously flabby interior—they are not equipped to sit on walls. This prohibition is not arbitrary any more than God's prohibitions against a sinful action are arbitrary. Rather, these prohibitions are a manifestation of God's wisdom, of the infinite power of God contrasted with the finite powers of man, of a recognition that in an ordered universe there can be no trespassing beyond prescribed limits. And "a great fall" certainly has specific theological and mythic connotations: one thinks of the fall of Adam, of Satan, of Icarus, of Phaeton. . . .

A NOTE BY THE EDITORS

Humpty Dumpty is a riddle of great antiquity, with equivalents to be found in German, French, Finnish, etc., not to mention variant English wordings which involve different situations but the same theme. See *The Oxford Dictionary of Nursery Rhymes*, edited by Iona and Peter Opie (Oxford, Clarendon, 1955). Here it is suggested that the lines may once have accompanied a game in which the players impersonated eggs. Though its origin is untraceable, the rhyme has been applied to several historical figures, including Richard III of England (1452–1485). The illustration in *The Tall Book of Mother Goose* (New York, Harper, 1942) clearly represents Adolf Hitler.

EMOTIONAL QUALITY IN POETRY

F. R. LEAVIS (1895–   )

HERACLITUS	*PROUD MAISIE*
They told me, Heraclitus, they told me you were dead,	Proud Maisie is in the wood, Walking so early;
They brought me bitter news to hear and bitter tears to shed.	Sweet Robin sits on the bush Singing so rarely.
I wept as I remembered how often you and I	
Had tired the sun with talking and sent him down the sky.	"Tell me, thou bonny bird, When shall I marry me?"
	"When six braw gentlemen Kirkward shall carry ye."
And now that thou art lying, my dear old Carian guest,	"Who makes the bridal bed, Birdie, say truly?" 10
A handful of grey ashes, long, long ago at rest,	"The grey-headed sexton That delves the grave duly.
Still are thy pleasant voices, thy nightingales, awake;	"The glow-worm o'er grave and stone Shall light thee steady;
For Death, he taketh all away, but them he cannot take.	The owl from the steeple sing Welcome, proud lady."
—WILLIAM JOHNSON CORY (1823–1892)	—SIR WALTER SCOTT (1771–1832)

When we look at "Heraclitus" we see that the directly emotional and personal insistence distinguishing it is associated with an absence of core or substance: the poem seems to be all emotional comment, the alleged justifying situation, the subject of comment, being represented by loosely evocative generalities, about which the poet feels vaguely if "intensely" (the "intensity" of this kind of thing is conditioned by vagueness). Again, the emotion seems to be out there on the page, whereas in reading "Proud Maisie" we never seem to be offered emotions as such; the emotion develops and defines itself as we grasp the dramatic elements the poem does offer—the data it presents (that is the effect) with emotional "disinterestedness." For "disinterestedness" we can substitute "impersonality," with which term we introduce a critical topic of the first importance.

Someone may comment that, on the one hand, for Scott, whose poetic impulse clearly came not from any inescapable pang experienced in his immediately personal life, but from an interest in ballads and in the ballad-convention, the impersonality of his poem was an easy achievement, while, on the other hand, absence of impersonality in the handling of poignant emotion needn't be accompanied by the self-cherishing emotionality, the wallowing complaisance, of "Heraclitus." These matters can be carried further, and the essential distinctions given force, only by close and varied reference to the concrete. Here is a contrast analogous to the last, but a contrast in which the "impersonal" poem unmistakably derives from a seismic personal experience, while the obviously emotional poem is not suspect, like "Heraclitus," of being a mere indulgence in the sweets of poignancy:

(a) A slumber did my spirit seal;
    I had no human fears:
She seemed a thing that could not feel
    The touch of earthly years.

No motion has she now, no force;
    She neither hears nor sees;
Roll'd round in earth's diurnal course,
    With rocks, and stones, and trees.
        —[WILLIAM WORDSWORTH (1770–1850)]

(b) Break, break, break,
    On thy cold grey stones, O Sea!
And I would that my tongue could utter
    The thoughts that arise in me.

O well for the fisherman's boy,
    That he shouts with his sister at play!
O well for the sailor lad,
    That he sings in his boat on the bay!

And the stately ships go on
    To their haven under the hill:
But O for the touch of a vanish'd hand,
    And the sound of a voice that is still!

Break, break, break,
    At the foot of thy crags, O Sea!
But the tender grace of a day that is dead
    Will never come back to me.
        —[ALFRED, LORD TENNYSON (1809–1892)]

No one can doubt that Wordsworth wrote his poem because of something profoundly and involuntarily suffered—suffered as a personal calamity, but the experience has been so impersonalized that the effect, as much as that of "Proud Maisie," is one of bare and disinterested presentment. Again, though the working this time doesn't so obviously prompt to a diagrammatic schematization, the emotional power is generated between juxtaposed opposites. It is generated between the two stanzas, or between the states represented by the stanzas: "she was, she is not"—the statement seems almost as bare and simple as that. But the statement is concrete, and once the reading has been completed the whole poem is seen to be a complex organization, charged with a subtle life. In retrospect the first stanza takes on new significance:

> A slumber did my spirit seal;
> I had no human fears

—the full force of that *human* comes out: the conditions of the human situation are inescapable and there is a certain *hubris* in the security of forgetful bliss. Again, the *human* enhances the ironic force of *thing* in the next line:

> She seemed a thing that could not feel
> The touch of earthly years.

In the second stanza she *is* a thing—a thing that, along with the rocks and stones and trees with which she is

> Roll'd round in earth's diurnal course,

cannot in reality feel the touch of earthly years and enjoys a real immunity from death. The *diurnal,* chosen apparently for its scientific nakedness and reinforcing as it does that stating bareness with which the diction and tone express the brutal finality of the fact, has actually, at the same time, a potent evocative force: it puts the fact in an astronomical setting and evokes the vast inevorable regularity of the planetary motions, the effect being analogous to that of the enclosing morning-night contrast of "Proud Maisie."

In "Break, break, break" we again have the poem that offers emotion directly—the poem in which the emotion seems to be "out there" on the page. If we read the poem aloud the emotion, in full force from the opening, asserts itself in the plangency of tone and movement that is compelled upon us. We do not, however, this time feel moved to a dismissing judgment. The poet is clearly one of distinguished gift, we cannot doubt that behind the poem there is a genuinely personal urgency, and we are not ready to accuse him of being moved primarily by the enjoyment of being poignantly moved—though we *can* very readily imagine a rendering of the poem that should betray too much enjoyment of the poignancy.

And here, in this last suggestion, we glimpse a way of getting beyond a neutrally descriptive account of the differences between the two poems. We can say that Wordsworth's poem is a securer kind of achievement. If someone should comment that to make it a point against a poem that it lends itself more readily to abuse is to assume a great deal, it will perhaps be best not to take up the challenge directly, but to advance another proposition: an emotional *habit* answering to the mode of "Break, break, break" would need to be regarded critically. The poet, we can say, whose habitual mode—whose emotional habit—was represented by that poem would not only be very limited; we should expect to find him noticeably given to certain weaknesses and vices. Further, the reader who cannot see that Tennyson's poem, with all its distinction and refinement, yields a satisfaction inferior in kind to that represented by Wordsworth, cannot securely appreciate the highest poetic achievement at its true worth and is not very likely to be at all strong or sure in the kind of judgment that discriminates between "Break, break, break" and "Heraclitus."

AN INTERPRETATION OF ROBERT HERRICK'S "UPON JULIA'S CLOTHES"

EARL DANIELS (1893–   )

UPON JULIA'S CLOTHES

When as in silks my Julia goes,
Then, then, me thinks, how sweetly flows
That liquefaction of her clothes.

Next, when I cast mine eyes, and see
That brave vibration, each way free;
O how that glittering taketh me!

—ROBERT HERRICK (1591–1674)

Superficially, the poem is obvious to the point of seeming to deprecate analysis, not to be worth it. A pretty girl moves through six lines, for a moment only catches an observer's eye, passes, and is gone. So slight is the impact of the experience that he writes not about the girl but about her clothes. Costume is defined by silks, and each stanza is centered in a single quality of silk in movement, and in light (*liquefaction,* line 3, and *glittering,* line 6). The positions of these words in the last lines of each stanza should be noted and, more particularly, the increased sharpness lent to *glittering* by the necessity, here, of pronunciation in two syllables only: the vowel sound of an acute and pointed short *i* is closed tightly in by consonants, *g* and *t* in one syllable, *tr* and *ng* in the other. The stab of that word, a superb mine-eyes-dazzle effect, suggests the poem is not so simple as it seems: that Julia-in-clothes is more important than clothes, the apparent subject; that the observer is more deeply moved than he wants a careless reader to suppose, possibly than he himself knows.

Attention to sound and movement reveals the implications of the single word *glittering* to be a clue worth following. The poem is Julia and Julia's clothes. But each stanza contains lines (I, 2; II, 1, 3) which turn to the observer, and seem to hint in sound and movement at a central ironic contrast between the states of mind of the observer and the girl. The Julia lines flow, as easy and as liquid as the smooth silks which dress and conceal a lovely body. But the observer lines throb unevenly; they start and stop; they image the excitement and disturbance of the poet. It may not be too farfetched to wonder if they are not symbol for the quickened beating of a heart, the surprised catch of breath, in the presence of beauty, especially beauty of a woman. An attentive reader now begins to understand it is not Julia's clothes but Julia herself who is the subject of the poem; and the poem begins to grow and to take on new richness of meaning. To be especially noted is the contrast in stanza I between lines 1 and 2: in line 1, word ripples into word, sound into sound, the caesural pause is so slight as to be almost not noticeable; in line 2, the opening repetition of "then, then," where each word must be distinctly separated by pauses, where vowels are imbedded between inescapable consonants, announces a change, farther stressed by the parenthetical "me thinks." (Even the parenthesis plays its part here.) Only as this line, toward the end, moves to Julia and her costume does it begin to glide, to be liquefied again. The point is Julia moves through the poem serene, untouched; she may not even know the poet has so much as seen her. But he is in a different situation, for though he is ostensibly doing nothing more than writing a pretty lyric about a pretty dress, yet he reveals, in the sound, the movement, the pace of his words, how deeply he has been stirred by what seems so unimportant.

This makes for a basic ironic contrast, central to the poem: the ironic contrast between the girl and the man. Is it the irony of man (male) set over against woman (female)—a contrast as old as the Garden of Eden itself—or is it the profounder suggestion of the situation of man (not *a man*) in the presence of beauty—beauty here, as so often, being symbolized by a woman? I am reasonably certain that by implication and suggestion, by the subtlest of overtones, both ideas are in their way present, contributing rich values for a poem too often looked upon as too slight for serious consideration. Herrick has too long suffered from that kind of treatment.

AN INTERPRETATION OF THOMAS CAREW'S
"A SONG"

MARK VAN DOREN (1894–   )

A SONG

Ask me no more where Jove bestows,
When June is past, the fading rose;
For in your beauty's orient deep
These flowers, as in their causes, sleep.

Ask me no more whither do stray
The golden atoms of the day;
For, in pure love, heaven did prepare
Those powders to enrich your hair.

Ask me no more whither doth haste
The nightingale, when May is past;   10
For in your sweet dividing throat
She winters, and keeps warm her note.

Ask me no more where those stars light
That downwards fall in dead of night;
For in your eyes they sit, and there
Fixèd become, as in their sphere.

Ask me no more if east or west
The Phoenix builds her spicy nest;
For unto you at last she flies,
And in your fragrant bosom dies.   20

—THOMAS CAREW (1598?–1639?)

In the five stanzas of this formal song a lover pays five compliments to his lady. She is not named; nor does the song itself have any name except this noncommittal one which begins, casually enough, with the indefinite article: "A Song"—as if any lover, anywhere or at any time, might be understood to have seized a musical instrument of some sort and, looking into his lady's eyes, strummed it five times as he sang five answers to five questions which she or someone else has asked. It is not necessarily she who has put the questions. Perhaps she is perfectly silent, smiling as she listens; or she may not be here at all; she may indeed not exist, though we should prefer to think she does. The questions may well be the lover's own, which he has invented for the sake of their answers. They are rhetorical; they assist statement.

The five statements to which they lead are all, if one pleases, extravagant. Where does Jove, the king of the universe, send roses when they fade? Into your beauty, where they sleep. What is the destination, if any, of the sunlight's particles? Your hair, which they were created to adorn. Where does the nightingale fly when she stops singing? Into your throat, where she continues to sing until another season returns. Where do falling stars go? Into your eyes, as into the place for which they were intended. Where does the phoenix, that fabulous Arabian bird which lives forever by alternately burning itself and rising newborn from the ashes, build its nest upon which this act of immortality may be accomplished? In your bosom, of course.

Doubtless it is the extravagance of the compliments at which the lady smiles. Yet she is pleased, for she knows that her lover is trying to be absolute in the expression of his love. The things he says are true for him because he loves her without qualification. If to an indifferent person they would sound exaggerated or fantastic, he trusts her not to find them so; he counts on her to understand, as of course he understands, that overstatement is adoration's natural language. Only too much love is love enough; or rather, only too strong a statement is strong at all. The exact truth about her, supposing it could be put into words, would be inadequate to his purpose, which is to suggest that this after all is the exact truth—for him, anyway. He too smiles as he sings, watching his lady's eyes for signs that she measures the playful force with which he overstates his case. Absolute eloquence is the minimum effect at which he aims. All or nothing, as with any lover in the world, is the motto of his words and music.

But whereas he is like any other lover in his feeling he is different in his art. He is formal to what might seem a fault if we did not become aware of the resources he is using. We might let the matter go with conventional terms, or hum some current song; he explores nature, science, and myth in search of symbols which will carry his meaning. And he composes his poem with the utmost care for its structure, metrically and otherwise. The five stanzas are highly regular in their rhythm, and each of them strictly honors a pattern of syntax as well as a pattern of rhyme. Each first line begins with "Ask me no more," and each third line with For. The punctuation almost never varies. The rhyme scheme is the couplet scheme; and yet it is proper that the poem should appear as stanzas, as quatrains, for each set of four lines, with its asking and its answering couplet, is complete in itself, bringing the poem to a pause from which it will start again.

When it starts again, will it be any farther along? Is the poem aiming to be more than a series of statements—five, as it happens, and this is the number of the fingers on the hand that strokes the instrument whence the music comes—strung as stationary beads are strung, one after another on the string? Or is there movement in the whole? Does the poem climb? Does it reach a conclusion? Does it have a climax?

A progression appears if we consider the successive stanzas in terms of the activity, or the amount of activity, each describes. The first stanza, for example, contains no activity at all. Nothing could be quieter than the act, if it is an act, of sleeping in one's cause as the oak sleeps in the acorn or the rose in its seed, its root, waiting patiently to become itself. If this is an act, it must be done in a deep place out of time's reach; for cause itself is not a temporal thing. The place, indeed, is as deep as the lady's beauty, which is an *orient* deep. A famous word, sufficient in itself to have created Carew's reputation. For it suggests many things: the East, the brilliant spaces out of which suns rise, radiance itself, and the more general idea of source or origin— wells or fountains out of which come forth again whatever things have descended into them, or life which can be where death once was. Yet the tangible activity is nil. All is potentiality, and the sweet promise of more in place of less. Nor is the promise lightly stated: Jove is the agent of its fulfilment, and his name alliterates powerfully, decisively, with *June*.

The second stanza, breaking the trance of the first, sets things in motion, but small things, and indeed the smallest we can conceive. Atoms of light are finer than even the motes we watch dancing in a sunbeam; yet those motes will do for an image, particularly if we think of them as golden, as gold dust floating. The irregular accents we hear in the word *whither* are in the interest of what now is to be achieved: our sense of irre- ducible, indivisible, and all but invisible particles of matter set free—"whither do stray"—to wander where they will. Their will, in fact, is to wander toward that place of which their creator was thinking when he ground them up so light and fine. They are to settle upon my lady's already golden hair, where they will be noticed only as perfection is noticed, gracing what once seemed, yet only seemed, to be sufficiently beautiful without it.

The third stanza follows a larger creature to its destination. The nightingale, which sounds as well as is seen—where is its song continued after music's season closes? For such a singer cannot really cease; something must keep her voice warm and sweet, ready to be heard again. And here the poet runs a risk. For his answer, which is that the bird flies into his lady's throat and remains there, could be grotesque or painful if he did not know how to manage the reader's responses. He manages them, among other ways too mysterious to understand, by the word *dividing* and by the alliteration of *winters* with *warm*. *Dividing* is a musical term of Carew's century, the seventeenth, and refers to the art of descant, or singing in harmony, or performing in parts. It is a technical term for the miracle by which the many divisions of a song melt finally into one sweet thing, the song itself. The lady's throat, like the whole body of the night- ingale, is where music may be said to live, singing for its own pleasure, making sound or no sound as it chooses; wintering, or waiting, in the warmth of its own notes until it chooses to sing so that all may hear. The lady is speaking or singing now; the night- ingale will sing in May; but both are the same in idea, and it is in fact idea that entertains us here, not fact, not feathers, not vocal cords, not flesh in any form, nor even any audible sound. Again it is the promise of sound, the certainty that music remains possible, which reassures us after the disappearance of the nightingale. She has not disappeared after all, any more than the flowers of Jove can be said to have died, or the atoms of day to have wandered nowhere.

The fourth stanza reaches far into the universe—a dark universe, too, for now it is the dead of night—and sees the most startling of all movements. Stars fall. And where? Into my lady's eyes, where the quietest of verbs is found for what they do. They *sit,* fixed as proper stars are fixed, in the spheres which an old astronomy assumed were there to contain them. These spheres made music, too, grander than that of th nightingale; but the poem, though it lets us think of this, says nothing further about it. Our attention is upon the lady's eyes, which are bright not merely as stars are bright in the conventional comparison, but happy in their brightness because they are the home to which celestial wanderers have come. Once more the image of motion has given way to the image of rest; the moving object has plunged into the medium best fitted to receive it and henceforth to display it.

In the final stanza the mythical phoenix, more potent to our imagination than even the brightest star, plunges also to her rest. But it is not the rest of death. It is a rest after which action will commence again as life recommences in new birth. Nor does it matter where this happens. East or west is immaterial now; we remember *orient* in the third line of the poem, but we are far away from even the remotest east, as we are far away fom any west. The phoenix, searching for that spicy place where she can seem to die and yet not die, speeds unerringly to my lady's fragrant bosom, whence she will spring into future flight that contrasts with the quiet power, stated itself so noiselessly in stanza one, exerted by the causes of things. The poem returns to its beginning; draws a circle back through the world of atoms, birds, and stars; and enters, so to speak, itself.

The lady, meanwhile, has not moved, nor has the rhythm of the song abandoned its stateliness, its all but monotonous march of heavy and light syllables, its iambic walk which only in the fifth, seventh, ninth, twelfth, and sixteenth lines shifts momentarily into trochaic. Nor has the singer for one instant relaxed the formality of his smile. He has never become personal. He has kept his mind among metaphysical things, letting science and philosophy do his work of praise. But it was not praise either; it was compliment, which is more intimate and fanciful a thing. The lady never deserved this much. Or did she? The music says she did, and so does the gravity which still lingers in the lover's face. She deserved all that words can say when words refer to the greatest and highest things in the world: immortal things, whose home she is. *Dies* is the last word of the poem, yet death is the last thing it suggests. If any love can last forever, this love will. If any poem can, then this one must.

AN INTERPRETATION OF JOHN KEATS' "ODE ON MELANCHOLY"

RALPH D. EBERLY

ODE ON MELANCHOLY

No, no! go not to Lethe, neither twist
  Wolf's-bane, tight-rooted, for its poisonous wine;
Nor suffer thy pale forehead to be kissed
  By nightshade, ruby grape of Proserpine;
Make not your rosary of yew-berries,
  Nor let the beetle nor the death-moth be
    Your mournful Psyche, nor the downy owl
A partner in your sorrow's mysteries;
  For shade to shade will come too drowsily,
    And drown the wakeful anguish of the soul.

But when the melancholy fit shall fall
   Sudden from heaven like a weeping cloud,
That fosters the droop-headed flowers all,
   And hides the green hill in an April shroud;
Then glut thy sorrow on a morning rose,
   Or on the rainbow of the salt sand-wave,
     Or on the wealth of globèd peonies;
Or if thy mistress some rich anger shows,
   Emprison her soft hand, and let her rave,
     And feed deep, deep upon her peerless eyes.   20

She dwells with Beauty—Beauty that must die;
   And Joy, whose hand is ever at his lips
Bidding adieu; and aching Pleasure nigh,
   Turning to poison while the bee-mouth sips:
Ay, in the very temple of Delight
   Veiled Melancholy has her sovran shrine,
     Though seen of none save him whose strenuous **tongue**
Can burst Joy's grape against his palate fine;
   His soul shall taste the sadness of her might,
     And be among her cloudy trophies hung.   30

                —JOHN KEATS (1795–1821)

This poem is constructed like contrapuntal music. Two "meanings," like melodies in counterpoint, run throughout the whole ode, harmonizing with each other, contrast-ing with each other, and qualifying each other.

The surface theme urges one not to turn to death or to the agents of death, lest these things "drown the wakeful anguish of the soul." Instead, when beset by melancholy, let him turn to beautiful objects—a flower, an iridescent wave, or a beloved woman—and reflect how quickly such things must perish. Thus only can he feel the full power of melancholy.

If this meaning were satisfactory, the search for a contrapuntal theme might be regarded as a mere exercise of ingenuity. But this reading is not satisfactory. Taken in these terms alone, the poem seems to assume that a person would want to induce, rather than to avoid, the most acute form of melancholy. Surely many readers would con-demn such an assumption on the ground of sentimentality, and declare the poem a decadent invitation to an emotional orgy. But most readers will agree that the poem does not submit itself to this hostile judgment.

The implications of the ode, carried by image-suggestions, actually reverse the super-ficial meaning. The poem begins with a repudiation of traditional "graveyard" senti-mentality, on the grounds that melancholy so induced causes stupefaction, dulling or obliterating genuine experience. The opening phrase, "No, no! go not to Lethe," is richly significant; the poisons, the death-moth, the downy owl all suggest not only death itself, but also the benumbing self-dramatization, a kind of life-in-death, that attends sentimental melancholy. The double force of darkness and ghostliness in the phrase "shade to shade," together with the adverb *drowsily* in line 9, reinforces the idea of stupefaction. In line 10 the reason for the repudiation of spiritual opiates becomes overt with the words, "drown the *wakeful* anguish of the soul."

In the second stanza, melancholy is specifically referred to for the first time. The terms of the reference (lines 11-14) are revealing: the "melancholy fit" falls from heaven like rain, soothing, cooling, life-giving: in simile it "fosters the droop-headed flowers." Melancholy, then, is not a pointless gloom, but an element necessary to the keen awareness of beauty, and even of life itself.

The remainder of the second stanza and the whole of the third stanza declare that the essence of melancholy is to be found in the contemplation of beautiful things. "Beauty . . . must die," Joy's "hand is ever at his lips bidding adieu," pleasure turns to poison even while one tastes it. An alert person, alive to transience, finds delight the saddest of all experience. Melancholy has become a "veil'd" goddess, inseparable sister of Delight: the true worshipper of one must necessarily be a devotee of the other also. But this image reads two ways; the implication is clear that if one refuses to recognize Melancholy, he cannot know Delight. The image in lines 27-28 reaffirms the intention of the poem: melancholy is "seen of none save him whose strenuous tongue can burst Joy's grape against his palate fine." But only this strong-tongued person can taste Joy! How can one savor a grape, pray, unless he bursts it against his palate and thus releases its juices? Note the word *strenuous:* Keats insists that the vigorous, fearless acceptance of experience is the key to rich living. This is a far cry from maudlin, sentimental melancholy.

It is not to be assumed that the ode, by declaring melancholy a necessary element of the experience of joy, thereby reduces melancholy to a non-entity. Far from it! Melancholy and Delight are co-equal goddesses: two equally important phases of the same thing. Though the melancholy fit *fosters* life, it is also intimately associated with death: it falls *weeping* from heaven "and hides the green hill in an April *shroud*." The phrase, "April shroud," with its associations of life and of death, epitomizes the poem: It makes melancholy a symbol of the interrelation between life and death. The ironic ending of the poem clarifies this interrelation. Since the person who is really alive will know the brevity of life and its joys, the melancholy awareness of death will claim him as a "cloudy trophy"; but this very awareness will sharpen his appreciation of joy and make him, of all men, relish life most.

DOVER BEACH REVISITED

THEODORE MORRISON (1901–   )

DOVER BEACH

The sea is calm to-night.
The tide is full, the moon lies fair
Upon the straits;—on the French coast the light
Gleams and is gone; the cliffs of England stand
Glimmering and vast, out in the tranquil bay.
Come to the window, sweet is the night-air!
Only, from the long line of spray
Where the sea meets the moon-blanch'd land,
Listen! you hear the grating roar
Of pebbles which the waves draw back, and fling,   10
At their return, up the high strand,
Begin, and cease, and then again begin,
With tremulous cadence slow, and bring
The eternal note of sadness in.

Sophocles long ago
Heard it on the Ægean, and it brought
Into his mind the turbid ebb and flow
Of human misery; we
Find also in the sound a thought,
Hearing it by this distant northern sea.　　　　　　　20

The Sea of Faith
Was once, too, at the full, and round earth's shore
Lay like the folds of a bright girdle furl'd.
But now I only hear
Its melancholy, long, withdrawing roar,
Retreating, to the breath
Of the night-wind, down the vast edges drear
And naked shingles of the world.

Ah, love, let us be true
To one another! for the world, which seems　　　　　　30
To lie before us like a land of dreams,
So various, so beautiful, so new,
Hath really neither joy, nor love, nor light,
Nor certitude, nor peace, nor help for pain;
And we are here as on a darkling plain
Swept with confused alarms of struggle and flight,
Where ignorant armies clash by night.
　　　　　　　　　　—MATTHEW ARNOLD (1822–1888)

Early in the year 1939 a certain Professor of Educational Psychology, occupying a well-paid chair at a large endowed university, conceived a plot. From his desk in the imposing Hall of the Social Sciences where the Research Institute in Education was housed he had long burned with resentment against teachers of literature, especially against English departments. It seemed to him that the professors of English stood square across the path of his major professional ambition. His great desire in life was to introduce into the study, the teaching, the critical evaluation of literature some of the systematic method, some of the "objective procedure" as he liked to call it, some of the certainty of result which he believed to be characteristic of the physical sciences. "You make such a fetish of science," a colleague once said to him, "why aren't you a chemist?"—a question that annoyed him deeply.

If such a poem as Milton's "Lycidas" has a value—and most English teachers, even to-day, would start with that as a cardinal fact—then that value must be measurable and expressible in terms that do not shift and change from moment to moment and person to person with every subjective whim. They would agree, these teachers of literature, these professors of English, that the value of the poem is in some sense objective; they would never agree to undertake any objective procedure to determine what that value is. They would not clearly define what they meant by achievement in the study of literature, and they bridled and snorted when anyone else attempted to define it. He remembered what had happened when he had once been incautious enough to suggest to a professor of English in his own college that it might be possible to establish norms for the appreciation of Milton. The fellow had simply exploded into a peal of histrionic laughter and then had tried to wither him with an equally histrionic look of incredulity and disgust.

He would like to see what would happen if the teachers of English were forced or lured, by some scheme or other, into a public exposure of their position. It would put them in the light of intellectual charlatanism, nothing less . . . and suddenly Professor Chartly (for so he was nicknamed) began to see his way.

It was a simple plan that popped into his head, simple yet bold and practical. It was a challenge that could not be refused. A strategically placed friend in one of the large educational foundations could be counted on: there would be money for clerical expenses, for travel if need be. He took his pipe from his pocket, filled it, and began to puff exultantly. To-morrow he must broach the scheme to one or two colleagues; to-night, over cheese and beer, would not be too soon. He reached for the telephone.

The plan that he unfolded to his associates that evening aroused considerable skepticism at first, but gradually they succumbed to his enthusiasm. A number of well-known professors of literature at representative colleges up and down the land would be asked to write a critical evaluation of a poem prominent enough to form part of the standard reading in all large English courses. They would be asked to state the criteria on which they based their judgment. When all the answers had been received the whole dossier would be sent to a moderator, a trusted elder statesman of education, known everywhere for his dignity, liberality of intelligence, and long experience. He would be asked to make a preliminary examination of all the documents and to determine from the point of view of a teacher of literature whether they provided any basis for a common understanding. The moderator would then forward all the documents to Professor Chartly, who would make what in his own mind he was frank to call a more scientific analysis. Then the jaws of the trap would be ready to spring.

Once the conspirators had agreed on their plot their first difficulty came in the choice of a poem. Suffice it to say that someone eventually hit on Arnold's "Dover Beach," and the suggestion withstood all attack. "Dover Beach" was universally known, almost universally praised; it was remote enough so that contemporary jealousies and cults were not seriously involved, yet near enough not to call for any special expertness, historical or linguistic, as a prerequisite for judgment; it was generally given credit for skill as a work of art, yet it contained also, in its author's own phrase, a "criticism of life."

Rapidly in the days following the first meeting the representative teachers were chosen and invited to participate in the plan. Professional courtesy seemed to require the inclusion of an Arnold expert. But the one selected excused himself from producing a value judgment of "Dover Beach" on the ground that he was busy investigating a fresh clue to the identity of "Marguerite." He had evidence that the woman in question, after the episode hinted at in the famous poems, had married her deceased sister's husband, thus perhaps affecting Arnold's views on a social question about which he had said a good deal in his prose writings. The expert pointed out that he had been given a half-year's leave of absence and a research grant to pursue the shadow of Marguerite through Europe, wherever it might lead him. If only war did not break out he hoped to complete this research and solve one of the vexing problems that had always confronted Arnold's biographers. His energies would be too much engaged in this special investigation to deal justly with the more general questions raised by Professor Chartly's invitation. But he asked to be kept informed, since the results of the experiment could not fail to be of interest to him.

After a few hitches and delays from other quarters, the scheme was ripe. The requests were mailed out, and the Professor of Educational Psychology sat back in grim confidence to await the outcome.

It chanced that the first of the representative teachers who received and answered Professor Chartly's letter was thought of on his own campus as giving off a distinct though not unpleasant odor of the ivory tower. He would have resented the imputation himself. At forty-five Bradley Dewing was handsome in a somewhat speciously virile style, graying at the temples, but still well-knit and active. He prided himself on being able to beat most of his students at tennis; once a year he would play the third or fourth man on the varsity and go down to creditable defeat with some elegiac phrases on the ravages of time. He thought of himself as a man of the world; it was well for his contentment, which was seldom visibly ruffled, that he never heard the class mimic reproducing at a fraternity house or beer parlor his manner of saying: "After all, gentlemen, it is pure poetry that lasts. We must never forget the staying power of pure art." The class mimic never represents the whole of class opinion but he can usually make everyone within earshot laugh.

Professor Dewing could remember clearly what his own teachers had said about "Dover Beach" in the days when he was a freshman in college himself, phrases rounded with distant professorial unction: faith and doubt in the Victorian era; disturbing influence of Darwin on religious belief; Browning the optimist; Tennyson coming up with firm faith after a long struggle in the waters of doubt; Matthew Arnold, prophet of skepticism. How would "Dover Beach" stack up now as a poem? Pull Arnold down from the shelf and find out.

Ah, yes, how the familiar phrases came back. The sea is calm, the tide is full, the cliffs of England stand. . . . And then the lines he particularly liked:

> Come to the window, sweet is the night air!
> Only, from the long line of spray
> Where the sea meets the moon-blanch'd land,
> Listen! you hear the grating roar
> Of pebbles which the waves draw back, and fling,
> At their return, up the high strand,
> Begin, and cease, and then again begin,
> With tremulous cadence slow . . .

Good poetry, that! No one could mistake it. Onomatopoeia was a relatively cheap effect most of the time. Poe, for instance: "And the silken sad uncertain rustling of each purple curtain." Anyone could put a string of s's together and make them rustle. But these lines in "Dover Beach" were different. The onomatopoeia was involved in the whole scene, and it in turn involved the whole rhythmical movement of the verse, not the mere noise made by the consonants or vowels as such. The pauses—only, listen, draw back, fling, begin, cease—how they infused a subdued melancholy into the moonlit panorama at the same time that they gave it the utmost physical reality by suggesting the endless iteration of the waves! And then the phrase "With tremulous cadence slow" coming as yet one more touch, one "fine excess," when it seemed that every phrase and pause the scene could bear had already been lavished on it: that was Miltonic, Virgilian.

But the rest of the poem?

The Sea of Faith
Was once, too, at the full, and round earth's shore
Lay like the folds of a bright girdle furl'd . . .

Of course Arnold had evoked the whole scene only to bring before us this metaphor of faith in its ebb-tide. But that did not save the figure from triteness and from an even more fatal vagueness. Everything in second-rate poetry is compared to the sea: love is as deep, grief as salty, passion as turbulent. The sea may look like a bright girdle sometimes, though Professor Dewing did not think it particularly impressive to say so. And in what sense is *faith* a bright girdle? Is it the function of faith to embrace, to bind, to hold up a petticoat, or what? And what is the faith that Arnold has in mind? The poet evokes no precise concept of it. He throws us the simple, undifferentiated word, unites its loose emotional connotations with those of the sea, and leaves the whole matter there. And the concluding figure of "Dover Beach":

we are here as on a darkling plain
Swept with confused alarms of struggle and flight,
Where ignorant armies clash by night.

Splendid in itself, this memorable image. But the sea had been forgotten now; the darkling plain had displaced the figure from which the whole poem tacitly promised to evolve. It would not have been so if John Donne had been the craftsman. A single bold yet accurate analogy, with constantly developing implications, would have served him for the whole poem.

Thus mused Professor Dewing, the lines of his verdict taking shape in his head. A critic of poetry of course was not at liberty to pass judgment on a poet's thought; he could only judge whether, in treating of the thought or sensibility he had received from his age, the poet had produced a satisfactory work of art. Arnold, Professor Dewing felt, had not been able to escape from the didactic tone or from a certain commonness and vagueness of expression. With deep personal misgivings about his position in a world both socially and spiritually barbarous, he had sought an image for his emotion, and had found it in the sea—a natural phenomenon still obscured by the drapings of conventional beauty and used by all manner of poets to express all manner of feelings. "Dover Beach" would always remain notable, Professor Dewing decided, as an expression of Victorian sensibility. It contained lines of ever memorable poetic skill. But it could not, he felt, be accepted as a uniformly satisfactory example of poetic art.

It was occasionally a source of wonder to those about him just why Professor Oliver Twitchell spent so much time and eloquence urging that man's lower nature must be repressed, his animal instincts kept in bounds by the exertion of the higher will. To the casual observer, Professor Twitchell himself did not seem to possess much animal nature. It seemed incredible that a desperate struggle with powerful bestial passions might be going on at any moment within his own slight frame, behind his delicate white face in which the most prominent feature was the octagonal glasses that focused his eyes on the outside world. Professor Twitchell was a good deal given to discipleship but not much to friendship. He had himself been a disciple of the great Irving Babbitt, and he attracted a small number of disciples among his own more earnest students. But no one knew him well. Only one of his colleagues, who took a somewhat sardonic interest in the mysteries of human nature, possessed a possible clue to the origin of his efforts to repress man's lower nature and vindicate his higher. This colleague had wormed his way sufficiently into Oliver Twitchell's confidence to learn about his family, which he did not often mention. Professor Twitchell, it turned out, had come of decidedly unacademic stock. One of his brothers was the chief salesman for a company that made domestic fire-alarm appliances. At a moment's notice he would whip out a sample from his bag or pocket, plug it into the nearest electric outlet, and while the bystanders waited in terrified suspense, would explain that in the dead of night, if the house caught fire, the thing would go off with a whoop loud enough to warn the soundest sleeper. Lined up with his whole string of brothers and sisters, all older than he, all abounding in spirits, Professor Twitchell looked like the runt of the litter. His colleague decided that he must have had a very hard childhood, and that it was not his own animal nature that he needed so constantly to repress, but his family's.

Whatever the reasons, Professor Twitchell felt no reality in the teaching of literature except as he could extract from it definitions and illustrations of man's moral struggle in the world. For him recent history had been a history of intellectual confusion and degradation, and hence of social confusion and degradation. Western thought had fallen into a heresy. It had failed to maintain the fundamental grounds of a true humanism. It had blurred the distinction between man, God, and nature. Under the influence of the sciences, it had set up a monism in which the moral as well as the physical constitution of man was included within nature and the laws of nature. It had, therefore, exalted man as naturally good, and exalted the free expression of all his impulses. What were the results of this heresy? An age, complained Professor Twitchell bitterly, in which young women talked about sexual perversions at the dinner table; an age in which everyone agreed that society was in dissolution and insisted on the privilege of being dissolute; an age without any common standards of value in morals or art; an age, in short, without discipline, without self-restraint in private life or public.

Oliver Twitchell when he received Professor Chartly's envelope sat down with a strong favorable predisposition toward his task. He accepted wholeheartedly Arnold's attitude toward literature: the demand that poetry should be serious, that it should present us with a criticism of life, that it should be measured by standards not merely personal, but in some sense *real*.

"Dover Beach" had become Arnold's best-known poem, admired as his masterpiece. It would surely contain, therefore, a distillation of his attitude. Professor Twitchell pulled down his copy of Arnold and began to read and as he read he felt himself overtaken by surprised misgiving. The poem began well enough. The allusion to Sophocles, who had heard the sound of the retreating tide by the Ægean centuries ago, admirably prepared the groundwork of high seriousness for a poem which would culminate in a real criticism of human experience. But did the poem so culminate? It was true that the world

> Hath really neither joy, nor love, nor light,
> Nor certitude, nor peace, nor help for pain

if one meant the world as the worldling knows it, the man who conducts his life by unreflective natural impulse. Such a man will soon enough encounter the disappointments of ambition, the instability of all bonds and ties founded on nothing firmer than passion or self-interest. But this incertitude of the world, to a true disciple of culture, should become a means of self-discipline. It should lead him to ask how life may be purified and ennobled, how we may by wisdom and self-restraint oppose to the accidents of the world a true human culture based on the exertion of a higher will. No call to such a positive moral will, Professor Twitchell reluctantly discovered, can be heard in "Dover Beach." Man is an ignorant soldier struggling confusedly in a blind battle. Was this the culminating truth that Arnold the poet had given men in his masterpiece? Professor Twitchell sadly revised his value-judgment of the poem. He could not feel that in his most widely admired performance Arnold had seen life steadily or seen it whole; rather he had seen it only on its worldly side, and seen it under an aspect of terror. "Dover Beach" would always be justly respected for its poetic art, but the famous lines on Sophocles better exemplified the poet as a critic of life.

As a novelist still referred to in his late thirties as "young" and "promising," Rudolph Mole found himself in a curious relation toward his academic colleagues. He wrote for the public, not for the learned journals; hence he was spared the necessity of becoming a pedant. At the same time the more lucrative fruits of pedantry were denied to him by his quiet exclusion from the guild. Younger men sweating for promotion, living in shabby genteel poverty on yearly appointments, their childless wives mimicking their academic shop-talk in bluestocking phrases, would look up from the stacks of five-by-three cards on which they were constantly accumulating notes and references, and would say to him, "You don't realize how lucky you are, teaching composition. You aren't expected to know anything." Sometimes an older colleague, who had passed through several stages of the mysteries of preferment, would belittle professional scholarship to him with an elaborate show of graciousness and envy, "We are all just pedants," he would say. "You teach the students what they really want and need." Rudolph noticed that the self-confessed pedant went busily on publishing monographs and being promoted, while he himself remained, year by year, the English Department's most eminent poor relation.

He was not embittered. His dealings with students were pleasant and interesting. There was a sense of reality and purpose in trying to elicit from them a better expression of their thoughts, trying to increase their understanding of the literary crafts. He could attack their minds on any front he chose, and he could follow his intellectual hobbies as freely as he liked, without being confined to the artificial boundaries of a professional field of learning.

Freud, for example. When Professor Chartly and his accomplices decided that a teacher of creative writing should be included in their scheme and chose Rudolph Mole for the post, they happened to catch him at the height of his enthusiasm for Freud. Not that he expected to psychoanalyze authors through their works; that, he avowed, was not his purpose. You can't deduce the specific secrets of a man's life, he would cheerfully admit, by trying to fit his works into the text-book patterns of complexes and psychoses. The critic, in any case, is interested only in the man to the extent that he is involved in his work. But everyone agrees, Rudolph maintained, that the man is involved in his work. Some part of the psychic constitution of the author finds expression in every line that he writes. We can't understand the work unless we can understand the psychic traits that have gained expression in it. We may never be able to trace back these traits to their ultimate sources and causes, probably buried deep in the author's childhood. But we need to gain as much light on them as we can, since they appear in the work we are trying to apprehend, and determine its character. This is what criticism has always sought to do. Freud simply brings new light to the old task.

Rudolph was fortunate enough at the outset to pick up at the college bookstore a copy of Mr. Lionel Trilling's recent study of Matthew Arnold. In this volume he found much of his work already done for him. A footnote to Mr. Trilling's text, citing evidence from Professors Tinker and Lowry, made it clear that "Dover Beach" may well have been written in 1850, some seventeen years before it was first published. This, for Rudolph's purposes, was a priceless discovery. It meant that all the traditional talk about the poem was largely null and void. The poem was not a repercussion of the bombshell that Darwin dropped on the religious sensibilities of the Victorians. It was far more deeply personal and individual than that. Perhaps when Arnold published it his own sense of what it expressed or how it would be understood had changed. But clearly the poem came into being as an expression of what Arnold felt to be the particular kind of affection and passion he needed from a woman. It was a love poem, and took its place with utmost naturalness, once the clue had been given, in the group of similar and related poems addressed to "Marguerite." Mr. Trilling summed up in a fine sentence one strain in these poems, and the principal strain in "Dover Beach," when he wrote that for Arnold "fidelity is a word relevant only to those lovers who see the world as a place of sorrow and in their common suffering require the comfort of constancy."

> Ah, love, let us be true
> To one another! for the world . . .
> Hath really neither joy, nor love, nor light . . .

The point was unmistakable. And from the whole group of poems to which "Dover Beach" belonged, a sketch of Arnold as an erotic personality could be derived. The question whether a "real Marguerite" existed was an idle one, for the traits that found expression in the poems were at least "real" enough to produce the poems and to determine their character.

And what an odd spectacle it made, the self-expressed character of Arnold as a lover! The ordinary degree of aggressiveness, the normal joy of conquest and possession, seemed to be wholly absent from him. The love he asked for was essentially a protective love, sisterly or motherly; in its unavoidable ingredient of passion he felt a constant danger, which repelled and unsettled him. He addressed Marguerite as "My sister!" He avowed and deplored his own womanish fits of instability:

> I too have wish'd, no woman more,
> This starting, feverish heart, away.

He emphasized his nervous anguish and contrary impulses. He was a "teas'd o'erlabour'd heart," "an aimless unallay'd Desire." He could not break through his fundamental isolation and submerge himself in another human soul, and he believed that all men shared this plight:

> Yes: in the sea of life enisl'd,
> With echoing straits between us thrown.
> Dotting the shoreless watery wild,
> We mortal millions live *alone*,

He never "without remorse" allowed himself

> To haunt the place where passions reign,

yet it was clear that whether he had ever succeeded in giving himself up wholeheartedly
to a passion, he had wanted to. There could hardly be a more telltale phrase than
"Once-long'd-for storms of love."

In short much more illumination fell on "Dover Beach" from certain other verses
of Arnold's than from Darwin and all his commentators:

> Truth—what is truth? Two bleeding hearts
> Wounded by men, by Fortune tried,
> Outwearied with their lonely parts,
> Vow to beat henceforth side by side.

> The world to them was stern and drear;
> Their lot was but to weep and moan.
> Ah, let them keep their faith sincere,
> For neither could subsist alone!

Here was the nub. "Dover Beach" grew directly from and repeated the same emotion, but no doubt generalized and enlarged this emotion, sweeping into one intense
and far-reaching conviction of insecurity not only Arnold's personal fortunes in love,
but the social and religious faith of the world he lived in. That much could be said
for the traditional interpretation.

Of course, as Mr. Trilling did not fail to mention, anguished love affairs, harassed
by mysterious inner incompatibilities, formed a well-established literary convention.
But the fundamental sense of insecurity in "Dover Beach" was too genuine, too often
repeated in other works, to be written off altogether to that account. The same sense
of insecurity, the same need for some rock of protection, cried out again and again, not
merely in Arnold's love poems but in his elegies, reflective pieces, and fragments of
epic as well. Whenever Arnold produced a genuine and striking burst of poetry, with
the stamp of true self-expression on it, he seemed always to be in the dumps. Everywhere dejection, confusion, weakness, contention of soul. No adequate cause could be
found in the events of Arnold's life for such an acute sense of incertitude; it must
have been of psychic origin. Only in one line of effort this fundamental insecurity did
not hamper, sadden, or depress him, and that was in the free play of his intelligence
as a critic of letters and society. Even there, if it did not hamper his efforts, it directed
them. Arnold valiantly tried to erect a barrier of culture against the chaos and squalor
of society, against the contentiousness of men. What was this barrier but an elaborate
protective device?

The origin of the psychic pattern that expressed itself in Arnold's poems could
probably never be discovered. No doubt the influence that Arnold's father exercised
over his emotions and his thinking, even though Arnold rebelled to the extent at least
of casting off his father's religious beliefs, was of great importance. But much more
would have to be known to give a definite clue—more than ever could be known.
Arnold was secure from any attempt to spy out the heart of his mystery. But if criticism
could not discover the cause, it could assess the result, and could do so (thought
Rudolph Mole) with greater understanding by an attempt, with up-to-date psychological aid, to delve a little deeper into the essential traits that manifested themselves in
that result.

In 1917 Reuben Hale, a young instructor in a Western college, had lost his job and done time in the penitentiary for speaking against conscription and for organizing pacifist demonstrations. In the twenties he had lost two more academic posts for his sympathies with Soviet Russia and his inability to forget his Marxist principles while teaching literature. His contentious, eager, lovable, exasperating temperament tried the patience of one college administration after another. As he advanced into middle age, and his growing family suffered repeated upheavals, his friends began to fear that his robust quarrels with established order would leave him a penniless outcast at fifty. Then he was invited to take a flattering post at a girls' college known for its liberality of views. The connection proved surprisingly durable; in fact it became Professor Hale's turn to be apprehensive. He began to be morally alarmed at his own security, to fear that the bourgeois system which he had attacked so valiantly had somehow out-witted him and betrayed him into allegiance. When the C.I.O. made its initial drive and seemed to be carrying everything before it, he did his best to unseat himself again by rushing joyfully to the nearest picket lines and getting himself photographed by an alert press. Even this expedient failed, and he reconciled himself, not without wonder, to apparent academic permanence.

On winter afternoons his voice could be heard booming out through the closed door of his study to girls who came to consult him on all manner of subjects, from the merits of Plekhanov as a Marxist critic to their own most personal dilemmas. They called him Ben; he called them Smith, Jones, and Robinson. He never relaxed his cheerful bombardment of the milieu into which they were born, and of the larger social structure which made bourgeois wealth, bourgeois art, morals, and religion possible. But when a sophomore found herself pregnant it was to Professor Hale that she came for advice. Should she have an abortion or go through with it and heroically bear the social stigma? And it was Professor Hale who kept the affair from the Dean's office and the news-papers, sought out the boy, persuaded the young couple that they were desperately in love with each other, and that pending the revolution a respectable marriage would be the most prudent course, not to say the happiest.

James Joyce remarks of one of his characters that she dealt with moral problems as a cleaver deals with meat. Professor Hale's critical methods were comparably simple and direct. Literature, like the other arts, is in form and substance a product of society, and reflects the structure of society. The structure of society is a class structure: it is conditioned by the mode of production of goods, and by the legal conventions of ownership and control by which the ruling class keeps itself in power and endows itself with the necessary freedom to exploit men and materials for profit. A healthy liter-ature, in a society so constituted, can exist only if writers perceive the essential economic problem and ally themselves firmly with the working class.

Anyone could see the trouble with Arnold. His intelligence revealed to him the chaos that disrupted the society about him; the selfishness and brutality of the ruling class; the ugliness of the world which the industrial revolution had created, and which imperialism and "liberalism" were extending. Arnold was at his best in his critical satire of this world and of the ignorance of those who governed it. But his intelligence far outran his will, and his defect of will finally blinded his intelligence. He was too much a child of his class to disown it and fight his way to a workable remedy for social injustice. He caught a true vision of himself and of his times as standing between "two worlds, one dead, one powerless to be born." But he had not courage or stomach enough to lend his own powers to the birth struggle. Had he thrown in his sympathies unreservedly with the working class, and labored for the inescapable revolution. "Dover

Beach" would not have ended in pessimism and confusion. It would have ended in a cheerful, strenuous, and hopeful call to action. But Arnold could not divorce himself from the world of polite letters, of education, of culture, into which he had been born. He did his best to purify them, to make them into an instrument for the reform of society. But instinctively he knew that "culture" as he understood the term was not a social force in the world around him. Instinctively he knew that what he loved was doomed to defeat. And so "Dover Beach" ended in a futile plea for protection against the hideousness of the darkling plain and the confused alarms of struggle and flight.

Professor Chartly's envelope brought Reuben Hale his best opportunity since the first C.I.O. picket lines to vindicate his critical and social principles. He plunged into his answer with complete zest.

When Peter Lee Prampton agreed to act as moderator in Professor Chartly's experiment he congratulated himself that this would be his last great academic chore. He had enjoyed his career of scholarship and teaching, no man ever more keenly. But now it was drawing to an end. He was loaded with honors from two continents. The universities of Germany, France, and Britain had first laid their formative hands on his learning and cultivation, then given their most coveted recognition to its fruits. But the honor and the glory seemed a little vague on the June morning when the expressman brought into his library the sizable package of papers which Professor Chartly had boxed and shipped to him. He had kept all his life a certain simplicity of heart. At seventy-four he could still tote a pack with an easy endurance that humiliated men of forty. Now he found himself giving in more and more completely to a lust for trout. Half a century of hastily snatched vacations in Cape Breton or the Scottish Highlands had never allowed him really to fill up that hollow craving to find a wild stream and fish it which would sometimes rise in his throat even in the midst of a lecture.

Well, there would be time left before he died. And meanwhile here was this business of "Dover Beach." Matthew Arnold during one of his American lecture tours had been entertained by neighbors of the Pramptons. Peter Lee Prampton's father had dined with the great man, and had repeated his conversation and imitated his accent at the family table. Peter himself, as a boy of nineteen or so, had gone to hear Arnold lecture. That, he thought with a smile, was probably a good deal more than could be said for any of these poor hacks who had taken Professor Chartly's bait.

At the thought of Arnold he could still hear the carriage wheels grate on the pebbly road as he had driven, fifty odd years ago, to the lecture in town, the prospective Mrs. Prampton beside him. His fishing rod lay under the seat. He chuckled out loud as he remembered how a pound-and-a-half trout had jumped in the pool under the clattering planks of a bridge, and how he had pulled up the horse, jumped out, and tried a cast while Miss Osgood sat scolding in the carriage and shivering in the autumn air. They had been just a little late reaching the lecture, but the trout, wrapped in damp leaves, lay safely beside the rod.

It was queer that "Dover Beach" had not come more recently into his mind. Now that he turned his thoughts in that direction the poem was there in its entirety, waiting to be put on again like a coat that one has worn many times with pleasure and accidentally neglected for a while.

The Sea of Faith was once, too, at the full.

How those old Victorian battles had raged about the Prampton table when he was a boy! How the names of Arnold, Huxley, Darwin, Carlyle, Morris, Ruskin had been pelted back and forth by the excited disputants! *Literature and Dogma, God and the Bible, Culture and Anarchy.* The familiar titles brought an odd image into his mind: the tall figure of his father stretching up to turn on the gas lamps in the evening as the family sat down to dinner; the terrific pop of the pilot light as it exploded into a net of white flame, shaped like a little beehive; the buzz and whine of a jet turned up too high.

> Ah, love, let us be true
> To one another! for the world, which seems
> To lie before us like a land of dreams,
> So various, so beautiful, so new,
> Hath really neither joy, nor love, nor light,
> Nor certitude, nor peace, nor help for pain . . .

Peter Lee Prampton shivered in the warmth of his sunny library, shivered with that flash of perception into the past which sometimes enables a man to see how all that has happened in his life, for good or ill, turned on the narrowest edge of chance. He lived again in the world of dreams that his own youth had spread before him, a world truly various, beautiful, and new; full of promise, adventure, and liberty of choice, based on the opportunities which his father's wealth provided, and holding out the prospect of a smooth advance into a distinguished career. Then, within six months, a lavish demonstration that the world has neither certitude, nor peace, nor help for pain: his mother's death by cancer, his father's financial overthrow and suicide, the ruin of his own smooth hopes and the prospect instead of a long, hampered, and obscure fight toward his perhaps impossible ambition. He lived again through the night hours when he had tramped out with himself the youthful question whether he could hold Miss Osgood to her promise in the face of such reversals. And he did not forget how she took his long-sleepless face between her hands, kissed him, and smiled away his anxiety with unsteady lips. Surely everyone discovers at some time or other that the world is not a place of certitude; surely everyone cries out to some other human being for the fidelity which alone can make it so. What more could be asked of a poet than to take so profound and universal an experience and turn it into lines that could still speak long after he and his age were dead?

The best of it was that no one could miss the human feeling, the cry from the heart, in "Dover Beach"; it spoke so clearly and eloquently, in a language everyone could understand, in a form classically pure and simple. Or did it? Who could tell what any job-lot of academicians might be trusted to see or fail to see? And this assortment in Chartly's package might be a queer kettle of fish! Peter Lee Prampton had lived through the *Yellow Book* days of Art for Art's sake; he had read the muckrakers, and watched the rise of the Marxists and the Freudians. Could "Dover Beach" be condemned as unsympathetic with labor? Could a neurosis or a complex be discovered in it? His heart sank at the sharp sudden conviction that indeed these and worse discoveries about the poem might be seriously advanced. Well, he had always tried to go on the principle that every school of criticism should be free to exercise any sincere claim on men's interest and attention which it could win for itself. When he actually applied himself to the contents of Professor Chartly's bale he would be as charitable as he could, as receptive to light from any quarter as he could bring himself to be.

But the task could wait. He felt the need of a period of adjustment before he could approach it with reasonable equanimity. And in the meanwhile he could indulge himself in some long-needed editorial work on his dry-fly book.

ON WILLIAM ERNEST HENLEY'S "INVICTUS"

HERBERT MARSHALL McLUHAN (1911–   )

INVICTUS

Out of the night that covers me,
  Black as the Pit from pole to pole,
I thank whatever gods may be
  For my unconquerable soul.

In the fell clutch of circumstance
  I have not winced nor cried aloud.
Under the bludgeonings of chance
  My head is bloody, but unbowed.

Beyond this place of wrath and tears
  Looms but the horror of the shade,   10
And yet the menace of the years
  Finds, and shall find, me unafraid.

It matters not how strait the gate,
  How charged with punishments the
    scroll,
I am the master of my fate:
  I am the captain of my soul.

—WILLIAM ERNEST HENLEY (1849–1903)

Henley is a by-product of that notorious coarsening of sensibility which develops in England with the patriotic verse of Tennyson. He is the link between the noisy inanity of "Bury the great duke" and the pathic patriotics of Kipling and Newbolt. Like Tennyson and Kipling, his interests were split between rebellious estheticism, which links them with the diabolics of Byron and Swinburne (Henley wrote *Hawthorn and Lavender*), and a pose of aggressive nationalism laughable in its crudity and basic insincerity.

"Invictus" unites both the pose of the "diabolical" esthete and the pose of the rugged Englishman. Of course, its rhetorical credo goes beyond the stoical *Courage* of Sir James Barrie (who was Henley's disciple) in its angry and inverted theology. Barrie substituted whimsy for theology.

Henley provides himself with a Satanic backdrop as he comes forward to announce his own virtues. (The image is vaguely nautical, evoking the common notion of man's wayfaring. But the main suggestion of *Pit* is that of hell-trap. This is reinforced by *Clutch*.) He is appealing oratorically for the sympathetic admiration of an audience which he well understands. Almost every line contains a hard-bitten cliché which propels the "thought" along to the shrill double emphasis on "I" in the last two lines.

Verse of this sort has no internal organization. It doesn't hang together by a poetic action, which always manifests itself in the interaction of the language and metaphors, but simply by an *external* appeal to audience assumptions. (Contrast it in this respect with a genuinely successful poem such as Hardy's "Neutral Tones" [see p. 677] or consider how the superficially rhetorical credo of Tennyson's "Ulysses" [see p. 780] succeeds as poetry by reason of the original pressures in the rhythms of its language and the adequacy of the dramatic situation from which it grows.) The lines

> Beyond this place of wrath and tears
> Looms but the horror of the shade,

are the least foolish of the whole series of hyperboles. There is a crude sort of surprise intended in calling this life hell and the next a relief. The only example of restraint or tension in the entire poem is in the *but* of that second line.

For their full effect one has to imagine these verses being recited by an actor employing extreme gestures and the utmost emphasis of delivery. The setting for the drama is Hell and Judgment, the posture is defiance, the imagery banal, the effect that of a terrified man screwing his courage to the sticking point.

AN INTERPRETATION OF W. B. YEATS' "SAILING TO BYZANTIUM"

ELDER OLSON (1909–   )

SAILING TO BYZANTIUM

That is no country for old men. The young
In one another's arms, birds in the trees,
—Those dying generations—at their song,
The salmon-falls, the mackerel crowded seas,
Fish, flesh, or fowl, commend all summer long
Whatever is begotten, born, and dies.
Caught in that sensual music all neglect
Monuments of unageing intellect.

An aged man is but a paltry thing,
A tattered coat upon a stick, unless   10
Soul clap its hands and sing, and louder sing
For every tatter in its mortal dress,
Nor is there singing school but studying
Monuments of its own magnificence;
And therefore I have sailed the seas and come
To the holy city of Byzantium.

O sages standing in God's holy fire
As in the gold mosaic of a wall,
Come from the holy fire, perne in a gyre,
And be the singing-masters of my soul.   20
Consume my heart away; sick with desire
And fastened to a dying animal
It knows not what it is; and gather me
Into the artifice of eternity.

Once out of nature I shall never take
My bodily form from any natural thing,
But such a form as Grecian goldsmiths make
Of hammered gold and gold enameling
To keep a drowsy Emperor awake;
Or set upon a golden bough to sing   30
To lords and ladies of Byzantium
Of what is past, or passing, or to come.
—W. B. YEATS (1865–1939)

In "Sailing to Byzantium" an old man faces the problem of old age, of death, and of regeneration, and gives his decision. Old age, he tells us, excludes a man from the sensual joys of youth; the world appears to belong completely to the young, it is no place for the old; indeed, an old man is scarcely a man at all—he is an empty artifice, an effigy merely, of a man; he is a tattered coat upon a stick. This would be very bad, except that the young also are excluded from something; rapt in their sensuality, they are ignorant utterly of the world of the spirit. Hence if old age frees a man from sensual passion, he may rejoice in the liberation of the soul; he is admitted into the realm of the spirit; and his rejoicing will increase according as he realizes the magnificence of the soul. But the soul can best learn its own greatness from the great works of art; hence he turns to those great works, but in turning to them, he finds that these are by no means mere effigies, or monuments, but things which have souls also; these live in the noblest element of God's fire, free from all corruption; hence he prays for death, for release from his mortal body; and since the insouled monuments exhibit the possibility of the soul's existence in some other matter than flesh, he wishes reincarnation, not now in a mortal body, but in the immortal and changeless embodiment of art.

There are thus the following terms, one might say, from which the poem suspends: the condition of the young, who are spiritually passive although sensually active; the condition of the merely old, who are spiritually and physically impotent; the condition of the old, who, although physically impotent, are capable of spiritual activity; the condition of art considered as inanimate—i.e., the condition of things which are merely monuments; and finally the condition of art considered as animate—as of such things as artificial birds which have a human soul. The second term, impotent and unspiritual old age, is a privative, a repugnant state which causes the progression through the other various alternative terms, until its contrary is encountered. The first and third terms are clearly contraries of each other; taken together as animate nature they are further contrary to the fourth term, inanimate art. None of these terms represents a wholly desirable mode of existence; but the fifth term, which represents such a mode, amalgamates the positive elements and eliminates the negative elements of both nature and art, and effects thus a resolution of the whole, for now the soul is present, as it would not be in art, nor is it passive, as it would be in the young and sensual mortal body, nor is it lodged in a "dying animal," as it would be in the body of the aged man; the soul is now free to act in its own supremacy and in full cognizance of its own excellence, and its embodiment is now incorruptible and secure from all the ills of flesh.

About these several oppositions the poem forms. The whole turns on the old man's realization, now that he is in the presence of the images of Byzantium, that these images have souls; there are consequently two major divisions which divide the poem precisely in half, the first two stanzas presenting art as inanimate, the second two, as animate; and that this is the case can be seen from such signs as that in the first half of the poem the images are stated as passive objects—they are twice called "monuments," they are merely objects of contemplation, they may be neglected or studied, visited or not visited, whereas in stanzas III and IV they are treated as gods which can be prayed to for life or death, as beings capable of motion from sphere to sphere, as instructors of the soul, as sages possessed of wisdom; and the curious shift in the manner of consideration is signalized by the subtle phrasing of the first two lines of stanza III: "O sages standing in God's holy fire / As in the gold mosaic of a wall." According to the first part, the images at Byzantium were images, and one should have expected at most some figurative apostrophe to them: "O images set in the gold mosaic of a wall, much as the sages stand in God's holy fire": but here the similitude is reversed, and lest there should be any error, the sages are besought to come from the holy fire and begin the tuition of the soul, the destruction of the flesh.

Within these two halves of the poem, further divisions may be found, coincident with the stanzaic divisions. Stanza I presents a rejection of passion, stanza II an acceptance of intellection; then, turning on the realization that art is insouled, stanza III presents a rejection of the corruptible embodiment, and stanza IV, an acceptance of the incorruptible. There is an alternation, thus, of negative and affirmative: out of passion into intellection, out of corruption into permanence, in clear balance, the proportion being I: II: III: IV; and what orders these sections is their dialectical sequence. That is, passion must be condemned before the intellect can be esteemed; the intellect must operate before the images can be known to be insouled; the realization that the images are insouled precedes the realization that the body may be dispensed with; and the reincarnation of the soul in some changeless medium can be recognized as a possibility only through the prior recognition that the flesh is not the necessary matter of the soul. The parallel opposition of contraries constitutes a sharp demarcation: in stanza I a mortal bird of nature amid natural trees sings a brief song of sensual joy in praise of mortal things, of "whatever is begotten, born, and dies"; in stanza IV an immortal and artificial bird set in an artificial tree sings an eternal song of spiritual joy in praise of eternal things, of "what is past, or passing, or to come"; and similarly, in stanza II a living thing is found to be an inanimate artifice, "a tattered coat upon a stick," incapable of motion, speech, sense or knowledge, whereas in stanza III what had appeared to be inanimate artifice is found to possess a soul, and hence to be capable of all these. A certain artificial symmetry in the argument serves to distinguish these parts even further: stanzas I and IV begin with the conclusions of their respective arguments, whereas II and III end with their proper conclusions, and I is dependent upon II for the substantiation of its premises, as IV is dependent upon III.

This much indication of the principal organization of the work permits the explication, in terms of this, of the more elementary proportions. The first line of stanza I presents immediately, in its most simple statement, the condition which is the genesis of the whole structure: "That is no country for old men"; old men are shut out from something, and the remainder of the first six lines indicates precisely what it is from which they are excluded. The young are given over to sensual delight, in which old men can no longer participate. But a wall, if it shuts out, also shuts in; if the old are excluded from something, so are the young; lines 7 and 8, consequently, exhibit a second sense in which "That is no country for old men," for the young neglect all intellectual things. Further, the use of "that" implies a possible "this"; that is, there is a country for the old as for the young; and, again, the use of "that" implies that the separation from the country of the young is already complete. The occupation of the young is shrewdly stated: at first sight the human lovers "in one another's arms" have, like the birds at their song, apparently a romantic and sentimental aura; but the curious interpolation of "Those dying generations" in the description of the birds foreshadows the significance they are soon to have; and the phrases immediately following remove all sentimentality: "the salmon-falls, the mackerel-crowded seas" intend the ascent of salmon to the headwaters, the descent of mackerel to the deep seas in the spawning season, and the ironic intention is clear: all—the human lovers, the birds, the fish, do but spawn, but copulate, and this is their whole being; and if the parallel statement does not make this sufficiently evident, the summation of all in terms merely of animal genera—"fish, flesh, or fowl"—is unmistakable. The country of the young, then, is in its air, in its waters, and on its earth, from headwaters to ocean, wholly given over to sensuality; its inhabitants "commend all summer long" anything whatsoever, so long as it be mortal and animal—they commend "whatever is begotten, born, and dies"; and while they "commend" because they have great joy, that which they praise, they who praise, and their praise itself are ephemeral, for these mortals praise the things of mortality, and their commendation, like their joy, lasts but a summer, a mating season. The concluding lines of the stanza remove all ambiguity, and cancel all possibility of a return to such a country; even if the old man could, he would not return to a land where "Caught in that sensual music, all neglect / Monuments of unageing intellect." The young are "caught," they are really passive and incapable of free action; and they neglect those things which are unageing.

Merely to end here, however, with a condemnation of youthful sensuality would be unsatisfactory; as the second stanza expounds, old age itself is no solution; the old man cannot justly say, like Sophocles when he was asked whether he regretted the loss of youth and love, "Peace; most gladly have I escaped the thing of which you speak; I feel as if I had escaped from a mad and furious master"; for merely to be old is merely to be in a state of privation, it is to be "a paltry thing / A tattered coat upon a stick," it is to be the merest scarecrow, the merest fiction and semblance of a man, an inanimate rag upon a dead stick. A man merely old, then, is worse off than youth; if the souls of the young are captive, the old have, in this sense at least, no souls at all. Something positive must be added; and if the soul can wax and grow strong as the body wanes, then every step in the dissolution of the body—"every tatter in its mortal dress"—is cause for a further augmentation of joy. But this can occur only if the soul can rejoice in its own power and magnificence; this rejoicing is possible only if the soul knows of its own magnificence, and this knowledge is possible only through the contemplation of monuments which recall that magnificence. The soul of the aged must be strong to seek that which youth neglects. Hence the old must seek Byzantium; that is the country of the old; it is reached by sailing the seas, by breaking utterly with the country of the young; all passion must be left behind, the soul must be free to study the emblems of unchanging things.

Here the soul should be filled with joy; it should, by merely "studying," commend changeless things with song, as youth commends the changing with song; it would seem that the problem has been resolved, and the poem hence must end; but the contemplation of the monuments teaches first of all that these are no mere monuments but living things, and that the soul cannot grow into likeness with these beings of immortal embodiment unless it cast off its mortal body utterly. Nor is joy possible until the body be dissolved; the heart is still sick with the impossible desires of the flesh, it is still ignorant of its circumstances, and no song is possible to the soul while even a remnant of passion remains. Hence the old man prays to the sages who really stand in God's holy fire and have merely the semblance of images in gold mosaic; let them descend, "perning in a gyre," that is, moving in the circular motion which alone is possible to eternal things, let them consume with holy fire the heart which is the last seat of passion and ignorance, let them instruct the soul, let them gather it into the artifice of eternity and make the old man like themselves; even Byzantium, so long as the flesh be present, is no country for old men.

What it is to be like these, the soul, as yet uninstructed, can only conjecture; at any rate, with the destruction of the flesh it will be free of its ills; and if, as in Plato's myth of Er, the soul after death is free to choose some new embodiment, it will never again elect the flesh which is so quickly corruptible and which enslaves it to passion; it will choose some such form of art as that of the artificial birds in Theophilus' garden;[1] it will be incorruptible and passionless gold; and it will dwell among leaves and boughs which are also of incorruptible and passionless metal. And now all sources of conflict are resolved in this last: the old has become the ageless; impotency has been exchanged for a higher power; the soul is free of passion and free for its joy, and it sings as youth once sang, but now of "What is past, and passing, and to come" —of the divisions of Eternity—rather than of "Whatever is begotten, born, and dies" —of the divisions of mortal time. And it has here its country, its proper and permanent habitation.

Although the argument as we have stated it clearly underlies the poem, it would be erroneous to suppose that this in itself constitutes the poem, for in that case there would be no difference between our paraphrase and the poem itself. The poem itself comprehends the argument and collocates with it many terms which, although they could scarcely be formulated into some order approximating the pattern of the argument, nevertheles qualify the argument and determine its course. The basic analogies of the poem—of the natural world to a country, of the aged man to a scarecrow, of the world of art to Byzantium, and of artificial to natural generation—all these function as do the definitions of terms in actual argument; they serve to delimit the sphere of discourse and to make the argument intelligible.

This point is worth some discussion. The criticism of poetry has often turned chiefly on the so-called psychological connotations of readers with single words or phrases; but one may doubt whether the reader is at liberty to intrude such irrelevances as the accidents of personal experience or the inevitable ambiguities of language would necessarily afford. Surely the ultimate consequence of such assumptions must be either that the poem becomes a mere stimulus to independent poetic activities on the part of the reader—that is, the reader becomes the true poet, his reading the true poem— or, on the other hand, that the reader becomes the matter or medium of art, in which case all the arts would have a common medium, the soul of the spectator. Neither of these consequences, it need scarcely be said, complies with the stipulations which initiated this discussion.

If the basic terms of a lyric poem do not receive their meanings from the chance associations of the reader, neither do they have their dictionary meanings; like terms in most discourse, they take their significance from their context, through justaposition to other terms with which they are equated, contrasted, correlated, or combined. In the present poem, for instance, the term "singing" is explicitly extended beyond its usual meaning to cover two kinds of jubilation, the rejoicing of the natural creature and that of the artificial; as a consequence, all the terms which relate to jubilation and song are affected; for example, "commend," "music," "singing-school," and "singing-masters" suffer an extention commensurate with that of singing. Similarly, the term "intellect" and all the terms associated with it suffer extention; and the monuments here are not ordinary monuments, but changeless embodiments of the changeless soul —by no means effigies, but truly living creatures, capable of will, of desire, of jubilation, of local motion, of intellection and instruction. Nor is Byzantium the historical

---

[1] In his note to the poem (*Collected Poems*, New York, 1933, p. 450) Yeats remarks: "I have read somewhere that in the Emperor's palace at Byzantium was a tree made of gold and silver, and artificial birds that sang." Undoubtedly the Emperor was Theophilus (829–842), and the birds conform to the descriptions of certain automata constructed for him by Leo Mathematicus and John Hylilas. Cf. *Hist. Byzan. Script. post Theoph.*, Anon. Cont. Theoph., 107; Constantini Monassis, *Brev. Hist.*, 107; and Michaeli Glycae, *Annales*, 292. See also Gibbon, *Decline and Fall*, Chapter LIII, and George Finlay, *History of the Byzantine Empire* (London, 1906), pp. 140, 148, where further references are given.

city; the tourist is not invited to recall that here once he was overcharged, nor is the historian invited to contribute such information as that this was a city visited by Hugh of Vermandois; Byzantium is not a place upon a map, but a term in the poem; a term signifying a stage of contemplation wherein the soul studies itself and so learns both what it is and in what consists true and eternal joy.

Furthermore, if the words of a poem have meanings which the poet may arbitrarily determine, the "objects" in poetry are also given whatever "properties" the poet sees fit to assign to them. That is, whereas the physical thing has its determinate nature and is subject to physical laws such as Newton's laws, the "things" of a poem —the artificial and natural creatures here, for instance—have only such properties as statement within the poem affords them. Poetic statements must not be confused, however, with propositions; since they are not statements about things which exist outside the poem, it would be meaningless to evaluate them as true or false; they have rather the status of definitions or resolutions; and while in certain poems the coordination is dialectical, as in this poem, no criteria of dialectic could be significantly applied to them, for a dialectic is necessarily regulated by the natures of things external to the dialectic and must ultimately be evaluated by references to those externals, whereas the coordination of elements in a poem cannot involve reference to anything outside the poem. Even when poetic statements are incidentally true propositions, even when their coordination is also cogent argument, these coincidences would not affect their poetic status. Thus, "To His Coy Mistress" is an excellent poem, whether the lover's argument is valid or not. In a sense, every poem is a microcosmos, a discrete and independent universe with its laws provided by the poet; his decision is absolute; he can make things good or bad, great or small, powerful or weak, just as he wills; he may make men taller than mountains or smaller than atoms, he may suspend whole cities in the air, he may destroy creation or re-form it; within his universe the impossible becomes the possible, the necessary the contingent—if he but says they do.

I have said that the bare argument of "Sailing to Byzantium" is not the poem; but I should argue that the argument (considered not as a real argument, but according to what I have said, as a certain collocation of terms) is the *principle* of this poem, in a sense analogous to that in which, for Aristotle, plot is the principle of tragedy. For if the principle is that for the sake of which all other things in the poem exist, and that, consequently, in terms of which all are intelligible, what could be the principle, other than the thing we have supposed? There is here no plot, no ordered tissue of incidents, for, first of all, the whole poem is of a moment—the moment in which the old man confronts the monuments and addresses them—whereas a tissue of incidents, a plot, must extend over a span of time. And second, there can be no plot because there are no incidents; the "events" in a lyric poem are never incidents as such, connected by necessity or probability, but devices for making poetic statements. Again, since there is no action, there is no agent, that is, *character,* in the sense in which there are differentiated agents in drama or epic, each duly discriminated for his distinct part in the action; rather, the character in the sense in which character may be said to exist here is almost completely universalized. Hence, if plot does not constitute the principle of the poem, neither does character; for not all the parts of the poem would be explicable in terms of character, nor are we presented with any precise depiction of character here, as we should be if it were the end. On the merely verbal level, again, we can account for nothing; the words must be explained in terms of something else, not the poem in terms of the words; and further, a principle must be a principle of something other than itself; hence the words cannot be a principle of their own arrangements.

Rather, it is clear as we look at the poem, that a certain problem orders the whole—the problem of finding a suitable compensation for the losses suffered in old age; the poem begins with exclusion from the pleasures of youth, develops among ordered dialectical alternatives, and ends when the problem is permanently solved. As the problem determines the limits of the poem, so it determines all else; the character is determined by it, for example, because—according to the very nature of the problem —a young man could not have conceived of the problem as it is stated, nor could a raging and sensual old man, nor could an old man who was contented with age, like Sophocles; since an ideal and permanent solution was to be given to the problem, a character conscious of loss, and capable of conceiving an ideal solution, was necessitated. Nothing beside this is indicated with respect to the speaker. Again, the words themselves are determined by the problem; while the choice of metaphors of a "country," or "song," and of modes of embodiment was initially arbitrary, once the metaphors have been stated they must be carried out according to the dictates of the problem; indeed, it is possible to trace variations in diction precisely proportional to the stages of the dialectic. For example, the stages are verbally signalized by the succession "flesh," "stick," "dying animal," "gold," in terms of expressions of embodiment, or "no country," "Byzantium," "the artifice of eternity," which is amid "holy fire," in terms of habitation; and the metaphor of the artificial bird in the fourth stanza bears such relation—in terms of setting, song, character of joy, object of joy, and "bodily form"—to the real birds—"those dying generations"—in stanza I as the solution of the problem bears to the element the negation of which generated the dialectic. In a similar manner the presence of nearly every word in the poem might be justified if space permitted.

On the basis of our examination, then, we may say that there exists a kind of poem (since we have here one instance of it) which has argument, in the sense we have stipulated, as its principle; not, let us remember, a dialectic referable to externals, but a certain formal collocation of terms which is referable to nothing outside itself and which may be called the soul of the poem in the sense in which Aristotle calls plot the soul of tragedy. This kind of poetry has the same means as tragedy, epic, and comedy, but whereas the latter are imitations of human action, so that their principle is a certain collocation of incidents organized by necessity and probability—whereas, that is, these are dynamic, for they imitate change—the kind which we have been scrutinizing is static; it abstracts from motion and change, and though it sometimes appears to recount events, these are not events as parts of a plot connected by probability or necessity, but events in the sense in which we speak of events in a philosophical dialogue—they are only dialectically separable stages in the treatment of a problem, and are reducible to statements within the problem. Whereas in the Aristotelian treatment of poems which have a plot as their principle, certain qualitative parts of the various species resulted from an analysis of the object of imitation, that is, the action, a different procedure is necessary here; the principle is a tissue not of events but of ideas, and the ordering of the poem will not be by necessity and probability, by the antecedents and consequents of action, but by dialectical priority and posteriority. Lastly, while character will be necessitated here as where a plot is the principle, it will be determined, not by its share in an action, but by its role in a drama, not of action, but of thought. That is, it is determined, as the characters in a Platonic dialogue are determined, by the nature of the discourse which they are to utter.

It would be a mistake, however, to assume that all lyrics are of the order considered here. The term lyric itself has been given an extraordinary variety of applications, and the scrupulous analyst and critic will attempt to keep the variety of critical approaches almost commensurate with these, on the assumption of great art—however familiar the pattern in which it is apparently laid—is always in the last analysis *sui generis*.

AN INTERPRETATION OF ROBERT FROST'S "STOPPING BY WOODS . . ."

EARL DANIELS (1893–   )

. . . If you are one of those taught to approach the presence of the poem in quest of vital lesson, of profound comment on man and the universe, the answer is, *Don't*. Here should be no halfway measures, no reducing the urge to philosophy by half, no gradual tapering-off. You may, after all, rest comfortable in the assurance that if philosophy and morals are present in any vital way, they will make themselves felt without your conscious searching for them, insistent on their share in your awareness of the complete poem.

The way of a group of college freshmen with a poem of Robert Frost illustrates how deadly this concern about morals may be. Here is the poem.

STOPPING BY WOODS ON A SNOWY EVENING

Whose woods these are I think I know.
His house is in the village though;
He will not see me stopping here
To watch his woods fill up with snow.

My little horse must think it queer
To stop without a farmhouse near
Between the woods and frozen lake
The darkest evening of the year.

He gives his harness bells a shake
To ask if there is some mistake.
The only other sound's the sweep
Of easy wind and downy flake.

The woods are lovely, dark and deep.
But I have promises to keep,
And miles to go before I sleep,
And miles to go before I sleep.

—ROBERT FROST (1874-1963)

Here are some interpretations of freshmen who were supposed to be better-than-average students.

a) In this poem the underlying thought seems to be that of suicide. . . . The last four lines of the poem indicate that the person decides he has more work to do on earth before he dies in order to fulfill a promise of some kind.

b) A man who has promised to leave town after committing some crime, and has been told "to get going and don't stop." The line, "The darkest evening of the year," might mean the disgrace he has brought on himself; and, "I have promises to keep," may mean he has promised to get out of the country.

c) If he didn't mention that the owner of the woods lived in the village, I would say he was talking about the life he has yet to live before he meets his Maker.

d) It deals with the thought of eternal rest. . . . But then the subject is brought back to reality with the thought of the things he has yet to do, and the rest of his life he has yet to spend.

e) It may represent one who is tired of life's hardships, and is tempted to drop by the wayside in some secluded retreat, but who must press on since he has many years of work ahead and many obligations to fulfill before such rest may be his.

f) Almost every day we find ourselves faced with the lures of temptation. We realize that we ought to keep on our way, yet the temptation to stay where all is peaceful and quiet is often too great for us to resist. While we are here in college we are often tempted to do the easiest thing. That is, to neglect our studies and to run around and have a good time. However we know that there are promises to be kept and obligations to be filled. We have been sent here by our parents for the purpose of receiving an education, and there is no doubt that our duty is to do all in our power to take advantage of this opportunity.

g) I am a college man. I am taking a pre-med course. I am away from home. I am open to temptations that college may offer me. Am I to take advantage of their owner's absence to sit and gaze in his woods—to take advantage of being away from my parents to stop by the wayside and admire the beautiful sirens? Or, am I to be a second Ulysses and have sufficient will power to overcome these temptations? Am I to stop where there is "easy wind and downy flake"—to sit back in my chair, just to dream and forget all hardships? Or am I to heed the impatience of the horse and the warning of the harness bell—to awaken to my will calling for me to go on? True, it is dark now, and I cannot see well, but do I not remember the vows that I have made—to go through at all costs? Yes, I must go through those long miles of roads rougher than *I* can imagine, before *I* call for time out.

Comments *f* and *g* are especially nauseous misunderstandings, and they represent the cardinal sin of personal application. To make a poem mean privately, to ourselves alone, to look first for directions about *our* life and *our* problems—no going wrong can be more abysmally bad. Like the old hocus-pocus magic-formula way in which the Bible used to be consulted, you put your question, open the book at random, drop an equally random finger on the page, and there you are—provided you are ingenious enough in twisting words to meet special situations and personal needs. The method is equally unintelligent with the Bible and with poetry, and to resort to it is to proclaim oneself part of an intellectual underworld of superstition and ignorance. The poet's message, so far as he has a message for the individual, is a message to the individual not in his private and peculiar selfhood, but in his representative capacity as a normal human being, as a man; it is part of the universality of the poet's speaking.

If facile talk about appreciation, concern with peripheral things, and preoccupation with morals and the meaning of life are heresies, what is sound doctrine in the reading of poetry? What is orthodox? What is a right approach to Frost's poem, or to any poem? The simple, natural approach, the easiest way. What is obvious in "Stopping by Woods on a Snowy Evening" is that the poet has had a perfectly everyday experience. On a snow-filled winter's afternoon, he has come to a patch of woodland; for no reason, save that he simply and unashamedly likes to, he has stopped, just to watch the woods fill up with snow. That is the experience, the start of the poem, which, from such an unassuming start, got itself written because *the poet enjoyed the experience,* remembered it, and something made him want to try to put it in words, *just for fun: the poem is a record of experience to be shared with a reader,* who must take it at this simple face value if he is to read the poem as it should be read. Most poems probably begin much like this. And if someone says, "It may never have happened to Frost; he may have imagined it all," the answer is that in literature and the arts there is no essential difference between experience in actuality and experience in imagination; both are the stuff of poems, in the broadest sense of the term, *experience.* It is really very little a reader's business whether a writer is using memory or imagination, so long as the reality of the result is not affected. Frost may, indeed, have imagined it all, so far as we have a right to know, or care.

But why should a poet want to share experience, if he has nothing "important" to say, no "lesson" to teach, if he is not intent on "improving society," and "bettering the conditions of the human race"? Like so many facts, this is a mystery, hid in elemental human nature. Men do act this way: human nature prompts them to want to tell others what has happened to them. All conversation is built on that ancient formula, "Have you heard this one?" The questioner hopes "this one" has not been heard, so that he can go on and tell his story, enjoy sharing his experience.

The woman in the parable is a case in point. She had lost her money. It is not significant that she went on an orgy of spring cleaning, turning the house upside down, or that she found her money. But when she found it, and this is the important thing, her next move was to give a party, inviting friends and neighbors for miles around, just that they might rejoice with her because she had found what had been lost: in other words, that they might share her experience. So the poet, though tangibilities like money may not be involved. Something emotionally stirring has happened, and he makes a poem, which is his invitation to his friends and neighbors to rejoice with him. How ungracious of the friends and neighbors of the woman, if they had hunted for lessons in the experience, emphasized, perhaps, the moral that in the future she must be more careful about her money, suggested it was all an illustration of the guidance of a good providence, enabling her to recover her fortune—or any other testimony a dyed-in-the-wool moralist might strain to discover. They had been invited to a party; the woman didn't want lessons; she wanted them to have a good time with her. No less ungracious is the reader who would deduce moral teaching from "Stopping by Woods on a Snowy Evening," and from many other poems, when what the poet wants is that we should have a good time at his party, along with him, because he, in the first place, had a good time with his experience. Such sharing is the request every good poet makes of his readers, and it leads straight to an idea at the heart of all poetry, the irrefragable cornerstone on which poetry rests. That idea, the center of this book, is that *poetry, reduced to its simplest, is only experience.* Experience moved the poet; he enjoyed it, and wanted to put it down on paper, as experience and nothing else, partly because writing is a self-contained action which is fun for the writer, partly because he wanted the reader to enjoy the experience with him. If we are to learn to read, we must begin with elemental, irreducible facts like this.

Of course poetry can be, often is, profound and philosophical, probing below surfaces, reaching far down to the depths of the spirit, anxious about Life, and Death, what is before Life, and after Death. In his *De Rerum Natura* (Of the Nature of

Things), Lucretius wrote thousands of lines devoted to the origin of the universe, to man's nature and his place within his world. He wrote a poem, which has lived for more than nineteen hundred years, admittedly one of the great things of all literatures. Milton set himself, in *Paradise Lost,* to

assert eternal Providence,
And justify the ways of God to men.

And whatever we may think of the success with which he resolved his problem, his poem is one of the few supremely great poems so far given to the world.

AN INTERPRETATION OF T. S. ELIOT'S "THE LOVE SONG OF J. ALFRED PRUFROCK"

CLEANTH BROOKS (1906–   ) and ROBERT PENN WARREN (1905–   )

THE LOVE SONG OF J. ALFRED PRUFROCK

> *S'io credesse che mia risposta fosse*
> *A persona che mai tornasse al mondo,*
> *Questa fiamma staria senza piu scosse.*
> *Ma perciocche giammai di questo fondo*
> *Non torno vivo alcun, s' i' odo il vero,*
> *Senza tema d' infamia ti rispondo.*

Let us go then, you and I,
When the evening is spread out against the sky
Like a patient etherised upon a table;
Let us go, through certain half-deserted streets,
The muttering retreats
Of restless nights in one-night cheap hotels
And sawdust restaurants with oyster-shells:
Streets that follow like a tedious argument
Of insidious intent
To lead you to an overwhelming question . . .   10
Oh, do not ask, "What is it?"
Let us go and make our visit.

In the room the women come and go
Talking of Michelangelo.

The yellow fog that rubs its back upon the window-panes,
The yellow smoke that rubs its muzzle on the window-panes
Licked its tongue into the corners of the evening,
Lingered upon the pools that stand in drains,
Let fall upon its back the soot that falls from chimneys,
Slipped by the terrace, made a sudden leap,   20
And seeing that it was a soft October night,
Curled once about the house, and fell asleep.

And indeed there will be time
For the yellow smoke that slides along the street,
Rubbing its back upon the window-panes;
There will be time, there will be time
To prepare a face to meet the faces that you meet;
There will be time to murder and create,
And time for all the works and days of hands
That lift and drop a question on your plate;   30
Time for you and time for me,
And time yet for a hundred indecisions,
And for a hundred visions and revisions,
Before the taking of a toast and tea.

In the room the women come and go
Talking of Michelangelo.

And indeed there will be time
To wonder, "Do I dare?" and, "Do I dare?"
Time to turn back and descend the stair,
With a bald spot in the middle of my hair—   40
(They will say: "How his hair is growing thin!")
My morning coat, my collar mounting firmly to the chin,
My necktie rich and modest, but asserted by a simple pin—
(They will say: "But how his arms and legs are thin!")
Do I dare
Disturb the universe?
In a minute there is time
For decisions and revisions which a minute will reverse.

For I have known them all already, known them all;
Have known the evenings, mornings, afternoons,   50
I have measured out my life with coffee spoons;
I know the voices dying with a dying fall
Beneath the music from a farther room.
    So how should I presume?

And I have known the eyes already, known them all—
The eyes that fix you in a formulated phrase,
And when I am formulated, sprawling on a pin,
When I am pinned and wriggling on the wall,
Then how should I begin
To spit out all the butt-ends of my days and ways?   60
    And how should I presume?

And I have known the arms already, known them all—
Arms that are braceleted and white and bare
(But in the lamplight, downed with light brown hair!)
Is it perfume from a dress

That makes me so digress?
Arms that lie along a table, or wrap about a shawl.
   And should I then presume?
   And how should I begin?

     .   .   .   .   .

Shall I say, I have gone at dusk through narrow streets   70
And watched the smoke that rises from the pipes
Of lonely men in shirt-sleeves, leaning out of windows? . . .

I should have been a pair of ragged claws
Scuttling across the floors of silent seas.

     .   .   .   .   .

And the afternoon, the evening, sleeps so peacefully!
Smoothed by long fingers,
Asleep . . . tired . . . or it malingers,
Stretched on the floor, here beside you and me.
Should I, after tea and cakes and ices,
Have the strength to force the moment to its crisis?   80
But though I have wept and fasted, wept and prayed,
Though I have seen my head (grown slightly bald) brought in
    upon a platter,
I am no prophet—and here's no great matter;
I have seen the moment of my greatness flicker,
And I have seen the eternal Footman hold my coat, and snicker,
And in short, I was afraid.

And would it have been worth it, after all,
After the cups, the marmalade, the tea,
Among the porcelain, among some talk of you and me,
Would it have been worth while,   90
To have bitten off the matter with a smile,
To have squeezed the universe into a ball
To roll it toward some overwhelming question,
To say: "I am Lazarus, come from the dead,
Come back to tell you all, I shall tell you all"—
If one, settling a pillow by her head,
   Should say: "That is not what I meant at all;
   That is not it, at all."

And would it have been worth it, after all,
Would it have been worth while,   100
After the sunsets and the dooryards and the sprinkled streets,
After the novels, after the teacups, after the skirts that trail
    along the floor—
And this, and so much more?—
It is impossible to say just what I mean!
But as if a magic lantern threw the nerves in patterns on a screen:

Would it have been worth while
If one, settling a pillow or throwing off a shawl,
And turning toward the window, should say:
  "That is not it at all,
  That is not what I mean, at all."   110

     .   .   .   .   .

No! I am not Prince Hamlet, nor was meant to be;
Am an attendant lord, one that will do
To swell a progress, start a scene or two,
Advise the prince; no doubt, an easy tool,
Deferential, glad to be of use,
Politic, cautious, and meticulous;
Full of high sentence, but a bit obtuse;
At times, indeed, almost ridiculous—
Almost, at times, the Fool.

I grow old . . . I grow old . . .   120
I shall wear the bottoms of my trousers rolled.

Shall I part my hair behind? Do I dare to eat a peach?
I shall wear white flannel trousers, and walk upon the beach.
I have heard the mermaids singing, each to each.

I do not think that they will sing to me.

I have seen them riding seaward on the waves
Combing the white hair of the waves blown back
When the wind blows the water white and black.

We have lingered in the chambers of the sea
By sea-girls wreathed with seaweed red and brown   130
Till human voices wake us, and we drown.

                —T. S. Eliot (1888–   )

    This poem is a dramatic monologue. As in Tennyson's "Ulysses" (p. 780) or Amy Lowell's "Patterns" (p. 783), a person utters a speech that implies his story and reveals his character. The implication of the story is fairly clear in the poems by Tennyson and Amy Lowell and the revelation is fairly simple, but in both the reader must depend to some extent upon his imagination to fill in what is unsaid. In "The Love Song of J. Alfred Prufrock" the reader must assume even more responsibility for filling in the unsaid. For one thing, the events are not as fully indicated in Eliot's poem as in the others, but for another and more important thing, the continuity is not as clear. In neither "Ulysses" nor "Patterns" are the transitions always strictly logical. Sometimes the speaker moves from one aspect of the subject to another by a process of association. One thing suggests another in the flow of consciousness. But the transitions in Prufrock's utterance are more violent, at first glance more unjustifiable. But can we make sense of them? Is the poem a mere jumble?

It is obviously not a mere jumble, for upon early reading a general impression of Prufrock comes through. He is a middle-aged man, somewhat over-sensitive and timid, yearning and procrastinating, fearful that life has passed him by and yet somehow resigned to the fact, very much a creature of his world of drawing rooms and yet feeling a vague dissatisfaction with that world. But only a closer inspection will give us the full significance of many details in the poem and permit us to realize the implications of the whole poem. To make this inspection, let us take up points in their order.

Who is the "you" of the poem? It is the same "you" who appears in many other poems, the generalized reader. But in this poem, the "you" is a little more—the person to whom Prufrock wishes to make his revelation, to tell his secret. In the end we shall return to this question.

The time is evening, when the "you" is invited to make the visit, and this evening world becomes more and more important as the poem proceeds. It is a world of neither night nor day. Twilight is the atmosphere of the poem. It is an evening "Like a patient etherised upon a table," and with this image the twilight world becomes also the world of twilight in another way, the realm between life and death. Here, too, enters the notion of a sick world, the atmosphere of the operating room: and we can say that, in one sense, Prufrock is performing an operation, or at least making a clinical examination. (The patient, however, is himself as well as his world.) He is seeking the answer to a question—the "overwhelming question," which the "you" must not ask about but can understand only by making his visit, by seeing Prufrock's world.

To reach Prufrock's proper world, the "you" must pass through a slum section of sinister streets. This provides the setting for Prufrock's world, a contrast that becomes more important later in the poem, but which for the moment points up the triviality of the conversation of the women upon whom we suddenly come. This is not to say that the subject of their conversation is trivial. On the contrary, the subject, Michelangelo, is in contrast with the triviality of the women, for he, a man of violent personality and an artist of epic grandeur, and furthermore an almost typical figure of the great creative period of the Renaissance, would scarcely be at home with the women of Prufrock's world.

With lines 15 to 22 we find more of the twilight atmosphere of the poem. But there is some development here, for the settling down of the smoke and fog tends to emphasize the isolation of the drawing room from the outside world. In addition, the image of the housecat falling asleep involves the relaxed, aimless quality of Prufrock's world.

In the next section (lines 23–34) two new motifs enter the poem, the motif of time and that of appearance-and-reality. For the first, there will be time for some great, as yet unnamed, decision to settle the "overwhelming question"—for the "visions and revisions." The word *vision* here is important, for it implies the possibility of some fundamental insight, a flash of truth, a glimpse of beauty. Mystics, saint, seers, poets have "visions." But this word is played off against *revision,* with its implication of the second thought, the calculated change, etc. For the second motif of this section, we see that Prufrock prepares a mask for the world. He cannot face the world directly, there is a need for disguise.

What this need is, does not yet emerge, but in the next section (lines 37–48) we see that the disguise is prompted by fear of the mocking, inimical eyes of the world that will avidly note all defects and failings. And here, too, the time motif changes its emphasis. In the section before, there was enough time to allow for postponement of vital decision, but now mixed with that idea is the idea of the closing in of time, of age. With this sense of the closing in of time, and with the fear, does Prufrock dare disturb the universe with the significant question?

The next three sections (lines 49–69) further explain why Prufrock may not disturb the universe. First, he himself belongs to that world, and therefore it would be a presumption for him to criticize it. On what grounds could he, the perfect product of that world, enervated by its sense of fatuity, offer a judgment against it? Second, he fears the world, and again the inimical eyes appear. This fear would prevent him from changing his "days and ways."

The last of these three sections (lines 62–69) has the same outline, as it were, as the other two: I have known this world, etc., therefore, how should I presume? But the content is new, the arms and the perfume, and cannot be accounted for as merely details of the Prufrock world. After all, the poem is called a "love song," and there has been no love story thus far. Now, not a woman, but women enter significantly. Prufrock is attracted by the sight of the bare arms, by the whiff of perfume, but in the midst of the lines recording the romantic attraction, we find the more realistic observation put as a parenthesis:

But in the lamplight, downed with light brown hair!

Is this a mere observation, or does it indicate something about Prufrock? The fact that the observation of the "real" arms is put in contrast with the "romantic" arms, modifies the attraction: against the attraction there is a hint of revulsion, a hint of neurotic repudiation of the real, the physical. In the face of this situation, how should Prufrock "begin"?

The next five lines (70–74), which are a kind of interpolation, develops the "love" motif. Prufrock remembers having passed through the mean streets and slums, as in the opening of the poem, and having seen the lonely men there, the old derelicts and discards of society. Why is this recollection relevant here? Why does it come now into Prufrock's mind, and into the poem? Prufrock, too, is a lonely man, a derelict and a discard, and he suddenly feels an identification with those other lonely men. But at the same time his condition is in contrast to theirs. They are lonely because of poverty, bad luck, sickness, or age, while Prufrock is lonely because of some shrinking from, and repudiation of, life.

This reading is supported by the lines about the ragged claws. The claws come as a kind of embodiment of blind appetite, the opposite end of the scale from the over-refined and neurotic existence of Prufrock. But Prufrock, in his despair, would prefer that life of the claws, no matter how low and rudimentary, merely because it *is* life and is purposeful. Both the glimpse of the slum and of the primitive sea-floor are in contrast with the Prufrock world; and we may notice how, with line 70, a flat, prosaic rhythm appears, very different from the fluent, relaxed rhythm characteristic of the rest of the poem.

With line 75, we return to the drawing room and the etherized, peaceful twilight world in which Prufrock does not have the strength to force the "crisis," the overwhelming question. The motif that dominates the section is the time motif, the sense of physical decay and impending death, the sense of there being, not too much time, but not enough time. In this sense of time having run out Prufrock's agony now seems of no account; it has led to nothing. He admits that he is no prophet, no announcer of a new dispensation like John the Baptist. And in the reference to John the Baptist we catch also an allusion to the love story, for the prophet's death was demanded by

Salome because he had rejected her love: Prufrock too, has rejected love, but not because he is a prophet with a burning message and faith. He is merely a product of his world, where even Death is a kind of footman who holds the coat and snickers at the slightly ridiculous guest. Even Prufrock's death will lack dignity and meaning.

In the two sections from line 87 to line 110 Prufrock asks would it have been worth it, even if he had forced the crisis. But what would the crisis have been? It seems to involve the love story, it involves some understanding with a woman. We have an allusion to Marvell's love poem "To His Coy Mistress" (p. 721) in the line "To have squeezed the universe into a ball." Marvell's lovers would squeeze up their strength and sweetness into a supreme moment, but with Prufrock it is the universe which is to be rolled toward the "overwhelming question." In other words, with Prufrock it is not merely the personal relationship, but the meaning of the world, of life, that is involved. But the two are to be somehow related: the personal relationship cannot be significant if life is without significance.

Prufrock, if he had been able to force the crisis, would have seemed, he feels, like Lazarus come from the dead. Let us examine what is implied in the allusion. There are two characters by this name in the Bible. One is the beggar (*Luke,* 16) who lay at the rich man's gate, and the other is the brother of Mary and Martha who died and was raised by Jesus (*John,* 11). When the first Lazarus died he was carried by angels to Abraham's bosom, while the rich man was sent to hell. The rich man, seeing Lazarus happy, asked that Lazarus be sent to give him water. When Abraham replied that this was impossible, the rich man asked that at least Lazarus be sent to warn the rich man's five brothers that they might not come to hell for their lack of charity. Abraham replied that the brothers already had the prophets.

And he [the rich man] said, Nay, father Abraham: but if one went unto them from the dead, they will repent.

And he [Abraham] said unto him, If they hear not Moses and the prophets, neither will they be persuaded, though one rose from the dead.

So both references involve a return from the dead, and we may say that elements of both are suggested by the allusion. To return from the dead would be for Prufrock to awaken from his meaningless existence. To tell all, as related to the raising of Lazarus by Jesus, would be to tell what it is like to be dead, to report the horror. In relation to the other Lazarus story, to tell all would mean to utter the warning to repentance. The story of the beggar Lazarus seems to have a little more weight in the allusion than the story of the other Lazarus. The warning from Prufrock, like that given to the rich men by the beggar Lazarus, would not be heeded by the lady of the drawing room; she simply would not understand what Prufrock was talking about if he should raise the "overwhelming question." (Neither of the Biblical stories gives an exact parallel to Prufrock's situation, for in the one from the *Gospel of John* the importance of the risen Lazarus to the living is not stressed, and in the one from the *Gospel of Luke,* the dead man, unlike Prufrock, is called back from bliss to the world. But the general import of the allusion is clear, and that is what matters.)

With the realization that even if he had had the strength to raise the question the lady would not have understood him, Prufrock is struck by his own inadequacy. He is not Prince Hamlet (lines 111–120). Hamlet suffered doubt and despair. Hamlet brought an "overwhelming question" to Ophelia, who could not understand what he meant. Hamlet postponed decisive action. But there the parallel ends. Hamlet struggled grandly and passionately with his problem. He was not a victim of neurotic shrinking and timidity. The world he confronted was evil and violent, it was not twilit and relaxed. The play *Hamlet,* like the work of Michelangelo, belongs to a great creative period in history, and the mere reference evokes that world in contrast to Prufrock's world. Prufrock, with sad self-irony, sees all this, and knows that if he corresponds to any character in the play it is to the sententious, empty, old Polonius, the sycophantic Rosenkrantz, or the silly, foppish Osric. Perhaps—though there is no fool in *Hamlet*—to the fool, that stock character of many Elizabethan tragedies.

So with line 121 we see Prufrock resigned to his rôle, resigned to the fact that he will never raise the overwhelming question, resigned to the fact of age which has overtaken his postponements. With this reference to the motif of time, we see him as an aging man on the beach wistfully watching the girls, who have no attention to spare for him. Suddenly this scene is transformed into a vision of beauty and vitality, in contrast to the world Prufrock has inhabited. The girls become mermaids, as it were, riding triumphantly and effortlessly seaward into their natural creative element. (We may notice how this refers also to the sea of the ragged claws: the brute vitality and the vision of beauty are both aspects of the sea, the life-source.)

The concluding reference to the mermaids (lines 129–31) gives us a kind of odd reversion to Prufrock's original situation: he has "lingered," not in the drawing-room surrounded by the women talking of Michelangelo, but in the "chambers of the sea," surrounded by "sea-girls." But such an experience can occur only in dream: "human voices wake us. . . ." And to wake is to return to the human world—is to suffocate and die: ". . . and we drown."

The concluding image thus summarizes brilliantly Prufrock's character and his plight: he can immerse himself in the life-giving sea only in dream, and even in that dream, it is essentially his passive, negative self that is projected: *he* does not ride "seaward on the waves"; he lingers in the "chambers"—he is wreathed by the "sea-girls." Yet, though he cannot live in the sea, or in a romantic dream of the sea, his desiccated "human" world suffocates him. He is a fish out of water indeed.

AN INTERPRETATION OF E. E. CUMMINGS' "ANYONE LIVED IN A PRETTY HOW TOWN"

R. W. STALLMAN (1911–   )

ANYONE LIVED IN A PRETTY HOW TOWN

anyone lived in a pretty how town
(with up so floating many bells down)
spring summer autumn winter
he sang his didn't he danced his did.

Women and men (both little and small)
cared for anyone not at all
they sowed their isn't they reaped their
   same
sun moon stars rain

children guessed (but only a few
and down they forgot as up they grew
autumn winter spring summer)   11
that noone loved him more by more

when by now and tree by leaf
she laughed his joy she cried his grief
bird by snow and stir by still
anyone's any was all to her

someones married their everyones
laughed their cryings and did their dance
(sleep wake hope and then) they
said their nevers they slept their dream 20

stars rain sun moon
(and only the snow can begin to explain
how children are apt to forget to
    remember
with up so floating many bells down)

one day anyone died i guess
(and noone stooped to kiss his face)

busy folk buried them side by side
little by little and was by was

all by all and deep by deep
and more by more they dream their sleep
noone and anyone earth by april   31
wish by spirit and if by yes.

Women and men (both dong and ding)
summer autumn winter spring
reaped their sowing and went their came
sun moon stars rain
            —E. E. CUMMINGS (1894–1962)

This poem, apparently obscure nonsense, is rich in meanings; and though it may appear difficult at first glance, it is actually very simple to understand. Cummings uses language "reflexively," every word being counterpointed against another. At the literal level of the language there is a narrative plot, a miniature short story. What makes the poem seem so strange or seemingly incomprehensible is its uncommon arrangement of common words, its wrenched syntax, and its coining of new words from old ones by reconverting their dictionary meaning and usage.

Cummings's case study is a certain anonymous fellow, a citizen of How * Town. The town disowns him. Why? Well, for one thing their conventions are shocked by his unconventional way of life. He simply does not conform. Of course they don't care for Mr. Anyone because they "cared for anyone not at all" (line 6): they care only selfishly for themselves alone. These people "both little [*i.e.,* children] and small" (5) are small spiritually; which is why *"noone* loved him more by more" (12). And socially he didn't count because "anyone" married "noone." As for Miss "noone," she "loved him more by more." The non-lovers are the Someones who "married their everyones" (17). They play the social game, which is why they are Someones, but in conforming like "everyones" they have lost out in living, in loving life for its own sake. These Someones and Everyones do the conventional things in the conventional ways, and their life is a deadness and a monotony—"sleep wake hope and then"—because they live not at all spontaneously. And that is what sets them apart from Mr. Anyone. They *"did* their dance" (18), whereas he *"danced* his did" (4). They *"said* their nevers" (20), said their neverthelesses, talked about what they didn't do and made excuses; whereas he *"sang* his didn't" (4). In short, "anyone *lived."* For him How Town was "pretty how town," beautiful; beautiful "with up so floating many bells down"—life in both its up's and down's, it was all singsong to him. Anyone and Noone lived happily forever in the point-present now—not in How Town so much

* The dictionary lists eight variant meanings for the word *how,* and all eight reverberate throughout the poem. Cummings uses the word as a noun. In the noun-sense the word means manner or method. But the meanings of *how* as adverb equally apply:—1. In what manner or way; 2. to what number or degree; 3. in what state or condition; 4. for what reason; 5. with what meaning, to what effect; 6. at what price, how dear; and 7. *how* meaning "what," as how about it? How Town is the conventional town of conformity to convention, where what counts is social manner or method, social degree, state or condition. In How Town what counts is how you do it, and the price is dear. In the sense of *how* as "why," the question asked by the poem is what meaning has this way of life?

as in Now Town. She loved him "by now and tree by leaf" (13), all of him by every part of him: "anyone's any [thing] was all to her" (16). She "laughed his joy she cried his grief" (14); whereas the Someones married to their Everyones "laughed [at] their cryings" (18); their marriage is no marriage, merely an empty form. Even in death the lovers "dream their sleep" (30), belong to eternity and are reborn ("earth by april"); whereas the non-lovers even while living seem dead—"they slept their dream" (20). Caring "for anyone not at all/they sowed their isn't they reaped their same" (6–8). Their routine clocked existence repeats itself through the cycles of time—"autumn winter spring summer"—with one season the same as another and later generations repeating the same old stenciled way of life (stanza 9). Time passes, mechanical time clocked by "sun moon stars rain" (lines 8 and 36), with the variant— "stars rain sun moon" (21)—to indicate the passing of time. The life of Someones and Everyones is never punctuated by memorable moments. No comma halts these "busy folk." And their children repeat the same blurred, indiscriminate, humdrum existence; they too "went their came" (35), wasting their coming by their busy going. Thus the bells, symbolizing Time, sound to them only as "dong and ding" (33), which is as dead men hear it, hollow; whereas to Mr. Anyone the bells sang, and he danced his life in lilt with them. Himself childlike in spontaneity, "children guessed" *how to live,* by his example—"but only a few / and down they forgot as up they grew" (9–10). Living is by loving, and loving is by losing oneself in another:

> little by little and was by was
>
> all by all and deep by deep
> and more by more they dream their sleep
> noone and anyone

But like Someones and Everyones, children become time-busy and "forget to remember" how to live, how to love. And that is how it goes in How to Live Town. The day Anyone died (stanza 7) "noone stooped to kiss his face."

AN INTERPRETATION OF JOHN PEALE BISHOP'S "PERSPECTIVES ARE PRECIPICES"

R. W. STALLMAN (1911–   )

PERSPECTIVES ARE PRECIPICES

Sister Anne, Sister Anne,
Do you see anybody coming?

I see a distance of black yews
Long as the history of the Jews.

I see a road sunned with white sand,
Wide plains surrounding silence. And

Far-off, a broken colonnade
That overthrows the sun with shade.

Sister Anne, Sister Anne,
Do you see nobody coming?   10

A man

Upon that road a man who goes
Dragging a shadow by its toes.

Diminishing he goes, head bare
Of any covering even hair.

A pitcher depending from one hand
Goes mouth down. And dry is sand

Sister Anne, Sister Anne,
What do you see?

His dwindling stride. And he seems blind   20
Or worse to the prone man behind.

Sister Anne! Sister Anne!

I see a road. Beyond nowhere
Defined by cirrus and blue air.

I saw a man but he is gone
His shadow gone into the sun.
                    —John Peale Bishop (1892–1944)

Like Keats, Bishop is a painting poet. "Perspectives" is the perfect poem as paint-ing. In his essay on "Poetry and Painting" (*Sewanee Review:* Spring 1945) Bishop, replying to Tate's strictures on the poem as painting (in *Reactionary Essays*), seems to assent that "in some of my poems I lean very far toward the painters, finding in an art not theirs solutions which are possibly proper only to them"; but he points out that the mixture of the *genres* has always existed. In painting, which is the control of space, "the spatial imitation of a moment . . . is still an imagination of time"; and in poetry, which is the control of time, the temporal is frequently converted into terms of space. "Perspectives," like MacLeish's "You, Andrew Marvell," (see p. 682) embodies in space-images its theme of time. The example Bishop cites in his essay is that section of T. S. Eliot's *The Waste Land* beginning:

Here is no water but only rock
Rock and no water and the sandy road . . .

This he explicates: "the dry rocks and the sandy road winding toward the mountain where there is still no water are but symbols of a spiritual drought, due to the dis-appearance of faith in the truth of Christianity, which is itself a disaster of time." This explication, observe, is itself an explication of Bishop's own Dali painting. In

"Perspectives" the symbols of that spiritual drought are the *dry sand* and the *dry pitcher* (replacing the *rock* in Eliot's landscape). Sister Anne's perspective of history is a perspective of broken colonnades (cultures and beliefs destroyed by the anti-religious attitude) and of a road—once the road of religious faith, now the road of scientific reason—down which man and his civilization disappear. "Beyond nowhere" is Sister Anne's single image of hope and consolation. The road of scientific reason ends ultimately in realms of the supernatural. Yet her images define a vacuum: the world of faith is as empty as the world of reason is desolate. Hence Sister Anne's discourse echoes with doubt, with despair, and with fear the questioning voice of doubt (*"Do you see nobody coming?"*), of despair (*"What do you see?"*), and of fear (*"Sister Anne! Sister Anne!"*). Questioner and Answerer personify the theme of the poem, and its dialogue form is thus determined. Ironically, it is Science (or Reason) as Questioner; it is Religion (or Faith) as Answerer. Sister Anne and her brother represent that faith-beyond-reason and that reason which together form the dichotomy in man's present spiritual being. Reason, the Questioner, is as blind as the figure depicted in the landscape Sister Anne reports in her discourse. (It is an aesthetic discourse in terms of pictures, not a scientific discourse in terms of statements.) That prone man is our dead past whose monument of time casts a shadow of belief, but that shadow of belief is but a mockery of solace from the sun. Blinded by the sun of disbelief and by the sunned road of reason, man sees neither before him that shadow of belief nor behind him that shadow of time he drags by its toes. Down that road "Diminishing he goes"—mankind with "head bare," with no faith to protect him and ("His dwindling stride") with but a dwindling belief in himself. His road is broken by precipices and disappears "Beyond nowhere."

The consecutive images spacing "Perspectives," though they occur successively and not as they would in a Dali painting simultaneously, define simultaneously a present-past-future disaster of time. Man's present spiritual drought (the picture is its emblem) is the resultant disaster of his tragic past ("a distance of black yews") and images his future wasteland. Tate, in his brilliant commentary, observes that the plastic technique of this poem is violated by the Metaphysical Wit of "Long as the history of the Jews." But despite this minor blemish, "Perspectives" is a rich poem. The problem of the poet as painter is to achieve within the plastic objectivity of his poem a framework of idea or meaning. Bishop's poem is the solution of that problem.

THREE INTERPRETATIONS OF DYLAN THOMAS' "THE FORCE THAT THROUGH THE GREEN FUSE DRIVES"

THE FORCE THAT THROUGH THE GREEN FUSE DRIVES

The force that through the green fuse drives the flower
Drives my green age; that blasts the roots of trees
Is my destroyer.
And I am dumb to tell the crooked rose
My youth is bent by the same wintry fever.

The force that drives the water through the rocks
Drives my red blood; that dries the mouthing streams
Turns mine to wax.
And I am dumb to mouth unto my veins
How at the mountain spring the same mouth sucks.   10

The hand that whirls the water in the pool
Stirs the quicksand; that ropes the blowing wind
Hauls my shroud sail.
And I am dumb to tell the hanging man
How of my clay is made the hangman's lime.

The lips of time leech to the fountain head;
Love drips and gathers, but the fallen blood
Shall calm her sores.
And I am dumb to tell a weather's wind
How time has ticked a heaven round the stars.   20

And I am dumb to tell the lover's tomb
How at my sheet goes the same crooked worm.
                    —Dylan Thomas (1914–1953)

1. G. GIOVANNINI (1906–   )

Thomas' poem, of which an explication is asked (Exp., Nov., 1949, VIII, Q3), has a highly wrought and closely knit metaphorical surface carefully disguising meaning, and in such poetry what is extracted as basic meaning may be only another surface disguising a meaning felt rather than understood conceptually. The explication which follows attempts to uncover the meaning next to the metaphorical surface of Thomas' poem, and it leaves to one side the felt implications, largely Freudian, which commentators have found in his early verse.

The character speaking in the poem is a youth ("my green age") who discovers that life predicates death, and stands bewildered and inarticulate ("I am dumb") before man and nature informed by a paradoxical principle. The meaning is a variation on an old theme: life (and love) cankered by death (cf. Blake's "The Sick Rose"). The variation consists of the predication that life and death issue from the same cause— "The force" in the poem, a force in an obscure way associated with God; for in the first line of stanza 2 there is an oblique allusion to *Exodus* XVII, 6, where God draws water out of a rock, and in the first line of stanza 3 an allusion to *John* V, 4, where the angel of God stirs the water in the pool of Bethesda. The theme may be seen developed in the first three lines of each of the first three stanzas in a powerful manner by a statement immediately followed, after the semicolon, by a counterstatement. The life-giving force driving through the stem ("green fuse") of the flower and the youth's body also "blasts" the tree (the verb echoes "fuse" now understood in its literal sense) and kills the man. The syntactic pattern of the first three lines carries the paradoxical meaning; for the counterstatement (death) is grammatically a coordinate and integral part of the statement (life), a conjunction of a meaningful kind seen in small in the phrases (e.g., the oxymoron "wintry fever"). This same pattern and meaning are repeated exactly in the next two stanzas. The force driving the water, traditionally a symbol of life, and the blood also dries the streams at their source ("mouthing") and congeals in death the speaker's life-streams ("turns mine to wax"). In the third stanza the dynamism of force, now "The hand," is in terms of rapid movement (whirlpool), and of swift time; for "The hand that whirls" seems to suggest a clock, and "quicksand" the swift passage of time as in an hourglass. But the same force checks ("ropes") the movement of the wind and kills ("Hauls my shroud sail"). In the fourth stanza the syntactic pattern is varied a little, and so is the meaning, the paradox of life-death being here translated as love-death. The theme is developed in its cosmic aspects: creation ("The lips of time") passionately suck ("leech") its being from a source, and love "gathers," possibly in the sense in which Hopkins uses the verb in "God's Grandeur": "The world is charged with the grandeur of God . . . It gathers to a greatness." But with reference to the counterstatement, where death ("fallen blood") again appears, "gathers" has an appropriate medical sense: love is imaged as a swollen suppurating wound, from which the issue of blood signifies the stillness of death ("Shall calm her sores").

The refrain, "And I am dumb," functions as illustration everywhere except in the fourth stanza: the speaker carries death within him; for though he is young and avidly experiences life ("at the mountain spring the same mouth sucks"), his body bends toward death, it is attacked by the "crooked worm" and is the making of the quicklime of the grave ("hangman's lime"). The refrain in the fourth stanza refers not to death, but to the ecstasy of love ticking "a heaven round the stars"; but the meaning here is countered by death in the final refrain which immediately follows, and the poem ends effectively with the two sides of the thematic paradox formally and precisely juxtaposed. All the refrains have in common the sense of the speaker's isolation, of his inability to communicate and establish a sympathetic contact with an inexplicable universe. The isolation is intense; for in the second refrain the young man is unable to communicate even with himself ("dumb to mouth unto my veins"). The theme of this poem is more succinctly and abstractly stated in a passage from Thomas' "A Process in the Weather": "the womb Drives in a death as life leaks out" —a theme which can be glossed by Donne's sermon *Death's Duell* (cf. J. L. Sweeney, Intro., Thomas' *Selected Writings*): "wee celebrate our own funeralls with cries, even at our birth."

2. S. F. JOHNSON (1918–   )

Thomas' "force" is a generalized *élan vital*, the natural vitality that both creates and destroys us. Human change is but a small part of the great cycle of natural change and is effected by the same simple cause. The opening lines of each stanza present four variations on this implied theme; the two-line refrains stress the limits of human communication by detailing the senses in which even a poet is "dumb."

I. The force is an explosive. Stalks of plants are fuses through which the explosive power is driven; flowers and foliage are products of an explosion which creates one condition of mortality. The poet is "green" (young) and, unlike non-human organisms, is aware that birth is the beginning of death. The refrain emphasizes his humanity, his ability to communicate complex meanings only to other humans. Here the explosive image is translated into human terms (fever). Fever is wintry since it hastens human age and death just as the first frost hastens vegetative age and death.

II. The vitality of growing things is extended to inanimate nature, where again the same force drives and dries (the omission of a phoneme is the difference between life and death). The poet's streams are bloodstreams; the pliability and stickiness of wax applies equally to the coagulation of the blood at death and to the drying-up of mud in a streambed. Refrain: the force is personified as a mouth (connecting with "leech" in stanza 4). "Mouth" is used in three ways here ("tell" is altered in this refrain alone in order to give scope to the play on words): streams "mouth" into larger streams, into the sea; the poet "mouths" (declaims) to those who can (will) hear him; the "mouth," adapted to giving out and taking in, symbolizes the elemental force that creates and destroys.

III. The force, here as the hand of God, keeps the elements in motion: water, earth, and air, connecting with fire in stanza 1. Of course it controls the poet, now a ship, consistent with the sea imagery of the stanza; the sail, the activated part, is the libido. Refrain: the poem can communicate only with the living, part of whose clay, in various excremental forms, has long since re-entered the natural cycle and helped compose its products.

IV. The force is time itself. The mouth symbol is developed in the verb "leech." The reduction of the life-force from anthropomorphic God to a voracious, blind mouth emphasizes the naturalistic attitude in the poem. Time's leeching lips are juxtaposed with love, the only emotion named in the poem. Love acts in such a way as to place it, with the life-force, at the very pulse of life; it drips and gathers, like blood at a leech wound, subject to involuntary pulsation of all nature. The sup-posedly beneficial effects of blood-letting are paralleled with the calming effect of the sexual manifestation of love. The refrain contrasts chillingly with the warmth of love and emphasizes man's small place in the well-integrated, clockwork universe.

Refrain: The facts of death support the poet's consistent view of man's place in nature. The refrain tightens the poem by drawing on the power of earlier elements (lover's tomb and hanging man, crooked worm and crooked rose, worm and leech, sheet and shroud sail) and by reiterating the central notion that everything is subject to decay.

The poem is saved from sentimentality, a risk it runs, by its tightly consistent atti-tude, which unifies images drawn from widely disparate spheres. The vocabulary, as in most of Thomas' poems, is largely restricted to common Anglo-Saxon words, pre-dominantly monosyllabic, arranged in a pattern so slowly paced that the reader is forced to explore the range of meanings of these words, revitalized by their unusual contexts. The poet is not dumb to tell his readers what he is about: "from the first declension of the flesh I learnt man's tongue . . . To shade and knit anew the patch of words Left by the dead who . . . Need no word's warmth" (from "Love's First Fever"); "I write . . . Not for the towering dead . . . But for the lovers . . . Who pay no praise or wages Nor heed my craft or art" ("In my Craft").

3. S. F. JOHNSON (1918–   )

Professor Giovannini, in his explication of this poem (*Exp.*, June, 1950, VIII, 59), sees allusions "in the first line of stanza 2 . . . to *Exodus*, XVII, 6, where God draws water out of a rock, and in the first line of stanza 3 . . . to *John,* V, 4, where the angel of God stirs the water in the pool of Bethesda." Thomas' poetry is indeed packed with Biblical allusions, but his style, which more frequently echoes the Hebraic lyrical mode than the diverse narrative modes of the Pentateuch and the Gospels, suggests that these allusions be looked for in the lyrical parts of the Old Testament. The force that "drives the water through the rocks," "dries the mouthing streams," "whirls the water in the pool," and "ropes the blowing wind" is paralleled in all these manifestations in the evidences of God's power cited by Job in his replies to the third cycle of speeches of his friends (*Job,* XXII–XXVII) and in the ancient poem of divine wisdom (*Job,* XXVII). In the order in which these echoes occur in Thomas' poem, compare:

"He cutteth out channels among the rocks" (XXVIII, 10) (stanza 2, line 1), "He bindeth the streams that they trickle not" (XXVIII, 11) (stanza 2, line 2), "Drought and heat consume the snow waters: So doth Sheol those that have sinned" (XXIV, 19) (stanza 2, lines 2–3), "He stirreth up the sea with his power" (XXVI, 12) (stanza 3, line 1), "To make a weight for the wind: Yea, he meteth out the waters by measure" (XXVIII, 25) (stanza 3, line 2).

Perhaps the "sores" (stanza 4, line 3) were suggested by those of Job. Even the conventional worm in the last line appears in Job's speeches, once in direct association with the third quotation above: "The worm shall feed sweetly on him" (XXIV, 20), "They lie down alike in the dust, And the worm covereth them" (XXI, 26). Thomas' force, like Job's God, is an inscrutable creator-destroyer. The lesson of Job, that the human mind is too limited to apprehend God, parallels Thomas' emphasis on the limits of human communication. . . .

NOTES AND QUESTIONS

I: The Poem

i. The Poem as Picture

675. "I HEAR AN ARMY CHARGING . . ."

JAMES JOYCE

What justifies the nightmare atmosphere of this poem? Could the final two lines just as well open the poem as close it? Do they explain the dream? What answer is there to the rhetorical question: "My heart, have you no wisdom to despair?" This poem, consciously or unconsciously, echoes Freudian symbolism. Examples? What is the motivating situation? Is the emotion expressed here excessive? Contrast the mood of Joyce's poem with that of Rossetti's "The Woodspurge" (p. 678).

675. THE TIDE RISES, THE TIDE FALLS

HENRY WADSWORTH LONGFELLOW

Of the 15 lines in this poem, nine of them end with the same rhyme. What effect is achieved by this? What is achieved by the repetition of the title as the last line in each of the three stanzas? What is the tone of the poem?

676. "LOVELIEST OF TREES . . ."

A. E. HOUSMAN

Does the second stanza provide contrast? How is the final stanza prepared for by the mathematics of lines 5-8? Is the cherry actually "hung with snow"? Or is it that the cherry wears white petals that appear as a mass of snow? Is the season winter or spring? Is there any allegorical intention in the final phrase: "hung with snow" (line 12)? Or in "Eastertide" (line 4)?

676. COME IN

ROBERT FROST

In the dark woods there is thrush music "like a call to come in/To the dark and

lament." It's the end of the day; it's the end of something evoking a lament. Even so, this bird "still could sing" (line 8). The speaker rejects the dark woods—"I was out for stars:/I would not come in." What is meant? Why can't the bird "better its perch for the night" (line 7)? Allegorically, what's the situation? Like all Frost poems, "Come In" is built upon a contrast; explain.

676. THE DARKLING THRUSH

THOMAS HARDY

1, coppice: small woods. 5, bine-stems: hop-stems. 10, Century's corpse: the poem is dated on the last day of the 19th century.

How does the diction in the first stanza prepare for the metaphor in lines 9-12? How do the figures of speech in lines 5-6 serve both as contrast and preparation for the third stanza? Comment on the appropriateness of *fervorless* (16) and *terrestrial* (27).

677. NEUTRAL TONES

THOMAS HARDY

Does the title describe the landscape, the mood of the speaker, or both? Does the speaker have a listener? Is the last stanza an effective conclusion? Why? What does the mental picture of that wintry scene come to symbolize? How do the specific details of that scene—gray leaves, white sun, dead smile, etc.—contribute to the symbolic meaning?

677. HEAT

ARCHIBALD LAMPMAN

A hot day usually produces lethargy of body and mind, yet the poet asserts that "In the full furnace of this hour/My thoughts grow keen and clear." What characteristics of the description seem designed to support this claim? Note the implied contrasts throughout the poem of such opposites as dry and wet, hot and cool, light and shade. What other contrasts can be found? Is the theme of contrast made too explicit in the first two lines of the last stanza? Explain.

678. THE WOODSPURGE
DANTE GABRIEL ROSSETTI

How does this poem use imagery to evoke a psychological state of mind? The time of the poem is the moment just after the movement of the wind has stopped. What has stopped is time. Time has stopped because the lover has lost his beloved. The poet creates this idea by symbol: "The wind flapped loose." Rossetti's image converts invisible wind into something visible, tangible, plastic. Like the wind, the beloved lies still, torn loose from him who had "walked on at the wind's will"; like the wind, she has been "Shaken out dead from tree and hill" (line 2). It is as though her death has paralyzed Nature.

The first stanza presents the scene as a painter would paint it. (Rossetti was himself a painter, and the founder of the Pre-Raphaelite Brotherhood of painters. Some of his paintings are analogies of his poems.) The influence of sculpture on Rossetti is evidenced in the second stanza of "The Woodspurge." The sculptured posture of the lover signifies his grief. The range of his view is restricted to a small space, and the time is restricted to a single moment. It is a moment of his perception of the woodspurge flowering "three cups in one." It is a moment of grief, and, at the same time, it is a moment of insight, if not wisdom, sprung from his grief, flowering like the woodspurge from the weeds. It is the moment of "perfect grief" because of this flowering, this insight which is his consolation for the lost beloved: "The woodspurge has a cup of three." This symbol resists paraphrase, but, according to one interpretation, a trinity of relationship is suggested —a mystic identity between Nature, the lost beloved, and the grief-stricken lover seems symbolized by the three-cupped woodspurge. Has the woodspurge flowered before his eyes, or is it that it was always there but had not been noticed until now? The ambiguity of lines 11-12 is purposeful: "The woodspurge *flowered*." One wonders

why "ten weeds"? Can you explain the meaning of: "My naked ears heard the day pass"?

Contrast the mood in this poem with those in the poems on daffodils by Herrick and Wordsworth (pp. 729, 820).

678. THIS AMBER SUNSTREAM
MARK VAN DOREN

It is twilight, which (to give the dictionary definition) is a faint light through which anything is viewed. And throughout the poem reality is viewed from the point of view of "This amber sunstream." The substance of things is created by light. Not till the light thickens from clear sunlight to amber does man comprehend its value: "No living man may know it till this hour" (line 7). Thus light is equated with time, the point-present now ("with an hour to live"), which expends itself freely: "Flows carelessly, and does not save itself" (line 2). What is thereby implied about life is How to Live It. *Versus* clock-time—"the clock upon a shelf,/Declaring the lone hour"—Time itself, which flows unclocked, is silent: "for where *it* goes/All space in a great silence ever flows" (lines 5-6). *It* is the sunstream of the Moment Now.

Continue the explication.

679. COMPOSED UPON WESTMINSTER BRIDGE
WILLIAM WORDSWORTH

Is this a generalized or particularized picture of a city? Explain. What is the poet's attitude towards his subject? How does the poet use both contrast and comparison? What is the effect of line 12, which mentions the only thing in the picture that moves? Why would this line be less effective if it occurred in the first eight lines rather than in the last six?

Show how the sonnet by Wordsworth resembles yet differs from the following extract from the *Journal* of his sister Dorothy, describing the same occasion: "We left London on Saturday morning at half past five or six. . . . We mounted the Dover Coach at Charing Cross. It was a beautiful morning. The city, St. Paul's, with the river, and a multitude of little boats, made a most beautiful sight as we crossed Westminster Bridge. The houses were not overhung by their cloud of smoke, and they were spread out endlessly, yet the sun shone so brightly, with such a fierce light, that there was something like the purity of one of nature's own grand spectacles."

679. THE CITY IN THE SEA
EDGAR ALLAN POE

The original title of this poem was "The Doomed City," changed to "The City of Sin," and finally to its present title. The vast lore of sunken cities—*e.g.,* Atlantis—undoubtedly contributed to the creation of Poe's phantom city in its stagnant sea, together with Scriptural allusions to Babylon, Gomorrah, and Tyre. The doom pronounced against Tyre, in chapters 26-28 of *Ezekiel,* presents some especially striking parallels.

680. ODE TO THE WEST WIND
PERCY BYSSHE SHELLEY

21, Maenad: female worshiper of Bacchus. **32, Baiae's bay:** in Campania, Italy.

In the first three sections of the ode Shelley pictures the West Wind in its effect upon leaves, clouds, and waves. Are the details in each section coherently related? Does Shelley interrelate the leaves, clouds, and waves? What function is performed by Section IV? In line 53 Shelley petitions the Wind to lift him "as a wave, a leaf, a cloud," but in Section V the imagery seems related to only one of these three. Is Shelley guilty of bad workmanship? Why, or why not? Is the West Wind employed as a symbol? Of what?

682. YOU, ANDREW MARVELL
ARCHIBALD MacLEISH

Is the picture created in this poem of the coming on of night as the earth turns from west to east as vivid and meaningful as the somewhat similar picture in Meredith's sonnet, "Lucifer in Starlight," on p. 683? Justify your answer. How consistently does MacLeish liken the oncoming of night to a rising of flood waters? Why does the poet change the rhythm in the last stanza? What is the theme of the poem? Is "the shadow of the night" used symbolically? (See the poem by Marvell on p. 778.)

683. THE EAGLE
ALFRED, LORD TENNYSON

In the first stanza, is the observer above, below, or beside the eagle? Where is he in the second stanza? Would the poem be as successful if three 2-line stanzas were used? Does the metre of line 6 suit the sense of the line? Explain why the phrases "he stands" and "he falls" are effectively placed. Is there a "theme" in this poem?

683. GOD'S GRANDEUR
GERARD MANLEY HOPKINS

Is this simply a poem of exalted wonder, or are other moods present also? What manifestations of the "grandeur" are suggested by line 2? By line 3? What reason does Hopkins suggest that may account for modern disregard of the deity (line 4)? What has happened to the world? To man? How does Hopkins use the night-morning image to suggest that man's abuse of the soil will not last? Is the word *foil* (line 2) borrowed from metalworking or from fencing, or both? Is it related to *rod* in line 4? What is the meaning of *spent* (line 9)? Why is the world described as *bent* (line 13)? What effect is obtained by repetition of words and sounds in lines 5, 6, and 7? By the interjection *ah!* in the last line of the poem?

683. LUCIFER IN STARLIGHT
GEORGE MEREDITH

1, Lucifer: The name given to the "morning star" and sometimes also to the "evening star"—both designations for the planet Venus. From the Biblical passage—"How art thou fallen from heaven, O Lucifer, son of the morning," (*Isaiah* 14:12)—the name Lucifer came to be interpreted as that of Satan before his fall. Milton's *Paradise Lost* contains an account of the battle between the heavenly hosts and the rebelling angels, led by the archangel Lucifer, and the subsequent expulsion from heaven and incarceration in hell. **8, planet:** the literal meaning of the word *planet* is "wandering," as contrasted with the "fixed" stars. Meredith's use of "Lucifer" as both the name of the planet and of the rebel archangel is obviously more appropriate than if he had used "Satan" or any other of his many names. **10, Awe,** *i.e.,* God. But the word *God* connotes "goodness," whereas Lucifer recognizes only Power.

How successfully does Meredith create his global picture? Are such details as those in lines 4 and 5 necessary? Why? What new aspect of the Deity does Satan discover? Is Meredith merely refurbishing an old religious myth, or is he making a comment on the nature of the universe? What dramatic quality appears in the poem? The word *unalterable* is often considered the keyword of the poem. Note that it is also the longest word in the poem. How are its vowel and consonant sounds related to those of the other words in the same line?

684. THE BLESSED DAMOZEL
DANTE GABRIEL ROSSETTI

1, damozel: Rossetti uses a variant of the Old French word from which *damsel* also comes. **9, Mary's:** The Virgin Mary's. **10, meetly:** fittingly, suitably. **13, Herseemed:** It seemed to her. **19, (To one . . . :** Parentheses are used to indicate a shift to the viewpoint of the lover on earth. **54, The stars sang:** The Ptolemaic astronomy taught that the stars and planets make music as they move about the earth in their concentric spheres. Cf. *Job* 38:7—"When the morning stars sang together. . . ." **86, That living mystic tree:** "the tree of life which bare twelve manner of fruits, and yieldeth her fruit every month" (*Revelation* 22:2). **87, Dove:** the Holy Spirit. **107-8, Cecily . . . Rosalys:** five saints. **126, citherns and citoles:** medieval stringed instruments.

Rossetti also painted a picture bearing the same title as this poem and on the same subject. Sir Hall Caine reported that Rossetti's poem was motivated by Poe's "The Raven" (p. 853) and quoted Rossetti as saying: "I saw that Poe had done the utmost possible to do with the grief of the lover on earth, and so I determined to reverse the conditions, and give utterance to the yearning of the loved one in heaven." Is the tone of the poem spiritual or sensuous? Explain. Who is describing the damozel and the setting? Why does the medievalism suggested in language and setting seem appropriate? Would this poem be as effective if the earthly lover did not appear in it? Compare this poem pictorially with the poems by Holmes (p. 687), Robinson (p. 689), and Ransom (p. 688) and with Poe's "The Raven" (p. 853).

685. ULALUME
EDGAR ALLAN POE

6, Auber: This, and the later "Weir" and "Mount Yaanek," are fictitious place-names created by Poe for their romantic overtones. **11, cypress:** A kind of tree often planted about tombs. An "alley" of cypresses would suggest what the narrator will find at the end. **19, Boreal:** northern—also suggests the eerie brightness of the aurora borealis. **37, Astarte:** Phoenician goddess of fertility and reproduction, of earthly love as distinct from heavenly love. **39, Dian:** Diana was the Roman goddess of pure or chaste love. **43, where the worm never dies:** See *Isaiah* 66:24. **44, stars of the Lion:** The constellation Leo, here implying danger. **46, Lethean:** The Lethe is the "river of forgetfulness" in hell. Dante makes it the boundary between purgatory and paradise.

For a while after "Ulalume" was first published (1847), Poe sometimes preferred the poem without its last (tenth) stanza. Though he included this stanza in the final published version, some readers contend that it is close to being ridiculous, and that it spoils the description in the preceding nine stanzas of gradually rising uneasiness culminating in the recognition of the cause of the uneasiness. Do you agree? Structurally the poem represents a "debate" between self and other-self, between the sensuous outer self and the deeper inner self—between flesh and spirit, in short. Note the similar contrast between Astarte and Diana. In the criticized tenth stanza, the "I" and "Psyche" are no longer opposed, but unite in a common utterance. Discuss the effect of the repetition of consonant sounds, especially the grouping of *l*-sounds, and the effect of the many polysyllabic adjectives from Latin roots (e.g., immemorial, senescent, nebulous, etc.).

687. MY AUNT
OLIVER WENDELL HOLMES

What creates the light tone of this poem? Would the lightness be possible if the poem were written from the point of view of the aunt? To what extent is this poem a satire of the aunt? Of her father? Compare the portrait of the aunt in this poem with that in "Aunt Helen" by T. S. Eliot.

688. AUNT HELEN
T. S. ELIOT

Now that Aunt Helen—protectress of the moral core—is dead, the second housemaid flirts with the footman. It's as though her death has brought about a loosening of the moral fibre of her civilization. What supports this reading? What do you make of the statement: "He was aware that this sort of thing had occurred before"? Can you establish any connection thematically between Eliot's poem and Holmes's "My Aunt"?

688. AN EPITAPH
WALTER DE LA MARE

That she was "the most beautiful lady" is stated, not created. In "Here Lies a Lady" Ransom's opening line almost paraphrases de la Mare's opening line. In what sense is Ransom's poem a kind of critique of de la Mare's "Epitaph"? Is "Epitaph" purely personal?

In contrast to "An Epitaph," Ransom's "Here Lies a Lady" and Robinson's "For a Dead Lady" bear points of kinship. What are they?

688. HERE LIES A LADY
JOHN CROWE RANSOM

Is this poem in its treatment of subject "romantic," sentimental, or ironical? Define the poet's treatment of subject, style or tone, and theme. Here the dead lady remains, we may suppose, in her coffin just before burial, or perhaps just after the funeral, but in either event she remains very much alive. What do we learn about her way of life from her way of death? What is revealed by the singsong style of line 2? Why was the lady "lucky" in her dying (line 14)?

How many voices or styles has the speaker of Ransom's poem? For instance, the matter-of-factness in the final line of the final stanza; or the final line in stanza 3. Is the speaker's voice here the voice of a friend, a doctor, or a poet? What pose does he take in the opening line of stanza 4? Trace the shifts in tone. Look in your dictionary for the definition of *bathos* and illustrate by examples in this poem. How does Ransom's style itself evoke a meaning?

What does the inquiry about the lady's fevered activity symbolize: "What was she making?" (line 7) or the answer: "Why, nothing"? What is the symbolic intention of "old scraps of laces, snipped into curious shreds"?

689. FOR A DEAD LADY
EDWIN ARLINGTON ROBINSON

How does Robinson use contrast to suggest the "shifting and many-shaded" qualities of the lady's character? Is her character wholly admirable? Does the poem raise any of the larger issues of life and death in general?

689. FROM THE HAZEL BOUGH
EARLE BIRNEY

Whose eyes are they—"eyes were trees / where boys leant out"—the lady's, or onlookers'? After the lady has been possessed, no man sees / "what leans out / from the hazel bough." What tells us that she has been possessed? What's her plight now? Is the poem an elegy? Is any criticism of the lady (or her morals) implied? The words *lazy* (line 2) in a transferred epithet. What are its implications?

690. MUSÉE DES BEAUX ARTS
W. H. AUDEN

A painting presents simultaneously details that in a poem can be presented only consecutively. Auden's poem *as* painting is not the same, of course, as an actual painting; the poem communicates or expresses a meaning in a way peculiar to the literary arts. What the painter means by his painting he must express by painting it; what the poet means by his poem is expressed by concrete images but frequently also by direct communication or statement. What is there in Auden's poem that could not appear in an actual painting? Single out these aspects. Is it necessary to acquaint oneself first of all with Brueghel's "Landscape With the Fall of Icarus" before comprehending Auden's poem? Does the poem exist in its own right as poem apart from its inspirational source? Brueghel's "Icarus" is at the Brussels Museum of the Fine Arts; hence the title "Musée des Beaux Arts" (Museum of the Fine Arts).

What does "the miraculous birth" refer to? And "the dreadful martyrdom [that] must run its course"? The fall of Icarus is epitomized by Auden's phrase as "the forsaken cry." What other event does "the forsaken cry" bring to mind? Both Greek and Christian allusions appear in the poem.

690. HUNTERS IN THE SNOW: BRUEGHEL

JOSEPH LANGLAND

Both this poem and the one that follows concern the same painting—a different one from the painting by Brueghel referred to in the preceding poem by Auden. How do the three poems differ in form, tone, theme, and treatment of the subject?

691. WINTER LANDSCAPE

JOHN BERRYMAN

This poem is based on the painting "The Hunters in the Snow" by Pieter Brueghel, the 16th century Flemish painter. In what way is the theme of the poem comparable to that of Keats' "Ode on a Grecian Urn" (p. 694)? Is it significant that the entire poem is composed of a single sentence? What use is made of repetition in the poem? Compare this poem with the two preceding poems, also based on paintings by Brueghel.

692. LEDA AND THE SWAN

W. B. YEATS

Zeus, in the form of a swan, ravished Leda, who eventually brought forth two eggs, from one of which came Castor and Clytemnestra, from the other Pollux and Helen. Helen became responsible for the destruction of Troy by fire (see line 10); Clytemnestra murdered her husband Agamemnon (line 11) upon his return from the Trojan War. In Yeats's cyclical theory of history, the visitation of Leda by Zeus symbolized the beginnings of classical civilization, paralleling the Virgin Mary and her dove—the Annunciation that ushered in the Christian cycle. Yeats once admitted that he had begun the poem with this symbolic conception in mind, "but as I wrote, bird and lady took such possession of the scene that all politics went out of it." (See Michelangelo's painting of Leda, a colored reproduction of which Yeats possessed.)

Is Yeats's "Leda and the Swan" more than a vivid description of a mythical event? What knowledge was engendered "in the loins" "Before the indifferent beak could let her drop"? What theme does this translate into? Does any of the author's own original conception remain? Any of his original symbolism? What accounts for changes in original intention or conception, whereby the finished work differs considerably from the projected groundplan? Rhyme, for instance? Yeats, incidentally, is a master in the functional use of "eye-rhyme," "ghost-rhyme," or half-rhymes, such as here in *up* and *drop*. What purpose does this half-rhyme serve in the context of that final stanza?

Notice that the poem is a sonnet with the conventional two-part division, octave and sestet, with the sestet rhyming *e, f, g, e, f, g.* Yet it also breaks away from the conventional form. Compare with the structure of sonnets by Shakespeare (pp. 705, 724–725); by Wordsworth (pp. 679, 717); by Meredith (pp. 683, 728).

693. SOLDIERS BATHING

F. T. PRINCE

24, Michelangelo's cartoon: The reference is to the "Bathing Soldiers" scene from the "Battle of Cascina." **33, Ucello or Pollaiuolo:** Paolo Ucello (1397–1475) and Antonio Pollaiuolo (1429–1498) are Italian painters. Pollaiuolo, who was also a sculptor and engraver, has left not only an engraving entitled "The Battle of the Nudes" but also a bas-relief on the same subject. **45, Lachrimae Christi:** Christ's tears.

Why is the contrast between the nakedness of the bathing soldiers and the machinery of war an effective one? Does the speaker refer to the painters to remind himself that men fought when the "machinery" was at a minimum, or for some other reason? What attitude towards their subject was held by the painters, according to the speaker? What, according to him, has caused our modern attitude to be different? Is love a "terror" to us because it involves responsibilities, a willingness to sacrifice ourselves, etc., which we refuse to assume? What is the "freedom" accompanying crimes and sin that does not accompany virtue and love? How many times is the word "freedom" used in the poem? What is meant by "the fright and shame of nakedness"? Does the speaker seem to find a symbolic meaning in the "streak of red" in line 66?

694. ODE ON A GRECIAN URN
JOHN KEATS

41, brede: embroidery, frieze.

The actual urn inspiring Keats has been identified as the Towneley vase, but in any case his imagination, contemplating the urn, attains for a moment a vision of truth and reality. What are the several group pictures on the urn? In what sense can the urn express "a flowery tale more sweetly than our rhyme"? What is suggested by the term "Cold Pastoral"? What does Keats seem to believe about the relation between art and life?

What is meant by the enigmatic proposi-

tion "Beauty is Truth, Truth Beauty"? Is it addressed to the reader of the poem or to the figures on the urn? Justify your answer. What is suggested by the poet's awareness of the desolate town, "emptied of this folk"?

The statuary forms on the urn are forever fixed in timeless immobility. Their ecstasy is arrested in pure present immediacy, motionless in a frozen moment. The imagined action immobilized on the urn is the moment just before fulfilment (line 15ff.). Contrast this poem with the following poems which also depict an arrested action or an action felt with similar pure present immediacy: Yeats's "Leda and the Swan" (p. 692), and MacLeish's "You, Andrew Marvell" (p. 682).

William Faulkner uses this poem as a key element in his story "The Bear" (see pp. 128–129).

ii. The Poem as Subject and Theme

---

696. ARS POETICA
ARCHIBALD MACLEISH

Divide the poem into its three parts. In part one the first couplet contains an abstract statement in the first line followed by a concrete image as illustration: "a globed fruit." What other couplets in the poem use this same pattern?

How many of the images are circular objects, or objects suggesting a curve? Lines 9 and 10 are repeated in lines 15 and 16. Can you justify the repetition of this couplet? Has the statement contained in the couplet anything to do with the reason for repeating this burden as refrain?

The title means, of course, *the art of poetry.* What are the three qualities a poem should possess, according to MacLeish? Does his *own* poem contain all three?

697. TO HOLD IN A POEM
A. J. M. SMITH

8, Laurentia: the Laurentian mountain region in northern Ontario and Quebec.

Much glaciated, the bare rock shows in long undulant lines.

Here is an *ars poetica,* a canon for poetry: let the poet use only those words which are "Sweet-smelling and bright / As new rain; as hard / And as smooth and as white / As a brook pebble cold and unmarred" (lines 9–12). What is implied in his preference for cold words and crisp and clear? For words having "The spirit of mountains" and "Of forests as pointed as grass"? In what sense are words *unbuyable* and *dear?* Or deeded *forever* (lines 19, 20)? For him the language of poetry is *austere* (line 17); why this preference for austerity of language? Does the language of the poem itself conform to the poet's stated canon for poetry? His bias is for "The North" (line 20), and since Smith is a Canadian poet the term could be read as indicating Canada. However, it can also be read as a preference for northern as opposed to southern cultures, for the language of northern peoples rather than southern. The vocabulary of the poem includes words derived from Latin as well as Anglo-Saxon roots. Does this fact contradict the poet's own canon?

Compare what MacLeish is saying in "Ars Poetica (p. 696) and *how* he says it. Which poem is more successful? Does not MacLeish's "Ars Poetica" contradict its own poetic canon? Notice that both MacLeish and Smith employ similes, whereas Glenway Wescott in "The Poet at Night-Fall" employs symbols.

697. THE POET AT NIGHT-FALL
GLENWAY WESCOTT

"Ah me, beauty does not enclose life, / But blows through it— / Like that idea, the wind" (lines 7–9). Beautiful is the wind—that "vocal wind" of our words, which alters every aspect of reality: "The scarred sea" (line 12), "The poplar, the splashing crest" (line 15), etc. That vocal wind, "Which goes and comes / Altering every aspect" (lines 13–14), is "unseen and useless, / Even superseded upon / The scarred sea" (lines 10–12). Why is it *useless?* It is useless because words have no equivalents in the realities of things: "I see no equivalents / For that which I see, / Among words."

Explicate now the final stanza.

697. "POET"
WILLIAM JAY SMITH

The Poet is José Garcia Villa, whose verse has appeared in many "little magazines" in the United States and is punctuated precisely as given in this parody.

698. POETRY
MARIANNE MOORE

Like MacLeish in "Ars Poetica" (p. 696), Miss Moore in "Poetry" provides a canon of poetic art. She defines art as "imaginary gardens with real toads in them," poetry being composed by "literalists of the imagination" (lines 22, 19–20). Yeats said of Blake: "he was a too literal realist of imagination, as others are of nature; and because he believed that the figures seen by the mind's eye, when exalted by inspiration, were 'eternal existences,' symbols or divine essences, he hated every grace of style that might obscure their lineaments." (*Essays*, 1924, p. 147.)

The real toads in the poem as imaginary garden are comprised of anything in the life we experience—anything is fit subject for poetry. For example: a "bat / holding on upside down or in quest of something to / eat, elephants pushing, a wild horse taking a roll, a tireless wolf under / a tree," etc. Other conceivable subjects for poetry include "the immovable critic twitching his skin like a horse that feels a flea, the base- / ball fan, the statistician." Miss Moore's aesthetic theory widens the boundaries of poetry to include what formerly was regarded as fit subject-matter only for prose: "nor is it valid / to discriminate against 'business documents and / school-books'; all these phenomena are important." And useful to poetry. They provide for the poem its "specifications" and make for density in texture.

What Miss Moore argues against is Tolstoy's notion that "poetry is everything with the exception of business documents and school books" (Tolstoy in his *Diary*). She is also sharply taking issue with Tolstoy's definition of the process of art:

"To evoke in oneself a feeling one has experienced, and having evoked it in oneself, then by means of movement, lines, colours, sounds, or forms expressed in words so to transmit that feeling that others experience the same feeling—this is the activity of art."

Tolstoy's definition is echoed by A. E. Housman in *The Name and Nature of Poetry* (1933): "to transfuse emotion—not to transmit thought but to set up in the reader's sense a vibration corresponding to what was felt by the writer—is the peculiar function of poetry." Housman's Recognition Test for Poetry?—when the skin bristles, when the spine shivers, when the hair stands up, when there's a constriction of the throat, or when there's a sensation in the pit of the stomach!

These sensations are useful to poetry, Miss Moore admits, but poetry is comprised not solely of sensations. Art aims to express feeling *and* transmit meaning. What Miss Moore dislikes is "all this fiddle" setting limitations to poetry in definitions about it: "I, too, dislike it"—*it* being any such limiting definition of the nature and purpose of poetry. Reading such discussions about poetry, one discovers in "all this fiddle," nevertheless something "genuine"—namely

> Hands that can grasp, eyes
> that can dilate, hair that can rise
> if it must. . . .

Sensations are necessary and important, but they are not to be exploited for their own sake—neither within the given poem nor within any critical theory of poetry:

> . . . these things are important not because a
> high-sounding interpretation can be put upon them but because they are useful.

They are the raw materials of poetry, but when misused they become the derivative and false ingredients of pseudo-poetry. It is pseudo-poetry that E. E. Cummings ridicules in "Poem, or Beauty Hurts Mr. Vinal" (see p. 789).

698. A NOISELESS PATIENT SPIDER
WALT WHITMAN

In this poem, does Whitman's interest lie in a peculiar biological phenomenon observable on the Atlantic coast—that of spiders floating on long filaments out to sea—or does it lie in himself as representative of mankind? How successful is the analogy between the isolated, helpless, exploring spider and the detached, musing, venturing soul? How does the very movement of lines 4 and 5 suggest the unreeling or outthrusting of the spider's filaments? What is suggested by the fact that the sentence started in line 6 is not syntactically complete? How many examples of parallel structure are to be found in the poem? How do these parallels relate to the analogy between spider and soul? What would be the difference if the *noiseless* of line 1 followed the word *patient*—or if *noiseless* were replaced by its synonym *silent?* What effect is accomplished by the use of the hard "c" sounds in *ductile, anchor,* and *catch?* Compare with the "l" sounds in lines 4 and 5.

699. THE SPIDER HOLDS A SILVER BALL
EMILY DICKINSON

In her mature years **Emily Dickinson** seldom left her house and garden, but she, also, was moved to poetic reflection by a spider—of the kind most familiar to her. How does her attitude differ from that of Whitman on the subject? What are the characteristics of the imagery she uses? Would the poem be "improved" if Miss Dickinson had used normal rhymes instead of consonance (*i.e.,* repetition of sounds

in the consonants but not in the vowels)? Is it possible to read this poem not as a description of the activities and fate of a spider, but as a symbol of human life?

700. SNAKE
D. H. LAWRENCE

66, the albatross: see Coleridge's "The Ancient Mariner" (p. 745).

This poem has the same "subject" as Emily Dickinson's poem "The Snake" (p. 699)—but what is the difference in theme? In mood? How much in each poem could be called description? Is Lawrence's poem the more "dramatic"? How appropriate in their contexts are Dickinson's "It wrinkled, and was gone" and Lawrence's "convulsed in undignified haste"? Explain. What other examples of diction in each poem seem particularly effective? Is symbolism present in either poem? Is there any similarity in the feeling towards snakes expressed in the two poems?

702. ODE TO A NIGHTINGALE
JOHN KEATS

2, hemlock: a poisonous plant which produces death by paralysis. **4, Lethe:** river of forgetfulness in Hades. **7, Dryad:** wood-nymph. **13, Flora:** goddess of flowers, here used for the flowers themselves. **14, Provençal:** a kingdom of medieval France, famous for its troubadours. **16, Hippocrene:** fountain of the Muses on Mt. Helicon. **32, pards:** leopards. Bacchus, god of wine, was sometimes represented in a chariot drawn by panthers or leopards. **33, viewless:** invisible. **43, embalmèd:** full of balm or perfume. **51, Darkling:** in the dark. **67, alien corn:** see *Ruth* 2. The corn was "alien" because Ruth had come to Judah from her native country of Moab. **68-70, Charm'd . . . forlorn:** In early versions these lines read as follows: "Charmed the wide casements, opening on the foam / Of keelless seas, in fairy lands forlorn."

Discuss this poem as a reverie, as a poem on life and death, as a poem on the role of the imagination in life and art.

704. PHILOMELA
MATTHEW ARNOLD

21, thy dumb sister: Procne, in the version Arnold followed. **27, Daulis:** in Thrace.

27, Cephissian vale: valley of the river Cephissus. **28, Eugenia:** an imaginary companion.

The legend which forms the basis of this poem appears in several variants, but the essentials of the most usual version may be summarized as follows: The King of Thrace, Tereus, married Procne, an Athenian. Afterwards he fell in love with Procne's sister, Philomela, ravished her, and then cut out her tongue so that the rape could not be told. Philomela, however, found means through needlework ("the too clear web" of line 21) to inform Procne of the deed. Thereupon the two sisters killed Procne's infant son, Itylus, and served the flesh to Tereus, the father, as food. In indignation, the gods changed Procne into a swallow, Philomela into a nightingale whose song forever bemoans the murdered child, and Tereus into a hawk forever pursuing the sisters. Arnold's version differs in that Procne is the victim of Tereus, who had wearied of her as his wife and who wished to silence her and pretend she was dead to enable him to marry Philomela.

704. PHILOMELA
JOHN CROWE RANSOM

What differences emerge in the subject and treatment of the three poems on a nightingale? In the first two poems, for instance, *mood* (*i.e.,* atmosphere) predominates; in the third, *tone.* What is this tone —that is, what is the speaker's attitude towards his own situation?
Although Greek myth is the surface subject of Ransom's poem—he addresses "Procne, Philomela, and Itylus"—his "hidden" subject is modern poetry and modern life: Whereas "The nightingale descanted unto Ovid," today no nightingale descants —no myth inspires us now. What is the attitude of the speaker in the poem towards the nightingale legend? What characteristics of the modern world—especially of America—make the legend an "improbable tale"? What is meant by the lines "Ah, but our numbers are not felicitous, / It goes not liquidly for us"? Why does the speaker seem to despair of our "inordinate race"? What is intended by the reference to America as "this other Thrace," and by the contrasting phrase "royal Attic"? How would you reply to the question "How could her delicate dirge run democratic?" Does the

speaker long for the "fabulous provinces," or reject them, or reveal an ironic combination of yearning and dismissal?

705. "WHEN TO THE SESSIONS . . ."
WILLIAM SHAKESPEARE

4, dear time's waste: precious time wasted in seeking what he did not find. **6, dateless:** without end, without a time fixed for termination. **8, expense:** passing away—also cost in time. **10, tell:** count.

How consistently does Shakespeare employ terms and metaphors drawn from legal language? How does this usage contribute to the tone of the poem?

706. MY LOST YOUTH
HENRY WADSWORTH LONGFELLOW

1, the beautiful town: Portland, Maine, where Longfellow was born. **13, the Hesperides:** the island on which was the garden containing the golden apples, guarded by the daughters of Hesperus. **37, sea-fight:** the American *Enterprise* and the British *Boxer* fought off Portland harbor in 1813, both captains being killed. The boy Longfellow attended the double funeral.

How justify the present sequence of stanzas? Is there any schemework informing the ordering of scenes and details? Does this poem recall the past or recreate the past? Is it a sentimental poem? Is the emotion or sentiment expressed in excess of the motivating situation? Is the refrain successful in its purpose? Why, or why not?

707. FERN HILL
DYLAN THOMAS

3, dingle: wooded valley. **8, daisies and barley:** usual in harvest festival decorations in Wales. **30, Adam and maiden:** the allusion is to the time immediately after the creation of Adam and Eve, and of animals (horses) newly created out of earth by the hand of God.

This poem, like Longfellow's, expresses a nostalgic yearning for lost youth, its freshness and its richness. But, as in many recent poems, the expository statements are simply omitted, forcing the reader to infer the "background" from slight hints. The poet is remembering boyhood days and nights on a Welsh farm. The sensations, activities, feelings of that past time are, throughout, so fused with the emotions and thoughts of the poet's present maturity that the texture of the poem is richly complex. In other words, this is not a poem of simple recall. Compare the tone of "Fern Hill" with that of "My Lost Youth." Notice the interweaving of such words as time, sun, moon, green, golden—and of such details as those involving birds and animals. Is verbal repetition used successfully? Does it serve a similar function in this poem to that served by the refrain in Longfellow's? Are the near-echoes in such phrases as "once below a time" and "happy as the grass was green" [cf., "once upon a time" and "happy as the day was long"] effective devices in this poem? Why does the personification of Time as a Pied Piper (cf., lines 42-45) seem particularly appropriate in a poem on this subject and theme? What use does Thomas make of symbolism?

708. PIANO
D. H. LAWRENCE

Compare this poem with the two preceding poems in terms of the feelings and attitudes of the poets. What does the contrast between the "tinkling piano" and "the great black piano appassionato" dramatize? In what way is the theme of this poem different from that of the two preceding poems?

709. O CAPTAIN! MY CAPTAIN!
WALT WHITMAN

Of the several poems Whitman wrote commemorating Lincoln, this soon became most widely known. Whitman often recited it, but once confessed he was "almost sorry" he had ever written it—an opinion he never voiced about his "When Lilacs Last in the Dooryard Bloom'd." Would you describe the captain-of-the-ship image as natural and effective, or obvious and trite? This poem, and the preceding one by Bryant, are written with rhyme and regular metre. What is gained (or lost) by Whitman in "When Lilacs Last . . ." by his avoidance of these ingredients?

710. WHEN LILACS LAST IN THE DOORYARD BLOOM'D
WALT WHITMAN

1, lilacs: Lilacs were in bloom at Whitman's Brooklyn home when Lincoln was shot in Washington on April 15, 1865. 32, journeys a coffin: A funeral train carried Lincoln's body to his home at Springfield, Illinois, stopping at the chief cities along the way. The burial took place on May 4. 121, companions: Whitman is distinguishing between awareness of the particular fact of Lincoln's individual death and awareness of the meaning of death in general.

Although this poem says little of Lincoln's achievement and does not even mention his name, it is generally conceded to be one of the greatest of elegies and the greatest poetic tribute to Lincoln. What characteristics of the traditional elegy are revealed in the poem? How does Whitman attempt to extend the emotion from the merely personal to the national, from the death of one man to the common fate of all men? What do the three symbols—the star, the lilac, and the song of the thrush—each represent? Show how Whitman interweaves these symbols throughout the poem—after each is introduced successively in sections 2, 3, and 4—in a kind of thematic organization which unifies the entire poem. How does section 13—which brings together the three symbols or motifs—serve as a transitional section between the preceding lamentation for the death of the man Lincoln and the following consolation in the thought that only the physical body dies? Explain how section 16 associates all three symbols simultaneously with Lincoln and with Whitman's elegy. In what way does Whitman employ parallelism and the periodic sentence as devices for binding together his "catalogues" of specific details?

716. SUNBURNED ULYSSES
FREDERICK PROKOSCH

This poem and the following one by Robert Graves portray Ulysses at an earlier period of his career than Tennyson's poem (p. 780). What similarities and differences are found in these three portraits of one man?

717. STEAMBOATS, VIADUCTS, AND RAILWAYS
WILLIAM WORDSWORTH

In what sense is this a poem on "steamboats, viaducts, and railways"? What is the poet's attitude towards these new inventions—which is what they were in 1833 when the poem was published? What is the theme of the poem? How suitable is the sonnet form? Is this a good poem? Why, or why not?

718. THE LOCOMOTIVE
EMILY DICKINSON

14, **Boanerges:** literally "sons of thunder," a name applied by Jesus to two vociferous preachers among his followers. See *Mark* 3:17.

In the preceding poem Wordsworth seemed of the opinion that certain phenomena of the machine age were "at war with old poetic feeling." Does Miss Dickinson share this view? What is the tone of her poem? Is the basic metaphor that of the locomotive as horse or as dragon, or a fusion of both? Are the actions attributed to the locomotive arranged in any special sequence, or could they be rearranged in another order without serious effect?

718. TO A LOCOMOTIVE IN WINTER
WALT WHITMAN

Unlike Miss Dickinson's poem, Whitman's offers not only description and emotion but also symbolic meaning or theme. Several interpretations of the symbolism have been advanced—that the locomotive represents the American people, modern cultural progress, and Whitman's own poetry. What phrases or ideas seem to support these three possibilities? Is the poem enriched or merely confused by this complexity? Does Whitman successfully fuse the precise details of the locomotive— *e.g.,* cylindric body, side bars, headlight— with his metaphorical epithets such as "Fierce-throated beauty!" and the abstractions of his symbolic generalizations? Is the phrase in the title, "in Winter," shown to be relevant?

719. THE EXPRESS
STEPHEN SPENDER

How does the tone of this poem compare with that of Whitman's or Miss Dickinson's? Which poem presents the most precise, most vivid, most emotionalized picture of a locomotive? What does Spender achieve by his repetition of "p" and "f" sounds in the opening lines? Contrast the metrical pattern of these lines with that in lines 8-9, for instance. What accounts for the shift from specific details like gasworks and cemeteries to allegorical abstractions like "eras of wild happiness" and "beyond the crest of the world"? Can the poem be read with the Express as a symbol of the "social revolution," with its slow start in the Manifesto of Marx and Engels in 1848, its growing movement and strength, with its progress culminating in a kind of universal Utopia? In this reading *Edinburgh* and *Rome* would suggest the Presbyterian (Protestant) and Roman Catholic assurances of the good life, which would be surpassed by that achieved through revolutionary social reform; the *comet* moving musically would suggest universal harmony, perhaps "music of the spheres"; the "honey buds" would connote a Utopian "land of milk and honey." Would such a reading "destroy" the pleasure found in the poem as simple description or picture? Why, or why not? (The fact that Stephen Spender is known to have been an ardent sympathizer with radical social reform does not prove the symbolic reading of his poem.)

720. AN IRISH AIRMAN FORESEES HIS DEATH
W. B. YEATS

How does Yeats communicate the "lonely impulse of delight" which was at least part of the motive for the speaker's becoming an airman? What is the theme of this poem? What is the mood? How does the poet employ *contrast* throughout the poem to culminate in the phrase "this life, this death"?

720. HIGH FLIGHT
JOHN GILLESPIE MAGEE

The writer of this sonnet was born in China of American missionary parents. He enlisted in the Royal Canadian Air Force in October, 1940; in December, 1941 he was killed on active service in Britain. The sonnet was found written on the back of an envelope.

Explain how the poet communicates his sense of exhilaration in flying. Are the last three lines a fitting conclusion? Why, or why not?

721. THE LANDSCAPE NEAR AN AERODROME
STEPHEN SPENDER

In this poem Spender's interest is obviously not focussed upon communicating a sense of flight, but nevertheless he uses such sensations for his own purposes. Explain how. What is Spender's theme? Compare this poem with Wordsworth's sonnet "Composed upon Westminster Bridge" (p. 679) for another and quite different description of an urban scene, and with Spender's own "The Express" (p. 719) for another example of his use of the mechanical phenomena of modern urban life.

722. NEXT PLEASE
PHILIP LARKIN

What literally are the "wretched stalks / Of disappointment" (lines 9-10)? Why is the speaker of the poem located on a *bluff:*

"Watching from a bluff" (line 5)? The ship's "figurehead with golden tits / Arching our way" (lines 13-14) has been prepared for in what line? What is it that's "No sooner present than it turns to past" (lines 15-16)?

723. THE FIGUREHEAD
R. W. STALLMAN

The grammatical subject of "Uprears against the museum-wall" (line 5) is the title of the poem. In what sense are "The relics of our history / Widowed like this figurehead" (lines 17-18)? That which is "Drowned in that past we voyage for" (line 14) is that "armada of promises" (to quote from Philip Larkin's poem "Next Please"). What paradox contrives the "conceit" of "The Figurehead"? Compare and contrast "Next Please" with "The Figurehead."

iii. The Poem as Comparison

724. THREE SONNETS
WILLIAM SHAKESPEARE

18. "SHALL I COMPARE THEE . . ." **7, every fair from fair:** every beauty from its beauty. **8, untrimm'd:** stripped, despoiled. **9, owest:** ownest.

33. "FULL MANY A GLORIOUS MORNING . . ." **12, region cloud:** cloud of the upper air.

73. "THAT TIME OF YEAR . . ." **12, Consumed . . . nourished by:** Choked by the ashes of the wood that has fed the fire.

In the first of these sonnets, is the person addressed *compared* with a summer's day? What is the paradox involved in the basic analogy? Why is it that her "eternal summer shall not fade" (line 8)? That it "shall not fade" is redundant since her summer is, the poet says, "eternal,"—but what makes her summer "eternal"?

Compare the various analogies employed in these three sonnets. Which seems to be the most successful poem? Explain. Compare the themes of the three poems.

725. "MY LOVE IS LIKE TO ICE . . ."
EDMUND SPENSER

Spenser's "Amoretti" is a sequence of love sonnets addressed to Elizabeth Boyle during the poet's courtship of her. Whereas Elizabeth Browning's love sonnet (p. 728) presents definitions, Spenser's poem defines love by metaphor, by concrete analogy. Here a single analogy suffices. How is the conclusion (lines 13-14) prepared for?

726. A VALEDICTION: FORBIDDING MOURNING
JOHN DONNE

9, Moving of th' earth: either earthquakes or the motion of the earth around the sun according to the new Copernican astronomy —both alarming to Donne's contemporaries. **11, trepidation of the spheres:** a concept from the old Ptolemaic astronomy, referring to the motion of the outermost sphere (that of the fixed stars) believed to cause the "innocent" or harmless variation in the date of the equinox. **13, sublunary:** below the sphere of the moon—that is, on earth— all is imperfect and mortal; above it, throughout the spheres. all is perfect, immortal, immutable. **16, elemented:** constituted, composed. **26, stiff twin compasses:** a pair of dividers. **35, just:** perfect.

The poem opens on a comparison between the manner of dying and the manner of loving. In what way is this comparison echoed in the remaining seven stanzas? How is the defining theme of the metaphysical poets, the theme of two in one, embodied in Donne's famous compass analogy in lines 21-36? And how again in the following poem, "The Definition of Love" (lines 25-28) by Andrew Marvell.

726. THE DEFINITION OF LOVE
ANDREW MARVELL

14, close: unite. **24, planisphere:** a map of the globe projected on a plane or flat surface. The opposite poles of the earth could be united only if the round globe was "compressed" into a flat two-dimensional disc. **31-32, conjunction . . . opposition:** terms from astrology. Stars in conjunction are close together in the sky and unite their influence; in opposition they are far apart and the influences clash. **32, the stars:** used also in the sense of "Fate."

Donne's poem on the same page depicts the union of lovers, united even in their division. Marvell's poem shows, as it were, the other side of the coin. In both poems an idea is embodied in astronomical and mathematical imagery.

Marvell's lovers share a "conjunction of the mind" (line 31), but also an "opposition of the stars" (line 32); the lover is thus divided in his union with his beloved. For what reason is their union in flesh an impossibility? What is his conception of love? And hers? How is the final line prepared for? Explain line 19: "love's whole world on us doth wheel." Why then "Two perfect loves" (line 14)? Notice that the "act of love-making" is *abstractly* imaged,

not sensuously so, in the ironic definition of his Love:

> It was begotten by Despair
> Upon Impossibility.

727. "THERE IS A GARDEN IN HER FACE"
THOMAS CAMPION

7, "Cherry ripe": the cry of London street vendors.

727. TO THE VIRGINS . . .
ROBERT HERRICK

Compare this poem with "To His Coy Mistress" by Andrew Marvell, p. 778.

727. TO HELEN
EDGAR ALLAN POE

2, Nicaean: various conjectures have been offered about the meaning of this term, but none has won universal acceptance. **7, hyacinth:** In his story "Ligeia," Poe uses "the Homeric epithet, 'hyacinthine' " to designate the "the raven-black . . . glossy . . . luxuriant, and naturally-curling tresses" of Ligeia (p. 106). **16, Psyche:** the soul.

Poe stated that the poem was addressed to Mrs. Jane Stith Stanard and commemorated "the first purely ideal love of my soul." Mrs. Stanard died in 1824, when Poe was in his middle teens. What is the subject of the poem? Is Poe describing Helen or his own "awakening" to several aspects of his own nature? In their first version, lines 9-10 read as follows: "To the beauty of fair Greece / And the grandeur of old Rome." Explain why these lines are inferior to the final version.

728. "HOW DO I LOVE THEE . . ."
ELIZABETH BARRETT BROWNING

Sonnets from the Portuguese, a sequence of sonnets about the poet's own life and love for Robert Browning, was published anonymously. The phrase "from the Portuguese" was used in an attempt to disguise the personal element in what pretended to be a translation. Are the intangibles and abstractions by which the poet tries to express the degree or intensity of her love successful in communicating sincerity of emotion? Would simpler, concrete images and analogies have been more convincing? Defend your opinion. Compare this poem with Marvell's "The Definition of Love" (p. 726), a poem on a very similar theme. Also with Spenser's sonnet on p. 725.

728. "THUS PITEOUSLY LOVE CLOSED . . ."
GEORGE MEREDITH

This is the fiftieth and concluding poem in a sequence of 16-line sonnets entitled "Modern Love" and depicting the tragic break-up of a marriage between two high-strung, imaginative persons. The narrator is the husband.

In subject (the "union of this ever-diverse pair") Meredith's poem bears resemblance to the Donne and Marvell poems discussed above. This poem, however, is a short story or novel compressed into sonnet form. Is it "dramatic" in the sense that Donne's and Marvell's poems are dramatic, namely in the sense of the drama of a mind thinking through an argument, a process of thought spinning upon a premise?

Where is the speaker situated? Why the phrase "buried day" (line 8)? What is suggested in the contrasted images of *falcon* and *bat* (lines 3, 4)? Is this poem a true sonnet? Explain.

729. AUTUMNUS
JOSHUA SYLVESTER

What is the analogy? Here a leaf, personified, images man's plight. Is personification employed in the following poem by Herbert? Whereas Herbert's "Virtue" presents three images by analogy, Sylvester's poem makes use of only one. The marvel here is how Sylvester has put to the utmost use his single analogy.

729. VIRTUE
GEORGE HERBERT

Herbert refers to three things for provoking reflection upon the commonplace: the impermanence of life. A contradiction or "reversal" sets the third line in each stanza turning upon or against the opening couplet, with the final line presenting an analogy. There is the same "turnabout" in stanza 4, but this one is unexpected. How has it been prepared for nevertheless?

729. TO DAFFODILS
ROBERT HERRICK

8, **even-song:** evening church service.

Are the analogies between the daffodils and human beings convincing? What other analogies are used? Compare the treatment of life's transience in this poem with that in the poem by Freneau which follows. Compare also Wordsworth's poem on daffodils, pp. 820–821.

729. THE WILD HONEYSUCKLE
PHILIP FRENEAU

What basis for analogy exists between Freneau's poem and Herrick's "To Daffodils"? What are the differences between this poem and Shakespeare's sonnets, or Spenser's sonnet (pp. 724, 725)? Is this poem "sentimental"—any more so than Herrick's?

730. THE RETURN
EDNA ST. VINCENT MILLAY

Millay's version of mortality "pictures Earth in a sort of Mother Hubbard character, receiving back the sons she sent forth to failure, but too busy to give them much attention, and unaware of any reason why they should have failed." (From *The World's Body* [1938], by John Crowe Ransom.)

Ransom complains that the last line is weak and even uncertain in meaning, whereas it ought to be clear and memorable. Millay "is not sure whether she is saying: A comforter who does not understand, or: A comfort that does not comprehend (or include) understanding. It is by a verbal accident that *comprehend* is ambiguous, and it is only by some wrenching that *comprehend* in the sense of *understand* (for which it substitutes poorly) can be predicated of the abstract term *comfort*."

730. DAYS
RALPH WALDO EMERSON

Is the fundamental image in the poem—that of a procession—consistently maintained? Why does Emerson call the Days "muffled and dumb" (line 2)? How does this phrase, in conjunction with their offering of gifts (line 5), help to explain the *hypocritic* attribute in the opening line? What is the theme of the poem?

731. BIRCHES
ROBERT FROST

Trace through the poem the alternation between the imaginative and the logical or scientific approaches to the subject matter. In what way are the birch trees employed as a symbol? Discuss the simile in lines 44-47. What verse-form does Frost use?

732. TREE AT MY WINDOW
ROBERT FROST

Explain "Vague dream-head" (line 5). The talk of the tree, says the speaker, could not be profound. Is his own speech profound, meaningful? Does stanza 3 indicate a theory about the source of poetic profundity? At what point does the analogy between tree and man begin in this poem? How is the analogy *structurally* the poem?

732. MENDING WALL
ROBERT FROST

Note the irony in the fact that the two men co-operate to keep themselves separate. Together they build a wall which serves no purpose. What is the essential difference between the two men? Why is the simile—"like an old-stone savage armed"—appropriate for the neighbor? If tradition—what father said—keeps people apart, what forces tend to unite them, according to Frost?

733. DOMINATION OF BLACK
WALLACE STEVENS

The very title of this poem implies both contrast and conflict. Black is the negation of both color and light. What is it that black, so to speak, seeks to "dominate"? What time of year is it? Time of day? List the things that represent light and color, from "fire" in the first line to the peacocks in the final line.

Notice the many repetitions in the poem —both of nouns and verbs—and in particular the verb-forms "turned" and "turning." Constant change is balanced by constant repetition. Compare the contexts of "came striding" in lines 9 and 34. Each time the speaker was somehow re-assured when he "remembered the cry of the peacocks." He is not sure, perhaps, against what the peacocks cry, but that they cry "against" something is made clear enough. Is the sense of companionable protest a result of the fact that the speaker and the peacocks are (in the poem) the only living creatures in a constantly changing and ominous world?

734. MINE NO. 6
MALCOLM COWLEY

On the source of "Mine No. 6," a note by the author:

"Mine No. 6 was on the south branch of Blacklick Creek, in Cambria County, Pennsylvania, about five miles from where I was born. The group of miners' cabins had no other name, no post office, no school at the time, no church, no place to buy anything except the mine commissary, no law except the mine superintendent, no fish in the poisoned stream, no tree within half a mile, and nobody except the superintendent who spoke English."—From a letter to R. W. Stallman (1960).

The mood evoked in the octave of this sonnet, evoked by the picture of the mine on the "ulcerated hill," is juxtaposed with the mood of the sestet: "Beauty, perfection, I have loved you fiercely/—even in this windy slum." The contrast between dream and reality elicits the irony. For other poems constructed by Double Mood see Arthur Rimbaud's *"Chanson de la plus Haut Tour"* (p. 806) and James Joyce's "I Hear an Army Charging" (p. 675).

735. MIRAGE
R. P. BLACKMUR

For the observers in "Mirage" the time is desolate noon because it is a time without movement or change. It is a "stricken time" because myth and dream are discredited. Only the speaker of the poem believes in the shared vision, the miraculous mirage. To the observers, the perspective is devoid of movement; the flux of things has stopped; their hearts are maimed by the nothingness of the world before them. What appears as change is but a mirage: a shining mountain rising from the sea in a spume-filled sky. "Somebody said mirage. and it was gone." The deadness and emptiness of the world remain, and that is our world of reality. Only a dream brings about change, and a dream is mere illusion, "but there I have been living ever since." Why so? Why does he alone believe in what he knows to be nonexistent?

Blackmur's poem is built upon the contrast of immobility (lines 1-8) and mobility (lines 8-14). Study this poem in relation to Rossetti's "Woodspurge" (p. 678), where images of *space* define, as here, a moment of *time*. In both poems time is fixed to one moment, whereas in MacLeish's "You, Andrew Marvell" (p. 682) the space images create the sense of time's cycles.

736. JUGGLER
RICHARD WILBUR

Why is the juggler described as "a sky-blue juggler" (line 6)? Why are the bouncing balls "red"? Well, they are "spheres" (line 9), stars "Grazing his finger ends" (line 10). The word *his* implies whom? Who else could "shake our gravity up"? For whom else do we "batter our hands" (line 29)? "Who has won for once over the world's weight" (line 30)? Where in the poem is the literal juggler depicted? In sum, the poem is built upon an implied comparison; explain. Why doesn't the poet flatly state the comparison?

737. CARGOES
JOHN MASEFIELD

What allegory is intended by the three pictures in the poem? In the final picture, which is set in opposition to the first two, what phrase discloses the poet's attitude? Is the impression you retain from the poem predominantly one of a series of pictures or of a theme advanced by the poet? Explain.

iv. The Poem as Narrative

738. THE THREE RAVENS
ANONYMOUS

Only lines 9-15 are spoken by the ravens. Who speaks in the rest of the poem? Should the material in lines 16-23 have been cast into dialogue form? What effect has the refrain?

739. THE TWA CORBIES
ANONYMOUS

"The Three Ravens" and "The Twa Corbies" provide two different versions of the same story. How does the behavior of the knight's hound, hawk, and "lady fair" in the second poem differ from that in the first? Is the conclusion of "The Three Ravens" better than that of "The Twa Corbies"? Why, or why not? What effect is achieved by having the birds serve as narrators and commentators? More of this poem is cast into the speech of the birds than in "The Three Ravens." How does this affect the emotions aroused by the poem?

739. SIR PATRICK SPENS
ANONYMOUS

In longer versions of this ballad the purpose of the voyage is said to be to bring back the king's daughter from Norway. This version concentrates upon the orders and the shipwreck, the heart of the tragedy. Is anything important lost by the omission of this "background"—or omission of transitions between the scenes which make up the poem? Can it be said that even if the "facts" are skimped, the emotional consequences are fully revealed? Why is the picture in lines 43-44 better than a prose statement such as: "And in the sea Sir Patrick and his men were drowned"? Why are the forebodings in lines 23-28 effective as a narrative device? What irony is suggested by the poet's selection of the blood-red wine, cork-heeled shoes, the fans, and the combs as details to mention? Is any contrast implied between Sir Patrick and the Scots lords? What is the effect of the repetition in lines 33, 37, 41?

740. THE WIFE OF USHER'S WELL
ANONYMOUS

Is there any connection between the mother's words in the fourth stanza and the return of the sons? What is the character of the mother? How is repetition used to heighten the emotional effect in the poem? Compare the mixture of exposition and dialogue in this poem with that in "Sir Patrick Spens."

740. THE UNQUIET GRAVE
ANONYMOUS

Unlike the preceding ballads which combine narration and dialogue, this poem is cast entirely into dialogue. Identify the speakers. Is there any reason for the use of the third person—"she"—in the fourth line rather than the second person—"you"? What is the theme of the poem? Could the lover be said to be courting death at the grave of his beloved? How appropriate is the flower symbol of line 23 in suggesting that death is natural and to be accepted unrepiningly? Is the idea of resurrection in heaven also implicit in the symbol? How successful are the opening two lines of the poem in establishing the mood of the poem?

741. BONNY BARBARA ALLAN
ANONYMOUS

As in "The Unquiet Grave," we have in this poem a dialogue between two lovers —but here the dialogue is set in a framework of exposition. What are some of the other differences? Are the characters of the protagonists revealed progressively, or all at once? How convincing is the ending?

741. BARBARA ALLEN'S CRUELTY
ANONYMOUS

Compare this version of this famous ballad with the preceding version. Which is the better poem? Explain why.

742. EDWARD
ANONYMOUS

Although the preceding ballads have used some question-and-answer dialogue, this is the first to rely entirely upon this method of presentation. Is this a gain or a loss? Could the preceding ballads have used this method as effectively, or is it effective mainly because of the "surprise ending"? Why is Edward *sad* (4)? Are the terms he applies to his hawk and horse really applicable to his father as he now sees him retrospectively? What is shown of the mother's character by each successive question? How is the ending—surprise though it is—prepared for by what is revealed of the mother by her attitude during the conversation? For example, what is shown by her dismissing the horse as *auld* and only one of many? What is achieved by the rather elaborate use of refrain and repetition?

743. LORD RANDAL
ANONYMOUS

How does the question-and-answer method in this poem compare with that in "Edward"? How does the parallelism of form in each stanza build to a cumulative effect? What is achieved by the surprise variation in the last line of the last stanza, as compared with the repetition in the other stanzas? Does this last line change, in retrospect, the meaning of the phrase "weary wi' hunting"? In this poem do we learn progressively more about the characters—as we did in "Edward"—or merely more about the situation? Should the balladist have told us *why* Lord Randal was poisoned? Would the emotional effect be increased if we knew? Would the stimulus to the imagination?

743. LA BELLE DAME SANS MERCI
JOHN KEATS

Title, La Belle Dame sans Merci: the beautiful lady without pity. 18, fragrant zone: girdle of flowers. 19, as: *i.e.,* as if. 32, kisses four: In a joking letter to his brother when enclosing the poem Keats wrote: "Why four kisses . . . why . . . because . . . I was obliged to choose an even number that both eyes might have fair play. . . . I think two a piece quite sufficient. Suppose I had seven; there would have been three and a half a piece—a very awkward affair. . . ."

Note that there are two speakers in the poem. At what point does the first speaker give place to the second? What parallel is established between the situation or plight of the knight and the season and setting? How does Keats make the one serve as a commentary upon the other? How justify the circular form of the poem, its ending returning us to its beginning?

"La Belle Dame sans Merci" is, as other critics have pointed out, the poem *par excellence* of romantic disillusionment. The lady in the meads appears to be "a faery's child": she lives in an elfin grot and she feeds on manna dew. Is she something more? Is she the symbol of what we long for—perfection in beauty, love, and warm devotion?

The crux of Keats' poem is the conflict between ideals or dreams and fact, between illusions and reality. The poem evokes this theme by its contrast of moods. Hawthorne's treatment of a similar theme is his short story: "My Kinsman, Major Molineux" (p. 93). Major Molineux in some ways is to the boy in Hawthorne's story what the lady in the meads is to the knight-at-arms. Compare and point out the differences between Hawthorne's story and Keats' poem.

744. LA BELLE DAME SANS MERCI
Rolfe Humphries

How justify the title of this poem? Humphries' poem, by its very title, is asking for comparison with Keats' famous ballad. How do the two poems differ—in situation, in mood, in theme, and in form? What kinship has the situation in Humphries' poem with the situation in Keats' In both poems the narrator is stripped of illusions. Keats' "lady in the meads" transposes into the mysterious woman of Humphries' ballad, the woman of the poem's burden: *"Who is the third who always walks beside you?"* As symbol, what is her identity? What does this poem *mean*? Could Humphries' poem have been constructed, like that of Keats, in circular form?

How do these two poems resemble the folk ballads, and how do they differ from that *genre?*

745. THE RIME OF THE ANCIENT MARINER
Samuel Taylor Coleridge

12, Eftsoons: Forthwith. **76, vespers:** Probably means simply "evenings," rather than "evening prayers." The meaning seems to be that the bird perched for nine consecutive evenings—and remained all night.

The murder would therefore be that of a creature who had for a time shared the sailors' home. [See the remarks by Arthur Dickson, *Explicator,* VI, 5 (June, 1948).] **184, gossameres:** filmy spider-webs which float in the air. **211, nether tip:** In discussing this famous astronomical "error" Professor J. L. Lowes has shown that Coleridge could have cited scientific authority for this remark. The strange phenomenon was twice reported by responsible astronomers in the *Philosophical Transactions of the Royal Society,* a publication of which Coleridge was an ardent reader. [See *The Road to Xanadu* (Boston: Houghton Mifflin Co., 1927), pp. 180, 510.] **314, fire-flags:** the aurora australis, perhaps. **489, rood:** Cross. **535, ivy-tod:** ivy bush.

What effect is achieved by the device of the detained Wedding Guest? What is significant about the Guest's question in lines 79-81? Part I of the poem sets the stage and provides necessary exposition leading up to the confession of the crime and sin—the shooting of the Albatross. What exactly does each of the other six parts contribute to the unfolding of the narrative? How many of the Seven Parts end with a stanza mentioning the Albatross? What is significant about this repetition? About the exceptions? What is the "theme" of the poem? What does the Albatross symbolize?

Is the Mariner a representative of the type of man who is a spiritual isolationist, unaware of the oneness of life? (See lines 232-235.) This interpretation is suggested by Louise Schutz Boas [*Explicator,* II, 7 (May, 1944)], who contends that when the Mariner feels kinship with the watersnakes he frees himself from the evil of isolationism, and that when he feels compulsion to tell his story to selected listeners, he is motivated by the desire to assert his feeling of being a part of God's universe. Do you agree with this interpretation? William Wordsworth, close friend of Coleridge, said in a note appended to the 1800 edition of *Lyrical Ballads* that Coleridge was conscious that the poem contained defects and had wished to omit it from further editions of *Lyrical Ballads.* Wordsworth says he prevailed upon Coleridge to allow it to remain, and then continues:

The Poem of my Friend has indeed great defects; first, that the principal person has no distinct character, either in his profession of Mariner, or as a human being who having been long under the controul of super-natural impressions might be supposed him-self to partake of something supernatural: secondly, that he does not act, but is con-tinually acted upon: thirdly, that the events having no necessary connection do not pro-duce each other; and lastly, that the imagery is somewhat too laboriously accumulated. Yet the Poem contains many delicate touches of passion, and indeed the passion is every where true to nature; a great number of the stanzas present beautiful images, and are expressed with unusual felicity of language; and the versification, though the metre is itself unfit for long poems, is harmonious and artfully varied, exhibiting the utmost powers of that metre, and every variety of which it is capable. It therefore appeared to me that these several merits (the first of which, namely that of the passion, is of the highest kind,) gave to the Poem a value which is not often possessed by better Poems. On this account I requested of my Friend to permit me to republish it.

How valid are Wordsworth's praise and censure of the poem? What characteristics of the folk ballad are found in Coleridge's poem?

Coleridge himself once wrote: "The romance-writer possesses an unlimited power over situations; but he must scrupu-lously make his characters act in congruity with them. Let him work *physical* wonders only, and we will be content to dream with him for a while; but by the first *moral* miracle which he attempts he disgusts us and awakens us." That the physical events in the *Ancient Mariner* are improbable no one will deny. But does the poem abide by Coleridge's own insistence upon truth to human nature, truth to the constitution of the universe—but especially psychological truth? In other words, while the incidents are those of fantasy, are the theme and characterization those of truth?

761. THE HAYSTACK IN THE FLOODS
WILLIAM MORRIS

45, **Poictiers:** site of defeat of French in 1356 by the heavily outnumbered English. 47, **Gascon frontier:** At this time Gascony was held by the English. 51, **those six men:** the judges in witchcraft trials. 52, **Chatelet:** a prison in Paris. 55-56, **my weak hands . . . swim:** an allusion to the "trial by water." If the accused sank he was inno-cent; if not, he was guilty. 61, **St. George:** patron saint of England. 153, **fitte:** canto, division of a narrative poem.

How successfully does Morris create set-ting and mood for this poem of the ambush of the English Robert de Marny by the French Godmar? What part in the poem is played by the rain and the haystack? Does the narrator compress his story too much—that is, does he omit any necessary information? How effective is the use of repetition? The use of dialogue? What is indicated by the phrase "gag me Robert" (line 109)? Do the characters of the three principals emerge clearly? How much weight should be placed on Jehane's fear of damnation (line 48) as influencing her decision? What is suggested in Godmar's remark in lines 154-155? Is the narrator impersonal in his presentation? How does this narrative poem compare with a folk ballad?

765. DAVID
EARLE BIRNEY

What examples of foreshadowing are found in this poem? Justify the division of the narrative into nine sections. Comment on the emotional and dramatic effectiveness of the concluding line of the poem.

v. The Poem as Drama

---

772. "I DIED FOR BEAUTY"
EMILY DICKINSON

Compare this poem with Keats' "Ode on a Grecian Urn" (p. 694), especially lines 49-50.

772. FUTILITY
WILFRED OWEN

W. B. Yeats' private opinion of Owen's poetry—"unworthy of the poet's corner of a country newspaper"—is refuted by the fact of Owen's importance in modern poetry, his achievement in two or three poems ("Futility" being one of these), and the acclaim he receives from other poets and critics. At his worst, Owen is imitative of Keats, but the war (World War 1, in which Owen was killed—just two weeks before the Armistice), as Louis MacNeice says, "dissolved the Keats in Owen and made him a far finer poet than he would—probably—otherwise have been. . . ." Yeats' label—"He is all blood, dirt & sucked sugar stick"—is unfair both to the man and his poetic talent. "Futility" has the blood and dirt in it, but where is the "sugar stick"?

If Owen is traditionally poetic in imagery and epithets, he is nevertheless an innovator in technique, particularly in experimentations in rhyme. Auden and other poets have studied Owen, whose "Futility" provides an early model of the use of consonance and assonance in place of conventional "true-rhyme." (An example of true or perfect rhyme is: *snow/ know.*) In "consonantal rhyme" there is a felt agreement or consonance of sounds in the syllables following the vowels of different words. (An example of consonance: *seeds/ sides.*) In assonance there is a felt identity in the vowel sounds of different words. (Example: *sun/ once.*) "Futility" employs

all three types of rhyming: *sun/ once; unsown/ know* (assonance); *once/ France; seeds/ sides; star/ stir; tall/ toil* (consonance); *snow/ know; tall/ all* (true-rhyme). Furthermore, it employs internal rhyme by the assonance of the vowel *o* in such words as *awoke* (lines 2, 4, and 9); and in *now* and *rouse* (line 5). These cross-patterns bind the words of the poem together, and subtly so. The point is worth making because the poem that does not seem to rhyme is for many readers no poem at all. If the rhymes in this poem are ambiguous, so is the metre and the meaning. What is the poet saying?

Why is the sun called "the kind old sun"? In what ways is the sun *kind?* Why are sunbeams given the epithet *fatuous?* Is the basic conceit or conceptual idea of the poem *fatuous* or ironic? Romantic or naturalistic, fantasy or fact? What is the mood of the poem?

772. "IS MY TEAM PLOUGHING"
A. E. HOUSMAN

Why is it that this dead man asks questions of the living? Other dead men do not stir from their graves; what stirs this one? Is this dramatic dialogue meaningful, or is it merely the device of the poet for evolving an ironic plot? The irony is rather obvious: "*No change* though you lie under / The land you used to plough." And the irony, too, in "Now I stand up no more"; but are the repetitions of the phrase "stand up" (in lines 15 and 16) merely technically clever parallelisms, or are they *morally* as well as ironically significant? Was the dead man, when he lived, a better man morally than his "friend"? How can this inference be proven? The living, like the dead, "lie down." Only "The goal stands up"—and the keeper (God?). But perhaps this dead man rises only in the mind of his friend?

Is this psychological interpretation of the drama founded on what the poem defines as fact?

Why does the friend try to stop the dead man's questions?—"Be still, my lad, and sleep." Was the dead man formerly the village goalkeeper? The question and answer form of this poem suggests comparison with such traditional ballads as "Edward" and "Lord Randal." (See pages 742–743.) Compare it also with "The Unquiet Grave" (p. 740).

773. TO AN ATHLETE DYING YOUNG
A. E. HOUSMAN

Who is speaking? To whom? Are the parallels between the youth's dying and his running, between the funeral and a victory parade, consistently maintained? How is the race between time and fame (lines 19-20) related to the theme of the poem? How does the tone help prevent the poem from lapsing into sentimentality? What are some of the principal symbols in the poem?

773. THE FUNERAL
JOHN DONNE

9, **sinewy thread my brain:** the spinal cord, nervous system. 20, **reliques:** relics are objects venerated because of their association with a saint or other sacred personage. 23, **bravery:** bravado.

What are the principal images used in this poem? What is the tone of the speaker?

774. THE CANONIZATION
JOHN DONNE

7, **stampèd face:** on coins. The contrast suggested is between a career at court and a career in business. 15, **plaguy bill:** the weekly list of persons who died of the plague. 22, **eagle and the dove:** symbols of strength and purity, respectively. 23, **phoenix:** a legendary bird, symbol of immortality, which lived a thousand years, burned itself to death in a nest of spices, and rose new-born from its own ashes. 30, **legend:** a term applied in Donne's day to the biographical account of a saint's life. It contrasts with "sonnets" (l. 32), frequently used in series by lovers—e.g., Spenser's *Amoretti*, etc.—to "chronicle" the

"history" of their love. 33, **becomes: suits.**

The fundamental analogy on which the poem is built is between lovers and holy anchorites who renounce the secular, practical world for a better one—but the better world for the lovers is one of love, not piety. To whom does the speaker address himself? How does the tone of his remarks change through the first three stanzas? How important in the poem is the symbol of the phoenix? Could the lovers be said to die to the mundane world in order to rise to a new and better one of their own? Note that in the closing lines of the poem the lovers are said to gain the whole world— "countries, towns, courts." Why, according to the speaker, will other lovers pray to them for assistance?

775. PIAZZA PIECE
JOHN CROWE RANSOM

In what ways is this sonnet an innovation on the conventional sonnet? Its form, obviously, is based upon a contrast. Is the voice of the "gentleman in a dustcoat" different in tone and style from the voice of the "lady young in beauty waiting"? What does the repeated burden of the first and final lines of the sestet tell us about the possibilities for fulfillment of the lady's expectation and hope? The word *waiting* tumbles into line 10, and in the final *waiting* the sense is suspended. Why is that word located as the end word of each line? The word *want* (line 4) has the double meaning of "desire" and "lacking." How are these meanings played upon in the final scene? Why is it that the roses on her trellis are dying? And, finally, what do the characters of this dialogue represent? With Ransom's sonnet compare Drayton's "Since there's no help." What similarity exists between these poems in their octaves, and what differences can you define in their sestets?

775. "SINCE THERE'S NO HELP . . ."
MICHAEL DRAYTON

The lover here says one thing and means the opposite. What is the ambiguity in "kiss *and part*"? In "Shake hands *for ever*"? And in "thou might'st him yet recover"? And the woman he bids farewell to, what is her stand in this matter? How is her attitude indicated?

776. "I WILL NOT LET THEE GO."
ROBERT BRIDGES

What basis of comparison has this poem with the preceding sonnet by Drayton? Is Bridges' poem "dramatic"? What is accomplished by using the same line as the first in every stanza? By varying the last lines of the stanzas? Are the references to natural phenomena—wind, sun, stars, etc. —arranged in a significant order? Explain.

776. SONG ("SWEETEST LOVE . . .")
JOHN DONNE

7, use: accustom, practice.

Compare this poem with Donne's "A Valediction: Forbidding Mourning" (p. 726) on the same subject. How does Donne's expression of the *oneness* of true lovers in this poem compare with that in the following poem "The Good-Morrow," and "A Valediction: Forbidding Mourning"?

777. THE GOOD-MORROW
JOHN DONNE

4, seven sleepers' den: a reference to the legend of the seven youths from Ephesus who hid in a cave about 250 A.D. to escape persecution as Christians and then slept for about two centuries before emerging in a world where Christianity was now honored. 12, other: *i.e.,* others; the plural without *s* was common in Donne's time. 17, hemispheres: half spheres, which together make one sphere; the sphere was considered to be the perfect shape. 19, was not mixt equally: A perfect mixture of the four elements— earth, air, fire, water—produced immortality. 21, none can die: If the form is perfect (a sphere) and the mixture perfect, the product (the union of the lovers) is immortal.

What is the theme of this poem? How are the images of new adulthood, new morning, and new world related to this theme? Compare the image (in lines 15-17) of the lovers' discovering their respective worlds or hemispheres in each other's eyes with the image in lines 39-44 of Donne's "The Canonization" (p. 774).

777. "WESTERN WIND, WHEN WILT THOU BLOW"
ANONYMOUS

How does the cry for rain relate to the mood of loneliness? The poem is built upon an analogy. Can you define it? The romantic invocation to the wind contrasts with the realistic cry. But what has the wind to do with the lover's plight?

778. TO HIS COY MISTRESS
ANDREW MARVELL

7, Humber: Marvell lived in Hull, on the Humber river. 10, conversion of the Jews: used to suggest a future time almost inconceivably remote and unlikely. 11, vegetable: placidly growing like a plant—as contrasted with "am'rous birds of prey" in line 38. 44, gates of life: the reference may be to the womb and birth passage.

What are the three stages of the lover's argument? What is the dominant tone of each? How does the imagery differ in each of the three sections of the poem? Why are images of vast time and space used in the first section? How do they relate to the image of time in line 22 and image of a narrow and restricted space in line 26? Show how Marvell sometimes employs overstatement, sometimes understatement. Is the theme of the poem broader than that of a lover's petition to his mistress? Compare this poem with Archibald MacLeish's "You, Andrew Marvell" (p. 682).

778. PORPHYRIA'S LOVER
ROBERT BROWNING

What is suggested of Porphyria's character by lines 16-19, 21-25? What is suggested by the fact that only after a number of actions on entering the cottage does she, "last," sit down by the lover's side? What is suggested of the lover's character by lines 42-44, 47-48, 53-55? To whom is the lover speaking? How does Browning use contrast for dramatic effect?

779. MY LAST DUCHESS
ROBERT BROWNING

3, Frà Pandolf: an imaginary painter. 45, I gave commands: When asked if this passage meant that the Duchess was put to death, Browning at first said yes, but then added "or he might have had her shut up in a convent." In any event she was, of course, now dead, or the Duke would be unable to marry again. **56, Claus of Innsbruck:** an imaginary sculptor.

To whom is the Duke speaking? What is to be inferred about the listener's character and behavior by the Duke's responses (see lines 12-13, 43, 53-54)? What is suggested of the character of the Duchess by lines 40-41? What is the function of the art treasures—such as the painting and the bronze statue—in the poem? What is the effect of our discovering, at the end of the poem, that the Duke is arranging a second marriage? What is the tone of the poem? What is the verse form? What are the similarities and differences between this dramatic monologue and "Porphyria's Lover"?

780. ULYSSES
ALFRED, LORD TENNYSON

10, rainy Hyades: a group of stars, in the constellation Taurus, believed to cause rainy weather.

Ulysses, one of the Greek leaders in the Trojan War, and a ten-years' wanderer afterwards (see Homer's *Odyssey*), is shown here some time after he finally reached home. To whom is he speaking? In what mood? What is his character? Is it wholly admirable? What are his attitudes towards his wife, his son, his people? Two contrasting interpretations seem possible. First, Ulysses may be a man unwilling to subside into complacent dotage, just "killing time," when he might yet, if he tried, do "some work of noble note," seek "a newer world," and so on. Second, Ulysses may be a man who shrugs off his duties and responsibilities, leaving them to others, in order to indulge his selfish yearning for new adventures and new knowledge—since there is no indication that he will return from this proposed journey "beyond the sunset" in order to help others benefit from the different discoveries he expects to make. The one view is, in short, that Ulysses is an individualist rightly pursuing his own salvation and interests, whereas the other is that Ulysses is a self-indulgent globetrotter who shirks his social obligations. [It should be stated that Tennyson would strongly repudiate this second view. He himself said of the poem (written soon after the death of

his close friend Hallam) that it gave "the feeling about the need of going forward and braving the struggle of life perhaps more simply than anything in *In Memoriam*." How far should a writer's "intention," even when definitely known, govern the interpretation and judgment of a poem?] Compare "Ulysses" with the preceding dramatic monologues by Browning. Is there any dramatic conflict in "Ulysses"? For a contrasting view of Ulysses as a character (and as a younger man) see the poems by Prokosch and Graves (p. 716).

782. SPRING AND FALL: TO A YOUNG CHILD
GERARD MANLEY HOPKINS

2, Goldengrove: a grove where autumn leaves are golden. The word expresses childhood fancy and wonderment. **8, wanwood:** a word coined by the poet to express the pale and sickly appearance of the grove losing its leaves. *Wan-* is a prefix (similar to *dis-* or *un-*) and, as adjective, it means gloomy, dark, or pale, or sad. **8, leafmeal:** another coined word, the idea being leaf by leaf or "piecemeal." It suggests the passing of time, life's departure. **8, worlds of wanwood leafmeal lie:** cf. *Revelations:* 10: 10-11. ". . . and there fell a great star from heaven . . . and it fell upon the third part of the rivers, and upon the fountains of waters; / And the name of the star is called Wormwood: and the third part of the waters became wormwood; and many men died of the waters, because they were made bitter." As *wanwood* suggests *wormwood,* so too it carries the burden of *wanhope.* And *leafmeal* relates to *leafmold,* which feeds growth in following seasons. **9, And yet you will weep and know why:** the accented word *will* pitches the meaning to "yet you will *to* weep and *to* know why." The poem pivots on this meaning. **13, ghost:** spirit.

What is "the blight man was born for"? List the words in the poem connotative of sadness—in *leaves* (transposed into a verb), for instance. The poem divides into four parts; what are they? Could the final line be relocated earlier in the poem? Why not? What prepares for it? What is the relationship between the metrics of the poem and what is said? "Sorrow's springs" equates with fall, and autumn's leaves with "things of man." And Goldengrove, the woods in autumn, is dispossessed of its precious gold (gold, a thing of man). What does *blight* (line 14) attach to? What, in fact, does Margaret mourn for? And how is what she mourns for symbolized? Why is it that when "heart grows older / It will come to such sights colder / By and by"? For what reason will Margaret *then* not "spare a sigh"?

782. THE LISTENERS
WALTER DE LA MARE

The literal Traveler knocks on the door, but nobody answers. There is nobody there to answer, except some "phantom listeners." So much for the literal Traveler; but who is the allegorical Traveler and who are these "phantom listeners"? Their stillness, he feels, *answers* his cry (line 22). The Traveler's eyes are gray; the door of the house is moonlit; its windowsill, like the sky, is leaf-fringed; and its dark stair goes down to an empty hall filled with invisible forms who, ghost-like, utter no sound. What is the allegorical meaning of all this? Is it possible to prove any single interpretation? What does this fable *mean*? As many things as there are readers?

783. NEW YEAR'S EVE
THOMAS HARDY

11-12, who in This tabernacle groan: See *II Corinthians* 5:4. The allusion is to man's "earthly house" as contrasted with the "building of God . . . eternal in the heavens." **30, unweeting:** (archaic) unknowing, unaware.

What does Hardy gain by using the dialogue form? What is the effect of the Biblical phrase in lines 11-12? Of the archaism "unweeting" in line 30? What is the theme of the poem? What is the tone?

783. PATTERNS
AMY LOWELL

What is the evidence that this poem is set in the 18th century? Is the narrator speaking or *thinking* the words of the poem? Although we are not informed of the cause of the woman's state of mind until the poem is more than half read, are there any foreshadowings that prepare us? Why is it psychologically convincing that a grieving woman might very well think of her garden and her gown in the manner shown? How many different kinds of "patterns" appear in the poem? Are there any forces, named or implicit, opposed to the various patterns? Trace the chronological pattern throughout the poem, the sequence of past, present, future. What is the theme of the poem? What are some of the symbols used? What use is made of repetition?

785. MR. FLOOD'S PARTY
EDWIN ARLINGTON ROBINSON

8, Tilbury Town: The name Robinson used in his poems for Gardiner, Maine. **11, the poet says:** See the *Rubaiyat of Omar Khayyám,* stanza 7. **20, like Roland's ghost:** This has been explained in different ways. One explanation is that the allusion is to the ending of Browning's "Childe Roland to the Dark Tower Came" (see p. 836). Another is that the reference is to Roland, the famous knight of medieval romance— and more particularly to Roland sounding his horn in the pass of Roncesvalles to summon Charlemagne and his army from the valley below. Whichever is right, Robinson's purpose is clear—to invoke a combination of incongruity and relevance, comedy and pathos, in a suggestive ambivalence.

What other examples of a similar nature are employed by the poet? Compare the tone of this poem with that of "Miniver Cheevy" by the same poet (p. 792).

786. MY PAPA'S WALTZ
THEODORE ROETHKE

What is the boy's attitude toward Papa? Any resentment? That the speaker of the poem calls the incident a waltz tells us what? Is there any irony in this poem?

vi. The Poem as Satire and Parody

---

787. "MY MISTRESS' EYES . . ."
WILLIAM SHAKESPEARE

5, damask'd: mingled pink and white

Is Shakespeare here ridiculing the extravagances of language in the love poems of his contemporaries, or satirizing his mistress? Explain. What is the mood of this sonnet? Comment on the word *reeks* (line 8).

787. [BELINDA PREPARES FOR DAY]
ALEXANDER POPE

5, knocked the ground: to summon the maid. **6, pressed watch:** a watch which repeats, when the stem is pressed, the strokes indicating the hours or parts of hours. **22, the Ring:** the circular promenade in London's Hyde Park. **49, Shock:** Belinda's lap dog. **57, inferior Priestess:** the maid, Betty. **68, Patches:** coloured court plaster, sometimes shaped like stars or crescents, stuck on the face ostensibly to emphasize such features as dimples or handsome eyes.

If the identity of the author were not known, by what evidence would we know that this is an 18th century poem? Compare Shakespeare's Ariel in *The Tempest* with Pope's Ariel (line 40). What meanings attach to *pious* in "pious maid" (line 46)? Compare the characterization given in Amy Lowell's "Patterns" (p. 783) with Pope's Belinda. After reading Pope on Belinda, turn to Marvell's "To His Coy Mistress" (p. 778); what contrasts exist?

789. POEM, OR BEAUTY HURTS MR. VINAL
E. E. CUMMINGS

Mr. Vinal: Harold Vinal, editor of *Voices,* a little poetry magazine founded in 1921.

Voices aimed to preserve poetry or to rescue it from the danger of modern attacks upon its sensibilities. Vinal's editorial program made much ado over the "surrender" of modern poetry to the harsh realities of "the modern distemper." Vinal insisted on the "subjective source and quality of poetry." (See *The Little Magazine,* by Frederick J. Hoffman and others, 1946.)

In view of the above note spell out what Cummings is up to. What literary allusions or echoes do you spot in Cummings' satire? What purpose is served by the Nationally Advertised Products? Cummings sometimes runs words together and sometimes he fractions a word or phrase. For what effect? Characterize the speaker—"take it from me kiddo," etc. Define the effect of the final line.

790. THE UNKNOWN CITIZEN
W. H. AUDEN

Is an individual or a society being satirized? Is the time the present or the future? Explain. Comment on the connection between line 4, lines 20-24, and 28-29. Explain the change of rhythm that begins in line 14. Compare the theme and tone of this poem with those of "Miniver Cheevy" and "Newsreel" (p. 792). Compare also with Cummings' "anyone lived in a pretty how town" (p. 942).

791. DIRGE
KENNETH FEARING

Define the activities, values, way of life, and the death of the stereotype whose dirge is here sung. What is suggested by the indication that the pall-bearers are strangers to one another and indifferent to the deceased? What is achieved by the use of such words as *wow, blooie, zowie, bong,* etc.? Compare this satire with the poem preceding it and the two which follow it. Can you justify the form of this poem as in keeping with its subject?

792. MINIVER CHEEVY
EDWIN ARLINGTON ROBINSON

11, Thebes: Greek city famous in the Peloponnesian and other wars. **11, Camelot:** King Arthur's capital. **12, Priam:** king of Troy during the Trojan War. **17, Medici:** A family in Florence during the Renaissance, famous both for their patronage of art and learning and for some unsavory activities.

What effect is achieved by the use of a shorter line to conclude each stanza? Is the subject of the poem an individual or a type?

792. NEWSREEL
C. DAY LEWIS

Is this a satire on moviegoers only? Why is the comparison between the moviehouse and an aquarium tank an effective one? What is achieved by the repetition in lines 19-20, and in 24-25? What is the theme of the poem?

793. TO A SINISTER POTATO
PETER VIERECK

1, earth-apple: the French term for potato, *pomme de terre,* literally means "apple of earth."

What indicates that the poet is using the potato symbolically? What does the "sinister potato" symbolize? Comment on *lours* (in the last line of the poem).

794. ON THE VANITY OF EARTHLY GREATNESS
ARTHUR GUITERMAN

Is there any logic in the selection of mastodon, Charlemagne, grizzly bear, and Caesar? Should there be any necessarily? Would other examples have served as well as the four selected? Explain.

794. "NEXT TO OF COURSE GOD"
E. E. CUMMINGS

What effect is achieved by the omission of capitalization and punctuation? By the

fragmentary phrases? By the last line? Is it significant that the poem is written as a sonnet?

794. WHITE CHRISTMAS
W. R. RODGERS

18, Feeds the five thousand: Refers to the miracle of the loaves and fishes; see *Mark* 6:35-44.

Compare this satirical comment on one aspect of modern Christian culture with that in Clough's "The Latest Decalogue." Which displays the greater emotion? Explain. What is achieved by the repetition of "punctually" at the beginning of each stanza? Comment on the diction and imagery of the poem.

795. THE LATEST DECALOGUE
ARTHUR HUGH CLOUGH

Compare the Ten Commandments—*Exodus* 20:3-17; *Deuteronomy* 5:7-21. Is the attitude shown in this poem one of mockery, cynicism, grief, or wrath? Explain.

796. "NEARING AGAIN THE LEGENDARY ISLE"
C. DAY LEWIS

This poem, like the following poem by Manifold, uses a legendary episode in Homer's *Odyssey* as the basis of satiric comment. Against what is the satire directed—the legend? the man? modern life? Is the target the same in both poems?

796. THE SIRENS
JOHN MANIFOLD

2, Wolf, Weinberger, Morley: Hugo Wolf (1860–1903), German composer; Jaromir Weinberger (1896–), Czech composer; and Thomas Morley (1557–1603), English composer.

What is the theme of this poem? What is its tone? Is the poet mocking Homer or commenting on modern life?

Contrast the portrait of Odysseus here with that of the same man in the poems by Prokosch and Graves (p. 716), and Tennyson (p. 780). [Ulysses is the Latin name for Odysseus.]

797. THE PASSIONATE SHEPHERD TO HIS LOVE
CHRISTOPHER MARLOWE

What characteristics of the pastoral convention are employed by Marlowe? What is the tone of the poem?

798. "COME LIVE WITH ME AND BE MY LOVE"
C. DAY LEWIS

Why does Lewis single out for parody the most famous of Elizabethan pastorals? Is it not because Marlowe's poem represents the most familiar and perfect example of "pure" poetry, of Art disengaged from Life? Lewis's mockery of Marlowe's theme of "the invitation to love"—the literary device which that poem initiated and which has persisted down to our own time—is *intended* as a criticism of the tradition of "pure" poetry. To Lewis, "The Passionate Shepherd" expresses the escapism of the poet of middle-class culture into a world of make-believe. His satire is directed against all poets who fashion a poetry of escape.

From the opening invitation to take an emotional trip to Arcadia we are shocked back to the reality

> Of peace and plenty, bed and board,
> That chance employment may afford.

The literary and social satire of Marlowe's facile optimism mocks at every word its counterpart. The ironies point to the intention of the parody: the irony in the prettiness of "dainties" and the mock alliteration (line 5); the irony in "thou shalt *read* [in advertisements] of summer frocks" (a humorous play on the original rhyme); the ironic disparity between pastoral and city life in the grotesque comedy of "madrigals" "by the sour canals" (a biting commentary on a civilization of shepherds in overalls);

the grim pun on the word "tire" (line 12) —a word often used in Elizabethan times for "attire" or "dress"; the grating discords of the parody as contrasted with the liquid music of the original; the mockery of the pure paintbox method of Marlowe, which Lewis discards in the last stanza for the bald facts:

> Hunger shall make thy modest zone
> And cheat fond death of all but bone.

For the modern shepherd there is no escape; the modern poet, Lewis insists, must face realities.

799. HEAVEN
RUPERT BROOKE

Brooke's poem is not strictly a parody of the preceding poem by Tennyson, but rather a parody of some ideas expressed in various parts of *In Memoriam*. The extract from Tennyson's poem given here is merely an illustration. Moreover, the literary echoes in Brooke's poem are not all from Tennyson. Is the impact of "Heaven" much reduced even if all the echoes are not positively identified? Why, or why not? What is the target of Brooke's satire?

799. "WHAT, STILL ALIVE . . ."
HUGH KINGSMILL

Like Brooke's "Heaven," Kingsmill's poem has its target not in a single poem but rather in the characteristic ideas and phrases exhibited in many poems by the "victim." The preceding poem by Housman is again merely illustrative of the kind of thing Kingsmill is aiming at. Consider also some of the other poems by Housman found in this book.

For an example of parody where the target *is* a specific poem, see the following pair of poems by Masefield and Guiterman.

vii. The Poem as Translation

---

801. [THE WYF OF BATHE]
GEOFFREY CHAUCER

In the introduction to his translation of Chaucer, Professor Lumiansky points out that the English Chaucer used was not "a stiff literary language" but usually "the direct, highly idiomatic, colloquial language of the streets." To reproduce for the modern reader this "conversational quality" is, he says, "almost impossible" in verse, rhymed or unrhymed, or in archaic prose. Since "most of the charm and effectiveness of Chaucer's rhymes and meters" must be lost in any translation, Professor Lumiansky claims, the use of a modern idiomatic prose might at least approximate "the conversational quality of the Middle English original."

Does his translation achieve the result he sought? What does Morrison's rhymed translation aim to emulate? Not Chaucer's speech, but ours?

What elements are gained by Morrison's use of rhymed couplets? Considering the poetic use of language, why is Morrison's "worthy woman" more effective than Lumiansky's literal translation "good wife"? Study Morrison's poetic use of language; do you find any counterpointing of word against word? Any in the Chaucer original? Do you consider the texture of Morrison's translation richer than the prose one? Explain.

803. EIN FICHTENBAUM STEHT EINSAM
HEINRICH HEINE

Where Kramer's translation is "ice and snowdrift / Quilt him in covers of white" (stanza 1), Leland writes: "the ice and snowdrifts / Enfold him in mantle white." Which is the more original phrasing?

Can you find faults in all three translations as poems in their own right? For example, comment on the intensive "so" in line 1 of Untermeyer's version. On Kramer's "covers of white." On Leland's "in mantle white." Also comment on the differing connotations of "the East," "an Orient land," and "the Eastern land," as renderings of Heine's "Morgenland."

806. CHANSON DE LA PLUS HAUTE TOUR
ARTHUR RIMBAUD

From Une Saison en Enfer. Not to be confused with Rimbaud's poem of same title and refrain in Les Illuminations.

Notice that the structure of Rimbaud's poem is retained in the translations. The opening couplet evokes a mood of hope, which is undercut by the juxtaposed mood of despair in the stanza following. Next the mood of hope is re-invoked in the repeated burden of the refrain (lines 9-10). The image which follows this (in stanza 3) contradicts the hope of the refrain by its mood of despair, and the contrasted mood creates the irony of the final couplet. The poem is thus constructed by alternating and contrasting moods, mood A cancelled out by mood B.

What the poem says has been created, not stated. What does the poem "say"? Is the connection between the parts of Rimbaud's poem psychological or logical?

For two other poems whose structure is that of contrasting moods, see James Joyce's "I Hear an Army . . ." (p. 675) and Malcolm Cowley's "Mine No. 6" (p. 734).

804. DIE BOTSCHAFT
HEINRICH HEINE

Which of the three translations of Heine's poem do you think best approximates spoken English?

II: The Poem and the Creative Process

814. POETRY AND THE POET
ELIZABETH DREW

814.9, "Q": Sir Arthur Quiller Couch (1863–1944), British professor, critic, and novelist. **815.5, la belle dame sans merci:** See the poem, by John Keats, on p. 743.

Though Elizabeth Drew focusses her discussion on poetry, her account of how the imaginative or creative mind operates on experience to produce literature is equally applicable to other forms of literary art, in prose as well as poetry. What are some of the similarities and differences between the factual and the literary expression of the experiences described in turn first by Clarke and Keats; by Dorothy Wordsworth and William Wordsworth; by Clarke and Dorothy Wordsworth; by Keats and William Wordsworth? (Note that in the two prose accounts some material has been omitted from the text because of irrelevancy, but even of what remains the two poets chose to ignore some material included by the two prose writers.) What kind of information do the poets consider irrelevant—and why?

815. ON FIRST LOOKING INTO CHAPMAN'S HOMER
JOHN KEATS

4, Apollo: the god of poetry. **8, Chapman:** George Chapman (1559?–1634), poet and dramatist. His translation of the *Iliad* was first published in 1611, the *Odyssey* in 1614–15. The book Keats read with Clarke was a folio edition of 1616.

Explain the effectiveness of the imagery of space and movement in the octave or first eight lines of the sonnet in contrast with that of space and immobility in the sestet. Why do you suppose Keats ended his poem with the image of Cortez rather than with that of the "watcher of the skies," even though stellar space is more "unlimited" than even the great Pacific? Why is the final version of line 7—"Yet never did I breathe its pure serene"—much better than the first version—"Yet could I never judge what men could mean"? The words *realm, fealty,* and *demesne* suggest medieval feudalism rather than ancient Greece; are they therefore inappropriate in the diction of the poem? It was Balboa, not Cortez, who discovered the Pacific. Does the error in fact affect the value of the poem? If not, why not?

820. "I WANDERED LONELY AS A CLOUD"
WILLIAM WORDSWORTH

Dorothy Wordsworth's journal shows that the poet was *not* alone at the time of seeing the daffodils. What dramatic effect is achieved by the poet's depicting himself as a lonely figure? From a study of the epithets applied to the daffodils and to the poet, show how the dramatization is accomplished. Why does the poet personify the daffodils? Compare the vowel sounds in lines 1 and 2 with those, for instance, in lines 23 and 24. Explain the difference in effect. Does the last stanza "draw a moral" or does it extend the experience being presented?

821. From CHAPMAN'S HOMER
GEORGE CHAPMAN

1, Samothrace: an island in the Aegean Sea, northeast of Troy. **3, Priam's city:** Priam was king of Troy. **3, Achive:** *i.e.,* Greek. **3, Ida:** mountain near Troy. **10, Aegas:** Neptune's palace was located in the depths of the sea near Ægae, a city on the Corinthian Gulf in Greece. **822.25, Phaeacia:** the Homeric island of Scheria, supposedly modern Corfu. **4, She:** Pallas Athene, powerful Greek goddess, patron of Ulysses.

In his translation of the *Iliad* Chapman uses a fourteen-syllable line, rhyming in couplets; in his *Odyssey* he uses ten-syllable couplets—basically the same form Pope used a little over a hundred years later. What are the weaknesses and strengths of each? It is possible that the *golden* and *gold* epithets applied to Neptune found an echo in Keats' phrase: *realms of gold.* Compare and contrast the kind of diction and use of detail in the descriptions by Chapman and Pope of Ulysses' adventure.

829. KUBLA KHAN
S. T. COLERIDGE

Does the visionary or dream origin of this poem affect its value? (If you think it does, would you say the same thing about a mathematical or chemical discovery in a dream? Such discoveries are part of the history of science. But only good poets and good scientists have dreams that turn out to be good poetry or good science.) Does the last section of the poem (lines 37 ff.) suggest that the poem is partly about the creative power of music and of song, the ability of poetry to recreate the wondrous but lost world of Kubla Khan? Comment on the shifts in rhythm in the poem, the use of repetition, and the character of the imagery. Can you reduce this poem to any theme or meaning?

831. "CHILDE ROLAND TO THE DARK TOWER CAME"
ROBERT BROWNING

Title: "Childe" is a title of gentility. **68, bents:** "bent" is a kind of grass. **114, bespate:** spattered. **135, mews:** an enclosure, den, etc. **142, Tophet:** outer darkness, hell. **160, Apollyon:** destroying angel, the Devil. **161, dragon-penned:** dragon-feathered; "pen" is (now) archaic for quill or feather. **202, slug-horn:** trumpet.

Is this poem a dream told by the dreamer on awakening, or is it a narrative of an experience told to a listener afterwards, or is it a kind of "stream of consciousness" taking place as Roland rides along? Various interpretations of the poem have been made, depending on the answers to such questions as: What does the Tower represent? Who is the "hoary cripple"? Is he

the figure of Death telling the reluctant individual that "this is where you turn off," so to speak—and therefore all Roland has left is to attempt an unfaltering and brave death? (In this interpretation the squat tower becomes the grave or crypt.) Is the cripple the Devil, leading men astray from the true path? (By this view the tower becomes the gates of hell.) Is the cripple, on the other hand, a beneficent figure, desiring to help the stalwart traveller? Are the regions through which Roland passes arranged in a significant sequence—each an area revealing signs of death from different causes (starvation, violence, torture, disease, etc.)?

What do we learn of Roland's character? What do you suppose happened after the "slug-horn's" challenge rang out? Does it matter that we are not enlightened? Does a knowledge of the probable sources of the poem help us understand its meaning?

For another poem inspired by the poet's reading, see the discussion of the writing of Keats' "On First Looking into Chapman's Homer" (pp. 814–819).

853. THE RAVEN
EDGAR ALLAN POE

41, Pallas: Pallas Athene, Greek goddess of wisdom. **47, Plutonian:** Pluto was king of the Underworld. **82, nepenthe:** a drug to relieve pain or sorrow. **89, balm in Gilead:** see *Jeremiah* 8:22. **93, Aidenn:** Eden, with spelling altered for the sake of the rhyme. **106, lamplight . . . shadow:** bracket candelabra were in Poe's day sometimes attached to a wall above the door.

Compare this poem with Rossetti's "The Blessed Damozel" (p. 684) and the note to that poem on p. 954.

867. THE TIGER
WILLIAM BLAKE

Who is the speaker in the poem? What is his attitude? Is this a description of a tiger, or is the tiger a symbol? If so, of what? In the process of creating his poem, as shown in the two drafts, did Blake revise his ideas as he wrote or merely strive for greater power and economy in expression? What ideas or phrases which appear in the original draft are omitted in the final version? Comment on these omissions.

III: The Poem and the Reader

899. HOW TO CRITICIZE A POEM
THEODORE SPENCER

What qualities in the methods and language of some contemporary critics does Spencer burlesque? Notice the errors in the allusions to *Oedipus Rex,* the *Iliad,* and the *Aeneid.* What other similar errors does Spencer introduce?

910. ODE ON MELANCHOLY
JOHN KEATS

1, **Lethe:** river of forgetfulness in Hades. **2ff., Wolf's-bane, etc.:** things traditionally associated with melancholy. **4, Proserpine:** the daughter of Demeter (goddess of earth) and of Jupiter. She was abducted by Pluto, king of the underworld, to be his queen, and as such became one of the deities of death. **7, Psyche:** soul. **8, mysteries:** here used in its meaning of the rites or practices of an esoteric cult. **17, globèd peonies:** the petals of a mature, apparently perfect peony can "collapse" all at once if shaken.

912. DOVER BEACH REVISITED
THEODORE MORRISON

What types of critics are represented by Chartly, Dewing, Twitchell, Mole, Hale, and Prampton? Is there significance in the passages singled out for special thought by each of them? What is the point of view of the author himself? Is the ending inconclusive? Why, or why not? Does the answer depend upon what kind of critic you yourself are? What is your opinion of Arnold's poem?

INDEX OF AUTHORS AND TITLES

Page numbers followed by "n" indicate locations of Notes and Questions.